DISPUTED MORAL ISSUES

A Reader

Second Edition

Mark Timmons
University of Arizona

New York   Oxford
OXFORD UNIVERSITY PRESS
2011

Oxford University Press, Inc., publishes works that further Oxford University's
objective of excellence in research, scholarship, and education.

Oxford   New York
Auckland   Cape Town   Dar es Salaam   Hong Kong   Karachi
Kuala Lumpur   Madrid   Melbourne   Mexico City   Nairobi
New Delhi   Shanghai   Taipei   Toronto

With offices in
Argentina   Austria   Brazil   Chile   Czech Republic   France   Greece
Guatemala   Hungary   Italy   Japan   Poland   Portugal   Singapore
South Korea   Switzerland   Thailand   Turkey   Ukraine   Vietnam

Copyright © 2011, 2007 by Oxford University Press, Inc.

Published by Oxford University Press, Inc.
198 Madison Avenue, New York, New York 10016
http://www.oup.com

Oxford is a registered trademark of Oxford University Press

Library of Congress Cataloging-in-Publication Data
Disputed moral issues : a reader / [edited by] Mark Timmons.—2nd ed.
    p. cm.
  Includes bibliographical references.
  ISBN 978–0–19–538872–5
  1. Ethics—Textbooks. 2. Ethical problems—Textbooks.   I. Timmons, Mark, 1951–
  BJ1012.D57 2010
  170—dc22   2010027668

Printing number: 9 8 7 6 5 4 3 2 1
Printed in the United States of America
on acid-free paper

CONTENTS

Preface   ix
User's Guide   xiii

1 A MORAL THEORY PRIMER   1

1. What Is a Moral Theory?   2
2. Six Essential Moral Theories   6
   A. Consequentialism   6
   B. Natural Law Theory   12
   C. Kantian Moral Theory   15
   D. Rights-Based Moral Theory   20
   E. Virtue Ethics   25
   F. Ethics of Prima Facie Duty   27
3. Coping with Many Moral Theories   29
   Appendix: Ethics by Authority?   33

2 MORAL THEORY SELECTIONS   38

JEREMY BENTHAM / *The Principle of Utility*   38
ST. THOMAS AQUINAS / *Treatise on Law*   43
IMMANUEL KANT / *The Moral Law*   47
JOHN LOCKE / *Natural Rights*   55
ARISTOTLE / *Virtue and Character*   58
W. D. ROSS / *What Makes Right Actions Right?*   67

Additional Resources   71

3 SEXUAL MORALITY AND MARRIAGE 73

Vatican Declaration on Some Questions of Sexual Ethics 78

JOHN CORVINO / Why Shouldn't Tommy and Jim Have Sex? A Defense of Homosexuality 84

THOMAS A. MAPPES / A Liberal View of Sexual Morality and the Concept of Using Another Person 90

RAJA HALWANI / Virtue Ethics and Adultery 101

MAGGIE GALLAGHER / Normal Marriage: Two Views 107

EVAN WOLFSON / Enough Marriage to Share 115

Additional Resources 120

4 PORNOGRAPHY, HATE SPEECH, AND CENSORSHIP 122

THE ATTORNEY GENERAL'S COMMISSION ON PORNOGRAPHY / Pornography and Harm 131

NADINE STROSSEN / Why Censoring Pornography Would Not Reduce Discrimination or Violence against Women 137

RONALD DWORKIN / Liberty and Pornography 147

JUDITH M. HILL / Pornography and Degradation 154

CHARLES R. LAWRENCE III / Racist Speech as the Functional Equivalent of Fighting Words 162

JOHN ARTHUR / Sticks and Stones 166

Additional Resources 174

5 DRUGS, GAMBLING, AND ADDICTION 176

DAVID BOAZ / Drug-Free America or Free America? 182

PETER DE MARNEFFE / Decriminalize, Don't Legalize 188

ROBERT E. GOODIN / Permissible Paternalism: Saving Smokers from Themselves 198

DANIEL SHAPIRO / Addiction and Drug Policy 204

PETER COLLINS / Is Gambling Immoral? A Virtue Ethics Approach 211

DAVID B. FLETCHER / Gambling and Character 220

Additional Resources 229

6 Sexism, Racism, and Reparation   231

Marilyn Frye / *Sexism*   236

J. L. A. Garcia / *Racism as a Model for Understanding Sexism*   242

Michael Philips / *Racist Acts and Racist Humor*   252

J. Angelo Corlett / *Reparations to Native Americans?*   262

Louis P. Pojman / *Why Affirmative Action Is Immoral*   274

Thomas E. Hill Jr. / *The Message of Affirmative Action*   283

Additional Resources   292

7 Euthanasia and Physician-Assisted Suicide   294

J. Gay-Williams / *The Wrongfulness of Euthanasia*   299

James Rachels / *Active and Passive Euthanasia*   303

Bonnie Steinbock / *The Intentional Termination of Life*   307

Dan W. Brock / *Voluntary Active Euthanasia*   313

Richard Doerflinger / *Assisted Suicide: Pro-Choice or Anti-Life?*   317

David T. Watts and Timothy Howell / *Assisted Suicide Is Not Voluntary Active Euthanasia*   323

Additional Resources   328

8 The Ethical Treatment of Animals   330

Gaverick Matheny / *Utilitarianism and Animals*   333

Tom Regan / *Are Zoos Morally Defensible?*   342

Carl Cohen / *Do Animals Have Rights?*   348

Mary Anne Warren / *Human and Animal Rights Compared*   356

Jordan Curnutt / *A New Argument for Vegetarianism*   362

Additional Resources   372

9 Abortion   373

Pope John Paul II / *The Unspeakable Crime of Abortion*   381

Mary Anne Warren / *On the Moral and Legal Status of Abortion*   384

Judith Jarvis Thomson / *A Defense of Abortion*   391

DAN MARQUIS / *Why Abortion Is Immoral*   400

L. W. SUMNER / *A Moderate View*   405

ROSALIND HURSTHOUSE / *Virtue Theory and Abortion*   411

Additional Resources   421

10 CLONING AND GENETIC ENHANCEMENT   423

JOHN ROBERTSON / *Liberty, Identity, and Human Cloning*   430

LEON R. KASS / *Preventing Brave New World*   437

GREGORY E. PENCE / *Will Cloning Harm People?*   446

MICHAEL J. SANDEL / *The Case against Perfection*   455

ARTHUR L. CAPLAN / *Good, Better, or Best?*   463

Additional Resources   470

11 THE DEATH PENALTY   472

IMMANUEL KANT / *Punishment and the Principle of Equality*   478

STEPHEN NATHANSON / *An Eye for an Eye?*   481

ERNEST VAN DEN HAAG / *A Defense of the Death Penalty*   487

JEFFREY H. REIMAN / *Civilization, Safety, and Deterrence*   492

JAMES S. LIEBMAN, JEFFREY FAGAN, VALERIE WEST, AND
JONATHAN LLOYD / *Capital Attrition: Error Rates in
Capital Cases, 1973–1995*   495

Additional Resources   503

12 WAR, TERRORISM, AND TORTURE   504

RICHARD A. WASSERSTROM / *Does Morality Apply to War?*   512

HAIG KHATCHADOURIAN / *Terrorism and Morality*   516

MICHAEL WALZER / *After 9/11: Five Questions about Terrorism*   524

JAMES P. STERBA / *Terrorism and International Justice*   530

HENRY SHUE / *Torture*   540

ALAN M. DERSHOWITZ / *Should the Ticking Bomb Terrorist Be Tortured?*   549

Additional Resources   560

13 WORLD HUNGER AND POVERTY   562

GARRETT HARDIN / *Lifeboat Ethics*   565

PETER SINGER / *The Life You Can Save*   571

JOHN ARTHUR / *World Hunger and Moral Obligation*   585

AMARTYA SEN / *Property and Hunger*   594

ONORA O'NEILL / *A Kantian Approach to World Hunger*   600

Additional Resources   606

14 THE ENVIRONMENT, CONSUMPTION, AND GLOBAL WARMING   607

WILLIAM F. BAXTER / *People or Penguins: The Case for Optimal Pollution*   614

ALDO LEOPOLD / *The Land Ethic*   619

THOMAS E. HILL JR. / *Ideals of Human Excellence and Preserving the Natural Environment*   624

PETER WENZ / *Synergistic Environmental Virtues: Consumerism and Human Flourishing*   631

WALTER SINNOTT-ARMSTRONG / *It's Not My Fault: Global Warming and Individual Moral Obligations*   642

BJØRN LOMBORG / *Let's Keep Our Cool about Global Warming*   658

Additional Resources   664

Appendix: Quick Guide to Moral Theories   666

Glossary   670

PREFACE

The guiding aim of this anthology is to connect various disputed moral issues with moral theory in order to help students better understand the nature of these disputes. The issues featured in this book include questions about the morality of various forms of sexual behavior; pornography, hate speech, and censorship; drugs, gambling, and addiction; sexism, racism, and reparations; euthanasia and suicide; the ethical treatment of animals; abortion; cloning and genetic enhancement; the death penalty; war, terrorism, and torture; world hunger and poverty; and ethical questions that relate to consumption, global warming, and the environment in general.

The connection between moral disputes over such issues and moral theory is that opposing moral viewpoints on some topics are very often grounded in one or another moral theory. Thus, to understand an author's arguments for her or his favored position, one must be able to recognize the author's deepest moral assumptions, which are reflected in the moral theory from which the author proceeds in reasoning about particular moral issues.

In editing this anthology, I have attempted to help readers connect moral issues with theory in the following ways:

- *A moral theory primer.* One way to connect issues and theory is to have students read compact summaries of the various moral theories—summaries that convey just enough detail about a moral theory to aid understanding without overwhelming the reader. This is what I have tried to do in the first chapter, "A Moral Theory Primer," in which I first explain what a moral theory is all about—its main concepts and guiding aims—and then proceed to present six types of moral theory that are essential for understanding moral disputes over the sorts of issues featured in this book. In the brief introduction and "User's Guide" immediately following this preface, I explain how one might integrate the moral theory primer into a moral problems course.
- *Chapter introductions.* In addition to the moral theory primer, I have also written introductions to each chapter that go over certain conceptual, historical, and theoretical issues that students must have in beginning their study of moral issues. These introductions include remarks about how the moral theories presented in the primer relate to the arguments of the authors whose writings are featured in the chapter.
- *Selection summaries.* Again, in order to aid one's understanding of the articles, each selection is preceded by a short summary of the article. Immediately after the summary I have, where relevant, included a cue to readers that indicates the relevant part of the moral theory primer that will aid in understanding the article in question.

- *Reading and discussion questions.* Following each selection, I have included a set of reading and discussion questions. The reading questions are meant to prompt students' understanding of each selection's content, whereas the discussion questions are meant to help stimulate critical thought about the issues and arguments in the selections.
- *Quick guide to moral theories.* I have also included an appendix, "Quick Guide to Moral Theories," which lists the various principles featured in each of the six theories featured in the primer. This is for readers who need a brief reminder of the key elements of one or more of the featured moral theories.

In addition, this anthology includes the following features that many will find useful:

- *Glossary.* For ease of reference, I have included a glossary of important terms that are defined in the moral theory primer and in the chapter introductions. Each term in the glossary appears in boldface type when it is first introduced in the text. The glossary entry for each term specifies the chapter and section in which the term is first introduced.
- *Additional resources.* Finally, at the end of each chapter, I have included a short list of resources, broken down into Web resources, authored books and articles, and edited collections. These resources are recommended to those who wish to explore a topic in more detail.

As mentioned earlier, the following "User's Guide" makes a few suggestions about integrating the study of moral theory and moral issues.

New to the Second Edition

In addition to adding reading and discussion questions for each selection and expanding the additional resources material to include Web resources, this edition features many selections that were not included in the first edition, twenty-one in all. Of particular note are the following:

- I have added an entirely new chapter, "Readings in Moral Theory," featuring selections from Jeremy Bentham, St. Thomas Aquinas, Immanuel Kant, John Locke, Aristotle, and W. D. Ross, which correspond, respectively, to those sections in "A Moral Theory Primer" on consequentialism, natural law theory, Kantian ethics, rights-based theory, virtue ethics, and the ethics of prima facie duty.
- The chapter from the first edition on sexual morality has been expanded to include the topic of same-sex marriage, featuring articles by Maggie Gallagher and Evan Wolfson debating its morality.
- The chapter on drugs, addiction, and gambling features an article on drug legalization written especially for this edition by Peter de Marneffe. I have also included a recent article on gambling by David B. Fletcher, "Gambling and Character," which provides a companion piece to the article by Peter Collins. Both authors view gambling from a virtue ethics perspective, but come to different conclusions about the morality of this practice.
- The chapter on the ethical treatment of animals includes an article by Gaverick Matheny who, I believe, makes the clearest utilitarian case for the claim that certain practices that involve harm to nonhuman animals is morally wrong. Also new to this edition is Tom

Regan's "Are Zoos Morally Defensible?" Replacing Carl Cohen's "In Defense of Speciesism" from the first edition of this book is Cohen's "Do Animals Have Rights?"

- I have replaced Peter Singer's well-known and often reprinted 1971 classic, "Famine,
Affluence, and Morality," with selections from his 2009 book, *The Life You Can Save*,
which features the same basic argument as the one in the 1971 article, but which I think
is better for teaching because it includes updated statistics about affluence and about
poverty, and it includes Singer's responses to various objections often raised against
his basic argument.

- The final chapter featuring topics often discussed in connection with the environment
now includes articles on consumption and global warming by Peter Wenz, "Synergistic
Environmental Virtues: Consumerism and Human Flourishing," Walter Sinnott-Armstrong, "It's Not *My* Fault: Global Warming and Individual Moral Obligations," and
Bjørn Lomborg, "Let's Keep Our Cool about Global Warming."

Finally, this second edition features an "Instructor's Manual" and "Testbank" on CD and
a companion Website for both students and instructors that I describe in more detail in the
"User's Guide" that follows this preface.

Acknowledgments and Dedication

Thanks go to Robert Miller and Christina Mancuso for their guidance and friendly advice
that helped me a great deal in editing this second edition. Gathering permissions for a project this size is a painstaking job, and I was extremely lucky to have Chris Kahn doing this.
Cyrena Sullivan composed the reading and discussion questions for each of the book's selections, and Chris Kahn was responsible for creating the "Instructor's Manual." Thank you,
Chris and Cyrena.

I received excellent advice and welcome encouragement from the following philosophers
who commented on the first edition of this book and whose collective input has helped make
this second edition better than the first: Susan J. Armstrong at Humboldt State University,
William J. Garland at The University of the South, Charles Edwin Harris at Texas A&M
University, Simon Keller at Boston University and University of Melbourne, Scott LaBarge
at Santa Clara University, Christopher Morris at University of Maryland, Valerie Tiberius at
University of Minnesota, Jon Tresan at University of Florida, and Leo Zaibert at University
of Wisconsin–Parkside.

Finally, once again, Betsy Timmons discussed with me many of the moral issues in this
book and was a constant source of good advice about the chapter introductions. It is to her
that I dedicate this second edition.

Mark Timmons
Tucson, AZ

User's Guide

In what follows, I suggest how instructors might approach teaching a course that is primarily focused on particular moral disputes but that also integrates moral theory into the teaching of those disputes. Following this discussion is a description of the various resources for both students and instructors that come with this book.

As mentioned in the preface, a central aim of this anthology is to connect a range of contemporary disputed moral issues to moral theory. Much of the philosophical literature on the morality of abortion, homosexuality, pornography, cloning, and the death penalty approaches these and other issues from the perspective of some *moral theory*. As I will explain more fully in the next chapter, a moral theory purports to answer general moral questions about the nature of the right and the good. So one way in which philosophers tackle disputed moral issues is by appealing to a moral theory—appealing, that is, to a general conception of the right and the good in examining some particular moral issue.

But this presents a challenge for students who are trying to understand and think about the moral controversies featured in this book and presents an associated challenge for instructors. Because of the important role that moral theory plays in the writings of both professional philosophers and nonphilosophers who write about contemporary moral issues, a full understanding of most of the readings in this book requires that one have a basic grasp of the various moral theories to which authors appeal in their writings. Some authors take the time to briefly explain whatever moral theory they are using in approaching some moral issue, but many do not—they assume a basic acquaintance with moral theory. And this means that a student not previously acquainted with moral theory is often at a disadvantage in trying to understand the position and arguments of an author. The associated challenge for an instructor is to teach just enough moral theory to aid students' understanding in a course devoted primarily to disputed moral issues.

In this anthology, I try to address this challenge in a number of related ways. First, I have written an introductory overview of moral theory, "A Moral Theory Primer," in which I first explain what a moral theory is all about and then present the basic elements of six types of moral theory that are featured throughout the readings in this book. These theories include the following:

- *Consequentialism* (including utilitarianism)
- *Natural law theory* (including the doctrine of double effect)
- *Kantian moral theory* (including Kant's Humanity and Universal Law formulations of the categorical imperative—Kant's fundamental moral principle)

- *Rights-based theory* (including an explanation of "rights-focused" approaches to moral problems that are very common but importantly distinct from a genuinely rights-*based* theory)
- *Virtue ethics* (including an explanation of the concepts of virtue and vice)
- *Ethics of prima facie duty* (including W. D. Ross's classic version and the more recent version defended by Robert Audi)

The moral theory primer, then, is meant to get readers up to basic speed on six essential moral theories, with an eye on their application to disputed moral issues. In addition, the primer addresses the following commonly voiced questions about moral theory and about the particular selection of theories featured in this book:

- What is the point of moral theory in thinking about disputed moral issues in light of the fact that there is a variety of competing moral theories whose application to some issue may yield conflicting moral verdicts?
- What about theories that appeal to the will of God or to the norms of society or culture in determining what is right or wrong?

I do not attempt to provide a full response to these questions, but I do think they are well worth addressing in a first course in ethics, even if only briefly.

The moral theory primer can be read straight through. But let me make a suggestion about how it might be used in a course devoted mainly to contemporary moral problems—a suggestion that incorporates additional ways in which I have tried to address the previously mentioned challenge. (What I am about to say reflects my own approach to teaching a contemporary moral problems course.)

The basic idea is to incorporate select readings from the moral theory primer as one proceeds to work through the readings in the chapters that follow. The motto here is: *Teach moral theory as needed* in working through the readings. I have written the primer so that the segments on each of the six types of moral theory are largely self-standing; they can be consulted as needed in learning about and teaching moral issues. I find that teaching moral theory as needed helps students to better digest and understand the somewhat abstract nature of a moral theory by immediately relating it to some concrete moral issue. And, of course, their coming to understand moral theory helps them more fully understand the readings.

Let me further suggest a way of implementing the teaching of theory on an as-needed approach.

- *Getting started.* Read the introduction and section 1 of the moral theory primer in which I provide a brief overview of what a moral theory is all about. That will be enough to get readers started.
- *Moving ahead to the moral issues.* Then I recommend proceeding to one of the chapters on a disputed moral issue—they can be taught in any order.[1]
- *Chapter introductions.* Read the chapter introduction on the selected topic. They are meant to explain basic concepts relevant to the chapter topic. Each of these chapters ends with a subsection entitled "Theory Meets Practice," in which I briefly relate the moral theories that are used in that chapter's readings to the topic of the chapter.
- *Cues for the integrated use of the moral theory primer.* Then proceed to work through the readings in the selected chapter. Each reading begins with a brief summary of the

article and, in those cases in which an author is appealing to, or relying on, some moral theory, the summaries are followed by a recommended reading, *which cues readers to go back (if needed) to the relevant sections of the moral theory primer where the theory in question is presented.* This is how I incorporate the teaching of various moral theories into the course as needed.

Let me add that not every reading appeals to one or another moral theory. Some articles are mainly concerned with conveying an understanding of some disputed concept like "sexism" or "racism." One of the articles in the chapter on the death penalty is concerned entirely with statistical evidence about error rates in capital cases, an issue that, of course, bears importantly on the morality of the death penalty. And in a few other cases, the readings do not clearly proceed from some moral theory. So, not every article summary includes a recommendation to consult the moral theory primer. But most of the reading selections do connect directly with one or more of the moral theories explained in the primer.

- *Quick reference guide to moral theories.* In order to make it easy to review the fundamental principles of each of the theories, I have included an appendix, "Quick Guide to Moral Theories" with this information. Once one has read the relevant sections of the moral theory primer, this guide may be consulted to refresh one's memory of the basics.

Again, the preceding steps reflect how I like to proceed. Users are invited to find ways that best fit their own style of teaching.

Resources for Students and Instructors

This second edition includes an "Instructor's Manual" and "Testbank" on CD and a Companion Website (www.oup.com/us/timmons) that offers resources for both students and instructors.

Instructor Resources both in the Instructor's Manual and in the Companion Website include the following:

- Sample syllabi
- Lecture notes in PowerPoint format
- Chapter goals and summaries
- A Testbank that includes essay, multiple choice, true/false, and fill-in-the-blank questions

Student Resources on the Companion Website include the following:

- Self-quizzes, which include multiple choice, true/false, and fill-in-the-blank questions
- Helpful Web links
- Suggested readings and media (articles, films, etc.)

NOTE

1. Of course, some topics naturally go well together because the moral issues they raise are deeply connected. For instance, chapter 4 on pornography, hate speech, and censorship raises issues about the morality of government interference in the lives of its citizens. The same sort of issue comes up in chapter 5 on drugs, gambling, and addiction. Chapters 8 and 9 on animals and abortion, respectively, go together because they raise important questions about the scope of moral standing, that is, about the boundaries of what should count in our moral deliberations.

1 } A Moral Theory Primer

In 1998, Dr. Jack Kevorkian helped Thomas Youk end his life by giving him a lethal injection of drugs—an incident that was videotaped and later broadcast on CBS's *60 Minutes.*[1] Youk had been suffering from amyotrophic lateral sclerosis (often called Lou Gehrig's disease), a progressive neurodegenerative disease that attacks nerve cells in the brain and spinal cord, eventually leading to death. In the later stages of the disease, its victims are completely paralyzed, as was Youk at the time of his death.

Kevorkian's killing Youk was a case of euthanasia, which is defined as the act of killing (or allowing to die) on grounds of mercy for the victim. In this case, because Youk consented to his own death and because Kevorkian brought about Youk's death by an act of lethal injection, Kevorkian's action was an instance of voluntary active euthanasia. Kevorkian was eventually tried and convicted of second degree murder for his active role in bringing about Youk's death. But even if Kevorkian did violate the law, was his action morally wrong? Youk's immediate family and many others saw nothing morally wrong with Youk's decision or with Kevorkian's act. They argued, for example, that proper respect for an individual's freedom of choice means that people in Youk's situation have a moral right to choose to die and that, therefore, Kevorkian was not acting immorally in helping Youk end his life. Of course, many others disagreed, arguing, for example, that euthanasia is morally wrong because of its possible bad effects over time on society, including the possibility that the practice of euthanasia could be abused, and vulnerable persons might be put to death without their consent. Which side of this moral dispute is correct? Is euthanasia at least sometimes morally right, or is this practice morally wrong?

Disputes over moral issues are a fact of our social lives. Most people, through television, the Internet, magazines, and conversing with others, are familiar with some of the general contours of such disputes—disputes, for example, over the death penalty, the ethical treatment of animals, human cloning, abortion. The same sort of moral question raised about the actions of Kervorkian can be raised about these and other moral issues. Thinking critically about such moral issues is where philosophy becomes especially important.

A *philosophical* approach to moral issues has as its guiding aim arriving at correct or justified answers to questions about the morality of the death penalty, the ethical treatment of animals, human cloning, abortion, and other issues of moral concern. Given the contested nature of such practices as cloning and abortion, one needs to be able to defend one's position with *reasons*. Just as those who dispute questions about, say, science or history are expected to give reasons for the scientific and historical beliefs they hold, those who seriously dispute moral questions are expected to give reasons for whatever moral position they take on a certain issue. If we examine how philosophers go about providing reasons for the moral positions they take on certain issues, we find that very often they appeal to a **moral theory.** That is, in arguing for a particular position on the topic of, say, euthanasia, philosophers often make their case by applying a moral theory to the practice of euthanasia. Applying moral theory to issues of practical concern—practical issues—is one dominant way in which reasoning in ethics proceeds, and this way of tackling moral issues by applying theory to cases is featured in this book of readings.

But what is a moral theory? What are its guiding aims? What moral theories are there? How is a moral theory used in reasoning about disputed moral issues? These are the main questions of concern in this moral theory primer.

1.   WHAT IS A MORAL THEORY?

According to philosopher John Rawls, "The two main concepts of ethics are those of the right and the good. . . . The structure of an ethical theory is, then, largely determined by how it defines and connects these two basic notions."[2]

In explaining what a moral theory is, then, the place to begin is by clarifying the two main concepts featured in such a theory.

The Main Concepts: The Right and the Good

In ethics, the terms "right" and "wrong" are used primarily to evaluate the morality of actions, and in this chapter we are mainly concerned with moral theories that address the nature of right and wrong action (or right action, for short). Here, talk of right action in contrast to wrong action involves using the term "right" broadly to refer to actions that aren't wrong. Used in this broad sense, to say of an action that it is right is to say that it is "all right" (not wrong) to perform, and we leave open the question of whether the act, in addition to being all right, is an action that we morally ought to perform—an obligation or duty. But we sometimes find "right" being used narrowly to refer to actions that are "the" morally right action for one to perform, and when so used, it refers to actions that are morally required or obligatory (one's obligation or duty). Actions that are all right to perform (right in the sense of merely being not wrong) and that are also not one's moral obligation to perform—actions that are all right to perform and all right not to perform—are morally optional. So, we have three basic categories of moral evaluation into which an action may fall: an action may be morally obligatory (something one morally ought to do, is morally required to do, is one's duty), or morally optional, or morally wrong. To help keep this terminology straight, I have summarized what I have been saying in Figure 1.1.

Again, in ethics, the terms "good" and "bad" are used primarily in assessing the value of persons (their character) as well as experiences, things, and states of affairs. Philosophers distinguish between something's having **intrinsic value** (that is, being intrinsically good or bad) and something's having **extrinsic value** (that is, being extrinsically good or bad). Something has intrinsic value when its value depends on features that are *inherent* to it,

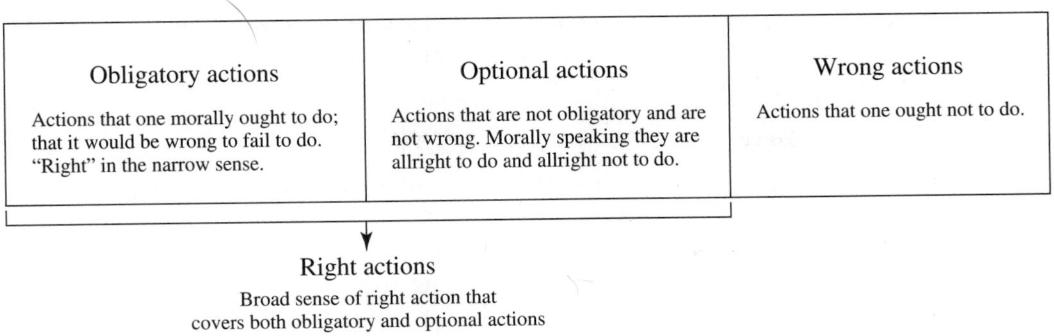

Obligatory actions	Optional actions	Wrong actions
Actions that one morally ought to do; that it would be wrong to fail to do. "Right" in the narrow sense.	Actions that are not obligatory and are not wrong. Morally speaking they are allright to do and allright not to do.	Actions that one ought not to do.

Right actions

Broad sense of right action that
covers both obligatory and optional actions

FIGURE 1.1   Basic Categories of Right Conduct

whereas something is extrinsically good when its goodness is a matter of how it is related to something else that is intrinsically good. For instance, some philosophers maintain that happiness is intrinsically good—its goodness depends on the inherent nature of happiness—and that things like money and power, while not intrinsically good, are nevertheless extrinsically good (valuable) because they can be used to bring about or contribute to happiness. Thus, the notion of intrinsic value is the more basic of the two notions, and so philosophical accounts of value are concerned with the nature of intrinsic value. And here we can recognize three basic value categories: the *intrinsically good,* the *intrinsically bad* (also referred to as the intrinsically *evil*), and what we may call the *intrinsically value-neutral*—that is, the category of all those things that are neither intrinsically good nor bad (though they may have extrinsic value).[3]

A moral theory, then, is a theory about the nature of the right and the good and about the proper method for making correct or justified moral decisions. Accordingly, here are some of the main questions that a moral theory attempts to answer:

1. What *makes* an action right or wrong—what *best explains why* right acts are right and wrong acts are wrong?
2. What *makes* something good or bad—what *best explains why* intrinsically good things are intrinsically good (and similarly for things that are intrinsically bad or evil)?
3. What is the *proper method* (supposing there is one) for reasoning our way to correct or justified moral conclusions about the rightness and wrongness of actions and the goodness and badness of persons, and other items of moral evaluation?

In order to understand more fully what a moral theory is and how it attempts to answer these questions, let us relate what has just been said to the two guiding aims of moral theory.

Two Main Aims of a Moral Theory

Corresponding to the first two questions about the nature of the right and the good is what we may call the theoretical aim of a moral theory:

The **theoretical aim** of a moral theory is to discover those underlying features of actions, persons, and other items of moral evaluation that *make* them right or wrong, good or bad and thus *explain why* such items have the moral properties they have. Features of this sort serve as *moral criteria* of the right and the good.

Our third main question about proper methodology in ethics is the basis for the practical aim of a moral theory:

> The **practical aim** of a moral theory is to offer *practical guidance* for how we might arrive at correct or justified moral verdicts about matters of moral concern—verdicts which we can then use to help guide choice.

Given these aims, we can evaluate a moral theory by seeing how well it satisfies them. We will return to the issue of evaluating moral theories in section 3. For the time being, we can gain a clearer understanding of these aims by considering the role that principles typically play in moral theories.

The Role of Moral Principles

In attempting to satisfy these two aims, philosophers typically propose **moral principles**— very general moral statements that specify conditions under which an action is right (or wrong) and something is intrinsically good (or bad). Principles that state conditions for an action's being right (or wrong) are **principles of right conduct,** and those that specify conditions under which something has intrinsic value are **principles of value.** Here is an example of a principle of right conduct (where "right" is being used in its broad sense to mean "not wrong"):

> P   An action is right if and only if (and because) it would, if performed, likely bring about at least as much overall happiness as would any available alternative action.[4]

This principle, understood as a moral criterion of right action, purports to reveal the underlying nature of right action—what *makes* a right action right. According to P, facts about how much overall happiness an action would bring about were it to be performed are what determine whether it is morally right. Although P addresses the rightness of actions, it has implications for wrongness as well. From P, together with the definitional claim that if an action is not morally right (in the broad sense of the term) then it is morally wrong, we may infer the following:

> P*   An action is wrong if and only if (and because) it would, if performed, likely not bring about at least as much overall happiness as would some available alternative action.

Since, as we have just seen, principles about moral wrongness can be derived from principles of rightness, I shall, in explaining a moral theory's account of right and wrong, simply formulate a theory's principles (there may be more than one) for right action.

In addition to serving as moral criteria, principles like P are typically intended to provide some practical guidance for coming to correct or justified moral verdicts about particular issues, thus addressing the practical aim of moral theory. The idea is that if P is a correct moral principle, then we should be able to use it to guide our moral deliberations in coming to correct conclusions about the rightness of actions, thus serving as a basis for moral decision making. In reasoning our way to moral conclusions about what to do, P has us focus on the consequences of actions and instructs us to consider in particular how much overall happiness actions would likely bring about.

To sum up, a moral theory can be understood as setting forth moral principles of right conduct and value that are supposed to explain what makes an action or other object of evaluation right or wrong, good or bad (thus satisfying the theoretical aim), as well as principles that can be used to guide moral thought in arriving at correct or justified decisions about what to do (thus satisfying the practical aim).

The Structure of a Moral Theory

Finally, what Rawls calls the "structure" of a moral theory is a matter of how a theory connects the right and the good. As we shall see, some theories take the concept of the good to be more basic than the concept of the right and thus define or characterize the rightness of actions in terms of considerations of intrinsic goodness. Call such theories value-based moral theories. **Value-based moral theories** include versions of consequentialism, natural law theory, and virtue ethics. However, some moral theories do not define rightness in terms of goodness. Some theories are **duty-based moral theories**—theories that take the concept of duty to be basic and so define or characterize the rightness of actions independently of considerations of goodness. These theories are often called "deontological" moral theories (from *deon,* the Greek term for duty). The moral theory of Immanuel Kant (see later in this chapter) and theories inspired by Kant (Kantian moral theories) are arguably deontological.[5] And what is called the ethics of prima facie duty, if not a pure deontological theory, contains deontological elements, as we shall see when we discuss this theory later in section 2.

Brief Summary

Now that we have reviewed a few basic elements of moral theory, let us briefly sum up.

- *Main concepts of moral theory.* The two main concepts featured in moral theory are the concepts of the right (and wrong) and the good (and bad).
- *Two aims of moral theory.* A moral theory can be understood as having two central aims. The theoretical aim is to explain the underlying nature of the right and the good—specifying those features of actions or other items of evaluation that *make* an action or whatever right or wrong, good or bad. We call such features "criteria." The practical aim is to offer practical guidance for how we might arrive at correct or justified moral verdicts about matters of moral concern.
- *The role of moral principles.* A moral theory is typically composed of moral principles (sometimes a single, fundamental principle) that are intended to serve as criteria of the right and the good (thus satisfying the theoretical aim) and are also intended to be useful in guiding moral thinking toward correct, or at least justified conclusions about some moral issue.
- *The structure of a moral theory.* Considerations of structure concern how a moral theory connects the concepts of the right and the good. Value-based theories make the good (intrinsic value) more basic than the right and define or characterize the right in terms of the good. Duty-based theories characterize the right independently of considerations of value.

In the next section, we briefly examine six moral theories that play a large role in philo-sophical discussions of disputed moral issues. After presenting these theories, I devote the remaining section and an appendix to questions that are likely to occur to readers. First, there is the question of why studying moral theories is helpful in thinking about disputed moral issues when there is no *one* moral theory that is accepted by all those who study moral theory. Rather, we find a variety of apparently competing moral theories that sometimes yield conflicting moral verdicts about the same issue. So, how can appealing to moral theory really help in trying to think productively about moral issues? This is a fair question that I address in section 3. In the appendix, I briefly present two moral theories whose guiding ideas will be familiar to most all readers—the divine command theory and ethical relativism—and I explain why they aren't featured in this book's readings. However, before going on, let me say something about how one might use this chapter in studying the moral issues featured in this book.

User's Guide Interlude

In the "User's Guide," I suggested that although this chapter can be read straight through, readers may want to stop here and go on to one of the following chapters and begin their study of disputed moral issues. In the chapter introductions and the brief article summaries that precede each reading selection, I prompt readers to read (or reread) my presentations of one or more of the six moral theories I describe in the next section of this chapter. And, of course, for those who wish to consult primary sources corresponding to the moral theories in question, there are the selections in the next chapter.

As I explained in the user's guide, I like to teach moral theory along with the readings. Seeing how a moral theory applies to a particular moral issue is helpful for understanding an author's position on the issue, which in turn helps readers gain a deeper understanding of and appreciation for moral theory. As for integrating section 3 and the appendix, I recommend consulting these parts of the chapter when the questions they address are prompted by one's thinking about and discussing the book's readings.

2.   SIX ESSENTIAL MORAL THEORIES

Six types of moral theory are prominently represented in our readings: consequentialism, natural law theory, Kantian moral theory, rights-based moral theory, virtue ethics, and the ethics of prima facie duty. Here, then, is an overview of these various theories that will pro-vide useful background for understanding our readings.

A. Consequentialism

In thinking about moral issues, one obvious thing to do is to consider the consequences or effects of various actions—the consequences or effects on matters that are of concern to us. **Consequentialism** is a type of moral theory according to which consequences of actions are all that matter in determining the rightness and wrongness of actions. Its guiding idea is this:

C   Right action is to be understood entirely in terms of the overall intrinsic value of the consequences of the action compared to the overall intrinsic value of the consequences associated with alternative actions an agent might perform instead. An action is right if and only if (and because) its consequences would be at least as good as the consequences of any alternative action that the agent might instead perform.

A number of important ideas are packed into C that we need to unpack—ideas that are present in the varieties of consequentialist moral theory presented next. Let us sort them out.

- First, consequentialist moral theory is a *value-based moral theory*: it characterizes or defines right action in terms of intrinsic value.
- Second, this sort of theory involves the fairly intuitive idea of *alternative actions* open to an agent: in circumstances calling for a moral choice, an agent is confronted by a range of alternative actions, any one of which she might choose to perform.
- Third (and relatedly), consequentialism is a *comparative* theory of right action: the rightness (or wrongness) of an action depends on how much intrinsic value it would likely produce (if performed) compared to how much intrinsic value alternative actions would likely produce (if performed).
- Fourth, the consequentialist account of right action is a *maximizing* conception: we are to perform that action, from among the alternatives, whose consequences will have *at least as much* overall value as any other.
- Fifth, and finally, consequentialism is a strongly *impartialist* moral theory in the sense that the rightness or wrongness of an action is made to depend on the values of the consequences for *everyone* who is affected by the action, where everyone affected counts *equally*. (This fifth point will become clearer when we consider particular versions of consequentialism.)

Consequentialism, we have noted, is a *general type* of moral theory that has a variety of species. For instance, consequentialists may differ over the issue of what has intrinsic value. Those versions that take happiness or welfare alone to have intrinsic value are versions of utilitarianism, whereas those that take human perfection to have intrinsic value are versions of perfectionism. Again, consequentialists may differ over the primary focus of consequentialist evaluation. Some versions focus on individual actions, other versions focus on rules. So, we can distinguish four main species of consequentialism. Let us explore further.

Utilitarianism has been perhaps the most prominent form of consequentialism, so let us begin with it.

Utilitarianism

Utilitarianism was originally developed and defended by Jeremy Bentham (1748–1832) and later refined by John Stuart Mill (1806–1873).[6] Their basic idea is that it is *human welfare* or *happiness* that alone is intrinsically valuable and that the rightness or wrongness of actions depends entirely on how they affect human welfare or happiness. As a consequentialist theory, utilitarianism requires that one *maximize* welfare where the welfare of *all* individuals who will be affected by some action counts. We can sharpen our characterization of this theory by introducing the technical term "utility," which refers to the *net value* of the consequences of actions—how much overall welfare or happiness would likely result from an action, taking into account both the short-term and long-term effects of the action on the welfare of all who will be affected. The basic idea is that the moral status of an action—its rightness or wrongness—depends both on how much happiness (if any) it would likely produce for each individual affected were it to be performed, as well as how much unhappiness (if any) it would likely produce for each affected person were it to be performed. For each alternative action, then, we can consider the *net balance* of overall happiness versus unhappiness associated with that action. Call this overall net value the **utility** of an action. We can now formulate a generic statement of the basic utilitarian principle—the **principle of utility:**

> **U**   An action is right if and only if (and because) it would (if performed) likely produce at least as high a utility (net overall balance of welfare) as would any other alternative action one might perform instead.[7]

Notice that the utility of an action might be negative. That is, all things considered, an action may produce a net balance of unhappiness over happiness were it to be performed. Moreover, since U (like all versions of C) is comparative, it may turn out that the right action in some unfortunate circumstance is the one that would likely bring about the least amount of overall negative utility.

As formulated, U leaves open questions about the nature of happiness and unhappiness about which there are different philosophical theories.[8] Bentham and (apparently) Mill held that happiness is entirely constituted by experiences of pleasure and unhappiness by experiences of displeasure or pain. And so their theory of intrinsic value is called **value hedonism:** *only* states of pleasure have positive intrinsic value and *only* states of pain have intrinsic negative value; anything else of value is of mere extrinsic value. So, for instance, for the value hedonist, any positive value that knowledge may have is extrinsic: it is only of positive value when it contributes to bringing about what has intrinsic value, namely pleasure (or the alleviation of pain). It should be noted that a value hedonist need not (and should not) take an excessively narrow view of pleasure and pain; the hedonist can follow Bentham and Mill in holding that in addition to such bodily pleasures of the sort one gets from eating delicious food or having a massage, there are aesthetic and intellectual pleasures such as appreciating a beautifully written poem. Moreover, the value hedonist will recognize not only passive pleasures of the sort just mentioned, but also active pleasures as when one plays a game or is involved in some creative activity. So value hedonism can recognize a broad range of pleasurable experiences that have positive intrinsic value and a broad range of painful experiences that have negative intrinsic value.

If we now combine the principle of utility (U) with value hedonism, we obtain **hedonistic utilitarianism:**

> **HU**   An action is right if and only if (and because) it would likely produce (if performed) at least as high a net balance of pleasure (or less pain) as would any other alternative action one might do instead.

But as I hope my presentation has made clear, one need not accept hedonism as a theory of value in order to be a utilitarian. In fact, many contemporary utilitarians reject value hedonism and accept some other conception of happiness or welfare. But, again, what makes a theory a version of utilitarianism is that the theory accepts the basic consequentialist claim, C, together with the idea that it is human happiness or human well-being that has intrinsic value and is to be promoted in what we do.

Perfectionist Consequentialism

But a consequentialist need not be a utilitarian—she might hold that there are items having intrinsic value other than happiness that are important in determining the rightness or wrongness of action. To illustrate, I have chosen what is called **perfectionist consequentialism**—a species of the generic view that accepts a perfectionist theory of value.[9] According to a **value perfectionist,** it is states of human perfection, including knowledge and achievement that have intrinsic value.[10] One might come to have a great deal of knowledge and achievement in one's life, yet not be happy. So a perfectionist theory of the good is not the same as a happiness theory of the good. We might formulate the basic principle of perfectionist consequentialism as follows:

> **PC**   An action is right if and only if (and because) it would (if performed) likely bring about a greater net balance of perfectionist goods than would any alternative action one might perform instead.

The distinction between utilitarianism and perfectionist consequentialism has to do with differences over what has intrinsic value for purposes of morally evaluating actions. And notice that the consequentialist principles presented thus far refer to particular concrete actions and their consequences, so the views (expressed in principles U, HU, and PC) are versions of **act consequentialism.** However, as mentioned at the outset, another important division within the ranks of consequentialists is between act and rule versions of the view. So let us turn from act versions to rule versions.

Rule Consequentialism

Moral rules—rules, for example, against lying, theft, and killing—are generally thought to be significant in thinking about particular moral issues. The importance of moral rules is emphasized by rule consequentialists. Whereas act consequentialism is the view that the rightness of a particular, concrete action—an actual or possible doing by a person at a time—depends on the value of its consequences, **rule consequentialism** is the view that the rightness or wrongness of an action depends on whether it is required, permitted, or prohibited by a rule whose consequences are best.[11] So rule consequentialism involves two levels of evaluation: first, rules that require, permit, or prohibit various courses of action are evaluated by reference to the values of their consequences, and second, a particular action is evaluated by determining whether it is required, permitted, or prohibited by a rule whose consequences are best. Let us explore this view a bit further.

The sense in which a rule can have consequences has to do with the fact that were people to accept the rule in question, this would influence what they do. So, we can evaluate a rule by asking what consequences would likely be brought about were it to be generally accepted in society. Call the value associated with rules their **acceptance value.** This idea is familiar. Think of debates in the sporting world about changing the rules of some sport. The focus in such debates is on the likely effects the proposed rule change would have on the game, were it to be accepted.

According to rule consequentialism, then, the morality of a particular action in some situation depends upon the acceptance values of various competing rules that are relevant to the situation in question. We can thus formulate this theory with the following principle of right conduct:

RC   An action is right if and only if (and because) it is permitted by a rule whose associated acceptance value is at least as high as the acceptance value of any other rule applying to the situation.

In order to better understand this principle, let us illustrate its application with a simple example.

Suppose that I have promised to help you move next Friday morning. Friday morning arrives, and many alternative courses of action are open to me. Among them are these:

A1. Keep my promise (and show up at your place),
A2. Break my promise (and do something else).

Corresponding to each of these alternative actions, we have these rules:

R1. Whenever one makes a promise, keep it,
R2. Whenever one makes a promise, break it if one feels like it.

Now consider the acceptance values associated with these rules. I think we can all agree that acceptance value of **R1** is far greater than that of **R2.** So (ignoring for the moment that there may be other competing rules to be considered in this situation) rule consequentialism implies that one ought to keep one's promise.

Finally notice that act and rule consequentialism may diverge in their moral implications. To stick with the previous example, suppose that by breaking my promise and instead hanging out with some friends at the local pool hall will likely produce a greater level of overall intrinsic value than would the backbreaking work of helping you move. Besides, you've lined up plenty of help; I won't be missed that much. Act consequentialism implies that it would be morally permissible to go ahead and break the promise; rule consequentialism by contrast implies that I am morally obliged to keep my promise.

Brief Summary

Let us pause for a moment to summarize (see Fig. 1.2) what we have covered. As we have seen, the basic consequentialist idea (C) can be developed in a variety of ways; we have considered four versions of this generic approach to ethics.

For now, the main idea to take away from this discussion is that for all varieties of consequentialism, the rightness or wrongness of an action depends entirely on the net intrinsic value of the consequences of either individual actions or rules. Consequentialist theories (and especially utilitarianism) are often discussed in articles and books about disputed moral issues. Some authors appeal to consequentialism to justify their particular views on some moral issue; other authors will contrast their approach with consequentialism.

Applying Consequentialism

To convey a sense of how one is to go about applying consequentialism to a particular moral issue, let us work with act utilitarianism as expressed earlier in U. And to make things fairly manageable, let us consider a rather simple case.

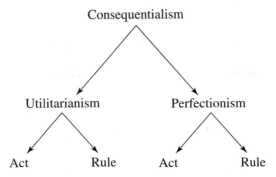

FIGURE 1.2   Some Forms of Consequentialism

Suppose that I am in charge of inviting a guest philosopher to speak at my university and that I've narrowed the choices to two. On the one hand, I can invite Dr. Brilliant, a very well-known and innovative philosopher but whose manner of presentation is decidedly dull. The philosophy faculty will no doubt take pleasure in his presentation and will benefit intellectually from what he has to say, but others will be bored stiff and get little out of the talk. On the other hand, I can invite Dr. Flash who is not nearly as accomplished as Dr. Brilliant but who I know is an extremely engaging speaker. Suppose that five professional philosophers and forty-five students are expected to attend the lecture no matter which of these two philosophers I invite.

Now if I apply U to my situation, it would have me invite the speaker whose talk will produce the greatest amount of overall happiness. A careful application of U would require that I consider each person who will be affected by the lecture of Dr. Brilliant and determine how much happiness (if any) that person would experience as a result of this lecture and then determine how much unhappiness (if any) that person would experience as a result of this lecture. Once I have done this calculation for each person, I then calculate how much total happiness the lecture would cause and how much total unhappiness it would cause in order to arrive at the overall net value associated with Dr. Brilliant's lecture. I do the same for Dr. Flash. The lecture I ought to sponsor and hence the philosopher I ought to invite depends on which talk will result in the greatest amount of intrinsic value.

Obviously, to apply U to one's own choices with any precision would require much factual information: information about one's circumstances, about the various alternative actions one might perform in one's particular circumstances, about the individuals who will be affected either negatively or positively were one to perform a particular action, and about the overall amount of happiness or unhappiness, both short term and long term, that would likely result from each of the various alternative actions. Some critics of consequentialism argue that when it comes to satisfying the practical aim of moral theory—the aim of providing practical guidance for arriving at correct or justified verdicts for the further aim of acting on such verdicts—consequentialism makes implausible demands on what one needs to know in order to apply it to particular cases. Defenders reply that even if *precise* application of this sort of moral theory is not feasible, we can and do make rough estimates of the values of the consequences of various alternative actions, and that in doing so we must realize that the moral verdicts we reach as a result are likely to be highly fallible. But this, say the defenders, is something we just have to live with given our limited information about the effects of our actions.

B. Natural Law Theory

The idea that certain actions or practices are "natural" while others are "unnatural" is commonly offered as a reason why certain "unnatural" actions are wrong and that we ought to do what is natural. Think of popular arguments against homosexuality. This idea of morality being natural is associated with the **natural law theory**.[12]

This type of moral theory is often traced to the thirteenth-century philosopher and theologian St. Thomas Aquinas (1225–1274). It gets its name from the guiding idea that there are objectively true moral principles that are grounded in human nature.[13] Because there are objective facts about human nature that determine what our good consists in, and because moral requirements have to do with maintaining and promoting the human goods, these requirements, unlike the rules of some club or made-up game, are part of the natural order. Because the natural law theory bases right action on considerations of intrinsic value, it is a value-based theory of right conduct, as is consequentialism. However, as we shall see in setting out this theory, natural law theory is opposed to consequentialism—it denies that the *only* considerations that matter when it comes to right action are consequences. So, to understand this theory let us proceed by first presenting its theory of intrinsic value and then presenting its theory of right conduct in two parts: (a) first, the "core" of theory and then (b) the doctrine of double effect.

Theory of Intrinsic Value[14]

According to Aquinas's version of natural law theory, there are four basic intrinsic goods:

- Human life
- Human procreation (which includes raising children)
- Human knowledge
- Human sociability (this value has to do with associations and bonds with others, including friendship, social organizations, and political organizations)

Each of these items, then, has intrinsic value and their destruction is intrinsically bad or evil. These four values are the basis for the core of natural law theory.

The Core

We can state the basic principle of natural law theory roughly as follows:

NLT   An action is right if and only if (and because) in performing the action one does not directly violate any of the basic values.

Thus, killing a human being (with some exceptions explained later) is morally wrong. If we suppose, as many natural law theorists do, that the use of contraceptives thwarts human procreation, then their use is morally wrong. Interfering with the good of knowledge by distorting information or by lying is morally wrong. Destroying legitimate social bonds through the advocacy of anarchy is morally wrong.

But what about hard cases in which no matter what one does, one will violate at least one of the basic values and thus bring about evil through whichever action one chooses? Let us consider a much discussed case involving abortion. Suppose that a pregnant woman has cancer of the uterus and must have a hysterectomy (removal of her uterus) to save her life.

Human life is one of the intrinsic goods, so having the operation will have at least one good effect. But suppose (just for the sake of the example) that from conception the fetus counts as a human life and so having the hysterectomy would bring about the death of the unborn human life. This effect, because it involves the destruction of something having intrinsic value—human life—is an evil. And let us suppose that this moral dilemma is unavoidable in this case because there is no other way to save the woman's life while also preserving the life of her fetus. How does the natural law theory deal with this kind of case? After all, the core of the theory seems to say that any action that violates one or more of the basic goods is wrong, period. But if it really does say this, then we have to conclude that her having the operation is wrong, but also her not having the operation is wrong (because she will fail to preserve her own life). How can natural law theory deal with this moral dilemma?

If we go back and inspect the basic principle of natural law theory, NLT, we notice that what it prohibits are actions that *directly* violate one or more of the basic goods, thereby bringing about evil. But what counts as a direct violation? Can there be morally permissible "indirect" violations? These questions bring us to the next major component of natural law ethics—the doctrine of double effect.

The Doctrine of Double Effect

In addition to the core principle (NLT), the natural law theory also embraces the following set of provisions that compose the **doctrine of double effect**—so named because it concerns cases in which performing an action would have at least one good effect and one bad effect (where good and bad have to do with the theory's list of intrinsic goods). So this doctrine is meant to address the question of whether it is ever morally permissible to knowingly bring about bad or evil consequences where one's aim in action is to bring about or preserve one or more of the basic human goods. Here, then, is a statement of the various provisions making up the doctrine:

> **DDE**   An action that would bring about at least one evil effect and at least one good effect is morally permissible if (and only if) the following conditions are satisfied:

Intrinsic permissibility: The action in question, apart from its effects, is morally permissible;
Necessity: It is not possible to bring about the good effect except by performing an action that will bring about the evil effect in question;
Nonintentionality: The evil effect is not intended—it is neither one's end nor a chosen means for bringing about some intended end;
Proportionality: The evil that will be brought about by the action is not out of proportion to the good being aimed at.

What this principle does is help define the idea of a direct violation of a human good which is the central idea in the core principle, NLT. We shall return to this point in a moment. For the time being, let us explain DDE by showing how it would apply to the case just described.

In applying DDE to our moral dilemma, we must ask whether all four of the doctrine's provisions are satisfied. Let us take them in order. (1) First, since having a hysterectomy is not an intrinsically wrong action, the first requirement is satisfied. (2) Furthermore, given my description of the case, the second requirement of DDE is met because having a hysterectomy is the *only* way to save her life. Were there some other operation or some medication that would both save the woman's life and preserve the life of the fetus, then the necessity condition would not be met and the hysterectomy would be wrong. But we are supposing that there are no such options in this case.

(3) The third requirement rests on the distinction between effects that one intends in action and effects that may be foreseen but are unintended. One intends some consequence or effect when either it is something one is aiming to bring about (an end) or it is one's chosen means for bringing about some desired end. Here is a simple, everyday example. I fire a rifle in order to hit the paper target, but in so doing I know that the noise from the rifle will frighten nearby wildlife. But even though I can foresee that my act of pulling the trigger will frighten those animals, this effect is not intended: it is not my purpose—my purpose is to hit the target, and their being frightened is not a means for achieving my end—the means is taking aim and firing. So the effect of my act of firing—frightening those animals—is not something I intend, rather it is a foreseen but unintended side effect of what I do.

Returning now to our example, we find that this third provision is satisfied because although the death of the unborn child is a foreseen effect of the hysterectomy, its death is not her chief aim or end (saving her own life), and it is not a means by which her life will be saved. After all, were she not pregnant, she would still have the operation to save her life, and so the death of the unborn is a mere unintended and unfortunate side effect of the operation. Removing the cancer is what will save her life.

(4) Finally, the evil that will result from the operation (loss of one innocent human life) is not grossly out of proportion to the good that will result (saving an innocent human life). (When DDE is applied to the morality of war activities, considerations of proportionality of evil to good become especially relevant. See the introduction to chapter 12 and the articles in that chapter by Haig Khatchadourian and James P. Sterba.)

Having explained the DDE, we can now return to the core principle, NLT, and explain how these two elements are related in natural law ethics. The idea is that, according to NLT, we are not to *directly* violate any of the basic human goods. The DDE helps define what counts as a direct violation: direct violations are those that cannot be justified by the doctrine of double effect.

Before going on, it will be useful to pause for a moment to compare the natural law theory with consequentialism. In response to our moral dilemma involving the hysterectomy, an act consequentialist will say that we should consider the value of the consequences of the alternative actions (having a hysterectomy or refraining from this operation) and choose the action with the best consequences. In short, for the act consequentialist good results justify the means. But not for the natural law theorist, because on her theory one may not act in direct violation of the basic goods even if by doing so one would produce better consequences. Good ends do not always justify an action that is a means to those ends. For instance, I am not permitted to intentionally kill one innocent human being (do evil) even if by doing so I can save five others (bring about good). To see how consequentialism and natural law theory yield different verdicts about a difficult moral case, consider the case of a woman who is pregnant, but this time she is suffering from a "tubal" pregnancy, which means that her fetus is lodged in her fallopian tube and thus has not implanted itself into the uterine wall. If nothing is done, both fetus and woman will die. The only thing that can be done to save the woman is to remove the fetus, which will bring about its death. Exercise: apply act consequentialism and the natural law theory to this case to see whether they differ in their moral implications.

Applying Natural Law Theory

In applying the natural law theory to some case in order to determine whether a particular course of action is morally right, one begins with the core principle, NLT, and asks whether the action in question would violate any of the basic goods. If not, then the action is not wrong. But if it would violate one or more of the basic goods, then one has to determine whether the action would constitute a *direct* violation. And to do that, one makes use of the DDE. If the action satisfies all four provisions of DDE, then the violation is not direct and the action is morally permissible. If the action does not pass DDE, then the action involves a direct violation of one or more of the intrinsic goods and is, therefore, wrong.

Of course, as with all moral theories, applying the natural law theory is not a mechanical process. For one thing, one must address questions about the proper interpretation of the four basic human goods. Surely coming to have knowledge of the basic laws that govern the physical universe is intrinsically valuable, if any knowledge is. But what if, for example, I spend my time counting the number of needles on a cactus plant for no particular reason; is the knowledge I acquire about the number of needles really of any intrinsic value? One can raise similar questions about the other three basic human goods. Furthermore, applying the doctrine of double effect raises questions of interpretation. For instance, the proportionality provision requires that the evil caused by an action not be "out of proportion" to the good effects of that action. But, of course, determining when things are out of proportion requires sensitivity to particular cases and the use of good judgment.

These points about interpretation are not meant as a criticism of natural law theory; rather they call attention to the fact that applying it to particular moral issues requires that we interpret its various elements. As we shall see, a similar point applies to Kantian moral theory.

C. Kantian Moral Theory

Most everyone has come across moral arguments that appeal to the **golden rule:** do unto others as you would have them do unto you. This rule encapsulates a kind of test for thinking about the morality of actions: it asks the individual making a moral choice that will affect others to consider how one would like it were one on the receiving end of the action in question. In the case of Thomas Youk with which we began the chapter, the golden rule would have Kevorkian consider what he would want done to (or for) him were he in Youk's situation. Various objections have been made to the golden rule—for instance, it suggests that the rightness or wrongness of an action depends simply on what one does or would desire. But people can have crazy desires. A masochist who inflicts pain on others might cheerfully say that he would have others do unto him as he is doing to them. Do we want to conclude that his causing others pain is morally right? Perhaps there is some interpretation of the golden rule that does not yield the wrong result in the case of the masochist or other examples that have been used against it. Nevertheless, there is something about the *spirit* of the golden rule that seems right. The idea suggested by this rule is that morality requires that we not treat people unfairly, that we respect other persons by taking them into account in our moral deliberations. This suggestion is quite vague but finds one articulation in Kantian moral theory to which we now turn.

Kantian moral theory derives from the moral writings of the German philosopher Immanuel Kant (1724–1804), which continue to have an enormous influence on contemporary ethics.[15]

Central to Kant's moral theory is the idea that moral requirements can be expressed as commands or imperatives that categorically bid us to perform certain actions—requirements that apply to us regardless of what we might happen to want or desire or how such actions bear on the production of our own happiness. Kant thought that specific moral requirements could be derived from a fundamental moral principle that he called the **categorical imperative.** Moreover, Kant offered various alternative formulations of his fundamental moral principle. The two I will consider are the ones that are most often applied to moral issues.

The Humanity Formulation

One of Kant's formulations of his categorical imperative is called the **Humanity formulation:**

> **H**   An action is right if and only if (and because) the action treats persons (including oneself) as ends in themselves and not as mere means.

Obviously, to make use of this principle, we need to know what it means to treat someone as an end and what it means to treat someone as a mere means. Space does not permit a thorough discussion of these ideas, so a few illustrations will have to suffice.[16]

Deception and coercion are two ways in which one can treat another person as a mere means—as an object to be manipulated. Deceiving someone in order to get him or her to do something he or she would otherwise not agree to do constitutes using the person as though that person were a mere instrument at one's disposal for promoting one's own ends. Again, many cases of coercing someone by threats involves attempting to manipulate that person for one's own purposes and hence constitutes an attempt to use him or her as a mere means to one's own ends.

But Kant's Humanity formulation requires not only that we not treat others as mere means to our own ends (a negative requirement), but also that we treat them as ends in themselves (a positive requirement). For Kant, to say that persons are ends in themselves is to say that they have a special worth or value that demands of us that we have a certain positive regard for them. Kant refers to this special worth as *dignity.*[17] So, for instance, if I fail to help those who need and deserve my help, I don't treat them as mere means, but I do fail to have a positive regard for their welfare and thus fail to properly recognize their worth as persons.

Applying Kant's Humanity Formulation

As just explained, applying the Humanity formulation requires consideration of the dual requirements that we not treat people as mere means and that we also not fail to treat them as ends in themselves—as individuals who have dignity. Interpreting these requirements is where the hard work comes in: what are the boundaries when it comes to treating people as *mere* means? If, in walking by, I see that you are wearing a watch and ask you for the time, I am using you as a means for finding out what time it is, but I am not thereby using you as a *mere* means to my own ends. We have noted that deception and coercion represent main ways in which one might use someone as a mere means—as something to be manipulated. So we have a good start on interpreting the idea of treatment as mere means. Here is not the place to consider other ways in which our actions might involve treating someone as a mere means. Rather, the point I wish to make is that we have some idea of what it means to treat someone as a mere means and we must build on this understanding to apply the Humanity formulation to a range of moral issues.

Similar remarks apply to the requirement that we positively treat others as ends in themselves. Here it is interesting to note that Kant argued that in satisfying this requirement, we are obligated to adopt two very general goals—the goal of promoting the (morally permissible) ends of others, and the goal of self-perfection. Such wide-open goals allow a person much latitude in deciding in what ways and on what occasions to promote the ends of others and one's own self-perfection. For Kant, then, applying the positive requirement embedded in H is a matter of figuring out how best to integrate the promotion of the well-being of others and one's own self-perfection into a moral life.

The Universal Law Formulation

Kant's other main formulation of the categorical imperative, the **Universal Law formulation**, expresses a test whereby we can determine whether our actions are right or wrong.

> **UL**   An action is right if and only if one can both (a) consistently conceive of everyone adopting and acting on the general policy (that, is the maxim) of one's action, and also (b) consistently will that everyone act on that maxim.[18]

This formulation will remind readers of the golden rule, though notice that UL does not refer to an agent's wants; rather it represents a kind of consistency test.[19] Unfortunately, interpreting Kant's two-part test requires some explanation. So let me say a bit more about UL and then, using some of Kant's own examples, show how it can be applied.

According to Kant, when we act, we act on a general policy that is called a "maxim." To determine the morality of an action, one formulates the general policy of one's action and asks whether one could consistently both conceive of and will that everyone act on the same policy or, to put it in Kant's terms, one asks whether one could consistently conceive and will that the maxim of one's action become a "universal law" governing everyone's behavior. If so, then the action is right; if not, then the action is wrong. So UL expresses a two-part test one can use to determine the rightness or wrongness of actions. To make Kant's tests more concrete, let us consider a few of Kant's own sample applications of UL.

One of Kant's examples involves making a lying promise—that is, a promise that one has no intention of keeping. Consider a case in which I desperately need money right away and the only way I can get it is by getting a loan which I must promise to repay. I know, however, that I won't be able to repay the loan. The maxim corresponding to the action I am considering is:

> **M1**   Whenever I need money and can get it only by making a lying promise, I will borrow the money by making a lying promise.

Kant's principle, UL, would have me test the morality of making a lying promise by asking whether I could *consistently conceive* and *will* that everyone act on M1—that everyone who needs money in such circumstances as mine make a lying promise. Let us first ask whether this is something I can consistently conceive. If it isn't, then I certainly can't consistently will that everyone adopt and act on it.

Kant claims that when I think through what would be involved in everyone acting on M1, I realize that I cannot even consistently conceive of a world in which everyone in need of money successfully makes lying promises. After all, a world in which everyone in need of money goes around trying to get the money by making a lying promise is one in which successful promising becomes impossible since, as Kant observes, "no one would believe what was promised him but would laugh at all such expressions as vain pretenses."[20] Thus, trying to even conceive of a world in which everyone in need of money acts on M1 involves an inconsistency: it is a world in which (1) *everyone* in need gets money by making a lying promise, but because of the breakdown in the institution of promising that would result, it is a world in which (2) *not everyone* in need gets money by making a lying promise for the reason Kant gives. But if I can't consistently conceive of everyone acting on M1, then my maxim fails the first test mentioned in UL. And if I can't consistently conceive that everyone act on M1, this shows me that, in making a lying promise, I am acting on an immoral policy and that my action is wrong.

But why is the fact that one cannot consistently conceive that everyone act on one's maxim an indication that the action in question is wrong? Kant's idea here seems to be that in performing an action whose maxim I cannot consistently conceive everyone adopting, I am, in effect, proposing to make an exception of myself—an exception that I cannot justify. In making an exception of myself, I am failing to respect others because I'm taking advantage of the fact that many others do not make lying promises. And so these reflections lead us to conclude that making a lying promise is morally wrong.

Here is another example Kant uses to illustrate the application of UL that has to do with clause (b) of UL. Suppose I am in a position to help someone in need but would rather not be bothered. The maxim Kant has us consider is:

M2   Whenever I am able to help others in need, I will refrain from helping them.

Using UL, I am to consider whether I can consistently conceive of a world in which everyone adopts and acts on this maxim. Is such a world conceivable? It would seem so. Granted, a world in which people in need did not receive help from others would be a very unpleasant place. Perhaps the human race would not survive in such a world. But we can certainly conceive of a world in which the human race ceases to exist. So, M2 passes the first part of Kant's UL test.

But can one *will* that M2 be adopted and acted upon by everyone? Upon reflection I realize that if I will that everyone adopt and act on M2, I am thereby willing that others refuse to help me when I am in need. But willing that others refuse to help me is inconsistent with the fact that as a rational agent I do will that others help me when I am in need. That is, as a rational agent, I embrace the following maxim:

RM   I will that others who are able to do so help me when I am in need.

But an implication of my willing that everyone adopt and act on M2 would be:

IM   I will that others who are able to help me, refuse to do so when I am in need.

RM is inconsistent with IM—and IM an implication of willing that everyone adopt and act on M2. Thus, I cannot consistently will that everyone adopt and act on M2. Since I cannot consistently will that everyone adopt M2, then according to clause (b) of Kant's UL, my action of refusing to help others in need is morally wrong.

What is the point of Kant's UL formulation involving two tests? Kant thought that these two tests could distinguish between what he called "narrow" or "perfect" duty and "wide" or "imperfect" duty: maxims that one cannot consistently conceive as adopted and acted on by everyone involve actions that are contrary to narrow duty, whereas those that can be so conceived but which one cannot consistently will involve actions that are contrary to wide duty.

The realm of narrow duty concerns those actions and omissions regarding which one has comparatively little room for when and how one complies with the duty. If I have promised to do something for you on a particular occasion—help you with your taxes—then to fulfill my obligation I must perform some rather specific action (helping you with your taxes) at a certain time. By contrast, a wide duty is one which can be fulfilled in a variety of ways and situations, giving one much leeway in how and when to fulfill the duty. Duties of charity—helping others—are like this.

It is important to notice that in his examples, Kant is not arguing that if everyone went around making lying promises the consequences would be bad and therefore making a lying promise is wrong. Again, he does not argue that the consequences of everyone refusing to help others in need would be bad and therefore refusing help to others is wrong. Such ways of arguing are characteristic of consequentialism, but Kant rejects consequentialism. He has us consider the implications of everyone acting on the general policy behind one's own action because he thinks doing so is a way of revealing any inconsistencies in what one wills, which in turn indicates whether an action fails to respect persons. So the test involved in the categorical imperative is meant to reveal whether one's action shows a proper respect for persons.

Applying the Universal Law Formulation

Since this formulation expresses tests for determining the rightness or wrongness of actions, I have been illustrating how it is to be applied in thinking through moral issues. If we step back from these illustrations, we can summarize the basic procedure to be followed. In applying UL to some actual or contemplated action of yours, here are the basic steps to follow:

- Formulate the maxim on which you are proposing to act, which will have the form "I will ____ whenever ____," where the blanks are filled with a description of your action and circumstances, respectively.
- Next, you consider the possibility of everyone in your circumstances adopting and acting on that same maxim. In particular, you ask yourself whether you can consistently *conceive* of a world in which everyone adopts and acts on the maxim in question. This is the test expressed in clause (a) of UL.
- If you cannot even conceive of such a world, then action on the maxim is morally wrong—a violation of narrow duty. The lying promise example illustrates this result.
- If you can consistently conceive of a world in which everyone adopts and acts on the maxim, then you are to ask yourself whether you could, even so, consistently will that everyone adopt and act on the maxim. This is the test expressed in clause (b) of UL.
- If you cannot consistently will that everyone adopt and act on that maxim, then action on the maxim is wrong—a violation of wide duty. The case of refusing to help others illustrates this result.
- Finally, if your maxim is such that you can both consistently conceive of a world in which everyone adopts and acts on your maxim and consistently will this to be the case—if the maxim passes both tests—then action on the maxim is morally right.

The two main challenges for anyone applying the UL formulation to a particular issue is to correctly formulate one's maxim and then carefully think through Kant's two consistency tests.

How are the two formulations of the categorical imperative—H and UL—related? They are supposed to be alternative formulations of the same basic principle, rather than two entirely distinct principles. One way to see how this might be so is to notice that in cases in which I cannot consistently conceive or will that my maxim be adopted by everyone, I am making an exception of myself, and in doing so either I am treating someone as a mere means or I am failing to treat others as ends in themselves. And, of course, treating others as mere means and failing to treat them as ends in themselves is precisely what the Humanity formulation rules out.

D. Rights-Based Moral Theory

In our brief survey of moral theories up to this point, we have seen how those theories attempt to give accounts of the nature of right (and wrong) action, where "right" is being used in its adjectival sense. Nothing so far has been said about the notion of *a right* or *rights*. However, in moral theory we distinguish between the adjectival use of "right" as in *right action* and its use as a noun as in *a right to life*. One can hold that actions may or may not be right—actions that are either permissible or impermissible to do—without also holding that there are things called rights. Perhaps the most basic idea of a **right** is that of an *entitlement* to be free to engage in some activity, to exercise a certain power, or to be provided with some benefit. One's having such an entitlement typically imposes duties on others (including governments) either to refrain from interfering with one's freedom (or exercise of power) or to provide one with some benefit, depending on the right in question. In explaining the idea of a right and how it figures both in moral theory and in moral controversies, it will be useful to briefly discuss the following topics: (1) some basic elements of a right, (2) categories of rights, (3) rights and moral theory, (4) the idea of a rights-based moral theory, (5) the application of rights-based theories in practice, and (6) so-called rights-focused approaches to moral issues.[21]

Rights: Some Basic Elements

A right has the following characteristics. First, there is the **rights holder**, the party who has or "holds" the right. If you own property, then as a property owner, then you hold a property right. A rights holder may be an individual or a group. Minority rights are one type of group rights. One of the most important philosophical questions about rights concerns the *scope* of rights holders—those beings that *have* rights. According to some views that would restrict the scope of rights holders, only those creatures that have a developed capacity to reason can be the holders of rights. Less restrictive views would allow that anything having interests, including certain nonhuman animals, can be rights holders. Among those who approach moral issues from the perspective of rights—including the issues of abortion, animals, and the environment—we find important differences in views about the requirements for holding rights and thus differences in views about the scope of rights holders.

A second element of a right is what we might call the **rights addressee**, that is, the individual or group with regard to whom the rights holder is entitled to certain treatment. If I have entered into a contract with you to provide you a service, then I am the addressee of your right; you are entitled to demand that I provide that service. The relationship between a rights holder and the corresponding rights addressee can most often be understood in terms of the idea of a *claim*. For instance, in light of a rights holder being entitled to certain treatment by others, we may say that the former has a valid *claim* on the behavior of the latter. And so, corresponding to a rights holder's claim, the addressee of a right has an obligation or duty to either perform or refrain from performing actions that would affect the rights holder and the treatment to which he or she is entitled. Thus, at least for most rights, there is a correlation between the rights of rights holders and certain duties on the part of addressees.

A third element is the **content** of a right, which refers to whatever action, states, or objects the right concerns. The right to freedom of expression differs in content from the right to life. And, of course, these rights differ in content from property rights, and so on.

Finally, another dimension of rights is that of **strength**. Think of a right as a claim on others that has a certain degree of strength in the sense that the stronger right, the stronger the justification needed to defeat the right in question. For instance, some hold the view that nonhuman animals as well as human beings have a right to life. Suppose this is correct. It may still be the case that the right to life of a human being is stronger than the right to life of, say, a dog or cat. The difference in strength here would be reflected, for example, by the fact that one would be arguably justified in euthanizing a dog or cat if the animal were no longer able to walk, while this same sort of reason would not be strong enough to euthanize a human being.

Related to the fact that rights come in degrees of strength is the fact that in some situations someone might be morally justified in performing an action that "goes against" another person's right. And when this occurs, let us say that the person's right has been infringed. So, for instance, suppose my property rights involve the claim that no one may enter my house and use my property without my consent. Now suppose that my next door neighbor's child has been seriously hurt and needs immediate medical attention, and so calling an ambulance is in order. Suppose also that the closest phone available to my neighbor is the one in my house, but I am not at home. Were the neighbor to break into my house to use my phone, he or she would be infringing upon my property rights. But assuming that the neighbor is morally justified in doing this, we may call this case of "going against" my right, a **rights infringement**. By contrast, **rights violations** involve cases where someone goes against another person's rights but is not morally justified in doing so. Thus, as we are using these terms, rights infringements involve actions that are not morally wrong given the circumstances, while rights violations involve actions that are morally wrong.

Categories of Rights

It is common to recognize both negative and positive rights. A **negative right** is an entitlement of noninterference and thus involves a claim by the rights holder that others refrain from interfering with her or his engaging in some activity. Because such rights require that others *not* act in certain ways, they impose what are called negative duties. Rights that are correlated with negative duties are called negative rights. A right to certain liberties such as free speech is an example of a negative right—a right that imposes a duty on others not to interfere with one's expressing one's ideas. A **positive right**, by contrast, involves the rights holder being entitled to something and thus having a valid claim that some other party do or provide something (some service or some good) to that rights holder. Because the duty in question requires positive action on the part of the addressee, the corresponding right is called a positive right. For instance, Article 25 of the United Nations 1948 *Universal Declaration of Human Rights* states:

> Everyone has a right to a standard of living adequate for the health and well-being of himself and of his family, including food, clothing, housing, and medical care and necessary social services, and the right to security in the event of unemployment, sickness, disability, widowhood, old age, or other lack of livelihood in circumstances beyond his control.

This (alleged) right is supposed to be held by all human beings and presumably it is a right that one be provided certain necessities by one's nation or perhaps other nations in a position to provide such goods.

In addition to the distinction between negative and positive rights, it is also important to distinguish **moral rights** from legal rights. This distinction has to do with the source of a right. A so-called moral right is a right that a being has independently of any legal system or other set of conventions.[22] So, for instance, it is often claimed that all human beings, in virtue of facts about humanity, have certain rights, including the rights to life, liberty, and well-being. Such alleged universal rights of humanity[23] are typically referred to as **human rights**. A **legal right** is something that results or comes into existence as the result of a legal statute or some other form of governmental activity. One reason why it is important to distinguish moral from legal rights is that controversies over moral issues are often framed in terms of whether some individual (including nonhumans) or group has certain moral rights—rights that may or may not be recognized by some particular legal system and thus not (at the time in question) count as legal rights within the system in question. So, in debates over the morality of various activities and practices where talk of rights enter the discussion, one is mainly concerned with moral rights.

Another common distinction, often associated with human rights, is the distinction between "basic" and "nonbasic" rights. Roughly, speaking, a **basic right** is a universal right that is especially important in the lives of individuals—rights such as the rights to life and to liberty, which arguably must be met in order to live a decent life. One's right to life and freedom from torture is clearly more important compared with one's right to be repaid a sum of money by a borrower. Just how to distinguish basic from nonbasic rights is controversial, and we need not examine various proposals here. It is enough for our purposes to leave the distinction at a more or less intuitive level and recognize that rights differ in their importance and thus in their comparative strengths.

Let us now turn from our general discussion of rights to their place in moral theory and in contemporary debates over particular moral issues.

Rights and Moral Theory

A great deal of contemporary discussion about moral issues is couched in terms of rights. Does a human fetus have a moral right to life? Does a terminally ill patient in severe pain have a moral right to die? Do people have a moral right to reproduce by cloning? Do animals have moral rights? In this subsection and the next, I want to explain how rights figure in moral theories. In doing so, I will make two main points: (1) All of the moral theories we have already surveyed (as well as the two that follow) can recognize moral rights. (2) However, what is distinctive of a rights-based moral theory is that it takes rights to be in some sense more basic than such notions as value (including utility), dignity, and right action (including duty). Let us take these points one by one.

First, a utilitarian who recognizes moral rights will attempt to explain rights on the basis of utility by claiming that a moral right is a kind of entitlement that imposes various claims on addressees justified by the fact that its recognition will contribute to the maximization of overall welfare. This means that for the utilitarian—who, as a consequentialist, embraces a value-based moral theory—rights are derivative rather than basic in her moral theory. Similar remarks apply to the moral theories featured in this chapter. For instance, according to Kantian ethics, all human beings possess moral rights in virtue of having a certain status—being the sort of creature that possesses dignity. Having this sort of status, according to the Kantian, demands that persons be treated in certain ways and thus that they enjoy certain moral rights. Thus, utilitarians and Kantians can agree that persons have moral rights. They disagree in how they explain the basis of such rights. And notice that because utilitarians and Kantians purport to explain moral rights in terms of more basic elements—utility in the case of utilitarianism, the possession of dignity in the case of Kantians—it would be incorrect to think of these theories as rights-based.

Rights-Based Moral Theory

Might there be a **rights-based moral theory**—a moral theory according to which rights are more basic than utility, dignity, and even duty? Unlike the other theories featured in this chapter, rights-based theories are relatively underdeveloped despite the fact that appeals to rights are very common in discussions of moral issues. What we find in the writings of authors who appeal to rights in discussing particular moral issues is that they often fail to indicate the nature of rights—whether they have a consequentialist, natural law, Kantian, or some other basis on the one hand, or whether, on the other hand, they are conceived as basic in the theory. So let us consider the idea of a rights-based moral theory.

According to such a theory, rights are even more basic than right action and duty. But one might think that duties must be more basic than rights and so there cannot be a rights-based moral theory. After all, as explained above, a typical moral right is a claim one party has against others that they do or refrain from some activity, and it is natural to think of these burdens as duties or obligations that are owed to the rights-holder. If I have a right to free speech, then this seems to entail that others have a duty not to interfere with me in certain ways and thus that the concept of duty must be used to explain what a right is. If so, then duty is more basic than a right and so a rights-based theory is conceptually impossible.

Granted, it is common to explain the idea of a moral right of one party in terms of certain corresponding duties on the part of others. But as J. L. Mackie, a defender of rights-based moral theory explains, instead of thinking of rights in terms of duties, "we could look at it the other way round: what is primary is A's having this right in a sense indicated by the prescription 'Let A be able to do X if he chooses,' and the duty of others not to interfere follows from this."[24]

So let us follow Mackie and suppose that there is no conceptual barrier to there being a rights-based theory of right and wrong action. How might it be developed? The idea would be to begin with a list of moral rights, perhaps distinguishing such basic rights, including for instance the rights to life and to liberty, from nonbasic rights. Once one has identified the various moral rights, one could then proceed to define or characterize the concepts of right and wrong action in terms of moral rights. Here, then, is how we might express the basic idea of right conduct for a rights-based theory:

R   An action is right if and only if (and because) in performing it either (a) one does not violate the moral rights of others, or (b) in cases where it is not possible to respect all such rights because they are in conflict, one's action is among the best ways to protect the most important rights in the case at hand.

This principle—it is more of a *scheme*—all by itself is too abstract to be of any practical use. What needs to be added, of course, is a specification of the moral rights that figure in this scheme and their relative importance. Mackie proposes a single basic moral right: the right of persons to "choose how they shall live."[25] But this right to choose is wide open, and to work our way from it to specific moral obligations, we will need to specify what sorts of more specific rights people have in virtue of having this most basic right. Perhaps we can begin by recognizing the Jeffersonian moral rights to life, liberty, and the pursuit of happiness. And then, for each of these general rights, we might specify them further by recognizing a set of specific moral rights including, for example, a right to free speech.

So, specifying a single basic and perhaps very general moral right (or set of them) and working toward a specification of more specific moral rights is one task of a rights-based moral theory. However one works out the details of what the moral rights are, we must keep in mind the obvious fact that in some contexts moral rights will come into conflict. My right of free speech may conflict with the rights that others have to be safe from harm. Suppose, for instance, that on some occasion, my speaking out would seriously jeopardize the personal safety of others. If so, then in such circumstances, it is plausible to suppose that people's right of personal safety overrides a person's right to free speech. How is one to determine whether one right overrides another in cases of conflict? This question brings us to the issue of applying a rights-based theory to moral issues.

Applying a Rights-Based Moral Theory

Principle (or scheme) R purports to explain an action's being morally right (and by implication morally wrong) in terms of respecting fundamental moral rights. Clause (a) of R covers the easy case in which one's action simply does not come into contact with the moral rights of others. I get up in the morning and decide to eat Cheerios for breakfast. Unusual cases aside, this action has nothing to do with the moral rights of others—I'm morally free to eat the Cheerios or not. Clause (b), however, is where a rights-based approach to moral problems is most relevant: one can frame many of the disputed moral issues featured in this book as a conflict of rights: right to life versus right to choice; right to express oneself in speech and writing versus right to public safety, and so on.

So in applying R (supplemented with a theory of rights) to moral issues, the challenge is to find the best way of properly balancing competing rights claims in arriving at a moral verdict about what ought to be done. As I will explain more thoroughly below in connection with the ethics of prima facie duty, it is very doubtful that there is some fixed mechanical procedure that one can use in arriving at a correct or justified moral verdict in particular cases based on a consideration of competing rights. Rather, what one needs is what philosophers call **moral judgment**—roughly, an acquired skill at discerning what matters the most morally speaking and coming to an all-things-considered moral verdict where this skill cannot be entirely captured by a set of rules. The point to stress here is that, as with the other moral theories we are considering, applying a moral theory—its principles—to particular issues is not a mechanical process. But this does not take away from the value of such theories in guiding one's moral deliberations and subsequent choices.

Rights-Focused Approaches to Moral Issues

We have noted that talk of rights is very common in moral thought and discussion. However, we have also noted that in thinking about a moral issue in terms of competing rights claims, one need not accept a rights-based moral theory as just described. As noted earlier, consequentialists, Kantians, and natural law theorists can and do recognize rights—although on these theories rights are not what is most morally basic in the theory. So, because one may appeal to rights in discussing a moral issue without accepting a rights-based moral theory, we must recognize what we may call **rights-focused** approaches to moral issues. To say that an author's approach to a moral issue is rights-focused is simply to say that the author appeals to rights as a basis for taking a stand on the issue at hand—the author may or may not also embrace a rights-based moral theory. In my article introductions, I have chosen to use the term "rights-focused" in summarizing the views of those authors who appeal primarily to rights in their article, unless the author makes it clear that he or she embraces a rights-based moral theory.

E. Virtue Ethics

Sometimes our moral thinking is dominated by thoughts about what sort of person one would be if one were to perform some action. The thought of living up to certain ideals or virtues of what a morally good person is like is crucial here. Being an unselfish person is an ideal that we may use in evaluating some course of action, and sometimes we may think, "Not helping her would be selfish on my part, so I'm going to help." When our moral thinking takes this turn, we are evaluating actions in terms of virtue and vice. The ideas of virtue and vice have played a negligible role in the moral theories we have surveyed (at least as I have presented them).[26] However, inspired primarily by the ethical views of the ancient Greek philosophers Plato and Aristotle, **virtue ethics** makes the concepts of virtue and vice central in moral theory. Such theories, as I will understand them, take the concepts of virtue and vice to be more basic than the concepts of right and wrong, and thus propose to define or characterize the latter in terms of the former.[27]

One might characterize right and wrong in terms of virtue and vice in different ways, but here (roughly) is how Rosalind Hursthouse, whose article on abortion is included in chapter 9, formulates a virtue ethical principle of right action:

> **VE**   An action is right if and only if (and because) it is what a virtuous agent (acting in character) would not avoid doing in the circumstances under consideration.

How are we to understand the concept of a virtuous agent featured in this principle? One straightforward way is to say that the virtuous agent is one who has the virtues. But what is a virtue? And which ones does the virtuous agent have?

A **virtue** is a trait of character or mind that typically involves dispositions to act, feel, and think in certain ways and that is central in the *positive* evaluation of persons. Honesty and loyalty are two commonly recognized virtues. The trait of honesty, for instance, involves at a minimum being disposed to tell the truth and avoid lying, as well as the disposition to have certain feelings about truth telling (positive ones) and about lying (negative ones). Honesty, as a virtue, is a trait that has positive value and contributes to what makes someone a good person. In contrast to a virtue, a **vice** is a trait of character or mind which typically involves dispositions to act, feel, and think in certain ways, and that is central in the *negative* evaluation of persons. So, for instance, opposed to the virtue of honesty is the vice of dishonesty which may be understood as having inappropriate dispositions of action and feeling regarding truth telling and lying. Furthermore, as a vice, dishonesty has negative value and contributes to what makes someone a morally bad person. So, in general, virtues and vices are character traits that are manifested in having certain dispositions to act and feel in certain ways and that bear on what makes a person morally good or bad. Here, then, is a short (and by no means complete) list of fairly commonly recognized moral virtues and their corresponding vices:[28]

- Honesty/Dishonesty
- Courage/Cowardice
- Justice/Injustice
- Temperance/Intemperance
- Beneficence/Selfishness
- Humility/Arrogance
- Loyalty/Disloyalty
- Gratitude/Ingratitude

Applying Virtue Ethics

To apply VE to a particular case, then, we must first determine which character traits are the virtues that are possessed by the virtuous agent (we may begin with the previous list), and then determine how, on the basis of such traits, this agent would be disposed to act in the circumstances in question. An action that a virtuous agent, acting in character, would not fail to perform in some circumstance is morally required, an action she might or might not do at her discretion is morally optional, and one that she would avoid doing is morally wrong.

Of course, in applying virtue ethics to disputed moral issues, we encounter the fact that more than one virtue is relevant to the case at hand and that one of them—say, honesty—favors telling the truth, whereas one of the others—say, loyalty—favors telling a lie. In such cases of conflict among the virtues, we must examine the particular details of the case at hand and ask such questions as, "What is at stake here?" "How important is telling the truth in this case?" "How important is loyalty to an organization?" It is only by examining the details of such cases of conflict that we can come to an all-things-considered moral evaluation of some particular action based on considerations of virtue. This point is reflected in VE's reference to a virtuous agent *acting in character.* Presumably, such an ideal agent has the sort of practical wisdom or judgment that is required in order for her to discern which virtue consideration, from among the competing virtue considerations in a particular case, has the most weight. As I have been noting all along in presenting the various moral theories—something that we explore a bit further in the next subsection—the application of moral theories to particular issues requires moral judgment.

F. Ethics of Prima Facie Duty

Whereas consequentialism, for instance, features a single moral principle of right conduct, what I am calling the **ethics of prima facie duty** features a plurality of basic moral principles of right conduct. The most famous version of this kind of view was developed by the twentieth-century British philosopher W. D. Ross (1877–1971). To understand the elements of Ross's view, we need to do the following: (1) explain what he means by talk of "prima facie duty"; (2) present his basic principles of prima facie duty; and then (3) explain the role of moral judgment in applying them in practice.

The Concept of a Prima Facie Duty

To say that one has a **prima facie duty** to perform some action is to say that one has *some* moral reason to perform the action, but the reason in question might be *overridden* by some other moral reason that favors not performing the action. The best way to understand the concept is with an example. Suppose I have promised to pick you up on Saturday by 10:00 A.M. so that you can get to a very important job interview (your car is in the shop). Ross would say that because of my having made a promise to you, I have a prima facie duty (of fidelity—see later discussion) to do what I said I would do: pick you up by 10:00 A.M. on Saturday. But now suppose that as I am about to leave to pick you up, my child falls off the roof of my house and needs immediate medical attention. Ross would say that here I have a prima facie duty to take my child to the emergency ward of the hospital. So, I have a prima facie duty to start out for your place and a conflicting prima facie duty to attend to my child: as things have turned out, I am not able to fulfill both prima facie duties. Now the point of calling a duty "prima facie" is that the moral reasons provided by such facts as that I've made a promise or that my child needs my help can be outweighed by other moral reasons that favor doing some other action. Ross puts this point by saying that a prima facie duty can be overridden—beat out—by a competing prima facie duty. In the case I've described, because it is my child and because she needs immediate medical attention, my prima facie duty to help her overrides my prima facie duty to come pick you up. When one prima facie duty prevails in some conflict of duties situation, it becomes one's *all-things-considered duty*—it is what you ought, all things considered, to do in that circumstance. So, for Ross, to say that one has a prima facie duty to perform action *A* on some occasion is to say that one has a moral reason to do *A,* and unless something comes up that is morally more important, one has an all-things-considered duty to do *A* on that occasion.

Ross's theory of right conduct, which is our main concern, is based partly on his theory of intrinsic value to which we now turn.

Ross's Theory of Intrinsic Value

Ross held that there are four basic intrinsic goods:

1. Virtue. The disposition to act from certain desires, including the desire to do what is morally right, is intrinsically good.
2. Pleasure. States of experiencing pleasure are intrinsically good.
3. Pleasure in proportion to virtue. The state of experiencing pleasure in proportion to one's level of virtue is intrinsically good.

4. Knowledge. Having knowledge (at least of a nontrivial sort) is intrinsically good.

The items on this list are the basis for some of Ross's basic prima facie duties—call them "value-based" prima facie duties. What Ross calls duties of "special obligation" are not based on his theory of intrinsic value.

Ross's Prima Facie Duties

Here, then, is Ross's list of basic prima facie duties, organized into the two categories just mentioned:

Basic Value-Based Prima Facie Duties

1. Justice: prima facie, one ought to ensure that pleasure is distributed according to merit.
2. Beneficence: prima facie, one ought to help those in need and, in general, increase the virtue, pleasure, and knowledge of others.
3. Self-improvement: prima facie, one ought to improve oneself with respect to one's own virtue and knowledge.
4. Nonmaleficence: prima facie, one ought to refrain from harming others.

Basic Prima Facie Duties of Special Obligation

5. Fidelity: prima facie, one ought to keep one's promises (including the implicit promise to be truthful).
6. Reparation: prima facie, one ought to make amends to others for any past wrongs one has done them.
7. Gratitude: prima facie, one ought to show gratitude toward one's benefactors.

The first four basic prima facie duties, then, make reference to what has intrinsic value according to Ross's theory of value. Ross himself points out that the prima facie duties of justice, beneficence, and self-improvement "come under the general principle that we should produce as much good as possible."[29] This part of Ross's theory fits the characterization of consequentialism.

The duties of special obligation do not make reference to what has intrinsic value; the duties of fidelity, reparation, and gratitude do not depend for their prima facie rightness on the values of the consequences of those actions. This part of Ross's theory is clearly duty-based or deontological. Overall, then, Ross's theory represents a hybrid: part consequentialist, part deontological.

Applying the Ethics of Prima Facie Duties

But how, on Ross's view, does one determine in some particular case that one prima facie duty overrides another, competing prima facie duty? Ross denies that there is any correct super-principle like the principle of utility or Kant's categorical imperative to which one might appeal to determine one's all-things-considered duty in cases of conflict. Nor is there any fixed ranking of the various prima facie duties such that the duty higher up on the list always beats out duties below it. Rather, according to Ross, in determining which prima facie duty is most "stringent" in some particular case and thus represents one's all-things-considered duty, one must examine the details of the case by using one's *judgment* about which of the competing duties is (in that situation) strongest. As mentioned earlier, moral judgment is a matter of discerning the morally important features of a situation and determining what ought or ought not to be done, where doing so cannot be fully captured in a set of rules. Judgment is largely a matter of skill that one may acquire through experience.

One final remark. One need not agree with Ross's own list of basic prima facie duties in order to accept the other tenets of Ross's view. For instance, Robert Audi has recently defended an ethic of prima facie duties that features ten basic prima facie duties.[30] Audi, unlike Ross, distinguishes duties not to lie from duties of fidelity, and he adds two additional duties to Ross's list. So were we to make the additions Audi proposes, we would have the following:

8. Veracity: prima facie, one ought not to lie.
9. Enhancement and preservation of freedom: prima facie, one ought to contribute to increasing or at least preserving the freedom of others with priority given to removing constraints over enhancing opportunities.
10. Respectfulness: prima facie, one ought, in the manner of our relations with other people, treat others respectfully.

The main point I wish to make here is that Ross's version of an ethic of prima facie duties is one version of this general sort of view. Audi's view attempts to build upon and improve Ross's view.

This completes our survey of some of the leading moral theories that figure importantly in many of this book's readings. As mentioned earlier, I recommend using these summaries of the six theories as an aid in understanding those writings in which an author appeals to one or other of them. The remaining section and the appendix address questions about moral theory that are likely to occur to the reader:

- What is the point of moral theory in thinking about disputed moral issues in light of the fact that there is a variety of competing moral theories?
- What about theories that appeal to the will of God or to the norms of society of culture in determining what is right or wrong?

3.   COPING WITH MANY MORAL THEORIES

This chapter began with a brief overview of the central concepts and guiding aims of moral theory and then proceeded to survey six types of moral theory. In working through the various moral problems featured in this book, one will find that different moral theories often yield different and conflicting answers to questions about the morality of some action. The natural law theory, for instance, arguably condemns all homosexual behavior as morally wrong; a consequentialist approach does not. So the application of one theory to an issue may yield one moral verdict, while the application of another theory may yield a conflicting moral verdict. What, then, a student may ask, is the point of thinking about disputed moral issues from the perspective of moral theory? It all seems rather arbitrary.

This is a completely understandable question whose answer requires that one move from a focus on particular moral issues to questions about the nature and evaluation of moral theories. It is not possible to fully address such questions in a chapter whose aim is to provide students with a basic understanding of a range of moral theories. But because of its importance, the question does deserve to be addressed, even if briefly. In so doing, I will first offer some remarks about evaluating a moral theory, and then I will suggest a way of looking at the various moral theories for the illumination I think they provide in thinking about moral issues.

Evaluating a Moral Theory

Philosophers who develop a moral theory do not just state some moral principle or other and leave it at that; rather, they *argue* for whatever principles they are proposing. And we can critically evaluate their arguments. So the first point I wish to make is that there can be rational debate about a moral theory—not any old moral theory is as good as any other.

Furthermore, there are standards for evaluating a moral theory—standards that are not arbitrary but rather have to do with the guiding aims of a moral theory that we discussed in section 1 of this chapter. Corresponding to the theoretical aim of moral theory—the aim of explaining what makes something right or wrong, good or bad—is the principle of **explanatory power:**

> A moral theory should feature principles that explain our more specific considered moral beliefs, thus helping us understand *why* actions, persons, and other objects of moral evaluation are right or wrong, good or bad. The better a theory's principles in providing such explanations, the better the theory.

This principle appeals to our "considered" moral beliefs, which may be defined as those moral beliefs that are *deeply held* and *very widely shared.* I hope that everyone reading this text believes that murder is wrong, that rape is wrong, and that child molestation is wrong. The list could be extended. Moreover, such moral beliefs are (for those who have them) very likely deeply held convictions. The principle of explanatory power tells us to evaluate a moral theory by determining whether its principles properly explain why such actions are morally wrong. Similar remarks apply to widely shared and deeply held beliefs about our obligations. So we can help confirm a moral theory by showing that it can properly explain the rightness or wrongness of actions about whose moral status we are virtually certain. Correlatively, we can criticize a moral theory by showing that it does not properly explain the rightness or wrongness of actions about whose moral status we are virtually certain. Applying this principle requires that we can tell what counts as a good explanation of the rightness or wrongness of actions. This is a topic of lively and ongoing philosophical inquiry whose study would take us far beyond the scope of this book. But in thinking about moral issues from the perspective of moral theory, the reader is invited to consider not only what a theory implies about some action or practice, but also what explanation it provides for whatever verdict it reaches about the action or practice under consideration. (I return briefly to this matter toward the end of this section.)

According to the practical aim of moral theory, we want moral principles that will help guide our moral deliberations and subsequent choices. Corresponding to this aim is the principle of **practical guidance:**

> A moral theory should feature principles that are useful in guiding moral deliberation toward correct or justified moral verdicts about particular issues which we can then use

to help guide choice. The better a theory's principles are in providing practical guidance, the better the theory.

Any moral theory that would yield inconsistent verdicts about some particular concrete action is obviously of no practical help on the issue at hand. Furthermore, a moral theory whose principles are so vague that it fails to have clear implications for a range of moral issues is again of no help in guiding thought about those issues. Finally, a moral theory whose principles are extremely difficult to apply because, for example, applying them requires a great deal of factual information that is humanly impossible to acquire, is at odds with the principle of practical guidance. These are three measures to consider in evaluating how well a moral theory does in satisfying the principle of practical guidance and thus how well it does in satisfying the practical aim of moral theory.

These brief remarks are only meant to indicate how one can begin to evaluate a moral theory. Hopefully, what I have said is enough to make a start on answering the challenge that began this section. Let us now move on to the second point I wish to make in response to the challenge.

Moral Theory and Moral Illumination[31]

I conclude with a plea for the importance of moral theory, even if there is no one theory that currently commands the allegiance of all philosophers who specialize in ethics. The plea is that moral theory can help focus and sharpen our moral thinking about particular issues, and it can thereby provide a kind of insight and illumination of moral issues that is otherwise easily missed. Let me explain.

No doubt readers of this chapter will have noticed that the various moral theories we have surveyed build on ideas that are very familiar. To see this, let us return to the case of euthanasia with which this chapter began. You may recall that in that case, Dr. Jack Kevorkian brought about the death of his patient Thomas Youk by a lethal injection. We described Kevorkian's action as an instance of voluntary active euthanasia. Now if one pays attention to on-line discussions and newspaper editorials that focus on this moral issue, and listens to the views of politicians and other social activists who discuss it, we find that some arguments appeal to the likely effects or consequences of allowing this practice. And of course, the idea that an action's rightness or wrongness is to be explained by reference to its likely consequences is the main idea of the various varieties of consequentialist moral theory. Similar remarks can be made about the other five types of moral theory presented in section 2. Some arguments over euthanasia focus on the intrinsic value of human life—one of the four basic human goods featured in natural law ethics. Related to questions about end-of-life moral decisions, some have argued that providing a terminal patient with painkilling drugs that will knowingly cause the patient to die of liver failure before succumbing to cancer is nevertheless permissible because death in this case is merely a foreseen side effect of the painkilling drug. Here we have a tacit appeal to the doctrine of double effect. Again, we find arguments that appeal to the special dignity and worth of human beings, as well as arguments that appeal to such alleged rights as the right to die or the right to die with dignity—arguments that tacitly appeal, respectively, to elements of Kantian moral theory and to rights-based moral theory (or at least rights-focused approaches to moral issues). Similar points can be made about virtue ethics and the ethics of prima facie duties.

So the first point I wish to make about studying moral issues from the perspective of moral theory is that one thereby gains greater insight and clarity into the kinds of arguments that one commonly reads and hears (and perhaps is disposed to give) over disputed moral issues. In fact, one may think of the various moral theories we have surveyed as attempts to develop such familiar ideas from moral thought and discourse in a rigorous philosophical manner. To really understand some moral issue for purposes of making up your own mind about it, you first have to understand the issue, which in turn requires that you consider the various reasons that reflective people bring to bear in thinking and debating the issue at hand. Such reasons, as I have just indicated, are often developed systematically in a moral theory. So coming to understand moral theory helps provide a kind of moral illumination or insight into moral issues.

The further point is this. Different moral theories differ partly because of how they propose to *organize* our moral thinking about practical issues. For instance, utilitarianism has us organize our moral thinking about some issue in terms of its likely effects on well-being or happiness. Virtue ethics, by contrast, has us organize our moral thinking around considerations of virtue and vice, asking us, for example, to view a proposed course of action in terms of what it would express about our characters. Rights-based moral theories have us think about an issue in terms of competing moral claims that can be made by various involved parties. Similar remarks apply to Kantian moral theory, natural law theory, and the ethics of prima facie duty. But let us put aside for the moment the fact that the various moral theories in question purport to provide competing answers to questions about the underlying nature of right and wrong, good and bad. If we do, we might then view these theories as providing different ways of diagnosing and thinking about a moral problem, where in some cases the best approach is utilitarian, whereas in others the best approach is from a virtue ethics perspective, and still in others, some other moral theory best gets at what is morally most important to consider. In other words, it strikes me that some practical moral questions are best approached from, say, the perspective of act utilitarianism, others not. Here is an example that comes up in the chapter on war, terrorism, and torture and is discussed in the reading from Alan M. Dershowitz. He considers a "ticking bomb" scenario in which a captured terrorist very likely knows the whereabouts of a powerful explosive set to go off in a heavily populated city. Would it be morally permissible to torture this (uncooperative) individual in an attempt to extract information that might be used to locate and defuse the explosive? Given what is at stake in *this* particular case, I can well understand why one's moral thinking would be guided by essentially act utilitarian reasoning. But in other cases, thinking in these terms seems morally askew. Thomas E. Hill Jr., in his article included in chapter 14, argues that in thinking about how we ought to relate to the environment, utilitarianism fails to properly diagnose what is wrong with certain ways of treating the environment. He also argues that thinking in terms of rights fails to get at what is really morally important about our dealings with the environment. His proposal is to think in terms of virtue—ideals of excellence—rather than in terms of utility or rights. As explained in section 1 of this chapter, a moral theory is partly in the business of providing practical guidance for moral thinking and decision making. My suggestion is that in some contexts it makes sense to think as an act utilitarian, in other contexts it makes most sense to think in terms of rights, and in still other contexts, thinking in terms of virtue and excellence seems most illuminating. The same can be said about the other moral theories we have surveyed. Thinking exclusively about all moral issues in terms of some one particular moral theory assumes a *one-size-fits-all* approach to moral thinking. I am suggesting that this probably isn't the best way to use theory to illuminate practice.[32]

Returning now to the challenge that began this section, I have tried to address it in two ways. First, moral theory is not arbitrary in the sense that you can just pick and choose your favorite or make up your own: there are standards for evaluating moral theories that have to do with the theoretical and practical aims of moral theory. Second, the variety of moral theories on offer can positively aid in one's moral thinking about controversial moral issues in two ways. First, it can do so by providing rigorous articulations of common ideas about morality. And second, it can do so if one views these theories as diagnostic tools for getting to the heart of moral problems. Some tools are better for some jobs than other tools. My suggestion is that a particular moral theory may be a better tool than others when it comes to thinking through some particular issue, though a different theory may be better at helping one think through other issues.

APPENDIX: ETHICS BY AUTHORITY?

DIVINE COMMAND THEORY AND ETHICAL RELATIVISM

The idea that morality depends on some authority—whether the will of God or the norms of one's culture—is well known, even if not generally well understood. The readings in this collection by and large reflect the impact of the six moral theories presented in section 2 on philosophical thinking about disputed moral issues. This does not mean that other moral theories or approaches to moral issues are not worthy of philosophical attention. My presentation has been selective. However, because what I am calling ethics by authority in one form or another will likely occur to readers, I think it is important to explain why many who think about moral issues have grave reservations about both divine command theory and ethical relativism.

According to the **divine command theory,** what is right or wrong depends on God's commands in the sense that what *makes* an action right or wrong are mere facts about God's commands, nothing more. On this view, an action is wrong whenever (and because) God commands that we not do the action. An action is morally obligatory whenever (and because) God commands that we do it. Otherwise an action is morally optional. So the fundamental moral principle of this sort of theory can be expressed as follows:

> **DCT** An action is right if and only if (and because) God does not command that we not do that action.

For many people, being told that God does or does not command some action is crucial in their thinking about moral issues. But surely if God commands that we perform some action, there must be some reason why God issues this command—some reason that explains *why* the action is something we ought or ought not to do. But then, as philosophers, we can ask what it is about the action in question that makes it wrong and is a basis for God's command. And once we put the question to ourselves in this way, we are simply raising the general moral questions about the right and the good that we began with. So, appealing to God's commands (at least for believers) may help the believer decide what to do, but the fact that God commands this or that action does not answer the deep question about the underlying nature of right and wrong that a moral theory attempts to answer—it does not plausibly address the main *theoretical aim* of moral theory explained earlier.

Of course, someone sympathetic to DCT may claim that it is just God's commands that make an action right or wrong. But this won't be acceptable to a theist who thinks that God's actions are rational. After all, if one says that there is no reason behind God's commands, then one is saying that God has no good reason for commanding that we keep our promises and not commit murder, that God's commands are completely arbitrary. But this can't be right. So, a theist must say that there are facts about an action that make it wrong and that since God knows all facts, and since God is all-good, God commands that we do what is (independently of his commands) right and not do what is wrong.

As for **ethical relativism,** there is a good deal of confusion generated by the vague (and unfortunately popular) talk of morality being relative. Surely anyone can agree that whether a particular action—say, addressing a professor by her first name—is morally right may be importantly affected by what a society considers to be insulting. In the United States at present, the social norms that help specify what constitutes an insult do not seem to consider a student addressing a university professor by her first name as an insult. If that's right, then a student in a U.S. university would not be insulting a professor in addressing her by her first name (unless, perhaps, the professor had expressed a desire not to be so addressed). But in other countries (at present), the social norms governing student–professor relationships are such that the sort of address in question does constitute an insult. If we agree that insults are morally wrong (see the chapters dealing with hate speech and with sexism, racism, and reparation for more about the morality of insults), then we can easily see that the action of addressing a professor by her first name is morally wrong in some social circumstances (when in certain countries) and not in others (when in the United States). But this kind of context-sensitivity of morality according to which one's circumstances, including the social norms of one's culture, may have a bearing on what is right or wrong to do in that culture is something that all of the moral theories we have considered do accept.

So if ethical relativism is to represent a moral theory that competes with the ones we have surveyed, what must it say? It must say something like this: (1) there are no correct moral norms or principles that are valid for all cultures at all times; rather (2) there are only the moral norms that some group or culture happens to accept, and these norms—*no matter what those norms say*—are what determine what is right or wrong for members of that group or culture. We can encapsulate these ideas in the following principle:

> **ER**   An action (performed by members of a group G) is right if and only if the moral norms that are accepted by G permit the performance of the action.

Thus, if some culture accepts the moral norm that the enslavement of other human beings is morally right, then (according to the relativist) enslavement really *is* right—for those people.

Now relativism has its popular allure. Some people seem to take ethical relativism as an enlightened view about the true nature of morality. In order to disabuse the reader of the kind of simple ethical relativism just described, consider abortion. Suppose we find out that a majority of current U.S. citizens accept a set of moral norms that find nothing wrong with abortion. If we suppose that the moral norms of some culture are those norms that are held by a majority of its members, then according to ethical relativism, we would have to conclude that abortion (for members of U.S. culture) is morally right. Even if you think that abortion is morally right, do you (the reader) really think that the actual moral rightness and wrong-ness of an action depends on majority opinion? If so, then you might think we can settle moral issues by a vote. But this would mean that no matter what the majority of some group accepts as part of that group's moral norms—genocide, slavery, infanticide, lying, cheating, whatever—those actions would be right for members of that group. Granted, the members of some group may honestly *think* that genocide is morally right, but thinking something is right does not *make* it right. Right?

So, we can agree to the following thesis of **context-sensitivity:**

CS   The rightness or wrongness of an action may depend in part on facts about the agent and her circumstances, where her circumstances may include facts about the norms for what counts as constituting insults, a person's privacy, proper respect for others, and so forth.

The example of insulting behavior illustrates how CS can be true. But as we have already noted, CS is compatible with all of the nonrelativist moral theories that we have surveyed in section 2. According to each of those theories, there are basic moral principles or norms whose correctness is objective and not dependent on whether they happen to be accepted by some culture. Of course, in applying one of these principles to some particular case, we must consider various details of the case including facts about particular agents and their circum-stances as well as facts about the society in which one happens to live.

Whether some version of ethical relativism can be defended is controversial and cannot be settled here. If so, it would have to improve upon ER. My main point was to note the important difference between CS and ER (they are often confused) and explain why CS is uncontroversial and why ER is problematic.

According to both divine command theory and ethical relativism, morality depends on the dictates of some authority—God or culture. I have tried to indicate very briefly why many moral philosophers are not satisfied with either of these theories.[33] In any case, in our readings, although a few authors appeal to theological premises in attempting to support a position on a disputed moral issue, none of these authors rest their case solely on a brute appeal to what they take to be God's commands. And none of the authors appeal to ethical relativism.

NOTES

1. A few paragraphs of material in this essay are taken from my "Ethics" in *Reflections on Philosophy,* 2nd ed., ed. L. McHenry and T. Yagisowa, (New York: Longman's Publishers, 2003), 103–25.
2. John Rawls, *A Theory of Justice* (Cambridge, MA: Harvard University Press, 1971), 24.
3. Given this understanding of the notions of intrinsic and extrinsic value, it is possible for some-thing to have value of both sorts. Suppose, for example, that both happiness and knowledge have intrinsic positive value. Since knowledge can be of use in promoting happiness, knowledge can also have extrinsic value.
4. The "if and only if (and because) . . ." is meant to make clear that what follows the "and because" is meant to be a moral criterion that explains *why* the item being evaluated has whatever moral property (e.g., rightness) is mentioned in the first part of the principle.
5. To categorize Kant's ethical theory as deontological in the sense of being fundamentally duty-based may be inaccurate. Arguably, the notion of dignity—a kind of status that all persons have—is the explanatory basis of duties in Kant's ethical theory. Since dignity is a kind of value, this would make Kant's theory a certain kind of value-based theory, but nevertheless distinct from consequentialist views.

6. See Jeremy Bentham, *An Introduction to the Principles of Morals and Legislation* (New York: Hafner Press, 1948, originally published in 1789), and J. S. Mill, *Utilitarianism* (Indianapolis, IN: Hackett Publishing, 1979, originally published in 1861).

7. Another important distinction within consequentialism is between versions that appeal to the *actual* consequences (and associated value) that would occur were some action to be performed and versions that appeal to the *likely* consequences (and associated value) of actions—those consequences and their associated value that can be reasonably expected to follow from an action were it to be performed. I have chosen to formulate consequentialist principles in terms of likely consequences, since in applying a consequentialist theory to practice, we have to rely on our *estimates* of the consequences and associated value of actions.

8. I have explained utilitarianism in terms of *human* happiness or welfare, but a utilitarian may expand the scope of moral concern to all creatures for whom it makes sense to talk about their happiness or welfare.

9. For a recent defense of perfectionist consequentialism, see Tom Hurka, *Perfectionism* (Oxford: Oxford University Press, 1993).

10. What I am describing is a pure perfectionist account of value. It is, of course, possible to accept a hybrid view of intrinsic value according to which both happiness and perfectionist goods such as knowledge and achievement have intrinsic value.

11. For a recent defense of rule consequentialism, see Brad Hooker, *Ideal Code, Real World* (Oxford: Oxford University Press, 2000).

12. This is not to say that the best form of the natural law theory embraces the idea that "unnatural" actions are wrong and "natural" actions are right. The version I am about to present does not feature such ideas.

13. For a recent defense of natural law theory, see John Finnis, *Natural Law and Natural Rights* (Oxford: Oxford University Press, 1980).

14. Here is an appropriate place to clarify what I am calling theories of intrinsic value that figure importantly in those moral theories which feature value-based theories of right conduct. Ideally, a complete theory of intrinsic value would accomplish two related tasks: (1) provide a complete list of those types of things that have intrinsic value and also (2) specify those underlying features of intrinsically good and bad things *in virtue of which* they have whatever intrinsic value they do have. However, since our main concern in this chapter is with that part of a moral theory having to do with right and wrong action, we need only consider how a theory of intrinsic value responds to the first task—a specification of the types of things that have intrinsic value. So, for example, in what immediately follows, I will simply list the most basic types of items that have positive intrinsic value according to the natural law theory.

15. Kant's major writings in ethics include *Groundwork of the Metaphysics of Morals* (1785), *Critique of Practical Reason* (1790), and *The Metaphysics of Morals* (1797). All of these writings are included in Mary E. Gregor, trans., *Kant's Practical Philosophy* (Cambridge: Cambridge University Press, 1997). Page references to Kant's writings are to this volume. For a recent defense of Kantian ethics, see Onora O'Neill, *Towards Justice and Virtue* (Cambridge: Cambridge University Press, 1996).

16. In her article on a Kantian approach to world hunger included in chapter 13, Onora O'Neill develops these ideas in more detail.

17. See *Groundwork of the Metaphysics of Morals,* section II, 84–85.

18. I have left out the "and because" since arguably this formulation does not purport to express a moral criterion of right action—what *makes* an action right for Kant is expressed by the Humanity formulation; a *test* of an action's rightness is provided by the Universal Law formulation. For more on this, see my *Moral Theory: An Introduction,* chap. 5.

19. In the *Groundwork,* section II, in the footnote on p. 80, Kant raises objections to the golden rule.

20. *Practical Philosophy,* 74.
21. Readers should be aware that the topic of rights is extremely complex and contentious. In what follows, my aim is to introduce readers to some distinctions and to some observations about rights, moral theory, and moral controversies which, although elementary and perhaps contentious, are useful for understanding moral disputes that are framed in terms of rights.
22. Such rights are sometimes referred to as "natural rights."
23. *Universal* human rights are rights that are enjoyed by all human beings regardless of nationality, sex, race, religion, or other such distinctions. Universal rights, as universal, are contrasted with the particular rights of particular individuals, such as the rights that come with owning a house or having a certain occupation.
24. J. L. Mackie, "Can There Be a Rights-Based Moral Theory?" *Midwest Studies in Philosophy* 3 (1978): 351.
25. Mackie, "Rights-Based Moral Theory," 355.
26. This does not mean that such theories have little to say about such matters. For instance, Kant elaborates a theory of virtue in the "Doctrine of Virtue" which makes up part 2 of his 1797 *Metaphysics of Morals.*
27. For a recent defense of virtue ethics, see Rosalind Hursthouse, *On Virtue Ethics* (Oxford: Oxford University Press, 1999).
28. Defenders of virtue ethics often attempt to explain the basis of the virtues and vices (why some trait is a virtue or a vice) by appealing to the idea of human flourishing. The idea is that a trait of character or mind is a virtue because it contributes to or partly constitutes the flourishing of its possessor. For more on this point, see Hursthouse's "Virtue Theory and Abortion" included in chapter 9.
29. W. D. Ross, *The Right and the Good* (Oxford: Oxford University Press, 1930), 27.
30. See Audi's *The Good in the Right* (Princeton, N.J.: Princeton University Press, 2004) for a recent defense of an ethic of prima facie duty that attempts to integrate this sort of view into a basically Kantian framework.
31. Special thanks to Jason Brennan and to Dave Schmidtz for very helpful conversations about moral theory and illumination.
32. These remarks suggest the possibility of combining certain elements from the various theories into one big super-theory featuring a plurality of principles, some having to do with duties, others with virtuous actions, others with rights, others with utility, and perhaps all of them unified by the Kantian idea of respect for persons, animals, and the environment. Doing so would still leave open the question of whether some one element of the theory—duties, virtues, rights, etc.—is most basic in the theory. One possibility (and the one that strikes me as initially plausible) is a theory according to which these notions are "interpenetrating"—a full understanding of any one of them requires appeal to the others.
33. For a more detailed presentation and critique of divine command theory and ethical relativism, see chapters 2 and 3 of my *Moral Theory: An Introduction* (Lanham, MD: Rowman & Littlefield, 2002). This book also has chapters on utilitarianism, natural law theory, Kantian ethics, the ethics of prima facie duty (what I there call ethical pluralism), and virtue ethics.

2) Moral Theory Selections

The following sections are from the writings of Jeremy Bentham, St. Thomas Aquinas, Immanuel Kant, John Locke, Aristotle, and W. D. Ross. Each selection focuses on key aspects of the philosopher's theory of morality. In each selection, one or both of the following questions are being addressed:

- What makes an action morally right or morally wrong?
- What kind of life is best for human beings to lead?

Bentham presents a classic utilitarian version of consequentialism. Aquinas sets forth the elements of natural law theory. Kant explains and illustrates what he takes to be the supreme moral principle of right conduct: the so-called categorical imperative. Locke articulates a conception of natural rights. Aristotle explains the connection between a flourishing life and virtuous action. Finally, Ross defends his ethic of prima facie duties.

An overview of the main concepts and aims of moral theory, in addition to brief overviews of the various types of moral theory featured in each of these selections, can be found in the previous chapter, "A Moral Theory Primer."

JEREMY BENTHAM

The Principle of Utility

Bentham is often referred to as the father of modern utilitarianism—a version of consequentialism. Utilitarianism makes the rightness and wrongness of an action depend entirely on the "utility" of the action, where utility for Bentham is understood entirely in terms of the net balance of pleasure versus pain that would be produced by an action, taking into account *all* creatures who will be affected by the action in question. Thus, Bentham defends a hedonist utilitarian principle, which can be stated as follows: "An action is right if and only if (and because) if it would produce (if performed) as least as high a net balance of pleasure (or reduction of pain) as would any other alternative action one might do instead."

In the following selection from his classic *The Principles of Morals and Legislation* (1789), Bentham first defends his principle of utility and then proceeds to set forth his famous "felicific calculus"—a list of seven considerations to be used in calculating the utility of actions.

Recommended Reading: See consequentialism, chap. 1, sec. 2A, for more detail on the varieties of consequentialist moral theory (including utilitarianism), as well as for more elaboration of Bentham's theory.

The principle of utility is the foundation of the present work: it will be proper therefore at the outset to give an explicit and determinate account of what is meant by it. By the principle of utility is meant that principle which approves or disapproves of every action whatsoever, according to the tendency which it appears to have to augment or diminish the happiness of the party whose interest is in question: or, what is the same thing in other words, to promote or to oppose that happiness. I say of every action whatsoever; and therefore not only of every action of a private individual, but of every measure of government.

By utility is meant that property in any object, whereby it tends to produce benefit, advantage, pleasure, good, or happiness (all this in the present case comes to the same thing), or (what comes again to the same thing) to prevent the happening of mischief, pain, evil, or unhappiness to the party whose interest is considered: if that party be the community in general, then the happiness of the community: if a particular individual, then the happiness of that individual.

The interest of the community is one of the most general expressions that can occur in the phraseology of morals: no wonder that the meaning of it is often lost. When it has a meaning, it is this. The community is a fictitious *body,* composed of the individual persons who are considered as constituting as it were

its *member*s. The interest of the community then is, what?—the sum of the interests of the several members who compose it.

It is in vain to talk of the interest of the community, without understanding what is the interest of the individual. A thing is said to promote the interest, or to be *for* the interest, of an individual, when it tends to add to the sum total of his pleasures: or, what comes to the same thing, to diminish the sum total of his pains.

An action then may be said to be conformable to the principle of utility, or, for shortness sake, to utility (meaning with respect to the community at large), when the tendency it has to augment the happiness of the community is greater than any it has to diminish it.

A measure of government (which is but a particular kind of action, performed by a particular person or persons) may be said to be conformable to or dictated by the principle of utility, when in like manner the tendency which it has to augment the happiness of the community is greater than any which it has to diminish it.

When an action, or in particular a measure of government, is supposed by a man to be conformable to the principle of utility, it may be convenient, for the purposes of discourse, to imagine a kind of law or dictate, called a law or dictate of utility: and to speak of the action in question, as being conformable to such law or dictate.

From Jeremy Bentham, *The Principles of Morals and Legislation* (New York: Hafner Press, 1948 reprint).

A man may be said to be a partisan of the principle of utility when the approbation or disapprobation he annexes to any action, or to any measure, is determined by and proportioned to the tendency which he conceives it to have to augment or to diminish the happiness of the community: or in other words, to its conformity or unconformity to the laws or dictates of utility.

Of an action that is conformable to the principle of utility one may always say either that it is one that ought to be done, or at least that it is not one that ought not to be done. One may say also, that it is right it should be done; at least that it is not wrong it should be done: that it is a right action; at least that it is not a wrong action. When thus interpreted, the words *ought*, and *right* and *wrong*, and others of that stamp, have a meaning: when otherwise, they have none.

Has the rectitude of this principle been ever formally contested? It should seem that it had, by those who have not known what they have been meaning. Is it susceptible of any direct proof? it should seem not: for that which is used to prove every thing else, cannot itself be proved: a chain of proofs must have their commencement somewhere. To give such proof is as impossible as it is needless.

Not that there is or ever has been that human creature breathing, however stupid or perverse, who has not on many, perhaps on most occasions of his life, deferred to it. By the natural constitution of the human frame, on most occasions of their lives men in general embrace this principle, without thinking of it: if not for the ordering of their own actions, yet for the trying of their own actions, as well as of those of other men. There have been, at the same time, not many, perhaps, even of the most intelligent, who have been disposed to embrace it purely and without reserve. There are even few who have not taken some occasion or other to quarrel with it, either on account of their not understanding always how to apply it, or on account of some prejudice or other which they were afraid to examine into or could not bear to part with. For such is the stuff that man is made of: in principle and in practice, in a right track and in a wrong one, the rarest of all human qualities is consistency.

When a man attempts to combat the principle of utility, it is with reasons drawn, without his being aware of it, from that very principle itself. His arguments, if they prove any thing, prove not that the principle is *wrong*, but that, according to the applications he supposes to be made of it, it is *misapplied.* Is it possible for a man to move the earth? Yes; but he must first find out another earth to stand upon.

To disprove the propriety of it by arguments is impossible; but, from the causes that have been mentioned, or from some confused or partial view of it, a man may happen to be disposed not to relish it. Where this is the case, if he thinks the setting of his opinions on such a subject worth the trouble, let him take the following steps, and at length, perhaps, he may come to reconcile himself to it.

Let him settle with himself, whether he would wish to discard this principle altogether; if so, let him consider what it is that all his reasonings (in matters of politics especially) can amount to?

If he would, let him settle with himself, whether he would judge and act without any principle, or whether there is any other he would judge and act by?

If there be, let him examine and satisfy himself whether the principle he thinks he has found is really any separate intelligible principle; or whether it be not a mere principle in words, a kind of phrase, which at bottom expresses neither more nor less than the mere averment of his own unfounded sentiments; that is, what in another person he might be apt to call caprice?

If he is inclined to think that his own approbation or disapprobation, annexed to the idea of an act, without any regard to its consequences, is a sufficient foundation for him to judge and act upon, let him ask himself whether his sentiment is to be a standard of right and wrong, with respect to every other man, or whether every man's sentiment has the same privilege of being a standard to itself?

In the first case, let him ask himself whether his principle is not despotical, and hostile to all the rest of human race?

In the second case, whether it is not anarchial, and whether at this rate there are not as many different standards of right and wrong as there are men? and whether even to the same man, the same thing, which is right today, may not (without the least change in its nature) be wrong tomorrow? and whether the same thing is not right and wrong in the same place at the same time? and in either case, whether all argument is not at an end? and whether, when two men have said, "I like this," and "I don't like it," they can (upon such a principle) have any thing more to say?

If he should have said to himself, No: for that the sentiment which he proposes as a standard must be grounded on reflection, let him say on what particulars the reflection is to turn? if on particulars having relation to the utility of the act, then let him say whether this is not deserting his own principle, and borrowing assistance from the very one in opposition to which he sets it up: or if not on those particulars, on what other particulars?

If he should be for compounding the matter, and adopting his own principle in part, and the principle of utility in part, let him say how far he will adopt it?

When he has settled with himself where he will stop, then let him ask himself how he justifies to himself the adopting it so far? and why he will not adopt it any farther?

Admitting any other principle than the principle of utility to be a right principle, a principle that it is right for a man to pursue; admitting (what is not true) that the word *right* can have a meaning without reference to utility, let him say whether there is any such thing as a *motive* that a man can have to pursue the dictates of it: if there is, let him say what that motive is, and how it is to be distinguished from those which enforce the dictates of utility: if not, then lastly let him say what it is this other principle can be good for?...

Pleasures then, and the avoidance of pains, are the *ends* which the legislator has in view: it behooves him therefore to understand their *value.* Pleasures and pains are the *instruments* he has to work with: it behooves him therefore to understand their force, which is again, in other words, their value.

To a person considered *by himself,* the value of a pleasure or pain considered *by itself* will be greater or less, according to the four following circumstances:

1. Its *intensity.*
2. Its *duration.*
3. Its *certainty* or *uncertainty.*
4. Its *propinquity* or *remoteness.*

These are the circumstances which are to be considered in estimating a pleasure or a pain considered each of them by itself. But when the value of any pleasure or pain is considered for the purpose of estimating the tendency of any *act* by which it is produced, there are two other circumstances to be taken into the account; these are,

5. Its *fecundity,* or the chance it has of being followed by sensations of the *same* kind: that is, pleasures, if it be a pleasure: pains, if it be a pain.
6. Its *purity,* or the chance it has of *not* being followed by sensations of the *opposite* kind: that is, pains, if it be a pleasure: pleasures, if it be a pain.

These two last, however, are in strictness scarcely to be deemed properties of the pleasure or the pain itself, they are not, therefore, in strictness to be taken into the account of the value of that pleasure or that pain. They are in strictness to be deemed properties only of the act, or other event, by which such pleasure or pain has been produced; and accordingly are only to be taken into the account of the tendency of such act or such event.

To a *number* of persons, with reference to each of whom the value of a pleasure or a pain is considered, it will be greater or less, according to seven circumstances: to wit, the six preceding ones; *viz.*

1. Its *intensity.*
2. Its *duration.*
3. Its *certainty* or *uncertainty.*
4. Its *propinquity* or *remoteness.*
5. Its *fecundity.*
6. Its *purity.*

And one other; to wit:

7. Its *extent*; that is, the number of persons to whom it *extends*; or (in other words) who are affected by it.

To take an exact account then of the general tendency of any act, by which the interests of a community are affected, proceed as follows. Begin with any one person of those whose interests seem most immediately to be affected by it: and take an account,

1. Of the value of each distinguishable *pleasure* which appears to be produced by it in the *first* instance.
2. Of the value of each *pain* which appears to be produced by it in the *first* instance.
3. Of the value of each pleasure which appears to be produced by it *after* the first. This constitutes the *fecundity* of the first *pleasure* and the *impurity* of the first *pain.*
4. Of the value of each *pain* which appears to be produced by it after the first. This constitutes *the fecundity* of the first *pain,* and the *impurity* of the first pleasure.
5. Sum up all the values of all the *pleasures* on the one side, and those of all the pains on the other. The balance, if it be on the side of pleasure, will give the *good* tendency of the act upon the whole, with respect to the interests of that *individual* person; if on the side of pain, the *bad* tendency of it upon the whole.
6. Take an account of the *number* of persons whose interests appear to be concerned; and repeat the above process with respect to each. Sum up the numbers expressive of the degrees of *good* tendency, which the act has, with respect to each individual, in regard to whom the tendency of it is *good* upon the whole: do this again with respect to each individual, in regard to whom the tendency of it is *good* upon the whole: do this again with respect to each individual, in regard to whom the tendency of it is *bad* upon the whole. Take the *balance;* which, if on the side of *pleasure,* will give the general *good tendency* of the act, with respect to the total number or community of individuals concerned; if on the side of pain, the general *evil tendency,* with respect to the same community.

It is not to be expected that this process should be strictly pursued previously to every moral judgment, or to every legislative or judicial operation. It may, however, be always kept in view: and as near as the process actually pursued on these occasions approaches to it, so near will such process approach to the character of an exact one.

The same process is alike applicable to pleasure and pain, in whatever shape they appear: and by whatever denomination they are distinguished: to pleasure, whether it be called *good* (which is properly the cause or instrument of pleasure) or *profit* (which is distant pleasure, or the cause or instrument of distant pleasure), or *convenience,* or *advantage, benefit, emolument, happiness,* and so forth: to pain, whether it be called *evil* (which corresponds to *good),* or *mischief* or *inconvenience,* or *disadvantage*, or *loss,* or *unhappiness,* and so forth.

Nor is this a novel and unwarranted, any more than it is a useless theory. In all this there is nothing but what the practice of mankind, wheresoever they have a clear view of their own interest, is perfectly conformable to. An article of property, an estate in land, for instance, is valuable, on what account? On account of the pleasures of all kinds which it enables a man to produce, and what comes to the same thing the pains of all kinds which it enables him to avert. But the value of such an article of property is universally understood to rise or fall according to the length or shortness of the time which a man has in it: the certainty or uncertainty of its coming into possession: and the nearness or remoteness of the time at which, if at all, it is to come into possession. As to the *intensity* of the pleasures which a man may derive from it, this is never thought of, because it depends upon the use which each particular person may come to make of it; which cannot be estimated till the particular pleasures he may come to derive from it, or the particular pains he may come to exclude by means of it, are brought to view. For the same reason, neither does he think of the *fecundity* or *purity* of those pleasures....

READING QUESTIONS

1. How does Bentham characterize *utility?*
2. Explain in your own words the elements that make up Bentham's seven-element felicific calculus.

DISCUSSION QUESTIONS

1. How do you think Bentham would respond to the suggestion that in addition to the good of pleasure, there are other goods such as artistic accomplishment and scientific knowledge?
2. Pick a particular moral issue that is represented in this anthology and explain what Bentham's principle of utility would imply about the rightness or wrongness of the issue in question.

St. Thomas Aquinas

Treatise on Law

In the following selection from his *Summa Theologiae* (Summary of Theology), thirteenth-century philosopher and theologian St. Thomas Aquinas presents a classical version of the natural law theory of morality. He defines law as "an ordinance of reason for the common good, promulgated by him who has care of the community." *Natural* law is that part of God's eternal law that concerns how human beings ought to conduct themselves. The first precept of natural law is that "good is to be done, evil is to be avoided." Human beings have natural inclinations to seek various ends that (according to Aquinas) indicate what has intrinsic value and thus ought to be protected and cultivated. Thus, for Aquinas, morality is ultimately grounded in facts about human nature that can be discovered by inquiring into the nature of human beings. Hence, the label, "natural law theory."

Recommended Reading: See natural law theory, chap. 1, sec. 2B, for an elaboration of the basic concepts and principles of Aquinas's version of natural law theory, including a presentation of the doctrine of double effect.

WHETHER LAW IS SOMETHING PERTAINING TO REASON?

...It belongs to the law to command and to forbid. But it belongs to reason to command, as was stated above. Therefore law is something pertaining to reason....Law is a rule and measure of acts, whereby man is induced to act or is restrained from acting; for *lex (law)* is derived from *ligare (to bind),* because it binds one to act. Now the rule and measure of human acts is the reason, which is the first principle of human acts, as is evident from what has been stated above. For it belongs to the reason to direct to the end, which is the first principle in all matters of action....

WHETHER LAW IS ALWAYS DIRECTED TO THE COMMON GOOD?

...As we have stated above, law belongs to that which is a principle of human acts, because it is their rule and measure. Now as reason is a principle of human acts, so in reason itself there is something which is the principle in respect of all the rest. Hence to this principle chiefly and mainly law must needs be referred. Now the first principle in practical matters, which are the object of the practical reason, is the last end: and the last end of human life is happiness or beatitude, as we have stated above. Consequently, law must needs concern itself mainly with the order that is in beatitude. Moreover, since every part is ordained to the whole as the imperfect to the perfect, and since one man is a part of the perfect community, law must needs concern itself properly with the order directed to universal happiness....Since law is chiefly ordained to the common good, any other precept in regard to some individual work must needs be devoid of the nature of a law, save in so far as it regards the common good. Therefore every law is ordained to the common good....

WHETHER PROMULGATION IS ESSENTIAL TO LAW?

...As was stated above, a law is imposed on others as a rule and measure. Now a rule or measure is imposed by being applied to those who are to be ruled and measured by it. Therefore, in order that a law obtain the binding force which is proper to a law, it must needs be applied to the men who have to be ruled by it. But such application is made by its being made known to them by promulgation. Therefore promulgation is necessary for law to obtain its force....Law is nothing else than an ordinance of reason for the common good, promulgated by him who has the care of the community....

The natural law is promulgated by the very fact that God has instilled it into man's mind so as to be known by him naturally....

WHETHER THERE IS AN ETERNAL LAW?

...As we have stated above, law is nothing else but a dictate of practical reason emanating from the ruler who governs a perfect community. Now it is evident, granted that the world is ruled by divine providence, as was stated in the First Part, that the whole community of the universe is governed by the divine reason. Therefore the very notion of the government of things in God, the ruler of the universe, has the nature of a law. And since the divine reason's conception of things is not subject to time, but is eternal, according to *Prov.* 8:23, therefore it is that this kind of law must be called eternal....

Promulgation is made by word of mouth or in writing, and in both ways the eternal law is promulgated, because both the divine Word and the writing of the Book of Life are eternal....

WHETHER THERE IS IN US A NATURAL LAW?

...As we have stated above, law, being a rule and measure, can be in a person in two ways: in one way, as in him that rules and measures; in another way, as in that which is ruled and measured, since a thing is ruled and measured in so far as it partakes of the rule or measure. Therefore, since all things subject to divine providence are ruled and measured by the eternal law, as was stated above, it is evident that all things partake in some way in the eternal law, in so far as, namely, from its being imprinted on them, they derive their respective inclinations to their proper acts and ends. Now among all others, the rational creature is subject to divine providence in a more excellent way, in so far as it itself partakes of a share of providence, by being provident both for itself and for others. Therefore it has a share of the eternal reason, whereby it has a natural inclination to its proper act and end; and this participation of the eternal law in the rational creature is called the natural law. Hence the Psalmist, after saying (Ps. 4:6): *Offer up the sacrifice of justice,* as though someone asked what the works of justice are, adds: *Many say, Who showeth us good things?* in answer to which question he says: *The light of Thy countenance, O Lord, is signed upon us.* He thus implies that the light of natural reason, whereby we discern what is good and what is evil, which is the function of the natural law, is nothing else than an imprint on us of the divine light. It is therefore evident that the natural law is nothing else than the rational creature's participation of the eternal law....

WHETHER THE NATURAL LAW CONTAINS SEVERAL PRECEPTS, OR ONLY ONE?

...The precepts of the natural law are to the practical reason what the first principles of demonstrations are to the speculative reason, because both are self-evident principles. Now a thing is said to be self-evident in two ways: first, in itself; secondly, in relation to us. Any proposition is said to be self-evident in itself, if its predicate is contained in the notion of the subject; even though it may happen that to one who does not know the definition of the subject, such a proposition is not self-evident. For instance, this proposition, *Man is a rational being,* is, in its very nature, self-evident, since he who says *man,* says *a rational being*; and yet to one who does not know what a man is, this proposition is not self-evident. Hence it is that, as Boethius says, certain axioms or propositions are universally self-evident to all; and such are the propositions whose terms are known to all, as, *Every whole is greater than its part,* and *Things equal to one and the same are equal to one another.* But some propositions are self-evident only to the wise, who understand the meaning of the terms of such propositions. Thus to one who understands that an angel is not a body, it is self-evident that an angel is not circumscriptively in a place. But this is not evident to the unlearned, for they cannot grasp it.

Now a certain order is to be found in those things that are apprehended by men. For that which first falls under apprehension, is *being,* the understanding of which is included in all things whatsoever a man apprehends. Therefore the first indemonstrable principle is that *the same thing cannot be affirmed and denied at the same time,* which is based on the notion of *being and not-being*: and on this principle all others are based.... Now as *being* is the first thing that falls under the apprehension absolutely, so *good* is the first thing that falls under the apprehension of the practical reason, which is directed to action (since every agent acts for an end, which has the nature of good). Consequently, the first principle in the practical reason is one founded on the nature of good, viz., that *good is that which all things seek after.* Hence, this is the first precept of law, that *good is to be done and promoted, and evil is to be avoided.* All other precepts of the natural law are based upon this; so that all the things which the practical reason naturally apprehends as man's good belong to the precepts of the natural law under the form of things to be done or avoided.

Since, however, good has the nature of an end, and evil, the nature of the contrary, hence it is that all those things to which man has a natural inclination are naturally apprehended by reason as being good, and consequently as objects of pursuit, and their contraries as evil, and objects of avoidance. Therefore, the order of the precepts of the natural law is according to the order of natural inclinations. For there is in man, first of all, an inclination to good in accordance with the nature which he has in common with all substances, inasmuch, namely, as every substance seeks the preservation of its own being, according to its nature; and by reason of this inclination, whatever is a means of preserving human life, and of warding off its obstacles, belongs to the natural law. Secondly, there is in man an inclination to things that pertain to him more specially, according to that nature which he has in common with other animals; and in virtue of this inclination, those things are said to belong to the natural law *which nature has taught to all animals*, such as sexual intercourse, the education of offspring, and so forth. Thirdly, there is in man an inclination to good according to the nature of his reason, which nature is proper to him. Thus man has a natural inclination to know the truth about God, and to live in society; and in this respect, whatever pertains to this inclination belongs to the natural law: *e.g.*, to shun ignorance, to avoid offending those among whom one has to live, and other such things regarding the above inclination....

All these precepts of the law of nature have the character of one natural law, inasmuch as they flow from one first precept....

WHETHER THE NATURAL LAW IS THE SAME IN ALL MEN?

...As we have stated above, to the natural law belong those things to which a man is inclined naturally; and among these it is proper to man to be inclined to act according to reason. Now it belongs to the reason to proceed from what is common to what is proper.... The speculative reason, however, is differently situated, in this matter, from the practical reason. For, since the speculative reason is concerned chiefly with necessary things, which cannot be otherwise than they are, its proper conclusions, like the universal principles, contain the truth without fail. The practical reason, on the other hand, is concerned with contingent matters, which is the domain of human actions; and, consequently, although there is necessity in the common principles, the more we descend towards the particular, the more frequently we encounter defects. Accordingly, then, in speculative matters truth is the same in all men, both as to principles and as to conclusions; although the truth is not known to all as regards the conclusions, but only as regards the principles which are called *common notions*. But in matters of action, truth or practical rectitude is not the same for all as to what is particular, but only as to the common principles; and where there is the same rectitude in relation to particulars, it is not equally known to all.

It is therefore evident that, as regards the common principles whether of speculative or of practical reason, truth or rectitude is the same for all, and is equally known by all. But as to the proper conclusions of the speculative reason, the truth is the same for all, but it is not equally known to all. Thus, it is true for all that the three angles of a triangle are together equal to two right angles, although it is not known to all. But as to the proper conclusions of the practical reason, neither is the truth or rectitude the same for all, nor, where it is the same, is it equally known by all. Thus, it is right and true for all to act according to reason, and from this principle it follows, as a proper conclusion, that goods entrusted to another should be restored to their owner. Now this is true for the majority of cases. But it may happen in a particular case that it would be injurious, and therefore unreasonable, to restore goods held in trust; for instance, if they are claimed for the purpose of fighting against one's country. And this principle will be found to fail the more, according as we descend further towards the particular, *e.g.*, if one were to say that goods held in trust should be restored with such and such a guarantee, or in such and such a way; because the greater the number of conditions added, the greater the number of ways in which the principle may fail, so that it be not right to restore or not to restore.

Consequently, we must say that the natural law, as to the first common principles, is the same for all, both as to rectitude and as to knowledge. But as to certain more particular aspects, which are conclusions, as it were, of those common principles, it is the same for all in the majority of cases, both as to rectitude and as to knowledge; and yet in some few cases it may fail, both as to rectitude, by reason of certain obstacles (just as natures subject to generation and corruption fail in some few cases because of some obstacle), and as to knowledge, since in some the reason is perverted by passion, or evil habit, or an evil disposition of nature. Thus at one time theft, although it is expressly contrary to the natural law, was not considered wrong among the Germans, as Julius Caesar relates.

READING QUESTIONS

1. What is "natural" about the natural law?
2. What are the fundamental human goods according to Aquinas? How does Aquinas attempt to support his claims that these are goods?
3. What moral obligations does Aquinas mention as following from each of the human goods?

DISCUSSION QUESTIONS

1. Do you think that Aquinas's list of fundamental human goods is complete? Why or why not?
2. Do you think that Aquinas's natural law theory allows for killing in self-defense? Why or why not?

IMMANUEL KANT

The Moral Law

Kant is one of the most important philosophers of the Western world. In the selection below from his 1785 *Groundwork (Foundations) of the Metaphysics of Morals,* he presents and illustrates what he takes to be the fundamental principle of morality, the Categorical Imperative, which (he argues) is implicit in the moral thinking of ordinary men and women. He first argues that this principle can be made explicit by reflecting on the concept of a good will. Kant then proceeds to explain the difference between two types of imperatives—hypothetical and categorical—the latter being distinctive of morality. Then, having explained the very idea of a categorical imperative, Kant formulates his fundamental principle in a variety of ways—in terms of *universal law, humanity as an end in itself,* and *the kingdom of ends,* providing sample applications of the Categorical Imperative to questions about the morality of suicide, making false promises, allowing one's talents to rust, and helping others in need.

Recommended Reading: See Kantian moral theory, chap. 1, sec. 2C, for further explanation of Kant's theory.

THE GOOD WILL

Nothing can possibly be conceived in the world, or even out of it, which can be called good, without qualification, except a Good Will. Intelligence, wit, judgment, and the other *talents* of the mind, however they may be named, or courage, resolution, perseverance, as qualities of temperament, are undoubtedly good and desirable in many respects; but these gifts of nature may also become extremely bad and mischievous if the will which is to make use of them, and which, therefore constitutes what is called *character,* is not good. It is the same with the *gifts of fortune.* Power, riches, honor, even health, and the general well-being and contentment with one's condition which is called *happiness*, inspire pride, and often presumption, if there is not a good will to correct the influence of these on the mind, and with this also to rectify the whole principle of acting, and adapt it to its end. The sight of a being who is not adorned with a single feature of a pure and good will, enjoying unbroken prosperity, can never give pleasure to an impartial rational spectator. Thus a good will appears to constitute the indispensable condition even of being worthy of happiness.

There are even some qualities which are of service to this good will itself, and may facilitate its action, yet which have no intrinsic unconditional value, but always presuppose a good will, and this qualifies the esteem that we justly have for them, and does not permit us to regard them as absolutely good. Moderation in the affections and passions, self-control, and calm deliberation are not only good in many respects, but even seem to constitute part of the intrinsic worth of the person; but they are far from deserving to be called good without qualification, although they have been so unconditionally praised by the ancients. For without the principles of a good will, they may become extremely bad; and the coolness of a villain not only makes him far more dangerous, but also directly makes him more abominable in our eyes than he would have been without it.

A good will is good not because of what it performs or effects, not by its aptness for the attainment of some proposed end, but simply by virtue of the volition, that is, it is good in itself, and considered by itself is to be esteemed much higher than all that can be brought about by it in favor of any inclination, nay, even of the sum-total of all inclinations. Even if it should happen that, owing to special disfavor of fortune, or the niggardly provision of a step-motherly nature, this will should wholly lack power to accomplish its purpose, if with its greatest efforts it should yet achieve nothing, and there should remain only the good will (not, to be sure, a mere wish, but the summoning of all means in our power), then, like a jewel, it would still shine by its own light, as a thing which has its whole value in itself. Its usefulness or fruitlessness can neither add to nor take away anything from this value....

...Thus the moral worth of an action does not lie in the effect expected from it, nor in any principle of action which requires to borrow its motive from this

From I. Kant, *The Foundations of the Metaphysics of Morals,* T. K. Abbott, trans. First published in 1873.

expected effect. For all these effects—agreeableness of one's condition, and even the promotion of the happiness of others—could have been also brought about by other causes, so that for this there would have been no need of the will of a rational being; whereas it is in this alone that the supreme and unconditional good can be found. The pre-eminent good which we call moral can therefore consist in nothing else than *the conception of law* in itself, *which certainly* is *only possible in a rational being*, in so far as this conception, and not the expected effect, determines the will. This is a good which is already present in the person who acts accordingly, and we have not to wait for it to appear first in the result.

THE SUPREME PRINCIPLE OF MORALITY: THE CATEGORICAL IMPERATIVE

But what sort of law can that be, the conception of which must determine the will, even without paying any regard to the effect expected from it, in order that this will may be called good absolutely and without qualification? As I have deprived the will of every impulse which could arise to it from obedience to any law, there remains nothing but the universal conformity of its actions to law in general, which alone is to serve the will as a principle, *i.e.* I am never to act otherwise than *so that I could also will that my maxim should become a universal law*. Here, now, it is the simple conformity to law in general, without assuming any particular law applicable to certain actions, that serves the will as its principle, and must so serve it, if duty is not to be a vain delusion and a chimerical notion. The common reason of men in its practical judgments perfectly coincides with this, and always has in view the principle here suggested. Let the question be, for example: May I when in distress make a promise with the intention not to keep it? I readily distinguish here between the

two significations which the question may have: Whether it is prudent, or whether it is right, to make a false promise? The former may undoubtedly often be the case. I see clearly indeed that it is not enough to extricate myself from a present difficulty by means of this subterfuge, but it must be well considered whether there may not hereafter spring from this lie much greater inconvenience than that from which I now free myself, and as, with all my supposed *cunning,* the consequences cannot be so easily foreseen but that credit once lost may be much more injurious to me than any mischief which I seek to avoid at present, it should be considered whether it would not be more *prudent* to act herein according to a universal maxim, and to make it a habit to promise nothing except with the intention of keeping it. But it is soon clear to me that such a maxim will still only be based on the fear of consequences. Now it is a wholly different thing to be truthful from duty, and to be so from apprehension of injurious consequences. In the first case, the very notion of the action already implies a law for me; in the second case, I must first look about elsewhere to see what results may be combined with it which would affect myself. For to deviate from the principle of duty is beyond all doubt wicked; but to be unfaithful to my maxim of prudence may often be very advantageous to me, although to abide by it is certainly safer. The shortest way, however, and an unerring one, to discover the answer to this question whether a lying promise is consistent with duty, is to ask myself, Should I be content that my maxim (to extricate myself from difficulty by a false promise) should hold good as a universal law, for myself as well as for others? and should I be able to say to myself, "Every one may make a deceitful promise when he finds himself in a difficulty from which he cannot otherwise extricate himself"? Then I presently become aware that while I can will the lie, I can by no means will that lying should be a universal law. For with such a law there would be no promises at all, since it would be in vain to allege my intention in regard to my future actions to those who would not believe this allegation, or if they over-hastily did so, would pay me back in my own coin. Hence my maxim, as soon as it should be made a universal law, would necessarily destroy itself....

IMPERATIVES: HYPOTHETICAL AND CATEGORICAL

Everything in nature works according to laws. Rational beings alone have the faculty of acting according *to the conception of laws*, that is according to principles, *i.e.,* have a *will*. Since the deduction of actions from principles requires *reason,* the will is nothing but practical reason. If reason infallibly determines the will, then the actions of such a being which are recognized as objectively necessary are subjectively necessary also, *i.e.,* the will is a faculty to choose *that only* which reason independent of inclination recognizes as practically necessary, *i.e.,* as good. But if reason of itself does not sufficiently determine the will, if the latter is subject also to subjective conditions (particular impulses) which do not always coincide with the objective conditions; in a word, if the will does not *in itself* completely accord with reason (which is actually the case with men), then the actions which objectively are recognized as necessary are subjectively contingent, and the determination of such a will according to objective laws is *obligation,* that is to say, the relation of the objective laws to a will that is not thoroughly good is conceived as the determination of the will of a rational being by principles of reason, but which the will from its nature does not of necessity follow.

The conception of an objective principle, in so far as it is obligatory for a will, is called a command (of reason), and the formula of the command is called an Imperative.

All imperatives are expressed by the word *ought* [or *shall*], and thereby indicate the relation of an objective law of reason to a will, which from its subjective constitution is not necessarily determined by it (an obligation). They say that something would be good to do or to forbear, but they say it to a will which

does not always do a thing because it is conceived to be good to do it. That is practically *good,* however, which determines the will by means of the conceptions of reason, and consequently not from subjective causes, but objectively, that is on principles which are valid for every rational being as such. It is distinguished from the *pleasant,* as that which influences the will only by means of sensation from merely subjective causes, valid only for the sense of this or that one, and not as a principle of reason, which holds for every one.

A perfectly good will would therefore be equally subject to objective laws (*viz.,* laws of good), but could not be conceived as *obliged* thereby to act lawfully, because of itself from its subjective constitution it can only be determined by the conception of good. Therefore no imperatives hold for the Divine will, or in general for a *holy* will; *ought* is here out of place, because the volition is already of itself necessarily in unison with the law. Therefore imperatives are only formulae to express the relation of objective laws of all volition to the subjective imperfection of the will of this or that rational being, *e.g.,* the human will.

Now all *imperatives* command either *hypothetically* or *categorically.* The former represent the practical necessity of a possible action as means to something else that is willed (or at least which one might possibly will). The categorical imperative would be that which represented an action as necessary of itself without reference to another end, *i.e.,* as objectively necessary....

FIRST FORMULATION OF THE CATEGORICAL IMPERATIVE: UNIVERSAL LAW

There is therefore but one categorical imperative, namely, this: *Act only on that maxim whereby thou canst at the same time will that it should become a universal law.*

Now if all imperatives of duty can be deduced from this one imperative as from their principle, then, although it should remain undecided whether what is called duty is not merely a vain notion, yet at least we shall be able to show what we understand by it and what this notion means.

Since the universality of the law according to which effects are produced constitutes what is properly called *nature* in the most general sense (as to form), that is the existence of things so far as it is determined by general laws, the imperative of duty may be expressed thus: *Act as if the maxim of thy action were to become by thy will a universal law of nature.*

FOUR ILLUSTRATIONS

We will now enumerate a few duties, adopting the usual division of them into duties to ourselves and to others, and into perfect and imperfect duties.

1. A man reduced to despair by a series of misfortunes feels wearied of life, but is still so far in possession of his reason that he can ask himself whether it would not be contrary to his duty to himself to take his own life. Now he inquires whether the maxim of his action could become a universal law of nature. His maxim is: From self-love I adopt it as a principle to shorten my life when its longer duration is likely to bring more evil than satisfaction. It is asked then simply whether this principle founded on self-love can become a universal law of nature. Now we see at once that a system of nature of which it should be a law to destroy life by means of the very feeling whose special nature it is to impel to the improvement of life would contradict itself, and therefore could not exist as a system of nature; hence that maxim cannot possibly exist as a universal law of nature, and consequently would be wholly inconsistent with the supreme principle of all duty.

2. Another finds himself forced by necessity to borrow money He knows that he will not be able to repay it, but sees also that nothing will be lent to him, unless he promises stoutly to repay it in a definite time. He desires to make this promise, but he has still so much conscience as to ask himself: Is it not unlawful and inconsistent with duty to get out of a difficulty in this way? Suppose, however, that he resolves to do so, then the maxim of his action would be expressed thus: When I think myself in want of money, I will borrow money and promise to repay it, although I know that I never can do so. Now this principle of self-love or of one's own advantage may perhaps be consistent with my whole future welfare; but the question now is, Is it right? I change then the suggestion of self-love into a universal law, and state the question thus: How would it be if my maxim were a universal law? Then I see at once that it could never hold as a universal law of nature, but would necessarily contradict itself. For supposing it to be a universal law that everyone when he thinks himself in a difficulty should be able to promise whatever he pleases, with the purpose of not keeping his promise, the promise itself would become impossible, as well as the end that one might have in view in it, since no one would consider that anything was promised to him, but would ridicule all such statements as vain pretenses.

3. A third finds in himself a talent which with the help of some culture might make him a useful man in many respects. But he finds himself in comfortable circumstances, and prefers to indulge in pleasure rather than to take pains in enlarging and improving his happy natural capacities. He asks, however, whether his maxim of neglect of his natural gifts, besides agreeing with his inclination to indulgence, agrees also with what is called duty. He sees then that a system of nature could indeed subsist with such a universal law although men (like the South Sea islanders) should let their talents rust, and resolve to devote their lives

merely to idleness, amusement, and propagation of their species—in a word, to enjoyment; but he cannot possibly will that this should be a universal law of nature, or be implanted in us as such by a natural instinct. For, as a rational being, he necessarily wills that his faculties be developed, since they serve him, and have been given him, for all sorts of possible purposes.

4. A fourth, who is in prosperity, while he sees that others have to contend with great wretchedness and that he could help them, thinks: What concern is it of mine? Let everyone be as happy as Heaven pleases, or as he can make himself; I will take nothing from him nor even envy him, only I do not wish to contribute anything to his welfare or to his assistance in distress! Now no doubt if such a mode of thinking were a universal law, the human race might very well subsist, and doubtless even better than in a state in which everyone talks of sympathy and good-will, or even takes care occasionally to put it into practice, but, on the other side, also cheats when he can, betrays the rights of men, or otherwise violates them. But although it is possible that a universal law of nature might exist in accordance with that maxim, it is impossible to *will* that such a principle should have the universal validity of a law of nature. For a will which resolved this would contradict itself, inasmuch as many cases might occur in which one would have need of the love and sympathy of others, and in which, by such a law of nature, sprung from his own will, he would deprive himself of all hope of the aid he desires....

SECOND FORMULATION OF THE CATEGORICAL IMPERATIVE: HUMANITY AS AN END IN ITSELF

...Now I say: man and generally any rational being *exists* as an end in himself, *not merely as*

a means to be arbitrarily used by this or that will, but in all his actions, whether they concern himself or other rational beings, must be always regarded at the same time as an end. All objects of the inclinations have only a conditional worth; for if the inclinations and the wants founded on them did not exist, then their object would be without value. But the inclinations themselves being sources of want are so far from having an absolute worth for which they should be desired, that, on the contrary, it must be the universal wish of every rational being to be wholly free from them. Thus the worth of any object which is *to be acquired* by our action is always conditional. Beings whose existence depends not on our will but on nature's, have nevertheless, if they are nonrational beings, only a relative value as means, and are therefore called *things;* rational beings, on the contrary, are called *persons,* because their very nature points them out as ends in themselves, that is as something which must not be used merely as means, and so far therefore restricts freedom of action (and is an object of respect). These, therefore, are not merely subjective ends whose existence has a worth *for us* as an effect of our action, but *objective ends,* that is things whose existence is an end in itself: an end moreover for which no other can be substituted, which they should subserve *merely* as means, for otherwise nothing whatever would possess *absolute worth*; but if all worth were conditioned and therefore contingent, then there would be no supreme practical principle of reason whatever.

If then there is a supreme practical principle or, in respect of the human will, a categorical imperative, it must be one which, being drawn from the conception of that which is necessarily an end for everyone because it is *an end in itself*, constitutes an *objective* principle of will, and can therefore serve as a universal practical law. The foundation of this principle is: *rational nature exists as an end in itself*. Man necessarily conceives his own existence as being so: so far then this is a *subjective* principle of human actions. But every other rational being regards its existence similarly, just on the same rational principle that holds for me: so that it is at the same time an objective principle from which as a supreme practical law all laws of the will must be capable of being deduced. Accordingly the practical imperative will be as follows: *So act as to treat humanity, whether in thine own person or in that of any other, in every case as an end withal, never as means only....*

We will now inquire whether this can be practically carried out.

To abide by the previous examples:

Firstly, under the head of the necessary duty to oneself: He who contemplates suicide should ask himself whether his action can be consistent with the idea of humanity *as an end in itself.* If he destroys himself in order to escape from painful circumstances, he uses a person merely as *a mean* to maintain a tolerable condition up to the end of life. But a man is not a thing, that is to say, something which can be used merely as a means, but must in all his actions be always considered as an end in himself. I cannot, therefore, dispose in any way of a man in my own person so as to mutilate him, to damage or kill him. (It belongs to ethics proper to define this principle more precisely so as to avoid all misunderstanding, *e.g.,* as to the amputation of the limbs in order to preserve myself; as to exposing my life to danger with a view to preserve it, &c. This question is therefore omitted here.)

Secondly, as regards necessary duties, or those of strict obligation, towards others; he who is thinking of making a lying promise to others will see at once that he would be using another man *merely as a mean,* without the latter containing at the same time the end in himself. For he whom I propose by such a promise to use for my own purposes cannot possibly assent to my mode of acting towards him, and therefore cannot himself contain the end of this action. This violation of the principle of humanity in other men is more obvious if we take in examples of attacks on the freedom and property of others. For then it is clear that he who transgresses the rights of men, intends to use the person of others merely as means, without considering that as rational beings they ought always to be esteemed also as ends, that is, as beings who must be capable of containing in themselves the end of the very same action.

Thirdly, as regards contingent (meritorious) duties to oneself; it is not enough that the action does not violate humanity in our own person as an end in itself, it must also *harmonize with* it. Now there are in humanity capacities of greater perfection which belong to the end that nature has in view in regard to humanity in ourselves as the subject: to neglect these might perhaps be consistent with the *maintenance* of humanity as an end in itself, but not with the *advancement* of this end.

Fourthly, as regards meritorious duties towards others: the natural end which all men have is their own happiness. Now humanity might indeed subsist, although no one should contribute anything to the happiness of others, provided he did not intentionally withdraw anything from it; but after all, this would only harmonize negatively not positively with *humanity as an end in itself,* if everyone does not also endeavor, as far as in him lies, to forward the ends of others. For the ends of any subject which is an end in himself, ought as far as possible to be *my* ends also, if that conception is to have its *full* effect with me.

...Looking back now on all previous attempts to discover the principle of morality, we need not wonder why they all failed. It was seen that man was bound to laws by duty, but it was not observed that the laws to which he is subject are *only those of his own giving,* though at the same time they are *universal,* and that he is only bound to act in conformity with his own will; a will, however, which is designed by nature to give universal laws. For when one has conceived man only as subject to a law (no matter what), then this law required some interest, either by way of attraction or constraint, since it did not originate as a law from his *own* will, but this will was according to a law obliged by *something else* to act in a certain manner. Now by this necessary consequence all the labor spent in finding a supreme principle of *duty* was irrevocably lost. For men never elicited duty, but only a necessity of acting from a certain interest. Whether this interest was private or otherwise, in any case the imperative must be conditional, and could not by any means be capable of being a moral command. I will therefore call this the principle of *Autonomy* of the will, in contrast with every other which I accordingly reckon as *Heteronomy*.

THE KINGDOM OF ENDS

The conception of every rational being as one which must consider itself as giving in all the maxims of its will universal laws, so as to judge itself and its actions from this point of view—this conception leads to another which depends on it and is very fruitful, namely, that of a *kingdom of ends*.

By a *kingdom* I understand the union of different rational beings in a system by common laws. Now since it is by laws that ends are determined as regards their universal validity, hence, if we abstract from the personal differences of rational beings, and likewise from all the content of their private ends, we shall be able to conceive all ends combined in a systematic whole (including both rational beings as ends in themselves, and also the special ends which each may propose to himself), that is to say, we can conceive a kingdom of ends, which on the preceding principles is possible.

For all rational beings come under the *law* that each of them must treat itself and all others *never merely as means*, but in every case *at the same time as ends in themselves*. Hence results a systematic union of rational beings by common objective laws, i.e., a kingdom which may be called a kingdom of ends, since what these laws have in view is just the relation of these beings to one another as ends and means....

READING QUESTIONS

1. Explain in your own words Kant's distinction between hypothetical and categorical imperatives. What makes an imperative hypothetical? What makes an imperative categorical?
2. The Universal Law formulation of the categorical imperative involves testing maxims, which Kant proceeds to illustrate with four examples. For each of his examples, try explaining in your own words how Kant's test is supposed to work in showing that certain maxims cannot be consistently willed as universal law.
3. Kant also applies the Humanity as an End in Itself formulation to the same four examples. For each of these examples, how does Kant use his principle to establish claims about the morality of type of action he considers?

DISCUSSION QUESTIONS

1. Suppose someone proposes to act on the following maxim: *Whenever I know that other athletes against whom I am competing are using performance-enhancing drugs, I too will take such drugs in order to have a chance at winning.* Apply Kant's Universal Law formula to this maxim to determine whether the action being proposed is morally right or wrong.
2. Suppose that Jones is terminally ill and he and his physicians are reasonably certain that he only has about a week to live. But his life during his remaining time will be *very* painful and misery-ridden. Jones and his family agree that it would be preferable for Jones to die a drug-induced painless death now than for him to linger on in misery for the next week or so. His physicians agree. Apply Kant's Universal Law and Humanity formulations to this case in order to determine whether (according to Kant's moral theory) it would be permissible for Jones to allow himself to be put to death in these circumstances.

JOHN LOCKE

Natural Rights

According to Locke, all men (humans) are created by God as equal and free, but subject to "the law of nature" which "teaches all mankind who will but consult it that, being all equal and independent, no one ought to harm another in his life, health, liberty, or possessions." Thus Locke, like Aquinas, accepts a natural law conception of morality. However, in the following selection from *Two Treatises of Government*, Locke emphasizes the "natural" rights that correspond to the obligations just mentioned.

Recommended Reading: See rights-based moral theory, chap. 1, sec. 2D, for further discussion of moral rights and how they figure in moral theory.

To understand political power aright, and derive it from its original, we must consider what state all men are naturally in, and that is a state of perfect freedom to order their actions and dispose of their possessions and persons as they think fit, within the bounds of the law of nature, without asking leave, or depending upon the will of any other man.

A state also of equality, wherein all the power and jurisdiction is reciprocal, no one having more than another; there being nothing more evident than that creatures of the same species and rank, promiscuously born to all the same advantages of nature, and the use of the same faculties, should also be equal one amongst another without subordination or subjection, unless the Lord and Master of them all should by any manifest declaration of His will set one above another, and confer on him by an evident and clear appointment an undoubted right to dominion and sovereignty....

But though this be a state of liberty, yet it is not a state of license; though man in that state have an uncontrollable liberty to dispose of his person or possessions, yet he has not liberty to destroy himself, or so much as any creature in his possession, but where some nobler use than its bare preservation calls for it. The state of nature has a law of nature

to govern it, which obliges everyone; and reason, which is that law, teaches all mankind who will but consult it, that, being all equal and independent, no one ought to harm another in his life, health, liberty, or possessions. For men being all the workmanship of one omnipotent and infinitely wise Maker—all the servants of one sovereign Master, sent into the world by His order, and about His business—they are His property, whose workmanship they are, made to last during His, not one another's pleasure; and being furnished with like faculties, sharing all in one community of nature, there cannot be supposed any such subordination among us, that may authorize us to destroy one another, as if we were made for one another's uses, as the inferior ranks of creatures are for ours. Everyone, as he is bound to preserve himself, and not to quit his station willfully, so, by the like reason, when his own preservation comes not in competition, ought he, as much as he can, to preserve the rest of mankind, and not, unless it be to do justice on an offender, take away or impair the life, or what tends to the preservation of the life, the liberty, health, limb, or goods of another.

And that all men be restrained from invading other rights, and from doing hurt to one another, and the

From John Locke, *Two Treatises of Government* (1690).

law of nature be observed, which willeth the peace and preservation of all mankind, the execution of the law of nature is in that state put into every man's hand, whereby everyone has a right to punish the transgressors of that law to such a degree as may hinder its violation. For the law of nature would, as all other laws that concern men in this world, be in vain if there were nobody that, in the state of nature, had a power to execute that law, and thereby preserve the innocent and restrain offenders. And if anyone in the state of nature may punish another for any evil he has done, everyone may do so. For in that state of perfect equality, where naturally there is no superiority or jurisdiction of one over another, what any may do in prosecution of that law, everyone must needs have a right to do.

And thus in the state of nature one man comes by a power over another; but yet no absolute or arbitrary power, to use a criminal, when he has got him in his hands, according to the passionate heats or boundless extravagance of his own will; but only to retribute to him so far as calm reason and conscience dictate what is proportionate to his transgression, which is so much as may serve for reparation and restraint. For these two are the only reasons why one man may lawfully do harm to another, which is that we call punishment. In transgressing the law of nature, the offender declares himself to live by another rule than that of common reason and equity, which is that measure God has set to the actions of men, for their mutual security; and so he becomes dangerous to mankind, the tie which is to secure them from injury and violence being sighted and broken by him. Which, being a trespass against the whole species, and the peace and safety of it, provided for by the law of nature, every man upon this score, by the right he hath to preserve mankind in general, may restrain, or, where it is necessary, destroy things noxious to them, and so may bring such evil on anyone who hath transgressed that law, as may make him repent the doing of it, and thereby deter him, and by his example others, from doing the like mischief. And in this case, and upon this ground, every man hath a right to punish the offender, and be executioner of the law of nature.

I doubt not but this will seem a very strange doctrine to some men: but before they condemn it, I desire them to resolve me by what right any prince or state can put to death or punish an alien, for any crime he commits in their country. 'Tis certain their laws, by virtue of any sanction they receive from the promulgated will of the legislative, reach not a stranger: they speak not to him, nor, if they did, is he bound to hearken them. The legislative authority, by which they are in force over the subjects of that commonwealth, hath no power over him. Those who have the supreme power of making laws in England, France, or Holland, are to an Indian but like the rest of the world—men without authority. And, therefore, if by the law of nature every man hath not a power to punish offenses against it, as he soberly judges the case to require, I see not how the magistrates of any community can punish an alien of another country; since in reference to him they can have no more power than what every man naturally may have over another.

Besides the crime which consists in violating the law, and varying from the right rule of reason, whereby a man so far becomes degenerate, and declares himself to quit the principles of human nature, and to be a noxious creature, there is commonly injury done, and some person or other, some other man receives damage by his transgression, in which case he who hath received any damage, has, besides the right of punishment common to him with other men, a particular right to seek reparation from him that has done it. And any other person who finds it just, may also join with him that is injured, and assist him in recovering from the offender so much as many make satisfaction for the harm he has suffered.

From these two distinct rights—the one of punishing the crime for restraint and preventing the like offense, which right of punishing is in everybody; the other of taking reparation, which belongs only to the injured party—comes it to pass that the magistrate, who by being magistrate hath the common right of punishing put into his hands, can often, where the public good demands not the execution of the law, remit the punishment of criminal offenses by his own authority, but yet cannot remit the satisfaction due to any private man for the damage he has received. That he who has suffered the damage has a right to demand in his own name, and he alone can remit. The damnified person has this power of appropriating to himself the goods or service of the offender, by right of self-preservation, as every man has a power to punish the crime, to prevent its being committed again, by the right he has of preserving all mankind, and doing all reasonable things he can in order to that end. And thus it is that every man in the state of nature has a power to kill a murderer, both to deter others from doing the like injury which no reparation can compensate, by the example of the punishment that attends it from everybody, and also to secure men from the attempts of a criminal who having renounced reason, the common rule and measure God hath given to mankind, hath by the unjust violence and slaughter he hath committed upon one, declared war against all mankind, and therefore may be destroyed as a lion or a tiger, one of those wild savage beasts with whom men can have no society nor security. And upon this is grounded that great law of nature. "Whoso sheddeth man's blood, by man shall his blood be shed." And Cain was so fully convinced that everyone had a right to destroy such a criminal, that after the murder of his brother he cries out, "Every one that findeth me shall slay me"; so plain was it writ in the hearts of mankind.

By the same reason may a man in the state of nature punish the lesser breaches of that law. It will perhaps be demanded, With death? I answer, each transgression may be punished to that degree, and with so much severity, as will suffice to make it an ill bargain to the offender, give him cause to repent, and terrify others from doing the like. Every offense that can be committed in the state of nature, may in the state of nature be also punished equally, and as far forth as it may, in a commonwealth. For though it would be beside my present purpose to enter here into the particulars of the law of nature, or its measures of punishment, yet it is certain there is such a law, and that, too, as intelligible and plain to a rational creature and a studier of that law as the positive laws of commonwealth; nay, possibly plainer, as much as reason is easier to be understood than the fancies and intricate contrivances of men, following contrary and hidden interests put into words; for truly so are a great part of the municipal laws of countries, which are only so far right as they are founded on the law of nature, by which they are to be regulated and interpreted.

To this strange doctrine—viz., that in the state of nature everyone has the executive power of the law of nature—I doubt not but it will be objected that it is unreasonable for men to be judges in their own cases, that self-love will make men partial to themselves and their friends. And on the other side, that ill-nature, passion, and revenge will carry them too far in punishing others; and hence nothing but confusion and disorder will follow; and that therefore God hath certainly appointed government to restrain the partiality and violence of men. I easily grant that civil government is the proper remedy for the inconveniences of the state of nature, which must certainly be great where men may be judges in their own case, since 'tis easy to be imagined that he who was so unjust as to do his brother an injury, will scarce be so just as to condemn himself for it. But I shall desire those who make this objection, to remember that absolute monarchs are but men, and if government is to be the remedy of those evils which necessarily follow from men's being judges in their own cases, and the state of nature is therefore not to be endured, I desire to know what kind of government that is, and how much better it is than the state of nature, where one man commanding a multitude, has the liberty to be judge in his own case, and may do to all his subjects whatever he pleases, without the least question or control of those who execute his pleasure; and in whatsoever he doth, whether led by reason, mistake, or passion, must be submitted to, which men in the state of nature are not bound to do one to another? And if he that judges, judges amiss in his own or any other case, he is answerable for it to the rest of mankind.

'Tis often asked as a mighty objection, Where are, or ever were there, any men in such a state of nature? To which it may suffice as an answer at present: That since all princes and rulers of independent governments all through the world are in a state of nature, 'tis plain the world never was, nor ever will be, without numbers of men in that state. I have named all governors of independent communities, whether they are or are not in league with others. For 'tis not every compact that puts an end to the state of nature between men, but only this one of agreeing together mutually to enter into one community, and make one body politic; other promises and compacts men may make one with another, and yet still be in the state of nature. The promises and bargains for truck, etc., between the two men in Soldania, in or between a Swiss and an Indian, in the woods of America, are binding to them, though they are perfectly in a state of nature in reference to one another. For truth and keeping of faith belong to men as men, and not as members of society.

To those that say there were never any men in the state of nature, I will not only oppose the authority of the judicious Hooker—(Eccl. Pol., lib. i., sect. 10), where he says, "The laws which have been hitherto mentioned," i.e., the laws of nature, "do bind men absolutely, even as they are men, although they have never any settled fellowship, and never any solemn agreement amongst themselves what to do or not to do; but forasmuch as we are not by ourselves sufficient to furnish ourselves with competent store of things needful for such a life as our nature doth desire—a life fit for the dignity of man—therefore to supply those defects and imperfections which are in us, as living single and solely by ourselves, we are naturally induced to seek communion and fellowship with others; this was the cause of men's uniting themselves at first in politic societies"—but I moreover affirm that all men are naturally in that state, and remain so, till by their own consents they make themselves members of some politic society; and I doubt not, in the sequel of this discourse, to make it very clear.

READING QUESTIONS

1. Explain in your own words the idea of a natural right.
2. In addition to the rights to life, health, liberty, and possession, what rights does Locke discuss in this selection?

DISCUSSION QUESTIONS

1. Assuming that there are natural rights, are they any such rights not mentioned by Locke in our selection?
2. Both Aquinas and Locke accept a natural law conception of morality. Does Locke's appeal to natural rights add anything to the natural law theory that is lacking in Aquinas?

ARISTOTLE

Virtue and Character

The writings of Aristotle have made a tremendous impact on the history of philosophy and continue to do so. The following selection is from *Nichomachean Ethics*, in which Aristotle begins by arguing that a happy or good life essentially involves a life of activity in accordance with virtue. He then goes on to define virtue as a disposition to avoid extremes in feeling and action. For example, in matters relating to money, the virtue of generosity stands between the extremes of extravagance and stinginess.

Recommended Reading: See virtue ethics, chap. 1, sec. 2E, for a presentation of a contemporary version of a virtue-based account of right and wrong action that is inspired by the work of Aristotle.

CHARACTERISTICS OF THE GOOD

1. The good is the end of action.

But let us return once again to the good we are looking for, and consider just what it could be, since it is apparently one thing in one action or craft, and another thing in another; for it is one thing in medicine, another in generalship, and so on for the rest.

What, then, is the good in each of these cases? Surely it is that for the sake of which the other things are done; and in medicine this is health, in generalship victory, in house-building a house, in another case something else, but in every action and decision it is the end, since it is for the sake of the end that everyone does the other things.

And so, if there is some end of everything that is pursued in action, this will be the good pursued in action; and if there are more ends than one, these will be the goods pursued in action.

Our argument has progressed, then, to the same conclusion [as before, that the highest end is the good]; but we must try to clarify this still more.

2. The good is complete.

Though apparently there are many ends, we choose some of them, e.g., wealth, flutes and, in general, instruments, because of something else; hence it is clear that not all ends are complete. But the best good is apparently something complete.

Hence, if only one end is complete, this will be what we are looking for; and if more than one are complete, the most complete of these will be what we are looking for.

CRITERIA FOR COMPLETENESS

An end pursued in itself, we say, is more complete than an end pursued because of something else; and an end that is never choiceworthy because of something else is more complete than ends that are choiceworthy both in themselves and because of this end; and hence an end that is always [choiceworthy, and also] choiceworthy in itself, never because of something else, is unconditionally complete.

3. Happiness meets the criteria for completeness, but other goods do not.

Now happiness more than anything else seems unconditionally complete, since we always [choose it, and also] choose it because of itself, never because of something else. Honor, pleasure, understanding and every virtue we certainly choose because of themselves, since we would choose each of them even if it had no further result, but we also choose them for the sake of happiness, supposing that through them we shall be happy. Happiness, by contrast, no one ever chooses for their sake, or for the sake of anything else at all.

From *Nicomachean Ethics*, trans. Terence Irwin (Hackett, 1974). Reprinted by permission of Hackett Publishing Company, Inc. All rights reserved.

4. The good is self-sufficient; so is happiness.

The same conclusion [that happiness is complete] also appears to follow from self-sufficiency, since the complete good seems to be self-sufficient.

Now what we count as self-sufficient is not what suffices for a solitary person by himself, living an isolated life, but what suffices also for parents, children, wife and in general for friends and fellow-citizens, since a human being is a naturally political [animal]. Here, however, we must impose some limit; for if we extend the good to parents' parents and children's children and to friends of friends, we shall go on without limit; but we must examine this another time.

Anyhow, we regard something as self-sufficient when all by itself it makes a life choiceworthy and lacking nothing; and that is what we think happiness does.

5. The good is most choiceworthy; so is happiness.

Moreover, [the complete good is most choiceworthy, and] we think happiness is most choiceworthy of all goods, since it is not counted as one good among many. If it were counted as one among many, then, clearly, we think that the addition of the smallest of goods would make it more choiceworthy; for [the smallest good] that is added becomes an extra quantity of goods [so creating a good larger than the original good], and the larger of two goods is always more choiceworthy. [But we do not think any addition can make happiness more choiceworthy; hence it *is* most choiceworthy.]

Happiness, then, is apparently something complete and self-sufficient, since it is the end of the things pursued in action.

A clearer account of the good: the human soul's activity expressing virtue.

But presumably the remark that the best good is happiness is apparently something [generally] agreed, and what we miss is a clearer statement of what the best good is.

1. If something has a function, its good depends on its function.

Well, perhaps we shall find the best good if we first find the function of a human being. For just as the good, i.e., [doing] well, for a flautist, a sculptor, and every craftsman, and, in general, for whatever has a function and [characteristic] action, seems to depend on its function, the same seems to be true for a human being, if a human being has some function.

2. What sorts of things have functions?

Then do the carpenter and the leatherworker have their functions and actions, while a human being has none, and is by nature idle, without any function? Or, just as eye, hand, foot and, in general, every [bodily] part apparently has its functions, may we likewise ascribe to a human being some functions besides all of theirs?

3. The human function.

What, then, could this be? For living is apparently shared with plants, but what we are looking for is the special function of a human being; hence we should set aside the life of nutrition and growth. The life next in order is some sort of life of sense-perception; but this too is apparently shared, with horse, ox and every animal. The remaining possibility, then, is some sort of life of action of the [part of the soul] that has reason.

Clarification of "has reason" and "life."

Now this [part has two parts, which have reason in different ways], one as obeying the reason [in the other part], the other as itself having reason and thinking. [We intend both.] Moreover, life is also spoken of in two ways [as capacity and as activity], and we must take [a human being's special function to be] life as activity, since this seems to be called life to a fuller extent.

4. The human good is activity expressing virtue.

(a) We have found, then, that the human function is the soul's activity that expresses reason [as itself having reason] or requires reason [as obeying reason].(b) Now the function of F, e.g., of a harpist, is the same in kind, so we say, as the function of an excellent F, e.g., an excellent harpist. (c) The same is true unconditionally in every case, when we add to the function the superior achievement that expresses the virtue; for a harpist's function, e.g., is to play the harp, and a good harpist's is to do it well. (d) Now we take the human function to be a certain kind of life, and take this life to be the soul's activity and actions that express reason. (e) [Hence by (c) and (d)] the excellent man's function is to do this finely and well. (f) Each function is completed well when its completion expresses the proper virtue. (g) Therefore [by (d), (e) and (f)] the human good turns out to be the soul's activity that expresses virtue.

5. The good must also be complete.

And if there are more virtues than one, the good will express the best and most complete virtue. Moreover, it will be in a complete life. For one swallow does not make a spring, nor does one day; nor, similarly, does one day or a short time make us blessed and happy....

VIRTUES OF CHARACTER IN GENERAL

How a Virtue of Character Is Acquired

Virtue, then, is of two sorts, virtue of thought and virtue of character. Virtue of thought arises and grows mostly from teaching, and hence needs experience and time. Virtue of character [i.e., of *ethos*] results from habit [*ethos*]; hence its name "ethical," slightly varied from "*ethos*."

Virtue comes about, not by a process of nature, but by habituation.

Hence it is also clear that none of the virtues of character arises in us naturally.

1. What is natural cannot be changed by habituation.

For if something is by nature [in one condition], habituation cannot bring it into another condition. A stone, e.g., by nature moves downwards, and habituation could not make it move upwards, not even if you threw it up ten thousand times to habituate it; nor could habituation make fire move downwards, or bring anything that is by nature in one condition into another condition.

Thus the virtues arise in us neither by nature nor against nature, but we are by nature able to acquire them, and reach our complete perfection through habit.

2. Natural capacities are not acquired by habituation.

Further, if something arises in us by nature, we first have the capacity for it, and later display the activity. This is clear in the case of the senses; for we did not acquire them by frequent seeing or hearing, but already had them when we exercised them, and did not get them by exercising them.

Virtues, by contrast, we acquire, just as we acquire crafts, by having previously activated them. For we learn a craft by producing the same product that we must produce when we have learned it, becoming builders, e.g., by building and harpists by playing the harp; so also, then, we become just by doing just actions, temperate by doing temperate actions, brave by doing brave actions.

3. Legislators concentrate on habituation.

What goes on in cities is evidence for this also. For the legislator makes the citizens good by habituating them, and this is the wish of every legislator; if he fails to do it well he misses his goal. [The right] habituation is what makes the difference between a good political system and a bad one.

4. Virtue and vice are formed by good and bad actions.

Further, just as in the case of a craft, the sources and means that develop each virtue also ruin it. For playing the harp makes both good and bad harpists, and it is analogous in the case of builders and all the rest; for building well makes good builders, building badly, bad ones. If it were not so, no teacher would be needed, but everyone would be born a good or a bad craftsman.

It is the same, then, with the virtues. For actions in dealings with [other] human beings make some people just, some unjust; actions in terrifying situations and the acquired habit of fear or confidence make some brave and others cowardly. The same is true of situations involving appetites and anger; for one or another sort of conduct in these situations makes some people temperate and gentle, others intemperate and irascible.

Conclusion: The Importance of Habituation.

To sum up, then, in a single account: A state [of character] arises from [the repetition of] similar activities. Hence we must display the right activities, since differences in these imply corresponding differences in the states. It is not unimportant, then, to acquire one sort of habit or another, right from our youth; rather, it is very important, indeed all-important....

But our claims about habituation raise a puzzle: How can we become good without being good already?

However, someone might raise this puzzle: "What do you mean by saying that to become just we must first do just actions and to become temperate we must first do temperate actions? For if we do what is grammatical or musical, we must already be grammarians or musicians. In the same way, then, if we do what is just or temperate, we must already be just or temperate."

First reply: Conformity versus understanding.

But surely this is not so even with the crafts, for it is possible to produce something grammatical by chance or by following someone else's instructions. To be a grammarian, then, we must both produce something grammatical and produce it in the way in which the grammarian produces it, i.e., expressing grammatical knowledge that is in us.

Second reply: Crafts versus virtues.

Moreover, in any case what is true of crafts is not true of virtues. For the products of a craft determine by their own character whether they have been produced well; and so it suffices that they are in the right state when they have been produced. But for actions expressing virtue to be done temperately or justly [and hence well] it does not suffice that they are themselves in the right state. Rather, the agent must also be in the right state when he does them. First, he must know [that he is doing virtuous actions]; second, he must decide on them, and decide on them for themselves; and, third, he must also do them from a firm and unchanging state.

As conditions for having a craft these three do not count, except for the knowing itself. As a condition for having a virtue, however, the knowing counts for nothing, or [rather] for only a little, whereas the other two conditions are very important, indeed all-important. And these other two conditions are achieved by the frequent doing of just and temperate actions.

Hence actions are called just or temperate when they are the sort that a just or temperate person would do. But the just and temperate person is not the one who [merely] does these actions, but the one who also does them in the way in which just or temperate people do them.

It is right, then, to say that a person comes to be just from doing just actions and temperate from doing temperate actions; for no one has even a prospect of becoming good from failing to do them.

Virtue requires habituation, and therefore requires practice, not just theory.

The many, however, do not do these actions but take refuge in arguments, thinking that they are doing philosophy, and that this is the way to become excellent people. In this they are like a sick person who listens attentively to the doctor, but acts on none of his instructions. Such a course of treatment will not improve the state of his body; any more than will the many's way of doing philosophy improve the state of their souls.

A VIRTUE OF CHARACTER IS A STATE INTERMEDIATE BETWEEN TWO EXTREMES, AND INVOLVING DECISION

The Genus

Feelings, capacities, states. Next we must examine what virtue is. Since there are three conditions arising in the soul—feelings, capacities and states—virtue must be one of these.

By feelings I mean appetite, anger, fear, confidence, envy, joy, love, hate, longing, jealousy, pity, in general whatever implies pleasure or pain.

By capacities I mean what we have when we are said to be capable of these feelings—capable of, e.g., being angry or afraid or feeling pity.

By states I mean what we have when we are well or badly off in relation to feelings. If, e.g., our feeling is too intense or slack, we are badly off in relation to anger, but if it is intermediate, we are well off; and the same is true in the other cases.

Virtue is not a feeling . . .

First, then, neither virtues nor vices are feelings. (a) For we are called excellent or base in so far as we have virtues or vices, not in so far as we have feelings. (b) We are neither praised nor blamed in so far as we have feelings; for we do not praise the angry or the frightened person, and do not blame the person who is simply angry, but only the person who is angry in a particular way. But we are praised or blamed in so far as we have virtues or vices. (c) We are angry and afraid without decision; but the virtues

are decisions of some kind, or [rather] require decision. (d) Besides, in so far as we have feelings, we are said to be moved; but in so far as we have virtues or vices, we are said to be in some condition rather than moved.

Or a capacity . . .

For these reasons the virtues are not capacities either; for we are neither called good nor called bad in so far as we are simply capable of feelings. Further, while *we* have capacities by nature, we do not become good or bad by nature; we have discussed this before.

But a state

If, then, the virtues are neither feelings nor capacities, the remaining possibility is that they are states. And so we have said what the genus of virtue is.

The Differentia

But we must say not only, as we already have, that it is a state, but also what sort of state it is.

Virtue and the Human Function

It should be said, then, that every virtue causes its possessors to be in a good state and to perform their functions well; the virtue of eyes, e.g., makes the eyes and their functioning excellent, because it makes us see well; and similarly, the virtue of a horse makes the horse excellent, and thereby good at galloping, at carrying its rider and at standing steady in the face of the enemy. If this is true in every case, then the virtue of a human being will likewise be the state that makes a human being good and makes him perform his function well . . . .

The Numerical Mean and the Mean Relative to Us

In everything continuous and divisible we can take more, less and equal, and each of them either in the object itself or relative to us; and the equal is some intermediate between excess and deficiency.

By the intermediate in the object I mean what is equidistant from each extremity; this is one and the same for everyone. But relative to us the intermediate is what is neither superfluous nor deficient; this is not one, and is not the same for everyone.

If, e.g., ten are many and two are few, we take six as intermediate in the object, since it exceeds [two] and is exceeded [by ten] by an equal amount, [four]; this is what is intermediate by numerical proportion. But that is not how we must take the intermediate that is relative to us. For if, e.g., ten pounds [of food] are a lot for someone to eat, and two pounds a little, it does not follow that the trainer will prescribe six, since this might also be either a little or a lot for the person who is to take it—for Milo [the athlete] a little, but for the beginner in gymnastics a lot; and the same is true for running and wrestling. In this way every scientific expert avoids excess and deficiency and seeks and chooses what is intermediate—but intermediate relative to us, not in the object.

Virtue seeks the mean relative to us: Argument from craft to virtue.

This, then, is how each science produces its product well, by focusing on what is intermediate and making the product conform to that. This, indeed, is why people regularly comment on well-made products that nothing could be added or subtracted, since they assume that excess or deficiency ruins a good [result] while the mean preserves it. Good craftsmen also, we say, focus on what is intermediate when they produce their product. And since virtue, like nature, is better and more exact than any craft, it will also aim at what is intermediate.

Arguments from the Nature of Virtue of Character

By virtue I mean virtue of character; for this [pursues the mean because] it is concerned with feelings and actions, and these admit of excess, deficiency and an intermediate condition. We can be afraid, e.g., or be confident, or have appetites, or get angry, or feel pity, in general have pleasure or pain, both too

much and too little, and in both ways not well; but [having these feelings] at the right times, about the right things, towards the right people, for the right end, and in the right way, is the intermediate and best condition, and this is proper to virtue. Similarly actions also admit of excess, deficiency and the intermediate condition.

Now virtue is concerned with feelings and actions, in which excess and deficiency are in error and incur blame, while the intermediate condition is correct and wins praise, which are both proper features of virtue. Virtue, then, is a mean, in so far as it aims at what is intermediate.

Moreover, there are many ways to be in error, since badness is proper to what is unlimited, as the Pythagoreans pictured it, and good to what is limited; but there is only one way to be correct. That is why error is easy and correctness hard, since it is easy to miss the target and hard to hit it. And so for this reason also excess and deficiency are proper to vice, the mean to virtue; "for we are noble in only one way, but bad in all sorts of ways."

Definition of Virtue

Virtue, then, is (a) a state that decides, (b) [consisting] in a mean, (c) the mean relative to us, (d) which is defined by reference to reason, (e) i.e., to the reason by reference to which the intelligent person would define it. It is a mean between two vices, one of excess and one of deficiency.

It is a mean for this reason also: Some vices miss what is right because they are deficient, others because they are excessive, in feelings or in actions, while virtue finds and chooses what is intermediate.

Hence, as far as its substance and the account stating its essence are concerned, virtue is a mean; but as far as the best [condition] and the good [result] are concerned, it is an extremity.

The definition must not he misapplied to cases in which there is no mean.

But not every action or feeling admits of the mean. For the names of some automatically include baseness, e.g., spite, shamelessness, envy [among feelings], and adultery, theft, murder, among actions. All of these and similar things are called by these names because they themselves, not their excesses or deficiencies, are base.

Hence in doing these things we can never be correct, but must invariably be in error. We cannot do them well or not well—e.g., by committing adultery with the right woman at the right time in the right way; on the contrary, it is true unconditionally that to do any of them is to be in error.

[To think these admit of a mean], therefore, is like thinking that unjust or cowardly or intemperate action also admits of a mean, an excess and a deficiency. For then there would be a mean of excess, a mean of deficiency, an excess of excess and a deficiency of deficiency.

Rather, just as there is no excess or deficiency of temperance or of bravery, since the intermediate is a sort of extreme [in achieving the good], so also there is no mean of these [vicious actions] either, but whatever way anyone does them, he is in error. For in general there is no mean of excess or of deficiency, and no excess or deficiency of a mean.

The Definition of Virtue as a Mean Applies to the Individual Virtues

However, we must not only state this general account but also apply it to the particular cases. For among accounts concerning actions, though the general ones are common to more cases, the specific ones are truer, since actions are about particular cases, and our account must accord with these. Let us, then, find these from the chart.

CLASSIFICATION OF VIRTUES OF CHARACTER

Virtues Concerned with Feelings

1. First in feelings of fear and confidence the mean is bravery. The excessively fearless person is nameless (and in fact many cases are nameless), while the one who is excessively confident is rash; the one who is excessively afraid and deficient in confidence is cowardly.

2. In pleasures and pains, though not in all types, and in pains less than in pleasures, the mean is temperance and the excess intemperance. People deficient in pleasure are not often found, which is why they also lack even a name; let us call them insensible.

Virtues Concerned with External Goods

3. In giving and taking money the mean is generosity, the excess wastefulness and the deficiency ungenerosity. Here the vicious people have contrary excesses and defects; for the wasteful person spends to excess and is deficient in taking, whereas the ungenerous person takes to excess and is deficient in spending. At the moment we are speaking in outline and summary....

4. In questions of money there are also other conditions. Another mean is magnificence; for the magnificent person differs from the generous by being concerned with large matters, while the generous person is concerned with small. The excess is ostentation and vulgarity, and the deficiency niggardliness, and these differ from the vices related to generosity....

5. In honor and dishonor the mean is magnanimity, the excess something called a sort of vanity, and the deficiency pusillanimity.

6. And just as we said that generosity differs from magnificence in its concern with small matters, similarly there is a virtue concerned with small honors, differing in the same way from magnanimity, which is concerned with great honors. For honor can be desired either in the right way or more or less than is right. If someone desires it to excess, he is called an honor-lover, and if his desire is deficient he is called indifferent to honor, but if he is intermediate he has no name. The corresponding conditions have no name either, except the condition of the honor-lover, which is called honor-loving.

This is why people at the extremes claim the intermediate area. Indeed, we also sometimes call the intermediate person an honor-lover, and sometimes call him indifferent to honor; and sometimes we praise the honor-lover, sometimes the person indifferent to honor....

Virtues Concerned with Social Life

7. Anger also admits of an excess, deficiency and mean. These are all practically nameless; but since we call the intermediate person mild, let us call the mean mildness. Among the extreme people let the excessive person be irascible, and the vice be irascibility, and let the deficient person be a sort of inirascible person, and the deficiency be inirascibility.

There are three other means, somewhat similar to one another, but different. For they are all concerned with association in conversations and actions, but differ in so far as one is concerned with truth-telling in these areas, the other two with sources of pleasure, some of which are found in amusement, and the others in daily life in general. Hence we should also discuss these states, so that we can better observe that in every case the mean is praiseworthy, while the extremes are neither praiseworthy nor correct, but blameworthy. Most of these cases are also nameless, and we must try, as in the other cases also, to make names ourselves, to make things clear and easy to follow.

8. In truth-telling, then, let us call the intermediate person truthful, and the mean truthfulness; pretense that overstates will be boastfulness, and the person who has it boastful; pretense that understates will be self-deprecation, and the person who has it self-deprecating.

9. In sources of pleasure in amusements let us call the intermediate person witty, and the condition wit; the excess buffoonery and the person who has it a buffoon; and the deficient person a sort of boor and the state boorishness.

10. In the other sources of pleasure, those in daily life, let us call the person who is pleasant in the right way friendly, and the mean state friendliness. If someone goes to excess with no [further] aim he will be ingratiating; if he does it for his own advantage, a flatterer. The deficient person, unpleasant in everything, will be a sort of quarrelsome and ill-tempered person.

Mean States that Are Not Virtues

11. There are also means in feelings and concerned with feelings: shame, e.g., is not a virtue, but the person prone to shame as well as the virtuous person we have described receives praise. For here also one person is called intermediate, and another—the person excessively prone to shame, who is ashamed about everything—is called excessive; the person who is deficient in shame or never feels shame at all is said to have no sense of disgrace; and the intermediate one is called prone to shame.

12. Proper indignation is the mean between envy and spite; these conditions are concerned with pleasure and pain at what happens to our neighbors. For the properly indignant person feels pain when someone does well undeservedly; the envious person exceeds him by feeling pain when anyone does well, while the spiteful person is so deficient in feeling pain that he actually enjoys [other people's misfortunes].

READING QUESTIONS

1. How does Aristotle defend the claim that the good for human beings is happiness?
2. According to Aristotle, how is virtue acquired?
3. How does Aristotle define virtue? What role does the idea of a "mean" play in his definition?
4. Review the various traits of character Aristotle lists.

DISCUSSION QUESTIONS

1. Are there any virtues that you think are missing from Aristotle's discussion?
2. Which of the virtues and vices Aristotle discusses strike you as distinctively ethical or moral virtues and vices? If you think that some of the virtue and vices are not ethical, what is the basis for distinguishing ethical from other types of virtue and vice?

W. D. Ross

What Makes Right Actions Right?

In contrast to the views of Bentham and Kant, Ross (1877–1971) denies that there is some single moral principle that can be used to derive more specific moral obligations. Rather, he defends a version of moral pluralism, according to which there is a plurality of irreducible moral rules that are basic in moral thought. There rules express what Ross calls *prima facie duties*—duties such as keeping promises and avoiding injury to others. Such duties may come into conflict in particular circumstances, and when they do, what is demanded (according to Ross) is that we use moral judgment in order to determine which prima facie duty is (in that circumstance) weightiest and should be obeyed.

Recommended Reading: See ethics of prima facie duty, chap. 1, sec. 2F, for an explication of Ross's moral theory, plus some remarks about how some contemporary philosophers have developed Ross's theory.

When a plain man fulfills a promise because he thinks he ought to do so, it seems clear that he does so with no thought of its total consequences, still less with any opinion that these are likely to be the best possible. He thinks in fact much more of the past than of the future. What makes him think it right to act in a certain way is the fact that he has promised to do so—that and, usually, nothing more. That his act will produce the best possible consequences is not his reason for calling it right. What lends color to the theory we are examining, then, is not the actions (which form probably a great majority of our actions) in which some such reflection as "I have promised" is the only reason we give ourselves for thinking a certain action right, but the exceptional cases in which the consequences of fulfilling a promise (for

From *The Right and the Good* by W. D. Ross (Oxford: Oxford University Press, 1930). Reprinted by permission of the publisher.

instance) would be so disastrous to others that we judge it right not to do so. It must of course be admitted that such cases exist. If I have promised to meet a friend at a particular time for some trivial purpose, I should certainly think myself justified in breaking my engagement if by doing so I could prevent a serious accident or bring relief to the victims of one. And the supporters of the view we are examining hold that my thinking so is due to my thinking that I shall bring more good into existence by the one action than by the other. A different account may, however, be given of the matter, an account which will, I believe, show itself to be the true one. It may be said that besides the duty of fulfilling promises I have and recognize a duty of relieving distress, and that when I think it right to do the latter at the cost of not doing the former, it is not because I think I shall produce more good thereby but because I think it the duty which is in the circumstances more of a duty. This account surely corresponds much more closely with what we really think in such a situation. If, so far as I can see, I could bring equal amounts of good into being by fulfilling my promise and by helping someone to whom I had made no promise, I should not hesitate to regard the former as my duty. Yet on the view that what is right is right because it is productive of the most good I should not so regard it ....

In fact the theory of ... utilitarianism ... seems to simplify unduly our relations to our fellows. It says, in effect, that the only morally significant relation in which my neighbors stand to me is that of being possible beneficiaries by my action. They do stand in this relation to me, and this relation is morally significant. But they may also stand to me in the relation of promisee to promiser, of creditor to debtor, of wife to husband, of child to parent, of friend to friend, of fellow countryman to fellow countryman, and the like; and each of these relations is the foundation of a *prima facie* duty, which is more or less incumbent on me according to the circumstances of the case. When I am in a situation, as perhaps I always am, in which more than one of these *prima facie* duties is incumbent on me, what I have to do is to study the situation as fully as I can until I form the considered opinion (it is never more) that in the circumstances one of them is more incumbent than any other; then I am bound to

think that to do this *prima facie* duty is my duty *sans phrase* in the situation.

I suggest "*prima facie* duty" or "conditional duty" as a brief way of referring to the characteristic (quite distinct from that of being a duty proper) which an act has, in virtue of being of a certain kind (e.g., the keeping of a promise), of being an act which would be a duty proper if it were not at the same time of another kind which is morally significant. Whether an act is a duty proper or actual duty depends on *all* the morally significant kinds it is an instance of ....

There is nothing arbitrary about these *prima facie* duties. Each rests on a definite circumstance which cannot seriously be held to be without moral significance. Of *prima facie* duties I suggest, without claiming completeness or finality for it, the following division.

(1) Some duties rest on previous acts of my own. These duties seem to include two kinds, (*a*) those resting on a promise or what may fairly be called an implicit promise, such as the implicit undertaking not to tell lies which seems to be implied in the act of entering into conversation (at any rate by civilized men), or of writing books that purport to be history and not fiction. These may be called the duties of fidelity. (*b*) Those resting on a previous wrongful act. These may be called the duties of reparation. (2) Some rest on previous acts of other men, i.e., services done by them to me. These may be loosely described as the duties of gratitude. (3) Some rest on the fact or possibility of a distribution of pleasure or happiness (or of the means thereto) which is not in accordance with the merit of the persons concerned; in such cases there arises a duty to upset or prevent such a distribution. These are the duties of justice. (4) Some rest on the mere fact that there are other beings in the world whose condition we can make better in respect of virtue, or of intelligence, or of pleasure. These are the duties of beneficence. (5) Some rest on the fact that we can improve our own condition in respect of virtue or of intelligence. These are the duties of self-improvement. (6) I think that we should distinguish from (4) the duties that may be summed up under the title of "not injuring others." No doubt to injure others is incidentally to fail to do them good; but it seems to me clear that non-maleficence is apprehended as a duty distinct

from that of beneficence, and as a duty of a more stringent character. It will be noticed that this alone among the types of duty has been stated in a negative way. An attempt might no doubt be made to state this duty, like the others, in a positive way. It might be said that it is really the duty to prevent ourselves from acting either from an inclination to harm others or from an inclination to seek our own pleasure, in doing which we should incidentally harm them. But on reflection it seems clear that the primary duty here is the duty not to harm others, this being a duty whether or not we have an inclination that if followed would lead to our harming them; and that when we have such an inclination the primary duty not to harm others gives rise to a consequential duty to resist the inclination. The recognition of this duty of non-maleficence is the first step on the way to the recognition of the duty of beneficence; and that accounts for the prominence of the commands "thou shalt not kill," "thou shalt not commit adultery," "thou shalt not steal," "thou shalt not bear false witness," in so early a code as the Decalogue. But even when we have come to recognize the duty of beneficence, it appears to me that the duty of non-maleficence is recognized as a distinct one, and as *prima facie* more binding. We should not in general consider it justifiable to kill one person in order to keep another alive, or to steal from one in order to give alms to another....

The essential defect of the...utilitarian theory is that it ignores, or at least does not do full justice to, the highly personal character of duty. If the only duty is to produce the maximum of good, the question who is to have the good—whether it is myself, or my benefactor, or a person to whom I have made a promise to confer that good on him, or a mere fellow man to whom I stand in no such special relation—should make no difference to my having a duty to produce that good. But we are all in fact sure that it makes a vast difference....

...That an act, *qua* fulfilling a promise, or *qua* effecting a just distribution of good, or *qua* returning services rendered, or *qua* promoting the good of others, or *qua* promoting the virtue or insight of the agent, is *prima facie* right, is self-evident; not in the sense that it is evident from the beginning of our lives, or as soon as we attend to the proposition for the first time, but in the sense that when we have reached sufficient mental maturity and have given sufficient attention to the proposition it is evident without any need of proof, or of evidence beyond itself. It is self-evident just as a mathematical axiom, or the validity of a form of inference, is evident. The moral order expressed in these propositions is just as much part of the fundamental nature of the universe (and, we may add, of any possible universe in which there were moral agents at all) as is the spatial or numerical structure expressed in the axioms of geometry or arithmetic. In our confidence that these propositions are true there is involved the same trust in our reason that is involved in our confidence in mathematics; and we should have no justification for trusting it in the latter sphere and distrusting it in the former. In both cases we are dealing with propositions that cannot be proved, but that just as certainly need no proof....

Our judgments about our actual duty in concrete situations have none of the certainty that attaches to our recognition of the general principles of duty. A statement is certain, i.e., is an expression of knowledge, only in one or other of two cases: when it is either self-evident, or a valid conclusion from self-evident premises.

And our judgments about our particular duties have neither of these characters. (1) They are not self-evident. Where a possible act is seen to have two characteristics, in virtue of one of which it is *prima facie* right, and in virtue of the other *prima facie* wrong, we are (I think) well aware that we are not certain whether we ought or ought not to do it; that whether we do it or not, we are taking a moral risk. We come in the long run, after consideration, to think one duty more pressing than the other, but we do not feel certain that it is so. And though we do not always recognize that a possible act has two such characteristics, and though there *may* be cases in which it has not, we are never certain that any particular possible act has not, and therefore never certain that it is right, nor certain that it is wrong. For, to go no further in the analysis, it is enough to point out that any particular act will in all probability in the course of time contribute to the bringing about of good or of evil for many human beings, and thus have a *prima facie* rightness or wrongness of which we know nothing. (2) Again, our judgments about our particular duties are not logical conclusions from self-evident premises. The only possible premises would be the general principles stating their *prima facie* rightness or wrongness *qua* having the different characteristics they do have; and even if we could (as we cannot) apprehend the extent to which an act will tend on the one hand, for example, to bring about advantages for our benefactors, and on the other hand to bring about disadvantages for fellow men who are not our benefactors, there is no principle by which we can draw the conclusion that it is on the whole right or on the whole wrong. In this respect the judgment as to the rightness of a particular act is just like the judgment as to the beauty of a particular natural object or work of art. A poem is, for instance, in respect of certain qualities beautiful and in respect of certain others not beautiful; and our judgment as to the degree of beauty it possesses on the whole is never reached by logical reasoning from the apprehension of its particular beauties or particular defects. Both in this and in the moral case we have more or less probable opinions which are not logically justified conclusions from the general principles that are recognized as self-evident.

There is therefore much truth in the description of the right act as a fortunate act. If we cannot be certain that it is right, it is our good fortune if the act we do is the right act. This consideration does not, however, make the doing of our duty a mere matter of chance. There is a parallel here between the doing of duty and the doing of what will be to our personal advantage. We never *know* what act will in the long run be to our advantage. Yet it is certain that we are more likely in general to secure our advantage if we estimate to the best of our ability the probable tendencies of our actions in this respect, than if we act on caprice. And similarly we are more likely to do our duty if we reflect to the best of our ability on the *prima facie* rightness or wrongness of various possible acts in virtue of the characteristics we perceive them to have, than if we act without reflection. With this greater likelihood we must be content....

In what has preceded, a good deal of use has been made of "what we really think" about moral questions....

...It might be said that this is in principle wrong; that we should not be content to expound what our present moral consciousness tells us but should aim at a criticism of our existing moral consciousness in the light of theory. Now I do not doubt that the moral consciousness of men has in detail undergone a good deal of modification as regards the things we think right, at the hands of moral theory. But ... we have to ask ourselves whether we really, when we reflect, *are* convinced that this is self-evident, and whether we really *can* get rid of our view that promise-keeping has a bindingness independent of productiveness of maximum good. In my own experience I find that I cannot, in spite of a very genuine attempt to do so....

I would maintain, in fact, that what we are apt to describe as "what we think" about moral questions contains a considerable amount that we do not think but know, and that this forms the standard by reference to which the truth of any moral theory has to be tested, instead of having itself to be tested by reference to any theory. I hope that I have in what precedes indicated what in my view these elements of knowledge are that are involved in our ordinary moral consciousness.

It would be a mistake to found a natural science on "what we really think," i.e., on what reasonably thoughtful and well-educated people think about the subjects of the science before they have studied them scientifically. For such opinions are interpretations, and often misinterpretations, of sense-experience; and the man of science must appeal from these to sense-experience itself, which furnishes his real data. In ethics no such appeal is possible. We have no more direct way of access to the facts about rightness and goodness and about what things are right or good, than by thinking about them; the moral convictions of thoughtful and well-educated people are the data of ethics just as sense-perceptions are the data of a natural science. Just as some of the latter have to be rejected as illusory, so have some of the former; but as the latter are rejected only when they are in conflict with other more accurate sense-perceptions, the former are rejected only when they are in conflict with other convictions which stand better the test of reflection. The existing body of moral convictions of the best people is the cumulative product of the moral reflection of many generations, which has developed an extremely delicate power of appreciation of moral distinctions; and this the theorist cannot afford to treat with anything other than the greatest respect. The verdicts of the moral consciousness of the best people are the foundation on which he must build; though he must first compare them with one another and eliminate any contradictions they may contain.

READING QUESTIONS

1. Explain in your own words what Ross means by "prima facie duty."
2. Ross claims that the utilitarian theory "ignores, or at least does not do full justice to, the highly personal character of duty." What does he mean by this?
3. What does Ross say about the need to prove his principles of prima facie duty? Do you find his claim plausible? Explain.

DISCUSSION QUESTIONS

1. What conclusions do you think follow from Ross's ethic of prima facie duty about the morality of meat eating?
2. What implications do you think Ross's theory has for certain sexual issues including homosexuality, adultery, and prostitution?

ADDITIONAL RESOURCES

Web Resources

Stanford Encyclopedia of Philosophy, <http://plato.stanford.edu/>. An excellent resource. See in particular the following entries:

- Aquinas's Moral, Political, and Legal Philosophy by John Finnis
- The Natural Law Tradition in Ethics by Mark Murphy
- Doctrine of Double Effect by Alison McIntyre
- Consequentialism by Walter Sinnott-Armstrong
- The History of Utilitarianism by Julia Driver
- Kant's Moral Theory by Robert Johnson
- Locke's Political Philosophy by Alex Tuckness
- Rights by Leif Wenar
- Aristotle's Ethics by Richard Kraut

Authored Books

The following are introductory texts.

Darwall, Stephen, *Philosophical Ethics* (Boulder, CO: Westview Press, 1998). Parts III and IV of this text include two chapters on Mill, two on Kant, and one on Aristotle.

Driver, Julia, *Ethics: The Fundamentals* (Oxford: Blackwell Publishing Ltd, 2007). Includes chapters on God, morality and human nature, utilitarianism, consequentialism, Kant's ethics, virtue ethics, and feminist ethics, social contract theory, intuitionism, and moral nihilism.

Harris, C. E., *Applying Moral Theories,* 5th ed. (Belmont, CA: Wadsworth, 2005). A text featuring chapters on egoism, natural law, utilitarianism, respect for persons, and virtue ethics with a special focus on the application of these theories to moral problems.

Timmons, Mark, *Moral Theory: An Introduction* (Rowman & Littlefield, 2002). A text entirely devoted to normative ethical theory. Includes chapters on divine command theory, relativism, natural law theory, utilitarianism (both classical and contemporary), Kantian moral theory, ethical pluralism (Ross), virtue ethics, and ethical particularism.

Edited Collections

There are many ethics anthologies that are either dedicated to or feature readings in moral theory. Here are two of them.

Shafer-Landau, Russ, *Ethical Theory: An Anthology* (Oxford: Blackwell, 2007). Approaching 800 pages, this anthology includes a wide range of classical and contemporary selections in both moral theory and applied ethics.

Timmons, Mark, *Conduct and Character: Readings in Moral Theory*, 6th ed. (Belmont, CA: Thomson Wadsworth, 2011). A compact reader with selections from classical and contemporary sources covering a wide variety of moral theories, including the six featured in chapters 1 and 2 of this anthology.

3 } Sexual Morality and Marriage

Moral questions about sexual activity including contraception, masturbation, simultaneous sex with multiple partners, homosexuality, adultery, premarital sex, and prostitution seem to be a permanent source of dispute. Some think that all such actions are inherently morally wrong; others disagree. Moral questions about sexual behavior are related to moral and legal questions about marriage. Some claim that marriage ought to be between one man and one woman; that any other form of interpersonal union involving sex among partners is both morally wrong and ought to be legally prohibited. Questions about the morality and legality of marriage have been hotly debated in recent years where the focus has been on same-sex marriage.

Debates over the morality of various forms of sexual behavior and over the morality and legality of same-sex marriage raise the following questions:

- For each type of sexual activity in question, are there any conditions under which it is morally wrong?
- For those sexual activities and practices that are morally wrong, what is the best explanation of their wrongness?
- Should same-sex marriage be permitted?
- If not, what is the best explanation of why it should not be permitted?

1. A SPECTRUM OF VIEWS

Often the terms **"conservative," "liberal,"** and **"moderate"** are used to characterize different positions one might take on some moral issue. Let us first explain these labels as they tend to be used in connection with issues about sexual behavior, and then I will issue a couple of warnings about their use.

The differences among conservative, liberal, and moderate views on most any moral issue have to do with the range of behavior that is taken to be morally permissible: conservative views restrict the range to a greater degree than do moderate or liberal views, and, of course, a moderate view imposes more restrictions than does a liberal one. When it comes to questions of sexual behavior, moral restrictions focus on the nature of the relationship that exists among those engaged in sexual activity. The motto of the conservative is "no sex without legal marriage," where it is assumed that marriage partners are of the opposite sex and that they are restricted in their sexual activity to having sex with each other and not, say, with partners from another marriage. Most obviously, a conservative sexual ethic rules out a number of sexual activities including premarital sex, adultery, prostitution, and homosexual behavior.

By contrast, a liberal on matters of sexual morality will hold that limits on sex have to do with the moral restrictions on human relationships generally—restrictions that are not specifically about sex. So, for example, on a standard liberal view, sexual behavior by an individual that is based on deceiving a sexual partner is wrong because it involves deception. Lying to someone about having a sexually transmittable disease in order to get them to agree to sexual intercourse is wrong because (according to the liberal view), lying in general is wrong. Again, sex involving coercion (including most obviously rape) is wrong on a liberal view because coercion is wrong. A conservative will agree with the liberal about cases involving deception and coercion, but where they differ is that the conservative holds that there are further restrictions on morally permissible sex besides those having to do with general moral rules that apply to all behavior. For a liberal, then, there is nothing inherently morally wrong with homosexuality, premarital sex, prostitution, simultaneous sex with multiple partners, adultery, prostitution—individual instances of all of these activities are permissible *so long as they are not in violation of general moral rules applying to all sorts of behavior—sexual and nonsexual.*

Finally, a moderate is someone who disagrees with a conservative in restricting morally permissible sex to partners who are legally married, but also disagrees with a liberal who thinks that the only moral restrictions on sex have to do with general moral rules. Rather, a typical moderate position claims that in order for sexual activity by an individual to be morally legitimate, that person must have a certain "bond" with her or his partner. Sometimes this view is expressed in the motto "no sex without love." Were a moderate to stick to this motto, her view would still allow many forms of sexual interaction ruled out by the typical conservative. For instance, going by this motto, homosexual behavior between gays or lesbians who love each other is morally permitted.

But let me issue two warnings about the use of these labels. First, speaking now about moral issues generally, these labels are here being used for general positions on the morality of some activity that differ in *the range of sexual activities that are thought to be morally permissible.* In other contexts, these same labels are used to classify views over economic policy and more generally over the role of government in the lives of its citizens.[1] And so the first warning is this: when using such labels, remember that it is possible to be, for example, a conservative about economic issues, but a liberal or moderate about moral issues. Additionally, if one is a liberal, say, about the morality of euthanasia, one need not be a liberal about all other moral issues. In short, taking a so-called liberal or conservative or moderate position on one issue need not commit you to taking the same type of position on other issues.

The second warning is this. There is no *one* conservative or liberal or moderate position on any one topic. These labels are names for general types of views, and within each type there will be a variety of more specific versions of the general type. Thus, two individuals might hold a conservative position with respect to sexual morality, but one of these positions may be more conservative than the other. For instance, in addition to holding that sexual partners must be legally married to each other, one might hold that there are moral limits to what sorts of sexual activity they may engage in. One possible further restriction might rule out anal intercourse or mutual masturbation or (even more restrictively) sexual intercourse that does not aim at producing children. Within each camp, we find a variety of possible views that are more or less restrictive. So, if one is going to use these labels, then it is best to think of there being a spectrum of views that blend into one another. Here is a simple visual aid:

| Liberal | Moderate | Conservative |

Let the farthest point on the left of the horizontal line represent the most extreme liberal view, and let the farthest point on the right of the same line represent the most extreme conservative view. A line is a series of points, and so think of there being possible views about the morality of sexual behavior that may be positioned anywhere along this line. Using these labels, one might hold an extremely conservative view, or instead one might hold a moderately conservative view, or perhaps a moderately liberal view, and so on. The view one holds on any moral issue should be based on one's assessment of the quality of the moral arguments that concern the issue in question, rather than based on whichever label applies to that view.

Let us now turn to the sorts of arguments featured in our readings. It is useful to sort the readings into two groups. First, there are "general approaches" to sexual morality that attempt to provide a general ethical framework for thinking about matters of sex. Second, there are "selected topics" including adultery, homosexuality, and same-sex marriage (among others) that are discussed in our readings.

2. THEORY MEETS PRACTICE: GENERAL APPROACHES

In the first and third readings that follow, we find sharply contrasting approaches to sexual morality. The "Vatican Declaration" presents a conservative sexual ethic based on some elements of natural law theory. In the second article, Thomas A. Mappes defends a liberal view based on one leading idea of Kant's ethics. And in his article on adultery, Raja Halwani embraces a version of virtue ethics. Let us briefly consider the natural law and Kantian approaches, saving the virtue ethics approach for our discussion of special topics.

Natural Law Theory

You may recall from chapter 1 that the basic idea of natural law ethics is that there is an objective human good, and the rightness or wrongness of actions is evaluated in terms of how they bear on the production and maintenance of what is good. According to Aquinas, one of the four basic human goods is procreation, proper respect for which imposes obligations regarding the use of sexual organs as well as obligations regarding the "natural" outcome of sexual intercourse, namely, child rearing.

Sometimes natural law theory is associated with the idea that an action is morally wrong if performing it would somehow go against nature. The idea is summed up in the formula: *an action is wrong if it is unnatural,* and it is the basis of the often-heard "unnaturalness" argument against homosexuality and other forms of sexual behavior. Problems with the unnaturalness argument are discussed in the reading from John Corvino. However, one should not suppose that all versions (or even the most plausible version) of natural law theory commit one to questionable ideas about what is and is not natural.

Kantian Moral Theory

One of the leading ideas of Kant's ethics is the general requirement to treat all persons as ends in themselves and never *merely* as means to an end. This is Kant's Humanity formulation of his fundamental moral principle—the categorical imperative. This principle was discussed briefly in the first chapter and is the basis of a liberal view on sexual morality defended by Mappes. What Mappes does is provide a characterization of what it means to treat someone as a mere means, and on that basis proceeds to draw out various moral implications for sexual activity. It should be noted that Kant himself held a fairly conservative view of sexual morality because he thought that sexual behavior outside the confines of marriage was inherently degrading to the worth or dignity of human beings. On this point Kant and Mappes differ significantly.

3. THEORY MEETS PRACTICE: SPECIAL TOPICS

Adultery

Adultery is the act of voluntary sexual intercourse between a married person and someone other than his or her legal spouse. Adulterous actions are widely considered to be morally wrong—either in all, or at least most, cases. But how best can we understand the wrongness of such actions—what best explains the wrongness of adulterous actions? This same question can be asked of infidelity between couples who are not legally married but who are involved in a romantic relationship that is understood by the partners to be sexually exclusive. Consequentialists will appeal to the overall badness of the consequences of sexual infidelity, while Kantians like Mappes will stress the fact that cases of infidelity where one partner deceives the other violates the requirement that partners treat each other not as a mere means but as ends in themselves. By contrast, virtue ethics approaches the morality of adultery in particular and sexual fidelity in general by focusing on ideals toward which a virtuous person would aspire. This is the approach that is defended by Raja Halwani in our readings. He argues that virtue ethics provides a better understanding of the morality of sexual fidelity than does either consequentialist or Kantian approaches.

Homosexuality

The morality of **homosexual behavior**—sexual activity, particularly intercourse, between members of the same sex—is a continuing source of moral and legal dispute. As noted above, one familiar kind of argument for the claim that homosexuality is morally wrong is that such sex is "unnatural." In addition, some critics argue that homosexuality (compared to heterosexuality) is harmful to those who engage in it as well as to other members of society. In addition to his critique of unnaturalness arguments concerning homosexuality, Corvino also discusses arguments that allege various sorts of harm.

Same-Sex Marriage

A related issue that has received much media attention in recent years is **same-sex marriage**. Same-sex marriage is to be distinguished from **civil unions**, which is a legal category that grants some rights to same-sex couples, and **domestic partnerships**, which is a legal category that extends some rights to unmarried couples, including same-sex couples. With respect to rights, the main difference between marriages that are recognized by the federal government and civil unions is that the former but not the latter offers *federal* benefits and protections.

However, in 1996, the United States Congress passed the "Defense of Marriage Act" (**DOMA**), which, for purposes of Federal law, defines "marriage" as "a legal union between one man and one woman as husband and wife." This definition implies that the federal benefits that opposite-sex married couples enjoy compared to those involved in civil unions are not available to same-sex married couples.

DOMA also affirms the power of U.S. states to refuse to grant and to recognize same-sex marriages. Many U.S. states have either passed laws that prohibit marrying same-sex couples in that state or have adopted state constitutional amendments prohibiting same-sex marriages. However, as of July 2009, six states (Connecticut, Iowa, Maine, Massachusetts, New Hampshire, and Vermont) had passed laws that legalize same-sex marriages, and prohibitions in many other states are currently being subject to legal challenge. However, in 2009, voters in Maine voted to repeal the state law permitting same-sex marriages. Should same-sex marriages be legalized? This question is debated in the selections by Maggie Gallagher, who opposes such unions, and Evan Wolfson, who favors them. Much of their disagreement stems from claims about the predicted consequences of allowing same-sex marriage.

NOTE

1. This usage of "liberal" and "conservative" should not be confused with the political ideologies that are referred to by the labels "Liberal*ism*" and "Conservat*ism.*" These views are briefly described in the introduction to the chapter on pornography, hate speech, and censorship, sec. 2.

Vatican Declaration on Some Questions of Sexual Ethics

This declaration affirms the traditional teachings of the Catholic Church on matters of sexual behavior. The basis of the church's teachings is the natural law approach to ethics, according to which there are objective standards of human behavior that are grounded in facts about human nature and are thus "perennial"—principles that can be known either through revelation or through the use of reason. The fundamental principles of sexual morality concern, then, the nature of the human being and the proper function of sexual behavior, which includes "mutual self-giving and human procreation in the context of true love." This principle is then used as a basis for arguing that premarital sex, homosexuality, and masturbation are morally wrong.

Recommended Reading: natural law theory, chap. 1, sec. 2B.

INTRODUCTION

Importance of Sexuality

1. The human person, according to the scientific disciplines of our day, is so deeply influenced by his sexuality that this latter must be regarded as one of the basic factors shaping human life. The person's sex is the source of the biological, psychological and spiritual characteristics which make the person male or female, and thus are extremely important and influential in the maturation and socialization of the individual. It is easy to understand, therefore, why matters pertaining to sex are frequently and openly discussed in books, periodicals, newspapers and other communications media.

Meanwhile, moral corruption is on the increase. One of the most serious signs of this is the boundless exaltation of sex. In addition, with the help of the mass media and the various forms of entertainment, sex has even invaded the field of education and infected the public mind.

In this situation, some educators, teachers and moralists have been able to contribute to a better understanding and vital integration of the special values and qualities proper to each sex. Others, however, have defended views and ways of acting which are in conflict with the true moral requirements of man, and have even opened the door to a licentious hedonism.

The result is that, within a few years' time, teachings, moral norms and habits of life hitherto faithfully preserved have been called into doubt, even by Christians. Many today are asking what they are to regard as true when so many current views are at odds with what they learned from the Church.

Occasion for This Declaration

2. In the face of this intellectual confusion and moral corruption the Church cannot stand by and do nothing.

The issue here is too important in the life both of the individual and of contemporary society.[1]

Bishops see each day the ever increasing difficulties of the faithful in acquiring sound moral teaching, especially in sexual matters, and of pastors in effectively explaining that teaching. The bishops know it is their pastoral duty to come to the aid of the faithful in such a serious matter. Indeed, some outstanding documents have been published on the subject by some bishops and some episcopal conferences. But, since erroneous views and the deviations they produce continue to be broadcast everywhere, the Sacred Congregation for the Doctrine of the Faith in accordance with its role in the universal Church[2] and by mandate of the Supreme Pontiff, has thought it necessary to issue this Declaration.

I. GENERAL CONSIDERATIONS

The Sources of Moral Knowledge

3. The men of our day are increasingly persuaded that their dignity and calling as human beings requires them to use their minds to discover the values and powers inherent in their nature, to develop these without ceasing and to translate them into action, so that they may make daily greater progress.

When it comes to judgments on moral matters, however, man may not proceed simply as he thinks fit. "Deep within, man detects the law of conscience—a law which is not self-imposed but which holds him to obedience. . . . For man has in his heart a law written by God. To obey it is the very dignity of man; according to it he will be judged."[3]

To us Christians, moreover, God has revealed his plan of salvation and has given us Christ, the Savior and sanctifier, as the supreme and immutable norm of life through his teaching and example. Christ himself has said: "I am the light of the world. No follower of mine shall ever walk in darkness; no, he shall possess the light of life."[4]

The authentic dignity of man cannot be promoted, therefore, except through adherence to the order which

is essential to his nature. There is no denying, of course, that in the history of civilization many of the concrete conditions and relationships of human life have changed and will change again in the future but every moral evolution and every manner of life must respect the limits set by the immutable principles which are grounded in the constitutive elements and essential relations proper to the human person. These elements and relations are not subject to historical contingency.

The basic principles in question can be grasped by man's reason. They are contained in "the divine law—eternal, objective and universal—whereby God orders, directs and governs the entire universe and all the ways of the human community by a plan conceived in wisdom and love. God has made man a participant in this law, with the result that, under the gentle disposition of divine Providence, he can come to perceive ever more fully the truth that is unchanging."[5] This divine law is something we can know.

The Principles of Morality Are Perennial

4. Wrongly, therefore, do many today deny that either human nature or revealed law furnishes any absolute and changeless norm for particular actions except the general law of love and respect for human dignity. To justify this position, they argue that both the so-called norms of the natural law and the precepts of Sacred Scripture are simply products of a particular human culture and its expressions at a certain point in history.

But divine revelation and, in its own order, natural human wisdom show us genuine exigencies of human nature and, as a direct and necessary consequence, immutable laws which are grounded in the constitutive elements of human nature and show themselves the same in all rational beings. . . .

The Fundamental Principles of Sexual Morality

5. Since sexual morality has to do with values which are basic to human and Christian life, the general doctrine we have been presenting applies to it. In this area there are principles and norms which the Church has always unhesitatingly transmitted as part

of her teaching, however opposed they might be to the mentality and ways of the world. These principles and norms have their origin, not in a particular culture, but in knowledge of the divine law and human nature. Consequently, it is impossible for them to lose their binding force or to be called into doubt on the grounds of cultural change.

These principles guided Vatican Council II when it provided advice and directives for the establishment of the kind of social life in which the equal dignity of man and woman will be respected, even while the differences between them also are preserved.[6]

In speaking of the sexual nature of the human being and of the human generative powers, the Council observes that these are "remarkably superior to those found in lower grades of life."[7] Then it deals in detail with the principles and norms which apply to human sexuality in the married state and are based on the finality of the function proper to marriage.

In this context the Council asserts that the moral goodness of the actions proper to married life, when ordered as man's true dignity requires, "does not depend only on a sincere intention and the evaluating of motives, but must be judged by objective standards. These are drawn from the nature of the human person and of his acts, and have regard for the whole meaning of mutual self-giving and human procreation in the context of true love."[8]

These last words are a brief summation of the Council's teaching (previously set forth at length in the same document[9]) on the finality of the sexual act and on the chief norm governing its morality. It is respect for this finality which guarantees the moral goodness of the act.

The same principle, which the Church derives from divine revelation and from her authentic interpretation of the natural law, is also the source of her traditional teaching that the exercise of the sexual function has its true meaning and is morally good only in legitimate marriage.[10]

Limits of This Declaration

6. It is not the intention of this declaration to treat all abuses of the sexual powers nor to deal with all that is involved in the practice of chastity but rather to recall the Church's norms on certain specific points, since there is a crying need of opposing certain serious errors and deviant forms of behavior.

II. SPECIFIC APPLICATIONS

Premarital Relations

7. Many individuals at the present time are claiming the right to sexual union before marriage, at least when there is a firm intention of marrying and when a love which both partners think of as already conjugal demands this further step which seems to them connatural. They consider this further step justified especially when external circumstances prevent the formal entry into marriage or when intimate union seems necessary if love is to be kept alive.

This view is opposed to the Christian teaching that any human genital act whatsoever may be placed only within the framework of marriage. For, however firm the intention of those who pledge themselves to each other in such premature unions, these unions cannot guarantee the sincerity and fidelity of the relationship between man and woman, and, above all, cannot protect the relationship against the changeableness of desire and determination.

Yet, Christ the Lord willed that the union be a stable one and he restored it to its original condition as founded in the difference between the sexes. "Have you not read that at the beginning the Creator made them male and female and declared., 'For this reason a man shall leave his father and mother and cling to his wife and the two shall become as one'? Thus they are no longer two but one flesh. Therefore, let no man separate what God has joined."[11] . . .

Such has always been the Church's understanding of and teaching on the exercise of the sexual function.[12] She finds, moreover, that natural human wisdom and the lessons of history are in profound agreement with her.

Experience teaches that if sexual union is truly to satisfy the requirements of its own finality and of human dignity, love must be safeguarded by the stability marriage gives. These requirements necessitate a contract which is sanctioned and protected by society: the contract gives rise to a new state of life and is of exceptional importance for the exclusive union of man and woman as well as for the good of their family and the whole of human society. Premarital relations, on the other hand, most often exclude any prospect of children. Such love claims in vain to be conjugal since it cannot, as it certainly should, grow into a maternal and paternal love; or, if the pair do become parents, it will be to the detriment of the children, who are deprived of a stable environment in which they can grow up in a proper fashion and find the way and means of entering into the larger society of men.

Therefore, the consent of those entering into marriage must be externally manifested, and this in such a way as to render it binding in the eyes of society. The faithful, for their part, must follow the laws of the Church in declaring their marital consent: it is this consent that makes their marriage a sacrament of Christ.

Homosexuality

8. Contrary to the perennial teaching of the Church and the moral sense of the Christian people, some individuals today have, on psychological grounds, begun to judge indulgently or even simply to excuse homosexual relations for certain people.

They make a distinction which has indeed some foundation: between homosexuals whose bent derives from improper education or a failure of sexual maturation or habit or bad example or some similar cause and is only temporary or at least is not incurable; and homosexuals who are permanently such because of some innate drive or a pathological condition which is considered incurable.

The propensity of those in the latter class is—it is argued—so natural that it should be regarded as justifying homosexual relations within a sincere and loving communion of life which is comparable to marriage inasmuch as those involved in it deem it impossible for them to live a solitary life.

Objective Evil of Such Acts

As far as pastoral care is concerned, such homosexuals are certainly to be treated with understanding and encouraged to hope that they can some day overcome their difficulties and their inability to fit into society in a normal fashion. Prudence, too, must be exercised in judging their guilt. However, no pastoral approach may be taken which would consider these individuals morally justified on the grounds that such acts are in accordance with their nature. For, according to the objective moral order, homosexual relations are acts deprived of the essential ordination they ought to have.

In Sacred Scripture such acts are condemned as serious deviations and are even considered to be the lamentable effect of rejecting God.[13] This judgment on the part of the divinely inspired Scriptures does not justify us in saying that all who suffer from this anomaly are guilty of personal sin but it does show that homosexual acts are disordered by their very nature and can never be approved.

Masturbation

9. Frequently today we find doubt or open rejection of the traditional Catholic teaching that masturbation is a serious moral disorder. Psychology and sociology (it is claimed) show that masturbation, especially in adolescents, is a normal phase in the process of sexual maturation and is, therefore, not gravely sinful unless the individual deliberately cultivates a solitary pleasure that is turned in upon itself ("ipsation"). In this last case, the act would be radically opposed to that loving communion between persons of different sexes which (according to some) is the principal goal to be sought in the use of the sexual powers.

This opinion is contrary to the teaching and pastoral practice of the Catholic Church. Whatever be the validity of certain arguments of a biological and philosophical kind which theologians sometimes use, both the magisterium of the Church (following a constant tradition) and the moral sense of the faithful have unhesitatingly asserted that masturbation is an intrinsically and seriously disordered act.[14] The chief reason for this stand is that, whatever the motive, the deliberate use of the sexual faculty outside of normal conjugal relations essentially contradicts its finality. In such an act there is lacking the sexual relationship which the moral order requires, the kind of relationship in which "the whole meaning of mutual self-giving and human procreation" is made concretely real "in the context of true love."[15] Only within such a relationship may the sexual powers be deliberately exercised.

Even if it cannot be established that Sacred Scripture condemns this sin under a specific name, the Church's tradition rightly understands it to be condemned in the New Testament when the latter speaks of "uncleanness" or "unchasteness" or the other vices contrary to chastity and continence.

Sociological research can show the relative frequency of this disorder according to places, types of people and various circumstances which may be taken into account. It thus provides an array of facts. But facts provide no norm for judging the morality of human acts.[16] The frequency of the act here in question is connected with innate human weakness deriving from original sin, but also with the loss of the sense of God, with the moral corruption fostered by the commercialization of vice, with the unbridled license to be found in so many books and forms of public entertainment and with the forgetfulness of modesty, which is the safeguard of chastity.

In dealing with masturbation, modern psychology provides a number of valid and useful insights which enable us to judge more equitably of moral responsibility. They can also help us understand how adolescent immaturity (sometimes prolonged beyond the adolescent years) or a lack of psychological balance or habits can affect behavior, since they may make an action less deliberate and not always a subjectively serious sin. But the lack of serious responsibility should not be generally presumed; if it is, there is simply a failure to recognize man's ability to act in a moral way.

In the pastoral ministry, in order to reach a balanced judgment in individual cases account must be taken of the overall habitual manner in which the person acts, not only in regard to charity and justice, but also in regard to the care with which he observes the precept of chastity in particular. Special heed must be paid to whether he uses the necessary natural and supernatural helps which Christian asceticism recommends, in the light of long experience, for mastering the passions and attaining virtue. . . .

NOTES

1. See Vatican II, *Pastoral Constitution on the Church in the World of Today,* no. 47: *Acta Apostolicae Sedis* 58 (1966) 1067 [*The Pope Speaks* XI, 289–290].

2. See the Apostolic Constitution *Regimini Ecclesiae universae* (August 15, 1967), no. 29: *AAS* 59 (1967) 897 [*TPS* XII, 401–402].

3. *Pastoral Constitution on the Church in the World of Today,* no. 16: *AAS* 58 (1966) 1037 [*TPS* XI, 268].

4. *Jn* 8, 12.

5. *Declaration on Religious Freedom,* no. 3: *AAS* 58 (1966) 931 [*TPS* XI, 86].

6. See Vatican II, *Declaration on Christian Education,* nos. 1 and 8: *AAS* 58 (1966) 729–730, 734–736 [*TPS* XI, 201–202, 206–207]; *Pastoral Constitution on the Church in the World of Today,* nos. 29, 60, 67: *AAS* 58 (1966) 1048–1049, 1080–1081, 1088–1089 [*TPS* XI, 276–277, 299–300, 304–305].

7. *Pastoral Constitution on the Church in the World of Today,* no. 51: *AAS* 58 (1966) 1072 [*TPS* XI, 293].

8. Loc. cit.: see also no. 49: *AAS* 58 (1966) 1069–1070 [*TPS* XI, 291–292].

9. See *Pastoral Constitution on the Church in the World of Today,* nos. 49–50: *AAS* 58 (1966) 1069–1072 [*TPS* XI, 291–293].

10. The present Declaration does not review all the moral norms for the use of sex, since they have already been set forth in the encyclicals *Casti Connubii* and *Humanae Vitae.*

11. *Mt* 19, 4–6.

12. See Innocent IV, Letter *Sub Catholicae professione* (March 6, 1254) (*DS* 835); Pius II. Letter *Cum sicut accepimus* (November 14, 1459) (*DS* 1367); Decrees of the Holy Office on September 24, 1665 (*DS* 2045) and March 2, 1679 (*DS* 2148); Pius XI, Encyclical *Casti Connubii* (December 31, 1930): *AAS* 22 (1930) 538–539.

13. *Rom* 1:24–27: "In consequence, God delivered them up in their lusts to unclean practices; they engaged

in the mutual degradation of their bodies, these men who exchanged the truth of God for a lie and worshiped and served the creature rather than the Creator—blessed be he forever, amen! God therefore delivered them to disgraceful passions. Their women exchanged natural intercourse for unnatural, and the men gave up natural intercourse with women and burned with lust for one another. Men did shameful things with men, and thus received in their own persons the penalty for their perversity." See also what St. Paul says of sodomy in *1 Cor* 6, 9; *1 Tm* 1, 10.

14. See Leo IX, Letter *Ad splendidum nitentes* (1054) (*DS* 687–688); Decree of the Holy Office on March 2, 1679 (*DS* 2149); Pius XII, Addresses of October 8, 1953: *AAS* 45 (1953) 677–678, and May 19, 1956: *AAS* 48 (1956) 472–473.

15. *Pastoral Constitution on the Church in the World of Today,* no. 51: *AAS* 58 (1966) 1072 [*TPS* XI, 293].

16. See Paul VI, Apostolic Exhortation *Quinque iam anni* (December 8, 1970): *AAS* 63 (1971) 102 [*TPS* XV, 329]: "If sociological surveys are useful for better discovering the thought patterns of the people of a particular place, the anxieties and needs of those to whom we proclaim the word of God, and also the oppositions made to it by modern reasoning through the widespread notion that outside science there exists no legitimate form of knowledge, still the conclusions drawn from such surveys could not of themselves constitute a determining criterion of truth."

READING QUESTIONS

1. Explain the sources of moral knowledge according to the Vatican.
2. How does the Vatican characterize morally good sexual activity?
3. Why does the Vatican object to premarital sexual relations? How is marriage intended to stabilize the relationship between two individuals?
4. What is the distinction recognized by the Vatican regarding the cause of homosexual behavior?
5. Why does the Vatican believe that homosexuality is objectively evil? How should pastors address specific cases of individual engagement in homosexual behavior according to the Vatican?

DISCUSSION QUESTIONS

1. The Vatican claims that the institution of marriage is designed to encourage stable relationships. Consider whether marriages generally succeed or fail in this regard. Can individuals that engage in sexual relations outside of the bonds of marriage maintain stable and lasting commitments to one another?
2. How might persons in the secular and scientific communities respond to the Vatican's objections to homosexuality and masturbation?

John Corvino

Why Shouldn't Tommy and Jim Have Sex?
A Defense of Homosexuality

Among the most commonly raised moral objections to homosexual behavior are that it is "unnatural" and that it is harmful either to those who engage in it or to others. Corvino considers a number of versions of both types of argument and concludes that none of them are defensible.

Recommended Reading: natural law theory, chap. 1, sec. 2B.

Tommy and Jim are a homosexual couple I know. Tommy is an accountant; Jim is a botany professor. They are in their forties and have been together fourteen years, the last five of which they've lived in a Victorian house that they've lovingly restored. Although their relationship has had its challenges, each has made sacrifices for the sake of the other's happiness and the relationship's long-term success.

I assume that Tommy and Jim have sex with each other (although I've never bothered to ask). Furthermore, I contend that they probably *should* have sex with each other. For one thing, sex is pleasurable. But it is also much more than that: a sexual relationship can unite two people in a way that virtually nothing else can. It can be an avenue of growth, of communication, and of lasting interpersonal fulfillment. These are reasons why most heterosexual couples have sex even if they don't want children, don't want children yet, or don't want additional children. And if these reasons are good enough for most heterosexual couples, then they should be good enough for Tommy and Jim.

Of course, having a reason to do something does not preclude there being an even better reason for not doing it. Tommy might have a good reason for drinking orange juice (it's tasty and nutritious) but an even better reason for not doing so (he's allergic). The point is that one would need a pretty good reason for denying a sexual relationship to Tommy and Jim, given the intense benefits widely associated with such relationships. The question I shall consider in this paper is thus quite simple: Why shouldn't Tommy and Jim have sex?[1]

HOMOSEXUAL SEX IS "UNNATURAL"

Many contend that homosexual sex is "unnatural." But what does that mean? Many things that people value—clothing, houses, medicine, and government, for example—are unnatural in some sense. On the other hand, many things that people detest—disease, suffering, and death, for example—are "natural" in the sense that they occur "in nature." If the unnaturalness charge is to be more than empty rhetorical flourish, those who levy it must specify what they mean. Borrowing from Burton Leiser, I will examine several possible meanings of "unnatural."[2]

From John Covino, "Why Shouldn't Tommy and Jim Have Sex? A Defense of Homosexuality," in John Covino, ed., *Same Sex: Debating the Ethics, Science, and Culture of Homosexuality* (Lanham, MD: Rowman and Littlefield, 1997). Reprinted by permission of the publisher.

What Is Unusual or Abnormal Is Unnatural

One meaning of "unnatural" refers to that which deviates from the norm, that is, from what most people do. Obviously, most people engage in heterosexual relationships. But does it follow that it is wrong to engage in homosexual relationships? Relatively few people read Sanskrit, pilot ships, play the mandolin, breed goats, or write with both hands, yet none of these activities is immoral simply because it is unusual. As the Ramsey Colloquium, a group of Jewish and Christian scholars who oppose homosexuality, writes, "The statistical frequency of an act does not determine its moral status."[3] So while homosexuality might be unnatural in the sense of being unusual, that fact is morally irrelevant.

What Is Not Practiced by Other Animals Is Unnatural

Some people argue, "Even animals know better than to behave homosexually; homosexuality must be wrong." This argument is doubly flawed. First, it rests on a false premise. Numerous studies—including Anne Perkins's study of "gay" sheep and George and Molly Hunt's study of "lesbian" seagulls—have shown that some animals do form homosexual pair-bonds.[4] Second, even if animals did not behave homosexually, that fact would not prove that homosexuality is immoral. After all, animals don't cook their food, brush their teeth, participate in religious worship, or attend college; human beings do all of these without moral censure. Indeed, the idea that animals could provide us with our standards—especially our sexual standards—is simply amusing.

What Does Not Proceed from Innate Desires Is Unnatural

Recent studies suggesting a biological basis for homosexuality have resulted in two popular positions. One side proposes that homosexual people are "born that way" and that it is therefore natural (and thus good) for them to form homosexual relationships. The other side maintains that homosexuality is a lifestyle choice, which is therefore unnatural (and thus wrong). Both sides assume a connection between the origin of homosexual orientation, on the one hand, and the moral value of homosexual activity, on the other. And insofar as they share that assumption, both sides are wrong.

Consider first the pro-homosexual side: "They are born that way: therefore it's natural and good." This inference assumes that all innate desires are good ones (i.e., that they should be acted upon). But that assumption is clearly false. Research suggests that some people are born with a predisposition toward violence, but such people have no more right to strangle their neighbors than anyone else. So while people like Tommy and Jim may be born with homosexual tendencies, it doesn't follow that they ought to act on them. Nor does it follow that they ought *not* to act on them, even if the tendencies are not innate. I probably do not have any innate tendency to write with my left hand (since I, like everyone else in my family, have always been right-handed), but it doesn't follow that it would be immoral for me to do so. So simply asserting that homosexuality is a lifestyle choice will not show that it is an immoral lifestyle choice.

Do people "choose" to be homosexual? People certainly don't seem to choose their sexual *feelings,* at least not in any direct or obvious way. (Do you? Think about it.) Rather, they find certain people attractive and certain activities arousing, whether they "decide" to or not. Indeed, most people at some point in their lives wish that they could control their feelings more—for example, in situations of unrequited love—and find it frustrating that they cannot. What they *can* control to a considerable degree is how and when they act upon those feelings. In that sense, both homosexuality and heterosexuality involve lifestyle choices. But in either case, determining the origin of the feelings will not determine whether it is moral to act on them.

What Violates an Organ's Principal Purpose Is Unnatural

Perhaps when people claim that homosexual sex is unnatural they mean that it cannot result in procreation. The idea behind the argument is that human organs have various natural purposes: eyes are for seeing, ears are for hearing, genitals are for procreating. According to this argument, it is immoral to use an organ in a way that violates its particular purpose.

Many of our organs, however, have multiple purposes. Tommy can use his mouth for talking, eating, breathing, licking stamps, chewing gum, kissing women, or kissing Jim; and it seems rather arbitrary to claim that all but the last use are "natural." (And if we say that some of the other uses are "unnatural, but not immoral," we have failed to specify a morally relevant sense of the term "natural.")

Just because people can and do use their sexual organs to procreate, it does not follow that they should not use them for other purposes. Sexual organs seem very well suited for expressing love, for giving and receiving pleasure, and for celebrating, replenishing, and enhancing a relationship—even when procreation is not a factor. Unless opponents of homosexuality are prepared to condemn heterosexual couples who use contraception or individuals who masturbate, they must abandon this version of the unnaturalness argument. Indeed, even the Roman Catholic Church, which forbids contraception and masturbation, approves of sex for sterile couples and of sex during pregnancy, neither of which can lead to procreation. The Church concedes here that intimacy and pleasure are morally legitimate purposes for sex, even in cases where procreation is impossible. But since homosexual sex can achieve these purposes as well, it is inconsistent for the Church to condemn it on the grounds that it is not procreative. . . .

What Is Disgusting or Offensive Is Unnatural

It often seems that when people call homosexuality "unnatural" they really just mean that it's disgusting. But plenty of morally neutral activities—handling snakes, eating snails, performing autopsies, cleaning toilets, and so on—disgust people. Indeed, for centuries, most people found interracial relationships disgusting, yet that feeling—which has by no means disappeared—hardly proves that such relationships

are wrong. In sum, the charge that homosexuality is unnatural, at least in its most common forms, is longer on rhetorical flourish than on philosophical cogency. At best it expresses an aesthetic judgment, not a moral judgment.

HOMOSEXUAL SEX IS HARMFUL

One might instead argue that homosexuality is harmful. The Ramsey Colloquium, for instance, argues that homosexuality leads to the breakdown of the family and, ultimately, of human society, and it points to the "alarming rates of sexual promiscuity, depression, and suicide and the ominous presence of AIDS within the homosexual subculture."[5] Thomas Schmidt marshals copious statistics to show that homosexual activity undermines physical and psychological health.[6] Such charges, if correct, would seem to provide strong evidence against homosexuality. But are the charges correct? And do they prove what they purport to prove?

One obvious (and obviously problematic) way to answer the first question is to ask people like Tommy and Jim. It would appear that no one is in a better position to judge the homosexual lifestyle than those who know it firsthand. Yet it is unlikely that critics would trust their testimony. Indeed, the more homosexual people try to explain their lives, the more critics accuse them of deceitfully promoting an agenda. (It's like trying to prove that you're not crazy. The more you object, the more people think, "That's exactly what a crazy person would say.")

One might instead turn to statistics. An obvious problem with this tack is that both sides of the debate bring forth extensive statistics and "expert" testimony, leaving the average observer confused. There is a more subtle problem as well. Because of widespread antigay sentiment, many homosexual people won't acknowledge their romantic feelings to themselves, much less to researchers. I have known a number of gay men who did not "come out" until their forties and fifties, and no amount of professional competence on the part of interviewers would have been likely to open their closets sooner. Such problems compound the usual difficulties of finding representative population samples for statistical study.

Yet even if the statistical claims of gay rights opponents were true, they would not prove what they purport to prove, for several reasons. First, as any good statistician realizes, correlation does not equal cause. Even if homosexual people were more likely to commit suicide, be promiscuous, or contract AIDS than the general population, it would not follow that their homosexuality causes them to do these things. An alternative—and very plausible—explanation is that these phenomena, like the disproportionately high crime rates among African Americans, are at least partly a function of society's treatment of the group in question. Suppose you were told from a very early age that the romantic feelings that you experienced were sick, unnatural, and disgusting. Suppose further that expressing these feelings put you at risk of social ostracism or, worse yet, physical violence. Is it not plausible that you would, for instance, be more inclined to depression than you would be without such obstacles? And that such depression could, in its extreme forms, lead to suicide or other self-destructive behaviors? (It is indeed remarkable that couples like Tommy and Jim continue to flourish in the face of such obstacles.)

A similar explanation can be given for the alleged promiscuity of homosexuals. The denial of legal marriage, the pressure to remain in the closet, and the overt hostility toward homosexual relationships are all more conducive to transient, clandestine encounters than they are to long-term unions. As a result, that which is challenging enough for heterosexual couples—settling down and building a life together—becomes far more challenging for homosexual couples.

Indeed, there is an interesting tension in the critics' position here. Opponents of homosexuality commonly claim that "marriage and the family . . . are fragile institutions in need of careful and continuing support."[7] And they point to the increasing prevalence of divorce and premarital sex among heterosexuals as evidence that such support is declining. Yet they refuse to concede that the complete absence of similar support for homosexual relationships might explain many of the alleged problems of homosexuals. The critics can't have it both ways: if heterosexual marriages are in trouble despite the various social, economic, and legal incentives for keeping them together, society should be little surprised that homosexual relationships—which not only lack such supports, but face overt hostility—are difficult to maintain.

One might object that if social ostracism were the main cause of homosexual people's problems, then homosexual people in more "tolerant" cities like New York and San Francisco should exhibit fewer such problems than their small-town counterparts; yet statistics do not seem to bear this out. This objection underestimates the extent of antigay sentiment in our society. By the time many gay and lesbian people move to urban centers, they have already been exposed to (and may have internalized) considerable hostility toward homosexuality. Moreover, the visibility of homosexuality in urban centers makes gay and lesbian people there more vulnerable to attack (and thus more likely to exhibit certain difficulties). Finally, note that urbanites *in general* (not just homosexual urbanites) tend to exhibit higher rates of promiscuity, depression, and sexually transmitted disease than the rest of the population.

But what about AIDS? Opponents of homosexuality sometimes claim that even if homosexual sex is not, strictly speaking, immoral, it is still a bad idea, since it puts people at risk for AIDS and other sexually transmitted diseases. But that claim is misleading: it is infinitely more risky for Tommy to have sex with a woman who is HIV-positive than with Jim, who is HIV-negative. Obviously, it's not homosexuality that's harmful, it's the virus; and the virus may be carried by both heterosexual and homosexual people.

Now it may be true (in the United States, at least) that homosexual males are statistically more likely to carry the virus than heterosexual females and thus that homosexual sex is *statistically* more risky than heterosexual sex (in cases where the partner's HIV status is unknown). But opponents of homosexuality need something stronger than this statistical claim. For if it is wrong for men to have sex with men because their doing so puts them at a higher AIDS risk than heterosexual sex, then it is also wrong for women to have sex with men because their doing so puts them at a higher AIDS risk than homosexual sex (lesbians as a group have the lowest incidence of AIDS). Purely from the standpoint of AIDS risk, women ought to prefer lesbian sex.

If this response seems silly, it is because there is obviously more to choosing a romantic or sexual partner than determining AIDS risk. And a major part of the decision, one that opponents of homosexuality consistently overlook, is considering whether one can have a mutually fulfilling relationship with the partner. For many people like Tommy and Jim, such fulfillment—which most heterosexuals recognize to be an important component of human flourishing—is only possible with members of the same sex.

Of course, the foregoing argument hinges on the claim that homosexual sex can only cause harm indirectly. Some would object that there are certain activities—anal sex, for instance—that for anatomical reasons are intrinsically harmful. But an argument against anal intercourse is by no means tantamount to an argument against homosexuality: neither all nor only homosexuals engage in anal sex. There are plenty of other things for both gay men and lesbians to do in bed. Indeed, for women, it appears that the most common forms of homosexual activity may be *less* risky than penile-vaginal intercourse, since the latter has been linked to cervical cancer.[8]

In sum, there is nothing *inherently* risky about sex between persons of the same gender. It is only risky under certain conditions: for instance, if they exchange diseased bodily fluids or if they engage in certain "rough" forms of sex that could cause tearing of delicate tissue. Heterosexual sex is equally risky under such conditions. Thus, even if statistical claims like those of Schmidt and the Ramsey Colloquium were true, they would not prove that homosexuality is immoral. At best, they would prove that homosexual people—like everyone else—ought to take great care when deciding to become sexually active.

Of course, there's more to a flourishing life than avoiding harm. One might argue that even if Tommy and Jim are not harming each other by

their relationship, they are still failing to achieve the higher level of fulfillment possible in a heterosexual relationship, which is rooted in the complementarity of male and female. But this argument just ignores the facts: Tommy and Jim are homosexual *precisely because* they find relationships with men (and, in particular, with each other) more fulfilling than relationships with women. Even evangelicals (who have long advocated "faith healing" for homosexuals) are beginning to acknowledge that the choice for most homosexual people is not between homosexual relationships and heterosexual relationships, but rather between homosexual relationships and celibacy. What the critics need to show, therefore, is that no matter how loving, committed, mutual, generous, and fulfilling the relationship may be, Tommy and Jim would flourish more if they were celibate. Given the evidence of their lives (and of others like them), this is a formidable task indeed.

Thus far I have focused on the allegation that homosexuality harms those who engage in it. But what about the allegation that homosexuality harms other, non-consenting parties? Here I will briefly consider two claims: that homosexuality threatens children and that it threatens society.

Those who argue that homosexuality threatens children may mean one of two things. First, they may mean that homosexual people are child molesters. Statistically, the vast majority of reported cases of child sexual abuse involve young girls and their fathers, stepfathers, or other familiar (and presumably heterosexual) adult males. But opponents of homosexuality argue that when one adjusts for relative percentage in the population, homosexual males appear more likely than heterosexual males to be child molesters. As I argued above, the problems with obtaining reliable statistics on homosexuality render such calculations difficult. Fortunately, they are also unnecessary.

Child abuse is a terrible thing. But when a heterosexual male molests a child (or rapes a woman or commits assault), the act does not reflect upon all heterosexuals. Similarly, when a homosexual male molests a child, there is no reason why that act should reflect upon all homosexuals. Sex with adults of the same sex is one thing; sex with *children* of the same sex is quite another. Conflating the two not only slanders innocent people, it also misdirects resources intended to protect children. Furthermore, many men convicted of molesting young boys are sexually attracted to adult women and report no attraction to adult men. To call such men "homosexual," or even "bisexual," is probably to stretch such terms too far.

Alternatively, those who charge that homosexuality threatens children might mean that the increasing visibility of homosexual relationships makes children more likely to become homosexual. The argument for this view is patently circular. One cannot prove that doing *X* is bad by arguing that it causes other people to do *X,* which is bad. One must first establish independently that *X* is bad. That said, there is not a shred of evidence to demonstrate that exposure to homosexuality leads children to become homosexual.

But doesn't homosexuality threaten society? A Roman Catholic priest once put the argument to me as follows: "Of course homosexuality is bad for society. If everyone were homosexual, there would be no society." Perhaps it is true that if everyone were homosexual, there would be no society. But if everyone were a celibate priest, society would collapse just as surely, and my friend the priest didn't seem to think that he was doing anything wrong simply by failing to procreate. . . .

From the fact that the continuation of society requires procreation, it does not follow that *everyone* must procreate. Moreover, even if such an obligation existed, it would not preclude homosexuality. At best, it would preclude *exclusive* homosexuality: homosexual people who occasionally have heterosexual sex can procreate just fine. And given artificial insemination, even those who are exclusively homosexual can procreate. In short, the priest's claim—if everyone were homosexual, there would be no society—is false; and even if it were true, it would not establish that homosexuality is immoral. . . .

I have argued that Tommy and Jim's sexual relationship harms neither them nor society. On the contrary, it benefits both. It benefits them because it makes them happier—not merely in a short-term, hedonistic sense, but in a long-term, "big picture" sort of way. And, in turn, it benefits society, since it makes Tommy and Jim more stable, more productive, and more generous than they would otherwise be. In short, their relationship—including its sexual component—provides the same kinds of benefits that infertile heterosexual relationships provide (and perhaps other benefits as well). Nor should we fear that accepting their relationship and others like it will cause people to flee in droves from the institution of heterosexual marriage. After all, . . . the usual response to a gay person is not "How come *he* gets to be gay and I don't?" . . .

NOTES

1. Although my central example in the paper is a gay male couple, much of what I say will apply mutatis mutandis to lesbians as well, since many of the same arguments are used against them. This is not to say gay male sexuality and lesbian sexuality are largely similar or that discussions of the former will cover all that needs to be said about the latter. Furthermore, the fact that I focus on a long-term, committed relationship should not be taken to imply any judgment about homosexual activity outside of such unions. If the argument of this paper is successful, then the evaluation of homosexual activity outside of committed unions should be largely (if not entirely) similar to the evaluation of *hetero*sexual activity outside of committed unions.

2. Burton M. Leiser, *Liberty, Justice, and Morals: Contemporary Value Conflicts* (New York: Macmillan, 1986), 51–57.

3. The Ramsey Colloquium, "The Homosexual Movement," *First Things* (March 1994), 15–20.

4. For an overview of some of these studies, see Simon LeVay, *Queer Science* (Boston: MIT Press, 1996), chap. 10.

5. The Ramsey Colloquium, "The Homosexual Movement," 19.

6. Thomas Schmidt, "The Price of Love" in *Straight and Narrow? Compassion and Clarity in the Homosexuality Debate* (Downers Grove, IL: InterVarsity Press, 1995), chap. 6.

7. The Ramsey Colloquium, "The Homosexual Movement," 19.

8. See S. R. Johnson, E. M. Smith, and S. M. Guenther, "Comparison of Gynecological Health Care Problems Between Lesbian and Bisexual Women," *Journal of Reproductive Medicine* 32 (1987), 805–811.

READING QUESTIONS

1. What are the five ways in which we might understand the use of the term "unnatural"? What are Corvino's objections to each of these possibilities?
2. Explain why opponents of homosexuality believe that homosexual sex is harmful.
3. What are some of the main problems Corvino notes for the statistical data on homosexuality? Even if the statistical information at hand is accurate, what reasons does Corvino give for thinking that the information doesn't prove what the opponents of homosexuality claim it does?
4. How does Corvino respond to the objection that social ostracism remains a problem in more "tolerant" cities like New York and San Francisco?
5. Explain the arguments given by opponents of homosexuality that homosexual behavior causes harm to other parties such as children and society in general. How does Corvino respond to these arguments?

DISCUSSION QUESTIONS

1. Are there any other ways we could understand the term "unnatural" other than the ones considered by Corvino?
2. Corvino argues that homosexuality is not harmful in the ways its opponents tend to claim. Has Corvino overlooked any ways in which homsexuality is potentially harmful?

Thomas A. Mappes

A Liberal View of Sexual Morality and the Concept of Using Another Person

Mappes develops an essentially Kantian sexual ethic by appealing to the idea that in our dealings with others, we ought never to treat someone as a mere means to our own ends; to so treat them is to immorally *use* them. Mappes defines using someone as intentionally treating them in a way that violates the requirement that our involvement with others be based on their *voluntary* and *informed* consent. If we focus now on sexual behavior, we arrive at a basic principle of sexual morality according to which A's sexual interaction with B is morally permissible only if A does not sexually treat B in a way that intentionally interferes with B's voluntary and informed consent. Since coercion is a main vehicle for interfering with someone's actions being voluntary, and deception is the means by which one interferes with another's actions being informed, we can use the basic principle just formulated to arrive at moral verdicts about certain forms of sexual behavior. In his article, Mappes develops this Kantian view by investigating specific cases of sexual interaction involving deception, coercion, and offers.

Recommended Reading: Kantian moral theory, chap. 1, sec. 2C.

The central tenet of *conventional* sexual morality is that nonmarital sex is immoral. A somewhat less restrictive sexual ethic holds that *sex without love* is immoral. If neither of these positions is philosophically defensible, and I would contend that neither is, it does not follow that there are no substantive moral restrictions on human sexual interaction. *Any* human interaction, including sexual interaction, may be judged morally objectionable to the extent that it transgresses a justified moral rule or principle. The way to construct a detailed account of sexual morality, it would seem, is simply to work out the implications of relevant moral rules or principles in the area of human sexual interaction.

As one important step in the direction of such an account, I will attempt to work out the implications of an especially relevant moral principle, the principle that it is wrong for one person to use another person. However ambiguous the expression "using another person" may seem to be, there is a determinate and clearly specifiable sense according to which using another person is morally objectionable. Once this morally significant sense of "using another person" is identified and explicated, the concept of using another person can play an important role in the articulation of a defensible account of sexual morality.

I. THE MORALLY SIGNIFICANT SENSE OF "USING ANOTHER PERSON"

Historically, the concept of using another person is associated with the ethical system of Immanuel Kant.

According to a fundamental Kantian principle, it is morally wrong for A to use B *merely as a means* (to achieve A's ends). Kant's principle does not rule out A using B as a means, only A using B *merely* as a means, that is, in a way incompatible with respect for B as a person. In the ordinary course of life, it is surely unavoidable (and morally unproblematic) that each of us in numerous ways uses others as a means to achieve our various ends. A college teacher uses students as a means to achieve his or her livelihood. A college student uses instructors as a means of gaining knowledge and skills. Such human interactions, presumably based on the voluntary participation of the respective parties, are quite compatible with the idea of respect for persons. But respect for persons entails that each of us recognize the rightful authority of other persons (as rational beings) to conduct their individual lives as they see fit. We may legitimately recruit others to participate in the satisfaction of our personal ends, but they are used merely as a means whenever we undermine the voluntary or informed character of their consent to interact with us in some desired way. A coerces B at knife point to hand over $200. A uses B merely as a means. If A had requested of B a gift of $200, leaving B free to determine whether or not to make the gift, A would have proceeded in a manner compatible with respect for B as a person. C deceptively rolls back the odometer of a car and thereby manipulates D's decision to buy the car. C uses D merely as a means.

On the basis of these considerations, I would suggest that the morally significant sense of "using another person" is best understood by reference to the notion of *voluntary informed consent*. More specifically, A immorally uses B if and only if A intentionally acts in a way that violates the requirement that B's involvement with A's ends be based on B's voluntary informed consent. If this account is correct, using another person (in the morally significant sense) can arise in at least two important ways: via *coercion,* which is antithetical to voluntary consent, and via *deception,* which undermines the informed character of voluntary consent. . . .

To illuminate the concept of using that has been proposed, I will consider . . . the matter of research involving human subjects. In the sphere of researcher-subject interaction, just as in the sphere of human sexual interaction, there is ample opportunity for immorally using another person. If a researcher is engaged in a study that involves human subjects, we may presume that the "end" of the researcher is the successful completion of the study. (The researcher may desire this particular end for any number of reasons: the speculative understanding it will provide, the technology it will make possible, the eventual benefit of humankind, increased status in the scientific community, a raise in pay, etc.) The work, let us presume, strictly requires the use (employment) of human research subjects. The researcher, however, immorally uses other people only if he or she intentionally acts in a way that violates the requirement that the participation of research subjects be based on their voluntary informed consent.

Let us assume that in a particular case participation as a research subject involves some rather significant risks. Accordingly, the researcher finds that potential subjects are reluctant to volunteer. At this point, if an unscrupulous researcher is willing to resort to the immoral using of other people (to achieve his or her own ends), two manifest options are available—deception and coercion. By way of deception, the researcher might choose to lie about the risks involved. For example, potential subjects could be explicitly told that there are no significant risks associated with research participation. On the other hand, the researcher could simply withhold a full disclosure of risks. Whether pumped full of false information or simply deprived of relevant information, the potential subject is intentionally deceived in such a way as to be led to a decision that furthers the researcher's ends. In manipulating the decision making process of the potential subject in this way, the researcher is guilty of immorally using another person.

To explain how an unscrupulous researcher might immorally use another person via coercion, it is helpful to distinguish two basic forms of coercion.[1]

"Occurrent" coercion involves the use of physical force. "Dispositional" coercion involves the threat of harm. If I am forcibly thrown out of my office by an intruder, I am the victim of occurrent coercion. If, on the other hand, I leave my office because an intruder has threatened to shoot me if I do not leave, I am the victim of dispositional coercion. The victim of occurrent coercion literally has no choice in what happens. The victim of dispositional coercion, in contrast, does intentionally choose a certain course of action. However, one's choice, in the face of the threat of harm, is less than fully voluntary.

It is perhaps unlikely that even an unscrupulous researcher would resort to any very explicit measure of coercion. Deception, it seems, is less risky. Still, it is well known that Nazi medical experimenters ruthlessly employed coercion. By way of occurrent coercion, the Nazis literally forced great numbers of concentration camp victims to participate in experiments that entailed their own death or dismemberment. And if some concentration camp victims "volunteered" to participate in Nazi research to avoid even more unspeakable horrors, clearly we must consider them victims of dispositional coercion. The Nazi researchers, employing coercion, immorally used other human beings with a vengeance.

II. DECEPTION AND SEXUAL MORALITY

To this point, I have been concerned to identify and explicate the morally significant sense of "using another person." On the view proposed, A immorally uses B if and only if A intentionally acts in a way that violates the requirement that B's involvement with A's ends be based on B's voluntary informed consent. I will now apply this account to the area of human sexual interaction and explore its implications. For economy of expression in what follows, "using" (and its cognates) is to be understood as referring only to the morally significant sense.

If we presume a state of affairs in which A desires some form of sexual interaction with B, we can say that this desired form of sexual interaction with B is A's end.

Thus A sexually *uses* B if and only if A intentionally acts in a way that violates the requirement that B's sexual interaction with A be based on B's voluntary informed consent. It seems clear then that A may sexually use B in at least two distinctive ways, (1) via coercion and (2) via deception. However, before proceeding to discuss deception and then the more problematic case of coercion, one important point must be made. In emphasizing the centrality of coercion and deception as mechanisms for the sexual using of another person, I have in mind sexual interaction with a fully competent adult partner. We should also want to say, I think, that sexual interaction with a child inescapably involves the sexual using of another person. Even if a child "consents" to sexual interaction, he or she is, strictly speaking, incapable of *informed* consent. It's a matter of being *incompetent* to give consent. Similarly, to the extent that a mentally retarded person is rightly considered incompetent, sexual interaction with such a person amounts to the sexual using of that person, unless someone empowered to give "proxy consent" has done so. (In certain circumstances, sexual involvement might be in the best interests of a mentally retarded person.) We can also visualize the case of an otherwise fully competent adult temporarily disordered by drugs or alcohol. To the extent that such a person is rightly regarded as temporarily incompetent, winning his or her "consent" to sexual interaction could culminate in the sexual using of that person.

There are a host of clear cases in which one person sexually uses another precisely because the former employs deception in a way that undermines the informed character of the latter's consent to sexual interaction. Consider this example. One person, A, has decided, as a matter of personal prudence based on past experience, not to become sexually involved outside the confines of a loving relationship. Another person, B, strongly desires a sexual relationship with A but does not love A. B, aware of A's unwillingness to engage in sex without love, professes love for A, thereby hoping to win A's consent to a sexual relationship. B's ploy is successful; A consents. When the smoke clears and A becomes aware of B's deception, it would be both appropriate and natural for A to complain, "I've been used."

In the same vein, here are some other examples. (1) Mr. A is aware that Ms. B will consent to sexual involvement only on the understanding that in time the two will be married. Mr. A has no intention of marrying Ms. B but says that he will. (2) Ms. C has herpes and is well aware that Mr. D will never consent to sex if he knows of her condition. When asked by Mr. D, Ms. C denies that she has herpes. (3) Mr. E knows that Ms. F will not consent to sexual intercourse in the absence of responsible birth control measures. Mr. E tells Ms. F that he has had a vasectomy, which is not the case. (4) Ms. G knows that Mr. H would not consent to sexual involvement with a married woman. Ms. G is married but tells Mr. H that she is single. (5) Ms. I is well aware that Ms. J is interested in a stable lesbian relationship and will not consent to become sexually involved with someone who is bisexual. Ms. I tells Ms. J that she is exclusively homosexual, whereas the truth is that she is bisexual.

If one person's consent to sex is predicated on false beliefs that have been intentionally and deceptively inculcated by one's sexual partner in an effort to win the former's consent, the resulting sexual interaction involves one person sexually using another. In each of the above cases, one person explicitly *lies* to another. False information is intentionally conveyed to win consent to sexual interaction, and the end result is the sexual using of another person.

As noted earlier, however, lying is not the only form of deception. Under certain circumstances, the simple withholding of information can be considered a form of deception. Accordingly, it is possible to sexually use another person not only by (deceptively) lying about relevant facts but also by (deceptively) not disclosing relevant facts. If A has good reason to believe that B would refuse to consent to sexual interaction should B become aware of certain factual information, and if A withholds disclosure of this information in order to enhance the possibility of gaining B's consent, then, if B does consent, A sexually uses B via deception. One example will suffice. Suppose that Mr. A meets Ms. B in a singles bar. Mr. A realizes immediately that Ms. B is the sister of Ms. C, a woman that Mr. A has been sexually involved with for a long time. Mr. A, knowing that it is very unlikely that Ms. B will consent to sexual interaction if she becomes aware of Mr. A's involvement with her sister, decides not to disclose this information. If Ms. B eventually consents to sexual interaction, since her consent is the product of Mr. A's deception, it is rightly thought that she has been sexually used by him.

III. COERCION AND SEXUAL MORALITY

We have considered the case of deception. The present task is to consider the more difficult case of coercion. Whereas deception functions to undermine the *informed* character of voluntary consent (to sexual interaction), coercion either obliterates consent entirely (the case of occurrent coercion) or undermines the voluntariness of consent (the case of dispositional coercion).

Forcible rape is the most conspicuous, and most brutal, way of sexually using another person via coercion.[2] Forcible rape may involve either occurrent coercion or dispositional coercion. A man who rapes a woman by the employment of sheer physical force, by simply overpowering her, employs occurrent coercion. There is literally no sexual *interaction* in such a case; only the rapist performs an action. In no sense does the woman consent to or participate in sexual activity. She has no choice in what takes place, or rather, physical force results in her choice being simply beside the point. The employment of occurrent coercion for the purpose of rape "objectifies" the victim in the strongest sense of that term. She is treated like a physical object. One does not interact with physical objects; one acts upon them. In a perfectly ordinary (not the morally significant) sense of the term, we "use" physical objects. But when the victim of rape is treated as if she were a physical object, there we have one of the most vivid examples of the immoral using of another person.

Frequently, forcible rape involves not occurrent coercion (or not *only* occurrent coercion) but dispositional coercion.[3] In dispositional coercion, the relevant factor is not physical force but the threat of harm. The rapist threatens his victim with immediate and serious bodily harm. For example, a man threatens to kill or beat a woman if she resists his sexual demands. She "consents," that is, she submits to his demands. He may demand only passive participation (simply not struggling against him) or he may demand some measure of active participation. Rape that employs dispositional coercion is surely just as wrong as rape that employs occurrent coercion, but there is a notable difference in the mechanism by which the rapist uses his victim in the two cases. With occurrent coercion, the victim's consent is entirely bypassed. With dispositional coercion, the victim's consent is not bypassed. It is coerced. Dispositional coercion undermines the *voluntariness* of consent. The rapist, by employing the threat of immediate and serious bodily harm, may succeed in bending the victim's will. He may gain the victim's "consent." But he uses another person precisely because consent is coerced.

The relevance of occurrent coercion is limited to the case of forcible rape. Dispositional coercion, a notion that also plays an indispensable role in an overall account of forcible rape, now becomes our central concern. Although the threat of immediate and serious bodily harm stands out as the most brutal way of coercing consent to sexual interaction, we must not neglect the employment of other kinds of threats to this same end. There are numerous ways in which one person can effectively harm, and thus effectively threaten, another. Accordingly, for example, consent to sexual interaction might be coerced by threatening to damage someone's reputation. If a person consents to sexual interaction to avoid a threatened harm, then that person has been sexually used (via dispositional coercion). In the face of a threat, of course, it remains possible that a person will refuse to comply with another's sexual demands. It is probably best to describe this sort of situation as a case not of coercion, which entails the *successful* use of threats to gain compliance, but of *attempted* coercion. Of course, the moral fault of an individual emerges with the *attempt* to coerce. A person who attempts murder is morally blameworthy even if the attempt fails. The same is true for someone who fails in an effort to coerce consent to sexual interaction.

Consider now each of the following cases:

Case 1

Mr. Supervisor makes a series of increasingly less subtle sexual overtures to Ms. Employee. These advances are consistently and firmly rejected by Ms. Employee. Eventually, Mr. Supervisor makes it clear that the granting of "sexual favors" is a condition of her continued employment.

Case 2

Ms. Debtor borrowed a substantial sum of money from Mr. Creditor, on the understanding that she would pay it back within one year. In the meantime, Ms. Debtor has become sexually attracted to Mr. Creditor, but he does not share her interest. At the end of the one-year period, Mr. Creditor asks Ms. Debtor to return the money. She says she will be happy to return the money so long as he consents to sexual interaction with her.

Case 3

Mr. Theatergoer has two tickets to the most talked-about play of the season. He is introduced to a woman whom he finds sexually attractive and who shares his interest in the theater. In the course of their conversation, she expresses disappointment that the play everyone is talking about is sold out; she would love to see it. At this point, Mr. Theatergoer suggests that she be his guest at the theater. "Oh, by the way," he says, "I always expect sex from my dates."

Case 4

Ms. Jetsetter is planning a trip to Europe. She has been trying for some time to develop a sexual relationship with a man who has shown little interest in her. She knows, however, that he has always wanted to go to Europe and that it is only lack of money that has deterred him. Ms. Jetsetter proposes that he come along as her traveling companion, all expenses paid, on the express understanding that sex is part of the arrangement.

Cases 1 and 2 involve attempts to sexually use another person whereas cases 3 and 4 do not. To see why this is so, it is essential to introduce a distinction between two kinds of proposals, viz., the distinction between *threats* and *offers*.[4] The logical form of a threat differs from the logical form of an offer in the following way. Threat: "If you *do not* do what I am proposing you do, I will bring about an *undesirable consequence* for you." Offer: "If you *do* what I am proposing you do, I will bring about a *desirable consequence* for you." The person who makes a threat attempts to gain compliance by attaching an undesirable consequence to the alternative of noncompliance. This person attempts to *coerce* consent. The person who makes an offer attempts to gain compliance by attaching a desirable consequence to the alternative of compliance. This person attempts not to coerce but to *induce* consent.

Since threats are morally problematic in a way that offers are not, it is not uncommon for threats to be advanced in the language of offers. Threats are represented as if they were offers. An armed assailant might say, "I'm going to make you an *offer.* If you give me your money, I will allow you to go on living." Though this proposal on the surface has the logical form of an offer, it is in reality a threat. The underlying sense of the proposal is this: "If you do not give me your money, I will kill you." If, in a given case, it is initially unclear whether a certain proposal is to count as a threat or an offer, ask the following question. Does the proposal in question have the effect of making a person *worse off upon noncompliance?* The recipient of an offer, upon noncompliance, *is not worse off* than he or she was before the offer. In contrast, the recipient of a threat, upon noncompliance, *is worse off* than he or she was before the threat. Since the "offer" of our armed assailant has the effect, upon noncompliance, of rendering its recipient worse off (relative to the preproposal situation of the recipient), the recipient is faced with a threat, not an offer.

The most obvious way for a coercer to attach an undesirable consequence to the path of noncompliance is by threatening to render the victim of coercion materially worse off than he or she has heretofore been. Thus a person is threatened with loss of life, bodily injury, damage to property, damage to reputation, etc. It is important to realize, however, that a person can also be effectively coerced by being threatened with the withholding of something (in some cases, what we would call a "benefit") to which the person is entitled. Suppose that A is mired in quicksand and is slowly but surely approaching death. When B happens along, A cries out to B for assistance. All B need do is throw A a rope. B is quite willing to accommodate A, "provided you pay me $100,000 over the next ten years." Is B making A an offer? Hardly! B, we must presume, stands under a moral obligation to come to the aid of a person in serious distress, at least when such assistance entails no significant risk, sacrifice of time, etc. A is entitled to B's assistance. Thus, in reality, B attaches an undesirable consequence to A's noncompliance with the proposal that A pay B $100,000. A is undoubtedly better off that B has happened along, but A is not rendered better off *by B's proposal.* Before B's proposal, A legitimately expected assistance from B, "no strings attached." In attaching a very unwelcome string, B's proposal effectively renders A worse off. What B proposes, then, is not an offer of assistance. Rather, B threatens A with the withholding of something (assistance) that A is entitled to have from B. . . .

With the distinction between threats and offers clearly in view, it now becomes clear why cases 1 and 2 do indeed involve attempts to sexually use another person whereas cases 3 and 4 do not. Cases 1 and 2 embody threats, whereas cases 3 and 4 embody offers. In case 1, Mr. Supervisor proposes sexual interaction with Ms. Employee and, in an effort to gain compliance, threatens her with the loss of her job. Mr. Supervisor thereby attaches an undesirable consequence to one of Ms. Employee's alternatives, the path of noncompliance. Typical of the threat situation, Mr. Supervisor's proposal has the effect of rendering Ms. Employee worse off upon noncompliance. Mr. Supervisor is attempting via (dispositional) coercion to sexually use Ms. Employee. The situation in case 2 is similar. Ms. Debtor, as *she* might be inclined to say, "offers" to pay Mr. Creditor the money she owes him *if* he consents to sexual interaction with her. In reality, Ms. Debtor is threatening Mr. Creditor, attempting to coerce his consent to sexual interaction, attempting to sexually use him. Though Mr. Creditor is not now in possession of the money Ms. Debtor owes him, he is *entitled* to receive it from her at this time. She threatens to deprive him of something to which he is entitled. Clearly, her proposal has the effect of rendering him worse off upon noncompliance. Before her proposal, he had the legitimate expectation, "no strings attached," of receiving the money in question.

Cases 3 and 4 embody offers; neither involves an attempt to sexually use another person. Mr. Theatergoer simply provides an inducement for the woman he has just met to accept his proposal of sexual interaction. He offers her the opportunity to see the play that everyone is talking about. In attaching a desirable consequence to the alternative of compliance, Mr. Theatergoer in no way threatens or attempts to coerce his potential companion. Typical of the offer situation, his proposal does not have the effect of rendering her worse off upon noncompliance. She now has a new opportunity; if she chooses to forgo this opportunity, she is no worse off. The situation in case 4 is similar. Ms. Jetsetter provides an inducement for a man that she is interested in to accept her proposal of sexual involvement. She offers him the opportunity to see Europe, without expense, as her traveling companion. Before Ms. Jetsetter's proposal, he had no prospect of a European trip. If he chooses to reject her proposal, he is no worse off than he has heretofore been. Ms. Jetsetter's proposal embodies an offer, not a threat. She cannot be accused of attempting to sexually use her potential traveling companion.

Consider now two further cases, 5 and 6, each of which develops in the following way. Professor Highstatus, a man of high academic accomplishment, is sexually attracted to a student in one of his classes. He is very anxious to secure her consent to sexual interaction. Ms. Student, confused and unsettled by his sexual advances, has begun to practice "avoidance behavior." To the extent that it is possible, she goes out of her way to avoid him.

Case 5

Professor Highstatus tells Ms. Student that, though her work is such as to entitle her to a grade of B in the class, she will be assigned a D unless she consents to sexual interaction.

Case 6

Professor Highstatus tells Ms. Student that, though her work is such as to entitle her to a grade of B, she will be assigned an A if she consents to sexual interaction.

It is clear that case 5 involves an attempt to sexually use another person. Case 6, however, at least at face value, does not. In case 5, Professor Highstatus *threatens* to deprive Ms. Student of the grade she deserves. In case 6, he *offers* to assign her a grade that is higher than she deserves. In case 5, Ms. Student would be worse off upon noncompliance with Professor Highstatus's proposal. In case 6, she would not be worse off upon noncompliance with his proposal. In saying that case 6 does not involve an attempt to sexually use another person, it is not being asserted that Professor Highstatus is acting in a morally legitimate fashion. In offering a student a higher grade than she deserves, he is guilty of abusing his institutional authority. He is under an obligation to assign the grades that students earn, as defined by the relevant course standards. In case 6, Professor Highstatus is undoubtedly acting in a morally reprehensible way, but in contrast to case 5, where it is fair to say that he both abuses his institutional authority *and* attempts to sexually use another person, we can plausibly say that in case 6 his moral failure is limited to abuse of his institutional authority.

There remains, however, a suspicion that case 6 might after all embody an attempt to sexually use another person. There is no question that the literal content of what Professor Highstatus conveys to Ms. Student has the logical form of an offer and not a threat. Still, is it not the case that Ms. Student may very well feel threatened? Professor Highstatus, in an effort to secure consent to sexual interaction, has announced that he will assign Ms. Student a higher grade than she deserves. Can she really turn him down without substantial risk? Is he not likely to retaliate? If she spurns him, will he not lower her grade or otherwise make it harder for her to succeed in her academic program? He does, after all, have power over her. Will he use it to her detriment? Surely he is not above abusing his institutional authority to achieve his ends; this much is abundantly clear from his willingness to assign a grade higher than a student deserves.

Is Professor Highstatus naive to the threat that Ms. Student may find implicit in the situation? Perhaps. In such a case, if Ms. Student reluctantly consents to sexual interaction, we may be inclined to say that he has *unwittingly* used her. More likely, Professor Highstatus is well aware of the way in which Ms. Student will perceive his proposal. He knows that threats need not be verbally expressed. Indeed, it may

even be the case that he consciously exploits his underground reputation. "Everyone knows what happens to the women who reject Professor Highstatus's little offers." To the extent, then, that Professor Highstatus intends to convey a threat in case 6, he is attempting via coercion to sexually use another person. . . .

IV. THE IDEA OF A COERCIVE OFFER

In section III, I have sketched an overall account of sexually using another person *via coercion*. In this section, I will consider the need for modifications or extensions of the suggested account. As before, certain case studies will serve as points of departure.

Case 7

Ms. Starlet, a glamorous, wealthy, and highly successful model, wants nothing more than to become a movie superstar. Mr. Moviemogul, a famous producer, is very taken with Ms. Starlet's beauty. He invites her to come to his office for a screen test. After the screen test, Mr. Moviemogul tells Ms. Starlet that he is prepared to make her a star, on the condition that she agree to sexual involvement with him. Ms. Starlet finds Mr. Moviemogul personally repugnant; she is not at all sexually attracted to him. With great reluctance, she agrees to his proposal.

Has Mr. Moviemogul sexually used Ms. Starlet? No. He has made her an offer that she has accepted, however reluctantly. The situation would be quite different if it were plausible to believe that she was, before acceptance of his proposal, *entitled* to his efforts to make her a star. Then we could read case 7 as amounting to his threatening to deprive her of something to which she was entitled. But what conceivable grounds could be found for the claim that Mr. Moviemogul, before Ms. Starlet's acceptance of his proposal, is under an obligation to make her a star? He does not threaten her; he makes her an offer. Even if there are other good grounds for morally condemning his action, it is a mistake to think that he is guilty of coercing consent.

But some would assert that Mr. Moviemogul's offer, on the grounds that it confronts Ms. Starlet with an overwhelming inducement, is simply an example of a *coercive offer.* The more general claim at issue is that offers are coercive precisely inasmuch as they are extremely enticing or seductive. Though there is an important reality associated with the notion of a coercive offer, a reality that must shortly be confronted, we ought not embrace the view that an offer is coercive merely because it is extremely enticing or seductive. Virginia Held is a leading proponent of the view under attack here. She writes:

> A person unable to spurn an offer may act as unwillingly as a person unable to resist a threat. Consider the distinction between rape and seduction. In one case constraint and threat are operative, in the other inducement and offer. If the degree of inducement is set high enough in the case of seduction, there may seem to be little difference in the extent of coercion involved. In both cases, persons may act against their own wills.[5]

Certainly a rape victim who acquiesces at knife point is forced to act *against her will.* Does Ms. Starlet, however, act against her will? We have said that she consents "with great reluctance" to sexual involvement, but she does not act against her will. She *wants* very much to be a movie star. I might want very much to be thin. She regrets having to become sexually involved with Mr. Moviemogul as a means of achieving what she wants. I might regret very much having to go on a diet to lose weight. If we say that Ms. Starlet acts against her will in case 7, then we must say that I am acting against my will in embracing "with great reluctance" the diet I despise.

A more important line of argument against Held's view can be advanced on the basis of the widely accepted notion that there is a moral presumption against coercion. Held herself embraces this notion and very effectively clarifies it:

> . . . [A]lthough coercion is not *always* wrong (quite obviously: one coerces the small child not to run across the highway, or the murderer to drop his weapon), there is a presumption against it. . . . This has the standing of a fundamental moral principle. . . .
>
> What can be concluded at the moral level is that we have a prima facie obligation not to employ coercion.[6] [all italics hers]

But it would seem that acceptance of the moral presumption against coercion is not compatible with the view that offers become coercive precisely inasmuch as they become extremely enticing or seductive. Suppose you are my neighbor and regularly spend your Saturday afternoon on the golf course. Suppose also that you are a skilled gardener. I am anxious to convince you to do some gardening work for me and it must be done this Saturday. I offer you $100, $200, $300, . . . in an effort to make it worth your while to sacrifice your recreation and undertake my gardening. At some point, my proposal becomes very enticing. Yet, at the same time in no sense is my proposal becoming morally problematic. If my proposal were becoming coercive, surely our moral sense would be aroused.

Though it is surely not true that the extremely enticing character of an offer is sufficient to make it coercive, we need not reach the conclusion that no sense can be made out of the notion of a coercive offer. Indeed, there is an important social reality that the notion of a coercive offer appears to capture, and insight into this reality can be gained by simply taking note of the sort of case that most draws us to the language of "coercive offer." Is it not a case in which the recipient of an offer is in circumstances of genuine need, and acceptance of the offer seems to present the only realistic possibility for alleviating the need? Assuming that this sort of case is the heart of the matter, it seems that we cannot avoid introducing some sort of distinction between *genuine needs* and *mere wants.* Though the philosophical difficulties involved in drawing this distinction are not insignificant, I nevertheless claim that we will not achieve any clarity about the notion of a coercive offer, at least in this context, except in reference to it. Whatever puzzlement we may feel with regard to the host of borderline cases that can be advanced, it is nevertheless true, for example, that I *genuinely need* food and that I *merely want* a backyard tennis court. In the same spirit, I think it can be acknowledged by all that Ms. Starlet, though she *wants* very much to be a star, does not in any relevant sense *need* to be a star. Accordingly, there is little plausibility in thinking that Mr. Moviemogul makes her a coercive offer. The following case, in contrast, can more plausibly be thought to embody a coercive offer.

Case 8

Mr. Troubled is a young widower who is raising his three children. He lives in a small town and believes that it is important for him to stay there so that his children continue to have the emotional support of other family members. But economic times are tough. Mr. Troubled has been laid off from his job and has not been able to find another. His unemployment benefits have ceased and his relatives are in no position to help him financially. If he is unable to come up with the money for his mortgage payments, he will lose his rather modest house. Ms. Opportunistic lives in the same town. Since shortly after the death of Mr. Troubled's wife, she has consistently made sexual overtures in his direction. Mr. Troubled, for his part, does not care for Ms. Opportunistic and has made it clear to her that he is not interested in sexual involvement with her. She, however, is well aware of his present difficulties. To win his consent to a sexual affair, Ms. Opportunistic offers to make mortgage payments for Mr. Troubled on a continuing basis.

Is Ms. Opportunistic attempting to sexually use Mr. Troubled? The correct answer is yes, even though we must first accept the conclusion that her proposal embodies an offer and not a threat. If Ms. Opportunistic were threatening Mr. Troubled, her proposal would have the effect of rendering him worse off upon noncompliance. But this is not the case. If he rejects her proposal, his situation will not worsen; he will simply remain, as before, in circumstances of extreme need. It might be objected at this point that Ms. Opportunistic does in fact threaten Mr. Troubled. She threatens to deprive him of something to which he is entitled, namely, the alleviation of a genuine need. But this approach is defensible only if, before acceptance of her proposal, he is entitled to have his needs alleviated *by her.* And whatever Mr. Troubled and his children are entitled to from their society as a whole—they are perhaps slipping through the "social safety net"—it cannot be plausibly maintained that Mr. Troubled is entitled to have his mortgage payments made *by Ms. Opportunistic.*

Yet, though she does not threaten him, she is attempting to sexually use him. How can this conclusion be reconciled with our overall account of sexually using another person? First of all, I want to suggest that nothing hangs on whether or not we decide to call Ms. Opportunistic's offer "coercive." More important than the label "coercive offer" is an appreciation of the social reality that inclines us to consider the label appropriate. The label most forcefully asserts itself when we reflect on what Mr. Troubled is likely to say after accepting the offer. "I really had no choice." "I didn't want to accept her offer but what could I do? I have my children to think about." Both Mr. Troubled and Ms. Starlet (in our previous case) *reluctantly* consented to sexual interaction, but I think it can be agreed that Ms. Starlet had a choice in a way that Mr. Troubled did not. Mr. Troubled's choice was *severely constrained by his needs,* whereas Ms. Starlet's was not. As for Ms. Opportunistic, it seems that we might describe her approach as in some sense exploiting or taking advantage of Mr. Troubled's desperate situation. It is not so much, as we would say in the case of threats, that she coerces him or his consent, but rather that she achieves her aim of winning consent by taking advantage of the fact that he is already "under coercion," that is, his choice is severely constrained by his need. If we choose to describe what has taken place as a "coercive offer," we should remember that Mr. Troubled is "coerced" (constrained) by his own need or perhaps by preexisting factors in his situation rather than by Ms. Opportunistic or her offer.

Since it is not quite right to say that Ms. Opportunistic is attempting to coerce Mr. Troubled, even if we are prepared to embrace the label "coercive offer," we cannot simply say, as we would say in the case of threats, that she is attempting to sexually use him *via coercion.* The proper account of the way in which Ms. Opportunistic attempts to sexually use Mr. Troubled is somewhat different. Let us say simply that she attempts to sexually use him *by taking advantage of his desperate situation.* The sense behind this distinctive way of sexually using someone is that a person's choice situation can sometimes be subject to such severe prior constraints that the possibility of *voluntary* consent to sexual interaction is precluded. A advances an offer calculated to gain B's reluctant consent to sexual interaction by confronting B, who has no apparent way of alleviating a genuine need, with an opportunity to do so, but makes this opportunity contingent upon consent to sexual interaction. In such a case, should we not say simply that B's need, when coupled with a lack of viable alternatives, results in B being incapable of *voluntarily* accepting A's offer? Thus A, in making an offer which B "cannot refuse," although not coercing B, nevertheless does intentionally act in a way that violates the requirement that B's sexual interaction with A be based upon B's voluntary informed consent. Thus A sexually uses B.

The central claim of this paper is that A sexually uses B if and only if A intentionally acts in a way that violates the requirement that B's sexual interaction with A be based on B's voluntary informed consent. Clearly, deception and coercion are important mechanisms whereby sexual using takes place. But consideration of case 8 has led us to the identification of yet another mechanism. In summary, then, limiting attention to cases of sexual interaction with a fully competent adult partner, A can sexually use B not only (1) by deceiving B or (2) by coercing B but also (3) by taking advantage of B's desperate situation.

NOTES

1. I follow here an account of coercion developed by Michael D. Bayles in "A Concept of Coercion," in J. Roland Pennock and John W. Chapman, eds., *Coercion: Nomos XIV* (Chicago: Aldine-Atherton, 1972), pp. 16–29.

2. Statutory rape, sexual relations with a person under the legal age of consent, can also be construed as the sexual using of another person. In contrast to forcible rape, however, statutory rape need not involve coercion. The victim of statutory rape may freely "consent" to sexual interaction but, at least in the eyes of the law, is deemed incompetent to consent.

3. A man wrestles a woman to the ground. She is the victim of occurrent coercion. He threatens to beat her unless she submits to his sexual demands. Now she becomes the victim of dispositional coercion.

4. My account of this distinction largely derives from Robert Nozick, "Coercion," in Sidney Morgenbesser, Patrick Suppes, and Morton White, eds., *Philosophy, Science, and Method* (New York: St. Martin's Press, 1969), pp. 440–472, and from Michael D. Bayles, "Coercive Offers and Public Benefits," *The Personalist* 55, no. 2 (Spring 1974), 139–144.

5. Virginia Held, "Coercion and Coercive Offers," in *Coercion: Nomos XIV,* p. 58.

6. Ibid., pp. 61, 62.

READING QUESTIONS

1. What is the morally significant sense of using another person according to Mappes?
2. Explain the difference between coercion and deception. What is the distinction between occurrent and dispositional coercion? Give examples of each.
3. How does Mappes distinguish between threats and offers?
4. What is a coercive offer? Why does Mappes find this idea problematic?

DISCUSSION QUESTIONS

1. Mappes describes several situations which are supposed to illustrate cases in which a person either is or is not being used by another. Should we accept the evaluations he makes about each of these cases? Are there any reasons why we might think that people are being used in the cases where Mappes claims they are not? Consider the situations Mappes suggests as cases of threats and offers as well.
2. How plausible is the idea of a coercive offer? How is taking advantage of someone similar to or different from a case of deception or coercion?

RAJA HALWANI

Virtue Ethics and Adultery

Halwani begins with a brief overview of virtue ethics, explaining some of its advantages over consequentialist and Kantian (deontological) "modern" moral theories. Although these modern moral theories take the concept of right action to be logically prior to the concept of virtue, virtue ethics, by contrast, understands right action in terms of virtue. Halwani then considers the moral issue of sexual fidelity in marriage and romantic commitments generally from a virtue ethics perspective. His central claim is that the goods of love, trust, and affection are central to these sorts of committed relationships—relationships which for many people partly constitute a flourishing life. A virtuous person, then, in protecting these goods would be a person who (with success) strives toward the ideal or virtue of fidelity. It follows on the virtue ethical conception of wrongness that adulterous actions are (at least typically) morally wrong because the person engaged in them fails to live up to this ideal. Halwani concludes by considering possible cases in which it would not be wrong (given a person's circumstances) to engage in adultery, even though doing so may be a kind of moral failure.

Recommended Reading: virtue ethics, chap. 1, sec. 2E. Also relevant are consequentialism, chap. 1, sec. 2A, and Kantian moral theory, chap. 1, sec. 2C.

. . . I would like to take a look at adultery from the standpoint of an ethics of virtue, the reason being that such an ethics allows better for the complexities surrounding the topic.

In the first section, I list and briefly explain some of the most important misgivings that the friends of virtue ethics have with Kantian theory (and consequentialism). I also briefly explain the salient features of an ethics of virtue, some of its salient problems, and some possible replies to these problems. In the second section, . . . I discuss what an ethics of virtue has to say on adultery.

1. VIRTUE ETHICS

Recently, there has been some dissatisfaction with modern moral philosophy, that is, Kantian ethics, consequentialism, and their offshoots, such as social contract ethics and rights theory. Elizabeth Anscombe, Philippa Foot, Alasdair MacIntyre, and Bernard Williams are among the first philosophers to inveigh against modern moral philosophy, and their views have prompted the search for an alternative ethical theory. . . .

Most philosophers who have attacked modern moral philosophy have gathered around an ethics of virtue, an ethics which is still in its infancy insofar as its theoretical articulation is concerned. The core idea in an ethics of virtue is that the basic judgments in ethics are not judgments about acts but about character. According to Gregory Trianosky, "a pure ethics of virtue makes two claims. First it claims that at least some judgments about virtue can be validated independently of any appeal to judgments about the rightness of actions. Second . . . it is this antecedent goodness of traits which ultimately makes any right

From Raja Halwani, "Virtue Ethics and Adultery," *Journal of Social Philosophy* 29 (1998). Reprinted by permission of *Journal of Social Philosophy.*

act right."[1] Under deontological and utilitarian conceptions, the notion of right behavior or acts is logically prior to that of virtues. An ethics of virtue flips such a conception around: it is right behavior which is justified in terms of the virtues.

The question now of course is from what do the virtues themselves derive their justification. The answer usually given is that the virtues derive their justification from the notion of well-being or human flourishing. The virtues can then be thought of as being either *necessary* for well-being or as *constitutive* of it. However, and according to Statman, the linkage between the virtues and well-being is not essential to an ethics of virtue. What is essential is the claim that judgments about character are prior to judgments about the rightness or wrongness of behavior.[2] Such a claim can be a moderate one—that although most judgments are judgments of character, still, some actions can be evaluated independently of character—or it can be an extreme one. Under an extreme formulation, we can hold either a reductionist view or a replacement one. The former states that deontic concepts such as rightness and duty are useful, but that they are nevertheless derived from concepts of character. The latter, which is the most extreme formulation, states that deontic notions should be entirely discarded by an ethics of virtue and be replaced by other concepts, such as those of courage, benevolence, and generosity—the "thick concepts" of Bernard Williams.[3]

A good person is someone who is good because of the virtues he or she possesses. So not only are acts justified in terms of the virtues, but also whether a person is good or not will depend on the virtues, or lack thereof, that she has. This raises the question of what kind of an account of the virtues can be given. Typically, the understanding of the virtues has been dispositional: to have a certain virtue is to be disposed to act in certain ways given certain conditions. Such an understanding has been attacked by Mary Ella Savarino on the grounds that virtues do not turn out to be fundamental: "the focus is not on the virtue itself (courage), but on the person's behavior."[4] Savarino herself favors an account of virtues which takes them to be first actualities in the Aristotelian sense. In any case, the issue is still open: an adequate account of the virtues is needed.

It is obvious that virtue ethics has a number of advantages. For example, it makes room for the idea that it is not the case that for any moral problem there is only one right answer. Two virtuous people may act differently from one another when faced with the same situation, and yet both their actions can be right. A mother in poor health who has to work in the fields, who has five children, and who has an abortion upon her sixth pregnancy is not to be described as self-indulgent. Another mother in a similar situation might decide to go ahead with the pregnancy, and she is surely heroic. Both the actions are right despite the fact that the mothers acted differently. Second, virtue ethics is not in tension with the phenomenon of moral luck. As Statman put it, "According to Virtue Ethics, judgments of character, such as, 'Barbara is a friendly woman,' 'Tom is unbearably arrogant,' are not touched by the discovery that these traits are the result of genes, education, and circumstances, over which the agent had very limited control."[5]

Another important advantage of an ethics of virtue is its rejection of the distinction between the moral and the nonmoral. For if virtue ethics is concerned with the evaluation of character, then other nonmoral traits would be important, especially if the notion of well-being is taken to be primary. What enters into the well-being or flourishing of a person is not only what has been traditionally dubbed as "moral," but also a host of other "nonmoral" considerations, such as love, marriage, and sexual relations. . . .

2. ADULTERY AND VIRTUE ETHICS

In *Having Love Affairs,*[6] Richard Taylor gives us an interesting case of a married couple, the upshot of which is that whereas it is the wife who commits adultery, she is not the one to be described as unfaithful. The husband has been married to the same woman for a long time, and he has never been sexually unfaithful to her. He believes that sexual fidelity is of utmost importance, and he frowns upon any act of adultery committed by others. However, it is not in his nature, so to speak, to be sexually active. As a matter of fact, "[h]is intimacy with his own wife is perfunctory, infrequent, dutiful, and quite devoid of joy for himself or his spouse" (pp. 59–60). Moreover, it appears to others that the couple are of moderate financial means but hard-working. However, the husband, in complete secrecy from his wife and others, has a number of savings accounts which collectively contain a huge sum of money accumulated over the years. The wife, on the other hand, gets sick with cancer and undergoes a mastectomy, "[w]hereupon whatever small affection her husband ever had for her evaporates completely" (p. 60). The husband neglects her to the point of being "dimly aware" of her presence. In addition, the wife has always been an ardent writer of good poetry, and she meets a man who appreciates her talents. The man is oblivious to her physical scars, and loves her for who she is. Although Taylor does not explicitly say it, it seems that the wife has an affair with this man. The question that Taylor poses is, "Who has been faithless to whom?" (p. 60). The answer, of course, is, "The husband."[7]

I have gone into the details of this story because it gives us a good starting point as to how an ethics of virtue would deal with the issue of adultery. The picture we get from Taylor's story is that of a man (the husband) who lies, deceives, and is not to be commended for his sexual fidelity. He is the kind of person who is calculative, cold, selfish, and emotionally distant. Moreover, the fact that he did not commit adultery has nothing to do with his amazing ability to withstand sexual temptations, and has everything to do with the facts that he has never been tempted and that he is of a sexually passive nature. The wife, out of sheer bad luck, gets sick with cancer, suffers from its effects, and suffers from her husband's increased neglect. That she has an affair with another man is not only understandable, but even recommended, given her need for affirmation and love.

Under a Kantian picture, we are at a loss as to how to deal with Taylor's case. Did the wife violate her promise of sexual fidelity? Yes. Was her violation permissible in this case, that is, did she have a duty that can override her duty to keep her promise to her husband? If yes, what duty would that be? The duty to be happy? That would surely be a very strange

duty, for under a Kantian scheme we do not have a duty to promote our own happiness. Does the fact that the husband violated his duty to love his wife justify her violation of the promise to sexual fidelity? Surely not, for if her violation is wrong, then, as the saying goes, two wrongs do not make a right, and if her violation is permissible, surely it is not because her husband violated his own promise. Perhaps a good way to think of this would be the following: had the husband done what he did, without having made any promises, he would still be a despicable person. The wife might very well have broken her promise of sexual fidelity and so violated a right that her husband has against her. But as Rosalind Hursthouse suggests in her paper on abortion and virtue ethics, "in exercising a moral right I can do something cruel, or callous, or selfish, light-minded, self-righteous, stupid, inconsiderate, disloyal, dishonest,—that is, act viciously."[8] Similarly but oppositely, in violating a right one might sometimes do what is morally correct. Violation of promises is not what is at stake here.

Does virtue ethics have any general picture to give us about adultery? Yes, and the answer can be approached from two perspectives: the nature of love and the nature of the virtuous person.

The wrongness of adultery stems from the fact that adultery occurs in the context of marriage or a love relationship, the basis of which is an emotional commitment. Although it is perhaps meaningful to speak of adultery when it occurs in the context of a purely sexual relationship between two people, the act of the adulterer does not appear to be so horrific in such a case. What seems to be horrible about adultery is that it indicates a more fundamental betrayal, namely, that of love. As Bonnie Steinbock puts it, "[s]exual infidelity has significance as a sign of a deeper betrayal—falling in love with someone else."[9] Logically speaking, of course, there is no necessary connection between sex and love, as gay male orgy rooms aptly demonstrate. Indeed, one can argue that given that it is possible for love and sex to be disconnected, the permissibility of adultery follows. An argument that tries to show the immorality of adultery by arguing that since sex is connected with love, then sexual betrayal is tantamount to emotional betrayal, and hence adultery is wrong, is an invalid one, because there is no necessary connection between love and sex. This kind of reasoning[10] is correct but naive. It is true that sex is a pleasurable activity in and of itself, but sex is also typically an intimate activity. It requires a substantial amount of trust, it involves a good amount of self-exposure, and it is accompanied by the exchange of affection. We do not typically have sex in ways that are depicted in pornography movies, in which the partners have sex purely for sex's sake. Moreover, sex is connected to love precisely because it is a pleasurable activity: "People naturally have feelings of affection for those who make them happy, and sex is a very good way of making someone extraordinarily happy" (Steinbock, p. 190).

The fact that sex is intimately connected with love indicates the wrongness of adultery in two important ways. On the part of the adulterous spouse, the spouse, upon committing adultery, puts himself in a position in which emotional betrayal might be involved, and in which there is the possibility of increased affection between himself and the person he is having sex with. On the part of the nonadulterous spouse, the amount of pain and hurt upon the discovery is bad in itself, and it could lead to the destruction of the marriage. It could destroy the trust and affection that have been built over the years, and it could leave either party, if not both, emotionally and mentally damaged. I then endorse Steinbock's conclusion that sexual fidelity is an ideal in a marriage or in a romantic commitment.

If fidelity is an ideal in marriage, then a virtuous person would strive to stick to this ideal in a relationship. Moreover, a virtuous spouse would strive to maintain and foster the love, trust, and affection that exist between him and his spouse. These are healthy emotions and are an important part, surely, of any conception of a virtuous and flourishing person. To this end, adultery is to be avoided. This is a difficult endeavor, for it seems that we are not by nature sexually monogamous: we find people other than our spouses to be also sexually desirable, and we sometimes fantasize about them. Moreover, it is a fact that with time, the novelty of sex with one person wears out, and the temptation to seek sexual encounters with new partners increases. These facts warn us that sometimes failure to conform to the ideal is understandable. Be this as it may, it is crucial to strive for the ideal of fidelity. If the person is in love with someone, and if the person wants to be with that person for an indefinite period of time, then it is essential to strive for fidelity, given that adultery can damage the relationship and the persons involved. But to maintain the ideal of fidelity requires one to be a certain kind of person, a sexually faithful person, not because being sexually faithful guarantees the flourishing of the relationship and the people involved, but because in most cases it is pre-required by such flourishing.

A virtuous person is one who is to a large extent wise, courageous, fair, honest, moderate, caring, compassionate, benevolent, loving. Some of these virtues go a long way in helping to maintain the ideal of fidelity: the wisdom not to put oneself in tempting situations and in situations in which one cannot easily resist temptation (e.g., drunkenness), the wisdom to know when one is ready for a commitment, the wisdom to know whether one is the kind of person who is capable of being in a committed relationship, the courage to resist temptation, the compassion, care, and love for one's spouse that would form one's basis for refusing to commit adultery, and the honesty to one's spouse in the case of committing adultery. Other virtues do not seem to have room with respect to adultery. Adultery does not, for example, admit of moderation.[11]

But perhaps the important question is what virtue ethics tells us about the failure to conform to the ideal.[12] If in a drunken moment a spouse goes ahead and commits adultery, this would be a sorry and sad situation, but it would not be a tragedy, for the chances of emotional betrayal here are minimal, and to throw away a marriage, especially if it is good, because of what one spouse did in a moment of drunkenness is uncalled for. The fact that one might commit adultery in a drunken moment does not indicate that the marriage was going sour (the question, "Why else would one commit adultery?" often embodies this mistaken reasoning). As I mentioned, it does not seem to be in our nature to be sexually monogamous, and being drunk can often unleash our inhibited desires. But this is no good reason to throw away a good marriage.

If a woman is abused by her spouse, treated as an object, neglected, or all of these, she cannot be described as self-indulgent if she has an affair with another person. Her self-worth and happiness are at stake, and an affair can go a long way in healing her scars. To argue that the wife should first get a divorce before she has an affair with another man is simplistic. Often there are important factors at play that block such a way out. The wife might have no independent economic means by which she can sustain herself. There might be children involved, and sometimes the wife reasons that it is not in their best interests if a divorce occurs. Also, the wife might wish to stay in the marriage in the hope that it will get better, even if she does not envision a clear way of how this would happen.

In communities, such as those of Renaissance Florence and some Middle Eastern countries, in which marriage is often not based on love, the risk that there is a mismatch between the two married people is high, and often in such communities dissolving the marriage is not an easy matter, given that much rests on the continuation of the marriage, such as family honor, money, and political alliances. If one of, or both, the spouses commits adultery, this would be understandable, and perhaps even encouraged. Being stuck with a person that one does not want to be with is not a trivial matter, and having an extramarital affair can make the situation a bit more bearable.

Furthermore, sometimes the decision to commit adultery is the right one, although it might still be a case of moral failing. A husband who thinks that his wife is not treating him well, who feels that his marital life falls short of what it should be, who is as a result miserable, but who fails to be honest about his thoughts and feelings because he is too cowardly to talk to his wife, or because he lacks the perception to realize that his wife is simply unaware of the results of her actions, might very well make the right decision in having an affair with someone who satisfies his psychological and emotional needs. But the husband has also failed by allowing the situation to reach the point where he feels the need for an affair. He lacked the requisite courage and honesty to deal with these problems with his wife.

A person who knows from experience that his sexual drive is very strong, and who feels unable to be sexually monogamous simply because he loves sex too much, and yet who desires to be in a relationship with some specific individual, should be quite honest about what the sexual expectations of such a relationship would be. A sexually open relationship might be the most desirable form. Many gay couples, for example, have such relationships. Yet the form of extramarital sex that they allow themselves to have is highly impersonal so as to avoid the possibility of emotional intimacy with the new sexual partner. Hence, they resort to cruising in parks, they resort to dark rooms in gay bars and discos, and these are places in which there is minimal or no verbal and emotional communication.

One last issue I would like to discuss briefly is the question of why utilitarianism cannot account, as successfully as virtue ethics, for the wrongness of adultery. After all, a utilitarian might advise married couples not to commit adultery because the consequences might be bad: loss of love between the spouses, possible anguish for the children, and so forth.[13]

As far as act utilitarianism goes, I find it unsuccessful to deal with this issue for two major reasons. The first is that act utilitarianism has certain undesirable consequences, and hence is in itself a bad theory *in general*. Act utilitarianism could justify acts of murder, of punishing the innocent, and of trampling on the rights of others if such acts proved to have a net effect of good consequences (typically, happiness) over bad ones. The second reason is that act utilitarianism, insofar as it is a utilitarian theory—which it is—is not concerned only with the effects that adultery has on the family in question. Insofar as it is a utilitarian theory, it is concerned with the effects it has on everyone. Hence, and at least in principle, act utilitarianism could justify an act of adultery by appealing to the overall consequences. For example, suppose that John is married to Judith, that they have no children because Judith cannot have them, and that they both refuse to adopt. Suppose further that on one dark night John finally succumbs to lust and has an affair with his secretary Jezebel. They fall in love with each other, and they get married after John and Judith get a divorce. John and Jezebel proceed to have three children, one who grows up to be a physicist and who ends up solving the problems of quantum mechanics, one who grows up to be a doctor and who finds a decisive cure for AIDS, and the third who grows up to be a famed economist who, solves the problem of the incompatibility of price inflation and high employment. It would seem, then, that act utilitarianism could justify wrong acts of adultery.

Rule utilitarianism, which states that certain kinds of acts are wrong because they violate certain rules, and which justifies these rules by appealing to the principle of utility, suffers from its own defects. In general, when certain rules conflict, a rule utilitarian, being a utilitarian, must resort to solving the problem by appealing to the consequences of each act. Hence, in cases when there is a conflict of rules, rule utilitarianism becomes act utilitarianism. Furthermore, when it comes to adultery, rule utilitarianism is not as well equipped as virtue ethics is to handle this problem. Rule utilitarianism becomes similar to Kantian ethics in telling us that adultery is wrong because it violates a certain rule (adultery is wrong; do not commit adultery). By not appealing to character traits, the history of the agents involved, and the circumstances at hand (because these are not part and parcel of this doctrine), rule utilitarianism is as ineffective as Kantian ethics. We have seen, however, that virtue ethics is equipped to give us good explanations and justifications for certain cases of adultery precisely because it is a theory which takes certain factors into account, factors that have hitherto been left out by deontological and consequentialist theories of ethics.[14]

There is no one single answer to the question, "Would a virtuous person refrain from committing adultery?" Part of what it is to be a virtuous person is to be sensitive to the details of the situation and to be sensitive to the fact that one is a member of a certain kind of community or culture. Virtue ethics does not lapse into a vicious form of relativism or particularism. It tells us that a virtuous spouse should strive to maintain the ideal of fidelity, difficult though this may be. But virtue ethics does not give us one formula for treating the issue, and this, I believe, is a positive aspect of virtue ethics. As Aristotle remarked,

we should not demand exactness from a subject that is not exact.

NOTES

1. Gregory Trianosky, "What is Virtue Ethics All About?" *American Philosophical Quarterly,* vol. 27, 1990, p. 336.

2. Daniel Statman, *Virtue Ethics: A Critical Reader* (Washington, D.C.: Georgetown University Press, 1997).

3. Ibid., p. 9 Michael Slote, *From Morality to Virtue,* advocates the moderate view. Anscombe advocates the replacement view. Williams seems to hold the reductionist view. See also Philipp Montague, "Virtue Ethics: A Qualified Success Story," *American Philosophical Quarterly,* vol. 29, no. 1, January 1992.

4. Mary Ella Savarino, "Toward an Ontology of Virtue Ethics," *Journal of Philosophical Research,* vol. 18, 1993, p. 245.

5. Statman, p. 17.

6. Buffalo: Prometheus Books, 1982. Page references in my paper are to this book.

7. It is debatable whether such a case can be dealt with from a Kantian standpoint by relying on the prima facie rider: adultery is permissible because the wife had a duty that overrides her promise of sexual fidelity to her husband. From Wreen's perspective, my guess is that he would not allow it. The case he gives is of a couple who experience sexual dysfunction, such that the only way to save their marriage is for one of them (the relevant party) to commit adultery. Crucial to this case is the goal (duty?) to save the marriage, a goal which is not operative in the case given by Taylor.

8. "Virtue Theory and Abortion," *Philosophy and Public Affairs,* vol. 20, no. 3, 1991, p. 235.

9. "Adultery," in *Philosophy of Sex,* p. 192. Page references in my paper are to this anthology.

10. This reasoning is used by Richard Wasserstrom, "Is Adultery Immoral?" in *Philosophy and Sex,* R. Barker and F. Elliston, eds. (Buffalo: Prometheus Books, 1984).

11. Except in some special cases. A couple in an open relationship might want to be moderate in their extramarital sexual activities perhaps to avoid the higher risk of contracting diseases, especially the potentially fatal HIV. A person who is allowed by his or her spouse (for some reason or another) to engage in extramarital sex might still want to be moderate in what they do during their sexual escapades and in the frequency of such escapades.

12. In what follows, I owe much to Steinbock's "Adultery" and Hursthouse's "Virtue Theory and Abortion."

13. This suggestion was given by a reader from *The Journal of Social Philosophy.*

14. The reader from the journal also mentioned character utilitarianism, and why such a view cannot explain the wrongness of adultery as well as virtue ethics. I have never been entirely clear on what character utilitarianism exactly amounts to. As far as I understand it, it is the view that we should strive to have good characters. Stated in this way, it would seem to be a species of virtue ethics, and so, on my view, benign. But I still need to find a more articulate and coherent formulation of the view.

READING QUESTIONS

1. What are the advantages of virtue ethics according to Halwani?
2. Explain the case of adultery that Halwani uses as his main illustration. How does the virtue ethical response to such a case differ from the Kantian and consequentialist responses?
3. What is the ideal toward which the virtuous person should strive in a relationship according to Halwani? What virtues should the virtuous person acquire in order to attain this ideal? Explain how each of these virtues could play a role in achieving an ideal relationship.
4. What reasons does Halwani give for rejecting both act and rule utilitarianism?

DISCUSSION QUESTIONS

1. Is a virtue ethical approach the best one to take with respect to the situation of adultery? Why or why not? Discuss whether certain aspects of the virtue ethical approach could be incorporated into either Kantian or utilitarian approaches to these sorts of problems.
2. One of Halwani's objections to act utilitarianism is that it is concerned with the effect an action has on everyone involved. Are there any reasons to think that a virtue ethical approach might have the same problem?

MAGGIE GALLAGHER

Normal Marriage: Two Views

Gallagher distinguishes two views of marriage, views that differ over what they take to be *fundamental* about the institution of marriage. According to the view of marriage as a public bond and sexual institution between members of the opposite sex, marriage is fundamentally about the reproduction of children and continuation of society. By contrast, according to what Gallagher calls the "relationship view," marriage is an essentially private relationship whose fundamental aim is to enhance the personal well-being of the married partners. According to Gallagher the campaign by some to legalize same-sex marriage is the "logical result" of the increasing acceptance of the relationship view of marriage. And one of the main problems Gallagher sees in the legalization of same-sex marriage (and in the relationship view of marriage generally) is an erosion of the idea that there is a special connection between a child and his or her biological parents that creates responsibilities by those parents for the care of the child. She also casts doubt on the alleged benefits to children and adults who are involved in same-sex marriages and suggests that the campaign for legalization of same-sex marriage is largely a cultural symbolic issue.

Recommended Reading: consequentialism, chap. 1, sec. 2A.

What is marriage for?[1]

Every known human society has some form of marriage. In every advanced society, marriage exists as a public, legal act and not merely a private romantic or religious rite. Why?

Advocates of same-sex unions have done us the favor of pushing the intellectual debate over marriage to the deepest questions. Before we can decide whether sex is irrelevant (or how it is relevant) to the public purposes of marriage, we have to decide what those public purposes are. Why does the state get involved in the intimate lives of its citizens?

There are two views at play in the public square, marriage as a public bond and sexual institution or marriage as a private emotional relationship. They are not mutually exclusive, in the sense that most Americans today draw their understanding of marriage from both streams. But ultimately these two competing visions of what marriage is for lead the law in dramatically opposing directions.

THE RELATIONSHIP VIEW

Here is one view: Marriage is an essentially private, intimate, emotional relationship created by two people for their own personal reasons to enhance their own personal well-being. Marriage is created by the couple for the couple.

It is wrong and discriminatory, as well as counterproductive, therefore, for the state to privilege certain kinds of intimate relations over others. Marriage has a legal form but no specific content. Each person has the right to socially express his or her own inner vision of family, sexuality, and intimacy on an equal basis.

Sometimes this argument is made in its strongest possible form. As Rutgers law professor Drucilla Cornell put it, "The state should have no right to privilege or impose one form of family structure or sexuality over another. This would mean that some adults could choose *consensual* polygamy. Mormon men could have more than one wife. Four women who worship the mother goddess could also recognize and form a unity and call their relationship a marriage. There would be no state-enforced single relationship—not monogamy, heterosexuality, polygamy, or polyandry.... [Legislating] love and [conscripting] men is a sign of the fear of, not a solution to, the crisis of families. Intimate associations are different undertakings. They always have been so. The freedom to form families opens up the possibility of people creating their own families in the way most suitable to them."[2]

More often, it is tempered with an acknowledgment that the state does have a potential interest in regulating intimate relations, including marriage, but it is limited to the protection of existing dependents. To the extent that marriage protects the weak (children), the state may prefer marriage. But it makes no sense in this view for the state to deny the benefits of marriage to any two people, especially any two people with children. The only goods of marriage that the state confers are a small number of practical advantages in inheritance, Social Security, and health insurance law. There is no rational reason, therefore, to withhold these benefits from any couple who wishes to claim them on behalf of themselves or (especially) their dependents. When it comes to same-sex unions, these advocates typically rely on social science to uphold their claim that there is no rational reason why marriage should be understood as an inherently sexual (rather than unisex) institution.

More recent reviews of this body of literature call these claims into question. Due to problems in sample selection and size, study design, and other technical flaws, the current body of social science literature on gay parenting cannot tell us whether or not there are any important differences between children raised by their own two married mothers and fathers and children raised by two same-sex parents. Social science evidence, as it now stands, certainly does not refute the idea that children do better raised by their own two married mothers and fathers.[3]...

In the larger sweep of history, despite significant countercurrents,[4] this view of marriage as emotional intimacy is gaining dramatic ground. In this sense, same-sex marriage is not an outlandish deviation; it is the logical result of the rather popular contemporary view of marriage as a personal right of the individual, created by the individual, for purposes that the individual alone defines. When two individuals who happen to have desires and tastes for each other coincide for a lifetime, that is beautiful. If not, it just is not anybody else's business.

Of course, if this is what marriage is for, many things about the state's traditional regulation of marriage become difficult to understand. It is difficult to understand in this scheme why the state would be involved in marriage at all, or why marriage must be confined to the couple, or why, even at the most basic level, the word *marriage* requires intimacy at all. If fairness is the issue, why can a worker give his health insurance benefits only to someone he or she is sleeping with? Why do you have to live together? Why

can't business partners declare their relationship a marriage and save on the insurance premiums?

Drucilla Cornell is correct, but she does not see far enough. If marriage is just another word for an intimate union, then the state has no legitimate reason to insist that it even be intimate unless the couple, or the quadruplets, want it so. For the individual to be truly free to make unconstrained intimate choices, marriage itself must be deconstructed.

What about the children? There the state will, as Cornell puts it, separate the parenting alliance from the sexual alliance. Adults will still have obligations to children, but they will be severed from their newly unfettered intimate adult lives. What then is the source of adult obligation to specific children? There are only two possible answers: biology and contract.

Advocates of the alternative have diligently pushed the idea that contract not biology, creates parental obligations, in part because it is the only possible way for same-sex couples to have children together. The old stubborn reality that the people who make the baby are its parents must be shoved aside to accommodate an infinite diversity of adult choice. The people who thought up the baby are its real parents. So, for example, a surrogate mother is not a mother—the baby she carries is not hers because she did not intend for it to be hers. The mind is more important than the body, especially to people with Ph.D.s.

Of course, this latter view coincides with one important reality. It is easy to make a baby, hard to love and protect and provide for children to adulthood. One important goal of state regulation of intimacy has been to ensure that children have what they need. Advocates of family diversity tell us that it is therefore cruel to deprive any actual child of whatever benefit can be milked from the state by having the law prefer any family form. If the adults have decided to be parents, the state should applaud and enforce this decision, no matter how or who or even how many. So a *New York Times* story in 2000 applauded the growing legal acceptance of gay families, like those Joseph DeFillipis and his partner, David Koteles, are in the process of making. "[T]he men entered into an arrangement to conceive a child with a lesbian couple and to raise him or her jointly... The arrangement could lead to a tangle of legal questions should the foursome pull in different directions." But "DeFillipis and his three prospective co-parents have not been to a lawyer.... Instead for the last two years, they have discussed every conceivable area of dispute, including religion, geography and finances."[5] Two parents are good, four parents are better, in this view.

But its advocates, narrowly focused as they are on the urgent desires of a small number of adults to make their unorthodox family dreams come true, ignore the implications of this argument for vast numbers of children. Even today, most children are created by acts of the body, not the will. The best data indicate that about half of all pregnancies are unintended (including about a fifth of marital births and 58 percent of unwed births). Close to half of all women will experience an unintended pregnancy.[6] Sex makes babies, sometimes on purpose, but frequently not. The womb also has its reasons, which reason knows not.

If it is choice and contract that create parental obligations, why do these mothers have any obligations for the creatures of their bodies? Why are they not legal strangers to their own babies unless they voluntarily choose to contract obligations? On a less theoretical plane, why are we hounding poor men for child support, for babies for which they never contracted? Why would any man ever feel an obligation to take care of—or even marry—the mother of the children his body created? If it is adult choice that creates parental obligation, we are imposing a monstrous injustice on some of the least privileged men in this society, as well as some of the better-off....

Once we sever, conceptually, the sexual alliance and the parenting alliance, we sever children from their uncontested claim on their parents'—especially their fathers'—care and protection. It is the fathers who disappear, because while fathers and mothers are equally beloved and important to their children, fatherhood and motherhood are not equally natural or inevitable. Far more than mothers, reliable fathers are cultural creations, products of specific ideals, norms, rituals, and mating and parenting practices. Today, after thirty years of sexual revolution, only 60 percent of American children now live with their own two married parents.[7] Of the remaining 40 percent, the overwhelming majority live with their single or remarried mothers.[8]

A vast body of social science evidence shows that children who are not raised by their own married mother and father are at increased risk[9] for just about every negative outcome social scientists know how to measure: including physical illness, mental illness, school failure, child abuse, substance abuse, early unwed pregnancy, and criminal misconduct.[10] There is no evidence from the social sciences (including the literature on gay parenting) that credibly disrupts the assumption that a child does better raised by his or her own married mother and father.[11] But even if better research showed that individual same-sex couples do a good job with their individual children, the institutionalization of same-sex unions as marriages still threatens the well-being of other children and the public purposes (or, to lapse into legal terminology, the state's interest) in marriage.

Good fathers are made, not born. When family and sexual norms are weakened, it is generally children's access to fathers, not mothers, that is at risk. When we tell adults that parenting obligations are created by free choices of adults that the law only sanctions after the fact, the well-being of children is put at risk.

Two questions are raised by the prospect of unisex marriage: (1) Can a society or culture reliably make men into good fathers while at the same time affirming in its governing family law that children do not need mothers and fathers, and that it is choice, not biology, that creates family obligations? (2) Can a society that adopts the set of ideas and ideals driving the postmodern family even survive? I think that the answer to both these questions is, demonstrably, no.

MARRIAGE AS A UNIVERSAL HUMAN INSTITUTION

What is the alternate view of marriage? Some might call it traditional, but this is really not the right term, in the sense that this broad view of marriage is not the product of some specific tradition—custom, religion, or culture. The specific contours of our own inherited marriage tradition, deeply rooted in Judeo-Christian culture, which include reciprocal pledges of lifelong monogamy and fidelity, are, of course, not universal. Defending these particular contours is a task for another day.

But what every known human society calls marriage shares certain basic, recognizable features, including most especially the privileging of the reproductive couple, in order to protect both the interests of children and the interests of the society. Marriage is everywhere the word we use to describe a public sexual union between a man and a woman that creates rights and obligations between the couple and any children the union may produce.[12] Marriage as a public tie obligates not only fathers, but fathers' kin to recognize the children of this union. Marriage is in every society the sexual union where childbearing and raising are not only tolerated but applauded and encouraged. Marriage is the way in which every society attempts to channel the erotic energies of men and women into a relatively narrow, but highly fruitful channel, to give every child the father his or her heart desires. Above all, normal marriage is normative. The society defines for its young what the relationship is and what purposes it serves. Successful societies do this not only because children need fathers, but also because societies need babies. It is a truism, frequently forgotten by large complex societies, that only societies that reproduce survive.

In the context of the contemporary Western family system, this point is not as academic as most people think. In addition to the direct pain and suffering caused by family breakdown (driven by the idea that, children do not need families consisting of mothers and fathers, and that the sexual desires and freedoms of adults are more important than family norms), the evidence of reproductive dysfunction in all societies that adopt these postmodern family ideas is, at this point, overwhelming. For two generations every Western, industrialized nation has had subreplacement birthrates. In America, the crisis is still many generations off because our birthrates are closer to replacement and our social tolerance of immigration is higher. But many European nations are on the road to dying out, absent dramatic changes in reproductive patterns. By the year 2050, Italy's population is projected to decline by more than a quarter. The political, economic, and cultural implications of European depopulation are likely to be profound.[13]

Normal marriage is normative. Marriage does not merely reflect individual desire; it shapes and channels it. Marriage as a social institution communicates that a certain kind of sexual union is, in fact, our shared ideal: one where a man and a woman join not only their bodies, but their hearts and their bank accounts, in a context where children are welcome. Of course, not everybody wants or achieves this social ideal. In important ways marriage regulates the relationships and sexual conduct even of people who are not married and may never even get married. Its social and legal prominence informs young lovers about the end toward which they aspire, the outward meaning of their most urgent, personal impulses. It signals to cohabitors the limitations of their own and/ or their partners' commitment.

Marriage, as a universal human idea, does not require the ruthless or puritanical suppression of alternatives. It is consistent with a variety of attitudes toward alternate forms of sexual expression, from stigma to acceptance. What it is not consistent with is a legal regime such as that suggested by the Vermont court: that there is no rational relation between the law of marriage and procreation.[14] Because some infertile people marry, and assisted reproductive technology is more common now, the court argued, marriage in Vermont now has nothing to do with its great universal anthropological imperative: family making in a way that encourages ties between fathers, mothers, and their children—and the successful reproduction of society.[15]

Marriage as a universal human institution is, as I have said, consistent with a variety of attitudes toward alternative intimate and sexual relations, from stigma to tolerance. But if we lose the idea that marriage is about, at some basic level, the reproduction of children and society, if our law rejects the presumption that children need mothers and fathers, and that marriage is the way in which we do our best to get them for children, then we cannot expect private tastes and opinions alone to sustain the marriage idea.

That is what same-sex marriage puts at risk. For what benefit? Responsible adults of all sexual orientations who care about children and society should be especially cautious about radical revisions of marriage law, given the extremely small number of couples on whose behalf we contemplate overturning normative marriage. The latest Census Bureau figures report that only about 0.5 percent of all households consist of same-sex couples. Most of these are likely to be gay or lesbian.[16] But many of them, like many opposite-sex cohabitors, are likely uninterested in marriage.

Could we use registered domestic partners to get an idea how many same-sex couples are being denied matrimony by current law? In August 2001, I called the domestic partnership registries of the ten largest U.S. cities that have domestic partner registries. In these ten cities, same-sex registered domestic partners account for about 0.1 percent of the population.[17]

How many domestic partners depend on one another for health benefits—another crude proxy for denial of marriage rights? I tried to obtain such data from the ten largest corporations that offer domestic partnership benefits: General Motors, Ford Motor Company, Citigroup, Enron Corporation, IBM, AT&T, Verizon Communications, Philip Morris, J.P. Morgan Chase and Company, and Bank of America Corporation. However, only one of these ten companies, General Motors, was willing to release the data: Out of a total of 1,330,000 employees, exactly 166 workers (or just over 0.01 percent) chose to extend their health insurance to a same-sex partner.

This is not surprising. No definitive research on the gay and lesbian population exists, but the majority of gay and lesbian individuals are likely not living with partners. Many who do live in sexual partnership may refuse financial responsibility for each other (just like many opposite-sex cohabitors). Even where same-sex couples do wish a financial union, most partners are likely working and maintaining their own insurance benefits.

Similarly, we suspect that the number of children who might benefit from, say, health insurance through same-sex marriage is quite small. Why? First, only

0.5 percent of households consist of same-sex couples. Only a minority of these have children from the union, through adoption or donor insemination. If the child is either the natural or adopted child of the parents, he or she is likely covered by the working parent's health insurance anyway. Finally, while married people's income is pooled for tax and welfare purposes, that of domestic partners (especially same-sex partners) is typically not. This means that unmarried partners are eligible for social insurance benefits unavailable to most married couples. So unlike married couples, if one parent in a domestic partnership drops out of the work force to care for a baby, he or she will likely qualify for Medicaid and other means-tested medical and financial benefits reserved for low-income and single parents.

The demand for same-sex-marriage benefits is not likely based on filling a huge unmet need for practical benefits. Children or adults are not being deprived of health care en masse because law and social policies favor married couples over unrelated cohabitors. Instead, the drive for same-sex marriage appears to be a largely symbolic cultural issue; the goal (or at any rate the main effect) is not filling a need for health insurance or other practical benefits, but making a powerful social statement: Same-sex unions are the functional equivalent of marriage, traditionally understood, and should be treated as such by law and public policy.

Is this a statement the law ought to make? Is it true? When it comes to child well-being, we could not begin to say that current social science research justifies this statement. To come to this conclusion, research following a nationally representative sample of children of same-sex couples over time, comparing children of same-sex couples to children living with their own mothers and fathers, with adequate controls for other background variables, would be necessary. This research has, as yet, not even been attempted. Meanwhile, a large body of social science evidence confirms the advantages of the intact mother–father family over alternate family forms, including other two-parent homes, such as remarriages.

Surely there can be no legal right to ask the law to, in essence, lie—to endorse unequivocally what we do not yet know to be true: that same-sex unions are the functional equivalents of marriages when it comes to child rearing. Nor should the law of marriage focus only on the well-being of individual children of individual unions, but on the broader social impact that legal presumptions of marriage and parenthood have on the conduct of all parents, and therefore all children. When the law assumes and promulgates the idea that either mothers or fathers are dispensable, and that marriage is an essentially private matter whose form is determined by private adult desires, marriage in general and children in particular will inevitably suffer.

Marriage is an institution in crisis. Close to half of new marriages end in divorce. A third of our children are born out of wedlock. The majority of children, at current estimates, will experience a fatherless or motherless household. Making substantial new progress in actually reversing the trend toward family fragmentation requires that law and society reject the deepest presumptions driving the movement toward gay marriage: the ideas that marriage is essentially a private choice created by and for the couple, that children do just fine in whatever family forms their parents choose to create, and that babies are irrelevant to the public purposes of marriage.

People who wish to legislate same-sex unions do so in the name of high ideals: fairness, justice, compassion. I do not doubt their sincerity. But I do not share their own high estimate of their actions. To take the already troubled institution most responsible for the protection of children and the continuation of society and to gut its most basic presumption in the name of furthering adult interests in sexual liberty seems to me morally and socially cavalier.

NOTES

1. I express my gratitude to E.J. Graff for posing the question so clearly. See E.J. Graff, 1999, *What Is Marriage For?* (Boston: Beacon Press).

2. Drucilia Cornell, 1998, "Fatherhood and Its Discontents: Men, Patriarchy, and Freedom," in Cynthia R. Daniels (ed.), *Lost Fathers: The Politics of Fatherlessness in America* (New York: St. Martin's Press): 199.

3. Most of these same-sex-parenting studies actually compare children of single heterosexual mothers to children of lesbian mothers. They may be relevant to other legal questions, such as custody, but they do not show that same-sex unions are the functional equivalent of mother–father unions.

4. See, for example, *The Marriage Movement: A Statement of Principles*, 2000 (New York: Institute for American Values), available at www.marriagemovement. org.

5. John Leland, 2000, "O.K. You're Gay. So? Where's My Grandchild?" *New York Times* (December 21): F1. See also accompanying story, John Leland, 2000, "State Laws Vary, but a Broad Trend Is Clear," *New York Times* (December 21): F4.

6. Stanley K. Henshaw, 1998, "Unintended Pregnancy in the United States," *Family Planning Perspectives* 30(1): 24–29.

7. Sharon Vandivere, Kristen Anderson Moore, and Martha Zaslow, 2001, *Children's Family Environments: Findings from the National Survey of America's Families* (Washington, DC: Urban Institute). The data on the proportion of children living with their own two married parents are from unpublished analyses provided to David Blankenhorn.

8. In 1997, 23 percent of family households were headed by a female single parent, while 5 percent were headed by a male single parent. U.S. Bureau of the Census, 1998, *Statistical Abstract of the United States: 1998*, 118th ed. (Washington, DC: U.S. Govt. Printing Office), p. 68.

9. The literature on this point now stretches into literally thousands of studies. For some important recent summaries, see Paul R. Amato and Alan Booth, 1997, *A Generation at Risk: Growing Up in an Era of Family Upheaval* (Cambridge, MA: Harvard University Press); Sara McLanahan and Gary D. Sandefur, 1994, *Growing Up with a Single Parent: What Hurts, What Helps* (Cambridge, MA: Harvard University Press); *The Marriage Movement: A Statement of Principles*, 2000 (New York: Institute for American Values), available at www.marriagemovement.org; and Linda J. Waite and Maggie Gallagher, 2000, *The Case for Marriage: Why Married People Are Happier, Healthier, and Better Off Financially* (New York: Doubleday).

10. For a review of the evidence see Linda J. Waite and Maggie Gallagher, 2000, *The Case for Marriage: Why Married People Are Happier, Healthier, and Better Off Financially* (New York: Doubleday); Norval Glenn et al., 2002, *Why Marriage Matters: 21 Conclusions from the Social Sciences* (New York: Institute for American Values).

11. See note 3.

12. But what of recent claims that same-sex marriages are in fact not anthropologically uncommon? Mostly

these involved reinterpreting other sorts of social ties as marriage, as John Boswell did when he speculated that blood-brother ceremonies blessed by the church in medieval Europe were the equivalent of contemporary same-sex unions. John Boswell, *Same-Sex Unions in Premodern Europe* (New York: Villard Books, 1994). [For a critique of Boswell's assertion that early Christian and medieval church attitudes to same-sex relationships were either affirming or not entirely negative, see David F. Greenberg, 1988, *The Construction of Homosexuality* (Chicago: University of Chicago Press).] When same-sex relations were institutionalized in small tribal societies, it was often for the purpose of sustaining marriage systems. Men who had to wait for their betrothed wife to mature sexually before marrying, for example, were often expected to engage in sexual relationships with their future wife's older brother to cement kinship ties. Homosexual relations between unmarried juveniles were often encouraged as an alternative to potentially disruptive, procreative sex with unmarried girls. Many tribal societies engage in ritual homosexuality for the purpose of strengthening male bonds. All members are expected to marry upon reaching sexual and social maturity, however. The handful of small tribal civilizations (such as those that practiced, the Native American custom of *berdache*) that allowed men to marry men required one partner to adopt a female social role. In polygamous societies, such marriages would not have affected the birthrate (which is determined by births per woman) and may have encouraged child survival by gaining the labor of two adult men for the polygamous family group. See David F. Greenberg, *The Construction of Homosexuality*, pp. 26–73.

13. See, for example, *Replacement Migration: Is It a Solution to Declining and Ageing Populations*? 2000 (New York: Population Division of the Department of Economic and Social Affairs, United Nations, March 17).

14. *Baker v. State*, 744 A.2d. 864 (Vt. 1999).

15. The state does not require fertility tests for marriage, but historically it has imposed a sexual performance requirement on men for marriage. For example, male impotence has always been a ground for annulling a marriage, and not, one supposes because the state viewed itself as having an interest in furthering the sexual gratification of women.

16. Census respondents who indicated that a same-sex adult was their unmarried partner or spouse were categorized as same-sex couples, since roommate or boarder was available to individuals who did not have a romantic relationship. "Households Headed by Gays Rose in the '90s, Data Shows," 2001, *New York Times*, August 21: A17.

17. Maggie Gallagher, forthcoming. *Why Supporting Marriage Makes Business Sense*.

READING QUESTIONS

1. Describe what Gallagher calls the "Relationship View" of marriage. What is the difference between the stronger and weaker forms of the typical arguments offered in favor of this view?

2. What are the two possible sources of adult obligation to specific children according to Gallagher? Which of these is endorsed by advocates of gay marriage?

3. Explain the potential problems Gallagher anticipates for a society where the relationship view of marriage is widespread.

4. Why does Gallagher think that children of gay couples would not be deprived of any potential state benefits even if their parents are prohibited from marrying?

DISCUSSION QUESTIONS

1. Should the state be involved in the regulation of marriage practices?

2. Gallagher claims that gay marriage is a symbolic and cultural issue rather than a practical one. Are there good reasons to accept this claim? To what extent should we take into account the practical issues surrounding the gay marriage debate?

3. Is Gallagher right to worry that the state's endorsement of gay marriage would contribute to the breakdown of the family?

Evan Wolfson

Enough Marriage to Share

Wolfson's article is a direct reply to the previous article by Gallagher, who appeals to the importance of raising children in arguing against same-sex marriage and in favor of more traditional opposite-sex marriages. In defense of same-sex marriage, Wolfson argues that most studies of the children being raised by gay and lesbian couples conclude that these children are not disadvantaged compared to children raised by heterosexual couples. He also questions Gallagher's appeal to the problems with sustaining good marriages (including, for example, high rates of divorce) as having any "logical connection" to the question of legalizing gay marriage.

Recommended Reading: consequentalism, chap. 1, sec. 2A.

I am always struck when opponents of marriage equality—who spend a good chunk of their time urging people to get married and advocating special rights for those who do—then turn around and argue that gay people alone should not be allowed to marry....

Maggie Gallagher, for example, together with coauthor Linda J. Waite, wrote a whole book titled *The Case for Marriage: Why Married People Are Happier, Healthier, and Better Off Financially*. Neither there nor in "Normal Marriage: Two Views" does she explain why gay people should not want and deserve to be happier, healthier, and financially secure, too.

To me, this is puzzling. It is not difficult to find real-life stories of gay parents and their kids, not difficult to hear about the harms and joys we experience, like any other human beings, with families and life's ups and downs.[1] Lambda Legal Defense and Education Fund's Web site, for example, details the experiences of couples such as Ivonne and Jeanette (a couple with two children who were threatened with eviction from their housing project because they are not married), Fred and Tim (who lost custody of their kids because they are not married), Ronnie and

Elaine (denied health benefits and leave from work because they are not married), and others.

Why would someone sincerely concerned with the well-being of people, including children, defend discriminatory exclusion from an institution that might bring these couples and these children support and protection in life? How does it help the children being raised by gay parents to deprive these children of the protections and support that would come to their families with marriage?

Actually, as courts in Hawaii and Vermont, among others, have found, perpetuating the denial of civil marriage does not help these kids—or any one—at all.[2] The unanimous Vermont Supreme Court concluded, "If anything, the exclusion of same-sex couples from the legal protections incident to marriage exposes their children to the precise risks that the State argues the marriage laws are designed to secure against."[3] Even if Gallagher were correct that one family configuration is "the best," the argument for discrimination fails. As an authoritative 1999 report out of Stanford University conclusively demonstrated, it simply makes no sense to say, "We care about children," and then punish some kids for having the "wrong parents" by denying their families the benefits of marriage.[4]

Moreover, contrary to her claim, there is no evidence to support the offensive proposition that only one size of family must fit all. Most studies—including ones that Gallagher relies on—reflect the common sense that what counts is not the family structure, but the quality of dedication, commitment, self-sacrifice, and love in the household. For example, the American Psychological Association surveyed the abundant and uncontroverted research and concluded that

> [n]ot a single study has found children of gay or lesbian parents to be disadvantaged in any significant respect relative to children of heterosexual parents. Indeed, the evidence to date suggests that home environments provided by gay and lesbian parents are as likely as those provided by heterosexual parents to support and enable children's psychosocial growth.[5]

As the highly respected American Academy of Pediatrics affirmed in February 2002, there is simply no evidence, scientific or otherwise, to suggest that gay parents are any less fit, or that their children are any less happy, healthy, and well adjusted.[6]

In fact, much of what preoccupies Gallagher—deficiencies in parenting, divorce and failures of existing marriages, "radical fatherless[ness]" and "making men good fathers," polygamy (!), society's "need [for] babies" in order to survive—does not have any logical connection to depriving gay people of the commitment, responsibilities, and support that come with marriage. Fencing gay people out of marriage does nothing to help nongay people treat their spouses better, or behave more responsibly, or spend more time with their kids. While I agree with Gallagher that we should not "ask the law to, in essence, lie," isn't it a lie to say that committed gay couples taking on the responsibilities of civil marriage threaten this most resilient of social institutions—when nongay convicted murderers, deadbeat dads, and, for that matter, even game-show contestants on *Who Wants to Marry a Millionaire?* who never met before are all free to marry at will?[7]

Given Gallagher's emphasis on married mothers and fathers, isn't having the law pretend that there is only one family model that works (let alone exists) a lie? Isn't it a lie to claim to be caring about the kids (Gallagher cites the importance of giving kids an "uncontested claim on their parents") and then deny marriage licenses to their parents if they happen to be gay? Isn't it a lie to use kids as the excuse to deny gay people the precious freedom to marry when we grant marriage licenses to senior citizens and those who do not wish to procreate, as well as childless couples such as Bob and Elizabeth Dole, Pat and Shelley Buchanan, or even George and Martha Washington? Isn't it a lie not to recognize that people have many reasons for wanting to marry?[8]

The denial of marriage to same-sex couples helps no one. But what it does do, as the title of Gallagher's book underscores, is harm lesbians and gay men, our children, and those who care about us. Gay youth are sent a message of inferiority and exclusion; often before they even know that they are gay, they can sense that their difference means that they will be excluded from an important part of life. Gay couples are deprived of important protections and support (as necessary for lesbian and gay human beings as for nongays); if these things matter for nongay lives, why are they trivial when gay people seek them? Moreover, our nongay parents, siblings, nieces and nephews, grandparents, and friends suffer, too, when we are treated unequally and are cast outside the law's protection. What good parent does not want the same opportunities, joys, and shelter for all his or her children, gay or nongay? The law should help support families and enlarge people's possibilities, not tear them apart or put barriers in their way.

Beyond that, the discriminatory restriction on marriage injures the American commitment to equality for all and respect for each person's pursuit of happiness. As California's Supreme Court noted in striking down discrimination in marriage, the "essence of the right to marry [is] the freedom to join in marriage with the person of one's choice. . . . Human beings are bereft of worth and dignity by a doctrine that would make them as interchangeable as trains."[9]

Our opponents sometimes seem to imply that there is something sinister about these American values of equal treatment and respect for individuals' choices. They truck in the usual gloom-and-doom that opponents of equality have always invoked to hold back such "radical" changes as women's advancement, interracial marriage, divorce, and contraception.[10] But their quarrel really ought not to be with gay people (who, after all, are seeking to take part in the responsibilities and commitment of marriage Gallagher extols), or with the Vermont Supreme Court (which stuck with the facts and found that "legal protection and security for [gay people's] avowed commitment to an intimate and lasting human relationship is simply, when all is said and done, a recognition of our common humanity").[11] Rather, our opponents' real quarrel is with modernity, pluralism, the separation of church and state, the U.S. Supreme Court, and our federal Constitution.

To read Gallagher's essay, one would not know that for decades the law of the land (America, that is, unlike, perhaps, more theocratic or women subordinating societies) has been to recognize that marriage is not just about procreation—indeed, is not necessarily about procreation at all. Many people, of course, choose to have children within the context of marriage and commentators are free to urge them to do so. Raising kids within marriage is precisely what many gay people are seeking to do, amid fierce (and unhelpful) right-wing attacks on their families.

But the law, the courts, and the Constitution have also long recognized that people marry for reasons other than procreation. The "important tributes of marriage," as Justice Sandra Day O'Connor wrote in one unanimous case, are its "expressions of emotional support and public commitment"; its "spiritual significance" for many; the sexual fulfillment it may entail; and its role as a "precondition to the receipt of government benefits . . . and other, less tangible benefits."[12] That same year, well before the Hawaii Supreme Court required the government to show a reason for excluding gay couples from marriage, a leading family law treatise observed that the American institution of marriage had changed "from the days when it was an economic producing unit of society with responsibilities for child rearing and training, to the present, when its chief functions seem to be furnishing opportunities for affection, companionship, and sexual satisfaction."[13]

As Judge Kevin Chang held in the historic 1996 Hawaii trial decision finding no valid reason for denying same-sex couples the freedom to marry:

> In Hawaii, and elsewhere, people marry for a variety of reasons, including . . . (1) having or raising children; (2) stability and commitment; (3) emotional closeness; (4) intimacy and monogamy; (5) the establishment of a framework for a long-term relationship; (6) personal significance; (7) legal and economic protections, benefits and obligations.[14]

"Gay men and lesbian women," the judge found, "share this same mix of reasons for wanting to be able to marry.[15] Nothing in Gallagher's pile of data, the meaningful as well as the dubious, refutes this central and basic point.

As former President Gerald Ford declared in October 2001 when asked about lesbian and gay families and marriage, "I think they ought to be treated equally. Period." Asked whether gay couples should get the same Social Security, tax, and other federal benefits as married couples, the Republican replied, "I don't see why they shouldn't. I think that's a proper goal."[16] Civil rights hero John Lewis, now a congressman from Georgia, decried attacks on gay people's freedom to marry, noting that the exclusion "denies gay men and women the right to liberty and the pursuit of happiness." Said Congressman Lewis:

> Marriage is a basic human right. You cannot tell people they cannot fall in love. Dr. Martin Luther King, Jr. used to say when people talked about interracial marriage and I quote, "Races do not fall in love and get married. Individuals fall in love and get married." . . . Mr. Chairman, I have known racism. I have known bigotry. This bill [the proposed federal antimarriage law of 1996, adding an overlay of federal discrimination against same-sex couples] stinks of the same fear, hatred and intolerance. It should not be called the Defense of Marriage Act. It should be called the defense of mean-spirited bigots act.[17]

Following September 11, 2001, Republican Governor George Pataki of New York, noting that no one asked the firefighters entering the World Trade Center whether they were gay or whom they loved, issued an executive order requiring the state Crime Victims

Compensation Board to treat surviving same-sex partners as equivalent to spouses.

More than thirty-five years ago, the Supreme Court rejected claims that allowing contraception would lead to the demise of society.[18] In its opinion, the Court also took a stand against those who sought to hijack other people's freedom to marry as a vehicle for imposing their own personal or parochial agendas. In America, under our Constitution, the Court held:

> Marriage is a coming together for better or for worse, hopefully enduring, and intimate to the degree of being sacred. *It is an association that promotes a way of life, not causes*; a harmony in living, not political faiths; a bilateral loyalty, *not* commercial or *social projects.*[19]

Whether she is sincere or not, it is wrong for Gallagher to deny gay people the freedom to marry in order to promote her views on how people should conduct their own affairs or behave in their own marriages or lives, or in order to somehow chasten nongay people into being better parents or partners....

In 2001, 2,000 same-sex couples got legally married in the Netherlands, our NATO ally and the United States' oldest, constant friend; the sky did not fall.[20] If marriage is, as Gallagher argues, good for individuals, communities, children, and our country, then surely it would be good for gay people, too.[21] It would also be good for the nation we are part of to welcome us across the threshold instead of barring the door.

NOTES

1. See, e.g., *Denying Access to Marriage Harms Families*, http://www.lambdalegal.org/cgi.bin/iowa/documents/record?record=873; *The Plaintiff Couples*, http://www.glad.org.

2. *Baehr v. Mike* (trial); *Baker v. State* (Vt. S.Ct).

3. *Baker*, cite.

4. Michael S. Wald, *Same-Sex Couples: Marriage, Families, and Children* (Stanford University, 1999),http://www.law.stanford.edu/faculty/wald/summary.shtml.

5. *Lesbian and Gay Parenting: A Resource for Psychologists* (American Psychological Association, 1995), p. 8. Gallagher takes social science data suggesting that kids do better with two involved parents (and the financial and emotional resources they can bring) and

transmutes that into an argument that this means "[their] own married mother and father," a conclusion that matches her agenda but for which there is no support.

6. "Children deserve to know that their relationships with both of their parents are stable and legally recognized. This applies to all children, whether their parents are of the same or opposite sex. The American Academy of Pediatrics recognizes that a considerable body of professional literature provides evidence that children with parents who are homosexual can have the same advantages and the same expectations for health, adjustment, and development as can children whose parents are heterosexual." "Technical Report: Coparent or Second-Parent Adoptions by Same-Sex Parents," *Pediatrics* (Feb. 2002), pp. 339–340, http://www.aap.org/policy/020008.html; APA, *ibid*.

7. One of Gallagher's arguments seems to be that there are so few gay couples that it is not worth ending the sex restriction in marriage. While the exact number of gay people, let alone same-sex couples, is unknown, the 2000 census showed gay people present in nearly every county of the country and a significant number of same-sex couples, despite its serious undercounting. D'Vera Cohn, "Count of Gay Couples Up 300%," *Washington Post*, Aug. 22, 2001, p. A3. Even more tellingly, the most authoritative comparison of married nongay, cohabiting nongay, lesbian, and gay couples concluded that " '[c]ouplehood,' either as a reality or an aspiration, is as strong among gay people as it is among heterosexuals." Blumstein and Schwartz, *American Couples: Money, Work, Sex* (New York: William Morrow, 1983), p. 45. Putting aside the question of numbers (as if the injury were not severe to each couple, no matter how many or how few), it is hard to see how allowing what Gallagher believes is such an ostensibly small group of families to partake of the protections of marriage threatens civilization's collapse.

8. The state has always licensed marriages between elderly, sterile, and even impotent parties. Indeed, a refusal to allow the elderly or infertile to marry would almost certainly be unconstitutional, and Gallagher does not seem to advocate such a restriction for these nonprocreating couples. The only people upon whom our opponents seek to impose a "procreation" requirement are same-sex couples.

9. *Perez v. Lippold*, 198 P.2d 17, 19 (Cal. 1948) (because of the different-race restriction, a person "find[s] himself barred by law from marrying the person of his choice and that person to him may be irreplaceable").

10. One court, for example, upheld restrictions on different-race marriage on the grounds that it was "unnatural," saying that it would lead to children who are "generally sickly, and effeminate...and inferior in physical

development and strength." *Scott v. Georgia*, 39 Ga. 321, 323 (1869). Dire claims such as Ms Gallagher's about the consequences of allowing gay people to marry were also made, for example, about contraception. See Evan Wolfson, "Crossing the Threshold: Equal Marriage Rights for Lesbians and Gay Men," 21 *N.Y.U. Rev. of Law & Soc. Change* 567, 610 n. 190 (1994) (e.g., one commentator declared, "Japanese birth control devices in the homes of America can be more destructive than Japanese bombers over Pearl Harbor"). For an appalling and yet sometimes amusing recital of such "jeremiads," see E.J. Graff, *What Is Marriage For?* (Boston: Beacon Press, 1999).

11. *Baker v. Vermont.*

12. *Turner v. Safley*, 482 U S. 78, 95–96 (1997) (even convicted felons have a constitutionally protected interest in their freedom to marry, even though they may not be able to enjoy all these enumerated attributes). The Court pointedly did not cite procreation as even one of the bases for the freedom to marry.

13. Homer H. Clark, Jr., *The Law of Domestic Relations in the United States*, 2d. ed. 1987, vol. 1, p. 74.

14. *Baehr v. Miike*, Finding of Fact 138.

15. *Id.*

16. Deb Price, "Gerald Ford: Treat Gay Couples Equally," *Detroit News*, Oct. 29, 2001.

17. Congressman John Lewis, U.S. House of Representatives, July 11, 1996.

18. Wolfson, "Crossing the Threshold," 610 n. 190.

19. *Griswold v. Connecticut*, 381 U.S. 479, 486 (1965) (emphasis added).

20. Associated Press, "Dutch Gay Marriage Stats Released," Dec. 12, 2001. The Dutch government reported that same-sex couples' marriages comprised 3.6 percent of all new marriages between the ending of marriage discrimination on April 1 and September 30, 2001. In Denmark, where "gay marriage" has been in existence for more than a decade, opponents are unable to cite any adverse consequences and, indeed, "acknowledge their concerns may have been overblown." L. Ingrassia, "Danes Don't Debate Morality of Same-Sex Marriage; Even Opponents Say '89 Law Brought No Social Ill," *Wall Street Journal*, June 8, 1994.

21. This was the conclusion of the official report from the Canadian government's Law Commission, which after years of study recently called on Parliament and provincial governments to eliminate discriminatory restrictions on civil marriage and allow same-sex couples the full and equal freedom to marry. Law Commission of Canada, "Beyond Conjugality" http://www.lcc.gc.ca/en/themes/pr/cpra/report.html#004e (Dec. 21, 2001).

READING QUESTIONS

1. What are some of the many reasons that persons may want to marry according to Wolfson and others?
2. Why does Wolfson think that Maggie Gallagher's view of a "one size should fit all" family structure harms rather than helps children?
3. Who is harmed by the denial of marriage rights to gay and lesbian couples other than the children of such unions according to Wolfson?
4. What does Wolfson suggest are the chief functions of marriage other than procreation?

DISCUSSION QUESTIONS

1. Should we agree with Wolfson that denying marriage to gay and lesbian couples does more harm than good to the children of these couples?
2. Wolfson denies Maggie Gallagher's claim that there is any logical connection between problematic family issues, such as the prevalence of fatherlessness and divorce in our society, and gay marriage. Are there any reasons to think that there might be some connection between the advocacy of gay marriage and these sorts of social problems?
3. Is Wolfson right in claiming that procreation is not one of the chief functions of marriage?

ADDITIONAL RESOURCES

Web Resources

The Pew Forum on Religion & Public Life <http://pewforum.org/docs/>. This site is an excellent resource for learning more about the history of the same-sex marriage movement as well as about the legal, political, and ethical issues regarding such marriage.

Brake, Elizabeth, "Marriage and Domestic Relationships," <http://plato.stanford.edu/entries/marriage/>. Includes discussion of the history of marriage, as well as the philosophical debates over marriage including same-sex marriage.

Pickett, Brent, "Homosexuality," <http://plato.stanford.edu/entries/homosexuality/>. Includes discussion of the history of same-sex attraction, natural law objections, and queer theory.

Authored Books

Rauch, Jonathan, *Gay Marriage: Why It Is Good for Gays, Good for Straights, and Good for America* (Holt Paperbacks, 2004). Rauch argues for same-sex marriage on moral grounds, claiming that such unions enable homosexuals to live a kind of fulfilling life that is otherwise not possible. (Rauch's defense contrasts with Wolfson's "civil rights" defense. See below.)

Stanton, Glenn T. and Bill Maier, *Marriage on Trial: The Case Against Same-Sex Marriage and Parenting* (InterVarsity Press, 2004). The authors oppose same-sex marriage by appealing to social science research in arguing that that same-sex marriage is likely to be harmful to society.

Wolfson, Evan, *Why Marriage Matters: America, Equality, and Gay People's Right to Marry* (Simon & Schuster, 2005). The author of this chapter's "Enough Marriage for All" defends same-sex marriage in the United States as a civil right.

Edited Collections

Baker, Robert B., Kathleen J. Wininger, and Frederick A. Elliston (eds.), *Philosophy and Sex*, 3rd ed. (Amherst, N.Y.: Prometheus Books, 1998). This anthology of forty-four essays is divided into three parts: (1) Love, Marriage, and Reproduction, (2) Gender, Sexuality, and Perversion, and (3) Desire, Pornography, and Rape.

Corvino, John (ed.), *Same Sex: Debating the Ethics, Science, and Culture of Homosexuality* (Lanham, MD: Rowman & Littlefield, 1997). This anthology includes twenty-one articles divided into four parts: Morality and Religion, Science and Identity, Identity and History, and Public Policy.

Sobel, Alan (ed.), *The Philosophy of Sex* (Lanham, MD: Rowman & Littlefield, 2001). This recent anthology is probably the best of its kind. It has thirty articles organized into the following six parts:(1) conceptual analysis, (2) homosexuality,(3) abortion,(4) Kant and sex, (5) rape and harassment, and (6) pornography and prostitution. It also includes an extensive bibliography on these and other topics.

Sullivan, Andrew, *Same-Sex Marriage: Pro and Con* (Vintage, revised edition, 2004). A wide-ranging collection of essays debating various aspects of same-sex marriage including historic, religious, legal, and public-policy issues. The collection is also notable for featuring essays by public figures, religious leaders, pundits, and essayists as well as by academics and legal experts.

Trevas, Robert, Arthur Zucker, and Donald Borchert (eds.), *Philosophy of Sex and Love*, 3rd ed. (Upper Saddle River, N.J.: Prentice Hall, 1997). A wide-ranging collection of essays covering historical, religious, and philosophical perspectives on sex, love, and their relationship. Marriage, adultery, prostitution, pornography, homosexuality, sexual harassment, and perversion are among the topics of contemporary interest that are discussed.

Wardle, Lynn D., Mark Strasser, William C. Duncan, and David Orgon Coolidge (eds.), *Marriage and Same-Sex Unions* (Westport, CT: Preager, 2003). An extensive anthology that addresses both moral and legal perspectives on same sex marriage. It includes the selections by Gallagher and Wolfson reprinted in this chapter.

4 }Pornography, Hate Speech, and Censorship

The Internet and the cable and satellite industries have brought growing concern about the seeming pervasiveness of language and images that many consider to be indecent, obscene, or pornographic. Censoring such language and images is one way that governments have attempted to control various forms of media and communication. For instance, in 2005 the Federal Communications Commission (FCC), an independent U.S. government agency, fined Clear Channel $495,000 for "indecent" comments made by Howard Stern on his radio show. In 2005, Stern announced that he would move his show from Clear Channel to satellite radio to avoid the indecency regulations of the FCC, whose rules do not currently apply to satellite and cable broadcasts. Should Congress extend the FCC rules to include such broadcasts? Critics worry that extending government regulation in this way will probably mean much stronger regulation affecting not only sexually oriented channels like Playboy Television but also many popular but controversial shows such as *The Sopranos.*

In recent years concern has also been growing over hate speech, especially racially motivated hate speech and related forms of harassment. For instance, in 1990 Stanford University enacted a harassment code (for those attending or employed by the university) that prohibits hate speech. Other universities have adopted similar policies. Critics argue that such censorship violates the right to free speech of U.S. citizens as guaranteed by the First Amendment to the Constitution.

The examples just mentioned all concern the issue of censorship. But in addition to whether pornography or hate speech is a proper target of censorship, one can raise questions about the morality of producing and consuming pornographic materials and about the morality of lewd, obscene, or hateful manners of speech. Concerning pornography and censorship, here are the basic questions to be raised:

- Is either the production or consumption of pornography morally wrong?
- For any such activities that are wrong, what explains why they are wrong?
- Would it be morally acceptable for a government to pass laws that make the production and consumption of pornography illegal?

Similar questions can be asked about hate speech, but let us first consider disputes concerning pornography and then turn to disputes about hate speech.

1. WHAT IS PORNOGRAPHY?

According to most dictionary definitions, **pornography** is "the depiction of erotic behavior (as in pictures or writing) intended to cause sexual excitement."[1] But for purposes of moral and legal discussion, it is important to notice that within the category of pornography, there are importantly different species. The 1986 Attorney General's Commission on Pornography (included as one of our readings) distinguishes four categories of pornography: (1) violent pornography, (2) nonviolent but degrading pornography, (3) nonviolent, nondegrading pornography, and (4) the special category of child pornography. In discussing the issue of pornography, then, it is important to be clear about which species of pornography is in question. If I announce that pornography ought not to be censored and you respond by saying that it ought to be censored, then we will be talking past one another if I am thinking exclusively about nonviolent, nondegrading pornography and you are thinking exclusively about pornography that is either violent or degrading.

Here is a related point. When one looks to recent literature on pornography, one often finds the term "pornography" being used for a certain restrictive class of sexually explicit material. For instance, Helen E. Longino distinguishes pornography from what she calls **erotica.** She defines pornography as "verbal or pictorial material which represents or describes sexual behavior that is degrading or abusive to one or more of the participants in such a way as to endorse the degradation."[2] On this definition, what makes something pornography is not just its sexual content or the fact that it is intended to cause sexual excitement, but (in addition) its degradation of one or more of those being depicted *and* its endorsement of that degradation. Erotica is then characterized as including sexually explicit material that either is not degrading to one or more of the participants or does not endorse such degradation. Notice that the class of items picked out by Longino's definition of "pornography" coincides with the Attorney General's Commission's first two categories—violent and nonviolent but degrading pornography—whereas "erotica" coincides with the commission's category of nonviolent, nondegrading pornography. So, again, in thinking about the morality and legality of pornography, it is important to be clear about what is being referred to by the term.[3]

2. LIBERTY-LIMITING PRINCIPLES

In order to provide a framework for thinking about censorship, it will help to introduce various principles—**liberty-limiting principles**—that figure prominently in debates over censorship. A "liberty-limiting" principle *purports* to specify considerations that may morally justify a government in passing laws that would interfere with the liberty of mentally competent adults (henceforth, "individuals"). Traditionally, the following four such principles have played an important role in moral and political philosophy.

The Harm Principle

According to the **harm principle**, a government may justifiably pass laws that interfere with the liberty of individuals in order to *prohibit individuals from causing harm to other individuals or to society.* To clarify this principle, we need to address the following three issues.

First, and mostly obviously, in applying the harm principle, we must determine what is going to count as harm (at least for purposes of justifying government interference). Certainly, physical harms such as killing, maiming, or inflicting physical pain on someone are to count, and we should also include psychological harms to one's mental health. Other harms include economic harms as well as harms to one's career and reputation. So, in applying the harm principle, we need to keep in mind the range of harms that might result from some activity.

Second, harms can vary in their seriousness. So, in applying the harm principle, we must also consider how serious would be the harm caused by some activity. Arguably, in order for the harm principle to justify government-backed prohibition of some activity, it must be the case that very serious harms would result from allowing citizens to engage in that activity.

Third, the harm principle can be viewed as an essentially consequentialist moral principle,[4] and therefore in applying it we must balance the likely good effects of passing and enforcing a law that prohibits some harmful behavior with the likely negative effects of not doing so. If the negative social consequences of enforcing a law against some activity would produce a greater level of harm than is produced by allowing the activity, then the harm principle cannot justify government legislation prohibiting the activity. With these points in mind, it is clear that laws against murder, maiming, severe physical injury, and theft are justified by appeal to the harm principle. But as we shall see, there is a good deal of controversy over whether this principle can justify government censorship of pornography.

The Offense Principle

According to the **offense principle**, a government may justifiably pass laws that interfere with individual liberty in order to *prohibit individuals from offending others,* where offensive behavior includes causing others shame, embarrassment, or discomfort. To distinguish this principle from the harm principle, we must distinguish psychological harms—harms to one's mental health—from unpleasant psychological states that do not constitute harms. Consider an example. Laws prohibiting public nudity seem to receive justification from the offense principle. Someone who appears naked in full public view may cause onlookers uneasiness and embarrassment, but normally such negative feelings do not constitute *harm* to those who have them. Notice that this principle is not meant to cover cases in which someone's mere knowledge of the behavior of others is offensive to that person. Rather, the principle is meant to apply to cases in which (1) "normal" or "average" persons would find the behavior deeply offensive—the *standard of universality,* and (2) encountering the offensive behavior cannot be reasonably avoided—the *standard of reasonable avoidability.* Obscene remarks over a loudspeaker, walking nude through a downtown, billboards and signage with obscene sexually explicit content are all examples of cases that fail the standard of reasonable avoidability.[5]

The Principle of Legal Paternalism

According to the principle of **legal paternalism,** a government may justifiably pass laws in order to *protect individuals from harming themselves.* Thus, for example, seat belt laws and motorcycle helmet laws might be defended on the basis of the principle of paternalism, as well as laws that prohibit the use of certain drugs—a subject of the next chapter.

Principle of Legal Moralism

The principle of **legal moralism** states that a government may justifiably pass laws that interfere with individual liberty in order to *protect common moral standards, independently of whether the activities in question are harmful to others or to oneself.* Of course, murder, rape, and theft are immoral, but because they are also harmful, laws against such actions can be sufficiently justified by the harm principle. Appeals to the principle of legal moralism typically arise in attempts to justify laws against certain so-called victimless violations of common morality. Sodomy laws are perhaps an example.

There are four points about these liberty-limiting principles that should be kept in mind. First, it is here assumed that an individual's liberty (freedom of choice and action) is of great value, and thus interference with one's liberty requires some *moral* justification.[6] These principles, then, are intended to state conditions under which a government may be *morally* justified in restricting individual liberty through law. Second, each of these principles states considerations (harm to others, offense to others, harm to oneself, and immoral behavior) that *may* justify a government in passing laws against some activity. The emphasis on "may" was implicit in our discussion of the harm principle. Whether a government *is* justified in passing laws against some form of behavior based on the harm principle requires not only that the behavior really is harmful, but also that the harms are serious and that the enforcement of laws against the behavior in question would not result in even greater harm than does the behavior itself.

Third, these principles are not mutually exclusive; one might accept more than one of them. Indeed, one might accept all four. Fourth, and finally, in claiming that these principles *purport* to specify considerations that may justify government interference with individual liberty, we leave open the question about which of them *ought* to serve as principles that morally justify such interference. Debate over the justification of these principles is a subject for social and political philosophy and hence beyond the scope of our present concerns. But a few brief remarks are in order here.

The most uncontroversial of the principles is the harm principle—certainly if a government is ever morally justified in using its coercive power to interfere with individual liberty, it is to protect individuals and society generally from being harmed by others. John Stuart Mill, in his influential classic *On Liberty* (1859), ardently defends the idea that the harm principle is the *only* legitimate liberty-limiting principle:

> [T]he only purpose for which power can be rightfully exercised over any member of a civilized community, against his will, is to prevent harm to others. His own good, either physical or moral, is not a sufficient warrant. He cannot rightfully be compelled to do or forbear because it will be better for him to do so, because it will make him happier, because, in the opinion of others, to do so would be wise or even right. These are good reasons for remonstrating with him, or reasoning with him, or persuading him, or entreating him, but not for compelling him or visiting him with any evil in case he do otherwise. To justify that, the conduct from which it is desired to deter him, must be

calculated to produce evil to someone else. The only part of the conduct of any one for which he is amenable to society, is that which concerns others. In the part which merely concerns himself, his independence is, of right, absolute.[7]

In this passage, Mill is clearly rejecting the principle of paternalism. Moreover, his remark about being compelled to forbear from some action because "in the opinion of others, to do so would be wise or even right," indicates his rejection of the principle of legal moralism.

Mill's position is representative of Liberalism. **Liberalism,** understood as a political ideology,[8] is associated with the idea of safeguarding individual liberties against government interference through a structure of equal rights. Of course, saying this does not distinguish Liberalism from all competing nonliberal ideologies. Ronald Dworkin has argued that the distinguishing idea of Liberalism is a certain conception of the equal treatment of citizens by a government as a fundamental moral ideal—a conception requiring that in order for a government to treat its citizens as equals, it must remain as neutral as possible on the question of the good life for human beings.[9] By contrast, nonliberal views, including versions of **Conservatism,** reject this particular conception of equal treatment, insisting that in treating their citizens equally, governments may (and perhaps must) make decisions based partly on some particular conception of what a truly good life for human beings requires.[10] On the basis of their conception of equality (as requiring government neutrality over the good life), liberals tend to be staunch defenders of a certain array of basic liberties, including those providing strong protection of speech, and a sphere of privacy to lead one's own life as one sees fit. Thus, liberal thinkers following in the tradition of Mill defend the harm principle (as well as the offense principle)[11] but tend to reject the principles of paternalism and legal moralism, since these principles (arguably) involve government interference based on a particular conception of the good life for human beings. Conservatives, by contrast, tend to accept the principles of paternalism and legal moralism, and so, for example, are not opposed to government interference on behalf of upholding standards of moral decency.

3. PORNOGRAPHY AND CENSORSHIP

Now that we have a rudimentary understanding of the various liberty-limiting principles, how might any of them serve as a basis for justifiably censoring at least some forms of pornography? In order for any of these principles to provide a good moral justification for censorship, two conditions must be met. First, the principle in question must be a *defensible* liberty-limiting principle. Second, it would have to be shown that pornography (its production or its consumption) has the characteristic mentioned in the principle. For example, to apply the harm principle, it would have to be shown that pornography causes serious harm to society. So let us briefly return to the liberty-limiting principles with these two questions in mind, taking each principle in turn.

Most disputes over pornography and censorship take place against the background of the right to freedom of speech. For example, according to First Amendment of the U.S. Constitution:

Congress shall pass no law respecting an establishment of religion, or prohibiting the free exercise thereof; or abridging the freedom of speech, or of the press; or the right of people to peaceably assemble, and to petition the Government for a redress of its grievances.

The first point to note about the First Amendment is that although it has sometimes been interpreted as placing an *absolute prohibition* on laws restricting free speech, more often it has been interpreted as placing a *very strong presumption* against laws that would restrict free speech. This is where the harm principle comes into play. The classic example here is yelling "Fire!" in a crowded theater. Since such speech puts others at immediate risk of serious harm, and since the harm principle is widely recognized as a defensible liberty-limiting principle (by Liberals and nonliberals alike), this kind of speech is legitimately prohibited by law.

With respect to disputes about pornography and censorship in relation to the U.S. Constitution, the main things to keep in mind are these. First, because the harm principle is relatively uncontroversial as a liberty-limiting principle, much of the debate over pornography in the past thirty years has focused on the question of its harmful effects on society. Second, since there is a strong presumption in favor of freedom of speech and expression, there is a strong burden of proof on those who are pro-censorship to show that pornography (at least certain forms of it) causes serious harm to society—serious enough to justify passing laws against its production and consumption.

The offense principle is perhaps more controversial than the harm principle (although it is widely accepted), and its role in pro-censorship arguments is primarily relevant in connection with, for example, public displays that are found offensive by nonconsenting individuals. Were a pornographic film to be shown outdoors at a public place where passersby might unavoidably see it, then the offense principle (assuming it is acceptable) might justify laws against such showings. Disputes over pornography have mainly to do with its production and use by *consenting* individuals, rather than cases in which nonconsenting individuals are subjected to it, and so the offense principle has not played as large a role in such disputes as has the harm principle.

As noted earlier, the principle of paternalism is controversial, and so appealing to it to justify antipornography laws is problematic; many people do not think the government ought to interfere in the liberty of its citizens for their own good. However, ignoring questions about its justification, if one were to use this principle in connection with censorship, one would have to show that producing or consuming pornography tends to seriously harm those who produce it, or those who participate in it, or those who consume it. One might claim that these individuals harm their own character by producing, participating in, or consuming pornography. But again, this claim would need to be shown, and even if it could be shown, one would also have to show that the principle of paternalism is an acceptable liberty-limiting principle.

Finally, the principle of legal moralism has played an important role in Conservative pro-censorship arguments. For example, some claim that pornographic magazines and films involve images and depictions of morally disgusting and "dirty" sexual activities and that to consume such images and depictions for purposes of sexual stimulation is immoral. One problem with this kind of argument is that there are questions about which moral standards should be imposed in applying the principle of legal moralism. But more importantly, the principle itself is highly disputed. As we saw earlier, many, following Mill, argue against it by claiming that it is not the proper role of government to get involved in the nonharmful personal lives of individuals.

These remarks help explain why, at least in debates having to do with U.S. First Amendment rights, claims about the harmfulness of pornography have been at the center of controversy over its censorship: the harm principle is uncontroversial, whereas the other principles are either not as relevant to the debate (offense) or are questionable (paternalism and legal moralism).

4. HATE SPEECH

In 1990, Robert A. Viktora was convicted under the St. Paul, Minnesota, city ordinance that prohibited forms of speech or expression that were likely to provoke "anger, alarm, or resentment in others on the basis of race, color, creed, religion, or gender." Viktora, together with several white teenagers, burned a cross on the lawn of a black family that had recently moved into a predominantly white neighborhood in St. Paul. Viktora challenged the conviction, arguing that it violated his freedom of speech. In the 1992 *R.A.V. v. St. Paul* decision, the U.S. Supreme Court struck down the St. Paul ordinance, arguing that while fighting words were not protected by the First Amendment, the sort of hateful expression engaged in by Viktora is protected, and that to outlaw such expression would amount to discrimination against speech on the basis of its content. The Court's ruling raises a battery of moral and legal issues that parallel the ones raised in connection with pornography.

Let us define **hate speech** as *language (oral or written) that expresses strong hatred, contempt, or intolerance for some social group, particularly social groups classified according to race, ethnicity, gender, sexual orientation, religion, disability, or nationality.*[12] Some characterizations also make explicit reference to the intentions of the speaker by adding that the aim of such speech is to degrade, dehumanize, intimidate, or incite violence against members of the group being targeted.

We can now raise a set of moral questions that parallel the ones raised earlier about pornography:

- Is hate speech morally wrong?
- If it is, what is the best explanation of why it is wrong?
- Furthermore, would it be morally permissible for a government to pass laws that would make hate speech illegal?

Now that we have some background for studying the topics of pornography, hate speech, and censorship, let us turn to the various moral arguments that we find represented in recent literature on these topics.

5. THEORY MEETS PRACTICE

Because much of the controversy over the censorship of pornography and hate speech focuses on the overall effects of such activities, let us begin with consequentialism.

Consequentialism

As we have seen, the claim that pornography causes substantial harm appeals to the alleged bad consequences of such expression as a basis for censorship. We may think of the harm principle as a specification of the general consequentialist theory of morality for use in connection with evaluating the morality of government interference with individual liberty.[13] And, as with all consequentialist approaches, it is important to consider the *overall* consequences of various alternative courses of action in determining which course is morally permissible. When it comes to the issue of censoring pornography, we have already noted the strong burden of proof on pro-censorship advocates to provide clear evidence of serious harm to society. Suppose that the evidence were very clear that pornography does cause substantial harm to society. This alone, however, would not be enough to justify censorship. We also noted that in applying the harm principle, one must consider the costs and benefits of passing and enforcing censorship laws against the costs and benefits of not doing so. Would passing and enforcing censorship laws have what is called a "chilling effect" on other forms of speech (e.g., political speech) that ought to be protected? That is, would passing laws against pornography make people more wary of other forms of unpopular speech and expression and discourage them from expressing themselves?[14] Another worry has to do with sliding down a slippery slope (a topic that is discussed more fully in the introduction to chapter 8). If we allow censorship of pornography, do we risk opening the door to the censorship of materials with sexual content that is merely unpopular or controversial from, say, certain religious perspectives? And if that happens, what about materials that are not sexual in content but unpopular?

The 1986 Meese Commission, whose report is included in our readings, cites what it takes to be evidence that certain forms of pornography cause harm, particularly to women. Moreover, some feminist writers have argued that pornography violates the basic civil rights of women, constituting harm to their interests, and is therefore subject to censorship.[15] However, Nadine Strossen, in a selection included in this chapter, attempts to rebut the Meese Commission's conclusions about pornography and harm, and she argues that censorship would likely result in more harm than good to women. Ronald Dworkin, in his essay included in this chapter, agrees with Strossen that a clear link between pornography (excluding, of course, child pornography) and harm remains controversial. He also argues at length that arguments focusing on the civil rights of women fail to justify censorship.

Turning briefly to hate speech, questions about its negative effects are central in the articles by Charles R. Lawrence III and John Arthur. Lawrence argues that hate speech (at least as it occurs in certain contexts) is equivalent to fighting words and thus is not protected by the First Amendment. Against Lawrence, Arthur argues that hate speech is protected and criticizes pro-censorship arguments based on the harm and offense principles.

Kantian Ethics

We do find Kantian, nonconsequentialist arguments for the claim that pornography is morally wrong. Judith M. Hill, in her article included in this chapter, argues that (most) pornography portrays women as mere means and thus as deserving less respect than what is owed to men. Given the Kantian principle that we ought never to treat persons as mere means and always as ends in themselves, it follows from Hill's analysis that pornography (its production and consumption) is morally wrong. Since hate speech expresses disrespect for members of some group, it seems to follow from Hill's interpretation of Kant's principle that such speech is morally wrong, although her article does not discuss this issue. Notice that these Kantian arguments concern only the morality of the practices in question and don't *directly* have implications for questions about censorship (unless one accepts the principle of legal moralism). Nevertheless, if as some feminists have argued, the production and consumption of pornography is degrading to women—portraying them as less worthy of respect than men—then because this representation of women is likely to have negative effects on how women are perceived and treated in society, Hill's observations are indeed important with respect to the debate over pornography and harm.

NOTES

1. From the *Merriam-Webster Online Dictionary.* Etymologically, the word *pornography* derives from the Greek word *pornographos,* which taken literally means "writing about the activities of prostitutes."

2. Helen E. Longino, "Pornography, Oppression, and Freedom: A Closer Look," in *Take Back the Night: Women on Pornography* (New York: Morrow, 1980).

3. The notion of obscenity is often used in characterizing pornography, but the ordinary concepts of the obscene and the pornographic are distinct. While pornography concerns forms of expression that have sexual content and are intended to arouse sexual excitement, obscenity (what is obscene) refers more generally to things that are morally repugnant. However, in U.S. law, the prevailing *legal* definition of "obscene" is to be found in *Miller v. California,* 413 U.S. 15, which involves a three-pronged test: material is obscene only if: "(a) the average person, applying contemporary community standards would find that the work, taken as a whole, appeals to the prurient interest, (b) . . . the work depicts or describes, in a patently offensive way, sexual conduct specifically defined by the applicable state law; and (c) . . . the work, taken as a whole, lacks serious literary, artistic, political, or scientific value" (25).

4. See chapter 1, section 2A, for a discussion of consequentialism.

5. These examples and general discussion of the offense principle are inspired by Joel Feinberg's discussion in his *Social Philosophy* (Englewood Cliffs, NJ: Prentice-Hall, 1973), 41–45.

6. This presumption of the value of liberty requires defense—a central topic in social and political philosophy.

7. J. S. Mill, *On Liberty* (1859), Elizabeth Rapaport (ed.), (Indianapolis, IN: Hackett Publishing Company, Inc., 1978), 9.

8. In the introduction to the previous chapter on sexual morality, I introduced the labels "conservative," "liberal," and "moderate" to classify general types of views one might take on some particular moral issue, where the difference between these views has to do with how restrictive they are about the morality of the issue in question. According to this usage, a conservative view is comparatively restrictive in what it considers to be morally permissible regarding the issue in question, a liberal view is comparatively unrestrictive, and a moderate view falls in between. But being a liberal or a conservative about some moral issue should not be confused with accepting the ideology of Liberalism or Conservatism, respectively. For instance, someone who holds a liberal view (small *l*) on some particular moral issue (abortion, for example) might be a political Conservative, maintaining that in general it is within the proper moral authority of a government to pass laws to protect morality. In addition to the essays by Ronald Dworkin cited in note 9, I recommend the essays "Liberalism" and "Conservatism" by Robert Eccleshall in his anthology *Political Ideologies: An Introduction,* 2nd ed. (London: Routledge, 1994), for a more thorough discussion of Liberalism and Conservatism.

9. See Ronald Dworkin's essays "Liberalism," "Why Liberals Should Care about Equality," and "What Justice Isn't," reprinted in his *A Matter of Principle* (Cambridge, MA: Harvard University Press, 1985).

10. Conservatism, as the label suggests, is often associated with preserving traditions (moral, religious, political) and being opposed to radical social change. Eccleshall, in his essay "Conservatism" (cited in note 8), argues that this conception is inaccurate. He claims that a "vindication of inequality" is the distinguishing feature of this ideology.

11. The offense principle is often recognized by liberals as a necessary supplement to the harm principle. On this point, see Feinberg, *Social Philosophy*, 41–45.

12. The term "hate speech" does not (yet) appear, for instance, in the *Merriam-Webster Online Dictionary*, but a Google search query for a definition turns up a number of sites that define the term in roughly the same way.

13. Strictly speaking, one need not embrace a consequentialist moral theory in order to accept the harm principle. For instance, one might hold that certain matters of personal morality are governed by such nonconsequentialist principles as Kant's Humanity version of the categorical imperative, while also claiming that matters of public policy ought to be decided on consequentialist grounds.

14. For a discussion of the chilling effect on speech brought about by recent actions of the FCC and U.S. Congress, see Katherine A. Fallow, "The Big Chill? Congress and the FCC Crack Down on Indecency," *Communications Lawyer* 22 (2004), 24–32.

15. See, for example, Catharine A. MacKinnon, "Francis Biddle's Sister Pornography, Civil Rights, and Speech," in Catharine A. MacKinnon, *Feminism Unmodified: Discourses on Lift and Law* (Cambridge, MA: Harvard University Press, 1987).

The Attorney General's Commission on Pornography

Pornography and Harm

In 1985, U.S. President Ronald Reagan appointed Attorney General Edwin Meese III to head an eleven-member commission whose purpose was to investigate the problem of pornography in the United States and, in particular, any role it might play in the production of harm. In 1986 the Meese Commission made its report in which it distinguishes four types of pornography: (1) violent, (2) nonviolent but degrading, (3) nonviolent and nondegrading, and (4) child pornography. After reviewing the available evidence about the causal effects of pornography, the commission concluded that there is sufficient evidence linking both violent and nonviolent but degrading pornography to violence against women. However,

Reprinted from *Final Report,* Washington, DC: United States Department of Justice, July 1986.

its members could not reach sufficient agreement about whether exposure to nonviolent and nondegrading pornography is linked to harm. Finally, the commission explains the "special horror" of child pornography, which by definition involves the sexual exploitation of children.

Recommended Reading: consequentialism, chap. 1, sec. 2A.

MATTERS OF METHOD

. . . The analysis of the hypothesis that pornography causes harm must start with the identification of hypothesized harms, proceed to the determination of whether those hypothesized harms are indeed harmful, and then conclude with the examination of whether a causal link exists between the material and the harm. When the consequences of exposure to sexually explicit material are not harmful, or when there is no causal relationship between exposure to sexually explicit material and some harmful consequence, then we cannot say that the sexually explicit material is harmful. But if sexually explicit material of some variety is causally related to, or increases the incidence of, some behavior that *is* harmful, then it is safe to conclude that the material is harmful. . . .

The Problem of Multiple Causation

The world is complex, and most consequences are "caused" by numerous factors. Are highway deaths caused by failure to wear seat belts, failure of the automobile companies to install airbags, failure of the government to require automobile companies to install airbags, alcohol, judicial leniency towards drunk drivers, speeding, and so on and on? Is heart disease caused by cigarette smoking, obesity, stress, or excess animal fat in our diets? As with most other questions of this type, the answers can only be "all of the above," and so too with the problem of pornography. We have concluded, for example, that some forms of sexually explicit material bear a causal relationship both to sexual violence and to sex discrimination, but we are hardly so naive as to suppose that were these forms of pornography to disappear the problems of sex discrimination and sexual violence would come to an end.

If this is so, then what does it mean to identify a causal relationship? It means that the evidence supports the conclusion that if there were none of the material being tested, then the incidence of the consequences would be less. We live in a world of multiple causation, and to identify a factor as a *cause* in such a world means only that if this factor were eliminated while everything else stayed the same then the problem would at least be lessened. In most cases it is impossible to say any more than this, although to say this is to say quite a great deal. But when we identify something as a cause, we do not deny that there are other causes, and we do not deny that some of these other causes might bear an even *greater* causal connection than does some form of pornography. That is, it may be, for example, and there is some evidence that points in this direction, that certain magazines focusing on guns, martial arts, and related topics bear a closer causal relationship to sexual violence than do some magazines that are, in a term we will explain shortly, "degrading." If this is true, then the amount of sexual violence would be reduced more by eliminating the weaponry magazines and keeping the degrading magazines than it would be reduced by eliminating the degrading magazines and keeping the weaponry magazines. . . .

OUR CONCLUSIONS ABOUT HARM

We present in the following sections our conclusions regarding the harms we have investigated with respect to the various subdividing categories we have found most useful. . . .

Sexually Violent Material

The category of material on which most of the evidence has focused is the category of material featuring actual or unmistakably simulated or unmistakably threatened violence presented in sexually explicit fashion with a predominant focus on the sexually explicit violence. Increasingly, the most prevalent forms of pornography, as well as an increasingly prevalent body of less sexually explicit material, fit this description. Some of this material involves sado-masochistic themes, with the standard accoutrements of the genre, including whips, chains, devices of torture, and so on. But another theme of some of this material is not sado-masochistic, but involves instead the recurrent theme of a man making some sort of sexual advance to a woman, being rebuffed, and then raping the woman or in some other way violently forcing himself on the woman. In almost all of this material, whether in magazine or motion picture form, the woman eventually becomes aroused and ecstatic about the initially forced sexual activity, and usually is portrayed as begging for more. There is also a large body of material, more "mainstream" in its availability, that portrays sexual activity or sexually suggestive nudity coupled with extreme violence, such as disfigurement or murder. The so-called "slasher" films fit this description, as does some material, both in films and in magazines, that is less or more sexually explicit than the proto-typical "slasher" film. . . .

When clinical and experimental research has focused particularly on sexually violent material, the conclusions have been virtually unanimous. In both clinical and experimental settings, exposure to sexually violent materials has indicated an increase in the likelihood of aggression. More specifically, the research, which is described in much detail later in this Report, shows a causal relationship between exposure to material of this type and aggressive behavior towards women.

Finding a link between aggressive behavior towards women and sexual violence, whether lawful or unlawful, requires assumptions not found exclusively in the experimental evidence. We see no reason, however, not to make these assumptions.

The assumption that increased aggressive behavior towards women is causally related, for an aggregate population, to increased sexual violence is significantly supported by the clinical evidence, as well as by much of the less scientific evidence. They are also to all of us assumptions that are plainly justified by our own common sense. This is not to say that all people with heightened levels of aggression will commit acts of sexual violence. But it is to say that over a sufficiently large number of cases we are confident in asserting that an increase in aggressive behavior directed at women will cause an increase in the level of sexual violence directed at women.

Thus we reach our conclusions by combining the results of the research with highly justifiable assumptions about the generalizability of more limited research results. Since the clinical and experimental evidence supports the conclusion that there is a causal relationship between exposure to sexually violent materials and an increase in aggressive behavior directed towards women, and since we believe that an increase in aggressive behavior towards women will in a population increase the incidence of sexual violence in that population, we have reached the conclusion, unanimously and confidently, that the available evidence strongly supports the hypothesis that substantial exposure to sexually violent materials as described here bears a causal relationship to antisocial acts of sexual violence and, for some subgroups, possibly to unlawful acts of sexual violence.

Although we rely for this conclusion on significant scientific empirical evidence, we feel it worthwhile to note the underlying logic of the conclusion. The evidence says simply that the images that people are exposed to bear a causal relationship to their behavior. This is hardly surprising. What would be surprising would be to find otherwise, and we have not so found. We have not, of course, found that the images people are exposed to are a greater cause of sexual violence than all or even many other possible causes the investigation of which has been beyond our mandate. Nevertheless, it would be strange indeed if graphic representations of a form of behavior, especially in a form that almost exclusively portrays such behavior as desirable, did not have at least some effect on patterns of behavior.

Sexual violence is not the only negative effect reported in the research to result from substantial exposure to sexually violent materials. The evidence is also strongly supportive of significant attitudinal changes on the part of those with substantial exposure to violent pornography. These attitudinal changes are numerous. Victims of rape and other forms of sexual violence are likely to be perceived by people so exposed as more responsible for the assault, as having suffered less injury, and as having been less degraded as a result of the experience. Similarly, people with a substantial exposure to violent pornography are likely to see the rapist or other sexual offender as less responsible for the act and as deserving of less stringent punishment.

These attitudinal changes have been shown experimentally to include a larger range of attitudes than those just discussed. The evidence also strongly supports the conclusion that substantial exposure to violent sexually explicit material leads to a greater acceptance of the "rape myth" in its broader sense—that women enjoy being coerced into sexual activity, that they enjoy being physically hurt in sexual context, and that as a result a man who forces himself on a woman sexually is in fact merely acceding to the "real" wishes of the woman, regardless of the extent to which she seems to be resisting. The myth is that a woman who says "no" really means "yes," and that men are justified in acting on the assumption that the "no" answer is indeed the "yes" answer. We have little trouble concluding that this attitude is both pervasive and profoundly harmful, and that any stimulus reinforcing or increasing the incidence of this attitude is for that reason alone properly designated as harmful.

. . . All of the harms discussed here, including acceptance of the legitimacy of sexual violence against women but not limited to it, are more pronounced when the sexually violent materials depict the woman as experiencing arousal, orgasm, or other form of enjoyment as the ultimate result of the sexual assault. This theme, unfortunately very common in the materials we have examined, is likely to be the major, albeit not the only, component of what it is in the materials in this category that causes the consequences that have been identified. . . .

Nonviolent Materials Depicting Degradation, Domination, Subordination, or Humiliation

. . . It appears that effects similar to, although not as extensive as that involved with violent material, can be identified with respect to . . . degrading material, but that these effects are likely absent when neither degradation nor violence is present.

An enormous amount of the most sexually explicit material available, as well as much of the material that is somewhat less sexually explicit, is material that we would characterize as "degrading," the term we use to encompass the undeniably linked characteristics of degradation, domination, subordination, and humiliation. The degradation we refer to is degradation of people, most often women, and here we are referring to material that, although not violent, depicts people, usually women, as existing solely for the sexual satisfaction of others, usually men, or that depicts people, usually women, in decidedly subordinate roles in their sexual relations with others, or that depicts people engaged in sexual practices that would to most people be considered humiliating. Indeed, forms of degradation represent the largely predominant proportion of commercially available pornography.

With respect to material of this variety, our conclusions are substantially similar to those with respect to violent material, although we make them with somewhat less assumption than was the case with respect to violent material. The evidence, scientific and otherwise, is more tentative, but supports the conclusion that the material we describe as degrading bears some causal relationship to the attitudinal changes we have previously identified. That is, substantial exposure to material of this variety is likely to increase the extent to which those exposed will view rape or other forms of sexual violence as less serious than they otherwise would have, will view the victims of rape and other forms of sexual violence as significantly more responsible, and will view the offenders as significantly less responsible. We also conclude that the evidence supports the conclusion that substantial exposure to material of this type will increase acceptance of the proposition that women like to be forced into sexual practices, and, once again, that the woman who says "no" really means "yes."

. . . We believe we are justified in drawing the following conclusions: Over a large enough sample of population that believes that many women like to be raped, that believes that sexual violence or sexual coercion is often desired or appropriate, and that believes that sex offenders are less responsible for their acts, [this population] will commit more acts of sexual violence or sexual coercion than would a population holding these beliefs to a lesser extent.

. . . Thus, we conclude that substantial exposure to materials of this type bears some causal relationship to the level of sexual violence, sexual coercion, or unwanted sexual aggression in the population so exposed.

We need mention as well that our focus on these more violent or more coercive forms of actual subordination of women should not diminish what we take to be a necessarily incorporated conclusion: Substantial exposure to materials of this type bears some causal relationship to the incidence of various nonviolent forms of discrimination against or subordination of women in our society. To the extent that these materials create or reinforce the view that women's function is disproportionately to satisfy the sexual needs of men, then the materials will have pervasive effects on the treatment of women in society far beyond the incidence of identifiable acts of rape or other sexual violence. . . .

Non-Violent and Non-Degrading Materials

Our most controversial category has been the category of sexually explicit materials that are not violent and are not degrading as we have used that term. They are materials in which the participants appear to be fully willing participants occupying substantially

equal roles in a setting devoid of actual or apparent violence or pain. This category is in fact quite small in terms of currently available materials. There is some, to be sure, and the amount may increase as the division between the degrading and the non-degrading becomes more accepted, but we are convinced that only a small amount of currently available highly sexually explicit material is neither violent nor degrading. We thus talk about a small category, but one that should not be ignored.

We have disagreed substantially about the effects of such materials, and that should come as no surprise. We are dealing in this category with "pure" sex, as to which there are widely divergent views in this society. That we have disagreed among ourselves does little more than reflect the extent to which we are representative of the population as a whole. In light of that disagreement, it is perhaps more appropriate to explain the various views rather than indicate a unanimity that does not exist, within this Commission or within society, or attempt the preposterous task of saying that some fundamental view about the role of sexuality and portrayals of sexuality was accepted or defeated by such-and-such vote. We do not wish to give easy answers to hard questions, and thus feel better with describing the diversity of opinion rather than suppressing part of it.

In examining the material in this category, we have not had the benefit of extensive evidence. Research has only recently begun to distinguish the non-violent but degrading from material that is neither violent nor degrading, and we have all relied on a combination of interpretation of existing studies that may not have drawn the same divisions, studies that did draw these distinctions, clinical evidence, interpretation of victim testimony, and our own perceptions of the effect of images on human behavior. Although the social science evidence is far from conclusive, we are, on the current state of the evidence, persuaded that material of this type does not bear a causal relationship to rape and other acts of sexual violence. . . .

That there does not appear from the social science evidence to be a causal link with sexual violence, however, does not answer the question of whether such materials might not themselves simply for some other reason constitute a harm in themselves, or bear a causal link to consequences other than sexual violence but still taken to be harmful. And it is here that we and society at large have the greatest differences in opinion.

One issue relates to materials that, although undoubtedly consensual and equal, depict sexual practices frequently condemned in this and other societies. In addition, level of societal condemnation varies for different activities; some activities are condemned by some people, but not by others. We have discovered that to some significant extent the assessment of the harmfulness of materials depicting such activities correlates directly with the assessment of the harmfulness of the activities themselves. Intuitively and not experimentally, we can hypothesize that materials portraying such an activity will either help to legitimize or will bear some causal relationship to that activity itself. With respect to these materials, therefore, it appears that a conclusion about the harmfulness of these materials turns on a conclusion about the harmfulness of the activity itself. As to this, we are unable to agree with respect to many of these activities. Our differences reflect differences now extant in society at large, and actively debated, and we can hardly resolve them here.

A larger issue is the very question of promiscuity. Even to the extent that the behavior depicted is not inherently condemned by some or any of us, the manner of presentation almost necessarily suggests that the activities are taking place outside of the context of marriage, love, commitment, or even affection. Again, it is far from implausible to hypothesize that materials depicting sexual activity without marriage, love, commitment, or affection bear some causal relationship to sexual activity without marriage, love, commitment, or affection. There are undoubtedly many causes for what used to be called the "sexual revolution," but it is absurd to suppose that depictions or descriptions of uncommitted sexuality were not among them. Thus, once again our disagreements reflect disagreements in society at large, although not to as great an extent. Although there are many members of this

society who can and have made affirmative cases for uncommitted sexuality, none of us believes it to be a good thing. A number of us, however, believe that the level of commitment in sexuality is a matter of choice among those who voluntarily engage in the activity. Others of us believe that uncommitted sexual activity is wrong for the individuals involved and harmful to society to the extent of its prevalence. Our view of the ultimate harmfulness of much of this material, therefore, is reflective of our individual views about the extent to whether sexual commitment is purely a matter of individual choice. . . .

THE SPECIAL HORROR OF CHILD PORNOGRAPHY

What is commonly referred to as "child pornography" is not so much a form of pornography as it is a form of sexual exploitation of children. The distinguishing characteristic of child pornography, as generally understood, is that actual children are photographed while engaged in some form of sexual activity, either with adults or with other children. To understand the very idea of child pornography requires understanding the way in which real children, whether actually identified or not, are photographed, and understanding the way in which the use of real children in photographs creates a special harm largely independent of the kinds of concerns often expressed with respect to sexually explicit materials involving only adults.

Thus, the necessary focus of an inquiry into child pornography must be on the process by which children, from as young as one week up to the age of majority, are induced to engage in sexual activity of one sort or another, and the process by which children are photographed while engaging in that activity. The inevitably permanent record of that sexual activity created by a photograph is rather plainly a harm to the children photographed. But even if the photograph were never again seen, the very activity involved in creating the photograph is itself an act of sexual exploitation of children, and thus the issues related to the sexual abuse of children and those related to child pornography are inextricably linked. Child pornography necessarily includes the sexual abuse of a real child, and there can be no understanding of the special problem of child pornography until there is understanding of the special way in which child pornography *is* child abuse. . . .

READING QUESTIONS

1. Explain the problem of multiple causation when it comes to identifying harms.
2. What are the four types of pornography that the commission describes in its report? What conclusion do they reach regarding the harm caused by each of these types?
3. Why is child pornography considered a "special horror" by the commission? In what ways does it differ from the other types of pornography they investigate?

DISCUSSION QUESTIONS

1. How useful is it to differentiate between various types of pornography in the way the commission does? Discuss whether there is any overlap between the various types.
2. Is the Attorney General right to suggest that child pornography is a particularly horrible instance of pornography? Why or why not? Consider whether there are instances of adult pornography that are worse than child pornography.

NADINE STROSSEN

Why Censoring Pornography Would Not Reduce Discrimination or Violence against Women

Strossen is critical of the 1986 Meese Commission's report about the alleged negative effects of pornography on the interests of women. In rebutting the claims of the commission, she considers four types of evidence alleging a causal link: (1) laboratory research,

From Nadine Strossen, *Defending Pornography. Free Speech, Sex, and the Fight for Women's Rights* (New York: Anchor Books, 1995).

(2) correlational data, (3) anecdotal data, and (4) studies of sex offenders, arguing that none of this work shows clearly that pornography is a cause of harm to women. She concludes that even if there were a causal link between pornography and harm to women, the negative effects of censorship would outweigh whatever positive benefits censorship would produce. In her view, "censoring pornography would do women more harm than good."

Recommended Reading: consequentialism, chap. 1, sec. 2A.

The only thing pornography is known to cause directly is the solitary act of masturbation. As for corruption, the only immediate victim is English prose.

—*Gore Vidal, writer*[1]

Even . . . [if] we could neutralize its negative side effects, would censorship "cure"—or at least reduce—the discrimination and violence against women allegedly caused by pornography? That is the assumption that underlies the feminist procensorship position, fueling the argument that we should trade in our free speech rights to promote women's safety and equality rights. In fact, though, the hoped-for benefits of censorship are as hypothetical as our exercise in wishing away the evils of censorship. I will show this by examining the largely unexamined assumption that censorship would reduce sexism and violence against women. This assumption rests, in turn, on three others:

- that exposure to sexist, violent imagery leads to sexist, violent behavior;
- that the effective suppression of pornography would significantly reduce exposure to sexist, violent imagery; and
- that censorship would effectively suppress pornography.

To justify censoring pornography on the rationale that it would reduce violence or discrimination against women, one would have to provide actual support for all three of these assumptions. Each presupposes the others. Yet the only one of them that has received substantial attention is the first—that exposure to sexist, violent imagery leads to sexist, violent behavior—and, as I show later in this chapter, there is no credible evidence to bear it out. Even feminist advocates of censoring pornography have

acknowledged that this asserted causal connection cannot be proven, and therefore fall back on the argument that it should be accepted "on faith." Catharine MacKinnon has well captured this fallback position through her defensive double negative: "There is no evidence that pornography does no harm."

Of course, given the impossibility of proving that there is *no* evidence of *no* harm, we would have no free speech, and indeed no freedom of any kind, were such a burden of proof actually to be imposed on those seeking to enjoy their liberties. To appreciate this, just substitute for the word "pornography" in MacKinnon's pronouncement any other type of expression or any other human right. We would have to acknowledge that "there is no evidence" that television does no harm, or that editorials criticizing government officials do no harm, or that religious sermons do no harm, and so forth. There certainly is no evidence that feminist writing in general, or MacKinnon's in particular, does no harm.

In its 1992 *Butler* decision, accepting the antipornography feminist position, the Canadian Supreme Court also accepted this dangerous intuitive approach to limiting sexual expression, stating:

> It might be suggested that proof of actual harm should be required . . . [I]t is sufficient . . . for Parliament to have a reasonable basis for concluding that harm will result and this requirement does not demand actual proof of harm.[2]

Even if we were willing to follow the Canadian Supreme Court and procensorship feminists in believing, without evidence, that exposure to sexist, violent imagery does lead to sexist, violent behavior, we still should not accept their calls for censorship. Even if we assumed that *seeing* pornography leads to committing sexist and violent actions, it still would not follow that *censoring* pornography would reduce sexism or violence, due to flaws in the remaining two assumptions: we still would have to prove that pornography has a corner on the sexism and violence market, and that pornography is in fact entirely suppressible.

Even if pornography could be completely suppressed, the sexist, violent imagery that pervades the mainstream media would remain untouched. Therefore, if exposure to such materials caused violence and sexism, these problems would still remain with us. But no censorship regime could completely suppress pornography. It would continue to exist underground. . . .

Let's now examine in more detail the fallacies in each of the three assumptions underlying the feminist procensorship stance. And let's start with the single assumption that has been the focus of discussion—the alleged causal relationship between exposure to sexist, violent imagery and sexist, violent behavior.

MONKEY SEE, MONKEY DO?

Aside from the mere fear that sexual expression might cause discrimination or violence against women, advocates of censorship attempt to rely on four types of evidence concerning this alleged causal link: laboratory research data concerning the attitudinal effects of showing various types of sexually explicit materials to volunteer subjects, who are usually male college students; correlational data concerning availability of sexually oriented materials and anti-female discrimination or violence; anecdotal data consisting of accounts by sex offenders and their victims concerning any role that pornography may have played in the offenses; and studies of sex offenders, assessing factors that may have led to their crimes.

As even some leading procensorship feminists have acknowledged, along with the Canadian Supreme Court in *Butler,* none of these types of "evidence" prove that pornography harms women. Rather than retracing the previous works that have reviewed this evidence and reaffirmed its failure to substantiate the

alleged causal connection, I will simply summarize their conclusions.

Laboratory Experiments

The most comprehensive recent review of the social science data is contained in Marcia Pally's 1994 book *Sex and Sensibility: Reflections on Forbidden Mirrors and the Will to Censor.*[3] It exhaustively canvasses laboratory studies that have evaluated the impact of exposing experimental subjects to sexually explicit expression of many varieties, and concludes that no credible evidence substantiates a clear causal connection between any type of sexually explicit material and any sexist or violent behavior. The book also draws the same conclusion from its thorough review of field and correlational studies, as well as sociological surveys, in the U.S., Canada, Europe, and Asia.

Numerous academic and governmental surveys of the social science studies have similarly rejected the purported link between sexual expression and aggression. The National Research Council's Panel on Understanding and Preventing Violence concluded, in 1993: "Demonstrated empirical links between pornography and sex crimes in general are weak or absent."[4]

Given the overwhelming consensus that laboratory studies do not demonstrate a causal tie between exposure to sexually explicit imagery and violent behavior, the Meese Pornography Commission Report's contrary conclusion, not surprisingly, has been the subject of heated criticism, including criticism by dissenting commissioners and by the very social scientists on whose research the report purportedly relied.

The many grounds on which the Commission's report was widely repudiated include that: six of the Commission's eleven members already were committed antipornography crusaders when they were appointed to it; the Commission was poorly funded and undertook no research; its hearings were slanted toward preconceived antipornography conclusions in terms of the witnesses invited to testify and the questions they were asked; and, in assessing the alleged harmful effects of pornography, the Commission's report relied essentially upon morality, expressly noting at several points that its conclusions were based on "common sense," "personal insight," and "intuition."

Two of the Meese Commission's harshest critics were, interestingly, two female members of that very Commission, Judith Becker and Ellen Levine. Becker is a psychiatrist and psychologist whose entire extensive career has been devoted to studying sexual violence and abuse, from both research and clinical perspectives. Levine is a journalist who has focused on women's issues, and who edits a popular women's magazine. In their formal dissent from the Commission's report, they concluded:

> [T]he social science research has not been designed to evaluate the relationship between exposure to pornography and the commission of sexual crimes; therefore efforts to tease the current data into proof of a casual [sic] link between these acts simply cannot be accepted.[5]

Three of the foremost researchers concerned with the alleged causal relationship between sexually explicit materials and sexual violence, Edward Donnerstein, Daniel Linz, and Steven Penrod, also have sharply disputed the Meese Commission's findings about a purported causal relationship.[6]

Since the feminist censorship proposals aim at sexually explicit material that allegedly is "degrading" to women, it is especially noteworthy that research data show no link between exposure to "degrading" sexually explicit material and sexual aggression.

Even two research literature surveys that were conducted for the Meese Commission, one by University of Calgary professor Edna Einseidel and the other by then–Surgeon General C. Everett Koop, also failed to find any link between "degrading" pornography and sex crimes or aggression. Surgeon General Koop's survey concluded that only two reliable generalizations could be made about the impact of exposure to "degrading" sexual material on its viewers: it caused them to think that a variety of sexual practices were more common than they had previously believed, and it caused them to more accurately estimate the prevalence of varied sexual practices.[7]

Experiments also fail to establish any link between women's exposure to such materials and their development of negative self-images. Carol Krafka found that, in comparison with other women, women who were exposed to sexually "degrading" materials did not engage in more sex-role stereotyping; nor did they experience lower self-esteem, have less satisfaction with their body image, accept more anti-woman myths about rape, or show greater acceptance of violence against women.[8] Similar conclusions have been reached by Donnerstein, Linz, and Penrod.[9]

Correlational Data

Both the Meese Commission and procensorship feminists have attempted to rely on studies that allegedly show a correlation between the availability of sexually explicit materials and sexual offense rates. Of course, though, a positive correlation between two phenomena does not prove that one causes the other. Accordingly, even if the studies did consistently show a positive correlation between the prevalence of sexual materials and sexual offenses—which they do not—they still would not establish that exposure to the materials *caused* the rise in offenses. The same correlation could also reflect the opposite causal chain—if, for example, rapists relived their violent acts by purchasing sexually violent magazines or videotapes.

Any correlation between the availability of sexual materials and the rate of sex offenses could also reflect an independent factor that causes increases in both. Cynthia Gentry's correlational studies have identified just such an independent variable in geographical areas that have high rates of both the circulation of sexually explicit magazines and sexual violence: namely, a high population of men between the ages of eighteen and thirty-four.[10] Similarly, Larry Baron and Murray Straus have noted that areas where both sexual materials and sexual aggression are prevalent are characterized by a "hypermasculated or macho culture pattern," which may well be the underlying causal agent.[11] Accordingly, Joseph Scott and Loretta Schwalm found that communities with higher rape rates experienced stronger sales not only of porn magazines, but also of *all* male-oriented magazines, including *Field and Stream*.[12]

Even more damning to the attempt to rest the "porn-causes-rape-or-discrimination" theory on alleged correlations is that there simply are no consistent correlations. While the asserted correlation would not be *sufficient* to prove the claimed causal connection, it is *necessary* to prove that connection. Therefore, the existence of the alleged causal relationship is conclusively refuted by the fact that levels of violence and discrimination against women are often *inversely* related to the availability of sexually explicit materials, including violent sexually explicit materials. This inverse relationship appears in various kinds of comparisons: between different states within the United States; between different countries; and between different periods within the same country.

Within the United States, the Baron and Straus research has shown no consistent pattern between the availability of sexual materials and the number of rapes from state to state. Utah is the lowest-ranking state in the availability of sexual materials but twenty-fifth in the number of rapes, whereas New Hampshire ranks ninth highest in the availability of sexual materials but only forty-fourth in the number of rapes.

The lack of a consistent correlation between pornography consumption and violence against women is underscored by one claim of the procensorship feminists themselves: they maintain that the availability and consumption of pornography, including violent pornography, have been increasing throughout the United States. At the same time, though, the rates of sex crimes have been decreasing or remaining steady. The Bureau of Justice Statistics reports that between 1973 and 1987, the national rape rate remained steady and the attempted rape rate decreased. Since these data were gathered from household surveys rather than from police records, they are considered to be the most accurate measures of the incidence of crimes. These data also cover the period during which feminists helped to create a social, political, and legal climate that should have encouraged higher percentages of rape victims to report their assaults. Thus, the fact that rapes reported to the Bureau of Justice Statistics have not increased provokes serious questions about the

procensorship feminists' theories of pornography-induced harm.[13] Similar questions are raised by data showing a decrease in wife battery between 1975 and 1985, again despite changes that should have encouraged the increased reporting of this chronically underreported crime.[14]

Noting that "[t]he mass-market pornography . . . industr[y] took off after World War II," Marcia Pally has commented:

> In the decades since the 1950s, with the marketing of sexual material . . . , the country has seen the greatest advances in sensitivity to violence against women and children. Before the . . . mass publication of sexual images, no rape or incest hot lines and battered women's shelters existed; date and marital rape were not yet phrases in the language. Should one conclude that the presence of pornography . . . has inspired public outrage at sexual crimes?[15]

Pally's rhetorical question underscores the illogicality of presuming that just because two phenomena happen to coexist, they therefore are causally linked. I have already shown that any correlation that might exist between the increased availability of pornography and *increased* misogynistic discrimination or violence could well be explained by other factors. The same is true for any correlation that might exist between the increased availability of pornography and *decreased* misogynistic discrimination or violence.

In a comparative state-by-state analysis, Larry Baron and Murray Straus have found a positive correlation between the circulation of pornographic magazines and the state's "index of gender equality," a composite of twenty-four indicators of economic, political, and legal equality.[16] As the researchers have observed, these findings may suggest that both sexually explicit material and gender equality flourish in tolerant climates with fewer restrictions on speech.

The absence of any consistent correlation between the availability of sexual materials and sexual violence is also clear in international comparisons. On the one hand, violence and discrimination against women are common in countries where sexually oriented material is almost completely unavailable, including Saudi Arabia, Iran, and China (where the sale and distribution of erotica is now a capital offense). On the other hand, violence against women is uncommon in countries where such material is readily available, including Denmark, Germany, and Japan.

Furthermore, patterns in other countries over time show no correlation between the increased availability of sexually explicit materials and increased violence against women. The 1991 analysis by University of Copenhagen professor Berl Kutchinsky revealed that, while nonsexual violent crime had increased up to 300 percent in Denmark, Sweden, and West Germany from 1964 to 1984, all three countries' rape rates either declined or remained constant during this same period, despite their lifting of restrictions on sexual materials. Kutchinsky's studies further show that sex crimes against girls dropped from 30 per 100,000 to 5 per 100,000 between 1965, when Denmark liberalized its obscenity laws, and 1982.

In the decade 1964–1974, there was a much greater increase in rape rates in Singapore, which tightly restricts sexually oriented expression, than in Sweden, which had liberalized its obscenity laws during that period. In Japan, where sexually explicit materials are easily accessible and stress themes of bondage, rape, and violence, rape rates decreased 45 percent during the same decade. Moreover, Japan reports a rape rate of 2.4 per 100,000 people, compared with 34.5 in the United States, although violent erotica is more prevalent in Japan.[17]

Anecdotes and Suspicions

As Seventh Circuit Court of Appeals Judge Richard Posner observed about MacKinnon's book *Only Words:*

> MacKinnon's treatment of the central issue of pornography as she herself poses it—the harm that pornography does to women—is shockingly casual. Much of her evidence is anecdotal, and in a nation of 260 million people, anecdotes are a weak form of evidence.[18]

Many procensorship advocates attempt to rest their case on self-serving "porn-made-me-do-it" claims by sexual offenders, as well as on statements by victims or police officers that sexual offenders had sexually

explicit materials in their possession at the time they committed their crimes.

The logical fallacy of relying on anecdotes to establish a general causal connection between exposure to sexual materials and violence against women was aptly noted by journalist Ellen Willis: "Anti-porn activists cite cases of sexual killers who were also users of pornography, but this is no more logical than arguing that marriage causes rape because some rapists are married."[19]

Even assuming that sexual materials really were the triggering factors behind some specific crimes, that could not justify restrictions on such materials. As former Supreme Court justice William O. Douglas wrote: "The First Amendment demands more than a horrible example or two of the perpetrator of a crime of sexual violence, in whose pocket is found a pornographic book, before it allows the Nation to be saddled with a regime of censorship."[20] If we attempted to ban all words or images that had ever been blamed for inspiring or instigating particular crimes by some aberrant or antisocial individual, we would end up with little left to read or view. Throughout history and around the world, criminals have regularly blamed their conduct on a sweeping array of words and images in books, movies, and television.

As noted by the 1979 report of the British Committee on Obscenity and Film Censorship, "For those who are susceptible to them, the stimuli to aggressive behavior are all around us."[21] To illustrate the innumerable crimes that have been incited by words or images, the Committee cited a young man who attempted to kill his parents with a meat cleaver after watching a dramatized version of Dostoyevsky's *The Brothers Karamazov,* and a Jamaican man of African descent in London who raped a white woman, saying that the televised showing of Alex Haley's *Roots* had "inspired" him to treat her as white men had treated black women. Additional examples cited by Ohio State University law professor Earl Finbar Murphy underscore that word blaming and image blaming extend to many religious works, too:

> Heinrich Pommerenke, who was a rapist, abuser, and mass slayer of women in Germany, was prompted to

his series of ghastly deeds by Cecil B. DeMille's *The Ten Commandments.* During the scene of the Jewish women dancing about the Golden Calf, all the doubts of his life became clear: Women were the source of the world's troubles and it was his mission to both punish them for this and to execute them. Leaving the theater, he slew the first victim in a park nearby. John George Haigh, the British vampire who sucked his victims' blood through soda straws and dissolved their drained bodies in acid baths, first had his murder-inciting dreams and vampire longings from watching the "voluptuous" procedure of—an Anglican High Church Service.[22]

Were we to ban words or images on the grounds that they had incited some susceptible individuals to commit crimes, the Bible would be in great jeopardy. No other work has more often been blamed for more heinous crimes by the perpetrators of such crimes. The Bible has been named as the instigating or justifying factor for many individual and mass crimes, ranging from the religious wars, inquisitions, witch burnings, and pogroms of earlier eras to systematic child abuse and ritual murders today.

Marcia Pally's *Sex and Sensibility* contains a lengthy litany of some of the multitudinous, horrific bad acts that have been blamed on the "Good Book." She also cites some of the many passages depicting the "graphic, sexually explicit subordination of women" that would allow the entire Bible to be banned under the procensorship feminists' antipornography law. Pally writes:

> [T]he Bible has unbeatable worldwide sales and includes detailed justification of child abuse, wife battery, rape, and the daily humiliation of women. Short stories running through the text serve as models for sexual assault and the mauling of children. The entire set of books is available to children, who are encouraged or required to read it. It is printed and distributed by some of the world's most powerful organizations. . . .
>
> With refreshing frankness, the Bible tells men it is their rightful place to rule women. . . . [It] specifies exactly how many shekels less than men women are worth. Genesis 19:1–8 tells one of many tales about fathers setting up their daughters to be gang raped. Even more prevalent are . . . glamorized war stories in which the fruits of victory are the local girls. . . . [P]erhaps most gruesome is the snuff story about the guy who set

his maid up to be gang raped and, after her death from the assault, cut her body up into little pieces. . . . Unlike movies and television programs, these tales are generally taken to be true, not simulated, accounts.[23]

In 1992, Gene Kasmar petitioned the Brooklyn Center, Minnesota, school board to ban the Bible from school classrooms and libraries on the ground that it is lewd, indecent, obscene, offensive, violent, and dangerous to women and children. He specifically complained about biblical references to concubines, explicit sex, child abuse, incest, nakedness, and mistreatment of women—all subjects, significantly, that would trigger the feminist-style antipornography laws.

In response, the chief counsel of Pat Robertson's American Center for Law and Justice in Virginia, Jay Sekulow, flew to Minnesota and argued that the Bible "is worthy of study for its literary and historic qualities."[24] While the Brooklyn Center School Board apparently agreed with this assessment, voting unanimously to reject Kasmar's petition, it must be recalled that Sekulow's argument would be unavailing under Dworkin-MacKinnon–type antipornography laws. Under the MacDworkin model law, any work could be banned on the basis of even one isolated passage that meets the definition of pornography, and the work could not be saved by any serious literary, historic, or other value it might offer. Consequently, the feminist antipornography law could be used by Kasmar and others to ban the Bible not only from public schools, but also from public libraries, bookstores, and all other venues.

The countless expressive works that have been blamed for crimes include many that convey profeminist messages. Therefore, an anecdotal, image-blaming rationale for censorship would condemn many feminist works. For example, the television movie *The Burning Bed,* which told the true story of a battered wife who set fire to her sleeping husband, was blamed for some "copycat" crimes, as well as for some acts of violence by men against women. The argument that such incidents would justify suppression would mark the end of any films or other works depicting—and deploring—the real violence that plagues the lives of too many actual women.

Under a censorship regime that permits anecdotal, book-blaming "evidence," all other feminist materials would be equally endangered, not "just" works that depict the violence that has been inflicted on women. That is because, as feminist writings themselves have observed, some sexual assaults are committed by men who feel threatened by the women's movement. Should feminist works therefore be banned on the theory that they might well motivate a man to act out his misogynistic aggression?

Studies of Sex Offenders

The scientists who have investigated the impact of exposure to sexual materials in real life have not found that either sexual materials or attitudes toward women play any significant role in prompting actual violence. In general, these studies show that sex offenders had less exposure to sexually explicit materials than most men, that they first saw such materials at a later age than nonoffenders, that they were overwhelmingly more likely to have been punished for looking at them as teenagers, and that they often find sexual images more distressing than arousing.[25]

While no evidence substantiates that viewing pornography leads to violence and discrimination against women, some evidence indicates that, if anything, there may well be an inverse causal relationship between exposure to sexually explicit materials and misogynistic violence or discrimination. One of the leading researchers in this area, Edward Donnerstein of the University of California at Santa Barbara, has written: "A good amount of research strongly supports the position that exposure to erotica can reduce aggressive responses in people who are predisposed to aggress."[26] Similarly, John Money, of Johns Hopkins Medical School, a leading expert on sexual violence, has noted that most people with criminal sexualities were raised with strict, antisexual, repressive attitudes. He predicts that the "current repressive attitudes toward sex will breed an ever-widening epidemic of aberrant sexual behavior."[27]

In one 1989 experiment, males who had been exposed to pornography were more willing to come to the aid of a female subject who appeared to be hurt than

were men who had been exposed to other stimuli.[28] Laboratory studies further indicate that there may well be an inverse causal relationship between exposure to violent sexually explicit material and sexual arousal. For example, in 1991, Howard Barbaree and William Marshall, of Queen's College in Ontario, found:

> For most men, hearing a description of an encounter where the man is forcing the woman to have sex, and the woman is in distress or pain, dampens the arousal by about 50 percent compared to arousal levels using a scene of consenting lovemaking. . . . Ordinarily violence inhibits sexual arousal in men. A blood flow loss of 50 percent means a man would not be able to penetrate a woman.[29]

The foregoing research findings are certainly more consistent with what many feminist scholars have been writing about rape than is the procensorship feminists' pornocentric analysis: namely, rape is not a crime about sex, but rather, about violence.[30]

SEE NO PORNOGRAPHY, SEE NO SEXIST AND VIOLENT IMAGERY?

Pornography constitutes only a small subset of the sexist or violent imagery that pervades our culture and media. New York Law School professor Carlin Meyer recently conducted a comprehensive survey of the views of women's sexuality, status, and gender roles that are purveyed in nonpornographic media:

> Today, mainstream television, film, advertising, music, art, and popular (including religious) literature are the primary propagators of Western views of sexuality and sex roles. Not only do we read, see and experience their language and imagery more often and at earlier ages than we do most explicit sexual representation, but precisely because mainstream imagery is ordinary and everyday, it more powerfully convinces us that it depicts the world as it is or ought to be.[31]

Other cultural and media analysts have likewise concluded that more-damaging sexist imagery is more broadly purveyed through mainstream, nonsexual representations. Thelma McCormack, director of York University's Feminist Studies Centre, has concluded that "the enemy of women's equality is our mainstream culture with its images of women as family-centered," rather than imagery of women as sexual. According to McCormack:

> Surveys and public opinion studies confirm the connection between gender-role traditionalism and an acceptance or belief in the normality of a stratified social system. The more traditional a person's views are about women, the more likely he or she is to accept inequality as inevitable, functional, natural, desirable and immutable. In short, if any image of woman can be said to influence our thinking about gender equality, it is the domestic woman not the Dionysian one.[32]

Social science researchers have found that acceptance of the rape myth and other misogynistic attitudes concerning women and violence are just as likely to result from exposure to many types of mass media— from soap operas to popular commercial films—as from even intense exposure to violent, misogynistic sexually explicit materials.[33] Accordingly, if we really wanted to purge all sexist, violent representations from our culture, we would have to cast the net far beyond pornography, notwithstanding how comprehensive and elastic that category is. Would even procensorship feminists want to deal such a death-blow to First Amendment freedoms?

CENSOR PORNOGRAPHY, SEE NO PORNOGRAPHY?

Procensorship feminists themselves have acknowledged that censorship would probably just drive pornography underground. Indeed, as recently as 1987, Catharine MacKinnon recognized that "pornography cannot be reformed or suppressed or banned."[34]

The assumption that censorship would substantially reduce the availability or impact of pornography also overlooks evidence that censorship makes some viewers more desirous of pornography and more receptive to its imagery. This "forbidden fruits" effect has been corroborated by historical experience and social science research. All recent studies of the suppression of sexual expression, including Walter Kendrick's 1987 book *The Secret Museum: Pornography in Modern Culture* and Edward de Grazia's 1992 book *Girls Lean Back Everywhere: The Law of Obscenity and the Assault on Genius,* demonstrate that any censorship effort simply increases the attention that a targeted work receives. Social scientific studies that were included in the report of the 1970 President's Commission on Obscenity and Pornography suggested that censorship of sexually explicit materials may increase their desirability and impact, and also that a viewer's awareness that sexually oriented parts of a film have been censored may lead to frustration and subsequent aggressive behavior.[35]

The foregoing data about the impact of censoring pornography are consistent with broader research findings: the evidence suggests that censorship of *any* material increases an audience's desire to obtain the material and disposes the audience to be more receptive to it.[36] Critical viewing skills, and the ability to regard media images skeptically and analytically, atrophy under a censorial regime. A public that learns to question everything it sees or hears is better equipped to reject culturally propagated values than is one that assumes the media have been purged of all "incorrect" perspectives.

Even assuming for the sake of argument that there were a causal link between pornography and anti-female discrimination and violence, the insignificant contribution that censorship might make to reducing them would not outweigh the substantial damage that censorship would do to feminist goals. From the lack of actual evidence to substantiate the alleged causal link, the conclusion follows even more inescapably: *Censoring pornography would do women more harm than good.*

NOTES

1. Quoted in David Futrelle, "The Politics of Porn, Shameful Pleasures," *In These Times,* 7 March 1994, pp. 14–17.

2. *Butler v. the Queen* 1 SCR 452 (199), p. 505.

3. Marcia Pally, *Sex and Sensibility: Reflections on Forbidden Mirrors and the Will to Censor* (Hopewell, N.J.: Ecco Press, 1994).

4. Albert J. Reiss, Jr. and Jeffrey A. Roth, eds., *Understanding and Preventing Violence* (Washington, D.C.: National Academy Press, 1993), p. 111. (A project for the National Research Council.)

5. Judith Becker and Ellen Levine, paper presented to a meeting of the National Coalition Against Censorship, New York, N.Y., 17 June 1986.

6. Daniel Linz, Steven D. Penrod, and Edward Donnerstein, "The Attorney General's Commission on Pornography: The Gaps between 'Findings' and Facts," *American Bar Foundation Research Journal* 4 (Fall 1987): 713–36, at 723.

7. Edward Mulvey and Jeffrey Haugaard, *Surgeon General's Workshop on Pornography and Public Health* (Arlington, Virginia: U.S. Department of Health and Human Services, 1986).

8. Carol Krafka, "Sexually Explicit, Sexually Violent, and Violent Media: Effects of Multiple Naturalistic Exposures and Debriefing on Female Viewers" (Ph.D. dissertation, University of Wisconsin, 1985), p. 29.

9. Daniel Linz, Edward Donnerstein, and Steven Penrod, "The Effects of Long-Term Exposure to Violent and Sexually Degrading Depictions of Women," *Journal of Personality and Social Psychology* 55 (1988): 758–68.

10. Cynthia Gentry, "Pornography and Rape: An Empirical Analysis," *Deviant Behavior: An Interdisciplinary Journal* 12 (1991): 277–88, at 284.

11. Larry Baron and Murray Straus, "Four Theories of Rape: A Macro-sociological Analysis," *Social Problems* 34, no. 5 (1987): 467–89.

12. Joseph Scott and Loretta Schwalm, "Pornography and Rape: An Examination of Adult Theater Rates and Rape Rates by State," in J. E. Scott and T. Hirchi (eds.), *Controversial Issues in Crime and Justice* (Beverly Hills: Sage, 1988).

13. Bureau of Justice Statistics, *Criminal Victimization in the United States* (Washington, D.C.: Government Printing Office, 1990); Pally, *Sex and Sensibility,* p. 22.

14. Richard J. Gelles and Murray Straus, *Intimate Violence: The Causes and Consequences of Abuse in the American Family* (New York: Touchstone, 1989), p. 112.

15. Pally, *Sex and Sensibility,* pp. 21, 23.

16. Baron and Straus, "Four Theories of Rape."

17. Pally, *Sex and Sensibility,* pp. 57–61.

18. Richard Posner, "Obsession," review of *Only Words* by Catharine MacKinnon, *New Republic,* 18 October 1993, pp. 31–36, at p. 34.

19. Ellen Willis, "An Unholy Alliance," *New York Newsday,* 25 February 1992, p. 78.

20. *Memoirs v. Massachusetts,* 383 U.S. 413, 432 (1966) (concurring).

21. Williams Committee, *The British Inquiry into Obscenity and Film Censorship* (London, England: Home Office Research and Planning Unit, 1979).

22. Earl Finbar Murphy, "The Value of Pornography," *Wayne Law Review* 10 (1964): 655–80, at 668.

23. Pally, *Sex and Sensibility,* pp. 99–100.

24. Associated Press, "Atheist Loses Fight to Ban Bible at School," *Chicago Tribune,* 11 November 1992.

25. Pally, *Sex and Sensibility,* pp. 25–61.

26. Edward Donnerstein, "Erotica and Human Aggression," in *Aggression: Theoretical and Empirical Reviews,* ed. Richard Green and Edward Donnerstein (New York: Academic Press, 1983), pp. 127–28.

27. Quoted in Jane Brody, "Scientists Trace Aberrant Sexuality," *New York Times,* 23 January 1990.

28. Pally, *Sex and Sensibility,* p. 50.

29. Howard Barbaree and William Marshall, "The Role of Male Sexual Arousal in Rape: Six Models," *Journal of Consulting and Clinical Psychology* 59, no. 5 (1991): 621–30; Pally, *Sex and Sensibility*, pp. 44–45.

30. Susan Brownmiller, *Against Our Will: Men, Women, and Rape* (New York: Simon & Schuster, 1975); Susan Estrich, *Real Rape* (Boston: Harvard University Press, 1987).

31. Carlin Meyer, "Sex, Censorship, and Women's Liberation" (unpublished), pp. 42–43. [A revised version of this manuscript was published in *Texas Law Review* 72 (1994): 1097–1201.]

32. Thelma McCormack, "If Pornography Is the Theory, Is Inequality the Practice?" (presented at public forum, *Refusing Censorship: Feminists and Activists Fight Back,* York, Canada, 12 November 1992), p. 12.

33. Edward Donnerstein, Daniel Linz, and Steven Penrod, *The Question of Pornography: Research Findings and Policy Implications* (New York: Free Press, 1987), p. 107.

34. Catharine MacKinnon, "Not a Moral Issue," *Yale Law & Policy Review* 2 (1984): 321–45, at 325.

35. Percy H. Tannenbaum, "Emotional Arousal as a Mediator of Communication Effects," *Technical Report of the U.S. Commission on Obscenity and Pornography* 8 (1971), p. 353.

36. Timothy C. Brock, "Erotic Materials: A Commodity Theory Analysis of Availability and Desirability," *Technical Report of the U.S. Commission on Obscenity and Pornography* 6 (1971), pp. 131–37.

READING QUESTIONS

1. What are the three assumptions on which the claim that censorship would reduce sexism and violence against women rests according to Strossen?
2. What are the four types of evidence that are used to justify the assumptions about the effects of pornography? Why does Strossen believe that none of these types of evidence proves that pornography harms women?
3. Explain Strossen's reasons for thinking that the mainstream media is just as damaging (if not more damaging) to women as is pornographic material.
4. How does Strossen argue for the view that censoring pornography would not reduce its availability or impact?

DISCUSSION QUESTIONS

1. What kinds of evidence should we rely on when trying to answer questions about whether pornography is harmful to women? Should we reject anecdotal evidence and common sense intuitions as Strossen suggests? Why or why not?
2. Suppose that Strossen is right to claim that none of the evidence commonly presented proves that pornography harms women. Consider and discuss whether there are any other reasons to censor pornographic materials.

RONALD DWORKIN

Liberty and Pornography

Dworkin, following Isaiah Berlin, distinguishes negative from positive liberty, and uses this distinction to address certain pro-censorship arguments, including feminist arguments that appeal to the idea that certain forms of pornography contribute to the false idea that women have less worth or dignity than do men. Negative liberty involves not being hindered from engaging in certain behavior including, for example, the exercise of one's right to free speech. Positive liberty, by contrast, involves the right to engage in certain activities that enable one to participate in public decisions and includes, for example, the right to vote. In terms of the distinction between negative and positive liberty, the pro-censorship feminist arguments in question can be understood as appealing to women's positive liberty to participate equally with men in community. The idea, then, is that the positive liberty in question ought to limit the negative liberty of free speech and expression when it comes to pornography. Against this line of argument, Dworkin claims that the "point of free speech [which we find in the U.S. Constitution] is . . . to allow ideas to have whatever consequences flow from their dissemination, including the undesirable consequences for positive liberty." He concludes that even if pornography interferes with women's positive liberty to participate in political processes, this would not justify censoring pornography. Dworkin also responds to a related pro-censorship argument based on the idea that because pornography, through its portrayal of women, tends to silence them, it thus violates their negative liberty to free speech.

Recommended Reading: consequentialism, chap. 1, sec. 2A, and rights-focused approach to moral issues, chap. 1, sec. 2D.

When Isaiah Berlin delivered his famous inaugural lecture as Chichele Professor of Social and Political Theory at Oxford, in 1958, he felt it necessary to acknowledge that politics did not attract the professional attention of most serious philosophers in Britain and America. They thought philosophy had no place in politics, and vice versa; that political philosophy could be nothing more than a parade of the theorist's own preferences and allegiances with no supporting arguments of any rigor or respectability. That gloomy picture is unrecognizable now. Political philosophy thrives as a mature industry; it dominates many distinguished philosophy departments and attracts a large share of the best graduate students almost everywhere.

Berlin's lecture, "Two Concepts of Liberty," played an important and distinctive role in this renaissance. It provoked immediate, continuing, heated, and mainly illuminating controversy. It became, almost at once, a staple of graduate and undergraduate reading lists, as it still is. Its scope and erudition, its historical sweep and evident contemporary force, its sheer interest, made political ideas suddenly seem exciting and fun. Its main polemical message—that it is fatally dangerous for philosophers to ignore either the complexity or the power of those ideas—was both compelling and overdue. But chiefly, or so I think, its importance lay in the force of its central argument. For though Berlin began by conceding to the disdaining philosophers that political philosophy could not match logic or the philosophy of language as a theater for "radical

discoveries," in which "talent for minute analyses is likely to be rewarded," he continued by analyzing subtle distinctions that, as it happens, are even more important now, in the Western democracies at least, than when he first called our attention to them.

I must try to describe two central features of his argument, though for reasons of space I shall have to leave out much that is important to them. The first is the celebrated distinction described in the lecture's title: between two (closely allied) senses of liberty. Negative liberty (as Berlin came later to restate it) means not being obstructed by others in doing what one might wish to do. We count some negative liberties—like the freedom to speak our minds without censorship—as very important and others—like driving at very fast speeds—as trivial. But they are both instances of negative freedom, and though a state may be justified in imposing speed limits, for example, on grounds of safety and convenience, that is nevertheless an instance of restricting negative liberty.

Positive liberty, on the other hand, is the power to control or participate in public decisions, including the decision how far to curtail negative liberty. In an ideal democracy—whatever that is—the people govern themselves. Each is master to the same degree, and positive liberty is secured for all.

In his inaugural lecture Berlin described the historical corruption of the idea of positive liberty, a corruption that began in the idea that someone's true liberty lies in control by his rational self rather than his empirical self, that is, in control that aims at securing goals other than those the person himself recognizes. Freedom, on that conception, is possible only when people are governed, ruthlessly if necessary, by rulers who know their true, metaphysical will. Only then are people truly free, albeit against their will. That deeply confused and dangerous, but nevertheless potent, chain of argument had in many parts of the world turned positive liberty into the most terrible tyranny. Of course, by calling attention to this corruption of positive liberty, Berlin did not mean that negative liberty was an unalloyed blessing, and should be protected in all its forms in all circumstances at all costs. He said later that on the contrary, the vices of excessive and indiscriminate negative liberty were so evident, particularly in the form of savage economic inequality, that he had not thought it necessary to describe them in much detail.

The second feature of Berlin's argument that I have in mind is a theme repeated throughout his writing on political topics. He insists on the complexity of political value, and the fallacy of supposing that all the political virtues that are attractive in themselves can be realized in a single political structure. The ancient Platonic ideal of some master accommodation of all attractive virtues and goals, combined in institutions satisfying each in the right proportion and sacrificing none, is in Berlin's view, for all its imaginative power and historical influence, only a seductive myth. He later summed this up:

> One freedom may abort another; one freedom may obstruct or fail to create conditions which make other freedoms, or a larger degree of freedom, or freedom for more persons, possible; positive and negative freedom may collide; the freedom of the individual or the group may not be fully compatible with a full degree of participation in a common life, with its demands for cooperation, solidarity, fraternity. But beyond all these there is an acuter issue: the paramount need to satisfy the claims of other, no less ultimate, values: justice, happiness, love, the realization of capacities to create new things and experiences and ideas, the discovery of the truth. Nothing is gained by identifying freedom proper, in either of its senses, with these values, or with the conditions of freedom, or by confounding types of freedom with one another.[1]

Berlin's warnings about conflating positive and negative liberty, and liberty itself, with other values seemed, to students of political philosophy in the great Western democracies in the 1950s, to provide important lessons about authoritarian regimes in other times and places. Though cherished liberties were very much under attack in both America and Britain in that decade, the attack was not grounded in or defended through either form of confusion. The enemies of negative liberty were powerful, but they were also crude and undisguised. Joseph McCarthy and his allies did not rely on any Kantian or Hegelian or Marxist concept of metaphysical selves to justify censorship or blacklists. They distinguished liberty not from itself, but from security; they claimed that too much free speech made us vulnerable to spies and intellectual saboteurs and ultimately to conquest.

In both Britain and America, in spite of limited reforms, the state still sought to enforce conventional sexual morality about pornography, contraception, prostitution, and homosexuality. Conservatives who defended these invasions of negative liberty appealed not to some higher or different sense of freedom, however, but to values that were plainly distinct from, and in conflict with, freedom: religion, true morality, and traditional and proper family values. The wars over liberty were fought, or so it seemed, by clearly divided armies. Liberals were for liberty, except, in some circumstances, for the negative liberty of economic entrepreneurs. Conservatives were for that liberty, but against other forms when these collided with security or their view of decency and morality.

But now the political maps have radically changed and some forms of negative liberty have acquired new opponents. Both in America and in Britain, though in different ways, conflicts over race and gender have transformed old alliances and divisions. Speech that expresses racial hatred, or a degrading attitude toward women, has come to seem intolerable to many people whose convictions are otherwise traditionally liberal. It is hardly surprising that they should try to reduce the conflict between their old liberal ideals and their new acceptance of censorship by adopting some new definition of what liberty, properly understood, really is. It is hardly surprising, but the result is dangerous confusion, and Berlin's warnings, framed with different problems in mind, are directly in point.

I shall try to illustrate that point with a single example: a lawsuit arising out of the attempt by certain feminist groups in America to outlaw what they consider a particularly objectionable form of pornography. I select this example not because pornography is more important or dangerous or objectionable than racist invective or other highly distasteful kinds of speech, but because the debate over pornography has been the subject of the fullest and most comprehensive scholarly discussion.

Through the efforts of Catharine MacKinnon, a professor of law at the University of Michigan, and other prominent feminists, Indianapolis, Indiana, enacted an antipornography ordinance. The ordinance defined pornography as "the graphic sexually explicit subordination of women, whether in pictures or words . . ." and it specified, as among pornographic materials falling within that definition, those that present women as enjoying pain or humiliation or rape, or as degraded or tortured or filthy, bruised or bleeding, or in postures of servility or submission or display. It included no exception for literary or artistic value, and opponents claimed that applied literally it would outlaw James Joyce's *Ulysses,* John Cleland's *Memoirs of a Woman of Pleasure,* various works of D. H. Lawrence, and even Yeats's "Leda and the Swan." But the groups who sponsored the ordinance were anxious to establish that their objection was not to obscenity or indecency as such, but to the consequences for women of a particular kind of pornography, and they presumably thought that an exception for artistic value would undermine that claim.[2]

The ordinance did not simply regulate the display of pornography so defined, or restrict its sale or distribution to particular areas, or guard against the exhibition of pornography to children. Regulation for those purposes does restrain negative liberty, but if reasonable it does so in a way compatible with free speech. Zoning and display regulations may make pornography more expensive or inconvenient to obtain, but they do not offend the principle that no one must be prevented from publishing or reading what he or she wishes on the ground that its content is immoral or offensive.[3] The Indianapolis ordinance, on the other

hand, prohibited any "production, sale, exhibition, or distribution" whatever of the material it defined as pornographic.

Publishers and members of the public who claimed a desire to read the banned material arranged a prompt constitutional challenge. The federal district court held that the ordinance was unconstitutional because it violated the First Amendment to the United States Constitution, which guarantees the negative liberty of free speech.[4] The Circuit Court for the Seventh Circuit upheld the district court's decision,[5] and the Supreme Court of the United States declined to review that holding. The Circuit Court's decision, in an opinion by Judge Easterbrook, noticed that the ordinance did not outlaw obscene or indecent material generally but only material reflecting the opinion that women are submissive, or enjoy being dominated, or should be treated as if they did. Easterbrook said that the central point of the First Amendment was exactly to protect speech from content-based regulation of that sort. Censorship may on some occasions be permitted if it aims to prohibit directly dangerous speech—crying fire in a crowded theater or inciting a crowd to violence, for example—or speech particularly and unnecessarily inconvenient—broadcasting from sound trucks patrolling residential streets at night, for instance. But nothing must be censored, Easterbrook wrote, because the message it seeks to deliver is a bad one, or because it expresses ideas that should not be heard at all.

It is by no means universally agreed that censorship should never be based on content. The British Race Relations Act, for example, forbids speech of racial hatred, not only when it is likely to lead to violence, but generally, on the grounds that members of minority races should be protected from racial insults. In America, however, it is a fixed principle of constitutional law that such regulation is unconstitutional unless some compelling necessity, not just official or majority disapproval of the message, requires it. Pornography is often grotesquely offensive; it is insulting, not only to women but to men as well. But we cannot consider that a sufficient reason for banning it without destroying the principle that the speech we hate is as much entitled to protection as any other. The essence of negative liberty is freedom to offend, and that applies to the tawdry as well as the heroic.

Lawyers who defend the Indianapolis ordinance argue that society does have a further justification for outlawing pornography: that it causes great harm as well as offense to women. But their arguments mix together claims about different types or kinds of harm, and it is necessary to distinguish these. They argue, first, that some forms of pornography significantly increase the danger that women will be raped or physically assaulted. If that were true, and the danger were clear and present, then it would indeed justify censorship of those forms, unless less stringent methods of control, such as restricting pornography's audience, would be feasible, appropriate, and effective. In fact, however, though there is some evidence that exposure to pornography weakens people's critical attitudes toward sexual violence, there is no persuasive evidence that it causes more actual incidents of assault. The Seventh Circuit cited a variety of studies (including that of the Williams Commission in Britain in 1979), all of which concluded, the court said, "that it is not possible to demonstrate a direct link between obscenity and rape. . . ."[6] A recent report based on a year's research in Britain said: "The evidence does not point to pornography as a cause of deviant sexual orientation in offenders. Rather, it seems to be used as part of that deviant sexual orientation."[7]

Some feminist groups argue, however, that pornography causes not just physical violence but a more general and endemic subordination of women. In that way, they say, pornography makes for inequality. But even if it could be shown, as a matter of causal connection, that pornography is in part responsible for the economic structure in which few women attain top jobs or equal pay for the same work, that would not justify censorship under the Constitution. It would plainly be unconstitutional to ban speech directly *advocating* that women occupy inferior roles, or none at all, in commerce and the professions, even if that speech fell on willing male ears and achieved its goals. So it cannot be a reason for banning pornography that it contributes to an unequal economic or social structure, even if we think that it does.

But the most imaginative feminist literature for censorship makes a further and different argument: that negative liberty for pornographers conflicts not just with equality but with positive liberty as well, because pornography leads to women's *political* as well as economic or social subordination. Of course pornography does not take the vote from women, or somehow make their votes count less. But it produces a climate, according to this argument, in which women cannot have genuine political power or authority because they are perceived and understood unauthentically—that is, they are made over by male fantasy into people very different from, and of much less consequence than, the people they really are. Consider, for example, these remarks from the work of the principal sponsor of the Indianapolis ordinance. "[Pornography] institutionalizes the sexuality of male supremacy, fusing the eroticization of dominance and submission with the social construction of male and female. . . . Men treat women as who they see women as being. Pornography constructs who that is. Men's power over women means that the way men see women defines who women can be."[8]

Pornography, on this view, denies the positive liberty of women; it denies them the right to be their own masters by recreating them, for politics and society, in the shapes of male fantasy. That is a powerful argument, even in constitutional terms, because it asserts a conflict not just between liberty and equality but within liberty itself, that is, a conflict that cannot be resolved simply on the ground that liberty must be sovereign. What shall we make of the argument understood that way? We must notice, first, that it remains a causal argument. It claims not that pornography is a consequence or symptom or symbol of how the identity of women has been reconstructed by men, but an important cause or vehicle of that reconstruction.

That seems strikingly implausible. Sadistic pornography is revolting, but it is not in general circulation, except for its milder, soft-porn manifestations. It seems unlikely that it has remotely the influence over how women's sexuality or character or talents are conceived by men, and indeed by women, that commercial advertising and soap operas have. Television and other parts of popular culture use sexual display and sexual innuendo to sell virtually everything, and they often show women as experts in domestic detail and unreasoned intuition and nothing else. The images they create are subtle and ubiquitous, and it would not be surprising to learn, through whatever research might establish this, that they indeed do great damage to the way women are understood and allowed to be influential in politics. Sadistic pornography, though much more offensive and disturbing, is greatly overshadowed by these dismal cultural influences as a causal force.

Judge Easterbrook's opinion for the Seventh Circuit assumed, for the sake of argument, however, that pornography did have the consequences the defenders of the ordinance claimed. He said that the argument nevertheless failed because the point of free speech is precisely to allow ideas to have whatever consequences follow from their dissemination, including undesirable consequences for positive liberty. "Under the First Amendment," he said, "the government must leave to the people the evaluation of ideas. Bald or subtle, an idea is as powerful as the audience allows it to be. . . . [The assumed result] simply demonstrates the power of pornography as speech. All of these unhappy effects depend on mental intermediation."

That is right as a matter of American constitutional law. The Ku Klux Klan and the American Nazi party are allowed to propagate their ideas in America, and the British Race Relations Act, so far as it forbids abstract speech of racial hatred, would be unconstitutional in the U.S. But does the American attitude represent the kind of Platonic absolutism Berlin warned against? No, because there is an important difference between the idea he thinks absurd, that all ideals attractive in themselves can be perfectly reconciled within a single utopian political order, and the different idea he thought essential, that we must, as individuals and nations, choose, among possible combinations of ideals, a coherent, even though inevitably and regrettably limited, set of these to define our own individual or national way of life. Freedom of speech, conceived and protected as a fundamental negative liberty, is the core of the choice modern democracies have made, a choice we must now honor in finding our own ways to combat the shaming inequalities women still suffer.

Of course it is fully recognized in First Amendment jurisprudence that some speech has the effect of silencing others. Government must indeed balance negative liberties when it prevents heckling or other demonstrative speech designed to stop others from speaking or being heard. But Michelman has something different in mind. He says that a woman's speech may be silenced not just by noise intended to drown her out but also by argument and images that change her audience's perceptions of her character, needs, desires, and standing, and also, perhaps, change her own sense of who she is and what she wants. Speech with that consequence silences her, Michelman supposes, by making it impossible for her effectively to contribute to the process Judge Easterbrook said the First Amendment protected, the process through which ideas battle for the public's favor. "[It] is a highly plausible claim," Michelman writes, "[that] pornography [is] a cause of women's subordination and silencing. . . . It is a fair and obvious question why our society's openness to challenge does not need protection against repressive private as well as public action."[9]

He argues that if our commitment to negative freedom of speech is consequentialist—if we want free speech in order to have a society in which no idea is barred from entry—then we must censor some ideas in order to make entry possible for other ones. He protests that the distinction that American constitutional law makes between the suppression of ideas by the effect of public criminal law and by the consequences of private speech is arbitrary, and that a sound concern for openness would be equally worried about both forms of control. But the distinction the law makes is not between public and private power as such, but between negative liberty and other virtues, including positive liberty. It would indeed be contradictory for a constitution to prohibit official censorship while protecting the right of private citizens physically to prevent other citizens from publishing or broadcasting specified ideas. That would allow private citizens to violate the negative liberty of other citizens by preventing them from saying what they wish.

But there is no contradiction in insisting that every idea must be allowed to be heard, even those whose consequence is that other ideas will be misunderstood, or given little consideration, or even not be spoken at all because those who might speak them are not in control of their own public identities and therefore cannot be understood as they wish to be. These are very bad consequences, and they must be resisted by whatever means our Constitution permits. But acts that have these consequences do not, for that reason, deprive others of their negative liberty to speak, and the distinction, as Berlin insisted, is very far from arbitrary or inconsequential.

It is of course understandable why Michelman and others should want to expand the idea of negative liberty in the way they try to do. Only by characterizing certain ideas as themselves "silencing" ideas—only by supposing that censoring pornography is the same thing as stopping people from drowning out other speakers—can they hope to justify censorship within the constitutional scheme that assigns a preeminent place to free speech. But the assimilation is nevertheless a confusion, exactly the kind of confusion Berlin warned against in his original lecture, because it obscures the true political choice that must be made. I return to Berlin's lecture, which put the point with that striking combination of clarity and sweep I have been celebrating:

> I should be guilt-stricken, and rightly so, if I were not, in some circumstances, ready to make [some] sacrifice [of freedom]. But a sacrifice is not an increase in what is being sacrificed, namely freedom, however great the moral need or the compensation for it. Everything is what it is: liberty is liberty, not equality or fairness or justice or culture, or human happiness or a quiet conscience.

NOTES

1. Isaiah Berlin, *Four Essays on Liberty* (Oxford University Press, 1968), p. lvi.

2. MacKinnon explained that "if a woman is subjected, why should it matter that the work has other value?" See her article "Pornography, Civil Rights, and Speech," in *Harvard Civil Rights–Civil Liberties Law Review.* Vol. 28, p. 21.

3. See my article "Do We Have a Right to Pornography?" reprinted as Chapter 17 in my book *A Matter of Principle* (Harvard University Press, 1985).

4. *American Booksellers Association, Inc. et al. v. William H. Hudnut, III, Mayor, City of Indianapolis, et al.,* 598 F. Supp. 1316 (S.D. Ind. 1984).

5. 771 F. 2d 323 (US Court of Appeals, Seventh Circuit).

6. That court, in a confused passage, said that it nevertheless accepted "the premises of this legislation," which included the claims about a causal connection with sexual violence. But it seemed to mean that it was accepting the rather different causal claim considered in the next paragraph, about subordination. In any case, it said that it accepted those premises only for the sake of argument, since it thought it had no authority to reject decisions of Indianapolis based on its interpretation of empirical evidence.

7. See the *Daily Telegraph,* December 23, 1990. Of course further studies might contradict this assumption. But it seems very unlikely that pornography will be found to stimulate physical violence to the overall extent that nonpornographic depictions of violence, which are much more pervasive in our media and culture, do.

8. See MacKinnon's article cited in note 2.

9. Frank Michelman, "Conceptions of Democracy in American Constitutional Argument: The Case of Pornography Regulation." *Tennessee Law Review,* Vol. 56, No. 291 (1989), pp. 303–304.

READING QUESTIONS

1. Explain the distinction between negative and positive liberty according to Dworkin's understanding of Isaiah Berlin's original proposal in "Two Concepts of Liberty."

2. Why was Indiana's antipornography ordinance declared unconstitutional?

3. What arguments were given by defenders of the ordinance to show that the pornography they found objectionable caused harm to women? How does Dworkin respond to each of these arguments?

4. Explain the argument that certain kinds of speech including pornography may be "silencing." Include in your explanation Dworkin's reply to this kind of argument.

DISCUSSION QUESTIONS

1. Do you agree with the court's ruling that the Indiana antipornography ordinance is unconstitutional? Are there any other grounds on which we might be able to claim that the type of speech in question is immoral even if it is unconstitutional?
2. Dworkin argues that the influence of the type of pornography prohibited by the Indiana ordinance is not as great as some might suspect. Is he right to suggest that such pornography is not as influential as the images of women portrayed in other forms of media like soap operas? What influences does this type of pornography actually have?

JUDITH M. HILL

Pornography and Degradation

Hill advances an essentially Kantian argument against what she calls "victim pornography." According to Hill, degradation is a public phenomenon in which some individual or group is overtly represented as not being worthy of a certain level of respect that they are due. Victim pornography, by its very nature, degrades women by representing them as members of a class of beings not entitled to an appropriate level of respect. Thus, since on the Kantian view, failing to treat others as deserving of respect is morally objectionable, victim pornography is morally objectionable. Hill concludes by considering the legal implications of her analysis of victim pornography.

Recommended Reading: Kantian moral theory, chap. 2, sec. 2C.

The issue of pornography has often been approached from a utilitarian point of view, with the discussion focusing on what the consequences of pornography might be. There is a great deal of literature concerning whether or not the availability of pornographic material is responsible for violence against women, or for promoting a depersonalized attitude toward sexual relationships. There is not a great deal of agreement on these empirical questions (Berger, 1977).

Recently, there have been several attempts to introduce city or county ordinances banning the sale of pornography, in Minneapolis, Indianapolis, Los Angeles, and Suffolk, New York. The proponents of these ordinances have argued that pornography violates the civil rights of women, apparently a non-utilitarian argument. However, their argument turns on the premise that *the effect* of pornography is to deny equal opportunities to women. Thus far, the courts have rejected this line of reasoning, and the constitutionality of the proposed statutes, largely because they are not convinced that the consequences of pornography are such as to warrant restrictions of First Amendment rights.

I am interested in presenting an argument that does not appeal to the consequences of pornography, a strictly nonutilitarian argument that rests on the hypothesis that pornography degrades women. I believe that pornography *does* degrade women. However, the concept of degradation is a slippery one, which, like other concepts of oppression, has not been examined as carefully as it must be if we are going to discuss oppression illuminatingly. In the first part of this article, therefore, I will offer an analysis of the concept of degradation. In the second part, I will show why and how pornography degrades women.

I

I propose that we begin with the assumption that degradation involves, literally, a de-grading. This proposition is, I realize, both vague and ambiguous. It is ambiguous because "de-grade" may suggest either (1) to *down*-grade, to lower the worth of, to de-value, or (2) to *assign* a lower grade to, to give a lower evaluation, to characterize as of lesser worth. In other words, de-gradation may be thought to entail either a real loss of worth, or an imputed loss of worth. In either case, the proposal is vague, because it gives no indication of the *kind* of value that must be lost, or imputed to be lost, in order for degradation to take place.

The following examples suggest a direction we might take in firming up this proposal.

In William Styron's novel, *Sophie's Choice,* Sophie mentions that although the Nazis routinely shaved the heads of all inmates at Auschwitz, those inmates who occupied positions of favor were permitted to

wear headscarves in order to hide their "degrading baldness."

In Emma Goldman's autobiography, recounting a period of time spent in prison, she describes as "degrading" the prisoners being forced to march in lockstep while carrying buckets of excrement from their cells to the river.

In both these cases, the writers are describing environments in which severe physical abuse was a commonplace. The horrors of the Nazi death camps are well-known. The plight of working class women in prisons in the late nineteenth and early twentieth centuries was also appalling: forced labor under sweatshop conditions, with inadequate food, crowded living quarters, and no medical facilities. Given the context of physical abuse in both cases, it is significant that what Goldman and Styron's Sophie focus on as degrading is not any physical abuse or deprivation at all, but on practices the importance of which (to both practitioner and victim) is largely symbolic. In both cases, it is a kind of public display of low status which is described as degrading.

Extrapolating from Styron and Goldman, I would suggest that the de-grading involved in degradation is a lowering of *moral* status. A person is not degraded merely by losing status as president of the company or as most valuable player or as woman of the year. Degradation is not to be confused with decline or defeat. It is not a matter of losing power or prestige or privilege, but of losing something considerably more central to one's personhood. To give this account a Kantian interpretation: degradation involves being treated as though one were a means only, as though one were not an end in herself, as though one were something less than a person.

However, degradation is not *simply* a matter of being treated as something less than a person. If this were true, then shaved heads and forced marches would be the least of the degradations inflicted upon Sophie and Goldman, for in much of the physical and mental abuse they suffered they were treated as less than persons. It is not a sufficient condition of degradation that a person be treated as something less than a person.

I am inclined to say that it is a necessary condition of degradation that a person *be perceived*—by herself or by others—as being treated as something less than a person. Degradation occurs with the creation of a public impression that a person is being treated as something less than a person. Thus, baldness was degrading within the context of Auschwitz because it marked one as a member of the class that was being treated as subhuman. Forced marches for prisoners doing housekeeping chores were degrading because their sole purpose was to exhibit—for the benefit of the prisoners and the guards, at least—the complete submissiveness and obedience of the prisoners and the complete control of the guards; forced marches served as a demonstration that the prisoners could be treated in whatever manner, however inhuman, that the guards desired.

In short, degradation is a public phenomenon. If there is no perception of a person being treated as though she were a means only, then she is not degraded, although she may be exploited or cheated or abused. For example, consider the difference between an employer who underpays employees while expressing contempt for them, and an employer who underpays employees while cultivating an image of benevolent concern. The former degrades her employees; the latter "merely" cheats them. Or, consider the difference between a man who publicly treats his wife as a servant, and a man who treats his wife as a means only while expressing love and affection for her. Again, the former degrades his wife; the latter "merely" takes advantage of her.

Although degradation requires a public perception of someone being treated as a means only, this perception need not be widely shared: it is often enough that the victim perceives it, i.e., that it be public in principle only. On the other hand, it may be true that the degradation is more severe if the perception is more widespread. To be actually observed in public being treated as less than a person is more degrading than being subjected to the same treatment in private.

This suggests, to return to a question raised above, that degradation involves a de-grading in the sense of imputing a lesser value to, rather than in the sense of lessening the value of. *Covert* treatment of a person as a means only—a matter of exploitation or abuse rather than of degradation, if my analysis is

correct—implies *no* conviction on the agent's part that his action is morally justifiable, that the other deserves to be treated as a means only. Such actions do not, therefore, impute a lesser moral worth to the victim. However, an agent who lets his victims know that he is intentionally treating her as a means only, exhibits a certain contempt for her, demonstrates a certain conviction that his action is justifiable, that she deserves to be treated as less than a person. Finally, an agent who treats his victim as something less than a person in public places, for the whole world to observe, demonstrates a conviction that her worthlessness is so extreme that all the world can be counted upon to regard him as justified in treating her accordingly. In short, the more public the display of contempt, the stronger is the imputation of moral worthlessness.

It may sometimes be thought that degradation degrades not only in the sense of imputing lesser moral worth to a person, but also in the sense of actively lessening the moral worth of a person. In particular, I suspect that people who degrade others often vaguely think of this as a kind of challenge or as a test. One meets the challenge, passes the test, by insisting (presumably at whatever cost) on being treated with respect. One fails the test by acquiescing; and the penalty for failure is the loss of one's right to be treated with respect. Thus, degradation carries with it its own justification: people who allow themselves to be treated as less than persons deserve to be treated as less than persons.

This is a mistake. A person does not have to earn the right to be treated as an end in himself, to be treated with fairness and consideration; and a person does not forfeit these rights by failing to insist that they be respected. These are rights a person has simply in virtue of being a person, in virtue of having the potential (in theory, at least) for certain kinds of behavior. Consequently, degradation is always morally wrong. It does not become less wrong because the degraded person acquiesces. . . .

To summarize: a person is degraded when she is publicly, or at least overtly, treated as a means only, as something less than a person. Degradation involves a de-grading at least in the sense that it entails a (false) imputation of a lower moral status than persons, as such, are ordinarily accorded; and sometimes also in the sense that it involves a diminution of the moral courage of the person degraded.

II

Now we may turn to the question of whether or not pornography degrades women.

Obviously, the answer to this question will depend in part on what we identify as pornography. The Indianapolis and Minneapolis city ordinances, which were framed primarily by Andrea Dworkin and Catherine MacKinnon, defined pornography as "the graphic sexually explicit subordination of women, whether in pictures or in words." The proposed ordinances listed six conditions, at least one of which would have to be present in order to qualify a work as pornographic. Among these conditions were: (1) presenting women as sexual objects "who enjoy pain and humiliation"; (2) presenting women as "experiencing pleasure in being raped"; (3) presenting women as objects for "domination, conquest, violation, exploitation, possession or use." (Shipp 1984)

It should be noted that Andrea Dworkin is of the opinion that, in fact, virtually all of what passes for "adult entertainment" falls into one or more of these categories. She points out that, etymologically, pornography is "the depiction of vile whores"; and that after extensive research on the content and nature of contemporary "adult entertainment," she has concluded that it is *still* best described as the depiction of vile whores. "The fact that pornography is widely believed to be 'sexual representation' or 'depictions of sex' emphasizes only that the valuation of women as low whores is widespread and that the sexuality of women is perceived as low and whorish in itself" (Dworkin 1981, 201). In short, although Dworkin's proposed ordinances do not mandate censorship of sexually explicit, or obscene, material, *as such,* it is probably fair to say that she expects them to have the effect of eliminating most of what is commonly regarded as pornography.

Perhaps for this reason, some critics of the Minneapolis and Indianapolis ordinances have drawn the conclusion that these ordinances threaten all sexually explicit material. Civil libertarian Nat Hentoff (1984), for example, decried the ordinances as endangering "such works as . . . *Dr Zhivago,* . . . *Lolita,* and of course, bountiful sections of the Old Testament." As I understand the proposed ordinances, they would *not* ban such works; and it is not *my* intention in this paper to object to such works as these. Therefore, in order to avoid this sort of misunderstanding, I will elaborate a bit on the Dworkin/ MacKinnon definition of pornography, narrowing in on a genre I shall call Victim Pornography.

Victim Pornography is the graphic depiction of situations in which women are degraded by sexual activity, viz., (a) situations in which a woman is treated by a man (or by another woman) as a means of obtaining sexual pleasure, while he shows no consideration for her pleasure or desires or well-being, and (b) situations in which a woman is not only subjected to such treatment, but suggests it to the man in the first place. Furthermore, Victim Pornography presents such activity as entertaining. There is no suggestion that women should not be treated as less than persons; and often there is no hint that a woman might dislike such treatment.[1]

I believe that Victim Pornography does comprise at least a very large part of what passes today for adult entertainment. Dworkin is right in maintaining that much of what is commonly regarded as pornography is a celebration of violence and exploitation. However, I want to emphasize that the issue I am addressing is *not* the morality of what is commonly regarded as pornography: I am not concerned here with material that is sexually explicit, or obscene, as such. The focus of my discussion is neither *Lady Chatterley's Lover* nor *Playboy's* "Ten Coeds At Home," but Victim Pornography: depictions of women being bound, beaten, raped, mutilated, and, as often as not, begging for more. . . .

However, this is not a *necessary* feature of the production of pornography, even of Victim Pornography. Although it would be naive to suppose that the producers of pornography typically show respect and consideration for their models, we can at least imagine a producer of pornography taking time to ensure that the model's job is no more painful than necessary; treating unpleasant aspects of her job *as* unpleasant aspects, rather than as opportunities for leering; treating the models as people doing a job for pay, rather than as so much meat. A producer of pornography who behaves in this way still treats the model as a means to making profits, and perhaps *only* as a means to making profits (and not as an artist, or as a friend, for example); but does not treat her as a means only, as though she were not an end in herself, as less than a person.

In other words, it is not a necessary feature of the production of Victim Pornography that the models be degraded. Certainly it *may* happen, and often *does* happen; and certainly it is morally reprehensible when it happens. But pornography, even Victim Pornography, can surely be produced without degradation to the models,[2] and therefore the potential for degradation to models is not a reason to end the production of pornography. . . .

The hypothesis that the women who act in pornographic films and pose for pornographic magazines are necessarily treated as means only by the *patrons* of pornography, is even less plausible than the hypothesis that they are necessarily treated as means only by the producers of pornography.

It is doubtlessly the case that many people use pornography as a means of obtaining pleasure. The women who act in pornographic films and pose for pornographic magazines are, therefore, indirectly, instruments of pleasure for patrons of pornography. However, although it may follow that the patrons of pornography treat the models in pornographic material only as means to their own ends, it does *not* follow that they treat them as means *only,* as though they were not ends in themselves. The relationship between the patrons and the women who model for pornography is not, as such, sufficiently personal—they do not actually interact—to allow of this description.

In short, it is not true that women who serve as models for pornography are treated as means only, as less than persons, by consumers of pornography. On the other hand, although it may be true that these women are only treated as means, this is not in itself degrading to them.

It becomes apparent that any sort of degradation attaching to pornography will not occur on the personal level suggested by the hypotheses we have just considered. However, we have not yet considered the hypothesis that the pornography industry degrades women as a class rather than this or that individual woman.

The pornography industry regularly publishes material which, speaking conservatively, tends to contribute to the perpetuation of derogatory beliefs about womankind. Victim Pornography, in particular, depicts women not simply as ill treated, but as eager to be used and abused, totally lacking in human dignity: as more or less worthless for any purpose other than casual sexual intercourse. Many pieces of pornography depict *all* female characters in such negative ways.

Of course pornography is fiction, and does not purport to be anything other than fiction. However, fiction is not supposed to be devoid of all factual truth; indeed, fiction *should* contain truths about human nature, about motivation, about power, and so on. Consequently, although pornographic material may make no claim to be describing actual states of affairs, we might say that it offers a perspective on the actual nature of womankind. The perspective offered by Victim Pornography is that, in general, women are narcissistic, masochistic, and not fully persons in the moral sense.

I would not suggest that it is the *intention* of pornographers to convey the message that all women may be, or should be, or like to be treated as less than persons. This is almost surely false. Most pornographers are not at all interested in influencing behavior, or in conveying universal truths; their intention is to titillate. Nevertheless, because pornography trades in stereotypes, shunning any careful or serious character development (by its very nature; this is what makes it bad literature), and because the stereotypes that titillate (at least, that titillate the patrons of Victim Pornography) are derogatory ones—the nymphomaniac, the masochist, the mindless playmate—much of Victim Pornography supports the idea that all women fall into one or another of these categories, whether or not this is its intention. The genre of Victim Pornography, taken as a whole, implies that most women are mindless, masochistic nymphomaniacs. That is to say, this would be the logical conclusion to draw on the basis of the characterization offered in Victim Pornography.[3]

The point I want to make here is *not* that Victim Pornography is responsible for negative attitudes and/or violent behavior towards women. If pornography were eliminated from the culture, there would probably be no discernible change in beliefs about, or attitudes towards women, unless many of its spiritual cognates were eliminated simultaneously. Conversely, if all aspects of the tradition of treating women as less than persons *except* pornography were eliminated, pornography would become more or less innocuous, would be difficult to take seriously. In other words, I am inclined to be quite conservative in estimating the degree of potential pornography has, in and of itself, to actually plant the seeds of derogatory beliefs about, and subsequent violent behavior toward, womankind. Pornography only contributes to the nurture of the plant.

Again, the point is *not* that Victim Pornography has negative consequences for women. The point is that Victim Pornography contains implications that defame womankind. The perspective on women offered by Victim Pornography is not only derogatory, it is false. Most women are *not* mindless, masochistic nymphomaniacs. Most women do not enjoy being beaten and raped. Most women do not want, or expect, to be treated as less than persons by their sexual partners. (This may seem so obvious that it should not have to be said. Indeed, it should not have to be said. However, a look at what goes on at rape trials will show that it is not, unfortunately, obvious.)

Nevertheless, the pornography industry routinely publishes material that supports this view of womankind. The pornography industry does not care that this view is false. This is what sells, to the tune of $7 billion a year. In short, the pornography industry is quite willing to defame womankind for the sake of making a profit.

In so doing, the pornography industry degrades womankind. It treats the class of women as nothing more than a means to its own financial ends. It treats the class of women as though such a smearing of its reputation is unimportant, trivial. In other words, pornography degrades women because it treats them as members of a class which has no honor and is not entitled to respect. The pornography industry treats women as though the truth about their nature may be ignored or distorted with impunity. The point is not that pornography may incite men to rape women. The point is that the pornography industry blithely perpetuates derogatory myths, blithely lies, about the nature of women, for its own financial gain.

In publishing Victim Pornography, the pornography industry treats women, as a class, as less than persons. In my view, this is sufficient to support the claim that Victim Pornography is morally objectionable.

A word about the legal implications of this analysis:

The anti-pornography ordinances proposed in Indianapolis and Minneapolis suggest that the sale of pornography be viewed as a violation of women's civil rights. I think this is more promising than the old approach of objecting to pornography on grounds of obscenity. The champions of free speech characterize all obscenity laws as attempts to curtail the free exchange of ideas simply because the most sensitive members of society are offended by them. However absurd it may be to characterize Victim Pornography as an exchange of ideas, the civil libertarians do not seem likely to relinquish this position any time soon. The approach taken by MacKinnon and Dworkin has the advantage of not lending itself to this interpretation. Even a cursory reading of their defense will show that they are not bluestockings imposing their personal subjective standards of decency on the rest of society.

Furthermore, treating pornography as a violation of civil rights rather than as an affront to people who are offended by obscenity, entails that it cannot be dealt with, as Joel Feinberg (1980, 89) suggests, by noting that people do not have to read what offends them. In other words, if pornography were objectionable simply in the sense that it offends some people, it might be appropriate to conclude that censorship is not warranted. As Feinberg argues, if the material that offends one is easily avoided, as obscene books and movies are, the fact that they are offensive to some does not constitute reason to censor them. However, if pornography is not simply obscene, but a violation of civil rights, the suggestion that people who find it objectionable should simply avoid it, is hardly appropriate. Violations of civil rights are not corrected by ignoring them.

The MacKinnon/Dworkin appeal to the civil rights of women rests on equal rights statutes. Their hypothesis is that pornography is a discriminatory practice based on sex because its effect is to deny women equal opportunities in society. This approach has the disadvantage of having to appeal to highly controversial studies concerning the consequences of pornography: its success depends on the plausibility of the claim that when pornography is offered for sale, the result is a significant negative influence on people's beliefs about women, and a subsequent negative influence on people's behavior towards women. To date, this claim has been treated by the courts as not providing sufficient reason to curtail first amendment rights. Whatever negative consequences the sale of pornography might have—and these are minimized—they are not thought to be serious enough to warrant censorship.

My analysis of Victim Pornography as degrading suggests a different unpacking of the MacKinnon/Dworkin hypothesis that pornography violates the civil rights of women. On my account, Victim Pornography *libels* women as a class, in impugning the nature of women. This approach would not have to rely on controversial empirical studies concerning the consequences of pornography. Libel can be established without demonstrating actual damage to the plaintiff. Libel laws originated in a time when a person's honor and reputation were valued for their own sake, and not simply because of their business value. Therefore, in proving libel, it is enough to show that a defamatory statement about the plaintiff is false.

Furthermore, this approach does not constitute a new challenge to free speech. Libel has *never* been protected by the First Amendment, and it is unlikely that even the most liberal of civil libertarians would be tempted to argue that it should be.

Would a case against Victim Pornography as libel stand up in court? . . .

The major difficulty I foresee in establishing that pornography libels women as a class is the problem of establishing that Victim Pornography does indeed imply that women are generally masochistic nymphomaniacs. The pornography industry will insist that it is dealing in fiction, that the material it sells depicting the degradation of women has nothing to do with reality; that its object is to entertain, not to inform.

It is beyond the scope of this paper to construct the legal case against pornography. I will only repeat that the fact that films or reading material are presented as fiction does not entail that they are supposed to be, expected to be, devoid of truth. Furthermore, it is not necessary to prove intent to injure in establishing libel; the fact that the producers of Victim Pornography do not intend to influence anyone's beliefs about the nature of women as a class (if it is a fact), is irrelevant. If the content of Victim Pornography carries the implication that, in general, women are masochistic, nymphomaniac, and not fully persons in the moral sense, the case for libel stands.

To conclude: The pornography industry makes a large share of its profit by selling material that displays a total lack of regard for the truth about womankind on the part of the industry. Pornographic material that depicts all or most women characters as masochists or nymphomaniacs or as mindless demipersons, carries with it the implication that this is the nature of womankind, and therefore of all individual women. *Whether or not* anyone believes that this is true of women, or acts accordingly, as a result of reading pornographic books or watching pornographic films, the implication itself is defamatory. In marketing such material, the pornography industry treats all women as nothing more than means to its own financial gain. This is not a matter of the pornography industry excusably treating women only as means in the course of a very limited business relationship (in the way in which an employer might excusably treat an employee only as a means).

The propagation of false and derogatory statements about a class of people, for the sake of profit, inexcusably treats all members of that class as though they were means only, as though they were not ends in themselves.

NOTES

1. I should acknowledge that men as well as women can be, and sometimes are, portrayed in pornographic material as being degraded. Nevertheless, we would do well to keep in mind a few significant differences between pornography that portrays men as degraded, and pornography that portrays women as degraded: (1) Material in which men are the victims of sexually aggressive women is the exception rather than the rule; (2) Very little else in the culture reinforces the idea of men being degraded by women; and (3) The victimized men and aggressive women in such material are usually depicted as homosexual, and therefore not "really" men and not "really" women, respectively, by the standards of the material itself; thus, it is still quasi-women who are victimized and pseudo-men who are victimizers.

2. I am not suggesting, of course, that women who participate in making Victim Pornography are *less degraded than other women by the sale of pornography,* but only that they are not necessarily degraded in their role as models.

3. A word about the importance of context. If we lived in a culture in which nothing supported the idea that women are less than full persons, I might be more reluctant to say that Victim Pornography has implications concerning the nature of womankind. If nothing in the culture supported the idea that women may be treated as though they were not ends in themselves, I might be willing to say that Victim Pornography is pure fantasy, no more to be taken seriously—no more to be generalized from—than a cartoon that portrays cats as indiscriminate eaters, or an advertisement that portrays auto mechanics as good natured and helpful, or a story that portrays men as enjoying abuse. But the fact is that there are many facets of our culture that tend to support the view that women like to be abused. Much of popular music romanticizes such relationships; advertisements tacitly give them a stamp of approval by describing abuse as the norm for the attractive upper-middle class family next door, or by giving it a slightly exotic flavor; some religious dogma openly prescribes treating women as less than persons. In light of this tradition, Victim Pornography can*not* be easily dismissed as mere fantasy, with no implications concerning the nature of women. Victim Pornography contributes to the tradition of viewing women as less than full persons, whatever the intention of its authors.

REFERENCES

Berger, Fred. "Pornography, Sex, and Censorship." *Social Theory and Practice* 4 (1977): 183–210.

Dworkin, Andrea. *Pornography: Men Possessing Women.* New York: Perigee Books, 1981.

Feinberg, Joel. "Harmless Immoralities and Offensive Nuisances." *In Rights, Justice and the Bounds of Liberty.* Princeton: Princeton University Press, 1980.

Goldman, Emma. *Living My Life.* New York: Knopf, 1983.

Hentoff, Nat. "War on Pornography." *The Washington Post* (31 August 1984): A21.

Shipp, E. R. "Federal Judge Hears Arguments on Validity of Indianapolis Pornography Measure." *New York Times* (31 July 1984): A10.

Styron, William. *Sophie's Choice.* New York: Random House, 1979.

READING QUESTIONS

1. What are the two types of degradation according to Hill? Explain the cases she uses to illustrate the concept of degradation.
2. What is the role of perception in degradation? How does public perception differ from private perception?
3. What kind of pornography degrades women according to Hill? Note the three conditions she mentions.
4. What is victim pornography? How does Hill argue that the pornography industry degrades women as a class?
5. What are the legal implications of pornography that is degrading to women and what is Hill's new analysis of the problem?

DISCUSSION QUESTIONS

1. What reasons might we have for thinking that pornography is not degrading to women in the way Hill describes? Are there any reasons other than the ones she considers for thinking that it is degrading to both men and women?

2. Suppose that victim pornography is a form of libel as Hill suggests. Who should go about bringing that particular charge against the pornography industry? Consider in particular whether the responsibility lies with any person or if it is the responsibility of the women who are degraded.

CHARLES R. LAWRENCE III

Racist Speech as the Functional Equivalent of Fighting Words

According to the 1990 Stanford University policy on free expression and discriminatory harassment, all Stanford students have a "right to equal access to a Stanford education without discrimination on the basis of sex, race, color, handicap, religion, sexual orientation or national and ethnic origin." The policy goes on to prohibit hate speech on campus because it interferes with this right of students. Lawrence defends the Stanford policy by arguing that hate speech used in face-to-face insults falls within the "fighting words" exception to First Amendment protection. In particular, he argues that because face-to-face hate speech is like receiving a slap in the face, its harm to the victim is "clear and present" and so is not protected by the First Amendment. He also argues that because racial insults are intended to injure the victim rather than discover truth or initiate discussion, such speech is at odds with the fundamental purpose of the First Amendment.

Recommended Reading: consequentialism, chap. 1, sec. 2A.

Much recent debate over the efficacy of regulating racist speech has focused on the efforts by colleges and universities to respond to the burgeoning incidents of racial harassment on their campuses. At Stanford, where I teach, there has been considerable controversy over whether racist and other discriminatory verbal harassment should be regulated and what form any regulation should take. Proponents of

From Charles R. Lawrence III, "If He Hollers Let Him Go: Regulating Hate Speech on Campus," *Duke Law Journal* 1990. Reprinted by permission of the author.

regulation have been sensitive to the danger of inhibiting expression, and the current regulation (which was drafted by my colleague Tom Grey) manifests that sensitivity. It is drafted somewhat more narrowly than I would have preferred, leaving unregulated hate speech that occurs in settings where there is a captive audience, but I largely agree with this regulation's substance and approach. I include it here as one example of a regulation of racist speech that I would argue violates neither First Amendment precedent nor principle. The regulation reads as follows:

Fundamental Standard Interpretation: Free Expression and Discriminatory Harassment

1. Stanford is committed to the principles of free inquiry and free expression. Students have the right to hold and vigorously defend and promote their opinions, thus entering them into the life of the University, there to flourish or wither according to their merits. Respect for this right requires that students tolerate even expression of opinions that they find abhorrent. Intimidation of students by other students in their exercise of this right, by violence or threat of violence, is therefore considered . . . a violation of the Fundamental Standard.

2. Stanford is also committed to principles of equal opportunity and nondiscrimination. Each student has the right to equal access to a Stanford education, without discrimination on the basis of sex, race, color, handicap, religion, sexual orientation, or national and ethnic origin. Harassment of students on the basis of any of these characteristics tends to create a hostile environment that makes access to education for those subjected to it less than equal. Such discriminatory harassment is therefore considered to be a violation of the Fundamental Standard.

3. This interpretation of the Fundamental Standard is intended to clarify the point at which protected free expression ends and prohibited discriminatory harassment begins. Prohibited harassment includes discriminatory intimidation by threats of violence, and also includes personal vilification of students on the basis of

their sex, race, color, handicap, religion, sexual orientation, or national and ethnic origin.

4. Speech or other expression constitutes harassment by vilification if it:

   a. is intended to insult or stigmatize an individual or a small number of individuals on the basis of their sex, race, color, handicap, religion, sexual orientation, or national and ethnic origin; and

   b. is addressed directly to the individual or individuals whom it insults or stigmatizes; and

   c. makes use of "fighting" words or nonverbal symbols.

In the context of discriminatory harassment, "fighting" words or nonverbal symbols are words, pictures, or symbols that, by virtue of their form, are commonly understood to convey direct and visceral hatred or contempt for human beings on the basis of their sex, race, color, handicap, religion, sexual orientation, and national and ethnic origin.[1]

This regulation and others like it have been characterized in the press as the work of "thought police," but the rule does nothing more than prohibit intentional face-to-face insults, a form of speech that is unprotected by the First Amendment. When racist speech takes the form of face-to-face insults, catcalls, or other assaultive speech aimed at an individual or a small group of persons, then it falls within the "fighting words" exception to First Amendment protection. The Supreme Court has held that words that "by their very utterance inflict injury or tend to incite an immediate breach of the peace"[2] are not constitutionally protected.

Face-to-face racial insults, like fighting words, are undeserving of First Amendment protection for two reasons. The first reason is the immediacy of the injurious impact of racial insults. The experience of being called "nigger," "spic," "Jap," or "kike" is like receiving a slap in the face. The injury is instantaneous. There is neither an opportunity for intermediary reflection on the idea conveyed nor an opportunity for responsive speech. The harm to be avoided is both clear and present. The second reason that racial insults should not fall under protected speech relates to the purpose underlying the First Amendment. The purpose of the First Amendment is to foster the greatest amount of speech. Racial insults disserve that purpose. Assaultive racist speech functions as a preemptive strike. The racial invective is experienced as a blow, not a proffered idea, and once the blow is struck, it is unlikely that dialogue will follow. Racial insults are undeserving of First Amendment protection because the perpetrator's intention is not to discover truth or initiate dialogue, but to injure the victim.

The fighting words doctrine anticipates that the verbal slap in the face of insulting words will provoke a violent response, resulting in a breach of the peace. When racial insults are hurled at minorities, the response may be silence or flight rather than a fight, but the preemptive effect on further speech is the same. Women and minorities often report that they find themselves speechless in the face of discriminatory verbal attacks. This inability to respond is not the result of oversensitivity among these groups, as some individuals who oppose protective regulation have argued. Rather it is the product of several factors, all of which evidence the nonspeech character of the initial preemptive verbal assault. The first factor is that the visceral emotional response to personal attack precludes speech. Attack produces an instinctive, defensive psychological reaction. Fear, rage, shock, and flight all interfere with any reasoned response. Words like "nigger," "kike," and "faggot" produce physical symptoms that temporarily disable the victim, and the perpetrators often use these words with the intention of producing this effect. Many victims do not find words of response until well after the assault, when the cowardly assaulter has departed.

A second factor that distinguishes racial insults from protected speech is the preemptive nature of such insults—words of response to such verbal attacks may never be forthcoming because speech is usually an inadequate response. When one is personally attacked with words that denote one's subhuman status and untouchability, there is little, if anything, that can be said to redress either the emotional or reputational injury. This is particularly true when the message and meaning of the epithet resonates with

beliefs widely held in society. This preservation of widespread beliefs is what makes the face-to-face racial attack more likely to preempt speech than other fighting words do. The racist name caller is accompanied by a cultural chorus of equally demeaning speech and symbols. Segregation and other forms of racist speech injure victims because of their dehumanizing and excluding message. Each individual message gains its power because of the cumulative and reinforcing effect of countless similar messages that are conveyed in a society where racism is ubiquitous.

The subordinated victims of fighting words also are silenced by their relatively powerless position in society. Because of the significance of power and position, the categorization of racial epithets as fighting words provides an inadequate paradigm; instead one must speak of their functional equivalent. The fighting words doctrine presupposes an encounter between two persons of relatively equal power who have been acculturated to respond to face-to-face insults with violence: The fighting words doctrine is a paradigm based on a white male point of view. It captures the "macho" quality of male discourse. It is accepted, justifiable, and even praiseworthy when "real men" respond to personal insult with violence. (Presidential candidate George Bush effectively emulated the most macho—and not coincidentally most violent—of movie stars, Clint Eastwood, when he repeatedly used the phrase, "Read my lips!" Any teenage boy will tell you the subtext of this message: "I've got nothing else to say about this and if you don't like what I'm saying we can step outside.") The fighting words doctrine's responsiveness to this male stance in the world and its blindness to the cultural experience of women is another example of how neutral principles of law reflect the values of those who are dominant.

Black men also are well aware of the double standard that our culture applies in responding to insult. Part of the culture of racial domination through violence—a culture of dominance manifested historically in thousands of lynchings in the South and more recently in the racial violence at Howard Beach and Bensonhurst—is the paradoxical expectation on the part of whites that Black males will accept insult from whites without protest, yet will become violent without provocation. These expectations combine two assumptions: First, that Blacks as a group—and especially Black men—are more violent; and second, that as inferior persons, Blacks have no right to feel insulted. One can imagine the response of universities if Black men started to respond to racist fighting words by beating up white students.

In most situations, minorities correctly perceive that a violent response to fighting words will result in a risk to their own life and limb. This risk forces targets to remain silent and submissive. This response is most obvious when women submit to sexually assaultive speech or when the racist name caller is in a more powerful position—the boss on the job or a member of a violent racist group. . . .

One of my students, a white gay male, related an experience that is quite instructive in understanding the fighting words doctrine. In response to my request that students describe how they experienced the injury of racist speech, Michael told a story of being called "faggot" by a man on a subway. His description included all of the speech-inhibiting elements I have noted. . . . He found himself in a state of semishock, nauseous, dizzy, unable to muster the witty, sarcastic, articulate rejoinder he was accustomed to making. He was instantly aware of the recent spate of gay bashing in San Francisco and that many of these incidents had escalated from verbal encounters. Even hours later when the shock subsided and his facility with words returned, he realized that any response was inadequate to counter the hundreds of years of societal defamation that one word—*faggot*—carried with it. Like the word *nigger* and unlike the word *liar,* it is not sufficient to deny the truth of the word's application, to say, "I am not a faggot." One must deny the truth of the word's meaning, a meaning shouted from the rooftops by the rest of the world a million times a day. The complex response "Yes, I am a member of the group you despise and [I reject] the degraded meaning of the word you use . . ." is not effective in a subway encounter. Although many of us constantly and in myriad ways seek to counter the lie spoken in the meaning of hateful words like *nigger* and *faggot,* it is a nearly impossible burden to bear when one

is ambushed by a sudden, face-to-face hate speech assault.

But there was another part of my discussion with Michael that is equally instructive. I asked if he could remember a situation when he had been verbally attacked with reference to his being a white male. Had he ever been called a "honkey," a "chauvinist pig," or "mick"? (Michael is from a working-class Irish family in Boston.) He said that he had been called some version of all three and that although he found the last one more offensive than the first two, he had not experienced—even in that subordinated role—the same disorienting powerlessness he had experienced when attacked for his membership in the gay community. The question of power, of the context of the power relationships within which speech takes place, and the connection to violence must be considered as we decide how best to foster the freest and fullest dialogue within our communities. Regulation of face-to-face verbal assault in the manner contemplated by the proposed Stanford provision will make room for more speech than it chills. The provision is clearly within the spirit, if not the letter, of existing First Amendment doctrine. . . .

NOTES

1. Interpretation of the Fundamental Standard defining when verbal or nonverbal abuse violates the student conduct code adopted by the Stanford University Student Conduct Legislative Council, March 14, 1990. "SCLC Offers Revised Reading of Standard," *Stanford Daily,* Apr. 4, 1990, §1, col. 4.

It is important to recognize that this regulation is not content-neutral. It prohibits "discriminatory harassment" rather than just plain harassment, and it regulates only discriminatory harassment based on "sex, race, color, handicap, religion, sexual orientation, and national and ethnic origin." It is arguably viewpoint neutral with respect to these categories, although its reference to "words . . . that, by virtue of their form, are commonly understood to convey direct and visceral hatred or contempt" probably means that there will be many more epithets that refer to subordinated groups than words that refer to superordinate groups covered by the regulation.

2. *Chaplinsky v. New Hampshire,* 315 U.S 568, 572 (1942).

READING QUESTIONS

1. Explain the three criteria for speech that constitutes harassment by vilification according to the Standard Interpretation adopted by Stanford University.
2. What two reasons does Lawrence give for why the sort of speech prohibited by the Standard Interpretation is undeserving of protection?
3. Why are people speechless in the face of certain insults according to Lawrence?

DISCUSSION QUESTIONS

1. Is Lawrence right to claim that there is really no response to discriminatory insults other than violence? Try to come up with possible verbal responses that could be made by the victims of such insults.
2. Should we agree with Lawrence and Stanford University that the sort of speech at issue makes use of "fighting" words? Does such language necessarily incite an immediate breach of peace?

JOHN ARTHUR

Sticks and Stones

Arthur first explains the basis for protecting freedom of speech and then, after reviewing the interpretation of the First Amendment by the U.S. Supreme Court, explains why the Court has been rightly reluctant to treat hate speech as unprotected. In defending hate speech as a protected form of speech, Arthur distinguishes between wrongs and harms. You are wronged but not harmed if someone breaks into your car, takes nothing, and does no damage. He then argues that hate speech, despite wronging its victims, has not been shown (at least by itself) to cause various sorts of harms, including harm to one's self-esteem and physical harm. (Arthur finds the same methodological problems with attempts to link hate speech to harm as are found in attempts to link pornography to harm.) But even supposing that there is a causal link between hate speech and harm, Arthur argues that on balance there is compelling reason for such speech to receive First Amendment protection. He reaches a similar conclusion regarding pro-censorship arguments that appeal to the offense principle.

Recommended Reading: consequentialism, chap. 1, sec. 2A.

From John Arthur, "Sticks and Stones," in *Ethics in Practice: An Anthology,* H. LaFollette, ed., Blackwell, 1997. Reprinted by permission of the author.

Proponents of limiting hate speech on college campuses and elsewhere have generally taken one of two approaches. One is to pass a "speech code" that identifies which words or ideas are banned, the punishment that may be imposed, and (as at the University of Michigan) an interpretive "Guide" meant to explain how the rules will be applied. The other approach has been to treat hate speech as a form of harassment. Here the censorship is justified on anti-discrimination grounds: hate speech, it is argued, subjects its victims to a "hostile" work environment, which courts have held constitutes job discrimination (*Meritor Savings Bank v. Vinson,* 1986).

. . . Rather than censoring all expressions of hatred, advocates of banning hate speech use the term narrowly, to refer to speech directed at people *in virtue of their membership in a (usually historically disadvantaged) racial, religious, ethnic, sexual or other group.*

Such a conception can be criticized, of course, on the ground that it arbitrarily narrows the field to one form of hate speech. Perhaps, however, there is reason to focus on a limited problem: if it turns out, for example, that hate speech directed against such groups is especially harmful, then it may seem reasonable to have created this special usage of the term. In this paper I consider some of the important issues surrounding hate speech and its regulation: the political and legal importance of free speech; the types of harm that might be attributed to it; and whether, even if no harm results, causing emotional distress and offense is by itself sufficient to warrant censorship.

WHY PROTECT FREEDOM OF SPEECH?

Respecting freedom of speech is important for a variety of reasons. First, as J. S. Mill argued long ago, free and unfettered debate is vital for the pursuit of truth. If knowledge is to grow, people must be free to put forth ideas and theories they deem worthy of consideration, and others must be left equally free to criticize them. Even false ideas should be protected, Mill argued, so that the truth will not become mere dogma, unchallenged and little understood. "However true [an opinion] may be," he wrote, "if it is not fully, frequently, and fearlessly discussed, it will be held as a dead dogma, not a living truth" (Mill, 1978, p. 34). . . .

Free speech is also an essential feature of democratic, efficient and just government. Fair, democratic elections cannot occur unless candidates are free to debate and criticize each other's policies, nor can government be run efficiently unless corruption and other abuses can be exposed by a free press. . . .

A third value, individual autonomy, is also served by free speech. In chapter III of *On Liberty,* "Of Individuality, as One of the Elements of Well Being," Mill writes that "He who lets the world, or his own portion of it, choose his plan of life for him, has no need of any other faculty than the ape-like one of imitation. . . . Among the works of man, which human life is rightly employed in perfecting and beautifying, the first in importance surely is man himself" (Mill, 1978, p. 56). Mill's suggestion is that the best life does not result from being forced to live a certain way, but instead is freely chosen without coercion from outside. But if Mill is right, then freedom of speech as well as action are important to achieve a worthwhile life. Free and open discussion helps people exercise their capacities of reasoning and judgment, capacities that are essential for autonomous and informed choices.

Besides these important social advantages of respecting free speech, . . . freedom of expression is important for its own sake, because it is a basic human right. Not only does free speech *promote* autonomy, as Mill argued, but it is also a *reflection* of individual autonomy and of human equality. Censorship denigrates our status as equal, autonomous persons by saying, in effect, that some people simply cannot be trusted to make up their own minds about what is right or true. Because of the ideas they hold or the subjects they find interesting, they need not be treated with the same respect as other citizens with whom they disagree; only we, not they, are free to believe as we wish. . . .

Because it serves important social goals, and also must be respected in the name of equal citizenship, the right to speak and write freely is perhaps the most important of all rights. But beyond that, two further points also need to be stressed. Free speech is fragile, in two respects. The first is the chilling effect that censorship poses. Language banning hate speech will inevitably be vague and indeterminate, at least to some extent: words like "hate" and "denigrate" and "victimize," which often occur in such rules, are not self-defining. When such bans bring strict penalties, as they sometimes do, they risk sweeping too broadly, capturing valuable speech in their net along with the speech they seek to prohibit. Criminal or civil penalties therefore pose a threat to speech generally, and the values underlying it, as people consider the potential risks of expressing their opinions while threatened by legal sanctions. Censorship risks having a chilling effect.

The second danger of censorship, often referred to as the "slippery slope," begins with the historical observation that unpopular minorities and controversial ideas are always vulnerable to political repression, whether by authoritarian regimes hoping to remain in power, or elected officials desiring to secure reelection by attacking unpopular groups or silencing political opponents. For that reason, it is important to create a high wall of constitutional protection securing the right to speak against attempts to limit it. Without strong, politically resistant constraints on governmental efforts to restrict speech, there is constant risk—demonstrated by historical experience—that what begins as a minor breach in the wall can be turned by governmental officials and intolerant majorities into a large, destructive exception. . . .

FREE SPEECH AND THE CONSTITUTION

The Supreme Court has not always interpreted the First Amendment's free speech and press clauses in a manner consistent with speech's importance. Early in the twentieth century people were often jailed, and their convictions upheld, for expressing unpopular political views, including distributing pamphlets critical of American military intervention in the Russian revolution (*Abrams* v. *United States,* 1919). Then, in the McCarthy era of the 1950s, government prosecuted over a hundred people for what was in effect either teaching Marxism or belonging to the Communist Party (*Dennis* v. *United States,* 1951). Beginning in the 1960s, however, the US Supreme Court changed direction, interpreting the Constitution's command that government not restrict freedom of speech as imposing strict limits on governmental power to censor speech and punish speakers.

Pursuing this goal, the [Court] first defined "speech" broadly, to include not just words but other forms of expression as well. Free speech protection now extends to people who wear arm bands, burn the flag, and peaceably march. The Court has also made a critically important distinction, between governmental regulations aimed at the *content* or *ideas* a person wishes to convey and content-neutral restrictions on the *time, place, and manner* in which the speech occurs. Thus, government is given fairly wide latitude to curtail speakers who use bull-horns at night, spray-paint their ideas on public buildings, or invade private property in order to get their messages across. But when governmental censors object not to how or where the speech occurs, but instead to the content itself, the Constitution is far more restrictive. Here, the Supreme Court has held, we are at the very heart of the First Amendment and the values it protects. Indeed, said the Court, there is "no such thing as a false idea" under the US Constitution (*Gertz* v. *Robert Welch, Inc.,* 1974).

Wary of the chilling effect and the slippery slope, the Supreme Court has therefore held that government cannot regulate the content of speech unless it falls within certain narrowly defined categories. These constitutionally "unprotected categories" include libel (but criticisms of public officials must not only be false but uttered "maliciously" to be libelous), incitement to lawlessness (if the incitement is "immanent," such as yelling "Let's kill the capitalist!" in front of an angry mob), obscenity (assuming that the speech also lacks substantial social value), and "fighting words" (like "fascist pig" that are uttered in a face-to-face context likely to injure or provoke immediate, hostile reaction). In that way, each of these unprotected categories is precisely defined so as not to endanger free expression in general. . . .

Applying these principles, the Supreme Court held in 1989 that a "flag desecration is constitutionally protected" (*Texas* v. *Johnson,* 1989). Texas's statute had defined "desecration" in terms of the tendency to "offend" someone who was likely to know of the act. But, said the Court in striking down the statute, not only does flag burning involve ideas, the statute is not viewpoint neutral. Because it singled out one side of a debate—those who are critical of government—the law must serve an especially clear and important purpose. Mere "offense," the justices concluded, was insufficiently important to warrant intrusion into free expression.

In light of this constitutional history, it is not surprising that attempts to ban hate speech have fared poorly in American courts. Responding to various acts of racist speech on its campus, the University of Michigan passed one of the most far-reaching speech codes ever attempted at an American university; it prohibited "stigmatizing or victimizing" either individuals or groups on the basis of "race, ethnicity, religion, sex, sexual orientation, creed, national origin, ancestry, age, marital status, handicap or Vietnam-era veteran status." According to a "Guide" published by the University to help explain the code's meaning, conduct that violates the code would include a male student who "makes remarks in class like 'Women just aren't as good in this field as men,' thus creating a hostile learning atmosphere for female classmates." Also punishable under the code were "derogatory" comments about a person's or group's "physical appearance or sexual orientation, or their cultural origins, or religious beliefs" (*Doe* v. *University of Michigan,* 1989, pp. 857–8). To almost nobody's surprise, the Michigan Code was rejected as unconstitutional, on grounds that it violated rights both to free speech and to due process of law. The case was brought by a psychology instructor who feared that his course in developmental psychology, which discussed biological differences between males and females, might be taken by some to be "stigmatizing and victimizing." The Court agreed with the professor, holding that the Michigan code was both "overbroad" and "unconstitutionally vague." A second code at the University of Wisconsin soon met a similar fate, even though it banned only slurs and epithets (*UMV Post* v. *Board of Regents of the University of Wisconsin,* 1991).

Confirming these lower court decisions, the Supreme Court in 1992 ruled unconstitutional a city ordinance making it a misdemeanor to place on public or private property any "symbol, object, appellation, characterization or graffiti" that the person knows or has reasonable grounds for knowing will arouse "anger, alarm or resentment" on the basis of race, color, creed, religion or gender (*R.A.V.* v. *City of St. Paul,* 1992, p. 2541). In overturning a juvenile's conviction for placing a burning cross on a black family's lawn, the majority held that even if the statute were understood very narrowly, to limit only "fighting words," it was nonetheless unconstitutional because it punished only some fighting words and not others. In so doing, argued one justice, the law violated the important principle of content neutrality: it censored some uses of fighting words, namely those focusing on race, color, creed, religion or gender, but not others. It prescribed political orthodoxy. Other justices emphasized that no serious harm had been identified that could warrant restrictions on speech. The law, wrote Justice White, criminalizes conduct that "causes only hurt feelings, offense, or resentment, and is protected by the First Amendment" (*R.A.V.* v. *City of St. Paul,* 1992, p. 2559).

Perhaps, however, the Court has gone too far in protecting hate speech. Advocates of banning hate speech commonly claim it harms its victims. "There is a great difference," writes Charles Lawrence, "between the offensiveness of words that you would rather not hear because they are labelled dirty, impolite, or personally demeaning and the injury [of hate speech]" (Lawrence, 1990, p. 74). Elsewhere he describes hate speech as "aimed at an entire group with the effect of causing significant *harm* to individual group members" (Lawrence, 1990, p. 57, emphasis added). Richard Delgado similarly claims that it would be rare for a white who is called a "dumb honkey" to be in a position to claim legal redress since, unlike a member of an historically oppressed group, it would be unlikely that a white person would "suffer *harm* from such an insult" (Delgado, 1982, p. 110, emphasis added).

But are these writers correct that various forms of hate speech cross the boundary from the distressing and offensive to the genuinely harmful?

HARM AND OFFENSE

To claim that someone has been harmed is different from claiming she has been wronged. I can break into your house undetected, do no damage, and leave. While I have wronged you, I might not have harmed you, especially if you didn't know about it and I didn't take anything.

What then must be the case for wronging somebody to also constitute a harm? First, to be harmed is not merely to experience a minor irritation or hurt, nor is it simply to undergo an unwanted experience. Though unwanted, the screech of chalk on the blackboard, an unpleasant smell, a pinch or slap, a brief but frightening experience, and a revolting sight are not harms. Harms are significant events. Following Joel Feinberg, I will assume that harms occur not when we are merely hurt or offended, but when our "interests" are frustrated, defeated or set back (Feinberg, 1984, pp. 31–51). By interests he means something in which we have a stake—just as we may have a "stake" in a company. So while many of our interests are obviously tied to our wants and desires, a mere want does not constitute an interest. A minor disappointment is not a frustration of interests in the relevant sense. Feinberg thus emphasizes the "directional" nature of interests that are "set back" when one is harmed, pointing out that the interests are "ongoing concerns" rather than temporary wants. Genuine harms thus impede or thwart people's future objectives or options, which explains why the unpleasant memory or smell and the bite's itch are not harms while loss of a limb, of freedom, and of health are. Harms can therefore come from virtually any source: falling trees, disease,

economic or romantic competitors, and muggers are only a few examples. . . .

We now turn to the question of whether hate speech causes harm. In discussing this, we will consider various types of harm that might result, as well as making important distinctions . . . between cumulative and individual harm and between direct and indirect harm.

CUMULATIVE VERSUS INDIVIDUAL HARM

. . . [W]e must first distinguish between harms flowing from *individual* actions and *cumulative* harms. Often what is a singly harmless act can be damaging when added to other similar acts. One person walking across a lawn does little damage, but constant walking will destroy the lawn. Indeed the single act might be entirely without negative effect. Pollution, for instance, is often harmful only cumulatively, not singly. Though one car battery's lead may do no harm to those who drink the water downstream, when added to the pollution of many others the cumulative harm can be disastrous.

Further, the fact that it was singly harmless is no justification for performing the act. The complete response to a person who insists that he had a right to pollute since his action did no damage is that if everyone behaved that way great harm would follow: once a legal scheme protecting the environment is in place, criminal law is rightly invoked even against individually harmless acts on grounds of cumulative harm.

It might then be argued that even if individual hate speech acts do not cause harm, it should still be banned because of its cumulatively harmful effects. What might that harm consist in? Defending hate speech codes, Mari J. Matsuda writes that "As much as one may try to resist a piece of hate propaganda, the effect on one's self-esteem and sense of personal security is devastating. To be hated, despised, and alone is the ultimate fear of all human beings.. . . [R]acial inferiority is planted in our minds as an idea that may hold some truth" (Matsuda, 1989, p. 25). Besides the distress caused by the hate speech, Matsuda is suggesting, hate speech victims may also be harmed in either of two ways: reduced self-esteem or increased risk of violence and discrimination. I will begin with self-esteem, turning to questions of violence and discrimination in the next section.

CUMULATIVE HARM TO SELF-ESTEEM

What then is self-esteem? Following Rawls, let us assume that by "self-esteem" or "self-respect" we mean the sense both that one's goals and life-plan are worthwhile and that one has talents and other characteristics sufficient to make their accomplishment possible (Rawls, 1971, pp. 440–6). Loss of self-esteem might therefore constitute harm because it reduces motivation and willingness to put forth effort. If hate-speech victims believe they have little or no chance of success, their future options will be reduced. . . .

Assuming loss of self-esteem is a harm, how plausible is Matsuda's suggestion that hate speech has the (cumulative) effect of reducing it? Many factors can reduce self-esteem. Demeaning portrayals of one's group in the media, widespread anti-social behavior of others in the group, family break-down, poor performance in school and on the job, drugs, and even well intended affirmative-action programs all may lessen self-esteem. Indeed, I suggest that, absent those other factors, simply being subject to hate speech would not significantly reduce self-esteem. An otherwise secure and confident person might be made angry (or fearful) by racial or other attacks, feeling the speaker is ignorant, rude, or stupid. But without many other factors it is hard to see that hate speech by itself would have much impact on self-esteem. . . .

But even assuming hate speech does reduce self-esteem to some degree, notice how far the argument has strayed from the original, robust claim that hate speech should be banned because it causes harm. First each individual act must be added to other acts of hate speech, but then it must also be added to the many other, more important factors that together reduce self-esteem. Given the importance of protecting speech I discussed earlier, and the presumption it creates against censorship, Matsuda's argument that it reduces self-esteem seems far too speculative and indirect to warrant criminalizing otherwise protected speech.

DISCRIMINATION AND VIOLENCE AS INDIRECT HARMS

But surely, it may be objected, the real issue is simply this: hate speech should be banned because it increases racial or other forms of hatred, which in turn leads to increased violence and discrimination—both of which are obviously harmful. That is a serious claim, and must be taken seriously. Notice first, however, that this effect of hate speech, if it exists, is only indirect; hate speech is harmful only because of its impact on others who are then led in turn to commit acts of violence or discrimination.

There are important problems with this as an argument for banning hate speech. One epistemological problem is whether we really know that the link exists between hate speech, increased hatred, and illegal acts. Suppose we discovered a close correlation between reading hate speech and committing acts of violence—what have we proved? Not, as might be thought, that hate speech causes violence. Rather, we would only know that *either* (A) reading such material increases hatred and violence, *or* (B) those who commit hate crimes also tend to like reading hate speech. The situation with respect to hate speech mirrors arguments about violence and pornography: the observation that rapists subscribe in greater proportion to pornographic magazines than do non-rapists does not show we can reduce rape by banning pornography. Maybe people who rape just tend also to like pornography. Similarly, reduction in hate speech might, or might not, reduce hate-related crime, even assuming that those who commit hate crimes are avid readers of hate literature.

. . . [W]e have on hand two different ways of dealing with acts of violence and discrimination motivated by hatred: by using government censorship in an effort at thought control, trying to eliminate hatred and prejudice, or by insisting that whether people like somebody or not they cannot assault them or discriminate against them. My suggestion is that passing and vigorously enforcing laws against violence and discrimination themselves is a better method of preventing indirect harm than curtailing speech. . . .

OFFENSIVE EXPRESSION AND EPITHETS

I have argued that hate speech should not be banned on the ground of preventing harm. But government often restricts behavior that is not strictly speaking harmful: it prevents littering, for instance, and limits how high we build our buildings, the drugs we take and the training our doctors receive, to mention only a few examples. Some of these restrictions are controversial, of course, especially ones that seem designed only to keep us from harming ourselves. But others, for example limiting alterations of historic buildings and preventing littering, are rarely disputed. Government also limits various forms of public behavior that are grossly offensive, revolting or shocking. An assault on the sense of smell and hearing, unusual or even common sexual activities in public, extreme provocations of anger, or threats that generate great anxiety or fear, are generally regarded as examples of behavior that can be restricted although they do not cause genuine harm.

Charles Lawrence suggests that this argument also applies to hate speech. The experience of being called "nigger," "spic," "Jap," or "kike," he writes, "is like receiving a slap in the face. The injury is instantaneous" (Lawrence, 1990, pp. 68–9). He describes the experience of a student who was called a "faggot" on a subway: "He found himself in a state of semi-shock, nauseous, dizzy, unable to muster the witty,

sarcastic, articulate rejoinder he was accustomed to making" (Lawrence, 1990, p. 70).

. . . [B]ecause of speech's critical importance and government's tendency to regulate and limit political discussion to suit its own ends, I have argued, it is important to limit governmental censorship to narrowly and precisely defined unprotected categories . . . Assuming that we might wish to keep this unprotected-categories approach, how might offensive hate speech be regulated? One possibility is to allow government to ban speech that "causes substantial distress and offense" to those who hear it. Were we to adopt such a principle, however, we would effectively gut the First Amendment. All kinds of political speech, including much that we would all think must be protected, is offensive to somebody somewhere. . . .

Nor would it work to limit the unprotected category to all speech that is distressing and offensive to members of historically stigmatized groups, for that too would sweep far too broadly. Speech critical of peoples, nations, and religious institutions and practices often offends group members, as do discussions of differences between the races and sexes. Social and biological scientists sometimes find themselves confronted by people who have been deeply wounded by their words, as the instructor who got in trouble at the University of Michigan over his comments about sex-linked abilities illustrates. Or what about psychologists who wish to do research into group IQ differences? Should only those who reach conclusions that are not offensive be allowed to publish?

Others, however, have suggested another, less sweeping approach: why not at least ban racial or other *epithets* since they are a unique form of "speech act" that does not deserve protection. Unlike other forms of protected speech, it is claimed that epithets and name calling are constitutionally useless; they constitute acts of "subordination" that treat others as "moral inferiors" (Altmann, 1993). Racial, religious and ethnic epithets are therefore a distinct type of speech act in which the speaker is subordinating rather than claiming, asserting, requesting, or any of the other array of actions we accomplish with language. So (it is concluded) while all the other types of speech acts deserve protection, mere epithets and slurs do not.

The problem with this argument, however, is that epithets are *not* simply acts of subordination, devoid of social and political significance or meaning, any more than burning a flag is simply an act of heating cloth. Besides "subordinating" another, epithets can also express emotion (anger or hatred, for example) or defiance of authority. And like burning or refusing to salute the flag (both protected acts), epithets also can be seen to express a political message, such as that another person or group is less worthy of moral consideration or is receiving undeserved preferences. That means, then, that however objectionable the content of such epithets is they go well beyond mere acts of "subordination" and therefore must be protected.

It is worth emphasizing, however, that although people have a political and constitutional *right* to use such language, it does not follow that they *should* use it or that they are behaving decently or morally when they exercise the right. A wrong remains a wrong, even if government may for good reason choose not to punish it. I am therefore in no way defending on moral grounds those who utter hate speech—an impossible task, in my view. . . .

But how, then, should others respond to those, on a university campus or off, who are offended and distressed when others exercise their right to speak? When children call each other names and cruelly tease each other, the standard adult response is to work on both sides of the problem. Teasers are encouraged to be more sensitive to others' feelings, and victims are encouraged to ignore the remarks. "Sticks and stones can break my bones, but names can never hurt me" was commonplace on the playground when I was a child. . . .

Like the sexual freedoms of homosexuals, freedom of speech is often the source of great distress to others. I have argued, however, that because of the risks and costs of censorship there is no alternative to accepting those costs, or more precisely to imposing the costs on those who find themselves distressed and offended by the speech. Like people who are offended by homosexuality or inter-racial couples, targets of hate speech can ask why they should have to suffer distress. The answer is the same in each case: nobody has the right to demand that government protect them against distress when doing so would violate others' rights. Many of us believe that racists would be better people and lead more worthwhile lives if they didn't harbor hatred, but that belief does not justify restricting their speech, any more than the Puritans' desire to save souls would warrant religious intolerance, or Catholics' moral disapproval of homosexuality justify banning homosexual literature.

REFERENCES

Abrams v. *United States,* 250 US 616 (1919).

Altmann, A.: "Liberalism and Campus Hate Speech," *Ethics,* 103 (1993).

Delgado, R.: "Words that Wound: A Tort Action for Racial Insults, Epithets, and Name Calling," 17, *Harvard Civil Rights—Civil Liberties Law Review,* 133 (1982); reprinted in Matsuda et al. (1993).

Dennis v. *United States,* 341 US 494 (1951).

Doe v. *University of Michigan,* 721 F. Supp. 852 (E. D. Mich. 1989).

Feinberg, J.: *The Moral Limits of the Criminal Law,* Volume I: *Harm to Others* (New York: Oxford University Press, 1984).

———:*The Moral Limits of the Criminal Law,* Volume II: *Offense to Others* (New York: Oxford University Press, 1985).

Gertz v. *Robert Welch, Inc.,* 418 US 323, 339 (1974).

Lawrence, C.: "If He Hollers Let Him Go: Regulating Racist Speech on Campus," *Duke Law Journal,* 431 (1990); reprinted in Matsuda et al. (1993).

Matsuda, M.: "Public Response to Racist Speech: Considering the Victim's Story," *Michigan Law Review,* 87 (1989); reprinted in Matsuda et al. (1993).

Matsuda, M., Lawrence, C. R., Delgado, R., and Crenshaw, K. W.: *Words that Wound: Critical Race Theory, Assaultive Speech, and the First Amendment* (Boulder, CO: Westview Press, 1993).

Meritor Savings Bank v. *Vinson,* 477 US 57 (1986).

Mill, J. S.: *On Liberty* (Indianapolis, IN: Hackett, 1978).

Rawls, J.: *A Theory of Justice* (Cambridge, MA: Harvard University Press, 1971).

Texas v. *Johnson,* 491 US 397 (1989).

UMV Post v. *Board of Regents of the University of Wisconsin,* 774 F. Supp. 1163 (1991).

READING QUESTIONS

1. How does Arthur define "hate speech"? What is the objection that he considers to this definition and how does he reply?
2. Explain the four different reasons offered by Arthur for why freedom of speech should be protected. Why does he think that freedom of speech is fragile? What are the four cases in which the government is permitted to regulate speech?
3. When is wronging someone harming them according to Arthur? How does he distinguish between cumulative and individual harm?
4. How does Arthur reply to those who advocate banning certain types of hate speech? How does he suggest we handle situations in which hate speech offends individuals?

DISCUSSION QUESTIONS

1. Discuss how the potential harmful aspects of hate speech compare to other forms of harm that individuals inflict and suffer. Should we accept Arthur's view that offensive speech is not always harmful? Why or why not?
2. Arthur suggests that overcoming the offensive nature of hate speech will require working with both the victims and the speakers. Does this suggestion offer a plausible solution to the problem? Why or why not? Consider and discuss some practical ways in which this sort of project could be carried out.

ADDITIONAL RESOURCES

Web Resources

American Civil Liberties Union, <www.aclu.org>. Organization devoted to protecting rights, among them, First Amendment rights to freedom of speech, association and assembly, press, and religion.

Feminists against Censorship (FAC), <http://www.fiawol.demon.co.uk/FAC/facfaq.htm>. Organization established in 1989 to fight censorship.

West, Caroline. "Pornography and Censorship," *The Stanford Encyclopedia of Philosophy,* 2004, Edward N. Zalta (ed.), <http://plato.stanford.edu/entries/pornography-censorship/>. An overview of the topic, including an extensive bibliography.

Authored Books

MacKinnon, Catharine, A. *Just Words* (Cambridge, MA: Harvard University Press, 1996). Feminist legal scholar, MacKinnon, advocates limiting freedom of speech to exclude hate speech and pornography based on considerations of equality.

Paul, Pamela, *Pornified How Pornography Is Damaging Our Lives, Our Relationships and Our Families* (New York: The Holt Company, 2006). As the title indicates, Paul explores the damaging effects of pornography.

Scheill, Timothy, *Campus Hate Speech on Trial* (Lawrence, KS: University Press of Kansas, 1999). An analysis of the historical, legal, and philosophical arguments regarding hate speech. The author is critical of hate speech restrictions, arguing that they are potential weapons against the groups they are designed to protect.

Edited Collections

Baird, Robert M. and Stuart E Rosenbaum (eds.), *Pornography: Public Right of Public Menace?* (Amherst, N.Y.: Promethesus Books, 1997). A collection of 25 essays (including an excerpt from the 1997 Supreme Court Case: *Reno v. American Civil Liberties Union*), divided into five sections: (1) The Communications Decency Act, (2) Feminist Perspectives, (3) Libertarian Perspectives, (4) Religious Perspectives, and (5) The Causal Issue.

Cornell, Drucilla (ed.), *Feminism and Pornography* (Oxford: Oxford University Press, 2000). A wide-ranging collection of essays organized into five parts: I, "Anti-Pornography Feminism," II, "Questioning Moralism," III, "An Historical and Cultural Analysis of Sexuality, Imperialism, and Modernity," IV, "Breaking Open the Ground of Sex and Gender," and V, "Erotic Hope, Feminine Sexuality, and the Beginnings of Sexual Freedom."

Dwyer, Susan (ed.), *The Problem of Pornography* (Belmont, CA: Wadsworth, 1995). An anthology of 14 essays by various authors divided into four parts: (1) Characterizing Pornography, (2) Rights, Equality, and Free Speech, (3) Pornography, Sexuality, and Politics, and (4) Pornography and Speech Acts. Dwyer's introductory essay, legal appendix, and bibliography are very useful.

Whillock, Rita Kirk and Slayden, David, eds., *Hate Speech* (London: Sage Press, 1995). Nine essays examine hate and intolerance in media, popular culture, and moral and political discourse.

Whisnant, Rebecca and Stark, Christine (eds.), *Not for Sale: Feminists Resisting Prostitution and Pornography* (Spinifex Press, 2005). A collection of essays exploring connections among pornography, prostitution, and such evils as racism, poverty, and militarism.

5 } Drugs, Gambling, and Addiction

In 1973, U.S. president Richard M. Nixon appointed Myles Ambrose to head up a new agency—the Drug Enforcement Administration (DEA)—which announced a war on drugs. How successful this "war" has been in its thirty-year history is a matter of dispute. According to some sources, the international trade in illegal drugs is now a thriving $400 billion a year business. The war on drugs—which most recently has focused on the production and use of methamphetamine—has brought to public attention various moral and legal questions about drug use, among them the following:

- Is it morally permissible to take drugs?
- In those cases (if any) in which taking drugs is morally wrong, what explains its wrongness?
- Is it morally acceptable for a government to pass laws that make the production and consumption of such drugs illegal?

The very same questions arise in connection with gambling, but for the time being let us focus exclusively on moral issues concerning drugs. Our questions refer simply to drugs, but there are all sorts of drugs that can be easily obtained over the counter (aspirin, cold medications, and so on), as well as drugs one can legally obtain by prescription. Moral disputes about drugs have only pertained to certain kinds of drugs. So let us begin by clarifying the sorts of drugs that are at issue.

1. DRUGS

Speaking most generally, a **drug** is any chemical substance that affects the functioning of living things (including the organisms that inhabit living things). *Medical uses* of drugs are for the purposes of prevention and treatment of disease, whereas *nonmedical uses* include uses for religious, aesthetic, political, and recreational purposes.[1] What is often called *drug use* refers to the nonmedical use of so-called **psychotropic drugs** that produce changes in mood, feeling, and perception. Psychotropic drugs (at least those that are the subject of moral and legal scrutiny) are often classified into these groups: opiates, hallucinogens, stimulants, cannabis, and depressants. Here is a short description of each of these types.

Opiates include opium, heroin, and morphine. Opium, obtained from the seed pods of the poppy plant, has as one of its main constituents morphine, from which heroin was developed. These drugs (also referred to as *narcotics*) are highly effective in reducing or eliminating pain and inducing sleep, but they are also highly addictive and strongly associated with drug abuse.

Hallucinogens are often referred to as "psychedelics" and include LSD, mescaline (the active ingredient in peyote cactus), and psilocybin and psilocin, which come from Mexican mushrooms. One effect of these drugs (for which they are sought) is their capacity to alter perception by inducing illusions and hallucinations.

Stimulants include cocaine (derived from cocoa plants), crack (a concentrated form of cocaine), caffeine, nicotine, amphetamines, methamphetamine ("meth"), and diet pills. When taken in small doses, these stimulants typically produce a sense of well-being, increased mental alertness, and physical strength, but large doses may produce increased excitement and mental confusion.

Cannabis is derived from a hemp plant (*Cannabis sativa*) and includes marijuana, hashish, and other related drugs. The effects of this drug vary in strength, depending on the preparation, and compare with those associated with hallucinogens.

Depressants include sedatives, barbiturates, and alcohol, which produce drowsiness and sedation.

In moral and legal discussions of drugs, drug abuse, and drug addiction, the term "drug" is meant to refer to the kinds of psychotropic drugs just described.[2] Because there are many types of (psychotropic) drugs, it is important to be aware of their differences, which may be important for sorting out the morality of drug use. Heroin, LSD, and cocaine differ in some ways from one another, and as a group they all differ markedly from nicotine. But like the "harder" drugs, nicotine is addictive. So, if one argues for the legal prohibition of hard drugs based on their alleged addictive powers, what about smoking? Should it be illegal too? Before getting to these questions, let us briefly consider the nature of addiction.

2. ADDICTION

Addiction is most closely associated with drug use, but the term is often used very broadly to refer to a type of compulsive behavior involving dependence on some substance or activity which, for whatever reason, is undesirable. Thus, we hear of sexual addiction and gambling addiction, as well as drug addiction. If we concentrate on drug addiction, it is common to distinguish *physical addiction* from *psychological addiction*. Addiction of both sorts involves a dependence on a drug despite its ill effects on one's health, work, activities, and general well-being. Physical addiction is indicated by physical withdrawal symptoms that occur when an individual ceases to use the drug—symptoms that include body aches, constant movement, and fitful sleeping. Psychological dependence involves a strong desire or perceived need to take the drug for its psychological effects (e.g., a sense of well-being), where withdrawal does not produce the physical effects characteristic of physical dependence. As mentioned earlier, opiates are highly physically addictive, whereas marijuana is psychologically addictive.

What is called **drug abuse** is the excessive nonmedical use of a drug that may cause harm to oneself or to others, including, for instance, abuse of alcohol by drinking too much on some one occasion. Here, we are focused on addiction. There are disputes about the nature of drug addiction. On what Daniel Shapiro calls a "standard view," addiction is caused by the pharmacological effects of the drug—the drug itself is the source of the addiction. On a nonstandard view defended by Shapiro, addiction results from the interplay of the drug, a user's personality, and social circumstances.

The dangers of drug addiction are often cited in disputes over the morality of government interference in the use of drugs for nonmedical reasons. So let us turn to questions about drugs and the law.

3. LIBERTY-LIMITING PRINCIPLES

In discussions of the morality of the legal restriction and prohibition of drugs for nonmedical uses, the same liberty-limiting principles that we discussed in the previous chapter on censorship are relevant here. Here, then, is a brief summary of the previous discussion of these principles. (For more detail, see section 2 of the introduction to pornography, hate speech, and censorship.)

A **liberty-limiting principle** purports to set forth conditions under which a government may be morally justified in passing laws that limit the liberty of its citizens. There are four such principles.

The Harm Principle

According to the **harm principle**, a government may justifiably pass laws that interfere with the liberty of individuals in order to *prohibit individuals from causing harm to other individuals or to society.* The harms in question include both serious physical harms (e.g., maiming, killing, inflicting injury) as well as serious psychological and economic harms.

The Offense Principle

According to the **offense principle**, a government may justifiably pass laws that interfere with individual liberty in order to *prohibit individuals from offending others,* where offensive behavior includes causing others shame, embarrassment, or discomfort. Laws against public nudity are often defended by appealing to this principle.

The Principle of Legal Paternalism

According to the principle of **legal paternalism**, a government is morally justified in passing laws in order to *protect individuals from harming themselves.* Motorcycle helmet laws and seat belt laws are often defended on the basis of this principle.

The Principle of Legal Moralism

The principle of **legal moralism** states that a government may justifiably pass laws that interfere with individual liberty in order to *protect common moral standards, independently* *of whether the activities in question are harmful to others or to oneself.* This principle is often used in the attempt to justify laws against so-called victimless violations of moral standards—violations that are (arguably) neither harmful to self or others and, because they are not done in public, are not offensive to the viewing public.

There are two points about the use of these principles worth noting. First, in order for a government to appeal to one of these principles in an attempt to morally justify laws that interfere with individual liberty of its citizens, two conditions must be met. First, the principle in question must be a correct liberty-limiting principle—it must correctly state a condition under which a government can (really) morally justify limiting the liberty of its citizens. Second, the activity or practice in question must satisfy the condition set forth in the principle. If, for instance, one appeals to the harm principle to prohibit the production and consumption of a type of drug, then one must show that the use of the drug in question does cause harm to other individuals or to society generally. (Additionally, one must show that the level of harm that would be caused by use of the drug under conditions where it is not prohibited by law would be higher than the level of harm that would result from passing and enforcing laws against its use.)

The second general point is that some of these principles are relatively uncontroversial, but others are not. The harm principle is relatively uncontroversial. And perhaps the same can be said of the offense principle. However, the principles of paternalism and legal moralism are quite controversial, particularly in liberal democratic countries such as the United States. In such countries that strongly value individual liberty of choice, it is widely believed that the proper role of government is limited to preventing harm (and perhaps offense) to others.

4. DRUGS, LIBERTY, AND THE LAW

Here it is important to distinguish the issue of **drug prohibition** versus **legalization** from the issue of **drug criminalization** versus **decriminalization**. Peter de Marneffe, in his selection included in this chapter, defines drug prohibition as referring to legal penalties for the manufacture, sale, and distribution of large quantities of drugs. Drug legalization refers to having no such penalties. By contrast, drug criminalization refers to criminal penalties for using drugs and possessing small quantities of drugs, while drug decriminalization refers to the opposite of criminalization. The importance of distinguishing prohibition from criminalization is that it is possible to defend the former but reject the latter (as we shall see in our readings).

In debates over the legalization and the decriminalization of nonmedical uses of drugs, the principles of harm, paternalism, and legal moralism are all relevant. To appeal to the harm principle requires demonstration of harm to others or to society generally caused by the use of the drug in question. It is widely believed that many of the drugs mentioned earlier are addictive and thereby lead to the commission of crimes that cause harm to others and society. However, as we shall see when we read the article by Daniel Shapiro, there is disagreement about whether drug use is the cause of crimes that are committed owing to addiction. Furthermore, in order to justify a law by the harm principle, one must show that the level of harm that would likely result from not having a law prohibiting use outweighs the level of harm that would likely result from having a law. Again, those in favor of the legalization of drugs often argue that given the crimes that are committed as a result of a black market in the production, distribution, and sale of drugs, existing drug laws ought to be repealed. David Boaz defends this view in the first selection, while Peter de Marneffe opposes legalization of the sale, manufacture and distribution of drugs, though he also argues that it ought not to be against the law for individuals to use drugs or possess small quantities of drugs.

Nicotine is an addictive drug, and so the legality of smoking has recently received some attention from philosophers. In the United States, laws prohibit smoking in certain public places including airports and shopping malls. And some states have laws that prohibit smoking in restaurants. All of these laws can be justified by the harm principle. However, in his article, Robert E. Goodin takes a more radical approach to smoking and the law: he advocates a principle of legal paternalism and explores the implications of this liberty-limiting principle for the activity of smoking.

Having reviewed some of the basic concepts and principles involved in questions over the morality of government interference in the nonmedical use of drugs, let us turn briefly to the issue of gambling.

5. GAMBLING

Gambling (at least roughly speaking) is betting on an uncertain outcome in which one risks something of value in the hope of receiving something of greater value. Playing lotteries and casino games are clear cases of gambling, which is sometimes said to be addictive and for this reason (among others) morally suspect. Thus, we can raise the very same sorts of questions about gambling that were just raised about drugs.

- Is gambling morally permissible?
- In those cases (if any) in which gambling is morally wrong, what explains its wrongness?
- Is it morally acceptable for a government to pass laws that make various sorts of gambling illegal?

Focusing on the first two questions, if one searches the Internet for articles about the morality of gambling, one finds many antigambling arguments that appeal to religious considerations. But there are secular antigambling arguments, including arguments that appeal to consequentialism, to Kantian moral theory, and to virtue ethics. Whether any of these arguments is persuasive is discussed in the article by Peter Collins.

6. THEORY MEETS PRACTICE

We have already considered arguments regarding the moral permissibility of passing laws that would interfere with an individual's liberty to obtain and use drugs. And arguments about gambling that would appeal to one or other of the liberty-limiting principles should be relatively clear from the previous discussion of drugs, liberty, and the law. So let us turn to issues of personal morality and consider the kinds of moral arguments that are grounded in some of the major moral theories.

Consequentialism

For the consequentialist, the morality of an action (or practice) depends on how much overall intrinsic value (or disvalue) it would bring about compared to alternative actions (including the alternative of simply refraining from the action under scrutiny). So this view implies that whether taking a drug is wrong depends on its effects—where we consider the effects both on the individual performing the action and on anyone else affected. Presumably for the consequentialist, the morality of some instance of taking a drug will vary from person to person depending on how much overall value would be brought about.[3] Applying the theory with any degree of accuracy will require some reliable information about one's own personality and circumstances—how taking a drug will likely affect you and others—and so will be no easy task.

Kantian Moral Theory

According to the Humanity formulation of Kant's categorical imperative, an action is morally right if and only if in performing it one does not treat persons as mere means to an end but as ends in themselves. What does this principle imply about the morality of drug use? Again, this will depend on the drug in question as well as the quantity used and the frequency of use. Of course, drug use that harms others constitutes a failure to treat those others as ends in themselves, as would any gratuitous harm. The same holds for gambling. But perhaps the more interesting question from a Kantian perspective is whether drug use or gambling represents a violation of one's duty to self. Arguably, if either drug use or gambling would hinder the development of those important physical, moral, aesthetic, or intellectual capacities that are part of a balanced human existence, then such activities would be wrong—a violation of one's duty to oneself. This same kind of point about Kantian moral theory is made by Peter Collins in his article on the morality of gambling.

Virtue Ethics

Enjoying oneself is certainly part of a flourishing human life, and so long as drug use and gambling do not interfere with (or threaten to interfere with) those ingredients of a good life, there is nothing wrong with such activities and perhaps some reason to engage in them. If temperance in food and drink and other pleasures is a virtue and intemperance a vice, then the virtuous agent will avoid engaging in any form of drug use or gambling that would express intemperance. So if we accept a virtue account of right action according to which an action is morally right or permissible if and only if a virtuous agent (one who has the virtues) may choose to engage in the action, then whether or not the use of some particular drug on some occasion is right will depend on facts about the exercise of temperance by that person on that occasion. The virtue ethics approach to the morality of gambling is defended by Collins, who argues that gambling can fit into a virtuous, flourishing life and thus (in some forms, on some occasions, and for some people) it is morally permissible. However, Collins's appeal to virtue ethics in defense of gambling is challenged by David B. Fletcher in "Gambling and Character," the final selection of the chapter. As the title of his paper suggests, Fletcher argues that the likely negative effects of gambling on character provide a basis for arguing that this practice is morally objectionable.

NOTES

1. In 2009, the U.S. Federal government issued new guidelines stating that patients and suppliers in states that legally allow the use of marijuana for medical purposes are not to be prosecuted under federal law for using or supplying this drug. As of 2009, fourteen states allow the medical use of marijuana.

2. There are also moral and legal issues about performance-enhancing drugs (anabolic and androgenetic steroids) as well as inhalants and solvents that are often used for nonmedical purposes.

3. This holds for an *act* consequentialist. A *rule* consequentialist, as explained in chap. 1, sec. 2A, will compare the likely effects of a rule prohibiting the use of certain drugs with the likely effects of not having a prohibitive rule as a basis for arriving at a conclusion about the morality of particular acts of drug use.

DAVID BOAZ

Drug-Free America or Free America?

Boaz favors the legalization of marijuana, heroin, and cocaine, arguing that individuals have a natural right to live as they choose so long as they do not violate the equal rights of others. Against those who argue that the right to take drugs is justifiably restricted in order to protect society from certain social harms, Boaz argues that drug prohibition has been a failure, creating greater social ills than would result from legalization.

Recommended Reading: rights-based moral theory, chap. 1, sec. 2D.

INTRODUCTION:
THE DRUG PROBLEM

Human beings have used mind-altering substances throughout recorded history. Why? . . . Perhaps because we fail to love one another as we should. Perhaps because of the social pressure for success. Perhaps because—and this is what really irks the prohibitionists—we enjoy drugs' mind-altering effects.

Though the reasons for drug use are numerous, the governmental response has been singular: almost as long as humans have used drugs, governments have tried to stop them. In the sixteenth century the Egyptian government banned coffee. In the seventeenth century the Czar of Russia and the Sultan of the Ottoman Empire executed tobacco smokers. In the eighteenth century England tried to halt gin consumption and China penalized opium sellers with strangulation.

The drug prohibition experiment most familiar to Americans is the prohibition of alcohol in the 1920s. The period has become notorious for the widespread illegal consumption of alcohol and the resultant crime. Movies such as *Some Like It Hot* typify the popular legend of the era. The failure of Prohibition, however, is not just legendary. Consumption of alcohol probably fell slightly at the beginning of Prohibition but then rose steadily throughout the period. Alcohol became more potent, and there were reportedly more illegal speakeasies than there had been legal saloons. More serious for nondrinkers, the per capita murder rate and the assault-by-firearm rate both rose throughout Prohibition.

Most of the same phenomena are occurring with today's prohibition of marijuana, cocaine, and heroin. Use of these drugs has risen and fallen during the seventy-seven years since Congress passed the Harrison Narcotics Act [designed to curb opium trafficking], with little relationship to the level of enforcement. In the past decade, the decade of the "War on Drugs," use of these drugs seems to have declined, but no faster than the decline in the use of the legal drugs, alcohol and tobacco. In the 1980s Americans became more health- and fitness-conscious, and use of all drugs seems to have correspondingly decreased. Drug prohibition, however, has not stopped thirty million people from trying cocaine and sixty million people from trying marijuana. Prohibition also has not stopped the number of heroin users from increasing by one hundred fifty percent and the number of cocaine users from increasing by ten thousand percent. Moreover, prohibition has not kept drugs out of the hands of children: in 1988 fifty-four percent of high school seniors admitted to having tried illicit drugs; eighty-eight percent said it was fairly easy or very easy to obtain marijuana; and fifty-four percent said the same about cocaine.

Although drug prohibition has not curtailed drug use, it has severely limited some fundamental American liberties. Programs such as "Zero Tolerance," which advocates seizing a car or boat on the mere allegation of a law enforcement official that the vehicle contains drugs, ignore the constitutional principle that a person is innocent until proven guilty.

In attempting to fashion a solution to "the drug problem," one first needs to define the problem society is trying to solve. If the problem is the age-old human instinct to use mind-altering substances, then the solution might be God, or evolution, or stronger families, or Alcoholics Anonymous. History suggests, however, that the solution is unlikely to be found in the halls of Congress. If, on the other hand, the problem is the soaring murder rate, the destruction of inner-city communities, the creation of a criminal subculture, and the fear millions of Americans experience on their own streets, then a solution may well be found in Congress—not in the creation of laws but in their repeal.

This Article proposes that the repeal of certain laws will force individuals to take responsibility for their actions; the repeal of other laws will provide individuals the right to make important decisions in their lives free from outside interference. Together these changes will create the society in which drugs can, and must, be legalized. Legalization of drugs, in turn, will end the need for the government to make the intrusions into our fundamental rights as it does so often in its War on Drugs.

THE FUTILITY OF PROHIBITION

A. The War on Drugs

Prohibition of drugs is not the solution to the drug problem. [Since 1981] the United States has waged a "War on Drugs." The goals of this War were simple: prohibit the cultivation or manufacture of drugs, prohibit the import of drugs, and prohibit the use of drugs. As the aforementioned statistics demonstrate, the War has not achieved its goals.

Prohibitionists, however, sometimes claim that the United States has not yet "really fought a drug war." The prohibitionists argue that a "true drug war" would sharply lower drug use. They feel that the government has not fully committed itself to winning this battle. One need only look at the War on Drugs record, however, to see the commitment.

- Congress passed stricter anti-drug laws in 1984, 1986, and 1988. Congress and state legislators steadily increased penalties for drug law violations, mandating jail time even for first offenders, imposing large civil fines, seizing property, denying federal benefits to drug law violators, and evicting tenants from public housing.
- Federal drug war outlays tripled between 1980 and 1988, and the federal government spent more than $20 billion on anti-drug activities during the decade. Adjusted for inflation, the federal government spends ten times as much on drug-law enforcement every year as it spent on Prohibition enforcement throughout the Roaring Twenties.
- Police officers made more than one million drug law arrests in 1989, more than two-thirds of them for drug possession.
- The number of drug busts tripled during the 1980s, and the number of convictions doubled.
- America's prison population more than doubled between 1981 and 1990, from 344,283 to 755,425. Prisons in thirty-five states and the District of Columbia are under court orders because of overcrowding or poor conditions. An increasing percentage of these prisoners are in jail for nonviolent drug law violations.

- The armed services, Coast Guard, and Civil Air Patrol became more active in the drug fight, providing search and pursuit planes, helicopters, ocean interdiction, and radar. Defense Department spending on the War on Drugs rose from $200 million in 1988 to $800 million in 1990.
- The Central Intelligence Agency (CIA) and National Security Agency began using spy satellites and communications listening technology as part of the drug war. The CIA also designed a special Counter Narcotics Center.
- The federal government forced drug testing upon public employees and required contractors to establish "drug-free" workplaces. Drug testing has also expanded among private companies.
- Seizures of cocaine rose from 2,000 kilograms in 1981 to 57,000 kilograms in 1988.

Despite this enormous effort, drugs are more readily available than ever before. The War on Drugs has failed to achieve its primary goal of diminishing the availability and use of drugs.

B. Prohibition Creates Financial Incentives

One reason for the failure of the War on Drugs is that it ignores the fact that prohibition sets up tremendous financial incentives for drug dealers to supply the demand. Prohibition, at least initially, reduces the supply of the prohibited substance and thus raises the price. In addition, a large risk premium is added onto the price. One has to pay a painter more to paint the Golden Gate Bridge than to paint a house because of the added danger. Similarly, drug dealers demand more money to sell cocaine than to sell alcohol. Those who are willing to accept the risk of arrest or murder will be handsomely—sometimes unbelievably—rewarded.

Drug dealers, therefore, whatever one may think of them morally, are actually profit-seeking entrepreneurs. Drug researcher James Ostrowski points out that "[t]he public has the false impression that drug enforcers are highly innovative, continually devising new schemes to catch drug dealers. Actually, the reverse is true. The dealers, like successful businessmen, are usually one step ahead of the 'competition.'"[1]

New examples of the drug dealers' entrepreneurial skills appear every day. For example, partly because the Supreme Court upheld surveillance flights over private property to look for marijuana fields, marijuana growers have been moving indoors and underground. The Drug Enforcement Administration seized about 130 indoor marijuana gardens in California in 1989; by November the figure for 1990 was 259.

Overseas exporters have also been showing off their entrepreneurial skills. Some have been sending drugs into the United States in the luggage of children traveling alone, on the assumption that authorities will not suspect children and will go easy on them if they are caught. Others have concealed drugs in anchovy cans, bean-sprout washing machines, fuel tanks, and T-shirts. At least one man surgically implanted a pound of cocaine in his thighs. Some smugglers swallow drugs before getting on international flights. Professor Ethan Nadelmann has explained the spread of overseas exporters as the "push-down/pop-up factor": push down drug production in one country, and it will pop up in another.[2] For example, Nadelmann notes that "Colombian marijuana growers rapidly expanded production following successful eradication efforts in Mexico during the mid-1970s. Today, Mexican growers are rapidly taking advantage of recent Colombian government successes in eradicating marijuana."

Prohibition of drugs creates tremendous profit incentives. In turn, the profit incentives induce drug manufacturers and dealers to creatively stay one step ahead of the drug enforcement officials. The profit incentives show the futility of eradication, interdiction, and enforcement and make one question whether prohibition will ever be successful. . . .

INDIVIDUAL RIGHTS

Many of the drug enforcement ideas the prohibitionists suggest trample upon numerous constitutional and natural rights. In any discussion of government policies, it is necessary to examine the effect on natural rights for one simple reason: Individuals have rights that governments may not violate. In the Declaration of Independence, Thomas Jefferson defined these rights as life, liberty, and the pursuit of happiness. I argue that these inviolable rights can actually be classified as one fundamental right: Individuals have the right to live their lives in any way they choose so long as they do not violate the equal rights of others. To put this idea in the drug context, what right could be more basic, more inherent in human nature, than the right to choose what substances to put in one's own body? Whether it is alcohol, tobacco, laetrile, AZT, saturated fat, or cocaine, this is a decision that the individual should make, not the government. This point seems so obvious to me that it is, to borrow Jefferson's words, self-evident.

The prohibitionists, however, fail to recognize this fundamental freedom. They advance several arguments in an effort to rebut the presumption in favor of liberty. First, they argue, drug users are responsible for the violence of the drug trade and the resulting damage to innocent people. The erstwhile Drug Czar, William Bennett, when asked how his nicotine addiction differed from a drug addiction, responded, "I didn't do any drive-by shootings."[3] Similarly former First Lady Nancy Reagan said, "The casual user may think when he takes a line of cocaine or smokes a joint in the privacy of his nice condo, listening to his expensive stereo, that he's somehow not bothering anyone. But there is a trail of death and destruction that leads directly to his door. I'm saying that if you're a casual drug user, you are an accomplice to murder."[4]

The comments of both Mr. Bennett and Mrs. Reagan, however, display a remarkable ignorance about the illegal-drug business. Drug use does not cause violence. Alcohol did not cause the violence of the 1920s, Prohibition did. Similarly drugs do not cause today's soaring murder rates, drug prohibition does. The chain of events is obvious: drug laws reduce the supply and raise the price of drugs. The high price causes addicts to commit crimes to pay for a habit that would be easily affordable if obtaining drugs was legal. The illegality of the business means that business disputes—between customers and suppliers or between rival suppliers—can be settled only through violence, not through the courts. The violence of the business then draws in those who have a propensity—or what economists call a comparative advantage—for violence. When Congress repealed Prohibition, the violence went out of the liquor business. Similarly, when Congress repeals drug prohibition, the heroin and cocaine trade will cease to be violent. As columnist Stephen Chapman put it, "the real accomplices to murder" are those responsible for the laws that make the drug business violent.[5]

Another prohibitionist argument against the right to take drugs is that drug use affects others, such as automobile accident victims and crack babies. With regard to the former, certainly good reasons exist to strictly penalize driving (as well as flying or operating machinery) while under the influence of drugs. It hardly seems appropriate, however, to penalize those who use drugs safely in an attempt to stop the unsafe usage. As for harm to babies, this is a heart-rending problem (though perhaps not as large a problem as is sometimes believed). Again, however, it seems unnecessary and unfair to ban a recreational drug just because it should not be used during pregnancy. Moreover, drug-affected babies have one point in common with driving under the influence: misuse of legal drugs (alcohol, tobacco, codeine, caffeine) as well as illegal drugs, contribute to both problems. Thus, if society wants to ban cocaine and marijuana because of these drugs' potential for misuse, society should logically also ban alcohol, tobacco, and similar legal drugs.

The question of an individual right to use drugs comes down to this: If the government can tell us what we can put into our own bodies, what can it not tell us? What limits on government action are there? We would do well to remember Jefferson's advice: "Was the government to prescribe to us our medicine and diet, our bodies would be in such keeping as our souls are now."[6]

THE SOLUTION: RE-ESTABLISH INDIVIDUAL RESPONSIBILITY

For the past several decades a flight from individual responsibility has taken place in the United States.

Intellectuals, often government funded, have concocted a whole array of explanations as to why nothing that happens to us is our own fault. These intellectuals tell us that the poor are not responsible for their poverty, the fat are not responsible for their overeating, the alcoholic are not responsible for their drinking. Any attempt to suggest that people are sometimes responsible for their own failures is denounced as "blaming the victim."

These nonresponsibility attitudes are particularly common in discussions of alcohol, tobacco, and other drugs. Development of these attitudes probably began in the 1930s with the formulation of the classic disease theory of alcoholism. The disease theory holds that alcoholism is a disease that the alcoholic cannot control. People have found it easy to apply the theory of addiction to tobacco, cocaine, heroin, even marijuana. In each case, according to the theory, people get "hooked" and simply cannot control their use. Author Herbert Fingarette, however, stated that "*no* leading research authorities accept the classic disease concept [for alcoholism]."[7] Many scientists, though, believe it is appropriate to mislead the public about the nature of alcoholism in order to induce what they see as the right behavior with regard to alcohol.

In the popular press the addiction theory has spread rapidly. Popular magazines declare everything from sex to shopping to video games an addiction that the addicted person has no power to control. As William Wilbanks said, the phrase "I can't help myself" has become the all-purpose excuse of our time.[8]

The addiction theory has also gained prominence in discussions of illegal drugs. Both prohibitionists and legalizers tend to be enamored of the classic notion of addiction. Prohibitionists say that because people cannot help themselves with respect to addictive drugs, society must threaten them with criminal sanctions to protect them from their own failings. Legalizers offer instead a "medical model": treat drug use as a disease, not a crime. The legalizers urge that the billions of dollars currently spent on drug enforcement be transferred to treatment programs so that government can supply "treatment on demand" for drug addicts.

Despite the popular affection for the addiction theory, numerous commentators denounce the theory. For example, addiction researcher Stanton Peele deplores the effects of telling people that addictive behavior is uncontrollable:

> [O]ne of the best antidotes to addiction is to teach children responsibility and respect for others and to insist on ethical standards for everyone—children, adults, addicts. Crosscultural data indicate, for instance, that when an experience is defined as uncontrollable, many people experience such loss of control and use it to justify their transgressions against society. For example, studies find that the "uncontrollable" consequences of alcohol consumption vary from one society to another, depending upon cultural expectations.[9]

. . . The United States requires . . . more reforms—in addition to drug legalization—to create the kind of society in which people accept responsibility for their actions. . . .

Americans might take . . . steps to restore traditional notions of individual responsibility. Laws regarding drugs should only punish persons who violate the rights of others; private actions should go unpunished. Thus, laws should strictly punish those who drive while under the influence of alcohol or other drugs. Intoxication, moreover, should not be a legal defense against charges of theft, violence, or other rights violations, nor should a claim of "shopping addiction" excuse people from having to pay their debts. Physicians, intellectuals, and religious leaders should recognize that the denial of responsibility has gone too far, and they should begin to stress the moral value of individual responsibility, the self-respect such responsibility brings, and the utilitarian benefits of living in a society in which all persons are held responsible for the consequences of their actions.

CONCLUSION

Society cannot really make war on drugs, which are just chemical substances. Society can only wage wars against people, in this case people who use and sell drugs. Before America continues a war that has cost many billions of dollars and many thousands of lives—more than eight thousand lives per year even before the skyrocketing murder rates of the past few years—Americans should be sure that the benefits exceed the costs. Remarkably, all of the high-ranking officers in the Reagan administration's drug war reported in 1988 that they knew of no studies showing that the benefits of prohibition exceeded the costs.

There is a good reason for the lack of such a study. Prohibition is futile. We cannot win the War on Drugs. We cannot even keep drugs out of our prisons. Thus, we could turn the United States into a police state, and we still would not win the War on Drugs. The costs of prohibition, however, are very real: tens of billions of dollars a year, corruption of law enforcement officials, civil liberties abuses, the destruction of inner-city communities, black-market murders, murders incident to street crime by addicts seeking to pay for their habit, and the growing sense that our major cities are places of uncontrollable violence.

Hundreds, perhaps thousands, of years of history teach us that we will never make our society drug-free. In the futile attempt to do so, however, we may well make our society unfree.

NOTES

1. Ostrowski, *Thinking About Drug Legalization*, 121 Pol'y Analysis, May 25, 1989, at 34. . . .

2. Nadelmann, *The Case for Legalization*, 92 Pub. Interest 3, 9 (1988). . . .

3. Isikoff, *Bennett Rebuts Drug Legalization Ideas*, Washington Post, Dec. 12, 1989, at A10, col. 1.

4. Chapman, *Nancy Reagan and the Real Villains in the Drug War*, Chicago Tribune, Mar. 6, 1988, § 4, at 3, col. 1. . . .

5. Chapman, supra note 4.

6. T. Jefferson, *Notes on Virginia*, in The Life and Selected Writings of Thomas Jefferson 187, 275 (1944).

7. H. Fingarette, Heavy Drinking at 3 (1988) (emphasis in original). . . .

8. Wilbanks, *The New Obscenity*, 54 Vital Speeches of the Day 658, 658–59 (1988).

9. See generally S. Peele, *Control Yourself*, Reason, Feb. 1990, at 25.

READING QUESTIONS

1. What reasons does Boaz give for thinking that prohibition of drugs like cocaine and marijuana has restricted liberty?
2. What are the three goals of the war on drugs? How has the government shown its commitment to fighting this war?
3. Why has the war on drugs failed according to Boaz? How, specifically, has the prohibition of certain drugs created financial incentives for dealers of illegal drugs?
4. In what ways does prohibition violate our natural and constitutional rights?
5. Explain Boaz's reasons for why drug use does not cause violence in the way suggested by supporters of prohibition and the war on drugs.
6. How does Boaz incorporate the notion of increased responsibility into a possible solution to the problems caused by the sale and use of illegal drugs?

DISCUSSION QUESTIONS

1. Boaz denies the claim that the benefits of the war on drugs has outweighed the costs. Is he right to deny this claim? If so, can you think of any changes to the way the war on drugs is waged that might make it more beneficial?
2. Should drug users be blamed for any of the violence that occurs as a result of their drug use? Try to come up with some examples of cases in which violence is caused by drug users that are either under the influence of a particular drug or otherwise as a result of their involvement with drugs.

PETER DE MARNEFFE

Decriminalize, Don't Legalize

De Marneffe defends the decriminalization of drugs but argues that this position is consistent with being against the legalization of such drugs. He bases his case for decriminalization largely on an appeal to respect for the autonomy of individuals, while he bases his case for the legal prohibition of the manufacture and sale of large quantities of drugs on the claim that legalization would likely dramatically increase the incidence of drug abuse, thus bringing about an increase in harm to drug users and society generally. In defending his view, de Marneffe argues that drug prohibition does not violate individual rights, that it does not represent an unacceptable form of paternalism, and that it does not imply that alcohol, fatty foods, or tobacco ought also to be prohibited.

Recommended Reading: Section 3 of this chapter's introduction to liberty-limiting principles. Also relevant are Kantian moral theory, chap. 1, sec. 2D, and consequentialism, chap. 1, sec. 2A.

Drugs should be decriminalized, but not legalized. There should be no criminal penalties for using drugs or for possessing small quantities for personal use, but there should be criminal penalties for the manufacture and sale of drugs and for the possession of large quantities. Isn't this inconsistent? If it is legal to use drugs, shouldn't it also be legal to make and sell them? Here I explain why not.

First, some terminology. Drug prohibition refers to criminal penalties for the manufacture, sale, and possession of large quantities of drugs. Its opposite is drug legalization. Drug criminalization refers to criminal penalties for using drugs and for possessing small quantities of drugs. Its opposite is drug decriminalization. Here I defend drug prohibition, not drug criminalization.

THE BASIC ARGUMENT

The basic argument for drug prohibition is that if drugs are legalized, there will be more drug abuse. People use drugs because they enjoy them; they find them fun and relaxing. If it is easier, safer, and less expensive to do something fun and relaxing, more people will do it and do it more often. If drugs are legalized, they will be easier to get, safer to use, and less expensive to buy. They will be easier to get because they will be sold at the local drug or liquor store. They will be safer to use because they will be sold in standard doses and will come with safety precautions. They will be less expensive because the supply will increase and the risk of making, transporting, and selling drugs will decrease. So if drugs are legalized, there will be more drug use and consequently more drug abuse.

Evidence comes from the study of drinking. Alcohol abuse declines with alcohol use, which declines with decreased availability and higher prices (Cook 2007). For example, alcohol abuse declined substantially during the early years of Prohibition, when alcohol became less easily available and more expensive (Miron and Zwiebel 1991). Evidence for this is that during Prohibition deaths from cirrhosis of the liver declined by about 50%, and admissions to state hospitals for alcoholic psychosis declined substantially as well (Warburton 1932). The study of alcohol regulation since Prohibition further supports the conclusion that alcohol abuse declines with an increase in price—resulting from excise taxes, for example—and that alcohol abuse also declines with availability—when, for example, the law restricts the times when alcohol can be legally sold and when it prohibits those under twenty-one from purchasing alcohol (Cook 2007). Another commonly cited piece of evidence that drug use declines with availability is that heroin use was much higher among army personnel in Vietnam where it was easily available than it was among veterans who returned to the U.S., where it was much less available (Robins, Davis, and Goodwin 1974). Another piece of evidence is that the percentage of physicians who use psychoactive drugs is much higher than the general population, which can be attributed to the fact that drugs are more available to doctors (Vaillant, Brighton, and McArthur 1970).

Critics of drug prohibition commonly argue that it does no good because there is still so much drug use even though drugs are illegal. This is a bad argument. It is true there is a lot of drug use in the U.S., but this is no reason to conclude that drug laws do no good or that drugs should be legalized. There is also a lot of theft in the U.S. and it doesn't follow that laws against larceny do no good or that theft should be decriminalized. This is because, although many things are now stolen, it is likely that many more things would be stolen if theft were decriminalized.

In fact almost everyone who studies the question agrees that drug abuse will probably increase if drugs are legalized. Where there is disagreement is on how much it will increase. Those who defend drug legalization believe that although drug abuse will probably increase with legalization, it will not increase by very much, and a moderate increase is justified by the benefits of drug legalization. What are these benefits? If drugs are legalized, the argument goes, there will no longer be a black market for drugs, and so the associated violence and police corruption will cease. There will be fewer drug overdoses because drugs will be safer, because they will be sold in standard, regulated doses. Drugs will also be cheaper, so drug addicts will not need to steal to support their habits. Finally, if drugs are legalized the government can tax drugs the way it taxes alcohol and tobacco and thereby raise needed revenue. These benefits are so great, the defender of drug legalization maintains, that they justify the cost of a moderate increase in drug abuse that will probably accompany drug legalization.

The defender of drug prohibition has a different view. He believes that if drugs are legalized there will be a dramatic increase in drug abuse. He then argues that the risks of violence to innocent bystanders caused by the illegal drug trade can be reduced to acceptable levels by adequate community policing; that police corruption can be adequately controlled by proper police training, monitoring, and compensation; that there will not be significantly fewer overdoses with legalization because drug abuse will increase dramatically as a result and because heavy drug use is inherently dangerous and often reckless; that although drugs will be cheaper with legalization, there will be more drug addicts as a result, some of whom will stop working to concentrate on drug use, and so who will steal to support their habits; and that the social cost of a dramatic increase in drug abuse is much greater than anything that could be paid for by taxing legalized drugs. The probable costs of legalizing drugs therefore outweigh any probable benefit, the argument for prohibition goes, and the costs of prohibiting drugs can be reduced by wise policies of

enforcement, by enough so that drug prohibition can be justified by its benefit in reducing drug abuse.

Who is right? No one is justified in feeling certain, but here I assume that the defenders of prohibition are right, partly because this is what I believe, but mostly because I want to explain how, on this assumption, it makes sense to support drug prohibition and not drug criminalization. Some people think that drug criminalization is wrong because it violates our rights to liberty. From this they naturally conclude that drugs should be legalized. This, however, is a non sequitur, because it makes perfect sense to hold that although drug criminalization violates our rights, drug prohibition does not, as I now explain.

The basic argument for drug prohibition is that drug abuse will increase substantially if drugs are legalized. By *drug abuse* I mean drug use that harms the user or others or that creates a significant risk of harm. The term "drug abuse" is sometimes used more broadly than this, to include the recreational use of any illegal drug. Since the drug is illegal, its use is abuse. This characterization is misleading, however, because recreational drug use, in itself, is not harmful, and does not always create a significant risk of harm. Usually nothing bad occurs when someone smokes marijuana, or snorts cocaine, or ingests a tablet of LSD. Only very rarely is the user harmed by a moderate dose of these drugs, and others are harmed even less often. Heavy drug use, in contrast, can have lasting negative effects on a person's life and on the lives of those who depend on him. If, for example, a young person uses heroin heavily, he is less likely to do his school work and finish high school. If a parent uses heroin heavily, he is more likely to neglect his children, and less likely to take care of his health and to meet other important obligations, such as showing up for work. When a child's parents neglect him due to heavy drug use or when a young person neglects his own education and career, this can have lasting bad consequences on his life. So it makes sense to want there to be less drug abuse of this kind.

It is natural to think that if this argument justifies drug prohibition, it also justifies drug criminalization. After all, if drug use is decriminalized, surely the amount of drug abuse will also increase. Isn't it inconsistent, then, to hold that drugs should be prohibited but not criminalized? No, because there are important differences between prohibition and criminalization.

One important difference is that whereas drug criminalization prohibits individuals from having certain experiences that are enjoyable and illuminating, drug prohibition does not do this. Drug prohibition is similar to alcohol prohibition of the 1920s, which prohibited the manufacture, sale, and transportation of alcohol for commercial purposes, but did not prohibit drinking or the making of alcoholic beverages for personal use. Likewise, drug prohibition prohibits the manufacture, sale and possession of large quantities, but it does not prohibit drug use or making drugs for personal use. Drug criminalization, in contrast, does prohibit this. It thus prohibits people from using their own minds and their own bodies for certain kinds of pleasure and adventure. It prohibits people from regulating their moods in certain ways. This seems overly intrusive. As adults we are entitled to determine what happens in our minds and to our bodies, unless our decisions pose a serious risk of harm to others or to ourselves. Because drug use in itself does not pose a serious risk of harm to anyone, respect for persons, as independent beings who are properly sovereign over their own minds and bodies, seems incompatible with drug criminalization.

Drug prohibition, in contrast, is compatible with respect for persons. Drug prohibition makes it illegal to operate a certain kind of business; but it does not prohibit anyone from experimenting with drugs or from regulating their moods in the ways that illegal drugs provide. It does not deprive anyone of control over their own minds and bodies. Where will people get drugs if others are not permitted to manufacture and sell them? In some cases they can safely make them on their own. In other cases they can receive them as a gift from friends who are good at chemistry, and, of course, people can still buy drugs illegally even if they are prohibited. What's the point of drug prohibition if people still buy drugs anyway? Well, what's the point of murder laws if people are still murdered? Presumably murder laws reduce the number of murders by enough to justify the costs of enforcement and the risks of wrongful conviction. If drug prohibition significantly reduces the amount

of drugs that are made and sold and thereby reduces drug abuse, it can likewise be justified as *reducing* drug abuse even if it does not *eliminate* it.

To the self-sovereignty argument against criminalization, we should add that adults have important interests in the freedom necessary to lead a life that seems worthwhile to them, a life that makes sense to them as the right sort of life for them to lead, provided that in doing so they do not seriously harm others or themselves or pose a serious risk of harm. Each of us has one earthly life to lead, and it is important that we determine how we lead this life, what experiences we have, what goals we pursue, what kinds of relationships we have, and what kinds of people we become. For some, drug use is an important part of the kind of life that makes most sense to them. This is true not only of those who use drugs in religious ceremonies. It is also true of those who orient their lives around certain kinds of social and aesthetic experiences. "Dead heads" used to orient their lives around attending Grateful Dead concerts, smoking marijuana, and sharing this experience with others. Assuming the use of marijuana does not pose a serious risk of harm to the user or others, the fact that marijuana played a central role in this kind of life is a strong argument against criminalizing its use.

It is not, however, a strong argument for *legalizing* marijuana. After all, a person who wants to orient his life in this way can do this perfectly well even if it is illegal to manufacture and sell marijuana for profit. He can grow his own or share with friends. No doubt some will want to live the life of a drug dealer; this is the kind of life they want to lead. What is distinctive, however, about the life of a drug dealer is a function of its illegality. Hence this career aspiration does not provide a compelling argument for legalization. If anything, it is a reason to prohibit drugs, because if drugs are legalized, those who value dealing drugs as part of an outlaw lifestyle will no longer have the opportunity to lead an outlaw life in this way. Nor is the loss of the opportunity to sell drugs legally a serious loss, because under drug prohibition similar job opportunities will continue to exist, such as the opportunity to legally sell pharmaceuticals and alcoholic beverages. (If you are tempted to argue that the opportunity to sell alcoholic beverages and pharmaceuticals is not in fact available to most of those who sell drugs now, you should understand that this counts in favor of drug prohibition, not legalization, since only prohibition offers this kind of business opportunity to those who otherwise have little chance of entering the corporate world.)

Drug criminalization threatens personal autonomy in a way that drug prohibition does not. This is the main point so far. The claim, however, that drug criminalization threatens autonomy might be jarring. Aren't some drugs highly addictive, and isn't drug addiction inconsistent with autonomy? Doesn't concern for autonomy therefore warrant the criminalization of drugs? No. For one thing, laws that criminalize drugs deprive people of the legal discretion to use drugs, whether for good reasons or bad, and so deprive them of a kind of personal authority, which is a form of personal autonomy. For another, only a small proportion of those who use drugs are addicts. This is true even of those who use heroin, cocaine, and methamphetamine (Goode 1999). For this reason, respect for the autonomy of the vast majority of drug users provides a strong reason against criminalization. Furthermore, the claim that drug addiction is incompatible with autonomy is based on a misunderstanding of what addiction is. In the imagination of some philosophers, an addict is like a zombie who has lost the capacity to choose or to act in accordance with his own judgment of what is best. This is not an accurate picture of any real drug addict. We call people drug addicts for one or more of the following reasons. (1) They use a drug to relieve a craving. (2) They use a drug even though they obviously shouldn't, because of the harm their drug use is likely to do them or others. (3) Although they believe they should use this drug at the moment they choose to use it, at other times when their judgment is more reliable and less distorted by temptation, they sincerely believe they should not use this drug any more. Even when all these things are true of a person, it is an error to characterize him as a zombie who has lost his power of choice. The addict is still someone who chooses, and chooses on the basis of his own judgment of what is best, just like the rest of us. If the drug addict were someone whose real self has decided not to use drugs, but who is then attacked by an alien desire that takes over his body and forces him to use drugs against his will, and if a person is less likely to be attacked in this way if drugs are criminalized, there might be a sense in which drug criminalization promotes the autonomy of addicts. But drug addiction is nothing like this. The addict's desire to use drugs is just as much a part of his real self as any desire he might have to stop. It's not an alien desire that forces him to do something against his will. It arises from his own sincere belief that the pleasure or relief of using this drug is a good reason to use it. So it is a mistake to suppose that drug use, even heavy drug use, is not autonomous.

Autonomy means different things and one thing it means is independence. In this sense a person might be less autonomous due to drug abuse. If a person drops out of high school due to drug abuse, he may be less intellectually and emotionally mature as a result and less capable of supporting himself. A person who abuses drugs may also be less capable of holding a job. So a person who abuses drugs may be less intellectually, emotionally, and financially independent as a result. If drug laws reduce this kind of drug abuse, there is therefore a sense in which they promote autonomy. This is not because drug abuse itself is not autonomous or because addicts are zombies who have lost the capacity for choice. It is because drug abuse is often infantilizing.

In evaluating drug laws, we must therefore consider whether the way in which they promote autonomy justifies the way in which they limit it. Because most drug users are not addicts and because even addicts use drugs as a matter of choice, respect for autonomy seems incompatible with a blanket prohibition of drug use. But drug prohibition does not threaten personal autonomy in the same way. To this we should add that those at risk of being harmed by drug abuse have a stronger complaint against those who manufacture and sell drugs than they do against those who use them privately or make them for their own use. When a person grows marijuana and smokes it by himself or with friends, he does little to significantly increase anyone else's risk of harm. In contrast, when a businessman sets up a lab to make heroin and then distributes this product to retailers who sell it to any willing buyer, this businessman increases others' risk of harm significantly. Others therefore have a stronger complaint against his activities. Because those at risk of harm from drug abuse have a stronger complaint against drug manufacturers and dealers than they have against private users, and because there are weighty reasons of personal autonomy against drug criminalization, but not against drug prohibition, it makes sense to make a distinction between these policies, and *to* support one and not the other.

DOES DRUG PROHIBITION VIOLATE INDIVIDUAL RIGHTS?

Even so, prohibition might violate our rights. I have suggested that if the benefits of prohibition outweigh the costs, then this policy is justifiable. But a policy can violate a person's rights even if its aggregated benefits outweigh its aggregated costs. "Each person," writes John Rawls, "possesses an inviolability founded on justice that even the welfare of society as a whole cannot override" (Rawls 1971, 3). Utilitarianism, which Rawls rejects, directs the government to adopt whatever policies will result in the most happiness, summed over individuals, and this principle may warrant policies that violate our moral rights. Because it is wrong for a government to sacrifice the individual in this way, a defender of drug prohibition must therefore explain why this policy violates no one's rights.

Part of the explanation has already been given: unlike drug criminalization, drug prohibition does not pose a serious threat to personal autonomy. Recognizing the value of autonomy, however, is not all there is to taking rights seriously. Taking rights seriously also involves commitment to *individualism*, according to which we may not evaluate government policies solely by subtracting aggregated costs from aggregated benefits, but must also make one-to-one comparisons of the burdens that individuals bear under these policies. In this way we take seriously the separateness of persons. It is possible, although unlikely, that a system of slavery could be justified by utilitarian reasoning, because, although a few are harmed by this system, so many benefit from it. To understand what would be wrong with this, we must make one-to-one comparisons and recognize that the worst burden imposed on the individual slave is substantially worse than the worst burden anyone would bear if this system were rejected or abolished.

Sometimes, however, it is permissible for the government to limit the liberty of the few for the benefit of the many. It is permissible, for example, for the government to imprison some people to protect society as a whole. To apply individualism to the assessment of government policies, we must therefore find a way of evaluating whether a government policy objectionably sacrifices an individual for the benefit of society. I offer the following hypothesis: the government *objectionably* sacrifices a person in limiting her liberty if and only if it violates the *burdens principle*. This principle is that the government may not limit a person's liberty in ways that impose a burden on her that is substantially worse than the worst burden anyone would bear in the absence of this policy. When the government violates this principle in adopting policies for the good of society, it objectionably sacrifices someone for the benefit of society; it fails to respect her inviolability; it violates her rights. To illustrate, even if a system of slavery maximizes economic productivity, it imposes a burden on the individual slave that is substantially worse than the worst burden anyone would bear if the government were not to maintain this system. So the government violates the burdens principle in maintaining this system, and consequently violates the rights of those enslaved.

Does the burdens principle prove too much? Consider the following objection. Surely it is worse to be in jail than to have something stolen from a store one owns, works at, or shops at. Don't laws prohibiting shoplifting therefore violate the burdens principle? Doesn't this show that this principle is invalid? This challenge can be addressed once we understand how burdens are to be compared. The relative weight of burdens is to be assessed by the relative weight of reasons that individuals have to want or want not to be in the relevant situations. The reasons there are for us to want to be free to take whatever we want from a store without paying are not very weighty.

Consequently, our reasons are not very weighty to want to avoid a situation in which we must either pay for what we take or risk criminal penalties. On the other hand, there are good reasons for each of us to want the government to enforce a rule prohibiting shoplifting, grounded partly in the fact that without this policy the availability of retail goods will decline sharply over time. A law that prohibits shoplifting therefore does not violate the burdens principle, provided this law is administered fairly, harsh penalties are avoided, and necessity is accepted as an excuse.

I now assume that the burdens principle provides the correct basis for assessing whether the government in limiting a person's liberty objectionably sacrifices her for the benefit of society as a whole. If so, a defender of drug prohibition should be able to explain why this policy does not violate this principle. Suppose, then, that if drugs are legalized, drug abuse by young people and parents will increase dramatically. Suppose, too, that drug abuse by young people commonly damages their future prospects, because it results in a failure to perform important tasks, such as finishing school, and to develop important habits, such as being a reliable employee, and that these failures early on have a lasting negative impact on a person's life. Suppose, too, that drug abuse by parents commonly damages the future prospects of their children because it results in serious forms of child neglect. On these assumptions, there are good reasons for some people to prefer their situations when drugs are less easily available. Some people will therefore bear a significant burden as a result of drug legalization: those who will be at a substantially higher risk of harm from drug abuse if drugs are legalized. These burdens appear to be at least as great as the burden that drug prohibition imposes on businessmen in prohibiting them from manufacturing and selling drugs. The burden on businessmen is equivalent to the choice of not going into the drug business or risking legal penalties. This is not a heavy burden because there are alternative business opportunities under drug prohibition that are similar to those that would exist in the drug trade if drugs were legalized. Hence drug prohibition does not objectionably sacrifice the liberty of businessmen for the benefit of society as a whole, and so does not violate their rights.

If the burdens principle is valid as a constraint on government policies that limit individual liberty, then someone who defends drug prohibition but not drug criminalization must defend one of the following positions: (1) Although drug criminalization violates the burdens principle, drug prohibition does not. (2) Although neither drug criminalization nor drug prohibition violates the burdens principle, drug prohibition can be justified by a cost–benefit analysis whereas drug criminalization cannot. Note here that although the burdens principle imposes an individualistic constraint on the justification of liberty-limiting government policies, it allows a policy to be justified by a cost–benefit analysis provided that this policy does not violate the burdens principle. If the worst burden that a policy imposes on someone is not substantially worse than the worst burden someone would bear in the absence of this policy, then this policy does not violate the burdens principle, and it can be justified provided that its benefits outweigh its costs, however this is properly determined.

Given the important differences between drug criminalization and drug prohibition identified above, it makes sense to argue that whereas drug criminalization violates the burdens principle, drug prohibition does not. But even if drug criminalization does not violate the burdens principle, it makes sense to defend drug prohibition and not drug criminalization. Suppose for the sake of argument that the burden that drug criminalization imposes on drug users, although significant, is not substantially worse than the worst burden someone would bear as the result of drug decriminalization. Perhaps some young people will be at a significantly higher risk of self-destructive drug abuse or drug-induced parental neglect if drugs are decriminalized than they are when drugs are criminalized. Perhaps this burden is comparable to the burden that drug users bear when drugs are criminalized. (Bear in mind that drug criminalization might be justified even if harsh penalties for drug possession are not.) It is still arguable that whereas the costs of criminalization outweigh the benefits, this is not true of drug prohibition. Perhaps the aggregate costs in restricting personal autonomy and in prohibiting a form of adventure and mood control outweigh the aggregate costs of increased risk of drug abuse that would result from decriminalization, even though the aggregated costs of increased drug abuse that would result from drug legalization outweigh its aggregated costs.

COMMON OBJECTIONS

1. Paternalism

Sometimes the government violates a person's rights even when it does not sacrifice him for the benefit of society as a whole. Sometimes it violates a person's rights when it limits his liberty for his own benefit. A common objection to drug laws is that they are paternalistic: they limit people's liberty for their own good. Because drug prohibition does not prohibit anyone from buying drugs for personal use, it does not limit the liberty of drug users in this way for their own good. Assuming, though, that this policy is effective, it does limit a drug user's opportunity to buy drugs. So if this policy is justified by the assumption that it is bad for some people to have these opportunities, there is arguably a sense in which this policy is paternalistic.

This kind of paternalism, however, is not the kind that defenders of individual liberty have found most objectionable. The most objectionable forms of paternalism are those that satisfy the following description: the policy prohibits a mature adult from doing what he sincerely and consistently believes it is best for him to do; this person is mentally competent and adequately informed about the possible negative consequences; this policy limits an important liberty of this person, such as religious or sexual freedom; this policy limits this liberty by imposing criminal penalties; this policy cannot be justified except as benefitting this person, by deterring him from doing something presumed by others to be unwise. Policies that satisfy this description seem to involve an unjustifiable restriction of personal autonomy. Drug prohibition, however, does not satisfy this description. For one thing, drug prohibition limits the liberty of businessmen for the benefit of others—those who would otherwise be at a higher risk of being harmed by drug abuse. It does not limit the liberty of businessmen for *their* own good. Furthermore, the primary intended beneficiaries of drug prohibition are young people—those who would otherwise be at a higher risk of self-destructive drug abuse and parental neglect—and not mature adults who enjoy using drugs and so would like to have a legal supply. Moreover, drug prohibition does not prohibit anyone from using drugs. So even granting, what might be questioned, that the freedom to use drugs is an important liberty, like religious and sexual freedom, drug prohibition does not restrict this liberty, since it does not prohibit anyone from using drugs. Finally, drug prohibition does not impose criminal penalties on anyone for drug use. One can therefore agree that any policy that satisfies the above description is objectionably paternalistic, and yet consistently defend drug prohibition, since this policy does not involve this kind of paternalism.

2. Prohibition and Harsh Penalties

Another common objection to drug laws is that it is terrible that so many people are in prison on drug offenses. This is terrible. It is important, however, to distinguish the question of drug prohibition from the question of penalties. It is possible that, although some drugs should be prohibited, our current penalties for drug dealing are too harsh. A defender of prohibition can hold that although there should be penalties of some sort for the manufacture and sale of drugs, the penalties for first offenses should be mild, and should increase only gradually, with stiffer penalties only for repeat offenses. Moreover, a defender of drug prohibition can consistently oppose any penalties for simple drug possession, which are the penalties most strongly protested by critics of U.S. drug laws. Observe, too, that someone who opposes the legalization of all drugs might nonetheless support the legalization of some. For example, someone who supports the prohibition of heroin, cocaine, and methamphetamine might nonetheless consistently support the legalization of marijuana and some hallucinogenic drugs, such as LSD, mescaline, peyote, and MDMA (Ecstasy). This makes sense because some drugs are more harmful than others.

3. Alcohol Prohibition?

Another common objection to drug laws is that it makes no sense to defend drug prohibition and not alcohol prohibition. After all, alcohol abuse is much more harmful than drug abuse, much more highly associated with violence, property crime, accidental injury and death. So if the government is justified in prohibiting drugs, it must also be justified in prohibiting the manufacture and sale of alcohol. Assuming that alcohol prohibition is unjustifiable, drug prohibition must be unjustifiable too.

One possible response is to hold, contrary to popular belief, that alcohol prohibition is justifiable. In fact, general opposition to alcohol prohibition is based on false beliefs about its effects, such as that it does nothing to reduce alcohol abuse and that it necessarily results in a huge increase in crime and corruption (Moore 1989). But it is not necessary to endorse alcohol prohibition in order to defend drug prohibition. One can argue instead that, although drinking is more harmful than drug use, the costs of now instituting alcohol prohibition would outweigh the benefits, whereas this is not true of continuing the policy of drug prohibition. A policy that reduces the availability of a socially stigmatized drug is likely to do more to reduce its abuse than a policy that reduces the availability of a socially accepted drug. Drinking is socially accepted and fully integrated into normal social life. This is not true of heroin, cocaine, and methamphetamine, which are widely regarded as evil. For this reason drug prohibition might be much more effective at reducing drug abuse than alcohol prohibition would now be at reducing alcohol abuse. It is also true that if alcohol prohibition is adopted now, many people who have built their livelihood around manufacturing, selling, and serving alcohol would be adversely affected. These are people who made certain decisions, for example, to open a restaurant, based on the assumption that it will be legal to sell alcohol. This is not true of continuing the policy of drug prohibition. Taking these and other considerations into account, it is arguable that whereas the benefits of continuing drug prohibition outweigh the costs, the costs of now instituting alcohol prohibition outweigh the benefits, even though alcohol abuse is generally more destructive than the abuse of other drugs.

4. Fatty Foods and Tobacco Prohibition?

A related objection is that the consumption of other goods is at least as harmful as drug use and we do not think that these other goods should be prohibited. For example, obesity and smoking cause far more deaths than drug use does, and we don't think that the manufacture and sale of fatty foods or cigarettes should be prohibited. Isn't this inconsistent? No, because one can reasonably argue that whereas the benefits of continuing to prohibit the manufacture and sale of drugs outweigh the costs, this is not true of now prohibiting these other products. Food production and the food service industry is a large sector of our economy, and the production, sale, and preparation of fatty foods is a large part of this sector. If the government were now to prohibit the manufacture and sale of all fatty foods this would have a huge negative impact on our economy, our way of life, and our habits of socializing. The same cannot be said for continuing (and properly modifying) drug prohibition. Tobacco prohibition is a harder case, but even here there are important differences between the case for drug prohibition and for laws prohibiting the manufacture and sale of cigarettes. A central concern in defending drug laws is the damage that drug abuse does to young people in limiting their future prospects, by causing the loss of important opportunities that will be difficult to recover. If a young person neglects his schoolwork and employment as a result of drug abuse, this is likely to have a lasting negative impact on his life. If a child is neglected by her parents due to drug abuse, this will increase her risk of serious injury and may have a lasting negative impact on her emotional and intellectual development. The availability of cigarettes does not have this same kind of negative impact. When a young person smokes, she increases her risk of certain serious diseases as an adult. Smoking, however, does not interfere with a person's intellectual and emotional development in the way that drug abuse and parental neglect do. Furthermore, the risks created by smoking as teenager can be effectively reduced later in life, by quitting as an adult. A similar point may be made about obesity. Finally, although cigarette smoking and obesity may be more likely to shorten a person's life, the kind of drug abuse that results in parental neglect or dropping out of school may have a greater negative impact on the overall quality of a person's life. The risk to a young person of being in an environment where drugs are easily available is thus different, and in some ways significantly worse, than being in an environment where cigarettes or fatty foods are easily available. Consequently there is no inconsistency in accepting this argument for drug prohibition and rejecting corresponding arguments for prohibiting cigarettes and fatty foods.

CONCLUSION

To conclude, support for drug prohibition is consistent with opposing drug criminalization; it is consistent with respect for personal autonomy; it is consistent with the principle that each person possesses an inviolability founded on justice that even the welfare of society as a whole cannot override; it is consistent with opposing the kind of paternalism that defenders of individual liberty have found most appalling; it is consistent with not supporting alcohol prohibition; it is consistent with not supporting cigarette and fatty food prohibition.

It remains an open question whether the benefits of drug prohibition really justify its costs. One cost I haven't considered is the negative impact that drug prohibition has on the political cultures of drug producing countries, such as Mexico, Colombia and Afghanistan. Because drugs are illegal in Europe and North America, drug wholesalers in drug producing countries can make huge profits by selling drugs to drug retailers in rich countries, which the drug wholesalers then use to bribe and intimidate local police, judges, and politicians, fostering government corruption. It is also true that because drugs are illegal in these countries those in the drug trade must settle their disputes with violence and intimidation,

and that innocent bystanders in these countries are sometimes harmed as a result. So it is arguable that drug prohibition harms the citizens of drug producing countries too much to be justified by the goal of reducing drug abuse in rich countries, even granting that drug abuse in rich countries would soar if drugs were legalized there.

This is a serious objection. Whether it is decisive depends on how much less corrupt the governments of drug producing nations would be and how much safer their citizens would be without drug prohibition. It depends, too, on how much drug abuse would increase in drug producing countries if drugs were legalized there. One of the most serious worries about legalizing drugs is the expected increase in drug abuse by relatively disadvantaged youth who already lack good educational and employment opportunities, and the expected increase in drug abuse by their parents. If there is reason to worry about the impact of drug legalization on the disadvantaged youth of rich countries, there is also reason to worry about the impact of drug legalization on the disadvantaged youth of drug producing nations, which are relatively poorer. When we consider the negative impact of drug prohibition on these countries, we must therefore also consider the likely negative impact of drug legalization. If drug abuse among young people and their parents in drug producing countries would increase dramatically with drug legalization, and if drug prohibition is not the primary cause of government corruption in these countries, and is not a major cause of violence to innocent bystanders, then it makes sense to believe that the overall benefits of drug prohibition to everyone outweigh the costs, and so to oppose drug legalization on this ground.

REFERENCES

Cook, Philip J. *Paying the Tab*. (Princeton: Princeton University Press, 2007).

Goode, Erich. *Drugs in American Society*, 5th ed. (New York: McGraw–Hill, 1999).

Miron, Jeffrey A. and Jeffrey Zwiebel. "Alcohol Consumption During Prohibition." *American Economic Review* 81 (1991): 242–47.

Moore, Mark. "Actually, Prohibition Was a Success." *New York Times*, October 16 (1989): A21.

Rawls, John. *A Theory of Justice.* (Cambridge, MA: Harvard University Press, 1971).

Robins, Lee N., Darlene H. Davis, and Donald Goodwin. "Drug Use by U.S. Army Enlisted Men in Vietnam: A Follow-Up on Their Return Home." *American Journal of Epidemiology* 99 (1974): 235–49.

Vaillant, George E., Jane R. Brighton, and Charles McArthur. "Physicians' Use of Mood-Altering Drugs." *The New England Journal of Medicine* 282 (1970): 365–70.

Warburton, Clark. *The Economic Results of Prohibition.* (New York: Columbia University Press, 1932).

READING QUESTIONS

1. According to de Marneffe, drug criminalization is incompatible with personal autonomy, but drug prohibition is not. How does de Marneffe argue for these claims?
2. In discussing drug prohibition and individual rights, de Marneffe invokes what he calls the "burdens principle." What is this principle and how does de Marneffe use it in defending his claim that drug prohibition is consistent with respecting individual rights?
3. What reasons does de Marneffe give for claiming that his position on drug prohibition does not automatically imply that prohibitions on alcohol, fatty foods and tobacco would be justified?

DISCUSSION QUESTIONS

1. Do you agree with de Marneffe that the legalization of drugs will result in a dramatic increase in serious and harmful drug abuse? Why or why not?
2. In the concluding section of his article, de Marneffe raises a potential objection to his view on drug prohibition, namely, that the benefits of prohibition are outweighed by the costs. What costs does de Marneffe mention? Do you think the costs in question are enough to outweigh the benefits of prohibition? (In thinking about this question, readers are advised to consult Web resources to gather information about drug-related violence and drug abuse.)

ROBERT E. GOODIN

Permissible Paternalism: Saving Smokers from Themselves

Contrary to the widely shared assumption that legal paternalism is at odds with the proper practices of liberal democracies, Goodin argues that some forms of control and interference may be morally justified on paternalist grounds. In defending legal paternalism, Goodin focuses on smoking, arguing that there may be good reasons, consistent with liberal democracy, for public officials to pass laws that would interfere with this activity. Goodin does recognize a presumption against paternalistic interference by government, and claims that public officials should refrain from paternalistic intervention in the lives of its citizens regarding any type of activity when they are convinced that persons engaging in that activity are acting on preferences that are *relevant, settled, preferred*, and perhaps *their own*. Using the case of Rose Cipollone (a smoker who successfully won a court case against a tobacco company) as an example, Goodin explains how the "manifest preferences" of smokers are often not relevant, not settled, not preferred, and not their own. Goodin concludes by considering the kinds of governmental regulation of smoking that might be paternalistically justified.

Recommended Reading: Section 3 of this chapter's introduction to liberty-limiting principles. Also relevant, chap. 1, sec. 2D, on rights.

Paternalism is desperately out of fashion. Nowadays notions of "children's rights" severely limit what even parents may do to their own offspring, in their children's interests but against their will. What public officials may properly do to adult citizens, in their interests but against their will, is presumably even more tightly circumscribed. So the project I have set for myself—carving out a substantial sphere of morally permissible paternalism—might seem simply preposterous in present political and philosophical circumstances.

Here I shall say no more about the paternalism of parents toward their own children. My focus will instead be upon ways in which certain public policies designed to promote people's interests might be morally justifiable even if those people were themselves opposed to such policies.

Neither shall I say much more about notions of rights. But in focusing upon people's interests rather than their rights, I shall arguably be sticking closely to the sorts of concerns that motivate rights theorists. Of course, what it is to have a right is itself philosophically disputed; and on at least one account (the so-called "interest theory") to have a right is nothing more than to have a legally protected interest. But on the rival account (the so-called "choice theory")

the whole point of rights is to have a legally protected choice. There, the point of having a right is that your choice in the matter will be respected, even if that choice actually runs contrary to your own best interests.

It is that understanding of rights which leads us to suppose that paternalism and rights are necessarily at odds, and there are strict limits in the extent to which we might reconcile the two positions. Still, there is some substantial scope for compromise between the two positions.

Those theorists who see rights as protecting people's choices rather than promoting their interests would be most at odds with paternalists who were proposing to impose upon people what is judged to be *objectively* good for them. That is to say, they would be most at odds if paternalists were proposing to impose upon people outcomes which are judged to be good for those people, whether or not there were any grounds for that conclusion in those people's own subjective judgments of their own good.

Rights theorists and paternalists would still be at odds, but less at odds, if paternalists refrained from talking about interests in so starkly objective a way. Then, just as rights command respect for people's choices, so too would paternalists be insisting that

From Robert E. Goodin, "Permissible Paternalism: Saving Smokers from Themselves," in William H. Shaw, ed., *Social and Personal Ethics*, 3rd edition, Wadsworth, 1999. Reprinted by permission of the author.

we respect choices that people themselves have or would have made. The two are not quite the same, to be sure, but they are much more nearly the same than the ordinary contrast between paternalists and rights theorists would seem to suggest.

That is precisely the sort of conciliatory gesture that I shall here be proposing. In paternalistically justifying some course of action on the grounds that it is in someone's interests, I shall always be searching for some warrant in that person's own value judgments for saying that it is in that person's interests.

"Some warrant" is a loose constraint, to be sure. Occasionally will we find genuine cases of what philosophers call "weakness of will": people being possessed of a powerful, conscious present desire to do something that they nonetheless just cannot bring themselves to do. Then public policy forcing them to realize their own desire, though arguably paternalistic, is transparently justifiable even in terms of people's own subjective values. More often, though, the subjective value to which we are appealing is one which is present only in an inchoate form, or will only arise later, or can be appreciated only in retrospect.

Paternalism is clearly paternalistic in imposing those more weakly-held subjective values upon people in preference to their more strongly held ones. But, equally clearly, it is less offensively paternalistic thanks to this crucial fact: at least it deals strictly in terms of values that are or will be subjectively present, at some point or another and to some extent or another, in the person concerned.

I. THE SCOPE OF PATERNALISM

When we are talking about public policies (and maybe even when we are talking of private, familial relations), paternalism surely can only be justified for the "big decisions" in people's lives. No one, except possibly parents and perhaps not even they, would propose to stop you from buying candy bars on a whim, under the influence of seductive advertising and at some marginal cost to your dental health.

So far as public policy is concerned, certainly, to be a fitting subject for public paternalism a decision must first of all involve high stakes. Life-and-death issues most conspicuously qualify. But so do those that substantially shape your subsequent life prospects. Decisions to drop out of school or to begin taking drugs involve high stakes of roughly that sort. If the decision is also substantially irreversible—returning to school is unlikely, the drug is addictive—then that further bolsters the case for paternalistic intervention.

The point in both cases is that people would not have a chance to benefit by learning from their mistakes. If the stakes are so high that losing the gamble once will kill you, then there is no opportunity for subsequent learning. Similarly, if the decision is irreversible, you might know better next time but be unable to benefit from your new wisdom.

II. EVALUATING PREFERENCES

The case for paternalism, as I have cast it, is that the public officials might better respect your own preferences than you would have done through your own actions. That is to say that public officials are engaged in evaluating your (surface) preferences, judging them according to some standard of your own (deeper) preferences. Public officials should refrain from paternalistic interference, and allow you to act without state interference, only if they are convinced that you are acting on:

- *relevant* preferences;
- *settled* preferences;
- *preferred* preferences; and, perhaps,
- *your own* preferences.

In what follows, I shall consider each of those requirements in turn. My running example will be the problem of smoking and policies to control it. Nothing turns on the peculiarities of that example, though. There are many others like it in relevant respects.

It often helps, in arguments like this, to apply generalities to particular cases. So, in what follows, I shall further focus in on the case of one particular smoker, Rose Cipollone. Her situation is nowise unique—in all the respects that matter here, she might be considered the proto-typical smoker. All that makes her case special is that she (or more precisely her heir) was the first to win a court case against the tobacco companies whose products killed her.

In summarizing the evidence presented at that trial, the judge described the facts of the case as follows.

> Rose...Cipollone...began to smoke at age 16,...while she was still in high school. She testified that she began to smoke because she saw people smoking in the movies, in advertisements, and looked upon it as something "cool, glamorous and grown-up" to do. She began smoking Chesterfields...primarily because of advertising of "pretty girls and movie stars," and because Chesterfields were described as "mild."...
>
> Mrs. Cipollone attempted to quit smoking while pregnant with her first child..., but even then she would sneak cigarettes. While she was in labor she smoked an entire pack of cigarettes, provided to her at her request by her doctor, and after the birth...she resumed smoking. She smoked a minimum of a pack a day and as much as two packs a day.
>
> In 1955, she switched...to L&M cigarettes... because...she believed that the filter would trap whatever was "bad" for her in cigarette smoking. She relied upon advertisements which supported that contention. She...switched to Virginia Slims...because the cigarettes were glamorous and long, and were associated with beautiful women—and the liberated woman....
>
> Because she developed a smoker's cough and heard reports that smoking caused cancer, she tried to cut down her smoking. These attempts were unsuccessful....
>
> Mrs. Cipollone switched to lower tar and nicotine cigarettes based upon advertising from which she concluded that those cigarettes were safe or safer...[and] upon the recommendation of her family physician. In 1981 her cancer was diagnosed, and even though her doctors advised her to stop she was unable to do so. She even told her doctors and her husband that she had quit when she had not, and she continued to smoke until June of 1982 when her lung was removed. Even thereafter she smoked occasionally—in hiding. She stopped smoking in 1983 when her cancer had metastasized and she was diagnosed as fatally ill.

This sad history contains many of the features that I shall be arguing make paternalism most permissible.

Relevant Preferences

The case against paternalism consists in the simple proposition that, morally, we ought to respect people's own choices in matters that affect themselves and by-and-large only themselves. But there are many questions we first might legitimately ask about those preferences, without in any way questioning this fundamental principle of respecting people's autonomy.

One is simply whether the preferences in play are genuinely *relevant* to the decision at hand. Often they are not. Laymen often make purely factual mistakes in their means-ends reasoning. They think—or indeed, as in the case of Rose Cipollone, are led by false advertising to suppose—that an activity is safe when it is not. They think that an activity like smoking is glamorous, when the true facts of the matter are that smoking may well cause circulatory problems requiring the distinctly unglamorous amputation of an arm or leg.

When people make purely factual mistakes like that, we might legitimately override their surface preferences (the preference to smoke) in the name of their own deeper preferences (to stay alive and bodily intact). Public policies designed to prevent youngsters from taking up smoking when they want to, or to make it harder (more expensive or inconvenient) for existing smokers to continue smoking when they want to, may be paternalistic in the sense of running contrary to people's own manifest choices in the matter. But this overriding of their choices is grounded in their own deeper preferences, so such paternalism would be minimally offensive from a moral point of view.

Settled Preferences

We might ask, further, whether the preferences being manifested are "settled" preferences or whether they are merely transitory phases people are going through. It may be morally permissible to let people commit euthanasia voluntarily, if we are sure they really want to die. But if we think that they may subsequently change their minds, then we have good grounds for supposing that we should stop them.

The same may well be true with smoking policy. While Rose Cipollone herself thought smoking was both glamorous and safe, youngsters beginning to smoke today typically know better. But many of them still say that they would prefer a shorter but more glamorous life, and that they are therefore more than happy to accept the risks that smoking entails. Say what they may at age sixteen, though, we cannot help supposing that they will think differently when pigeons eventually come home to roost. The risk-courting preferences of youth are a characteristic product of a peculiarly dare-devil phase that virtually all of them will, like their predecessors, certainly grow out of.

Insofar as people's preferences are not settled—insofar as they choose one option now, yet at some later time may wish that they had chosen another—we have another ground for permissible paternalism. Policymakers dedicated to respecting people's own choices have, in effect, two of the person's own choices to choose between. How such conflicts should be settled is hard to say. We might weigh the strength or duration of the preferences, how well they fit with the person's other preferences, and so on.

Whatever else we do, though, we clearly ought not privilege one preference over another just because it got there first. Morally, it is permissible for policymakers to ignore one of a person's present preferences (to smoke, for example) in deference to another that is virtually certain later to emerge (as was Rose Cipollone's wish to live, once she had cancer).

Preferred Preferences

A third case for permissible paternalism turns on the observation that people have not only multiple and conflicting preferences but also preferences for preferences. Rose Cipollone wanted to smoke. But, judging from her frequent (albeit failed) attempts to quit, she also wanted *not to want* to smoke.

In this respect, it might be said, Rose Cipollone's history is representative of smokers more generally.

The US Surgeon General reports that some 90 percent of regular smokers have tried and failed to quit. That recidivism rate has led the World Health Organization to rank nicotine as an addictive substance on a par with heroin itself.

That classification is richly confirmed by the stories that smokers themselves tell about their failed attempts to quit. Rose Cipollone tried to quit while pregnant, only to end up smoking an entire pack in the delivery room. She tried to quit once her cancer was diagnosed, and once again after her lung was taken out, even then only to end up sneaking an occasional smoke.

In cases like this—where people want to stop some activity, try to stop it but find that they cannot stop—public policy that helps them do so can hardly be said to be paternalistic in any morally offensive respect. It overrides people's preferences, to be sure. But the preferences which it overrides are ones which people themselves wish they did not have.

The preferences which it respects—the preferences to stop smoking (like preferences of reformed alcoholics to stay off drink, or of the obese to lose weight)—are, in contrast, preferences that the people concerned themselves prefer. They would themselves rank those preferences above their own occasional inclinations to backslide. In helping them to implement their own preferred preferences, we are only respecting people's own priorities.

Your Own Preferences

Finally, before automatically respecting people's choices, we ought to make sure that they are really their *own* choices. We respect people's choices because in that way we manifest respect for them as persons. But if the choices in question were literally someone else's—the results of a post-hypnotic suggestion, for example—then clearly there that logic would provide no reason for our respecting those preferences.

Some people say that the effects of advertising are rather like that. No doubt there is a certain informational content to advertising. But that is not all there is in it. When Rose Cipollone read the tar and nicotine content in advertisments, what she was getting was information. What she was getting when looking at the accompanying pictures of movie stars and glamorous, liberated women was something else altogether.

Using the power of subliminal suggestion, advertising implants preferences in people in a way that largely or wholly bypasses their judgment. Insofar as it does so, the resulting preferences are not authentically that person's own. And those implanted preferences are not entitled to the respect that is rightly reserved for a person's authentic preferences, in consequence.

Such thoughts might lead some to say that we should therefore ignore altogether advertising-induced preferences in framing our public policy. I demur. There is just too much force in the rejoinder that, "Wherever those preferences came from in the first instance, they are mine now." If we want our policies to respect people by (among other things) respecting their preferences, then we will have to respect all of those preferences with which people now associate themselves.

Even admitting the force of that rejoinder, though, there is much that still might be done to curb the preference-shaping activities of, for example, the tobacco industry. Even those who say "they're my preferences now" would presumably have preferred, ahead of time, to make up their own minds in the matter. So there we have a case, couched in terms of people's own (past) preferences, for severely restricting the advertising and promotion of products—especially ones which people will later regret having grown to like, but which they will later be unable to resist.

III. CONCLUSIONS

What, in practical policy terms, follows from all that? Well, in the case of smoking, which has served as my running example, we might ban the sale of tobacco altogether or turn it into a drug available only on prescription to registered users. Or, less dramatically, we might make cigarettes difficult and expensive to obtain—especially for youngsters, whose purchases are particularly price-sensitive. We might ban all promotional advertising of tobacco products, designed as it is to attract new users. We might prohibit smoking in all offices, restaurants, and other public places, thus making it harder for smokers to find a place to partake and providing a further inducement for them to quit.

All of those policies would be good for smokers themselves. They would enjoy a longer life expectancy and a higher quality of life if they stopped smoking. But that is to talk the language of interests rather than of rights and choices. In those latter terms, all those policies clearly go against smokers' manifest preferences, in one sense or another. Smokers want to keep smoking. They do not want to pay more or drive further to get their cigarettes. They want to be able to take comfort in advertisements constantly telling them how glamorous their smoking is.

In other more important senses, though, such policies can be justified even in terms of the preferences of smokers themselves. They do not want to die, as a quarter of them eventually will (and ten to fifteen years before their time) of smoking-related diseases; it is only false beliefs or wishful thinking that make smokers think that continued smoking is consistent with that desire not to avoid a premature death. At the moment they may think that the benefits of smoking outweigh the costs, but they will almost certainly revise that view once those costs are eventually sheeted home. The vast majority of smokers would like to stop smoking but, being addicted, find it very hard now to do so.

Like Rose Cipollone, certainly in her dying days and intermittently even from her early adulthood, most smokers themselves would say that they would have been better off never starting. Many even agree that they would welcome anything (like a workplace ban on smoking) that might now make them stop. Given the internally conflicting preferences here in play, smokers also harbor at one and the same time preferences pointing in the opposite direction; that is what might make helping them to stop seem unacceptably paternalistic. But in terms of other of their preferences—and ones that deserve clear precedence, at that—doing so is perfectly well warranted.

Smoking is unusual, perhaps, in presenting a case for permissible paternalism on all four of the fronts here canvassed. Most activities might qualify under only one or two of the headings. However, that may well be enough. My point here is not that paternalism is always permissible but merely that it may always be.

In the discourse of liberal democracies, the charge of paternalism is typically taken to be a knock-down objection to any policy. If I am right, that knee-jerk response is wrong. When confronted with the charge of paternalism, it should always be open to us to say, "Sure, this proposal is paternalistic—but is the paternalism in view permissible or impermissible, good or bad?" More often than not, I think we will find, paternalism might prove perfectly defensible along the lines sketched here.

READING QUESTIONS

1. What should the scope of paternalism be according to Goodin?
2. When should public officials refrain from paternalistic interference according to Goodin?
3. Explain the case of Rose Cipollone and the differences among relevant, settled, preferred, and one's own preferences.
4. What are some of the public policies that Goodin thinks might be justified in the light of his considerations about the interests and preferences of smokers?

DISCUSSION QUESTION

1. Kant and many other philosophers hold that one has duties to oneself, including a duty to refrain from harmful activities. Can there be duties that one owes to oneself? If not, why not? If so, is refraining from smoking one of them?

DANIEL SHAPIRO

Addiction and Drug Policy

According to the "standard view" of addiction, certain drugs are highly addictive largely because of their pharmacological effects—effects on the brain owing to the chemical constitution of the drug. This kind of pharmacological explanation plays a significant role in some arguments in favor of legal bans on certain drugs, especially "hard drugs." Shapiro challenges the standard view, arguing that factors such as an individual's mind-set as well as an individual's social and cultural setting importantly contribute to drug addiction. According to Shapiro, then, cravings, increased drug tolerance, and withdrawal symptoms cannot explain drug addiction. He bolsters his case against the standard view by examining nicotine addiction.

Most people think that illegal drugs, such as cocaine and heroin, are highly addictive. Usually their addictiveness is explained by pharmacology: their chemical composition and its effects on the brain are such that, after a while, it's hard to stop using them. This view of drug addiction—I call it the standard view—underlies most opposition to legalizing cocaine and heroin. James Wilson's (1990) arguments are typical: legalization increases access, and increased access to addictive drugs increases addiction. The standard view also underlies the increasingly popular opinion, given a philosophical defense by Robert Goodin (1989), that cigarette smokers are addicts in the grip of a powerful drug.

However, the standard view is false: pharmacology, I shall argue, does not by itself do much to explain drug addiction. I will offer a different explanation of drug addiction and discuss its implications for the debate about drug legalization.

PROBLEMS WITH THE STANDARD VIEW

We label someone as a drug addict because of his behavior. A drug addict uses drugs repeatedly, compulsively, and wants to stop or cut back on his use but finds it's difficult to do so; at its worst, drug addiction dominates or crowds out other activities and concerns. The standard view attempts to explain this compulsive behavior by the drug's effects on the brain. Repeated use of an addictive drug induces cravings and the user comes to need a substantial amount to get the effect she wants, i.e., develops tolerance. If the user tries to stop, she then suffers very disagreeable effects, called withdrawal symptoms. (For more detail on the standard view, see American Psychiatric Association 1994, 176–81.)

Cravings, tolerance, and withdrawal symptoms: do these explain drug addiction? A craving or strong desire to do something doesn't *make* one do something: one can act on a desire or ignore it *or* attempt to extinguish it. Tolerance explains why the user increases her intake to get the effect she wants, but that doesn't explain why she would find it difficult to *stop wanting* this effect. Thus, the key idea in the standard view is really withdrawal symptoms, because that is needed to explain the difficulty in extinguishing the desire to take the drug or to stop wanting the effects the drug produces. However, for this explanation to work, these symptoms have to be really bad, for if they aren't, why not just put up with them as a small price to pay for getting free of the drug? However, withdrawal symptoms aren't *that* bad. Heroin is considered terribly addictive, yet pharmacologists describe its withdrawal symptoms as like having a bad flu for about a week: typical withdrawal symptoms include fever, diarrhea, sneezing, muscle cramps, and vomiting (Kaplan 1983, 15, 19, 35). While a bad flu is quite unpleasant, it's not so bad that one has little choice but to take heroin rather than experience it. Indeed, most withdrawal symptoms for any drug cease within a few weeks, yet most heavy users who relapse do so after that period and few drug addicts report withdrawal symptoms as the reason for their relapse (Peele 1985, 19–20, 67; Schacter 1982, 436–44; Waldorf, Reinarman, and Murphy 1991, 241).

Thus, cravings, tolerance, and withdrawal symptoms cannot explain addiction. An additional problem for the standard view is that most drug users, whether they use legal or illegal drugs, do not become addicts, and few addicts remain so permanently. (Cigarette smokers are a partial exception, which I discuss later.) Anonymous surveys of drug users by the Substance Abuse and Mental Health Services Administration indicate that less than 10 percent of those who have tried powder cocaine use it monthly (National Household Survey of Drug Abuse 2001, tables H1 and H2). Furthermore, most monthly users are not addicts; a survey of young adults, for example (Johnston, O'Malley, and Bachman for the National Institute on Drug Abuse 1996, 84–5), found that less than 10 percent of monthly cocaine users used it daily. (Even a daily user need not be an addict; someone who drinks daily is not thereby an alcoholic.) The figures are not appreciably different for crack cocaine (Erickson, Smart, and Murray 1994, 167–74, 231–32, Morgan and Zimmer 1997, 142–44) and only slightly higher for heroin (Husak 1992, 125; Sullum 2003, 228). These surveys have been confirmed by longitudinal studies—studies of a set of users over time—which indicate that moderate and/or controlled use of these drugs is the norm, not the exception, and that even heavy users do not inevitably march to addiction, let alone remain permanent addicts (Waldorf, Reinarman, and Murphy 1991, Erickson, Smart, and Murray 1994; Zinberg 1984, 111–34, 152–71). The standard view has to explain the preeminence of controlled use by arguing that drug laws reduce access to illegal drugs. However, I argue below that even with easy access to drugs most people use them responsibly, and so something other than the law and pharmacology must explain patterns of drug use.

AN ALTERNATIVE VIEW

I will defend a view of addiction summed up by Norman Zinberg's book, *Drug, Set, and Setting* (1984). "Drug" means pharmacology; "set" means the individual's mindset, his personality, values, and expectations; and "setting" means the cultural or social surroundings of drug use. This should sound like common sense. Humans are interpretative animals, and so what results from drug use depends not just on the experience or effects produced by the drug but *also* on the interpretation of that experience or effects. And how one interprets or understands the experience depends on one's individuality and the cultural or social setting. I begin

with setting. Hospital patients that get continuous and massive doses of narcotics rarely get addicted or crave the drugs after release from the hospital (Peele 1985, 17; Falk 1996, 9). The quantity and duration of their drug use pales in significance compared with the setting of their drug consumption: subsequent ill effects from the drug are rarely interpreted in terms of addiction. A study of Vietnam veterans, the largest study of untreated heroin users ever conducted, provides more dramatic evidence of the role of setting. Three-quarters of Vietnam vets who used heroin in Vietnam became addicted, but after coming home, only half of heroin users in Vietnam continued to use, and of those only 12 percent were addicts (Robins, Heltzer, Hesselbrock, and Wish 1980). Wilson also mentions this study and says that the change was because heroin is illegal in the U.S. (1990, 22), and while this undoubtedly played a role, so did the difference in social setting: Vietnam, with its absence of work and family, as well as loneliness and fear of death, helped to promote acceptance of heavy drug use.

Along the same lines, consider the effects of alcohol in different cultures. In Finland, for example, violence and alcohol are linked, for sometimes heavy drinkers end up in fights; in Greece, Italy, and other Mediterranean countries, however, where almost all drinking is moderate and controlled, there is no violence-alcohol link (Peele 1985, 25). Why the differences? Humans are social or cultural animals, not just products of their biochemistry, and this means, in part, that social norms or rules play a significant role in influencing behavior. In cultures where potentially intoxicating drugs such as alcohol are viewed as supplements or accompaniments to life, moderate and controlled use will be the norm—hence, even though Mediterranean cultures typically consume large amounts of alcohol, there is little alcoholism—while in cultures where alcohol is also viewed as a way of escaping one's problems, alcoholism will be more prevalent, which may explain the problem in Finland and some other Scandinavian cultures. In addition to cultural influences, most people learn to use alcohol responsibly by observing their parents. They see their parents drink at a ball game or to celebrate special occasions or with food at a meal, but rarely on an empty stomach; they learn it's wrong to be drunk at work, to drink and drive; they learn that uncontrolled behavior with alcohol is generally frowned upon; they absorb certain norms and values such as "know your limit," "don't drink alone," "don't drink in the morning," and so forth. They learn about rituals which reinforce moderation, such as the phrase "let's have a drink." These informal rules and rituals teach most people how to use alchohol responsibly (Zinberg 1987, 258–62).

While social controls are harder to develop with illicit drugs—accurate information is pretty scarce, and parents feel uncomfortable teaching their children about controlled use—even here sanctions and rituals promoting moderate use exist. For example, in a study of an eleven-year follow-up of an informal network of middle-class cocaine users largely connected through ties of friendship, most of whom were moderate users, the authors concluded that:

> Rather than cocaine overpowering user concerns with family, health, and career, we found that the high value most of our users placed upon family, health, and career achievement . . . mitigated against abuse and addiction. Such group norms and the informal social controls that seemed to stem from them (e.g., expressions of concern, warning about risks, the use of pejorative names like "coke hog," refusal to share with abusers) mediated the force of pharmacological, physiological, and psychological factors which can lead to addiction (Murphy 1989: 435).

Even many heavy cocaine users are able to prevent their use from becoming out of control (or out of control for significant periods of time) by regulating the time and circumstances of use (not using during work, never using too late at night, limiting use on weekdays), using with friends rather than alone, employing fixed rules (paying bills before spending money on cocaine), etc. (Waldorf, Reinarman, and Murphy 1991). Unsurprisingly, these studies of controlled cocaine use generally focus on middle-class users: their income and the psychological support of friends and family put them at less of a risk of ruining their lives by drug use than those with little income or hope (Peele 1991, 159–60).

I now examine the effects of set on drug use, that is, the effect of expectations, personality, and values.

Expectations are important because drug use occurs in a pattern of ongoing activity, and one's interpretation of the drug's effects depends upon expectations of how those effects will fit into or alter those activities. Expectations explain the well-known placebo effect: if people consume something they mistakenly believe will stop or alleviate their pain, it often does. Along the same lines, in experiments with American college-age men, aggression and sexual arousal increased when these men were told they were drinking liquor, even though they were drinking 0 proof, while when drinking liquor and told they were not, they acted normally (Peele 1985, 17). The role of expectations also explains why many users of heroin, cocaine, and other psychoactive drugs do not like or even recognize the effects when they first take it and have to be taught to or learn how to appreciate the effects (Peele 1985, 13–14; Waldorf, Reinarman, and Murphy 1991, 264; Zinberg 1984, 117). The importance of expectations means that those users who view the drug as overpowering them will tend to find their lives dominated by the drug, while those who view it as an enhancement or a complement to certain experiences or activities will tend not to let drugs dominate or overpower their other interests (Peele 1991, 156–58, 169–70).

As for the individual's personality and values, the predictions of common sense are pretty much accurate. Psychologically healthy people are likely to engage in controlled, moderate drug use, or if they find themselves progressing to uncontrolled use, they tend to cut back. On other hand, drug addicts of all kinds tend to have more psychological problems before they started using illicit drugs (Peele 1991, 153–54, 157; Zinberg 1984, 74–76). People who are motivated to control their own lives will tend to make drug use an accompaniment or an ingredient in their lives, not the dominant factor. Those who place a high value on responsibility, work, family, productivity, etc., will tend to fit drug use into their lives rather than letting it run their lives (Waldorf, Reinarman, and Murphy 1991, 267; Peele 1991, 160–66). That's why drug use of all kinds, licit or illicit, tends to taper off with age: keeping a job, raising a family, and so forth leave limited time or motivation for uncontrolled or near continuous drug use (Peele 1985, 15). And it's why it's not uncommon for addicts to explain their addiction by saying that they drifted into the addict's life; with little to compete with their drug use, or lacking motivation to substitute other activities or interests, drug use comes to dominate their lives (DeGrandpre and White 1996, 44–46). Those with richer lives, or who are motivated on an individual and/or cultural level to get richer lives, are less likely to succumb to addiction. To summarize: even with easy access to intoxicating drugs, most drug users don't become addicts, or if they do, don't remain addicts for that long, because most people have and are motivated to find better things to do with their lives. These better things result from their individual personality and values and their social or cultural setting.

CIGARETTE SMOKING AND THE ROLE OF PHARMACOLOGY

I've discussed how set and setting influence drug use, but where does pharmacology fit in? Its role is revealed by examining why it is much harder to stop smoking cigarettes—only half of smokers that try to stop smoking succeed in quitting—than to stop using other substances. (For more detail in what follows, see Shapiro 1994 and the references cited therein.)

Smokers smoke to relax; to concentrate; to handle anxiety, stress, and difficult interpersonal situations; as a way of taking a break during the day; as a social lubricant; as a means of oral gratification—and this is a partial list. Since smoking is a means to or part of so many activities, situations, and moods, stopping smoking is a major life change and major life changes do not come easily. Part of the reason smoking is so integrated into people's lives is pharmacological. Nicotine's effects on the brain are mild and subtle: it doesn't disrupt your life. While addicts or heavy users of other drugs such as cocaine, heroin, or alcohol *also* use their drugs as a means to or part of a variety of activities, situations, and moods, most users of these drugs are not lifelong addicts or heavy users, because these drugs are not so mild and heavy use has a stronger tendency over time to disrupt people's lives.

The pharmacology of smoking, however, cannot be separated from its social setting. Smoking doesn't disrupt people's lives in part because it is legal. Even with increasing regulations, smokers still can smoke in a variety of situations (driving, walking on public streets, etc.), while one cannot use illegal drugs except in a furtive and secretive manner. Furthermore, the mild effects of nicotine are due to its mild potency—smokers can carefully control their nicotine intake, getting small doses throughout the day—and its mild potency is due partly to smoking being legal. Legal drugs tend to have milder potencies than illegal ones for two reasons. First, illegal markets create incentives for stronger potencies, as sellers will favor concentrated forms of a drug that can be easily concealed and give a big bang for the buck. Second, in legal markets different potencies of the same drug openly compete, and over time the weaker ones come to be preferred—consider the popularity of low tar/nicotine cigarettes and wine and beer over hard liquor.

Thus, pharmacology and setting interact: smoking is well integrated into people's lives because the nicotine in cigarettes has mild pharmacological effects and because smoking is legal, and nicotine has those mild effects in part because smoking is legal. Pharmacology also interacts with what I've been calling set. The harms of smoking are slow to occur, are cumulative, and largely affect one's health, not one's ability to perform normal activities (at least prior to getting seriously ill). Furthermore, to eliminate these harms requires complete smoking cessation; cutting back rarely suffices (even light smokers increase their chances of getting lung cancer, emphysema, and heart disease). Thus, quitting smoking requires strong motivation, since its bad effects are not immediate and it does not disrupt one's life. Add to this what I noted earlier, that stopping smoking means changing one's life, and it's unsurprising that many find it difficult to stop.

Thus, it is a mistake to argue, as Goodin did, that the difficulty in quitting is mainly explicable by the effects of nicotine. Smokers are addicted to smoking, an *activity*, and their being addicted to it is not reducible to their being addicted to a *drug*. If my explanation of the relative difficulty of quitting smoking is correct, then the standard view of an addictive drug is quite suspect. That view suggests that knowledge of a drug's pharmacology provides a basis for making reasonable predictions about a drug's addictiveness. However, understanding nicotine's effects upon the brain (which is what Goodin stressed in his explanation of smokers' addiction) does not tell us that it's hard to stop smoking; we only know that once we add information about set and setting. Generalizing from the case of smoking, all we can say is:

> The milder the effects upon the brain, the easier for adults to purchase, the more easily integrated into one's life, and the more the bad effects are cumulative, slow-acting and only reversible upon complete cessation, the more addictive the drug.

Besides being a mouthful, this understanding of drug addiction requires introducing the *interaction* of set and setting with pharmacology to explain the addictiveness potential of various drugs. It is simpler and less misleading to say that people tend to *addict themselves* to various substances (and activities), this tendency varying with various cultural and individual influences.

CONCLUSION

My argument undercuts the worry that legalizing cocaine and heroin will produce an explosion of addiction because people will have access to inherently and powerfully addictive drugs. The standard view that cocaine and heroin are *inherently* addictive is false, because no drug is inherently addictive. The desire of most people to lead responsible and productive lives in a social setting that rewards such desires is what controls and limits most drug use. Ironically, if cocaine and heroin in a legal market would be as disruptive as many drug prohibitionists fear, then that is an excellent reason why addiction would not explode under legalization—drug use that

tends to thrive is drug use that is woven into, rather than disrupts, responsible people's lives.

ADDENDUM

After I wrote this article, some of my students raised the following objection. I argue that drug addiction that disrupts people's lives would not thrive under legalization because most people's desire and ability to lead responsible lives would break or prevent such addiction. However, suppose that legalization of cocaine and heroin makes the use of those drugs similar to the use of cigarettes—small, mild doses throughout the day which are well integrated into people's lives. If legalization brings it about that those who addict themselves to these drugs are like those who addict themselves to smoking—their addiction does not disrupt their lives, but is integrated into it—wouldn't that mean that addiction to these drugs would become as prevalent as cigarette addiction?

It is possible that legalizing heroin and cocaine would make its use similar to the current use of cigarettes. However, if this happened, the main worry about heroin and cocaine addiction would be gone. We would not have a problem of a large increase in the number of people throwing away or messing up their lives. At worst, if legalizing cocaine and heroin produced as bad health effects as cigarette smoking does (which is dubious—see Carnwath and Smith 2002, 137–39; Morgan and Zimmer 1997, 131, 136, 141), then we would have a new health problem. Of course, someone might argue that one should not legalize a drug which could worsen the health of a significant percentage of its users, even if that use does not mess up most of its users' lives. It is beyond the scope of this paper to evaluate such arguments (however, see Shapiro 1994), but notice that the implications of my essay cut against the claim that these health risks were not voluntarily incurred. Since one's drug use partly depends on one's values and personality, then to the extent that one can be said to be responsible for the choices influenced by one's values and personality, then to that extent those who addict themselves to a certain drug can be said to have voluntarily incurred the risks involved in that drug use.

REFERENCES

American Psychiatric Association. 1994. *Diagnostic and Statistical Manual of Mental Disorders.* 4th ed. Washington, D.C.: American Psychiatric Association.

Carnwath, T., and I. Smith. 2002. *Heroin Century.* London: Routledge.

DeGrandpre, R., and E. White. 1996. "Drugs: In Care of the Self." *Common Knowledge* 3: 27–48.

Erickson, P., E. Edward, R. Smart, and G. Murray. 1994. *The Steel Drug: Crack and Cocaine in Perspective.* 2nd ed. New York: MacMillan.

Falk, J. 1996. "Environmental Factors in the Instigation and Maintenance of Drug Abuse." In W. Bickel and R. DeGrandpre, eds., *Drug Policy and Human Nature.* New York: Plenum Press.

Goodin, R. 1989. "The Ethics of Smoking." *Ethics* 99: 574–624.

Husak, D. 1992. *Drugs and Rights.* New York: Cambridge University Press.

Johnston, L. D., P. M. O'Malley, and J. G. Bachman. 1996. *Monitoring the Future Study, 1975–1994: National Survey Results on Drug Use.* Volume II: *College Students and Young Adults.* Rockville, Md.: National Institute on Drug Abuse.

Kaplan, J. 1983. *The Hardest Drug: Heroin and Public Policy.* Chicago: University of Chicago Press.

Morgan, J., and L. Zimmerman. 1997. "The Social Pharmacology of Smokeable Cocaine: Not All It's Cracked Up to Be." In C. Reinarman and H. Levine, eds., *Crack in America: Demon Drugs and Social Justice.* Berkeley: University of California Press.

Murphy, S., C. Reinarman, and D. Waldorf. 1989. "An 11 Year Follow-Up of a Network of Cocaine Users." *British Journal of Addiction* 84: 427–36.

Peele, S. 1985. *The Meaning of Addiction: Compulsive Experience and Its Interpretation.* Lexington, Mass.: D.C. Heath and Company.

Peele, S. 1991. *The Diseasing of America: Addiction Treatment Out of Control.* Boston: Houghton Mifflin Company.

Robins, L., J. Helzer, M. Hesselbrock, and E. Wish. 1980. "Vietnam Veterans Three Years After Vietnam: How Our Study Changed Our View of Heroin." In L. Brill and C. Winick, eds., *The Yearbook of Substance Use and Abuse.* Vol. 2. New York: Human Sciences Press.

Schacter, S. 1982. "Recidivism and Self-Cure of Smoking and Obesity." *American Psychologist* 37: 436–44.

Shapiro, D. 1994. "Smoking Tobacco: Irrationality, Addiction and Paternalism." *Public Affairs Quarterly* 8: 187–203.

Substance Abuse and Mental Health Services Administration. 2002. *Tables from the 2001 National Household Survey on Drug Abuse*, Department of Health and Human Services, available online at http://www.samhsa.gov/oas/NHSDA/2klNHSDA/vol2/appendixh_1.htm.

Sullum, J. 2003. *Saying Yes: In Defense of Drug Use.* New York: Tarcher/Putnam.

Waldorf, D., C. Reinarman, and S. Murphy. 1991. *Cocaine Changes: The Experience of Using and Quitting.* Philadelphia: Temple University Press.

Wilson, J. 1990. "Against the Legalization of Drugs." *Commentary* 89: 21–28.

Zinberg, N. 1984. *Drug, Set, and Setting.* New Haven, Conn.: Yale University Press.

Zinberg, N. 1987. "The Use and Misuse of Intoxicants." In R. Hamowy, ed., *Dealing with Drugs.* Lexington, Mass.: D. C. Heath and Company.

READING QUESTIONS

1. How does Shapiro characterize the "standard view" of addiction as it relates to drugs like heroin and cocaine?
2. Explain the problems with the standard view according to Shapiro.
3. What is the alternative view of addiction suggested by Shapiro? What is meant by the terms "drug," "set," and "setting" in the context of this view?
4. How does Shapiro contrast the case of cigarette smoking with the cases of addiction predicted by the standard view?

DISCUSSION QUESTIONS

1. Are there any remaining merits of the standard view of addiction rejected by Shapiro?
2. Do you think that Shapiro overestimates the positive influences of social and individual controls on the use of illicit drugs like heroin and cocaine?
3. Are there any downsides to the legalization of illicit drugs that Shapiro fails to consider?

PETER COLLINS

Is Gambling Immoral? A Virtue Ethics Approach

After explaining what gambling is, Collins proceeds to consider various kinds of arguments for the conclusion that commercial (rather than social) gambling is morally wrong. In particular, he considers and rejects arguments based on utilitarian (consequentialist) moral theory and on Kantian moral theory. He also critically considers moral arguments against gambling based on what he calls "puritan" considerations, including appeal to the idea of stewardship, which we find in Lisa Newton's anti-gambling argument from the previous article. Approaching this issue from an essentially Aristotelian virtue-based approach to ethics—according to which considerations of human eudaimonia (flourishing or happiness) play a central role in ethical decision making—Collins argues that gambling and its pleasures may play a morally acceptable role in a flourishing human life.

Recommended Reading: virtue ethics, chap. 1, sec. 2E. Also relevant are consequentialism, chap. 1, sec. 2A, and Kantian moral theory, chap. 1, sec. 2B.

1. INTRODUCTION

The question of whether gambling should be prohibited or legalised and, if legalised, how it should be regulated has received considerable attention from people who think about public policy. It is no part of my purpose here to try to contribute to answering those questions. Clearly, in as far as these questions raise moral issues, they are issues of public rather than private morality. That is, they are about what governments should or should not use their coercive powers to do rather than about how we individually should conduct our lives in conformity with what morality requires.

Historically, gambling along with other activities deemed to constitute vices has been legally proscribed because two beliefs were widely held: first that gambling is immoral and second, that it is the business of government to try to stamp out activities which are immoral. The second of these beliefs, however, has for better or for worse been largely discredited in pluralist societies committed to the principles of liberal democracy, on the grounds that it is neither morally defensible nor politically practicable. As a consequence, advocates of banning or limiting legal gambling tend to avoid invoking the claim that gambling is intrinsically immoral even though this is a belief which many of them hold. Instead they focus on trying to show that prohibition or legal restriction is justified on the basis of the illegitimate harm that legalised gambling does to gamblers themselves, to third parties and to society as a whole.

But is gambling immoral? Suppose it were agreed, on the purest libertarian grounds, that the State should do absolutely nothing to try to prevent or discourage people from gambling as much as they like; would there still be any good reasons why you and I should nevertheless decide on moral grounds that gambling ought to play little or no part in the way we conduct our daily lives?

I want to anchor this discussion by identifying [two] reasons why this question deserves substantial attention from moral philosophers and certainly more attention than it has recently received.[1] . . .

First, the role which pleasure and pleasures should play in our lives is a fundamental issue in moral philosophy to the extent that it addresses the question of how ordinary people ought to conduct their everyday lives. Gambling furnishes a particularly good case study for this kind of philosophising since it not only tends to consume considerable time and money which could arguably be better spent but also has a propensity to become addictive. For reasons which may be largely self-serving we tend to avoid reflection on this kind of question when it applies to our own pleasures or those of our friends. But it becomes inescapable when we think about the need to offer rational guidance to children about how they should conduct themselves in relation to different kinds of pleasure. And as soon as we ask: "What should we teach children about gambling?" we confront the question of the morality or otherwise of gambling.

Secondly, it is clear that gambling provides an interesting case against which to test different types of ethical theory. As we shall see, some people argue that gambling violates the principle of utility. Others claim on Kantian grounds that it is inconsistent with conduct of a rational and autonomous person. Gambling has also, of course, been condemned by those who espouse a puritan ethic whether based on religious convictions or on secular considerations.

Finally we need to consider the claim that gambling is incompatible with living the best or most fulfilling kind of life of which human beings are capable. . . .

2. WHAT IS GAMBLING?

Before we can properly address questions about the morality of gambling we need to make some conceptual points about the nature of the activity we are discussing.

The standard definition of gambling is that it involves three components:

• Something valuable is placed at risk (staked).
• With the prospect of winning something more valuable if one set of events occurs and of losing one's stake if another set of events occurs.
• Where the outcome is wholly or partly unpredictable by the gambler.

This definition, however, seems to leave some important questions unanswered amongst which I wish to single out two because of their relevance to the moral issues.

First there is the question of whether buying stocks and shares is gambling. The thought here is that a pro-gambling argument might be developed along the following lines. If there is no difference between speculating on the stock market and gambling in a casino, the latter activity can only be morally culpable if the former is too. But it would obviously be absurd to condemn investing on the stock exchange as immoral. Therefore it is absurd to condemn gambling in casinos as immoral.

In order to refute this argument it is not necessary to rebut the full (and considerable) force of Marx's arguments to the effect that those who make money out of the mere ownership of capital in the form of shares are robbing workers of the private property which is rightfully theirs because it was created by their labour. All that is necessary is to point out that the stock exchange is not in its essence a provider of gambling services but rather of opportunities for genuine investment. The stock exchange thus differs from a casino or lottery in at least two crucial ways. First, success on the stock exchange depends primarily on the exercise of rational judgment. Second, investing in the stock market is not a zero sum game. That is, making profits on the stock exchange does not necessitate the making of losses by others: in the normal case it depends on the creation of new wealth. It is true that some investing on the stock exchange is, from the point of view of the investor, exactly like gambling—for example, if they pick their investments using a pin. Similarly, some gambling is indeed like investing on the stock exchange: the professional poker player or the bettor on horse races who is an expert on form is trying to make money out of superior knowledge and judgment. But the essence of investing in the stock market does not consist in people literally "trying their luck" in circumstances where one person's gain is always another's loss. The essence of gambling—or at least of the most widespread forms of gambling with whose morality this essay is mainly concerned—consists in just this.

This is why some of the most telling arguments against gambling are that, unlike investing, it is an irrational activity which is unproductive, at best, and destructive of wealth, at worst.

The second distinction which needs to be added to the standard definition of gambling is that between social gambling and commercial gambling. In the heyday of temperance movements, opponents of gambling argued that playing low-stakes social bridge was no less to be condemned on moral grounds than betting on horses, playing roulette or going to a gambling den. For the purposes of the present discussion,

however, I shall assume that there could be a great deal of difference from a moral point of view between:

- games of skill engaged in as a social pastime and spiced up with wagers which all participants have a formally equal chance of winning, and
- gambling on games where the outcome is unavoidably and mainly dependent on luck, in commercial contexts where the games are set up so as to make it certain that the players will in the long run lose.

Thus the morality of gambling on slot machines, as opposed to having a bet on a game of golf, may be significantly affected by the fact that anyone who plays gaming machines ought to know that over time they are bound to lose. This may, for example, strengthen the claim that such gambling must be irrational and as such morally wrong. Note also that such an argument would not be affected by whether the amount wagered was large or small.

A very important question for conceptual analysis which underlies the question of what principles we should adopt in shaping both personal conduct and public policy in regard to gambling is: "To what extent is gambling like and unlike other pleasures which have historically been banned on the grounds that they are immoral?" At one extreme some would claim that gambling is like taking hard drugs and should be eschewed on the grounds that it is immoral and banned on the grounds that it is highly dangerous. At the other extreme, people argue that gambling is no more vicious or dangerous than going to the theatre or cinema which was also once much disapproved of by puritans. Rather than discussing these questions fully here, I simply note that to the extent that gambling is both similar to and different from other pleasurable activities to which we devote time and money we will benefit in our thinking about both public and private morality if we accept the demands of consistency in this area, i.e., if we accept that we should take the same position with respect to all pleasures except to the extent that we can demonstrate relevant differences between them. The discussion which follows, therefore, is implicitly though not explicitly concerned that a satisfactory answer can be given to the question: "What are the morally relevant differences, if any, between gambling and, say, dancing, playing golf (on the Sabbath), watching sexually exciting movies or consuming psychotropic drugs for pleasure?"

To summarise these considerations, then, I shall be here predominantly concerned with the morality of individuals' playing games of chance in commercial contexts where the odds are systematically stacked against them. The paradigm will be games like roulette or slot machine gambling. I shall also be concerned with table games played in casinos such as poker or blackjack where the opportunities to exercise skill are rendered systematically nugatory, as well as with lotteries and other number games like keno and bingo. With respect to most sports- and other event-betting I take it that ignorance of the relevant facts for most punters is sufficient to make the outcome the equivalent to one which is predominantly determined by luck. By contrast, I shall not concern myself with the morality of either professional gamblers who rely on superior knowledge and skill in order to make money or of the suppliers of gambling services who earn their money by offering only games in which the odds always favour the House.

I shall proceed by considering what light may be shed on the first question I identify above, namely how does gambling relate to a general moral theory of pleasure, by considering what light may be shed on this question by the four types of ethical theory alluded to above. Not only does applying these theories illuminate the ethics of gambling but we also learn something about the power of the theories by testing them against the case of gambling.

In general, I shall argue that a strong puritan position—it is always good to deny oneself pleasure—is indefensible. I shall also argue against a weaker puritan position which says that it is wrong to engage in any wasteful and addictive activities of which gambling is clearly one. On the other hand, I do not take the view—though I do take it seriously—that gambling is unconditionally good for one's moral health. Perhaps rather tamely, I conclude by adopting what I take to be an Aristotelian view of the morality of gambling and I hope that this position is sustainable with respect to all those pleasures which have been and continue to be deemed by some to be "vices."

3. MILL, UTILITARIANISM AND VICE

A good place to begin considering whether we ought to refrain from or restrict our indulgence in gambling even if the law does not oblige us to do so is with John Stuart Mill's extraordinarily rich, subtle and sensible Chapter 5 of *On Liberty*. Here he treats of each of fornicating, gambling, drunkenness and drugs. Under the title "Applications," Mill addresses the question of what would happen in terms of actual policy and legislation if his two great principles were adopted by government. The principles are:

- "That the individual is not accountable to society for his actions, in so far as these concern the interests of no person but himself"
- "That for such actions as are prejudicial to the interests of others, the individual is accountable and may be subjected either to social or to legal punishment if society is of the opinion that the one or the other is requisite for its protection"[2]

Clearly on Mill's view, we cannot outlaw consensual fornication, gambling or self-intoxication. Nor, according to Mill can we subject people who engage in such activities to social sanctions such as ostracism. This is because in an ideal libertarian society, the State makes no attempt to stop people enjoying themselves in whatever way they choose provided only that they do not illegitimately harm others. In such a state anyone may do as they please within the limits of the harm proviso; and in particular, there are no restrictions on indulgence in all manner of pleasures deemed to be vices, no matter how widespread and deeply ingrained the conviction may be that these activities are immoral. But this does not mean, according to Mill, that there are no good moral grounds for refraining from indulgence in vicious pleasures. His felicific ethics as expounded in *Utilitarianism* allow him at least two arguments.

The first is that vicious self-indulgence may be contrary to the principle of utility to the extent that it is self-damaging and conducive for the individual to a preponderance of misery over pleasure in the long run. The second is that fornication, gambling and drunkenness are "lower pleasures" which ought to be abstained from in favour of higher pleasures such as enjoying works of great art.

Neither of these reasons is very convincing as they stand. The first turns on matters of empirical fact: for example, will my indulgence in drugs or gambling ultimately lead to the madness and misery of addiction? The answer in at least many cases is "No" and as Mill himself says, "no-one but the person himself can judge of the motive which may prompt him to incur the risk."[3] Consequently, the most others may legitimately do is to ensure that "he be warned of the danger."[4]

With regard to the argument from higher pleasures, apart from the well-known difficulty which this notion creates for the utilitarian calculus generally, it is also far from clear that the vices would always fail Mill's own test. This test consists in asking moral or hedonic experts who have experience of both higher pleasures such as reading poetry and lower pleasures such as playing pushpin, which of the two activities afford them the greater pleasure. Unfortunately for puritans, however, plenty of people who thoroughly appreciate Picasso's paintings, nevertheless rate the pleasures of fornication even more highly. (Perhaps Picasso himself did.)

On the other hand, I think both kinds of argument have some force in relation to at least the commonest forms of gambling, namely wagering on mechanical devices like roulette wheels or slot machines. Even non-pathological gambling consumes significant amounts of time and money on an activity which arguably affords no significant intellectual or physical stimulation, which, in other words is literally mechanical and mindless. On a purely utilitarian calculus of maximising personal pleasure it is probably easy for most people to get a bigger bang for their leisure buck. I also think that gambling fares poorly in relation to the question of higher pleasures and that it ought to be possible for most people to get a better as well as a bigger bang for their buck.

However, as far as Mill is concerned, the truth is, I believe, that the logic of his position really supports the hedonistic, "whatever-turns-you-on" permissivism. However, Mill didn't embrace such an ethic himself partly because he was concerned to defend utilitarianism against criticism from high-minded Victorian moralists but more because he was himself largely in sympathy with their puritanism, at least in relation to traditional vices. He would almost certainly have regarded modern permissivism as decadent.

However, even if Mill's arguments against vices in general are inadequate to shore up a general defence of puritanism against permissivism, there may be some other and better arguments against unrestrained self-indulgence at least in relation to gambling even though these arguments do not support stronger forms of puritanism or a moral requirement for teetotalism in respect of gambling. Kantian moral reasoning might furnish such arguments.

4. KANTIAN ARGUMENTS AND GAMBLING

The general form of Kantian arguments vetoing particular practices is that one could not rationally desire the world to be a place in which everyone acted in accordance with the principle of conduct which informs the particular practice under discussion. Thus, one could not rationally want the world to be a place where everyone told lies or broke promises whenever it suited them. This seems plausible to the extent that there does seem to be something very like a piece of self-contradiction in asserting: "It would be a good thing if people always told lies when they felt like it" or "Everyone ought to break their promises if they think they will gain thereby." It also seems plausible to claim that there would be something not just bad but mad about someone who asserted without any further explanation that it is just or right for blue-eyed people to be paid much more than brown-eyed people for doing the same job.

The most plausible way in which Kantian reasoning has been used against gambling is by focussing on the fact the whole point of gambling is to distribute property randomly: to make some people richer who have done nothing to deserve it and others poorer simply as a consequence of chance. Allied to this is the thought that gamblers are people who want something for nothing. A Kantian might then argue that one could not rationally desire a world in which what people possess bears no relation to what they deserve in terms of their natural endowments, the talents they cultivate and deploy, theft industry and/or their general contribution to the welfare of society.

One objection to this line of reasoning would be a sort of socialist argument which pointed out that, as a matter of fact, property in society mostly has been and mostly still is distributed according to accidents of birth. It might then be further urged that it would be much fairer and perhaps less divisive if, instead of allowing people to inherit wealth (and otherwise benefit materially from fortunate accidents of birth), differences in at least unearned wealth should be entirely determined by a literal lottery rather than the so-called "lottery of life."

This is perhaps fanciful. A more down-to-earth objection to the Kantian anti-gambling argument is to deny that gambling is all about wanting something for nothing. On the contrary, it may plausibly be urged, gambling is merely a pastime in which some people take pleasure and for which they are willing to pay in the form of the losses which they incur as a result of the fact that the odds are set, to a modest degree, against the player and in favour of the House. Surely, there is nothing irrational about the principle that people should be able to spend their own time and money on entertainments of their own choosing. . . .

There may, however, be a more persuasive and subtle argument against at least the forms of gambling whose paradigm is the gambling machine. This argument is usually couched in Kantian terms and suggests that gambling is an anti-rational activity which runs counter to our character as autonomous agents and, in some sense, requires us to surrender our freedom of will, something which it can no more be rationally right to do than to choose to submit to a condition of slavery. It can, however, also be articulated in utilitarian terms, employing Bentham's notion of the importance of the fecundity of pleasures and pains in doing the felicific calculus as well as noting the role of the principle of diminishing returns. On this view, we should judge pleasures and pains in respect of their propensity to spawn other pleasures and pains, as well as in the tendency of pleasures to grow stale on us the more we indulge in them.

Thus, the kinds of reason that one is intuitively most disposed to urge against regularly gambling on slot machines is that it is a vapid, pointless and mindless activity. As such, it may actually undermine or degrade the intelligence, given that there is no skill involved and that perhaps one becomes inveigled into deceiving oneself into believing that one may actually win in the long run. From a Kantian point of view, this may be thought to be inconsistent with living as a fully rational and autonomous human being. From a utilitarian point of view, it is at least a waste of time and money which could be more usefully employed. It may also actually blunt one's capacity for more profound pleasures.

The difficulty with this line of reasoning is partly that so are many of the other activities—playing solitaire, watching soap operas, etc.—which human beings divert themselves in their moments of leisure in the interval between birth and death. It is not obvious that it is more *rational* to spend time listening to Beethoven rather than playing roulette. On the other hand for many people who enjoy gambling, Beethoven's music sadly remains mere noise no matter how sincerely they attempt to appreciate it. What is obviously true as a matter of fact is that lots of people actually do get a lot of pleasure from gambling, that it does them no harm, and that they get as much benefit from it as others (such as Wittgenstein) get from other forms of recreation such as reading thrillers.

Of course, any time or money whatsoever which we spend on enjoying ourselves could in principle be used to improve ourselves or the lot of our fellow human beings, often in a manner that would be required of a fairly narrowly construed felicific calculus. Perhaps this means that we should regard gambling as indeed but one among many available diversions. However, in this case we might say, with Pascal, that any diversion which serves to distract us from the business of contemplating our ultimate destiny and thereby learning the truths which are necessary for the salvation of our immortal souls is *eo ipso* sinful. This brings us directly to a consideration of the religious case against gambling and secular versions of the same case.

5. PURITAN ARGUMENTS AND GAMBLING

The view that all indulgence in worldly pleasures is immoral is associated with the more fundamentalist and ascetic strands of all religions. It has a secular counterpart in the views of people who ascribe to political commitment the same importance as others ascribe to religious faith: the pursuit of private pleasure distracts from the work of establishing the political kingdom of heaven. An interesting, if eccentric, puritan view about gambling is to be found in Freud's claim that gambling is really a substitute for masturbation and, as such, an impediment to achieving the ideal of full genitality.

It is perhaps also worth mentioning that some people are puritanical about some pleasures on grounds that are more akin to aesthetic than moral ones. Very obviously people have objections of this kind to all sorts of sexual practices probably preferring to describe those who engage in them as disgusting rather than wicked. It is certainly true that many people who disapprove of Las Vegas would now be inclined to describe it as a monument to crassness and vulgarity rather than as a den of iniquity.

It must be conceded that by far the most common objections to gambling come from people who are in principle opposed to it on religious grounds which they take to possess the self-evidence of revealed truth. Typically they feel the same about sexual activity outside marriage as well as about getting drunk or high. Since, in the nature of the case, puritans tend to appeal either to contested authority or to faith or to taste, it is not clear what arguments could effectively be urged against them. Clearly, they would be right if in fact it turns out that those who indulge themselves in certain kinds of pleasure are going to suffer greatly after they are dead while those who abstain receive great blessings. But this seems equally clearly to be in the realm of the publicly unshowable even if it is not strictly unknowable.

Against puritanism one can urge but not demonstrate that pleasure is always a good and, as such, always a good prima facie reason for action. Thus, if there is anything morally wrong about indulging in any alleged vice, this cannot be a function of the character of the pleasure it offers, let alone of the fact that it offers pleasure at all. It is difficult to see how gambling could be rationally adjudged immoral merely on the grounds that people enjoy it. Like any other activity in which people take pleasure, if it is immoral this must be because of its propensity for corrupting character or otherwise doing damage to those who engage in it or to others. This must be to a significant extent an empirical issue and on this the evidence seems to be that in most cases gambling does not do any harm including harm to people's character.

A much more persuasive basis for arguments against dissipation of all sorts derives from the idea of stewardship. Here the religious version claims that our minds and bodies, our time and our talents, are all gifts of God. We are the stewards of our lives and our nature is such that we can only find true fulfillment and happiness by living in a manner befitting the creatures of God. We do this by attending to the workings of divine grace within us and engaging in works which are pleasing in the sight of our Creator. At all events we should not squander our lives in trivialities and we should acknowledge that a life given over to self-indulgence is an ultimately unsatisfying one.

The secular version of the stewardship argument sometimes appeals to the general economic well-being of society which allegedly requires a good deal of self-denial. More generally it appeals to our alleged obligations to future generations. In its simplest and, I think, strongest form it asserts that this life is all we have. Consequently, we should do everything in our power to ensure that we live it as well as we can and do not waste the only chance at living which we shall ever get.

Thinking in either of these ways enables us to make sense of what people have been getting at in their hostility to drugs, gambling and promiscuity. In each case a plausible argument can be made for the view that loveless sex is not a right use of the body, that consigning one's property to chance is improper stewardship of one's possessions, and that altering one's state of mind with chemicals is an abuse of one's mind. Arguments of this kind will never be decisive but that does not mean they are without rational force. And the force of these stewardship arguments is to alert us in what may be a very salutary way to the dangers of squandering our lives. It does not, however, support the view, nor is it usually taken as supporting the view, that any particular pleasures are in themselves wrong, including gambling.

6. EUDAIMONIC ETHICS AND THE PLACE OF PLEASURE IN THE GOOD LIFE

At this point I think the stewardship argument becomes part of what I take to be the most convincing of all ethical theories, namely what I call eudaimonic ethical theory which most explicitly characterises Greek ethical thought but which is also at the basis of all moral systems which derive from religious creeds or secular belief systems such as Marxism or Psychoanalysis. The fundamental tenet of this kind of theory is that the answers to ethical questions are to be found by discovering what is the best kind of life that a human being can lead. Here the best kind of life is understood as the one which is most conducive to true inner well-being or happiness. This may be thought to have a different answer for different people or a general answer which is true for everyone. It is also clear that there are many different views about what constitutes the summum bonum or supreme good for human beings.

The great strength of such theories is that they make all ethical judgments ultimately a matter of enlightened self-interest and thus render the facts about human nature and human experience crucial for determining how we ought to live. In technical terms, it is analytic that one ought to live the best possible life of which one is capable and it is also analytic that the best possible life is the one which most conduces to eudaimonia or true happiness.

If this line of reasoning is to be helpful in answering the question: "Is gambling immoral?" we need to ask the question which is asked by the Greeks in a self-consciously philosophical way and to which all religions and secular ideologies offer (usually dogmatic) answers, namely: "What is the role of pleasure generally and of individual pleasures specifically in the life of a truly happy man?"

At this point I want to claim that, in general, the view of Aristotle is superior to that, not only of later religious puritans, but also to that of other secular philosophers in both the ancient and the modern worlds. For Aristotle, pleasure is indeed an important part of the best kind of life which a human being can lead, as is wealth. A life in which there is no fun can no more be accounted a happy life than a life of grinding poverty.

But pleasure, like money, is not the only ingredient in a truly happy human life nor is it the most important ingredient. And indeed a life which is exclusively devoted to the pursuit of either pleasure or money will not be a happy one. Hence the famous doctrine of the golden mean which in this case would require finding the right median course between the opposing vices of an excessive asceticism, on the one hand, and of hedonistic over-indulgence on the other.

Obviously for many people gambling will not be an important source of pleasure in their lives. But for those who do derive significant pleasure from gambling, what Aristotle defends in respect of pleasure generally seems to be a sensible view to take in respect of gambling. This is the Delphic injunction: "Nothing in excess."

The virtue of temperance which this maxim recommends is one which it is highly plausible to see as an essential ingredient in living the best kind of life of which we are capable, especially in respect of the commonest sources of pleasurable recreation. Not only does temperance obviously avoid the dangers of addiction but it is not unreasonable to suppose that it issues in a life which is better than one of total abstinence. Thus it may in fact be the case that more people who drink in moderation, have temperate sex lives, and even enjoy the occasional game of chance have lives which are not only more enviable but also more admirable than those who eschew all such pleasures. Their obvious advantages over both the hedonist and the ascetic is that their wants are tempered to their ability to satisfy them. Moreover, they do not find themselves in the condition of permanent tantalization which Schopenhauer believed to be our natural lot.

At least this is a way I can imagine we might talk to our children about "adult pleasures" with honesty and helpfulness.

7. CONCLUSION

I want to conclude by first trying to express as forcefully as I can what I take to be a synthesis of all the anti-gambling views we have considered from all philosophical standpoints and then to say some things which seem to me to be relevant to a defence of gambling against these charges.

The worst that can be said about the sort of gambling which is typified by repetitively inserting money into gambling machines is that as a way of spending time and money it is mindless, anti-social, boring, dehumanizing, vulgar, ugly, degrading, depraving, cretinising, soul-destroying, feckless and stupid.

Against this need to be set a number of considerations which relate to why people actually engage in this activity and what the actual effect on their character may be supposed to be.

In the first place people who spend money on gambling are buying three distinct kinds of product. The first is the pleasure of play. People play slot machines and table games pretty much as they play pinball machines or games of patience. Precisely because it is not intellectually or physically taxing, some people find this an especially relaxing form of amusement. It is hard to make a serious moral case against indulging in the pleasures of playing games for recreation or entertainment. Secondly, people who gamble on machines which offer large jackpots, who buy lottery tickets or do the pools are really buying (through theft losses) fuel for their fantasies of getting suddenly and fabulously rich beyond the dreams of avarice. In itself this puts gambling in the same morally trivial category as other forms of innocuous escapism such as watching soap operas or reading sex-and-shopping novels. From one

point of view, indeed, buying a lottery ticket may not only be a harmless form of escapism but also a rational investment. For the poor who have no other prospect of ever becoming really rich no matter how hard they work, it is better to have a very remote chance of attaining great wealth than no chance at all. Thirdly, people pay for the ancillary pleasures they associate with gambling—the conviviality of the bingo hall or the betting shop, the glamour of the casino or the racetrack, and in all cases the defence against loneliness. This seems to be not just harmless but positively benign.

We should perhaps also consider the view that gambling may actually be good for the character. Perhaps gambling accustoms us to sit more loosely than we otherwise would towards money and material possessions and this may be morally desirable. Perhaps, too, gambling inculcates the virtues of courage, equanimity, and graciousness in adversity and good fortune alike. . . .

In some ways it would be nice to conclude with the suggestion that not only is gambling generally good for the moral character but that gambling for very high stakes is particularly likely to develop moral heroism. The truth of the matter, however, is almost certainly much duller. This is that for the vast majority of people who engage in it gambling has no significant impact on their moral character at all. Moreover, when it appears to, it is more likely to be an expression of character traits which for better or worse are already established rather than being the cause of the emergence of new vices or virtues which otherwise would not have developed.

If this is so, then it looks as if the truth about gambling is that, despite all the passion which continues to inform the attacks of opponents of gambling, it is in fact for the most part a morally trivial issue. What is of course not morally trivial is that no one ought to devote too much of their time, their talents, their energies and their resources to activities which are morally trivial, and that includes gambling.

NOTES

1. Amongst the articles which have addressed recently this issue, the following deserve mention: Barrett, Will: "Gambling and Public Policy" *Public Affairs Quarterly*. Vol. 14. No 1, January 2000; Lorenz, Valerie C: "Gambling" in *Encyclopaedia of Applied Ethics*. San

Diego Academic Press. 1998; Newton, Lisa: "Gambling, A Preliminary Inquiry." *Business Ethics Quarterly.* Vol. 3. Issue 4. 1993. Murphy, Jeffrie. "Indian Casinos and the Morality of Gambling." *Public Affairs Quarterly.* Vol. 12. Jan 1998. Versions of all the anti-gambling arguments discussed here can also be found in a form which repays philosophical analysis in MacKenzie, W. Douglas: *The Ethics of Gambling.* (4th Edition). The Sunday School Union. London 1899.

2. J.S. Mill: *On Liberty.* (1859) Everyman's Library Edition Edited by H.B. Acton. 1910. New Edition 1972. pp. 162–3.

3. Ibid., p. 165.

4. Ibid.

READING QUESTIONS

1. What are the three standard components of gambling according to Collins?
2. Explain the two ways in which investing in the stock market is different from gambling. How does Collins distinguish between social and commercial gambling?
3. Explain the utilitarian and Kantian arguments against gambling. What objections does Collins raise against each of these types of arguments?
4. What is the stewardship argument against gambling?
5. What should the role of pleasure be in the life of the happy man according to Collins?

DISCUSSION QUESTIONS

1. Collins briefly considers how gambling is like or unlike other pleasures such as taking drugs and going to the theater. Are there any pleasurable activities Collins fails to consider? Discuss some of the differences and similarities between gambling and these other pleasures.
2. What should the role of pleasure be in a good life? Should we agree with Collins that gambling in moderation is a pleasurable activity that is morally permissible in a happy life?

DAVID B. FLETCHER

Gambling and Character

Fletcher presents five arguments for the claim that gambling is morally objectionable, all of which focus on the negative effects of gambling on one's character. Fletcher's position therefore contrasts sharply with Peter Collins's virtue-based defense of gambling.

Recommended Reading: virtue ethics, chap. 1, sec. 2E.

From David B. Fletcher, "Gambling and Character," *International Journal of Applied Philosophy* Vol. 17, no. 1 (Spring 2003): 1–15.

"Seven deadly sins. One convenient location."
—*Las Vegas Advertiserment*[1]

Is there any inconsistency in a champion of moral virtue being a high stakes gambler? In May 2003, William Bennett—conservative commentator, former government official, advocate of ethical reform, and author of such best selling titles as *The Book of Virtues*—admitted to large-scale gambling after reports surfaced that he had lost as much as $8 million in casino gambling in the past decade. Earnings of as much as half a million dollars from speaking engagements in which he extolled virtues and excoriated vices were funneled into the coffers of such casinos as Caesars in Atlantic City and the Bellagio in Las Vegas. Bennett defends his gambling and states that "it's never been a moral issue with me."[2]

Is Bennett correct that it is not inconsistent to gamble while preaching virtue, or is gambling, in fact, morally problematic? Legalized gambling has been expanding exponentially in American society in the past few years to become a highly prominent feature of our social landscape. While it has all the hallmarks of a large-scale moral and social concern, remarkably, philosophers have paid scarce attention to the moral issues surrounding this phenomenon. Despite the fact that gambling historically has been regarded as immoral in American society, or perhaps in part because of this fact, today's moral and social philosophers have given the topic wide berth.

About a decade ago, philosopher Lisa Newton referred to the "tradition of moral censure of gambling"[3] and wrote what announced itself to be a "preliminary inquiry" on the subject of gambling considered from the standpoint of applied ethics, an attempt "to provide an account of the blameworthiness of gambling itself."[4] At that time, she reported that she was only able to locate one article on the ethics of gambling. Philosophers, indeed, have not added significantly to that number in the decade that followed, and I believe that this neglect is unjustified. While much could be said about gambling from the perspective of *social* ethics, I here seek like Newton to give an account of the moral status of gambling itself. I wish however to avoid the temptation to give a "thin" account in simply categorizing gambling as "permissible" or "impermissible"; instead, I will

attempt to assess the impact of this practice on character and the moral life.

In terms of its scale and social impact, gambling is indeed worthy of the attention of moral philosophers. "From 1974 to 1994—20 years—the amount of money Americans legally wagered has risen 2,800 percent, from $17 billion to $482 billion."[5] Gambling revenues are $60 billion per year, up from $1 billion in 1980. This comes to a figure of $164 million dollars *per day* spent on gambling.[6] Today's figure is a sum greater than the Federal government spends on Medicare and Medicaid combined.[7] Amazingly, as PBS's *Frontline* reports, "Gambling generates more revenue than movies, spectator sports, theme parks, cruise ships and recorded music combined."[8]

The Gambling Impact and Behavior Study[9] has estimated, using DSM-IV criteria developed by the American Psychiatric Association, that 5.5 million Americans are problem or pathological gamblers, and another 15 million are deemed to be "at risk." The rate of at-risk gambling among 16- and 17-year-old children is twice the adult rate. The study estimates that problem and pathological gamblers "cost society approximately $5 billion per year and an additional $40 billion in lifetime costs for productivity reductions, social services, and creditor losses."[10] In light of the staggering impact on individuals, families, communities, and the nation, truly it is high time that philosophers turn their attention to gambling....

No observer of moral philosophy in the past two decades can miss the impact of the renewed perspective of virtue ethics, although the development of this perspective in areas of applied ethics still is at a underdeveloped stage. One way to do applied virtue ethics is to evaluate types of action in terms of their impact on character. Joel J. Kupperman defines character this way:

> X's character is X's normal pattern of thought and action, especially with respect to concerns and commitments in matters affecting the happiness of others or of X, and most especially in relation to moral choices.[11]

While the subject of character is complex, it at least can be said that an individual must possess practical rationality and an adequate set of virtues to have a good character and be a morally well functioning individual. I contend that gambling either directly harms the character of the gambler or puts it at significant risk. Since individuals ought to safeguard and develop their character, they should avoid gambling. While gambling may not be without its benefits, these are not worth the negative impact on one's character. . . .

Now to turn to the question whether or not gambling is indeed "an addictive vice that degrades character." Which aspects of character are jeopardized by the practice of gambling, and to what extent? Apparently, the effects on character are variable with the individual, depending on one's moral stamina, the extent to which one gambles, and other factors. Even gambling foe William Temple could argue that "gambling is not necessarily a practice springing directly from an evil character; it is compatible with a high level of moral attainment."[12] I would argue, however, that gambling typically and frequently impairs the character of many gamblers in the following ways: A) injures self-control; B) involves greed; C) is careless with money; D) cultivates indifference; and E) compromises practical rationality.

A) Self Control—The excitement that gives gambling its appeal raises questions about its effect on character. The gambler is truly a "player," and gambling is a form of play, often of an intense nature. But play, of course, can be good. Is there a respect in which the play of gambling is morally objectionable?

R.H. Charles roots the appeal of gambling in "man's (sic) inherent love of sport or adventure."[13] Part of the tremendous appeal of gambling owes no doubt to its value as a form of entertainment. Gambling's supporters have long defended it in terms of this value, and today its promoters refer to the "gaming-entertainment industry." ' Early in the twentieth century, William Temple expressed, but did not hold, the view that "If a man can afford it why should he not spend, or risk, his money on the pleasure of that excitement as another spends his on going to a concert of a play?"[14] Or, as another early twentieth century writer put it, "I am convinced, therefore, that within limits indulgence in gambling is legitimate. . . . [I]t fills legitimately enough a humble position in the economy of our lives, side by side with the watching of football matches and the attendance at picture houses."[15]

Is gambling a vice, or an innocent amusement? Can a moral difference be shown to exist between spending money on entertainment, such as dinner and a play, and betting and losing the same amount of money at a casino?

Among the "traditional arguments" for the immorality of gambling that Richard Lippke rejects is one based on "the lingering cultural reluctance to defend activities simply because individuals find them enjoyable," which he sees as an American ambivalence about "individuals just having fun."[16] Whether Americans are as dour and joyless as Lippke suggests, and whether our centuries-old discomfort with gambling is mere Puritanism, I believe that the particular form of entertainment represented by gambling argues against its innocence.

The gambling opponent does not, as Lippke suggests, object to the fact that gambling is fun, but *how* it is fun, that it involves a sort of fun that is hazardous to the moral life. One does not need to be puritanical to realize that fun can be bad, as seen in the examples of the fun had at a cockfight, as a voyeur, or on a destructive spree. Fun can be faulted morally if it is obtained at the expense of the suffering of others, or in violation of their rights, or in violation of other moral duties. In those cases, part of the objection to the fun is that one not only takes part in an objectionable activity but that one enjoys it and finds fun in it. Such enjoyment itself can be grounds for moral disapproval. Likewise, there are moral perils in the fun of gambling. The enjoyment obtained in gambling is worsened morally by the intensity of an enjoyment that works against prudence, restraint, and self control.

Gambling advocate David Spanier complains that "the individual pleasures and psychic rewards of gambling have been generally underappreciated," and cites a number of such benefits.[17] Foremost among these for Spanier is "the action." For Spanier the term "entertainment" would be too mild for the excitement he finds in the activity. Spanier informs us that the commonplace phrase "Where the action is" used to denote excitement and pleasure from gambling, derives from a 1947 story by Damon Runyon. For Spanier, "Action expresses, in a word, the whole gambling experience." But what is meant by "the action"? For Spanier, "It means playing with chance, taking a challenge, the excitement of living in top gear. In gambling, this is the payoff."

Spanier's description of the pleasures of being caught up in casino gambling is lurid and revealing enough to quote at length:

> The gambling games offered by casinos act like a drug. It's part physical, part psychological, highs and lows, over and over, in rapid succession. These fluctuations of loss and gain, the glint of light and action, awareness of other people gambling, the sense underneath it all of playing with risk, of living on the edge of danger, are exciting. This is what the expression "getting the adrenalin going" means. The physical sensation—dryness in the throat, sweaty palms, butterflies in the stomach, the feeling of every nerve on full alert—is, for many people, highly pleasurable. Some psychologists have suggested a parallel between gambling and sexual excitement: build-up, climax, release of tension, repeated over and over. There is no need to press the analogy too far to make the point that gambling carries a strong emotional charge.

Spanier notes that casinos carefully calculate how to enhance this pleasurable experience and to keep everyday reality at bay:

> To increase the sense of indulgence, of fantasy, of losing hold of reality, casinos create an ambience far removed from the surround of ordinary life. No clocks. No daylight. Seductive lighting. Flashes of surreal color. The whir of the slots. The beat of music, pulsing under the noise of greetings, shouts, ringing jackpots, whoops from the winners. Drinks on the house—"Keep 'em coming, baby!"—and on every side, the half-open sexual turn-on of cutey-pie dealers in party dress or cowboy gear. What a heady, glamorous mix! How can anyone long resist it? All of it designed to disorient the gamblers and keep them playing. The whole operation driven—this is most important—by easy credit. "Another 2,000, Mr. Ashuro, just sign this slip, sir."[18]

Is there anything wrong with the sort of fun in which Spanier revels? Can the "entertainment argument" justify the expenditure of money for that sort of enjoinment? Compare the pleasure of gambling with the pleasure of attending a play, as in Temple's example. At the theater, one is entertained, perhaps, but not in a way that is a simple waste of time. The entertainment is in a context of an experience in which one enters imaginatively into the world of strangers and their lives, experiences empathy, and

is enriched. Similar benefits can be obtained from attending concerts, films, and having dinner with friends. Any impact that such entertainments might have upon character is likely to be at least neutral if not positive.

However, at the gambling table, the pleasures obtained are not personality-enriching enjoyments but the thrills of the danger that one might lose one's property and of the hope of obtaining that of others. It is the enjoyment of leaving one's welfare and that of others to chance, of seeking "unrealistic" goals as Campbell tells us, "bucking the odds and finding excitement in doing so."[19] The thrill of gambling is a delight in irrationality and placing valuables at unnecessary risk. Borna and Lowry criticize the irrationality of the gambling experience. For them, to gamble is

> [T]o will not to have a will [which] is similar to getting drunk where the individual temporarily yields the control of his reason, affections, conscience, and thus prostitutes his nature for the pleasure of getting drunk.[20]

In a similar vein, the prominent legal philosopher Lon Fuller has argued that gambling ought to be legally prohibited because it is "a form of conduct unbefitting a human being with rational capacities," and contends that while the law cannot compel a person to live rationally, it can "seek to exclude from his life the grosser and most obvious manifestations of chance and irrationality."[21]

I would submit that engaging in risky, irrational behavior in the attempt to gain control over another's property, and finding excitement in it, is objectionable. It is also hazardous to the moral life to engage in such activity in a context in which one is inclined, even encouraged, to lose sight of the implications of what one is doing.

Not surprisingly, enjoyment of this nature can be addictive. As the National Gambling Impact Study has found, "Pathological and problem gamblers are much more likely than low-risk gamblers to gamble for the excitement." Such gamblers number about fifteen million Americans, mostly male and a disproportionate number African-American, who "are more likely than other gamblers or nongamblers to have been on welfare, declared bankruptcy, and to have been arrested or incarcerated." These gamblers cost society financially, as noted above, but as the study noted, "these calculations are inadequate to capture the intrafamilial costs of divorce and family disruption associated with problem and pathological gambling."[22]

While most gamblers do not become addicted, a great many do, and the gambler is both running a risk of doing so and contributing to a system in which this might befall others. Because the damages of addiction are so great for the individual, her loved ones, and others, gambling would seem to be out of place in a well-lived life.

B) Greed—It is paradoxical that the gambler may be both casually irresponsible with his own money and greedy for money he does not have. Most commentators agree that the desire to win money is a major component of gambling. William Temple expresses the objection in religious terms when he states, "The persistent appeal to covetousness is fundamentally opposed to the unselfishness which was taught by Jesus Christ and by the New Testament as a whole." Besides traditional religious opposition to greed, it has been condemned by philosophers at least since Aristotle.

C) Indifference to Others—Gambling is inconsistent with an appropriate concern for the welfare of others, whether it is those to whom one is financially responsible or those against whom one is playing. Because gambling is a zero-sum game, one can only win if another loses. If the gambler is to win she gains property at another's expense. This is more obvious in wagers between individuals, as opposed to lottery and casino gambling. R. H. Charles alleges, "The real interest of the gambler is to get hold of his neighbour's property, and make no equivalent return."[23] Temple states, "The attempt (inseparable from gambling) to make profit out of the inevitable loss and possible suffering of others is the antithesis of that love of one's neighbor on which our Lord insisted."

While the gambler has so little regard for the stranger that he wants to "get hold of his … property, and make no equivalent return," he damages most directly the interests of his family and others of his immediate circle. Lisa Newton considers and rejects the argument that gambling is wrong because of the harms it inflicts on one's own circle. She admits that "others are surely injured" and recognizes "the miseries of the gamblers' families and friends as they struggle to survive themselves, cover for the gambler and pay the debts."[24] Yet, she argues, this regrettable situation does not support a charge of immorality for two reasons. First, these individuals do not suffer a "violation of their rights," since, in some sense, they remain in their situation voluntarily. Second, she argues that there is really no injury to these individuals, since

> Whatever the peculiar mental anguish of the gambler's family, the only material damage they suffer is impoverishment, and they might suffer that from any number of causes (if the family breadwinner is laid off from work, for instance), without anyone thinking an injury has been done.

Newton deals too cavalierly with what the National Commission lamented as the "intrafamilial costs of divorce and family disruption" associated with problem gambling. Newton's first claim is that the psychological and financial damage that gamblers do to others is not a wrong, and not a rights violation, since in some sense those others "accept the situation overall and voluntarily remain in it—*voluntas non fit iniuira*." Yet, as a general principle, we do not accept that A may freely harm B as long as B fails to absent himself from the situation. No doubt victims of domestic abuse are well advised to get free of the relationship and seek shelter and help, but should they fail to do this, the abuse does not somehow become "consensual" and therefore permitted. Similarly, a man who learns that his wife is gambling away the family resources is being wronged, and she is morally guilty.

In any case, Newton's argument only bears on those cases in which the victims of the gamblers' losses are consenting adults who are aware of the gambling and the losses. It doesn't begin to address the wrongs done by gamblers who conceal their activity, nor those injuries done to children. Among the most obvious young victims are those identified by researcher Earl L. Grinols when he notes that "it is not uncommon for problem gamblers to abandon their young children in parked automobiles or casino lobbies for hours and even days as they gamble."[25]

The second part of Newton's argument is that the financial ruin that the gambler brings upon the family is not grounds for a moral objection, since ruin can come in many ways other than gambling. This is a peculiar argument because it is so vulnerable to counterexamples. For example, we might say that a company that pollutes the local water supply and causes cancer to a local residents has done no wrong, since they could have contracted cancer or other serious illnesses in many other ways as well.

In her example, Newton compares the gambler's loss of family resources to a similar loss resulting from an involuntary layoff from work. Clearly, though, those cases are markedly different, as the gambler has brought about the losses by her voluntary action, while the laid-off worker is a victim that is in no way responsible for her woes. I conclude that the gambler who loses money needed by the family has wronged her family, particularly so if the family members are unaware of the losses, or if they are children.

D) Disregard for Money—Gambling is the textbook example of what can be called poor stewardship of one's resources. Again, William Temple puts the issue in religious terms when he says, "To risk money haphazardly is to disregard the insistence of the Church in every age of living faith that possessions are a trust, and that men must account to God for their use."

Concern over the poor stewardship involved in gambling can also be expressed in nonreligious terms, in terms of responsibility to society and the state rather than to God. Lisa Newton has objected to gambling that it is an "egregious violation" of the duty of stewardship.[26] Newton offers what she calls "a secular version" of the traditional theistic argument, based on the "strong social interest" that applies to the way members handle their property. This interest requires us to spend money on things we might not want, such as casualty insurance, and prohibits us from purchasing things we do want, such as controlled substances and non-approved medications. It also requires that we maintain our property "in accordance with zoning and other regulations." There is a "strong state interest in the

management of property as a whole," which, in general, is only opposed by "diehard libertarians." As a further attack on the libertarian defense of gambling, she notes that those who bankrupt themselves will require welfare assistance at taxpayer expense

Newton's stewardship argument has met with opposition in the literature. Richard L. Lippke has objected that her argument "seems to overstate society's interest in the care and conservation of property," particularly in societies that are above a subsistence level. He argues that "it is no longer the case that risking any measure of property through gambling places individuals, families, or communities in jeopardy."[27] Similarly, Will Barrett would apply her argument "only on occasions where relatively large amounts of property are being placed at risk, without being reduced to absurdity."[28]

Does society have an interest in the gambler's financial irresponsibility? Gambling small amounts of money in the course of a year may be unwise, but it is unlikely to affect society for the worse, and perhaps it would even benefit the state since gambling revenues are taxed. However, for many individuals, including the over twenty million adult problem gamblers, gambling is poor stewardship indeed and entails costs far beyond any value gambling yields to them. Gambling as a whole is poor stewardship for the country, not only in the fact there are far better uses for $60 billion, but in the many millions spent to deal with problem gambling. The stewardship argument, properly considered, has force, even in its secular version.

E) Practical Irrationality—To gamble one's resources in the hopes of winning money is unwise, and the reliance on luck so characteristic of gamblers is an abdication of reason. The glorification of chance is criticized by W. Douglas Mackenzie, who argued that in gambling the individual yields the control of his reason to chance, and hence betrays his nature as a rational being.[29] Charles condemns the appeal to chance in the strongest terms:

> Since, then, gambling is essentially an appeal to chance, or the element of the irrational and unknown in life, it follows that gambling belongs intrinsically to the savage or uncivilized type of character.[30]

In the highly routinized world of the "organization man" or woman, some gambling advocates would find much to applaud in this appeal to the "uncivilized." What we have called the irrationality of gambling is celebrated in a fascinating existential argument for gambling offered by Felicia Campbell based on insights from Karl Jaspers.[31] Jaspers had said, "whenever people are reduced to the position of those who merely have to perform an allotted task, the problem of the cleavage between being a human creature and being a worker plays a decisive part in the individual's fate."

It is just such an alienated worker who, for Campbell, can find an opportunity for self-expression in gambling. Her argument is reminiscent of the ruminations of Dostoevsky's Underground Man, who rails against social expectations to such a degree that he refuses to see a doctor when ill, because that is what a reasonable person would be expected to do. Campbell argues that gambling offers "brief freedom from an unrewarding occupation," providing an opportunity for alienated people to seek adventure and uncertainty and to engage in decision-making that affects their lives. For her, gambling is "striking out" motivated by the "preservative impulse," an impulse necessary for "the preservation of the self." By gambling "the individual strives to sustain energy and courage." To gamble is to engage in adventure.

However alienated she might be in her workaday world, in gambling the player can pursue "the wooing of the unknown, chance, danger, and all that is new." Gambling satisfies the "need to get out of line," rebel, and provides an "artificial crisis," which enables a person "to function fully in the moment." Gambling is

> [A] means of surmounting impotence, of feeling that he has a hand in his own destiny. Having little opportunity for decision making in his job, he feels that if he wins he has in some way controlled his world; if he loses, it is simply a tough break.[32]

Campbell's arguments are interesting because they seek not merely to excuse or defend gambling but to commend it, at least for a certain category of impotent, alienated worker. For Campbell, the impulse to gamble is life affirming, an opportunity to make up for what is lacked in terms of excitement, autonomy, and interest.

This is not the place to take up the empirical claim implicit in her argument, that there are many people who find their work lives wretched and who presumably find no extracurricular outlets in family, avocations, religious activity, and community involvement. I would like to counter, however, that gambling is an inappropriate way to deal with the existential crisis of work-induced wretchedness. If one feels like a "loser" in one's life, it would be unwise to seek escape in an activity in which one is exceedingly likely to have that status powerfully reiterated.

Will Barrett argues that "Gambling with the primary aim of winning is irrational when the long term odds are less than half, just because they are less than half."[33] He also believes that someone knowing the odds against increasing her property in gambling who yet gambles for that purpose exhibits "a failure of practical reasoning," while a person who gambles an amount she can afford knowing that winning is a "mere possibility" is not guilty of such irrationality.[34] "The failure of rationality is built into the activity."[35]

However, for Barrett there may be "peripheral reasons" for gambling, fitting into the three categories of "excitement, sociability, and business and related entertainment." To gamble for those reasons, with no real hope of gain, is not irrational (although it is not truly gambling, many gamblers would add).

The irrationality of gambling as a way to realize a return on investment is argued by James Walsh, who states:

> All forms of legalized gambling are bad investments. The odds for most games are slanted in favor of the casino. But people are drawn to casinos and other betting outlets in growing numbers. Buying a lottery ticket is just about the worst investment anyone can make. The odds against winning anything substantial are astronomical.[36]

In gambling, the worker, oppressed by economic actors far larger than herself, loses again to the very oppressors to whom she owes her problems, large corporations and the government. The average casino gambler spends almost $600 in a casino visit and usually leaves with nothing,[37] while the casinos themselves, divisions of major Fortune 500 corporations such as Park Place Entertainment, MGM Mirage, and Harrah's Entertainment, make a staggering profit. Park Place Entertainment, the highest earning casino company in the country, posted 2001 sales of $4,631,000,000, while MGM Mirage earned $4,009,600,000. The gambler would be well advised to find a means of self validation that is more likely to achieve its goals and not work directly contrary to them.

At the extreme, gambling can create its own problems significant enough to encourage suicide. In a grim echo of the film, *Leaving Las Vegas,* sociologist David Phillips and his associates studied the connection between suicide and gambling. They found that suicide accounts for only .97 percent of all visitor deaths in the other American counties they studied, yet in Las Vegas it accounts for 4.28 percent of visitor deaths. Las Vegas has the highest suicide rate in the United States, both for visitors and for residents, including gamblers and others affected by their gambling. Phillips and his collaborators report that

> In general, visitors to and residents of major gaming communities experience significantly elevated suicide levels. In Atlantic City, abnormally high suicide levels for visitors and residents appeared only after gambling casinos were opened. The findings do not seem to result merely because gaming settings attract suicidal individuals.[38]

Campbell's defense of gambling is based on the idea that it increases the autonomy of the oppressed worker. However, in reality it damages autonomy, since as Barrett argues,

> People who choose irrationally fail to act in the light of beliefs they would have if they were better informed, and if they persist in choosing irrationality in the face of evidence that their desires will not be satisfied, do not act autonomously.[39]

Barrett argues that "being irrational often undermines a person's capacity for freedom of choice."[40] Thus, gambling undermines the practical rationality needed for autonomous living and strikes a telling blow against character.

V

Gambling is among those behaviors traditionally considered "bad habits" or "minor vices" in this country, according to historian John C. Burnham.[41] Among Protestants, at least, gambling trifled with God's will in its reliance on chance and showed a casual attitude toward property and was associated with "idlers who were unproductive and got into other mischief as well."[42] At least in English speaking societies, gambling has been at best a "guilty pleasure," publicly opposed and privately tolerated to an extent. Gambling can still bring disgrace or disapproval to a Pete Rose or Michael Jordan, and gambling scandals can rock such preeminent institutions as Northwestern University, yet social condemnation seems to be on the wane. Although only just over a decade ago, some form of gambling was legal in only two states, today, only two states forbid it.[43] Today's older adults, according to psychologist Dennis P. McNeilly, have "seen gambling change in our society from something considered a sin or a vice to mainstream entertainment and socially acceptable."[44]

In this essay, we have attempted to indicate certain aspects of gambling that seem to injure character and interfere with a well-lived life. We have seen how the sort of excitement and pleasure it offers works against self-control and courts addiction. It is both motivated by greed and, paradoxically, is dangerously reckless with resources. It encourages attitudes and practices that are indifferent to the well being both of loved ones and of strangers. Finally, while it seems to offer freedom and an opportunity for authenticity, it actually enslaves by gravely damaging practical rationality and the basis of autonomy. While many regard it as at worst foolish or uncouth, on closer examination it is seen to be toxic to character.

NOTES

1. Advertisement for *vegashotspots.com, Chicago Tribune Magazine*, June 9, 2002, 29.

2. Jonathan Alter and Joshua Green, "The Man of Virtues Has a Vice," *Newsweek online*, May 2, 2003, http://www.msnbc.com/news/908430.asp#BODY.

3. Lisa Newton, "Gambling: a Preliminary Inquiry," *Business Ethics Quarterly* 3, 4 (October 1993): 415.

4. Newton, "Gambling," 405–418.

5. *Frontline*, "Easy Money," Gambling Facts and Stats, June 10, 1997. http://www.pbs.org/wgbh/pages/frontline/shows/gamble/etc/facts.html.

6. Timothy A. Kelly, "A Researcher Looks at Gambling," Address delivered to the National Coalition against Legalized Gambling, September 28, 2001 (Dr. Kelly is Executive Director, National Gambling Impact Study Committee).

7. Timothy L. O'Brien, *Bad Bet: The Inside Story of the Glamour, Glitz, and Danger of America's Gambling Industry* (Times Books: 1998), 4; David P. Phillips, Ward R. Welty, Marisa M. Smith, "Elevated Suicide Levels Associated With Legalized Gambling," *Suicide & Life-Threatening Behavior* 27, 4 (Winter 1997): 373–378.

8. PBS, *Frontline*, Gambling Facts and Stats.

9. See the NGISC website at http://govinfo.library.unt.edu/ngisc/ and the NORC website at http://www.norc.uchicago.edu/.

10. National Opinion Research Council, *Gambling Impact and Behavior Study: A Report to the National Gambling Impact Study Commission*, April 1, 1999, viii–x.

11. Joel J. Kupperman, *Character* (Oxford University Press, 1991), 17.

12. William Temple, "Gambling and Ethics," in *Essays in Christian Politics and Kindred Subjects*, (Longmans, Green, and Co, 1927): 121–130.

13. R. H. Charles, *Gambling & Betting: A Short Study Dealing With Their Origin And Their Relation To Morality And Religion* (Edinburgh, T & T Clark, 1925), 1.

14. William Temple, "Gambling," in *Essays in Christian Politics and Kindred Subjects*, (Longmans, Green, and Co. Ltd, 1927), 127.

15. R. C. Mortimer, "Gambling," *Personal Ethics* ed. Kenneth E. Kirk, (Clarendon Press, 1934): 144.

16. Richard L. Lippke, "Should States Be in the Gambling Business?" *Public Affairs Quarterly* 11, 1 (January 1997): 59.

17. David Spanier, "The Joy of Gambling," *The Wilson Quarterly* 19 (Autumn 1995): 34–40.

18. Spanier, "The Joy of Gambling," 34–40.

19. Felicia Campbell, "The Future of Gambling," *The Futurist* (1976), cited in "Easy Money," *Frontline,* June 10, 1997, http://www.pbs.org/wgbh/pages/frontline/shows/gamble/procon/future.html.

20. Shaheen Borna and James Lowry, "Gambling and Speculation," *Journal of Business Ethics* 6 (1987): 219–224.

21. Lon Fuller, *The Morality of Law* (Yale University Press, 1964): 8–9, cited in Will Barrett, "Gambling and Public Policy," *Public Affairs Quarterly* 14, 1 (January 2000): 69.

22. National Opinion Research Center, *Highlights*.

23. Charles, *Gambling & Betting,* 19.

24. Newton, "Gambling," 405.

25. Quoted in "Gambling on Gambling," *The Futurist* 31 (January/February 1997): 38.

26. Newton, "Gambling," 407.

27. Lippke, "Should States Be in the Gambling Business," 59.

28. Barrett, "Gambling and Public Policy," 68.

29. W. Douglas Mackenzie, cited in Borna and Lowry, "Gambling and Speculation."

30. Charles, *Gambling & Betting*.

31. Felicia Campbell, "Gambling: A Positive View," in William R. Eadington, *Gambling and Society*, (Charles C. Thomas, 1976), 218–228.

32. Felicia F. Campbell, "The Virtues of Gambling," *Business and Society Review*, in "Easy Money," *Frontline*, June 10, 1997, http://www.pbs.org/wgbh/pages/frontline/shows/gamble/procon/virtues.html.

33. Will Barrett, "Gambling and Public Policy," *Public Affairs Quarterly*, vol. 14, No. 1 (January 2000), 57–71.

34. Barrett, "Gambling and Public Policy," 64.

35. Barrett, "Gambling and Public Policy," 66.

36. James Walsh, "What are the odds?" *True Odds* (Merritt Publishing, 1996), cited in "Easy Money," *Frontline,* June 10, 1997, http://www.pbs.org/wgbh/pages/frontline/shows/gamble/odds/intro.html.

37. "Taking Chances," *The Wilson Quarterly* 19 (Autumn, 1995): 21, *Frontline*, "Easy Money," Gambling Facts and Stats, June 10, 1997. http://www.pbs.org/wgbh/pages/frontline/shows/gamble/etc/ facts.html.

38. David P. Phillips, Ward Welty, and Marisa Smith, "Elevated suicide levels associated with legalized gambling," *Suicide and Life-Threatening Behavior* 27 (1997).

39. Barrett, "Gambling and Public Policy," 67.

40. Barrett, "Gambling and Public Policy," 65.

41. John C. Burnham, *Bad Habits: Drinking, Smoking, Taking Drugs, Gambling, Sexual Misbehavior, And Swearing In American History* (New York University Press, 1993).

42. Ibid., 147–48.

43. Rod L. Evans and Mark Hance, "The Background to the Debate," *Legalized Gambling: For and Against* ed. Rod L. Evans and Mark Hance, (Open Court, 1998): 1–7.

44. Cited in John W. Kennedy, "Gambling Away the Golden Years," *Christianity Today* (May 24, 1999) 43, 6.

READING QUESTIONS

1. What five aspects of an individual's character does Fletcher think are jeopardized by gambling?
2. What are the rewards of gambling according to its advocates?
3. How does Fletcher respond to what he calls the "Entertainment Argument" for gambling?
4. Explain the reasons Fletcher offers for why the practice of gambling contributes to and represents a failure of rationality. Provide concrete examples of gambling behavior that exhibits the irrationality he attempts to characterize.
5. What is Fletcher's argument for the claim that gambling promotes indifference toward others? What arguments does he consider in opposition to this view and what is his response?

DISCUSSION QUESTIONS

1. Does the practice of gambling jeopardize our character in the several ways Fletcher suggests? If so, is the detriment inflicted on a person's character by gambling a necessary result of the practice or is it somehow avoidable?
2. Suppose Fletcher is right to recognize the differences between forms of entertainment like gambling and going to a film or a play. The former represents a moral hazard while the latter is often morally neutral if not rewarding. Do we have any reasons to think that engaging in the latter sorts of activities is ever morally hazardous? What, if any, other forms of entertainment or activity can threaten our moral character in the ways Fletcher describes?

ADDITIONAL RESOURCES

Web Resources

The U.S. Drug Enforcement Administration (DEA) <www.usdoj.gov/dea>, providing information on drugs, drug laws, and drug prevention.

The National Institute on Drug Abuse (NIDA) <www.nida.gov>. NIDA's main objective is to bring to bear on drug abuse the results of scientific inquiry. It also provides detailed information about specific drugs and drug prevention.

The National Organization for the Reform of Marijuana Laws (NORML) <www.norml.org>. A site with information about marijuana and dedicated to its legalization.

Authored Books & Articles

Butler, Keith, "The Moral Status of Smoking," *Social Theory and Practice* 19 (1993): 1–26. Argues that smoking routinely violates the harm principle.

Collins, Peter D., *Gambling and the Public Interest* (Westport, CT: Praeger Publishers, 2003). Collins examines the issue of gambling from a public policy perspective and argues that although for liberal democratic societies there is no moral justification for banning gambling, nevertheless there is a place for various public policy measures regarding the gambling industry aimed at minimizing any ill social effects of gambling.

de Marneffe, Peter, "Do We Have a Right to Use Drugs?" *Public Affairs Quarterly* 10 (1996): 229–47. de Marneffe argues that democratic countries are justified in passing some laws against the sale and use of certain drugs.

Husak, Douglas, N., *Drugs and Rights* (New York: Cambridge University Press, 1992). Husak argues that the "war on drugs" violates basic human rights to take drugs for recreational purposes.

Husak, Douglas, and Peter de Marneffe, *The Legalization of Drugs: For and Against* (Cambridge: Cambridge University Press, 2005). Husak defends the "for" position while de Marneffe defends the "against" position in this very readable and highly recommended book.

Miron, Jeffrey A., and Jeffrey Zwiebel, "The Economic Case Against Drug Prohibition," *Journal of Economic Perspectives* 9 (1995): 175–92. Authors argue that a free market in drugs is preferable to the current policy of drug prohibition.

Murphy, Jeffrie, G., "Indian Casinos and the Morality of Gambling," *Public Affairs Quarterly* 12 (1998): 119–36. Murphy considers the morality and justice of gambling, arguing that objections to its morality and justice are not compelling.

Newton, Lisa H., "Gambling: A Preliminary Inquiry," *Business Ethics Quarterly* 3 (1993): 405–18. Newton argues that the wrongness of gambling can be explained by appeal to the duty of steward-ship—the duty to protect and take care of property. Her argument is discussed in both the Collins and the Fletcher articles included in this chapter.

Shapiro, Daniel, "Smoking Tobacco," *Public Affairs Quarterly* 8 (1994): 187–203. Critical of Goodin's case in favor of paternalistic laws aimed at regulating smoking.

Slone, Frank A., J. Ostermann, G. Picone, C. Conover, and D. H. Taylor, Jr., *The Price of Smoking* (Boston: The MIT Press, 2006). Discussion of the social effects of smoking.

Wilson, James Q., "Against the Legalization of Drugs," *Commentary* 89 (1990): 21–8. Wilson presents arguments that appeal to both the harm principle and the principle of legal moralism in arguing against legalization.

Edited Collections

Belenko, Steven R. (ed.), *Drugs and Drug Policy in America* (Westport, Conn.: Greenwood Press, 2000). A collection of over 250 primary documents including court cases, speeches, laws, and opinion pieces that usefully trace the history of drugs and drug policy in America from the 19th century to the present.

Schaler, Jeffrey A. (ed.), *Shall We Legalize, Decriminalize, or Regulate?* (Buffalo, NY: Prometheus Books, 1998). Twenty-nine essays divided into eight parts: 1. Those Who Cannot Remember the Past. 2. A War on Drugs or a War on People? 3. Just Say "No" to Drug Legalization. 4. Medical Marijuana: What Counts as Medicine? 5. Drug War Metaphors and Additions: Drugs are Property. 6. Addiction is a Behavior: The Myth of Loss of Control. 7. Do Drugs Cause Crime? 8. State-Supported and Court-Ordered Treatment for Addiction Is Unconstitutional.

6 } Sexism, Racism, and Reparation

Since 1880 there have been roughly five thousand reported incidents in the United States of lynchings, most of them perpetrated against African Americans. On June 15, 2005, the U.S. Senate issued a formal apology for its history of not having passed any one of approximately two hundred bills that would have made lynching a federal crime, the first of which was proposed over one hundred years ago. Blockage in the Senate of antilynching laws was mainly due to opposition from senators from the U.S. South. This one-hundred-year failure to make what was a terrible racially biased practice a federal crime is but one manifestation of deeply racist attitudes that mar the history of the United States. Many people believe that the history of racism in the United States morally demands some form of reparation (and not just apology) be made to those citizens who have either directly or indirectly suffered or been disadvantaged by racist practices.

As we shall see in this chapter, moral questions about sexism and racism are not concerned with whether such discriminatory actions and practices are wrong—calling some action or practice racist or sexist entails that the action or practice in question is at least presumptively morally wrong. There are, however, important questions about the scope of racist and sexist actions and practices, and there are moral questions about what (if anything) is owed to victims of gender-based and race-based discrimination. Here, then, are some of the main moral questions about sexism and racism:

- What best explains why sexism and racism are morally wrong?
- Given a history of racism and/or sexism in a country, is some sort of reparation or compensation owed to members of the victimized group?
- Supposing that some form of reparation or compensation is owed, what form should it take? For example, are affirmative action policies that we find in universities and other organizations morally justified?

In order to set the stage for understanding these questions and the moral controversies they involve, let us begin with some remarks about the concepts of sexism and racism.

1. SEXISM AND RACISM

The *Merriam-Webster Online Dictionary* defines these terms in the following way:

Sexism

1: prejudice or discrimination based on sex; *especially*: discrimination against women

2: behavior, conditions, or attitudes that foster stereotypes of social roles based on sex.

Racism

1: a belief that race is the primary determinant of human traits and capacities and that racial differences produce an inherent superiority of a particular race
2: racial prejudice or discrimination.

Both definitions mention prejudice and discrimination as part of the common meaning of these terms, so let us work with these notions, keeping in mind the differences between sexism and racism revealed in these definitions.[1]

First, let us distinguish between someone being a sexist or a racist and someone engaging in sexist or racist activities. To be a sexist is to have negative beliefs or attitudes about some individual because she or he is of a particular sex. To be a racist is to have negative beliefs or attitudes about some individual because that individual belongs to some ethnic group. These definitions of being a sexist or racist only require that one have a certain prejudice toward members of some group even if one never acts in a discriminatory way toward its members. If, for example, someone believes that someone else is inferior in some way because the latter person is, say, black (about whom the person has negative beliefs or attitudes), then the person in question has racist attitudes and counts as a racist. Similarly for someone being a sexist. To have sexist or racist beliefs or attitudes is to have a *prejudice* against the members of some group.

While being a sexist or a racist is a matter of being prejudiced, actions and practices directed against individuals belonging to a sex or ethnic group are *discriminatory*. For an action or activity to be sexist or racist is for it to be directed against some individual because one believes (whether truly or not) that the individual belongs to a sex or an ethnic group. An act of sexism or racism may be intentional—as when a person's hatred for members of a certain sex or race motivates the person to knowingly engage in the sexist or racist activity. But there can be cases of unintentional sexist or racist acts as when someone does not intend to act in a racist way, but unwittingly says something or does something that is prejudicial toward a member of some ethnic group that results from the person's prejudicial beliefs about the group in question. For instance, someone might tell a joke and not intend for it to be harmful or prejudicial toward members of some ethnic group, even though in fact the joke is racist. One way in which the importance of unintentional sexist and racist acts can be brought out is by focusing on humor. In his article, Michael Philips considers the morality of humor (his focus is on racist humor, but as he points out, what he says applies also to sexist humor) and defines what he calls a "basic racist act" as one in which *either* (1) the actor performs the action in order to harm a member of some group because of a negative attitude toward the group *or* (2) regardless of the actor's intentions, the action in question may reasonably be expected to mistreat a member of an ethnic group. The second clause of his definition allows for unintentional race-based discrimination. In a similar way, we can distinguish intentional from unintentional sex-based acts of discrimination.

My characterizations of sexism and racism have focused on the beliefs, attitudes, and actions of individuals that constitute what we may call *interpersonal* sexism and racism. But institutions, legal systems, economic systems, and cultures can be sexist or racist if those institutions, systems, and cultures are partly constituted by rules, laws, regulations, and expectations that serve to promote sexist or racist beliefs, attitudes, and actions. These are cases of *institutional* sexism and racism, the main focus of the contribution by Marilyn Frye.

2. REPARATION

One of the main moral issues dealt with in some of the selections in this chapter is repara-tion for past wrongs against members of a sex or ethnic group. Roughly speaking, **repa-ration** involves making up for some past wrong. As J. Angelo Corlett points out in his article, often the wrongs in question were done to people who are now deceased, and so making up to them is not literally possible. Moreover, in some cases it is not possible to make up the past wrong to the descendants of the wronged victims. In such cases, accord-ing to Corlett, we may engage in *reparative compensation,* which attempts to rectify past wrongs by providing to those wronged or their descendants some form of compensation in the form of money, tax breaks, property, or other goods that is in proportion to the degree of evil that resulted from the wrong. While some sort of financial compensation may be called for as a response to sexism and racism, affirmative action policies that have to do with a person's opportunities may also be a fitting response to such discriminatory practices.

3. THEORY MEETS PRACTICE

Let us conclude by considering how the following four moral theories address the moral questions we have raised about sexism and racism.

Consequentialism

A consequentialist will explain the wrongness of sexism and racism in terms of the purported (overall) negative consequences of such actions and practices. Slavery and ethnic cleansing are but two clear cases of racist practices that have resulted in the maiming, murdering, and marginalization of members of various ethnic groups. It is very doubtful according to the consequentialist that the net value of the consequences of such activities is anything but extremely negative.

As for reparation generally and affirmative action policies in particular, the consequen-tialist will claim that such practices are morally required if they are more likely to have a greater net value for everyone affected than the value that would result from not engaging in these activities. These are matters that may divide consequentialists, since there may be doubts about the overall net value of at least certain forms of reparation and certain affirma-tive action policies.

Kantian Moral Theory

For a Kantian, all persons regardless of ethnicity and sex are deserving of equal respect in the sense that it is not permissible to treat anyone in a discriminatory manner, since doing so fails to treat them as ends in themselves. (This is an application of Kant's Humanity formula-tion of the categorical imperative presented in chapter 1, section 2C.) Moreover, a Kantian can claim that sexist and racist beliefs and attitudes are wrong (regardless of whether they result in the racist ever acting on his prejudicial beliefs or attitudes) because having them constitutes a failure to have a proper regard for the equal moral status of persons regardless of their sex or ethnicity.

If one uses Kant's Universal Law formulation of the categorical imperative, then whether a Kantian will claim that reparation or affirmative action policies are morally permissible (and perhaps morally required) will depend on whether the reparation or policies in question can be universalized. Can one consistently conceive and will that such practices be adopted by all? If so, then they are morally permissible. Can one consistently will that no such practices be adopted by all? If not, then not having such practices is morally wrong. Interestingly, Louis P. Pojman, in an article included in this chapter, argues that Kant's Humanity formulation can be used to argue against affirmative action policies. Kant's Universal Law and Humanity formulations of the categorical imperative are supposed to agree in their moral implications. If the Universal Law formulation conflicts in its verdict about affirmative action with the verdict reached by the Humanity formulation, this would reveal a deep incoherence in Kant's own moral theory. Whether these principles really do yield opposing verdicts about the morality of affirmative action is controversial and cannot be settled here.

Ethics of Prima Facie Duties

On W. D. Ross's moral theory (presented in chapter 1, section 2F), we have a prima facie duty of nonmaleficence—a prima facie duty not to harm others. This duty is not absolute—it can be overridden—however, it is clear that gross instances of sexism and racism are cases of maleficence that are not overridden by any other prima facie duty on Ross's list of seven such duties. Does Ross's view address sexist and racist prejudice even when having such beliefs and attitudes does not result in discriminatory actions? Ross's theory of prima facie duties may not clearly deal with this kind of case, since all of his prima facie duties have to do with actions and omissions. Robert Audi's version of an ethic of prima facie duties includes a duty of respectfulness: "We should, in the manner of our relations with other people, treat them respectfully."[2] But Audi's formulation of the duty of respectfulness does not address the morality of a person's attitudes; rather it concerns how we treat others. But we can easily revise Audi's principle so that it does make reference to one's beliefs and attitudes: we should, in the manner of our relations with other people *and in our attitudes toward them,* treat them and regard them respectfully. In having sexist or racist attitudes, one fails to have a proper respect for members of some sex or some ethnic group.

Both Ross and Audi recognize a prima facie duty of reparation: "We should make amends for our wrong-doing."[3] This principle, as stated, most directly applies to cases in which an individual has engaged in wrongdoing—she ought to make amends to the person(s) she has wronged. But what about cases in which the main perpetrators are our ancestors and the individuals directly wronged are now dead? Arguably, this is the case in contemporary North America in relation to the practice of slavery. Nevertheless, one can understand the "we" and "our" in the stated principle of reparation as the historical "we" and "our." If we are beneficiaries of past sexism or racism, then it may be morally incumbent on us to make reparations for past wrongs to those individuals of oppressed groups who (as a group) are less well off than they would be had their group not been a historical target of sexism or racism. In his article included in this chapter, J. Angelo Corlett makes a case for the claim that non-native

U.S. citizens have a prima facie duty of reparation toward Native Americans and that this prima facie duty is not overridden by other moral considerations.

Virtue Ethics

One might approach moral questions about racism by first asking what sort of character traits are best to have and which are best to avoid—the virtues and the vices, respectively—and then asking whether racist activities (and being a racist) are expressions of some vice. If so, then such activities and attitudes are wrong. And here it seems that the virtue ethicist is going to be able to argue that this kind of moral theory does provide a basis for the moral condemnation of racist actions *and* racist attitudes. The kinds of motives from which racism and racist acts arise—for example, hatred and fear—are characteristic of the vices of hatred and arrogance, respectively. With regard to reparations and affirmative action policies, again, the virtue ethicist will want to evaluate the morality of particular policies by considering whether such policies are those that a virtuous agent would advocate.

One way to understand Thomas E. Hill Jr.'s defense of affirmative action is through the lens of the virtue approach to moral deliberation. Hill is critical of consequentialist ("forward-looking") approaches and also critical of essentially "backward-looking" approaches that would appeal to a prima facie duty of reparation. Instead, Hill argues that there are certain ideals (we might say virtues) that we ought to aspire to achieve, including mutual respect and trust.

NOTES

1. It should be noted that although there are important similarities between sexism and racism, particularly with respect to the psychological and social mechanisms that make them possible, there are also important differences. For instance, Ann Cudd and Leslie E. Jones in their article "Sexism" point out that racism "is based on dubious theories about the differences between races, while sexual difference can hardly be denied" (104). Their article is included in R. G. Frey and Christopher Heath Wellman, eds., *A Companion to Applied Ethics* (Oxford: Blackwell, 2003).

2. Robert Audi, *The Good in the Right* (Princeton, NJ: Princeton University Press, 2004), 195.

3. Audi, *The Good in the Right,* 191.

MARILYN FRYE

Sexism

According to Frye, sex identification is an all-pervasive feature of our lives, and in contemporary culture it confers advantages upon men and disadvantages upon women. Sex identification is present in what Frye calls "sex marking"—how people respond to members of a sex—and in "sex announcement"—the ways in which, through, for example, manner, clothing, and hair style, we announce our sex. The various forces that require us to mark and announce sex, then, are forces that partly constitute the oppression of women. According to Frye, the term "sexist" refers to those cultural and economic structures that create and enforce elaborate patterns of marking and announcement that divide the species into sexes, one dominant over the other.

The first philosophical project I undertook as a feminist was that of trying to say carefully and persuasively what sexism is, and what it is for someone, some institution or some act to be sexist. This project was pressed on me with considerable urgency because, like most women coming to a feminist perception of themselves and the world, I was seeing sexism everywhere and trying to make it perceptible to others. I would point out, complain and criticize, but most frequently my friends and colleagues would not see that what I declared to be sexist was sexist, or at all objectionable.

As the critic and as the initiator of the topic, I was the one on whom the burden of proof fell—it was I who had to explain and convince. Teaching philosophy had already taught me that people cannot be persuaded of things they are not ready to be persuaded of; there are certain complexes of will and prior experience which will inevitably block persuasion, no matter the merits of the case presented. I knew that even if I could explain fully and clearly what I was saying when I called something sexist, I would not necessarily be able to convince various others of the correctness of this claim. . . .

Sex-identification intrudes into every moment of our lives and discourse, no matter what the supposedly primary focus or topic of the moment is. Elaborate, systematic, ubiquitous and redundant marking of a distinction between two sexes of humans and most animals is customary and obligatory. One *never* can ignore it.

Examples of sex-marking behavior patterns abound. A couple enters a restaurant; the headwaiter or hostess addresses the man and does not address the woman. The physician addresses the man by surname and honorific (Mr. Baxter, Rev. Jones) and addresses the woman by given name (Nancy, Gloria). You congratulate your friend—a hug, a slap on the back, shaking hands, kissing; one of the things which determines which of these you do is your friend's sex. In everything one does one has two complete repertoires of behavior, one for interactions with women and one for interactions with men. Greeting, storytelling, order-giving and order-receiving, negotiating, gesturing deference or dominance, encouraging, challenging, asking for information: one does all of these things differently depending upon whether the relevant others are male or female. . . .

From Marilyn Frye, *The Politics of Reality* (Freedom, CA: The Crossing Press, 1983), 17, 19–20, 23–24, 31–38.

The pressure on each of us to guess or determine the sex of everybody else both generates and is exhibited in a great pressure on each of us to *inform* everybody all the time of our sex. For, if you strip humans of most of their cultural trappings, it is not always that easy to tell without close inspection which are female, which are male. The tangible and visible physical differences between the sexes are not particularly sharp or numerous. Individual variation along the physical dimensions we think of as associated with maleness and femaleness are great, and the differences between the sexes could easily be obscured by bodily decoration, hair removal and the like. One of the shocks, when one does mistake someone's sex, is the discovery of how easily one can be misled. We could not ensure that we could identify people by their sex virtually anytime and anywhere under any conditions if they did not announce themselves, did not *tell* us in one way or another.

We do not, in fact, announce our sexes "in one way or another." We announce them in a thousand ways. We deck ourselves from head to toe with garments and decorations which serve like badges and buttons to announce our sexes. For every type of occasion there are distinct clothes, gear and accessories, hairdos, cosmetics and scents, labeled as "ladies'" or "men's" and labeling us as females or males, and most of the time most of us choose, use, wear or bear the paraphernalia associated with our sex. It goes below the skin as well. There are different styles of gait, gesture, posture, speech, humor, taste and even of perception, interest and attention that we learn as we grow up to be women or to be men and that label and announce us as women or as men. It begins early in life: even infants in arms are color coded.

That we wear and bear signs of our sexes, and that this is compulsory, is made clearest in the relatively rare cases when we do not do so, or not enough. Responses ranging from critical to indignant to hostile meet mothers whose small children are not immediately sex-identifiable, and hippies used to be accosted on the streets (by otherwise reserved and polite people) with criticisms and accusations when their clothing and style gave off mixed and contradictory sex-announcements. Anyone in any kind of job placement service and any Success Manual will tell you that you cannot expect to get or keep a job if your clothing or personal style is ambiguous in its announcement of your sex. You don't go to a job interview wearing the other sex's shoes and socks. . . .

Sex-marking and sex-announcing are equally compulsory for males and females; but that is as far as equality goes in this matter. The meaning and import of this behavior is profoundly different for women and for men.

Whatever features an individual male person has which tend to his social and economic disadvantage (his age, race, class, height, etc.), one feature which never tends to his disadvantage in the society at large is his maleness. The case for females is the mirror image of this. Whatever features an individual female person has which tend to her social and economic advantage (her age, race, etc.), one feature which always tends to her disadvantage is her femaleness. Therefore, when a male's sex-category is the thing about him that gets first and most repeated notice, the thing about him that is being framed and emphasized and given primacy is a feature which in general is an asset to him. When a female's sex-category is the thing about her that gets first and most repeated notice, the thing about her that is being framed and emphasized and given primacy is a feature which in general is a liability to her. Manifestations of this divergence in the meaning and consequences of sex-announcement can be very concrete.

Walking down the street in the evening in a town or city exposes one to some risk of assault. For males the risk is less; for females the risk is greater. If one announces oneself male, one is presumed by potential assailants to be more rather than less likely to defend oneself or be able to evade the assault and, if the male-announcement is strong and unambiguous, to be a noncandidate for sexual assault. If one announces oneself female, one is presumed by potential assailants to be less rather than more likely to defend oneself or to evade the assault and, if the female-announcement is strong and unambiguous, to be a prime candidate for sexual assault. Both the man and the woman "announce" their sex through style of gait, clothing, hair style, etc., but they are not equally or identically affected by announcing their sex. The male's announcement tends toward his protection or safety, and the female's announcement tends toward her victimization. It could not be more immediate or concrete; the meaning of the sex-identification could not be more different.

The sex-marking behavioral repertoires are such that in the behavior of almost all people of both sexes addressing or responding to males (especially within their own culture/race) generally is done in a manner which suggests basic respect, while addressing or responding to females is done in a manner that suggests the females' inferiority (condescending tones, presumptions of ignorance, overfamiliarity, sexual aggression, etc.). So, when one approaches an ordinary well-socialized person in such cultures, if one is male, one's own behavioral announcement of maleness tends to evoke supportive and beneficial response and if one is female, one's own behavioral announcement of femaleness tends to evoke degrading and detrimental response.

The details of the sex-announcing behaviors also contribute to the reduction of women and the elevation of men. The case is most obvious in the matter of clothing. As feminists have been saying for two hundred years or so, ladies' clothing is generally restrictive, binding, burdening and frail; it threatens to fall apart and/or to uncover something that is supposed to be covered if you bend, reach, kick, punch or run. It typically does not protect effectively against hazards in the environment, nor permit the wearer to protect herself against the hazards of the human environment. Men's clothing is generally the opposite of all this—sturdy, suitably protective, permitting movement and locomotion. The details of feminine manners and postures also serve to bind and restrict. To be feminine is to take up little space, to defer to others, to be silent or affirming of others, etc. It is not necessary here to survey all this, for it has been done many times and in illuminating detail in feminist writings. My point here is that though both men and women must behave in sex-announcing ways, the behavior which announces femaleness is in itself both physically and socially binding and

limiting as the behavior which announces maleness is not.

The sex-correlated variations in our behavior tend systematically to the benefit of males and the detriment of females. The male, announcing his sex in sex-identifying behavior and dress, is both announcing and acting on his membership in a dominant caste—dominant within his subculture and to a fair extent across subcultures as well. The female, announcing her sex, is both announcing and acting on her membership in the subordinated caste. She is obliged to inform others constantly and in every sort of situation that she is to be treated as inferior, without authority, assaultable. She cannot move or speak within the usual cultural norms without engaging in self-deprecation. The male cannot move or speak without engaging in self-aggrandizement. Constant sex-identification both defines and maintains the caste boundary without which there could not be a dominance-subordination structure.

The forces which make us mark and announce sexes are among the forces which constitute the oppression of women, and they are central and essential to the maintenance of that system.

Oppression is a system of interrelated barriers and forces which reduce, immobilize and mold people who belong to a certain group, and effect their subordination to another group (individually to individuals of the other group, and as a group, to that group). Such a system could not exist were not the groups, the categories of persons, well defined. Logically, it presupposes that there are two distinct categories. Practically, they must be not only distinct but relatively easily identifiable; the barriers and forces could not be suitably located and applied if there were often much doubt as to which individuals were to be contained and reduced, which were to dominate.

It is extremely costly to subordinate a large group of people simply by applications of material force, as is indicated by the costs of maximum security prisons and of military suppression of nationalist movements. For subordination to be permanent and cost effective, it is necessary to create conditions such that the subordinated group acquiesces to some extent in the subordination. Probably one of the most efficient ways to secure acquiescence is to convince the people that their subordination is inevitable. The mechanisms by which the subordinate and dominant categories are defined can contribute greatly to popular belief in the inevitability of the dominance/subordination structure.

For efficient subordination, what's wanted is that the structure not appear to be a cultural artifact kept in place by human decision or custom, but that it appear *natural*—that it appear to be a quite direct consequence of facts about the beast which are beyond the scope of human manipulation or revision. It must seem natural that individuals of the one category are dominated by individuals of the other and that as groups, the one dominates the other. To make this seem natural, it will help if it seems to all concerned that members of the two groups are *very* different from each other, and this appearance is enhanced if it can be made to appear that within each group, the members are very like one another. In other words, the appearance of the naturalness of the dominance of men and the subordination of women is supported by anything which supports the appearance that men are very like other men and very unlike women, and that women are very like other women and very unlike men. All behavior which encourages the appearance that humans are biologically sharply sex-dimorphic encourages the acquiescence of women (and, to the extent it needs encouragement, of men) in women's subordination.

That we are trained to behave so differently as women and as men, and to behave so differently toward women and toward men, itself contributes mightily to the appearance of extreme natural dimorphism, but also, the *ways* we act as women and as men, and the *ways* we act toward women and toward men, mold our bodies and our minds to the shapes of subordination and dominance. We do become what we practice being.

Throughout this essay I have seemed to beg the question at hand. Should I not be trying to prove that there are few and insignificant differences between females and males, if that is what I believe, rather than assuming it? What I have been doing is offering observations which suggest that if one thinks there are biologically deep differences between women and men which cause and justify divisions of labor and responsibility such as we see in the modern patriarchal family and male-dominated workplace, one may *not* have arrived at this belief because of direct experience of unmolested physical evidence, but because our customs serve to construct that appearance; and I suggest that these customs are artifacts of culture which exist to support a morally and scientifically insupportable system of dominance and subordination.

But also, in the end, I do not want to claim simply that there are not socially significant biologically-grounded differences between human females and males. Things are much more complex than that.

Enculturation and socialization are, I think, misunderstood if one pictures them as processes which apply layers of cultural gloss over a biological substratum. It is with that picture in mind that one asks whether this or that aspect of behavior is due to *nature* or *nurture*. One means, does it emanate from the biological substratum or does it come from some layer of the shellac? A variant on this wrong picture is the picture according to which enculturation or socialization is something mental or psychological, as opposed to something physical or biological. Then one can think of attitudes and habits of perception, for instance, as *learned* versus *biologically determined*. And again, one can ask such things as whether men's aggressiveness is learned or biologically determined, and if the former is asserted, one can think in terms of changing them while if the latter is asserted, one must give up all thought of reform.

My observations and experience suggest another way of looking at this. I see enormous social pressure on us all to act feminine or act masculine (and not both), so I am inclined to think that if we were to break the habits of culture which generate that pressure, people would not act particularly masculine or feminine. The fact that there are such penalties threatened for deviations from these patterns strongly suggests that the patterns would not be there but for the threats. This leads, I think, to a skeptical conclusion: we do not know whether human behavior patterns would be dimorphic along lines of chromosomal sex if we were not threatened and bullied; nor do we know, if we assume that they would be dimorphous, *what* they would be, that is, *what* constellations of traits and tendencies would fall out along that genetic line. And these questions are odd anyway, for there is no question of humans growing up *without* culture, so we don't know what other cultural variables we might imagine to be at work in a culture in which the familiar training to masculinity and femininity were not going on.

On the other hand, as one goes about in the world, and in particular as one tries out strategies meant to alter the behaviors which constitute and support male dominance, one often has extremely convincing experiences of the *inflexibility* of people in this respect, of a resistance to change which seems to run much, much deeper than willingness or willfulness in the face of arguments and evidence. As feminist activists, many of us have felt this most particularly in the case of men, and it has sometimes seemed that the relative flexibility and adaptability of women and the relative rigidity of men are so widespread within each group respectively, and so often and convincingly encountered, that they must be biologically given. And one watches men and women on the streets, and their bodies seem so different—one hardly can avoid thinking there are vast and profound differences between women and men without giving up the hard won confidence in one's powers of perception.

The first remedy here is to lift one's eyes from a single culture, class and race. If the bodies of Asian women set them apart so sharply from Asian men, see how different they are also from black women; if white men all look alike and very different from white women, it helps to note that black men don't look so like white men.

The second remedy is to think about the subjective experience we have of our *habits*. If one habitually twists a lock of one's hair whenever one is reading and has tried to break this habit, one knows how *bodily* it is; but that does not convince one it is genetically determined. People who drive to work every day often take the same route every day, and if they mean to take another route one day in order to do an errand on the way, they may find themselves at work, conveyed along the habitual route, without having revised the decision to do the errand. The habit of taking that course is mapped into one's body; it is not a matter of a decision—a mental event—that is repeated each day upon a daily re-judgment of the reasonableness of the course. It is also not genetic. We are animals. Learning is physical, bodily. There is not a separate, nonmaterial "control room" where socialization, enculturation and habit formation take place and where, since it is nonmaterial, change is independent of bodies and easier than in bodies.

Socialization molds our bodies; enculturation forms our skeletons, our musculature, our central nervous systems. By the time we are gendered adults, masculinity and femininity *are biological.* They are structural and material features of how our bodies are. My experience suggests that they are changeable just as one would expect bodies to be—slowly, through constant practice and deliberate regimens designed to remap and rebuild nerve and tissue. This is how many of us *have* changed when we chose to change from "women" as culturally defined to *women* as we define ourselves. Both the sources of the changes and the resistances to them are bodily—are among the possibilities of our animal natures, whatever those may be.

But now *biological* does not mean *genetically determined* or *inevitable.* It just means *of the animal.*

It is no accident that feminism has often focused on our bodies. Rape, battering, reproductive self-determination, health, nutrition, self-defense, athletics, financial independence (control of the means of feeding and sheltering ourselves). And it is no accident that with varying degrees of conscious intention, feminists have tried to create separate spaces where women could exist somewhat sheltered from the prevailing winds of patriarchal culture and try to stand up straight for once. One needs space to *practice* an erect posture; one cannot just will it to happen. To retrain one's body one needs physical freedom from what are, in the last analysis, physical forces misshaping it to the contours of the subordinate.

The cultural and economic structures which create and enforce elaborate and rigid patterns of sex-marking and sex-announcing behavior, that is, create gender as we know it, mold us as dominators and subordinates (I do not say "mold our minds" or "mold our personalities"). They construct two classes of animals, the masculine and the feminine, where another constellation of forces might have constructed three or five categories, and not necessarily hierarchically related. Or such a spectrum of sorts that we would not experience them as "sorts" at all.

The term *sexist* characterizes cultural and economic structures which create and enforce the elaborate and rigid patterns of sex-marking and sex-announcing which divide the species, along lines of sex, into dominators and subordinates. Individual acts and practices are sexist which reinforce and support those structures, either as culture or as shapes taken on by the enculturated animals. Resistance to sexism is that which undermines those structures by social and political action and by projects of reconstruction and revision of ourselves.

READING QUESTIONS

1. How does Frye characterize "sex-marking" and "sex-announcement"? Give examples of each for both males and females.
2. How do males and females differ with respect to their treatment and standing in society according to Frye?
3. What is the source of female oppression according to Frye?
4. How does Frye respond to the objection that she is begging the question? What is her solution for breaking the habit of seeing differences between males and females?

DISCUSSION QUESTIONS

1. Consider whether classifying an individual as either a male or a female is inherently wrong. How might the oppression of women in society be overcome without having to avoid gender division?
2. To what extent are society and culture responsible for the differences between men and women? Discuss some other possible sources of these differences.

J. L. A. GARCIA

Racism as a Model for Understanding Sexism

As Garcia explains, the term "sexism" was introduced by feminists in the 1960s to refer to something that is supposed to be analogous to racism. Garcia is concerned with determining whether this understanding of sexism is correct. He does so by considering certain influential analyses of sexism and racism, including the analyses offered by Richard Wasserstrom and Marilyn Frye, arguing that these accounts fail in one way or another to properly characterize sexism and racism. Garcia then proposes an understanding of racism according to which it consists of either race-based ill will or race-based lack of goodwill, and uses this analysis to vindicate the feminist idea that sexism is analogous to racism.

INTRODUCTION:
RACISM AND SEXISM

According to the *OED*, the term "sexism" entered English in the middle and late 1960s. It is generally allowed that the term was conceived as an analogue of racism, and the first recorded use of any cognate term makes this derivation explicit: "When you argue that since fewer women write good poetry this justifies their total exclusion, you are taking a position analogous to that of the racist—I might call you in this case a 'sexist'—who says that since so few negroes [*sic*] have held positions of importance . . . their exclusion from history books is a matter of good judgment rather than discrimination."[1]

Those who devised the term "sexism," then, took it to be the same kind of thing as racism with the notion of sex replacing that of race in marking out the victims and women replacing Black people as the most salient targets of victimization (in the actual current and historical situations, if not necessarily).[2] Sexism was held to be formally, structurally similar to racism, but with different content. What appear to be among

the first recorded uses of this and related terms bring this out. Thus: "A sexist is one who proclaims or justifies or assumes the supremacy of one sex (guess which) over the other." Or, again: "Sexism is judging people by their sex where sex doesn't matter."[3] These remarks clearly adapt, to relations between the sexes, understandings of racism then (and now) current. The former formally resembles a typical definition of racism as "an explicit and systematic ideology of racial superiority," changing content by the substitution of sex for race. The latter is a formal match for the common view that racism consists in irrelevantly taking race into account.[4]

Even a quick examination of some survey literature shows that this close formal connection is still widely assumed. One social critic says racism "suggests first and foremost a negative external view, that is, a negative view held toward members of another group." She thinks both 'sexism' and 'racism' "refer . . . to oppressive behaviors, policies, and attitudes ranging from institutionalized murder to unwitting support of insensitive practices by the well-intentioned."[5] A second relates what she thinks of as "the dual discriminations of sexism and racism,"

From J. L. A. Garcia, "Racism as a Model for Understanding Sexism," in Naomi Zack, ed., *Race/Sex* (New York and London: Routledge, 1977).

explaining that "*Racism* refers to the ideological, structural, and behavioral systems in society which deny and limit opportunities for some groups because of their racial identity in order to create and maintain a racial hierarchy. *Sexism* refers to a system of control which maintains and legitimates a sexual hierarchy in which males are dominant."[6] Plainly, her intent is to draw on the detail provided in the understanding of racism she offers to elucidate that she provides for sexism. The "system of control" in the latter must comprise the society's "ideological, structural, and ideological systems" mentioned in the former, and the way in which this system "maintains and legitimates sexual hierarchy" is, presumably, by "deny[ing] and limit[ing] opportunities" for women, in the same manner that, she has explained, racism acts thereby to "create and maintain . . . racial hierarchy." Some even go on to rebut claims of "reverse sexism," mirroring responses to current complaints against race preferential affirmative action policies as "reverse racism," and to level charges of "institutionalized sexism," mirroring common talk of "institutional racism."[7]

Our examination also reveals that among these same writers, all of whom are sure that sexism structurally resembles racism, there is no agreement on just what sexism is. This is because they disagree about that in which the prior notion of racism itself consists. Some feminists understand racism and sexism as ways of thinking and talking about people; others see both as ways of treating people: one group maintains they lie within individuals, while a different one maintains they can be found only in institutions and social systems. To understand sexism we should begin by analyzing racism, first to see what it is; second, to assess its suitability as a conceptual model for understanding sexism; and third, to consider in what sexism will consist if the term's originators were correct in seeing sexism as structurally, formally similar to racism.

My procedure here will be, in section 1, to investigate an influential analysis of racism, which promises application also to sexism. In section 2, I propose a different account of racism, in light of difficulties found in others. In section 3, I examine an important account of the nature of sexism, to see if the topic is better grasped by confronting it directly, rather than through the model of racism. In section 4, I sketch what sexism is if it really is structurally like racism. In section 5, I elaborate one element of this reconceptualization of sexism to deal with a salient form of sexism whose analogous form of racism has been little examined.

I. WASSERSTROM ON RACISM AND SEXISM

In an early, but oft-reprinted and still highly influential, article on racism and sexism, Richard Wasserstrom offers a promisingly unified picture of the two phenomena. He writes:

> "[R]acism and sexism consist in taking race and sex into account in a certain way, in the context of a specific set of institutional arrangements and a specific ideology, which together create [a system of unjust institutions and unwarranted beliefs and attitudes] and [which together] maintain a system of unjust institutions and unwarranted beliefs and attitudes. That system is and has been one in which political, economic, and social power are concentrated in the hands of those who are white and male."[8]

Wasserstrom allows that there are differences between racism and sexism, but stresses that "the mode of analysis I propose serves as well . . . for an analogous analysis of the sexism of the legal system. . . . In theory, the foregoing analysis can be applied as readily to the social realities of sexual oppression as to racism." Nonetheless, his more detailed explanation focuses on law's racism. Unfortunately, his promise of a unified account, in which the claimed structural similarity of racism and sexism is maintained and explained, remains unrealized on examination. His account of racism's nature tries but fails, for several reasons, to provide necessary conditions for racism. First, there may be racism in individuals' attitudes even if there are no surrounding racist institutional arrangements or general ideology. Consider the solitary old anti-Black bigot, alone in her room, raging within over the signs of Black advancement she sees on TV, reads about in magazines, witnesses even in the evident prosperity of some of the Black people she sees walking or driving along beneath her window. She is a racist, if anyone is, irrespective of the ideology and institutions that surround her. Indeed, it is grotesque to maintain she gets off the hook of racism, merely when and because, contrary to her heartfelt desires, all such embodiments of racism have been eliminated.[9] Second, racism can exist if the institutions and beliefs are maintained but only unsystematically—in a haphazard, disconnected, sporadic, hit-and-miss, discontinuous way. For example, a group of racists may succeed in getting the athletic office—but not the principal's—at public school #1 to discriminate, the promotions office—but not the hiring officer—in company #35, and so on. This would be institutionalized but, nonetheless, nonsystematic racism. Third, if the claims about racism's successful concentration of power at the end of Wasserstrom's account are meant to be part of the definition or essence of racism, then they constitute another unnecessary condition, for racism also exists when the system tries but fails to concentrate power racially.[10]

Nor does Wasserstrom's account of the nature of racism provide sufficient conditions. Suppose that the causal connections he supposes exist, but are accidental, neither intended to harm nor born of callous disregard. Perhaps a group of institutions and beliefs do work together to form a system and this system operates to maintain itself to the disadvantage of one racial group. Imagine, however, that this occurs by accident. In that case, I want to say, there is no racism, although there is an oppressive system. This hypothesis might seem so far-fetched it is not worth attending to. However, what I am imagining has serious consequences for the real world, consequences that attend any account of racism that makes something racist depending simply on what it happens to "create," "maintain," or "concentrate." Imagine Twin Earth, where some of the complaints that conservatives raise against "the new (self-) segregation," "reverse discrimination," etc., really hold true. On Twin Earth, these antiracist efforts really do work to undermine self-confidence and self-esteem among those in the oppressed racial group; really do perpetuate racial

stereotypes and the belief that members of the group are unable to "make it" economically, or socially or academically on their own; really do generate hostility and resentment among those in the favored group; really do undermine self-confidence and the "work ethic" among intended beneficiaries. Wasserstrom's account implies that on Twin Earth such measures, undertaken by those on the bottom socially and economically are not only ill-advised and counter-productive, but are themselves racist, simply because, quite contrary to their purpose, they have the systematic effect of confirming unwarranted beliefs ("those people can't make it on their own"), promoting unwarranted attitudes ("I never feel comfortable about those people, they're so clique-ish"), perpetuating unjust institutions ("there's nothing wrong with our White Male's Party, segregated clubs, etc., if there's nothing wrong with their Women's Bank, Black Engineers' Association, etc."), and thus have the effect of further concentrating power in white male hands. Moreover, his account of what racism is unacceptably implies that, on Real Earth, we have to wait and see how things turn out before we know whether such self-help measures are counterproductive and therefore themselves racist!

Wasserstrom completes his account of racism by adding to his claims about its nature a discussion of three types: overt, such as Jim Crow laws; "covert but intentional," such as "grandfather clauses"; and institutional. Institutional racism resides either in "sub-institutions" with the law, such as mechanisms leading Black defendants to have disproportionately White juries, or consists in "conceptual institutional racism . . . [wherein,] often without [our] realizing it, the concepts used [in law] take for granted certain objectionable aspects of racist ideology."

Wasserstrom's account of the types and subtypes of racism is also problematic. First, what distinguishes "institutional racism" from "overt" and from "covert" racism within a legal system? Is not all state action *eo ipso* institutional? For that matter, is not any intentional (or unintentional) institutional racism necessarily either overt or covert?[11] *Tertium datur*? Second, the examples of institutional racism that Wasserstrom offers, e.g., selecting jurors from voting lists whose segregation leads to segregated juries, seem to consist in *not* taking race into account in cases where, Wasserstrom thinks, it should be. Suppose that this is a defect in these procedures and that it even makes them racist? They still cannot count as racist by Wasserstrom's account. That account requires that racism consist in taking race into account in certain ways and contexts. It says nothing of things being racist because of the ways in which race is *not* taken into account.

I conclude that Wasserstrom's understanding of racism cannot provide us the philosophical understanding of racism we should need to vindicate the view—held by those who coined the term "sexism"—that sexism is structurally similar to the social phenomena they identified in order to oppose. I shall suggest a different conceptualization.

II. RACISM RECONCEIVED

One of the many strengths of Wasserstrom's proposed account of racism and sexism is that it encompasses the principal types of phenomena with which people have identified racism and sexism: oppressive institutional practices and prejudiced individual beliefs. Oppressive institutional practices, however, turned out neither necessary nor sufficient for racism. What, then, of prejudiced beliefs? Again, someone may hold such a belief without properly incurring the charge of racism—for example, some *naif* hoodwinked by Plato's "noble lie" about the origins of the golden, silver, and bronze races.[12] Likewise, racism can characterize someone without her holding prejudiced beliefs—for example, when someone acts from or is filled with racial animosity neither derived from prior unfavorable beliefs about the hated race nor rationalized by later adoption of such beliefs.[13]

Some respond to these counterexamples to the sufficiency of prejudice for racism by conceding that it is not *what* a racist believes but *how* she believes it that makes her a racist. Kwame Anthony Appiah, for instance, maintains that a racist holds her prejudices in an ideological way, immunizing them from counter-argument. Lewis Gordon, legitimately

worried that Appiah's account threatens to exculpate the racist by assigning her ugly beliefs to irrationality, insists that what characterizes the racist is that she self-deceptively chooses to hold her prejudiced beliefs as a matter of what existentialists call "bad faith."[14]

I think none of these efforts to defend the view that racism is a matter of what one believes and how she believes it succeeds.[15] However, they suggest a different way of understanding racism. The person who holds to her "anti-Black" (or anti-whatever) prejudices regardless of counterevidence, or who deceives herself into holding onto them, is committed to opposing the advancement of those whose race she makes her enemy. She wants, and thinks she needs, those of the targeted race to suffer, at least to suffer in comparison to her. That indicates that the core of her racism lies not in her beliefs, and still less in social systems, but in her desires, hopes, and goals. Similarly, common sense indicates that the most egregious racists are race-haters. Certainly, the paradigmatic racist is: the Nazi, the Klansman, the White-supremacist "Skinhead," the slave-driver. Hatred, I think, is not itself necessary; some lesser forms of racial disregard—contempt and callous indifference, for instance—suffice for racism. The fact remains that racism lies primarily in the heart, that is, in hopes, fears, joys, desires, and intentions. Of course, it need not remain there. Normally, racism gets out to infect the racist's behavior, and when the racist exercises institutional authority, or when racists design social practices, the racial disregard that constitutes racism can become institutionalized and corrupt the operations of social systems and practices as well.

Understanding racism as race-based ill will (or a race-based deficiency in goodwill) has advantages. It explains how racism, while having its primary occurrence in individuals' hearts, can also infect their beliefs and actions. Moreover, it explains how group and institutional behavior, policies, and practices can be racist. It correctly classifies such paradigms of racism as the Nazi and the Klansman. Unlike attempts to understand racism in terms of effects, however, it need not extend the charge to cover anti-racist groups and undertakings simply because they prove counterproductive. Before we proceed to see how sexism would look if modeled on such an understanding of racism, however, we should examine how feminists have understood sexism. Since they do not agree on what sexism is, as with racism I will closely investigate one especially sophisticated, influential, and time-honored philosophical suggestion on how to conceptualize it.

III. FRYE ON SEXISM AND SEXISTS

In an article early in the career of the new academic feminism, and reprinted since, Marilyn Frye offers distinct and seemingly independent accounts of (1) some*thing*'s being sexist and of (2) some*one*'s being *a* sexist. About what makes a thing to be sexist, she writes, "The term 'sexist' in its core and perhaps most fundamental meaning is a term that characterizes anything that creates, constitutes, promotes, or exploits any irrelevant or impertinent marking of the distinctions between the sexes." She adds it "is commonly applied to specific acts or behavior or to certain institutional processes, laws, customs, and so forth."[16] About what it is for someone to be a sexist, she writes, "One would standardly characterize a person as a sexist in virtue of his sexist beliefs, opinions, convictions, and principles. A person might also be called a sexist in virtue of his acts and practices, but in general only if they are seen as associated with sexist beliefs. . . . Speaking quite generally, sexists are those who hold certain sorts of general beliefs about sexual differences and their consequences." These beliefs "would, for instance, support the view that physical differences between the sexes must always make for significant social and economic differences between them in any human society" and can be summed up in the "simple proposition: Males are innately superior to females."

Frye offers sophisticated accounts of what sexism is and of what a sexist is. Unfortunately, these accounts may not be consistent in their implications. The two accounts seem to lead to different and potentially inconsistent accounts of, at least, X's (i) being a sexist belief, (ii) being a sexist person, and (iii) being a sexist action. Should we say, for example, that a belief is a sexist belief when it "creates [or] promotes" irrelevant consideration of sex, as Frye's account of what makes a thing sexist implies? Or should we call it a sexist belief just when it can be "represented by the simple proposition: Males are innately superiority to females," as the account of what makes someone to be a sexist requires? In short, is a belief sexist because of what it *is* (that is, by the proposition that "represents" it) or because of what it *causes?* Frye winds up committed to both; but they are plainly different and open to inconsistent implications.

Similar questions arise for her account of what makes people sexists. Let us assume that a person who is a sexist is a sexist person. Is someone a sexist person because of what she "promotes or creates"? Or is it what she believes that makes her a sexist? An affirmative answer to the former follows from Frye's account of what it is for something to be a sexist such-and-such, and an affirmative answer to the latter follows from her account of what it is for someone to be a sexist.

In addition to problems of inconsistency in her accounts of sexist belief and sexist persons, consider her view of sexist conduct. Frye says, "A person might also be called a sexist in virtue of his acts and practices, but in general only if they are seen as associated with sexist beliefs." But must not the actions on whose basis a person is properly called a sexist themselves be sexist actions? It seems so, and Frye herself at this point speaks of "sexist behavior" even in non-sexists (agents who are not sexists). However, if so, then our question arises again. Is my behavior sexist when it is duly associated with my sexist beliefs, as what she says here suggests? Or when it "promotes [or] creates" irrelevant marking of sex difference, as her general account of what makes things sexist commits her to?

Finally, notice, that Frye's account of sexism, like Wasserstrom's, implausibly allows that someone and her efforts can be sexist simply because of bad luck in their unintended and perhaps unforeseeable effects. Even feminists' antisexist measures (e.g., forming an all-women's support group or a pro-woman advocacy group) might counterproductively create or promote an irrelevant (marking of) sexual difference. That might make them ill-advised, but it does not mean that they are sexist, *pace* Frye. Whether a person and her conduct are sexist is never just a matter of bad luck.

IV. WHAT IS SEXISM, IF IT IS LIKE RACISM?

Alison Jaggar has suggested a more promising account of sexism. She writes that in addition to "institutional sexism [which] is a social disadvantage which attaches to individuals of one sex or the other as a result of a certain way of institutionalizing activity," there is also "individual sexism which occurs when a certain individual or group of individuals express hatred or contempt for an individual or group of (usually) the other sex by an act of hostility which may or may not be violent but which is not part of a socially stabilized pattern of discrimination."[17] We need not endorse Jaggar's view that individual sexism need, for some reason, exclude institutionalized sexism, nor with her assumption that sexism need be something that "occurs." What is appealing in Jaggar's view is her suggestion that sexism is necessarily connected to something like "hatred or contempt." However, I see no reason to follow her in thinking the attitude must be expressed for there to be sexism. Sexism, if it is like racism, exists in the attitudes of someone filled with hatred or contempt, whether or not she expresses it in acts of hostility. It is enough that she be hostile in a certain way. If a man hates or disdains women as such, but never has opportunity to express this attitude in hostile acts towards them (perhaps he is part of an all-male ship's crew or prison population), this does not get him off the hook of *being* a sexist, even if he never treats women hostilely.

If sexism is like racism, then, it consists in sex-based disregard or ill will. Such an understanding of sexism has certain advantages. Feminists aim to improve the lot of women, and since they see sexism as their special enemy we can reasonably expect sexism to be a stance of opposition to women's welfare.

What is important for our purposes here is that it is only when so conceived that sexism is, as those who coined the term thought of it as being, a close structural relative of racism. That important fact highlights a second advantage to this sort of approach. When thought of as a certain kind of ill will (or, again like racism, as a deficit of goodwill), sexism is—like racism, xenophobia, and anti-Semitism—something that is obviously immoral. Appreciation of the central moral significance of such attitudes is one of the chief contributions of the recent revival of virtues-based moral theory. Since sexism was identified in order to condemn it and provide a clearer focus on what it is that demands censure, reform, and elimination, taking sexism as a vicious attitude helps the concept do its work.

Thought of as hostility to women in the form of hatred or contempt, "sexism" seems to be merely a new name for misogyny. This result, however, need not trouble us. Though the term "sexism" is new, it is no part of feminist thought to insist that what the term refers to is itself new. Quite the contrary. However, there is a problem in that sexism appears to include phenomena not usually considered parts or types of misogyny. Some people count insensitivity to women's needs, feelings, etc., as forms of sexism; yet it seems excessively severe to characterize much of this as "hatred or contempt." These people may need reminding that much insensitivity has moral import only in that it is something the morally virtuous person will try to eliminate from her attitude as undesirable, not in the stronger sense that it is itself vicious. Moreover, sometimes the fault lies less in X's insensitivity than in Y's oversensitivity. Still, the term "insensitivity" itself means a lack of feeling, and any adequate account of virtues and the moral life will sometimes fault people not only for how they do or do not think and act, but also for how they do or do not feel.

A related, but more complicated, problem is that sexism is also thought to include paternalistic attitudes towards women, attitudes or solicitude and even protection. Yet this is not the way we think of misogynists. (Nor racists.) As Laurence Thomas trenchantly reminds us, while the sexist may plausibly claim to be trying to protect women, to shield them from adult responsibilities, the White racist is not normally trying to protect Black people, even on her own (perhaps perverse) understanding of their interest.[18] So we shall need briefly to examine the nature of sexist paternalism before we can say whether reconceiving sexism along the lines I have sketched really can adequately delineate the social phenomenon with which it is concerned or successfully model that phenomenon on racism.

V. PATERNALISM, DISRESPECT, AND SELF-DECEPTION IN SEXISM

The root idea of paternalism is that A treats B paternalistically when A treats B as if B were a child under A's authority, overriding B's preferences, making the principal decisions in B's life. (Not merely like A's (possibly full-grown) offspring, that is, but like A's child.) Paternalism is not always objectionable. Children need to be treated paternalistically by those responsible for them. It is easy to see why paternal treatment breeds frustration and resentment, but what makes it immoral? When B is a responsible adult and A treats her as if she were something less than that, then A may be violating B's dignity by degrading her. Then A's act violates the virtue of justice in its disrespect. However, A only violates justice by treating B paternalistically if A does or should see B's true stature. When A is innocently unaware of B's status as a responsible moral agent, then neither A nor her action is unjust, for there is no viciousness through mere accident, mistake, or error.

Paternalistic behavior, then, is sometimes unjust. It is when someone who treats a responsible adult paternalistically knows what she is doing or is morally at fault in not knowing it. How is this sort of injustice related to something like Jaggar's "hatred or contempt"? I think that, like them, it is a type of ill will. Hatred is the opposite of love. Since loving someone is devoting one's will, affection, and desires to her welfare—in short, goodwill—hating her is comparably devoting oneself to depriving her of goods—that is, ill will. On that basis, we can say that the kind of disrespect and degradation that

characterizes such paternalism as that of Thomas' condescending, "protective" sexism is vicious insofar as it is rooted in disrespect, a failure to *regard* and to *treat* members of one sex, S1, as having the full rights and status that it is one of the marks of the virtuous to accord all people. Such lack of respect, as such, is a failure of goodwill and thus an offense against the moral virtue of benevolence, in that it manifests morally insufficient concern that S1s enjoy such goods of status, deference, and opportunity. The paternalist sexist acts viciously insofar as she is uninterested in securing to those in one sex these autonomy goods, and this failure to will goods of a certain sort is a failure in (and offense against) that moral virtue we call goodwill or benevolence.

When paternalism is immoral, then, the paternalist aims to secure another some good by depriving her of others. It is goodwill pursued through willing evils: doing evil that good may come. This way of understanding the morality of paternalism does more than provide a conception of sexist paternalism that fits a wider account of sexism as modeled on racism. It also is preferable for theoretical reasons both to understanding immoral paternalism as pursuing benevolence by violating an independent principle of autonomy—a conception now common in medical ethics—and to understanding vicious paternalism as embodying an "excess" of benevolence in violation of some quasi-Aristotelian mean. The former account, insofar as it leaves us with a conflict among basic principles, threatens to deprive us of rational ways of resolving the controversies surrounding paternalism. The latter account, inspired by Aristotle's doctrine of the mean, fails because benevolence itself is a moral virtue—not an Aristotelian one, of course, but a close relative of what Christians call charity—and thus not the sort of thing of which Aristotle said there could be a vicious excess.

This approach to sexism works well in explaining the immorality of failing to treat as an adult someone we know to be one. It threatens, however, to exculpate and even exonerate us in acting paternalistically toward those whose status as responsible, capable adults we do not recognize. What can be the *moral* fault in this mere *cognitive* lapse? Here, I think, some remarks of Frye's can help. We criticized her analysis of sexism above. However, she is at pains to distinguish sexism from a supposedly different phenomenon, which she initially calls "male chauvinism." "[T]he feminist" who used this (now somewhat dated) term, according to Frye, was "accusing the male chauvinist of . . . acting as though what really is *only* a group of human beings [viz., males] were all there is to the human race. . . ." For reasons that need not concern us here, Frye prefers the term 'phallism' to the then-current 'male chauvinism.' She bluntly attributes to 'phallism' "a picture of humanity as consisting [only] of males."[19] She elucidates, "The phallist approaches females with a superiority and condescension that we all take more or less appropriate to encounters with members of other species. . . . The phallist does not treat women as persons."

While Frye thinks some phallists are simply malicious, "it is more common for a person to shrink from such blatant immorality, guarding his conscience with a protective membrane of self-deception. The phallist can arrange things so he does not experience females as persons. . . ." After summarizing some strategies for so arranging things, Frye talks of "the phallist's *refusal* to experience women as persons." (Emphasis added.) This reference to a refusal to face the facts ties Frye's account of so-called "phallism" to Gordon's account of racism as involving "bad faith," which he sees as a way of hiding from oneself. Plainly, self-deception is an attractive way of hiding from truths whose recognition threatens our interests, as recognition of women as equals threatens the interests of those (of both sexes) who benefit in various ways from the degradation of women. This self-deception to which Frye and Gordon direct our attention, then, can be seen as rooted in the sexist's or the racist's perceived self-interest and, more important, mediated through the sexist's or racist's disregard for, and even hostility to the competing interests of others. Such self-deception would secure the connection we needed between the sexist (or racist) paternalist's failure to see those of another sex (or race) as fully responsible and offenses against the moral virtue or benevolences.[20] If this is correct, such sexism can now be understood as immoral for the same reason other forms are: it is infected by vicious disregard for others, that is, by a form of ill will, such as hatred or contempt, where contempt includes that form of ill will or non-benevolence directed especially against

someone's enjoying the goods of status and their requisite deference.

I have suggested that, once we properly understand racism as race-based ill will (or a racially-based deficit in goodwill), it follows that, if we are to vindicate the early feminists' view that sexism is structurally similar to racism, then sexism must also consist not in a social system, practice, or belief, but in sex-based contempt or other ill will. The good news in this is that the immorality of sexism is insured and clarified. It consists in vicious failures in the moral virtue of benevolence.

This understanding of sexism has implications for social discussion. If sexism, that is, misogyny, consists in having certain hostile feelings, desires, and intentions toward those of one of the sexes, then, while this may explain in some instances why this or that person believes a certain proposition about the differences between women and men and their proper social implications, by itself it generally does nothing to show the truth or falsity of these propositions. Of course, some such propositions—as that the rights of women are systematically less important than those of men—may seem plausible only to the vicious. Such theses aside, there remain many currently controversial claims about sex differences. That means that, as far as morality and sexism are concerned, the jury may still be out on the supposed complementarity of the sexes, on the special suitability of those of one or the other sex for certain roles, on the need of society or of individuals for sex-differentiation in how children are reared, directed, educated, and so on. There need be nothing on its face insulting or hostile to women in entertaining these ideas. On those matters of fact, we really are dealing with opinions—not vices—and we will need to hear various views with an unprejudiced mind. I think Dinesh D'Souza is wrong in thinking that racism (and, therefore, sexism, if it is like racism) is ultimately just an opinion.[21] However, he is right to insist that opinions are best combatted on their merits rather than through impugning, with charges of sexism or racism, the morality of those who may offer them. A given person S's holding a proposition p may be a matter of S's vicious self-deception. (Though normally S is entitled to the benefit of the doubt.) Whether it is or is not, we will need to marshal epistemic reasons against (the truth of) *p* itself. If we are to feel secure in rejecting *p*, not just moral reasons against holding *p* true. To do otherwise is to prove the critics of 'political correctness' right when they complain that oversensitivity to sex (and race) stifles intellectual freedom and much-needed social inquiry.[22,23]

NOTES

1. Attributed to a 1965 comment of D.M. Leet's, in Jane Mills, *Womanwords: a Dictionary of Words about Women* (New York: Macmillan, 1989), *s.v.* "Sexism/Sexist," p. 214. On the analogy with racism, "[S]exism . . . [is a t]erm constructed by analogy with racism . . ." Lisa Tuttle, ed., *Encyclopedia of Feminism* (New York: Facts on File/Pletus, 1986), *s.v.* 'sexism,' p. 292. "[The term 'sexism' was] coined during the feminist renaissance of the sixties, probably by analogy with the term racism." Mary Anne Warren, *The Nature of Woman* (Inverness: Edgepress, 1980), p. 424. (I owe this quotation to Cheris Kramarae and Paula Treichler, eds., *A Feminist Dictionary* (Boston: Pandora, 1985), *s.v.* "sexism," p. 412.)

2. Many would nowadays prefer to say "gender" where I have said "sex." I will not get into the issues surrounding the supposed "social construction" of gender and its supposed difference from sex, and will use the terms interchangeably.

3. Mills, *Womanwords,* attributes the former quotation to S. Vanauken and the latter to C. Bird. Both remarks are dated 1968.

4. The former quotation is attributed to Ambalvaner Sivanandan in Robert Miles, *Racism* (London: Routledge, 1989), p. 53. David Theo Goldberg critically treats the widely held view that racism must be irrational because it consists in attending to race in cases where it should be clear that race is irrelevant, in Goldberg, *Racist Culture* (Cambridge: Blackwell, 1993).

5. Claudia Card, "On Race, Racism, and Ethnicity," in *Overcoming Racism and Sexism,* Linda Bell and David Blumenfeld, eds., (Lanham, MD: Rowman and Littlefield, 1994) pp. 141–152.

6. Deborah King, "Double Jeopardy," in Helen Tierney, ed., *Women's Studies Encyclopedia* vol. I (New York: Greenwood, 1989), pp. 111–113.

7. "Although men also claim to be victims of sexism, either in personal relationships or in regard to affirmative action programmes, this is more accurately known as 'inverse sexism' or 'reverse sexism,' and is actually a response to the institutionalized sexism which oppresses all women." Tuttle, *Encyclopedia,* p. 292.

On institutional racism, see Kwame Ture and Charles Hamilton, *Black Power* (New York: Vintage, 1992); reissue, with new Afterwards, of 1967 edition.

8. Richard Wasserstrom, "Racism, Sexism, and Preferential Treatment: an Approach to the Topics," *UCLA Law Review* (February, 1977), pp. 581–615.

9. It seems there may be racism in individuals' attitudes even when there are such institutional and ideological arrangements, should those arrangements fail in either their task of creating or that of maintaining such an institutional and ideological system (despite their being meant to do harm). Maybe the system fails to be self-perpetuating, as Wasserstrom requires, either because it passes away or because it is maintained only by external forces operating independently of the system of beliefs and institutions itself.

10. In any case, these remarks about power would need to be generalized before they were acceptable, so that, in another possible world, at least, racism might work to concentrate power in the hands of white females, or black males, or black females.

11. Wasserstrom defines "overt racism" so that it "assign[s] benefits and burdens in such a way as to bestow an unjust benefit upon a member or members of the racially dominant group or an unjustified burden upon members of the racial groups that are oppressed." This seems to exclude any *possibility* of state racism against the disadvantaged group. So-called "reverse discrimination," then, *cannot* be racist in principle and of necessity. To see the moral absurdity of restricting racism to the powerful, consider Dinesh D'Souza's nice point that such a restriction immediately exonerates Klansmen and "skinheads" (who are unlikely nowadays to serve, say, as CEOs, DAs, etc., less likely, at least, than are African Americans) from the charge of racism. Dinesh D'Souza, *The End of Racism* (New York: Free Press, 1995), p. 410.

12. See Plato, *The Republic,* 415.

13. For additional discussion of this, see the more developed argument in J.L.A. Garcia, "Current Conceptions of Racism," *Journal of Social Philosophy* 28, no. 2, 1997: 5–42.

14. See Kwame Anthony Appiah, "Racisms," in David Theo Goldberg, ed., *Anatomy of Racism* (Minneapolis: University of Minnesota Press, 1990), pp. 3–17; Kwame Anthony Appiah, *In My Father's House* (New York: Oxford University Press, 1992); and Lewis Gordon, Jr., *Bad Faith and Antiblack Racism* (Atlantic Highlands: Humanities, 1995).

15. I develop such an account of racism and tie it to the moral virtues and virtues-based moral theory in Garcia,

"The Heart of Racism," *Journal of Social Philosophy* 27, 1996: 5–45, and in Leonard Harris, ed., *Racism* (Amherst: Prometheus/Humanity Books), 398–434.

16. Marilyn Frye, "Male Chauvinism: a Conceptual Analysis," in Robert Baker and Frederick Elliston, eds., *Philosophy and Sex* (Buffalo: Prometheus, 1975). Reprinted in Bishop and Weinzweig, eds., *Philosophy and Women,* pp. 26–33.

17. Alison Jaggar, "On Sexual Equality," *Ethics* 84 (1974); reprinted in Bishop and Weinzweig, eds., *Philosophy and Women,* pp. 77–87.

18. Laurence Thomas, "Sexism and Racism: Some Conceptual Differences," *Ethics* 90 (1980), pp. 239–250.

19. Frye, "Male Chauvinism."

20. Self-deception is a problematic concept. For discussion of some difficulties, see Brian McLaughlin, "Exploring the Possibility of Self-Deception in Belief," in Brian McLaughlin and Amelie Rorty, eds., *Perspectives on Self-Deception* (Berkeley: University of California Press, 1988), pp. 29–62.

21. D'Souza, *End of Racism,* pp. 525–556.

22. See Glenn Loury, "Self-Censorship in Public Discourse," in Glenn Loury, *One By One, From the Inside Out,* (New York: Free Press, 1995) chap. 8, pp. 145–182.

23. I am grateful to Catherine McKeen for bibliographic information; and to George Rudebusch for discussion of these topics, especially his suggestions about, and objections to, my understanding of paternalism.

READING QUESTIONS

1. What is Wasserstrom's account of racism? How is Garcia's Twin Earth example supposed to show that Wasserstrom's view does not provide sufficient conditions for racism?
2. According to Garcia, what are the advantages of understanding racism as race-based ill will (as opposed to understanding it as the possession of prejudiced beliefs)?
3. How does Garcia argue that Frye's accounts of what sexism is and what a sexist is may have inconsistent implications?
4. On Garcia's view, "sexism" and "misogyny" refer to the same thing, even though, as he notes, sexism appears to include phenomena not usually considered parts or types of misogyny. How does Garcia address this problem?
5. On Garcia's view, what makes sexism immoral?

DISCUSSION QUESTIONS

1. Can Garcia's account provide an explanation for why certain systems, institutions, or practices (rather than individual people) are racist? If so, how? If not, is that a problem?
2. What would Garcia say about cases where an apparently sexist person seems to have only good intentions?

MICHAEL PHILIPS

Racist Acts and Racist Humor

Philips contrasts two models for understanding racist humor: the agent-centered model and the act-centered model. According to the former model, in order for an action such as telling a joke to be racist, the actor must be a racist whose action is motivated by racist beliefs or feelings. Philips raises a number of objections to the agent-centered model and goes on to defend the act-centered model according to which what makes a joke racist is that it involves a basic racist act. A basic racist act is one in which either (1) the actor performs the action in order to harm someone else (the target of the joke) because the target is a member of a certain ethnic group, or (2) regardless of the actor's intentions, the act can be expected to mistreat the target. In cases in which ethnic humor meets either of these two conditions, it is racist and thus prima facie wrong.

Although Philips does not explicitly appeal to Ross's ethic of prima facie duties in defending his act-centered approach to the racist humor, his approach, with its emphasis on the prima facie wrongness of racist humor, can be understood from within Ross's moral theory.

Recommended Reading: ethics of prima facie duty, chap. 1, sec. 2F.

I

Racist jokes are often funny. And part of this has to do with their racism. Many Polish jokes, for example, may easily be converted into moron jokes but are not at all funny when delivered as such. Consider two answers to "What has an I.Q. of 100?": (a) a nation of morons; or (b) Poland. Similarly, jokes portraying Jews as cheap, Italians as cowards, and Greeks as dishonest may be told as jokes about how skinflints, cowards, or dishonest people get on in the world. But they are less funny as such (at least if one is not Jewish, Greek, or Italian). As this suggests, racist humor is "put down" humor. We laugh, in part, because we find put-downs funny, sometimes even if they are about us. In many contexts, this tendency is relatively harmless; indeed, within reason, it may be

therapeutic to join others in a good laugh at oneself. Why, then, all the commotion about racist humor?

"Racist" is a moral pejorative. To say that an act is racist is to say that it is prima facie wrong. Our problem, then, is to determine the range of cases that deserve this description. That is, we are trying to decide what forms of race-related behavior to discourage by means of this moral pejorative. In relation to humor, we face a nest of problems. Much racist humor, for example, attributes an unflattering characteristic to its target group. What if members of that group really have or tend statistically to have that characteristic? Surely we are allowed to notice this and to communicate this information to one another. Is truth a defense against the charge of racism? Also, what of the good-natured interplay between friends of different ethnic groups in which such jokes may play an important part? And what of exchanges of

From Michael Philips, "Racist Acts and Racist Humor," *Canadian Journal of Philosophy* 14 (1984). Reprinted by permission of the University of Calgary Press.

such jokes between members of ethnic groups about whom they are told? This paper will present an account of racist humor in relation to which we can answer these and related questions. What is said here about racist humor will also apply to sexist humor and to humor about national groups.

II

Not all humor that takes an ethnic group as its subject matter is racist. Some such humor is morally unobjectionable. Our first task, then, is to distinguish this sort of humor from racist humor. In other words, we need to determine why some humor about ethnic groups is morally unobjectionable while other humor is not.

Let me begin with a popular theory; or, in any case, a theory that is presupposed by a very common defense against the charge of having made a racist joke. This defense denies, in effect that joking remarks are racist so long as they are made by persons whose souls are pure. According to this view, a racist act presupposes a racist actor, and a racist actor is a person who acts from racist beliefs and/or racist feelings. I call this the Agent-Centered Account. Although a complete account of this view requires an account of the nature of racist beliefs and feelings, my purposes do not require this here. For now, suffice it to say that on this account one may innocently entertain one's fellow Rotarians with jokes like "After shaking hands with a Greek, count your fingers," so long as one harbors no racist beliefs or feelings about Greeks. If one's soul is pure, such jokes are all in good fun and ought to be accepted as such.

Before attacking this theory, I want to contrast it with my own account. The term "racist" is used of books, attitudes, societies, epithets, actions, persons, feelings, policies, laws, etc., as well as of humor. Any account of "racist" will explain some of these uses in relation to others. The Agent-Centered Theory explains racist humor in relation to racist persons, and racist persons in relation to racist beliefs and attitudes. And, to the extent that it can be generalized,

moreover it explains all other uses of "racist" in this way as well. On my own view, "racist" is used in its logically primary sense when it is attributed to actions. All other uses of "racist," I believe, must be understood directly or indirectly *in relation to* this one. Accordingly, racist beliefs are (roughly) beliefs about an ethnic group used to "justify" racist acts, racist feelings are feelings about an ethnic group that typically give rise to such acts, and racist epithets are the stings and arrows by means of which certain such acts are carried out. Books and films are said to be racist, on the other hand, if they perpetuate and stimulate racist beliefs or feelings (which are in turn understood in relation to racist acts).

More precisely, on my view, "racist" is used in its logically primary sense when it is used of what I shall call Basic Racist Acts. Roughly, P performs a Basic Racist Act by doing A when: (a) P does A in order to harm Q because Q is a member of a certain ethnic group; or (b) (regardless of P's intentions or purposes) P's doing A can reasonably be expected to mistreat Q as a consequence of Q's being a member of a certain ethnic group.[1] Note that, on this account, P's motives, beliefs, feelings, or intentions need not be taken into account in determining that P performed a racist act. If you refer to someone as "a stinking little kike" in my company, I am harmed by your action because I am Jewish, whether you intended this result or not. If this harm counts as mistreatment, then, in my account, your remark is racist, And, I shall argue, this is so even if you have nothing at all against Jews, e.g., you are merely attempting to discredit a competitor in the eyes of an anti-Semite. I call my view the Act-Centered Theory.

Before arguing for the superiority of this view to the Agent-Centered view, two observations are in order. To begin with, condition (a), in effect, acknowledges an element of truth in the Agent-Centered Theory. For if P does A in order to harm Q simply because Q is Hispanic, P must have racist beliefs or feelings against Hispanics. And it follows from this that P's acting on such beliefs or feelings—i.e., P's acting as a racist by doing A—is a sufficient condition of A's being a racist act. Nonetheless, it is mistaken to focus on P's beliefs or feelings in our account of why P's act is wrong. Rather, we ought focus on what P's act means for its victims. For roughly, it is not the fact that racists act on mistaken beliefs or irrational feelings that make their actions wrong, i.e., it is not the state of mind of the actor that corrupts the act. Rather, it is the meaning of the act for the victims that makes us condemn both the act and the state of mind that prompted it. Indeed, if condition (b) is correct, P's being a racist—or even acting as a racist on some particular occasion—is not a necessary condition of P's act being a racist act. It is sufficient that his act can reasonably be expected to mistreat in the appropriate way. This is not, of course, to say that an act must succeed in mistreating someone in order to be racist. Were this the case, condition (a) would be unnecessary. But, in general, because we are entitled to assume a certain competence on the part of wrong-doers, it makes sense for us morally to condemn acts that would mistreat or victimize were their intention realized. Accordingly, we condemn lies that fail to deceive, assaults that fail to harm, and robberies that yield no stolen goods. We do not condemn these acts because they spring from some intention or state of mind that can be identified as morally corrupt independently of its likelihood of giving rise to some form of mistreatment. On the contrary, it is precisely in virtue of this likelihood that we condemn the intention.

In the second place, it is worth pointing out that the Act-Centered Theory and the Agent-Centered Theory each reflect a certain point of view. Roughly, the Agent-Centered Theory reflects the perspective of the morally troubled member of a persecuting group. Such persons are loathe to acknowledge their contributions to what they agree to be a morally indefensible system. The Agent-Centered Account permits them to escape unblemished so long as they are able to purge themselves of racist beliefs and feelings. Once purged, they may do what is "necessary" to get on in a racist society without fear of moral censure. For example, they may prohibit their daughter to date a Black classmate on the grounds that this will jeopardize her future; or they may ask her not to invite her Black friends to her wedding on the grounds that this will be unsettling to old family friends. On the Agent-Centered Theory, if these are in fact their motives, they needn't think of their actions as racist, and they needn't think of themselves as complicit in a racist system. Indeed, this permits them to feel morally superior to those who discriminate out of feeling or conviction.

The Act-Centered conception, on the other hand, adopts the perspective of the victim, the accuser. The victim experiences racism as so many forms of mistreatment. If she is not invited to a friend's wedding because she is Black, she takes this to be a racist act. Since racist acts are wrong only prima facie, this does not necessarily mean that she condemns the act as wrong, or even that she considers her friend a racist (the relationship between racist acts and racist persons is more complex than this). Still, she is deprived of an invitation to which she is entitled as a friend because of her ethnicity. Accordingly, even if the act is justified, *she* is wronged. And since this is so, the act is racist.

As this suggests, the term "racism" marks a contested concept. Established English use places outside limits on what counts as an acceptable definition ("racist" can not be defined as ice cream) but there is plenty of room for disagreement within these parameters. Established English use does not and should not determine how we are to decide between the alternatives. When we choose between competing patterns of use we are deciding what forms of race-related behavior it is important for us as a society morally to disparage. In effect, then, a defense of an "analysis" of this concept is a defense of a moral standard (or set of related standards). My defense of an act-centered account, then, is really a defense of the claim that that account yields the sorts of moral judgments we should be making in relation to race-related conduct. More specifically, I am arguing that this pattern of use better serves the purposes of combating racial injustice than its alternatives.[2]

III

To begin with, the Agent-Centered Theory has difficulty making sense of certain important uses of "racist." Consider racial epithets ("nigger," "kike," "wop," etc.). On the Agent-Centered Theory, use of such epithets to insult or to assert undeserved power are racist *only if* the users have racist beliefs or feelings. But suppose that a white man calls a Black travelling-companion "nigger" to remind him of his social status, e.g., as an insult or as a power move ("Look nigger, if push comes to shove, nobody's going to take your side here"). In determining whether this use is racist, do we need to consider what the White man believes or feels about Blacks in general? Suppose that he harbors no beliefs or feelings to the effect that Blacks are inferior or deserve inferior treatment, and that he is "putting his companion in his place" *merely* to have his own way. Still, he has used this epithet unfairly to threaten, insult, or assume unwarranted power over another person; and, obviously, his act has this consequence because of his companion's race. Accordingly, I believe, we would call such acts "racist." In any case, we should speak this way. For we want morally to condemn forms of victimization that are made possible by the victims' ethnic identity and this seems an unobjectionable way to do so.

The Agent-Centered Theory, moreover, prevents us from saying that certain paradigm cases of racist acts are racist. Consider the German soldier who volunteers to march Jewish victims to the gas ovens *out of simple patriotism,* or the Klansman who ties nooses at lynchings for *business reasons.* Each may (in principle) act with heart and mind uncorrupted by racist beliefs or feelings (though obviously this is unlikely). Does this mean that they have not acted in a racist manner? Suppose that all the German soldiers at Dachau acted out of patriotism and all the Klansmen at the lynching were there for business reasons. Would this mean that none of those who participated in such events were guilty of racist acts?

Note that I am not arguing that participants in such events are racists; only that they act in a racist manner. Indeed, there may be good reason to deny they are racist since we want to distinguish those who participate in victimization out of patriotism or self-interest from those participate in victimization out of race hate or authentic conviction. Still, it is the victimization, not the persons, we are primarily concerned to condemn and eliminate, and if we refuse to condemn acts of victimization as racist, it is unclear what moral category we could invoke to this end.

Racist societies encourage racist victimization by a system of rewards and punishments. Sometimes these are formal and explicit (e.g., apartheid laws), sometimes they are informal and subtle (e.g., subtle forms of social exclusion). In any case, this system creates a set of prudential reasons for *all* members of the victimizing race to participate in victimization, i.e., to be complicit in the mistreatment of the victimized group. By calling these forms of complicity "racist," we make them a matter of moral concern whatever their motivation, i.e., whether they are motivated by race hate or by prudence. It is important that we do this. Were we morally to condemn only those forms of victimization motivated by race hate or racist beliefs, we would leave equally important forms of victimization outside the realm of moral concern; or, at best, subject to moral evaluation only on utilitarian grounds. Suppose, for example, that Alice excludes a Black friend from her wedding list in order to not to upset one of Daddy's business associates. And suppose that this action produces just a little more happiness than unhappiness. If we do not describe this sort of complicity in the general pattern of victimization of Blacks as prima facie wrong, in itself, her action will be immune from moral criticism. Moreover, to the extent that we discount utilitarian considerations in our ethics such acts of complicity will be regarded simply as questions of prudence. . . .

IV

Before applying my account to the question of racist humor, I would like to anticipate one further objection, viz., that on my account too many actions which seem entirely unobjectionable turn out to be racist. The objector recognizes that on my account racist acts are wrong prima facie, and that there may be occasions on which one is morally justified in acting in a racist manner. His concern is that in other cases of prima facie wrongs it is *typically* wrong to act in the proscribed manner, but that this does not appear to be so in the case of racism. For once we begin to think about it, it is clear that there are myriad ways we may contribute to the victimization of members of victimized groups without doing anything wrong. Consider, for example, cases of distrust. You are walking down a dark street in a poor Black neighborhood at night. A large Black man approaches you from the opposite direction. You cross the street to avoid contact. You recognize that the odds are slim that this particular man will attack you (25 to 1?). But the consequences of being attacked are so great that you would be foolish to take the risk. By so acting, however, you exhibit distrust of a *particular* person. Moreover, chances are excellent that this person has been treated with fear and distrust by Whites throughout his adolescence and adulthood simply in virtue of his size and race. To be treated in such a way is to be victimized, and by crossing the street you are contributing to this victimization. Examples of this sort of distrust are commonplace. And, in many cases at least, this distrustful attitude—though unfair to the overwhelming majority who pose no threat—is nonetheless rational. For, though the odds against any particular attack may be much in one's favor—e.g., 25 to 1—if one is not distrustful in this way and one lives in an urban environment, it is likely that one will be attacked sooner or later. And again, the consequences of an attack are so severe that it is foolish to take the risk in any case. According to the objection, acts of this sort are not typically wrong. And if they are not typically wrong, the victimization they involve ought not be regarded as prima facie wrong either.

This objection is not a strong one. It is interesting, however, in that it brings into relief an important fact about moral relations in racist societies. The fact is that in any society in which racism is pervasive there will be a social chasm between the races that forces most members of every ethnic group to relate to members of other groups through racial stereotypes, at least most of the time. There is too little opportunity for most people to get to know members of other groups well enough to permit anything else. Moreover, as the present example suggests, there may be good reason to act on stereotypes, even where it is recognized that a stereotype applies to only a small number of persons within a group. Now where the treatment dictated by the stereotype is negative, most persons in the victimized group (e.g., twenty-four or twenty-five) will be treated unfairly *as a matter of course* by most members of the victimizing group. The fact that this treatment *is* unfair, however, makes it prima facie wrong. The objector makes an obvious mistake in denying that victimization is prima facie wrong merely because it may typically

be justified by overriding considerations. But he is correct in emphasizing the high price—perhaps even the impossibility—of avoiding complicity in this victimization. If we are members of a victimizing race, it is virtually certain that we will be complicit. It is the genius of a racist society to arrange that this is so. This does not mean that we are all racists. Nor does it mean that we are moral monsters. Again, there are times that even the best intentioned of us have no real choice. But in this case, what we have no choice about is whether to commit a racist act. This is the tragedy of living in a racist society for the morally sensitive members of the victimizing race.

V

. . . Agent-Centered theories tend to direct our attention to the cognitive aspect of racist acts. In relation to humor, they incline us to focus on content. Accordingly, they direct our attention primarily to one form of humor—humor based on racist stereotypes and they incline us to consider such humor in a certain way, viz., in relation to the beliefs it may promote or express. Thus, if we adopt such an account, we are likely to consider the problem of characterizing racist humor as the problem of describing the sorts of beliefs such humor portrays or expresses. Accordingly, we shall probably begin by characterizing racist humor as humor which expresses false and unflattering beliefs about an ethnic group. And this beginning leads us inevitably to questions of truthfulness. For we must now decide how to characterize humor based on stereotypes which have some foundation in truth. For example, if it is statistically true that Blacks are significantly less literate than Whites, we will be inclined to ask whether it is racist to make jokes about problems created by Black illiteracy. It is likely, moreover, that we see in this question a conflict between truth, on the one hand, and social justice, on the other. By freeing us from focusing narrowly on content, the Act-Centered Theory frees us from focusing on questions of truth. Moreover, in many cases, at least, it enables us to avoid formulating the question of the morality of certain jokes as questions that involve deciding in favor of truth, on the one hand, or of social justice, on the other.

Roughly speaking, then, the Act-Centered Theory holds that ethnic humor is racist: (a) when it is used with the intent to victimize a member of an ethnic group in virtue of her ethnicity; and (b) when it in fact promotes such victimization or can reasonably be expected to promote it (e.g., by contributing to an atmosphere in which it is more likely to occur).

To be more precise, let us use the expression "a bit of humor" for a particular occurrence of humor, e.g., the telling of a joke, the mimicking of an accent, the appearance of a cartoon in a particular time and place. On my account, a bit of ethnic humor is racist if: (1) it is a Basic Racist Act, or (2) it can reasonably be expected to promote an atmosphere in which Basic Racist Acts are more likely to occur, or (3) it is intended to promote such an atmosphere. Of course, we also speak of jokes, books, films, etc. as racist "in themselves," i.e., apart from their particular occurrences. But if I am correct, this way of speaking is parasitic on the other. Roughly, we say that a joke "itself" is racist because a typical act of telling it will be racist in at least one of the ways described; and analogous points hold for films, books, laws, etc. (though, of course, we may need to express these points somewhat differently). A consequence of this view is that a joke which embodies a discarded and forgotten racist stereotype—e.g., a scheming Phoenician—is not now racist. Indeed, where stereotypes have been forgotten, stereotyped characters in jokes (books and movies) will not be identified as such; their actions will be construed as the acts of individuals rather than as representative of ethnic groups. Upon discovering that these characters were stereotypes, we may decide to call the work in question "racist." But here we mean only that the work was racist *in its time.* This use of "racist" does not have the same moral significance as our ordinary use. We do not mean to suggest by this, for example, that there is anything wrong with exhibiting or distributing this material now.

As suggested at the outset of this paper, at least much racist humor is "put down" humor. Racial "put downs," of course, are at least often Basic Racist Acts. In any case, it is clear that they are when they are used to insult, humiliate, ridicule, or otherwise assault someone in consequence of his ethnic identity. Such bits of humor need not make use of ethnic stereotypes. It is sometimes enough merely to humiliate a member of a victimized group in some manner thought to be funny (e.g., in the American West, to cut the "Chinaman's" pigtail). Such humor is often extremely cruel. Moreover, even where stereotypes are incorporated in ridicule or humiliation, use of these stereotypes is not racist merely because they promote racist beliefs. Indeed, their chief use may be to identify the form of insult or humiliation thought appropriate to the member of the victimized group. This form of humiliation, moreover, may be rather far removed from any racist belief that "justifies" mistreatment. Thus, though Jews were not *mistreated* on the ground that they were believed (or said) to have large noses, some think it quite amusing to make jokes about "Jewish noses." Note that insults, ridicule, and humiliation do not, *in general,* require justification—or even a sham of justification—to do their work. All that is required is an attitude of derision on the part of the victimizer toward some characteristic that the victim is said to have (however insincere the attribution). Again, some stereotypes do not function so much to promote beliefs but to ridicule or humiliate in just this way. The main point of portraying Jews with enormous noses and Blacks with huge lips is not to perpetuate the belief that Jews or Blacks tend to look *that* way. Rather, it is to promote an *attitude* about looking that way, and *to take the position* that Jews and Blacks look that way *as a way of* insulting Jews and Blacks. What goes on here is similar to what goes on in the school yard when a group of children decide to humiliate another child by taunting him with accusations that are insulting merely in virtue of the attitudes expressed toward him. Again, almost any characteristic will do here and it doesn't really matter to anyone whether or not the victim *is* that way. In fact, it may be more effective if he is not. Then, in addition to insult, he suffers a further miscarriage of justice. The difference between school yard tauntings and the caricatures of Jews and Blacks in question is that the tone of school yard tauntings is often deadly earnest while the caricatures in question taunt through comic ridicule.

Moreover, jokes and cartoons which on some occasions create or reinforce racist stereotypes may be racist in contexts where they do not serve this end. For they may be used *simply* to insult, humiliate, or ridicule. The most obvious example is that of a stereotyping joke told with gleeful hostility to a member of a victimized group. If the victim and the victimizer are alone, there may be no question of spreading or perpetrating racist beliefs here. What is racist about expressing such stereotypes is their use to insult or to humiliate. Where such jokes are told before "mixed audiences," they may be racist both because they insult and because they help to reinforce racist beliefs.

It is important to notice, moreover, that bits of humor that insult by the use of stereotypes may do so *however* close or far that stereotype is from a relevant statistical truth. As suggested, ridicule, insult, and humiliation are what they are whether or not the victims are as they are said to be; and, indeed, whether or not there is in fact something deficient about being as the victim is said to be. Note that children and insensitive adults may ridicule or humiliate retarded persons and spastics by imitating them *accurately.* In general, it may be insulting merely to point out some truth about a person that someone with respect for the feelings and well-being of others would pass over in silence.

Precisely what determines the conditions under which a person is humiliated, insulted, or ridiculed—as opposed to merely feeling that way—is a complex question that I cannot hope to answer here. It is clear, however, that context is extremely important. And here, two points are worthy of comment.

First, although it may occasionally be possible to exchange what would ordinarily be considered racial insults in an atmosphere of good will and comraderie, good will does not preclude the possibility of insults. One may insult or humiliate another with the purest of hearts and the best of intentions, so long as one is sufficiently stupid or insensitive (consider the high school principal who introduces a Japanese commencement speaker by "assuling" the audience that he "explesses the freerings of his frerrow immiglants").

Secondly, one may insult without saying or doing anything that is "objectively insulting." Sometimes it is enough simply to probe what ought to be recognized as a sensitive area. Typically, if we know that a friend is very touchy about, e.g., some characteristic, we avoid referring to it, even in jest. Indeed, unless there is some strong countervailing reason to refer to it, we insult him by so doing. And it does not matter whether or not we believe that our friend's sensitivity is rational, i.e., whether such remarks *ought to be* considered insulting or humiliating. If it is no great burden to respect his sensitivity, to fail to do so is insulting. And what holds for friends in this regard ought also to hold for acquaintances or even strangers. Typically, if we know that members of a victimized group are insulted by certain jokes made about them, we ought not to make such jokes in their presence (unless, e.g., we do this for therapeutic purpose). This standard, however, is too restrictive to govern communications before mass audiences, e.g., television. But even here we ought not require that sensitivities be perfectly rational in order to be respected. If a substantial number of the victimized group—say, a majority—is known to be offended by certain ways of portraying them, then it may be insulting to them to portray them in these ways simply because we ignore their sensitivities by so doing. If there is no overriding reason for portraying them in this way, we ought not to do so. Moreover, we ought to give special weight to the opinion of the victimized group that such portrayals *are* insulting in and of themselves. For it requires more empathy on the part of an outsider fully to appreciate the position of a victimized group than many of us have a right to claim. Consider, for example, the glee that the most educated among us take in telling Polish jokes.

But it is not only the immediate impact of racist humor on victimized groups that makes it racist. The impact on victimizers and potential victimizers is also important. Typically, discussion of this impact focuses on the cognitive side, i.e., on how racist humor spreads and reinforces racist beliefs. At least as important, I think, are the affective consequences. For, insofar as racist humor constitutes an assault on members of an ethnic group, it joins together those who participate—both performers and audience—in a community of feeling against that group. By appreciating such humor together, we take common joy in putting *them* down, e.g., in turning them into objects of scorn or contempt or into beings not to be taken seriously (wife jokes). Our mutual participation in this through shared laughter legitimizes this way of feeling about them. Those among us who fail to laugh—or who object to laughter—are immediately outsiders, perhaps even traitors. In general, the price of objecting is a small exile. By participating, however, one accepts membership in a racist association (albeit a temporary one). The seriousness of so doing, of course, is far less than, e.g., the seriousness of joining an official white supremacist organization. But notice that the difference in seriousness diminishes the greater one's participation in such informal communities of feeling.

It is important to note that this creation of a community of feeling is not contingent on the creation of a community of belief. Many people who entertain one another with Polish jokes do not thereby implicitly accept Polish slovenliness or stupidity as a fact. What they share is the pleasure of ridiculing Poles and they legitimize this pleasure by sharing it with one another. Typically, because they are innocent of racist beliefs and of hatred against Poles, they take this pleasure to be innocent (an Agent-Centered understanding). But one wonders how the Poles think of it. How do American philosophers of Polish descent feel knowing that their colleagues entertain themselves in this "innocent" way? (Imagine a Black philosopher in a department of Whites who told Sambo and Rastus jokes.) . . .

Most racist jokes do not persuade *by argument* that a certain stereotype is true of a certain ethnic group. Rather, they promote such stereotypes by repeated assertion. At least part of what gives such assertions their power to establish and to reinforce belief is that they are invested with the authority of those who make them. Roughly, one promotes racist beliefs by means of racist humor when one lends one's authority to a joke that embodies some racist stereotype. One may do this simply by telling such a joke in the way jokes are ordinarily told (as one may lend one's authority to what one asserts merely by asserting it). However, if one's audience has antecedent reason to believe that one does not hold such beliefs, or if one provides it with such reasons, this relationship will not hold. In this case, one may tell a joke that embodies some such stereotype without committing a racist act. Whether one lends one's authority to a stereotype by telling a joke (or displaying a cartoon) depends in part on the context. Typically, for example, one does not lend one's authority to such stereotypes by telling such jokes where the context is scholarly, e.g., where the purpose is to examine the means by which racist beliefs are perpetuated (though it is *possible* to lend one's authority even here by telling such jokes with obvious glee and approval).

It is worth pointing out, moreover, that we cannot determine by an abstract or acontextual analysis of content whether a joke could reasonably be expected to promote a racist stereotype.

Consider the following Polish joke:

Q: How do you tell the groom at a Polish wedding?

A: He's the one in the clean bowling shirt.

To an audience familiar with the current American Polish stereotype, this joke will be understood to assert that Poles are deficient in the categories of style and hygiene. An audience unfamiliar with this stereotype—e.g., an audience that believes that Poles are reputed to be elegant and cultured—cannot be expected to understand these sentences in this way. Indeed, such an audience would be at a loss to see any joke here at all. Many jokes are like this. Still other jokes can reasonably be expected to be understood differently depending on who tells them, to whom they are told, in what spirit they are told, and under what circumstances. Consider:

White Foreman: Washington, what the hell are you doing lying down on the job again? When I hired you, you said you never get tired.

Black Worker: That's how I do it, sir.

White Foreman: Don't talk in riddles, boy.

Black Worker: I ain't. You see, the reason I never gets tired is as soon as I begins to get tired I jes lies down and takes myself a rest.

Depending on who tells this joke to whom and on how it is told, it may reasonably be expected to be understood as a joke about Blacks in general, a joke about Black laborers, or a joke about a particular

Black man named Washington. Moreover, the joke may be understood to mean that Blacks are lazy, sly, or shiftless; or it may be understood to show how a clever Black worker can talk his way out of a tough spot; or, if Washington is an established character, it may be understood as another illustration of how Washington gets on in the world.[3] If we focus narrowly on content—if we focus on what is presupposed by "the joke itself"—it is easy to miss the importance of context here. . . .

VI

Let me conclude by summarizing my position and by applying it to the question of truth raised in the introductory section of this paper. To begin with, then, bits of humor may be racist in three ways: (1) They may insult (or be intended to insult), humiliate, or ridicule members of victimized groups in relation to their ethnic identity; (2) They may create (or be intended to create) a community of feelings against such a group; and (3) They may promote (or be intended to promote) beliefs that are used to "justify" the mistreatment of such a group.

Whether a particular bit of humor is racist in one or more of these ways depends on a variety of contextual features. On this view, when we describe a joke or cartoon as racist "in itself" we mean that a typical use of it will be racist in our culture. In making this judgment we presuppose a background of contextual features so familiar in our culture that they need not be specified. Given the history of racist cartoon caricatures of Blacks, a political cartoon that portrayed a prominent Black American with huge lips and bug eyes is a racist insult, despite the fact that he may have rather large lips and somewhat bulging eyes. Were it not for this history, however, such a caricature would be no more racist than any political cartoon that exaggerated the unusual anatomical features of its subject. And since it would not insult, it would not help to perpetuate a community of feeling against Blacks as well. Our judgment that any such cartoon is racist "in itself" presupposes this history. As we have seen, moreover,

a corresponding point holds in relation to the promotion of racist beliefs. Polish jokes cannot reasonably be expected to perpetuate or reinforce racist beliefs against Poles where the audience is familiar with a much different Polish stereotype (e.g., Poles as cultured and intelligent). In general, how an audience can reasonably be expected to understand such jokes will depend on what the audience already believes about the group in question.

Compare:

Question: What has an I.Q. of 100?

Answer 1: Poland

Answer 2: Israel

In general, to determine whether a bit of humor is racist in virtue of being insulting to a member of the relevant group may require a good deal of intelligence and sensitivity to feelings and to social dynamics. And the same may be said in relation to the creation of communities of feeling. For the formation of social alliances—and the use of humor to form them—may be very obvious or very subtle. Again, it may take a good deal of sensitivity to detect it.

Applying these findings to the questions raised in the introduction to this paper, it should be clear by now that truth is not a sufficient defense against the charge of racism. To begin with, racist victimization in a society may be supported by an ideology that consists—in part—of statistically true beliefs. For example, Blacks are statistically less literate than Whites. Such statistical truths, however, are abused in racist ideologies in two ways. First, they are used to support factual inferences that would not follow from them were all the evidence in (e.g., Blacks are genetically less capable of literacy than Whites); and secondly, they are used as premises in moral arguments for conclusions that do not follow from them (e.g., Blacks should have fewer rights than Whites). Most of us agree that it is racist to help to promote this ideology. Accordingly, we would judge ourselves amiss were we to mention the rate of Black literacy to someone who might come to be influenced by this ideology *and also* fail to give him an explanation of this fact. But this is just what we do when we tell such a person a joke in which Blacks are portrayed as illiterates. Even jokes that are grounded in statistically true stereotypes, then, may be racist in virtue of promoting racist ideology. Whether such jokes are racist for this reason, of course, is dependent on the audience to whom they are addressed. Where there is no question that the audience will be influenced in the direction of this racist ideology—e.g., where the audience consists of Black sociologists—the telling of such jokes need not be racist at all. Indeed, they could be used as a way of portraying just how bad things are (e.g., how Blacks have been deprived of educational opportunities).

As we saw, moreover, one can use the truth to insult, humiliate, or ridicule members of a victimized group, whether or not the truth ought to be considered shameful. Thus, Blacks are ridiculed for having big lips, Jews for having big noses, etc. It does not matter here whether or not this is true. Again, what is insulting here is the attitude of derision adopted toward the trait. Once members of a group are made to feel ashamed of being certain ways, it is insulting and humiliating to "remind" them that they are—whether they are or not or whether the trait is shameworthy or not. Moreover, it is clear that a community of feeling against a group is created when members of another group adopt an attitude of derision toward some trait alleged in the first, whether or not this allegation is true. Accordingly, bits of humor may be racist in all three ways despite the fact that they are grounded in some truth.

NOTES

1. I am using "mistreatment" in (b) to include any morally objectionable injury to someone's interests. Note that "harm" is not sufficient here. Affirmative Action, for example, may harm White males in virtue of their race, but is not "reverse racism" unless it can be established that it mistreats them. I use "harm" instead of "mistreatment" in condition (a) to avoid counterexamples in which A acts within his rights by harming B, but would not harm B were B's race different (e.g. White landlord A evicts Black tenant B for delinquency, in paying the rent, but would not do so were B White). Although I would argue that this constitutes mistreatment, I do not want my criteria to depend on the arguable point that one may mistreat someone by choosing to exercise one's rights.

2. For an account of how moral standards are properly defended and criticized see chapters 4–6 of my book *Between Universalism and Skepticism,* Oxford University Press, 1994.

3. Of course, Washington could be an established character who, in effect, represented a Black "type" or Blacks in general. Were this the case, the joke in question might be racist. Whether or not it is would depend, e.g., on what else is true of Washington as a character, and perhaps, on where the joke appears (e.g., whether in a predominantly Black or a predominantly White publication). Note that members of a victimized group are far less likely to mistake a survival strategy for a character trait than members of a victimizing group.

READING QUESTIONS

1. Explain the difference between the agent-centered and act-centered views of racist humor according to Philips.
2. What is a Basic Racist Act according to Philips?
3. What problems does Philips raise for the Agent-Centered theory of racist humor?
4. How does Philips respond to the possible objections he considers against the Act-Centered view?
5. What is a "bit of humor" and what are the three ways in which a "bit of humor" may be racist?

DISCUSSION QUESTIONS

1. Is Philips right to dismiss the Agent-Centered account of the morality of racist humor in its entirety? Is there a way to incorporate beliefs and feelings into the Act-Centered account that he proposes?
2. To what extent do you think that racist humor or bits of racist humor are perceived as insulting or harmful when told by members of the ethnic group in question to either audiences that consist of only that particular ethnic group or mixed audiences?

J. ANGELO CORLETT

Reparations to Native Americans?

Corlett argues that the history of rights violations by the U.S. government against Native Americans justifies reparations to Native Americans. To defend his argument, Corlett critically examines a number of possible objections that might be used to defeat his pro-reparations argument and finds none of them convincing. He concludes by considering various reparations policies that might be pursued.

Recommended Reading: consequentialism, chap. 1, sec. 2A, rights-based moral theory.

North American history is replete with accounts of atrocities being inflicted by members of one group on members of another. Some such examples include the seizure by the French, the British, the Spanish, the Dutch governments (and later by the United States and Canadian governments, respectively) of millions of acres of land inhabited by Native (North) Americans; the genocide (or attempt therein) of various Native American nations[1] by the U.S. military at the order of, among others, former U.S. president Andrew Jackson; the enslavement of several Native Americans in the United States, and other acts of oppression. These and other significant harms have found little justice in the form of reparations. This chapter seeks to clarify the nature of reparations and analyzes philosophically objections to policies of reparations to historically and seriously wronged groups with the primary focus being on the Native American experiences in the United States.

It is an embarrassing fact that major Western political philosophies by and large ignore (or, at best, give short shrift to) the claims of Native Americans to property. And given the importance of the concept of private property rights in historic and contemporary Western political philosophy, it is vital to delve into problems which, among other things, question who ought to be seen as having the overriding moral claim or right to, say, the lands on which entire countries and their respective citizens reside, such as with the United States. For the moral legitimacy of a country, it is assumed, is contingent on at least the extent to which that country acquires justly the land on which it and its citizens reside. The problem of reparations to Native Americans raises queries concerning the fundamental moral legitimacy of the United States. For it challenges the moral basis of putative U.S. rights to lands which, it is assumed, are necessary for its economic and political survival.

What *are* reparations? And are reparations to Native Americans by the U.S. government morally required? This chapter seeks to answer these and related questions as they concern the Native American lives and lands lost to the United States by means of crimes committed against various Native American nations by the U.S. government and its military.

Reparations, according to *Black's Law Dictionary,* involve "payment for an injury; redress for a wrong done." They are payments "made by one country to another for damages done during war." Reparations involve restitution, which is the "act of restoring . . . anything to its rightful owner; the act of making good or giving equivalent for any loss, damage or injury and indemnification. . . . A person who has been unjustly enriched at the expense of another is required

From J. Angelo Corlett, *Race, Racism, and Reparations* (Ithaca and London: Cornell University Press), 2003, ch. 8, "Reparations to Native Americans?" pp. 147–60, 164–65, 168–73, 185–90.

to make restitution to the other."[2] Those receiving reparations are typically groups, though there seems to be no moral or logical preclusion to individuals receiving them. Often the evils perpetrated are such that there is no "just" or genuinely sufficient manner by which to rectify matters between the wrongdoer (or her descendants) and the party wronged (or her descendants): *Reparative compensation* is the main form of reparations. It seeks to rectify severe wrongs of the distant past by providing the wronged parties or their descendants a sum of money (often collected by general tax revenues), property, and other tangible goods that might be (roughly) proportional to the harms experienced by them. *Reparative punishment,* if it is ever morally justified, should be reserved for those who are themselves guilty of intentionally not paying substantial compensatory reparations. Moreover, reparative compensation/punishment must, I argue, always conform to the principle of proportional compensation and/or punishment: *Compensation and/or punishment for significant wrongdoing is always to be meted out in (albeit rough) proportion to the wrongdoing(s) committed.*

Although reparations are for the most part a compensatory matter, they share much in common with some of the "expressive functions" of punishment articulated by Joel Feinberg.[3] Feinberg describes four expressive functions of punishment as "hard treatment." Punishment involves "authoritative disavowal" of a society of a criminal act. It says publicly that the criminal had no right to act as she did, that she did not truly represent society's best aims and aspirations in committing the criminal deed. Punishment also involves a society's "symbolic nonacquiescence" or its speaking in the name of the people (when it is a democratic society) against the criminal's wrongful deed. Punishment involves "vindication of the law" as a society goes on record by way of its statutes to reinforce the genuine standards of law. Finally, punishment "absolves the innocent" of blame for what a criminal does. Reparations, I argue, share with punishment these expressive features. Like punishment, reparations disavow the wrong(s) committed and charges that the wrongdoers had no right to perform such evil(s). Reparations, like punishment, say publicly that wrongdoings do not represent society's highest aims and aspirations. In

democratic regimes, reparations speak in the name of the people against the wrongdoings in question, and they uphold the genuine standards of law in the face of past failures of the legal system to carry out true justice. In addition, reparations alienate a reasonably just society from its corrupt past, absolving society of its historic evils. These are some of the specific expressive functions of reparations. Some of these expressive functions of reparations are articulated by Feinberg when he states that "reparation can express sympathy, benevolence, and concern, but, in addition, it is always the acknowledgment of a past wrong, a 'repayment of a debt,' and hence, like an apology, the redressing of the moral balance or the restoring of the status quo ante culpum."[4]

More generally, the expressive feature of reparations is to make public society's *own* liability concerning the wrongs it has wrought upon a group or individuals. It is to offer an unqualified and unambiguous *apology* to the wronged parties (or their successors) without presumption of forgiveness or mercy. Moreover, it is to acknowledge, in a public way, the moral wrongness of the act(s) in question and to never forget them. For as George Santayana encourages, those who do not remember the errors of the past are doomed to repeat them. . . .

The foregoing suggests the following reparations argument:

1. As much as is humanly possible, instances of clear and substantial historic rights violations ought to be rectified by way of reparations.
2. The U.S. government has clearly committed substantial historic rights violations against millions of Native Americans.
3. Therefore, the historic rights violations of the U.S. government against Native Americans ought to be rectified by way of reparations, as much as humanly possible.

The basis for (1) might be a desert-based (retributivist) one that insists that there is either a perfect duty or an imperfect duty to rectify past injustices of a substantial nature. Or, to the extent that it is humanly possible to rectify substantial wrongs for which a wrongdoer is responsible, the wrongdoer ought to rectify the wrongdoing. The locution, "as much as humanly possible" in (1) and (3) is meant to capture the idea of reparations being proportional to the harms they are meant to rectify.

OBJECTIONS TO THE REPARATIONS ARGUMENT AND REPLIES

If the reparations agument is plausible, then wherever there is significant injustice there is at least a prima facie reason to believe that such injustice deserves compensation or rectification. Moreover, where the facts of the guilt, fault, harm, and identity of the perpetrators and victims are clear reparations ought to be pursued for the sake of corrective justice. Hence, there is a presumptive case in favor of reparations to Native Americans by the U.S. government, given the substantial wrongs many Native Americans have experienced at the hands of the United States.

Precisely what is/was the harm perpetrated against Native Americans? . . . The campaigns against various Native American nations by the U.S. military serve as examples here. One specific instance of U.S. crimes against the Lakota Sioux was the massacre at Wounded Knee, which in turn culminated in the retaliatory violence against the U.S. military at Little Big Horn. Examples of U.S. torts against Native Americans are the fraudulent takings of lands, often followed by the U.S. government's refusal to honor its treaties made with various Native American nations. Yet for all of the several instances of unjustified violence and other crimes, torts and contract violations committed by the U.S. against various Native Americans, few, if any, apologies or reparations have been issued by the U.S. government. These are some reasons that form the presumptive case for reparations to Native Americans. But such a presumption can be overridden if it can be shown that considerations against such reparations outweigh the strength of the prima facie case for them where the instances in question are not "hard cases."[5] Hence it is important to consider the plausibility of various of the strongest objections to reparations to Native Americans . . .

THE OBJECTION FROM HISTORICAL COMPLEXITY

Given the above understanding of the nature of reparations, are reparations to Native Americans by the U.S. government morally required? Ought the U.S. government to provide reparations to Native Americans? A number of arguments can be marshaled against the imposition of reparations, and they deserve close scrutiny. First, there is the *objection from historical complexity*. This objection avers that history contains far too many and complex situations of conflict such that it would be impossible to figure out all of the injustices that would putatively require reparations. Where the perpetrators of the evils are dead and cannot be punished for their horrors it would be sheer dogmatic idealism to think that respecting rights requires or even permits the kind of complex legal casework that would be required to rectify all past wrongs. To award reparations to the wronged party or her descendants would end up forcing innocent parties (perhaps the descendants of the wrongdoers) to pay for what they themselves did not do. Among other things, the objection from historical complexity seems to assume that past injustices should not forever burden future putatively "innocent" generations. The objection from historical complexity challenges (1) of the reparations argument, suggesting that there are some instances of historic injustice that ought not to be rectified by way of reparations.

THE PRINCIPLE OF MORALLY JUST ACQUISITIONS AND TRANSFERS

In response to this objection to the reparations argument, it might be pointed out that the inability to figure out with precise accuracy *all there is to know* about *every case* that putatively involves reparations hardly prohibits a juridical system from awarding some measure of significant reparations where cases are clear (based on unambiguous historical records, for example). Even if it were true that a full-blown policy of reparations would involve reparations to Native Americans by not only the U.S. government, but by the governments of Spain, Portugal, England, France, the Netherlands, among others, and even if it proved overly difficult to figure out the extent to which each said government contributed to harms against Native Americans, this would hardly show that clear cases of U.S. harms to Native Americans ought not to be compensated by the United States. Moreover, though the parties to a putative case of reparations would involve those who themselves did no harm to the victims in question, such "innocent" parties who currently reside on or "own" lands that were once resided on by Native Americans are in violation of the principle of morally just acquisitions and transfers:

> Whatever is acquired or transferred by morally just means is itself morally just; whatever is acquired or transferred by morally unjust means is itself morally unjust.[6]

Basically, the intended meaning of this principle is that to the extent that property is acquired or transferred in a morally justified way (i.e., without force, fraud, or other kinds of coercion or deceit), the acquisition or transfer of that property carries with it a genuine moral claim or entitlement to occupy it without interference from others. To the extent that the principle of morally just acquisitions and transfers is violated, there is no legitimate claim or entitlement to occupy the property being acquired or transferred. . . .

Although the locutions "morally just" and "morally unjust" are somewhat vague, relatively clear cases of unjust acquisition or transfer, for instance, exist: when such acquisitions or transfers occur as the result of significant nonvoluntariness (the violent use of force, for example) on the part of those relinquishing property, when acquisitions or transfers involve fraud, or severe misunderstanding between principal parties. In the case of Native American lands (then a part of the United States) most of which were taken from them forcibly by the U.S. military at the direction of the U.S. president Andrew Jackson and other U.S. officials (many of which lands were encroached

upon illegally by U.S. citizens or civilians), there is no question who the wrongdoer was (the U.S. government, along with its citizen trespassers) and who the harmed parties were (Native Americans of various nations). In other cases, Native Americans were believed to have "given away" their land to invaders, interpreted as such, presumably, because of the hospitality of the Native peoples toward the invaders. In such cases, the questions are not who is the guilty party and who was the victim, but precisely how ought the victims to be "reparated" for the wrongdoings. In still other instances, such as our own, U.S. citizens have purchased in good faith lands from other non-Native peoples to which the former may not in fact have an overriding moral right. That a person purchased in good faith a stolen item in no wise entitles him to that item, as even the law stipulates. She who is truly entitled to the item has a right to it, and that right must be respected by all who take seriously what morality requires. Note that this argument is *not* contingent on the status of wellbeing of either the perpetrators or the victims of the evils inflicted that might require reparations. For reparations are morally required even if, say, the United States and its citizens were not well-off and if Native Americans were indeed relatively better-off. Reparative justice does not depend on the ability of perpetrators of wrongdoing to enrich their lives by inflicting wrongdoings on others. It is concerned primarily with rectifying past injustices regardless of whether or not perpetrators have been enriched at all by their wrong-doings. Thus the attempt of the objection from historical complexity to defeat (1) fails.

THE OBJECTION TO COLLECTIVE RESPONSIBILITY

This raises the issue of collective moral retrospective liability responsibility of, say, the U.S. government for severe wrongs committed in *its* name or on *its* behalf against Native Americans. *The objection to collective responsibility* challenges the morality of reparations to Native Americans on the grounds that it is problematic to hold the current U.S. government and its citizenry morally accountable for wrongs committed by previous generations of people who acted or failed to act, as the case may be, to harm Native Americans and on behalf of the U.S. government, its agencies, and/or on behalf of themselves as actual or putative U.S. citizens. Thus the objection to collective responsibility challenges (2) of the reparations argument insofar as (2) seeks to hold the U.S. *government* responsible for certain substantial wrongs against Native Americans.

However, the objection to collective responsibility falls prey to at least two weaknesses. First, the fundamental documents that form at least the basis of U.S. government are still those which govern the United States. Even though the atrocities committed against Native Americans generations ago were not the direct responsibility of today's U.S. citizens, the fact is that the U.S. government has persisted over time, and still exists.

Furthermore, it is plausible to think that when the U.S. army and government committed genocidal acts of violence against various Native American nations they rendered the United States collectively guilty and at fault because such acts were committed knowingly, intentionally, and voluntarily. Thus *we* (since it is *our* government, acting on *our* behalves) *are* justified in inferring that they were both causally responsible and morally liable (culpable) for those harms committed by them against the Native American nations. Additionally, though legally speaking it is not required that a guilty party apologize to the victim(s) of its wrongdoing(s), the extent of the harms committed by the U.S. government against various Native American nations would seem to suggest that an apology is needed. If this is true, then it would appear that both U.S. governmental (collective) feelings and expressions of guilt and remorse are suggested. That is, we would expect that the U.S. government would, in some official manner, express its genuine feelings of guilt and remorse to Native Americans, publicly renouncing its history of racially motivated oppression and holocaust against Native Americans and vowing that it never occur again. Of course, a clear record of governmental policies should reflect a support for such genuine feelings of guilt and remorse.

It is reasonable, then, to hold *it* (the U.S. government) accountable for its past wrongdoings, pending some adequate argumentation in support of the morality of a statute of limitations on trying and punishing/compensating such crimes. If it was just "discovered" that a corporation committed a gross wrongdoing (including murders) in 1900, would not justice dictate that the courts seek rectification in such a case, especially if that corporation is still in operation? The reasoning behind this might be either that the putatively guilty corporation is simply deserving of being forced to compensate some parties for the wrongdoing in question (a retributivist rationale) and/or that the corporation has gained an unfair advantage in committing such acts. In either case, where matters are clear, past wrongs of such magnitude as what happened to many Native Americans require that justice be realized and there appears to be no adequate reason why past wrongs against Native Americans by U.S. governmental representatives should not be treated in a similar manner as those in which we treat gross corporate wrongdoings that result from corporate representatives' actions or inactions. As for the individuals or aggregate mobs who committed theft, violent crimes, and other illegal acts against Native Americans, in some cases some criminals' transfers of assets/fortunes can be traced to current U.S. citizens or institutions, thereby providing a source of reparations. Of course, one who inherits what has been acquired or transferred to her hardly deserves what she inherits if possession of it is in violation of the principle of morally just acquisitions and transfers. The burden of argument, then, seems to be on those who would suggest that there is a moral statute of limitations on injustice. Furthermore, this burden of argument must be satisfied absent question-begging and/or self-serving reasoning.

A second problem with the objection to collective responsibility is that the principle of morally just acquisitions and transfers renders irrelevant the issue of whether or not the current U.S. government and its citizenry can legitimately be held accountable for the past injustices committed against Native Americans. In other words, the principle of morally just acquisitions and transfers renders otiose the objection to collective responsibility. And the principle does this in the following way: if, say, most or all of the lands currently occupied by the U.S. government and its citizens are in fact occupied in violation of the principle, then it matters not whether current occupants of those lands are actually liable for the illegitimate transfer of the lands. What truly matters here is whether or not the lands in question have indeed been transferred legitimately. Since most or all of them have not been legitimately transferred to current occupants, then no such occupants can have a legitimate and overriding moral claim to the lands they occupy. The problem of collective responsibility simply does not affect this fact. It is a red herring given the plausibility of the principle of morally just acquisitions and transfers. This rebuttal to the objection to collective responsibility relies on a "weak" form of compensation.

The significance of these replies to the objection to collective responsibility is that one provides a link between the U.S. government and many of the serious wrongs committed against Native Americans, satisfying the legal criteria of privity, standing, and nexus, each of which is necessary to establish a legal case for reparations. The second reply renders the objection to collective responsibility impotent insofar as Native Americans' moral rights to the lands in question are concerned. Thus the objection to collective responsibility fails to defeat (2) of the reparations argument, unless, of course, it can be shown by way of independent argument that there is a moral statute of limitations on injustice. . . .

THE AFFIRMATIVE ACTION OBJECTION

There is another objection to reparations: the *affirmative action objection*. This argument states that reparations are otiose given the existence of affirmative action in the hiring of underrepresented groups in the United States, typically, those which have been victimized by racial discrimination. Such support of historically wronged/underrepresented groups takes the form of affirmative action programs. With affirmative action programs in place, there is no need for reparations policies to Native Americans since Native Americans qualify for affirmative action programs.

However, affirmative action legislation is designed to assist in the providing of equal opportunities in employment and education for Native Americans, African Americans, and other minority groups. Yet in the case of employment opportunities, it would seem that affirmative action alone serves as a cruel form of mockery when construed as compensation for the numerous and harsh civil rights violations of these groups by the U.S. government and its citizens. Moreover, if distributive justice is the reason for the grounding of affirmative action, then affirmative action cannot serve as a challenge to reparations. For the recipients of such programs earn the wages or salaries they receive. This can hardly be seen as a legitimate form of compensation for damages. Affirmative action programs, whatever their legitimacy status, cannot and should not be construed as a form of reparations. As pointed out in previous chapters, to think that affirmative action programs can take the place of reparations to Native and African Americans is to commit a category mistake by conflating two essentially distinct policies with distinct functions. . . .

THE OBJECTION FROM THE INDETERMINACY OF NATIVE AMERICAN IDENTITY

Another objection to the awarding of reparations to Native Americans is the *objection from the indeterminacy of Native American identity*. This argument states that, even if there is no moral statute of limitations on otherwise legitimate Native American claims to reparations, such reparations are unwarranted because of the overly difficult task of determining the boundaries of ethnic group membership in general, and of Native American tribal affiliations in particular. For example, does it make moral sense to provide reparations to those who are, say, 10 percent Cherokee and 90 percent European American? What are the boundaries of ethnic group identity for purposes of reparations in particular and corrective justice more generally?

However, the objection from the indeterminacy of Native American identity is too pessimistic concerning the abilities of history, the law, and Native

Americans themselves to trace ethnic ties within and between Native peoples. Today's Native American nations (such as the Navajo or Diné nation in Window Rock, Arizona, or Six Nations in Brantford, Ontario, Canada) keep reasonably successful or accurate track of membership within their respective nations. Thus to the extent that a person is able to be clearly identified as someone belonging to a particular Native American nation (or to more than one nation, for that matter), and to the extent that that nation (or members of it) are owed reparations, that is the extent to which each member of the nation, as a descendant of the victims of gross forms of wrongdoing, are deserving of reparations. It is irrelevant to the moral status of reparations (or the moral desert notion of reparations) that such reparations might impinge on the privacy of persons in regards to their ethnicities, or that a "Balkanization" of ethnic groups might ensue. Insofar as the boundaries of Native American identity are concerned, perhaps these possible problems are, in the end, insoluable in any absolutely precise or totally uncontroversial sense. But these factors hardly render unrequired reparations to Native Americans. For many Native Americans are 50 percent or greater Native Americans of one or more such nations. And the fact that some people's Native American identity is dubious in no way serves as a reasonable consideration to refuse reparations to those who are clearly of substantially Native American ethnicity and who are otherwise deserving of them. . . .

THE HISTORICAL REPARATIONS OBJECTION

Yet another objection to reparations to Native Americans is that reparations have already been paid to Native American nations in the past for wrongs committed by the U.S. government. I shall refer to this objection as the *historical reparations objection.* In the case of those awarded to Native Americans by the United States, there are the examples of the state of Georgia's restoration of many Cherokee landmarks, a newspaper plant, and other buildings in New Echota, and the state of Georgia's repealing of its repressive anti-Native American laws of 1830. (It took until 1962 for this to occur, however.) Moreover, in 1956 the Pawnees were awarded more than $1 million in a suit they brought before the Indian Claims Commission for land taken from them in Iowa, Kansas, and Missouri. In 1881, the Poncas were compensated by Congress for their ill-treatment by the Court of Omaha, Kansas. For the illegal seizure of the Black Hills in 1876, then owned by the Sioux, compensation was paid. In 1927, the Shoshonis were paid over $6 million for land illegally seized from them (the amount was for the appraised value of *half* of their land, however). There are a few other instances of reparations to Native Americans, as history tells us.[7]

However, the historical reparations objection is based on evidence of reparations to a few Native American nations for property rights violations. There is a threefold difficulty here. First, such reparations were hardly sufficient to serve as anywhere close to adequate compensations for the property, "maltransfers," damages, and other malfeasances in question. Furthermore, the objection ignores completely the question of reparations for undeserved violence in the form of human rights violations against Native Americans, much of such violence was inflicted on various Native Americans by the U.S. military. Finally, it ignores the fact that the vast majority of property rights violations and civil rights violations against Native Americans in general are as of yet *un*compensated. Not unlike the objection from historical progress, the historical reparations objection, then, seems to be more of a non sequitur than a genuine concern.

THE OBJECTION FROM SOCIAL UTILITY

There is another objection to the argument for reparations to Native Americans, and it concerns whether or not the awarding of reparations to Native Americans by the United States would significantly decrease overall social utility. It would render the United States and its citizens—not to mention Native Americans themselves—worse off. For, as Locke argues, the European-based commercial system makes life better for everyone than the primitive hunting and gathering ways of life enjoyed by the Native American nations.[8] I shall refer to this as the *objection from social utility.* This utilitarian-based concern is that, strictly speaking, the awarding to Native Americans of the lands that were acquired from them in violation of the principle of morally just acquisitions and transfers would surely mean the dissolution of the United States as we know it, as mostly each U.S. citizen resides on land which would, presumably, be relinquished to Native peoples should reparations be enforced. The economic, political, and social implications of this action would be unthinkable, even if the awarding of reparations in this fashion were required by the balance of human reason. So social utility requires that reparations not be awarded because of the undue disruption that would certainly be experienced by the majority of citizens of each of the countries in question. Where would such citizens go if forced by, say, international law, to vacate the premises? Which countries would be in economic and political positions to admit these newly homeless persons? Thus reparations to Native Americans are morally unjustified, it is argued, because they would violate some acceptable principle of social utility.

However, the objection from social utility does not take seriously what people deserve and what retributive justice requires. For even if, strictly speaking, the balance of human reason permitted or required reparations that would then force U.S. citizens from the land on which they reside, this would not mean that the moral prerogative of the reparations in question would lead to the disbanding of the current citizens of the United States. For Native peoples might very well settle for sovereignty rights to the existing lands, yet lease such lands to the rest of the inhabitants. This mode of reparations would most likely dissolve the United States as we know it. But perhaps the United States, insofar as it was founded on the clear, repeated, and intentional violations of the content of the principle of morally just acquisitions and transfers, deserves to be dissolved in favor of taking much more

seriously (than it currently does) morality and justice. Nonetheless, the sovereignty over certain lands by Native Americans to others satisfies the concern for morality and justice in that it gives back to Native peoples the lands to which they had and have ultimate ("trumping") moral rights. But it also does not unduly affect those currently living on those lands in violation of the principle of morally just acquisitions and transfers. For they are not left without a place of residence, evading the aforementioned concern. (But they would be alienated from what is not really theirs to begin with, morally speaking.) Thus the objection from social utility does not pose an insoluble problem for reparations to Native Americans, though at least one strict form of reparations to Native Americans does imply the dissolution of the United States as we know it. . . .

SOME POSSIBLE REPARATIONS POLICIES

What sorts of specific compensatory measures ought to be imposed and against whom? Let us consider the plausibility of a range of possible policies of U.S. reparations to Native Americans. I will consider a number of such possible policies, from some of the more demanding ones to some of the least demanding. I assume that the crimes of unjust land takings, murders, and political repression by the U.S. government contain a minimal amount of moral and historical ambiguity: that the identities of the collective perpetrators, victims, and those targeted for reparations are knowable within reasonable clarity and precision.

Strict Justice, the Complete Restitution of Lands and Compensation for Personal Injuries/Loss of Personal Property

It might be argued that, strictly speaking, morality and justice require the complete return of the lands of North America that were gotten from Native peoples in violation of the principle of morally just acquisitions and transfers. Such a measure of reparations would not only return all such lands outright to Native peoples, but would require the U.S. government (along with British, Dutch, Spanish, French and Canadian governments, among others) to pay native peoples significant sums of money as compensation for damages for the crimes (murders, rapes, mayhems, and robbery by the thousands) committed against Native Americans in the "settling" of the "New World." It is plausible to believe that at least trillions of dollars would be rightly owed to Native Americans by these governments (perhaps respectively, especially considering punitive damages, unpaid interest accrued, and penalties!), each of which participated in the massacre and near complete genocide of all Native Americans over periods of generations. This form of reparations to surviving Native American nations would surely bring to economic demise each of the governments paying such reparations and would tilt rather severely the balance of global economic power in favor of Native Americans (and other indigenous peoples receiving similar such settlements).

In response to this proposed policy of reparations, it might be argued that a certain utilitarian consideration outweighs strict retributive justice, namely, that the millions of U.S. citizens not be made significantly worse-off in the process of rectifying past wrongs committed against native peoples. This is especially true since those who would be made worse-off are the clear numerical majority of people residing in the United States. Considerations of utility require that a less extreme and demanding policy of reparations be adopted. Thus the argument from social utility, refuted above, is reinvoked here.

But one question is whether or not such U.S. citizens are in a moral position to deny the legitimacy of a policy that would place them in economic ruins. The reason why such citizens are not in a moral position is that they are residing on lands to which they have no genuine and overriding moral right, that is, a moral right that (all things considered) trumps other competing moral claims to and/or interests in the lands in question. Does Andrew, who knowingly or unknowingly purchases or otherwise receives stolen property, have a moral claim to it? If so, does

Andrew's moral claim trump the moral right of the victim (the original moral right holder of the property) to the same? Consider the following example of a wealthy person whose *entire* fortune was contingent on and amounted to that which she inherited in violation of the principle of morally just acquisitions and transfers. Even if she is not morally entitled to that which was obtained unjustly, is she not entitled to the fruits of her labor/investments above and beyond the basic value of the inheritance. Even if it is true that she mixed her labor with some of the ill-gotten fortune to increase the fortune over time, her increase in fortune might be offset by the balance of leasing or interest payments owed for the land ill-acquired or the fortune acquired unjustly. Yet we would not think it correct that she remain in possession of "her" fortune but that she return it to the rightful heir or owner, namely the person who has a valid moral claim to the fortune.

Complete Restitution of Lands

Another policy of reparations to Native Americans would be the complete restitution of lands to them. Although it is impossible to return to particular Native American nations the lands that were theirs originally due to the fact that some such nations no longer exist, it would be possible to provide Native American nations, *as a coalition*, all such lands that were acquired or transferred in violation of the principle of morally just acquisitions and transfers. Presumably, this would mean that most or all U.S. occupied lands would be transferred to Native American nations, and that Native Americans would, as a coalition, become a sort of "landlord" over those who currently reside on the lands.

One difficulty with this proposed policy of reparations is that it does not account for the crimes against persons and is thus an insufficient form of reparations to Native Americans who as a group not only lost their native lands, but also were in many cases enslaved, killed, suffered severe damage to forms of livelihood, and so forth. So the restitution of lands to Native Americans simply repays them for the lands which is theirs by moral right. However, it does not compensate them for the damage to the land and resources, nor for the crimes against persons committed against them by the U.S. government.

Complete Compensation for Harms to Persons and Property

Another policy of reparations to Native Americans would involve complete compensation for harms against Native Americans and their personal property. This would surely entail the payment of billions of dollars over several years, especially in light of the millions of such native persons who were murdered, mutilated, tortured, and enslaved, and those who survived but often had their belongings and livelihoods ruined by marauding U.S. citizens (even by the U.S. army!). A complete compensation program for Native Americans would likely involve a continual payment of a substantial sum of money to Native American nations, with the idea that such payments would in themselves hardly serve as adequate compensation for the crimes perpetrated.

The difficulty with this form of reparations is that it does nothing to provide restitution to native peoples for their land that was taken from them in violation of the principle of morally just acquisitions and transfers. In fact, such a "complete" compensation policy leaves untouched the very social structure and government and forces that subdued the Native Americans in the first place, standing as a continual reminder of how evil can mock true justice. Even compensation with restitution of lands is hardly adequate for justice in this case. The same would follow, then, regarding policies of partial compensation for harms to persons and property, partial restitution of lands, partial compensation for harms to persons and property, and partial compensation for lands.

The "Buffalo Commons" Proposal

Short of complete restoration of lands and/or compensation for personal injuries of Native Americans, there lies another proposal. It is the partial but significant restoration of lands to Native Americans, lands that have, it is argued, never played an important role in the economic viability of the United States. Thus the restoring of such lands to Native Americans by way of reparations would pose no real threat to the U.S. economy. This is what has been referred to as the "Buffalo Commons" proposal.[9]

> What you end up with is a huge territory lying east of Denver, west of Lawrence, Kansas, and extending from the Canadian border to southern Texas, all of it "outside the loop" of United States business as usual.
>
> The bulk of this area is unceded territory owned by the Lakota, Pawnee, Arikara, Hidatsa, Mandan, Crow, Shoshone, Assiniboine, Cheyenne, Arapaho, Kiowa, Comanche, Jicarilla, and Mescalero Apache nations. There would be little cost to the United States, and virtually no arbitrary dispossession or dislocation of non-Indians, if the entire Commons were restored to these peoples.[10]

The reasons given in favor of this proposal are twofold. First, it provides Native Americans a means of tangible sovereignty and self-determination. Secondly, it provides "alternative socioeconomic models" for possible adaptation by those who are not Native Americans.

Of course, this proposal, however reasonable in its attempt to not disrupt the lives of U.S. citizens, is grossly inadequate as a form of reparations for the remainder of the territories taken by force and fraud from Native Americans. Nor does it begin to compensate Native Americans for the murders and other personal injuries indicted on them by the U.S. government. Nonetheless, the Buffalo Commons proposal is a reasonable attempt to balance the application of some plausible principle of utility to current U.S. society over against the demand for some degree of rectification for injustice to Native Americans. Although reasonable, the Buffalo Commons proposal is insufficient as a means for providing adequate reparations to Native Americans.

Substantial Reparations Tax

The previously discussed policies of reparations to Native Americans would come in the form of court-ordered settlements. But that is not the only way in which such reparations might be made. Instead, a tax might be levied on U.S. citizens, one that would be paid to various Native American nations. A substantial tax might amount to, say, 25 percent of each non–Native American's annual gross income in perpetuity.

An objection to this substantial reparations tax might be that it is overly substantial and demanding on U.S. citizens. However, it is hard to understand this concern in light of the fact that current U.S. citizens are residing on lands to which they have no moral right, given the foregoing arguments. Sometimes justice and morality demand what we in our less honorable moments find too difficult to do. If anything is problematic about the nature and scope of the substantial reparations tax, it is rather that it is insufficiently substantial, not that it is overly substantial.

Minimal Reparations Tax

A minimal reparations tax might amount to, say, 1 percent of each U.S. citizen's gross annual income. But if the substantial reparations tax is properly deemed as insufficient to adequately compensate for the harms committed against Native Americans by the U.S. government, then surely this minimal reparations tax would be nothing more than an insult to Native Americans and to justice and fairness itself.

The points of criticism of each of the above sketched reparations policies are meant to convey the idea that the fact that the U.S. citizenry does not desire to compensate Native Americans for the wrongs that the U.S. Government has committed against the latter shows a certain amount of moral ineptitude on the part of the U.S. citizenry in general. Moreover, if the principle of morally just acquisitions and transfers is correct in regards to the Native American experiences, then one is hardly in a moral position to deny the plausibility of any of these policies of reparations so long as they are acceptable to Native Americans. For neither policy is adequate to compensate Native Americans for the wrongs their people have suffered at the hands of the very government that persists today. Yet one wonders why, except for reasons of

racism and lack of moral character, even today most U.S. citizens would balk at even the hint of a *minimal* reparations tax to cover a fraction of the costs of arguably the worst evils ever perpetrated by a modern government.

If the arguments against reparations to Native Americans in the United States are defeasible for the reasons given herein, then the presumptive case in favor of reparations to Native Americans gains strength. Barring further argumentation that would render morally problematic such reparations, then, a case for such reparations has been made along the following lines. To the extent that history is unambiguous concerning the extent of guilt, fault, wrongdoing, and the identities of perpetrators and victims of historic injustices, policies of reparations to Native Americans should be enacted according to some fundamentally sound principle of proportional compensation.

If the foregoing analysis is sound, then one hope that the United States has of dragging itself out of the mire of its own perpetration of historic injustices against Native Americans is for it to institute adequate policies of reparations to Native Americans. Even so, such policies must receive far more commitment by the U.S. government than the treaties made by the U.S. government with Native American nations had received in the past. What is also needed is a national sense of shame-based guilt and collective remorse for the roles that the U.S. government and its citizenry played in founding the United States. Yet if such shame requires a higher-level self-consciousness, this might well be precisely what U.S. society lacks, providing its critics with ammunition for claims of the fundamental immorality of the United States in general. For a society that is based on unrectified injustice is itself unjust. But a society that simply refuses to admit its unjust history toward others not only remains unjust on balance, but serves as a stark reminder of the unabashed arrogance of its unspeakable badness.

NOTES

1. Similar points might well apply to Native Americans in Central and South America. Indeed, Native Americans in (former) island nations of the Americas, for example, the

Hawai'ian islands were victimized (accompanied in the end by threat of military force) by unjust takings by the United States and others. See Michael Dougherty, *To Steal a Kingdom: Probing Hawai'ian History* (Waimanalo: Island Style Press, 1992). That Hawai'ian culture was significantly affected by the intrusion of Europeans is noted in Martha Beckwith, *Hawai'ian Mythology* (Honolulu: University of Hawai'i Press, 1976).

2. Note that nothing in this conception of reparations requires that the reparations be "paid" or rendered by the perpetrators of wrongdoing only. (Compare the conception of reparations set forth in D. N. MacCormick, "The Obligation of Reparations," *Proceedings of the Aristotelian Society* 78 [1977–78]: 175). Contrast this notion of reparations with one articulated by Bernard Boxill: "Part of what is involved in rectifying an injustice is an acknowledgement on the part of the transgressor that what he is doing is required of him because of his prior error." Bernard Boxill. "The Morality of Reparations," in Barry R. Gross, ed., *Reverse Discrimination* (New York: Prometheus. 1977). p. 274.

3. Feinberg, *Doing and Deserving* (Princeton: Princeton University Press, 1970), chapter 5.

4. Feinberg, *Doing and Deserving,* p. 76.

5. For a discussion of hard cases in the context of law, see Ronald Dworkin, *Taking Rights Seriously* (Cambridge: Harvard University Press, 1978), chapter 4.

6. This principle bears a keen resemblance to the principle of just acquisitions, transfers and rectification found in Robert Nozick, *Anarchy, State, and Utopia* (New York: Basic Books, 1974), p. 150. However, the principle of morally just acquisitions and transfers makes no particular theoretical commitments to Nozick's entitlement theory or its implications.

7. Debo, *A History of the Indians in the United States* (Norman, OK: The University of Oklahoma Press, 1970).

8. Locke, *Second Treatise on Government,* sections 34, 37, 40–43.

9. Ward Churchill, *From a Native Son* (Boston: South End Press, 1996), pp. 528–30.

10. Ibid., p. 529.

READING QUESTIONS

1. What is Corlett's central argument for the claim that the historic rights violations of the U.S. government against Native Americans ought to be rectified by way of reparations?
2. What are the six objections to Corlett's reparations argument that Corlett discusses?
3. How does Corlett argue that affirmative action programs should not be understood as a form of reparations?
4. What is Corlett's response to the argument from social utility?
5. In his discussion of the "strict justice" reparations policy, how does Corlett use the case of the wealthy person to argue that U.S. citizens who would be economically ruined by the policy are not in a moral position to deny its legitimacy?

DISCUSSION QUESTIONS

1. Which of Corlett's six possible reparations policies seems the most reasonable? Why?
2. Does Corlett successfully defend his reparations argument? Are there any possible objections to the argument that he fails to address?

Louis P. Pojman

Why Affirmative Action Is Immoral

Pojman critically evaluates two common pro–affirmative action arguments: the forward-looking "level playing field" argument and the backward-looking "compensation" argument and concludes that neither of them succeeds in morally justifying what he calls "preferential affirmative action." He further argues that affirmative action policies are immoral because they involve unjust discrimination against innocent white males.

The underlying moral principle guiding Pojman's position is the Kantian principle that respect for persons requires that we treat each person as an end in him- or herself and never merely as a means to social purposes.

Recommended Reading: Kantian moral theory, chap. 1, sec. 2C.

The state shall not discriminate against, or grant preferential treatment to, any individual or group on the basis of race, sex, color, ethnicity, or national origin in the operation of public employment, public education, or public contracting
—(California Civil Rights Initiative, *Proposition 209*).

When affirmative action was first proposed in the early 1960s, as a civil rights activist and member of CORE, I supported it. The shackled runner metaphor, set forth by President Lyndon Johnson in his 1965 Howard University speech, seemed to make moral sense. An opportunity gap existed between White and Black societies which greatly handicapped Blacks. This was my *forward-looking* reason for supporting affirmative action. But I had a *backward-looking* argument, as well. America owed compensation to Blacks who had been hideously oppressed in our society. The reasons that caused me to change my mind on this issue will be discussed in this paper, in which I will argue that *preferential* affirmative action is immoral. I have given comprehensive critiques of affirmative action (henceforth AA) elsewhere, and space prevents a repetition of that material.[1] In this short paper I limit my

arguments to AA regarding race, since if any group deserves AA it is African-Americans. Also I concentrate on university admittance and hiring, since these are the areas with which I am most familiar.

First some definitional preliminaries: By *Affirmative Action* I refer to preferential treatment based on race, gender or ethnicity. We might call this *Preferential Affirmative Action* as opposed to *Procedural Affirmative Action,* which requires that special attention be given to insure that everything reasonable is done to recruit and support equally qualified minorities and women. I support *Procedural Affirmative Action* even to the point of allowing the properties in question to function as tie-breakers. In my experience, however, *Procedural Affirmative Action* tends to slip into *Preferential Affirmative Action.* Bureaucracies in general cannot be trusted to abide by the rules, hence the present need to eliminate AA altogether. Recall how race-norming procedures and AA admittance policies were kept secret for years. In the early 1990s, the University of Delaware withdrew Linda Gottfriedson's fellowship because she exposed the practice of race-norming. If and when

From Louis P. Pojman, "Why Affirmative Action Is Immoral," in L. Hinman, ed., *Contemporary Moral Issues: Diversity and Consensus*, 2nd ed. (Upper Saddle River, NJ: Prentice Hall, 2000).

we are committed to fair evaluations, *Procedural Affirmative Action* will be morally acceptable.

Let me turn to the two arguments that once persuaded me of the soundness of *Preferential Affirmative Action,* which I now believe to be unsound.

THE LEVEL PLAYING FIELD ARGUMENT

This is a version of President Johnson's Howard University "Shackled Runner" speech. Here is how Mylan Engel puts the argument:

> Consider a race, say a hundred yard dash. Mr. White starts at the 50 yard mark, while Mr. Black starts at the 0 yard mark. The gun goes off and sure enough Mr. White wins. Now very few people would think that sort of race was fair. . . . They certainly wouldn't think that Mr. White deserved significant economic gain for beating Mr. Black in such a race. Now, it seems to me that a similar sort of argument can be made in defense of strong AA. One need not appeal to compensation for past injustices, etc. The fact is that many white males have an unfair head start in the education and employment game. Consider a statistic reported on NPR today: 27% of Blacks and Latinos currently are living below the poverty line (the poverty line is now $16,400 for a family of four), whereas only 11% of (non-Asian) whites are living below the poverty line. And at each level above the poverty line, there is a disproportionate number of whites. The economic advantage experienced by whites is that more whites can afford to send their children to exclusive college preparatory private schools, and even those whites who can't afford to send their children to private schools, still have a better chance of living in a wealthy school district with better public schools. So, by the time the Young Mr. Whites and the Young Mr. Blacks are ready to start the university application process, more often than not, the young Mr. Whites already have the equivalent of a 50 or at least a 25-yard head start in the college application game.[2]

First of all, more should be done for poor families and poor neighborhoods, as well as poor schools. Economic disparities between the rich and the poor should be reduced. Programs, such as the East German youth program and President Clinton's Youth Corps, which has unfortunately foundered, in which every American youth gives 2 years to national service, either in the military or in community service, much of which would be geared toward improving the lot of the economically and educationally disadvantaged. The reward would be free college or grad school tuition or job/career training.

Secondly, I gradually came to see that the Level Playing Field Argument could best support a class-based approach to AA, rather than a race-based one. On current poverty statistics, 74 percent of Blacks and Hispanics are not living in poverty and 11 percent of Whites are, so this kind of AA would cut across racial and gender lines. I am sympathetic to class-based AA. The question is: what kind of help should be given?

Financial assistance would seem to be the best kind. Candidates would be accepted into universities on the basis of their qualifications, but would then be assisted according to need.[3] There is nothing new about this kind of program, it has traditionally been used (Pell Grants, etc.). Tie breakers could be used too. If Mr. Poor and Mr. Rich both had similar scores, it would be reasonable to take the disadvantage into consideration and award a place to Mr. Poor.

Engel points out, as an objection to this argument, that AA actually harms the very people it seeks to help, especially by stigmatizing them with the label "AA admittee" = "inferior student." But isn't the point that AA admittees are often not equipped to handle the rigors of the top schools? So we are doubly harming them. Even Bok and Bowen's new book *The Shape of the River,* which advocates AA in college admittance, concedes that blacks with identical SAT scores as whites get (on average) lower grades. The Center for Civil Rights has shown that in every state university examined (Michigan, North Carolina, Washington, etc.), Black admittance rates are based on much lower SAT scores and their failure and drop out rates are usually more than double those of whites. So AA actually is counterproductive, contributing to harming those it would help. Moreover, some schools have had to lower their standards to accommodate less qualified Blacks. While I was teaching at the University of Mississippi, a strong AA program was implemented. The Math Department had to switch to a high school algebra text in order to teach that course. The Affirmative Action handbook stated that any qualified minority (and female) candidate had a presumptive claim on any open academic position in the university. Sidney Hook relates an incident where a Religious Studies Department was instructed by an accrediting association to drop the requirements of Hebrew and Greek, since it was discouraging members of minorities groups to major in that discipline.

It gradually dawned on me that affirmative action was guilty of enacting the Peter Principle, which states that we should promote people to positions beyond their present abilities, where they will very likely fail. So Black students with SATs of 1150 are admitted to Harvard or Berkeley, from which they drop out or fail, whereas they would have done very well at a first rate state university or less prestigious small college.

My own experience is that of a poor teen-ager who started off at mediocre Morton High and Morton Jr. College in Cicero, Illinois, and who worked his way up to Columbia University and Union Seminary, then fellowships to the University of Copenhagen, and finally to Oxford University. I didn't get into Oxford until my 30s and would have failed had I gone right out of high school or junior college. I saw my community college, not as a stigma, but as an opportunity to improve myself so that I might be worthy of a more rigorous challenge.

Furthermore, it isn't Mr. Rich who is likely to be affected by AA. It's Mr. Poor-but-talented-White who is likely to be harmed. Mr. Rich has had such support, coaching and early advantages that he's on his way to success. Neither Mr. Poor Black nor Mr. Poor White is normally helped by AA. Mr. and Miss Middle Class Black is the main beneficiary.

There is another problem with the Level Playing Field Argument. It supposes that if everything were just, we'd have equal results in every area of life. But why should we expect this? Anyone who is familiar with Irish, Italian and Jewish ethnic patterns in New York City can attest to the fact that people from different ethnic communities (with the same economic status) turn out very differently: the Irish and Italian tended to go into the fire department and police force;

the Jews into academics, science and technology. There is evidence that Ashkanazy Jews have on average higher intelligence (measured in terms of academic ability, at least) than other ethnic groups. Both genetically and culturally differences exist between people and may exist between groups. This point may be uncomfortable to egalitarians, but, as philosophers, we should be concerned with the evidence, which, at least, gives us no reason to think that every group has the same average abilities.[4]

There is one other argument that caused me to give up the Leveling Argument. It can function as a disincentive to responsible parenting. If you and I both have the same economic opportunities but you save your money and dedicate your life to producing two excellent children with the best advantages, whereas I gamble, drink, spend enormous amounts of money on expensive cars, and neglect my 10 children, why should your two better qualified children be denied admission to Yale simply because my children are more needy (or are Black)? This seems to me to be a disincentive to good parenting as well as a denial of the merit attained by the better qualified. AA programs aren't fine grained enough to sort out these nuances.[5]

In conclusion, while many Middle Class Blacks and other minorities may be helped by AA policies, these policies do little to help the truly disadvantaged. The Leveling Argument is unsound. But even if it were sound, since it is basically a utilitarian argument, other considerations of justice could still override it. I turn to the second argument that once led me to support AA.

THE COMPENSATION ARGUMENT FOR PREFERENTIAL AFFIRMATIVE ACTION

The argument goes like this: historically Blacks have been wronged and severely harmed by Whites. Therefore white society should compensate Blacks for the injury caused them. Reverse discrimination in terms of preferential hiring, contracts, and scholarships seemed a fitting way to compensate for the past wrongs.[6] I was a member of Riverside Church in New York City when at a Sunday service in May of 1969, James Foreman pushed aside the minister and issued the Black Manifesto, demanding $500 million from the American religious establishment for reparations to Blacks. Foreman's disruption caused me to reassess my support of this argument, and gradually I began to realize that it involves a distorted notion of compensation.

Normally, we think of compensation as owed by a specific person A to another person B whom A has wronged in a specific way C. For example, if I have stolen your car and used it for a period of time to make business profits that would have gone to you, it is not enough that I return your car. I must pay you an amount reflecting your loss and my ability to pay. If I have made $5,000 and only have $10,000 in assets, it would not be possible for you to collect $20,000 in damages—even though that is the amount of loss you have incurred.

Sometimes compensation is extended to groups of people who have been unjustly harmed by the greater society. For example, the United States government has compensated the Japanese-Americans who were interred during the Second World War, and the West German government has paid reparations to the survivors of Nazi concentration camps. But here specific individuals have been identified who were wronged in an identifiable way by the government of the nation in question.

On the face of it, demands by Blacks for compensation do not fit the usual pattern. Southern states with Jim Crow laws could be accused of unjustly harming blacks, but it is hard to see that the United States government was involved in doing so. Much of the harm done to Blacks was the result of private discrimination, rather than state action. So the Germany/US analogy doesn't hold. Furthermore, it is not clear that all blacks were harmed in the same way or whether some were *unjustly* harmed or harmed more than poor Whites and others (e.g., Jews, Poles, short people). Finally, even if identifiable blacks were harmed by identifiable social practices, it is not clear that most forms of Affirmative

Action are appropriate to restore the situation. The usual practice of a financial payment, as I noted earlier, seems more appropriate than giving a high level job to someone unqualified or only minimally qualified, who, speculatively, might have been better qualified had he not been subject to racial discrimination. If John is the star tailback of our college team with a promising professional future, and I accidentally (but culpably) drive my pick-up truck over his legs, and so cripple him, John may be due compensation, but he is not due the tailback spot on the football team.

Still, there may be something intuitively compelling about compensating members of an oppressed group who are minimally qualified. Suppose that the Hatfields and the McCoys are enemy clans and some youths from the Hatfields go over and steal diamonds and gold from the McCoys, distributing it within the Hatfield economy. Even though we do not know which Hatfield youths did the stealing, we would want to restore the wealth, as far as possible, to the McCoys. One way might be to tax the Hatfields, but another might be to give preferential treatment in terms of scholarships and training programs and hiring to the McCoys.

This is perhaps the strongest argument for Affirmative Action, and it may well justify some weaker versions of AA, but it is doubtful whether it is sufficient to justify strong versions with quotas and goals and time tables in skilled positions. There are at least three reasons for this. First, we have no way of knowing how many people of any given group would have achieved some given level of competence had the world been different. Secondly, the normal criterion of competence is a strong prima facie consideration when the most important positions are at stake. There are three reasons for this: (1) treating people according to their merits respects them as persons, as ends in themselves, rather than as means to social ends (if we believe that individuals possess a dignity which deserves to be respected, then we ought to treat that individual on the basis of his or her merits, not as a mere instrument for social policy); (2) society has given people expectations that if they attain certain levels of excellence they will be rewarded appropriately;

and (3) filling the most important positions with the best qualified is the best way to ensure efficiency in job-related areas and in society in general. These reasons are not absolutes. They can be overridden.[7] But there is a strong presumption in their favor, so that a burden of proof rests with those who would override them.

The third reason against using affirmative action to compensate has to do with the arbitrariness of using preferential treatment in a market-driven process. Take the hiring of professors according to affirmative action guidelines. Should we hire (or admit into professional schools) minimally qualified AA candidates over better qualified candidates because they have suffered injustice as *individuals* or because they belong to a *group* that has suffered? If it is because they have suffered injustice, then it is irrelevant that they are members of minority groups. We should treat them as individuals and compensate them accordingly. So race and gender are really irrelevant. What counts is the injustice done to them. But if we reward them because they are members of an oppressed group, then we may do injustice by not rewarding individuals of other groups who have suffered injustice. Poor coal miners of West Virginia, railroad workers who worked under oppressive conditions to build the transcontinental railroads, short people, ugly people, people from abusive homes, and so forth all deserve some compensation from a society that has dealt them a raw deal. But hiring or admitting to special professional schools is arbitrary compensation in that it compensates only a few of the oppressed, and, generally, not the worst off. It compensates the best off Blacks and women, many who come from relatively wealthy families, leaving the truly disadvantaged, impoverished Blacks and Whites, males and females, in the same situation they already were in.[8]

At this point we face the objection that "innocent" White males have enormously profited from racism and sexism, so that while some of the above has merit, it doesn't acquit White males altogether. Preferential treatment to previously oppressed people may still be justified, all things considered. We turn to this argument.

THE ARGUMENT FOR COMPENSATION FROM THOSE WHO INNOCENTLY BENEFITTED FROM PAST INJUSTICE

Young White males as innocent beneficiaries of unjust discrimination against blacks and women have no grounds for complaint when society seeks to level the tilted field. They may be innocent of oppressing blacks, other minorities, and women, but they have unjustly benefitted from that oppression or discrimination. So it is perfectly proper that less qualified women and blacks be hired before them.

The operative principle is: He who knowingly and willingly benefits from a wrong must help pay for the wrong. Judith Jarvis Thomson puts it this way: "Many [white males] have been direct beneficiaries of policies which have down-graded blacks and women . . . and even those who did not directly benefit . . . had, at any rate, the advantage in the competition which comes of the confidence in one's full membership [in the community], and of one's right being recognized as a matter of course."[9] That is, white males obtain advantages in self-respect and self-confidence deriving from a racist/sexist system which denies these to blacks and women.

Here is my response to this argument: As I noted in the previous section, compensation is normally individual and specific. If A harms B regarding X, B has a right to compensation from A in regards to X. If A steals B's car and wrecks it, A has an obligation to compensate B for the stolen car, but A's son has no obligation to compensate B. Suppose A is unable to compensate B himself but he could steal C's car (roughly similar to B's). A has no right to steal C's car to compensate A. Furthermore, if A dies or disappears, B has no moral right to claim that society compensate him for the stolen car, though if he has insurance, he can make such a claim to the insurance company. Sometimes a wrong cannot be compensated, and we just have to make the best of an imperfect world.

Recently (mid-September, 1998), an umpire called what would have been Mark McGwire's

66th home run of the season a ground-rule double on the grounds that a fan caught the ball before it made it to the stands. A replay showed that the ball had already cleared the stands, so that it was a home run. The commissioner of baseball refused to over-rule the umpire's decision. Two days later Sammy Sosa hit two home runs, thus tying McGwire for the home run lead. McGwire was the victim of an unintended injustice (if the fact that it was an hon-est mistake bothers you, suppose the umpire did it on purpose). Should Sosa give up one of his home runs in order to rectify the injustice to McGwire? Morally, McGwire deserves to hold the record for home runs, but according to the rules, he has a right only to a tie at this point.

Suppose my parents, divining that I would grow up to have an unsurpassable desire to be a basket-ball player, bought an expensive growth hormone for me. Unfortunately, a neighbor stole it and gave it to little Michael, who gained the extra 13 inches—my 13 inches—and shot up to an enviable 6 feet 6 inches. Michael, better known as Michael Jordan, would have been a runt like me but for his luck. As it is he prof-ited from the injustice, and excelled in basketball, as I would have done had I had my proper dose.

Do I have a right to the millions of dollars that Jordan made as a professional basketball player—the unjustly accused innocent beneficiary of my growth hormone? I have a right to something from the neigh-bor who stole the hormone, and it might be kind of Jordan to give me free tickets to the Bull's basketball games, and remember me in his will. As far as I can see, however, he does not owe me anything, either legally or morally.

Suppose further that Michael Jordan and I are in high school together and we are both qualified to play basketball, only he is far better than I. Do I deserve to start in his position because I would have been as good as he is had someone not cheated me as a child? Again, I think not. But if being the lucky ben-eficiary of wrongdoing does not entail that Jordan (or the coach) owes me anything in regard to basketball, why should it be a reason to engage in preferential hiring in academic positions or highly coveted jobs? If minimal qualifications are not adequate to override excellence in basketball, even when the minimality

is a consequence of wrongdoing, why should they be adequate in other areas?

AFFIRMATIVE ACTION REQUIRES DISCRIMINATION AGAINST A DIFFERENT GROUP

Here is the third reason why I changed my mind on AA. Weak or procedural AA weakly discriminates against new minorities, mostly innocent young White males, and strong or preferential Affirmative Action strongly discriminates against these new minorities. As I argued earlier, this discrimination is unwar-ranted, since, even if some compensation to Blacks were indicated, it would be unfair to make innocent white males bear the whole brunt of the payments. Recently I had this experience. I knew a brilliant young philosopher, with outstanding publications in first level journals, who was having difficulty get-ting a tenure-track position. For the first time in my life I offered to make a phone call on his behalf to a university to which he had applied. When I reached the Chair of the Search Committee, he offered that the committee was under instructions from the Administration to hire a woman or a Black. They had one of each on their short-list, so they weren't even considering the applications of White males. At my urging he retrieved my friend's file, and said, "This fellow looks far superior to the two candidates we're interviewing, but there's nothing I can do about it." Cases like this come to my attention regularly. In fact, it is poor White youth who become the new pariahs on the job market. The children of the wealthy have little trouble getting into the best private grammar schools and, on the basis of superior early education, into the best universities, graduate schools, manage-rial and professional positions. Affirmative Action simply shifts injustice, setting Blacks, Hispanics, Native Americans, Asians and women against young White males, especially ethnic and poor white males. It makes no more sense to discriminate in favor of a rich Black or female who had the opportunity of the best family and education available against a poor White, than it does to discriminate in favor of White males against Blacks or women. It does little to rectify the goal of providing equal opportunity to all.

At the end of his essay supporting Affirmative Action, Albert Mosley points out that other groups besides Blacks have been benefited by AA, "women, the disabled, the elderly."[10] He's correct in including the elderly, for through powerful lobbies, such as the AARP, they do get special benefits, including Medicare, and may sue on the grounds of being discriminated against due to *Ageism,* prejudice against older people. Might this not be a reason to reconsider Affirmative Action? Consider the sheer rough percentages of those who qualify for some type of AA programs.

Group	Percentage in Population
1. Women	52
2. Blacks	12
3. Hispanics	9
4. Native Americans	2
5. Asian-Americans	4
6. Physically and Mentally Disabled	10
7. Welfare recipients	6
8. The Elderly	25 (est. Adults over 60)
9. Italians (in New York City)	3
Total	123

The Office of Federal Contract Compliance (OFCC) includes as protected categories not only Blacks but "all persons of Mexican, Puerto Rican, Cuban or Spanish origin or ancestry." The Small Business Administration adds Eskimos and Aleuts. Federal contracting programs include the following groups as meriting preferential treatment: People from Burma, Thailand, Malaysia, Indonesia, Singapore, Brunei, Japan, China, Taiwan, Laos, Cambodia, Vietnam, Korea, the Philippines, U.S. Trust Territory of the Pacific Islands, Republic of the Marshall Islands, federated States of Micronesia, the Commonwealth of the Northern Mariana Islands, Guam, Samoa, Macao, Hong Kong, Fiji, Tonga, Kiribati, Tuvalu, Mauru, India, Pakistan, Bangladesh,

Sri Lanka, Bhutan, the Maldives Islands, and Nepal.[11] Recent immigrants from these countries sometimes are awarded contracts in preference to lower bids by White male owned firms. Recently, it has been proposed that homosexuals be included in oppressed groups deserving Affirmative Action.[12] At Northeastern University in 1996 the faculty governing body voted to grant homosexuals Affirmative Action status at this university. How many more percentage points would this add? Several authors have advocated putting all poor people on the list.[13] And if we took handicaps seriously, would we not add ugly people, obese people, people who stammer, color-blind people, people with genetic liabilities, and, especially, short people, for which there is ample evidence of discrimination? How about left-handed people (about 9% of the population), they can't play short-stop or third base and have to put up with a right-handedly biased world. The only group not on the list is that of White males. Are they, especially healthy, middle-class young White males, becoming the new "oppressed class"? Should we add them to our list?

Respect for persons entails that we treat each person as an end in himself or herself, not simply as a means to be used for social purposes. What is wrong about discrimination against Blacks is that it fails to treat Black people as individuals, judging them instead by their skin color not their merit. What is wrong about discrimination against women is that it fails to treat them as individuals, judging them by their gender, not their merit. What is equally wrong about *Affirmative Action* is that it fails to treat White males with dignity as individuals, judging them by *both their race and gender,* instead of their merit. *Current Strong Affirmative Action is both racist and sexist.*

CONCLUSION

Let me sum up my discussion. The goal of the Civil Rights movement and of moral people everywhere has been justice for all, for a color-blind society, where people will not be judged by their race or gender but by their moral character and abilities. The question is: How best to get there? Civil rights legislation removed the unjust legal barriers, opening the way towards equal opportunity, but it did not tackle other factors, causes that result in unjust discrimination. Procedural Affirmative Action aims at encouraging minorities and women to strive for excellence in all areas of life, without unduly jeopardizing the rights of other groups, such as White males and Asians. The problem of Procedural Affirmative Action is that it easily slides into Preferential Affirmative Action where quotas, "goals and time-tables," "equal results,"—in a *word reverse discrimination*—prevail and are forced onto groups, thus promoting mediocrity, inefficiency, and resentment. My argument has been that, if we are serious about attaining a color-blind society, with a large amount of opportunity for all, we should shape our lives and our institutions in ways that make that more likely. AA vitiates that goal by setting up a new class of pariah, young White males, depriving them of the opportunities that they merit. Furthermore, AA frequently aims at the higher levels of society—universities and skilled jobs, but, if we want to improve our society, the best way to do it is to concentrate on families, children, early education, and the like, so that all are prepared to avail themselves of opportunity. Affirmative Action, on the one hand, is arbitrary, compensating a few of the better-off members of AA groups, and doing nothing for the truly disadvantaged, and on the other hand, is doubly arbitrary in exacting a penalty from unlucky talented young white males, who themselves may have been victims of oppression, while leaving better-off members of society untouched by its policies.

In addition to the arguments I have offered, Affirmative Action, rather than unite people of good will in the common cause of justice, tends to balkanize us into segregation-thinking. Professor Derrick Bell of Harvard Law School recently said that the African-American Supreme Court Judge Clarence Thomas, in his opposition to Affirmative Action, "doesn't think black."[14] Does Bell really claim that there is a standard and proper "Black" (and presumably a White) way of thinking? Ideologues like Bell, whether radical Blacks like himself, or Nazis who advocate "think Aryan," both represent the same thing: cynicism about rational debate, the very antithesis of the quest for impartial truth and justice. People of good will, who believe in reason to resolve our differences will oppose this kind of balkanization of ethnic groups.

Martin Luther said that humanity is like a man mounting a horse who always tends to fall off on the other side of the horse. This seems to be the case with Affirmative Action. Attempting to redress the discriminatory iniquities of our history, our well-intentioned social engineers now engage in new forms of discriminatory iniquity and thereby think that they have successfully mounted the horse of racial harmony. They have only fallen off on the other side of the issue.[15]

NOTES

1. See "The Moral Status of Affirmative Action" in *Public Affairs Quarterly,* vol. 6:2 (1992) and "The Case against Strong Affirmative Action" in *International Journal for Applied Philosophy,* vol. 12 (1998).

2. Mylan Engel, Correspondence, September 24, 1998.

3. Objective measures, such as SAT and ACT scores, along with high school grade point average, have considerable validity. The charge of being prejudicial has been adequately refuted. Actually, they predict better for Blacks than for Whites. Wherever possible recommendations and personal interviews should be used to supplement these measures.

4. Also, many Haitian and Latinos are recent immigrants to the USA (sometimes illegally so). Why should they be given preference over young white males? Why should the university be made to carry the heavy burden of leveling society when people come to our land voluntarily? Note too that poor Blacks and Hispanics typically have larger families than Whites and middle-class Blacks. If the poor are to be given special benefits, don't procreative responsibilities go along with them?

5. Many people think that it is somehow unjust if one community (or family) spends more money or resources on its children's education than another. A few years ago the New Jersey legislature passed a bill prohibiting communities from spending more than the average amount of money on its children's public education, lest inequalities emerge. But, if we believe that parents should have considerable freedom on how they use their resources, why is disparity unjust? Suppose you choose to have only 2 children

and make enormous sacrifices for their education and upbringing (say 40 units on each child) and I (with similar resources) have 10 children and spend less total resources to all 10 (averaging 5 units on each child). Why, should society have to make up the difference between what is spent on the 10 children. Surely, such supplementary aid, beyond a certain minimal limit, is a disincentive to be a responsible parent. Yet we don't want the children to suffer either. This may be a prima facie reason to require licenses for parenting (which has its own serious problems).

6. For a good discussion of this argument see B. Boxill, "The Morality of Reparation" in *Social Theory and Practice* 2:1(1972) and Albert G. Mosley in his and Nicholas Capaldi, *Affirmative Action; Social Justice or Unfair Preference?* (Totawa, NJ: Rowman and Littlefield, 1996), pp. 23–27.

7. Merit sometimes may be justifiably overridden by need, as when parents choose to spend extra earnings on special education for their disabled child rather than for their gifted child. Sometimes we may override merit for utilitarian purposes. For example, suppose you are the best shortstop on a baseball team but are also the best catcher. You'd rather play shortstop, but the manager decides to put you at catcher because, while your friend can do an adequate job at short, no one else is adequate at catcher. It's permissible for you to be assigned the job of catcher. Probably, some expression of appreciation would be due you.

8. I am indebted to Robert Simon's "Preferential Hiring" *Philosophy and Public Affairs* 3 (1974) for helping me to formulate this argument.

9. Judith Jarvis Thomson, "Preferential Hiring" in Marshall Cohen, Thomas Nagel, and Thomas Scanlon, eds., *Equality and Preferential Treatment* (Princeton: Princeton University Press, 1977).

10. Albert Mosley, op. cit., p. 53.

11. For a discussion of these figures, see Terry Eastland, *Ending Affirmative Action* (New York: Basic Books, 1996), p. 5Sf and 140f.

12. J. Sartorelli, "The Nature of Affirmative Action, Anti-Gay Oppression, and the Alleviation of Enduring Harm" *International Journal of Applied Philosophy* (vol. 11. No. 2, 1997).

13. For example, Iddo Landau, "Are You Entitled to Affirmative Action?" *International Journal of Applied Philosophy* (vol. 11. No. 2, 1997) and Richard Kahlenberg "Class Not Race" (*The New Republic* April 3, 1995).

14. See L. Gordon Crovitz, "Borking Begins, but Mudballs Bounce Off Judge Thomas, "*The Wall Street Journal,* July 17, 1991. Have you noticed the irony in this mudslinging at Judge Thomas? The same blacks and whites who oppose Judge Thomas, as not the best person for the job, are themselves the strongest proponents of Affirmative Action, which embraces the tenet that minimally qualified Blacks and women should get jobs over White males.

15. Some of the material in this essay appeared in "The Moral Status of Affirmative Action" *Public Affairs Quarterly,* vol. 6:2 (1992). I have not had space to consider all the objections to my position or discuss the issue of freedom of association which, I think, should be given much scope in private but not in public institutions. Barbara Bergmann (*In Defense of Affirmative Action* (New York: Basic Books, 1996, pp. 122–125)) and others argue that we already offering preferential treatment for athletes and veterans, especially in university admissions, so, being consistent, we should provide it for women and minorities. My answer is that I am against giving athletic scholarships, and I regard scholarships to veterans as a part of a contractual relationship, a reward for service to one's country. But I distinguish entrance programs from actual employment. I don't think that veterans should be afforded special privilege in hiring practices, unless it be as a tie breaker.

I should also mention that my arguments from merit and respect apply more specifically to public institutions than private ones, where issues of property rights and freedom of association carry more weight.

READING QUESTIONS

1. Explain the "level playing field" and "compensation" arguments in favor of affirmative action. What objections does Pojman raise for each of these arguments?
2. How does Pojman distinguish between preferential and procedural affirmative action?
3. Why does Pojman think that affirmative action encourages discrimination against different groups? What group in particular does he think affirmative action discriminates against?
4. Explain Pojman's reasons for thinking that affirmative action policies fail to show respect for persons and to treat them with dignity.

DISCUSSION QUESTIONS

1. Is Pojman's worry that preferential affirmative action would slide into procedural affirmative action justified? Why or why not?
2. Should we accept Pojman's claim that affirmative action discriminates against innocent white males? Why or why not? Suppose that affirmative action does discriminate against innocent white males in the way Pojman describes. Consider and discuss whether discrimination against one group of people is any more or less wrong than discrimination against another.

THOMAS E. HILL JR.

The Message of Affirmative Action

Hill is critical of "forward-looking" consequentialist attempts to justify affirmative action policies, and he is also critical of standard "backward-looking" attempts that would appeal, for example, to Ross's principle of reparation to justify such policies. Both approaches, argues Hill, convey the wrong message about the nature of racism and sexism and affirmative actions policies. In order to properly address the morality of affirmative action, Hill sketches a "narrative" framework for thinking about racism and sexism that emphasizes one's historical and cultural context and, in particular, the idea that many of our values are "cross-time wholes, with past, present, and future parts united in certain ways." Emphasizing the cross-time ideals or virtues of mutual respect and trust and the value of equal opportunity, Hill explains how affirmative action policies such as we find in many universities can be morally justified.

Recommended Reading: virtue ethics, chap. 1, sec. 2E. Also relevant are consequentialism, chap. 1, sec. 2A, and the ethics of prima facie duty, chap. 1, sec. 2F.

Affirmative Action Programs remain controversial, I suspect, partly because the familiar arguments for and against them start from significantly different moral perspectives. Thus I want to step back for a while from the details of debate about particular programs and give attention to the moral viewpoints presupposed in different *types* of argument. My aim, more specifically, is to compare the "messages" expressed when affirmative action is defended from different moral perspectives. Exclusively forward-looking (for example, utilitarian) arguments, I suggest, tend to express the wrong message, but this is also true of exclusively backward-looking (for example, reparation-based) arguments. However, a moral outlook that focuses on cross-temporal narrative values (such as mutually respectful social relations) suggests a more appropriate account of what affirmative action should try to express. Assessment of the message, admittedly, is only one aspect of a complex issue, but it is a relatively neglected one. My discussion takes for granted some common-sense ideas about the communicative function of action, and so I begin with these.

Actions, as the saying goes, often *speak* louder than words. There are times, too, when only actions can effectively communicate the message we want to convey and times when giving a message is a central part of the purpose of action. What our actions say to others depends largely, though not entirely, upon our avowed reasons for acting; and this is a matter for reflective decision, not something we discover later by looking back at what we did and its effects. The decision is important because "the same act" can have very different consequences, depending upon how we choose to justify it. In a sense, acts done for different reasons are not "the same act" even if they are otherwise similar, and so not merely the consequences but also the moral nature of our acts depends in part on our decisions about the reasons for doing them.

Unfortunately, the message actually conveyed by our actions does not depend only on our intentions and reasons, for our acts may have a meaning for others quite at odds with what we hoped to express. Others may misunderstand our intentions, doubt our sincerity, or discern a subtext that undermines the primary message. Even if sincere, well-intended, and successfully conveyed, the message of an act or policy does not by itself justify the means by which it is conveyed; it is almost always a relevant factor, however, in the moral assessment of an act or policy. . . .

I shall focus attention for a while upon this relatively neglected issue of the message of affirmative action. In particular, I want to consider what messages we *should try* to give with affirmative action programs and what messages we should try to avoid.

What is the best way to convey the intended message, and indeed whether it is likely to be heard, are empirical questions that I cannot settle; but the question I propose to consider is nonetheless important, and it is a *prior* question. What do we want to say with our affirmative action programs, and why? Since the message that is received and its consequences are likely to depend to some extent on what we decide, in all sincerity, to be the rationale for such programs, it would be premature and foolish to try to infer or predict these outcomes without adequate reflection on what the message and rationale should be. Also, for those who accept the historical/narrative perspective described in [this essay], there is additional reason to focus first on the desired message; for that perspective treats the message of affirmative action not merely as a minor side effect to be weighed in, for or against, but rather as an important part of the legitimate purpose of affirmative action.

Much useful discussion has been devoted to the constitutionality of affirmative action programs, to the relative moral rights involved, and to the advantages and disadvantages of specific types of programs. By deemphasizing these matters here, I do not mean to suggest that they are unimportant. Even more, my remarks are not meant to convey the message, "It doesn't matter what we do or achieve, all that matters is what we *say.*" To the contrary, I believe that mere gestures are insufficient and that universities cannot even communicate what they should by affirmative action policies unless these are sincerely designed to result in increased opportunities for those disadvantaged and insulted by racism and sexism. . . .

STRATEGIES OF JUSTIFICATION: CONSEQUENCES AND REPARATIONS

Some arguments for affirmative action look exclusively to its future benefits. The idea is that what has happened in the past is not in itself relevant to what we should do; at most, it provides clues as to what acts and policies are likely to bring about the best future. The philosophical tradition associated with this approach is utilitarianism, which declares that the morally right act is whatever produces the best consequences. Traditionally, utilitarianism evaluated consequences in terms of happiness and unhappiness, but the anticipated consequences of affirmative action are often described more specifically. For example, some argue that affirmative action will ease racial tensions, prevent riots, improve services in minority neighborhoods, reduce unemployment, remove inequities in income distribution, eliminate racial and sexual prejudice, and enhance the self-esteem of blacks and women. Some have called attention to the fact that women and minorities provide alternative perspectives on history, literature, philosophy, and politics, and that this has beneficial effects for both education and research.

These are important considerations, not irrelevant to the larger responsibilities of universities. For several reasons, however, I think it is a mistake for advocates of affirmative action to rest their case exclusively on such forward-looking arguments. First, critics raise reasonable doubts about whether affirmative action is necessary to achieve these admirable results. The economist Thomas Sowell argues that a free-market economy can achieve the same results more efficiently; his view is therefore that even if affirmative action has beneficial results (which he denies), it is not necessary for the purpose.[1] Though Sowell's position can be contested, the controversy itself tends to weaken confidence in the entirely forward-looking defense of affirmative action.

An even more obvious reason why affirmative action advocates should explore other avenues for its defense is that the exclusively forward-looking approach must give equal consideration to possible negative consequences of affirmative action. It may be, for example, that affirmative action will temporarily increase racial tensions, especially if its message is misunderstood. Even legitimate use of race and sex categories may encourage others to abuse the categories for unjust purposes. If applied without sensitive regard to the educational and research purposes of the university, affirmative action might severely undermine its efforts to fulfill these primary

responsibilities. If affirmative action programs were to lower academic standards for blacks and women, they would run the risk of damaging the respect that highly qualified blacks and women have earned by leading others to suspect that these highly qualified people lack the merits of white males in the same positions. This could also be damaging to the self-respect of those who accept affirmative action positions. Even programs that disavow "lower standards" unfortunately arouse the suspicion that they don't really do so, and this by itself can cause problems. Although I believe that well-designed affirmative action programs can minimize these negative effects, the fact that they are a risk is a reason for not resting the case for affirmative action on a delicate balance of costs and benefits.

Reflection on the *message* of affirmative action also leads me to move beyond entirely forward-looking arguments. For if the sole purpose is to bring about a brighter future, then we give the wrong message to both the white males who are rejected and to the women and blacks who are benefited. To the latter what we say, in effect, is this: "Never mind how you have been treated. Forget about the fact that your race or sex has in the past been actively excluded and discouraged, and that you yourself may have had handicaps due to prejudice. Our sole concern is to bring about certain good results in the future, and giving you a break happens to be a useful means for doing this. Don't think this is a recognition of your rights as an individual or your disadvantages as a member of a group. Nor does it mean that we have confidence in your abilities. We would do the same for those who are privileged and academically inferior if it would have the same socially beneficial results."

To the white male who would have had a university position but for affirmative action, the exclusively forward-looking approach says: "We deny you the place you otherwise would have had simply as a means to produce certain socially desirable outcomes. We have not judged that others are more deserving, or have a right, to the place we are giving them instead of you. Past racism and sexism are irrelevant. The point is just that the sacrifice of your concerns is a useful means to the larger end of the future welfare of others."

This, I think, is the wrong message to give. It is also unnecessary. The proper alternative, however, is not to ignore the possible future benefits of affirmative action but rather to take them into account as a part of a larger picture.

A radically different strategy for justifying affirmative action is to rely on backward-looking arguments. Such arguments call our attention to certain events in the past and assert that *because* these past events occurred, we have certain duties now. The modern philosopher who most influentially endorsed such arguments was W. D. Ross.[2] He argued that there are duties of fidelity, justice, gratitude, and reparation that have a moral force independent of any tendency these may have to promote good consequences. The fact that you have made a promise, for example, gives you a strong moral reason to do what you promised, whether or not doing so will on balance have more beneficial consequences. The Rossian principle that is often invoked in affirmative action debates is a principle of reparation. This says that those who wrongfully injure others have a (prima facie) duty to apologize and make restitution. Those who have wronged others owe reparation. . . .

There are, however, serious problems in trying to justify affirmative action by this backward-looking argument, especially if it is treated as the exclusive or central argument. Degrees of being advantaged and disadvantaged are notoriously hard to measure. New immigrants have not shared our history of past injustices, and so the argument may not apply to them in any straightforward way. The argument appeals to controversial ideas about property rights, inheritance, and group responsibilities. Some argue that affirmative action tends to benefit the least disadvantaged blacks and women; though this does not mean that they are owed nothing, their claims would seem to have lower priority than the needs of the most disadvantaged. Some highly qualified blacks and women object that affirmative action is damaging to their reputations and self-esteem, whereas the reparation argument seems to assume that it is a welcome benefit to all blacks and women.

If we focus on the message that the backward-looking argument sends, there are also some potential problems. Though rightly acknowledging past injustice, the argument (by itself) seems to convey the message that racial and sexual oppression consisted primarily in the loss of tangible goods, or the deprivation of specific rights and opportunities, that can be "paid back" in kind. The background idea, which goes back at least to Aristotle, is that persons wrongfully deprived of their "due" can justly demand an "equivalent" to what they have lost.[3] But, while specific deprivations were an important part of our racist and sexist past, they are far from the whole story. Among the worst wrongs then, as now, were humiliations and contemptuous treatment of a type that cannot, strictly, be "paid back." The problem was, and is, not just that specific rights and advantages were denied, but that prejudicial attitudes damaged self-esteem, undermined motivations, limited realistic options, and made even "officially open" opportunities seem undesirable. Racism and sexism were (and are) *insults*, not merely tangible *injuries*.[4] These are not the sort of thing that can be adequately measured and repaid with equivalents. The trouble with treating insulting racist and sexist practices on a pure reparation model is not merely the practical difficulty of identifying the offenders, determining the degree of guilt, assessing the amount of payment due, etc. It is also that penalty payments and compensation for lost benefits are not the only, or primary, moral responses that are called for. When affirmative action is defended exclusively by analogy with reparation, it tends to express the misleading message that the evils of racism and sexism are all tangible losses that can be "paid off;" by being silent on the insulting nature of racism and sexism, it tends to add insult to insult.

The message suggested by the reparation argument, by itself, also seems objectionable because it conveys the idea that higher education, teaching, and doing research are mainly benefits awarded in response to self-centered demands. The underlying picture too easily suggested is that applicants are a group of self-interested, bickering people, each grasping for limited "goodies" and insisting on a right to them. When a university grants an opportunity through affirmative action, its message would seem to be this. "We concede that you have a valid claim to this benefit and we yield to your demand, though this is not to suggest that we have confidence in your abilities or any desire to have you here." This invitation seems too concessive, the atmosphere too adversarial, and the emphasis too much on the benefits rather than the responsibilities of being a part of the university.

PHILOSOPHICAL INTERLUDE: AN ALTERNATIVE PERSPECTIVE

Here I want to digress from the explicit consideration of affirmative action in order to consider more abstract philosophical questions about the ways we evaluate acts and policies. At the risk of oversimplifying, I want to contrast some assumptions that have, until recently, been dominant in ethical theory with alternatives suggested by contemporary philosophers who emphasize historical context, narrative unity, and community values.[5] Although these alternatives, in my opinion, have not yet been adequately developed, there seem to be at least four distinguishable themes worth considering.

First, when we reflect on what we deeply value, we find that we care not merely about the present moment and each future moment in isolation but also about how our past, present, and future cohere or fit together into a life and a piece of history. Some of our values, we might say, are cross-time wholes, with past, present, and future parts united in certain ways. Thus, for example, the commitments I have made, the projects I have begun, what I have shared with those I love, the injuries I have caused, and the hopes I have encouraged importantly affect both whether I am satisfied with my present and how I want the future to go.

Second, in reflecting on stretches of our lives and histories, we frequently use evaluative concepts drawn more from narrative literature than from accounting. Thus, for example, we think of our lives as having significant beginnings, crises, turning points, dramatic tension, character development, climaxes, resolutions, comic interludes, tragic disruptions, and eventually fitting (or unfitting) endings. The value of any moment often depends on what came before and what we anticipate to follow. And since our lives are intertwined with others in a common history, we also care about how our moments cohere with others' life stories. The past is seen as more than a time of accumulated debts and assets, and the future is valued as more than an opportunity for reinvesting and cashing in assets.

Third, evaluation must take into account one's particular historical context, including one's cultural, national, and ethnic traditions, and the actual individuals in one's life. Sometimes this point is exaggerated, I think, to suggest a dubious cultural relativism or "particularism" in ethics: for example, the thesis that what is valuable for a person is defined by the person's culture or that evaluations imply no general reasons beyond particular judgments, such as "That's *our* way" and "John is *my* son." But, construed modestly as a practical or epistemological point, it seems obvious enough, on reflection, that we should take into account the historical context of our acts and that we are often in a better position to judge what is appropriate in particular cases than we are to articulate universally valid premises supporting the judgment. . . .

Fourth, when we evaluate particular acts and policies as parts of lives and histories, what is often most important is the value of the whole, which cannot always be determined by "summing up" the values of the parts. Lives, histories, and interpersonal relations over time are what G. E. Moore called "organic unities"—that is, wholes the value of which is not necessarily the sum of the values of the parts.[6] The point here is not merely the obvious practical limitation that we cannot measure and quantify values in this area. More fundamentally, the idea is that it would be a mistake even to try to evaluate certain unities by assessing different parts in isolation from one another, then adding up all their values. Suppose, for example, a woman with terminal cancer considered two quite different ways of spending her last days. One way, perhaps taking a world cruise, might seem best when evaluated in terms of the quality of each future moment, in isolation from her past and her present ties; but another way, perhaps seeking closure in projects and with estranged family members, might seem more valuable when seen as a part of her whole life.

Taken together, these ideas cast doubt on both the exclusively forward-looking method of assessment and the standard backward-looking alternative. Consequentialism, or the exclusively forward-looking method, attempts to determine what ought to be done at present by fixing attention entirely on future results. To be sure, any sensible consequentialist will consult the past for lessons and clues helpful in predicting future outcomes: for example, recalling that you offended someone yesterday may enable you to predict that the person will be cool to you tomorrow unless you apologize. But beyond this, consequentialists have no concern with the past, for their "bottom line" is always "what happens from now on," evaluated independently of the earlier chapters of our lives and histories. For the consequentialist, assessing a life or history from a narrative perspective becomes impossible or at least bizarre, as what must be evaluated at each shifting moment is "the story from now on" independently of what has already been written.[7]

The standard Rossian alternative to this exclusively forward-looking perspective is to introduce certain, (prima facie) *duties* to respond to certain past events in specified ways—for example, pay debts, keep promises, pay reparation for injuries. These duties are supposed to be self-evident and universal (though they are prima facie), and they do not hold because they tend to promote anything good or valuable. Apart from aspects of the acts mentioned in the principles (for example, fulfilling a promise, returning favors, not injuring, etc.), details of historical and personal context are considered irrelevant.

By contrast, the narrative perspective sketched above considers the past as an integral part of the valued unities that we aim to bring about, not merely as a source of duties. If one has negligently wronged another, Ross regards this past event as generating a duty to pay reparations even if doing so will result in nothing good. But from the narrative perspective, the past becomes relevant in a further way. One may say, for example, that the *whole* consisting of your life and your relationship with that person from the time of the injury into the future will be a better thing if you acknowledge the wrong and make efforts to restore what you have damaged. For Ross, the duty is

generated by the past and unrelated to bringing about anything good; from the narrative perspective, however, the requirement is just what is required to bring about a valuable connected whole with past, present, and future parts—the best way to complete a chapter, so to speak, in two intersecting lifestories.

So far, neither the Rossian nor the narrative account has told us much about the ultimate reasons for their evaluations, but they reveal ways to consider the matter. The Rossian asks us to judge particular cases in the light of "self-evident" general principles asserting that certain past events tend to generate present (or future) duties. The alternative perspective calls for examining lives and relationships, over time, in context, as organic unities evaluated (partly) in narrative terms.

To illustrate, consider two persons, John and Mary. John values having Mary's trust and respect, and conversely, Mary values having John's; moreover, John values the fact that Mary values being trusted and respected by him, and conversely Mary values the same about John.

Now suppose that other people have been abusive and insulting to Mary, and that John is worried that Mary may take things he had said and done as similarly insulting, even though he does not think that he consciously meant them this way. Though he is worried, Mary does not seem to suspect him; he fears that he may only make matters worse if he raises the issue, creating suspicions she did not have or focusing on doubts that he cannot allay. Perhaps, he thinks, their future relationship would be better served if he just remained silent, hoping that the trouble, if any, will fade in time. If so, consequentialist thinking would recommend silence. Acknowledging this, he might nonetheless feel that duties of friendship and fidelity demand that he raise the issue, regardless of whether or not the result will be worse. Then he would be thinking as a Rossian.

But, instead, he might look at the problem from an alternative perspective, asking himself what response best affirms and contributes to the sort of ongoing relationship he has and wants to continue with Mary. Given their history together, it is important to him to do his part towards restoring the relationship if it indeed has been marred by perceived insults or suspicions.

To be sure, he wants *future* relations of mutual trust and respect, but not at any price and not by just any means. Their history together is not irrelevant, for what he values is not merely a future of a certain kind, but that their relationship over time be of the sort he values. He values an ongoing history of mutual trust and respect that *calls for* an explicit response in this current situation, not merely as a means to a brighter future but as a present affirmation of what they value together. Even if unsure which course will be best for the future, he may be reasonably confident that the act that best expresses his respect and trust (and his valuing hers, etc.) is to confront the problem, express his regrets, reaffirm his respect, ask for her trust, be patient with her doubts, and welcome an open dialogue. If the insults were deep and it is not entirely clear whether or not he really associated himself with them, then mere words may not be enough to convey the message or even to assure himself of his own sincerity. Positive efforts, even at considerable cost, may be needed to express appropriately and convincingly what needs to be said. How the next chapter unfolds is not entirely up to him, and he would not be respectful if he presumed otherwise by trying to manipulate the best future unilaterally.

The example concerns only two persons and their personal values, but it illustrates a perspective that one can also take regarding moral problems involving many persons.

MUTUAL RESPECT, FAIR OPPORTUNITY, AND AFFIRMATIVE ACTION

Turning back to our main subject, I suggest that some of the values that give affirmative action its point are best seen as cross-time values that fall outside the exclusively forward-looking and backward-looking perspectives. They include having a history of racial and gender relations governed, so far as possible, by the ideals of mutual respect, trust, and fair opportunity for all.

Our national history provides a context of increasing recognition and broader interpretation of the democratic ideal of the equal dignity of all human beings—an ideal that has been flagrantly abused from the outset, partially affirmed in the bloody Civil War, and increasingly extended in the civil rights movement, but is still far from being fully respected. More specifically, blacks and women were systematically treated in an unfair and demeaning way by public institutions, including universities, until quite recently, and few could confidently claim to have rooted out racism and sexism even now.[8] The historical context is not what grounds or legitimates democratic values, but it is the background of the current problem, the sometimes admirable and often ugly way the chapters up until now have been written.

Consider the social ideal of mutual respect and trust among citizens. The problem of implementing this in the current context is different from the problem in the two-person example discussed above, for the history of our racial and gender relations is obviously not an idyllic story of mutual respect and trust momentarily interrupted by a crisis. Even so, the question to ask is not merely, "What will promote respectful and trusting racial and gender relations in future generations?", but rather, "Given our checkered past, how can we appropriately express the social value of mutual respect and trust that we want, so far as possible, to characterize our history?" We cannot change our racist and sexist past, but we also cannot express full respect for those present individuals who live in its aftermath if we ignore it. What is called for is not merely repayment of tangible debts incurred by past injuries, but also a message to counter the deep insult inherent in racism and sexism. . . .

CONCLUSION

The message is called for not just as a means to future good relations or a dutiful payment of a debt incurred by our past. It is called for by the ideal of being related to other human beings over time, so that our histories and biographies reflect the responses of those who deeply care about fair opportunity, mutual trust, and respect for all.

If so, what should public universities try to say to those offered opportunities through affirmative action? Perhaps something like this: "Whether we individually are among the guilty or not, we acknowledge that you have been wronged—if not by specific injuries which could be named and repaid, at least by the humiliating and debilitating attitudes prevalent in our country and our institutions. We deplore and denounce these attitudes and the wrongs that spring from them. We acknowledge that, so far, most of you have had your opportunities in life diminished by the effects of these attitudes, and we want no one's prospects to be diminished by injustice. We recognize your understandable grounds for suspicion and mistrust when we express these high-minded sentiments, and we want not only to ask respectfully for your trust but also to give concrete evidence of our sincerity. We welcome you respectfully into the university community and ask you to take a full share of the responsibilities as well as the benefits. By creating special opportunities, we recognize the disadvantages you have probably suffered; we show our respect for your talents and our commitment to the ideals of the university however, by not faking grades and honors for you. Given current attitudes about affirmative action, accepting this position will probably have drawbacks as well as advantages. It is an opportunity and a responsibility offered neither as charity nor as entitlement, but rather as part of a special effort to welcome and encourage minorities and women to participate more fully in the university at all levels. We believe that this program affirms some of the best ideals implicit in our history without violating the rights of any applicants. We hope that you will choose to accept the position in this spirit as well as for your own benefit."

The appropriate message is no doubt harder to communicate to those who stand to lose some traditional advantages under a legitimate affirmative action program. But if we set aside practical difficulties and suppose that the proper message could be sincerely given and accepted as such, what would it say? Ideally, it would convey an understanding of the moral reasoning for the program; perhaps,

in conclusion, it would say something like the following.

"These are the concerns that we felt made necessary the policy under which the university is temporarily giving special attention to women and minorities. We respect your rights to formal justice and to a policy guided by the university's education and research mission as well as its social responsibilities. Our policy in no way implies the view that your opportunities are less important than others', but we estimate (roughly, as we must) that as a white male you have probably had advantages and encouragement that for a long time have been systematically, unfairly, insultingly unavailable to most women and minorities. We deplore invidious race and gender distinctions; we hope that no misunderstanding of our program will prolong them. Unfortunately, nearly all blacks and women have been disadvantaged to some degree by bias against their groups, and it is impractical for universities to undertake the detailed investigations that would be needed to assess how much particular individuals have suffered or gained from racism and sexism. We appeal to you to share the historical values of fair opportunity and mutual respect that underlie this policy; we hope that, even though its effects may be personally disappointing, you can see the policy as an appropriate response to the current situation."

Unfortunately, as interests conflict and tempers rise, it is difficult to convey this idea without giving an unintended message as well. White males unhappy about the immediate effects of affirmative action may read the policy as saying that "justice" is the official word for giving preferential treatment to whatever group one happens to favor. Some may see a subtext insinuating that blacks and women are naturally inferior and "cannot make it on their own." Such cynical readings reveal either misunderstanding or the willful refusal to take the moral reasoning underlying affirmative action seriously. They pose serious obstacles to the success of affirmative action—practical problems that may be more intractable than respectful moral disagreement and counter-argument. But some types of affirmative action invite misunderstanding and suspicion more than others. For this reason, anyone who accepts the general case for affirmative action suggested here would do well to reexamine in detail the means by which they hope to communicate its message.[9]

NOTES

1. Thomas Sowell, *Race and Economics*. (New York: David McKay Co., 1975), ch. 6; *Markets and Minorities* (New York: Basic Books, Inc., 1981) pp. 114–15.

2. W. D. Ross, *The Right and the Good* (Oxford: Clarendon Press, 1930).

3. Aristotle, *Nicomachean Ethics,* tr. A. K. Thomson (Baltimore: Penguin Books, Inc., 1955), bk. V, esp. pp. 143–55.

4. See Boxill, *Blacks and Social Justice* (Totowa: Rowman & Allenheld, 1984), pp. 132ff., and Ronald Dworkin, "Reverse Discrimination," in *Taking Rights Seriously* (Cambridge: Harvard University Press, 1978), pp. 231ff.

5. See, for example, Alasdair MacIntyre, *After Virtue* (Notre Dame: Notre Dame University Press, 1981). Similar themes are found in Carol Gilligan's *In A Different Voice* (Cambridge: Harvard University Press, 1982) and in Lawrence Blum, *Friendship, Altruism, and Morality* (Boston: Routledge and Kegan Paul, 1980).

6. G. E. Moore, *Principia Ethica* (Cambridge University Press, 1912), pp. 27ff.

7. That is, the evaluation is independent of the past in the sense that the past makes no intrinsic difference to the final judgment and the future is not evaluated as a part of a temporal whole including the past. As noted, however, consequentialists will still look to the past for lessons and clues about how to bring about the best future.

8. Racism and sexism present significantly different problems, but I shall not try to analyze the differences here. For the most part my primary focus is on racism, but the relevance of the general type of moral thinking considered here to the problems of sexism should nonetheless be evident.

9. Although my aim in this essay has been to survey general types of arguments for thinking that some sort of affirmative action is needed, rather than to argue for any particular program, one cannot reasonably implement the general idea without considering many contextual factors that I have set aside here. Thus, the need for more detailed discussion is obvious.

READING QUESTIONS

1. Explain the backward- and forward-looking perspectives on affirmative action. What are some of the objections that Hill raises for each of these views? Consider in particular his problems with the messages they send.
2. Explain Hill's cross-temporal narrative value perspective. Focus on the four themes he lays out concerning the assumptions dominant in ethical theory. How does this view offer an advantage over the two views he rejects?
3. What sort of message does Hill believe ought to be sent by a successful affirmative action policy? What is one of the potential problems facing this message?

DISCUSSION QUESTIONS

1. To what extent should we be concerned with the message sent by policies and perspectives on affirmative action? How important should considerations such as motivations and results be in the affirmative action debate?
2. Suppose that Hill is correct about the importance of sending the right kind of message with an affirmative action policy. Reread his suggestion for an affirmative action statement that could be issued by a university and consider what messages it sends and whether those messages are in accord with the one he thinks is appropriate. What message should an affirmative action policy send?

ADDITIONAL RESOURCES

Web Resources

Civilrights.org, <http://www.civilrights.org/>. A civil rights advocacy organization involving the Leadership Conference on Civil Rights and the Leadership Conference on Civil Rights Education Fund.

Fullinwider, Robert, "Affirmative Action," <http://plato.stanford.edu/entries/affirmative-action/>. An overview of the legal and social controversy regarding affirmative action.

James, Michael, "Race," <http://plato.stanford.edu/entries/race/>. Includes discussion of the history of the concept of race, race as a social construction, and moral, legal, and social dimensions of the concept.

Haslanger, Sally and Tuana, Nancy, "Topics in Feminism," <http://plato.stanford.edu/entries/feminism-topics/>. An overview of feminist understandings of sexism and how properly to address it. This article also includes an extensive list of Internet resources on feminism and related topics.

National Organization of Women, <http://www.now.org/>. An organization of feminists whose chief goal is to bring about equality for all women.

Race, Gender and Affirmative Action, <http://www-personal.umich.edu./~eandersn/biblio.htm.>. A very useful annotated bibliography for teachers and students on the topics featured in this chapter.

Race Project, <http://www.understandingrace.org/home.html>. A project of the American Anthropological Association providing information about the nature of race.

Racism Review, <http://www.racismreview.com/>. A site aimed primarily at educators and researchers. It describes itself as "intended to provide a credible and reliable source of information for journalists, students and members of the general public who are seeking solid evidence-based research and analysis of race, racism, ethnicity, and immigration issues."

Southern Poverty Law Center, <http://www.splcenter.org/>. This center, founded in 1971, engages in legal and educational activities to combat intolerance and hate crimes.

Authored Books and Articles

Blum, Lawrence, *I'm not a racist, but...* (Ithaca and London: Cornell University Press, 2002). A critical examination of the concepts of race and racism as they have affected our ways of looking at things, including our moral interactions with others.

Corlett, J. Angelo, *Race, Racism, and Reparations* (Ithaca and London: Cornell University Press, 2003). A careful analysis of race, ethnic identity, and related matters of public policy.

Glasgow, Joshua, "Racism as Disrespect," *Ethics* 120 (2009): 64–93. A defense of the claim that racism should be understood in terms of disrespect.

Lippert-Rasmussen, Kaspar, *Ethical Theory and Moral Practice* 9 (2006): 167–85. Argues that the badness of discrimination is explained by its harmfulness. Critical of accounts that would explain the badness by appeal to disrespect-based views, according to which the badness is owing to the disrespect that discrimination expresses regardless of its harmful effects.

Shelby, Tommy, "Is Racism in the Heart?" *Journal of Social Philosophy* 33 (2002): 411–20. Traces racism to racist social ideology. (Glasgow's article is critical of this and similar "ideological" approaches.)

Edited Collections

Anderson, Jami, L. (ed.), *Race, Gender, and Sexuality* (Upper Saddle Creek, N.J.: Prentice Hall, 2003). An extensive collection of essays organized into chapters on Sex and Gender, Sex and Sexuality, Race and Ethnicity, Racism, Sexism, Heterosexism and Homophobia, Equality and Preferential Treatment, Discriminatory Harassment, Identity Speech and Political Speech, Sexual Speech, and Sexual Assault.

Crosby, Faye, J., and Cheyrl Van DeVeer, *Sex, Race, and Merit: Debating Affirmative Action in Education and Employment* (Ann Arbor: University of Michigan Press, 2000). A wide ranging collection of articles from newspapers, essays by scholars from various academic fields, and important legal and political documents that have shaped debate and policy over affirmative action.

Zack, Naomi (ed.), *Race/Sex: Their Sameness, Difference, and Interplay* (London and New York: Routledge, 1997). A collection of 16 essays by different authors exploring the analysis, comparison, phenomenology, and issues of performance regarding sex and race.

7 } Euthanasia and Physician-Assisted Suicide

The sad case of Terri Schiavo was intermittently in the news for a number of years. Schiavo suffered severe brain damage in 1990 owing to cardiac arrest. She was diagnosed by many physicians as being in a "persistent vegetative state," in which the individual is arguably not consciously experiencing anything, but unlike being in a coma, the individual undergoes periods of wakefulness. Most recently Schiavo's case was the subject of an intense public debate after her feeding tube was removed on March 18, 2005, at the request of her husband and after many legal battles with the parents of Schiavo. On March 21, Congress passed special legislation that would allow the parents of Schiavo to seek a review of their case in federal court to have a feeding tube reinserted, legislation that was signed that same day by President George W. Bush. Various federal courts turned down the appeal from Schiavo's parents to have the case reviewed further. Terri Schiavo died from dehydration on March 31, 2005.

As we shall see shortly, the decision to remove Schiavo's feeding tube, thus allowing her to die of dehydration, is a case of passive euthanasia. A number of legal and constitutional issues were raised by the Schiavo case, but no doubt what stirred such intense public interest in this case are the moral issues concerning euthanasia and suicide. Some of the most basic questions are these:

- Is euthanasia or suicide ever morally permissible?
- In those cases in which either of these activities is wrong, what best explains their wrongness?

Here, as with the issue of abortion, we (unfortunately) find parties to the debate being labeled as pro-life or pro-choice, which, of course, frames the issue as though one must (or should) respond to the first question with a simple yes or a simple no. But, as with most all controversial moral issues, there is a range of possible views, including moderate views which, in the case of euthanasia (and suicide), would reject simple answers and insist that details of specific cases do matter morally. In order to make progress in our understanding of the moral disputes over euthanasia and suicide, let us first explain what practices and types of action are the subject of these disputes, and then we will be prepared to understand how various ethical theories approach the moral questions just mentioned.

1. EUTHANASIA

Euthanasia is typically defined as the act or practice of killing or allowing someone to die on grounds of mercy. Because this definition covers a number of importantly different types of activity that may differ in their moral status, let us begin by calling attention to these types. There are two dimensions, so to speak, to be considered. First there is what we may call the "mode of death" dimension, which has to do with whether the death results from actively intervening to bring about the death of the patient or whether the death results from (or is hastened by) withholding some form of treatment which, had it been administered, would likely have prolonged the life of the patient. The former type of case is one of **active euthanasia,** whereas the latter type is often called **passive euthanasia.**

The other dimension has to do with matters concerning the consent or nonconsent of the patient. And here we need to distinguish three importantly different cases. Cases of **voluntary euthanasia** are those in which the patient has consented to the active bringing about of her death or to some means of passively allowing her to die. There are various ways in which a patient might consent, including the making of a living will in which the person specifies how he is to be treated under conditions in which his consent in that situation is not possible. Cases of **nonvoluntary euthanasia** are those in which the patient has not given his consent to be subject to euthanasia because the patient has not expressed a view about what others may do in case, for example, he goes into a persistent vegetative state. Cases of **involuntary euthanasia** are those in which the patient expresses (or may be presumed to have) a desire not to be the subject of euthanasia.

Although these distinctions are commonly made in the literature on euthanasia, the active/passive distinction, as I've explained it, seems to leave out, or at least does not clearly include, cases like that of Terri Schiavo in which treatment (the feeding tube) is withdrawn. On the one hand, withdrawing treatment is doing something active, but on the other hand, in withdrawing treatment one is allowing nature to take its course, and so rather than actively bringing about the death, one is passively allowing it to come about. Because space does not allow us to pursue this matter in any detail, I propose that because there does seem to be an important moral difference between clear cases of actively bringing about the death of a patient (e.g., by way of lethal injection) on the one hand, and cases of withholding and withdrawing treatment on the other, we ought to classify cases of withdrawing treatment as a type of passive euthanasia, making sure that within that category we recognize the two cases in question.

If we now combine the various modes of death with the various modes bearing on consent, we have nine distinct types of euthanasia. On the next page, is a visual aid that charts the types of cases just explained (Fig. 7.1). (As an exercise, the reader is encouraged to fill in the cells with examples.)

In light of this taxonomy, we can now formulate moral questions about euthanasia more precisely by asking, for each type of euthanasia (e.g., nonvoluntary passive withholding), whether it is ever morally permissible and if so under what conditions. Clearly, whether or not someone has given their consent to be a subject of euthanasia has an important bearing on the morality of euthanasia. The same may be true as to the mode of death—whether it is active or passive euthanasia.

Mode of Death

		Active	Passive	
			Withdrawing	Withholding
	Voluntary			
Mode of Consent	Nonvoluntary			
	Involuntary			

FIGURE 7.1   Types of Euthanasia

2. SUICIDE

Whereas euthanasia, by definition, involves the termination of someone's life by some-one else, **suicide** involves intentionally and thus voluntarily ending one's own life. This definition, then, rules out the possibility of there being nonvoluntary or involuntary cases of suicide. But this definition does not rule out the possibility of passive suicide—suicide in which one either withdraws some means of life support or refrains from intervening to save oneself from death. However, most discussion of the morality of suicide is focused on cases of active suicide.

Assisted suicides are those cases in which another person is involved to some degree in assisting an individual to commit suicide. Much recent discussion on this topic has focused on the role of physicians in helping a patient to commit suicide.[1] Often, the distinction between voluntary active euthanasia and assisted suicide is ignored or perhaps considered irrelevant for purposes of moral discussion. However, as we shall see in the reading from David T. Watts and Timothy Howell, there are some who think that these practices are impor-tantly different and that the moral and legal status of the one is different (or should differ) from the other.

Having clarified the concepts of euthanasia and suicide, let us now briefly consider some of the moral controversy about these issues.

3. THEORY MEETS PRACTICE

Together, the readings included in this chapter represent four theoretical approaches to the topics of euthanasia and suicide: Kantian moral theory, consequentialism, natural law theory, and the ethics of prima facie duty. Let us consider them in order.

Kantian Moral Theory

Kant argued that suicide is morally wrong because it violates the dignity of the human being who commits it. The problem with his argument is that he assumes that suicide in all (or most) cases represents a violation of human dignity, but this assumption needs defense—more than Kant provides. If my life is close to an end and I am in excruciating pain about which physicians can do nothing, is it a violation of my dignity if I end my life rather than pointlessly live on for a month or two? Perhaps so, but the case needs to be argued. The same general point holds in any attempt to apply Kant's Humanity formulation of the categorical imperative to cases of euthanasia: whether any such case fails to treat the patient as an end in herself requires supporting argument.

Consequentialism

Many discussions of euthanasia and suicide focus exclusively on the likely consequences of these practices, thus appealing, at least implicitly, to consequentialist moral theory. And here, as with many other issues featured in this book, worries about slippery slopes are raised. A slippery slope argument may take various forms, but behind all such arguments is the idea that if we allow some action or practice *P*, then we will open the door to other similar actions and practices that will eventually lead us down a slope to disastrous results. So, the argument concludes, *P* should not be permitted. Any such argument, in order to be good, must meet two requirements. First, it must be true that the envisioned results really are bad. But second, the central idea of the argument—that allowing one action or practice will likely lead us down a path to disaster—must be plausible. If either of these conditions is not met, the argument is said to commit the "slippery slope *fallacy.*"

Used in connection with euthanasia and assisted suicide (see the article by Richard Doerflinger in this chapter), one common slippery slope worry is that if we allow voluntary euthanasia, we will put ourselves on the road to permitting (or encouraging) *in*voluntary euthanasia—cases of murder. This particular slippery slope argument apparently meets the first condition of any good slippery slope argument, but does it meet the second? And if so, will the same worries apply to assisted suicide? These are difficult questions because to answer them, we must rely on predictions about the likely effects (within a culture over a particular span of time) of engaging in, say, voluntary euthanasia. And for predictions to be reliable (and not just a prejudice based on one's antecedent views about the morality of these practices), we need solid empirical evidence—evidence that we probably lack at this time. Many opponents of euthanasia will, at this point, appeal to what we may call the "moral safety" argument, according to which when we are in doubt about such matters, it is better to play it safe and not start out on a road that *may* lead to disaster. As with any consequentialist approach to moral issues, the crucial factor in determining the rightness or wrongness of some action or practice depends on how much net intrinsic value the action or practice will likely bring about compared to alternative actions and practices. Consequentialist defenders of euthanasia (and/or assisted suicide) will stress the great benefits of such practices in relation to relieving great human suffering. And, of course, consequentialists might be opposed to some forms of euthanasia but in favor of some forms of assisted suicide. This is roughly the view defended in the article by Watts and Howell.

Natural Law Theory

Part of the natural law approach to matters of life and death rests on the distinction between intentionally bringing about the death of someone and unintentionally but foreseeably doing so. (This distinction is central in the doctrine of double effect explained in chapter 1, section 2B.) Intentionally taking innocent human life is always wrong, according to the natural law theory, though if certain conditions are met, one may be justified in foreseeably bringing about the death of an innocent person unintentionally, where roughly this means that the person's death is not one's aim in action nor is it a means to achieving some end. Thus, according to natural law thinking, any form of euthanasia that involves intentionally bringing about the death of a patient, even for reasons of mercy, is morally forbidden. In developing this aspect of natural law theory, its defenders make use of the distinction between "ordinary" and "extraordinary" means of preserving life, which itself is a subject of some controversy. (For more on this, see the articles in this chapter by James Rachels and especially Bonnie Steinbock.) Related to the natural law approach to ethics is the idea that certain modes of action are wrong because they go against human nature and thus are "unnatural." The selection by J. Gay-Williams appeals to this idea in arguing against euthanasia.

Ethics of Prima Facie Duty

Finally, one might approach the moral issues of euthanasia and suicide from the perspective of an ethic of prima facie duties. Both W. D. Ross and Robert Audi, defenders of this sort of moral theory, hold that we have a prima facie duty to avoid harming ourselves and others, and they both recognize a prima facie duty of self-improvement, which, as formulated by Audi, involves the prima facie duty to sustain, as well as develop, our distinctively human capacities.[2] If euthanasia and suicide count as harms, then one has a prima facie obligation to not engage in such actions. Additionally, since being alive is a necessary condition for sustaining our distinctively human capacities, one may conclude we have a prima facie duty of self-improvement to not participate in euthanasia or commit suicide. From these two basic prima facie duties we may derive a further prima facie duty—the prima facie duty to not engage in euthanasia or in suicide.

But as we learned in the moral theory primer, the very idea of prima facie duty allows that in a particular case it can be overridden by some other, more stringent prima facie duty that also applies to the case. So the fundamental moral question for this theoretical approach to these topics is whether there are cases in which the prima facie duty prohibiting euthanasia and suicide is overridden. If we recognize that we have a prima facie duty to relieve horrible suffering in the world, then we have a basis for arguing that there may be morally permissible cases of euthanasia and suicide. One might do so by arguing that the only way of relieving the horrible suffering of certain patients—perhaps patients who are terminally ill—is to bring about their death mercifully. If one adds that we also have a prima facie duty to respect the autonomy of patients, we can build a case for the claim that some cases of voluntary euthanasia are morally permissible because the duty of relieving suffering outweighs the prima facie duty prohibiting euthanasia and suicide. Dan W. Brock, in one of our readings, defends voluntary active euthanasia by stressing the importance of autonomy and well-being in our moral thinking.

NOTES

1. In 1997, the state of Oregon enacted the only U.S. physician-assisted suicide law, the Death with Dignity Act. In 2001, U.S. attorney general John D. Ashcroft issued a directive that stated that the use of federally controlled substances to assist suicides violates the Controlled Substances Act. One aim of Ashcroft's directive was to allow federal criminal prosecution of physicians in Oregon who assisted in suicides. After legal battles between Ashcroft and lower courts, the case made it all the way to the U.S. Supreme Court. In 2006, in the case *Gonzales v. State of Oregon* (No. 04-623), the Court upheld Oregon's law allowing physician-assisted suicide. As of 2009, Montana and Washington have joined Oregon in legalizing assisted suicide. All three states impose certain restrictions on allowable assisted suicide, among them that the patient must be terminally ill and mentally competent and must make a voluntary request to die.

2. See Robert Audi, *The Good in the Right* (Princeton, NJ: Princeton University Press, 2004), 193–94.

J. GAY-WILLIAMS

The Wrongfulness of Euthanasia

After defining "euthanasia" as the "intentional taking the life of a presumably hopeless person," Gay-Williams proceeds to argue that not only is euthanasia inherently wrong, but also it is wrong when judged from the perspective of self-interest and judged in terms of its potentially negative effects on the quality of medical treatment.

Recommended Reading: natural law theory, chap. 1., sec. 2B, and consequentialism, chap. 1, sec. 2A.

My impression is that euthanasia—the idea, if not the practice—is slowly gaining acceptance within our society. Cynics might attribute this to an increasing tendency to devalue human life, but I do not believe this is the major factor. The acceptance is much more likely to be the result of unthinking sympathy and benevolence. Well-publicized, tragic stories like that of Karen Quinlan elicit from us deep feelings of compassion. We think to ourselves, "She and her family would be better off if she were dead." It is an easy step from this very human response to the view that if someone (and others) would be better off dead, then it might be all right to kill that person. Although I respect the compassion that leads to this conclusion, I believe the conclusion is wrong. I want to show that euthanasia

From J. Gay-Williams, "The Wrongfulness of Euthanasia," in Ronald Munson, ed., *Intervention and Reflection: Basic Issues in Medical Ethics*, 5th ed. © Wadsworth, 1996.

is wrong. It is inherently wrong, but it is also wrong judged from the standpoints of self-interest and of practical effects.

Before presenting my arguments to support this claim, it would be well to define "euthanasia." An essential aspect of euthanasia is that it involves taking a human life, either one's own or that of another. Also, the person whose life is taken must be someone who is believed to be suffering from some disease or injury from which recovery cannot reasonably be expected. Finally, the action must be deliberate and intentional. Thus, euthanasia is intentionally taking the life of a presumably hopeless person. Whether the life is one's own or that of another, the taking of it is still euthanasia.

It is important to be clear about the deliberate and intentional aspect of the killing. If a hopeless person is given an injection of the wrong drug by mistake and this causes his death, this is wrongful killing but not euthanasia. The killing cannot be the result of accident. Furthermore, if the person is given an injection of a drug that is believed to be necessary to treat his disease or better his condition and the person dies as a result, then this is neither wrongful killing nor euthanasia. The intention was to make the patient well, not kill him. Similarly, when a patient's condition is such that it is not reasonable to hope that any medical procedures or treatments will save his life, a failure to implement the procedures or treatments is not euthanasia. If the person dies, this will be as a result of his injuries or disease and not because of his failure to receive treatment.

The failure to continue treatment after it has been realized that the patient has little chance of benefiting from it has been characterized by some as "passive euthanasia." This phrase is misleading and mistaken. In such cases, the person involved is not killed (the first essential aspect of euthanasia), nor is the death of the person intended by the withholding of additional treatment (the third essential aspect of euthanasia). The aim may be to spare the person additional and unjustifiable pain, to save him from the indignities of hopeless manipulations, and to avoid increasing the financial and emotional burden on his family. When I buy a pencil it is so that I can use it to write, not to contribute to an increase in the gross national product. This may be the unintended consequence of my action, but it is not the aim of my action. So it is with failing to continue the treatment of a dying person. I intend his death no more than I intend to reduce the GNP by not using medical supplies. His is an unintended dying, and so-called "passive euthanasia" is not euthanasia at all.

1. THE ARGUMENT FROM NATURE

Every human being has a natural inclination to continue living. Our reflexes and responses fit us to fight attackers, flee wild animals, and dodge out of the way of trucks. In our daily lives we exercise the caution and care necessary to protect ourselves. Our bodies are similarly structured for survival right down to the molecular level. When we are cut, our capillaries seal shut, our blood clots, and fibrogen is produced to start the process of healing the wound. When we are invaded by bacteria, antibodies are produced to fight against the alien organisms, and their remains are swept out of the body by special cells designed for clean-up work.

Euthanasia does violence to this natural goal of survival. It is literally acting against nature because all the processes of nature are bent towards the end of bodily survival. Euthanasia defeats these subtle mechanisms in a way that, in a particular case, disease and injury might not.

It is possible, but not necessary, to make an appeal to revealed religion in this connection. Man as trustee of his body acts against God, its rightful possessor, when he takes his own life. He also violates the commandment to hold life sacred and never to take it without just and compelling cause. But since this appeal will persuade only those who are prepared to accept that religion has access to revealed truths, I shall not employ this line of argument.

It is enough, I believe, to recognize that the organization of the human body and our patterns of behavioral responses make the continuation of life a natural goal. By reason alone, then, we can recognize that euthanasia sets us against our own nature. Furthermore, in doing so, euthanasia does violence to our dignity. Our dignity comes from seeking our ends. When one of our goals is survival, and actions are taken that eliminate that goal, then our natural dignity suffers. Unlike animals, we are conscious through reason of our nature and our ends. Euthanasia involves acting as if this dual nature— inclination towards survival and awareness of this as an end—did not exist. Thus, euthanasia denies our basic human character and requires that we regard ourselves or others as something less than fully human.

2. THE ARGUMENT FROM SELF-INTEREST

The above arguments are, I believe, sufficient to show that euthanasia is inherently wrong. But there are reasons for considering it wrong when judged by standards other than reason. Because death is final and irreversible, euthanasia contains within it the possibility that we will work against our own interest if we practice it or allow it to be practiced on us.

Contemporary medicine has high standards of excellence and a proven record of accomplishment, but it does not possess perfect and complete knowledge. A mistaken diagnosis is possible, and so is a mistaken prognosis. Consequently, we may believe that we are dying of a disease when, as a matter of fact, we may not be. We may think that we have no hope of recovery when, as a matter of fact, our chances are quite good. In such circumstances, if euthanasia were permitted, we would die needlessly. Death is final and the chance of error too great to approve the practice of euthanasia.

Also, there is always the possibility that an experimental procedure or a hitherto untried technique will pull us through. We should at least keep this option open, but euthanasia closes it off. Furthermore, spontaneous remission does occur in many cases. For no apparent reason, a patient simply recovers when those all around him, including his physicians, expected him to die. Euthanasia would just guarantee their expectations and leave no room for the "miraculous" recoveries that frequently occur.

Finally, knowing that we can take our life at any time (or ask another to take it) might well incline us to give up too easily. The will to live is strong in all of us, but it can be weakened by pain and suffering and feelings of hopelessness. If during a bad time we allow ourselves to be killed, we never have a chance to reconsider. Recovery from a serious illness requires that we fight for it, and anything that weakens our determination by suggesting that there is an easy way out is ultimately against our own interest. Also, we may be inclined towards euthanasia because of our concern for others. If we see our sickness and suffering as an emotional and financial burden on our family, we may feel that to leave our life is to make their lives easier. The very presence of the possibility of euthanasia may keep us from surviving when we might.

3. THE ARGUMENT FROM PRACTICAL EFFECTS

Doctors and nurses are, for the most part, totally committed to saving lives. A life lost is, for them, almost a personal failure, an insult to their skills and knowledge. Euthanasia as a practice might well alter this. It could have a corrupting influence so that in any case that is severe doctors and nurses might not try hard enough to save the patient. They might decide that the patient would simply be "better off dead" and take the steps necessary to make that come about. This attitude could then carry over to their dealings with patients less seriously ill. The result would be an overall decline in the quality of medical care.

Finally, euthanasia as a policy is a slippery slope. A person apparently hopelessly ill may be allowed to take his own life. Then he may be permitted to deputize others to do it for him should he no longer be able to act. The judgment of others then becomes the ruling factor. Already at this point euthanasia is not personal and voluntary, for others are acting "on behalf of" the patient as they see fit. This may well incline them to act on behalf of other patients who have not authorized them to exercise their judgment. It is only a short step, then, from voluntary euthanasia (self-inflicted or authorized), to directed euthanasia administered to a patient who has given no authorization, to involuntary euthanasia conducted as part of a social policy. Recently many psychiatrists and sociologists have argued that we define as "mental illness" those forms of behavior that we disapprove of. This gives us license then to lock up those who display the behavior. The category of the "hopelessly ill" provides the possibility of even worse abuse. Embedded in a social policy, it would give society or its representatives the authority to eliminate all those who might be considered too "ill" to function normally any longer. The dangers of euthanasia are too great to all to run the risk of approving it in any form. The first slippery step may well lead to a serious and harmful fall.

I hope that I have succeeded in showing why the benevolence that inclines us to give approval of euthanasia is misplaced. Euthanasia is inherently wrong because it violates the nature and dignity of human beings. But even those who are not convinced by this must be persuaded that the potential personal and social dangers inherent in euthanasia are sufficient to forbid our approving it either as a personal practice or as a public policy.

Suffering is surely a terrible thing, and we have a clear duty to comfort those in need and to ease their suffering when we can. But suffering is also a natural part of life with values for the individual and for others that we should not overlook. We may legitimately seek for others and for ourselves an easeful death . . . Euthanasia, however, is not just an easeful death. It is a wrongful death. Euthanasia is not just dying. It is killing.

READING QUESTIONS

1. What are the three essential aspects of euthanasia according to Gay-Williams?
2. Why does Gay-Williams think the term "passive euthanasia" is misleading?
3. Explain the argument from nature against the practice of euthanasia. How does Gay-Williams appeal to religion in order to reinforce this argument?
4. Describe the ways in which the practice of euthanasia might work against our own self-interest.
5. Explain the reasons Gay-Williams offers for why euthanasia could result in an overall decline in the quality of medical care.

DISCUSSION QUESTIONS

1. Is Gay-Williams right to claim that the death of a patient that results from "a failure to implement . . . procedures or treatments" is unintentional?
2. Should we agree with Gay-Williams that the chance of error in medical practice is "too great" to approve the practice of euthanasia? Would the practice of euthanasia keep people from surviving when they might as he suggests?
3. How worried should we be about the slippery slope of euthanasia?

JAMES RACHELS

Active and Passive Euthanasia

James Rachels is critical of the 1973 American Medical Association (AMA) policy regarding euthanasia, which he understands as forbidding all mercy killing but permitting some cases of allowing a patient to die. Rachels argues that this policy would force physicians to sometimes engage in the inhumane treatment of patients and that it would allow life-and-death decisions to be made on morally irrelevant grounds. He then proceeds to argue that the policy is based on the false assumption that killing is intrinsically morally worse than letting someone die.

Recommended Reading: natural law theory, esp. doctrine of double effect, chap. 1, sec. 2B. Rachels does not mention this doctrine, but it is relevant for thinking about the AMA's policy that he criticizes.

The distinction between active and passive euthanasia is thought to be crucial for medical ethics. The idea is that it is permissible, at least in some cases, to withhold treatment and allow a patient to die, but it is never permissible to take any direct action designed to kill the patient. This doctrine seems to be accepted by most doctors, and it is endorsed in a statement adopted by the House of Delegates of the American Medical Association on December 4, 1973:

> The intentional termination of the life of one human being by another—mercy killing—is contrary to that for which the medical profession stands and is contrary to the policy of the American Medical Association.
>
> The cessation of the employment of extraordinary means to prolong the life of the body when there is irrefutable evidence that biological death is imminent is the decision of the patient and/or his immediate family. The advice and judgment of the physician should be freely available to the patient and/or his immediate family.

However, a strong case can be made against this doctrine. In what follows, I will set out some of the relevant arguments, and urge doctors to reconsider their views on this matter.

To begin with a familiar type of situation, a patient who is dying of incurable cancer of the throat is in terrible pain, which can no longer be satisfactorily alleviated. He is certain to die within a few days, even if present treatment is continued, but he does not want to go on living for those days since the pain is unbearable. So he asks the doctor for an end to it, and his family joins in the request.

Suppose the doctor agrees to withhold treatment, as the conventional doctrine says he may. The justification for his doing so is that the patient is in terrible agony, and since he is going to die anyway, it would be wrong to prolong his suffering needlessly. But now notice this. If one simply withholds treatment, it may take the patient longer to die, and so he may suffer more than he would if more direct action were taken and a lethal injection given. This fact provides strong reason for thinking that, once the initial decision not to prolong his agony has been made, active euthanasia is actually preferable to passive euthanasia, rather than the reverse. To say otherwise is to endorse the option that leads to more suffering rather than less, and is contrary to the humanitarian impulse

From James Rachels, "Active and Passive Euthanasia," *New England Journal of Medicine* 292 (1975): 78–80.

that prompts the decision not to prolong his life in the first place.

Part of my point is that the process of being "allowed to die" can be relatively slow and painful, whereas being given a lethal injection is relatively quick and painless. Let me give a different sort of example. In the United States about one in 600 babies is born with Down's syndrome. Most of these babies are otherwise healthy—that is, with only the usual pediatric care, they will proceed to an otherwise normal infancy. Some, however, are born with congenital defects such as intestinal obstructions that require operations if they are to live. Sometimes, the parents and the doctor will decide not to operate, and let the infant die. Anthony Shaw describes what happens then:

> . . . When surgery is denied [the doctor] must try to keep the infant from suffering while natural forces sap the baby's life away. As a surgeon whose natural inclination is to use the scalpel to fight off death, standing by and watching a salvageable baby die is the most emotionally exhausting experience I know. It is easy at a conference, in a theoretical discussion, to decide that such infants should be allowed to die. It is altogether different to stand by in the nursery and watch as dehydration and infection wither a tiny being over hours and days. This is a terrible ordeal for me and the hospital staff—much more so than for the parents who never set foot in the nursery.[1]

I can understand why some people are opposed to all euthanasia, and insist that such infants must be allowed to live. I think I can also understand why other people favor destroying these babies quickly and painlessly. But why should anyone favor letting "dehydration and infection wither a tiny being over hours and days"? The doctrine that says that a baby may be allowed to dehydrate and wither, but may not be given an injection that would end its life without suffering, seems so patently cruel as to require no further refutation. The strong language is not intended to offend, but only to put the point in the clearest possible way.

My second argument is that the conventional doctrine leads to decisions concerning life and death made on irrelevant grounds.

Consider again the case of the infants with Down's syndrome who need operations for congenital defects unrelated to the syndrome to live. Sometimes, there is no operation, and the baby dies, but when there is no such defect, the baby lives on. Now, an operation such as that to remove an intestinal obstruction is not prohibitively difficult. The reason why such operations are not performed in these cases is, clearly, that the child has Down's syndrome and the parents and doctor judge that because of that fact it is better for the child to die.

But notice that this situation is absurd, no matter what view one takes of the lives and potentials of such babies. If the life of such an infant is worth preserving, what does it matter if it needs a simple operation? Or, if one thinks it better that such a baby should not live on, what difference does it make that it happens to have an unobstructed intestinal tract? In either case, the matter of life and death is being decided on irrelevant grounds. It is the Down's syndrome, and not the intestines, that is the issue. The matter should be decided, if at all, on that basis, and not be allowed to depend on the essentially irrelevant question of whether the intestinal tract is blocked.

What makes this situation possible, of course, is the idea that when there is an intestinal blockage, one can "let the baby die," but when there is no such defect there is nothing that can be done, for one must not "kill" it. The fact that this idea leads to such results as deciding life or death on irrelevant grounds is another good reason why the doctrine should be rejected.

One reason why so many people think that there is an important moral difference between active and passive euthanasia is that they think killing someone is morally worse than letting someone die. But is it? Is killing, in itself, worse than letting die? To investigate this issue, two cases may be considered that are exactly alike except that one involves killing whereas the other involves letting someone die. Then, it can be asked whether this difference makes any difference to the moral assessments. It is important that the cases be exactly alike, except for this one difference, since otherwise one cannot be confident that it is this difference and not some other that accounts for any variation in the assessments of the two cases. So, let us consider this pair of cases:

In the first, Smith stands to gain a large inheritance if anything should happen to his six-year-old cousin. One evening while the child is taking his bath, Smith sneaks into the bathroom and drowns the child, and then arranges things so that it will look like an accident.

In the second, Jones also stands to gain if anything should happen to his six-year-old cousin. Like Smith, Jones sneaks in planning to drown the child in his bath. However, just as he enters the bathroom Jones sees the child slip and hit his head, and fall face down in the water. Jones is delighted; he stands by, ready to push the child's head back under if it is necessary, but it is not necessary. With only a little thrashing about the child drowns all by himself, "accidentally," as Jones watches and does nothing.

Now Smith killed the child, whereas Jones "merely" let the child die. That is the only difference between them. Did either man behave better, from a moral point of view? If the difference between killing and letting die were in itself a morally important matter, one should say that Jones's behavior was less reprehensible than Smith's. But does one really want to say that? I think not. In the first place, both men acted from the same motive, personal gain, and both had exactly the same end in view when they acted. It may be inferred from Smith's conduct that he is a bad man, although that judgment may be withdrawn or modified if certain further facts are learned about him—for example, that he is mentally deranged. But would not the very same thing be inferred about Jones from his conduct? And would not the same further considerations also be relevant to any modification of this judgment? Moreover, suppose Jones pleaded, in his own defense, "After all, I didn't do anything except just stand there and watch the child drown. I didn't kill him; I only let him die." Again, if letting die were in itself less bad than killing, this defense should have at least some weight. But it does not. Such a "defense" can only be regarded as a grotesque perversion of moral reasoning. Morally speaking, it is no defense at all.

Now, it may be pointed out, quite properly, that the cases of euthanasia with which doctors are concerned are not like this at all. They do not involve personal gain or the destruction of normally healthy children. Doctors are concerned only with cases in which the patient's life is of no further use to him, or

in which the patient's life has become or will soon become a terrible burden. However, the point is the same in these cases: the bare difference between killing and letting die does not, in itself, make a moral difference. If a doctor lets a patient die, for humane reasons, he is in the same moral position as if he had given the patient a lethal injection for humane reasons. If his decision was wrong—if, for example, the patient's illness was in fact curable—the decision would be equally regrettable no matter which method was used to carry it out. And if the doctor's decision was the right one, the method used is not in itself important.

The AMA policy statement isolates the crucial issue very well; the crucial issue is "the intentional termination of the life of one human being by another." But after identifying this issue, and forbidding "mercy killing," the statement goes on to deny that the cessation of treatment is the intentional termination of a life. This is where the mistake comes in, for what is the cessation of treatment, in these circumstances, if it is not "the intentional termination of the life of one human being by another?" Of course, it is exactly that, and if it were not, there would be no point to it.

Many people will find this judgment hard to accept. One reason, I think, is that it is very easy to conflate the question of whether killing is, in itself, worse than letting die, with the very different question of whether most actual cases of killing are more reprehensible than most actual cases of letting die. Most actual cases of killing are clearly terrible (think, for example, of all the murders reported in the newspapers), and one hears of such cases every day. On the other hand, one hardly ever hears of a case of letting die, except for the actions of doctors who are motivated by humanitarian reasons. So one learns to think of killing in a much worse light than of letting die. But this does not mean that there is something about killing that makes it in itself worse than letting die, for it is not the bare difference between killing and letting die that makes the difference in these cases. Rather, the other factors—the murderer's motive of personal gain, for example, contrasted with the doctor's humanitarian motivation—account for different reactions to the different cases.

I have argued that killing is not in itself any worse than letting die; if my contention is right, it follows that active euthanasia is not any worse than passive euthanasia. What arguments can be given on the other side? The most common, I believe, is the following:

"The important difference between active and passive euthanasia is that, in passive euthanasia, the doctor does not do anything to bring about the patient's death. The doctor does nothing, and the patient dies of whatever ills already afflict him. In active euthanasia, however, the doctor does something to bring about the patient's death: he kills him. The doctor who gives the patient with cancer a lethal injection has himself caused his patient's death; whereas if he merely ceases treatment, the cancer is the cause of the death."

A number of points need to be made here. The first is that it is not exactly correct to say that in passive euthanasia the doctor does nothing, for he does do one thing that is very important: he lets the patient die. "Letting someone die" is certainly different, in some respects, from other types of action—mainly in that it is a kind of action that one may perform by way of not performing certain other actions. For example, one may let a patient die by way of not giving medication, just as one may insult someone by way of not shaking his hand. But for any purpose of moral assessment, it is a type of action nonetheless. The decision to let a patient die is subject to moral appraisal in the same way that a decision to kill him would be subject to moral appraisal: it may be assessed as wise or unwise, compassionate or sadistic, right or wrong. If a doctor deliberately let a patient die who was suffering from a routinely curable illness, the doctor would certainly be to blame for what he had done, just as he would be to blame if he had needlessly killed the patient. Charges against him would then be appropriate. If so, it would be no defense at all for him to insist that he didn't "do anything." He would have done something very serious indeed, for he let his patient die.

Fixing the cause of death may be very important from a legal point of view, for it may determine whether criminal charges are brought against the doctor. But I do not think that this notion can be used to show a moral difference between active and passive euthanasia. The reason why it is considered bad to be the cause of someone's death is that death is regarded as a great evil—and so it is. However, if it has been decided that euthanasia—even passive euthanasia—is desirable in a given case, it has also been decided that in this instance death is no greater an evil than the patient's continued existence. And if this is true, the usual reason for not wanting to be the cause of someone's death simply does not apply.

Finally, doctors may think that all of this is only of academic interest—the sort of thing that philosophers may worry about but that has no practical bearing on their own work. After all, doctors must be concerned about the legal consequences of what they do, and active euthanasia is clearly forbidden by the law. But even so, doctors should also be concerned with the fact that the law is forcing upon them a moral doctrine that may well be indefensible, and has a considerable effect on their practices. Of course, most doctors are not now in the position of being coerced in this matter, for they do not regard themselves as merely going along with what the law requires. Rather, in statements such as the AMA policy statement that I have quoted, they are endorsing this doctrine as a central point of medical ethics. In that statement, active euthanasia is condemned not merely as illegal but as "contrary to that for which the medical profession stands," whereas passive euthanasia is approved. However, the preceding considerations suggest that there is really no moral difference between the two, considered in themselves (there may be important moral differences in some cases in their *consequences,* but, as I pointed out, these differences may make active euthanasia, and not passive euthanasia, the morally preferable option). So, whereas doctors may have to discriminate between active and passive euthanasia to satisfy the law, they should not do any more than that. In particular, they should not give the distinction any added authority and weight by writing it into official statements of medical ethics.

NOTE

1. A. Shaw: "Doctor, Do We Have a Choice?" *The New York Times Magazine,* Jan. 30, 1972, p. 54.

READING QUESTIONS

1. What is the AMA's 1973 policy regarding euthanasia? What are some of the differences between passive and active forms of euthanasia according to Rachels? Describe some cases of allowing a patient to die and killing a patient directly.
2. What is Rachels' main concern with allowing a patient to die? How does direct action by a doctor differ from cases where treatment is withheld from a patient?
3. Explain Rachels' argument for the claim that decisions to let patients die are made on morally irrelevant grounds. What objections are raised against this view and how does Rachels respond?
4. Why does Rachels think that doctors accepted the AMA's policy? How does he think that doctors should act with respect to policy and the law?

DISCUSSION QUESTIONS

1. Rachels presents hypothetical cases of individuals drowning to illustrate the difference between killing and letting die. Are there any reasons to think that an individual who allows another to drown while looking on is not like the case of a doctor who allows a patient to die by withholding treatment? Consider the morally relevant features of such situations which incline us to make the evaluations that we do.
2. What are the morally relevant differences between allowing someone to die and killing someone directly? Is allowing someone to die always a slow and painful process as Rachels suggests? Is taking direct action in order to kill someone always quick and painless?

BONNIE STEINBOCK

The Intentional Termination of Life

Steinbock's article is a reply to Rachels. She argues that Rachels is mistaken in supposing that the 1973 AMA policy is based on the thesis that killing is intrinsically morally worse than letting die. Instead, she explains that the policy is based on a set of overlapping distinctions including the difference between intending and foreseeing and between ordinary and extraordinary care. Consequently, according to Steinbock, the AMA policy does not have the kinds of practical consequences (inhumane treatment and irrelevant life-and-death decisions) that Rachels alleges.

Recommended Reading: natural law theory, esp. doctrine of double effect, chap. 1, sec. 2B.

From Bonnie Steinbock, "The Intentional Termination of Life," *Ethics in Science and Medicine* (now *Social Science and Medicine*) 6 (1979). © Pergamon Press PLC. Reprinted by permission.

According to James Rachels[1] a common mistake in medical ethics is the belief that there is a moral difference between active and passive euthanasia. This is a mistake, [he] argues, because the rationale underlying the distinction between active and passive euthanasia is the idea that there is a significant moral difference between intentionally killing and letting die. . . . Whether the belief that there is a significant moral difference (between intentionally killing and intentionally letting die) is mistaken is not my concern here. For it is far from clear that this distinction is the basis of the doctrine of the American Medical Association which Rachels attacks. And if the killing/letting die distinction is not the basis of the AMA doctrine, then arguments showing that the distinction has no moral force do not, in themselves reveal in the doctrine's adherents either "confused thinking" or "a moral point of view unrelated to the interests of individuals." Indeed, as we examine the AMA doctrine, I think it will become clear that it appeals to and makes use of a number of overlapping distinctions, which may have moral significance in particular cases, such as the distinction between intending and foreseeing, or between ordinary and extraordinary care. Let us then turn to the statement, from the House of Delegates of the AMA, which Rachels cites:

> The intentional termination of the life of one human being by another—mercy-killing—is contrary to that for which the medical profession stands and is contrary to the policy of the AMA.
>
> The cessation of the employment of extraordinary means to prolong the life of the body when there is irrefutable evidence that biological death is imminent is the decision of the patient and/or his immediate family. The advice and judgment of the physician should be freely available to the patient and/or his immediate family.[2]

Rachels attacks this statement because he believes that it contains a moral distinction between active and passive euthanasia. . . .

I intend to show that the AMA statement does not imply support of the active/passive euthanasia distinction. In forbidding the intentional termination of life, the statement rejects both active and passive euthanasia. It does allow for " . . . the cessation of the employment of extraordinary means . . ." to prolong life. The mistake Rachels makes is in identifying the cessation of life-prolonging treatment with passive euthanasia, or intentionally letting die. If it were right to equate the two, then the AMA statement would be self-contradictory, for it would begin by condemning, and end by allowing, the intentional termination of life. But if the cessation of life-prolonging treatment is not always or necessarily passive euthanasia, then there is no confusion and no contradiction.

Why does Rachels think that the cessation of life-prolonging treatment is the intentional termination of life? He says:

> The AMA policy statement isolates the crucial issue very well: The crucial issue is "the intentional termination of the life of one human being by another." But after identifying this issue, and forbidding "mercy-killing," the statement goes on to deny that the cessation of treatment is the intentional termination of a life. This is where the mistake comes in, for what is the cessation of treatment, in these circumstances, if it is not "the intentional termination of the life of one human being by another"? Of course it is exactly that, and if it were not, there would be no point to it.[3]

However, there *can* be a point (to the cessation of life-prolonging treatment) other than an endeavor to bring about the patient's death, and so the blanket identification of cessation of treatment with the intentional termination of a life is inaccurate. There are at least two situations in which the termination of life-prolonging treatment cannot be identified with the intentional termination of the life of one human being by another.

The first situation concerns the patient's right to refuse treatment. Rachels gives the example of a patient dying of an incurable disease, accompanied by unrelievable pain, who wants to end the treatment which cannot cure him but can only prolong his miserable existence. Why, they ask, may a doctor accede to the patient's request to stop treatment, but not provide a patient in a similar situation with a lethal dose? The answer lies in the patient's right to refuse treatment. In general, a competent adult has the right to refuse treatment, even where such treatment is necessary to prolong life. Indeed, the right to refuse treatment has been upheld even when the patient's reason for refusing treatment is generally agreed to be inadequate.[4] This right can be over-ridden (if, for example, the patient has dependent children) but, in general, no one may legally compel you to undergo treatment to which you have not consented, "Historically, surgical intrusion has always been considered a technical battery upon the person and one to be excused or justified by consent of the patient or justified by necessity created by the circumstances of the moment. . . ."[5]

At this point, it might be objected that if one has the right to refuse life-prolonging treatment, then consistency demands that one have the right to decide to end his life, and to obtain help in doing so. The idea is that the right to refuse treatment somehow implies a right to voluntary euthanasia, and we need to see why someone might think this. The right to refuse treatment has been considered by legal writers as an example of the right to privacy or, better, the right to bodily self-determination. You have the right to decide what happens to your own body, and the right to refuse treatment is an instance of that more general right. But if you have the right to determine what happens to your body, then should you not have the right to choose to end your life, and even a right to get help in doing so?

However, it is important to see that the right to refuse treatment is not the same as, nor does it entail, a right to voluntary euthanasia, even if both can be derived from the right to bodily self-determination. The right to refuse treatment is not itself a "right to die"; that one may choose to exercise this right even at the risk of death, or even *in order to die,* is irrelevant. The purpose of the right to refuse medical treatment is not to give persons a right to decide whether to live or die, but to protect them from the unwanted interferences of others. Perhaps we ought to interpret the right to bodily self-determination more broadly so as to include a right to die: But this would be a substantial extension of our present understanding of the right to bodily self-determination, and not a consequence of it. Should we recognize a right to voluntary euthanasia, we would have to agree that people have the right not merely to be left alone, but also the right to be killed. I leave to one side that substantive moral issue. My claim is simply that there can be a reason for terminating life-prolonging

treatment other than "to bring about the patient's death."

The second case in which termination of treatment cannot be identified with intentional, termination of life is where continued treatment has little chance of improving the patient's condition and brings greater discomfort than relief.

The question here is what treatment is appropriate to the particular case. A cancer specialist describes it in this way:

> My general rule is to administer therapy as long as a patient responds well and has the potential for a reasonably good quality of life. But when all feasible therapies have been administered and a patient shows signs of rapid deterioration, the continuation of therapy can cause more discomfort than the cancer. From that time I recommend surgery, radiotherapy, or chemotherapy only as a means of relieving pain. But if a patient's condition should once again stabilize after the withdrawal of active therapy and if it should appear that he could still gain some good time, I would immediately reinstitute active therapy. The decision to cease anticancer treatment is never irrevocable, and often the desire to live will push a patient to try for another remission, or even a few more days of life.[6]

The decision here to cease anticancer treatment cannot be construed as a decision that the patient die, or as the intentional termination of life. It is a decision to provide the most appropriate treatment for that patient at that time. Rachels suggests that the point of the cessation of treatment is the intentional termination of life. But here the point of discontinuing treatment is not to bring about the patient's death but to avoid treatment that will cause more discomfort than the cancer and has little hope of benefiting the patient. Treatment that meets this description is often called "extraordinary."[7] The concept is flexible, and what might be considered "extraordinary" in one situation might be ordinary in another. The use of a respirator to sustain a patient through a severe bout with a respiratory disease would be considered ordinary; its use to sustain the life of a severely brain-damaged person in an irreversible coma would be considered extraordinary.

Contrasted with extraordinary treatment is ordinary treatment, the care a doctor would normally be expected to provide. Failure to provide ordinary care constitutes neglect, and can even be construed as the intentional infliction of harm, where there is a legal obligation to provide care. The importance of the ordinary/extraordinary care distinction lies partly in its connection to the doctor's intention. The withholding of extraordinary care should be seen as a decision not to inflict painful treatment on a patient without reasonable hope of success. The withholding of ordinary care, by contrast, must be seen as neglect. Thus, one doctor says, "We have to draw a distinction between ordinary and extraordinary means. We never withdraw what's needed to make a baby comfortable, we would never withdraw the care a parent would provide. We never kill a baby. . . . But we may decide certain heroic intervention is not worthwhile."[8]

We should keep in mind the ordinary/extraordinary care distinction when considering an example given by Rachels to show the irrationality of the active/passive distinction with regard to infanticide. The example is this: A child is born with Down's syndrome and also has an intestinal obstruction which requires corrective surgery. If the surgery is not performed, the infant will starve to death, since it cannot take food orally. This may take days or even weeks, as dehydration and infection set in. Commenting on this situation, Rachels says:

> I can understand why some people are opposed to all euthanasia, and insist that such infants must be allowed to live. I think I can also understand why other people favor destroying these babies quickly and painlessly. But why should anyone favor letting "dehydration and infection wither a tiny being over hours and days"? The doctrine that says that a baby may be allowed to dehydrate and wither, but may not be given an injection that would end its life without suffering, seems so patently cruel as to require no further refutation.[9]

Such a doctrine perhaps does not need further refutation; but this is not the AMA doctrine. For the AMA statement criticized by Rachels allows only for the cessation of extraordinary means to prolong life when death is imminent. Neither of these conditions is satisfied in this example. Death is not imminent in this situation, any more than it would be if a normal child had an attack of appendicitis. Neither the corrective surgery to remove the intestinal obstruction, nor the

intravenous feeding required to keep the infant alive until such surgery is performed, can be regarded as extraordinary means, for neither is particularly expensive, nor does either place an overwhelming burden on the patient or others. (The continued existence of the child might be thought to place an overwhelming burden on its parents, but that has nothing to do with the characterization of the means to prolong its life as extraordinary. If it had, then *feeding* a severely defective child who required a great deal of care could be regarded as extraordinary.) The chances of success if the operation is undertaken are quite good, though there is always a risk in operating on infants. Though the Down's syndrome will not be alleviated, the child will proceed to an otherwise normal infancy.

It cannot be argued that the treatment is withheld for the infant's sake, unless one is prepared to argue that all mentally retarded babies are better off dead. This is particularly implausible in the case of Down's syndrome babies who generally do not suffer and are capable of giving and receiving love, of learning and playing, to varying degrees.

In a film on this subject entitled, "Who Should Survive?," a doctor defended a decision not to operate, saying that since the parents did not consent to the operation, the doctor's hands were tied. As we have seen, surgical intrusion requires consent, and in the case of infants, consent would normally come from the parents. But, as their legal guardians, parents are required to provide medical care for their children, and failure to do so can constitute criminal neglect or even homicide. In general, courts have been understandably reluctant to recognize a parental right to terminate life-prolonging treatment.[10] Although prosecution is unlikely, physicians who comply with invalid instructions from the parents and permit the infant's death could be liable for aiding and abetting, failure to report child neglect, or even homicide. So it is not true that, in this situation, doctors are legally bound to do as the parents wish.

To sum up, I think that Rachels is right to regard the decision not to operate in the Down's syndrome example as the intentional termination of life. But there is no reason to believe that either the law or the AMA would regard it otherwise. Certainly the decision to withhold treatment is not justified by the

AMA statement. That such infants have been allowed to die cannot be denied; but this, I think, is the result of doctors misunderstanding the law and the AMA position.

Withholding treatment in this case is the intentional termination of life because the infant is deliberately allowed to die; that is the point of not operating. But there are other cases in which that is not the point. If the point is to avoid inflicting painful treatment on a patient with little or no reasonable hope of success, this is not the intentional termination of life. The permissibility of such withholding of treatment, then, would have no implications for the permissibility of euthanasia, active or passive.

The decision whether or not to operate, or to institute vigorous treatment, is particularly agonizing in the case of children born with spina bifida, an opening in the base of the spine usually accompanied by hydrocephalus and mental retardation. If left unoperated, these children usually die of meningitis or kidney failure within the first few years of life. Even if they survive, all affected children face a life-time of illness, operations, and varying degrees of disability. The policy used to be to save as many as possible, but the trend now is toward selective treatment, based on the physician's estimate of the chances of success. If operating is not likely to improve significantly the child's condition, parents and doctors may agree not to operate. This is not the intentional termination of life, for again the purpose is not the termination of the child's life but the avoidance of painful and pointless treatment. Thus, the fact that withholding treatment is justified does not imply that killing the child would be equally justified.

Throughout the discussion. I have claimed that intentionally ceasing life-prolonging treatment is not the intentional termination of life unless the doctor has, as his or her purpose in stopping treatment, the patient's death.

It may be objected that I have incorrectly characterized the conditions for the intentional termination of life. Perhaps it is enough that the doctor intentionally ceases treatment, foreseeing that the patient will die; perhaps the reason for ceasing treatment is irrelevant to its characterization as the intentional termination of life. I find this suggestion implausible,

but am willing to consider arguments for it. Rachels has provided no such arguments: Indeed, he apparently shares my view about the intentional termination of life. For when he claims that the cessation of life-prolonging treatment *is* the intentional termination of life, his reason for making the claim is that "if it were not, there would be no point to it," Rachels believes that the point of ceasing treatment, "in these cases," is to bring about the patient's death. If that were not the point, he suggests, why would the doctor cease treatment? I have shown, however, that there can be a point to ceasing treatment which is not the death of the patient. In showing this, I have refuted Rachels's reason for identifying the cessation of life-prolonging treatment with the intentional termination of life, and thus his argument against the AMA doctrine.

Here someone might say: Even if the withholding of treatment is not the intentional termination of life, does that make a difference, morally speaking? If life-prolonging treatment may be withheld, for the sake of the child, may not an easy death be provided, for the sake of the child, as well? The unoperated child with spina bifida may take months or even years to die. Distressed by the spectacle of children "lying around waiting to die," one doctor has written, "It is time that society and medicine stopped perpetuating the fiction that withholding treatment is ethically different from terminating a life. It is time that society began to discuss mechanisms by which we can alleviate the pain and suffering for those individuals whom we cannot help."[11]

I do not deny that there may be cases in which death is in the best interests of the patient. In such cases, a quick and painless death may be the best thing. However, I do not think that, once active or vigorous treatment is stopped, a quick death is always preferable to a lingering one. We must be cautious about attributing to defective children *our* distress at seeing them linger. Waiting for them to die may be tough on parents, doctors, and nurses—it isn't necessarily tough on the child. The decision not to operate need not mean a decision to neglect, and it may be possible to make the remaining months of the child's life comfortable, pleasant, and filled with love. If this alternative is possible, surely it is more decent and humane than killing the child. In such a situation, withholding treatment, foreseeing the child's death, is not ethically equivalent to killing the child, and we cannot move from the permissibility of the former to that of the latter. I am worried that there will be a tendency to do precisely that if active euthanasia is regarded as morally equivalent to the withholding of life-prolonging treatment.

CONCLUSION

The AMA statement does not make the distinction Rachels wishes to attack, i.e., that between active and passive euthanasia. Instead, the statement draws a distinction between the intentional termination of life, on the one hand, and the cessation of the employment of extraordinary means to prolong life, on the other. Nothing said by Rachels shows that this distinction is confused. It may be that doctors have misinterpreted the AMA statement, and that this has led, for example, to decisions to allow defective infants slowly to starve to death. I quite agree with Rachels that the decisions to which they allude were cruel and made on irrelevant grounds. Certainly it is worth pointing out that allowing someone to die can be the intentional termination of life, and that it can be just as bad as, or worse than, killing someone. However, the withholding of life-prolonging treatment is not necessarily the intentional termination of life, so that if it

is permissible to withhold life-prolonging treatment, it does not follow that, other things being equal, it is permissible to kill. Furthermore, most of the time, other things are not equal. In many of the cases in which it would be right to cease treatment, I do not think that it would also be right to kill.

NOTES

1. James Rachels, "Active and passive euthanasia." *New England Journal of Medicine,* 292, 78–80, 1975.
2. Rachels, p. 78.
3. Rachels, p. 79–80.
4. For example, *In re Yetter,* 62 Pa. D. & C. 2d 619, C.P., Northampton County Ct., 1974.
5. David W. Meyers, "Legal aspects of voluntary euthanasia." In *Dilemmas of Euthanasia* (edited by John Behnke and Sissela Bok), p. 56. Anchor Books, New York, 1975.
6. Ernest H. Rosenbaum. *Living with Cancer,* p. 27. Praeger, New York, 1975.
7. Cf. Tristam Engelhardt, Jr. "Ethical issues in aiding the death of young children." In *Beneficent Euthanasia* (edited by Marvin Kohl), Prometheus Books, Buffalo, N.Y., 1975.
8. B. D. Colen, *Karen Ann Quinlan: Living and Dying in the Age of Eternal Life,* p. 115. Nash, 1976.
9. Rachels, p. 79.
10. Cf. Norman Cantor, "Law and the termination of an incompetent patient's life-preserving care." *Dilemmas of Euthanasia,* op. cit., pp. 69–105.
11. John Freeman, "Is there a right to die—quickly?" *Journal of Pediatrics,* 80, 905.

READING QUESTIONS

1. How does Steinbock believe that Rachels has misinterpreted the AMA's policy concerning euthanasia? What potentially mistaken view does Rachels believe the policy is based on? What are the distinctions the policy appeals to according to Steinbock?
2. Explain the differences between intended and foreseeable consequences and between ordinary and extraordinary care.
3. Explain Steinbock's objection that there may be reasons for the cessation of treatment other than the death of a patient. Why does she believe that the right to refuse treatment is not the same as the right to die?
4. When is a case of ceasing treatment a case of intentionally terminating a life according to Steinbock? When is it not? Give examples of each case.
5. How does Steinbock respond to the objection that there is no relevant moral difference between ceasing treatment and intentionally terminating a life?

DISCUSSION QUESTIONS

1. Suppose that Steinbock is right that the AMA's policy regarding euthanasia is not based on the view that killing is more wrong than letting die. What reasons are there for thinking that killing is more wrong than letting die? Discuss whether there are good reasons to support the view that letting die is either as wrong or worse than killing.
2. What are the morally relevant differences between ceasing treatment and intentionally terminating a life if any? How relevant is Steinbock's distinction between ordinary and extraordinary care?

DAN W. BROCK

Voluntary Active Euthanasia

Brock defends the moral permissibility of voluntary active euthanasia by appealing to two widely held values: the value of autonomy and the value of well-being. He then proceeds to respond to the objection that voluntary active euthanasia is contrary to the "moral center" of the practice of medicine, which, so the critics allege, requires physicians to preserve human life and never intentionally take it. According to Brock, this "moral center" objection misrepresents the true moral aim of medicine, which he claims is consistent with voluntary active euthanasia.

One might understand Brock's approach in terms of an ethics of prima facie duty featuring a prima facie duty to protect the autonomy of ourselves and others and a prima facie obligation to protect and perhaps promote the well-being of ourselves and others.

Recommended Reading: ethics of prima facie duty, chap. 1, sec. 2F.

My concern here will be with voluntary euthanasia only—that is, with the case in which a clearly competent patient makes a fully voluntary and persistent request for aid in dying. . . . I emphasize as well that I am concerned with active euthanasia, not withholding or withdrawing life-sustaining treatment, which some commentators characterize as "passive euthanasia." Finally, I will be concerned with euthanasia where the motive of those who perform it is to respect the wishes of the patient and to provide the patient with a "good death," though one important issue is whether a change in legal policy could restrict the performance of euthanasia to only those cases. . . .

From Dan W. Brock, "Voluntary Active Euthanasia," *Hastings Center Report* 22 (1992): 16, 20.

THE CENTRAL ETHICAL ARGUMENT FOR VOLUNTARY ACTIVE EUTHANASIA

The central ethical argument for euthanasia is familiar. It is that the very same two fundamental ethical values supporting the consensus on patient's rights to decide about life-sustaining treatment also support the ethical permissibility of euthanasia. These values are individual self-determination or autonomy and individual well-being. By self-determination as it bears on euthanasia, I mean people's interest in making important decisions about their lives for themselves according to their own values or conceptions of a good life, and in being left free to act on those decisions. Self-determination is valuable because it permits people to form and live in accordance with their own conception of a good life, at least within the bounds of justice and consistent with others doing so as well. In exercising self-determination people take responsibility for their lives and for the kinds of persons they become. A central aspect of human dignity lies in people's capacity to direct their lives in this way. The value of exercising self-determination presupposes some minimum of decisionmaking capacities or competence, which thus limits the scope of euthanasia supported by self-determination; it cannot justifiably be administered, for example, in cases of serious dementia or treatable clinical depression.

Does the value of individual self-determination extend to the time and manner of one's death? Most people are very concerned about the nature of the last stage of their lives. This reflects not just a fear of experiencing substantial suffering when dying, but also a desire to retain dignity and control during this last period of life. Death is today increasingly preceded by a long period of significant physical and mental decline, due in part to the technological interventions of modern medicine. Many people adjust to these disabilities and find meaning and value in new activities and ways. Others find the impairments and burdens in the last stage of their lives at some point sufficiently great to make life no longer worth living.

For many patients near death, maintaining the quality of one's life, avoiding great suffering, maintaining one's dignity, and insuring that others remember us as we wish them to become of paramount importance and outweigh merely extending one's life. But there is no single, objectively correct answer for everyone as to when, if at all, one's life becomes all things considered a burden and unwanted. If self-determination is a fundamental value, then the great variability among people on this question makes it especially important that individuals control the manner, circumstances, and timing of their dying and death.

The other main value that supports euthanasia is individual well-being. It might seem that individual well-being conflicts with a person's self-determination when the person requests euthanasia. Life itself is commonly taken to be a central good for persons, often valued for its own sake, as well as necessary for pursuit of all other goods within a life. But when a competent patient decides to forgo all further life-sustaining treatment then the patient, either explicitly or implicitly, commonly decides that the best life possible for him or her with treatment is of sufficiently poor quality that it is worse than no further life at all. Life is no longer considered a benefit by the patient, but has now become a burden. The same judgment underlies a request for euthanasia: continued life is seen by the patient as no longer a benefit, but now a burden. Especially in the often severely compromised and debilitated states of many critically ill or dying patients, there is no objective standard, but only the competent patient's judgment of whether continued life is no longer a benefit.

Of course, sometimes there are conditions, such as clinical depression, that call into question whether the patient has made a competent choice, either to forgo life-sustaining treatment or to seek euthanasia, and then the patient's choice need not be evidence that continued life is no longer a benefit for him or her. Just as with decision about treatment, a determination of incompetence can warrant not honoring the patient's choice; in the case of treatment, we then transfer decisional authority to a surrogate, though in the case of voluntary active euthanasia a determination that the patient is incompetent means that choice is not possible.

The value or right of self-determination does not entitle patients to compel physicians to act contrary to their own moral or professional values. Physicians are moral and professional agents whose own self-determination or integrity should be respected as well. If performing euthanasia became legally permissible, but conflicted with a particular physician's reasonable understanding of his or her moral or professional responsibilities, the care of a patient who requested euthanasia should be transferred to another. . . .

Some of the arguments against permitting euthanasia are aimed specifically against physicians. . . . Permitting physicians to perform euthanasia, it is said, would be incompatible with their fundamental moral and professional commitment as healers to care for patients and to protect life. Moreover, if euthanasia by physicians became common, patients would come to fear that a medication was intended not to treat or care, but instead to kill, and would thus lose trust in their physicians. This position was forcefully stated in a paper by Willard Gaylin and his colleagues:

> The very soul of medicine is on trial. . . . This issue touches medicine at its moral center; if this moral center collapses, if physicians become killers or are even licensed to kill, the profession—and, therewith, each physician—will never again be worthy of trust and respect as healer and comforter and protector of life in all its frailty.

These authors go on to make clear that, while they oppose permitting anyone to perform euthanasia, their special concern is with physicians doing so:

> We call on fellow physicians to say that they will not deliberately kill. We must also say to each of our fellow physicians that we will not tolerate killing of patients and that we shall take disciplinary action against doctors who kill. And we must say to the broader community that if it insists on tolerating or legalizing active euthanasia, it will have to find nonphysicians to do its killing.[1]

If permitting physicians to kill would undermine the very "moral center" of medicine, then almost certainly physicians should not be permitted to perform euthanasia. But how persuasive is this claim? Patients should not fear, as a consequence of permitting voluntary active euthanasia, that their physicians will substitute a lethal injection for what patients want and believe is part of their care. If active euthanasia is restricted to cases in which it is truly voluntary, then no patient should fear getting it unless she or he has voluntarily requested it. . . . Patient's trust of their physicians could be increased, not eroded, by knowledge that physicians will provide aid in dying when patients seek it.

Might Gaylin and his colleagues nevertheless be correct in their claim that the moral center of medicine would collapse if physicians were to become killers? This question raises what at the deepest level should be the guiding aims of medicine, a question that obviously cannot be fully explored here. But I do want to say enough to indicate the direction that I believe an appropriate response to this challenge should take. In spelling out above what I called the . . . [central] argument for voluntary active euthanasia, I suggested that two principal values—respecting patients' self-determination and promoting their well-being—underlie the consensus that competent patients, or the surrogates of incompetent patients, are entitled to refuse any life-sustaining treatment and to choose from among available alternative treatments. It is the commitment to these two values in guiding physicians' actions as healers, comforters, and protectors of their patients' lives that should be at the "moral center" of medicine, and these two values support physicians' administering euthanasia when their patients make competent requests for it.

What should not be at that moral center is a commitment to preserving patients' lives as such, without regard to whether those patients want their lives preserved or judge their preservation a benefit to them. Vitalism has been rejected by most physicians, and despite some statements that suggest it, is almost certainly not what Gaylin and colleagues intended. One of them, Leon Kass, has elaborated elsewhere the view that medicine is a moral profession whose proper aim is "the naturally given end of health," understood as the wholeness and well-working of the human being; "for the physician, at least human life in living bodies commands respect and reverence—by its very nature." Kass continues, "the deepest ethical principle restraining the physician's power is not the autonomy or freedom of the patient; neither is it his own compassion or good intention. Rather, it is the dignity and mysterious power of human life itself."[2] I believe Kass is in the end mistaken about the proper account of the aims of medicine and the limits on physicians'

power, but this difficult issue will certainly be one of the central themes in the continuing debate about euthanasia.

NOTES

1. Willard Gaylin, Leon M. Kass, Edmund D. Pellegrino, and Mark Siegler, "Doctors Must Not Kill," *JAMA* 259 (1988): 2139–40.

2. Leon M. Kass, "Neither for Love nor Money: Why Doctors Must Not Kill," *The Public Interest* 94 (1989): 25–46.

READING QUESTIONS

1. How does Brock characterize voluntary active euthanasia?
2. What is the central ethical argument for voluntary active euthanasia according to Brock?
3. Explain in detail the two values Brock thinks are at issue in questions that concern the morality of euthanasia as well as his argument for why they do not conflict with one another.
4. Why do opponents of voluntary active euthanasia think that the performance of such actions by physicians is incompatible with their moral and professional commitment as healers? How does Brock respond to their arguments?
5. What is the moral center of the physician's profession according to the opponents of voluntary active euthanasia?

DISCUSSION QUESTIONS

1. Is Brock's characterization of the moral center of the physician's profession correct? Why or why not? How does his view compare to the view that opponents of voluntary active euthanasia support?
2. What values other than individual autonomy and well-being are relevant when discussing the morality of euthanasia, if any? Should physicians be committed to upholding the two values Brock thinks are at issue?

RICHARD DOERFLINGER

Assisted Suicide: Pro-Choice or Anti-Life?

Richard Doerflinger objects to the permissibility of assisted suicide (which, for him, includes active euthanasia) by raising two objections to the pro-choice position on this topic. First, the logic of the pro-choice position, which appeals to the value of autonomy, is at odds with itself in its defense of assisted suicide. Second, pro-choice advocates fail to appreciate the risks of a slippery slope: various facts about human nature and society are likely (if not certain) to move us from allowing voluntary active euthanasia to wrongful practices of killing.

Recommended Reading: consequentialism, chap. 1, sec. 2A.

The intrinsic wrongness of directly killing the innocent, even with the victim's consent, is all but axiomatic in the Jewish and Christian worldviews that have shaped the laws and mores of Western civilization and the self-concept of its medical practitioners. This norm grew out of the conviction that human life is sacred because it is created in the image and likeness of God, and called to fulfillment in love of God and neighbor.

With the pervasive secularization of Western culture, norms against euthanasia and suicide have to a great extent been cut loose from their religious roots to fend for themselves. Because these norms seem abstract and unconvincing to many, debate tends to dwell not on the wrongness of the act as such but on what may follow from its acceptance. Such arguments are often described as claims about a "slippery slope," and debate shifts to the validity of slippery slope arguments in general.

Since it is sometimes argued that acceptance of assisted suicide is an outgrowth of respect for personal autonomy, and not lack of respect for the inherent worth of human life, I will outline how autonomy-based arguments in favor of assisting suicide do entail a statement about the value of life. I will

also distinguish two kinds of slippery slope argument often confused with each other, and argue that those who favor social and legal acceptance of assisted suicide have not adequately responded to the slippery slope claims of their opponents.

ASSISTED SUICIDE VERSUS RESPECT FOR LIFE

Some advocates of socially sanctioned assisted suicide admit (and a few boast) that their proposal is incompatible with the conviction that human life is of intrinsic worth. Attorney Robert Risley has said that he and his allies in the Hemlock Society are "so bold" as to seek to "overturn the sanctity of life principle" in American society. A life of suffering, "racked with pain," is "not the kind of life we cherish."[1]

Others eschew Risley's approach, perhaps recognizing that it creates a slippery slope toward practices almost universally condemned. If society is to help terminally ill patients to commit suicide because it agrees that death is objectively preferable to a life

From Richard Doerflinger, "Assisted Suicide: Pro-Choice or Anti-Life?" *Hastings Center Report,* Special Supplement (1989): 16–19. Reprinted by permission. © The Hastings Center.

of hardship, it will be difficult to draw the line at the seriously ill or even at circumstances where the victim requests death.

Some advocates of assisted suicide therefore take a different course, arguing that it is precisely respect for the dignity of the human person that demands respect for individual freedom as the noblest feature of that person. On this rationale a decision as to when and how to die deserves the respect and even the assistance of others because it is the ultimate exercise of self-determination—"ultimate" both in the sense that it is the last decision one will ever make and in the sense that through it one takes control of one's entire self. What makes such decisions worthy of respect is not the fact that death is chosen over life but that it is the individual's own free decision about his or her future.

Thus Derek Humphry, director of the Hemlock Society, describes his organization as "pro-choice" on this issue. Such groups favor establishment of a constitutional "right to die" modeled on the right to abortion delineated by the U.S. Supreme Court in 1973. This would be a right to choose whether or not to end one's own life, free of outside government interference. In theory, recognition of such a right would betray no bias toward choosing death.

LIFE VERSUS FREEDOM

This autonomy-based approach is more appealing than the straight-forward claim that some lives are not worth living, especially to Americans accustomed to valuing individual liberty above virtually all else. But the argument departs from American traditions on liberty in one fundamental respect.

When the Declaration of Independence proclaimed the inalienable human rights to be "life, liberty, and the pursuit of happiness," this ordering reflected a long-standing judgment about their relative priorities. Life, a human being's very earthly existence, is the most fundamental right because it is the necessary condition for all other worldly goods including freedom; freedom in turn makes it possible to pursue (without guaranteeing that one will attain) happiness.

Safeguards against the deliberate destruction of life are thus seen as necessary to protect freedom and all other human goods. This line of thought is not explicitly religious but is endorsed by some modern religious groups:

> The first right of the human person is his life. He has other goods and some are more precious, but this one is fundamental—the condition of all the others. Hence it must be protected above all others.[2]

On this view suicide is not the ultimate exercise of freedom but its ultimate self-contradiction: A free act that by destroying life, destroys all the individual's future earthly freedom. If life is more basic than freedom, society best serves freedom by discouraging rather than assisting self-destruction. Sometimes one must limit particular choices to safeguard freedom itself, as when American society chose over a century ago to prevent people from selling themselves into slavery even of their own volition.

It may be argued in objection that the person who ends his life has not truly suffered loss of freedom, because unlike the slave he need not continue to exist under the constraints of a loss of freedom. But the slave does have some freedom, including the freedom to seek various means of liberation or at least the freedom to choose what attitude to take regarding his plight. To claim that a slave is worse off than a corpse is to value a situation of limited freedom less than one of no freedom whatsoever, which seems inconsistent with the premise of the "pro-choice" position. Such a claim also seems tantamount to saying that some lives (such as those with less than absolute freedom) are objectively not worth living, a position that "pro-choice" advocates claim not to hold.

It may further be argued in objection that assistance in suicide is only being offered to those who can no longer meaningfully exercise other freedoms due to increased suffering and reduced capabilities and lifespan. To be sure, the suffering of terminally ill patients who can no longer pursue the simplest everyday tasks should call for sympathy and support from everyone in contact with them. But even these hardships do not constitute total loss of freedom of choice. If they did, one could hardly claim that the patient is in a position to make the ultimate free choice about suicide. A dying person capable of making a choice of that kind is also capable of making less monumental free choices about coping with his or her condition. This person generally faces a bewildering array of choices regarding the assessment of his or her past life and the resolution of relationships with family and friends. He or she must finally choose at this time what stance to take regarding the eternal questions about God, personal responsibility, and the prospects of a destiny after death.

In short, those who seek to maximize free choice may with consistency reject the idea of assisted suicide, instead facilitating all choices except that one which cuts short all choices.

In fact proponents of assisted suicide do not consistently place freedom of choice as their highest priority. They often defend the moderate nature of their project by stating, with Derek Humphry, that "we do not encourage suicide for any reason except to relieve unremitting suffering." It seems their highest priority is the "pursuit of happiness" (or avoidance of suffering) and not "liberty" as such. Liberty or freedom of choice loses its value if one's choices cannot relieve suffering and lead to happiness; life is of instrumental value, insofar as it makes possible choices that can bring happiness.

In this value system, choice as such does not warrant unqualified respect. In difficult circumstances, as when care of a suffering and dying patient is a great burden on family and society, the individual who chooses life despite suffering will not easily be seen as rational, thus will not easily receive understanding and assistance for this choice.

In short, an unqualified "pro-choice" defense of assisted suicide lacks coherence because corpses have no choices. A particular choice, that of death, is given priority over all the other choices it makes impossible, so the value of choice as such is not central to the argument.

A restriction of this rationale to cases of terminal illness also lacks logical force. For if ending a brief life of suffering can be good, it would seem that ending a long life of suffering may be better. Surely the approach of the California "Humane and Dignified Death Act"—where consensual killing of a patient expected to die in six months is presumably good medical practice, but killing the same patient a month

or two earlier is still punishable as homicide—is completely arbitrary.

SLIPPERY SLOPES, LOOSE CANNONS

Many arguments against sanctioning assisted suicide concern a different kind of "slippery slope": Contingent factors in the contemporary situation may make it virtually inevitable in practice, if not compelling at the level of abstract theory, that removal of the taboo against assisted suicide will lead to destructive expansions of the right to kill the innocent. Such factors may not be part of euthanasia advocates' own agenda; but if they exist and are beyond the control of these advocates, they must be taken into account in judging the moral and social wisdom of opening what may be a Pandora's box of social evils.

To distinguish this sociological argument from our dissection of the conceptual logic of the rationale for assisted suicide, we might call it a "loose cannon" argument. The basic claim is that socially accepted killing of innocent persons will interact with other social factors to threaten lives that advocates of assisted suicide would agree should be protected. These factors at present include the following:

> The psychological vulnerability of elderly and dying patients. Theorists may present voluntary and involuntary euthanasia as polar opposites; in practice there are many steps on the road from dispassionate, autonomous choice to subtle coercion. Elderly and disabled patients are often invited by our achievement-oriented society to see themselves as useless burdens on younger, more vital generations. In this climate, simply offering the option of "self-deliverance" shifts a burden of proof, so that helpless patients must ask themselves why they are not availing themselves of it. Society's offer of death communicates the message to certain patients that they may continue to live if they wish but the rest of us have no strong interest in their survival. Indeed, once the choice of a quick and painless death is officially accepted as rational, resistance to this choice may be seen as eccentric or even selfish.[3]

The crisis in health care costs. The growing incentives for physicians, hospitals, families, and insurance companies to control the cost of health care will bring additional pressures to bear on patients. Curt Garbesi, the Hemlock Society's legal consultant, argues that autonomy-based groups like Hemlock must "control the public debate" so assisted suicide will not be seized upon by public officials as a cost-cutting device. But simply basing one's own defense of assisted suicide on individual autonomy does not solve the problem. For in the economic sphere also, offering the option of suicide would subtly shift burdens of proof.

Adequate health care is now seen by at least some policymakers as a human right, as something a society owes to all its members. Acceptance of assisted suicide as an option for those requiring expensive care would not only offer health care providers an incentive to make that option seem attractive—it would also demote all other options to the status of strictly private choices by the individual. As such they may lose their moral and legal claim to public support—in much the same way that the U.S. Supreme Court, having protected abortion under a constitutional "right of privacy," has quite logically denied any government obligation to provide public funds for this strictly private choice. As life-extending care of the terminally ill is increasingly seen as strictly elective, society may become less willing to appropriate funds for such care, and economic pressures to choose death will grow accordingly.

Legal doctrines on "substituted judgment." American courts recognizing a fundamental right to refuse life-sustaining treatment have concluded that it is unjust to deny this right to the mentally incompetent. In such cases the right is exercised on the patient's behalf by others, who seek either to interpret what the patient's own wishes might have been or to serve his or her best interests. Once assisted suicide is established as a fundamental right, courts will almost certainly find that it is unjust not to extend this right to those unable to express their wishes: Hemlock's political arm, Americans Against Human Suffering, has underscored continuity between "passive" and "active" euthanasia by offering the Humane and Dignified Death Act as an amendment to California's

"living will" law, and by including a provision for appointment of a proxy to choose the time and manner of the patient's death. By such extensions our legal system would accommodate nonvoluntary, if not involuntary, active euthanasia.

Expanded definitions of terminal illness. The Hemlock Society wishes to offer assisted suicide only to those suffering from terminal illnesses. But some Hemlock officials have in mind a rather broad definition of "terminal illness." Derek Humphry says "two and a half million people alone are dying of Alzheimer's disease."[4] At Hemlock's 1986 convention, Dutch physician Pieter Admiraal boasted that he had recently broadened the meaning of terminal illness in his country by giving a lethal injection to a young quadriplegic woman—a Dutch court found that he acted within judicial guidelines allowing euthanasia for the terminally ill, because paralyzed patients have difficulty swallowing and could die from aspirating their food at any time.

The medical and legal meaning of terminal illness has already been expanded in the United States by professional societies, legislatures, and courts in the context of so-called passive euthanasia. A Uniform Rights of the Terminally Ill Act proposed by the National Conference of Commissioners on Uniform State Laws in 1986 defines a terminal illness as one that would cause the patient's death in a relatively short time if life-preserving treatment is not provided—prompting critics to ask if all diabetics, for example, are "terminal" by definition. Some courts already see comatose and vegetative states as "terminal" because they involve an inability to swallow that will lead to death unless artificial feeding is instituted. In the Hilda Peter case, the New Jersey Supreme Court declared that the traditional state interest in "preserving life" referred only to "cognitive and sapient life" and not to mere "biological" existence, implying that unconscious patients are terminal, or perhaps as good as dead, so far as state interests are concerned. Is there any reason to think that American law would suddenly resurrect the older, narrower meaning of "terminal illness" in the context of active euthanasia?

Prejudice against citizens with disabilities. If definitions of terminal illness expand to encompass states of severe physical or mental disability, another social reality will increase the pressure on patients to choose death: long-standing prejudice, sometimes bordering on revulsion, against people with disabilities. While it is seldom baldly claimed that disabled people have "lives not worth living," able-bodied people often say they could not live in a severely disabled state or would prefer death. In granting Elizabeth Bouvia a right to refuse a feeding tube that preserved her life, the California Appeals Court bluntly stated that her physical handicaps led her to "consider her existence meaningless" and that "she cannot be faulted for so concluding." According to disability rights expert Paul Longmore, in a society with such attitudes toward the disabled, "talk of their 'rational' or 'voluntary' suicide is simply Orwellian newspeak."[5]

Character of the medical profession. Advocates of assisted suicide realize that most physicians will resist giving lethal injections because they are trained, in Garbesi's words, to be "enemies of death." The California Medical Association firmly opposed the Humane and Dignified Death Act, seeing it as an attack on the ethical foundation of the medical profession.

Yet California appeals judge Lynn Compton was surely correct in his concurring opinion in the Bouvia case, when he said that a sufficient number of willing physicians can be found once legal sanctions against assisted suicide are dropped. Judge Compton said this had clearly been the case with abortion, despite the fact that the Hippocratic Oath condemns abortion as strongly as it condemns euthanasia. Opinion polls of physicians bear out the judgment that a significant number would perform lethal injections if they were legal.

Some might think this division or ambivalence about assisted suicide in the medical profession will restrain broad expansions of the practice. But if anything, Judge Compton's analogy to our experience with abortion suggests the opposite. Most physicians still have qualms about abortion, and those who perform abortions on a full-time basis are not readily accepted by their colleagues as paragons of the healing art. Consequently they tend to form their own professional societies, bolstering each other's positive self-image and developing euphemisms to blunt the moral edge of their work.

Once physicians abandon the traditional medical self-image, which rejects direct killing of patients in all circumstances, their new substitute self-image may require ever more aggressive efforts to make this killing more widely practiced and favorably received. To allow killing by physicians in certain circumstances may create a new lobby of physicians in favor of expanding medical killing.

The human will to power. The most deeply buried yet most powerful driving force toward widespread medical killing is a fact of human nature: Human beings are tempted to enjoy exercising power over others; ending another person's life is the ultimate exercise of that power. Once the taboo against killing has been set aside, it becomes progressively easier to channel one's aggressive instincts into the destruction of life in other contexts. Or as James Burtchaell has said: "There is a sort of virginity about murder; once one has violated it, it is awkward to refuse other invitations by saying, 'But that would be murder!'"[6]

Some will say assisted suicide for the terminally ill is morally distinguishable from murder and does not logically require termination of life in other circumstances. But my point is that the skill and the instinct to kill are more easily turned to other lethal tasks once they have an opportunity to exercise themselves. Thus Robert Jay Lifton has perceived differences between the German "mercy killings" of the 1930s and the later campaign to annihilate the Jews of Europe, yet still says that "at the heart of the Nazi enterprise . . . is the destruction of the boundary between healing and killing."[7] No other boundary separating these two situations was as fundamental as this one, and thus none was effective once it was crossed. As a matter of historical fact, personnel who had conducted the "mercy killing" program were quickly and readily recruited to operate the killing chambers of the death camps.[8] While the contemporary United States fortunately lacks the anti-Semitic and totalitarian attitudes that made the Holocaust possible, it has its own trends and pressures that may combine with acceptance of medical killing to produce a distinctively American catastrophe in the name of individual freedom.

These "loose cannon" arguments are not conclusive. All such arguments by their nature rest upon a reading and extrapolation of certain contingent factors in society. But their combined force provides a serious case against taking the irreversible step of sanctioning assisted suicide for any class of persons, so long as those who advocate this step fail to demonstrate why these predictions are wrong. If the strict philosophical case on behalf of "rational suicide" lacks coherence, the pragmatic claim that its acceptance would be a social benefit lacks grounding in history or common sense.

REFERENCES

1. Presentation at the Hemlock Society's Third National Voluntary Euthanasia Conference, "A Humane and Dignified Death," September 25–27, 1986, Washington, DC. All quotations from Hemlock Society officials are from the proceedings of this conference unless otherwise noted.

2. Vatican Congregation for the Doctrine of the Faith, Declaration on Procured Abortion (1974), para. 11.

3. I am indebted for this line of argument to Dr. Eric Chevlen.

4. Denis Herbstein, "Campaigning for the Right to Die," International Herald Tribune, 11 September 1986.

5. Paul K. Longmore, "Elizabeth Bouvia, Assisted Suicide and Social Prejudice," Issues in Law & Medicine 3:2 (1987), 168.

6. James T. Burtchaell, Rachel Weeping and Other Essays on Abortion (Kansas City: Andrews & McMeel, 1982), 188.

7. Robert Jay Lifton, The Nazi Doctors: Medical Killing and the Psychology of Genocide (New York: Basic Books, 1986), 14.

8. Yitzhak Rad, Belzec, Sobibor, Treblinka (Bloomington, IN: Indiana University Press, 1987), 11, 16–17.

READING QUESTIONS

1. How does Doerflinger distinguish between life and freedom? What reasons does Doerflinger give for thinking that life is the most fundamental right that we have?
2. How does Doerflinger respond to the objection that slavery is worse than death? What are some of the other objections he considers to his view?
3. Doerflinger argues that the practice of euthanasia is a slippery slope that would result in numerous negative outcomes. Explain in detail the seven possible results of permitting the practice of euthanasia according to Doerflinger.

DISCUSSION QUESTIONS

1. Should we agree with Doerflinger that life is the most fundamental of our rights? Why or why not? What other rights might be more or as equally fundamental?
2. How worried should we be that the practice of euthanasia will cause the negative results suggested by Doerflinger? What are some of the positive results of such a practice? Consider and discuss the potentially negative consequences of disallowing the practice of euthanasia.

DAVID T. WATTS AND TIMOTHY HOWELL

Assisted Suicide Is Not Voluntary Active Euthanasia

David T. Watts and Timothy Howell distinguish between voluntary active euthanasia and physician-assisted suicide and then proceed to distinguish three types of the latter practice which differ in how involved the physician is in the suicide of the patient: *providing information, providing the means of suicide,* and *supervising* or *directly aiding.* They argue that the various objections to voluntary active euthanasia are not compelling against physician-assisted suicide. They go on to defend the practice of what they call "limited" physician-assisted suicide, which would permit a physician to provide patients with information and means, but would prohibit the physician from supervising or directly helping a patient commit suicide.

Their article can be read as a response to the slippery slope objections raised by Doerflinger in the previous reading.

Recommended Reading: consequentialism, chap. 1, sec. 2A.

. . . [Ongoing] developments highlight some of the confusion emerging from discussions of voluntary active euthanasia (V.A.E.) and assisted suicide. A significant source of confusion has been the tendency to join these concepts or even to consider them synonymous. For example, the AGS Position Statement on V.A.E. and a recent article by Teno and Lynn in the *Journal of the American Geriatrics Society* both reject easing restrictions on V.A.E. and assisted suicide while making arguments *only* against euthanasia.[1,2] The National Hospice Organization also opposes euthanasia and assisted suicide, but it, too, appears to blur the distinction between them in stating that "euthanasia encompasses . . . in some settings, physician-assisted suicide."[3] Others appear to use the terms euthanasia and assisted suicide synonymously in arguing against both.

In contrast, the AMA Ethics and Health Policy Counsel argues against physician-assisted suicide and distinguishes this from euthanasia.[4] The AMA Council on Ethical and Judicial Affairs also acknowledges there is "an ethically relevant distinction between euthanasia and assisted suicide that makes assisted suicide a more attractive option." Yet it then goes on to assert that "the ethical concerns about physician-assisted suicide are similar to those of euthanasia since both are essentially interventions intended to cause death."[5]

In order to weigh and appreciate the merits of the different arguments for and against V.A.E. and physician-assisted suicide, it is critical that appropriate distinctions be made. For example, we believe the arguments made in the references cited above and by others[6,7] against euthanasia are telling. However, we find that these same arguments are substantially weaker when used against assisted suicide. And while we agree with the AMA Council on Ethical and Judicial Affairs that an ethically relevant distinction exists between euthanasia and assisted suicide, we think it is important to distinguish further between different forms of

From David T. Watts and Timothy Howell, "Assisted Suicide Is Not Voluntary Active Euthanasia," *Journal of the American Geriatrics Society* 40 (1992): 1043–1046.

assisted suicide. Only by doing so can we begin to sort out some of the apparent confusion in attitudes toward these issues. We caution our readers that the literature on this topic, while growing, remains preliminary, with little empirical research yet completed. Our arguments, however, are philosophical in nature and do not ultimately stand or fall on empirical data.

DEFINITIONS

Voluntary active euthanasia: Administration of medications or other interventions intended to cause death at a patient's request.

Assisted suicide: Provision of information, means, or direct assistance by which a patient may take his or her own life. Assisted suicide involves several possible levels of assistance: *providing information,* for example, may mean providing toxicological information or describing techniques by which someone may commit suicide; *providing the means* can involve written prescriptions for lethal amounts of medication; *supervising or directly aiding* includes inserting an intravenous line and instructing on starting a lethal infusion.

These levels of assistance have very different implications. Providing only information or means allows individuals to retain the greatest degree of control in choosing the time and mode of their deaths. Physician participation is only indirect. This type of limited assistance is exemplified by the widely reported case of Dr. Timothy Quill, who prescribed a lethal quantity of barbiturates at the request of one of his patients who had leukemia.[8] By contrast, supervising or directly aiding is the type of physician involvement characterizing the case of Dr. Jack Kevorkian and Janet Adkins. Adkins was a 54-year-old woman with a diagnosis of Alzheimer-type dementia who sought Kevorkian's assistance in ending her life. Dr. Kevorkian inserted an intravenous catheter and instructed Mrs. Adkins on activating a lethal infusion of potassium following barbiturate sedation, a process personally monitored by Kevor-

kian. This form of assisted suicide carries significant potential for physician influence or control of the process, and from it there is only a relatively short step to physician initiation (i.e., active euthanasia). We therefore reject physician-supervised suicide for the arguments commonly made against V.A.E., namely, that legalization would have serious adverse consequences, including potential abuse of vulnerable persons, mistrust of physicians, and diminished availability of supportive services for the dying.[2,3,5–7] We find each of these arguments, however, insufficient when applied to more limited forms of physician-assisted suicide (i.e., providing information or means).

WILL ASSISTED SUICIDE LEAD TO ABUSE OF VULNERABLE PERSONS?

A major concern is that some patients will request euthanasia or assisted suicide out of convenience to others.[2,4] It is certainly possible that a patient's desire to avoid being a burden could lead to such a request. With euthanasia, there is danger that a patient's request might find too ready acceptance. With assisted suicide, however, the ultimate decision, and the ultimate action, are the patient's, not the physician's. This places an important check and balance on physician initiation or patient acquiescence in euthanasia. As the AMA Council on Ethical and Judicial Affairs acknowledges, a greater level of patient autonomy is afforded by physician-assisted suicide than by euthanasia.[5]

Culturally or socially mediated requests for assisted suicide would remain a significant concern. Patients might also request aid in suicide out of fear, pain, ambivalence, or depression. The requirement that patients commit the ultimate act themselves cannot alone provide a sufficient safeguard. It would be incumbent on physicians to determine, insofar as possible, that requests for assisted suicide were not unduly influenced and that reversible conditions were optimally treated. As to how physicians might respond to such requests, data from the Netherlands indicate that about 75% of euthanasia requests in that country are refused.[9] It is our impression that most requests for assisted suicide, therefore, appear to represent opportunities for improved symptom control. We believe most serious requests would likely come from patients experiencing distressing symptoms of terminal illness.[10] By opening the door for counseling or treatment of reversible conditions, requests for assisted suicide might actually lead to averting some suicides which would have otherwise occurred.

Another concern regarding euthanasia is that it could come to be accepted without valid consent and that such a practice would more likely affect the frail and impoverished. The Remmelink Commission's investigation of euthanasia in the Netherlands appeared to justify such concerns in estimating that Dutch physicians may have performed 1,000 acts of involuntary euthanasia involving incompetent individuals.[11] But while euthanasia opens up the possibility of invalid consent, with assisted suicide consent is integral to the process. Because the choice of action clearly rests with the individual, there is substantially less likelihood for the abuse of assisted suicide as a societal vehicle for cost containment. And there is little basis for assuming that requests for assisted suicide would come primarily from frail and impoverished persons. Prolonged debilitation inherent in many illnesses is familiar to an increasing number of patients, family members, and health professionals. Such illnesses represent a greater financial threat to the middle- and upper-middle class, since the poor and disenfranchised have less to spend down to indigency. Thus, we suspect requests for assisted suicide might actually be more common from the educated, affluent, and outspoken.

Patients diagnosed with terminal or debilitating conditions are often vulnerable. We agree that such patients might request assisted suicide out of fear of pain, suffering, or isolation, and that too ready acceptance of such requests could be disastrous. Yet, we believe that patients' interests can be safeguarded by requirements for persistent, competent requests as well as thorough assessments

for conditions, such as clinical depression, which could be reversed, treated, or ameliorated. Foley recently outlined an approach to the suicidal cancer patient.[12] We share her view that many such patients' requests to terminate life are altered by the availability of expert, continuing hospice services. We concur with Foley and others in calling for the wider availability of such services,[1,2] so that requests for assisted suicide arising from pain, depression, or other distressing symptoms can be reduced to a minimum.

WOULD ASSISTED SUICIDE UNDERMINE TRUST BETWEEN PATIENTS AND PHYSICIANS?

The cardinal distinction between V.A.E. and assisted suicide is that V.A.E. is killing by physicians, while suicide is self-killing. Prohibiting both euthanasia and physician-supervised suicide (i.e., with direct physician involvement) should diminish worries that patients might have about physicians wrongly administering lethal medicine. At present, physician-patient trust is compromised by widespread concern that physicians try too hard to keep dying patients alive. The very strength of the physician-patient relationship has been cited as a justification for physician involvement in assisted suicide.[13]

A number of ethicists have expressed concern that both euthanasia and assisted suicide, if legalized, would have a negative impact on the way society perceives the role of physicians.[2,4,6,7] Limited forms of assisted suicide, however, have been viewed more positively.[14] Public and professional attitudes appear to be evolving on this issue. A 1990 Gallup poll found that 66% of respondents believed someone in great pain, with "no hope of improvement," had the moral right to commit suicide; in 1975 the figure was 41%.[15] A panel of distinguished physicians has stated that it is not immoral for a physician to assist in the rational suicide of a terminally ill person.[16] The recent publication of a book on techniques of committing or assisting suicide evoked wide interest and significant support for the right of people to take control of their dying.[17] For a significant segment of society, physician involvement in assisted suicide may be welcomed, not feared. Furthermore, while relatively few might be likely to seek assistance with suicide if stricken with a debilitating illness, a substantial number might take solace knowing they could request such assistance.

There is another argument raised against V.A.E. that we believe also falters when used to object to assisted suicide. It has been maintained that prohibiting euthanasia forces physicians to focus on the humane care of dying patients, including meticulous attention to their symptoms.[2,10] This argument implies that physicians find it easier to relieve the suffering of dying patients by ending their lives rather than attempting the difficult task of palliating their symptoms. But for some patients, the suffering may not be amenable to even the most expert palliation. Even in such instances, some argue that limited forms of assisted suicide should be prohibited on the grounds that not to forbid them would open the door for more generalized, less stringent applications of assisted suicide.

To us, this "slippery slope" argument seems to imply that the moral integrity of the medical profession must be maintained, even if at the cost of prolonged, unnecessary suffering by at least some dying patients. We believe such a posture is itself inhumane and not acceptable. It contradicts a fundamental principle that is an essential ingredient of physician-patient trust: that patient comfort should be a primary goal of the physician in the face of incurable illness. Furthermore, by allowing limited physician involvement in assisted suicide, physicians can respect both the principle of caring that guides them and the patients for whom caring alone is insufficient. We concede that there is another alternative: terminally ill patients who cannot avoid pain while awake may be given continuous anesthetic levels of medication.[2] But this is exactly the sort of dying process we believe many in our society want to avoid.

WILL ASSISTED SUICIDE AND EUTHANASIA WEAKEN SOCIETAL RESOLVE TO INCREASE RESOURCES ALLOCATED TO CARE OF THE DYING?

This argument assumes that V.A.E. and assisted suicide would both be widely practiced, and that their very availability would decrease tangible concern for those not choosing euthanasia or suicide. However, euthanasia is rarely requested even by terminal cancer patients.[2] In the Netherlands, euthanasia accounts for less than 2% of all deaths.[9] These data suggest that even if assisted suicide were available to those with intractable pain or distressing terminal conditions, it would likely be an option chosen by relatively few. With assisted suicide limited to relatively few cases, this argument collapses. For with only a few requesting assisted suicide, the vast number of patients with debilitating illnesses would be undiminished, and their numbers should remain sufficient to motivate societal concern for their needs. Furthermore, to withhold assisted suicide from the few making serious, valid requests would be to subordinate needlessly the interests of these few to those of the many. Compounding their tragedy would be the fact that these individuals could not even benefit from any increase in therapeutic resources prompted by their suffering, insofar as their conditions are, by definition, not able to be ameliorated.

CONCLUSION

We have argued that assisted suicide and voluntary active euthanasia are different and that each has differing implications for medical practice and society. Further discussion should consider the merits and disadvantages of each, a process enhanced by contrasting them. We have further argued that different forms of assisted suicide can be distinguished both clinically and philosophically. Although some may argue that all forms of assisted suicide are fundamentally the same, we believe the differences can be contrasted as starkly as a written prescription and a suicide machine.

We do not advocate ready acceptance of requests for suicide, nor do we wish to romanticize the concept of rational suicide.[18] In some situations, however, where severe debilitating illness cannot be reversed, suicide may represent a rational choice. If this is the case, then physician assistance could make the process more humane. Along with other geriatricians, we often face dilemmas involving the management of chronic illnesses in late life. We believe we can best serve our patients, and preserve their trust, by respecting their desire for autonomy, dignity, and quality, not only of life, but of dying.

REFERENCES

1. AGS Public Policy Committee. Voluntary active euthanasia. J Am Geriatr Soc 1991;39:826.

2. Teno J, Lynn J. Voluntary active euthanasia: The individual case and public policy. J Am Geriatr Soc 1991;39:827–830.

3. National Hospice Organization. Statement of the National Hospice Organization Opposing the Legalization of Euthanasia and Assisted Suicide. Arlington, VA: National Hospice Organization, 1991.

4. Orentlicher D. Physician participation in assisted suicide. JAMA 1989;262:1844–1845.

5. AMA. Report of the Council on Ethical and Judicial Affairs: Decisions Near the End of Life. Chicago, IL: American Medical Association, 1991.

6. Singer PA. Should doctors kill patients? Can Med Assoc J 1988;138:1000–1001.

7. Singer PA, Siegler M. Euthanasia—a critique. N Engl J Med 1990,322:1881–1883.

8. Quill TE. Death and dignity: A case of individualized decision making. N Engl J Med 1991;324:691–694.

9. Van der Maas PJ, Van Delden JJM, Pijnenborg L, Looman CWN. Euthanasia and other medical decisions concerning the end of life. Lancet 1991;338:669–74.

10. Palmore EB. Arguments for assisted suicide (letter). Gerontologist 1991;31:854.

11. Karel R. Undertreatment of pain, depression needs to be addressed before euthanasia made legal in U.S. Psychiatric News, December 20, 1991, pp 5, 13, 23.

12. Foley KM. The relationship of pain and symptom management to patient requests for physician-assisted suicide. J Pain Symptom Manag 1991;6:289–297.

13. Jecker NS. Giving death a hand. When the dying and the doctor stand in a special relationship. J Am Geriatr Soc 1991;39:831–835.

14. American College of Physicians. ACP to DA, Grand Jury: Dr. Quill acted "humanely." ACP Observer, September, 1991, p. 5.

15. Ames K, Wilson L, Sawhill R et al. Last rights. Newsweek August 26, 1991, pp. 40–41.

16. Wanzer SH, Federman DD, Adelstein SJ et al. The physician's responsibility toward hopelessly ill patients: A second look. N Engl J Med 1989;320:844–849.

17. Humphry D. Final Exit: The Practicalities of Self-Deliverance and Assisted Suicide for the Dying. Eugene, OR: The Hemlock Society, (distributed by Carol Publishing, Secaucus, NJ), 1991.

18. Conwell Y, Caine ED. Rational suicide and the right to die: Reality and myth. N Engl J Med 1991;325:1100–1103.

READING QUESTIONS

1. How do Watts and Howell define voluntary active euthanasia and assisted suicide?
2. What are the three levels of assistance a physician can provide in cases of physician-assisted suicide according to Watts and Howell?
3. Explain the three arguments normally used against voluntary active euthanasia that Watts and Howell claim are not compelling when applied to cases of physician-assisted suicide.
4. What arguments do Watts and Howell give against the claims that assisted suicide will lead to abuse of vulnerable persons and will undermine trust between patients and physicians?

DISCUSSION QUESTIONS

1. How might opponents of voluntary active euthanasia and assisted suicide respond to Watt's and Howell's claim that physician involvement is merely indirect in any of the three levels of assistance?
2. Consider whether there are any other potential problems that might be associated with physician-assisted suicide that Watts and Howell do not mention or address.
3. Discuss whether Watts and Howell are correct to draw the distinctions they do between voluntary active euthanasia and physician-assisted suicide.

ADDITIONAL RESOURCES

Web Resources

Pew Research Center <http://pewresearch.org/>. A nonpartisan site that conducts public opinion polls on public policy issues. One can find numerous links from this site to articles about attitudes toward physician-assisted suicide.

Young, Robert, "Voluntary Euthanasia," <http://plato.stanford.edu/entries/voluntary-euthanasia/>. An overview of the debate over voluntary euthanasia.

Authored Books

Dworkin, Gerald, R. G. Frey, and Sissela Bok (eds.) *Euthanasia and Physician Assisted Suicide: For and Against* (Cambridge: Cambridge University Press, 1998). In this two part book Dworkin and Frey defend the practices of euthanasia and physician-assisted suicide, and Bok argues against these practices.

Keown, John, *Euthanasia, Ethics and Public Policy: An Argument Against Legalisation* (Cambridge: Cambridge University Press, 2002). As the title indicates, Keown makes a case for not legalizing euthanasia and assisted suicide.

Edited Collections & Articles

Battin, Margaret P., Rosamond Rhodes, and Anita Silvers (eds.), *Physician Assisted Suicide: Expanding the Debate* (New York: Routledge, 1998). This collection features 23 essays, mostly by philosophers, debating the moral, social, and legal implications of physician-assisted suicide. The essays are organized into five parts: (1) Conceptual Issues, (2) Considering Those at Risk, (3) Considering the Practice of Medicine, (4) Considering the Impact of Legalization, and (5) Considering Religious Perspectives.

Birnbacher, Dieter, and Edgar Dahl (eds.), *Giving Death a Helping Hand: Physician-Assisted Suicide and Public Policy: An International Perspective*. International Library of Ethics, Law, and the New Medicine. (New York: Springer, 2008). This anthology includes 13 essays by a broad array of authors, including academics and health care practitioners, and incorporates various international perspectives on physician-assisted suicide.

Hastings Center Report, vol. 22, March–April, 1992. This issue of HCR includes the entire version of Dan Brock's defense of voluntary active euthanasia, an excerpt of which is included in this chapter. Brock's position is opposed in an essay by Daniel Callahan in that same issue.

Moreno, Jonathan D. (ed.), *Arguing Euthanasia: The Controversy Over Mercy Killing, Assisted Suicide, And The "Right To Die"* (New York: Touchstone, 1995). This collection features both outspoken advocates and critics debating the moral and social implications of euthanasia and assisted suicide.

8 } The Ethical Treatment of Animals

Nonhuman animals are used by humans as sources of food, clothing, entertainment, experimentation, and companionship. Most everyone thinks that there are moral limits to how we use animals, that cruelty to animals is morally wrong. To take one recent instance, in 2004, California governor Arnold Schwarzenegger signed into law a bill which, when it takes effect, will completely ban the production and sale of foie gras in California. Considered a gourmet delicacy, foie gras (French for "fatty liver") is produced by force-feeding ducks or geese so that their livers enlarge up to ten times their normal size. In the process, these animals experience ruptured necks as well as painful enlargement and rupturing of internal organs owing to the intense pressure caused by the forced feeding. Other cases are more difficult. In 2008 U.S. military researchers dressed pigs in armor and subjected them to various explosions in order to study the link between roadside bombs and brain damage. The point of the study, of course, was to help benefit U.S. soldiers fighting in Iraq and Afghanistan. Pigs were selected because their brains, hearts, and lungs are similar to those of humans. Are such experiments aimed at benefitting humans morally justified? Furthermore, what about the many other uses humans have for (nonhuman) animals, uses that do not necessarily inflict extreme pain on animals? Is there anything wrong with, say, painlessly killing and eating an animal for the taste of the meat?

In order to properly focus the ethical dispute over the use of animals, let us consider these two questions:

- Do any animals have direct moral standing?
- If so, what does this imply about various practices such as eating meat and using animals as subjects for experimentation?

In order to introduce the readings in this chapter, let us first explain what is meant in the first question by talk of "direct moral standing."

1. DIRECT MORAL STANDING

For purposes of introducing the selections both in this chapter and in the next, let us distinguish between two types of moral standing: *direct* and *indirect*. Roughly, for something to have **direct moral standing** is for it, independently of its relation to other things or creatures, to possess features in virtue of which it deserves to be given moral consideration by agents who are capable of making moral choices. Different moral theories represent direct moral standing in different ways. To claim that a creature has rights is one way of explaining how it is that it has direct moral standing. So is the claim that something has intrinsic or inherent value. And to claim that we have duties *to* something and not just duties *with regard* to it is yet another way of representing the idea that the item in question has direct moral standing. Of course, if something has direct moral standing—whether because it has rights, intrinsic value, or is something toward which we have duties—there must be some features or properties of the item in question in virtue of which it has such standing. Just what those features are is what is most philosophically contentious in debates about the ethical treatment of animals. As we shall see in the next chapter, this same general issue arises in the controversy over abortion.

Direct moral standing contrasts with indirect moral standing. For something to have mere **indirect moral standing** is for it to deserve moral consideration only because it is related to something with direct moral standing. Such items, including most obviously one's material possessions, do not themselves have features that would make taking, changing, or destroying them a wrong that is done *to or against* them. Rather, whatever moral requirements we have *with regard to* our treatment of material possessions is dependent upon their relation to beings that have direct moral standing.

As mentioned at the outset of this chapter, most everyone agrees that animals ought not to be treated cruelly. But being against the cruel treatment of animals does not require one to think that they have direct moral standing. The real philosophical dispute, then, which is reflected in the first question listed earlier, is whether any of them have what we are calling direct moral standing. If they do, then presumably it will be possible to launch arguments against various forms of treatment including killing and eating them and using them for certain sorts of experimentation.[1] But do they?

2. SPECIESISM?

Racism and sexism are familiar forms of morally unjustified prejudice. These practices involve the systematic discrimination against the interests of members of some racial groups because of their race in the case of racism and against the members of one sex because of their sex in the case of sexism, respectively. Because people of all races and both men and women have direct moral standing, the sort of discrimination characteristic of racism and sexism is morally unjustified. These types of discrimination are the subject of chapter 6.

The basic idea of systematic discrimination against the interests of members of some group has been extended by some philosophers to the treatment of animals. **Speciesism**, then, refers to the systematic discrimination against the members of some species by the members of another species. And certainly such discrimination goes on today. But whether such discrimination is morally wrong depends upon such questions as whether any of the nonhuman animals who are the victims of discrimination have direct moral standing. The articles included in this chapter are focused on this central issue.

3. THEORY MEETS PRACTICE

In our chapter's readings, we find appeals to consequentialism, rights, the ethics of prima facie duty, and virtue ethics prominent in debates about the ethical treatment of animals. Let us briefly consider each of these approaches.

Consequentialism

Utilitarianism is the most familiar form of consequentialism that has played an important role in arguments over the ethical treatment of animals. According to one standard version of the principle of utility, an action is wrong just in case (and because) performing it will likely fail to maximize happiness impartially considered. Moreover, for traditional utilitarians, happiness (and unhappiness) over a period of time in a creature's life is a matter of its experiences of pleasure and experiences of displeasure or pain. Further, since many nonhuman animals can experience pleasure and pain, these utilitarians conclude that they have direct moral standing and must be factored into our decision making. Utilitarian arguments, of course, depend heavily on factual claims about the overall comparative effects of contemplated courses of action. Gaverick Matheny argues on utilitarian grounds that when we estimate overall net happiness for all sentient creatures, we ought to conclude that many of our present practices involving the use of animals are morally wrong. Critics of this line of argument, whether or not they share a commitment to utilitarianism, challenge the utility calculation. In our readings, Tom Regan and Jordan Curnutt raise this calculation worry. And, of course, there are those who reject a strictly utilitarian approach to moral issues.

Rights Approaches

According to a rights-focused approach that would accord animals direct moral standing, the nonhuman animals in question possess the relevant characteristics that qualify them for having rights, including a right to life, to some kinds of liberty, and perhaps to whatever kind of life would allow them some measure of happiness. This approach is famously defended by Tom Regan, but its plausibility requires a defense of the nature of rights, their content, and their relative strengths—topics that are controversial. Carl Cohen argues that Regan's defense fails and that moral rights remain exclusively within the human realm. Mary Ann Warren attempts to answer various questions about rights, arguing that although animals do have rights and thus have direct moral standing, their rights are generally weaker than the corresponding rights of human beings. Nevertheless, disputes over basic questions about rights are often taken as a sticking point for rights-based approaches to the ethical treatment of animals.

Ethics of Prima Facie Duty

One might attempt to dodge the worries just raised against utilitarian and rights approaches by working with an ethic of prima facie duty. Certainly, if there are prima facie duties, one of them is the duty not to cause harm. And in our readings, Jordan Curnutt appeals to this duty in his defense of vegetarianism. His argument, then, requires defending certain factual claims about animals (they can be harmed), as well as claims about their treatment in meat production. Furthermore, since the whole point of a duty's being prima facie is that it can be overridden, Curnutt's argument requires defense of the claim (which he offers) that the prima facie duty not to harm, as applied to animals, is not overridden by various competing concerns.

Virtue Ethics

Although none of the readings in this chapter appeal to a virtue-based moral theory and its application to the ethical treatment of animals, the article by Thomas E. Hill Jr. in the final chapter on the environment does take a virtue approach to environmental issues. His approach, which appeals specifically to vices that represent a lack of the virtue of humility, could easily be extended to the case of animals.

NOTE

1. Although, even if some animals do have direct moral standing, it does not automatically fol-low that using them for such things as food and experimentation is wrong. For instance, direct moral standing may come in degrees so that the members of some species only have it to some small degree, in which case perhaps their use by humans under certain circumstances is not, all things considered, morally wrong.

GAVERICK MATHENY

Utilitarianism and Animals

Matheny defends what he calls a "strong principle of equal consideration of interests" according to which, in making correct moral decisions, one must give equal weight to the like interests of all creatures who will be affected by one's actions. Given that many nonhu-man animals have interests, it follows from the principle just mentioned that they deserve to have their interests in being free from pain and suffering count as much as the like interests of human beings. Matheny proceeds to explain what implications his principle has for such practices as meat eating, experimental use of animal subjects, and our treatment of wildlife.

Recommended Reading: consequentialism, chap. 1, sec. 2A.

Gaverick Matheny, "Utilitarianism and Animals," in Peter Singer, ed., *In Defense of Animals: The Second Wave* (Oxford: Blackwell Publishing, 2006).

In North America and Europe, around 17 billion land animals were raised and killed during 2001 to feed us. Somewhere between 50 and 100 million other animals were killed in laboratories, while another 30 million were killed in fur farms. The vast majority of these animals were forced to live and die in conditions most of us would find morally repugnant. Yet their use—and the use of comparable numbers of animals every year—has been justified by the belief that nonhuman animals do not deserve significant moral consideration. Several plausible ethical theories argue that this belief is mistaken. Utilitarianism is one such theory that condemns much of our present use of animals. If this theory is reasonable, then most of us should change the way we live.

ETHICS

There is broad consensus within both religious and secular ethics that an ethical life respects virtues like fairness, justice, and benevolence. At the heart of these virtues lies a more basic principle: I cannot reasonably claim that my interests matter more than yours simply because my interests are *mine*. My interests may matter more to *me*, but I cannot claim they matter more in any objective sense. From the ethical point of view, everyone's interests deserve equal consideration.

In the Judeo-Christian tradition, this sentiment is embodied in "The Golden Rule" attributed to Moses: "Love your neighbor as you love yourself" (Matthew 22:39) and in the Talmud, "What is hateful to you, do not to your fellow men" (Shabbat 31a). In the secular tradition, this sentiment is embodied in the "principle of equal consideration of interests": "Act in such a way that the like interests of everyone affected by your action are given equal weight." This phrase may lack the elegance of Scripture but conveys the same general idea. The principle of equal consideration of interests asks that we put ourselves in the shoes of each person affected by an action and compare the strengths of her or his interests to those of our own—regardless of *whose* interests they are. To be

fair, just, and benevolent, any ethical rule we adopt should respect this principle.

UTILITARIANISM

Utilitarianism is an ethical theory with the rule, "act in such a way as to maximize the expected satisfaction of interests in the world, equally considered." This rule is a logical extension of the principle of equal consideration of interests in that it says I should sum up the interests of all the parties affected by all my possible actions and choose the action that results in the greatest net satisfaction of interests. Another way of thinking about this is to imagine which actions I would choose if I had to live the lives of all those affected by me. Because the rule of utilitarianism represents a simple operation upon a principle of equality, it is perhaps the most minimal ethical rule we could derive. Utilitarianism is said to be universalist, welfarist, consequentialist, and aggregative. Each of these properties needs some explanation.

Utilitarianism is *universalist* because it takes into account the interests of all those who are affected by an action, regardless of their nationality, gender, race, or other traits that we find, upon reflection, are not morally relevant. The rule "act in such a way as to maximize the expected satisfaction of interests" is one we would be willing to have everyone adopt. Some writers have even claimed, forcefully, this is the only such rule.

Utilitarianism is *welfarist* because it defines what is ethically "good" in terms of people's welfare, which we can understand as the satisfaction (or dissatisfaction) of people's interests. Most of us are interested in good health, a good job, and our friends and family, among other things. We could reduce many if not all of these interests to something more general, such as an interest in a happy, pleasurable, relatively painless life. I will use the word "interests" to describe whatever it is that we value here—all those things that matter to us. We can safely say we all have an interest, at a minimum, in a pleasurable life, relatively free of pain. And from experience, we know when our happiness is decreased, as when we suffer acute pain, any other interests we may have tend to recede into the background. That being so, utilitarianism promotes an ethical rule that seeks to satisfy our interests, particularly those in a pleasurable, relatively painless life.

Utilitarianism is *consequentialist* because it evaluates the rightness or wrongness of an action by that action's expected consequences: the degree to which an action satisfies interests. These consequences can often be predicted and compared accurately with little more than common sense.

Finally, utilitarianism is said to be *aggregative* because it adds up the interests of all those affected by an action. To make a decision, I need to weigh the intensity, duration, and number of interests affected by all of my possible actions. I choose the action that results in the greatest net satisfaction of interests—"the greatest good for the greatest number." Utilitarian decisions thus involve a kind of accounting ledger, with our like interests serving as a common currency. This is no easy exercise. But, as we'll see, in many of our most important moral judgments, even a rough comparison of interests is enough to make a wise decision.

THE ADVANTAGES OF UTILITARIANISM

Utilitarianism has several advantages over other ethical theories. First, its consequentialism encourages us to make full use of information about the world as it is. If you have access to the same information as I do, you can argue with me about how I ought to act. This lends utilitarianism a greater degree of empirical objectivity than most ethical theories enjoy.

Some ethical theories hold less regard for consequences than does utilitarianism and address their ethical rules either to actions themselves or to the motivations prompting them. These rules would often lead to misery if they were followed without exception. For instance, we would not have praised Miep Gies, the woman who hid Anne Frank and

her family from the Nazis, had she followed the rule "never tell a lie" and turned the Franks over to the Nazis. Most of us believe the kind of deception Gies engaged in was justified, even heroic. So when should you tell a lie? When the consequences of not telling the lie are worse than the consequences of telling it. To decide otherwise would be to engage in a kind of rule worship at the expense of other people's interests. Because we are often forced to choose between the lesser of two evils, any rule about particular actions—lying, promising, killing, and so on—can lead to terrible results.

At the same time, it would be foolhardy to live without any general principles. I would not be an efficient utilitarian if, every time I approached a stoplight, I weighed the consequences of respecting traffic laws. This would waste time and regularly lead to poor results. It would be best if I adopted "rules of thumb" that, in general, promote the greatest satisfaction of interests by guiding my actions in ordinary situations. Such rules of thumb would likely include most of our common views about right and wrong. However, in extraordinary situations, these rules of thumb should be overridden, as in the case of Miep Gies. In this way, utilitarianism supports most of our common moral intuitions while, at the same time, overriding them in important cases where following them could be catastrophic.

Utilitarianism's aggregative properties offer additional advantages. Our moral decisions regularly benefit one individual at the expense or neglect of another. For instance, in North America and Europe, some citizens are taxed in order to provide financial support to the disabled, among others. Is it ethical to benefit one group with this tax while another suffers some expense? While such conflicts arise regularly in public policy, they also arise in our personal choices. In deciding to spend $1,000 on a piece of artwork instead of on a donation to a charity, I know a charity now has less money with which to help those in need than it would had I given it my $1,000. Is it ethical to have benefited myself while neglecting others? Utilitarianism, in allowing some exchange of costs and benefits, can help us answer questions like these, whereas many other ethical theories cannot.

Many of the moral stances implied by utilitarianism are familiar and widely accepted. Historically, utilitarians were among the most outpoken opponents of slavery and the strongest proponents of women's suffrage, public education, public health, and other social democratic institutions. In recent years, utilitarians have advanced some of the strongest moral arguments for charity to the poor and sick. At the same time, however, utilitarianism leads us to moral views many of us do not already accept. Prominent among these are moral views regarding nonhuman animals.

DO ANY NONHUMANS HAVE INTERESTS?

By the principle of equal consideration of interests, interests matter, regardless of *whose* interests they are. We can agree that we all have an interest, at a minimum, in a pleasurable life, relatively free of pain. Pleasure and pain *matter* to all of us who feel them. As such, it follows that we are obliged to consider, at a minimum, the interests of all those who are capable of feeling pleasure and pain—that is, all those who are sentient. We can then say that sentience is a sufficient condition for having interests and having those interests considered equally.

Are any nonhuman animals sentient? That is, are any nonhumans biologically capable of feeling pleasure and pain? There are few people today, including biologists, who seriously doubt the answer is yes. For most of us, our common sense and experience with animals, especially dogs and cats, are sufficient to let us answer affirmatively. However, our common sense and experience cannot always be trusted, and so we should look for further evidence that animals other than ourselves are sentient.

How do we know that other *human beings* are sentient? We cannot know for certain. My friend who shrieks after burning himself on the stove could be a very sophisticated robot, programmed to respond to certain kinds of stimuli with a shriek. But, because my friend is biologically similar to me, his awareness of pain would offer a biological advantage, his behavior is similar to my own when I am in pain, and his behavior is associated with a stimulus that would be painful for me, I have good reason to believe my friend feels pain.

We have similar reasons for believing that many nonhuman animals feel pain. Human beings evolved from other species. Those parts of the brain involved in sensing pleasure and pain are older than human beings and common to mammals and birds, and probably also to fish, reptiles, and amphibians. For most of these animals, awareness of pain would serve important functions, including learning from past mistakes.

Like my potentially robotic friend, these animals also respond to noxious stimuli much the same way we do. They avoid these stimuli and shriek, cry, or jerk when they can't escape them. The stimuli that cause these behaviors are ones we associate with pain, such as extreme pressure, heat, and tissue damage. These biological and behavioral indications do not guarantee sentience, but they are about as good as those that we have for my human friend.

Whether invertebrates such as insects feel pain is far less certain, as these animals do not possess the same equipment to feel pain and pleasure that we have; and, by their having short life-cycles in stereotyped environments, the biological advantages of being sentient are less obvious.

That some nonhuman animals feel pain needn't imply that their *interests* in not feeling pain are as intense as our own. It's possible that ordinary, adult humans are capable of feeling more intense pain than some nonhumans because we are self-conscious and can anticipate or remember pain with greater fidelity than can other animals. It could also be argued, however, that our rationality allows us to distance ourselves from pain or give pain a purpose (at the dentist's office, for instance) in ways that are not available to other animals. Moreover, even if other animals' interests in not feeling pain are less intense than our own, the sum of a larger number of interests of lesser intensity (such as 100,000 people's interests in $1 each) can still outweigh the sum of a smaller number of interests of greater intensity (such as my interest in $100,000).

So it is possible, even in those cases where significant human interests are at stake, for the interests of animals, considered equally, to outweigh our own. As we will see, however, in most cases involving animals, there are no significant human interests at stake, and the right course of action is easy to judge.

SOME REBUTTALS

Philosophers have never been immune to the prejudices of their day. In the past, some advanced elaborate arguments against civil rights, religious tolerance, and the abolition of slavery. Similarly, some philosophers today seek to justify our current prejudices against nonhuman animals, typically not by challenging the claim that some nonhumans are sentient, but rather by arguing that sentience is not a sufficient condition for moral consideration. Common to their arguments is the notion that moral consideration should be extended only to those individuals who also possess certain levels of rationality, intelligence, or language, or to those capable of reciprocating moral agreements, which likewise implies a certain level of rationality, intelligence, or language.

It is not clear how these arguments could succeed. First, why would an animal's lack of normal human levels of rationality, intelligence, or language give us license to ignore her or his pain? Second, if rationality, intelligence, or language were necessary conditions for moral consideration, why could we not give moral preference to humans who are more rational, intelligent, or verbose than other humans? Third, many adult mammals and birds exhibit greater rationality and intelligence than do human infants. Some nonhuman animals, such as apes, possess language, while some humans do not. Should human infants, along with severely retarded and brain-damaged humans, be excluded from moral consideration, while apes, dolphins, dogs, pigs, parrots, and other nonhumans are included? Efforts to limit moral consideration to human beings based on the possession of certain traits succeed neither in including all humans nor in excluding all nonhuman animals.

The most obvious property shared among all human beings that excludes all nonhuman animals is our membership of a particular biological group: the species *Homo sapiens*. What is significant about species membership that could justify broad differences in moral consideration? Why is the line drawn at species, rather than genus, subspecies, or some other biological division? There have been no convincing answers to these questions. If species membership is a justification for excluding sentient animals from moral consideration, then why not race or gender? Why could one not argue that an individual's membership of the biological group "human female" excludes that individual from moral consideration? One of the triumphs of modern ethics has been recognizing that an individual's membership of a group, alone, is not morally relevant. The cases against racism and sexism depended upon this point, as the case against speciesism does now.

If a nonhuman animal can feel pleasure and pain, then that animal possesses interests. To think otherwise is to pervert the sense in which we understand pleasure and pain, feelings that matter to us and to others who experience them. At a minimum, a sentient animal has an interest in a painless, pleasurable life. And if he or she possesses this interest, then he or she deserves no less consideration of his or her interests than we give to our own. This view, while modern in its popularity, is not new. The utilitarian Jeremy Bentham held it at a time when black slaves were treated much as we now treat nonhuman animals:

> The day may come when the rest of the animal creation may acquire those rights which never could have been witholden from them but by the hand of tyranny. The French have already discovered that the blackness of the skin is no reason why a human being should be abandoned without redress to the caprice of a tormentor. It may one day come to be recognized that the number of the legs, the villosity of the skin, or the termination of the *os sacrum*, are reasons equally insufficient for abandoning a sensitive being to the same fate. What else is it that should trace the insuperable line? Is it the faculty of reason, or perhaps the faculty

of discourse? But a full-grown horse or dog is beyond comparison a more rational, as well as a more conversable animal, than an infant of a day, or a week, or even a month, old. But suppose they were otherwise, what would it avail? The question is not, Can they reason? nor Can they talk? but, Can they suffer? (1988 [1823]: 1988: 310–11)

The principle of equal consideration of interests requires we count the interests of any individual equally with the like interests of any other. The racist violates this rule by giving greater weight to the interests of members of her own race. The sexist violates this rule by giving greater weight to the interests of members of his own sex. Similarly, the speciesist violates this rule by giving greater weight to the interests of members of his own species.

If an animal is sentient and if sentience is a sufficient condition for having interests, then we should consider that animal's interests equal to our own when making ethical decisions.… Animals are used in a wide range of human activities, including agriculture, product testing, medical and scientific research, entertainment, hunting and fishing, the manufacture of clothing, and as our pets. In most of these activities, we treat animals in ways that do not show proper regard for their interests and thereby are unethical. I will limit discussion here to our treatment of animals in agriculture, laboratories, and the wild.

FOOD

It is difficult…to convey factory farming practices in print, so I encourage you either to visit a factory farm or to watch video footage from these facilities at the website listed at the end of this essay. Factory farm conditions are believed by many to be so inhumane that it would be better if animals living in these facilities had not existed. Deciding what makes a life worth living is no simple matter, but we can think how we consider whether or not to euthanize a hopelessly sick dog or cat.

The pain experienced by animals in factory farms is likely greater than that experienced by many of those sick dogs and cats we choose to euthanize, as factory-farmed animals often experience an entire lifetime of pain, compared with a few weeks or months. If, for instance, we knew that our dog or cat would have no choice but to be confined in a cage so restrictive that turning around or freely stretching limbs is difficult if not impossible; live in his own excrement; be castrated or have her teeth, tail, or toes sliced off without anesthesia, I suspect most of us would believe that euthanizing the animal is the humane choice. It would be better, then, if farmed animals who endure these conditions did not exist.

One is hard-pressed to find, even among philosophers, any attempt to justify these conditions or the practice of eating factory-farmed animals. We have no nutritional need for animal products. In fact, vegetarians are, on average, healthier than those who eat meat. The overriding interest we have in eating animals is the pleasure we get from the taste of their flesh. However, there are a variety of vegetarian foods available, including ones that taste like animal products, from meat to eggs to milk, cheese, and yogurt. So, in order to justify eating animals, we would have to show that the pleasure gained from consuming them *minus* the pleasure gained from eating a vegetarian meal is greater than the pain caused by eating animals.

Whatever pleasure we gain from eating animals cannot be discounted. However, equal consideration of interests requires that we put ourselves in the place of a farmed animal as well as in the place of a meat-eater. Does the pleasure we enjoy from eating a chicken outweigh the pain we would endure were we to be raised and killed for that meal? We would probably conclude that our substantial interest in not being raised in a factory farm and slaughtered is stronger than our trivial interest in eating a chicken instead of chickpeas. There is, after all, no shortage of foods that we can eat that don't require an animal to suffer in a factory farm or slaughterhouse. That our trivial interest in the taste of meat now trumps the pain endured by 17 *billion* farmed animals may be some measure of how far we are from considering their interests equally.

Accordingly, equal consideration of interests requires that we abstain, at a minimum, from eating factory-farmed products—particularly poultry and eggs, products that seem to cause the most pain per unit of food. Ideally, we should not consume products from any animal that we believe is sentient. This is the least we can do to have any real regard for the pain felt by other animals. Eating animals is a habit for most of us and, like other habits, can be challenging to break. But millions of people have made the switch to a vegetarian diet and, as a result, have enjoyed better health and a clearer conscience.

The use of animals for food is by far the largest direct cause of animal abuse in North America and Europe; and our consumption of animal flesh, eggs, and milk probably causes more pain than any other action for which each of us is responsible. The average North American or European eats somewhere between 1,500 and 2,500 factory-farmed animals in his or her lifetime. If we ended our discussion here and all became vegans, we would effectively abolish 99 percent of the present use of animals. Still, there are other ways in which animals are abused that deserve discussion. The use of animals in laboratories, in particular, provides a testing ground for the principle of equal consideration of interests.

LABORATORIES

Somewhere between 50 and 100 million animals are killed each year in North American and European laboratories. As Richard Ryder (2006) describes, these include animals used in testing new products, formulations, and drugs as well as those used in medical and scientific research. U.S. law does not require research or testing facilities to report numbers of most of these animals—primarily rats, mice, and birds—so there is considerable uncertainty about the statistics.

There are potentially non-trivial benefits to human beings and other animals in using nonhuman animals for testing and in medical and veterinary research. That being so, utilitarianism cannot provide as simple an objection to the use of animals in experiments as it did to the use of animals for food. It can, however, provide a yardstick by which to judge whether a particular experiment is ethical.

We should first ask whether the experiment is worth conducting. Most product tests on animals involve household or personal care products that are only superficially different from existing products. How many different formulations of laundry detergent or shampoo does the world need? And much basic research involving animals may answer intellectually interesting questions but promise few benefits to either human or nonhuman animals. Do we need to know what happens to kittens after their eyes are removed at birth, or to monkeys when deprived of all maternal contact from infancy? In every case, we should ask if the pain prevented by an experiment is greater than the pain caused by that experiment. As experiments routinely involve thousands of animals with an uncertain benefit to any human or nonhuman animal, in most cases these experiments are not justified. It is difficult to imagine that the pain experienced by 100 million animals each year is *averting* an equivalent amount of pain.

However, if we believe that an experiment is justified on utilitarian grounds, there is another question we should ask to check our prejudices. Most adult mammals used in lab research—dogs, cats, mice, rabbits, rats, and primates—are more aware of what is happening to them than and at least as sensitive to pain as any human infant. Would researchers contemplating an animal experiment be willing, then, to place an orphaned human infant in the animal's place? If they are not, then their use of an animal is simple discrimination on the basis of species, which, as we found above, is morally unjustifiable. If the researchers are willing to place an infant in the animal's place, then they are at least morally consistent. Perhaps there are cases in which researchers believe an experiment is so valuable as to be worth an infant's life, but I doubt that many would make this claim.

WILDLIFE

Except for those hunted and fished, wild animals are often ignored in discussions of animal protection and seen as the domain of environmental protection.

Part of this neglect is probably justified. I would certainly choose to be an animal in the wild over being an animal in a factory farm. Nevertheless, animals in the wild deserve as much moral consideration as do those animals in farms or laboratories. Likewise, wild animals raise important questions for those interested, as we are, in the proper moral consideration of animals' interests.

There are few human activities that do not affect the welfare of wild animals. Particularly in developed countries, humans consume a tremendous amount of energy, water, land, timber, minerals, and other resources whose extraction or use damages natural habitats—killing or preventing from existing untold billions of wild animals. Many of these activities may well be justified. Nevertheless, most of us can take steps to reduce the impact we have on wild animals without sacrificing anything of comparable moral significance.

Most of these steps are familiar ones encouraged by environmental protection groups. We should drive less, use public transit more, adopt a vegetarian or preferably vegan diet, reduce our purchases of luxury goods, buy used rather than new items, and so on. For decades, environmentalists in Europe and North America have also encouraged couples to have smaller families. In Europe, it is not uncommon to find one-child families, and the same is beginning to be true in North America. Smaller families not only carry many social and economic advantages to parents and nations, they also significantly reduce the resources used and the number of animals threatened by human consumption. Of course, most of these measures help humans, too. Investments in family planning, for instance, are probably the most cost-effective measures to reduce global warming.

CONCLUSIONS

I have argued that utilitarianism is a reasonable ethical theory, that this theory includes animals in its moral consideration, and that it obliges us to make dramatic changes in our institutions and habits—most immediately, that we become vegetarian or preferably vegan. While my aim here has been to present a *utilitarian* argument, similar arguments regarding our mistreatment of animals have been put forward on the basis of all of the major secular and religious ethical theories.... But even less ambitious ethical arguments should convince us that much of our present treatment of animals is unethical.

Take, for instance, what I will call the "weak principle" of equal consideration of interests. Under the weak principle, we will consider the interests of non-human animals to be equal *only* to the like interests of other nonhuman animals. I don't believe there is any good reason to adopt the weak principle in place of the strong one discussed earlier. But, even if we were to adopt the weak principle, we would reach many of the same conclusions.

Almost all of us agree that we should treat dogs and cats humanely. There are few opponents, for instance, of current anti-cruelty laws aimed at protecting pets from abuse, neglect, or sport fighting. And therein lies a bizarre contradiction. For if these anti-cruelty laws applied to animals in factory farms or laboratories, the ways in which these animals are treated would be illegal throughout North America and Europe. Do we believe dogs and cats are so different from apes, pigs, cows, chickens, and rabbits that one group of animals—pets—deserve legal protection from human abuse, while the other group—animals in factory farms and in labs—deserve to have their abuse institutionalized? We cannot justify this contradiction by claiming that the abuse of farmed animals, for example, serves a purpose, whereas the abuse of pets does not. Arguably, the satisfaction enjoyed by someone who fights or otherwise abuses dogs and cats is just as great as that enjoyed by someone who eats meat.

What separates pets from the animals we abuse in factory farms and in labs is physical proximity. Our disregard for "food" or "lab" animals persists because we don't see them. Few people are aware of the ways in which they are mistreated and even fewer actually see the abuse. When people become aware, they are typically appalled—not because they have adopted a new ethical theory, but because they believe animals feel pain and they believe morally decent people should want to prevent pain whenever possible. The utilitarian argument for considering animals helps us to return to this common-sense view.

There are remarkably few contemporary defenses of our traditional treatment of animals. This may suggest that the principal obstacles to improving the treatment of animals are not philosophical uncertainties about their proper treatment but, rather, our ignorance about their current abuse and our reluctance to change deeply ingrained habits. Even the most reasonable among us is not invulnerable to the pressures of habit. Many moral philosophers who believe that eating animals is unethical continue to eat meat. This reflects the limits of reasoned argument in changing behavior. While I can't overcome those limits here, I encourage you, as you read this [chapter], to replace in your mind the animals being discussed with an animal familiar to you, such as a dog or cat, or, better yet, a human infant. If you do this, you are taking to heart the principle of equal consideration of interests and giving animals the consideration they deserve.

REFERENCES

Bentham, Jeremy (1988 [1828]) *The Principles of Morals and Legislation*, Amherst, N.Y.: Prometheus.

Ryder, Richard D. (2006) "Speciesism in the Laboratory," in *In Defense of Animals: The Second Wave*, P. Singer, ed., Oxford: Blackwell Publishing.

RECOMMENDATION

The reader is encouraged to watch video footage from factory farms such as *Meet Your Meat*. www.goveg.com/meetmeat.html.

READING QUESTIONS

1. Explain the basic ethical principle that Matheny focuses on in this article. What are some of the variations of this principle? Explain in particular the secular principle of equal consideration of interests.
2. How does Matheny define utilitarianism? Explain the four different properties of utilitarianism. What are the advantages of utilitarianism according to Matheny?
3. How does Matheny argue for the view that nonhuman animals have interests? What objections does he consider against his view and how does he respond to each objection?
4. What are some of the ways that we use and treat animals? Which of these are unethical according to Matheny? What arguments does he give to support his view that some of these practices are unethical?
5. Explain the utilitarian assessment offered by Matheny for whether experiments on nonhuman animals are worth conducting.

DISCUSSION QUESTIONS

1. Do any of the suggested advantages of utilitarianism introduce potential disadvantages for the view, especially as it relates to the treatment of nonhuman animals?
2. To what extent should the interests of nonhuman animals be taken into consideration in order to answer questions about how we ought to treat them? Should we adopt a strong or a weak principle of equal consideration of interests with respect to nonhuman animals?

Tom Regan

Are Zoos Morally Defensible?

Regan considers both utilitarian and rights approaches to the title question. He argues that because the utilitarian approach to the moral question about zoos requires far more information about the good and bad effects of zoos than can possibly be acquired, the view does not yield a determinate answer to the question. Regan favors the rights view according to which animals do have rights and therefore leads to the conclusion that zoos are not morally defensible.

Recommended Reading: rights-focused approach to moral issues, chap. 1, sec. 2D.

A great deal of recent work by moral philosophers— much of it in environmental ethics, for example, but much of it also in reference to questions about obligations to future generations and international justice—is directly relevant to the moral assessment of zoos. (Here and throughout I use the word "zoo" to refer to a professionally managed zoological institution accredited by the AZA and having a collection of live animals used for conservation, scientific studies, public education, and public display.) Yet most of this work has been overlooked by advocates of zoological parks. Why this is so is unclear, but certainly the responsibility for this lack of communication needs to be shared. Like all other specialists, moral philosophers have a tendency to converse only among themselves, just as, like others with a shared, crowded agenda, zoo professionals have limited discretionary time, thus little time to explore current tendencies in academic disciplines like moral philosophy. The present essay attempts to take some modest steps in the direction of better communication between the two professions....

CHANGING TIMES

Time was when philosophers had little good to say about animals other than human beings. "Nature's automata," writes Descartes (Regan and Singer 1976, 60). Morally considered, animals are in the same category as "sticks and stones," opines the early twentieth-century Jesuit Joseph Rickaby (179). True, there have been notable exceptions, throughout history, who celebrated the intelligence, beauty, and dignity of animals: Pythagoras, Cicero, Epicurus, Herodotus, Horace, Ovid, Plutarch, Seneca, Virgil—hardly a group of ancient-world animal crazies. By and large, however, a dismissive sentence or two sufficed or, when one's corpus took on grave proportions, a few paragraphs or pages. Thus we find Immanuel Kant, for example, by all accounts one of the most influential philosophers in the history of ideas, devoting almost two full pages to the question of our duties to nonhuman animals, while Saint Thomas Aquinas, easily the most important philosopher-theologian in the Roman Catholic tradition, bequeaths perhaps ten pages to this topic.

Times change. Today even a modest bibliography of the past decade's work by philosophers on the moral status of nonhuman animals (Magel 1989) would easily equal the length of Kant's and Aquinas's treatments combined (Regan and Singer 1976, 122–124, 56–60, 118–122), a quantitative symbol of the changes that have taken place, and continue to take place, in philosophy's attempt to excise the cancerous prejudices lodged in the anthropocentric belly of Western thought.

With relatively few speaking to the contrary (Saint Francis always comes to mind in this context), theists and humanists, rowdy bedfellows in most quarters, have gotten along amicably when discussing questions about the moral center of the terrestrial universe: human interests form the center of this universe. Let the theist look hopefully beyond the harsh edge of bodily death, let the humanist denounce, in Freud's terms, this "infantile view of the world," at least the two could agree that the moral universe revolves around us humans—our desires, our needs, our goals, our preferences, our love for one another. An intense dialectic now characterizes philosophy's assaults on the traditions of humanism and theism, assaults aimed not only at the traditional account of the moral status of nonhuman animals but also at the foundations of our moral dealings with the natural environment, with Nature generally. These assaults should not be viewed as local skirmishes between obscure academicians each bent on occupying a deserted fortress. At issue are the validity of alternative visions of the scheme of things and our place in it. The growing philosophical debate over our treatment of the planet and the other animals with whom we share it is both a symptom and a cause of a culture's attempt to come to critical terms with its past as it attempts to shape its future.

At present moral philosophers are raising a number of major challenges against moral anthropocentrism. I shall consider two. The first comes from utilitarians, the second from proponents of animal rights…. This essay offers a brief summary of each position with special reference to how it answers our central question—the question, again, Are zoos morally defensible?

UTILITARIANISM

The first fairly recent spark of revolt against moral anthropocentrism comes, as do other recent protests against institutionalized prejudice, from the pens of the nineteenth-century utilitarians Jeremy Bentham and John Stuart Mill. In an oft-quoted passage Bentham enfranchises sentient animals in the utilitarian moral community by declaring, "The question is not, Can they talk?, or Can they reason?, but, Can they suffer?" (Regan and Singer 1976, 130). Mill goes even further, writing that utilitarians "are perfectly willing to stake the whole question on this one issue. Granted that any practice causes more pain to animals than it gives pleasure to man: is that practice moral or immoral? And if, exactly in proportion as human beings raise their heads out of the slough of selfishness, they do not with one voice answer 'immoral' let the morality of the principle of utility be forever condemned" (132). Some of our duties are direct duties to other animals, not indirect duties to humanity. For utilitarians, these animals are themselves involved in the moral game.

Viewed against this historical backdrop, the position of the influential contemporary moral philosopher Peter Singer can be seen to be an extension of the utilitarian critique of moral anthropocentrism (Singer 1990). In Singer's hands utilitarianism requires that we consider the interests of everyone affected by what we do, and also that we weigh equal interests equally. We must not refuse to consider the interests of some people because they are Catholic, or female, or black, for example. Everyone's interests must be considered. And we must not discount the importance of equal interests because of whose interests they are. Everyone's interests must be weighed equitably. Now, to ignore or discount the importance of a woman's interests because she is a woman is an obvious example of the moral prejudice we call sexism, just as to ignore or discount the importance of the interests of African or Native Americans, Hispanics, etc. is an obvious form of racism. It remained for Singer to argue, which he does with great vigor, passion, and skill, that a similar moral prejudice lies at the heart of moral anthropocentrism, a prejudice that Singer, borrowing a term coined by the English author and animal activist Richard Ryder, denominates speciesism (Ryder 1975).

Like Bentham and Mill before him, therefore, Singer denies that humans are obliged to treat other animals equitably in the name of the betterment of humanity and also denies that acting dutifully toward these animals is a warm-up for the real moral game played between humans or, as theists would add, between humans and God. We owe it to those animals who have interests to take their interests into account, just as we also owe it to them to count their interests equitably. In these respects we have direct duties to them, not indirect duties to humanity. To think otherwise is to give sorry testimony to the very prejudice—speciesism—Singer is intent upon silencing.

UTILITARIANISM AND THE MORAL ASSESSMENT OF ZOOS

From a utilitarian perspective, then, the interests of animals must figure in the moral assessment of zoos. These interests include a variety of needs, desires, and preferences, including, for example, the interest wild animals have in freedom of movement, as well as adequate nutrition and an appropriate environment. Even zoos' most severe critics must acknowledge that in many of the most important respects, contemporary zoos have made important advances in meeting at least some of the most important interests of wild animals in captivity.

From a utilitarian perspective, however, there are additional questions that need to be answered before we are justified in answering our central question. For not only must we insist that the interests of captive animals be taken into account and be counted equitably, but we must also do the same for all those people whose interests are affected by having zoos—and this involves a very large number of people indeed, including those who work at zoos, those who visit them, and those (for example, people in the hotel and

restaurant business, as well as local and state governments) whose business or tax base benefits from having zoos in their region. To make an informed moral assessment of zoos, given utilitarian theory, in short, we need to consider a great deal more than the interests of those wild animals exhibited in zoos (though we certainly need to consider their interests). Since everyone's interests count, we need to consider everyone's interests, at least insofar as these interests are affected by having zoos—or by not having them.

Now, utilitarians are an optimistic, hearty breed, and what for many (myself included) seems to be an impossible task, to them appears merely difficult. The task is simple enough to state—namely, to determine how the many, the varied, and the competing interests of everyone affected by having zoos (or by not having them) are or will be affected by having (or not having) them. That, as I say, is the easy part. The hard (or impossible) part is actually to carry out this project. Granted, a number of story lines are possible (for example, stories about how much people really learn by going to zoos in comparison with how much they could learn by watching National Geographic specials). But many of these story lines will be in the nature of speculation rather than of fact, others will be empirical sketches rather than detailed studies, and the vital interests of some individuals (for example, the interests people have in having a job, medical benefits, a retirement plan) will tend not to be considered at all or to be greatly undervalued.

Moreover, the utilitarian moral assessment of zoos requires that we know a good deal more before we can make an informed assessment. Not only must we canvass all the interests of all those individuals who are affected, but we must also add up all the interests that are satisfied as well as all the interests that are frustrated, given the various options (for example, keeping zoos as they are, changing them in various ways, or abolishing them altogether). Then, having added all the pluses and minuses—and only then—are we in a position to say which of the options is the best one.

But (to put the point as mildly as possible) how we rationally are to carry out this part of the project (for example, how we rationally determine what an equitable trade-off is between, say, a wild animals' interest in roaming free and a tram operator's interest in a steady job) is far from clear. And yet unless we have comprehensible, comprehensive, and intellectually reliable instructions regarding how we are to do this, we will lack the very knowledge that, given utilitarian theory, we must have before we can make an informed moral assessment of zoos. The suspicion is, at least among utilitarianism's critics, the theory requires knowledge that far exceeds what we humans are capable of acquiring. In the particular case before us, then, it is arguable that utilitarian theory, conscientiously applied, would lead to moral skepticism—would lead, that is, to the conclusion that we just don't know whether or not zoos are morally defensible. At least for many people, myself included, this is a conclusion we would wish to avoid.

In addition to problems of this kind, utilitarianism also seems open to a variety of damaging moral criticisms, among which the following is representative. The theory commits us to withholding our moral assessment of actions or practices until everyone's interests have been taken into account and treated equitably. Thus the theory implies that before we can judge, say, whether the sexual abuse of very young children is morally wrong, we need to consider the interests of everyone involved—the very young child certainly, but also those of the abuser. But this seems morally outrageous. For what one wants to say, it seems to me, is that the sexual abuse of children is wrong independently of the interests of abusers, that their interests should play absolutely no role whatsoever in our judgment that their abuse is morally wrong, so that any theory that implies that their interests should play a role in our judgment must be mistaken. Thus, because utilitarianism does imply this, it must be mistaken.

Suppose this line of criticism is sound. Then it follows that we should not make our moral assessment of anything, whether the sexual abuse of children or the practice of keeping and exhibiting wild animals in zoos, in the way this theory recommends. If the theory is irredeemably flawed—and that it is, is what the example of child abuse is supposed to illustrate—then its answer to any moral question, including in particular our question about the defensibility of zoos, should carry no moral weight, one

way or the other (that is, whether the theory would justify zoos or find them indefensible). Despite its historic importance and continued influence, we are, I think, well advised to look elsewhere for an answer to our question.

THE RIGHTS VIEW

An alternative to the utilitarian attack on anthropocentrism is the rights view. Those who accept this view hold that (1) the moral assessment of zoos must be carried out against the backdrop of the rights of animals and that (2) when we make this assessment against this backdrop, zoos, as they presently exist, are not morally defensible. How might one defend what to many people will seem to be such extreme views? This is not a simple question by any means, but something by way of a sketch of this position needs to be presented here (Regan 1983).

The rights view rests on a number of factual beliefs about those animals humans eat, hunt, and trap, as well as those relevantly similar animals humans use in scientific research and exhibit in zoos. Included among these factual beliefs are the following: These animals are not only in the world, but they are also aware of it—and of what happens to them. And what happens to them matters to them. Each has a life that fares experientially better or worse for the one whose life it is. As such, all have lives of their own that are of importance to them apart from their utility to us. Like us, they bring a unified psychological presence to the world. Like us, they are somebodies, not somethings. They are not our tools, not our models, not our resources, not our commodities.

The lives that are theirs include a variety of biological, psychological, and social needs. The satisfaction of these needs is a source of pleasure, their frustration or abuse, a source of pain. The untimely death of the one whose life it is, whether this be painless or otherwise, is the greatest of harms since it is the greatest of losses: the loss of one's life itself. In these fundamental ways these nonhuman animals are the same as human beings. And so it is that according to the rights view, the ethics of our dealings with them and with one another must rest on the same fundamental moral principles.

At its deepest level an enlightened human ethic, according to the rights view, is based on the independent value of the individual: the moral worth of any one human being is not to be measured by how useful that person is in advancing the interests of other human beings. To treat human beings in ways that do not honor their independent value—to treat them as tools or models or commodities, for example—is to violate that most basic of human rights: the right of each of us to be treated with respect.

As viewed by its advocates, the philosophy of animal rights demands only that logic be respected. For any argument that plausibly explains the independent value of human beings, they claim, implies that other animals have this same value, and have it equally. Any argument that plausibly explains the right of humans to be treated with respect, it is further alleged, also implies that these other animals have this same right, and have it equally, too.

Those who accept the philosophy of animal rights, then, believe that women do not exist to serve men, blacks to serve whites, the rich to serve the poor, or the weak to serve the strong. The philosophy of animal rights not only accepts these truths, its advocates maintain, but also insists upon and justifies them. But this philosophy goes further. By insisting upon the independent value and rights of other animals, it attempts to give scientifically informed and morally impartial reasons for denying that these animals exist to serve us. Just as there is no master sex and no master race, so (animal rights advocates maintain) there is no master species.

ANIMAL RIGHTS AND THE MORAL ASSESSMENT OF ZOOS

To view nonhuman animals after the fashion of the philosophy of animal rights makes a truly profound difference to our understanding of what we may do to them. Because other animals have a moral right to respectful treatment, we ought not reduce their moral status to that of being useful means to our ends. That being so, the rights view excludes from consideration many of those factors that are relevant to the utilitarian moral assessment of zoos. As explained earlier, conscientious utilitarians need to ask how having zoos affects the interests people have in being gainfully employed, how the tourist trade and the local and state tax base are impacted, and how much people really learn from visiting zoos. All these questions, however, are irrelevant if those wild animals confined in zoos are not being treated with appropriate respect. If they are not, then, given the rights view, keeping these animals in zoos is wrong, and it is wrong independently of how the interests of others are affected.

Thus, the central question: Are animals in zoos treated with appropriate respect? To answer this question, we begin with an obvious fact—namely, the freedom of these animals is compromised, to varying degrees, by the conditions of their captivity. The rights view recognizes the justification of limiting another's freedom but only in a narrow range of cases. The most obvious relevant case would be one in which it is in the best interests of a particular animal to keep that animal in confinement. In principle, therefore, confining wild animals in zoos can be justified, according to the rights view, but only if it can be shown that it is in their best interests to do so. That being so, it is morally irrelevant to insist that zoos provide important educational and recreational opportunities for humans, or that captive animals serve as useful models in important scientific research, or that regions in which zoos are located benefit economically, or that zoo programs offer the opportunity for protecting rare or endangered species, or that variations on these programs insure genetic stock, or that any other consequence arises from keeping wild animals in captivity that forwards the interests of other individuals, whether humans or nonhumans.

Now, one can imagine circumstances in which such captivity might be defensible. For example, if the life of a wild animal could be saved only by temporarily removing the animal from the threat of human predation, and if, after this threat had abated, the animal was reintroduced into the wild, then this temporary confinement arguably is not disrespectful and thus might be justified. Perhaps there are other circumstances in which a wild animal's liberty could be limited temporarily, for that animal's own good. Obviously, however, there will be comparatively few such cases, and no less obviously, those cases that satisfy the requirements of the rights view are significantly different from the vast majority of cases in which wild animals are today confined in zoos, for these animals are confined and exhibited not because temporary captivity is in their best interests but because their captivity serves some purpose useful to others. As such, the rights view must take a very dim view of zoos, both as we know them now and as they are likely to be in the future. In answer to our central question—Are zoos morally defensible?—the rights view's answer, not surprisingly, is No, they are not....

REFERENCES

Magel, C. 1989. *Keyguide to Information Sources in Animal Rights*. London: Mansell.

Regan, T. 1983. *The Case for Animal Rights*. Berkeley: University of California Press.

Regan, T., and P. Singer, eds. 1976. *Animal Rights and Human Obligations*. Englewood Cliffs, N.J.: Prentice-Hall.

Ryder, R. 1975. *Victims of Science*. London: Davis-Poynter.

Singer, P. 1990. *Animal Liberation*. 2d ed. New York: Random House.

READING QUESTIONS

1. How does Regan define a "zoo"?
2. How would a utilitarian provide a moral assessment of zoos according to Regan? What are his objections to the utilitarian task in this particular case? What other criticisms does he raise against the utilitarian view generally?
3. What defense does Regan offer for the claim that zoos are not morally defensible according to the right's view?
4. In what cases does Regan claim that captivity of a nonhuman animal would be morally defensible?
5. Provide examples of the interests of nonhuman animals according to Regan.

DISCUSSION QUESTIONS

1. Should we reject utilitarianism as a way to assess the morality of zoos as Regan suggests? How might a utilitarian respond to the criticisms he raises?
2. Suppose that nonhuman animals have rights. Should nonhuman animal rights be respected as equal to those of humans? Describe cases where the rights of humans might trump the rights of nonhuman animals.

CARL COHEN

Do Animals Have Rights?

Cohen's negative answer to his title question involves two parts. First, he explains why non-human animals lack moral rights, even though humans have moral obligations with regard to them. Second, he critically evaluates Tom Regan's argument (from his 1983 book, *The Case for Animal Rights*) for the claim that nonhuman animals have rights. Regan's argument depends crucially on the claim that nonhuman animals, like human beings, have inherent value, and that therefore they have moral rights. Cohen argues that Regan's argument commits the fallacy of equivocation owing to multiple meanings of the term "inherent value."

Recommended Reading: rights-focused approaches, chap. 1, sec. 2D.

Whether animals have rights is a question of great importance because if they do, those rights must be respected, even at the cost of great burdens for human beings. A right (unlike an interest) is a valid claim, or potential claim, made by a moral agent, under principles that govern both the claimant and the target of the claim. Rights are precious; they are dispositive; they count.

You have a right to the return of money you lent me; we both understand that. It may be very convenient for me to keep the money, and you may have no need of it whatever; but my convenience and your needs are not to the point. You have a *right* to it, and we have courts of law partly to ensure that such rights will be respected.

If you make me a promise, I have a moral right to its fulfillment—even though there may be no law to enforce my right. It may be very much in your interest to break that promise, but your great interests and the silence of the law cut no mustard when your solemn promise—which we both well understood—had been given. Likewise, those holding power may have a great and benevolent interest in denying my rights to travel or to speak freely—but their interests are overridden by my rights.

A great deal was learned about hypothermia by some Nazi doctors who advanced their learning by soaking Jews in cold water and putting them in refrigerators to learn how hypothermia proceeds. We have no difficulty in seeing that they may not advance medicine in that way; the subjects of those atrocious experiments had rights that demanded respect. For those who ignored their rights we have nothing but moral loathing.

Some persons believe that animals have rights as surely as those Jews had rights, and they therefore look on the uses of animals in medical investigations just as we look at the Nazi use of the Jews, with moral loathing. They are consistent in doing so. If animals have rights they certainly have the right not to be killed, even to advance our important interests.

Some may say, "Well, they have rights, but we have rights too, and our rights override theirs." That may be true in some cases, but it will not solve the problem because, although we may have a weighty *interest* in learning, say, how to vaccinate against polio or other diseases, we do not have a *right* to learn such things. Nor could we honestly claim that we kill research animals in self-defense; they did not attack us. If animals have rights, they certainly have

Reprinted from *Ethics and Behavior*, 1997, vol. 7, no. 2, pp. 91–102.

the right not to be killed to advance the interests of others, whatever rights those others may have.

In 1952 there were about 58,000 cases of polio reported in the United States, and 3,000 polio deaths; my parents, parents everywhere, trembled in fear for their children at camp or away from home. Polio vaccination became routine in 1955, and cases dropped to about a dozen a year; today polio has been eradicated completely from the Western Hemisphere. The vaccine that achieved this, partly developed and tested only blocks from where I live in Ann Arbor, could have been developed *only* with the substantial use of animals. Polio vaccines had been tried many times earlier, but from those earlier vaccines children had contracted the disease; investigators had become, understandably, exceedingly cautious.

The killer disease for which a vaccine now is needed most desperately is malaria, which kills about 2 million people each year, most of them children. Many vaccines have been tried—not on children, thank God—and have failed. But very recently, after decades of effort, we learned how to make a vaccine that does, with complete success, inoculate mice against malaria. A safe vaccine for humans we do not yet have—but soon we will have it, thanks to the use of those mice, many of whom will have died in the process. To test that vaccine first on children would be an outrage, as it would have been an outrage to do so with the Salk and Sabin polio vaccines years ago. We use mice or monkeys *because there is no other way*. And there never will be another way because untested vaccines are very dangerous; their first use on a living organism is inescapably experimental; there is and will be no way to determine the reliability and safety of new vaccines without repeated tests on live organisms. Therefore, because we certainly may not use human children to test them, we will use mice (or as we develop an AIDS vaccine, primates) *or we will never have such vaccines*.

But if those animals we use in such tests have rights as human children do, what we did and are doing to them is as profoundly wrong as what the Nazis did to those Jews not long ago. Defenders of animal rights need not hold that medical scientists are vicious; they simply believe that what medical investigators are doing with animals is morally wrong.

Most biomedical investigations involving animal subjects use rodents: mice and rats. The rat is the animal appropriately considered (and used by the critic) as the exemplar whose moral stature is in dispute here. Tom Regan is a leading defender of the view that rats do such rights, and may not be used in biomedical investigations. He is an honest man. He sees the consequences of his view and accepts them forthrightly. In *The Case for Animal Rights* (Regan, 1983) he wrote,

> The harms others might face as a result of the dissolution of [some] practice or institution is no defense of allowing it to continue....No one has a right to be protected against being harmed if the protection in question involves violating the rights of others....No one has a right to be protected by the continuation of an unjust practice, one that violates the rights of others....Justice *must* be done, though the...heavens fall. (pp. 346–347)

That last line echoes Kant, who borrowed it from an older tradition. Believing that rats have rights as humans do, Regan (1983) was convinced that killing them in medical research was morally intolerable. He wrote,

> On the rights view, [he means, of course, the Regan rights view] we cannot justify harming a single rat *merely* by aggregating "the many human and humane benefits" that flow from doing it....Not even a single rat is to be treated as if that animal's value were reducible to his *possible utility* relative to the interests of others. (p. 384)

If there are some things that we cannot learn because animals have rights, well, as Regan (1983) put it, so be it.

This is the conclusion to which one certainly is driven if one holds that animals have rights. If Regan is correct about the moral standing of rats, we humans can have no right, ever, to kill them—unless perchance a rat attacks a person or a human baby, as rats sometimes do; then our right of self-defense may enter, I suppose. But medical investigations cannot honestly be described as self-defense, and medical investigations commonly require that many mice and rats be killed. Therefore, all medical investigations relying on them, or any other animal subjects—which includes most studies and all the most important studies of certain kinds—will have to stop. Bear in mind that the replacement of animal subjects by computer simulations, or tissue samples, and so on, is in most research a phantasm, a fantasy. Biomedical investigations using animal subjects (and of course all uses of animals as food) will have to stop.

This extraordinary consequence has no argumentative force for Regan and his followers; they are not consequentialists. For Regan the interests of humans, their desire to be freed of disease or relieved of pain, simply cannot outweigh the rights of a single rat. For him the issue is one of justice, and the use of animals in medical experiments (he believes) is simply not just. But the consequences of his view will give most of us, I submit, good reason to weigh very carefully the arguments he offers to support such far-reaching claims. Do you believe that the work of Drs. Salk and Sabin was morally right? Would you support it now, or support work just like it saving tens of thousands of human children from diphtheria, hepatitis, measles, rabies, rubella, and tetanus (all of which relied essentially on animal subjects)—as well as, now, AIDS, Lyme disease, and malaria? I surely do. If you would join me in this support we must conclude that the defense of animal rights is a gigantic mistake. I next aim to explain why animals cannot possess rights.

WHY ANIMALS DO NOT HAVE RIGHTS

Many obligations are owed by humans to animals; few will deny that. But it certainly does not follow from this that animals have rights because it is certainly not true that every obligation of ours arises from the rights of another. Not at all. We need to be clear and careful here. Rights entail obligations. If you have a right to the return of the money I borrowed, I have an obligation to repay it. No issue. If we have the right to speak freely on public policy matters, the community has the obligation to respect our right to do so. But

the proposition *all rights entail obligations* does not convert simply, as the logicians say. From the true proposition that all trees are plants, it does not follow that all plants are trees. Similarly, not all obligations are entailed by rights. Some obligations, like mine to repay the money I borrowed from you, do arise out of rights. But many obligations are owed to persons or other beings who have no rights whatever in the matter.

Obligations may arise from commitments freely made: As a college professor I accept the obligation to comment at length on the papers my students submit, and I do so; but they have not the right to *demand* that I do so. Civil servants and elected officials surely ought to be courteous to members of the public, but that obligation certainly is not grounded in citizens' rights.

Special relations often give rise to obligations: Hosts have the obligation to be cordial to their guests, but the guest has not the right to demand cordiality. Shepherds have obligations to their dogs, and cowboys to their horses, which do not flow from the rights of those dogs or horses. My son, now 5, may someday wish to study veterinary medicine as my father did; I will then have the obligation to help him as I can, and with pride I shall—but he has not the authority to demand such help as a matter of right. My dog has no right to daily exercise and veterinary care, but I do have the obligation to provide those things for her.

One may be obliged to another for a special act of kindness done; one may be obliged to put an animal out of its misery in view of its condition—but neither the beneficiary of that kindness nor that dying animal may have had a claim of right.

Beauchamp and Childress (1994) addressed what they called the "correlativity of rights and obligations" and wrote that they would defend an "untidy" (pp. 73–75) variety of that principle. It would be very untidy indeed. Some of our most important obligations—to members of our family, to the needy, to neighbors, and to sentient creatures of every sort—have no foundation in rights at all. Correlativity appears critical from the perspective of one who holds a right; your right correlates with my obligation to respect it. But the claim that rights and obligations are reciprocals, that every obligation flows from another's right, is false, plainly inconsistent with our general understanding of the differences between what we think we ought to do, and what others can justly *demand* that we do.

I emphasize this because, although animals have no rights, it surely does not follow from this that one is free to treat them with callous disregard. Animals are not stones; they feel. A rat may suffer; surely we have the obligation not to torture it gratuitously, even though it be true that the concept of a right could not possibly apply to it. We humans are obliged to act humanely, that is, being aware of their sentience, to apply to animals the moral principles that govern us regarding the gratuitous imposition of pain and suffering; which is not, of course, to treat animals as the possessors of rights.

Animals cannot be the bearers of rights because the concept of rights is essentially *human*; it is rooted in, and has force within, a human moral world. Humans must deal with rats—all too frequently in some parts of the world—and must be moral in their dealing with them; but a rat can no more be said to have rights than a table can be said to have ambition. To say of a rat that it has rights is to confuse categories, to apply to its world a moral category that has content only in the human moral world.

Try this thought experiment. Imagine, on the Serengeti Plain in East Africa, a lioness hunting for her cubs. A baby zebra, momentarily left unattended by its mother, is the prey; the lioness snatches it, rips open its throat, tears out chunks of its flesh, and departs. The mother zebra is driven nearly out of her wits when she cannot locate her baby; finding its carcass she will not even leave the remains for days. The scene may be thought unpleasant, but it is entirely natural, of course, and extremely common. If the zebra has a right to live, if the prey is just but the predator unjust, we ought to intervene, if we can, on behalf of right. But we do not intervene, of course—as we surely would intervene if we saw the lioness about to attack an unprotected human baby or you. What accounts for the moral difference? We justify different responses to humans and to zebras on the ground (implicit or explicit) that their moral stature is very different. The human has a right not

to be eaten alive; it is, after all, a human being. Do you believe the baby zebra has the right not to be slaughtered by that lioness? That the lioness has the *right* to kill that baby zebra for her cubs? If you are inclined to say, confronted by such natural rapacity—duplicated with untold variety millions of times each day on planet earth—that neither is right or wrong, that neither has a *right* against the other, I am on your side. Rights are of the highest moral consequence, yes; but zebras and lions and rats are totally amoral; there is no morality for them; they do no wrong, ever. In their world there are no rights.

A contemporary philosopher who has thought a good deal about animals, referring to them as "moral patients," put it this way:

> A moral patient lacks the ability to formulate, let alone bring to bear, moral principles in deliberating about which one among a number of possible acts it would be right or proper to perform. Moral patients, in a word, cannot do what is right, nor can they do what is wrong....Even when a moral patient causes significant harm to another, the moral patient has not done what is wrong. Only moral agents can do what is wrong. (Regan, 1983, pp. 152–153)

Just so. The concepts of wrong and right are totally foreign to animals, not conceivably within their ken or applicable to them, as the author of that passage clearly understands.

When using animals in our research, therefore, we ought indeed be humane—but we can never violate the rights of those animals because, to be blunt, they have none. Rights do not *apply* to them.

But humans do have rights. Where do our rights come from? Why are we not crudely natural creatures like rats and zebras? This question philosophers have struggled to answer from earliest times. A definitive account of the human moral condition I cannot here present, of course. But reflect for a moment on the kinds of answers that have been widely given:

- Some think our moral understanding, with its attendant duties, to be a divine gift. So St. Thomas said: The moral law is binding, and humans have the power, given by God, to grasp its binding character, and must therefore respect the rights that other humans possess. God makes us (Saint Augustine said before him) in his own image, and therefore with a will that is free, and gives us the power to recognize that, and therefore, unlike other creatures, we must choose between good and evil, between right and wrong.

- Many philosophers, distrusting theological justifications of rights and duties, sought the ground of human morality in the membership, by all humans, in a moral community. The English idealist, Bradley, called it an organic moral community; the German idealist, Hegel, called it an objective ethical order. These and like accounts commonly center on human inter-relations, on a moral *fabric* within which human agents always act, and within which animals never act and never can possibly act.

- The highly abstract reasoning from which such views emerge has dissatisfied many; you may find more nearly true the convictions of ethical intuitionists and realists who said, as H. A. Prichard, Sir David Ross, and my friend and teacher C. D. Broad, of happy memory, used to say, that there is a direct, underivative, intuitive cognition of rights as possessed by other humans, but not by animals.

- Or perhaps in the end we will return to Kant, and say with him that critical reason reveals at the core of human action a uniquely moral will, and the unique ability to grasp and to lay down moral laws for oneself and for others—an ability that is not conceivably within the capacity of any nonhuman animal whatever.

To be a moral agent (on this view) is to be able to grasp the generality of moral restrictions on our will. Humans understand that some things, which may be in our interest, *must not be willed*; we lay down moral laws for ourselves, and thus exhibit, as no other animal can exhibit, moral autonomy. My dog knows that there are certain things she must not do—but she knows this only as the outcome of her learning about her interests, the pains she may suffer if she does what had been taught forbidden. She does not know, cannot know (as Regan agrees) that any conduct is wrong. The proposition *It would be highly advantageous to act in such-and-such a way, but I may not because it would be wrong* is one that no dog or mouse or rabbit, however sweet and endearing, however loyal or attentive to its young, can ever entertain, or intend, or begin to grasp. Right is not in their world. But right and wrong are the very stuff of human moral life, the ever-present awareness of human beings who can do wrong, and who by seeking (often) to avoid wrong conduct prove themselves members of a moral community in which rights may be exercised and must be respected.

Some respond by saying, "This can't be correct, for human infants (and the comatose and senile, etc.) surely have rights, but they make no moral claims or judgments and can make none—and any view entailing that children can have no rights must be absurd." Objections of this kind miss the point badly. It is not individual persons who qualify (or are disqualified) for the possession of rights because of the presence or absence in them of some special capacity, thus resulting in the award of rights to some but not to others. Rights are universally human; they arise in a *human moral world*, in a moral *sphere*. In the human world moral judgments are pervasive; it is the fact that all humans including infants and the senile are members of that moral community—not the fact that as individuals they have or do not have certain special capacities, or merits—that makes humans bearers of rights. Therefore, it is beside the point to insist that animals have remarkable capacities, that they really have a consciousness of self, or of the future, or make plans, and so on. And the tired response that because infants plainly cannot make moral claims they must have no rights at all, or rats must have them too, we ought forever put aside. Responses like these arise out of a misconception of right itself. They mistakenly suppose that rights are tied to some identifiable individual abilities or sensibilities, and they fail to see that rights arise only in a community of moral beings, and that therefore there are spheres in which rights do apply and spheres in which they do not.

Rationality is not at issue; the capacity to communicate is not at issue. My dog can reason, if rather weakly, and she certainly can communicate. Cognitive criteria for the possession of rights,…are morally perilous. Indeed they are. Nor is the capacity to suffer here at issue. And, if *autonomy* be understood only as the capacity to choose this course rather than that, autonomy is not to the point either. But *moral autonomy*—that is, *moral self-legislation*—is to the point, because moral autonomy is uniquely human and is for animals out of the question, as we have seen, and as Regan and I agree. In talking about autonomy, therefore, we must be careful and precise.

Because humans do have rights, and these rights can be violated by other humans, we say that some humans commit *crimes*. But whether a crime has been committed depends utterly on the moral state of mind of the actor. If I take your coat, or your book, honestly thinking it was mine, I do not steal it. The *actus reus* (the guilty deed) must be accompanied, in a genuine crime, by a guilty mind, a *mens rea*. That recognition, not just of possible punishment for an act, but of moral duties that govern us, no rat or cow ever can possess. In primitive times humans did sometimes bring cows and horses to the bar of human justice. We chuckle at that practice now, realizing that accusing cows of crimes marks the primitive moral view as inane. Animals never can be criminals because they have no moral state of mind....

WHY ANIMALS ARE MISTAKENLY BELIEVED TO HAVE RIGHTS

From the foregoing discussion it follows that, if some philosophers believe that they have proved that animals have rights, they must have erred in the alleged proof. Regan is a leader among those who claim to *argue* in defense of the rights of rats; he contends that the best arguments are on his side. I aim next to show how he and others with like views go astray....

[Regan's] case is built entirely on the principle that allegedly *carries over* almost everything earlier claimed about human rights to rats and other animals. What principle is that? It is the principle, put in italics but given no name, that equates moral agents with moral patients:

The validity of the claim to respectful treatment, and thus the case for the recognition of the right to such

treatment, cannot be any stronger or weaker in the case of moral patients than it is in the case of moral agents. (Regan, p. 279)

But hold on. Why in the world should anyone think this principle to be true? Back in Section 5.2, where Regan first recounted his view of moral patients, he allowed that some of them are, although capable of experiencing pleasure and pain, lacking in other capacities. But he is interested, he told us there, in those moral patients—those animals—that are like humans in having *inherent value*. This is the key to the argument for animal rights, the possession of inherent value. How that concept functions in the argument becomes absolutely critical. I will say first briefly what will be shown more carefully later: *Inherent value* is an expression used by Regan (and many like him) with two very different senses—in one of which it is reasonable to conclude that those who have inherent value have rights, and in another sense in which that inference is wholly unwarranted. But the phrase, *inherent value* has some plausibility in both contexts, and thus by sliding from one sense of inherent value to the other Regan appears to succeed, in two pages, in making the case for animal rights.

The concept of inherent value first entered the discussion in the seventh chapter of Regan's (1983) book, at which point his principal object is to fault and defeat utilitarian arguments. It is not (he argued there) the pleasures or pains that go "into the cup" of humanity that give value, but the "cups" themselves; humans are equal in value because they are humans, having inherent value. So we are, all of us, equal—equal in being moral agents who have this inherent value. This approach to the moral stature of humans is likely to be found quite plausible. Regan called it the "postulate of inherent value"; all humans, "The lonely, forsaken, unwanted, and unloved are no more nor less inherently valuable than those who enjoy a more hospitable relationship with others" (p. 237). And Regan went on to argue for the proposition that all moral agents are "equal in inherent value." Holding some such views we are likely to say, with Kant, that all humans are beyond price. Their inherent value gives them moral dignity, a unique role in the moral world, as agents having the capacity to act morally and make moral judgments. This is inherent value in Sense 1.

The expression *inherent value* has another sense, however, also common and also plausible. My dog has inherent value, and so does every wild animal, every lion and zebra, which is why the senseless killing of animals is so repugnant. Each animal is unique, not replaceable in itself by another animal or by any rocks or clay. Animals, like humans, are not just things; they live, and as unique living creatures they have inherent value. This is an important point, and again likely to be thought plausible; but here, in Sense 2, the phrase *inherent value* means something quite distinct from what was meant in its earlier uses.

Inherent value in Sense 1, possessed by all humans but not by all animals, which warrants the claim of human rights, is very different from inherent value in Sense 2, which warrants no such claim. The uniqueness of animals, their intrinsic worthiness as individual living things, does not ground the possession of rights, has nothing to do with the moral condition in which rights arise. Regan's argument reached its critical objective with almost magical speed because, having argued that beings with inherent value (Sense 1) have rights that must be respected, he quickly asserted (putting it in italics lest the reader be inclined to express doubt) that rats and rabbits also have rights because they, too, have inherent value (Sense 2).

This is an egregious example of the fallacy of equivocation: the informal fallacy in which two or more meanings of the same word or phrase have been confused in the several premises of an argument (Cohen & Copi, 1994, pp. 143–144). Why is this slippage not seen at once? Partly because we know the phrase inherent value often is used loosely, so the reader is not prone to quibble about its introduction; partly because the two uses of the phrase relied on are both common, so neither signals danger; partly because inherent value in Sense 2 is indeed shared by those who have it in Sense 1; and partly because the phrase *inherent value* is woven into accounts of what Regan (1983) elsewhere called the *subject-of-a-life criterion*, a phrase of his own

devising for which he can stipulate any meaning he pleases, of course, and which also slides back and forth between the sphere of genuine moral agency and the sphere of animal experience. But perhaps the chief reason the equivocation between these two uses of the phrase *inherent value* is obscured (from the author, I believe, as well as from the reader) is the fact that the assertion that animals have rights appears only indirectly, as the outcome of the application of the principle that moral patients are entitled to the same respect as moral agents—a principle introduced at a point in the book long after the important moral differences between moral patients and moral agents have been recognized, with a good deal of tangled philosophical argument having been injected in between....

Animals do not have rights. Right does not apply in their world. We do have many obligations to animals, of course, and I honor Regan's appreciation of their sensitivities. I also honor his seriousness of purpose, and his always civil and always rational spirit. But he is, I submit, profoundly mistaken. I conclude with the observation that, had his mistaken views about the rights of animals long been accepted, most successful medical therapies recently devised—antibiotics, vaccines, prosthetic devices, and other compounds and instruments on which we now rely for saving and improving human lives and for the protection of our children—could not have been developed; and were his views to become general now (an outcome that is unlikely but possible) the consequences for medical science and for human well-being in the years ahead would be nothing less than catastrophic.

Advances in medicine absolutely require experiments, many of which are dangerous. Dangerous experiments absolutely require living organisms as subjects. Those living organisms (we now agree) certainly may not be human beings. Therefore, most advances in medicine will continue to rely on the use of nonhuman animals, or they will stop. Regan is free to say in response, as he does, "so be it." The rest of us must ask if the argument he presents is so compelling as to force us to accept that dreadful result.

REFERENCES

Beauchamp, T.L., & Childress, J.F. (1994). *Principles of biomedical ethics* (4th ed.). New York: Oxford University Press.

Cohen, C., & Copi, I. M. (1994). *Introduction to logic* (9th ed.). New York: Macmillan.

Regan, T. (1983). *The case for animal rights*. Berkeley: University of California Press.

READING QUESTIONS

1. Explain Cohen's distinction between interests and rights, giving examples of each.
2. Cohen claims that although rights entail obligations, the converse obligations entail rights is not true. Give your own example to support Cohen's negative claim.
3. What are the ways in which obligations arise according to Cohen?
4. Describe the four different views about where human rights come from according to Cohen.
5. What is Cohen's response to those who argue that humans such as infants have rights but can't make moral judgments?
6. What reasons does Cohen give for claiming that nonhuman animals lack moral rights?
7. Explain the particular fallacy of equivocation that Cohen claims Regan's argument for animal rights commits.

DISCUSSION QUESTIONS

1. Suppose that Cohen is correct in claiming that Regan's argument commits the fallacy of equivocation. Can you think of another argument for the claim that nonhuman animals have rights?
2. Suppose nonhuman animals do have some rights. How do they compare in content and strength to the basic rights of typical human beings?
3. Cohen admits that human beings do have obligations toward nonhuman animals even if those animals do not have rights. What sorts of obligations do we have toward nonhuman animals? Do these obligations differ in any significant ways from the obligations we have toward other human beings?
4. Cohen argues that human beings are the only kind of thing for which morality is an issue and that nonhuman animals are essentially amoral. What evidence do we have, if any, that nonhuman animals understand the difference between right and wrong? Is their understanding any different from our own?

Mary Anne Warren

Human and Animal Rights Compared

Warren distinguishes between the *content* of a right (the sphere of activity the right protects) and their *strength* (the strength of reasons required for it to be legitimately overridden). The content of the rights of members of a species depends on what its members require to pursue the needs and satisfactions of a life that is natural to its species. Thus, sentient nonhuman animals, according to Warren, have some rights to life, liberty (including freedom of movement), and happiness. However, she further argues that (1) because humans desire liberty and life more strongly than do nonhuman animals and (2) because humans possess moral autonomy whereas nonhuman animals do not, the rights of animals are weaker than the corresponding rights of humans. If moral autonomy is a basis for assigning stronger rights to typical human beings, what about nonparadigm humans including infants, small children, and those who are severely brain damaged? Warren answers that (1) the potential (of infants) and partial autonomy (of children) is a proper basis for assigning strong moral rights to them and that (2) the fact that typical humans place a very high value on nonparadigm humans is itself a further reason for assigning strong moral rights to nonparadigm humans.

Recommended Reading: rights-focused approach to moral issues, chap. 1, sec. 2D.

None of the animal liberationists have thus far provided a clear explanation of how and why the moral status of (most) animals differs from that of (most) human beings; and this is a point which must be clarified if their position is to be made fully persuasive. That there is such a difference seems to follow from some very strong moral intuitions which most of us share. A man who shoots squirrels for sport may or may not be acting reprehensibly; but it is difficult to believe that his actions should be placed in *exactly* the same moral category as those of a man who shoots women, or black children, for sport. So too it is doubtful that the Japanese fishermen who slaughtered dolphins because the latter were thought to be depleting the local fish populations were acting quite *as* wrongly as if they had slaughtered an equal number of their human neighbours for the

same reason. . . . There are two dimensions in which we may find differences between the rights of human beings and those of animals. The first involves the *content* of those rights, while the second involves their strength; that is, the strength of the reasons which are required to override them.

Consider, for instance, the right to liberty. The *human* right to liberty precludes imprisonment without due process of law, even if the prison is spacious and the conditions of confinement cause no obvious physical suffering. But it is not so obviously wrong to imprison animals, especially when the area to which they are confined provides a fair approximation of the conditions of their natural habitat, and a reasonable opportunity to pursue the satisfactions natural to their kind. Such conditions, which often result in an increased lifespan, and which may exist in wildlife

From Mary Anne Warren, "The Rights of the Nonhuman World," in *Environmental Philosophy: A Collection of Readings,* Robert Elliot and Arran Gare, eds., 1983. Reprinted by permission of Queensland University Press.

sanctuaries or even well-designed zoos, need not frustrate the needs or interests of animals in any significant way, and thus do not clearly violate their rights. Similarly treated human beings, on the other hand (e.g., native peoples confined to prison-like reservations), do tend to suffer from their loss of freedom. Human dignity and the fulfillment of the sorts of plans, hopes and desires which appear (thus far) to be uniquely human, require a more extensive freedom of movement than is the case with at least many nonhuman animals. Furthermore, there are aspects of human freedom, such as freedom of thought, freedom of speech and freedom of political association, which simply do not apply in the case of animals.

Thus, it seems that the human right to freedom is more extensive; that is, it precludes a wider range of specific ways of treating human beings than does the corresponding right on the part of animals. The argument cuts both ways, of course. *Some* animals, for example, great whales and migratory birds, may require at least as much physical freedom as do human beings if they are to pursue the satisfactions natural to their kind, and this fact provides a moral argument against keeping such creatures imprisoned. And even chickens may suffer from the extreme and unnatural confinement to which they are subjected on modern "factory farms." Yet it seems unnecessary to claim for *most* animals a right to a freedom quite as broad as that which we claim for ourselves.

Similar points may be made with respect to the right to life. Animals, it may be argued, lack the cognitive equipment to value their lives in the way that human beings do. Ruth Cigman argues that animals have *no* right to life because death is no misfortune for them.[1] In her view, the death of an animal is not a misfortune, because animals have no desires which are *categorical;* that is which do not "merely presuppose being alive (like the desire to eat when one is hungry), but rather answer the question whether one wants to remain alive."[2] In other words, animals appear to lack the sorts of long-range hopes, plans, ambitions and the like, which give human beings such a powerful interest in continued life. Animals, it seems, take life as it comes and do not specifically desire that it go on. True, squirrels store nuts for the winter and deer run from wolves; but these may be

seen as instinctive or conditioned responses to present circumstances, rather than evidence that they value life as such.

These reflections probably help to explain why the death of a sparrow seems less tragic than that of a human being. Human lives, one might say, have greater intrinsic value, because they are worth more *to their possessors.* But this does not demonstrate that no nonhuman animal has *any* right to life. Premature death may be a less *severe* misfortune for sentient nonhuman animals than for human beings, but it is a misfortune nevertheless. In the first place, it is a misfortune in that it deprives them of whatever pleasures the future might have held for them, regardless of whether or not they ever *consciously anticipated* those pleasures. The fact that they are not here afterwards, to *experience* their loss, no more shows that they have not lost anything than it does in the case of humans. In the second place, it is (possibly) a misfortune in that it frustrates whatever future-oriented desires animals *may* have, unbeknownst to us. Even now, in an age in which apes have been taught to use simplified human languages and attempts have been made to communicate with dolphins and whales, we still know very little about the operation of nonhuman minds. We know much too little to assume that nonhuman animals never consciously pursue relatively distant future goals. To the extent that they do, the question of whether such desires provide them with *reasons for living* or merely *presuppose* continued life, has no satisfactory answer, since they cannot contemplate these alternatives—or, if they can, we have no way of knowing what their conclusions are. All we know is that the more intelligent and psychologically complex an animal is, the more *likely* it is that it possesses specifically future-oriented desires, which would be frustrated even by *painless* death.

For these reasons, it is premature to conclude from the apparent intellectual inferiority of nonhuman animals that they have no right to life. A more plausible conclusion is that animals do have a right to life but that it is generally somewhat weaker than that of human beings. It is, perhaps, weak enough to enable us to justify killing animals when we have no other ways of achieving such vital goals as feeding or clothing ourselves, or obtaining knowledge which is necessary to save human lives. Weakening their right to life in this way does not render meaningless the assertion that they have such a right. For the point remains that *some* serious justification for the killing of sentient nonhuman animals is always necessary; they may not be killed merely to provide amusement or minor gains in convenience.

If animals' rights to liberty and life are somewhat weaker than those of human beings, may we say the same about their right to *happiness;* that is, their right not to be made to suffer needlessly or to be deprived of the pleasures natural to their kind? If so, it is not immediately clear why. There is little reason to suppose that pain or suffering are any less unpleasant for the higher animals (at least) than they are for us. Our large brains *may* cause us to experience pain more intensely than do most animals, and *probably* cause us to suffer more from the anticipation or remembrance of pain. These facts might tend to suggest that pain is, on the whole, a worse experience for us than for them. But it may also be argued that pain may be *worse* in some respects for nonhuman animals, who are presumably less able to distract themselves from it by thinking of something else, or to comfort themselves with the knowledge that it is temporary. Brigid Brophy points out that "pain is likely to fill the sheep's whole capacity for experience in a way it seldom does in us, whose intellect and imagination can create breaks for us in the immediacy of our sensations."[3]

The net result of such contrasting considerations is that we cannot possibly claim to know whether pain is, on the whole, worse for us than for animals, or whether their pleasures are any more or any less intense than ours. Thus, while we may justify assigning them a somewhat weaker right to life or liberty, on the grounds that they desire these goods less intensely than we do, we cannot discount their rights to freedom from needlessly inflicted pain or unnatural frustration on the same basis. There may, however, be *other* reasons for regarding all of the moral rights of animals as somewhat less stringent than the corresponding human rights.

A number of philosophers who deny that animals have moral rights point to the fact that nonhuman animals evidently lack the capacity for moral autonomy. Moral autonomy is the ability to act as a moral agent; that is, to act on the basis of an understanding of, and adherence to, moral rules or principles. H. J. McCloskey, for example, holds that "it is the capacity for moral autonomy . . . that is basic to the possibility of possessing a right."[4] McCloskey argues that it is inappropriate to ascribe moral rights to any entity which is not a moral agent, or *potentially* a moral agent, because a right is essentially an entitlement granted to a moral agent, licensing him or her to *act* in certain ways and to *demand* that other moral agents refrain from interference. For this reason, he says, "Where there is no possibility of [morally autonomous] action, potentially or actually . . . and where the being is not a member of a kind which is normally capable of [such] action, we withhold talk of rights."[5]

If moral autonomy—or being *potentially* autonomous, or a member of a kind which is *normally* capable of autonomy—is a necessary condition for having moral rights, then probably no nonhuman animal can qualify. For moral autonomy requires such probably uniquely human traits as "the capacity to be critically self-aware, manipulate concepts, use a sophisticated language, reflect, plan, deliberate, choose, and accept responsibility for acting."[6]

But why, we must ask, should the capacity for autonomy be regarded as a precondition for possessing moral rights? Autonomy is clearly crucial for the *exercise* of many human moral or legal rights, such as the right to vote or to run for public office. It is less clearly relevant, however, to the more basic human rights, such as the right to life or to freedom from unnecessary suffering. The fact that animals, like many human beings, cannot *demand* their moral rights (at least not in the words of any conventional human language) seems irrelevant. For, as Joel Feinberg points out, the interests of non-morally autonomous human beings may be defended by others, for example, in legal proceedings; and it is not clear why the interests of animals might not be represented in a similar fashion.[7]

It is implausible, therefore, to conclude that because animals lack moral autonomy they should be accorded *no moral rights whatsoever.* Nevertheless, it may be argued that the moral autonomy of (most) human beings provides a second reason, in addition to their more extensive interests and desires, for according somewhat *stronger* moral rights to human beings. The fundamental insight behind contractualist theories of morality is that, for morally autonomous beings such as ourselves, there is enormous mutual advantage in the adoption of a moral system designed to protect each of us from the harms that might otherwise be visited upon us by others. Each of us ought to accept and promote such a system because, to the extent that others also accept it, we will all be safer from attack by our fellows, more likely to receive assistance when we need it, and freer to engage in individual as well as cooperative endeavours of all kinds.

Thus, it is the possibility of *reciprocity* which motivates moral agents to extend *full and equal* moral rights, in the first instance, only to other moral agents. I respect your rights to life, liberty and the pursuit of happiness in part because you are a sentient being, whose interests have intrinsic moral significance. But I respect them as *fully equal to my own* because I hope and expect that you will do the same for me. Animals, insofar as they lack the degree of rationality necessary for moral autonomy, cannot agree to respect our interests as equal in moral importance to their own, and neither do they expect or demand such respect from us. Of course, domestic animals may expect to be fed, etc. But they do not, and cannot, expect to be treated as moral equals, for they do not understand that moral concept or what it implies. Consequently, it is neither pragmatically feasible nor morally obligatory to extend to them the same *full and equal* rights which we extend to human beings.

Is this a speciesist conclusion? Defenders of a more extreme animal-rights position may point out that this argument, from the lack of moral autonomy, has exactly the same form as that which has been used for thousands of years to rationalize denying equal moral rights to women and members of "inferior" races. Aristotle, for example, argued that women and slaves are naturally subordinate beings, because they lack the capacity for moral autonomy and self-direction,[8] and contemporary versions of this argument, used to support racist or sexist conclusions, are easy to find. Are we simply repeating Aristotle's mistake, in a different context?

The reply to this objection is very simple: animals, unlike women and slaves, really *are* incapable of moral autonomy, at least to the best of our knowledge. Aristotle certainly *ought* to have known that women and slaves are capable of morally autonomous action; their capacity to use moral language alone ought to have alerted him to this likelihood. If comparable evidence exists that (some) nonhuman animals are moral agents we have not yet found it. The fact that some apes (and, possibly, some cetaceans, are capable of learning radically simplified human languages, the terms of which refer primarily to objects and events in their immediate environment, in no way demonstrates that they can understand abstract moral concepts, rules or principles, or use this understanding to regulate their own behaviour.

On the other hand, this argument implies that if we *do* discover that certain nonhuman animals are capable of moral autonomy (which is certainly not impossible), then we ought to extend full and equal moral rights to those animals. Furthermore, if we someday encounter extraterrestrial beings, or build robots, androids or supercomputers which function as self-aware moral agents, then we must extend full and equal moral rights to these as well. Being a member of the human species is not a necessary condition for the possession of full "human" rights. Whether it is nevertheless a *sufficient* condition is the question to which we now turn.

THE MORAL RIGHTS OF NONPARADIGM HUMANS

If we are justified in ascribing somewhat different, and also somewhat stronger, moral rights to human beings than to sentient but non-morally autonomous animals, then what are we to say of the rights of human beings who happen not to be capable of moral autonomy, perhaps not even potentially? Both Singer and Regan have argued that if any of the superior intellectual capacities of normal and mature human beings are used to support a distinction between the moral status of *typical,* or paradigm, human beings, and that of animals, then consistency will require us to place certain "nonparadigm" humans, such as infants, small children and the severely retarded or incurably brain damaged, in the same inferior moral category.[9] Such a result is, of course, highly counterintuitive.

Fortunately, no such conclusion follows from the autonomy argument. There are many reasons for extending strong moral rights to nonparadigm humans; reasons which do not apply to most nonhuman animals. Infants and small children are granted strong moral rights in part because of their *potential* autonomy. But *potential* autonomy, as I have argued elsewhere,[10] is not in itself a sufficient reason for the ascription of full moral rights; if it were, then not only human foetuses (from conception onwards) but even ununited human sperm-egg pairs would have to be regarded as entities with a right to life the equivalent of our own—thus making not only abortion, but any intentional failure to procreate, the moral equivalent of murder. Those who do not find this extreme conclusion acceptable must appeal to reasons other than the *potential* moral autonomy of infants and small children to explain the strength of the latter's moral rights.

One reason for assigning strong moral rights to infants and children is that they possess not just *potential* but *partial* autonomy, and it is not clear how much of it they have at any given moment. The fact that, unlike baby chimpanzees, they are already learning the things which will enable them to *become* morally autonomous, makes it likely that their minds have more subtleties than their speech (or the lack of it) proclaims. Another reason is simply that most of us tend to place a very high value on the lives and well-being of infants. Perhaps we are to some degree "programmed" by nature to love and protect them; perhaps our reasons are somewhat egocentric; or perhaps we value them for their potential. Whatever the explanation, the fact that we do feel this way about them is in itself a valid reason for extending to them stronger moral and legal protections than we extend to nonhuman animals, even those which may have just as well or better-developed psychological capacities. A third, and perhaps the most important, reason is that if we did *not* extend strong moral rights to infants, far too few of them would ever *become* responsible, morally autonomous adults; too many would be treated "like animals" (i.e., in ways that it is generally wrong to treat even animals), and would consequently become socially crippled, antisocial or just very unhappy people. If any part of our moral code is to remain intact, it seems that infants and small children *must* be protected and cared for.

Analogous arguments explain why strong moral rights should also be accorded to other nonparadigm humans. The severely retarded or incurably senile, for instance, may have no potential for moral autonomy, but there are apt to be friends, relatives or other people who care what happens to them. Like children, such individuals may have more mental capacities than are readily apparent. Like children, they are more apt to achieve, or return to moral autonomy if they are valued and well cared for. Furthermore, any one of us may someday become mentally incapacitated to one degree or another, and we would all have reason to be anxious about our own futures if such incapacitation were made the basis for denying strong moral rights.

There are, then, sound reasons for assigning strong moral rights even to human beings who lack the mental capacities which justify the general distinction between human and animal rights. Their rights are based not only on the value which they themselves place upon their lives and well-being, but also on the value which other human beings place upon them.

But is this a valid basis for the assignment of moral rights? . . . Regan argues that we cannot justify the ascription of stronger rights to nonparadigm humans than to nonhuman animals in the way suggested, because "what underlies the ascription of rights to any given X is that X has value independently of anyone's valuing X."[11] After all, we do not speak of expensive paintings or gemstones as having rights, although many people value them and have good reasons for wanting them protected.

There is, however, a crucial difference between a rare painting and a severely retarded or senile human being; the latter not only has (or may have) value for other human beings but *also* has his or her own needs and interests. It may be this which leads us to say that such individuals have intrinsic value. The sentience of nonparadigm humans, like that of sentient nonhuman animals, gives them a place in the sphere of rights holders. So long as the moral rights of all sentient beings are given due recognition, there should be no objection to providing some of them with *additional* protections, on the basis of our interests as well as their own. Some philosophers speak of such additional protections, which are accorded to X on the basis of interests other than X's own, as *conferred* rights, in contrast to *natural* rights, which are entirely based upon the properties of X itself. But such "conferred" rights are not necessarily any weaker or less binding upon moral agents than are "natural" rights. Infants, and most other nonparadigm humans have the *same* basic moral rights that the rest of us do, even though the reasons for ascribing those rights are somewhat different in the two cases. . . .

NOTES

1. Ruth Cigman, "Death, Misfortune, and Species Inequality," *Philosophy and Public Affairs* 10, no. 1 (Winter 1981): p. 48.

2. Ibid., pp. 57–58. The concept of a categorical desire is introduced by Bernard Williams, "The Makropoulous Case," in his *Problems of the Self* (Cambridge: Cambridge University Press), 1973.

3. Brigid Brophy, "In Pursuit of a Fantasy," in *Animals, Men and Morals,* ed. Stanley and Rosalind Godlovitch (New York: Taplinger Publishing Co., 1972), p. 129.

4. H. J. McCloskey, "Moral Rights and Animals," *Inquiry* 22, nos. 1–2 (1979): 31.

5. Ibid., p. 29.

6. Michael Fox, "Animal Liberation: A Critique," *Ethics* 88, no. 2 (January 1978): 111.

7. Joel Feinberg, "The Rights of Animals and Unborn Generations," in *Philosophy and Environmental Crisis,* ed. William T. Blackstone (Athens, Ga.: University of Georgia Press), 1974, pp. 46–47.

8. Aristotle, *Politics* I. 1254, 1260, and 1264.

9. Peter Singer, *Animal Liberation: A New Ethics for Our Treatment of Animals* (New York: Avon, 1975), pp. 75–76; Tom Regan, "One Argument Concerning Animal Rights," *Inquiry* 22, nos. 1–2 (1979): 189–217.

10. Mary Anne Warren, "Do Potential People Have Moral Rights?" *Canadian Journal of Philosophy* 7, no. 2 (June 1977): 275–89.

11. Regan, "One Argument Concerning Animal Rights," p. 189.

READING QUESTIONS

1. Explain the difference between the content and strength of rights according to Warren.
2. Why does Warren believe that nonhuman animals lack a strong right to life? Why might death be a more severe misfortune for a human being than a nonhuman animal?
3. What is Warren's argument against the view that moral autonomy is required in order to possess certain rights? How does she argue for the view that nonhuman animals possess weaker rights than humans? What is Warren's response to the objection that her view is speciesist?
4. What is a nonparadigm human according to Warren? What reasons does she give for thinking that we should grant full moral rights to nonparadigm humans?

DISCUSSION QUESTIONS

1. Suppose that Warren is right to claim that nonparadigm humans should have full moral rights. What reasons could be given in favor of the view that nonhuman animals should have full moral rights as well? Consider some possible objections to Warren's argument for the view that nonparadigm humans should have full moral rights.
2. How relevant should moral autonomy be in the discussion of moral rights? Discuss whether autonomy is ever irrelevant to the ascription of an individual's standing in the moral community.

JORDAN CURNUTT

A New Argument for Vegetarianism

Curnutt argues that attempts by utilitarians and rights-based moral theorists to defend vegetarianism fail. He defends a new argument for vegetarianism based on the prima facie duty
against inflicting harm. In outline, his argument goes as follows. Since many nonhuman
animals are harmed by the practice of killing and eating them, such treatment is prima facie
morally wrong. Moreover, other considerations including those of cultural practices, aesthetic preferences, convenience, and nutrition do not provide reasons that override this prima
facie duty. Thus, killing and eating animals is all-things-considered wrong (in most cases),
and thus being a vegetarian is morally required.

Recommended Reading: ethics of prima facie duty, chap. 1, sec. 2F.

Philosophical discussion of vegetarianism has been
steadily decreasing over the last ten years or so. This
follows a prolific period in the 1970s and 1980s
when a veritable flood of books and journal articles appeared, devoted wholly or in part to various
defenses and rejections of vegetarianism. What has
happened? Have the relevant problems been solved?
Have philosophers simply lost interest in the topic? I
don't think so. My hypothesis is that the major theoretical approaches to the issue which have been most
rigorously pursued have produced a stalemate: appeal
to some form of utilitarian theory, or to rights-based
theories, or to pain and suffering, have not proved
fruitful for resolving the problems.

I would like to present an alternative to these traditional approaches. This alternative avoids the difficulties which result in the stalemate, successfully
eludes subsequent objections, and justifies a moral
requirement to refrain from eating animals. I will first
briefly explain why the old arguments have not been
helpful. The remainder of the paper is devoted to the
explanation and defense of a new argument for vegetarianism, one which does not depend on calculations

of utility, any particular conception of rights, or the
imposition of pain and suffering.

OLD ARGUMENTS
FOR VEGETARIANISM

Peter Singer has been the leading utilitarian defender
of vegetarianism for more than twenty years.[1] He has
often cited the vast amounts of pain and suffering
experienced by domesticated animals "down on the
factory farm" as they await and inevitably succumb
to their fate as food for human consumption.[2] A utilitarian of any species is required to produce that state
of affairs in which aggregations of certain positive
and negative mental states exceed (or at least equal)
such aggregations of any alternative state of affairs.
Singer has argued that factory farming woefully
fails to meet this standard. Vegetarianism is morally
obligatory simply because it maximizes utility, precisely what utilitarians say we are supposed to do.

From Jordan Curnutt, "A New Argument for Vegetarianism," *Journal of Social Philosophy* 28 (1997). Reprinted by permission
of *Journal of Social Philosophy*.

Animal-eating promotes disutility, precisely what we are supposed to avoid.

But several philosophers have urged that utilitarianism is a perilous ally for the vegetarian. One major problem is that the end of animal-eating produces disutilities which must be accounted for in the utilitarian ledger. When that is done, animal-eating may not emerge as morally wrong after all. For example, R. G. Frey has claimed that the demise of the meat industry and its satellites which would attend a wholesale conversion to vegetarianism would be catastrophic to human welfare, and so could not be given a utilitarian justification.[3] Frey lists fourteen different ways in which rampant vegetarianism would deleteriously affect human affairs, mainly in the form of economic losses for those employed in the industry. In the face of this, his utilitarian calculation yields the result that we are permitted to eat animals at will, but we must strive to reduce the amount of suffering they experience.[4]

Not only does vegetarianism produce disutilities, but animal-eating can actually maximize utility: utilitarianism may *require* animal-eating. Roger Crisp contends that this theory leads to what he calls the "Compromise Requirement view."[5] According to Crisp, "nonintensively-reared animals lead worthwhile lives: and humans derive gustatory pleasure, satisfaction, or some other positive mental state from eating them. Vegetarianism would put an end to these two sources of utility. Thus, given the requirement to maximize utility, raising and eating animals in these circumstances becomes a utilitarian obligation.[6]

These philosophers, among others, have pinpointed why the utilitarian case for vegetarianism is a shaky one. Like any other utilitarian calculation, the issue here is an empirical and hence contingent one: vegetarianism is at the mercy of such capricious factors as the number of humans who eat meat relative to the number of animals eaten, and the negative and positive mental states attendant on a wide variety of animal husbandry situations and human living conditions. A similar contingency concerning methods of livestock-rearing also obtains for any argument premised on the pain and suffering caused to the animals eaten, whether or not these experiences are deployed

in a utilitarian schema. Moreover, this theory requires summing and comparing the positive and negative mental states of *billions* of individuals of several different species. That prospect alone certainly makes it appear as though the problem is an intractable one. The lesson to be learned is that a successful argument for vegetarianism must be independent of any current or possible method of livestock-rearing and must appeal to factors which are fairly clear and manageable.

The leading contender to utilitarian theory in this area has been the rights-based perspective of Tom Regan. His dedication to defending animals in general and vegetarianism in particular nearly matches Singer's in duration and production.[7] In brief, Regan's position is that mammals of at least one year old are "subjects-of-a-life": they are conscious beings with a wide variety of mental states, such as preferences, beliefs, sensations, a sense of self and of the future. These features identify animals as rightsholders and possessors of "inherent" value. One implication of this view is that killing animals for food, whether or not this is done painlessly and independently of the quality of the animals' life, is a violation of their right to respectful treatment, since it uses them as a means to our own ends. Hence, vegetarianism is morally required.

Regan is one of many philosophers who advocate the view that nonpersons in general or animals in particular (or both) qualify as moral rightsholders. These philosophers tend to identify rightsholders according to their possession of certain affective capacities, such as interests or desires, and a number of them argue that animals do have these capacities. On the other hand, many other philosophers prefer cognitive criteria, confining rightsholders to beings with certain more advanced mental capacities—rationality and autonomy are the favorites—and explicitly or by implication disqualifying animals from this category.

The Case for Animal Rights represents the *opus classicus* of the deontological approach to animal issues. Through more than four hundred pages of dense and tightly argued text, Regan has canvassed the philosophical problems of human-animal relationships more thoroughly than anyone has ever done. Even so, his view has been subjected to some quite damaging criticisms, ranging from concern over the mysterious and controversial nature of "inherent value" to charges of inconsistency and implausibility when the rights of humans and those of animals come into conflict.[8] This fact, along with the formidable arguments marshaled by those who champion cognitive requirements for rights-holding, suggest that basing a case for vegetarianism upon the foundation of moral rights is an onerous task. The major problem is that the topic is exceedingly complex. A study of rights must address such daunting question as: What are rights? Are they real independently existing entities (natural rights) or human inventions (political, legal) or both? What is needed to qualify as a rights-holder? Exactly what rights are held by whom and why? How are conflicts among rights settled?

Thus, we have a very complicated theoretical endeavor marked by profound differences, yielding an area of philosophical debate which is highly unsettled. This tells us that a new argument for vegetarianism should traverse a relatively uncontroversial theoretical region which is stable and fixed.

A NEW ARGUMENT FOR VEGETARIANISM (NEW)

NEW makes no appeal to utility, rights, or pain and suffering:

[1] Causing harm is prima facie morally wrong.
[2] Killing animals causes them harm.
[3] Therefore, killing animals is prima facie morally wrong.
[4] Extensive animal-eating requires the killing of animals.
[5] Therefore, animal-eating is prima facie morally wrong.
[6] The wrongness of animal-eating is not overridden.
[7] Therefore, animal-eating is ultima facie morally wrong.

Premise [1] is an assumption: harming is wrong, not because it violates some right or because it fails to maximize utility, but simply because it is wrong. As "prima facie," however, the wrongness may be overridden in certain cases. I discuss premise [6] in the last section of the paper, and there I argue that the wrongness of the harm which eating animals causes them is not overridden, that it is "all things considered" or ultima facie wrong.

The term "extensive" in premise [4] indicates that the target of NEW is the industrialized practice of killing billions of animals as food for hundreds of millions of people, what has been referred to as "factory farming." NEW allows small-scale subsistence hunting, and eating animals who died due to accidents, natural causes, or other sources which do not involve the deliberate actions of moral agents.

The term "animal" used here and throughout this paper refers to any vertebrate species. For reasons I will make clear, NEW is more tentative with regard to invertebrate species. NEW is concerned with the harm caused by the killing and eating of animals, so it does not prohibit uses of animals which do not directly result in their deaths, in particular, those characteristic of the egg and dairy industries. Thus, the argument claims that "ovolacto vegetarianism" is not morally required.

I now proceed to defend the remainder of NEW: how killing animals causes them harm (premise [2]); why the prima facie wrongness of killing animals (conclusion [3]) means that eating animals is also prima facie wrong (conclusion [5]); and why the wrongness is not overridden (premise [6]).

KILLING AND HARM

The claim that killing animals causes them harm might seem too obvious to warrant much discussion. However, its importance here is to distance NEW more clearly from other defenses of vegetarianism. As we will see, killing is harmful—and therefore morally wrong—whether or not any rights are violated, and whether or not any pain or suffering occurs or some other conception of utility fails to be maximized.

Joel Feinberg's analysis of harm is especially useful here. To harm a being is to do something which adversely affects that individual's *interests*. According to Feinberg, harming amounts to "the thwarting, setting back, or defeating of an interest."[9] Interests are not univocal. Some interests are more important than others depending on their function in maintaining the basic well-being or welfare of the individual concerned. The most critical and essential interests that anyone can have are what Feinberg calls "welfare interests":

> In this category are the interests in the continuance for a foreseeable interval of one's life, the interests in one's own physical health and vigor, the integrity and normal functioning of one's body, the absence of absorbing pain and suffering . . . , emotional stability, the absence of groundless anxieties and resentments, the capacity to engage normally in social intercourse . . . , a tolerable social and physical environment, and a certain amount of freedom from interference and coercion.[10]

Welfare interests are "the very most important interests . . . cry[ing] out for protection" not only because they are definitive of basic well-being, but also because their realization is necessary before one can satisfy virtually any other interest or do much of anything with one's life. We cannot achieve our (ulterior) interests in a career or personal relationships or material goods if we are unhealthy, in chronic pain, emotionally unstable, living in an intolerable social and physical environment, and are constantly interfered with and coerced by others. Feinberg concludes that when welfare interests are defeated, a very serious harm indeed has been done to the possessor of those interests.[11]

What does it take to have an interest? Feinberg points out that there is a close connection between interests and desires: if A does in fact have an interest in x, we would typically not deny that A wants x.[12] However, we do speak of x *being in* A's interest, whether A wants x or not; this seems to be especially so when we are considering the welfare interests described above. We believe that normally an individual's life, physical and mental health, and personal freedom are in his or her interest even if these things are not wanted by that individual. This suggests to Feinberg that interests of this kind obtain independently of and are not derived from desires.[13]

We have here all that is needed to defend the claim that killing an animal causes it harm and is therefore (by the moral principle assumed in premise [1]) morally wrong. Moreover, killing is perhaps the most serious sort of harm that can be inflicted upon an animal by a moral agent; this is so not only because of the defeat of an animal's welfare interests—in life, health, and bodily integrity—but also because these are likely the only kind of interests animals have. One understanding of such interests appeals to the desire the animal has to live in a healthy, normal state of well-being. On Feinberg's analysis, another understanding of these interests makes no appeal to any such desire. This implies that killing defeats welfare interests independently of whether or not animals have a desire for life and well-being. They have an interest in this which is defeated when agents cause their deaths.

Some might object here that this is much too fast. Although it is true that x can be in A's interest even when A does not desire x, still x cannot be in A's interest if A has no desires whatever. Otherwise, we would be allowing that plants have interests, and that, some might think, is clearly absurd. Therefore, in order for this analysis of harm to be applicable to animals, it must be shown that they have some desires, preferably desires for that which agents are defeating.

DESIRE

Let us agree that the morally relevant sense of interest we want here is one constituted by certain desires. So why would anyone think that animals do not have desires? We attribute desires to animals routinely on much the same basis that we attribute desires to other people: as an explanation of their behavior. To say that some animal A wants x, uttered because A is doing something, is an extremely common locution for those who are in contact with animals everyday and seems to cause no problem for those who rarely ever encounter an animal. This creates a strong presumption in favor of animal desire. Since nobody denies that humans have desires, what do we have which animals do not have?

An answer that has been given, and perhaps the only answer available, is that animals do not have language. R. G. Frey holds this view that it is linguistic ability which makes desires possible. He maintains that for A to desire x, A must believe that something about x obtains.[14] However, "in expressions of the form '[A] believes that . . .' what follows the 'that' is a sentence, and what [A] believes is that the sentence is true."[15] Since animals do not have a language, they cannot believe that any sentence is true. It follows that animals have neither beliefs nor desires.

This argument has serious defects. Consider first: Frey does not give us any reason to accept the implication that belief is a necessary condition for desire. This is not obvious: the relationship between belief and desire is a complex one which has not been thoroughly investigated by philosophers. Some have held that the relation is one of correlativity, while others argue against it. And what can be called "primitive" desires do not seem to be attended by any particular beliefs: if I desire food or drink or sex or sleep, just what is it that I believe? That I am hungry, thirsty, aroused, or tired? But are these distinguishable from the desires themselves? I might believe that satisfying the desire will bring pleasure or satiation. But I might not. It is by no means clear that there must be some belief lurking about in order to genuinely have a desire.

Consider next Frey's claim that when A believes something, what A believes is that a certain sentence is true. So, for example, Harry's belief that the Chicago Cubs will win the pennant is his believing that the sentence "The Cubs will win the pennant" is true. But in that case, his belief that this sentence is true must itself be the belief that some other sentence is true, namely, the sentence "The sentence 'The Cubs will win the pennant' is true" is true. But then if Harry believes *that* sentence is true, he has to believe another sentence about this sentence about a

sentence is true, and so on. What Frey needs is some way to stop this regress.

Assume there is some nonarbitrary and convincing way to stop the regress; the belief under consideration is Harry's believing that the sentence "The Cubs will win the pennant" is true. But this is not what Harry believes. What he believes is *the Cubs will win the pennant,* that is, he believes that a group of men playing baseball will win more games than any team in their division over the course of the entire season, and then beat the winner of the other division four times in a playoff series. Harry's belief is about certain states of affairs in the world involving complex sets of persons, objects, and events, extended over a significant amount of time. His belief is clearly not about the truth value of a sentence.

So Frey has not shown that belief is a necessary condition for desire, and his argument that animals do not have desires fails. The next move would be to attack the specific desire in question. I have argued that killing an animal is morally wrong because of the harm the killing does; this harm is constituted by the defeat of welfare interests, and this interest is primarily a desire to live. One could then deny that animals have *this* desire. Ruth Cigman takes this approach when she denies that animals have "categorical desires," these being required to genuinely suffer death as a harm or "misfortune":

> to discover whether [death] is a misfortune for an animal, we must ask whether, or in what sense, animals don't want to die. . . . [A categorical desire] . . . answers the question whether one wants to remain alive . . . I reject the suggestion that a categorical desire is attributable to animals [because] . . . animals would have to possess essentially the same conceptions of life and death as persons do [and] . . . understand death as a condition which closes a possible future forever. . . .[16]

Cigman is denying that animals have this desire because it requires understanding certain *concepts:* life, death, the future, the value of life, and others.

The difficulties with Frey's argument suggest that concepts, or language generally, are not required in order to have desires (or beliefs), but these "categorical" kind are presumably supposed to be very special and hard to obtain. Let us assume that there really are these sorts of desires and they are as Cigman has described them. The question is: Why does a being need "categorical desires" in order to have a desire to live?

Cigman does not say. She simply notes that Bernard Williams says the desire to remain alive is a categorical desire and then proceeds to detail what such a desire involves in a way which excludes animals. She has given us no argument for the view that the observations we make of animal activities are not enough to attribute a desire to live to them: fleeing from predators and enemies, seeking cover from severe weather, tending to injuries (such as they can), struggling to extricate themselves from potentially fatal situations, and exhibiting palpable fear in the face of threats to their lives are just the sorts of behaviors which exhibit this desire. Cigman might respond here that such actions only show that animals are "blindly clinging on to life"[17] rather than manifesting a genuine desire to live; it is instinct or some automatic response, not intentional action. But these activities are not blind clutchings, they are purposive and deliberate with a particular point to them, namely, to maintain that life. We would make precisely the same attributions to humans who acted in this way, without pausing to consider whether or not they had the concepts Cigman asserts are requisite. And if we were to learn that these humans did not have these concepts, we would not and should not withdraw our judgment and chalk it all up to instinct. . . .

RECAPITULATION AND ELABORATION

At this point in the defense of NEW, we have firmly established the following:

[1] Causing harm is prima facie morally wrong.
[2] Killing animals causes them harm.
[3] Therefore, killing animals is prima facie morally wrong.

We have seen why killing animals harms them, and we have successfully countered challenges to the analysis of animal harms. We understand why this is one of the worst harms an animal can undergo, which indicates that this is a very serious (though prima facie) wrong when perpetrated by a moral agent. We can also now see the advantages of NEW over the old arguments for vegetarianism. NEW is not contingent upon any current or possible methods of raising animals for humans to eat: no matter how it is done, supplying food for millions of animal-eaters means the defeat of animal welfare interests. NEW does not employ any theoretical constructs which are unsettled and divisive: the analysis of harm in terms of interests and desires which are exhibited by certain behaviors is widely accepted and intuitively appealing. NEW does not introduce any indeterminacy or unwieldy ratiocination into the discussion: the desires and interests of animals, and the wrongness of defeating them, are plainly evident for all those who would simply look and see.

We can also now understand two further aspects of the vegetarianism required by NEW. Killing any creature with certain desires defeats its welfare interests, and is therefore harmful, but not all living things have such desires and interests. The judgment that some being has the requisite mental states must be formed on the basis of behavior and physiological evidence. Since invertebrates and plants either do not exhibit the appropriate behavior or they do not possess the appropriate physiological equipment (or both), consuming them is permitted. Although I do not hold that "interest-less" forms of life have no moral status whatever, I cannot here develop the notion of degrees of moral value or consider what else besides interests would qualify an entity for a moral status. It will have to suffice to say that beings with certain mental states are of greater moral worth than those without them, from the moral point of view it is better (ceteris paribus) to kill and eat a plant than an animal. Moreover, much vegetable matter can be eaten without killing anything: most vegetarian fare consists of the fruits and flowers of plants which are not killed or are harvested at the end of annual life cycles.

THE MORAL WRONGNESS OF EATING ANIMALS

The next step is to link the wrongness of *killing* animals with the wrongness of *eating* them:

[3] Therefore, killing animals is prima facie morally wrong.

[4] Animal-eating requires the killing of animals.

[5] Therefore, animal-eating is prima facie morally wrong.

Many might regard this step as especially problematic. All that has been shown so far is that moral agents who kill animals are engaged in actions which are prima facie wrong; how can it follow from this that different actions, done by different agents, are also prima facie wrong? After all, very few of those who consume animal flesh have personally killed the animals they eat. Those who actually do the killing—slaughterhouse workers—act impermissibly, while those who merely eat the body parts of dead animals supplied by those workers do not. How could the wrongness of one set of agents and actions *transfer* to an entirely different set?

One response would point out that purchasing and consuming the products of "factory farming" contributes to a morally abhorrent practice and thus perpetuates future wrongdoing. So although it is the killing which constitutes what is wrong with the practice of animal-eating, and conceding that very few animal-eaters actually kill what they eat, this contribution to and perpetuation of the killing should prompt us to act *as if* eating the animals is itself wrong. . . .

[But] we must not make this concession. Animal-eating is itself wrong, but this is not due to any "transference" of wrongness from the act of killing to the act of purchasing and eating animal flesh. The purchasing and consuming are two parts of the same wrong.

To see this, consider this [argument]:

This is a lovely lamp. You say its base is made from the bones and its shade from the skin of Jews killed in concentration camps? Well, so what? I didn't kill them.

Of course what the Nazis did was wrong, a very great moral evil. But my not buying the lamp is obviously not going to bring any of them back. Nor will it prevent any future harm: this sort of thing doesn't even occur any more, so there is no future wrongdoing to prevent even if my refusal to buy were effective in this way, which of course it wouldn't be. So what's wrong with buying and using the lamp?

. . . We do not need to find some way to understand this activity which will allow it to be construed "as if" it were wrong (but really isn't). Animal-eating is wrong for much the same reason that purchasing and using the products of a concentration camp or those of slave labor generally is wrong; it is wrong for the same reason that buying stolen property or accepting any of the ill-gotten gains of another is wrong: a person who eats animals, or buys and uses lamps from Auschwitz or cotton clothing from the antebellum South, or a hot stereo from a hoodlum is profiting from, benefiting from a morally nefarious practice. Doing so, and especially doing so when morally innocuous alternatives are readily available, not only indicates support for and the endorsement of moral evil, it is also to participate in that evil. It is an act of complicity, partaking in condemnable exploitation, reaping personal advantages at a significant cost to others. This is so whether or not an individual's abstinence from the practice has any effect whatsoever on its perpetuation. It strikes me as quite uncontroversial to say that one who concurs and cooperates with wrongdoing, who garners benefits through the defeat of the basic welfare interests of others, is himself doing something which is seriously morally wrong.

OVERRIDING THE MORAL WRONGNESS OF EATING ANIMALS

The final step in the defense of NEW is to support premise [6]: the prima facie wrongness of animal-eating is not defeated by additional factors which serve as overriding reasons; from this it will follow that animal-eating is ultima facie morally wrong (the conclusion [7]). There are at least four grounds for overriding this wrong: [1] traditional-cultural; [2] esthetic; [3] convenience; [4] nutrition. Do any of these supply an overriding reason which would morally justify the very serious harm that killing animals for food causes them?

[1] People eat animals because they have been raised on that diet, as have their parents and grandparents and on back through the generations. Animal-eating is a social practice which is deeply embedded into modern culture. Slavery, the oppression of women, and institutionalized racism also once had this status; however, few if any suppose that this status is what makes practices morally right or wrong. Slavery, for example, is wrong because it requires the persistent exploitation, coercion, and degradation of innocent people, not because it happens to be extinct in our society. The fact that a practice has the weight of tradition on its side and a prominent place in a given culture does not in itself carry any moral weight.[18]

[2] Animal flesh is regarded by most people as esthetically pleasing. Animal body parts are prepared for consumption in hundreds of different ways, employing many cooking techniques, spices, and accompaniments. Yet the esthetic attractions of other practices are regarded as irrelevant to their moral appraisal. Heliogabalus had masses of people gathered in fields, only to be mercilessly slaughtered solely for the pleasing effect he found in the sign of red blood on green grass.[19] Or consider "snuff films" whose "plot" is centered around the filming of an actual murder of a person apparently chosen at random. Who would not condemn such cinema in the strongest possible terms, even if it were directed by Orson Welles or Martin Scorcese and starred Dustin Hoffman or Meryl Streep? Yet one has only to enter the nearest slaughterhouse with a video camera on any given day of the week to produce a movie every bit as horrific as the most polished "snuff film."

[3] The convenience of animal-eating is largely a function of the other two factors. The pervasiveness of the desire to eat animals and its prominence within a variety of social functions naturally provokes free market economies to supply meat relatively cheaply and easily. Again, this seems to say nothing about whether or not animal-eating is morally permissible. It is often quite inconvenient and very difficult to keep a promise or discharge a parental duty or make a sacrifice for a stranger—or a friend; it is often quite convenient and very easy to conceal the trust or pocket merchandise without paying or take advantage of powerless persons. Few of us believe that convenience and ease have much of anything to do with whether these actions are morally right or wrong. Why should it be any different when it comes to killing animals for food?

It might be said that the difference is that human interests in convenience, in tradition, and esthetic pleasure override animal interests in life and well-being. This is because the defeat of an *animal* welfare interest, though morally wrong, is not a serious moral wrong. But what is it about humans which gives these nonbasic interests a moral priority over the most basic and important interests an animal can have? And what is it about animals which prevents a severe harm to them from being a serious moral problem? Certainly the nonbasic interests of some humans do not have a moral priority over the welfare interests of other humans, and there is no question that the gravity of a wrong increases with the severity of harm caused to humans. So in order to sustain the objection, some feature, unique to our species, must be identified which accounts for the disparity between human and animal harms and wrongs. Two such distinguishing features, already encountered, immediately present themselves as possibilities: rationality and language. However, appeal to one or both of these capacities raises two immediate problems. First, neither feature is uniquely absent in animal species. No one would seriously contend that a taste for human baby flesh morally overrides anything, nor would anyone claim that the defeat of a child's welfare interest was not a serious moral wrong. Second, why does the proposed feature make such an enormous moral difference? The suggestion is that rationality or language justifies a gap in treatment so vast that it means utmost respect and consideration for humans but allows killing animals out of habit and pleasure. This seems very implausible. The lack of the requisite capacities might reasonably justify *some* difference in treatment, but not a difference which requires a dignified life for those who are favored and permits an ignominious death for those who are not.

[4] Nutrition. Most recent debate about vegetarianism has focused on the question of the adequacy of a meatless diet for human nutrition. This could provide the best reason for overriding the wrongness of killing animals. Let us assume as a fundamental principle that no moral agent can be required to destroy his or her own health and basic welfare for the sake of others; therefore, a diet having this consequence is not morally justified. Does vegetarianism seriously endanger an individual's health and well-being?

Kathryn Paxton George has argued that a vegetarian diet would make large numbers of humans worse off than they would otherwise be if they ate animals. She lists seven groups of people for whom such abstinence possess a significant risk to personal health.[20] Evelyn Pluhar has disputed many of George's findings, especially those regarding the benefits of iron and the threat of osteoporosis. Supported by numerous nutrition studies, she argues that vitamin and mineral supplementation, as well as the utilization of appropriate plant sources, will alleviate any deficiencies; furthermore, Pluhar contends that the correlation between consuming animal products and meeting certain health requirements is a dubious one.[21] George responded that Pluhar had either misinterpreted or willfully ignored certain facts of the studies she had herself cited.[22] The exchange continues; a journal has devoted an entire issue to their disagreement.[23]

Fortunately, we need not enter this particular debate; George's target is what she calls "strict vegetarianism," the vegan diet totally devoid of any animal product. Both George and Pluhar admit that eggs and dairy products, which are allowed by NEW, would fulfill all or most of the required protein, vitamin, and mineral intake. I am not aware of any humans who, as a matter of basic welfare, must consume animal flesh in addition to eggs and dairy products, but if there are any such people, NEW would allow them to eat animals: we are under no moral requirement to significantly harm ourselves so that others, human or non-human, may benefit. . . .

I conclude that none of [1]–[4] serve as a sufficiently compelling reason to override the wrongness of harming the animals eaten. If there are any individuals who must eat animal flesh (rather than just eggs and dairy products) in order to avoid a pronounced deterioration of their health, they are not prohibited from doing so by NEW. This possible case notwithstanding, the eating of animal flesh is ultima facie morally wrong.

The success of NEW indicates the direction in which future philosophical discussion of vegetarianism ought to proceed. That path avoids the intractable, contingent, and highly controversial nature of rights-based theories and utilitarianism, focusing instead on the more manageable and less contentious areas of the wrongness of harming as a basic moral principle, the analysis of harm as a defeat of interests, and the understanding of interests in terms of certain desires. Much work remains to be done: the philosophy of mind which accounts plausibly for attributions of the appropriate mental states to animals needs to be specified; a fuller analysis of moral status (especially regarding the status of plant life) and the respective natures of basic and nonbasic interests will go a long way toward explaining the conditions under which various moral judgments are overridden; that project will lead to a certain ontological understanding of moral value and the general metaethical underpinnings of the normative ethic employed here. For now, the failure of arguments intended to deny animals the requisite interests and desires, and the failure of those intended to undermine NEW by appeal to overriding reasons and the wrong done by the consumer of animal flesh, means that vegetarianism emerges as a moral requirement as compelling as many of those that are more readily acknowledged and more assiduously practiced.

NOTES

1. In many works, but most notably *Animal Liberation,* Avon, 1st ed., 1975, 2nd ed., 1990; and *Practical Ethics,* Cambridge, 1st ed., 1979, 2nd ed., 1993.

2. For example, *Animal Liberation,* chap. 3. See also *Animal Factories,* Harmony Books, rev. ed., 1990, coauthored with Jim Mason.

3. *Rights, Killing, and Suffering,* Basil Blackwell, 1983.

4. Frey: 197–202.

5. "Utilitarianism and Vegetarianism," *International Journal of Applied Philosophy* 4 (1988): 41–49.

6. Crisp: 44. However, utility is not maximized by eating the products of factory farming. Crisp argues against Frey, that utilitarian considerations do not permit us to eat "intensively-reared" animals. But Frey asserts that "millions upon millions" of animals are not intensively-reared anyway (pp. 33–34).

7. Principally in a series of papers beginning with "The Moral Basis of Vegetarianism," *Canadian Journal of Philosophy* 5 (1975): 181–214, and culminating in *The Case for Animal Rights,* University of California Press, 1983.

8. For example: Paul Taylor, "Inherent Value and Moral Rights," and Jan Narveson, "On a Case for Animal Rights," both in *The Monist* 70 (1987): 15–49; David Ost, "The Case Against Animal Rights," *The Southern Journal of Philosophy* 24 (1986): 365–73; Mary Anne Warren, "Difficulties with the Strong Animal Rights Position," *Between the Species* 2 (1987): 163–73; and J. Baird Callicott, "Review of Tom Regan, *The Case For Animal Rights:* repr. in *In Defense of the Land Ethic,* State University of New York Press, 1989: 39–47.

9. *Harm to Others,* Oxford University Press, 1984: 33.

10. Feinberg: 37. Welfare interests are contrasted with "ulterior interests," which presuppose but also require as a necessary condition that certain welfare interests are satisfied. Feinberg lists raising a family, building a dream house, advancing a social cause, and others as examples of ulterior interests.

11. Ibid.

12. Ibid.: 38.

13. Ibid.: 42.

14. *Interests and Rights,* Clarendon, 1980: 72. Actually, Frey holds that desiring x requires that "I believe that I am deficient in respect of" x. This is too strong. I have amended the belief statement to a weaker claim, leaving it open what exactly A believes about x.

15. Frey: 87.

16. "Death, Misfortune, and Species Inequality," *Philosophy and Public Affairs* 10 (1980): 57–58. The concept of a "categorical desire" is adopted from Bernard Williams. I am taking "misfortune" and "harm" as synonymous, though Cigman herself never equates the two.

17. Cigman: 57.

18. A point forcefully made by means of a macabre device in the classic short story by Shirley Jackson, "The Lottery."

19. As reported by R. M. Hare in *Freedom and Reason,* Clarendon Press, 1963: 161.

20. "So Animal a Human . . . , or the Moral Relevance of Being An Omnivore," *Journal of Agricultural Ethics* 3 (1990): 172–186. Her list (pp. 175–78) includes children, pregnant and lactating women, the elderly, the poor, and the "undereducated."

21. "Who Can be Morally Obligated to be a Vegetarian?" *Journal of Agricultural and Environmental Ethics* 5 (1992): 189–215.

22. "The Use and Abuse of Scientific Studies," *Journal of Agricultural and Environmental Ethics* 5 (1992): 217–33.

23. *Journal of Agricultural and Environmental Ethics* 7 (1994).

READING QUESTIONS

1. Explain the old arguments for vegetarianism according to Curnutt. What are the problems he raises for Peter Singer and Tom Regan's arguments?

2. What is Curnutt's new argument? What does this argument not appeal to according to Curnutt? Why is the first premise problematic?

3. Explain the objection to the view that nonhuman animals have interests of a certain kind. How are interests and desires related according to Curnutt? What reasons does he consider for the view that nonhuman animals lack certain desires that humans have?

4. What are the four considerations that could potentially override the view that it is morally wrong to eat nonhuman animals? How does Curnutt respond to the problems raised by each consideration?

DISCUSSION QUESTIONS

1. Is Curnutt's argument an improvement over the arguments offered by Peter Singer and Tom Regan? Why or why not? What reasons might we have for thinking that Curnutt's new argument does appeal to utility, rights, or pain and suffering?

2. Consider whether there are any morally relevant differences between killing or harming animals and the act of eating them. Could eating animals be morally permitted even though killing and harming them is impermissible?

ADDITIONAL RESOURCES

Web Resources

People for the Ethical Treatment of Animals, <http://www.peta.org/>. Site of one of the most prominent animal advocacy organizations.

Gruen, Lori, "The Moral Status of Animals," <http://plato.stanford.edu/entries/moral-animal/>. An overview of the debate over the moral standing of nonhuman animals.

Authored Books

Regan, Tom, *The Case for Animal Rights*, 2nd ed. (Berkeley: University of California Press, 2004). An elaboration and defense of the view presented in his article in this chapter.

Singer, Peter, *Animal Liberation*, 2nd ed. (New York: Harper Perennial, 2002). Citing a wealth of empirical information, Singer's classic book (first published in 1975) defends the equal treatment of all sentient creatures.

Scully, Matthew, *Dominion*: *The Power of Man, the Suffering of Animals, and the Call to Mercy* (New York: St. Martin's Griffin, 2003). Journalist and former speechwriter for President George W. Bush, Scully argues against affording rights to animals and instead holds that the same goals of those who advocate animal rights can be obtained by appealing to the proper respect we ought to have toward animals.

Edited Collections

Armstrong, Susan J., and Richard G. Botzler (eds.), *The Animal Ethics Reader* (London: Routledge, 2003). An encyclopedic anthology covering all facets of the ethical treatment of animals, including for example, articles on animal experimentation, animals and entertainment, and animals and biotechnology.

Baird, Robert M., and Stuart E. Rosenbaum (eds.), *Animal Experimentation*: The Moral Issues (Amherst, N.Y.: Prometheus Books, 1991). A collection of sixteen essays including articles about the utilitarian and rights approaches to the issues.

Singer, Peter, (ed.), *In Defense of Animals: The Second Wave* (Oxford: Blackwell, 2006). A collection of eighteen essays, most of them appearing here for the first time, representing the most recent wave of thinking about the ethical treatment of animals.

Sunstein, Cass R., and Martha C. Nussbaum (eds.), *Animal Rights: Current Debates and New Directions* (Oxford: Oxford University Press, 2004). A collection of essays addressing ethical questions about ownership, protection against unjustified suffering, and the ability of animals to make their own choices free from human control.

9 Abortion

Perhaps the most hotly disputed of the moral questions represented in this book is the one over abortion. Here, unfortunately, is one topic where, in much of the public debate, passions run high while reason often goes on holiday. Some of the recent moral and legal controversy over abortion has focused on second-trimester abortions that involve a particular medical procedure known as *intact dilation and extraction* (I-D&E) and is referred to by its opponents as "partial-birth abortion."[1] In 2003, U.S. President George W. Bush signed into law the "Partial-Birth Abortion Ban Act," which makes I-D&E abortions illegal. While this particular legal and moral controversy is over a particular method of terminating a woman's pregnancy in the middle stages of pregnancy, there are controversies over first-trimester abortions including nonsurgical abortions that make use of the so-called abortion pill.[2]

As a start, we can raise the moral question of abortion in a simple way with this question:

- Is abortion ever morally permissible?

In order to clarify these disputed issues concerning abortion, let us consider some basic matters of biology, after which we will be in a better position to understand the abortion controversy. (Later in this introduction, I will suggest a more precise way of raising the central moral question over abortion.)

1. SOME BASICS ABOUT FETAL DEVELOPMENT

Certainly having some basic information about the biological facts of fetal development is important for coming to have a justified view about the morality of abortion. Below is a chart that summarizes what seem to be the most important biological facts that are often discussed in the literature on the morality of abortion.

The terminology in the following chart (**zygote, embryo,** and **fetus**) reflects strict medical usage, and so a fetus is not present until (roughly) the eighth week of pregnancy. But this medical use of the term is almost always ignored in ethical discussions of abortion where the term "fetus" is used also to refer to both the zygote and the embryo. My label for the chart reflects this broader usage, and henceforth I will be using the term in this way.

Stage	Time	Terminology	Comments
Fertilization/conception	Beginning of pregnancy	"zygote" (fertilized ovum). Also called a "conceptus."	Sperm unites with fertile ovum (egg) in the fallopian tube. 23 chromosomes of the female nucleus combine with 23 chromosomes contributed by the male nucleus resulting in a one-cell zygote with a human genetic code.
Cell division	Roughly every 22 hours		The process continues in the fallopian tube for about 72 hours until the zygote reaches the uterus.
Implantation	Day 5 or 6	60-cell berrylike cluster called a "morula." (Morum is Latin for "mulberry.") The morula develops into what is called the "blastocyst" consisting of two types of cells: the inner cell mass and the outer, enveloping layer of cells.	At implantation, the outer layer of cells ("trophoblast") connects with the maternal uterus, thus stimulating the formation of the placenta. The placenta transfers nutrients through the umbilical cord from the woman to the developing conceptus.
Embryonic stage	Weeks 2–4	Referred to as the "embryo" until week 8.	During this period, the embryo undergoes cell differentiation into three cell types: the ectoderm (producing skin and nervous system); the mesoderm (producing connective tissues, muscles, circulatory system, and bones); and the endoderm (producing the digestive system, lungs, and urinary system). The embryo divides into head and trunk and the internal organs (heart, brain) begin to develop. Limb buds begin to appear.

FIGURE 9.1   Stages of Fetal Development

Embryonic stage continued	Weeks 4–8		Continuation of development
Fetal stage	Week 8–birth	Name changed to "fetus" (also spelled "foetus")	Used in a strict biological sense, a fetus is an unborn vertebrate animal that has developed to the point of having the basic structure that is characteristic of its kind. This stage is characterized by growth and full development of its organs.
	Week 21 (roughly)	"Viability" refers to the stage in fetal development wherein it is possible for the fetus to survive outside the uterus.	
	Weeks 24–28		Developed capacity to feel pain (**sentience**)

FIGURE 9.1   Stages of Fetal Development (*continued*)

Having covered some of the biology of fetal development, let us proceed to clarify the dispute over abortion, beginning with a definition of what it is.

2. WHAT IS ABORTION?

Unfortunately, the term **abortion** is defined in importantly different ways. On some definitions, abortion refers to the *termination of a pregnancy before viability*.[3] Notice that although this definition does not explicitly refer to the death of the fetus, its death is implied given the definition of **viability** as the stage wherein it is possible for the fetus to survive outside the uterus. Notice also that this definition allows us to distinguish between spontaneous abortions and induced abortion. Spontaneous abortions (also called "miscarriages") result from "natural causes" and without the aid of deliberate interference. It is estimated that around 40 percent of pregnancies end in spontaneous abortion, many of them occurring very early in pregnancy and often mistaken for a delayed menstrual period. Induced abortions, then, are those that are brought about as a result of deliberate intervention.

But, then, if abortion is defined as the termination of a pre-viable fetus, what should we call the termination of a pregnancy after viability has been reached? Some post-viable terminations are due to premature birth. However, others are medically induced where the aim is to preserve the life of the fetus, as in cases of caesarean sections. Such cases are normally not a matter of moral dispute. The problematic cases are so-called partial birth abortions, which are defined as abortions in the second or third trimester of pregnancy in which the death of the fetus is induced after it has passed partway through the birth canal. Since viability occurs roughly in the middle of the second trimester, the definition of abortion with which we began would not classify many such cases as those of abortion. So, in order to recognize all cases that are of concern in the controversy over abortion, let us broaden the definition of "abortion" and use the term to refer to all cases in which *a pregnancy is intentionally interrupted and involves (as part of the process or aim of interruption) the intentional killing of the fetus.* This definition rules out so-called spontaneous abortions as being abortions, which we may instead refer to as miscarriages.

3. THE FETUS AND MORAL STANDING

Now that we have before us some information about fetal development and a working definition of abortion, let us focus for a moment on questions about the moral standing of the fetus.

Roughly, to say that something has moral standing is to say that it counts morally, that it needs to be taken into account in moral decision making. This idea is sometimes expressed by claiming that the thing or creature in question has rights, or that it has intrinsic value, or that we have duties *to* it and not just duties *with regard to* it. In order to clarify this idea a bit more, we can distinguish between something's having **direct moral standing** and something's having merely **indirect moral standing**. (This distinction was introduced in the previous chapter on the ethical treatment of animals.) Something possesses direct moral standing when it possesses properties in virtue of which it has moral standing. The rough idea here is that there is something inherent in the item in question that grounds its standing. By contrast, something has mere indirect moral standing when its standing depends entirely on its being related to something else that has direct moral standing. One might hold, for instance, that to have direct moral standing, a creature must be capable of rational, deliberate action and that (at least on Earth) only human beings and perhaps some higher primates have this property. It would then follow that all other creatures and nonliving things that have any moral standing will have it only because of how their existence bears on the lives of beings with direct moral standing.

Does a human fetus, at least at some stage of development, have direct moral standing? If we assume that direct moral standing can come in degrees, does it ever come to have strong direct moral standing—moral standing strong enough to make abortion seriously wrong? Answers to these questions require that one explain what it is about the fetus in virtue of which it has moral standing and in what degree: we need to specify some "marks" of direct moral standing. And much of the literature on abortion concerns the plausibility of various proposed criteria. Among the criteria that are often mentioned, we find having an immortal soul, having a human genetic code, having personhood, sentience, readable brain activity, being a potential person, having a future like that of an adult human being, viability, and birth. As we shall see, many of these criteria will be considered in the readings in this chapter.

In thinking clearly about the various proposed criteria of direct moral standing, it is useful to be aware of the distinction between necessary and sufficient conditions. To say that something X is a necessary condition for Y is to say that Y will not occur (exist or come to be) unless X is present. A necessary condition for someone's committing suicide is that they die. But clearly dying is not sufficient for having committed suicide. To say that X is a sufficient condition for Y is to say that if X occurs, its occurrence is enough for (sufficient for) Y's occurring. Dying is necessary but not sufficient for suicide. Jumping from a fifty-story building under normal conditions and landing on the pavement below is sufficient for committing suicide, but not necessary; there are many other ways to commit suicide.

Return now to questions about the moral standing of the fetus. Those who defend a conservative view (see section 5) about the morality of abortion often argue that in early pregnancy, the fetus possesses certain features that are *sufficient* for having strong direct moral standing. Nonconservatives often cite features that fetuses lack (either early on or perhaps throughout the entire pregnancy) that they take to be *necessary* for having strong direct moral standing, and thereby arrive at moderate or liberal positions on abortion. In thinking about what people say and write about the moral standing of the fetus, it is always a good idea to be clear about what claim is being made: is the claim that such and so feature is sufficient for having direct moral standing? If so, then in order to test the proposal, you try to think of something that clearly has the feature in question but that does not have moral standing. Is the claim that such and so feature is necessary for having direct moral standing? If so, then to test the proposal, you try to think of something that has moral standing but that lacks the feature in question.

4. REASONS FOR SEEKING AN ABORTION

Besides questions about the moral status of the fetus, there are questions about the reasons someone might propose for having an abortion. Often such reasons fall into one of the following categories (the list is not meant to be exhaustive):

- *Therapeutic* reasons: reasons relating to the life and health of the pregnant woman.
- *Eugenic* reasons: reasons relating to fetal abnormality.
- *Humanitarian* reasons: reasons that deal with a pregnancy due to incest or rape.
- *Socioeconomic* reasons: reasons relating, for example, to poverty, social stigma, or family size.

- *Personal* reasons: these include reasons other than any of the ones just mentioned that relate to a woman's preferences and projects. Two such reasons would be the desire to devote time to a professional career and just not wanting to be inconvenienced by the pregnancy.

The obvious point to be made here is that in thinking carefully about the morality of abortion, it is important to consider what reasons someone might propose for having an abortion and whether the reason in question is a genuinely good reason. Considerations of self-defense where a woman's life is endangered by her pregnancy presumably justify her having an abortion, and many conservative positions on abortion recognize this. What is controversial is whether any of the other kinds of considerations on the prior list can justify having an abortion. (And notice that putting the issue in this way—whether such and so reason can justify abortion—already seems to assume that at some stage of its development, the fetus has some moral standing.)

5. A RANGE OF VIEWS ON THE MORALITY OF ABORTION

In light of the preceding discussion, we can make our leading question about the morality of abortion more precise by restating it as follows:

- At what stage in fetal development (if any) and for what reasons (if any) is abortion ever morally permissible?

This way of posing the issue calls attention to the two main areas of moral dispute just described. First, there is dispute over the moral standing of the fetus at various stages in fetal development. One might hold, for instance, that at conception a human fetus (technically, a zygote) has no moral standing, and thus aborting the fetus very early in pregnancy is not morally wrong, although later in pregnancy (because of changes in the developing fetus), it does have moral standing and therefore later-stage abortions are wrong. The second area of dispute is over what sorts of reasons for having an abortion (if any) would morally justify such a procedure. One might hold, for instance, that the fact that the pregnant woman will die unless she aborts her fetus would justify having an abortion but that, say, economic reasons would not. And, of course, it is possible to hold the view that as the fetus develops its moral standing becomes stronger, and thus the reasons that would justify having an abortion must be correspondingly strong.

The labels "pro-life" and "conservative" are often used to refer to those who morally oppose abortion, whereas the terms "pro-choice" and "liberal" are often used to characterize those who do not. But such labels grossly oversimplify the complexity of the abortion issue and thereby falsely suggest that there are only two positions one might take on the issue. Given the way in which the main ethical question about abortion was formulated earlier, together with the discussion of the moral standing of the fetus and reasons for seeking an abortion, it should be clear that there is a range of views that one might hold about the morality of abortion. We can distinguish three broad categories of views: liberal, moderate, and conservative, so long as we keep in mind that each of these categories allows for a "more or less" version. Referring to our central moral question about abortion, an extreme liberal view would be one according to which abortion is morally permissible at any stage of moral development for any reason, whereas an extreme conservative view would hold that abortions are morally wrong at any stage of fetal development and for any reason. But, of course, there are liberal and conservative views that are not this extreme. And many people hold views that are most appropriately seen as moderate: some abortions are wrong and some aren't depending on the stage of fetal development and kind of reason one might have for having an abortion. So rather than think of the abortion dispute as between pro-life (conservative) and pro-choice (liberal), we should rather think in terms of a spectrum of possible views one might hold about the morality of abortion, as indicated by the following visual aid.[4]

| Liberal | Moderate | Conservative |

6. THE LEGALITY OF ABORTION

The 1973 U.S. Supreme Court decision in *Roe v. Wade* made many abortions legal.[5] In that case, a Texas resident, under the fictitious name of Jane Roe, challenged the then Texas law that made abortion illegal except in cases in which the woman's life was threatened by her pregnancy. Although the Court recognized a woman's right to privacy, including a right to decide to terminate her pregnancy, it also recognized a state's legitimate interest in protecting the life and health of the pregnant woman as well as a legitimate interest in protecting prenatal life. The decision in the case of *Roe* represented an attempt by the Court to balance these interests and resulted in striking down the Texas law. The ruling in effect gave a woman a constitutionally guaranteed right to an abortion throughout the first two-thirds of pregnancy, allowing some restrictions on the methods and circumstances of abortion for medical reasons. The *Roe* decision continues to be a source of heated moral and legal debate in the United States. In 1992 in the case *Planned Parenthood of Southeastern Pennsylvania v. Casey*,[6] the Court upheld the basic right to abortion established in *Roe*, but overturned the trimester formula of *Roe*, replacing it with viability as the stage of pregnancy at which a state's interest in prenatal life may override a pregnant woman's right to choose abortion. As noted above, in 2003 the Partial-Birth Abortion Ban Act was signed into law that prohibits partial-birth abortions (defined in note 1). In 2007 this Act was upheld as constitutional by the U.S. Supreme Court in *Gonzales, Attorney General v. Carhart et al.*[7] by a 5-to-4 vote.

7. THEORY MEETS PRACTICE

The various readings in this chapter reflect arguments about abortion from the perspectives of natural law theory, rights approaches, Kantian moral theory, and virtue ethics. Although none of the authors in this chapter approach the issue from a utilitarian or consequentialist perspective, let us begin with this perspective and then briefly consider how representatives of the other moral theories approach abortion.

Consequentialism

The consequentialist will approach the morality of abortion by considering how much overall intrinsic value is likely to be brought about by abortion. And, of course, claims about the overall consequences of any single abortion as well as claims about the practice of abortion are very controversial, and consequentialists will thus differ over abortion when they differ in their beliefs about its consequences.

Natural Law Theory

Although the selection by Pope John Paul II does not explicitly mention natural law doctrine, the idea that human life and human procreation are among the basic intrinsic goods is evident in what the pope says about abortion. According to natural law theory, the intentional killing of an innocent human being is always morally wrong. Based partly on biological claims about the human genetic code, the pope infers that a fetus is an innocent human being and that therefore abortion is murder.

Rights Approaches

The abortion dispute is often cast as a battle of rights: the (alleged) rights of the fetus versus the rights of the pregnant woman. Such disputes involve an inquiry into the basis of rights and a determination of the strengths of various rights of the woman compared to any rights a fetus may have. The articles by Mary Anne Warren and Judith Jarvis Thomson are concerned with such issues and their implications for the morality of abortion.

Virtue Ethics

Rosalind Hursthouse approaches the abortion issue from the perspective of virtue ethics, according to which rightness and wrongness depend on considerations of virtue and vice. This approach makes questions about a person's motives and questions of overall character salient in thinking about the morality of abortion. Such questions as whether having an abortion would be callous or self-centered, or rather whether, in some cases, it would be an expression of humility or modesty, are central in a virtue ethics approach for deciding whether some case of abortion would be morally right or wrong.

NOTES

1. Intact dilation and extraction involves removing or partially removing the fetus from the woman's cervix, after which the fetus is killed. It is defined as follows: "An abortion in which the person performing the abortion (A) deliberately and intentionally vaginally delivers a living fetus until, in the case of the head-first presentation, the entire fetal head is outside the body of the mother, or, in the case of breech presentation, any part of the fetal trunk past the navel is outside the body of the mother, for the purpose of performing an overt act that the person knows will kill the partially delivered living fetus; and (B) performs the overt act, other than completion of the delivery, that kills the partially

delivered living fetus." This method of D&E is distinguished from "standard D&E" in which the fetus is torn apart and thus dies before its body parts are extracted. The Partial-Birth Abortion Ban Act does not prohibit standard D&E abortions.

2. Nonsurgical abortions, which may be performed in the first 63 days of pregnancy, involve the use of RU-486 (the generic name for mifepristone), which is taken either in pill form or by injection (methotrexate).

3. See, for example, the *Merriam-Webster Online Dictionary* entry.

4. See the introduction to chapter 3 on sexual morality (section 1) for a related discussion of the spectrum of views one might hold about the morality of sexual behavior. Readers should be aware that taking a conservative moral position on some issue does not commit one to the political ideology of Conservatism, nor does taking a liberal view on some issue commit one to the ideology of Liberalism. For more on these ideologies, see chapter 4 on pornography, hate speech, and censorship, section 1.

5. 410 U.S. 113 (1973).

6. 505 U.S. 833.

7. 550 U.S. 124.

POPE JOHN PAUL II

The Unspeakable Crime of Abortion

According to Pope John Paul II, a human fetus from conception is an innocent human being and "is to be respected and treated as a person" and thus has the same right to life (and in the same degree) as any other person. Thus, abortions that kill the fetus are instances of murder, and various considerations that are often given in defense of abortion, including the health of the pregnant woman, cannot justify killing the innocent fetus.

Recommended Reading: Although Pope John Paul II does not appeal directly to natural law theory (chap. 1, sec. 2B), it is often the basis of the positions that the Catholic Church takes on moral issues. This is particularly evident in the Vatican Declaration included in the chapter on sexual morality.

Among all the crimes which can be committed against life, procured abortion has characteristics making it particularly serious and deplorable. The Second Vatican Council defines abortion, together with infanticide, as an "unspeakable crime."[1]

But today, in many people's consciences, the perception of its gravity has become progressively obscured. The acceptance of abortion in the popular mind, in behaviour and even in law itself, is a telling sign of an extremely dangerous crisis of the moral sense, which is becoming more and more incapable of distinguishing between good and evil, even when the fundamental right to life is at stake. Given such a grave situation, we need now more than ever to have the courage to look the truth in the eye and to *call things by their proper name,* without yielding to convenient compromises or to the temptation of self-deception. In this regard the reproach of the Prophet is extremely straightforward: "Woe to those who call evil good and good evil, who put darkness for light and light for darkness" (*Is* 5:20). Especially in the case of abortion there is a widespread use of ambiguous terminology, such as "interruption of pregnancy," which tends to hide abortion's true nature and to attenuate its seriousness in public opinion. Perhaps this linguistic phenomenon is itself a symptom of an uneasiness of conscience. But no word has the power to change the reality of things: procured abortion is *the deliberate and direct killing, by whatever means it is carried out, of a human being in the initial phase of his or her existence, extending from conception to birth.*

The moral gravity of procured abortion is apparent in all its truth if we recognize that we are dealing with murder and, in particular, when we consider the specific elements involved. The one eliminated is a human being at the very beginning of life. No one more absolutely *innocent* could be imagined. In no way could this human being ever be considered an aggressor, much less an unjust aggressor! He or she is *weak,* defenseless, even to the point of lacking that minimal form of defence consisting in the poignant power of a newborn baby's cries and tears. The unborn child is *totally entrusted* to the protection and care of the woman carrying him or her in the womb.

And yet sometimes it is precisely the mother herself who makes the decision and asks for the child to be eliminated, and who then goes about having it done.

It is true that the decision to have an abortion is often tragic and painful for the mother, insofar as the decision to rid herself of the fruit of conception is not made for purely selfish reasons or out of convenience, but out of a desire to protect certain important values such as her own health or a decent standard of living for the other members of the family. Sometimes it is feared that the child to be born would live in such conditions that it would be better if the birth did not take place. Nevertheless, these reasons and others like them, however serious and tragic, *can never justify the deliberate killing of an innocent human being.*

As well as the mother, there are often other people too who decide upon the death of the child in the womb. In the first place, the father of the child may be to blame, not only when he directly pressures the woman to have an abortion, but also when he indirectly encourages such a decision on her part by leaving her alone to face the problems of pregnancy:[2] in this way the family is thus mortally wounded and profaned in its nature as a community of love and in its vocation to be the "sanctuary of life." Nor can one overlook the pressures which sometimes come from the wider family circle and from friends. Sometimes the woman is subjected to such strong pressure that she feels psychologically forced to have an abortion: certainly in this case moral responsibility lies particularly with those who have directly or indirectly obliged her to have an abortion. Doctors and nurses are also responsible, when they place at the service of death skills which were acquired for promoting life.

But responsibility likewise falls on the legislators who have promoted and approved abortion laws, and, to the extent that they have a say in the matter, on the administrators of the health-care centres where abortions are performed. A general and no less serious responsibility lies with those who have encouraged the spread of an attitude of sexual permissiveness and a lack of esteem for motherhood, and with those who should have ensured—but did not—effective family and social policies in support of families, especially larger families and those with particular financial and educational needs. Finally, one cannot overlook the network of complicity which reaches out to include international institutions, foundations and associations which systematically campaign for the legalization and spread of abortion in the world. In this sense abortion goes beyond the responsibility of individuals and beyond the harm done to them, and takes on a distinctly social dimension. It is a most serious *wound* inflicted on society and its culture by the very people who ought to be society's promoters and defenders. As I wrote in my *Letter to Families,* "we are facing an immense threat to life: not only to the life of individuals but also to that of civilization itself."[3] We are facing what can be called a *"structure of sin"* which opposes human life not yet born.

Some people try to justify abortion by claiming that the result of conception, at least up to a certain number of days, cannot yet be considered a personal human life. But in fact, "from the time that the ovum is fertilized, a life is begun which is neither that of the father nor the mother; it is rather the life of a new human being with his own growth. It would never be made human if it were not human already. This has always been clear, and . . . modern genetic science offers clear confirmation. It has demonstrated that from the first instant there is established the programme of what this living being will be: a person, this individual person with his characteristic aspects already well determined. Right from fertilization the adventure of a human life begins, and each of its capacities requires time—rather lengthy time—to find its place and to be in a position to act."[4] Even if the presence of a spiritual soul cannot be ascertained by empirical data, the results themselves of scientific research on the human embryo provide "a valuable indication for discerning by the use of reason a personal presence at the moment of the first appearance of a human life: how could a human individual not be a human person?"[5]

Furthermore, what is at stake is so important that, from the standpoint of moral obligation, the mere probability that a human person is involved would suffice to justify an absolutely clear prohibition of any intervention aimed at killing a human embryo. Precisely for this reason, over and above all scientific debates and those philosophical affirmations to which the Magisterium has not expressly committed itself, the Church has always taught and continues to teach that the result of human procreation, from the first moment of its existence, must be guaranteed that unconditional respect which is morally due to the human being in his or her totality and unity as body and spirit: "*The human being is to be respected and treated as a person from the moment of conception*; and therefore from that same moment his rights as a person must be recognized, among which in the first place is the inviolable right of every innocent human being to life."[6]

NOTES

1. Pastoral Constitution on the Church in the Modern World *Gaudium et Spes*, 51: "Abortus necnon infanticidium nefanda sunt crimina."

2. Cf. John Paul II, Apostolic Letter *Mulieris Dignitatem* (15 August 1988), 14: *AAS* 80 (1988), 1686.

3. No. 21: *AAS* 86 (1994), 920.

4. Congregation for the Doctrine of the Faith, *Declaration on Procured Abortion* (18 November 1974), Nos. 12–13: *AAS* 66 (1974), 738.

5. Congregation for the Doctrine of the Faith, Instruction on Respect for Human Life in Its Origin and on the Dignity of Procreation *Donum Vitae* (22 February 1987), I, No. 1: *AAS* 80 (1988), 78–79.

6. Ibid., loc. cit., 79.

READING QUESTION

1. The Pope's main antiabortion argument is presented in the second to last paragraph of the selection. Try stating the argument's premises and its conclusion.

DISCUSSION QUESTIONS

1. Is it possible to agree with the Pope's genetic code argument regarding the moral status of the human fetus and yet reject the Pope's claim that all abortions are morally wrong?

2. Suppose a woman in early pregnancy finds out that she has cancer of the uterus and that she needs an immediate operation—a hysterectomy—to survive. This operation will inevitably bring about the death of the fetus and both woman and physicians know this. Would this procedure be morally permissible according to the Pope's stance on abortion? Why or why not? (In thinking about this question, it is important to consider the Pope's claim that abortion is "deliberate and direct killing" of the fetus. Readers are also advised to review the discussion of the principle of double effect in chap. 1, sec. 2E.)

MARY ANNE WARREN

On the Moral and Legal Status of Abortion

Warren first argues that the so-called genetic code argument—the argument that attempts to establish the moral standing of the fetus by appealing to biological facts—is fallacious. She then goes on to consider the issue of whether the fetus (at some stage of development) is a person by developing an account of the nature of personhood. According to Warren's analysis, a fetus is not a person at any stage in its development, and from this she concludes that abortion is not morally wrong. In arguing for her view, she considers and rejects opposing arguments that appeal to facts about fetal development, potentiality, and infanticide.

Recommended Reading: rights-focused approach to moral issues, chap. 1, sec. 2E.

The question which we must answer in order to produce a satisfactory solution to the problem of the moral status of abortion is this: How are we to define the moral community, the set of beings with full and equal moral rights, such that we can decide whether a human fetus is a member of this community or not?

What sort of entity, exactly, has the inalienable rights to life, liberty, and the pursuit of happiness? Jefferson attributed these rights to all *men,* and it may or may not be fair to suggest that he intended to attribute them *only* to men. Perhaps he ought to have attributed them to all human beings. If so, then we arrive, first, at [John] Noonan's problem of defining what makes a being human, and, second, at the equally vital question which Noonan does not consider, namely, What reason is there for identifying the moral community with the set of all human beings, in whatever way we have chosen to define that term?

1. ON THE DEFINITION OF "HUMAN"

One reason why this vital second question is so frequently overlooked in the debate over the moral status of abortion is that the term "human" has two distinct, but not often distinguished, senses. This fact results in a slide of meaning, which serves to conceal the fallaciousness of the traditional argument that since (1) it is wrong to kill innocent human beings, and (2) fetuses are innocent human beings, then (3) it is wrong to kill fetuses. For if "human" is used in the same sense in both (1) and (2) then, whichever of the two senses is meant, one of these premises is question-begging. And if it is used in two different senses then of course the conclusion doesn't follow.

Thus, (1) is a self-evident moral truth,[1] and avoids begging the question about abortion, only if "human being" is used to mean something like "a full-fledged member of the moral community." (It may or may not also be meant to refer exclusively to members of the species *Homo sapiens.*) We may call this the *moral* sense of "human." It is not to be confused with what we will call the *genetic* sense, i.e., the sense in which *any* member of the species is a human being, and no member of any other species could be. If (1) is acceptable only if the moral sense is intended, (2) is non-question-begging only if what is intended is the genetic sense.

In "Deciding Who Is Human," Noonan argues for the classification of fetuses with human beings by pointing to the presence of the full genetic code, and the potential capacity for rational thought.[2] It is clear that what he needs to show, for his version of the traditional argument to be valid, is that fetuses

are human in the moral sense, the sense in which it is analytically true that all human beings have full moral rights. But, in the absence of any argument showing that whatever is genetically human is also morally human, and he gives none, nothing more than genetic humanity can be demonstrated by the presence of the human genetic code. And, as we will see, the *potential* capacity for rational thought can at most show that an entity has the potential for *becoming* human in the moral sense.

2. DEFINING THE MORAL COMMUNITY

Can it be established that genetic humanity is sufficient for moral humanity? I think that there are very good reasons for not defining the moral community in this way. I would like to suggest an alternative way of defining the moral community, which I will argue for only to the extent of explaining why it is, or should be, self-evident. The suggestion is simply that the moral community consists of all and only *people*, rather than all and only human beings;[3] and probably the best way of demonstrating its self-evidence is by considering the concept of personhood, to see what sorts of entity are and are not persons, and what the decision that a being is or is not a person implies about its moral rights.

What characteristics entitle an entity to be considered a person? This is obviously not the place to attempt a complete analysis of the concept of personhood, but we do not need such a fully adequate analysis just to determine whether and why a fetus is or isn't a person. All we need is a rough and approximate list of the most basic criteria of personhood, and some idea of which, or how many, of these an entity must satisfy in order to properly be considered a person.

In searching for such criteria, it is useful to look beyond the set of people with whom we are acquainted, and ask how we would decide whether a totally alien being was a person or not. (For we have no right to assume that genetic humanity is necessary for personhood.) Imagine a space traveler who lands on an unknown planet and encounters a race of beings utterly unlike any he has ever seen or heard of. If he wants to be sure of behaving morally toward these beings, he has to somehow decide whether they are people, and hence have full moral rights, or whether they are the sort of thing which he need not feel guilty about treating as, for example, a source of food.

How should he go about making this decision? If he has some anthropological background, he might look for such things as religion, art, and the manufacturing of tools, weapons, or shelters, since these factors have been used to distinguish our human from our prehuman ancestors, in what seems to be closer to the moral than the genetic sense of "human." And no doubt he would be right to consider the presence of such factors as good evidence that the alien beings were people, and morally human. It would, however, be overly anthropocentric of him to take the absence of these things as adequate evidence that they were not, since we can imagine people who have progressed beyond, or evolved without ever developing, these cultural characteristics.

I suggest that the traits which are most central to the concept of personhood, or humanity in the moral sense, are, very roughly, the following:

1. consciousness (of objects and events external and/or internal to the being), and in particular the capacity to feel pain;
2. reasoning (the *developed* capacity to solve new and relatively complex problems);
3. self-motivated activity (activity which is relatively independent of either genetic or direct external control);
4. the capacity to communicate, by whatever means, messages of an indefinite variety of types, that is, not just with an indefinite number of possible contents, but on indefinitely many possible topics;
5. the presence of self-concepts, and self-awareness, either individual or racial, or both.

Admittedly, there are apt to be a great many problems involved in formulating precise definitions of these criteria, let alone in developing universally valid behavioral criteria for deciding when they apply. But I will assume that both we and our explorer know approximately what (1)–(5) mean, and that he is also able to determine whether or not they apply. How, then, should he use his findings to decide whether or not the alien beings are people? We needn't suppose that an entity must have *all* of these attributes to be properly considered a person; (1) and (2) alone may well be sufficient for personhood, and quite probably (1)–(3) are sufficient. Neither do we need to insist that any one of these criteria is *necessary* for personhood, although once again (1) and (2) look like fairly good candidates for necessary conditions, as does (3), if "activity" is construed so as to include the activity of reasoning.

All we need to claim, to demonstrate that a fetus is not a person, is that any being which satisfies *none* of (1)–(5) is certainly not a person. I consider this claim to be so obvious that I think anyone who denied it, and claimed that a being which satisfied none of (1)–(5) was a person all the same, would thereby demonstrate that he had no notion at all of what a person is—perhaps because he had confused the concept of a person with that of genetic humanity. If the opponents of abortion were to deny the appropriateness of these five criteria, I do not know what further arguments would convince them. We would probably have to admit that our conceptual schemes were indeed irreconcilably different, and that our dispute could not be settled objectively.

I do not expect this to happen, however, since I think that the concept of a person is one which is very nearly universal (to people), and that it is common to both proabortionists and antiabortionists, even though neither group has fully realized the relevance of this concept to the resolution of their dispute. Furthermore, I think that on reflection even the antiabortionists ought to agree not only that (1)–(5) are central to the concept of personhood, but also that it is a part of this concept that all and only people have full moral rights. The concept of a person is in part a moral concept; once we have admitted that *x* is a person we have recognized, even if we have not agreed to respect, *x*'s right to be treated as a member of the moral community. It is true that the claim that *x is a human being* is more commonly voiced as part of an appeal to treat *x* decently than is the claim that *x* is a person, but this is either because "human being" is here used in the sense which implies personhood, or because the genetic and moral senses of "human" have been confused.

Now if (1)–(5) are indeed the primary criteria of personhood, then it is clear that genetic humanity is neither necessary nor sufficient for establishing that an entity is a person. Some human beings are not people, and there may well be people who are not human beings. A man or woman whose consciousness has been permanently obliterated but who remains alive is a human being which is no longer a person; defective human beings, with no appreciable mental capacity, are not and presumably never will be people; and a fetus is a human being which is not yet a person, and which therefore cannot coherently be said to have full moral rights. Citizens of the next century should be prepared to recognize highly advanced, self-aware robots or computers, should such be developed, and intelligent inhabitants of other worlds, should such be found, as people in the fullest sense, and to respect their moral rights. But to ascribe full moral rights to an entity which is not a person is as absurd as to ascribe moral obligations and responsibilities to such an entity.

3. FETAL DEVELOPMENT AND THE RIGHT TO LIFE

Two problems arise in the application of these suggestions for the definition of the moral community to the determination of the precise moral status of a human fetus. Given that the paradigm example of a person is a normal adult human being, then (1) How like this paradigm, in particular how far advanced since conception, does a human being need to be before it begins to have a right to life by virtue, not of being fully a person as of yet, but of being *like* a person? and (2) To what extent, if any, does the fact that a fetus has the *potential* for becoming a person endow it with some of the same rights? Each of these questions requires some comment.

In answering the first question, we need not attempt a detailed consideration of the moral rights of organisms which are not developed enough, aware enough, intelligent enough, etc., to be considered people, but which resemble people in some respects. It does seem reasonable to suggest that the more like a person, in the relevant respects, a being is, the stronger is the case for regarding it as having a right to life, and indeed the stronger its right to life is. Thus we ought to take seriously the suggestion that, insofar as "the human individual develops biologically in a continuous fashion... the rights of a human person might develop in the same way."[4] But we must keep in mind that the attributes which are relevant in determining whether or not an entity is enough like a person to be regarded as having some of the same moral rights are no different from those which are relevant to determining whether or not it is fully a person— i.e., are no different from (1)–(5)—and that being genetically human, or having recognizably human facial and other physical features, or detectable brain activity, or the capacity to survive outside the uterus, are simply not among these relevant attributes.

Thus it is clear that even though a seven- or eight-month fetus has features which make it apt to arouse in us almost the same powerful protective instinct as is commonly aroused by a small infant, nevertheless it is not significantly more personlike than is a very small embryo. It is *somewhat* more personlike; it can apparently feel and respond to pain, and it may even have a rudimentary form of consciousness, insofar as its brain is quite active. Nevertheless, it seems safe to say that it is not fully conscious, in the way that an infant of a few months is, and that it cannot reason, or communicate messages of indefinitely many sorts, does not engage in self-motivated activity, and has no self-awareness. Thus, in the *relevant* respects, a fetus, even a fully developed one, is considerably less personlike than is the average mature mammal, indeed the average fish. And I think that a rational person must conclude that if the right to life of a fetus is to be based upon its resemblance to a person, then it cannot be said to have any more right to life than, let us say, a newborn guppy (which also seems to be capable of feeling pain), and that a right of that magnitude could never override a woman's right to obtain an abortion, at any stage of her pregnancy.

There may, of course, be other arguments in favor of placing legal limits upon the stage of pregnancy in which an abortion may be performed. Given the relative safety of the new techniques of artificially inducing labor during the third trimester, the danger to the woman's life or health is no longer such an argument. Neither is the fact that people tend to respond to the thought of abortion in the later stages of pregnancy with emotional repulsion, since mere emotional responses cannot take the place of moral reasoning in determining what ought to be permitted. Nor, finally, is the frequently heard argument that legalizing abortion, especially late in the pregnancy, may erode the level of respect for human life, leading, perhaps, to an increase in unjustified euthanasia and other crimes. For this threat, if it is a threat, can be better met by educating people to the kinds of moral distinctions which we are making here than by limiting access to abortion (which limitation may, in its disregard for the rights of women, be just as damaging to the level of respect for human rights).

Thus, since the fact that even a fully developed fetus is not personlike enough to have any significant right to life on the basis of its personlikeness shows that no legal restrictions upon the stage of pregnancy in which an abortion may be performed can be justified on the grounds that we should protect the rights of the older fetus, and since there is no other apparent justification for such restrictions, we may conclude that they are entirely unjustified. Whether or not it would be *indecent* (whatever that means) for a woman in her seventh month to obtain an abortion just to avoid having to postpone a trip to Europe, it would not, in itself, be *immoral*, and therefore it ought to be permitted.

4. POTENTIAL PERSONHOOD AND THE RIGHT TO LIFE

We have seen that a fetus does not resemble a person in any way which can support the claim that it has even some of the same rights. But what about its *potential*, the fact that if nurtured and allowed to develop naturally it will very probably become a person? Doesn't that alone give it at least some right to life? It is hard to deny that the fact that an entity is a potential person is a strong prima facie reason for not destroying it; but we need not conclude from this that a potential person has a right to life, by virtue of that potential. It may be that our feeling that it is better, other things being equal, not to destroy a potential person is better explained by the fact that potential people are still (felt to be) an invaluable resource, not to be lightly squandered. Surely, if every speck of dust were a potential person, we would be much less apt to conclude that every potential person has a right to become actual.

Still, we do not need to insist that a potential person has no right to life whatever. There may well be something immoral, and not just imprudent, about wantonly destroying potential people, when doing so isn't necessary to protect anyone's rights. But even if a potential person does have some prima facie right to life, such a right could not possibly outweigh the right of a woman to obtain an abortion, since the rights of any actual person invariably outweigh those of any potential person, whenever the two conflict. Since this may not be immediately obvious in the case of a human fetus, let us look at another case.

Suppose that our space explorer falls into the hands of an alien culture, whose scientists decide to create a few hundred thousand or more human beings, by breaking his body into its component cells, and using these to create fully developed human beings, with, of course, his genetic code. We may imagine that each of these newly created men will have all of the original man's abilities, skills, knowledge, and so on, and also have an individual self-concept, in short that each of them will be a bona fide (though hardly unique) person. Imagine that the whole project will take only seconds, and that its chances of success are extremely high, and that our explorer knows all of this, and also knows that these people will be treated fairly. I maintain that in such a situation he would have every right to escape if he could, and thus to deprive all of these potential people of their potential lives; for his right to life outweighs all of theirs together, in spite of the fact that they are all genetically human, all innocent, and all have a very high probability of becoming people very soon, if only he refrains from acting.

Indeed, I think he would have a right to escape even if it were not his life which the alien scientists planned to take, but only a year of his freedom, or, indeed, only a day. Nor would he be obligated to stay if he had gotten captured (thus bringing all these people-potentials into existence) because of his own carelessness, or even if he had done so deliberately, knowing the consequences. Regardless of how he got captured, he is not morally obligated to remain in captivity for *any* period of time for the sake of permitting any number of potential people to come into actuality, so great is the margin by which one actual person's right to liberty outweighs whatever right to life even a hundred thousand potential people have. And it seems reasonable to conclude that the rights of a woman will outweigh by a similar margin whatever right to life a fetus may have by virtue of its potential personhood.

Thus, neither a fetus's resemblance to a person, nor its potential for becoming a person provides any basis whatever for the claim that it has any significant right to life. Consequently, a woman's right to protect her health, happiness, freedom, and even her life,[5] by terminating an unwanted pregnancy, will always override whatever right to life it may be appropriate to ascribe to a fetus, even a fully developed one. And thus, in the absence of any overwhelming social need for every possible child, the laws which restrict the right to obtain an abortion, or limit the period of pregnancy during which an abortion may be performed, are a wholly unjustified violation of a woman's most basic moral and constitutional rights.[6]

POSTSCRIPT ON INFANTICIDE

Since the publication of this article, many people have written to point out that my argument appears to justify not only abortion, but infanticide as well. For a newborn infant is not significantly more personlike than an advanced fetus, and consequently it would

seem that if the destruction of the latter is permissible so too must be that of the former. Inasmuch as most people, regardless of how they feel about the morality of abortion, consider infanticide a form of murder, this might appear to represent a serious flaw in my argument.

Now, if I am right in holding that it is only people who have a full-fledged right to life, and who can be murdered, and if the criteria of personhood are as I have described them, then it obviously follows that killing a newborn infant isn't murder. It does *not* follow, however, that infanticide is permissible, for two reasons. In the first place, it would be wrong, at least in this country and in this period of history, and other things being equal, to kill a newborn infant, because even if its parents do not want it and would not suffer from its destruction, there are other people who would like to have it, and would, in all probability, be deprived of a great deal of pleasure by its destruction. Thus, infanticide is wrong for reasons analogous to those which make it wrong to wantonly destroy natural resources, or great works of art.

Secondly, most people, at least in this country, value infants and would much prefer that they be preserved, even if foster parents are not immediately available. Most of us would rather be taxed to support orphanages than allow unwanted infants to be destroyed. So long as there are people who want an infant preserved, and who are willing and able to provide the means of caring for it, under reasonably humane conditions, it is ceteris paribus, wrong to destroy it.

But, it might be replied, if this argument shows that infanticide is wrong, at least at this time and in this country, doesn't it also show that abortion is wrong? After all, many people value fetuses, are disturbed by their destruction, and would much prefer that they be preserved, even at some cost to themselves. Furthermore, as a potential source of pleasure to some foster family, a fetus is just as valuable as an infant. There is, however, a crucial difference between the two cases: so long as the fetus is unborn, its preservation, contrary to the wishes of the pregnant woman, violates her rights to freedom, happiness, and self-determination. Her rights override the rights of those who would like the fetus preserved, just as if someone's life or limb is threatened by a wild animal, his right to protect himself by destroying the animal overrides the rights of those who would prefer that the animal not be harmed.

The minute the infant is born, however, its preservation no longer violates any of its mother's rights, even if she wants it destroyed, because she is free to put it up for adoption. Consequently, while the moment of birth does not mark any sharp discontinuity in the degree to which an infant possesses the right to life, it does mark the end of its mother's right to determine its fate. Indeed, if abortion could be performed without killing the fetus, she would never possess the right to have the fetus destroyed, for the same reasons that she has no right to have an infant destroyed.

On the other hand, it follows from my argument that when an unwanted or defective infant is born into a society which cannot afford and/or is not willing to care for it, then its destruction is permissible. This conclusion will, no doubt, strike many people as heartless and immoral; but remember that the very existence of people who feel this way, and who are willing and able to provide care for unwanted infants, is reason enough to conclude that they should be preserved.

NOTES

1. Of course, the principle that it is (always) wrong to kill innocent human beings is in need of many other modifications, e.g., that it may be permissible to do so to save a greater number of other innocent human beings, but we may safely ignore these complications here.

2. John Noonan, "Deciding Who Is Human," *Natural Law Forum,* 13 (1968), 135.

3. From here on, we will use "human" to mean genetically human, since the moral sense seems closely connected to, and perhaps derived from, the assumption that genetic humanity is sufficient for membership in the moral community.

4. Thomas L. Hayes, "A Biological View," *Commonweal,* 85 (March 17, 1967), 677–78; quoted by Daniel Callahan, in *Abortion: Law, Choice and Morality* (London: Macmillan & Co., 1970).

5. That is, insofar as the death rate, for the woman, is higher for childbirth than for early abortion.

6. My thanks to the following people, who were kind enough to read and criticize an earlier version of this paper: Herbert Gold, Gene Glass, Anne Lauterbach, Judith Thomson, Mary Mothersill, and Timothy Binkley.

READING QUESTIONS

1. How does Warren criticize what she refers to as the "traditional argument" against abortion? (Readers should compare the argument in question with the Pope's main antiabortion argument from the previous chapter.)
2. Warren claims that being genetically human is not sufficient for moral humanity (personhood). How does she defend this claim?
3. Warren also claims that being genetically human is not necessary for moral humanity. How does she defend this claim?
4. What argument does Warren give for claiming that being a potential person cannot be used to defend an antiabortion position?
5. What reasons does Warren give for claiming that the gradualist approach to moral standing fails to show that even middle- to late-stage abortions are wrong?
6. How does Warren attempt to show that infanticide is morally wrong?

DISCUSSION QUESTIONS

1. Should we find Warren's account of personhood plausible? If not, why not?
2. Should we find Warren's explanation of the wrongness of infanticide convincing? Why or why not?

JUDITH JARVIS THOMSON

A Defense of Abortion

In what is perhaps the most famous of philosophical articles on abortion, Thomson argues for the claim that even if a fetus is a person from conception (and hence has a full right to life), a pregnant woman still has a right to have an abortion. If her argument is cogent, then those who think that the abortion issue can be settled by determining at what stage (if any) the fetus is a person are mistaken. Nevertheless, as Thomson explains, even if a pregnant woman has a right to an abortion, it does not follow that there would be nothing morally problematic about her choosing to act on this right. She claims that in some cases, depending on the circumstances, choosing an abortion would be callous or self-centered, and thus in such cases a woman ought not to choose abortion even if she has a right to.

Thomson's appeal to the vices of callousness and self-centeredness is a major theme in the virtue approach to abortion defended in the article by Rosalind Hursthouse.

Recommended Reading: rights-focused approach to moral issues, chap. 1, sec. 2D. Also relevant is virtue ethics, chap. 1, sec. 2E.

Most opposition to abortion relies on the premise that the fetus is a human being, a person, from the moment of conception. The premise is argued for, but, as I think, not well. Take, for example, the most common argument. We are asked to notice that the development of a human being from conception through birth into childhood is continuous; then it is said that to draw a line, to choose a point in this development and say "before this point the thing is not a person, after this point it is a person" is to make an arbitrary choice, a choice for which in the nature of things no good reason can be given. It is concluded that the fetus is, or anyway that we had better say it is, a person from the moment of conception. But this conclusion does not follow. Similar things might be said about the development of an acorn into an oak tree, and it does not follow that acorns are oak trees, or that we had better say they are. Arguments of this form are sometimes called "slippery slope arguments"—the phrase is perhaps self-explanatory—and it is dismaying that opponents of abortion rely on them so heavily and uncritically.

I am inclined to agree, however, that the prospects for "drawing a line" in the development of the fetus look dim. I am inclined to think also that we shall probably have to agree that the fetus has already become a human person well before birth. Indeed, it comes as a surprise when one first learns how early in its life it begins to acquire human characteristics. By the tenth week, for example, it already has a face, arms and legs, fingers and toes; it has internal organs, and brain activity is detectable.[1] On the other hand, I think that the premise is false, that the fetus is not a person from the moment of conception. A newly fertilized ovum, a newly implanted clump of cells, is no more a person than an acorn is an oak tree. But I

From Judith Jarvis Thomson, "A Defense of Abortion," *Philosophy and Public Affairs* 1 (1971). Reprinted by permission of Princeton University Press.

shall not discuss any of this. For it seems to me to be of great interest to ask what happens if, for the sake of argument, we allow the premise. How, precisely, are we supposed to get from there to the conclusion that abortion is morally impermissible? Opponents of abortion commonly spend most of their time establishing that the fetus is a person, and hardly any time explaining the step from there to the impermissibility of abortion. Perhaps they think the step too simple and obvious to require much comment. Or perhaps instead they are simply being economical in argument. Many of those who defend abortion rely on the premise that the fetus is not a person, but only a bit of tissue that will become a person at birth; and why pay out more arguments than you have to? Whatever the explanation, I suggest that the step they take is neither easy nor obvious, that it calls for closer examination than it is commonly given, and that when we do give it this closer examination we shall feel inclined to reject it.

I propose, then, that we grant that the fetus is a person from the moment of conception. How does the argument go from here? Something like this, I take it. Every person has a right to life. So the fetus has a right to life. No doubt the mother has a right to decide what shall happen in and to her body; everyone would grant that. But surely a person's right to life is stronger and more stringent than the mother's right to decide what happens in and to her body, and so outweighs it. So the fetus may not be killed; an abortion may not be performed.

It sounds plausible. But now let me ask you to imagine this. You wake up in the morning and find yourself back to back in bed with an unconscious violinist. A famous unconscious violinist. He has been found to have a fatal kidney ailment, and the Society of Music Lovers has canvassed all the available medical records and found that you alone have the right blood type to help. They have therefore kidnapped you, and last night the violinist's circulatory system was plugged into yours, so that your kidneys can be used to extract poisons from his blood as well as your own. The director of the hospital now tells you, "Look, we're sorry the Society of Music Lovers did this to you—we would never have permitted it if we had known. But still, they

did it, and the violinist now is plugged into you. To unplug you would be to kill him. But never mind, it's only for nine months. By then he will have recovered from his ailment, and can safely be unplugged from you." Is it morally incumbent on you to accede to this situation? No doubt it would be very nice of you if you did, a great kindness. But do you *have* to accede to it? What if it were not nine months, but nine years? Or longer still? What if the director of the hospital says, "Tough luck, I agree, but you've now got to stay in bed, with the violinist plugged into you, for the rest of your life. Because remember this. All persons have a right to life, and violinists are persons. Granted you have a right to decide what happens in and to your body, but a person's right to life outweighs your right to decide what happens in and to your body. So you cannot ever be unplugged from him." I imagine you would regard this as outrageous, which suggests that something really is wrong with that plausible-sounding argument I mentioned a moment ago.

In this case, of course, you were kidnapped; you didn't volunteer for the operation that plugged the violinist into your kidneys. Can those who oppose abortion on the ground I mentioned make an exception for a pregnancy due to rape? Certainly. They can say that persons have a right to life only if they didn't come into existence because of rape; or they can say that all persons have a right to life, but that some have less of a right to life than others, in particular, that those who came into existence because of rape have less. But these statements have a rather unpleasant sound. Surely the question of whether you have a right to life at all, or how much of it you have, shouldn't turn on the question of whether or not you are the product of a rape. And in fact the people who oppose abortion on the ground I mentioned do not make this distinction, and hence do not make an exception in case of rape.

Nor do they make an exception for a case in which the mother has to spend the nine months of her pregnancy in bed. They would agree that would be a great pity, and hard on the mother; but all the same, all persons have a right to life, the fetus is a person, and so on. I suspect, in fact, that they would not make an exception for a case in which, miraculously enough, the pregnancy went on for nine years, or even the rest of the mother's life.

Some won't even make an exception for a case in which continuation of the pregnancy is likely to shorten the mother's life; they regard abortion as impermissible even to save the mother's life. Such cases are nowadays very rare, and many opponents of abortion do not accept this extreme view....

Where the mother's life is not at stake, the argument I mentioned at the outset seems to have a much stronger pull. "Everyone has a right to life, so the unborn person has a right to life." And isn't the child's right to life weightier than anything other than the mother's own right to life, which she might put forward as ground for an abortion?

This argument treats the right to life as if it were unproblematic. It is not, and this seems to me to be precisely the source of the mistake.

For we should now, at long last, ask what it comes to, to have a right to life. In some views having a right to life includes having a right to be given at least the bare minimum one needs for continued life. But suppose that what in fact *is* the bare minimum a man needs for continued life is something he has no right at all to be given? If I am sick unto death, and the only thing that will save my life is the touch of Henry Fonda's cool hand on my fevered brow, then all the same, I have no right to be given the touch of Henry Fonda's cool hand on my fevered brow. It would be frightfully nice of him to fly in from the West Coast to provide it. It would be less nice, though no doubt well meant, if my friends flew out to the West Coast and carried Henry Fonda back with them. But I have no right at all against anybody that he should do this for me. Or again, to return to the story I told earlier, the fact that for continued life that violinist needs the continued use of your kidneys does not establish that he has a right to be given the continued use of your kidneys. He certainly has no right against you that *you* should give him continued use of your kidneys. For nobody has any right to use your kidneys unless you give him such a right; and nobody has the right against you that you shall give him this right—if you do allow him to go on using your kidneys, this is a kindness on your part, and not something he can claim from

you as his due. Nor has he any right against anybody else that *they* should give him continued use of your kidneys. Certainly he had no right against the Society of Music Lovers that they should plug him into you in the first place. And if you now start to unplug yourself, having learned that you will otherwise have to spend nine years in bed with him, there is nobody in the world who must try to prevent you, in order to see to it that he is given something he has a right to be given.

Some people are rather stricter about the right to life. In their view, it does not include the right to be given anything, but amounts to, and only to, the right not to be killed by anybody. But here a related difficulty arises. If everybody is to refrain from killing that violinist, then everybody must refrain from doing a great many different sorts of things. Everybody must refrain from slitting his throat, everybody must refrain from shooting him—and everybody must refrain from unplugging you from him. But does he have a right against everybody that they shall refrain from unplugging you from him? To refrain from doing this is to allow him to continue to use your kidneys. It could be argued that he has a right against us that *we* should allow him to continue to use your kidneys. That is, while he had no right against us that we should give him the use of your kidneys, it might be argued that he anyway has a right against us that we shall not now intervene and deprive him of the use of your kidneys. I shall come back to third-party interventions later. But certainly the violinist has no right against you that *you* shall allow him to continue to use your kidneys. As I said, if you do allow him to use them, it is a kindness on your part, and not something you owe him.

The difficulty I point to here is not peculiar to the right to life. It reappears in connection with all the other natural rights; and it is something which an adequate account of rights must deal with. For present purposes it is enough just to draw attention to it. But I would stress that I am not arguing that people do not have a right to life—quite to the contrary, it seems to me that the primary control we must place on the acceptability of an account of rights is that it should turn out in that account to be a truth that all persons have a right to life. I am arguing only that having a right to life does not guarantee having either a right to be given the use of or a right to be allowed continued use of another person's body—even if one needs it for life itself. So the right to life will not serve the opponents of abortion in the very simple and clear way in which they seem to have thought it would.

There is another way to bring out the difficulty. In the most ordinary sort of case, to deprive someone of what he has a right to is to treat him unjustly. Suppose a boy and his small brother are jointly given a box of chocolates for Christmas. If the older boy takes the box and refuses to give his brother any of the chocolates, he is unjust to him, for the brother has been given a right to half of them. But suppose that, having learned that otherwise it means nine years in bed with that violinist, you unplug yourself from him. You surely are not being unjust to him, for you gave him no right to use your kidneys, and no one else can have given him any such right. But we have to notice that in unplugging yourself, you are killing him; and violinists, like everybody else, have a right to life, and thus in the view we were considering just now, the right not to be killed. So here you do what he supposedly has a right you shall not do, but you do not act unjustly to him in doing it.

The emendation which may be made at this point is this: the right to life consists not in the right not to be killed, but rather in the right not to be killed unjustly. This runs a risk of circularity, but never mind: it would enable us to square the fact that the violinist has a right to life with the fact that you do not act unjustly toward him in unplugging yourself, thereby killing him. For if you do not kill him unjustly, you do not violate his right to life, and so it is no wonder you do him no injustice.

But if this emendation is accepted, the gap in the argument against abortion stares us plainly in the face: it is by no means enough to show that the fetus is a person, and to remind us that all persons have a right to life—we need to be shown also that killing the fetus violates its right to life, i.e., that abortion is unjust killing. And is it?

I suppose we may take it as a datum that in a case of pregnancy due to rape the mother has not given the unborn person a right to the use of her body for food and shelter. Indeed, in what pregnancy could it be supposed that the mother has given the unborn person such a right? It is not as if there were unborn persons drifting about the world, to whom a woman who wants a child says "I invite you in."

But it might be argued that there are other ways one can have acquired a right to the use of another person's body than by having been invited to use it by that person. Suppose a woman voluntarily indulges in intercourse, knowing of the chance it will issue in pregnancy, and then she does become pregnant; is she not in part responsible for the presence, in fact the very existence, of the unborn person inside her? No doubt she did not invite it in. But doesn't her partial responsibility for its being there itself give it a right to the use of her body? If so, then her aborting it would be more like the boy's taking away the chocolates, and less like your unplugging yourself from the violinist—doing so would be depriving it of what it does have a right to, and thus would be doing it an injustice.

And then, too, it might be asked whether or not she can kill it even to save her own life: If she voluntarily called it into existence, how can she now kill it, even in self-defense?

The first thing to be said about this is that it is something new. Opponents of abortion have been so concerned to make out the independence of the fetus, in order to establish that it has a right to life, just as its mother does, that they have tended to overlook the possible support they might gain from making out that the fetus is *dependent* on the mother, in order to establish that she has a special kind of responsibility for it, a responsibility that gives it rights against her which are not possessed by any independent person—such as an ailing violinist who is a stranger to her.

On the other hand, this argument would give the unborn person a right to its mother's body only if her pregnancy resulted from a voluntary act, undertaken in full knowledge of the chance a pregnancy might result from it. It would leave out entirely the unborn person whose existence is due to rape. Pending the availability of some further argument, then, we would be left with the conclusion that unborn persons whose existence is due to rape have no right to the use of their mothers' bodies, and thus that aborting them is not depriving them of anything they have a right to and hence is not unjust killing.

And we should also notice that it is not at all plain that this argument really does go even as far as it purports to. For there are cases and cases, and the details make a difference. If the room is stuffy, and I therefore open a window to air it, and a burglar climbs in, it would be absurd to say, "Ah, now he can stay, she's given him a right to the use of her house—for she is partially responsible for his presence there, having voluntarily done what enabled him to get in, in full knowledge that there are such things as burglars, and that burglars burgle." It would be still more absurd to say this if I had had bars installed outside my windows, precisely to prevent burglars from getting in, and a burglar got in only because of a defect in the bars. It remains equally absurd if we imagine it is not a burglar who climbs in, but an innocent person who blunders or falls in. Again, suppose it were like this: people-seeds drift about in the air like pollen, and if you open your windows, one may drift in and take root in your carpets or upholstery. You don't want children, so you fix up your windows with fine mesh screens, the very best you can buy. As can happen, however, and on very, very rare occasions does happen, one of the screens is defective; and a seed drifts in and takes root. Does the person-plant who now develops have a right to the use of your house? Surely not—despite the fact that you voluntarily opened your windows, you knowingly kept carpets and upholstered furniture, and you knew that screens were sometimes defective. Someone may argue that you are responsible for its rooting, that it does have a right to your house, because after all you *could* have lived out your life with bare floors and furniture, or with sealed windows and doors. But this won't do—for by the same token anyone can avoid a pregnancy due to rape by having a hysterectomy, or anyway by never leaving home without a (reliable!) army.

It seems to me that the argument we are looking at can establish at most that there are *some* cases in which the unborn person has a right to the use of its mother's body, and therefore *some* cases in which abortion is unjust killing. There is room for much

discussion and argument as to precisely which, if any. But I think we should side-step this issue and leave it open, for at any rate the argument certainly does not establish that all abortion is unjust killing.

There is room for yet another argument here, however. We surely must all grant that there may be cases in which it would be morally indecent to detach a person from your body at the cost of his life. Suppose you learn that what the violinist needs is not nine years of your life, but only one hour: all you need do to save his life is to spend one hour in that bed with him. Suppose also that letting him use your kidneys for that one hour would not affect your health in the slightest. Admittedly you were kidnapped. Admittedly you did not give anyone permission to plug him into you. Nevertheless it seems to me plain you *ought* to allow him to use your kidneys for that hour—it would be indecent to refuse.

Again, suppose pregnancy lasted only an hour, and constituted no threat to life or health. And suppose that a woman becomes pregnant as a result of rape. Admittedly she did not voluntarily do anything to bring about the existence of a child. Admittedly she did nothing at all which would give the unborn person a right to the use of her body. All the same it might well be said, as in the newly emended violinist story, that she *ought* to allow it to remain for that hour—that it would be indecent of her to refuse.

Now some people are inclined to use the term "right" in such a way that it follows from the fact that you ought to allow a person to use your body for the hour he needs, that he has a right to use your body for the hour he needs, even though he has not been given that right by any person or act. They may say that it follows also that if you refuse, you act unjustly toward him. This use of the term is perhaps so common that it cannot be called wrong; nevertheless it seems to me to be an unfortunate loosening of what we would do better to keep a tight rein on. Suppose that box of chocolates I mentioned earlier had not been given to both boys jointly, but was given only to the older boy. There he sits, stolidly eating his way through the box, his small brother watching enviously. Here we are likely to say "You ought not to be so mean. You ought to give your brother some of those chocolates." My own view is that it just does not follow from the truth of this that the brother has any right to any of the chocolates. If the boy refuses to give his brother any, he is greedy, stingy, callous—but not unjust. I suppose that the people I have in mind will say it does follow that the brother has a right to some of the chocolates, and thus that the boy does act unjustly if he refuses to give his brother any. But the effect of saying this is to obscure what we should keep distinct, namely the difference between the boy's refusal in this case and the boy's refusal in the earlier case, in which the box was given to both boys jointly, and in which the small brother thus had what was from any point of view clear title to half.

A further objection to so using the term "right" is that from the fact that A ought to do a thing for B, it follows that B has a right against A that A do it for him, is that it is going to make the question of whether or not a man has a right to a thing turn on how easy it is to provide him with it; and this seems not merely unfortunate, but morally unacceptable. Take the case of Henry Fonda again. I said earlier that I had no right to the touch of his cool hand on my fevered brow, even though I needed it to save my life. I said it would be frightfully nice of him to fly in from the West Coast to provide me with it, but that I had no right against him that he should do so. But suppose he isn't on the West Coast. Suppose he has only to walk across the room, place a hand briefly on my brow—and lo, my life is saved. Then surely he ought to do it, it would be indecent to refuse. Is it to be said "Ah, well, it follows that in this case she has a right to the touch of his hand on her brow, and so it would be an injustice in him to refuse"? So that I have a right to it when it is easy for him to provide it, though no right when it's hard? It's rather a shocking idea that anyone's rights should fade away and disappear as it gets harder and harder to accord them to him.

So my own view is that even though you ought to let the violinist use your kidneys for the one hour he needs, we should not conclude that he has a right to do so—we should say that if you refuse, you are, like the boy who owns all the chocolates and will give none away, self-centered and callous, inde-cent in fact, but not unjust. And similarly, that even

supposing a case in which a woman pregnant due to rape ought to allow the unborn person to use her body for the hour he needs, we should not conclude that he has a right to do so; we should conclude that she is self-centered, callous, indecent, but not unjust, if she refuses. The complaints are no less grave; they are just different. However, there is no need to insist on this point. If anyone does wish to deduce "he has a right" from "you ought," then all the same he must surely grant that there are cases in which it is not morally required of you that you allow that violin-ist to use your kidneys, and in which he does not have a right to use them, and in which you do not do him an injustice if you refuse. And so also for mother and unborn child. Except in such cases as the unborn person has a right to demand it—and we were leaving open the possibility that there may be such cases—nobody is morally *required* to make large sacrifices, of health, of all other interests and concerns, of all other duties and commitments, for nine years, or even for nine months, in order to keep another person alive.

We have in fact to distinguish between two kinds of Samaritan: the Good Samaritan and what we might call the Minimally Decent Samaritan. The story of the Good Samaritan, you will remember, goes like this:

> A certain man went down from Jerusalem to Jericho, and fell among thieves, which stripped him of his raiment, and wounded him, and departed, leaving him half dead.
>
> And by chance there came down a certain priest that way; and when he saw him, he passed by on the other side.
>
> And likewise a Levite, when he was at the place, came and looked on him, and passed by on the other side.
>
> But a certain Samaritan, as he journeyed, came where he was; and when he saw him he had compas-sion on him.
>
> And went to him, and bound up his wounds, pour-ing in oil and wine, and set him on his own beast, and brought him to an inn, and took care of him.
>
> And on the morrow, when he departed, he took out two pence, and gave them to the host, and said unto him, "Take care of him; and whatsoever thou spendest more, when I come again, I will repay thee."
>
> (Luke 10:30–35)

The Good Samaritan went out of his way, at some cost to himself, to help one in need of it. We are not told what the options were, that is, whether or not the priest and the Levite could have helped by doing less than the Good Samaritan did, but assuming they could have, then the fact they did nothing at all shows they were not even Minimally Decent Samaritans, not because they were not Samaritans, but because they were not even minimally decent.

These things are a matter of degree, of course, but there is a difference, and it comes out perhaps most clearly in the story of Kitty Genovese, who, as you will remember, was murdered while thirty-eight people watched or listened, and did nothing at all to help her. A Good Samaritan would have rushed out to give direct assistance against the murderer. Or perhaps we had better allow that it would have been a Splendid Samaritan who did this, on the ground that it would have involved a risk of death for himself. But the thirty-eight not only did not do this, they did not even trouble to pick up a phone to call the police. Minimally Decent Samaritanism would call for doing at least that, and their not having done it was monstrous.

After telling the story of the Good Samaritan, Jesus said "Go, and do thou likewise." Perhaps he meant that we are morally required to act as the Good Samaritan did. Perhaps he was urging people to do more than is morally required of them. At all events it seems plain that it was not morally required of any of the thirty-eight that he rush out to give direct assistance at the risk of his own life, and that it is not morally required of anyone that he give long stretches of his life—nine years or nine months—to sustaining the life of a person who has no special right (we were leaving open the possibility of this) to demand it.

Indeed, with one rather striking class of exceptions, no one in any country in the world is *legally* required to do anywhere near as much as this for anyone else. The class of exceptions is obvious. My main concern here is not the state of the law in respect to abortion, but it is worth drawing attention to the fact that in no state in this country is any man compelled by law to be even a Minimally Decent Samaritan to any person; there is no law under which charges could be brought against the thirty-eight who stood by while Kitty Genovese died. By contrast, in most states in this country women are compelled by law to be not merely Minimally Decent Samaritans, but Good Samaritans to unborn persons inside them. This doesn't by itself settle anything one way or the other, because it may well be argued that there should be laws in this country—as there are in many European countries—compelling at least Minimally Decent Samaritanism.[2] But it does show that there is a gross injustice in the existing state of the law. And it shows also that the groups currently working against liberalization of abortion laws, in fact working toward having it declared unconstitutional for a state to permit abortion, had better start working for the adoption of Good Samaritan laws generally, or earn the charge that they are acting in bad faith.

I should think, myself, that Minimally Decent Samaritan laws would be one thing, Good Samaritan laws quite another, and in fact highly improper. But we are not here concerned with the law. What we should ask is not whether anybody should be compelled by law to be a Good Samaritan, but whether we must accede to a situation in which somebody is being compelled—by nature, perhaps—to be a Good Samaritan. We have, in other words, to look now at third-party interventions. I have been arguing that no person is morally required to make large sacrifices to sustain the life of another who has no right to demand them, and this even where the sacrifices do not include life itself; we are not morally required to be Good Samaritans or anyway Very Good Samaritans to one another. But what if a man cannot extricate himself from such a situation? What if he appeals to us to extricate him? It seems to me plain that there are cases in which we can, cases in which a Good Samaritan would extricate him. There you are, you were kidnapped, and nine years in bed with that violinist lie ahead of you. You have your own life to lead. You are sorry, but you simply cannot see giving up so much of your life to the sustaining of his. You cannot extricate yourself, and ask us to do so. I should have thought that—in light of his having no right to the use of your body—it was obvious that we do not have to accede to your being forced to give up so much. We can do what you ask. There is no injustice to the violinist in our doing so.

Following the lead of the opponents of abortion, I have throughout been speaking of the fetus merely as a person, and what I have been asking is whether or not the argument we began with, which proceeds only from the fetus' being a person, really does establish its conclusion. I have argued that it does not.

But of course there are arguments and arguments, and it may be said that I have simply fastened on the wrong one. It may be said that what is important is not merely the fact that the fetus is a person, but that it is a person for whom the woman has a special kind of responsibility issuing from the fact that she is its mother. And it might be argued that all my analogies are therefore irrelevant—for you do not have that special kind of responsibility for that violinist, Henry Fonda does not have that special kind of responsibility for me. And our attention might be drawn to the fact that men and women both *are* compelled by law to provide support for their children.

I have in effect dealt (briefly) with this argument above; but a (still briefer) recapitulation now may be in order. Surely we do not have any such "special responsibility" for a person unless we have assumed it, explicitly or implicitly. If a set of parents do not try to prevent pregnancy, do not obtain an abortion, and then at the time of birth of the child do not put it out for adoption, but rather take it home with them, then they have assumed responsibility for it, they have given it rights, and they cannot *now* withdraw support from it at the cost of its life because they now find it difficult to go on providing for it. But if they have taken all reasonable precautions against having a child, they do not simply by virtue of their biological relationship to the child who comes into existence have a special responsibility for it. They may wish to assume responsibility for it, or they may not wish to. And I am suggesting that if assuming responsibility for it would require large sacrifices, then they may refuse. A Good Samaritan would not refuse—or anyway, a Splendid Samaritan, if the sacrifices that had to be made were enormous. But then so would a Good Samaritan assume responsibility for that violinist; so would Henry Fonda, if he is a Good Samaritan, fly in from the West Coast and assume responsibility for me.

My argument will be found unsatisfactory on two counts by many of those who want to regard abortion as morally permissible. First, while I do argue that abortion is not impermissible, I do not argue that it is always permissible. There may well be cases in which carrying the child to term requires only Minimally Decent Samaritanism of the mother, and this is a standard we must not fall below. I am inclined to think it a merit of my account precisely that it does *not* give a general yes or a general no. It allows for and supports our sense that, for example, a sick and desperately frightened fourteen-year-old schoolgirl, pregnant due to rape, may of *course* choose abortion, and that any law which rules this out is an insane law. And it also allows for and supports our sense that in other cases resort to abortion is even positively indecent. It would be indecent in the woman to request an abortion, and indecent in a doctor to perform it, if she is in her seventh month, and wants the abortion just to avoid the nuisance of postponing a trip abroad. The very fact that the arguments I have been drawing attention to treat all cases of abortion, or even all cases of abortion in which the mother's life is not at stake, as morally on a par ought to have made them suspect at the outset.

Secondly, while I am arguing for the permissibility of abortion in some cases, I am not arguing for the right to secure the death of the unborn child. It is easy to confuse these two things in that up to a certain point in the life of the fetus it is not able to survive outside the mother's body; hence removing it from her body guarantees its death. But they are importantly different. I have argued that you are not morally required to spend nine months in bed, sustaining the life of that violinist; but to say this is by no means to say that if, when you unplug yourself, there is a miracle and he survives, you then have a right to turn round and slit his throat. You may detach yourself even if this costs him his life; you have no right to be guaranteed his death, by some other means, if unplugging yourself does not kill him. There are some people who will feel dissatisfied by this feature of my argument. A woman may be utterly devastated by the thought of a child, a bit of herself, put out for adoption and never seen or heard of again. She may therefore want not merely that the child be detached from her, but more, that it die. Some opponents of abortion are inclined to regard this as beneath contempt—thereby showing insensitivity to what is surely a powerful source of despair. All the same, I agree that the desire for the child's death is not one which anybody may gratify, should it turn out to be possible to detach the child alive.

At this place, however, it should be remembered that we have only been pretending throughout that the fetus is a human being from the moment of conception. A very early abortion is surely not the killing of a person, and so is not dealt with by anything I have said here.

NOTES

I am very much indebted to James Thomson for discussion, criticism, and many helpful suggestions.

1. Daniel Callahan, *Abortion: Law, Choice and Morality* (New York, 1970), p. 373. This book gives a fascinating survey of the available information on abortion. The Jewish tradition is surveyed in David M. Feldman, *Birth Control in Jewish Law* (New York, 1968), Part 5, the Catholic tradition in John T. Noonan, Jr., "An Almost Absolute Value in History," in *The Morality of Abortion,* ed. John T. Noonan, Jr. (Cambridge, Mass., 1970).

2. For a discussion of the difficulties involved, and a survey of the European experience with such laws, see *The Good Samaritan and the Law,* ed. James M. Ratcliffe (New York, 1966).

READING QUESTIONS

1. What is the main point Thomson makes with her "famous violinist" example?
2. How does Thomson propose to understand the right to life?
3. What is Thomson's response to the following argument? If a woman engages in voluntarily sexual intercourse with the knowledge that she might become pregnant as a result, then if she does become pregnant, she has in effect given over the use of her body to the fetus and so the fetus has a right to the use of her body. But since (in such circumstances) the fetus has a right to the use of her body in order to survive, having an abortion would be morally wrong.
4. Consider this claim: If you ought to give another person something A, then that other person has a right against you that you give him or her A. How would Thomson respond to this claim? (Focus on what Thomson says about the box of chocolates and the Henry Fonda examples.)
5. In cases of pregnancy, what (according to Thomson) would constitute being a Good Samaritan? What would constitute being a Minimally Decent Samaritan?

DISCUSSION QUESTION

1. How (if at all) does Thomson's view address cases in which a woman becomes pregnant despite the fact that although she used reliable birth control methods, they failed to prevent her pregnancy through no fault of hers?

Dan Marquis

Why Abortion Is Immoral

Marquis's approach to the morality of abortion is to begin by asking what it is that makes killing a normal adult human being presumptively morally wrong. His proposal is that the wrongness of such killing is best explained by the fact that it deprives the individual of all future experiences and activities of value. He then argues that because a fetus has a "future like ours," killing it would be presumptively morally wrong for the same reason that it is wrong to kill a normal adult human being. He concludes by explaining why his argument does not entail that contraception is presumptively morally wrong.

Recommended Reading: ethics of prima facie duty, chap.1, sec. 2F.

The view that abortion is, with rare exceptions, seriously immoral has received little support in the recent philosophical literature. No doubt most philosophers affiliated with secular institutions of higher education believe that the anti-abortion position is either a symptom of irrational religious dogma or a conclusion generated by seriously confused philosophical argument. The purpose of this essay is to undermine this general belief. This essay sets out an argument that purports to show, as well as any argument in ethics can show, that abortion is, except possibly in rare cases, seriously immoral, that it is in the same moral category as killing an innocent adult human being.

This argument is based on a major assumption: If fetuses are in the same category as adult human beings with respect to the moral value of their lives, then the *presumption* that any particular abortion is immoral is exceedingly strong. Such a presumption could be overridden only by considerations more compelling than a woman's right to privacy. The defense of this assumption is beyond the scope of this essay.[1]

Furthermore, this essay will neglect a discussion of whether there are any such compelling considerations and what they are. Plainly there are strong candidates: abortion before implantation, abortion when the life of a woman is threatened by a pregnancy or abortion after rape. The casuistry of these hard cases will not be explored in this essay. The purpose of this essay is to develop a general argument for the claim that, subject to the assumption above, the overwhelming majority of deliberate abortions are seriously immoral....

...A necessary condition of resolving the abortion controversy is a...theoretical account of the wrongness of killing. After all, if we merely believe, but do not understand, why killing adult human beings such as ourselves is wrong, how could we conceivably show that abortion is either immoral or permissible?...

In order to develop such an account, we can start from the following unproblematic assumption concerning our own case: it is wrong to kill *us*. Why is it wrong? Some answers can be easily eliminated. It might be said that what makes killing us wrong is that a killing brutalizes the one who kills. But the brutalization consists of being inured to the performance of an act that is hideously immoral; hence, the brutalization does not explain the immorality. It might be said that what makes killing us wrong is the great loss others would experience due to our absence. Although

From Don Marquis, "Why Abortion Is Immoral," *Journal of Philosophy* 86 (1989). Reprinted by permission of the author and the publisher.

such hubris is understandable, such an explanation does not account for the wrongness of killing hermits, or those whose lives are relatively independent and whose friends find it easy to make new friends.

A more obvious answer is better. What primarily makes killing wrong is neither its effect on the murderer nor its effect on the victim's friends and relatives, but its effect on the victim. The loss of one's life is one of the greatest losses one can suffer. The loss of one's life deprives one of all the experiences, activities, projects, and enjoyments that would otherwise have constituted one's future. Therefore, killing someone is wrong, primarily because the killing inflicts (one of) the greatest possible losses on the victim. To describe this as the loss of life can be misleading, however. The change in my biological state does not by itself make killing me wrong. The effect of the loss of my biological life is the loss to me of all those activities, projects, experiences, and enjoyments which would otherwise have constituted my future personal life. These activities, projects, experiences, and enjoyments are either valuable for their own sakes or are means to something else that is valuable for its own sake. Some parts of my future are not valued by me now, but will come to be valued by me as I grow older and as my values and capacities change. When I am killed, I am deprived both of what I now value which would have been part of my future personal life, but also what I would come to value. Therefore, when I die, I am deprived of all of the value of my future. Inflicting this loss on me is ultimately what makes killing me wrong. This being the case, it would seem that what makes killing *any* adult human being prima facie seriously wrong is the loss of his or her future.[2]

How should this rudimentary theory of the wrongness of killing be evaluated? It cannot be faulted for deriving an "ought" from an "is," for it does not. The analysis assumes that killing me (or you, reader) is prima facie seriously wrong. The point of the analysis is to establish which natural property ultimately explains the wrongness of the killing, given that it is wrong. A natural property will ultimately explain the wrongness of killing, only if (1) the explanation fits with our intuitions about the matter and (2) there is no other natural property that provides the basis for a better explanation of the wrongness of killing. This analysis rests on the intuition that what makes killing a particular human or animal wrong is what it does to that particular human or animal. What makes killing wrong is some natural effect or other of the killing. Some would deny this. For instance, a divine-command theorist in ethics would deny it. Surely this denial is, however, one of those features of divine-command theory which renders it so implausible.

The claim that what makes killing wrong is the loss of the victim's future is directly supported by two considerations. In the first place, this theory explains why we regard killing as one of the worst of crimes. Killing is especially wrong, because it deprives the victim of more than perhaps any other crime. In the second place, people with AIDS or cancer who know they are dying believe, of course, that dying is a very bad thing for them. They believe that the loss of a future to them that they would otherwise have experienced is what makes their premature death a very bad thing for them. A better theory of the wrongness of killing would require a different natural property associated with killing which better fits with the attitudes of the dying. What could it be?

The view that what makes killing wrong is the loss to the victim of the value of the victim's future gains additional support when some of its implications are examined. In the first place, it is incompatible with the view that it is wrong to kill only beings who are biologically human. It is possible that there exists a different species from another planet whose members have a future like ours. Since having a future like that is what makes killing someone wrong, this theory entails that it would be wrong to kill members of such a species. Hence, this theory is opposed to the claim that only life that is biologically human has great moral worth, a claim which many anti-abortionists have seemed to adopt. This opposition, which this theory has in common with personhood theories, seems to be a merit of the theory.

In the second place, the claim that the loss of one's future is the wrong-making feature of one's being killed entails the possibility that the futures of some actual non-human mammals on our own planet are sufficiently like ours that it is seriously wrong to kill them also. Whether some animals do have the same right to life as human beings depends on adding to the account of the wrongness of killing some additional account of just what it is about my future or the futures of other adult human beings which makes it wrong to kill us. No such additional account will be offered in this essay. Undoubtedly, the provision of such an account would be a very difficult matter. Undoubtedly, any such account would be quite controversial. Hence, it surely should not reflect badly on this sketch of an elementary theory of the wrongness of killing that it is indeterminate with respect to some very difficult issues regarding animal rights.

In the third place, the claim that the loss of one's future is the wrong-making feature of one's being killed does not entail, as sanctity of human life theories do, that active euthanasia is wrong. Persons who are severely and incurably ill, who face a future of pain and despair, and who wish to die will not have suffered a loss if they are killed. It is, strictly speaking, the value of a human's future which makes killing wrong in this theory. This being so, killing does not necessarily wrong some persons who are sick and dying. Of course, there may be other reasons for a prohibition of active euthanasia, but that is another matter. Sanctity-of-human-life theories seem to hold that active euthanasia is seriously wrong even in an individual case where there seems to be good reason for it independently of public policy considerations. This consequence is most implausible, and it is a plus for the claim that the loss of a future of value is what makes killing wrong that it does not share this consequence.

In the fourth place, the account of the wrongness of killing defended in this essay does straightforwardly entail that it is prima facie seriously wrong to kill children and infants, for we do presume that they have futures of value. Since we do believe that it is wrong to kill defenseless little babies, it is important that a theory of the wrongness of killing easily account for this. Personhood theories of the wrongness of killing, on the other hand, cannot straightforwardly account for the wrongness of killing infants and young children. Hence, such theories must add special ad hoc accounts of the wrongness of killing the young. The plausibility of such ad hoc theories seems to be a function of how desperately one wants such theories to work. The claim that the primary wrong-making feature of a killing is the loss to the victim of the value of its future accounts for the wrongness of killing young children and infants directly; it makes the wrongness of such acts as obvious as we actually think it is. This is a further merit of this theory. Accordingly, it seems that this value of a future-like-ours theory of the wrongness of killing shares strengths of both sanctity-of-life and personhood accounts while avoiding weaknesses of both. In addition, it meshes with a central intuition concerning what makes killing wrong.

The claim that the primary wrong-making feature of a killing is the loss to the victim of the value of its future has obvious consequences for the ethics of abortion. The future of a standard fetus includes a set of experiences, projects, activities, and such which are identical with the futures of adult human beings and are identical with the futures of young children. Since the reason that is sufficient to explain why it is wrong to kill human beings after the time of birth is a reason that also applies to fetuses, it follows that abortion is prima facie seriously morally wrong.

This argument does not rely on the invalid inference that, since it is wrong to kill persons, it is wrong to kill potential persons also. The category that is morally central to this analysis is the category of having a valuable future like ours; it is not the category of personhood. The argument to the conclusion that abortion is prima facie seriously morally wrong proceeded independently of the notion of person or potential person or any equivalent. Someone may wish to start with this analysis in terms of the value of a human future, conclude that abortion is, except perhaps in rare circumstances, seriously morally wrong, infer that fetuses have the right to life, and then call fetuses "persons" as a result of their having the right to life. Clearly, in this case, the category of person is being used to state the *conclusion* of the analysis rather than to generate the *argument* of the analysis.

The structure of this anti-abortion argument can be both illuminated and defended by comparing it to what appears to be the best argument for the wrongness of the wanton infliction of pain on animals. This latter argument is based on the assumption that it is prima facie wrong to inflict pain on me (or you, reader). What is the natural property associated with the infliction of pain which makes such infliction wrong? The obvious answer seems to be that the infliction of pain causes suffering and that suffering is a misfortune. The suffering caused by the infliction of pain is what makes the wanton infliction of pain on me wrong. The wanton infliction of pain on other adult humans causes suffering. The wanton infliction of pain on animals causes suffering. Since causing suffering is what makes the wanton infliction of pain wrong and since the wanton infliction of pain on animals causes suffering, it follows that the wanton infliction of pain on animals is wrong.

This argument for the wrongness of the wanton infliction of pain on animals shares a number of structural features with the argument for the serious prima facie wrongness of abortion. Both arguments start with an obvious assumption concerning what it is wrong to do to me (or you, reader). Both then look for the characteristic or the consequence of the wrong action which makes the action wrong. Both recognize that the wrong-making feature of these immoral actions is a property of actions sometimes directed at individuals other than postnatal human beings. If the structure of the argument for the wrongness of the wanton infliction of pain on animals is sound, then the structure of the argument for the prima facie serious wrongness of abortion is also sound, for the structure of the two arguments is the same. The structure common to both is the key to the explanation of how the wrongness of abortion can be demonstrated without recourse to the category of person. In neither argument is that category crucial....

Of course, this value of a future-like-ours argument, if sound, shows only that abortion is prima facie wrong, not that it is wrong in any and all circumstances. Since the loss of the future to a standard fetus, if killed, is, however, at least as great a loss as the loss of the future to a standard adult human being who is killed, abortion, like ordinary killing, could be justified only by the most compelling reasons. The loss of one's life is almost the greatest misfortune that can happen to one. Presumably abortion could be justified in some circumstances, only if the loss consequent on failing to abort would be at least as great. Accordingly, morally permissible abortions will be rare indeed unless, perhaps, they occur so

early in pregnancy that a fetus is not yet definitely an individual. Hence, this argument should be taken as showing that abortion is presumptively very seriously wrong, where the presumption is very strong—as strong as the presumption that killing another adult human being is wrong....

In this essay, it has been argued that the correct ethic of the wrongness of killing can be extended to fetal life and used to show that there is a strong presumption that any abortion is morally impermissible. If the ethic of killing adopted here entails, however, that contraception is also seriously immoral, then there would appear to be a difficulty with the analysis of this essay.

But this analysis does not entail that contraception is wrong. Of course, contraception prevents the actualization of a possible future of value. Hence, it follows from the claim that futures of value should be maximized that contraception is prima facie immoral. This obligation to maximize does not exist, however; furthermore, nothing in the ethics of killing in this paper entails that it does. The ethics of killing in this essay would entail that contraception is wrong only if something were denied a human future of value by contraception. Nothing at all is denied such a future by contraception, however.

Candidates for a subject of harm by contraception fall into four categories: (1) some sperm or other, (2) some ovum or other, (3) a sperm and an ovum separately, and (4) a sperm and an ovum together. Assigning the harm to some sperm is utterly arbitrary, for no reason can be given for making a sperm the subject of harm rather than an ovum. Assigning the harm to some ovum is utterly arbitrary, for no reason can be given for making an ovum the subject of harm rather than a sperm. One might attempt to avoid these problems by insisting that contraception deprives both the sperm and the ovum separately of a valuable future like ours. On this alternative, too many futures are lost. Contraception was supposed to be wrong, because it deprived us of one future of value, not two. One might attempt to avoid this problem by holding that contraception deprives the combination of sperm and ovum of a valuable future like ours. But here the definite article misleads. At the time of contraception, there are hundreds of millions of sperm, one (released) ovum and millions of possible combinations of all of these. There is no actual combination at all. Is the subject of the loss to be a merely possible combination? Which one? This alternative does not yield an actual subject of harm either. Accordingly, the immorality of contraception is not entailed by the loss of a future-like-ours argument simply because there is no non-arbitrarily identifiable subject of the loss in the case of contraception. . . .

The purpose of this essay has been to set out an argument for the serious presumptive wrongness of abortion subject to the assumption that the moral permissibility of abortion stands or falls on the moral status of the fetus. Since a fetus possesses a property, the possession of which in adult human beings is sufficient to make killing an adult human being wrong, abortion is wrong. This way of dealing with the problem of abortion seems superior to other approaches to the ethics of abortion, because it rests on an ethics of killing which is close to self-evident, because the crucial morally relevant property clearly applies to fetuses, and because the argument avoids the usual equivocations on "human life," "human being," or "person." The argument rests neither on religious claims nor on

Papal dogma. It is not subject to the objection of "speciesism." Its soundness is compatible with the moral permissibility of euthanasia and contraception. It deals with our intuitions concerning young children.

Finally, this analysis can be viewed as resolving a standard problem—indeed, *the* standard problem—concerning the ethics of abortion. Clearly, it is wrong to kill adult human beings. Clearly, it is not wrong to end the life of some arbitrarily chosen single human cell. Fetuses seem to be like arbitrarily chosen human cells in some respects and like adult humans in other respects. The problem of the ethics of abortion is the problem of determining the fetal property that settles this moral controversy. The thesis of this essay is that the problem of the ethics of abortion, so understood, is solvable.

NOTES

1. Judith Jarvis Thomson has rejected this assumption in a famous essay, "A Defense of Abortion," *Philosophy and Public Affairs* 1, #1 (1971), 47–66.

2. I have been most influenced on this matter by Jonathan Glover, *Causing Death and Saving Lives* (New York: Penguin, 1977), ch. 3; and Robert Young, "What Is So Wrong with Killing People?" *Philosophy*, LIV, 210 (1979): 515–528.

READING QUESTIONS

1. According to Marquis, what is wrong with the claim that what explains why killing an innocent adult human being is wrong is that the death of the victim would be a great loss to his or her family and friends?

2. According to Marquis, there are two considerations that "directly" support his claim about what makes killing an innocent adult human being wrong. What are those considerations?

3. Marquis also claims that his view about the wrongness of killing gains additional support when its various implications are examined. What are the implications in question?

4. What reasons does Marquis give for claiming that his view on the morality of abortion does not imply that contraception is morally wrong?

DISCUSSION QUESTIONS

1. Should we find Marquis's claim that his view on the morality of abortion does not imply that contraception is wrong plausible? Explain why or why not.

2. How does Marquis's "future like ours" explanation of the wrongness of abortion differ from views that attempt to explain the wrongness of abortion by appealing to the idea that the fetus is a potential person?

L. W. Sumner

A Moderate View

Sumner faults conservative and liberal views on abortion for assuming that the moral status of a fetus remains the same throughout pregnancy. Rejecting this assumption, claims Sumner, allows for the development of a moderate view, according to which early-stage abortions are generally less morally problematic than abortions in the later stages of pregnancy. To support his moderate position, he defends a criterion of moral standing which, when applied to the issue of abortion, yields an in-between, moderate view.

Recommended Reading: consequentialism, chap. 1, sec. 2A.

A complete view of abortion, one that answers the main moral questions posed by the practice of abortion, is an ordered compound of three elements: an account of the moral status of the fetus, which grounds an account of the moral status of abortion, which in turn grounds a defense of an abortion policy. It is not enough, however, that a view of abortion be complete—it must also be well grounded. If we explore what is required to support an account of the moral status of the fetus, we will discover what it means for a view of abortion to be well grounded. The main requirement at this level is a *criterion of moral standing* that will specify the (natural) characteristic(s) whose possession is both necessary and sufficient for the possession of moral standing. A criterion of moral standing will therefore have the following form: all and only beings with characteristic C have moral standing. (Characteristic C may be a single property or a conjunction or disjunction of such properties.) A criterion of moral standing thus determines, both exhaustively and exclusively, the membership of the class of beings with such standing. Such a criterion will define the proper scope of our moral concern, telling us for all moral contexts

which beings must be accorded moral consideration in their own right. Thus it will determine, among other things, the moral status of inanimate natural objects, artifacts, nonhuman animals, body parts, superintelligent computers, androids, and extraterrestrials. It will also determine the moral status of (human) fetuses. An account of the moral status of the fetus is well grounded when it is derivable from an independently plausible criterion of moral standing. The independent plausibility of such a criterion is partly established by following out its implications for moral contexts other than abortion. But a criterion of moral standing can also be given a deeper justification by being grounded in a moral theory. The function of a moral theory is to identify those features of the world to which we should be morally sensitive and to guide that sensitivity. By providing us with a picture of the content and structure of morality, a moral theory will tell us, among other things, which beings merit moral consideration in their own right and what form this consideration should take. It will thereby generate and support a criterion of moral standing, thus serving as the last line of defense for a view of abortion.

From L. W. Sumner, "Abortion," in D. VanDeVeer & T. Regan, eds. *Health Care Ethics* (Philadelphia, PA: Temple University Press, 1987). Reprinted with permission of the author.

THE ESTABLISHED VIEWS

We are seeking a view of abortion that is both complete and well grounded. These requirements are not easily satisfied. The key elements remain an account of the moral status of the fetus and a supporting criterion of moral standing. Our search will be facilitated if we begin by examining the main contenders. The abortion debate in most of the Western democracies has been dominated by two positions that are so well entrenched that they may be called the established views. The liberal view supports what is popularly known as the "pro-choice" position on abortion.[1] At its heart is the contention that the fetus at every stage of pregnancy has no moral standing. From this premise it follows that although abortion kills the fetus it does not wrong it, since a being with no moral standing cannot be wronged. Abortion at all stages of pregnancy lacks a victim; circumstantial differences aside, it is the moral equivalent of contraception. The decision to seek an abortion, therefore, can properly be left to a woman's discretion. There is as little justification for legal regulation of abortion as there is for such regulation of contraception. The only defensible abortion policy is a permissive policy. The conservative view, however, supports what is popularly known as the "pro-life" position on abortion. At its heart is the contention that the fetus at every stage of pregnancy has full moral standing—the same status as an adult human being. From this premise it follows that because abortion kills the fetus it also wrongs it. Abortion at all stages of pregnancy has a victim; circumstantial differences aside, it is the moral equivalent of infanticide (and of other forms of homicide as well). The decision to seek an abortion, therefore, cannot properly be left to a woman's discretion. There is as much justification for legal regulation of abortion as there is for such regulation of infanticide. The only defensible abortion policy is a restrictive policy.

Before exploring these views separately, we should note an important feature that they share. On the substantive issue that is at the heart of the matter, liberals and conservatives occupy positions that are logical contraries, the latter holding that all fetuses have standing and the former that none do. Although contrary positions cannot both be true, they can both be false. From a logical point of view, it is open to someone to hold that some fetuses have standing while others do not. Thus while the established views occupy the opposite extremes along the spectrum of possible positions on this issue, there is a logical space between them. This logical space reflects the fact that each of the established views offers a uniform account of the moral status of the fetus—each, that is, holds that all fetuses have the same status, regardless of any respects in which they might differ. The most obvious respect in which fetuses can differ is in their gestational age and thus their level of development. During the normal course of pregnancy, a fetus gradually evolves from a tiny one-celled organism into a medium-sized and highly complex organism consisting of some six million differentiated cells. Both of the established views are committed to holding that all of the beings at all stages of this transition have precisely the same moral status. The gestational age of the fetus at the time of abortion is thus morally irrelevant on both views. So also is the reason for the abortion. This is irrelevant on the liberal view because no reason is necessary to justify abortion at any stage of pregnancy and equally irrelevant on the conservative view because no reason is sufficient to do so. The established views, therefore, despite their differences, agree on two very important matters: the moral irrelevance of both when and why an abortion is performed. . . .

A MODERATE VIEW

We can now catalogue the defects of the established views. The common source of these defects lies in their uniform accounts of the moral status of the fetus. These accounts yield three different sorts of awkward implications. First, they require that all abortions be accorded the same moral status regardless of the stage of pregnancy at which they are performed. Thus, liberals must hold that late abortions are as morally innocuous as early ones, and conservatives must hold that early abortions are as morally serious as late ones. Neither view is able to support the common conviction that late abortions are more serious than early ones. Second, these accounts require that all abortions be accorded the same moral status regardless of the reason for which they are performed. Thus, liberals must hold that all abortions are equally innocuous whatever their grounds, and conservatives must hold that all abortions are equally serious whatever their grounds. Neither view is able to support the common conviction that some grounds justify abortion more readily than others. Third, these accounts require that contraception, abortion, and infanticide all be accorded the same moral status. Thus, liberals must hold that all three practices are equally innocuous, while conservatives must hold that they are all equally serious. Neither view is able to support the common conviction that infanticide is more serious t abortion, which is in turn more serious than contraception.

Awkward results do not constitute a refutation. The constellation of moral issues concerning human reproduction and development is dark and mysterious. It may be that no internally coherent view of abortion will enable us to retain all of our common moral convictions in this landscape. If so, then perhaps the best we can manage is to embrace one of the established views and bring our attitudes (in whatever turns out to be the troublesome area) into line with it. However, results as awkward as these do provide a strong motive to seek an alternative to the established views and thus to explore the logical space between them.

There are various obstacles in the path of developing a moderate view of abortion. For one thing, any such view will lack the appealing simplicity of the established views. Both liberals and conservatives begin by adopting a simple account of the moral status of the fetus and end by supporting a simple abortion policy. A moderate account of the moral status of the fetus and a moderate abortion policy will inevitably be more complex. Further, a moderate account of the moral status of the fetus, whatever its precise shape, will draw a boundary between those fetuses that have moral standing and those that do not. It will then have to show that the location of this boundary is not arbitrary. Finally, a moderate view may seem nothing more than a compromise between the more extreme positions that lacks any independent rationale of its own.

These obstacles may, however, be less formidable than they appear. Although the complexity of a moderate view may render it harder to sell in the marketplace of ideas, it may otherwise be its greatest asset. It should be obvious by now that the moral issues raised by the peculiar nature of the fetus, and its peculiar relationship with its mother, are not simple. It would be surprising therefore if a simple resolution of them were satisfactory. The richer resources of a complex view may enable it to avoid some of the less palatable implications of its simpler rivals. The problem of locating a nonarbitrary threshold is easier to deal with when we recognize that there can be no sharp breakpoint in the course of human development at which moral standing is suddenly acquired. The attempt to define such a breakpoint was the fatal mistake of the naive versions of the liberal and conservative views. If, as seems likely, an acceptable criterion of moral standing is built around some characteristic that is acquired gradually during the normal course of human development, then moral standing will also be acquired gradually during the normal course of human development. In that case, the boundary between those beings that have moral standing and those that do not will be soft and slow rather than hard and fast. The more sophisticated and credible versions of the established views also pick out stages of development rather than precise breakpoints as their thresholds of moral standing; the only innovation of a moderate view is to locate this stage somewhere during pregnancy. The real challenge to a moderate view, therefore, is to show that it can be well grounded, and thus that it is not simply a way of splitting the difference between two equally unattractive options.

Our critique of the established views has equipped us with specifications for the design of a moderate alternative to them. The fundamental flaw of the established views was their adoption of a uniform account of the moral status of the fetus. A moderate view of abortion must therefore be built on a *differential* account of the moral status of the fetus, awarding moral standing to some fetuses and withholding it from others. The further defects of the established views impose three constraints on the shape of such a differential account. It must explain the moral relevance of the gestational age of the fetus at the time of abortion and thus must correlate moral status with level of fetal development. It must also explain the moral relevance, at least at some stages of pregnancy, of the reason for which an abortion is performed. And finally it must preserve the distinction between the moral innocuousness of contraception and the the moral seriousness of infanticide. When we combine these specifications, we obtain the rough outline of a moderate view. Such a view will identify the stage of pregnancy during which the fetus gains moral standing. Before that threshold, abortion will be as morally innocuous as contraception and no grounds will be needed to justify it. After the threshold, abortion will be as morally serious as infanticide and some special grounds will be needed to justify it (if it can be justified at this stage at all).

A moderate view is well grounded when it is derivable from an independently plausible criterion of moral standing. It is not difficult to construct a criterion that will yield a threshold somewhere during pregnancy.[2] Let us say that a being is sentient when it has the capacity to experience pleasure and pain and thus the capacity for enjoyment and suffering. Beings that are self-conscious or rational are generally (though perhaps not necessarily) also sentient, but many sentient beings lack both self-consciousness and rationality. A sentience criterion of moral standing thus sets a lower standard than that shared by the established views. Such a criterion will accord moral standing to the mentally handicapped regardless of impairments of their cognitive capacities. It will also accord moral standing to many, perhaps most, nonhuman animals.

The plausibility of a sentience criterion would be partially established by tracing out its implications for moral contexts other than abortion. But it would be considerably enhanced if such a criterion could also be given a deeper grounding. Such a grounding can be supplied by what seems a reasonable conception of the nature of morality. The moral point of view is just one among many evaluative points of view. It appears to be distinguished from the others in two respects: its special concern for the interest, welfare, or well-being of creatures and its requirement of impartiality. Adopting the moral point of view requires in one way or another according equal consideration to the interests of all beings. If this is so, then a being's having an interest to be considered is both necessary and sufficient for its having moral standing. While the notion of interest or welfare is far from transparent, its irreducible core appears to be the capacity for enjoyment and suffering: all and only beings with this capacity have an interest or welfare that the moral point of view requires us to respect. But then it follows easily that sentience is both necessary and sufficient for moral standing.

A criterion of moral standing is well grounded when it is derivable from some independently plausible moral theory. A sentience criterion can be grounded in any member of a class of theories that share the foregoing conception of the nature of morality. Because of the centrality of interest or welfare to that conception, let us call such theories welfare based. A sentience criterion of moral standing can be readily grounded in any welfare-based moral theory. The class of such theories is quite extensive, including everything from varieties of rights theory on the one hand to varieties of utilitarianism on the other. Whatever their conceptual and structural differences, a sentience criterion can be derived from any one of them. The diversity of theoretical resources available to support a sentience criterion is one of its greatest strengths. In addition, a weaker version of such a criterion is also derivable from more eclectic theories that treat the promotion and protection of welfare as one of the basic concerns of morality. Any such theory will yield the result that sentience is sufficient for moral standing, though it may also be necessary, thus providing partial support for a moderate view of abortion. Such a view is entirely unsupported only by moral theories that find no room whatever for the promotion of welfare among the concerns of morality.

When we apply a sentience criterion to the course of human development, it yields the result that the threshold of moral standing is the stage during which the capacity to experience pleasure and pain is first required. This capacity is clearly possessed by a newborn infant (and a full-term fetus) and is clearly not possessed by a pair of gametes (or a newly fertilized ovum). It is therefore acquired during the normal course of gestation. But when? A definite answer awaits a better understanding than we now possess of the development of the fetal nervous system and thus of fetal consciousness. We can, however, venture a provisional answer. It is standard practice to divide the normal course of gestation into three trimesters of thirteen weeks each. It is likely that a fetus is unable to feel pleasure or pain at the beginning of the second trimester and likely that it is able to do so at the end of that trimester. If this is so, then the threshold of sentience, and thus also the threshold of moral standing, occurs sometime during the second trimester.

We can now fill in our earlier sketch of a moderate view of abortion. A fetus acquires moral standing when it acquires sentience, that is to say at some stage in the second trimester of pregnancy. Before that threshold, when the fetus lacks moral standing, the decision to seek an abortion is morally equivalent to the decision to employ contraception; the effect in both cases is to prevent the existence of a being with moral standing. Such decisions are morally innocuous and should be left to the discretion of the parties involved. Thus, the liberal view of abortion, and a permissive abortion policy, are appropriate for early (prethreshold) abortions. After the threshold, when the fetus has moral standing, the decision to seek an abortion is morally equivalent to the decision to commit infanticide; the effect in both cases is to terminate the existence of a being with moral standing. Such decisions are morally serious and should not be left to the discretion of the parties involved (the fetus is now one of the parties involved).

It should follow that the conservative view of abortion and a restrictive abortion policy are appropriate for late (post-threshold) abortions. But this does not follow. Conservatives hold that abortion, because it is homicide, is unjustified on any grounds. This absolute position is indefensible

even for post-threshold fetuses with moral standing. Of the four categories of grounds for abortion, neither humanitarian nor socioeconomic grounds will apply to post-threshold abortions, since a permissive policy for the period before the threshold will afford women the opportunity to decide freely whether they wish to continue their pregnancies. Therapeutic grounds will however apply, since serious risks to maternal life or health may materialize after the threshold. If they do, there is no justification for refusing an abortion. A pregnant woman is providing life support for another being that is housed within her body. If continuing to provide that life support will place her own life or health at serious risk, then she cannot justifiably be compelled to do so, even though the fetus has moral standing and will die if deprived of that life support. Seeking an abortion in such circumstances is a legitimate act of self-preservation.[3]

A moderate abortion policy must therefore include a therapeutic ground for post-threshold abortions. It must also include a eugenic ground. Given current technology, some tests for fetal abnormalities can be carried out only in the second trimester. In many cases, therefore, serious abnormalities will be detected only after the fetus has passed the threshold. Circumstantial differences aside, the status of a severely deformed post-threshold fetus is the same as the status of a severely deformed newborn infant. The moral issues concerning the treatment of such newborns are themselves complex, but there appears to be a good case for selective infanticide in some cases. If so, then there is an even better case for late abortion on eugenic grounds, since here we must also reckon in the terrible burden of carrying to term a child that a woman knows to be deformed.

A moderate abortion policy will therefore contain the following ingredients: a time limit that separates early from late abortions, a permissive policy for early abortions, and a policy for late abortions that incorporates both therapeutic and eugenic grounds. This blueprint leaves many smaller questions of design to be settled. The grounds for late abortions must be specified more carefully by determining what is to count as a serious risk to maternal life or health and what is to count as a serious fetal abnormality. While no general formulation of a policy can settle these matters in detail, guidelines can and should be supplied. A policy should also specify the procedure that is to be followed in deciding when a particular case has met these guidelines.

But most of all, a moderate policy must impose a defensible time limit. As we saw earlier, from the moral point of view there can be no question of a sharp breakpoint. Fetal development unfolds gradually and cumulatively, and sentience like all other capacities is acquired slowly and by degrees. Thus we have clear cases of presentient fetuses in the first trimester and clear cases of sentient fetuses in the third trimester. But we also have unclear cases, encompassing many (perhaps most) second-trimester fetuses. From the moral point of view, we can say only that in these cases the moral status of the fetus, and thus the moral status of abortion, is indeterminate. This sort of moral indeterminacy occurs also at later stages of human development, for instance when we are attempting to fix the age of consent or of competence to drink or drive. We do not pretend in these latter cases that the capacity in question is acquired overnight on one's sixteenth or eighteenth birthday, and yet for legal purposes we must draw a sharp and determinate line. Any such line will be somewhat arbitrary, but it is enough if it is drawn within the appropriate threshold stage. So also in the case of a time limit for abortion, it is sufficient if the line for legal purposes is located within the appropriate threshold stage. A time limit anywhere in the second trimester is therefore defensible, at least until we acquire the kind of information about fetal development that will enable us to narrow the threshold stage and thus to locate the time limit with more accuracy.

CONCLUSIONS

…While both of the established views have obvious and serious defects, many people seem to feel that there is no coherent third alternative available to them. But a moderate view does appear to provide such an alternative. It does less violence than either of the established views to widely shared convictions about contraception, abortion, and infanticide, and it can be grounded upon a criterion of moral standing that seems to generate acceptable results in other moral contexts and is in turn derivable from a wide range of moral theories sharing a plausible conception of the nature of morality. Those who are dissatisfied with the established views need not therefore fear that in moving to the middle ground they are sacrificing reason for mere expediency.

NOTES

1. The terms 'liberal' and 'conservative,' as used in the chapter generally, refer respectively to those who think abortion permissible and those who believe it impermissible. Thus, 'liberal' here is not synonymous with 'political liberal' and 'conservative' is not synonymous with 'political conservative.'

2. The sentience criterion is defended in my *Abortion and Moral Theory* (Princeton, N.J.: Princeton University Press, 1981), 128–46.

3. This position is defended in Judith Jarvis Thomson, "A Defense of Abortion," in *The Rights and Wrongs of Abortion*, ed. Marshall Cohen et al. (Princeton, N.J.: Princeton University Press, 1974); for contrary views, see John Finnis, "The Rights and Wrongs of Abortion," in *The Rights and Wrongs of Abortion*, and Baruch Brody, *Abortion and the Sanctity of Human Life*: A Philosophical View (Cambridge, Mass.: MIT Press, 1975), Chapters 1 and 2.

READING QUESTIONS

1. According to Sumner, what important feature do both conservative and liberal views on abortion share?
2. What are the so-called awkward implications of both conservative and liberal views on abortion according to Sumner?
3. How does Sumner attempt to "ground" his sentience criterion of moral standing?
4. What sorts of considerations would justify a third-trimester abortion according to Sumner?

DISCUSSION QUESTION

1. Is sentience an acceptable criterion of moral standing? (To address this question, you should break it down into questions: Is sentience necessary for having moral standing? Is it sufficient?)

ROSALIND HURSTHOUSE

Virtue Theory and Abortion

After laying out the basic structure of a version of virtue ethics, Hursthouse proceeds to explain how this kind of moral theory can be useful in guiding moral thought and decision making generally and how, in particular, it can be used to think about the morality of abortion. According to Hursthouse, thinking about the morality of abortion in terms of virtues and vices transforms the debate about abortion. This debate is typically cast in terms of the apparent and conflicting rights of the fetus and the pregnant woman, but according to Hursthouse, approaching the issue from the perspective of virtue ethics makes appealing to rights largely irrelevant to the moral issue properly understood. By contrast, a virtue theoretic approach to abortion understands the morality of some act of abortion in terms of whether it would (in the circumstances) express certain character traits with regard to various goods and evils. In Hursthouse's view, some abortions are wrong because they express such vices as callousness, greediness, or selfishness, though other abortions are not wrong because they may express such virtues as humility or modesty.

Recommended Reading: virtue ethics, chap. 1, sec. 2E.

The sort of ethical theory derived from Aristotle, variously described as virtue ethics, virtue-based ethics, or neo-Aristotelianism, is becoming better known, and is now quite widely recognized as at least a possible rival to deontological and utilitarian theories. With recognition has come criticism, of varying quality. In this article I shall discuss . . . criticisms that I have frequently encountered, most of which seem to me to betray an inadequate grasp either of the structure of virtue theory or of what would be involved in thinking about a real moral issue in its terms. In the first half I aim particularly to secure an understanding that will reveal that many of these criticisms are simply misplaced, and to articulate what I take to be the major criticism of virtue theory. I reject this criticism, but do not claim that it is necessarily misplaced.

From Rosalind Hursthouse, "Virtue Theory and Abortion," *Philosophy and Public Affairs* 20 (1990).

In the second half I aim to deepen that understanding and highlight the issues raised by the criticisms by illustrating what the theory looks like when it is applied to a particular issue, in this case, abortion.

VIRTUE THEORY

Now let us consider what a skeletal virtue theory looks like. It begins with a specification of right action:

> P.1. An action is right if it is what a virtuous agent would do in the circumstances.[1]

This ... is a purely formal principle ... that forges the conceptual link between *right action* and *virtuous agent*. ... [I]t must, of course, go on to specify what the latter is. The first step toward this may appear quite trivial, but is needed to correct a prevailing tendency among many critics to define the virtuous agent as one who is disposed to act in accordance with a deontologist's moral rules.

> P.1a. A virtuous agent is one who acts virtuously, that is, one who has and exercises the virtues.

This subsidiary premise lays bare the fact that virtue theory aims to provide a nontrivial specification of the virtuous agent *via* a nontrivial specification of the virtues, which is given in its second premise:

> P.2. A virtue is a character trait a human being needs to flourish or live well.

This premise forges a conceptual link between *virtue* and *flourishing* (or *living well* or *eudaimonia*). . . . [V]irtue ethics, in theory, [then] goes on to argue that each favored character trait meets its [specification].

These are the bare bones of virtue theory. Following are five brief comments directed to some misconceived criticisms that should be cleared out of the way.

First, the theory does not have a peculiar weakness or problem in virtue of the fact that it involves the concept of *eudaimonia* (a standard criticism being that this concept is hopelessly obscure). Now no virtue theorist will pretend that the concept of human flourishing is an easy one to grasp. I will not even claim here (though I would elsewhere) that it is no more obscure than the concepts of *rationality* and *happiness,* since, if our vocabulary were more limited, we might, *faute de mieux,* call it (human) *rational happiness,* and thereby reveal that it has at least some of the difficulties of both. But virtue theory has never, so far as I know, been dismissed on the grounds of the *comparative* obscurity of this central concept; rather, the popular view is that it has a problem with this which deontology and utilitarianism in no way share. This, I think, is clearly false. Both *rationality* and *happiness*, as they figure in their respective theories, are rich and difficult concepts—hence all the disputes about the various tests for a rule's being an object of rational choice, and the disputes, dating back to Mill's introduction of the higher and lower pleasures, about what constitutes happiness.

Second, the theory is not trivially circular; it does not specify right action in terms of the virtuous agent and then immediately specify the virtuous agent in terms of right action. Rather, it specifies her in terms of the virtues, and then specifies these, not merely as dispositions to right action, but as the character traits (which are dispositions to feel and react as well as act in certain ways) required for *eudaimonia.*

Third, it does answer the question "What should I do?" as well as the question "What sort of person should I be?" (That is, it is not, as one of the catchphrases has it, concerned only with Being and not with Doing.)

Fourth, the theory does, to a certain extent, answer this question by coming up with rules or principles (contrary to the common claim that it does not come up with any rules or principles). Every virtue generates a positive instruction (act justly, kindly, courageously, honestly, etc.) and every vice a prohibition (do not act unjustly, cruelly, like a coward, dishonestly, etc.). So trying to decide what to do within the framework of virtue theory is not, as some people seem to imagine, necessarily a matter of taking one's favored candidate for a virtuous person and asking oneself, "What would they do in these circumstances?" (as if the raped fifteen-year-old girl might be supposed to say to herself, "Now would Socrates have an abortion if he were in my circumstances?" and as if someone who had never known or heard of anyone very virtuous were going to be left, according to the theory, with no way to decide what to do at all). The agent may instead ask herself, "If I were to do such and such now, would I be acting justly or unjustly (or neither), kindly or unkindly [and so on]?" I shall consider below the problem created by cases in which such a question apparently does not yield an answer to "What should I do?" (because, say, the alternatives are being unkind or being unjust); here my claim is only that it sometimes does—the agent may employ her concepts of the virtues and vices directly, rather than imagining what some hypothetical exemplar would do.

Fifth (a point that is implicit but should be made explicit), virtue theory is not committed to any sort of reductionism involving defining all of our moral concepts in terms of the virtuous agent. On the contrary, it relies on a lot of very significant moral concepts. Charity or benevolence, for instance, is the virtue whose concern is the *good* of others; that concept of *good* is related to the concept of *evil* or *harm,* and they are both related to the concepts of the *worthwhile,* the *advantageous,* and the *pleasant.* If I have the wrong conception of what is worthwhile and advantageous and pleasant, then I shall have the wrong conception of what is good for, and harmful to, myself and others, and, even with the best will in the world, will lack the virtue of charity, which involves getting all this right....

Finally, I want to articulate, and reject, what I take to be the major criticism of virtue theory. Perhaps because it is *the* major criticism, the reflection of a very general sort of disquiet about the theory, it is hard to state clearly—especially for someone who does not accept it—but it goes something like this.[2] My interlocutor says:

> Virtue theory can't *get* us anywhere in real moral issues because it's bound to be all assertion and no argument. You admit that the best it can come up with in the way of action-guiding rules are the ones that rely on the virtue and vice concepts, such as "act charitably," "don't act cruelly," and so on; and, as if that weren't bad enough, you admit that these virtue concepts, such as charity, presuppose concepts such as the *good,* and the

worthwhile, and so on. But that means that any virtue theorist who writes about real moral issues must rely on her audience's agreeing with her application of all these concepts, and hence accepting all the premises in which those applications are enshrined. But some other virtue theorist might take different premises about these matters, and come up with very different conclusions, and, within the terms of the theory, there is no way to distinguish between the two. While there is agreement, virtue theory can repeat conventional wisdom, preserve the status quo, but it can't get us anywhere in the way that a normative ethical theory is supposed to, namely, by providing rational grounds for acceptance of its practical conclusions.

My strategy will be to split this criticism into two: one...addressed to the virtue theorist's employment of the virtue and vice concepts enshrined in her rules—act charitably, honestly, and so on—and the other...addressed to her employment of concepts such as that of the *worthwhile.* Each objection, I shall maintain, implicitly appeals to a certain *condition of adequacy* on a normative moral theory, and in each case, I shall claim, the condition of adequacy, once made explicit, is utterly implausible.

It is true that when she discusses real moral issues, the virtue theorist has to assert that certain actions are honest, dishonest, or neither; charitable, uncharitable, or neither. And it is true that this is often a very difficult matter to decide; her rules are not always easy to apply. But this counts as a criticism of the theory only if we assume, as a condition of adequacy, that any adequate action-guiding theory must make the difficult business of knowing what to do if one is to act well easy, that it must provide clear guidance about what ought and ought not to be done which any reasonably clever adolescent could follow if she chose. But such a condition of adequacy is implausible. Acting rightly *is* difficult, and *does* call for much moral wisdom, and the relevant condition of adequacy, which virtue theory meets, is that it should have built into it an explanation of a truth expressed by Aristotle,[3] namely, that moral knowledge—unlike mathematical knowledge—cannot be acquired merely by attending lectures and is not characteristically to be found in people too young to have had much experience of life. There are youthful mathematical geniuses, but rarely, if ever, youthful moral geniuses, and this tells us something significant about the sort of knowledge that moral knowledge is. Virtue ethics builds this in straight off precisely by couching its rules in terms whose application may indeed call for the most delicate and sensitive judgment....

What about the virtue theorist's reliance on concepts such as that of the *worthwhile?* If such reliance is to count as a fault in the theory, what condition of adequacy is implicitly in play? It must be that any good normative theory should provide answers to questions about real moral issues whose truth is in no way determined by truths about what is worthwhile, or what really matters in human life. Now although people are initially inclined to reject out of hand the claim that the practical conclusions of a normative moral theory have to be based on premises about what is truly worthwhile, the alternative, once it is made explicit, may look even more unacceptable. Consider what the condition of adequacy entails. If truths about what is worthwhile (or truly good, or serious, or about what matters in human life) do *not* have to be appealed to in order to answer questions about real moral issues, then I might sensibly seek guidance about what I ought to do from someone who had declared in advance that she knew nothing about such matters, or from someone who said that, although she had opinions about them, these were quite likely to be wrong but that this did not matter, because they would play no determining role in the advice she gave me.

I should emphasize that we are talking about real moral issues and real guidance; I want to know whether I should have an abortion, take my mother off the life-support machine, leave academic life and become a doctor in the Third World, give up my job with the firm that is using animals in its experiments, tell my father he has cancer. Would I go to someone who says she has *no* views about what is worthwhile in life? Or to someone who says that, as a matter of fact, she tends to think that the only thing that matters is having a good time, but has a normative theory that is consistent both with this view and with my own rather more puritanical one, which will yield the guidance I need?

I take it as a premise that this is absurd. The relevant condition of adequacy should be that the practical conclusions of a good normative theory *must* be in part determined by premises about what is worthwhile, important, and so on. Thus I reject this "major criticism" of virtue theory, that it cannot get us anywhere in the way that a normative moral theory is supposed to. According to my response, a normative theory that any clever adolescent can apply, or that reaches practical conclusions that are in no way determined by premises about what is truly worthwhile, serious, and so on, is guaranteed to be an inadequate theory....

As promised, I now turn to an illustration of such discussion, applying virtue theory to abortion. Before I embark on this tendentious business, I should remind the reader of the aim of this discussion. I am not, in this article, trying to solve the problem of abortion; I am illustrating how virtue theory directs one to think about it....

ABORTION

As everyone knows, the morality of abortion is commonly discussed in relation to just two considerations: first, and predominantly, the status of the fetus and whether or not it is the sort of thing that may or may not be innocuously or justifiably killed; and second, and less predominantly (when, that is, the discussion concerns the *morality* of abortion rather than the question of permissible legislation in a just society), women's rights. If one thinks within this familiar framework, one may well be puzzled about what virtue theory, as such, could contribute. Some people assume the discussion will be conducted solely in terms of what the virtuous agent would or would not do (cf. the third, fourth, and fifth criticisms above). Others assume that only justice, or at most justice and charity, will be applied to the issue, generating a discussion very similar to Judith Jarvis Thomson's.[4]

Now if this is the way the virtue theorist's discussion of abortion is imagined to be, no wonder people think little of it. It seems obvious in advance that in any such discussion there must be either a great deal of extremely tendentious application of the virtue terms *just, charitable,* and so on or a lot of rhetorical appeal to "this is what only the virtuous agent knows." But these are caricatures; they fail to appreciate the way in which virtue theory quite transforms the discussion of abortion by dismissing the two familiar dominating considerations as, in a way, fundamentally irrelevant. In what way or ways, I hope to make both clear and plausible.

Let us first consider women's rights. Let me emphasize again that we are discussing the *morality* of abortion, not the rights and wrongs of laws prohibiting or permitting it. If we suppose that women do have a moral right to do as they choose with their own bodies, or, more particularly, to terminate their pregnancies, then it may well follow that a *law* forbidding abortion would be unjust. Indeed, even if they have no such right, such a law might be, as things stand at the moment, unjust, or impractical, or inhumane: on this issue I have nothing to say in this article. But, putting all questions about the justice or injustice of laws to one side, and supposing only that women have such a moral right, *nothing* follows from this supposition about the morality of abortion, according to virtue theory, once it is noted (quite generally, not with particular reference to abortion) that in exercising a moral right I can do something cruel, or callous, or selfish, light-minded, self-righteous, stupid, inconsiderate, disloyal, dishonest—that is, act viciously.[5] Love and friendship do not survive their parties' constantly insisting on their rights, nor do people live well when they think that getting what they have a right to is of preeminent importance; they harm others, and they harm themselves. So whether women have a moral right to terminate their pregnancies is irrelevant within virtue theory, for it is irrelevant to the question "In having an abortion in these circumstances, would the agent be acting virtuously or viciously or neither?"

What about the consideration of the status of the fetus—what can virtue theory say about that? One might say that this issue is not in the province of *any* moral theory; it is a metaphysical question, and an extremely difficult one at that. Must virtue theory then wait upon metaphysics to come up with the answer?

At first sight it might seem so. For virtue is said to involve knowledge, and part of this knowledge consists in having the *right* attitude to things. "Right" here does not just mean "morally right" or "proper" or "nice" in the modern sense; it means "accurate, true." One cannot have the right or correct attitude to something if the attitude is based on or involves false beliefs. And this suggests that if the status of the fetus is relevant to the rightness or wrongness of abortion, its status must be known, as a truth, to the fully wise and virtuous person.

But the sort of wisdom that the fully virtuous person has is not supposed to be recondite; it does not call for fancy philosophical sophistication, and it does not depend upon, let alone wait upon, the discoveries of academic philosophers. And this entails the following, rather startling, conclusion: that the status of the fetus—that issue over which so much ink has been spilt—is, according to virtue theory, simply not relevant to the rightness or wrongness of abortion (within, that is, a secular morality).

Or rather, since that is clearly too radical a conclusion, it is in a sense relevant, but only in the sense that the familiar biological facts are relevant. By "the familiar biological facts" I mean the facts that most human societies are and have been familiar with—that, standardly (but not invariably), pregnancy occurs as the result of sexual intercourse, that it lasts about nine months, during which time the fetus grows and develops, that standardly it terminates in the birth of a living baby, and that this is how we all come to be. . . .

Now if we are using virtue theory, our first question is not "What do the familiar biological facts show—what can be derived from them about the status of the fetus?" but "How do these facts figure in the practical reasoning, actions and passions, thoughts and reactions, of the virtuous and the nonvirtuous? What is the mark of having the right attitude to these facts and what manifests having the wrong attitude to them?" This immediately makes essentially relevant not only all the facts about human reproduction I mentioned above, but a whole range of facts about our emotions in relation to them as well. I mean such facts as that human parents, both male and female, tend to care passionately about their offspring, and that family relationships are among the deepest and strongest in our lives—and, significantly, among the longest-lasting.

These facts make it obvious that pregnancy is not just one among many other physical conditions; and hence that anyone who genuinely believes that an abortion is comparable to a haircut or an appendectomy is mistaken. The fact that the premature termination of a pregnancy is, in some sense, the cutting off of a new human life, and thereby, like the procreation of a new human life, connects with all our thoughts about human life and death, parenthood, and family relationships, must make it a serious matter. To disregard this fact about it, to think of abortion as nothing but the killing of something that does not matter, or as nothing but the exercise of some right or rights one has, or as the incidental means to some desirable state of affairs, is to do something callous and light-minded, the sort of thing that no virtuous and wise person would do. It is to have the wrong attitude not only to fetuses, but more generally to human life and death, parenthood, and family relationships.

Although I say that the facts make this obvious, I know that this is one of my tendentious points. In partial support of it I note that even the most dedicated proponents of the view that deliberate abortion is just like an appendectomy or haircut rarely hold the same view of spontaneous abortion, that is, miscarriage. It is not so tendentious of me to claim that to react to people's grief over miscarriage by saying, or even thinking, "What a fuss about nothing!" would be callous and light-minded, whereas to try to laugh someone out of grief over an appendectomy scar or a botched haircut would not be. It is hard to give this point due prominence within act-centered theories, for the inconsistency is an inconsistency in attitude about the seriousness of loss of life, not in beliefs about which acts are right or wrong. Moreover, an act-centered theorist may say, "Well, there is nothing wrong with *thinking* 'What a fuss about nothing!' as long as you do not say it and hurt the person who is grieving. And besides, we cannot be held responsible for our thoughts, only for the intentional actions they give rise to." But the character traits that virtue theory emphasizes are not simply dispositions to intentional actions, but a seamless disposition to certain actions and passions, thoughts and reactions.

To say that the cutting off of a human life is always a matter of some seriousness, at any stage,

is not to deny the relevance of gradual fetal development. Notwithstanding the well-worn point that clear boundary lines cannot be drawn, our emotions and attitudes regarding the fetus do change as it develops, and again when it is born, and indeed further as the baby grows. Abortion for shallow reasons in the later stages is much more shocking than abortion for the same reasons in the early stages in a way that matches the fact that deep grief over miscarriage in the later stages is more appropriate than it is over miscarriage in the earlier stages (when, that is, the grief is solely about the loss of *this* child, not about, as might be the case, the loss of one's only hope of having a child or of having one's husband's child). Imagine (or recall) a woman who already has children; she had not intended to have more, but finds herself unexpectedly pregnant. Though contrary to her plans, the pregnancy, once established as a fact, is welcomed—and then she loses the embryo almost immediately. If this were bemoaned as a tragedy, it would, I think, be a misapplication of the concept of what is tragic. But it may still properly be mourned as a loss. The grief is expressed in such terms as "I shall always wonder how she or he would have turned out" or "When I look at the others, I shall think, 'How different their lives would have been if this other one had been part of them.'" It would, I take it, be callous and light-minded to say, or think, "Well, she has already *got* four children; what's the problem?"; it would be neither, nor arrogantly intrusive in the case of a close friend, to try to correct prolonged mourning by saying, "I know it's sad, but it's not a tragedy; rejoice in the ones you have." The application of *tragic* becomes more appropriate as the fetus grows, for the mere fact that one has lived with it for longer, conscious of its existence, makes a difference. To shrug off an early abortion is understandable just because it is very hard to be fully conscious of the fetus's existence in the early stages and hence hard to appreciate that an early abortion is the destruction of life. It is particularly hard for the young and inexperienced to appreciate this, because appreciation of it usually comes only with experience.

I do not mean "with the experience of having an abortion" (though that may be part of it) but, quite generally, "with the experience of life." Many women who have borne children contrast their later pregnancies with their first successful one, saying that in the later ones they were conscious of a new life growing in them from very early on. And, more generally, as one reaches the age at which the next generation is coming up close behind one, the counterfactuals "If I, or she, had had an abortion, Alice, or Bob, would not have been born" acquire a significant application, which casts a new light on the conditionals "If I or Alice have an abortion then some Caroline or Bill will not be born."

The fact that pregnancy is not just one among many physical conditions does not mean that one can never regard it in that light without manifesting a vice. When women are in very poor physical health, or worn out from childbearing, or forced to do very physically demanding jobs, then they cannot be described as self-indulgent, callous, irresponsible, or light-minded if they seek abortions mainly with a view to avoiding pregnancy as the physical condition that it is. To go through with a pregnancy when one is utterly exhausted, or when one's job consists of crawling along tunnels hauling coal, as many women in the nineteenth century were obliged to do, is perhaps heroic, but people who do not achieve heroism are not necessarily vicious. That they can view the pregnancy only as eight months of misery, followed by hours if not days of agony and exhaustion, and abortion only as the blessed escape from this prospect, is entirely understandable and does not manifest any lack of serious respect for human life or a shallow attitude to motherhood. What it does show is that something is terribly amiss in the conditions of their lives, which make it so hard to recognize pregnancy and childbearing as the good that they can be.

In relation to this last point I should draw attention to the way in which virtue theory has a sort of built-in indexicality. Philosophers arguing against anything remotely resembling a belief in the sanctity of life (which the above claims clearly embody) frequently appeal to the existence of other communities in which abortion and infanticide are practiced. We should not automatically assume that it is impossible that some other communities could be morally inferior to our own; maybe some are, or have been, precisely insofar as their members are, typically, callous or light-minded or unjust. But in communities in which life is a great deal tougher for everyone than it is in ours, having the right attitude to human life and death, parenthood, and family relationships might well manifest itself in ways that are unlike ours. When it is essential to survival that most members of the community fend for themselves at a very young age or work during most of their waking hours, selective abortion or infanticide might be practiced either as a form of genuine euthanasia or for the sake of the community and not, I think, be thought callous or light-minded. But this does not make everything all right; as before, it shows that there is something amiss with the conditions of their lives, which are making it impossible for them to live really well.

The foregoing discussion, insofar as it emphasizes the right attitude to human life and death, parallels to a certain extent those standard discussions of abortion that concentrate on it solely as an issue of killing. But it does not, as those discussions do, gloss over the fact, emphasized by those who discuss the morality of abortion in terms of women's rights, that abortion, wildly unlike any other form of killing, is the termination of a pregnancy, which is a condition of a woman's body and results in *her* having a child if it is not aborted. This fact is given due recognition not by appeal to women's rights but by emphasizing the relevance of the familiar biological and psychological facts and their connection with having the right attitude to parenthood and family relationships. But it may well be thought that failing to bring in women's rights still leaves some important aspects of the problem of abortion untouched.

Speaking in terms of women's rights, people sometimes say things like, "Well, it's her life you're talking about too, you know; she's got a right to her own life, her own happiness." And the discussion stops there. But in the context of virtue theory, given that we are particularly concerned with what constitutes a good human life, with what true happiness or *eudaimonia* is, this is no place to stop. We go on to ask, "And is this life of hers a good one? Is she living well?"

If we are to go on to talk about good human lives, in the context of abortion, we have to bring in our thoughts about the value of love and family life, and our proper emotional development through a natural life cycle. The familiar facts support the view that parenthood in general, and motherhood and child-bearing in particular, are intrinsically worthwhile, are among the things that can be correctly thought to be partially constitutive of a flourishing human life.[6] If this is right, then a woman who opts for not being a mother (at all, or again, or now) by opting for abortion may thereby be manifesting a flawed grasp of what her life should be, and be about—a grasp that is childish, or grossly materialistic, or shortsighted, or shallow.

I said "*may* thereby": this *need* not be so. Consider, for instance, a woman who has already had several children and fears that to have another will seriously affect her capacity to be a good mother to the ones she has—she does not show a lack of appreciation of the intrinsic value of being a parent by opting for abortion. Nor does a woman who has been a good mother and is approaching the age at which she may be looking forward to being a good grandmother. Nor does a woman who discovers that her pregnancy may well kill her, and opts for abortion and adoption. Nor, necessarily, does a woman who has decided to lead a life centered around some other worthwhile activity or activities with which motherhood would compete.

People who are childless by choice are some-times described as "irresponsible," or "selfish," or "refusing to grow up," or "not knowing what life is about." But one can hold that having children is intrinsically worthwhile without endorsing this, for we are, after all, in the happy position of there being more worthwhile things to do than can be fitted into one lifetime. Parenthood, and motherhood in partic-ular, even if granted to be intrinsically worthwhile, undoubtedly take up a lot of one's adult life, leav-ing no room for some other worthwhile pursuits. But some women who choose abortion rather than have their first child, and some men who encourage their partners to choose abortion, are not avoiding par-enthood for the sake of other worthwhile pursuits, but for the worthless one of "having a good time," or for the pursuit of some false vision of the ideals of freedom or self-realization. And some others who say "I am not ready for parenthood yet" are making some sort of mistake about the extent to which one can manipulate the circumstances of one's life so as to make it fulfill some dream that one has. Perhaps one's dream is to have two perfect children, a girl and a boy, within a perfect marriage, in financially secure circumstances, with an interesting job of one's own. But to care too much about that dream, to demand of life that it give it to one and act accordingly, may be both greedy and foolish, and is to run the risk of missing out on happiness entirely. Not only may fate make the dream impossible, or destroy it, but one's own attachment to it may make it impossible. Good marriages, and the most promising children, can be destroyed by just one adult's excessive demand for perfection.

Once again, this is not to deny that girls may quite properly say "I am not ready for motherhood yet," especially in our society, and, far from manifesting irresponsibility or light-mindedness, show an appro-priate modesty or humility, or a fearfulness that does not amount to cowardice. However, even when the decision to have an abortion is the right decision—one that does not itself fall under a vice-related term and thereby one that the perfectly virtuous could recommend—it does not follow that there is no sense in which having the abortion is wrong, or guilt inappropriate. For, by virtue of the fact that a human life has been cut short, some evil has probably been brought about,[7] and that circumstances make the decision to bring about some evil the right decision will be a ground for guilt if getting into those cir-cumstances in the first place itself manifested a flaw in character.

What "gets one into those circumstances" in the case of abortion is, except in the case of rape, one's sexual activity and one's choices, or the lack of them, about one's sexual partner and about contra-ception. The virtuous woman (which here of course does not mean simply "chaste woman" but "woman with the virtues") has such character traits as strength, independence, resoluteness, decisiveness, self-confidence, responsibility, serious-minded-ness, and self-determination—and no one, I think, could deny that many women become pregnant in circumstances in which they cannot welcome or cannot face the thought of having *this* child precisely because they lack one or some of these character traits. So even in the cases where the decision to have an abortion is the right one, it can still be the reflection of a moral failing—not because the decision itself is weak or cowardly or irresolute or irresponsible or light-minded, but because lack of the requisite opposite of these failings landed one in the circumstances in the first place. Hence the common universalized claim that guilt and remorse are never appropriate emotions about an abortion is denied. They may be appropriate, and appropriately inculcated, even when the decision was the right one.

Another motivation for bringing women's rights into the discussion may be to attempt to correct the implication, carried by the killing-centered approach, that insofar as abortion is wrong, it is a wrong that only women do, or at least (given the preponderance of male doctors) that only women instigate. I do not myself believe that we can thus escape the fact that nature bears harder on women than it does on men,[8] but virtue theory can certainly correct many of the injustices that the emphasis on women's rights is rightly concerned about. With very little amendment, everything that has been said above applies to boys and men too. Although the abortion decision is, in a natural sense, the woman's decision, proper to her, boys and men are often party to it, for well or ill, and even when they are not, they are bound to have been party to the circumstances that brought it up. No less than girls and women, boys and men can, in their actions, manifest self-centeredness, callousness, and light-mindedness about life and parenthood in relation to abortion. They can be self-centered or courageous about the possibility of disability in their offspring; they need to reflect on their sexual activity and their choices, or the lack of them, about their sexual partner and contraception; they need to grow up and take responsibility for their own actions and life in relation to fatherhood. If it is true, as I maintain, that insofar as motherhood is intrinsically worthwhile, being a mother is an important purpose in women's lives, being a father (rather than a mere generator) is an important purpose in men's lives as well, and it is adolescent of men to turn a blind eye to this and pretend that they have many more important things to do.

CONCLUSION

Much more might be said, but I shall end the actual discussion of the problem of abortion here, and conclude by highlighting what I take to be its significant features. These hark back to many of the criticisms of virtue theory discussed earlier.

The discussion does not proceed simply by our trying to answer the question "Would a perfectly virtuous agent ever have an abortion and, if so, when?"; virtue theory is not limited to considering "Would Socrates have had an abortion if he were a raped, pregnant fifteen-year-old?" nor automatically stumped when we are considering circumstances into which no virtuous agent would have got herself. Instead, much of the discussion proceeds in the virtue- and vice-related terms whose application, in several cases, yields practical conclusions (cf. the third and fourth criticisms above). These terms are difficult to apply correctly, and anyone might challenge my application of any one of them. So, for example, I have claimed that some abortions, done for certain reasons, would be callous or light-minded; that others might indicate an appropriate modesty or humility; that others would reflect a greedy and foolish attitude to what one could expect out of life. Any of these examples may be disputed, but what is at issue is, should these difficult terms be there, or should the discussion be couched in terms that all clever adolescents can apply correctly? (Cf. the first half of the "major objection" above.)

Proceeding as it does in the virtue- and vice-related terms, the discussion thereby, inevitably, also contains claims about what is worthwhile, serious and important, good and evil, in our lives. So, for example, I claimed that parenthood is intrinsically worthwhile, and that having a good time was a worthless end (in life, not on individual occasions); that losing a fetus is always a serious matter (albeit not a tragedy in itself in the first trimester) whereas acquiring an appendectomy scar is a trivial one; that (human) death is an evil. Once again, these are difficult matters, and anyone might challenge any one of my claims. But what is at issue is, as before, should those difficult claims be there or can one reach practical conclusions about real moral issues that are in no way determined by premises about such matters? (Cf. the fifth criticism, and the second half of the "major criticism.")

The discussion also thereby, inevitably, contains claims about what life is like (e.g., my claim that love and friendship do not survive their parties' constantly insisting on their rights; or the claim that to demand perfection of life is to run the risk of missing out on happiness entirely). What is at issue is, should those disputable claims be there, or is our knowledge (or are our false opinions) about what life is like irrelevant to our understanding of real moral issues? (Cf. both halves of the "major criticism.")

Naturally, my own view is that all these concepts should be there in any discussion of real moral issues and that virtue theory, which uses all of them, is the right theory to apply to them. . . .

NOTES

Versions of this article have been read to philosophy societies at University College, London, Rutgers University, and the Universities of Dundee, Edinburgh, Oxford, Swansea, and California–San Diego; at a conference of the Polish and British Academies in Cracow in 1988 on "Life, Death and the Law," and as a symposium paper at the Pacific Division of the American Philosophical Association in 1989. I am grateful to the many people who contributed to the discussions of it on these occasions, and particularly to Philippa Foot and Anne Jaap Jacobson for private discussion.

1. It should be noted that this premise intentionally allows for the possibility that two virtuous agents, faced with the same choice in the same circumstances, may act differently. For example, one might opt for taking

her father off the life-support machine and the other for leaving her father on it. The theory requires that neither agent thinks that what the other does is wrong . . . but it explicitly allows that no action is uniquely right in such a case—both are right. It also intentionally allows for the possibility that in some circumstances—those into which no virtuous agent could have got herself—no action is right. I explore this premise at greater length in "Applying Virtue Ethics," [in *Virtue and Reason: Philippa Foot and Moral Theory,* R. Hursthouse, G. Lawrence, W. Quinn, eds. (Oxford: Clarendon Press, 1995)].

2. Intimations of this criticism constantly come up in discussion; the clearest statement of it I have found is by Onora O'Neill, in her review of Stephen Clark's *The Moral Status of Animals,* in *Journal of Philosophy* 77 (1980): 440–46. For a response I am much in sympathy with, see Cora Diamond, "Anything But Argument?" *Philosophical Investigations* 5 (1982): 23–41.

3. Aristotle, *Nicomachean Ethics* 1142a12–16.

4. Judith Jarvis Thomson, "A Defense of Abortion," *Philosophy & Public Affairs* 1, no. 1 (Fall 1971): 47–66. One could indeed regard this article as proto-virtue theory (no doubt to the surprise of the author) if the concepts of callousness and kindness were allowed more weight.

5. One possible qualification: if one ties the concept of justice very closely to rights, then if women do have a moral right to terminate their pregnancies it *may* follow that in doing so they do not act unjustly. (Cf. Thomson, "A Defense of Abortion.") But it is debatable whether even that much follows.

6. I take this as a premise here, but argue for it in some detail in my *Beginning Lives* (Oxford: Basil Blackwell, 1987). In this connection I also discuss adoption and the sense in which it may be regarded as "second best," and the difficult question of whether the good of parenthood may properly be sought, or indeed bought, by surrogacy.

7. I say "some evil has probably been brought about" on the ground that (human) life is (usually) a good and hence (human) death usually an evil. The exceptions would be (*a*) where death is actually a good or a benefit, because the baby that would come to be if the life were not cut short would be better off dead than alive, and (*b*) where death, though not a good, is not an evil either because the life that would be led (e.g., in a state of permanent coma) would not be a good.

8. I discuss this point at greater length in *Beginning Lives.*

READING QUESTIONS

1. Husthouse claims that even if a woman has a moral right to an abortion, "*nothing* follows from this supposition." How does she defend this claim?
2. Hursthouse claims that questions about the status of the fetus are not relevant (or not especially relevant) according to virtue ethics in determining whether abortion is right or wrong. How does she defend this claim?
3. According to Hursthouse's view on abortion, how are facts about the gradual development of the fetus relevant to the morality of abortion?
4. What does Hursthouse say about those who would seek an abortion saying, "I am not ready for parenthood/motherhood yet"?
5. Explain why Husthouse claims that even in cases where having an abortion is not morally wrong, having an abortion can still reflect a moral failing.

DISCUSSION QUESTIONS

1. Is Husthouse's virtue ethics approach to abortion superior to Thomson's rights-focused approach? Why or why not?
2. Should we agree with Hursthouse that questions about the moral status of the fetus are not as relevant to the abortion issue as many have supposed?

ADDITIONAL RESOURCES

Web Resources

The Centers for Disease Control and Prevention, <www.cdc.gov>. Includes information about health safety and abortion.

Emedicine Health, <http://www.emedicinehealth.com/abortion/article em.htm>. Features basic information on abortion including its legal status in the United States.

The National Right to Life Organization, <www.nric.org>. Advocates of the pro-life position.

NARAL Pro-Choice America, <www.prochoiceamerica.org>. Advocates of the pro-choice position.

Authored Books and Articles

Beckwith, Francis, J., *Politically Correct Death: Answering the Arguments for Abortion Rights* (Cedar Rapids, MI: Baker Book House, 1994). A defense of a conservative "pro-life" position with criticisms of what Beckwith takes to be the "pro-choice agenda."

Boonin, David, *A Defense of Abortion* (Cambridge: Cambridge University Press, 2003). A thorough and careful defense of the morality of abortion.

English, Jane, "Abortion and the Concept of a Person," *Canadian Journal of Philosophy* 5 (1975): 233–43. Argues that the concept of a person is not precise enough to determine whether the fetus is clearly a person or clearly not a person (considering all stages of fetal development). English also argues that a woman's right to self-defense justifies abortions even on the assumption that the fetus is a person.

Hare, R. M., "Abortion and the Golden Rule," *Philosophy and Public Affairs* 4 (1975): 210–22. An appeal to a version of the golden rule in defense of a moderate position on abortion.

Harman, Elizabeth, "The Potentiality Problem," *Philosophical Studies* 114 (2003): 173–98. Argues against the claim that potentiality confers moral standing on a fetus.

Luker, Kristin, *Abortion and the Politics of Motherhood* (Berkeley, CA: University of California Press, 1984). Contains an illuminating discussion of the history and sociology of the debate over abortion that began in the 19th century.

Shrage, Laurie, *Abortion and Social Responsibility: Depolarizing the Debate* (New York: Oxford University Press, 2003). A critical examination of *Roe v. Wade*'s regulatory scheme with a proposed alternative scheme that aims to depolarize the debate, win broader public support, and thus make legal abortion services more accessible to women in the United States.

Sherwin, Susan, "Abortion through a Feminist Ethics Lens," *Dialogue* 30 (1990): 327–42. Defense of a woman's right to choose abortion grounded in the importance of sexual and reproductive freedom for women.

Sinnott-Armstrong, Walter, "You Can't Lose What You Ain't Never Had: A Reply to Marquis on Abortion," *Philosophical Studies* 96 (1997): 59–72. Argues that Marquis's argument for the claim that abortion is seriously morally wrong commits the fallacy of equivocation.

Tooley, Michael, "Abortion and Infanticide," *Philosophy and Public Affairs* 2 (1972): 37–65. Defense of the moral permissibility of abortion and infanticide.

Tooley, Michael, Celia Wolf-Devine, Philip E. Devine, and Alison M. Jaggar, *Abortion: Three Perspectives* (New York: Oxford University Press, 2009). Four philosophers present three different positions concerning the moral permissibility of abortion, with point and counterpoint responses to one another.

Edited Anthologies

Beckwith, Francis J., and Louis P. Pojman (eds.), *The Abortion Controversy* (Belmont, CA: Wadsworth, 1988). Wide-ranging collection of articles debating abortion.

Baird, Robert M., and Stuart E. Rosenbaum (eds.), *The Ethics of Abortion: Pro-Life Vs. Pro-Choice*, 3rd ed. (New York: Prometheus Books, 2001). Twenty-two essays by various scholars organized into five parts: (1) The Issue, (2) Abortion and the Constitution, (3) Abortion and Feminism, (4) Abortion and Christianity, and (5) Abortion and Moral Philosophy.

Dwyer, Susan, and Joel Feinberg (eds.), *The Problem of Abortion*, 3rd ed. (Belmont, CA: Wadsworth, 1996). A collection of essays, mostly by philosophers, representing a spectrum of views about the morality of abortion.

10) Cloning and Genetic Enhancement

Reproductive technology has made significant advances in the past forty years. For instance, **in vitro** ("under glass") **fertilization** (IVF) through which a sperm fertilizes an egg in a petri dish and, after a few days of growth, is then implanted in a woman's uterus, is available to otherwise infertile couples. In 1978, Louise Brown, the first "test tube" baby, was born using in vitro fertilization, and since then over three million children have been born using this procedure. And just as this procedure was subject to intense moral scrutiny when it came on the scene, so also have cloning and the prospect of genetic enhancement, the subjects of this chapter. In order to gain a basic understanding of what is at stake in the moral controversy over these developments, let us focus first on the issue of cloning—what it is and the moral controversy it has caused—and then turn briefly to the ethics of genetic enhancement.

In 1997, a research team, led by Dr. Ian Wilmut of the Roslin Institute in Scotland, produced a cloned sheep named Dolly. The significance of Dolly is that she was the first mammal ever cloned, making it very probable that cloning other mammals, including humans, is possible. The apparently real prospect of cloning a human being—**reproductive cloning**—has generated much recent scientific and ethical debate. And so has **therapeutic cloning**, whose purpose is the production of embryos for use in medical research. If we turn our attention to *human* reproductive and therapeutic cloning, the central moral questions are the following:

- Is either type of human cloning (therapeutic or reproductive) ever morally permissible?
- If not, what best explains why such activities are morally wrong?

In order to appreciate the significance of these questions, we will need to review some very elementary scientific facts about the two types of cloning in question. After we understand what cloning is, we will proceed to recount recent attempts to ban this type of biotechnology and then return to the ethical issues just raised.

1. WHAT IS CLONING?

If we consider **cloning** an organism as an activity that we may choose to perform, then we can say that it involves the process of "asexually" producing a biological organism that is virtually genetically identical to another organism.[1] (The terms "asexual" and "sexual" have technical scientific meanings that are explained later.) The process in question involves **somatic cell**[2] **nuclear transfer** (SCNT for short), and the basic idea here is easy to understand. So, let us begin with what we are calling reproductive cloning and then turn to therapeutic cloning.

In sexual reproduction an unfertilized egg (called an **oocyte**, pronounced, oh-oh-site) is fertilized by a sperm resulting in what is called a **zygote**—a one-cell organism whose nucleus contains genetic information contributed by the individual who produced the egg and by the individual who produced the sperm. A one-cell zygote then undergoes cellular division, and many cells later we have what is commonly called an **embryo**. As the embryo develops, its cells begin to differentiate, forming cells with different functions—nerve cells, blood cells, fat cells, and so on. A complex organism is the eventual result.[3] Here is it important to notice that the process just described refers to cases in which reproduction takes place entirely in a woman's reproductive system *and* to cases in which fertilization is made to occur *in vitro*. Both count as "sexual" in the technical sense of the term, because both involve the genetic contribution from two individuals.

Cloning involves asexual reproduction in which (1) the nucleus of an unfertilized egg is removed and (2) the nucleus of another cell—the "donor" nucleus—is removed and then (3) inserted into the "hollow" unfertilized egg, (4) which is then implanted in a female's uterus. In this process, incidentally, the unfertilized egg and the donor nucleus may be contributed by different individuals, neither of whom may be the individual in whom the embryo is implanted. The resulting individual will be virtually genetically identical—will have nearly the same genetic makeup—as the individual from whom the donor nucleus was taken.[4] The crucial difference between sexual and asexual reproduction, then, is that in the former, the genetic makeup of the zygote and the resulting offspring are the direct result of the genetic contributions of two individuals—the produced offspring is not genetically identical to either of the other two individuals. However, individuals produced asexually by the process of nuclear transfer are virtually genetically identical to the nuclear donor. Let us call the offspring produced by what we are calling reproductive cloning **SCNT individuals**.

We now turn from reproductive cloning to therapeutic cloning. They differ mainly in the purposes for which the process of nuclear transfer is being used. But to understand the therapeutic use of cloning, we need to explain the nature and importance of **stem cells**. Stem cells are found throughout the body and are significant because they have the capability of developing into various kinds of cells or tissues in the body. Stem cells have three general properties: (1) Unlike muscle cells, blood cells, and nerve cells, stem cells have the capacity to renew themselves for long periods of time. (2) Stem cells are "undifferentiated" in that they do not have a specific function as do, for instance, red blood cells whose job is to carry oxygen through the bloodstream. (3) Stem cells can result in specialized cells through a process called differentiation. There are two main types of stem cells that we need to distinguish.

Adult stem cells are undifferentiated cells found among differentiated cells in a tissue or organ. Adult stem cells function to help maintain and repair damaged differentiated cells of the same organ or tissue type in which they are found. This would appear to limit their therapeutic use, since, for example, a heart adult stem cell could only be used to generate heart cells and thus not cells of any other type.[5]

Embryonic stem cells are found in embryos and are "pluripotent," that is, they can become any cell type found in the body. The use of embryonic stem cells, derived from human embryos created by *in vitro* fertilization, has generated moral controversy because extracting these pluripotent cells from embryos inevitably resulted in the destruction of the embryos. However, the use of embryonic stem cells, given that they can be manipulated to become a particular body cell type, makes them particularly valuable for treating disease and other medical conditions. Indeed, cloning makes it possible for a patient who, let us say, is suffering from heart disease, to have the nucleus of one of her body cells injected into an enucleated egg, which could then be induced to multiply, thereby producing an embryo. From the embryo, stem cells could be extracted and used for purposes of producing heart cells that would be used to treat one's heart disease. Because the embryonic stem cells produced in this way match your genetic makeup, there is reduced risk of tissue rejection and thus greater chance of success.

Until recently, use of embryonic stem cells for purposes of research required the destruction of the embryos from which these stem cells were derived. And the destruction of embryos has been a basis of moral objection to such research by those who consider the embryo to have direct moral standing. However, in 2006, scientists developed a technique for extracting embryonic stem cells without destroying the embryos. This breakthrough was greeted by some as removing any serious moral objections to the use of such cells in research.[6]

So, although both types of human cloning—reproductive and therapeutic—involve the process of nuclear transfer, the former has as its aim the bringing about of a child, while the latter aims only at producing a human embryo, stem cells from which might then be used for medical purposes. And, as we have just seen, although there have been moral objections to therapeutic cloning of the sort that involves the destruction of embryos, with new advances in the extraction of stem cells from human embryos that do not destroy the embryo, therapeutic cloning promises to become less morally problematic. In any case, it is the issue of reproductive cloning that has stirred most of the recent moral controversy over cloning and is the topic of concern in our selections dealing with cloning.

2. THE MOVE TO BAN CLONING

In the United States, one immediate response to the announcement of Dolly (the cloned sheep mentioned earlier) was the creation by President William Clinton of the National Bioethics Advisory Council (NBAC), whose task it was to investigate American public policy on the topic of cloning. After conducting hearings during which religious and secular moral arguments were presented and discussed, the NBAC called on Congress to pass laws that would make reproductive cloning a federal crime. To date, Congress has not been able to pass any such law.

On August 9, 2001, President George W. Bush announced that federal funding for stem cell research would be restricted to stem cell lines already in existence on the date of his announcement. This was generally seen as a compromise between factions that oppose therapeutic cloning and those in favor of it. On March 9, 2009, President Barack Obama issued an executive order ("Removing Barriers to Responsible Research Involving Human Stem Cells") that lifted the funding restrictions that President Bush's directive prohibited. Obama's order lifted the ban on the use of federal funding for research on stem cells created with private money, but did not address the ban on the use of federal funds to develop new stem cell lines.

As of January 2008, fifteen U.S. states have passed laws to ban reproductive cloning of humans, while six states also ban human therapeutic cloning.[7] According to the Center for Genetics and Society based in California, as of December of 2009 approximately fifty countries had passed laws banning reproductive cloning.

3. GENETIC ENHANCEMENT

Our developed capacity to manipulate human genetic material not only promises to provide ways to treat disease and other human maladies, but also may enable us to enhance our bodies and our minds. **Genetic enhancement** differs from cloning in that the latter is a form of asexual reproduction as explained earlier, whereas (human) genetic enhancement refers to manipulating genetic material in order to "improve" the talents and capacities of living humans or to produce offspring with certain desirable traits. For instance, the Genetics and IVF Institute in Fairfax, Virginia, already offers a process of sperm separation through which the sex of offspring can be selected. Creating "designer babies," as they are often called, is now an option for those who can afford it. There are further implications. For instance, **eugenics,** the project of "improving" humanity by bringing about genetic changes in future generations, is now very much a possibility.

Let us suppose that therapeutic (medical) genetic manipulation is at least sometimes morally permissible. So the controversy that has generated much recent discussion concerns these questions:

- Is genetic manipulation *for purposes of enhancement* ever morally permissible?
- If they are not, why is such manipulation for such purposes morally impermissible?

4. THEORY MEETS PRACTICE

Let us now turn to some of the moral arguments about cloning and genetic enhancement that are grounded in various moral theories.

Natural Law Theory

One kind of natural law argument against reproductive cloning begins with the thought that cloning (and other forms of assisted reproduction such as in vitro fertilization), because they are asexual, break the natural connection between sex and reproduction—they represent "unnatural" activities. If one then thinks that "unnatural" activities are morally wrong, one will conclude that cloning is morally wrong.[8] (For a critical assessment of arguments that appeal to the idea of "unnaturalness," see the article in chapter 3 by John Corvino.)

But a natural law approach need not appeal to the alleged unnaturalness of actions. Instead, natural law theorists often take reproduction to be intrinsically good and thus something that we are morally obliged to preserve and protect. Our moral obligations regarding reproduction are also taken to include proper child rearing—child rearing that fully respects the dignity of the child. Worries about respecting the worth of the child are a basis for natural law objections to cloning. And here is one place where natural law theory and Kantian ethics coincide in their moral concern about cloning. Let us pursue this line of thought further by turning to the Kantian perspective on this issue.

Kantian Moral Theory

The idea that morality requires that we respect the humanity in both ourselves and others is a guiding idea of the Kantian approach to moral issues. One of the most commonly voiced arguments against reproductive cloning is that it violates the dignity of the SCNT individual—it involves treating the individual as a mere means to some end. The specific manner in which this form of argument is expressed may differ from author to author, but we find a representative example of it in the article from Leon R. Kass included in this chapter.

The plausibility of this line of argument depends on the crucial claim that cloning represents or necessarily involves treating someone as a mere means. But this claim is contested by those who otherwise accept a Kantian approach. For instance, one might argue that there is nothing about cloning that necessarily involves treating anyone as a mere means.[9] Rather, so the argument might continue, whether a child is treated as a mere means and is thus treated immorally depends on the details of how he or she is treated, regardless of how that child was produced.

Consequentialism

Consequentialist thinking about ethical issues is guided by judgments about the likely consequences of actions and practices. Those who oppose cloning point to what they think are likely negative consequences of cloning including, in particular, physical and psychological harms they think are likely be to be suffered by SCNT individuals.

One particular consequentialist argument is called the "slippery slope." A slippery slope argument may take various forms, but behind all such arguments is the idea that if we allow some action or practice *P*, then we will open the door to other similar actions and practices that will eventually lead us down a slope to disastrous results. So, the argument concludes, we morally ought not to allow *P*. Any such argument, in order to be good, must meet two requirements. First, it must be true that the envisioned results really are bad. But second, the central idea of the argument—that allowing one action or practice will be likely to lead us down a path to disaster—must be plausible. If either of these conditions is not met, the argument is said to commit the slippery slope *fallacy*.

With regard to cloning, the argument is that if we allow certain forms of reproductive cloning for what may seem like acceptable reasons, this will open the door to further and further cases of cloning, leading eventually to its abuse and thus to disaster.[10] Perhaps the most vivid portrayal of what might happen is to be found in Aldous Huxley's 1932 novel, *Brave New World,* in which cloning is the chief means of reproduction through which the majority of humans in that world are genetically engineered for various purposes. Huxley's novel portrays a world in which cloning plays a central role in the loss of human dignity and individuality. In light of the recent advances in biotechnology and the very real possibility of reproductive cloning, Francis Fukuyama writes that "Huxley was right, that the most significant threat posed by contemporary biotechnology is the possibility that it will alter human nature and thereby move us into a 'posthuman' stage in history."[11] Voicing similar worries, Leon R. Kass, in an article included in this chapter, explicitly raises the specter of *Brave New World* in his opposition to cloning.

How forceful are such consequentialist arguments? Their plausibility depends crucially on the estimates of the likely consequences of cloning. Gregory Pence, in one of the selections included in this chapter, attempts to rebut the claims of the anticloning consequentialists. Still, many people who oppose reproductive cloning seem to base their opposition at least partly on what they take to be its likely consequences. Notice that those whose opposition to cloning depends *entirely* on an appeal to consequences will have to retract their moral stance on this topic if we have good reason (now or in the future) to believe that the effects of cloning are no more disastrous than, say, IVF.

Rights Approaches

Approaching the moral issues of both therapeutic and reproductive cloning from the perspective of rights has led to various opposing conclusions about such practices. For instance, in his article included in this chapter, John Robertson argues that various forms of assisted reproduction are plausibly included within a general right to reproductive liberty. On this basis, he concludes that cloning should be regarded as something we may choose and which is presumptively morally permissible, unless there are compelling reasons against exercising this form of reproductive liberty. Thus, unlike many writers on the ethics of cloning who think that the burden of moral justification rests with those who favor cloning, Robertson thinks that the burden of moral justification rests with those who think that there is something morally wrong with it.

But rights are often center stage in arguments that oppose therapeutic as well as reproductive cloning. A main ethical objection to therapeutic cloning is based on the fact that extracting stem cells from a human embryo inevitably destroys the embryo. Those who think that a human embryo has a right to life are against therapeutic cloning for the same reason they are against abortion—such activities involve the killing of an innocent human being with a right to life. Of course, whether this argument is sound depends on the crucial moral claim that a human embryo has a right to life, an issue discussed in the chapter on abortion.

Virtue Ethics

The ethical issues that genetic enhancement raises are much like the ones implicated in the debate over cloning. Consequentialist worries about the likely negative effects of this practice, Kantian worries about whether it is somehow dehumanizing, and natural law questions about its "naturalness" are all represented in the literature on the ethics of enhancement. In addition, ethical concerns that focus on the dispositions and attitudes that would be expressed through engaging in or condoning genetic enhancement—concerns that focus on virtue, vice, and the morality of character—have been raised by some critics of the practice. Michael J. Sandel, whose essay is included here, is one such critic whose approach to the ethics of enhancement is perhaps best viewed as an example of applied virtue ethics. Sandel's position is subjected to critical scrutiny by Arthur L. Caplan in the final selection in this chapter.

NOTES

1. Strictly speaking "cloning" refers very generally to the process of duplicating genetic material. There are different types of cloning: DNA cloning, reproductive cloning, and therapeutic cloning. The Human Genome Project has information on types of cloning. See Additional Resources for reference.

2. A **somatic cell** is any cell in the body other than an egg or sperm (gametes).

3. For more detail about human fetal development, see the introduction to the chapter on abortion.

4. The clone's chromosomal or nuclear DNA is the same as the donor's. Some of the clone's genetic material is contributed by the mitochondrial DNA in the cytoplasm of the enucleated egg, hence the claim that clones are "nearly" genetically identical to the cell donor.

5. Through a process of what is called "transdifferentiation" it may be possible for an adult stem cell to differentiate into a different cell type. For example, an adult brain stem cell might differentiate into a blood cell. However, whether this process does actually occur in humans is controversial.

6. Very recently scientists have been able to "reprogram" adult somatic cells so that they come to be like embryonic stem cells—cells that can become differentiated cells of most any type. Such genetically reprogrammed cells are called **induced pluripotent stem (iPS) cells**. If adult cells can be used for the same purposes of embryonic stem cells, then there is no need to engage in the process of cloning to produce an embryo from which embryonic stem cells are then extracted. For more information about iPS cells, consult "Stem Cell Information" to be found on the National Institutes of Health Web site mentioned in Additional Resources for this chapter.

7. This statistic is reported by the National Conference of State Legislatures (NCSL). See <http://www.ncsl.org/issuesresearch/health/humancloninglaws/tabid/14284/default.aspx>

8. This form of argument can be found in Leon Kass's "The Wisdom of Repugnance," *The New Republic* 2, June 1997. Notice that this argument, if sound, would also show that IVF is morally wrong, since sexual intercourse is not involved in the process. One might respond to this argument by pointing out that although there is a "natural" connection between eating and nutrition, breaking this connection by intravenous feeding would not be morally wrong. Thus, the mere breaking of a "natural" connection cannot make an action morally wrong. See also the Vatican declaration pertaining to bioethical issues mentioned in Additional Resources for this chapter.

9. This argument is to be found in Philip Kitcher's *The Lives to Come* mentioned in Additional Resources for this chapter.

10. This same slippery slope argument is often used to oppose therapeutic cloning. What forms of cloning might be understood as at least initially acceptable? There is some dispute over whether there are such cases.

11. Frances Fukuyama, *Our Posthuman Future* (New York: Farrar, Straus and Giroux, 2002), 7.

JOHN ROBERTSON

Liberty, Identity, and Human Cloning

In the following excerpted article, Robertson defends cloning by arguing that this practice is legitimately included within the scope of a right to reproductive liberty. He first argues that current forms of assisted reproduction including in vitro fertilization (IVF) and genetic selection are part of our reproductive liberty. He continues by then arguing that because cloning is similar in morally relevant respects to forms of assisted reproduction, we may conclude that cloning, too, is morally permissible, a practice to which we have a moral right. In defending this view, Robertson considers the cases of cloning a couple's embryos, cloning one's children, cloning third parties, and cloning oneself. He concludes with a proposal for public policy that would require that the moral freedom to clone be restricted by a willingness to rear cloned offspring on the part of those seeking to exercise this freedom.

Toward the end of his article, Robertson provides a brief reply to worries about sliding down a slippery slope, a slope that some writers like to compare to the disconcerting vision of a possible post-human future described in Aldous Huxley's 1932 novel *Brave New World*. This vision and the slippery slope concern about cloning are well represented in the article by Leon R. Kass that follows Robertson's.

Recommended Reading: rights-focused approach to moral issues, chap. 1, sec. 2D.

A proper assessment of human cloning requires that it be viewed in light of how it might be actually used once it is shown to be safe and effective. The most likely uses would involve extending current reproductive and genetic selection technologies. Several plausible uses can be articulated, quite different from the horrific scenarios currently imagined. The question becomes: Do these uses fall within mainstream understandings of why procreative freedom warrants special respect as one of our fundamental liberties? Investigation of this question will set the stage for examining what public policy toward human cloning ought to be.

THE DEMAND FOR HUMAN CLONING

Legitimate, family-centered uses of cloning are likely precisely because cloning is above all a commitment to have and rear a child. It will involve obtaining eggs, acquiring the DNA to be cloned, transfer of that DNA to a denucleated egg, placement of the activated embryo in a uterus, gestation, and the nurturing and rearing that the birth of any child requires. In addition, it will require a psychological commitment and ability to deal with the novelty of raising a child whose genome has

From "Liberty, Identity, and Human Cloning," John Robertson, *Texas Law Review* 1371, 1998. Reprinted by permission.

been chosen, and who may be the later-born identical twin of another person, living or dead.

The most bizarre or horrific scenarios of cloning conveniently overlook the basic reality that human cloning requires a gestating uterus and a commitment to rear. The gestating mother is eliminated through the idea of total laboratory gestation as imagined in Huxley's *Brave New World,* or through high-tech surgery as in the movie *Multiplicity.* In other scenarios, it is thought that an evildoer can hire several women to gestate copies, with little thought given to how they would be reared or molded to be like the clone source. Nearly all of them overlook the impact of environmental influences on the cloned child, and the duties and burdens that rearing any child requires. They also overlook the extent to which the cloned child is not the property or slave of the initiator, but a person in her own right with all the rights and duties of other persons.

Because cloning is first and foremost the commitment to have and rear a child, it is most likely to appeal to those who wish to have a family but cannot easily do so by ordinary coital means. In some cases, they would turn to cloning because of the advantages that it offers over other assisted reproductive techniques. Or they would choose cloning because they have a need to exercise genetic choice over offspring, as in the desire for a healthy child or for a child to serve as a tissue donor. Given the desire to have healthy children, it is unlikely that couples will be interested in cloning unless they have good reason for thinking that the procedure is safe and effective, and that only healthy children will be born.

The question for moral, legal, and policy analysis is to assess the needs that such uses serve—both those expected to be typical and those that seem more bizarre—and their importance relative to other reproductive and genetic selection endeavors. Can cloning be used responsibly to help a couple achieve legitimate reproductive or family formation goals? If so, are these uses properly characterized as falling within the procreative liberty of individuals, and thus not subject to state restriction without proof of compelling harm?

To assess these questions, we must first investigate the meaning of procreative liberty, and then ask whether uses of cloning to enhance fertility, substitute for a gamete or embryo donor, produce organs or tissue for transplant, or pick a particular genome fall within common understandings of that liberty.

HUMAN CLONING AND PROCREATIVE LIBERTY

Procreative liberty is the freedom to decide whether or not to have offspring. It is a deeply accepted moral value, and pervades many of our social practices.[1] Its importance stems from the impact which having or not having offspring has in our lives. This is evident in the case of a choice to avoid reproduction. Because reproduction imposes enormous physical burdens for the woman, as well as social, psychological, and emotional burdens on both men and women, it is widely thought that people should not have to bear those burdens unless they voluntarily choose to.

But the desire to reproduce is also important. It connects people with nature and the next generation, gives them a sense of immortality, and enables them to rear and parent children. Depriving a person of the ability or opportunity to reproduce is a major burden and also should not occur without their consent.

Reproductive freedom—the freedom to decide whether or not to have offspring—is generally thought to be an important instance of personal liberty. Indeed, given its great impact on a person, it is considered a fundamental personal liberty. In recent years the emergence of assisted reproduction, noncoital means of conception, and prebirth genetic selection has also raised controversies about the limits of procreative freedom. The question of whether cloning is part of procreative liberty is a serious one only if noncoital, assisted reproduction and genetic selection are themselves part of that liberty. A strong argument exists that the moral right to reproduce does include the right to use noncoital or assisted means of reproduction. Infertile couples have the same interests in reproducing as coitally fertile couples, and the same abilities to rear children. That they are coitally infertile should no more bar them from reproducing with technical assistance than visual blindness should bar a person from reading with Braille or the aid of a reader. It thus follows that married couples (and arguably single persons as well) have a moral right to use noncoital assisted reproductive techniques, such as in vitro fertilization (IVF) and artificial insemination with spouse or partner's sperm, to beget biologically related offspring for rearing. It should also follow—though this is more controversial—that the infertile couple would have the right to use gamete donors, gestational surrogates, and even embryo donors if necessary. Although third-party collaborative reproduction does not replicate exactly the genes, gestation, and rearing unity that ordinarily arises in coital reproduction, they come very close and should be treated accordingly. Each of them, with varying degrees of closeness, enables the couple to have or rear children biologically related to at least one of them.

Some right to engage in genetic selection would also seem to follow from the right to decide whether or not to procreate.[2] People make decisions to reproduce or not because of the package of experiences that they think reproduction or its absence would bring. In many cases, they would not reproduce if it would lead to a packet of experiences X, but they would if it would produce packet Y. Since the makeup of the packet will determine whether or not they reproduce, a right to make reproductive decisions based on that packet should follow. Some right to choose characteristics, either by negative exclusion or positive selection, should follow as well, for the decision to reproduce may often depend upon whether the child will have the characteristics of concern.

If most current forms of assisted reproduction and genetic selection fall within prevailing notions of procreative freedom, then a strong argument exists that some forms of cloning are aspects of procreative liberty as well. For cloning shares many features with assisted reproduction and genetic selection, though there are also important differences. For example, the most likely uses of cloning would enable a married couple, usually infertile, to have healthy, biologically related children for rearing.[3] Or it would enable them to obtain a source of tissue for transplant to enable an existing child to live.

Cloning, however, is also different in important respects. Unlike the various forms of assisted reproduction, cloning is concerned not merely with producing a child, but rather with the genes that the resulting child will have. Many prebirth genetic selection techniques are now in wide use, but they operate negatively by excluding undesirable genetic characteristics, rather than positively, as cloning does. Moreover, none of them are able to select the entire nuclear genome of a child as cloning does.[4]

DNA SOURCES AND PROCREATIVE LIBERTY

To assess whether cloning is protected as part of a married couple's procreative liberty, we must examine the several situations in which they might use nuclear transfer cloning to form a family. This will require addressing both the reasons or motivations driving a couple to clone, and the source of the DNA that they select for replication. It argues that cloning embryos, children, third parties, self, mate, or parents is an activity so similar to coital and noncoital forms of reproduction and family formation that they should be treated equivalently.

a. Cloning a couple's embryos. Cloning embryos, either by embryo splitting or nuclear transfer, would appear to be closely connected to procreative liberty. It is intended to enable a couple to rear a child biologically related to each, either by increasing the number of embryos available for transfer or by reducing the need to go through later IVF cycles.[5] Its reproductive status is clear whether the motivation for transfer of cloned embryos to the wife's uterus is simply to have another child or to replace a child who has died. In either case, transfer leads to the birth of a child from the couple's egg and sperm that they will rear.

Eventually, couples might seek to clone embryos, not to produce a child for rearing, but to produce an embryo from which tissue stem cells can be obtained for an existing child. In that case, cloning will not lead to the birth of another child. However, it involves use of their reproductive capacity. It may also enable existing children to live. It too should be found to be within the procreative or family autonomy of the couple.

b. Cloning one's children. The use of DNA from existing children to produce another child would also seem to fall within a couple's procreative liberty. This action is directly procreative because it leads to birth of a child who is formed from the egg and sperm of each spouse, even though it occurs asexually with the DNA of an existing child and not from a new union of egg and sperm.[6] Although it is novel to create a twin after one has already been born, it is still reproductive for the couple. The distinctly reproductive nature of their action is reinforced by the fact that they will gestate and rear the child that they clone.

The idea of cloning any existing child is plausibly foreseeable in several circumstances. One is where the parents want another child, and are so delighted with the existing one, that they simply want to create a twin of her, rather than take a chance on the genetic lottery.[7] A second is where an existing child might need an organ or tissue transplant. A third scenario would be to clone an existing child who has died, so that it might continue to live in another form with the parents.

The parental motivations in these cases are similar to parental motivations in coital reproduction. No one condemns parents who reproduce because they wanted a child as lovely as the first, they thought that a new child might be a tissue source for an existing child, or because they wanted another child after an earlier one had died. Given that the new child is cloned from the DNA of one of their own children, cloning one's own embryos or children to achieve those goals should also be regarded as an exercise of procreative liberty that deserves the special respect usually accorded to procreative choice.

c. Cloning third parties. A couple that seeks to use the DNA of a third party should also be viewed as forming a family in a way similar to family formation through coital conception. The DNA of another might be sought in lieu of gamete or embryo donation, though it could be chosen because of the source's characteristics or special meaning for the couple. The idea of "procreating" with the DNA of another raises several questions about the meaning and scope of procreative liberty that requires a more extended analysis. I begin with the initiating couple's rights or interests, and then ask whether the DNA source or her parents also have procreative interests and rights at stake.

(i) The initiating couple's cloning rights. We now ask whether the rights of procreation and family formation of a couple seeking to clone another's DNA would extend to use of a third party's DNA to create a child. Whether rearing is also intended turns out to be a key distinction. Let us first consider the situation where rearing is intended, and then the situation where no rearing is intended.

A strong case for a right to clone another person (assuming that that person and her parents have consented) is where a married couple seeks to clone in order to have a child to rear. Stronger still is the case in which the wife will gestate the resulting embryo and commits to rearing the child. Is this an exercise of their procreative liberty that deserves the special protection that procreative choice generally receives?

The most likely requests to clone a third party would arise from couples that are not reasonably able to reproduce in other ways. A common situation would be where the couple both lack viable gametes, though the wife can gestate, and thus are candidates for embryo donation. Rather than obtain an embryo generated by an unknown infertile couple, through cloning they could choose the genotype of the child they will carry and rear.

Whose DNA might they choose? The DNA could be obtained from a friend or family member, although parents pose a problem. It could come from a sperm, egg, or DNA bank that provides DNA for a fee. Perhaps famous people would be willing to part with their DNA, in the same way that a sperm bank from Nobel Prize winners was once created. Rather than choose themselves, the couple might delegate the task of choosing the genome to their doctor or to some other party.

A strong argument exists that a couple using the DNA of a third party in lieu of embryo donation is engaged in a legitimate exercise of procreative liberty. The argument rests on the view that embryo donation is a protected part of that liberty. That view rests in turn on the recognition of the right of infertile couples to use gamete donation to form a family. As we have seen, coital infertility alone does not deprive one of the right to reproduce. Infertile persons have the same interests in having and rearing offspring and are as well equipped to rear as fertile couples. If that is so, the state could not ban infertile couples from using noncoital techniques to have children without a showing of tangible or compelling harm.

The preceding discussion is premised on the initiating couple's willingness to raise the cloned child. If no rearing is intended, however, their claim to clone the DNA of another should not be recognized as part of their procreative liberty, whether or not they have other means to reproduce. In this scenario an initiator procures the DNA and denucleated eggs, has embryos created from the DNA, and then either sells or provides the embryos to others, or commissions surrogates to gestate the embryos. The resulting children are then reared by others.

The crucial difference here is absence of intention to rear. If one is not intending to rear, then one's claim to be exercising procreative choice is much less persuasive. One is not directly reproducing because one's genes are not involved—they are not even being replicated. Nor is one gestating or rearing. Indeed, such a practice has many of the characteristics that made human cloning initially appear to be such a frightening proposition. It seems to treat children like fungible commodities produced for profit without regard to their well-being. It should not be deemed part of the initiating couple's procreative liberty.

(ii) The clone source's right to be cloned. Mention of the procreative rights of the person providing the DNA to be cloned is also relevant. I will assume that the clone source has consented to use of their DNA. If so, does she independently have the right to have a later-born genetic twin, such that a ban on cloning would violate her procreative rights as well?

The fact that she will not be rearing the child is crucial. Her claim to be cloned then is simply a claim to have another person exist in the world with her DNA (and note that if anonymity holds, she may never learn that her clone was born, much less ever meet her). If so, the only interest at stake is her interest in possibly having her DNA replicated without her gestation, rearing, or even perhaps her knowledge that a twin has been born. It is difficult to argue that this is a strong procreative interest, if it is a procreative interest at all. Thus, unless she undertook to rear the resulting child, the clone source would not have a fundamental right to be cloned.

But this assumes that being cloned is not itself reproduction. One could argue that cloning is quintessentially reproductive for the clone source because her entire genome is replicated. In providing the DNA for another child, she will be continuing her DNA into another generation. Given that the goal of sexual and asexual reproduction is the same—the continuation of one's DNA—and that individuals who are cloned might find or view it as a way of maintaining continuity with nature, we could plausibly choose to consider it a form of reproduction.

But even if we view the clone source as fully and clearly reproducing, she still is not rearing. Her claim of a right to be cloned is still a claim of a right to reproduction *tout court*—the barest and least protected form of reproduction.[8] If there is no rearing or gestation her claim merely to have her genes replicated will not qualify for moral or legal rights protection. If the clone source has a right here to be cloned, it would have to be derivative of the initiators' right to select source DNA for the child whom they will rear.

d. Cloning oneself. Another likely cloning scenario will involve cloning oneself. A strong case can be made that the use of one's own DNA to have and rear a child should be protected by procreative liberty.

As we have just seen, the right to clone oneself is weakest if rearing is not intended. Even if we grant that self-cloning is in some sense truly reproductive, rather than merely replicative, it would still be reproduction *tout court,* the minimal and least protected form of reproduction. Thus cloning oneself with no rearing intended would have no independent claim to be an exercise of procreative liberty. If it is protected at all, it would be derivative of the couple who then gestate and rear the cloned child.

The claim of a right to clone oneself is different if one plans to gestate and rear the resulting child. The situation is best viewed as a joint endeavor of the couple. As in embryo donation, the couple would gestate and rear. In this case, however, there would be a genetic relation between one of the rearing partners and the child—the relation of later-born identical twin.

The idea of a right to parent one's own later-born sibling is also plausibly viewed as a variation on the right to use a gamete donor. If such a right exists, it plausibly follows that that they would have the right to choose the gametes or gamete source they wish to use. A right to use their own DNA to have a child whom they then rear should follow. Using their own DNA has distinct advantages over the gametes purchased from commercial sperm banks or paid egg donors. One is more clearly continuing her own genetic line, one knows the gene source, and one is not buying gametes. Some persons might plausibly insist that they would have a family only if they could clone one of themselves because they are leery of the gametes of anonymous strangers.[9]

One might also argue for a right to have and rear one's own identical twin—the right to clone oneself—as a direct exercise of the right to reproduce. If one is free to reproduce, then one should also have the right to be cloned, because the genetic replication involved in cloning is directly and quintessentially reproductive. Duplicating one's entire DNA by nuclear cell transfer enables a person to survive longer than if cloning did not occur. To use Richard Dawkins' evocative term, the selfish gene wants to survive as long as possible, and will settle for cloning if that will do the job.[10] If rearing is intended, a person's procreative liberty should include the right to clone oneself. Only tangible harm to the child or others would then justify restrictions on self-cloning.

CONSTITUTING PROCREATIVE LIBERTY

The analysis has produced plausible arguments for finding that cloning is directly involved with procreative liberty in situations where the couple initiating

the cloning intends to rear the resulting child. This protected interest is perhaps clearest when they are splitting embryos or using DNA from their own embryos or children, but it also holds when one of the rearing partner's DNA is used. Using the DNA of another person is less directly reproductive, but still maintains a gestational connection between the cloned child and its rearing parents, as now occurs in embryo donation.

In considering the relation between cloning and procreative liberty, we see once again how blurred the meanings of reproduction, family, parenting, and children become as we move away from sexual reproduction involving a couple's egg and sperm. Blurred meanings, however, can be clarified. The test must be how closely the marginal or deviant case is connected with the core. On this test, several plausible cases of a couple seeking to clone the DNA of embryos, children, themselves, or consenting third parties, can be articulated. In all instances they will be seeking a child whom they will gestate and rear. We do no great violence to prevailing understandings of procreative choice when we recognize DNA cloning to produce children whom we will rear as a legitimate form of family or procreative choice. Unless all selection is to be removed from reproduction, their interest in selecting the genes of their children deserves the same protection accorded other reproductive choices.

PUBLIC POLICY

Having discussed the scientific questions and social controversies surrounding cloning, and the likely demand for it once it is shown to be safe and effective, we are now in a position to discuss public policy for human cloning. In formulating policy, however, we must take account of the state of the cloning art. One set of policy options applies when human applications are still in the research and development or experimental stage. Another set exists when research shows that human cloning is safe and effective. The birth of a sheep clone after 277 tries at somatic cell nuclear transfer has shown that much more research is needed before somatic cell cloning by nuclear transfer will be routinely available in sheep and other species, much less in humans. But an important set of policy issues will arise if animal and laboratory research shows that cloning is safe and effective in humans. Should all cloning then be permitted? Should some types of cloning be prohibited? What regulations will minimize the harms that cloning could cause?

Based on the analysis in this article, a ban on all human cloning, including the family-centered uses described above, is overbroad. But we must also ask if some uses of cloning should be forbidden and whether some regulation of permitted uses is desirable once human cloning becomes medically safe and feasible.

No cloning without rearing. A ban on human cloning unless the parties requesting the cloning will also rear is a much better policy than a ban on all cloning. The requirement of having to rear the clone addresses the worse abuses of cloning. It prevents a person from creating clones to be used as subjects or workers without regard for their own interests. For example, situations like that in *Boys from Brazil* or *Brave New World* would be prohibited, because the initiator is not rearing. This rule will assure the child a two-parent rearing situation—a prime determinant of a child's welfare. Furthermore, the rule would not violate the initiator's procreative liberty because merely producing children for others to rear is not an exercise of that liberty.

Ensuring that the initiating couple rears the child given the DNA of another prevents some risks to the child, but still leaves open the threats to individuality, autonomy, and kinship that many persons think that cloning presents. I have argued that parents who intend to have and rear a healthy child might not be as prey to those concerns as feared, yet some cloning situations, because of the novelty of choosing a genome, might still produce social or psychological problems.

Those risks should be addressed in terms of the situations most likely to generate them, and the regulations, short of prohibition, that might minimize their occurrence. It hardly follows that all cloning should be banned, because some undesirable cloning situations might occur. Like other slippery slope arguments, there is no showing that the bad uses are so likely to occur, or that if they did, their bad effects would so clearly outweigh the good, that one is justified in suffering the loss of the good to prevent the bad.

NOTES

1. The moral and legal arguments for procreative liberty are presented in John A. Robertson, *Children of Choice: Freedom and the New Reproductive Technologies* (Princeton 1994), pp. 22–42.

2. For elaboration of this argument, see John A. Robertson, "Genetic Selection of Offspring Characteristics," 76 *B.U.L Rev.* 421, 424–432 (1996).

3. The article emphasizes the rights of married couples because they will be perceived as having a stronger claim to have children than unmarried persons. If their rights to clone are recognized, then the claims of unmarried persons to clone might follow.

4. Since only nuclear DNA is transferred in cloning, DNA contained in the egg's cytoplasm in the form of mitochondria is not cloned or replicated (it is in the case of cloning by embryo splitting). The resulting child is thus not a true clone, for its mitochondrial DNA will have come from the egg source, who will not usually also be providing the nucleus for transfer. Mitochondrial DNA is only a small portion of total DNA, perhaps 5%. However, malfunctions in it can still cause serious disease. See Douglas C. Wallace, "Mitochondrial DNA in Aging and Disease," 277 *Scientific American* 40 (August 1997).

5. It might also be done to provide an embryo or child from whom tissue or organs for transplant for an existing child.

6. Again, it might be used to create an embryo or child from whom tissue or organs for transplant into an existing child might be obtained.

7. I am grateful to my colleague Charles Silver for this suggestion. However, other colleagues with children inform me that they would not clone an existing child, because they would want to see how the next child would differ.

8. Reproduction *tout court* (without more) refers to genetic transmission without any rearing rights or duties in the resulting child, and in some cases, not even knowledge that a child has been born. The courts have not yet determined whether engaging in or avoiding reproduction *tout court* deserves the same protection that more robust

or involved forms of reproduction have. For further discussion, see *Children of Choice,* pp. 108–109.

9. Of course, this means that the other partner will have no DNA connection with the child she rears, unless she also provides the egg and mitochondria.

10. In the long run, cloning might not be adaptive, because genetic diversity is needed. However, if the alternative is no genetic continuation at all—say because no reproduction occurs, or a gamete donor is chosen—then cloning increases the chance of long-term survival of the cloned DNA more than no cloning at all. Richard Dawkins would clone himself purely out of curiosity. "I find it a personally riveting thought that I could watch a small copy of myself nurtured through the early decades of the twenty-first century." (Peter Steinfels, "Beliefs," *New York Times,* July 12, 1997, p. A8).

READING QUESTIONS

1. What is the central aim of Robertson's article?
2. How does Robertson characterize reproductive liberty?
3. What restrictions on reproductive cloning does Robertson favor (if any)?

DISCUSSION QUESTIONS

1. How might a critic best respond to Robertson's defense of a right to reproductive cloning?
2. Despite Robertson's claim that a person has a right to clone herself or himself, are there good reasons for being morally opposed to this use of reproductive cloning?

LEON R. KASS

Preventing Brave New World

Kass has been a vocal and longtime opponent of cloning. In the selection that follows, he begins by describing the dystopian world envisioned in Aldous Huxley's 1932 *Brave New World* and then proceeds to raise four moral arguments against reproductive cloning. In addition to objections based on likely bad consequences of cloning, Kass argues that cloning is "unethical in itself" because in various ways it represents a degradation of our human nature and thus is not in accord with respect for humanity—this latter sort of reasoning representative of Kantian and natural law ethics. Kass concludes by raising a slippery slope objection to defenders of cloning who, like John Robertson, base their defense on "reproductive liberty."

Recommended Reading: Kantian moral theory, chap. 1, sec. 2C, particularly the humanity formulation of Kant's categorical imperative. Also relevant is natural law theory, chap. 1, sec. 2B.

I.

The urgency of the great political struggles of the twentieth century, successfully waged against totalitarianisms first right and then left, seems to have blinded many people to a deeper and ultimately darker truth about the present age: all contemporary societies are travelling briskly in the same utopian direction. All are wedded to the modern technological project; all march eagerly to the drums of progress and fly proudly the banner of modern science; all sing loudly the Baconian anthem, "Conquer nature, relieve man's estate." Leading the triumphal procession is modern medicine, which is daily becoming ever more powerful in its battle against disease, decay, and death, thanks especially to astonishing achievements in biomedical science and technology—achievements for which we must surely be grateful.

Yet contemplating present and projected advances in genetic and reproductive technologies, in neuroscience and psychopharmacology, and in the development of artificial organs and computer-chip implants for human brains, we now clearly recognize new uses for biotechnical power that soar beyond the traditional medical goals of healing disease and relieving suffering. Human nature itself lies on the operating table, ready for alteration, for eugenic and psychic "enhancement," for wholesale re-design. In leading laboratories, academic and industrial, new creators are confidently amassing their powers and quietly honing their skills, while on the street their evangelists are zealously prophesying a post-human future. For anyone who cares about preserving our humanity, the time has come to pay attention.

Some transforming powers are already here. The Pill. In vitro fertilization. Bottled embryos. Surrogate wombs. Cloning. Genetic screening.

Genetic manipulation. Organ harvesting. Mechanical spare parts. Chimeras. Brain implants. Ritalin for the young, Viagra for the old, Prozac for everyone. And, to leave this vale of tears, a little extra morphine accompanied by Muzak.

Years ago Aldous Huxley saw it coming. In his charming but disturbing novel, *Brave New World* (it appeared in 1932 and is more powerful on each re-reading), he made its meaning strikingly visible for all to see. Unlike other frightening futuristic novels of the past century, such as Orwell's already dated *Nineteen Eighty-Four,* Huxley shows us a dystopia that goes with, rather than against, the human grain. Indeed, it is animated by our own most humane and progressive aspirations. Following those aspirations to their ultimate realization, Huxley enables us to recognize those less obvious but often more pernicious evils that are inextricably linked to the successful attainment of partial goods.

Huxley depicts human life seven centuries hence, living under the gentle hand of humanitarianism rendered fully competent by genetic manipulation, psychoactive drugs, hypnopaedia, and high-tech amusements. At long last, mankind has succeeded in eliminating disease, aggression, war, anxiety, suffering, guilt, envy, and grief. But this victory comes at the heavy price of homogenization, mediocrity, trivial pursuits, shallow attachments, debased tastes, spurious contentment, and souls without loves or longings. The Brave New World has achieved prosperity, community, stability and nigh-universal contentment, only to be peopled by creatures of human shape but stunted humanity. They consume, fornicate, take "soma," enjoy "centrifugal bumble-puppy," and operate the machinery that makes it all possible. They do not read, write, think, love, or govern themselves. Art and science, virtue and religion, family and friendship are all passe. What matters most is bodily health and immediate gratification: "Never put off till tomorrow the fun you can have today." Brave New Man is so dehumanized that he does not even recognize what has been lost.

Huxley's novel, of course, is science fiction. Prozac is not yet Huxley's "soma"; cloning by nuclear transfer or splitting embryos is not exactly "Bokanovskification"; MTV and virtual-reality parlors are not quite the "feelies"; and our current safe and consequenceless sexual practices are not universally as loveless or as empty as those in the novel. But the kinships are disquieting, all the more so since our technologies of bio-psycho-engineering are still in their infancy, and in ways that make all too clear what they might look like in their full maturity. Moreover, the cultural changes that technology has already wrought among us should make us even more worried than Huxley would have us be.

In Huxley's novel, everything proceeds under the direction of an omnipotent—albeit benevolent—world state. Yet the dehumanization that he portrays does not really require despotism or external control. To the contrary, precisely because the society of the future will deliver exactly what we most want—health, safety, comfort, plenty, pleasure, peace of mind and length of days—we can reach the same humanly debased condition solely on the basis of free human choice. No need for World Controllers. Just give us the technological imperative, liberal democratic society, compassionate humanitarianism, moral pluralism, and free markets, and we can take ourselves to a Brave New World all by ourselves—and without even deliberately deciding to go. In case you had not noticed, the train has already left the station and is gathering speed, but no one seems to be in charge.

Some among us are delighted, of course, by this state of affairs: some scientists and biotechnologists, their entrepreneurial backers, and a cheering claque of sci-fi enthusiasts, futurologists, and libertarians. There are dreams to be realized, powers to be exercised, honors to be won, and money—big money—to be made. But many of us are worried, and not, as the proponents of the revolution self-servingly claim, because we are either ignorant of science or afraid of the unknown. To the contrary, we can see all too

clearly where the train is headed, and we do not like the destination. We can distinguish cleverness about means from wisdom about ends, and we are loath to entrust the future of the race to those who cannot tell the difference. No friend of humanity cheers for a post-human future.

Yet for all our disquiet, we have until now done nothing to prevent it. We hide our heads in the sand because we enjoy the blessings that medicine keeps supplying, or we rationalize our inaction by declaring that human engineering is inevitable and we can do nothing about it. In either case, we are complicit in preparing for our own degradation, in some respects more to blame than the bio-zealots who, however misguided, are putting their money where their mouth is. Denial and despair, unattractive outlooks in any situation, become morally reprehensible when circumstances summon us to keep the world safe for human flourishing. Our immediate ancestors, taking up the challenge of their time, rose to the occasion and rescued the human future from the cruel dehumanizations of Nazi and Soviet tyranny. It is our more difficult task to find ways to preserve it from the soft dehumanizations of well-meaning but hubristic biotechnical "re-creationism"—and to do it without undermining biomedical science or rejecting its genuine contributions to human welfare. . . .

Not the least of our difficulties in trying to exercise control over where biology is taking us is the fact that we do not get to decide, once and for all, for or against the destination of a post-human world. The scientific discoveries and the technical powers that will take us there come to us piecemeal, one at a time and seemingly independent from one another, each often attractively introduced as a measure that will "help [us] not to be sick." But sometimes we come to a clear fork in the road where decision is possible, and where we know that our decision will make a world of difference—indeed, it will make a permanently different world. Fortunately, we stand now at the point of such a momentous decision. Events have conspired to provide us with a perfect opportunity to seize the initiative and to gain some control of the biotechnical project. I refer to the prospect of human cloning, a practice absolutely central to Huxley's fictional world. Indeed, creating and manipulating life in the laboratory is the gateway to a Brave New World, not only in fiction but also in fact.

"To clone or not to clone a human being" is no longer a fanciful question. Success in cloning sheep, and also cows, mice, pigs, and goats, makes it perfectly clear that a fateful decision is now at hand: whether we should welcome or even tolerate the cloning of human beings. If recent newspaper reports are to be believed, reputable scientists and physicians have announced their intention to produce the first human clone in the coming year. Their efforts may already be under way. . . .

But we dare not be complacent about what is at issue, for the stakes are very high. Human cloning, though partly continuous with previous reproductive technologies, is also something radically new in itself and in its easily foreseeable consequences—especially when coupled with powers for genetic "enhancement" and germline genetic modification that may soon become available, owing to the recently completed Human Genome Project. I exaggerate somewhat, but in the direction of the truth: we are compelled to decide nothing less than whether human procreation is going to remain human, whether children are going to be made to order rather than begotten, and whether we wish to say yes in principle to the road that leads to the dehumanized hell of *Brave New World*.

[W]e have here a golden opportunity to exercise some control over where biology is taking us. The technology of cloning is discrete and well defined, and it requires considerable technical know-how and dexterity; we can therefore know by name many of the likely practitioners. The public demand for cloning is extremely low, and most people are decidedly against it. Nothing scientifically or medically important would be lost by banning clonal reproduction; alternative and non-objectionable means are available to obtain some of the most important medical benefits claimed for (nonreproductive) human cloning. The commercial interests in human cloning are, for now, quite limited; and the nations of the world are actively seeking to prevent it. Now may be as good a chance as we will ever have to get our hands on the wheel of the runaway train now headed for a post-human world and to steer it toward a more dignified human future.

II.

What is cloning? Cloning, or asexual reproduction, is the production of individuals who are genetically identical to an already existing individual. The procedure's name is fancy—"somatic cell nuclear transfer"—but its concept is simple. Take a mature but unfertilized egg; remove or deactivate its nucleus; introduce a nucleus obtained from a specialized (somatic) cell of an adult organism. Once the egg begins to divide, transfer the little embryo to a woman's uterus to initiate a pregnancy. Since almost all the hereditary material of a cell is contained within its nucleus, the re-nucleated egg and the individual into which it develops are genetically identical to the organism that was the source of the transferred nucleus.

An unlimited number of genetically identical individuals—the group, as well as each of its members, is called "a clone"—could be produced by nuclear transfer. In principle, any person, male or female, newborn or adult, could be cloned, and in any quantity; and because stored cells can outlive their sources, one may even clone the dead. Since cloning requires no personal involvement on the part of the person whose genetic material is used, it could easily be used to reproduce living or deceased persons without their consent—a threat to reproductive freedom that has received relatively little attention.

Some possible misconceptions need to be avoided. Cloning is not Xeroxing: the clone of Bill Clinton, though his genetic double, would enter the world hairless, toothless, and peeing in his diapers, like any other human infant. But neither is cloning just like natural twinning: the cloned twin will be identical to an older, existing adult; and it will arise not by chance but by deliberate design; and its entire genetic makeup will be preselected by its parents and/or scientists. Moreover, the success rate of cloning, at least at first, will probably not be very high: the Scots transferred two hundred seventy-seven adult nuclei into sheep eggs, implanted twenty-nine clonal embryos, and achieved the birth of only one live lamb clone.

For this reason, among others, it is unlikely that, at least for now, the practice would be very popular;

and there is little immediate worry of mass-scale production of multicopies. Still, for the tens of thousands of people who sustain more than three hundred assisted-reproduction clinics in the United States and already avail themselves of in vitro fertilization and other techniques, cloning would be an option with virtually no added fuss. Panos Zavos, the Kentucky reproduction specialist who has announced his plans to clone a child, claims that he has already received thousands of e-mailed requests from people eager to clone, despite the known risks of failure and damaged offspring. Should commercial interests develop in "nucleus-banking," as they have in sperm-banking and egg-harvesting; should famous athletes or other celebrities decide to market their DNA the way they now market their autographs and nearly everything else; should techniques of embryo and germline genetic testing and manipulation arrive as anticipated, increasing the use of laboratory assistance in order to obtain "better" babies—should all this come to pass, cloning, if it is permitted, could become more than a marginal practice simply on the basis of free reproductive choice.

What are we to think about this prospect? Nothing good. Indeed, most people are repelled by nearly all aspects of human cloning: the possibility of mass production of human beings, with large clones of look-alikes, compromised in their individuality; the idea of father-son or mother-daughter "twins"; the bizarre prospect of a woman bearing and rearing a genetic copy of herself, her spouse, or even her deceased father or mother; the grotesqueness of conceiving a child as an exact "replacement" for another who has died; the utilitarian creation of embryonic duplicates of oneself, to be frozen away or created when needed to provide homologous tissues or organs for transplantation; the narcissism of those who would clone themselves, and the arrogance of others who think they know who deserves to be cloned; the Frankensteinian hubris to create a human life and increasingly to control its destiny; men playing at being God. Almost no one finds any of the suggested reasons for human cloning compelling, and almost everyone anticipates its possible misuses and abuses. And the popular belief that human cloning cannot be prevented makes the prospect all the more revolting.

Revulsion is not an argument; and some of yesterday's repugnances are today calmly accepted—not always for the better. In some crucial cases, however, repugnance is the emotional expression of deep wisdom, beyond reason's power completely to articulate it. Can anyone really give an argument fully adequate to the horror that is father-daughter incest (even with consent), or bestiality, or the mutilation of a corpse, or the eating of human flesh, or the rape or murder of another human being? Would anybody's failure to give full rational justification for his revulsion at those practices make that revulsion ethically suspect?

I suggest that our repugnance at human cloning belongs in this category. We are repelled by the prospect of cloning human beings not because of the strangeness or the novelty of the undertaking, but because we intuit and we feel, immediately and without argument, the violation of things that we rightfully hold dear. We sense that cloning represents a profound defilement of our given nature as procreative beings, and of the social relations built on this natural ground. We also sense that cloning is a radical form of child abuse. In this age in which everything is held to be permissible so long as it is freely done, and in which our bodies are regarded as mere instruments of our autonomous rational will, repugnance may be the only voice left that speaks up to defend the central core of our humanity. Shallow are the souls that have forgotten how to shudder.

III.

Yet repugnance need not stand naked before the bar of reason. The wisdom of our horror at human cloning can be at least partially articulated, even if this is finally one of those instances about which the heart has its reasons that reason cannot entirely know. I offer four objections to human cloning: that it constitutes unethical experimentation; that it threatens identity and individuality; that it turns procreation into manufacture (especially when understood as the harbinger of manipulations to come); and that it means despotism over children and perversion of parenthood. Please note: I speak only about so-called reproductive cloning, not about the creation of cloned embryos for research. The objections that may be raised against creating (or using) embryos for research are entirely independent of whether the research embryos are produced by cloning. What is radically distinct and radically new is reproductive cloning.

Any attempt to clone a human being would constitute an unethical experiment upon the resulting child-to-be. In all the animal experiments, fewer than two to three percent of all cloning attempts succeeded. Not only are there fetal deaths and stillborn infants, but many of the so-called "successes" are in fact failures. As has only recently become clear, there is a very high incidence of major disabilities and deformities in cloned animals that attain live birth. Cloned cows often have heart and lung problems; cloned mice later develop pathological obesity; other live-born cloned animals fail to reach normal developmental milestones.

The problem, scientists suggest, may lie in the fact that an egg with a new somatic nucleus must re-program itself in a matter of minutes or hours (whereas the nucleus of an unaltered egg has been prepared over months and years). There is thus a greatly increased likelihood of error in translating the genetic instructions, leading to developmental defects some of which will show themselves only much later. (Note also that these induced abnormalities may also affect the stem cells that scientists hope to harvest from cloned embryos. Lousy embryos, lousy stem cells.) Nearly all scientists now agree that attempts to clone human beings carry massive risks of producing unhealthy, abnormal, and malformed children. What are we to do with them? Shall we just discard the ones that fall short of expectations? Considered opinion is today nearly unanimous, even among scientists: attempts at human cloning are irresponsible and unethical. We cannot ethically even get to know whether or not human cloning is feasible.

If it were successful, cloning would create serious issues of identity and individuality. The clone may experience concerns about his distinctive identity not only because he will be, in genotype and in appearance, identical to another human being, but because he may also be twin to the person who is his "father" or his "mother"—if one can still call them that. Unaccountably, people treat as innocent the homey case of intra-familial cloning—the cloning of husband or wife (or single mother). They forget about the unique dangers of mixing the twin relation with the parent-child relation. (For this situation, the relation of contemporaneous twins is no precedent; yet even this less problematic situation teaches us how difficult it is to wrest independence from the being for whom one has the most powerful affinity.) Virtually no parent is going to be able to treat a clone of himself or herself as one treats a child generated by the lottery of sex. What will happen when the adolescent clone of Mommy becomes the spitting image of the woman with whom Daddy once fell in love? In case of divorce, will Mommy still love the clone of Daddy, even though she can no longer stand the sight of Daddy himself?

Most people think about cloning from the point of view of adults choosing to clone. Almost nobody thinks about what it would be like to be the cloned child. Surely his or her new life would constantly be scrutinized in relation to that of the older version. Even in the absence of unusual parental expectations for the clone—say, to live the same life, only without its errors—the child is likely to be ever a curiosity, ever a potential source of deja vu. Unlike "normal" identical twins, a cloned individual—copied from whomever—will be saddled with a genotype that has already lived. He will not be fully a surprise to the world: people are likely always to compare his doings in life with those of his alter ego, especially if he is a clone of someone gifted or famous. True, his nurture and his circumstance will be different; genotype is not exactly destiny. But one must also expect parental efforts to shape this new life after the original—or at least to view the child with the original version always firmly in mind. For why else did they clone from the star basketball player, the mathematician, or the beauty queen—or even dear old Dad—in the first place?

Human cloning would also represent a giant step toward the transformation of begetting into making, of procreation into manufacture (literally, "hand-made"), a process that has already begun with in vitro fertilization and genetic testing of embryos. With cloning, not only is the process in hand, but the total genetic blueprint of the cloned individual is selected and determined by the human artisans. To be sure, subsequent development is still according to natural processes; and the resulting children will be recognizably human. But we would be taking a major step into making man himself simply another one of the man-made things.

How does begetting differ from making? In natural procreation, human beings come together to give existence to another being that is formed exactly as we were, by what we are—living, hence perishable, hence aspiringly erotic, hence procreative human beings. But in clonal reproduction, and in the more advanced forms of manufacture to which it will lead, we give existence to a being not by what we are but by what we intend and design.

Let me be clear. The problem is not the mere intervention of technique, and the point is not that "nature knows best." The problem is that any child whose being, character, and capacities exist owing to human design does not stand on the same plane as its makers. As with any product of our making, no matter how excellent, the artificer stands above it, not as an equal but as a superior, transcending it by his will and creative prowess. In human cloning, scientists and prospective "parents" adopt a technocratic attitude toward human children: human children become their artifacts. Such an arrangement is profoundly dehumanizing, no matter how good the product.

Procreation dehumanized into manufacture is further degraded by commodification, a virtually inescapable result of allowing baby-making to proceed under the banner of commerce. Genetic and reproductive biotechnology companies are already growth industries, but they will soon go into commercial orbit now that the Human Genome Project has been completed. "Human eggs for sale" is already a big business, masquerading under the pretense of "donation." Newspaper advertisements on elite college campuses offer up to $50,000 for an egg "donor" tall enough to play women's basketball and with SAT scores high enough for admission to Stanford; and

to nobody's surprise, at such prices there are many young coeds eager to help shoppers obtain the finest babies money can buy. (The egg and womb-renting entrepreneurs shamelessly proceed on the ancient, disgusting, misogynist premise that most women will give you access to their bodies, if the price is right.) Even before the capacity for human cloning is perfected, established companies will have invested in the harvesting of eggs from ovaries obtained at autopsy or through ovarian surgery, practiced embryonic genetic alteration, and initiated the stockpiling of prospective donor tissues. Through the rental of surrogate-womb services, and through the buying and selling of tissues and embryos priced according to the merit of the donor, the commodification of nascent human life will be unstoppable.

Finally, the practice of human cloning by nuclear transfer—like other anticipated forms of genetically engineering the next generation—would enshrine and aggravate a profound misunderstanding of the meaning of having children and of the parent-child relationship. When a couple normally chooses to procreate, the partners are saying yes to the emergence of new life in its novelty—are saying yes not only to having a child, but also to having whatever child this child turns out to be. In accepting our finitude, in opening ourselves to our replacement, we tacitly confess the limits of our control.

Embracing the future by procreating means precisely that we are relinquishing our grip in the very activity of taking up our own share in what we hope will be the immortality of human life and the human species. This means that our children are not our children: they are not our property, they are not our possessions. Neither are they supposed to live our lives for us, or to live anyone's life but their own. Their genetic distinctiveness and independence are the natural foreshadowing of the deep truth that they have their own, never-before-enacted life to live. Though sprung from a past, they take an uncharted course into the future.

Much mischief is already done by parents who try to live vicariously through their children. Children are sometimes compelled to fulfill the broken dreams of unhappy parents. But whereas most parents normally have hopes for their children, cloning parents will have expectations. In cloning, such overbearing parents will have taken at the start a decisive step that contradicts the entire meaning of the open and forward-looking nature of parent-child relations. The child is given a genotype that has already lived, with full expectation that this blueprint of a past life ought to be controlling the life that is to come. A wanted child now means a child who exists precisely to fulfill parental wants. Like all the more precise eugenic manipulations that will follow in its wake, cloning is thus inherently despotic, for it seeks to make one's children after one's own image (or an image of one's choosing) and their future according to one's will.

Is this hyperbolic? Consider concretely the new realities of responsibility and guilt in the households of the cloned. No longer only the sins of the parents, but also the genetic choices of the parents, will be visited on the children—and beyond the third and fourth generation; and everyone will know who is responsible. No parent will be able to blame nature or the lottery of sex for an unhappy adolescent's big nose, dull wit, musical ineptitude, nervous disposition, or anything else that he hates about himself. Fairly or not, children will hold their cloners responsible for everything, for nature as well as for nurture. And parents, especially the better ones, will be limitlessly liable to guilt. Only the truly despotic souls will sleep the sleep of the innocent.

IV.

The defenders of cloning are not wittingly friends of despotism. Quite the contrary. Deaf to most other considerations, they regard themselves mainly as friends of freedom: the freedom of individuals to reproduce, the freedom of scientists and inventors to discover and to devise and to foster "progress" in genetic knowledge and technique, the freedom of entrepreneurs to profit in the market. They want largescale cloning only for animals, but they wish to preserve cloning as a human option for exercising our "right to reproduce"—our right to have children, and

children with "desirable genes." As some point out, under our "right to reproduce" we already practice early forms of unnatural, artificial, and extra-marital reproduction, and we already practice early forms of eugenic choice. For that reason, they argue, cloning is no big deal.

We have here a perfect example of the logic of the slippery slope. The principle of reproductive freedom currently enunciated by the proponents of cloning logically embraces the ethical acceptability of sliding all the way down: to producing children wholly in the laboratory from sperm to term (should it become feasible), and to producing children whose entire genetic makeup will be the product of parental eugenic planning and choice. If reproductive freedom means the right to have a child of one's own choosing by whatever means, then reproductive freedom knows and accepts no limits.

Proponents want us to believe that there are legitimate uses of cloning that can be distinguished from illegitimate uses, but by their own principles no such limits can be found. (Nor could any such limits be enforced in practice: once cloning is permitted, no one ever need discover whom one is cloning and why.) Reproductive freedom, as they understand it, is governed solely by the subjective wishes of the parents-to-be. The sentimentally appealing case of the childless married couple is, on these grounds, indistinguishable from the case of an individual (married or not) who would like to clone someone famous or talented, living or dead. And the principle here endorsed justifies not only cloning but also all future artificial attempts to create (manufacture) "better" or "perfect" babies. . . .

If you think that such scenarios require outside coercion or governmental tyranny, you are mistaken. Once it becomes possible, with the aid of human genomics, to produce or to select for what some regard as "better babies"—smarter, prettier, healthier, more athletic—parents will leap at the opportunity to "improve" their offspring. Indeed, not to do so will be socially regarded as a form of child neglect. Those who would ordinarily be opposed to such tinkering will be under enormous pressure to compete on behalf of their as yet unborn children—just as some now plan almost from their children's birth how to get them into Harvard. Never mind that, lacking a standard of "good" or "better," no one can really know whether any such changes will truly be improvements.

Proponents of cloning urge us to forget about the science-fiction scenarios of laboratory manufacture or multiple-copy clones, and to focus only on the sympathetic cases of infertile couples exercising their reproductive rights. But why, if the single cases are so innocent, should multiplying their performance be so off-putting? (Similarly, why do others object to people's making money from that practice if the practice itself is perfectly acceptable?) The so-called science-fiction cases—say, Brave New World—make vivid the meaning of what looks to us, mistakenly, to be benign. They reveal that what looks like compassionate humanitarianism is, in the end, crushing dehumanization.

V.

Whether or not they share my reasons, most people, I think, share my conclusion: that human cloning is unethical in itself and dangerous in its likely consequences, which include the precedent that it will establish for designing our children. Some reach this conclusion for their own good reasons, different from my own: concerns about distributive justice in access to eugenic cloning; worries about the genetic effects of asexual "in-breeding"; aversion to the implicit premise of genetic determinism; objections to the embryonic and fetal wastage that must necessarily accompany the efforts; religious opposition to "man playing God." But never mind why: the overwhelming majority of our fellow Americans remain firmly opposed to cloning human beings. . . .

READING QUESTIONS

1. According to Kass, What significance does a person's feeling of repugnanace at the thought of reproductive cloning have for questions about the morality of this practice?
2. According to Kass, why would reproductive cloning involve unethical experimentation?
3. According to Kass, why would reproductive cloning "create serious issues for identity and individuality"?
4. Kass claims that reproductive cloning would represent "a giant step toward transformation of begetting into making." What does he mean in saying this? What reasons does he give in support of this claim?
5. According to Kass, why is reproductive cloning "inherently despotic"?

DISCUSSION QUESTIONS

1. Consider how a critic might respond to each of Kass's four objections to reproductive cloning.
2. How would Kass respond to Robertson's appeal to reproductive liberty in defense of reproductive cloning?

GREGORY E. PENCE

Will Cloning Harm People?

Many object to reproductive cloning on consequentialist grounds—they claim that this sort of cloning will have bad or even disastrous effects on the individuals who are cloned and on society generally. Pence argues that such objections are often a combination of ignorance about, and unwarranted fear of, the realities of cloning. Of particular interest here are the claims about predicted psychological harm to cloned children. For instance, some worry that reproductive cloning will severely limit the cloned individual's future, since in the process of cloning some decision is made about the clone's genotype. Wouldn't choosing a genotype limit a child's future, genetically determining her or his future life? Pence argues that this sort of reasoning is based on the false view of "genetic determinism" and thus fails to consider the fact that differences in gestation, parents, and environment importantly contribute to the personality, interests, and future prospects of any child. Pence's article thus represents a rebuttal of consequentialist arguments against reproductive cloning, including the various objections brought up in the previous article by Leon Kass.

Recommended Reading: consequentialism, chap. 1, sec. 2A.

The most important moral objection to originating a human by cloning is the claim that the resulting person may be unnecessarily harmed, either by something in the process of cloning or by the unique expectations placed upon the resulting child. This essay considers this kind of objection.

By now the word "cloning" has so many bad associations from science fiction and political demagoguery that there is no longer any good reason to continue to use it. A more neutral phrase, meaning the same thing, is "somatic cell nuclear transfer" (SCNT), which refers to the process by which the genotype of an adult, differentiated cell can be used to create a new human embryo by transferring its nucleus to an enucleated human egg. The resulting embryo can then be gestated to create a baby who will be a delayed twin of its genetic ancestor.

For purposes of clarity and focus, I will only discuss the simple case where a couple wants to originate a single child by SCNT and not the cases of multiple origination of the same genotype. I will also not discuss questions of who would regulate reproduction of genotypes and processes of getting consent to reproduce genotypes.

PARALLELS WITH
IN VITRO FERTILIZATION:
REPEATING HISTORY?

Any time a new method of human reproduction may occur, critics try to prevent it by citing possible harm to children. The implicit premise: before it is allowed, any new method must prove that only healthy children will be created. Without such proof, the new method amounts to "unconsented to" experimentation on the

From "Will Cloning Harm People?" Gregory E. Pence, *Flesh of My Flesh: The Ethics of Cloning Humans*, G. E. Pence (Lanham, MD: Rowman and Littlefield, 1998).

unborn. So argued the late conservative, Christian bioethicist Paul Ramsey in the early 1970s about in vitro fertilization (IVF).[1]

Of course, ordinary sexual reproduction does not guarantee healthy children every time. Nor can a person consent until he is born. Nor can he really consent until he is old enough to understand consent. The requirement of "consent to be born" is silly.

Jeremy Rifkin, another critic of IVF in the early 1970s, seemed to demand that new forms of human reproduction be risk-free.[2] Twenty years later, Rifkin predictably bolted out the gate to condemn human cloning, demanding its world-wide ban, with penalties for transgressions as severe as those for rape and murder: "It's a horrendous crime to make a Xerox of someone," he declared ominously. "You're putting a human into a genetic straitjacket. For the first time, we've taken the principles of industrial design— quality control, predictability—and applied them to a human being."[3]

Daniel Callahan, a philosopher who had worked in the Catholic tradition and who founded the Hastings Center for research in medical ethics, argued in 1978 that the first case of IVF was "probably unethical" because there was no possible guarantee that Louise Brown would be normal.[4] Callahan added that many medical breakthroughs are unethical because we cannot know (using the philosopher's strong sense of "know") that the first patient will not be harmed. Two decades later, he implied that human cloning would also be unethical: "We live in a culture that likes science and technology very much. If someone wants something, and the rest of us can't prove they are going to do devastating harm, they are going to do it."[5]

Leon Kass, a social conservative and biologist-turned-bioethicist, argued strenuously in 1971 that babies created by artificial fertilization might be deformed: "It doesn't matter how many times the baby is tested while in the mother's womb," he averred, "they will never be certain the baby won't be born without defect."[6]

What these critics overlooked is that no reasonable approach to life avoids all risks. Nothing in life is risk-free, including having children. Even if babies are born healthy, they do not always turn out

as hoped. Taking such chances is part of becoming a parent.

Without some risk, there is no progress, no advance. Without risk, pioneers don't cross prairies, astronauts don't walk on the moon, and Freedom Riders don't take buses to integrate the South. The past critics of assisted reproduction demonstrated a psychologically normal but nevertheless unreasonable tendency to magnify the risk of a harmful but unlikely result. Such a result—even if very bad—still represents a very small risk. A baby born with a lethal genetic disease is an extremely bad but unlikely result; nevertheless, the risk shouldn't deter people from having children.

HUMANITY WILL NOT BE HARMED

Human SCNT is even more new and strange-sounding than in vitro fertilization (IVF). All that means is that it will take longer to get used to. Scaremongers have predicted terrible harm if children are born by SCNT, but in fact very little will change. Why is that?

First, to create a child by SCNT, a couple must use IVF, which is an expensive process, costing about $8,000 per attempt. Most American states do not require insurance companies to cover IVF, so IVF is mostly a cash-and-carry operation. Second, most IVF attempts are unsuccessful. The chances of any couple taking home a baby is quite low— only about 15%.

Only about 40,000 IVF babies have been born in America since the early 1980s. Suppose 50,000 such babies are born over the next decade. How many of these couples would want to originate a child by SCNT? Very few—at most, perhaps, a few hundred.

These figures are important because they tamp down many fears. As things now stand, originating humans by SCNT will never be common. Neither evolution nor old-fashioned human sex is in any way threatened. Nor is the family or human society. Most fears about human cloning stem from ignorance.

Similar fears linking cloning to dictatorship or the subjugation of women are equally ignorant. There are no artificial wombs (predictions, yes; realities, no—otherwise we could save premature babies born before 20 weeks). A healthy woman must agree to gestate any SCNT baby and such a woman will retain her right to abort. Women's rights to abortion are checks on evil uses of any new reproductive technology.

NEW THINGS MAKE US FEAR HARMS IRRATIONALLY

SCNT isn't really so new or different. Consider some cases on a continuum. In the first, the human embryo naturally splits in the process of twinning and produces two genetically-identical twins. Mothers have been conceiving and gestating human twins for all of human history. Call the children who result from this process Rebecca and Susan.

In the second case a technique is used where a human embryo is deliberately twinned in order to create more embryos for implantation in a woman who has been infertile with her mate. Instead of a random quirk in the uterus, now a physician and an infertile couple use a tiny electric current to split the embryo. Two identical embryos are created. All embryos are implanted and, as sometimes happens, rather than no embryo implanting successfully or only one, both embryos implant. Again, Rebecca and Susan are born.

In the third case, one of the twinned embryos is frozen (Susan) along with other embryos from the couple and the other embryo is implanted. In this case, although several embryos were implanted, only the one destined to be Rebecca is successful. Again, Rebecca is born.

Two years pass, and the couple desires another child. Some of their frozen embryos are thawed and implanted in the mother. The couple knows that one of the implanted embryos is the twin of Rebecca. In this second round of reproductive assistance, the embryo destined to be Susan successfully implants and a twin is born. Now Susan and Rebecca exist as twins, but born two years apart. Susan is the delayed twin of Rebecca. (Rumors abound that such births have already occurred in American infertility clinics.)

Suppose now that the "embryo that could become Susan" was twinned, and the "non-Susan" embryo is frozen. The rest of the details are then the same as the last scenario, but now two more years pass and the previously-frozen embryo is now implanted, gestated, and born. Susan and Rebecca now have another identical sister, Samantha. They would be identical triplets, born two and four years apart. In contrast to SCNT, where the mother's contribution of mitochondrial genes introduces small variations in nearly-identical genotypes, these embryos would have identical genomes.

Next, suppose that the embryo that could have been Rebecca miscarried and never became a child. The twinned embryo that could become Susan still exists. So the parents implant this embryo and Susan is born. Query to National Bioethics Advisory Commission: have the parents done something illegal? A child has been born who was originated by reproducing an embryo with a unique genotype. Remember, the embryo-that-could-become Rebecca existed first. So Susan only exists as a "clone" of the non-existent Rebecca.

Now, as bioethicist Leroy Walters emphasizes, let us consider an even thornier but more probable scenario.[7] Suppose we took the embryo-that-could-become Susan and transferred its nucleus to an enucleated egg of Susan's mother. Call the person who will emerge from this embryo "Suzette," because she is like Susan but different, because of her new mitochondrial DNA. Although the "Susan" embryo was created sexually, Suzette's origins are through somatic cell nuclear transfer. It is not clear that this process is illegal. The NBAC *Report* avoids taking a stand on this kind of case.[8]

Now compare all the above cases to originating Susan asexually by SCNT from the genotype of the adult Rebecca. Susan would again have a nearly-identical genome with Rebecca (identical except for mitochondrial DNA contributed by the gestating woman). Here we have nearly identical female genotypes, separated in time, created by choice. But how is this so different from choosing to have a delayed twin-child? Originating a child by SCNT is not a breakthrough in kind but a matter of degree along a continuum invoking twins and a special kind of reproductive choice.

COMPARING THE HARMS OF HUMAN REPRODUCTION

The question of multiple copies of one genome and its special issues of harm are ones that will not be discussed in this essay, but one asymmetry in our moral intuitions should be noticed.

The increasing use of fertility drugs has expanded many times the number of humans born who are twins, triplets, quadruplets, quintuplets, sextuplets, and even (in November of 1997 to the McCaugheys of Iowa) septuplets. If an entire country can rejoice about seven humans who are gestated in the same womb, raised by the same parents, and simultaneously created randomly from the same two sets of chromosomes, why should the same country fear deliberately originating copies of the same genome, either at once or over time? Our intuitions are even more skewed when we rejoice in the statistically-unlikely case of the seven healthy McCaughey children and ignore the far more likely cases where several of the multiply-gestated fetuses are disabled or dead.

People exaggerate the fears of the unknown and downplay the very real dangers of the familiar. In a very important sense, driving a car each day is far more dangerous to children than the new form of human reproduction under discussion here. Many, many people are hurt and killed every day in automobile wrecks, yet few people consider not driving.

In SCNT, there are possible dangers of telomere shortening, inheritance of environmental effects on adult cells passed to embryonic cells, and possible unknown dangers. Mammalian animal studies must determine if such dangers will occur in human SCNT origination. Once such studies prove that there are no special dangers of SCNT, the crucial question will arise: how safe must we expect human SCNT to be before we allow it?

In answering this question, it is very important to ask about the baseline of comparison. How safe is ordinary, human sexual reproduction? How safe is assisted reproduction? Who or what counts as a subject of a safety calculation about SCNT?

At least 40% of human embryos fail to implant in normal sexual reproduction.[9] Although this fact is not widely known, it is important because some discussions tend to assume that every human embryo becomes a human baby unless some extraordinary event occurs such as abortion. But this is not true. Nature seems to have a genetic filter, such that malformed embryos do not implant. About 50% of the rejected embryos are chromosomally abnormal, meaning that if they were somehow brought to term, the resulting children would be mutants or suffer genetic dysfunction.

A widely-reported but misleading aspect of Ian Wilmut's work was that it took 277 embryos to produce one live lamb. In fact, Wilmut started with 277 eggs, fused nuclei with them to create embryos, and then allowed them to become the best 29 embryos, which were allowed to gestate further. He had three lambs almost live, with one true success, Dolly. Subsequent work may easily bring the efficiency rate to 25%. When the calves "Charlie" and "George" were born in 1998, four live-born calves were created from an initial batch of only 50 embryos.[10]

Wilmut's embryo-to-birth ratio only seems inefficient or unsafe because the real inefficiency fate of accepted forms of human assisted reproduction is so little known. In in vitro fertilization, a woman is given drugs to stimulate superovulation so that physicians can remove as many eggs as possible. At each cycle of attempted in vitro fertilization, three or four embryos are implanted. Most couples make several attempts, so as many as nine to twelve embryos are involved for each couple. As noted, only about 15–20% of couples undergoing such attempts ever take home a baby.

Consider what these numbers mean when writ large. Take a hundred couples attempting assisted reproduction, each undergoing (on average) three attempts. Suppose there are unusually good results and that 20%

of these couples eventually take home a baby. Because more than one embryo may implant, assume that among these 20 couples, half have non-identical twins. But what is the efficiency rate here? Assuming a low number of three embryos implanted each time for the 300 attempts, it will take 900 embryos to produce 30 babies, for an efficiency rate of 1 in 30.

Nor is it true that all the loss of human potential occurred at the embryonic stage. Unfortunately, some of these pregnancies will end in miscarriages of fetuses, some well along in the second trimester.

Nevertheless, such loss of embryos and fetuses is almost universally accepted as morally permissible. Why is that? Because the infertile parents are trying to conceive their own children, because everyone thinks that is a good motive, and because few people object to the loss of embryos and fetuses *in this context of trying to conceive babies.* Seen in this light, what Wilmut did, starting out with a large number of embryos to get one successful lamb at birth, is not so novel or different from what now occurs in human assisted reproduction.

SUBJECTS AND NONSUBJECTS OF HARM

One premise that seems to figure in discussions of the safety of SCNT and other forms of assisted reproduction is that loss of human embryos morally matters. That premise should be rejected.

As the above discussion shows, loss of human embryos is a normal part of human conception and, without this process, humanity might suffer much more genetic disease. This process essentially involves the loss of human embryos as part of the natural state of things. Indeed, some researchers believe that for every human baby successfully born, there has been at least one human embryo lost along the way.

In vitro fertilization is widely-accepted as a great success in modern medicine. As said, over 40,000 American babies have been born this way. But calculations indicate that as many as a million human embryos may have been used in creating such successes.

Researchers often create embryos for subsequent cycles of implantation, only to learn that a pregnancy has been achieved and that such stored embryos are no longer needed. Thousands of such embryos can be stored indefinitely in liquid nitrogen. No one feels any great urgency about them and, indeed, many couples decline to pay fees to preserve their embryos.

The above considerations point to the obvious philosophical point that embryos are not persons with rights to life. Like an acorn, their value is all potential, little actual. Faced with a choice between paying a thousand dollars to keep two thousand embryos alive for a year in storage, or paying for an operation to keep a family pet alive for another year, no one will choose to pay for the embryos. How people actually act says much about their real values.

Thus an embryo cannot be harmed by being brought into existence and then being taken out of existence. An embryo is generally considered such until nine weeks after conception, when it is called a "fetus" (when it is born, it is called a "baby"). Embryos are not sentient and cannot experience pain. They are thus not the kind of subjects that can be harmed or benefitted.

As such, whether it takes one embryo to create a human baby or a hundred does not matter morally. It may matter aesthetically, financially, emotionally, or in time spent trying to reproduce, but it does not matter morally. As such, new forms of human reproduction such as IVF and SCNT that involve significant loss of embryos cannot be morally criticized on this charge.

Finally, because embryos don't count morally, they could be tested in various ways to eliminate defects in development or genetic mishaps. Certainly, if four or five SCNT embryos were implanted, only the healthiest one should be brought to term. As such, the risk of abnormal SCNT babies could be minimized.

SETTING THE STANDARD ABOUT THE RISK OF HARM

Animal tests have not yet shown that SCNT is safe enough to try in humans, and extensive animal testing should be done over the next few years. That means that, before we attempt SCNT in humans, we will need to be able to routinely produce healthy offspring by SCNT in lambs, cattle, and especially, non-human primates. After this testing is done, the time will come when a crucial question must be answered: how safe must human SCNT be before it is allowed? This is probably the most important, practical question before us now.

Should we have a very high standard, such that we take virtually no risk with a SCNT child? Daniel Callahan and Paul Ramsey, past critics of IVF, implied that unless a healthy baby could be guaranteed the first time, it was unethical to try to produce babies in a new way. At the other extreme, a low standard would allow great risks.

What is the appropriate standard? How high should be the bar over which scientists must be made to jump before they are allowed to try to originate a SCNT child? In my opinion, the standard of Callahan and Ramsey is too high. In reality, only God can meet that Olympian standard. It is also too high for those physicians trying to help infertile couples. If this high standard had been imposed on these people in the past, no form of assisted reproduction—including in vitro fertilization—would ever have been allowed.

On the other end of the scale, one could look at the very worst conditions for human gestation, where mothers are drug-dependent during pregnancy or exposed to dangerous chemicals. Such worst-case conditions include parents with a 50% chance of passing on a lethal genetic disease. The lowest standard of harm allows human reproduction even if there is such a high risk of harm ("harm" in the sense that the child would likely have a sub-normal future). One could argue that since society allows such mothers and couples to reproduce sexually, it could do no worse by allowing a child to be originated by SCNT.

I believe that the low standard is inappropriate to use with human SCNT. There is no reason to justify down to the very worst conditions under which society now tolerates humans being born. If the best we can do by SCNT is to produce children as good as those born with fetal-maternal alcohol syndrome, we shouldn't originate children this way.

Between these standards, there is the normal range of risk that is accepted by ordinary people in sexual reproduction. Human SCNT should be allowed when the predicted risk from animal studies falls within this range. "Ordinary people" refers to those who are neither alcoholic nor dependent on an illegal drug and where neither member of the couple knowingly passes on a high risk for a serious genetic disease.

This standard seems reasonable. It does not require a guarantee of a perfect baby, but it also rejects the "anything goes" view. For example, if the rate of serious deformities in normal human reproduction is 1%, and if the rate of chimpanzee SCNT reproduction were brought down to this rate, and if there were no reason to think that SCNT in human primates would he any higher, it should be permissible to attempt human SCNT. . . .

PSYCHOLOGICAL HARM TO THE CHILD

Another concern is about psychological harm to a child originated by SCNT. According to this objection, choosing to have a child is not like choosing a car or house. It is a moral decision because another being is affected. Having a child should be a careful, responsible choice and focused on what's best for the child. Having a child originated by SCNT is not morally permissible because it is not best for the child.

The problem with this argument is the last six words of the last sentence, which assumes bad motives on the part of parents. Unfortunately, SCNT is associated with bad motives in science fiction, but until we have evidence that it will be used this way, why assume the worst about people?

Certainly, if someone deliberately brought a child into the world with the intention of causing him harm, that would be immoral. Unfortunately, the concept of harm is a continuum and some people have very high standards, such that not providing a child a stay-at-home parent constitutes harming the child. But there is nothing about SCNT per se that is necessarily linked to bad motives. True, people would have certain expectations of a child created by SCNT, but parents-to-be already have certain expectations about children.

Too many parents are fatalistic and just accept whatever life throws at them. The very fact of being a parent for many people is something they must accept (because abortion was not a real option). Part of this acceptance is to just accept whatever genetic combination comes at birth from the random assortment of genes.

But why is such acceptance a good thing? It is a defeatist attitude in medicine against disease; it is a defeatist attitude toward survival when one's culture or country is under attack; and it is a defeatist attitude toward life in general. "The expectations of parents will be too high!" critics repeat. "Better to leave parents in ignorance and to leave their children as randomness decrees." The silliness of that view is apparent as soon as it is made explicit.

If we are thinking about harm to the child, an objection that comes up repeatedly might be called the argument for an open future. "In the case of cloning," it is objected, "the expectations are very specifically tied to the life of another person. So in a sense, the child's future is denied to him because he will be expected to be like his ancestor. But part of the wonder of having children is surprise at how they turn out. As such, some indeterminacy should remain a part of childhood. Human SCNT deprives a person of an open future because when we know how his previous twin lived, we will know how the new child will live."

It is true that the adults choosing this genotype rather than that one must have some expectations. There has to be some reason for choosing one genotype over another. But these expectations are only half based in fact. As we know, no person originated by SCNT will be identical to his ancestor because of mitochondrial DNA, because of his different gestation, because of his different parents, because of his different time in history, and perhaps, because of his different country and culture. Several famous pairs of conjoined twins, such as Eng and Chang, with both identical genotypes and identical uterine/childhood environments, have still had different personalities.[11] To assume that a SCNT child's future is not open is to assume genetic reductionism.

Moreover, insofar as parents have specific expectations about children created by SCNT, such expectations will likely be no better or worse than the normal expectations by parents of children created sexually. As said, there is nothing about SCNT per se that necessitates bad motives on the part of parents.

Notice that most of the expected harm to the child stems *from the predicted, prejudicial attitudes of other people to the SCNT child.* ("Would you want to be a cloned child? Can you imagine being called a freak and having only one genetic parent?") As such, it is important to remember that social expectations are *merely* social expectations. They are malleable and can change quickly. True, parents might initially have expectations that are too high and other people might regard such children with prejudice. But just as such inappropriate attitudes faded after the first cases of in vitro fertilization, they will fade here too.

Ron James, the Scottish millionaire who funded much of Ian Wilmut's research, points out that social attitudes change fast. Before the announcement of Dolly, polls showed that people thought that cloning animals and gene transfer to animals were "morally problematic," whereas germ-line gene therapy fell in the category of "just wrong." Two months after the announcement of Dolly, and after much discussion of human cloning, people's attitudes had shifted to accepting animal cloning and gene transfer to humans as "morally permissible," whereas germ-line gene therapy had shifted to being merely "morally problematic."[12]

James Watson, the co-discoverer of the double helix, once opposed in vitro fertilization by claiming that prejudicial attitudes of other people would harm children created this way. . . .[13] In that piece, the prejudice was really in Watson, because the way that he was stirring up fear was doing more to create the prejudice than any normal human reaction. Similarly, Leon Kass's recent long essay in *The New Republic* (see this volume), where he calls human asexual reproduction "repugnant" and a "horror," creates exactly the kind of prejudiced reaction that he predicts.[14] Rather than make a priori, self-fulfilling prophecies, wouldn't it be better to be empirical about such matters? To be more optimistic about the reactions of ordinary parents?

Children created by SCNT would not *look* any different from other children. Nobody at age two looks like he does at age 45 and, except for his parents, nobody knows what the 45-year-old man looked liked at age two. And since ordinary children often look like their parents, no one would be able to tell a SCNT child from others until he had lived a decade.

Kass claims that a child originated by SCNT will have "a troubled psychic identity" because he or she will be "utterly" confused about his social, genetic, and kinship ties.[15] At worst, this child will be like a child of "incest" and may, if originated as a male from the father, have the same sexual feelings towards the wife as the father. An older male might in turn have strong sexual feelings toward a young female with his wife's genome.

Yet if this were so, any husband of any married twin might have an equally troubled psychic identity because he might have the same sexual feelings toward the twin as his wife. Instead, those in relationships with twins claim that the individuals are very different.

Much of the above line of criticism simply begs the question and assumes that humans created by SCNT will be greeted by stigma or experience confusion. It is hard to understand why, once one gets beyond the novelty, because a child created asexually would know *exactly* who his ancestor was. No confusion there. True, prejudicial expectations could damage children, but why make public policy based on that?

Besides, isn't this kind of argument hypocritical in our present society? Where no one is making any serious effort to ban divorce, despite the overwhelming evidence that divorce seriously damages children, even teenage children. It is always far easier to concentrate on the dramatic, far-off harm than the ones close-at-hand. When we are really concerned about minimizing harm to children, we will pass laws requiring all parents wanting to divorce to go through counseling sessions or to wait a year. We will pass a federal law compelling child-support from fathers who flee to other states, and make it

impossible to renew a professional license or get paid in a public institution in another state until all child-support is paid. After that is done, then we can non-hypocritically talk about how much our society cares about not harming children who may be originated in new ways.

In conclusion, the predicted harms of SCNT to humans are wildly exaggerated, lack a comparative baseline, stem from irrational fears of the unknown, overlook greater dangers of familiar things, and are often based on the armchair psychological speculation of amateurs. Once studies prove SCNT as safe as normal sexual reproduction in non-human mammals, the harm objection will disappear. Given other arguments that SCNT could substantially benefit many children, the argument that SCNT would harm children is a weak one that needs to be weighed against its many potential benefits.16

NOTES

1. Paul Ramsey, *Fabricated Man: The Ethics of Genetic Control* (New Haven, Conn.: Yale University Press, 1970).

2. "What are the psychological implications of growing up as a specimen, sheltered not by a warm womb but by steel and glass, belonging to no one but the lab technician who joined together sperm and egg? In a world already populated with people with identity crises, what's the personal identity of a test-tube baby?" J. Rifkin and T. Howard, *Who Shall Play God?* (New York: Dell, 1977), 15.

3. Ehsan Massod, "Cloning Technique 'Reveals Legal Loophole'," *Nature* 38, 27 February 1987.

4. *New York Times,* 27 July 1978, A16.

5. Knight-Ridder newspapers, 10 March 1997.

6. Leon Kass, "The New Biology: What Price Relieving Man's Estate?" *Journal of the American Medical Association,* vol. 174, 19 November 1971, 779–788.

7. Leroy Walters, "Biomedical Ethics and Their Role in Mammalian Cloning," Conference on Mammalian Cloning: Implications for Science and Society, 27 June 1997, Crystal City Marriott, Crystal City, Virginia.

8. National Bioethics Advisory Commission (NBAC), *Cloning Human Beings: Report and Recommendations of the National Bioethics Advisory Commission,* Rockville, Md., June 1997.

9. A. Wilcox et al., "Incidence of Early Loss of Pregnancy," *New England Journal of Medicine* 319, no. 4, 28 July 1988, 189–194. See also J. Grudzinskas and A. Nysenbaum, "Failure

of Human Pregnancy after Implantation," *Annals of New York Academy of Sciences* 442, 1985, 39–44; J. Muller et al., "Fetal Loss after Implantation," *Lancet* 2, 1980, 554–556.

10. Rick Weiss, "Genetically Engineered Calves Cloned," 21 January 1998, *Washington Post,* A3.

11. David R. Collins, *Eng and Chang: The Original Siamese Twins* (New York: Dillon Press, 1994). Elaine Landau, *Joined at Birth: The Lives of Conjoined Twins* (New York: Grolier Publishing, 1997). See also Geoffrey A. Machin, "Conjoined Twins: Implications for Blastogenesis," *Birth Defects: Original Articles Series* 20, no. 1, 1993, March of Dimes Foundation, 142.

12. Ron James, Managing Director, PPL Therapeutics, "Industry Perspective: The Promise and Practical Applications," Conference on Mammalian Cloning: Implications for Science and Society, 27 June 1997, Crystal City Marriott, Crystal City, Virginia.

13. James D. Watson, "Moving Towards the Clonal Man," *Atlantic,* May 1971, 50–53.

14. Leon Kass, "The Wisdom of Repugnance," *The New Republic,* 2 June 1997.

15. Kass, "The Wisdom of Repugnance," 22–23.

16. Thanks to Mary Litch for comments on this essay.

READING QUESTIONS

1. What is the primary aim of Pence's article?
2. Why does Pence think that reproductive cloning will not harm humanity?
3. How does Pence defend the claim that an embryo cannot be the subject of harm?
4. One argument against reproductive cloning is that individuals who are brought about by this method will lack an "open future." Explain this argument. How does Pence criticize the argument?
5. How does Pence criticize Kass's "troubled psychic identity" objection to reproductive cloning?

DISCUSSION QUESTIONS

1. Pence claims that objections to reproductive cloning based on alleged psychological harms to cloned individuals are not good objections. Should we agree with him about this matter?
2. Given that infertile couples can try to have children by means of IVF (in vitro fertilization), can you think of any situations in which someone has good reason to prefer reproductive cloning to IVF as a method of assisted reproduction?

MICHAEL J. SANDEL

The Case against Perfection

Sandel's article is concerned with the ethics of genetic engineering and, in particular, with the prospect of enhancing human beings through such processes as sex selection; in short, it is concerned with the "ethics of enhancement," including eugenics. Sandel argues that such enhancement is morally questionable, not because of its likely consequences but because of the attitudes toward human beings that it expresses and promotes. As Sandel puts it, "The deepest moral objection to enhancement lies less in the perfection it seeks than in the human disposition it expresses and promotes." Enhancement, claims Sandel, devalues the moral significance of what he calls "giftedness," which "honors the cultivation and display of natural talents." From a religious perspective, enhancement devalues natural gifts because by allowing our talents and powers to be subject to human design, we "confuse our role with God's." From a secular perspective, if we come to see our talents as up to us, we damage the virtues of humility, responsibility, and solidarity. He explains why this is so in his discussion of eugenics.

Sandel's moral case against genetic engineering can be viewed as grounded in considerations of virtue and hence a virtue ethics approach to this issue. Here, it is important to recall from the moral theory primer that some consequentialists in ethics (perfectionists) make considerations of human perfection the basis of their theory of right conduct. Morally right actions are ones that best promote such human perfections as knowledge and achievement. This is not Sandel's approach to the ethics of enhancement. Rather, he stresses the kinds of dispositions of character and associated attitudes toward human life that loss of a sense of giftedness would bring in its wake.

Recommended Reading: virtue ethics, chap. 1, sec. 2E. Also relevant is consequentialism, chap. 1, sec. 2A.

Breakthroughs in genetics present us with a promise and a predicament. The promise is that we may soon be able to treat and prevent a host of debilitating diseases. The predicament is that our newfound genetic knowledge may also enable us to manipulate our own nature—to enhance our muscles, memories, and moods; to choose the sex, height, and other genetic traits of our children; to make ourselves "better than well." When science moves faster than moral understanding, as it does today, men and women struggle to articulate their unease. In liberal societies they reach first for the language of autonomy, fairness, and individual rights. But this part of our moral vocabulary is ill equipped to address the hardest questions posed by genetic engineering. The genomic revolution has induced a kind of moral vertigo.

Consider cloning. The birth of Dolly the cloned sheep, in 1997, brought a torrent of concern about

From Michael J. Sandel, "The Case Against Perfection: What's Wrong with Designer Children, Bionic Athletes, and Genetic Engineering," *Atlantic Monthly*, April 2004.

the prospect of cloned human beings. There are good medical reasons to worry. Most scientists agree that cloning is unsafe, likely to produce offspring with serious abnormalities. (Dolly recently died a premature death.) But suppose technology improved to the point where clones were at no greater risk than naturally conceived offspring. Would human cloning still be objectionable? Should our hesitation be moral as well as medical? What, exactly, is wrong with creating a child who is a genetic twin of one parent, or of an older sibling who has tragically died—or, for that matter, of an admired scientist, sports star, or celebrity?

Some say cloning is wrong because it violates the right to autonomy: by choosing a child's genetic makeup in advance, parents deny the child's right to an open future. A similar objection can be raised against any form of bioengineering that allows parents to select or reject genetic characteristics. According to this argument, genetic enhancements for musical talent, say, or athletic prowess, would point children toward particular choices, and so designer children would never be fully free.

At first glance the autonomy argument seems to capture what is troubling about human cloning and other forms of genetic engineering. It is not persuasive, for two reasons. First, it wrongly implies that absent a designing parent, children are free to choose their characteristics for themselves. But none of us chooses his genetic inheritance. The alternative to a cloned or genetically enhanced child is not one whose future is unbound by particular talents but one at the mercy of the genetic lottery.

Second, even if a concern for autonomy explains some of our worries about made-to-order children, it cannot explain our moral hesitation about people who seek genetic remedies or enhancements for themselves. Gene therapy on somatic (that is, nonreproductive) cells, such as muscle cells and brain cells, repairs or replaces defective genes. The moral quandary arises when people use such therapy not to cure a disease but to reach beyond health, to enhance their physical or cognitive capacities, to lift themselves above the norm.

Like cosmetic surgery, genetic enhancement employs medical means for nonmedical ends—ends unrelated to curing or preventing disease or repairing injury. But unlike cosmetic surgery, genetic enhancement is more than skin-deep. If we are ambivalent about surgery or Botox injections for sagging chins and furrowed brows, we are all the more troubled by genetic engineering for stronger bodies, sharper memories, greater intelligence, and happier moods. The question is whether we are right to be troubled, and if so, on what grounds.

In order to grapple with the ethics of enhancement, we need to confront questions largely lost from view—questions about the moral status of nature, and about the proper stance of human beings toward the given world. Since these questions verge on theology, modern philosophers and political theorists tend to shrink from them. But our new powers of biotechnology make them unavoidable. To see why this is so, consider four examples already on the horizon: muscle enhancement, memory enhancement, growth-hormone treatment, and reproductive technologies that enable parents to choose the sex and some genetic traits of their children. In each case what began as an attempt to treat a disease or prevent a genetic disorder now beckons as an instrument of improvement and consumer choice.

Muscles

Everyone would welcome a gene therapy to alleviate muscular dystrophy and to reverse the debilitating muscle loss that comes with old age. But what if the same therapy were used to improve athletic performance? Researchers have developed a synthetic gene that, when injected into the muscle cells of mice, prevents and even reverses natural muscle deterioration. The gene not only repairs wasted or injured muscles but also strengthens healthy ones. This success bodes well for human applications. H. Lee Sweeney, of the University of Pennsylvania, who leads the research, hopes his discovery will cure the immobility that afflicts the elderly. But Sweeney's bulked-up mice have already attracted the attention of athletes seeking a competitive edge. Although the therapy is not yet approved for human use, the prospect of genetically enhanced weight lifters, home-run sluggers, linebackers, and sprinters is easy to imagine. The widespread use of steroids and other performance-improving drugs in professional sports suggests that many athletes will be eager to avail themselves of genetic enhancement.

Suppose for the sake of argument that muscle-enhancing gene therapy, unlike steroids, turned out to be safe—or at least no riskier than a rigorous weight-training regimen. Would there be a reason to ban its use in sports? There is something unsettling about the image of genetically altered athletes lifting SUVs or hitting 650-foot home runs or running a three-minute mile. But what, exactly, is troubling about it? Is it simply that we find such superhuman spectacles too bizarre to contemplate? Or does our unease point to something of ethical significance?

It might be argued that a genetically enhanced athlete, like a drug-enhanced athlete, would have an unfair advantage over his unenhanced competitors. But the fairness argument against enhancement has a fatal flaw: it has always been the case that some athletes are better endowed genetically than others, and yet we do not consider this to undermine the fairness of competitive sports. From the standpoint of fairness, enhanced genetic differences would be no worse than natural ones, assuming they were safe and made available to all. If genetic enhancement in sports is morally objectionable, it must be for reasons other than fairness.

Memory

Genetic enhancement is possible for brains as well as brawn. In the mid-1990s scientists managed to manipulate a memory-linked gene in fruit flies, creating flies with photographic memories. More recently researchers have produced smart mice by inserting extra copies of a memory-related gene into mouse embryos. The altered mice learn more quickly and remember things longer than normal mice. The extra copies were programmed to remain active even in old age, and the improvement was passed on to offspring.

Human memory is more complicated, but biotech companies, including Memory Pharmaceuticals, are in hot pursuit of memory-enhancing drugs, or "cognition enhancers," for human beings. The obvious market for such drugs consists of those who suffer from Alzheimer's and other serious memory disorders. The companies also have their sights on a bigger market: the 81 million Americans over fifty, who are beginning to encounter the memory loss that comes naturally with age. A drug that reversed age-related memory loss would be a bonanza for the pharmaceutical industry: a Viagra for the brain. Such use would straddle the line between remedy and enhancement. Unlike a treatment for Alzheimer's, it would cure no disease; but insofar as it restored capacities a person once possessed, it would have a remedial aspect. It could also have purely nonmedical uses: for example, by a lawyer cramming to memorize facts for an upcoming trial, or by a business executive eager to learn Mandarin on the eve of his departure for Shanghai.

Some who worry about the ethics of cognitive enhancement point to the danger of creating two classes of human beings: those with access to enhancement technologies, and those who must make do with their natural capacities. And if the enhancements could be passed down the generations, the two classes might eventually become subspecies—the enhanced and the merely natural. But worry about access ignores the moral status of enhancement itself. Is the scenario troubling because the unenhanced poor would be denied the benefits of bioengineering, or because the enhanced affluent would somehow be dehumanized? As with muscles, so with memory: the fundamental question is not how to ensure equal access to enhancement but whether we should aspire to it in the first place.

Height

Pediatricians already struggle with the ethics of enhancement when confronted by parents who want to make their children taller. Since the 1980s human growth hormone has been approved for children with a hormone deficiency that makes them much shorter than average. But the treatment also increases the height of healthy children. Some parents of healthy children who are unhappy with their stature (typically boys) ask why it should make a difference whether a child is short because of a hormone deficiency or because his parents happen to be short. Whatever the cause, the social consequences are the same.

In the face of this argument some doctors began prescribing hormone treatments for children whose short stature was unrelated to any medical problem. By 1996 such "off-label" use accounted for 40 percent of human-growth-hormone prescriptions. Although it is legal to prescribe drugs for purposes not approved by the Food and Drug Administration, pharmaceutical companies cannot promote such use. Seeking to expand its market, Eli Lilly & Co. recently persuaded the FDA to approve its human growth hormone for healthy children whose projected adult height is in the bottom one percentile—under five feet three inches for boys and four feet eleven inches for girls. This concession raises a large question about the ethics of enhancement: If hormone treatments need not be limited to those with hormone deficiencies, why should they be available only to very short children? Why shouldn't all shorter-than-average children be able to seek treatment? And what about a child of average height who wants to be taller so that he can make the basketball team?

Some oppose height enhancement on the grounds that it is collectively self-defeating; as some become taller, others become shorter relative to the norm. Except in Lake Wobegon, not every child can be above average. As the unenhanced began to feel shorter, they, too, might seek treatment, leading to a hormonal arms race that left everyone worse off, especially those who couldn't afford to buy their way up from shortness.

But the arms-race objection is not decisive on its own. Like the fairness objection to bioengineered muscles and memory, it leaves unexamined the attitudes and dispositions that prompt the drive for enhancement. If we were bothered only by the injustice of adding shortness to the problems of the poor, we could remedy that unfairness by publicly subsidizing height enhancements. As for the relative height deprivation suffered by innocent bystanders, we could compensate them by taxing those who buy their way to greater height. The real question is whether we want to live in a society where parents feel compelled to spend a fortune to make perfectly healthy kids a few inches taller.

Sex selection

Perhaps the most inevitable nonmedical use of bioengineering is sex selection. For centuries parents have been trying to choose the sex of their children. Today biotech succeeds where folk remedies failed.

One technique for sex selection arose with prenatal tests using amniocentesis and ultrasound. These medical technologies were developed to detect genetic abnormalities such as spina bifida and Down syndrome. But they can also reveal the sex of the fetus—allowing for the abortion of a fetus of an undesired sex. Even among those who favor abortion rights, few advocate abortion simply because the parents do not want a girl. Nevertheless, in traditional societies with a powerful cultural preference for boys, this practice has become widespread.

Sex selection need not involve abortion, however. For couples undergoing in vitro fertilization (IVF), it is possible to choose the sex of the child before the fertilized egg is implanted in the womb. One method makes use of preimplantation genetic diagnosis (PGD), a procedure developed to screen for genetic diseases. Several eggs are fertilized in a petri dish and grown to the eight-cell stage (about three days). At that point the embryos are tested to determine their sex. Those of the desired sex are implanted; the others are typically discarded. Although few couples are likely to undergo the difficulty and expense of IVF simply to choose the sex of their child, embryo screening is a highly reliable means of sex selection. And as our genetic knowledge increases, it may be possible to use PGD to cull embryos carrying undesired genes, such as those associated with obesity, height, and skin color. The science-fiction movie *Gattaca* depicts a future in which parents routinely screen embryos for sex, height, immunity to disease, and even IQ. There is something troubling about the *Gattaca* scenario, but it is not easy to identify what exactly is wrong with screening embryos to choose the sex of our children.

One line of objection draws on arguments familiar from the abortion debate. Those who believe that an embryo is a person reject embryo screening for the same reasons they reject abortion. If an eight-cell embryo growing in a petri dish is morally equivalent to a fully developed human being, then discarding it is no better than aborting a fetus, and both practices are equivalent to infanticide. Whatever its merits, however, this "pro-life" objection is not an argument against sex selection as such.

The latest technology poses the question of sex selection unclouded by the matter of an embryo's moral status. The Genetics & IVF Institute, a for-profit infertility clinic in Fairfax, Virginia, now offers a sperm-sorting technique that makes it possible to choose the sex of one's child before it is conceived. X-bearing sperm, which produce girls, carry more DNA than Y-bearing sperm, which produce boys; a device called a flow cytometer can separate them. The process, called MicroSort, has a high rate of success.

If sex selection by sperm sorting is objectionable, it must be for reasons that go beyond the debate about the moral status of the embryo. One such reason is that sex selection is an instrument of sex discrimination—typically against girls, as illustrated by the chilling sex ratios in India and China. Some speculate that societies with substantially more men than women will be less stable, more violent, and more prone to crime or war. These are legitimate worries—but the sperm-sorting company has a clever way of addressing them. It offers MicroSort only to couples who want to choose the sex of a child for purposes of "family balancing." Those with more sons than daughters may choose a girl, and vice versa. But customers may not use the technology to stock up on children of the same sex, or even to choose the sex of their firstborn child. (So far the majority of MicroSort clients have chosen girls.) Under restrictions of this kind, do any ethical issues remain that should give us pause?

The case of MicroSort helps us isolate the moral objections that would persist if muscle-enhancement, memory-enhancement, and height-enhancement technologies were safe and available to all.

It is commonly said that genetic enhancements undermine our humanity by threatening our capacity to act freely, to succeed by our own efforts, and to consider ourselves responsible—worthy of praise or blame—for the things we do and for the way we are. It is one thing to hit seventy home runs as the result

of disciplined training and effort, and something else, something less, to hit them with the help of steroids or genetically enhanced muscles. Of course, the roles of effort and enhancement will be a matter of degree. But as the role of enhancement increases, our admiration for the achievement fades—or, rather, our admiration for the achievement shifts from the player to his pharmacist. This suggests that our moral response to enhancement is a response to the diminished agency of the person whose achievement is enhanced.

Though there is much to be said for this argument, I do not think the main problem with enhancement and genetic engineering is that they undermine effort and erode human agency. The deeper danger is that they represent a kind of hyperagency—a Promethean aspiration to remake nature, including human nature, to serve our purposes and satisfy our desires. The problem is not the drift to mechanism but the drive to mastery. And what the drive to mastery misses and may even destroy is an appreciation of the gifted character of human powers and achievements.

To acknowledge the giftedness of life is to recognize that our talents and powers are not wholly our own doing, despite the effort we expend to develop and to exercise them. It is also to recognize that not everything in the world is open to whatever use we may desire or devise. Appreciating the gifted quality of life constrains the Promethean project and conduces to a certain humility. It is in part a religious sensibility. But its resonance reaches beyond religion.

It is difficult to account for what we admire about human activity and achievement without drawing upon some version of this idea. Consider two types of athletic achievement. We appreciate players like Pete Rose, who are not blessed with great natural gifts but who manage, through striving, grit, and determination, to excel in their sport. But we also admire players like Joe DiMaggio, who display natural gifts with grace and effortlessness. Now, suppose we learned that both players took performance-enhancing drugs. Whose turn to drugs would we find more deeply disillusioning? Which aspect of the athletic ideal—effort or gift—would be more deeply offended?

Some might say effort: the problem with drugs is that they provide a shortcut, a way to win without striving. But striving is not the point of sports; excellence is. And excellence consists at least partly in the display of natural talents and gifts that are no doing of the athlete who possesses them. This is an uncomfortable fact for democratic societies. We want to believe that success, in sports and in life, is something we earn, not something we inherit. Natural gifts, and the admiration they inspire, embarrass the meritocratic faith; they cast doubt on the conviction that praise and rewards flow from effort alone. In the face of this embarrassment we inflate the moral significance of striving, and depreciate giftedness. This distortion can be seen, for example, in network-television coverage of the Olympics, which focuses less on the feats the athletes perform than on heartrending stories of the hardships they have overcome and the struggles they have waged to triumph over an injury or a difficult upbringing or political turmoil in their native land.

But effort isn't everything. No one believes that a mediocre basketball player who works and trains even harder than Michael Jordan deserves greater acclaim or a bigger contract. The real problem with genetically altered athletes is that they corrupt athletic competition as a human activity that honors the cultivation and display of natural talents. From this standpoint, enhancement can be seen as the ultimate expression of the ethic of effort and willfulness—a kind of high-tech striving. The ethic of willfulness and the biotechnological powers it now enlists are arrayed against the claims of giftedness.

The ethic of giftedness, under siege in sports, persists in the practice of parenting. But here, too, bio-engineering and genetic enhancement threaten to dislodge it. To appreciate children as gifts is to accept them as they come, not as objects of our design or products of our will or instruments of our ambition. Parental love is not contingent on the talents and attributes a child happens to have. We choose our friends and spouses at least partly on the basis of qualities we find attractive. But we do not choose our children. Their qualities are unpredictable, and even the most conscientious parents cannot be held wholly responsible for the kind of children they have. That is why parenthood, more than other human relationships, teaches what the theologian William F. May calls an "openness to the unbidden."

May's resonant phrase helps us see that the deepest moral objection to enhancement lies less in the perfection it seeks than in the human disposition it expresses and promotes. The problem is not that parents usurp the autonomy of a child they design. The problem lies in the hubris of the designing parents, in their drive to master the mystery of birth. Even if this disposition did not make parents tyrants to their children, it would disfigure the relation between parent and child, and deprive the parent of the humility and enlarged human sympathies that an openness to the unbidden can cultivate. . . .

The mandate to mold our children, to cultivate and improve them, complicates the case against enhancement. We usually admire parents who seek the best for their children, who spare no effort to help them achieve happiness and success. Some parents confer advantages on their children by enrolling them in expensive schools, hiring private tutors, sending them to tennis camp, providing them with piano lessons, ballet lessons, swimming lessons, SAT-prep courses, and so on. If it is permissible and even admirable for parents to help their children in these ways, why isn't it equally admirable for parents to use whatever genetic technologies may emerge (provided they are safe) to enhance their children's intelligence, musical ability, or athletic prowess?

The defenders of enhancement are right to this extent: improving children through genetic engineering is similar in spirit to the heavily managed, high-pressure child-rearing that is now common. But this similarity does not vindicate genetic enhancement. On the contrary, it highlights a problem with the trend toward hyperparenting. One conspicuous example of this trend is sports-crazed parents bent on making champions of their children. Another is the frenzied drive of overbearing parents to mold and manage their children's academic careers.

As the pressure for performance increases, so does the need to help distractible children concentrate on the task at hand. This may be why diagnoses of attention deficit and hyperactivity disorder have increased so sharply. Lawrence Diller, a pediatrician and the author of *Running on Ritalin,* estimates that five to six percent of American children under eighteen (a total of four to five million kids) are currently prescribed Ritalin,

Adderall, and other stimulants, the treatment of choice for ADHD. (Stimulants counteract hyperactivity by making it easier to focus and sustain attention.) The number of Ritalin prescriptions for children and adolescents has tripled over the past decade, but not all users suffer from attention disorders or hyperactivity. High school and college students have learned that prescription stimulants improve concentration for those with normal attention spans, and some buy or borrow their classmates' drugs to enhance their performance on the SAT or other exams. Since stimulants work for both medical and nonmedical purposes, they raise the same moral questions posed by other technologies of enhancement. . . .

This demand for performance and perfection animates the impulse to rail against the given. It is the deepest source of the moral trouble with enhancement.

Some see a clear line between genetic enhancement and other ways that people seek improvement in their children and themselves. Genetic manipulation seems somehow worse—more intrusive, more sinister—than other ways of enhancing performance and seeking success. But morally speaking, the difference is less significant than it seems. Bioengineering gives us reason to question the low-tech, high-pressure child-rearing practices we commonly accept. The hyperparenting familiar in our time represents an anxious excess of mastery and dominion that misses the sense of life as a gift. . . .

Why not shake off our unease about genetic enhancement as so much superstition? What would be lost if biotechnology dissolved our sense of giftedness?

From a religious standpoint the answer is clear: To believe that our talents and powers are wholly our own doing is to misunderstand our place in creation, to confuse our role with God's. Religion is not the only source of reasons to care about giftedness, however. The moral stakes can also be described in secular terms. If bioengineering made the myth of the "self-made man" come true, it would be difficult to view our talents as gifts for which we are indebted, rather than as achievements for which we are responsible. This would transform three key features of our moral landscape: humility, responsibility, and solidarity.

In a social world that prizes mastery and control, parenthood is a school for humility. That we care deeply about our children and yet cannot choose the kind we want teaches parents to be open to the unbidden. Such openness is a disposition worth affirming, not only within families but in the wider world as well. It invites us to abide the unexpected, to live with dissonance, to rein in the impulse to control. A *Gattaca*-like world in which parents became accustomed to specifying the sex and genetic traits of their children would be a world inhospitable to the unbidden, a gated community writ large. The awareness that our talents and abilities are not wholly our own doing restrains our tendency toward hubris.

Though some maintain that genetic enhancement erodes human agency by overriding effort, the real problem is the explosion, not the erosion, of responsibility. As humility gives way, responsibility expands to daunting proportions. We attribute less to chance and more to choice. Parents become responsible for choosing, or failing to choose, the right traits for their children. Athletes become responsible for acquiring, or failing to acquire, the talents that will help their teams win.

One of the blessings of seeing ourselves as creatures of nature, God, or fortune is that we are not wholly responsible for the way we are. The more we become masters of our genetic endowments, the greater the burden we bear for the talents we have and the way we perform. Today when a basketball player misses a rebound, his coach can blame him for being out of position. Tomorrow the coach may blame him for being too short. Even now the use of performance-enhancing drugs in professional sports is subtly transforming the expectations players have for one another; on some teams players who take the field free from amphetamines or other stimulants are criticized for "playing naked."

The more alive we are to the chanced nature of our lot, the more reason we have to share our fate with others. Consider insurance. Since people do not know whether or when various ills will befall them, they pool their risk by buying health insurance and life insurance. As life plays itself out, the healthy wind up subsidizing the unhealthy, and those who live to a ripe old age wind up subsidizing the families of those who die before their time. Even without a sense of mutual obligation, people pool their risks and resources and share one another's fate.

But insurance markets mimic solidarity only insofar as people do not know or control their own risk factors. Suppose genetic testing advanced to the point where it could reliably predict each person's medical future and life expectancy. Those confident of good health and long life would opt out of the pool, causing other people's premiums to skyrocket. The solidarity of insurance would disappear as those with good genes fled the actuarial company of those with bad ones.

The fear that insurance companies would use genetic data to assess risks and set premiums recently led the Senate to vote to prohibit genetic discrimination in health insurance. But the bigger danger, admittedly more speculative, is that genetic enhancement, if routinely practiced, would make it harder to foster the moral sentiments that social solidarity requires.

Why, after all, do the successful owe anything to the least-advantaged members of society? The best answer to this question leans heavily on the notion of giftedness. The natural talents that enable the successful to flourish are not their own doing but, rather, their good fortune—a result of the genetic lottery. If our genetic endowments are gifts, rather than achievements for which we can claim credit, it is a mistake and a conceit to assume that we are entitled to die full measure of the bounty they reap in a market economy. We therefore have an obligation to share this bounty with those who, through no fault of their own, lack comparable gifts.

A lively sense of the contingency of our gifts—a consciousness that none of us is wholly responsible for his or her success—saves a meritocratic society from sliding into the smug assumption that the rich are rich because they are more deserving than the poor. Without this, the successful would become even more likely than they are now to view themselves as self-made and self-sufficient, and hence wholly responsible for their success. Those at the bottom of society would be viewed not as disadvantaged, and thus worthy of a measure of compensation, but as simply unfit, and thus worthy of eugenic repair. The meritocracy, less chastened by chance, would become harder, less forgiving. As perfect genetic knowledge would end the simulacrum of solidarity in insurance markets, so perfect genetic control would erode the actual solidarity that arises when men and women reflect on the contingency of their talents and fortunes. . . .

It is often assumed that the powers of enhancement we now possess arose as an inadvertent by-product of biomedical progress—the genetic revolution came, so to speak, to cure disease, and stayed to tempt us with the prospect of enhancing our performance, designing our children, and perfecting our nature. That may have the story backwards. It is more plausible to view genetic engineering as the ultimate expression of our resolve to see ourselves astride the world, the masters of our nature. But that promise of mastery is flawed. It threatens to banish our appreciation of life as a gift, and to leave us with nothing to affirm or behold outside our own will.

READING QUESTIONS

1. Why does Sandel claim that the main ethical problem with genetic enhancement does not have to do with human autonomy?
2. In his discussion of various types of enhancement (muscles, memory, and height) Sandel asks readers to set aside questions about fairness and equal access to the means of such enhancements in reflecting on the morality of genetic enhancement. Why does he do this?
3. What is the difference between what Sandel calls the "ethic of giftedness" and the "ethic of willfulness"?
4. According to Sandel, what is the main moral objection to human genetic enhancement?

DISCUSSION QUESTIONS

1. Should we agree with Sandel that among the likely effects of human genetic enhancement will be a diminished sense of humility and solidarity?
2. Are there reasons, besides the ones that Sandel gives, for thinking that human genetic enhancement is morally wrong?

ARTHUR L. CAPLAN

Good, Better, or Best?

According to Caplan, the core of the so-called anti-meliorist moral stance regarding the use of biomedical techniques to improve human beings is composed of arguments to the effect that allowing such improvements will violate or perhaps destroy human nature. One such argument is Michael Sandel's appeal to the idea of giftedness featured in the previous selection. Caplan argues that none of the core arguments in question are successful.

Recommended Reading: natural law theory, chap. 1, sec. 2B.

THE RISE OF ANTI-MELIORISM

Excellence has come in for a lot of bad press recently. A torrent of books and articles have appeared [see list of References, 1–10, 20] all raising serious ethical questions about the wisdom and morality of trying to use new biomedical knowledge to perfect ourselves or our offspring. Of course, beating up on the literal pursuit of perfection is silly. As the artist Salvador Dali famously pointed out, "Have no fear of perfection—you'll never reach it."

Critics of those who allegedly seek to perfect human beings by means of bioengineering know this. Nonetheless, they often invoke the rhetoric of "perfection" in their critiques since the pursuit of perfection seems arrogant at best and silly at worst. Perfection, however, while an easy target, is not their real target. What they really are attacking is the far more frequently expressed, albeit far less lofty, and, notably, far less controversial goal—improvement. The critics are very concerned about the drive to improve or enhance particular human behaviors, traits or features by the application of emerging biomedical

From Arthur L. Caplan, "Good, Better, or Best?" in Julian Savulescu & Nick Bostrom, eds., *Human Enhancement* (2009). By permission of Oxford University Press, Inc.

knowledge in genetics, neuroscience, pharmacology and physiology.

Those who I will lump together as "anti-meliorists" wonder how we will ever resist the obvious temptation to put the explosion of biomedical knowledge to use for the aim of improving ourselves. They are quick to note that we are already edging down the melioristic road. Breasts are being augmented, wrinkles smoothed, fat suctioned, blood doped and moods calmed. Where, the anti-meliorists wonder, will this all end?

Why is the drive to improve ourselves so disturbing to anti-meliorists? Their arguments cluster around these key worries: that the pursuit of perfection by biomedical means is vain, selfish and unrewarding [1–3, 6, 7], that improving ourselves is unfair [1, 3, 4, 10], that the happiness achieved through engineering with an eye toward improvement will lead to a deformation of our character and spirit [1, 2, 4, 9], improvement in performance that is bioengineered is not authentic and therefore not morally proper [1, 2, 9, 10], accepting enhancement will undermine and deform the role of parent [9] and, that enhancement or improvement violate human nature [2, 4, 5, 7–9] or worse still, may actually destroy it [2, 5, 7, 9].

I am going to spend little time examining concerns about vanity. Vanity and self-regard are not the same things. Self-regard, in moderation, is not a moral evil. And when examined carefully the anti-meliorist invocation of vanity seems to me to be based on the assertion that the pursuit of improvement by means of bioengineering is of necessity vain rather than simply an instance of legitimate self-regard. Wanting to look better or function more efficiently cannot justifiably be dismissed as mere vanity. The anti-meliorist must first tell us how to recognize morally suspect vanity from morally legitimate self-regard.

I will also pass over anti-meliorist arguments about inequity since they miss the relevant mark. When it comes to worries about fair access to melioristic biotechnologies, those concerned about equity worry either about the creation of more "haves" and "have nots"—as the rich get better, the poor will languish—or, the inequity of private companies earning massive profits by seducing us all into frivolous efforts to improve ourselves [10].

Equity and fairness are major problems in this and every society. But, concerns about equity do not speak to why improvement is wrong. Rather, equity arguments tell us whether a pattern of inequality or a particular distribution of resources is right or wrong. It is important to decide what is fair in the distribution of access to enhancement technologies or what to do about greedy, manipulative pharmaceutical or cosmetics industries that fool us into wasting our money on silly things when real health needs go unmet—but these are matters that are quite distinct from and hardly unique to improvement via new biological knowledge. Equity arguments do not show what is inherently wrong with the desire to use biotechnology to improve ourselves and our children [11].

The remaining arguments of anti-meliorism do engage improvement on its own terms and thus do merit a response. It is the last of these arguments, which I believe is at the core of anti-meliorist concerns. So I will engage the view that it is wrong to tamper with human nature first and then return to the remaining concerns of anti-meliorists. I do not think that any of the arguments that have been brought forward provide a convincing case against improvement.

HUMAN NATURE INVIOLATE?

It cannot simply be the pursuit of improvement that is making anti-meliorists nervous. Many religious traditions, self-help, and spiritual movements seek improvement, even perfection [12–14] but these evoke no negative commentary from the anti-meliorists. Nor, interestingly enough, do recent and sustained efforts to improve animals and plants using biotechnology evoke much more than an ethical yawn (with the exception of McKibben [2]). Rather, it is the use of biomedical knowledge applied to you and me that is the crux of their concern. Those who worry about what will become of human nature fear that in applying new biomedical knowledge to improve human beings something essential about humanity will be lost. If biomedical tinkering is allowed we will destroy the very thing that makes us human—our nature.

Anti-meliorism rests, however, on a very shaky foundation. To support their position the anti-meliorists must state what human nature is. Despite a great deal of hand-waving about this they do not. They must also be very clear about why they see human nature as static. They are not. And they must advance an argument about why human nature, which has evolved in response to an enormous array of random forces, accidental environmental contingencies, and stochastic genetic events, tells us anything about what is good or desirable in terms of the traits humans should possess. They cannot.

The products of the "random walk" of evolution, where a series of contingent events intersect to produce the patterns of life we call organisms, do not teach any lessons about what we should become any more than they can tell us what is right or wrong, good or bad. They merely are what they are.

Is there a "nature" that is common to all humans, both those that exist now and those that have existed in the past? The fight over whether there is any such thing as human nature is a long-standing one [15, 16]. But one can concede that we have been shaped by a causally powerful set of genetic influences and selection forces and still remain skeptical as to whether these have produced a single "nature" that all members of humanity possess. What exactly is the single trait or fixed, determinate set of traits that defines the nature of who humans are and have been throughout our entire existence as a species on this planet? Unless they can articulate this Platonic essence, anti-meliorists who invoke the sanctity of human nature as the basis for their moral concerns about improvement lack a foundation for their argument. If one surveys all humans, across cultures, those of all ages and varieties of congenital defects, and those from different times in the past it becomes hard to believe any single trait is defining of human nature.

Without a demonstration of a "nature" there is no basis for the claim that change, improvement, and betterment always represent grave threats to our essential humanity. In fact, perhaps the only lesson

that evolution teaches is that adaptation to change is the key requirement for life on this planet.

Worse still for anti-meliorists, even if there is an amalgam of traits that might be roughly described as constituting human nature, that does not show that it is wrong to tamper with those traits to try and improve upon them. We are creatures who have long tinkered with ourselves using all manner of technologies from clothing to medicines to agriculturally produced foods to telescopes to computers to airplanes.

Our view of our "nature" is closely linked to the technologies that we have invented and to which we have adapted [17]. We don't think of ourselves as being engineered for improvement but we are. We have already engaged in systematic meliorism using science and technology. We are traveling, eating, flying, computing, and perceiving in ways that are distinct improvements upon what would be possible using only our natural endowments. Each of these "improvements" comes at a price but it is not clear that it is a price not worth paying [18]. And more to the point, there is no reason to think that this creative manipulation of our environment, including our own bodies and minds, is any less worthy of inclusion as part of human "nature" [19].

Nor is there any normative guidance offered by our evolutionary history that shows why we should not try to improve upon the biological design with which we are endowed. Augmenting breasts or prolonging erections may be vain, self indulgent, trivial, and a waste of scarce resources but seeking to use our knowledge to enhance our vision, memory, strength, learning skills, immunity, or metabolism are not obviously any of these things.

Ultimately, anti-meliorism posits a static vision of human nature to which the anti-meliorists mandate we reconcile ourselves. If anything is clear about human nature it is that this is not an accurate view of who we have been or what we are now, or a view which should determine what we become [16]. So, if human nature does not provide a foundation for anti-meliorism what other arguments are there? The inadvisability of settling for "cheap" thrills and the importance of resisting the lure of the inauthentic are two prominent lines of argument in the anti-meliorist camp.

The "Loss" of Authenticity

It is estimated that nearly one and a half million Americans have undergone laser surgery to improve their vision. The purveyors of this procedure often promise that those who have it will see better than they ever have before, even with the aid of glasses or contact lenses. Laser surgery sometimes can give eyes better than 20–20 vision. So, have those who have undergone this type of procedure and achieved enhanced vision done something immoral? If you were to read the report of the President's Council on Bioethics entitled *Beyond Therapy: Biotechnology and the Pursuit of Happiness* [1] you might think so.

Admittedly the eye is not the only part of the brain that people want to improve. Interest in brain enhancement is enormous. Already a number of pharmaceutical companies are interested in selling drugs such as Provigil, that allow individuals to go without sleep for longer periods of time than they otherwise could or Ambien that provides sleep with fewer side-effects than older sleeping aids. Herbal and nutritional companies are also peddling substances that allegedly can improve memory, mood, or sexual enjoyment. Many students are keenly interested in any drug, say Atavan or Ritalin or Prozac, that might improve their performance on tests or in musical, dramatic, or athletic performances by allowing for greater attention span, increased short-term memory, fewer muscle twitches or reduced anxiety. The military has an interest in seeing mental performance improved so as to increase the combat effectiveness of individuals or entire units. And not a few of us drink coffee, tea, colas, and other stimulants to try and enhance our cognitive performance. Many take various drugs, foods and herbs, or utilize technology such as virtual reality to try to enhance their mood, emotional state, or sexual enjoyment. While these activities can and sometimes are abused, it would hardly seem self evident that it is morally wrong to seek to try and improve one's mental abilities. Surely it is the critics of efforts to improve or enhance what the brain can do that bear the burden of showing why this is wrong.

So what is the basis for the moral concern of those who authored the Council's Report about efforts to improve, enhance or optimize our brains, vision, or any other human trait? To some extent they worry that since the brain is the seat of our nature then altering it is to alter our very nature. But as we have already seen this argument presumes both a clear, static, and inviolate nature that is not consistent with any evolutionary view of how our brains came to be what they are. So what other arguments do the anti-meliorists make? Among other concerns are these:

1. the happiness or satisfaction achieved through engineering is seductive and will lead to a deformation of our character and spirit;
2. improvement in performance that is engineered is not authentic and is, thus, not earned and is, therefore, not morally commendable.

Neither of these arguments provides a sufficient reason to oppose enhancement or optimization of our vision or our brains, our own or our children's. Each argument carries some emotive force, but is not a sound basis for rejecting choices that individuals or parents might make to improve or optimize their children. That is not to say that every choice for enhancement or optimization is beyond moral criticism or even morally valid. But it is to say that those who would have us turn away in principle from all forms of enhancement or optimization have not made a convincing case.

Consider these questions from the President's Council which suggest that all efforts at enhancement will distort or deform the nature of our experience:

> Indeed, why would one need to discipline one's passions, refine one's sentiments, and cultivate one's virtues, in short, to organize one's soul for action in the world, when one's aspiration to happiness could be satisfied by drugs in a quick, consistent, and cost-effective manner? [1]

The concern expressed here is that, if we enhance ourselves and our pleasures, achievements and enjoyments come easily, then why would we strive to be good or virtuous people?

The problem with this argument is that many people now do not strive to be virtuous or good, and they are not biologically or biotechnologically enhanced or optimized in any way. Laying the blame for vice, sloth, or the willingness to settle for cheap thrills at the feet of enhancement ignores the inconvenient fact that the desire for quick returns, easy money, and instant gratification have nothing at all to do with whether some or all of us choose to use biotechnology to become enhanced beings with different experiences. Vice is a trait of many if not all human beings. The notion of what we must seek and what we must avoid to facilitate character development and what that character should be that is implicit in the President's Council report has deeper roots in fictionalized accounts of young men at boarding schools, than anything that accurately describes how human beings actually evolve the character traits that they manifest or what psychologists and social scientists tell us about the process [18].

Still, the Council broods in *Beyond Therapy*, easy pleasures and cheap thrills will likely make us weak and spineless. There is nothing like misery to make us stronger. Sorrow, courageously confronted, can make us stronger, wiser, and more compassionate.

To what extent might the new antidepressants, the serotonin reuptake inhibitors or SSRIs, when used to reduce our troubles and sorrows, endanger this aspect of affective life? Although they do not prevent psychic pain, SSRIs may generally dull our capacity to feel it, rendering us less capable of experiencing and learning from misfortune or tragedy. They may make it difficult to empathize with the miseries of others. If some virtues can only be taught through experiencing very trying circumstances, those virtues might be lost, or at least less developed in a world of biological enhancement.

Put aside the fact that sorrow can also drive some to suicide and bring others to dysfunction and despair. And ignore the fact that using drugs to dull or blunt experience is not clearly linked in any way to the goals of enhancement or improvement. After all one might use drugs to intensify experiences that lead to the formation of virtue or empathy rather than to avoid such experiences. Putting these points aside, is it really true that improvement and virtue cannot co-exist?

This argument is a bit like those who worried what the airplane would do to the virtues of the combat ground soldier. The improved technology would make obsolete the kind of courage needed for a frontal assault. Oh really? Tell that to the fighter pilot who needs to evade a ground to air missile or land on an aircraft carrier at night, or to the helicopter pilot evacuating a wounded soldier under a barrage of ground fire. Improving performance is not necessarily toxic to virtue. It simply shifts how virtue is manifest. It is highly unlikely that those with enhanced vision, muscles, or brains would lack for challenges in the real world.

So the case is not made that improving our brains will destroy our "authentic" character. What then? The Council wring their collective hands at the prospect that enhancement of the brain or optimization of brain performance will cheapen the value of our experiences:

> But seldom do those who win by cheating or who love by deceiving cease to long for the joy and fulfillment that come from winning fair and square or being loved for who one truly is. Many stoop to fraud to obtain happiness, but none want their feeling of flourishing itself to be fraudulent. Yet a fraudulent happiness is just what the pharmacological management of our mental lives threatens to confer upon us. [1]

Translation: If you don't really earn your performance, if you do not sweat and toil at it, then it will not be authentic and it will ultimately prove unsatisfying. One is tempted to ask who is writing this stuff—is the Council somehow psychically channeling our Puritan ancestors?

Certainly it is exciting to achieve satisfaction by testing one's limits, by seeing what one can achieve by striving, struggling, and working to overcome innate limits. But it is also very satisfying to have benefits that simply come from out of the blue or through good fortune. No one who has enhanced vision as a result of laser surgery whom I have ever encountered feels the least bit of guilt, shame, or doubt that the improved vision they enjoy is fraudulent because they did nothing to deserve or earn it except pay their money and let a laser do its thing. Life is full of many pleasures that are not earned by testing our limits but which are fully and thoroughly enjoyed. Think of the joy in winning the lottery, or in finding out that your friends like you even though you cheat at cards, cannot stop smoking, eat too much, or are sometimes boring, or the pleasure you can find in solving problems using computers and every form of technological assistance you can muster to aid your fallible brain.

We do not always have to "earn" our happiness to be really and truly happy. Nor do we always reject as fraudulent those things that make us happy that we do nothing to earn. In fact it could be argued that a mix of both types of experiences, the happiness that is earned and the happiness that we enjoy as a matter of good fortune, is a more accurate reflection of authentic human experience. An enhanced brain or improved cognitive functioning would not in principle undermine the ethos of authenticity that undergirds human satisfaction because that infrastructure is not as the Council depicts it. Nor is it clear that improvement through bioengineering must always be inimical to authenticity.

NEUROTIC PARENTING AND IMPROVEMENT

Lastly, consider the concerns of Harvard's Michael Sandel [9, 21]…He is worried that if we seek to perfect our children, to enhance them and optimize them we will no longer see them as "gifts." They will instead become objects, things to manufacture.

> In a social world that prizes mastery and control, parenthood is a school for humility. That we care deeply about our children and yet cannot choose the kind we want teaches parents to be open to the unbidden. Such openness is a disposition worth affirming…it invites us to abide the unexpected, to live with dissonance, to rein in the impulse to control. [9, p. 60]

Put aside the irony of a Professor at a school to which parents devote enormous resources to enhance their children's capacities and abilities so that they may enter there counseling acceptance of the impulse to control the fate of their children. Ignore the fact that the vision of parenting that is put forward seems unduly bound by an upper class, American vision of what makes for desirable parenthood—no collective

parenting or parent–child estrangement cloud this vision. Is there value to be found in accepting the random draw of the genetic lottery with respect to one's children? Should a point mutation that produces a slight change in a trait or a recombination of genetic material really be seen as the source of value in creating the unexpected in our offspring? If the genetic endowment of our children is a gift then to whom ought we feel grateful—our microbial forebears, the dinosaurs, Neanderthals for not wiping our ancestors out? The metaphor of the gift makes no sense in the secular context such as Sandel proposes. Gifts require a giver but nature offers no likely suspects to occupy this role.

Much of what parents try to do is shape and control their children. They do not value much about their design but rather try to work with the tools and abilities that nature has given to parent a child that can be happy and productive. Would changing what the accidents of nature produce in terms of a child's endowment of traits and behaviors at birth really result in a child that is less the object of parental design or less on parental affection for a child [21]? Is it self evident that this must be so?

No doubt there are neurotic parents. And no doubt some parents can and do get caught up in trying to "perfect" their children. We are all familiar with the stereotypes of the demanding soccer parent or the overbearing parent who forces their child to do piano, math, tennis, or gymnastics regardless of the child's own wishes and even at the cost of the child's emotional and physical health.

But, adding more bioengineering possibilities to what is already there in terms of environmental and social tools that parents can use does nothing except broaden the armamentarium available to parents. The parents who are neurotic, overly demanding, and compulsively driven to change and shape their children according to their own values will be trying to do this with or without biological tools. The fact that there are some neurotic parents around should not be enough to prohibit the use of biological engineering to improve eyesight, enhance memory, or allow a child to learn languages with greater facility. The problem is bad parenting, not bad technology.

The case against all enhancements, in adults or children, is not made. Which, again, is not to say that all enhancement is, of necessity, good or desirable. But it is to say that, in principle, objections to perfection and enhancement should not deter those who seek to improve or make better use of biotechnology for themselves or their children. What we must do is take each proposed enhancement technology under consideration and decide whether what it can do is worth whatever price it might exact.

REFERENCES

1. President's Council on Bioethics. *Beyond Therapy: Biotechnology and the Pursuit of Happiness*, Harper Collins, 2003.

2. W. McKibben. *Enough: Staying Human in an Engineered Age*, Times Books, 2003.

3. D. Callahan. *What Price Better Health*, University of California Press, 2003.

4. C. Elliott. *Better Than Well: American Medicine Meets the American Dream*, W. W. Norton & Company, 2003.

5. F. Fukuyama. *Our Posthuman Future: Consequences of the Biotechnology Revolution*, Picador, 2003.

6. S. Rothman and D. Rothman. *The Pursuit of Perfection: The Promise and Perils of Medical Enhancement*, Pantheon, 2003.

7. L. R. Kass. "Life, Liberty and the Defense of Dignity: The Challenge for Bioethics," *Encounter*, 2002.

8. W. Kristol and E. Cohen (eds.), *The Future Is Now*, Rowman & Littlefield, 2002.

9. M. Sandel. "The Case Against Perfection," *The Atlantic Monthly*, April 2004, 51–62.

10. C. Elliott. "Pharma's Gain May Be Our Loss," PLOS *Medicine* 1:3, 2004, 52–3.

11. A. L. Caplan. "Nobody is perfect—but why not try to be better," PLOS *Medicine*, 1:3, 2004, 52–4.

12. W. Isaacson. *Benjamin Franklin: An American Life*, Simon and Schuster, 2003.

13. J. Whorton. *Crusaders for Fitness: The History of American Health Reformers*, Princeton University Press, 1984.

14. "Saint Teresa of Avila: The Way of Perfection." Available at: www.ccel.org/t/teresa/way/main.html

15. S. Pinker. *The Blank Slate: the modern denial of human nature*, Viking, 2002.

16. H. W. Baillie and T. K. Casey (eds.), *Is Human Nature Obsolete?*, MIT Press, 2005.

17. E. Tenner. *Our Own Devices: The past and future of body technology*, Knopf, 2003.

18. A. L. Caplan. "Is biomedical research too dangerous to pursue?" *Science* 303, 2004, 1142.

19. J. C. Gibbs. *Moral Development and Reality*, Sage, 2003.

20. J. C. L. Wells, S. Strickland, K. Laland (eds.), *Social Information Transmission and Human Biology*, Taylor and Frances, 2006.

21. M. Sandel. "The Case Against Perfection: What's Wrong with Designer Children, Bionic Athletes, and Genetic Engineering," in J. Savulescu and N. Bostrom (eds.), *Human Enhancement*, Oxford: Oxford University Press, 2008 and *The Case Against Perfection*, Harvard University Press, 2007.

22. M. Sagoff. "Nature and human nature," in H. W. Baillie and T. K. Casey (eds.), *Is Human Nature Obsolete?*, MIT Press, 2005.

READING QUESTIONS

1. What are the six key worries that anti-meliorists have about the improvement of humans through the use of biomedical knowledge? Which of these worries does Caplan attack directly in his article?
2. What does evolution teach us about the essence of human nature according to Caplan? Give some examples of ways in which evolution has affected humans.
3. List some of the ways in which human beings have already employed systematic meliorism to improve and enhance their lives.
4. Explain Caplan's objections to the anti-meliorist argument that the satisfaction achieved through biomedical engineering will lead to the deformation of human character and the loss of authenticity.
5. How does Caplan respond to the claim that meliorism will affect the way that parents see and treat their children?

DISCUSSION QUESTIONS

1. Caplan points out that anti-meliorists have failed to offer any characterization of an essential nature shared by all human beings. Consider whether there is something like an essential and shared human nature. Discuss the aspects and traits that might constitute human nature.
2. Caplan admits that some improvements to human traits and behavior may not be morally defensible. Describe the sorts of improvements that you think would be immoral. Consider Caplan's potential responses to your suggestions.
3. Suppose that systematic meliorism does pose a threat to human character and authenticity. How could individuals guard against this outcome while still engaging in the practice of biomedical engineering?
4. In his article, "The Case against Perfection," Sandel worries that human genetic enhancement will likely have negative effects on humility, responsibility, and solidarity. Do Caplan's remarks about Sandel's anti-meliorist position provide an adequate reply to Sandel's worries?

ADDITIONAL RESOURCES

Web Resources

Note: the first three of the following Web resources were selected mainly for their information about genetics, cloning, and stem cell research.

Center for Genetics and Society, <www.geneticsandsociety.org>. A nonprofit organization that disseminates information about reproductive technologies. According to its site, "The Center supports benign and beneficent medical applications of the new human genetic and reproductive technologies, and opposes those applications that objectify and commodify human life and threaten to divide human society."

Genomics.Energy.Gov, <http://genomics.energy.gov>. Site of the genome programs of the U.S. Department of Energy Office of Science. Includes information about cloning.

The National Institutes of Health, <www.nih.gov>. Includes information about stem cells, stem cell research, ethical issues raised by such research, and information on U.S. policy regarding the use of stem cells in research.

Devolder, Katrien, "Cloning," <http://plato.stanford.edu/entries/cloning>. An overview of the ethical dispute over therapeutic and reproductive cloning, including some discussion of religious perspectives.

Siegel, Andrew, "The Ethics of Stem Cell Research," <http://plato.stanford.edu/entries/stem-cells>. An overview of the ethical controversy over use of stem cells for therapeutic and reproductive purposes.

Authored Books

Agar, Nicholas, *Liberal Eugenics: In Defense of Human Enhancement* (Oxford: Blackwell, 2004). As the title indicates, Agar defends the morality of human enhancement employing what he calls the "method of moral images" that appeals to the idea of treating like cases alike.

Congregation for the Doctrine of the Faith, *Instruction* Dignitas Personae *on Certain Bioethical Questions*, 2008. An update of the Vatican's stance on biomedical issues in which it condemns *in vitro* fertilization, human cloning, genetic testing on embryos, embryonic stem cell research (that involves destruction of the embryos), and use of the RU-486 pill.

Kass, Leon R., *Human Cloning and Human Dignity: The Report of the President's Council on Bioethics* (New York: PublicAffairs Reports, 2002). A report from President George W. Bush's bioethics council with Kass as its chairman in which the ethical issues raised by cloning and matters of public policy are discussed.

Kitcher, Philip, *The Lives to Come: The Genetic Revolution and Human Possibilities* (New York: Simon & Schuster, 1997). A guide to advances in biomedical research including discussion of important moral and political questions such research raises.

Pence, Gregory, E., *Flesh of My Flesh: The Ethics of Cloning Humans* (Lanham, MD: Rowman & Littlefield, 1998). An examination of the ethical arguments over cloning and a qualified defense of the practice.

Pence, Gregory, E., *Cloning After Dolly: Who's Still Afraid?* (Lanham, MD: Rowman & Littlefield, 2005). A follow up to his 1998 book, extending his case in favor of cloning.

Stock, Gregory, *Redesigning Humans: Our Inevitable Genetic Future* (New York: Houghton Mifflin Co, 2002). Examines the emerging reproductive technologies for selection and alteration of human embryos. Stock argues that ethical objections to such selection and alteration are much like the objections formerly raised against in vitro fertilization.

Wilkinson, Stephen, *Choosing Tomorrow's Children* (New York: Oxford University Press, 2010). An examination of the moral issues raised by the prospects of selective reproduction.

Edited Collections

Klotzko, Arlene Judith (ed.), *The Cloning Sourcebook* (Oxford: Oxford University Press, 2001). Twenty-eight essays divided into four parts: (1) The Science of Cloning, (2) The Context of Cloning, (3) Cloning: The Ethical Issues, and (4) Cloning and Germ-Line Intervention: Policy Issues.

McGee, Glenn (ed.), *The Human Cloning Debate* (Berkeley, CA: Berkeley Hills Books, 2002). This anthology has nineteen selections debating the morality of cloning and includes five articles representing various religious (Jewish, Catholic, Protestant, Buddhist, and Islamic) perspectives on the issue.

Nussbaum, Martha C. and Cass R. Sunstein (eds.), *Clones and Clones: Facts and Fantasies about Human Cloning* (New York: W. W. Norton, 1998). A collection of twenty-four contributions organized into five sections: (1) Science, (2) Commentary, (3) Ethics and Religion, (4) Law and Public Policy, and (5) Fiction and Fantasy.

Rantala, M. L., and Arthur J Milgram (eds.), *Cloning: For and Against* (Chicago: Open Court, 1999). A wide-ranging collection of fifty-four essays by scientists, journalists, philosophers, religious leaders, and legal experts debating the ethical issues and matters of public policy regarding the prospect of cloning.

Ruse, Michael, and Christopher A. Pynes (eds.), *The Stem Cell Controversy*, 2nd ed. (Amherst, NY: Prometheus Books, 2006). Twenty-eight essays organized into five parts: (1) The Science of Stem Cells, (2) Medical Cures and Promises, (3) Moral Issues, (4) Religious Issues, and (5) Policy Issues.

Savulescu, Julian, and Nick Bostrom, (eds.), *Human Enhancement* (Oxford: Oxford University Press, 2009). Eighteen essays debating the general topic of human enhancement as well as specific applications including, for example, the issue of selection of children and the use of enhancements to improve athletic performance.

11 ⟩ The Death Penalty

As of 2008, the death penalty was legal in thirty-five U.S. states. In what is often called "the modern era" of the death penalty in the United States from 1976—when the 1972 moratorium on the death penalty was lifted by the U.S. Supreme Court—over 1000 individuals have been executed in the United States.[1] Although traditionally there has been wide support among U.S. citizens for the death penalty, this support has been declining in recent years. A Gallup Poll conducted in 1988 indicated that 79% of U.S. citizens favored the death penalty for the crime of murder. A 2008 Gallup Poll indicated that 64% of U.S. citizens support the death penalty for the crime of murder, while 30% are opposed. Another Gallup Poll conducted in 2006 is perhaps more revealing. This poll indicated that when presented with the option of sentencing someone to life in prison *without parole* for the crime of murder or sentencing that person to die, only 47% favored the death penalty, 48% favored life without parole, and 5% had no opinion.[2] At least in the United States, the death penalty continues to be a source of moral controversy.[3]

This controversy was further fueled in 2009 by the case of Cameron Todd Willingham, who in 2004 was executed in the state of Texas for setting fire to his house in 1991, which killed his three children. Willingham denied setting the fire and refused to enter a plea of guilty in exchange for a life sentence. In 2004 and after a detailed arson report concluded that the evidence against Willingham was "flimsy and inconclusive," Texas governor Rick Perry nevertheless denied a reprieve and Willingham was executed. In 2009, the Forensic Fire Commission hired an arson expert to review the evidence in the Willingham case. The expert, Craig L. Beyler, reported that the evidence in the case did not support the claim that the fire was a case of arson. In October of 2009, Beyler was set to testify before the Texas Forensic Science Commission, but two days before the commission was to hear this testimony, Governor Perry replaced the head and two other members of the commission. The newly appointed head, John M. Bradley, then canceled the meeting. The matter is still under consideration by the commission. Many are convinced that Texas executed an innocent man, and in his article, "Trial by Fire," about the Willingham case published in the The New Yorker, David Grann notes that Texas may be the first state forced to acknowledge that it carried out the execution of an innocent person.[4] Perhaps the most forceful moral argument against the death penalty is based on the claim that some people innocent of the crimes for which they are sentenced to die (Willingham may have been such a person) have been and likely will continue to be wrongly put to death. In recent years the use of DNA testing has also played a large role in exonerating some death row convicts and thus calling into question the death penalty. According to the *Innocence Project*, 245 individuals convicted of crimes have been exonerated by the use of DNA testing, 17 of whom were at one time sentenced to death.[5]

In addition to questions about the morality of the death penalty, there are also questions about its legality. The Eighth Amendment to the U.S. Constitution forbids "cruel and unusual" punishment, and some argue that the death penalty, because it is cruel and unusual, is unconstitutional and hence ought to be made illegal. This question of the constitutionality of the death penalty is the leading *general* question about its legality; but there are also *specific* legal questions about its use. For instance, in March 2005, the U.S. Supreme Court ruled it unconstitutional to execute juveniles—those under the age of eighteen who commit murder—a decision[6] in which the Court stressed the importance of appealing to "the evolving standards of decency that mark the progress of a maturing society" in determining which punishments are cruel and unusual.

But our concern here is with the *morality* of the death penalty, and the main questions are these:

- Is the death penalty ever a morally permissible form of punishment?
- If it is ever morally permitted, what best explains why such killing is permissible?

Those who answer the first question negatively are often referred to as **abolitionists,** and those who think that the death penalty is (or could be) morally justified (or perhaps even required) are often referred to as **retentionists.**[7] Of course, a retentionist need not and typically will not think that use of the death penalty is morally justified under *all* conditions. And so anyone who answers the first question affirmatively must address the second question.

In the remainder of this introduction, we shall consider important theoretical background that one must understand to be in a position to follow the moral controversy over the death penalty. We begin with some remarks about the idea of legal punishment and then proceed to outline two general approaches to the morality of punishment that influence moral discussion and debate over the specific punishment of execution.

1. LEGAL PUNISHMENT

The focus of this chapter is **legal punishment**—punishment administered by a legal authority. So, it is important at the outset to begin with a working definition of legal punishment, which will enable us to clarify the moral issues connected with legal punishment generally and the death penalty in particular.

Obviously, legal punishment presupposes a legal system, involving a set of laws and some mechanism of enforcement of those laws. Here, then, is a list of requirements that serve to define the very idea of a legal punishment.[8]

1. It must involve pain or other consequences normally considered unpleasant;
2. It must be for an offense against legal rules;
3. It must be of an actual or supposed offender for his or her offense;
4. It must be intentionally administered by human beings other than the offender;
5. It must be imposed and administered by an authority constituted by a legal system against which the offense is committed.

Because there is a moral presumption against the intentional infliction of pain or other unpleasant consequences on human beings, the practice of legal punishment calls for a moral justification. This moral question is addressed by theories about the morality of punishment.

2. THEORY MEETS PRACTICE

Two theories about the morality of punishment inform much of the debate over the death penalty. One theory is the **retributive theory of punishment**, which is basically Kantian in flavor; the other is the **consequentialist theory of punishment**. These theories attempt to answer two basic questions about the morality of punishment:

- What (if anything) morally justifies the practice of punishment?
- How much and what kinds of punishment are morally justified for various legal offenses?

The retributive and consequentialist theories provide competing answers to these two questions.

The Retributive Theory

The retributive theory in effect looks to the deeds of wrongdoers—both the fact that such deeds break laws and the specific nature of the deeds performed—in order to answer the two questions. So, the retributivist answer to the first question is

R1   What morally justifies punishment of wrongdoers is that those who break the law (and are properly judged to have done so) *deserve* to be punished.

A sense of fairness or justice prevails here. Wrongdoers are viewed as attempting to take unfair advantage of others and law-governed society generally, and the idea behind R1 is simply that justice demands that in response to crime, the wrongdoer suffer some sort of deprivation.

The retributivist response to the second question is

R2   The punishment for a particular offense against the law should "fit" the crime.

The task for the retentionist who accepts the retributive theory is to show that the death penalty is either required by, or at least consistent with, these two basic retributive principles (properly interpreted); opponents of the death penalty who accept the retributive theory must show that there is something about the death penalty that violates one or both of these principles (properly interpreted).

It is clear that R1 is neutral with regard to the moral justification of the death penalty—both retentionists and abolitionists, who otherwise accept the retributivist theory, can agree that punishment in general is justified because the wrongdoer deserves it. So the main focus of the retentionist's strategy in arguing about the death penalty will be R2. And here we find a variety of interpretations of R2, owing to the fact that there is more than one way of understanding the idea of a punishment *fitting* the crime. I will briefly mention two of them.

According to the principle expressed by **lex talionis** (law of retribution), making the punishment fit the crime is a matter of doing to the wrongdoer the *same kind of action* that he or she did to his or her victim(s). This "eye for an eye" principle implies that the appropriate punishment for the crime of murder is the death penalty, and finds a classic defense in the selection from Immanuel Kant included in our readings in this chapter.

An alternative interpretation of what it means to make the punishment fit the crime is the **principle of proportionality**, according to which the appropriate moral measure of specific punishments requires that they be in "proportion" to the crime: that the severity of the punishment should "be commensurate" with the gravity of the offense.

Thus, the task of the retributivist who wants to defend the death penalty is to provide an interpretation of R2 that (1) represents a philosophically defensible principle of punishment *and* that (2) implies or at least is consistent with having the death penalty. This challenge is discussed by Stephen Nathanson in one of the readings in this chapter, and he argues that it cannot plausibly be met.

Although Kant famously defends the death penalty by appealing to retributivist ideas about the morality of punishment, some abolitionists appeal (rather ironically) to Kant's Humanity formulation of the categorical imperative: *an action is right if and only if (and because) it is consistent with treating human beings as ends in themselves—as beings with an inherent worth or dignity.* Nathanson, for instance, appeals to Kant's principle in arguing against the morality of the death penalty, claiming that execution fails to comport with what he calls "personal desert" grounded in one's innate dignity as a human being.

So, in our selections here, we find both retentionists (Kant) and abolitionists (Nathanson) who accept a basically retributivist view of punishment, using that view to come to opposing conclusions about the morality of execution. What this shows is that in applying Kant's Humanity formulation to some specific issue, the main task for the Kantian is to provide and defend a plausible interpretation of treating humanity as ends and never as mere means.

The Consequentialist Theory

The consequentialist theory of the morality of punishment follows fairly directly from the basic idea of the consequentialist moral theory of right conduct that was presented in chapter 1: *an action or practice is right if and only if (and because) the overall value of the consequences of the action or practice would be at least as great as the overall value of the consequences of alternative actions and practices.* If we now appeal to this basic principle in responding to the two questions about the morality of punishment, we have

> **C1** Punishment as a response to crime is morally justified if and only if this practice, compared to any other response to crime, will likely produce as much overall intrinsic value as would any other response.

> **C2** A specific punishment for a certain crime is morally justified if and only if it would likely produce at least as much overall intrinsic value as would any other alternative punishment.

Consequentialist thinking about the death penalty focuses on C2 and thus on an assessment of the values of the consequences that are likely to result from having the death penalty compared to the values of the consequences that are likely to result from eliminating the death penalty. (Again, in cases in which a society does not currently have the death penalty, the comparison will be between instituting this punishment and not instituting it.)

Three things should be kept in mind about consequentialism as it bears on the morality of the death penalty. First, those who accept the consequentialist approach to the morality of punishment may or may not be committed thereby to the claim that the death penalty is morally justified—it all depends on what the values of the likely consequences of having the death penalty are compared with not having it. Second, this issue about values of the likely consequences is partly a moral issue but also partly a complicated empirical issue. The moral issue is this. What sorts of states of affairs (that might be consequences of some action or practice) have positive value, and what sorts have negative value? As we noted in the general introduction to this book, some consequentialists are utilitarians who think that happiness (welfare) is what has positive intrinsic value. But other consequentialists are perfectionists who hold that in addition to human happiness, such items as knowledge and achievement are intrinsically good. However, all parties to the dispute over the death penalty can agree that preserving human life—at least innocent human life, because it is necessary for achieving anything of intrinsic value—has a very high value, that the loss of human life is intrinsically bad or evil. If we agree, then, to focus on the value of human life when it comes to assessing the rightness of the death penalty, there is still the complicated empirical issue of determining whether employing this form of punishment will produce overall good enough consequences for society. This is an issue that criminologists and social scientists have studied and that is still being disputed.[9]

The third observation is that for purposes of evaluating the morality of some action or practice in terms of the values of its likely consequences, it is important to keep in mind that in so doing, one must consider not only the possible positive effects of the death penalty but also any negative effects that are likely to occur in allowing the death penalty. The same point applies when considering the possibility of abolishing the death penalty. So if we are to compare having the death penalty with not having it on strictly consequentialist grounds, then we have to consider the pluses and minuses of both options before we can move to a moral verdict about the morality of the death penalty.

Among the possible positive effects of having the death penalty are the following:

- **Deterrence:** Someone is *deterred* from committing murder by the threat of the death penalty only if his recognition of the death penalty as a possible consequence of committing murder explains why he doesn't commit it. Those who defend the death penalty on deterrence grounds argue that this punishment is *uniquely* effective in its deterrence effects in that there are some people who would be (or are) deterred by the threat of the death penalty, but would not be (or are not) deterred by a lesser punishment such as life without parole.

- **Prevention:** Someone is *prevented* by execution from committing a murder only if *had he not been executed, he would have gone ahead and committed the murder.* The point to be made about prevention and the death penalty is that even though someone's death prevents him from any further activity, it does not follow that he has thereby been prevented from performing certain specific acts. If, had he lived on, he would not have performed some action (for example, running for a seat in Congress), then it is not strictly correct to say that his death prevented him from running for a seat in Congress..

Among the possible negative consequences of having the death penalty are the following:

- Executing the innocent: The risk of executing innocent individuals owing to errors in the legal process that lead to conviction and "capital" (death penalty) sentencing.
- Incitement effect: Some argue that the death penalty may actually incite murder.[10]
- Financial cost: The death penalty cases cost more than other cases, and imposing the death penalty generally costs more than a sentence of life imprisonment without parole.[11]

These considerations about the consequences of the death penalty are taken up in the articles by Ernest van den Haag, Jeffrey H. Reiman, and the authors of the report on the evidence of errors in capital sentencing. Van den Haag defends the retentionist position on both retributivist and consequentialist grounds. Reiman is critical of the so-called common sense argument for the claim that the death penalty is a crime deterrent, an argument advanced by van den Haag. The final selection in this chapter is a report of an empirical study which, according to the authors, provides evidence of a significant error rate in the sentencing in death penalty cases.

NOTES

1. In the 1972 landmark decision *Furman v. Georgia* (408 U.S. 238), the U.S. Supreme Court ruled that the death penalty was unconstitutional *as then administered* because state statutes failed to provide guidelines for its use that would guard against its being imposed in an arbitrary and capricious manner. As a result of the Court's 1972 decision, states wanting to impose the death penalty worked to devise standards for its use that would provide safeguards against arbitrariness. In the 1976 case *Gregg v. Georgia* (428 U.S. 153), the Court approved Georgia's revised statutes governing the death penalty, thus lifting the moratorium.

2. The statistics just cited are taken from the Web site Death Penalty Information Center, www.deathpenaltyinfo.org.

3. According to *Amnesty International* (http://web.amnesty.org/pages/deathpenalty-countries-eng), as of 2008 more than two-thirds of the world's countries have abolished the death penalty either by law or by practice.

4. Grann's article was published in the September 7, 2009, edition. It can be found online at http://www.newyorker.com.

5. The *Innocence Project*, established in 1992, is devoted to "exonerating wrongfully convicted people through DNA testing and reforming the criminal justice system to prevent future injustice." <innocenceproject.org>.

6. *Roper v. Simmons,* No. 03-633.

7. Of course, this terminology is apt only if we are considering the morality of the death penalty in a country or state that currently allows it. Otherwise, those who are pro–death penalty are in favor of instituting it where it does not exist, and those against it are against its being instituted.

8. This list is taken from H. L. A. Hart, "Prolegomenon to the Principles of Punishment," in *Punishment and Responsibility* (Oxford: Oxford University Press, 1968).

9. See, for example, Richard A. Berk, "New Claims about Executions and General Deterrence: Déjà Vu All Over Again?" *Journal of Empirical Legal Studies* (July 19, 2004). Available at http://preprints.stat.ucla.edu/396/JELS.pap.pdf.

10. See for example, Mark Costonzo, *Just Revenge* (New York: St. Martin's Press, 1997).

11. See Richard C. Dieter, "Millions Misspent," in *The Death Penalty in America,* ed. Hugo Adam Bedau (Oxford: Oxford University Press, 1997).

IMMANUEL KANT

Punishment and the Principle of Equality

In this short excerpt from his 1997 *The Metaphysics of Morals,* part I, "The Doctrine of Right," Kant defends a version of the retributive theory of punishment and expresses opposition to consequentialist approaches. In particular, Kant argues that the appropriate moral principle for determining specific punishments is what he calls the "principle of equality," which expresses the idea that "the undeserved evil which any one commits on another, is to be regarded as perpetrated on himself." This idea in turn, claims Kant, implies that when someone slanders, steals, strikes, or kills another person, he or she (in effect) calls for those things to be done to him or her. Thus, on retributivist grounds, Kant argues that the death penalty for the crime of murder is morally required.

Recommended Reading: Kantian moral theory, chap. 1, sec. 2C.

The right of administering punishment, is the right of the sovereign as the supreme power to inflict pain upon a subject on account of a crime committed by him. The head of the state cannot therefore be punished: but his supremacy may be withdrawn from him. Any transgression of the public law which makes him who commits it incapable of being a citizen, constitutes a *crime,* either simply as a private crime (*crimen*), or also as a *public* crime (*crimen publicum*). Private crimes are dealt with by a civil court; public crimes by a criminal court.—Embezzlement or peculation of money or goods entrusted in trade, fraud in purchase or sale, if done before the eyes of the party who suffers, are private crimes. On the other hand, coining false money or forging bills of exchange, theft, robbery, etc., are public crimes, because the commonwealth, and not merely some particular individual, is endangered thereby. Such crimes may be divided into those of a *base* character (*indolis abjectae*) and those of a *violent* character (*indolis violentiae*).

Judicial or juridical punishment (*poena forensis*) is to be distinguished from natural punishment (*poena naturalis*), in which crime as vice punishes itself, and does not as such come within the cognizance of the legislator. Juridical punishment can

From Immanuel Kant, *The Philosophy of Law*, translated by W. Hastie (1887).

never be administered merely as a means for promoting another good, either with regard to the criminal himself or to civil society, but must in all cases be imposed only because the individual on whom it is inflicted *has committed a crime.* For one man ought never to be dealt with merely as a means subservient to the purpose of another, nor be mixed up with the subjects of real right. Against such treatment his inborn personality has a right to protect him, even though he may be condemned to lose his civil personality. He must first be found guilty and *punishable,* before there can be any thought of drawing from his punishment any benefit for himself or his fellow-citizens. The penal law is a categorical imperative; and woe to him who creeps through the serpent-windings of utilitarianism to discover some advantage that may discharge him from the justice of punishment, or even from the due measure of it, according to the pharisaic maxim: "It is better that *one* man should die than that the whole people should perish." For if justice and righteousness perish, human life would no longer have any value in the world.—What, then, is to be said of such a proposal as to keep a criminal alive who has been condemned to death, on his being given to understand that if he agreed to certain dangerous experiments being performed upon him, he would be allowed to survive if he came happily through them? It is argued that physicians might thus obtain new information that would be of value to the commonweal. But a court of justice would repudiate with scorn any proposal of this kind if made to it by the medical faculty; for justice would cease to be justice, if it were bartered away for any consideration whatever.

But what is the mode and measure of punishment which public justice takes as its principle and standard? It is just the principle of equality, by which the pointer of the scale of justice is made to incline no more to the one side than the other. It may be rendered by saying that the undeserved evil which any one commits on another, is to be regarded as perpetrated on himself. Hence it may be said: "If you slander another, you slander yourself; if you steal from another, you steal from yourself; if you strike another, you strike yourself; if you kill another, you kill yourself." This is the right of retaliation (*jus talionis*); and

properly understood, it is the only principle which in regulating a public court, as distinguished from mere private judgment, can definitely assign both the quality and the quantity of a just penalty. All other standards are wavering and uncertain; and on account of other considerations involved in them, they contain no principle conformable to the sentence of pure and strict justice. It may appear, however, that difference of social status would not admit the application of the principle of retaliation, which is that of "like with like." But although the application may not in all cases be possible according to the letter, yet as regards the effect it may always be attained in practice, by due regard being given to the disposition and sentiment of the parties in the higher social sphere. Thus a pecuniary penalty on account of a verbal injury, may have no direct proportion to the injustice of slander; for one who is wealthy may be able to indulge himself in this offence for his own gratification. Yet the attack committed on the honour of the party aggrieved may have its equivalent in the pain inflicted upon the pride of the aggressor, especially if he is condemned by the judgment of the court, not only to retract and apologize, but to submit to some meaner ordeal, as kissing the hand of the injured person. In like manner, if a man of the highest rank has violently assaulted an innocent citizen of the lower orders, he may be condemned not only to apologize but to undergo a solitary and painful imprisonment, whereby, in addition to the discomfort endured, the vanity of the offender would be painfully affected, and the very shame of his position would constitute an adequate retaliation after the principle of like with like. But how then would we render the statement: "If you *steal* from another, you steal from yourself"? In this way: that whoever steals anything makes the property of all insecure; he therefore robs himself of all security in property, according to the right of retaliation. Such a one has nothing, and can acquire nothing, but he has the will to live; and this is only possible by others supporting him. But as the state should not do this gratuitously, he must for this purpose yield his powers to the state to be used in penal labour; and thus he falls for a time, or it may be for life, into a condition of slavery.—But whoever has committed murder, must *die.* There is, in this case, no juridical substitute or surrogate, that can be given or taken for the satisfaction of justice. There is no *likeness* or proportion between life, however painful, and death; and therefore there is no equality between the crime of murder and the retaliation of it but what is judicially accomplished by the execution of the criminal. His death, however, must be kept free from all maltreatment that would make the humanity suffering in his person loathsome or abominable. Even if a civil society resolved to dissolve itself with the consent of all its members—as might be supposed in the case of a people inhabiting an island resolving to separate and scatter themselves throughout the whole world—the last murderer lying in the prison ought to be executed before the resolution was carried out. This ought to be done in order that every one may realize the desert of his deeds, and that bloodguiltiness may not remain upon the people; for otherwise they might all be regarded as participators in the murder as a public violation of justice.

The equalization of punishment with crime, is therefore only possible by the cognition of the judge extending even to the penalty of death, according to the right of retaliation.

READING QUESTIONS

1. How does Kant define "crime"? What are the differences between private and public crimes?
2. What is the distinction between judicial and natural punishment according to Kant?
3. Explain the Principle of Equality. How is it applied in cases where an individual commits the crimes of theft and murder according to Kant?
4. Explain the Right of Retaliation. How does Kant reply to the objection that there may be a difference in social status between a criminal and a victim that makes the Principle of Equality impossible to apply?

DISCUSSION QUESTIONS

1. Is Kant right to reject the utilitarian arguments against the death penalty? Why or why not? How might a utilitarian respond to the objections Kant raises?
2. Should we accept the Principle of Equality? Why or why not? Are there any other potential problems for the application of this principle other than the concern regarding the social status of the individuals involved in a crime?

STEPHEN NATHANSON

An Eye for an Eye?

Stephen Nathanson is critical of attempts to defend the morality of the death penalty on retributivist grounds. Focusing on the retributivist idea that a morally justified punishment must "fit" the crime, he considers two versions of what he calls the "equality" interpretation of this idea—a strict version of *lex talionis* and a version that would require that we make the punishment equivalent in the harm it brings to the wrongdoer as was done to the wrongdoer's victims. Against both versions of the equality interpretation Nathanson raises moral and practical objections. Nathanson then argues that the proportionality interpretation of "fit" also cannot be used to morally justify the death penalty. In the final section of his paper, Nathanson presents two arguments against the death penalty.

Recommended Reading: Kantian moral theory, chap. 1, sec. 2C.

AN EYE FOR AN EYE?

Suppose we . . . try to determine what people deserve from a strictly moral point of view. How shall we proceed?

The most usual suggestion is that we look at a person's actions because what someone deserves would appear to depend on what he or she does. A person's actions, it seems, provide not only a basis for a moral appraisal of the person but also a guide to how he should be treated. According to the *lex talionis* or principle of "an eye for an eye," we ought to treat people as they have treated others. What people deserve as recipients of rewards or punishments is determined by what they do as agents.

This is a powerful and attractive view, one that appears to be backed not only by moral common sense but also by tradition and philosophical thought. The most famous statement of philosophical support for this view comes from Immanuel Kant, who linked it directly with an argument for the death penalty. Discussing the problem of punishment, Kant writes,

> What kind and what degree of punishment does legal justice adopt as its principle and standard? None other than the principle of equality . . . the principle of not treating one side more favorably than the other. Accordingly, any undeserved evil that you inflict on someone else among the people is one that you do to yourself. If you vilify, you vilify yourself: if you steal from him, you steal from yourself; if you kill him, you kill yourself. Only the law of retribution (*jus talionis*) can determine exactly the kind and degree of punishment.[1]

Kant's view is attractive for a number of reasons. First, it accords with our belief that what a person deserves is related to what he does. Second, it appeals to a moral standard and does not seem to rely on any particular legal or political institutions. Third, it seems to provide a measure of appropriate punishment that can be used as a guide to creating laws and instituting punishments. It tells us that the punishment is to be identical with the crime. Whatever the criminal did to the victim is to be done in turn to the criminal.

From Stephen Nathanson, *An Eye for an Eye?* 2nd ed. (Lanham, MD: Rowman and Littlefield, 2001). Reprinted by permission.

In spite of the attractions of Kant's view, it is deeply flawed. When we see why, it will be clear that the whole "eye for an eye" perspective must be rejected.

PROBLEMS WITH THE EQUAL PUNISHMENT PRINCIPLE

There are two main problems with this view. First, appearances to the contrary, it does not actually provide a measure of moral desert. Second, it does not provide an adequate criterion for determining appropriate levels of punishment.

Let us begin with the second criticism, the claim that Kant's view fails to tell us how much punishment is appropriate for particular crimes. We can see this, first, by noting that for certain crimes, Kant's view recommends punishments that are not morally acceptable. Applied strictly, it would require that we rape rapists, torture torturers, and burn arsonists whose acts have led to deaths. In general, where a particular crime involves barbaric and inhuman treatment, Kant's principle tells us to act barbarically and inhumanly in return. So, in some cases, the principle generates unacceptable answers to the question of what constitutes appropriate punishment.

This is not its only defect. In many other cases, the principle tells us nothing at all about how to punish. While Kant thought it obvious how to apply his principle in the case of murder, his principle cannot serve as a general rule because it does not tell us how to punish many crimes. Using the Kantian version or the more common "eye for an eye" standard, what would we decide to do to embezzlers, spies, drunken drivers, airline hijackers, drug users, prostitutes, air polluters, or persons who practice medicine without a license? If one reflects on this question, it becomes clear that there is simply no answer to it. We could not in fact design a system of punishment simply on the basis of the "eye for an eye" principle.

In order to justify using the "eye for an eye" principle to answer our question about murder and the death penalty, we would first have to show that it worked for a whole range of cases, giving acceptable answers to questions about amounts of punishment. Then, having established it as a satisfactory general principle, we could apply it to the case of murder. It turns out, however, that when we try to apply the principle generally, we find that it either gives wrong answers or no answers at all. Indeed, I suspect that the principle of "an eye for an eye" is no longer even a principle. Instead, it is simply a metaphorical disguise for expressing belief in the death penalty. People who cite it do not take it seriously. They do not believe in a kidnapping for a kidnapping, a theft for a theft, and so on. Perhaps "an eye for an eye" once was a genuine principle, but now it is merely a slogan. Therefore, it gives us no guidance in deciding whether murderers deserve to die.

In reply to these objections, one might defend the principle by saying that it does not require that punishments be strictly identical with crimes. Rather, it requires only that a punishment produce an amount of suffering in the criminal which is equal to the amount suffered by the victim. Thus, we don't have to hijack airplanes belonging to airline hijackers, spy on spies, etc. We simply have to reproduce in them the harm done to others.

Unfortunately, this reply really does not solve the problem. It provides no answer to the first objection, since it would still require us to behave barbarically in our treatment of those who are guilty of barbaric crimes. Even if we do not reproduce their actions exactly, any action which caused equal suffering would itself be barbaric. Second, in trying to produce equal amounts of suffering, we run into many problems. Just how much suffering is produced by an airline hijacker or a spy? And how do we apply this principle to prostitutes or drug users, who may not produce any suffering at all? We have rough ideas about how serious various crimes are, but this may not correlate with any clear sense of just how much harm is done.

Furthermore, the same problem arises in determining how much suffering a particular punishment would produce for a particular criminal. People vary in their tolerance of pain and in the amount of unhappiness that a fine or a jail sentence would cause them. Recluses will be less disturbed by banishment than extroverts. Nature lovers will suffer more in prison than people who are indifferent to natural beauty. A literal application of the principle would require that we tailor punishments to individual sensitivities, yet this is at best impractical. To a large extent, the legal system must work with standardized and rather crude estimates of the negative impact that punishments have on people.

The move from calling for a punishment that is identical to the crime to favoring one that is equal in the harm done is no help to us or to the defense of the principle. "An eye for an eye" tells us neither what people deserve nor how we should treat them when they have done wrong.

PROPORTIONAL RETRIBUTIVISM

The view we have been considering can be called "equality retributivism," since it proposes that we repay criminals with punishments equal to their crimes. In the light of problems like those I have cited, some people have proposed a variation on this view, calling not for equal punishments but rather for punishments which are proportional to the crime. In defending such a view as a guide for setting criminal punishments, Andrew von Hirsch writes:

> If one asks how severely a wrongdoer deserves to be punished, a familiar principle comes to mind: Severity of punishment should be commensurate with the seriousness of the wrong. Only grave wrongs merit severe penalties; minor misdeeds deserve lenient punishments. Disproportionate penalties are undeserved— severe sanctions for minor wrongs or vice versa. This principle has variously been called a principle of "proportionality" or "just deserts"; we call it commensurate deserts.[2]

Like Kant, von Hirsch makes the punishment which a person deserves depend on that person's actions, but he departs from Kant in substituting proportionality for equality as the criterion for setting the amount of punishment.

In implementing a punishment system based on the proportionality view, one would first make a list of crimes, ranking them in order of seriousness. At one end would be quite trivial offenses like parking meter violations, while very serious crimes such as murder would occupy the other. In between, other crimes would be ranked according to their relative gravity. Then a corresponding scale of punishments would be constructed, and the two would be correlated. Punishments would be proportionate to crimes so long as we could say that the more serious the crime was, the higher on the punishment scale was the punishment administered.

This system does not have the defects of equality retributivism. It does not require that we treat those guilty of barbaric crimes barbarically. This is because we can set the upper limit of the punishment scale so as to exclude truly barbaric punishments. Second, unlike the equality principle, the proportionality view is genuinely general, providing a way of handling all crimes. Finally, it does justice to our ordinary belief that certain punishments are unjust because they are too severe or too lenient for the crime committed.

The proportionality principle does, I think, play a legitimate role in our thinking about punishments. Nonetheless, it is no help to death penalty advocates, because it does not require that murderers be executed. All that it requires is that if murder is the most serious crime, then murder should be punished by the most severe punishment on the scale. The principle does not tell us what this punishment should be, however, and it is quite compatible with the view that the most severe punishment should be a long prison term.

This failure of the theory to provide a basis for supporting the death penalty reveals an important gap in proportional retributivism. It shows that while the theory is general in scope, it does not yield any *specific* recommendations regarding punishment. It tells us, for example, that armed robbery should be punished more severely than embezzling and less severely than murder, but it does not tell us how much to punish any of these. This weakness is, in effect, conceded by von Hirsch, who admits that if we want to implement the "commensurate deserts" principle, we must supplement it with information about what level of punishment is needed to deter crimes.[3] In a later discussion of how to "anchor" the punishment system, he deals with this problem in more depth, but the factors he cites as relevant to making specific judgments (such as available prison space) have nothing to do with what people deserve. He also seems to suggest that a range of punishments may be appropriate for a particular crime. This runs counter to the death penalty supporter's sense that death alone is appropriate for some murderers.[4]

Neither of these retributive views, then, provides support for the death penalty. The equality principle fails because it is not in general true that the appropriate punishment for a crime is to do to the criminal what he has done to others. In some cases this is immoral, while in others it is impossible. The proportionality principle may be correct, but by itself it cannot determine specific punishments for specific crimes. Because of its flexibility and open-endedness, it is compatible with a great range of different punishments for murder.[5] . . .

THE SYMBOLISM OF ABOLISHING THE DEATH PENALTY

What is the symbolic message that we would convey by deciding to renounce the death penalty and to abolish its use?

I think that there are two primary messages. The first is the most frequently emphasized and is usually expressed in terms of the sanctity of human life, although I think we could better express it in terms of respect for human dignity. One way we express our respect for the dignity of human beings is by abstaining from depriving them of their lives, even if they have done terrible deeds. In defense of human well-being, we may punish people, for their crimes, but we ought not to deprive them of everything, which is what the death penalty does.

If we take the life of a criminal, we convey the idea that by his deeds he has made himself worthless and totally without human value. I do not believe that we are in a position to affirm that of anyone. We may hate such a person and feel the deepest anger against him, but when he no longer poses a threat to anyone, we ought not to take his life.

But, one might ask, hasn't the murderer forfeited whatever rights he might have had to our respect? Hasn't he, by his deeds, given up any rights that he had to decent treatment? Aren't we morally free to kill him if we wish?

These questions express important doubts about the obligation to accord any respect to those who have acted so deplorably, but I do not think that they prove that any such forfeiture has occurred. Certainly, when people murder or commit other crimes, they do forfeit some of the rights that are possessed by the law-abiding. They lose a certain right to be left alone. It becomes permissible to bring them to trial and, if they are convicted, to impose an appropriate—even a dreadful—punishment on them.

Nonetheless, they do not forfeit all their rights. It does not follow from the vileness of their actions that we can do anything whatsoever to them. This is part of the moral meaning of the constitutional ban on cruel and unusual punishments. No matter how terrible a person's deeds, we may not punish him in a cruel and unusual way. We may not torture him, for example. His right not to be tortured has not been forfeited. Why do these limits hold? Because this person remains a human being, and we think that there is something in him that we must continue to respect in spite of his terrible acts.

One way of seeing why those who murder still deserve some consideration and respect is by reflecting again on the idea of what it is to deserve something. In most contexts, we think that what people deserve depends on what they have done, intended, or tried to do. It depends on features that are qualities of individuals. The best person for the job deserves to be hired. The person who worked especially hard deserves our gratitude. We can call the concept that applies in these cases *personal* desert.

There is another kind of desert, however, that belongs to people by virtue of their humanity itself and does not depend on their individual efforts or achievements. I will call this impersonal kind of desert *human* desert. We appeal to this concept when we think that everyone deserves a certain level of treatment no matter what their individual qualities are. When the signers of the Declaration of Independence affirmed that people had inalienable rights to "life, liberty, and the pursuit of happiness," they were, appealing to such an idea. These rights do not have to be earned by people. They are possessed "naturally," and everyone is bound to respect them.

According to the view that I am defending, people do not lose all of their rights when they commit terrible crimes. They still deserve some level of decent treatment simply because they remain living, functioning human beings. This level of moral desert need not be earned, and it cannot be forfeited. This view may sound controversial, but in fact everyone who believes that cruel and unusual punishment should be forbidden implicitly agrees with it. That is, they agree that even after someone has committed a terrible crime, we do not have the right to do anything whatsoever to him.

What I am suggesting is that by renouncing the use of death as a punishment, we express and reaffirm our belief in the inalienable, unforfeitable core of human dignity.

Why is this a worthwhile message to convey? It is worth conveying because this belief is both important and precarious. Throughout history, people have found innumerable reasons to degrade the humanity of one another. They have found qualities in others that they hated or feared, and even when they were not threatened by these people, they have sought to harm them, deprive them of their liberty, or take their lives from them. They have often felt that they had good reasons to do these things, and they have invoked divine commands, racial purity, and state security to support their deeds.

These actions and attitudes are not relics of the past. They remain an awful feature of the contemporary world. By renouncing the death penalty, we show our determination to accord at least minimal respect even to those whom we believe to be personally vile or morally vicious. This is, perhaps, why we speak of the *sanctity* of human life rather than its value or worth. That which is sacred remains, in some sense, untouchable, and its value is not dependent on its worth or usefulness to us. Kant expressed this ideal of respect in the famous second version of the Categorical Imperative: "So act as to treat humanity, whether in thine own person or in that of any other, in every case as an end withal, never as a means only."[6] . . .

THE MORALITY OF RESTRAINT

I have argued that the first symbolic meaning conveyed by a renunciation of the death penalty is that human dignity must be respected in every person. To execute a person for murder is to treat that person as if he were nothing but a murderer and to deprive him of everything that he has. Therefore, if we want to convey the appropriate message about human dignity, we will renounce the death penalty.

One might object that, in making this point, I am contradicting the claim that killing in defense of oneself or others can be morally justified. If it is wrong to execute a person because this violates his dignity as a human being and deprives him of everything, it would seem to be equally wrong to kill this person as a means of defense. Defensive killing seems to violate these ideals in the same way that I claim punishing by death does. Isn't this inconsistent? Mustn't I either retreat to the absolute pacifist view or else allow that the death penalty is permissible?

. . . What I need to do now is to show that defensive killing is compatible with respect for human dignity. We can easily see that it is by recalling the central fact about killing to ward off an assault on one's own life. In this circumstance, someone will die. The only question open is whether it will be the attacker or the intended victim. We cannot act in any way that shows the very same respect and concern for both the attacker and the intended victim. Although we have no wish to harm the attacker, this is the only way to save the innocent person who is being attacked. In this situation, assuming that there are no alternative means of preventing the attack from succeeding, it is permissible to kill the attacker.

What is crucial here is that the choice is forced on us. If we do not act, then one person will be destroyed. There is no way of showing equal concern for both attacker and victim, so we give preference to the intended victim and accept the morality of killing the attacker.

The case of punishing by death is entirely different. If this punishment will neither save the life of the victim nor prevent the deaths of other potential victims, then the decision to kill the murderer is avoidable. We can restrain ourselves without sacrificing the life or well-being of other people who are equally deserving of respect and consideration. In this situation, the restrained reaction is the morally right one.

In addition to providing an answer to the objection, this point provides us with the second important message conveyed by the renunciation of punishing by death. When we restrain ourselves and do not take the lives of those who kill, we communicate the importance of minimizing killing and other acts of violence. We reinforce the idea that violence is morally legitimate only as a defensive measure and should be curbed whenever possible. . . .

When the state has a murderer in its power and could execute him but does not, this conveys the idea that even though this person has done wrong and even though we may be angry, outraged, and indignant with him, we will nonetheless control ourselves in a way that he did not. We will not kill him, even though we could do so and even though we are angry and indignant. We will exercise restraint, sanctioning killing only when it serves a protective function.

Why should we do this? Partly out of a respect for human dignity. But also because we want the state to set an example of proper behavior. We do not want to encourage people to resort to violence to settle conflicts when there are other ways available. We want to avoid the cycle of violence that can come from retaliation and counter-retaliation. Violence is a contagion that arouses hatred and anger, and if unchecked, it simply leads to still more violence.

The state can convey the message that the contagion must be stopped, and the most effective principle for stopping it is the idea that only defensive violence is justifiable. Since the death penalty is not an instance of defensive violence, it ought to be renounced.

We show our respect for life best by restraining ourselves and allowing murderers to live, rather than by following a policy of a life for a life. Respect for life and restraint of violence are aspects of the same ideal. The renunciation of the death penalty would symbolize our support of that ideal.

NOTES

1. Kant, *Metaphysical Elements of Justice,* translated by John Ladd (Indianapolis: Bobbs-Merrill, 1965), 101.

2. *Doing Justice* (New York: Hill & Wang, 1976), 66; reprinted in *Sentencing,* edited by H. Gross and A. von Hirsch (Oxford University Press, 1981), 243. For a more recent discussion and further defense by von Hirsch, see his *Past or Future Crimes* (New Brunswick, N.J.: Rutgers University Press, 1985).

3. von Hirsch, *Doing Justice,* 93–94. My criticisms of proportional retributivism are not novel. For helpful discussions of the view, see Hugo Bedau, "Concessions to Retribution in Punishment," in *Justice and Punishment,* edited by J. Cederblom and W. Blizek (Cambridge, Mass.: Bellinger, 1977), and M. Golding, *Philosophy of Law* (Englewood Cliffs, N.J.: Prentice Hall, 1975), 98–99.

4. See von Hirsch, *Past and Future Crimes,* ch. 8.

5. For more positive assessments of these theories, see Jeffrey Reiman, "Justice, Civilization, and the Death Penalty," *Philosophy and Public Affairs* 14 (1985): 115–48; and Michael Davis, "How to Make the Punishment Fit the Crime," *Ethics* 93 (1983).

6. *Fundamental Principles of the Metaphysics of Morals,* translated by T. Abbott (New York: Liberal Arts Press, 1949), 46.

READING QUESTIONS

1. Why is an eye for an eye an attractive view according to Nathanson? What are the two main problems he raises for this view, and what are the possible replies an advocate of such a view might make?

2. What is proportional retributivism and how does it differ from an eye for an eye?

3. What are the two messages that would be sent by abolishing the death penalty according to Nathanson? How does he reply to the objection that murderers forfeit their right to be respected as human beings?

4. How does Nathanson argue that killing in self defense is compatible with respect for the dignity of human life?

DISCUSSION QUESTIONS

1. Consider whether proportional retributivism is really an improvement on the view of an eye for an eye. How could an advocate of an eye for an eye respond to the claim that equality retributivism provides an adequate criterion for determining appropriate levels of punishment? Are there any other objections to the view that Nathanson fails to consider?
2. Would abolishing the death penalty send the messages that Nathanson suggests? What other messages, positive or negative, might the abolition of the death penalty send? What messages should be sent and how could we ensure that the right messages are sent?

ERNEST VAN DEN HAAG

A Defense of the Death Penalty

In response to various abolitionist arguments of the sort featured in the articles by Nathanson and Bedau, van den Haag defends the morality of the death penalty. In particular, he responds to these objections to the death penalty: (1) that it is unfairly administered, (2) that it is irreversible, (3) that it does not deter, (4) that its financial costs are prohibitive, (5) that it endorses and perhaps encourages unlawful killing, and (6) that it is degrading. Van den Haag then argues that the death penalty can be justified from both consequentialist and retributivist perspectives.

Recommended Reading: consequentialism, chap. 1, sec. 2A.

In an average year about 20,000 homicides occur in the United States. Fewer than 300 convicted murderers are sentenced to death. But because no more than 30 murderers have been executed in any recent year, most convicts sentenced to death are likely to die of old age. Nonetheless, the death penalty looms large in discussions: it raises important moral questions independent of the number of executions.

The death penalty is our harshest punishment. It is irrevocable: it ends the existence of those punished,

From Ernest van den Haag, "The Ultimate Punishment: A Defense," *Harvard Law Review* 99 (1986): 1662–69. Reprinted by permission of the author.

instead of temporarily imprisoning them. Further, although not intended to cause physical pain, execution is the only corporal punishment still applied to adults. These singular characteristics contribute to the perennial, impassioned controversy about capital punishment.

DISTRIBUTION

Consideration of the justice, morality, or usefulness, of capital punishment is often conflated with objections to its alleged discriminatory or capricious distribution among the guilty. Wrongly so. If capital punishment is immoral *in se*, no distribution among the guilty could make it moral. If capital punishment is moral, no distribution would make it immoral. Improper distribution cannot affect the quality of what is distributed, be it punishments or rewards. Discriminatory or capricious distribution thus could not justify abolition of the death penalty. Further, maldistribution inheres no more in capital punishment than in any other punishment.

Maldistribution between the guilty and the innocent is, by definition, unjust. But the injustice does not lie in the nature of the punishment. Because of the finality of the death penalty, the most grievous maldistribution occurs when it is imposed upon the innocent. However, the frequent allegations of discrimination and capriciousness refer to maldistribution among the guilty and not to the punishment of the innocent.

Maldistribution of any punishment among those who deserve it is irrelevant to its justice or morality. Even if poor or black convicts guilty of capital offenses suffer capital punishment, and other convicts equally guilty of the same crimes do not, a more equal distribution, however desirable, would merely be more equal. It would not be more just to the convicts under sentence of death.

Punishments are imposed on persons, not on racial or economic groups. Guilt is personal. The only relevant question is: does the person to be executed deserve the punishment? Whether or not others who deserved the same punishment, whatever their economic or racial group, have avoided execution is irrelevant. If they have, the guilt of the executed convicts would not be diminished, nor would their punishment be less deserved. To put the issue starkly, if the death penalty were imposed on guilty blacks, but not on guilty whites, or, if it were imposed by a lottery among the guilty, this irrationally discriminatory or capricious distribution would neither make the penalty unjust, nor cause anyone to be unjustly punished, despite the undue impunity bestowed on others.

Equality, in short, seems morally less important than justice. And justice is independent of distributional inequalities. The ideal of equal justice demands that justice be equally distributed, not that it be replaced by equality. Justice requires that as many of the guilty as possible be punished, regardless of whether others have avoided punishment. To let these others escape the deserved punishment does not do justice to them, or to society. But it is not unjust to those who could not escape.

These moral considerations are not meant to deny that irrational discrimination, or capriciousness, would be inconsistent with constitutional requirements. But I am satisfied that the Supreme Court has in fact provided for adherence to the constitutional requirement of equality as much as is possible. Some inequality is indeed unavoidable as a practical matter in any system. But, *ultra posse nemo obligatur.* (Nobody is bound beyond ability.)

Recent data reveal little direct racial discrimination in the sentencing of those arrested and convicted of murder. The abrogation of the death penalty for rape has eliminated a major source of racial discrimination. Concededly, some discrimination based on the race of murder victims may exist; yet, this discrimination affects criminal victimizers in an unexpected way. Murderers of whites are thought more likely to be executed than murderers of blacks. Black victims, then, are less fully vindicated than white ones. However, because most black murderers kill blacks, black murderers are spared the death penalty more often than are white murderers. They fare better than most white murderers. The motivation behind unequal distribution of the death penalty may well have been to discriminate against blacks, but the result has favored them. Maldistribution is thus a straw man for empirical as well as analytical reasons.

MISCARRIAGES OF JUSTICE

In a recent survey Professors Hugo Adam Bedau and Michael Radelet found that 7,000 persons were executed in the United States between 1900 and 1985 and that 25 were innocent of capital crimes. Among the innocents they list Sacco and Vanzetti as well as Ethel and Julius Rosenberg. Although their data may be questionable, I do not doubt that, over a long enough period, miscarriages of justice will occur even in capital cases.

Despite precautions, nearly all human activities, such as trucking, lighting, or construction, cost the lives of some innocent bystanders. We do not give up these activities, because the advantages, moral or material, outweigh the unintended losses. Analogously, for those who think the death penalty just, miscarriages of justice are offset by the moral benefits and the usefulness of doing justice. For those who think the death penalty unjust even when it does not miscarry, miscarriages can hardly be decisive.

DETERRENCE

Despite much recent work, there has been no conclusive statistical demonstration that the death penalty is a better deterrent than are alternative punishments. However, deterrence is less than decisive for either side. Most abolitionists acknowledge that they would continue to favor abolition even if the death penalty were shown to deter more murders than alternatives could deter. Abolitionists appear to value the life of a convicted murderer or, at least, his non-execution, more highly than they value the lives of the innocent victims who might be spared by deterring prospective murderers.

Deterrence is not altogether decisive for me either. I would favor retention of the death penalty as retribution even if it were shown that the threat of execution could not deter prospective murderers not already deterred by the threat of imprisonment. Still, I believe the death penalty, because of its finality, is more feared than imprisonment, and deters some prospective murderers not deterred by the threat of imprisonment. Sparing the lives of even a few prospective victims by deterring their murderers is more important than preserving the lives of convicted murderers because of the possibility, or even the probability, that executing them would not deter others. Whereas the lives of the victims who might be saved are valuable, that of the murderer has only negative value, because of his crime. Surely the criminal law is meant to protect the lives of potential victims in preference to those of actual murderers.

Murder rates are determined by many factors; neither the severity nor the probability of the threatened sanction is always decisive. However, for the long run, I share the view of Sir James Fitzjames Stephen: "Some men, probably, abstain from murder because they fear that if they committed murder they would be hanged. Hundreds of thousands abstain from it because they regard it with horror. One great reason why they regard it with horror is that murderers are hanged." Penal sanctions are useful in the long run for the formation of the internal restraints so necessary to control crime. The severity and finality of the death penalty is appropriate to the seriousness and the finality of murder.

INCIDENTAL ISSUES: COST, RELATIVE SUFFERING, BRUTALIZATION

Many nondecisive issues are associated with capital punishment. Some believe that the monetary cost of appealing a capital sentence is excessive. Yet most comparisons of the cost of life imprisonment with the cost of execution, apart from their dubious relevance, are flawed at least by the implied assumption that life prisoners will generate no judicial costs during their imprisonment. At any rate, the actual monetary costs are trumped by the importance of doing justice.

Others insist that a person sentenced to death suffers more than his victim suffered, and that this (excess) suffering is undue according to the *lex talionis* (rule of retaliation). We cannot know whether the murderer on death row suffers more than his victim suffered; however, unlike the murderer, the victim deserved none of the suffering inflicted. Further, the limitations of the *lex talionis* were meant to restrain private vengeance, not the social retribution that has taken its place. Punishment—regardless of the motivation—is not intended to revenge, offset, or compensate for the victim's suffering, or to be measured by it. Punishment is to vindicate the law and the social order undermined by the crime. This is why a kidnapper's penal confinement is not limited to the period for which he imprisoned his victim; nor is a burglar's confinement meant merely to offset the suffering or the harm he caused his victim; nor is it meant only to offset the advantage he gained.

Another argument heard at least since Beccaria is that, by killing a murderer, we encourage, endorse, or legitimize unlawful killing. Yet, although all punishments are meant to be unpleasant, it is seldom argued that they legitimize the unlawful imposition of identical unpleasantness. Imprisonment is not thought to legitimize kidnapping; neither are fines thought to legitimize robbery. The difference between murder and execution, or between kidnapping and imprisonment, is that the first is unlawful and undeserved, the second a lawful and deserved punishment for an unlawful act. The physical similarities of the punishment to the crime are irrelevant. The relevant difference is not physical, but social.

JUSTICE, EXCESS, DEGRADATION

We threaten punishments in order to deter crime. We impose them not only to make the threats credible but also as retribution (justice) for the crimes that were not deterred. Threats and punishments are necessary to deter and deterrence is a sufficient practical justification for them. Retribution is an independent moral justification. Although penalties can be unwise, repulsive, or inappropriate, and those punished can be pitiable, in a sense the infliction of legal punishment on a guilty person cannot be unjust. By committing the crime, the criminal volunteered to assume the risk of receiving a legal punishment that he could have avoided by not committing the crime. The punishment he suffers is the punishment he voluntarily risked suffering and, therefore, it is no more unjust to him than any other event for which one knowingly volunteers to assume the risk. Thus, the death penalty cannot be unjust to the guilty criminal.

There remain, however, two moral objections. The penalty may be regarded as always excessive as retribution and always morally degrading. To regard the death penalty as always excessive, one must believe that no crime—no matter how heinous—could possibly justify capital punishment. Such a belief can be neither corroborated nor refuted; it is an article of faith.

Alternatively, or concurrently, one may believe that everybody, the murderer no less than the victim, has an imprescriptible (natural?) right to life. The law therefore should not deprive anyone of life. I share Jeremy Bentham's view that any such "natural and imprescriptible rights" are "nonsense upon stilts."

Justice Brennan has insisted that the death penalty is "uncivilized," "inhuman," inconsistent with "human dignity" and with "the sanctity of life," that it "treats members of the human race as nonhumans, as objects to be toyed with and discarded," that it is "uniquely degrading to human dignity" and "by its very nature, [involves] a denial of the executed person's humanity." Justice Brennan does not say why he thinks execution "uncivilized." Hitherto most civilizations have had the death penalty, although it has been discarded in Western Europe, where it is currently unfashionable probably because of its abuse by totalitarian regimes.

By "degrading," Justice Brennan seems to mean that execution degrades the executed convicts. Yet philosophers, such as Immanuel Kant and G. F. W. Hegel, have insisted that, when deserved, execution, far from degrading the executed convict, affirms his humanity by affirming his rationality and his responsibility for his actions. They thought that execution, when deserved, is required for the sake of the convict's dignity. (Does not life imprisonment violate human dignity more than execution, by keeping alive a prisoner deprived of all autonomy?)

Common sense indicates that it cannot be death—our common fate—that is inhuman. Therefore, Justice Brennan must mean that death degrades when it comes not as a natural or accidental event, but as a deliberate social imposition. The murderer learns through his punishment that his fellow men have found him unworthy of living; that because he has murdered, he is being expelled from the community of the living. This degradation is self-inflicted. By murdering, the murderer has so dehumanized himself that he cannot remain among the living. The social recognition of his self-degradation is the punitive essence of execution. To believe, as Justice Brennan appears to, that the degradation is inflicted by the execution reverses the direction of causality.

Execution of those who have committed heinous murders may deter only one murder per year. If it does, it seems quite warranted. It is also the only fitting retribution for murder I can think of.

READING QUESTIONS

1. Why does van den Haag think that equality of distribution would not make the death penalty any more just to convicts?
2. What reasons does van den Haag give for thinking that miscarriages of justice are not enough to justify the claim that the death penalty is an unjust practice?
3. Why is deterrence not a decisive factor in the debate about the morality of the death penalty according to van den Haag?
4. How does van den Haag respond to the objections that the penalty of death is always excessive and always morally degrading?

DISCUSSION QUESTIONS

1. Should we agree with van den Haag's claims regarding the death penalty and miscarriages of justice? How many miscarriages of this kind do you believe would have to occur before they would fail to be offset by the moral benefit of the death penalty?
2. van den Haag claims that "if execution deters only one murderer a year, it is still warranted." He also claims that the death penalty is the only fitting retribution for murder. Does he provide sufficient reasons to accept each of these claims? Why or why not? If not, consider cases in which the death penalty would be warranted or what might be a fitting retribution for murder instead of the death penalty.

Jeffrey H. Reiman

Civilization, Safety, and Deterrence

Some defenders of the death penalty, including Ernest van den Haag, argue that even if we currently lack good scientific evidence that the death penalty is a uniquely effective deterrent, common sense tells us that this penalty is a crime deterrent. Against this common sense argument, Reiman raises four objections.

Recommended Reading: consequentialism, chap. 1, sec. 2A.

Were the death penalty clearly proven a better deterrent to the murder of innocent people than life in prison, we might have to admit that we had not yet reached a level of civilization at which we could protect ourselves without imposing this horrible fate on murderers, and thus we might have to grant the necessity of instituting the death penalty. But this is far from proven. The available research by no means clearly indicates that the death penalty reduces the incidence of homicide more than life imprisonment does. Even the econometric studies of Isaac Ehrlich, which purport to show that each execution saves seven or eight potential murder victims, have not changed this fact, as is testified to by the controversy and objections from equally respected statisticians that Ehrlich's work has provoked.[1]

Conceding that it has not been proven that the death penalty deters more murders than life imprisonment, van den Haag has argued that neither has it been proven that the death penalty does *not* deter more murders, and thus we must follow common sense which teaches that the higher the cost of something, the fewer people will choose it, and therefore at least some potential murderers who would not be deterred by life imprisonment will be deterred by the death penalty. Van den Haag writes:

> ...our experience shows that the greater the threatened penalty, the more it deters.

...Life in prison is still life, however unpleasant. In contrast, the death penalty does not just threaten to make life unpleasant—it threatens to take life altogether. This difference is perceived by those affected. We find that when they have the choice between life in prison and execution, 99% of all prisoners under sentence of death prefer life in prison....

From this unquestioned fact a reasonable conclusion can be drawn in favor of the superior deterrent effect of the death penalty. Those who have the choice in practice...fear death more than they fear life in prison....If they do, it follows that the threat of the death penalty, all other things equal, is likely to deter more than the threat of life in prison. One is most deterred by what one fears most. From which it follows that whatever statistics fail, or do not fail, to show, the death penalty is likely to be more deterrent than any other.[2]

Those of us who recognize how common-sensical it was, and still is, to believe that the sun moves around the earth, will be less willing than Professor van den Haag to follow common sense here, especially when it comes to doing something awful to our fellows. Moreover, there are good reasons for doubting common sense on this matter. Here are four:

1. From the fact that one penalty is more feared than another, it does not follow that the more feared penalty will deter more than the less feared, unless we know that the less feared penalty is not fearful enough to deter everyone who can

From Jeffrey H. Reiman, "Justice, Civilization, and the Death Penalty: Answering van den Haag," *Philosophy and Public Affairs* 14 (1985), pp. 115–48.

be deterred—and this is just what we don't know with regard to the death penalty. Though I fear the death penalty more than life in prison, I can't think of any act that the death penalty would deter me from that an equal likelihood of spending my life in prison wouldn't deter me from as well. Since it seems to me that whoever would be deterred by a given likelihood of death would be deterred by an *equal* likelihood of life behind bars, I suspect that the common-sense argument only seems plausible because we evaluate it unconsciously assuming that potential criminals will face larger likelihoods of death sentences than of life sentences. If the likelihoods were equal, it seems to me that where life imprisonment was improbable enough to make it too distant a possibility to worry much about, a similar low probability of death would have the same effect. After all, we are undeterred by small likelihoods of death every time we walk the streets. And if life imprisonment were sufficiently probable to pose a real deterrent threat, it would pose as much of a deterrent threat as death. And this is just what most of the research we have on the comparative deterrent impact of execution versus life imprisonment suggests.

2. In light of the fact that roughly 500 to 700 suspected felons are killed by the police in the line of duty every year, and the fact that the number of privately owned guns in America is substantially larger than the number of households in America, it must be granted that anyone contemplating committing a crime *already* faces a substantial risk of ending up dead as a result.[3] It's hard to see why anyone *who is not already deterred by this* would be deterred by the addition of the more distant risk of death after apprehension, conviction, and appeal. Indeed, this suggests that people consider risks in a much cruder way than van den Haag's appeal to common sense suggests—which should be evident to anyone who contemplates how few people use seatbelts (14% of drivers, on some estimates), when it is widely known that wearing them can spell the difference between life (outside prison) and death.[4]

3. Van den Haag has maintained that deterrence doesn't work only by means of cost–benefit calculations made by potential criminals. It works also by the lesson about the wrongfulness of murder that is slowly learned in a society that subjects murderers to the ultimate punishment. But if I am correct in claiming that the refusal to execute even those who deserve it has a civilizing effect, then the refusal to execute also teaches a lesson about the wrongfulness of murder. My claim here is admittedly speculative, but no more so than van den Haag's to the contrary. And my view has the added virtue of accounting for the failure of research to show an increased deterrent effect from executions *without having to deny the plausibility of van den Haag's common-sense argument that at least some additional potential murderers will be deterred by the prospect of the death penalty*. If there is a deterrent effect from *not executing*, then it is understandable that while executions will deter some murderers, this effect will be balanced out by the weakening of the deterrent effect of not executing, such that no net reduction in murders will result.[5] And this, by the way, also disposes of van den Haag's argument that, in the absence of knowledge one way or the other on the deterrent effect of executions, we should execute murderers rather than risk the lives of innocent people whose murders might have been deterred if we had. If there is a deterrent effect of not executing, it follows that we risk innocent lives either way. And if this is so, it seems that the only reasonable course of action is to refrain from imposing what we know is a horrible fate.[6]

4. Those who still think that van den Haag's common-sense argument for executing murderers is valid will find that the argument proves more than they bargained for. Van den Haag maintains that, in the absence of conclusive evidence on the relative deterrent impact of the death penalty versus life imprisonment, we must follow common sense and assume that if one punishment is more fearful than another, it will deter some potential criminals not deterred by the less fearful punishment. Since people sentenced to death will almost universally try to get their sentences changed to life in prison, it follows that death is more fearful than life imprisonment, and thus that it will deter some additional murderers. Consequently, we should institute the death penalty to save the lives these additional murderers would have taken. But, since people

sentenced to be tortured to death would surely try to get their sentences changed to simple execution, the same argument proves that death-by-torture will deter still more potential murderers. Consequently, we should institute death-by-torture to save the lives these additional murderers would have taken. Anyone who accepts van den Haag's argument is then confronted with a dilemma: Until we have conclusive evidence that capital punishment is a greater deterrent to murder than life imprisonment, he must grant *either* that we should not follow common sense and not impose the death penalty; *or* we should follow common sense and torture murderers to death. In short, either we must abolish the electric chair or reinstitute the rack. Surely, this is the *reductio ad absurdum* of van den Haag's common-sense argument.

NOTES

1. Isaac Ehrlich, "The Deterrent Effect of Capital Punishment: A Question of Life or Death," *American Economic Review 65* (June 1975):397–417. For reactions to Ehrlich's work, see Alfred Blumstein, Jacqueline Cohen, and Daniel Nagin, eds., *Deterrence and Incapacitation: Estimating the Effects of Criminal Sanctions on Crime Rates* (Washington, D.C.: National Academy of Sciences, 1978), esp. pp. 59–63 and 336–60; Brian E. Forst, "The Deterrent Effect on Capital Punishment: A Cross-State Analysis," *Minnesota Law Review 61* (May 1977):743–67, Deryck Beyleveld, "Ehrlich's Analysis of Deterrence," *British Journal of Criminology 22* (April 1982):101–23, and Isaac Ehrlich, "On Positive Methodology, Ethics and Polemics in Deterrence Research," *British Journal of Criminology 22* (April 1982):124–39.

2. Ernest van den Haag and John P. Conrad, *The Death Penalty: A Debate* (New York: Plenum Press, 1983), 68, 69.

3. On the number of people killed by the police, see Lawrence W. Sherman and Robert H. Langworthy, "Measuring Homicide by Police Officers," *Journal of Criminal Law and Criminology 70*, no. 4 (Winter 1979):546–60; on the number of privately owned guns, see Franklin Zimring, *Firearms and Violence in American Life* (Washington, D.C.: U.S. Government Printing Office, 1968), pp. 6–7.

4. *AAA World* (Potomac ed.) 4, no. 3 (May–June 1984), pp. 18c and 18i.

5. A related claim has been made by those who defend the so-called brutalization hypothesis by presenting evidence to show that murders *increase* following an execution. See, for example, William J. Bowers and Glenn L. Pierce, "Deterrence or Brutalization: What is the Effect of Executions?" *Crime & Delinquency 26*, no. 4 (October 1980):453–84. They conclude that each execution gives rise to two additional homicides in the month following, and that these are real additions, not just a change in timing of the homicides (ibid., p. 481). My claim, it should be noted, is not identical to this, since, as I indicate in the text, what I call "the deterrence effect of not executing" is not something whose impact is to be seen immediately following executions but over the long haul, and, further, my claim is compatible with finding no net increase in murders due to executions. Nonetheless, should the brutalization hypothesis be borne out by further studies, it would certainly lend support to the notion that there is a deterrent effect of not executing.

6. Van den Haag writes: "If we were quite ignorant about the marginal deterrent effects of execution, we would have to choose—like it or not—between the certainty of the convicted murderer's death by execution and the likelihood of the survival of future victims of other murderers on the one hand, and on the other his certain survival and the likelihood of the death of new victims. I'd rather execute a man convicted of having murdered others than put the lives of innocents at risk. I find it hard to understand the opposite choice" (p. 69). Conway was able to counter this argument earlier by pointing out that the research on the marginal deterrent effects of execution was not *inconclusive* in the sense of *tending to point both ways*, but rather in the sense of *giving us no reason to believe that capital punishment saves more lives than life imprisonment*. He could then answer van den Haag by saying that the choice is not between risking the lives of murderers and risking the lives of innocents, but between killing a murderer with no reason to believe lives will be saved, and sparing a murderer with no reason to believe lives will be lost (David A. Conway, "Capital Punishment and Deterrence: Some Considerations in Dialogue Form," *Philosophy & Public Affairs*, 3 (1974), pp. 442–43). This, of course, makes the choice to spare the murderer more understandable than van den Haag allows. Events, however, have overtaken Conway's argument. The advent of Ehrlich's research, contested though it may be, leaves us in fact with research that tends to point both ways.

READING QUESTIONS

1. How does Reiman characterize van den Haag's argument for the death penalty?
2. What are the four reasons Reiman offers for thinking that we should doubt some of our common sense intuitions about the nature of the death penalty as a deterrent?
3. Explain in detail why Reiman thinks that the refusal to execute has a civilizing effect and that it teaches the wrongfulness of murder. Explain also why he believes that van den Haag's argument proves more than it might seem to.

DISCUSSION QUESTIONS

1. Is Reiman right to claim that the refusal to execute individuals would have a civilizing effect? Why or why not? What reasons could we offer for thinking that refusing to execute murderers does not teach the wrongfulness of murder?
2. To what extent do you think criminals take the consequences of their actions into consideration, especially in the case of murder? Discuss how the answers to this question could affect the debate about the moral status of capital punishment.

JAMES S. LIEBMAN, JEFFREY FAGAN, VALERIE WEST, AND JONATHAN LLOYD

Capital Attrition: Error Rates in Capital Cases, 1973–1995[1]

The authors of this report studied the error rate in U.S. cases from 1975 to 1995 involving "capital sentences" (cases in which the sentence was the death penalty). One of the central findings of this research is that in 68 percent of capital cases that underwent judicial review, the death sentences were overturned owing to various errors including incompetent legal representation of the accused and suppression by the prosecution of evidence that the accused was in fact innocent of the crime in question. One implication that the authors draw from this research is that the public's awareness of such error rates would lower the public's confidence in the credibility of the death penalty.

Capital Attrition: Error Rates in Capital Cases, 1973–1995. Reprinted with permission from *Texas Law Review*, 1839 (2000).

I. INTRODUCTION

Americans seem to be of two minds about the death penalty. In the last several years, the overall number of executions has risen steeply, reaching a fifty-year high this year. Although two-thirds of the public support the penalty, this figure represents a sharp decline from the four-fifths of the population that endorsed the death penalty only six years ago, leaving support for capital punishment at a twenty-year low. When life without parole is offered as an alternative, support for the penalty drops even more—often below a majority. Grants of executive clemency reached a twenty-year high in 1999.

In 1999 and 2000, governors, attorneys general, and legislators in Alabama, Arizona, Florida, and Tennessee fought high-profile campaigns to increase the speed and number of executions. In the same period, however:

- The Republican Governor of Illinois, with support from a majority of the electorate, declared a moratorium on executions in that state.
- The Nebraska Legislature attempted to enact a similar moratorium. Although the Governor vetoed the legislation, the legislature appropriated money for a comprehensive study of the even-handedness of the state's exercise of capital punishment.
- Similar studies have been ordered in Illinois by the Chief Justice, task forces of both houses of the state legislature, and the governor. Indiana, Maryland, and the Attorney General of the United States have followed suit.
- Serious campaigns to abolish the death penalty are under way in New Hampshire and (with the support of the governor and a popular former Republican senator) in Oregon.
- The Florida Supreme Court and Mississippi Legislature recently acted to improve the quality of counsel in capital cases, and bills with bipartisan sponsorship aiming to do the same and to improve capital prisoners' access to DNA evidence have been introduced in both houses of the United States Congress.

Observers in the *Wall Street Journal, New York Times Magazine, Salon,* and on *ABC This Week* see "a tectonic shift in the politics of the death penalty."

In April 2000 alone, George Will and Reverend Pat Robertson—both strong death penalty supporters—expressed doubts about the manner in which government officials carry out the penalty in the United States, and Robertson subsequently advocated a moratorium on *Meet the Press.* In response, Reverend Jerry Falwell called for continued—even swifter—execution of death sentences.

Fueling these competing initiatives are two beliefs about the death penalty: One is that death sentences move too slowly from imposition to execution, undermining deterrence and retribution, subjecting our criminal laws and courts to ridicule, and increasing the agony of victims. The other is that death sentences are fraught with error, causing justice too often to miscarry, and subjecting innocent and other undeserving defendants—mainly, racial minorities and the poor—to execution.

Some observers attribute these seemingly conflicting events and opinions to "America's own schizophrenia. . . . We believe in the death penalty, but shrink from it as applied." These views may not conflict, however, and Americans who hold *both* may not be irrational. It may be that capital sentences spend too much time under review *and* that they are fraught with disturbing amounts of error. Indeed, it may be that capital sentences spend so much time under judicial review precisely *because* they are persistently and systematically fraught with alarming amounts of error, and that the expanding production of death sentences may compound the production of error. We are led to this conclusion by a study of all 4,578 capital sentences that were finally reviewed by stale direct appeal courts and all 599 capital sentences that were finally reviewed by federal habeas corpus courts between 1973 and 1995.

II. SUMMARY OF CENTRAL FINDINGS

In *Furman v. Georgia* in 1972, the Supreme Court reversed all existing capital statutes and death sentences. The modern death-sentencing era began the next year with the implementation of new capital statutes designed to satisfy *Furman.* In order to collect information about capital sentences imposed and reviewed after 1973 (no central repository exists), we conducted a painstaking search, beginning in 1995, of all published state and federal judicial opinions in the United States conducting direct and habeas review of capital judgments, and many of the available opinions conducting state post-conviction review of those judgments. We then (1) checked and catalogued all cases the opinions revealed, (2) collected hundreds of items of information about each case from the published decisions and the NAACP Legal Defense Fund's quarterly death row census, (3) tabulated the results, and (4) (still in progress) conducted multivariate statistical analyses to identify factors that may contribute to those results.

Six years in the making, our central findings thus far are these:

- Between 1973 and 1995, approximately 5,760 death sentences were imposed in the United States. Only 313 (5.4 percent; one in 19) of those resulted in an execution during the period.
- Of the 5,760 death sentences imposed in the study period, 4,578 (79 percent) were finally reviewed on "direct appeal" by a state high court. Of those, 1,885 (41 percent) were thrown out on the basis of "serious error" (error that substantially undermines the reliability of the outcome).
- Most of the remainder of the death sentences were then inspected by state post-conviction courts. Although incomplete, our data (reported in *A Broken System*) reveal that state post-conviction review is an important source of review in some states, including Florida, Georgia, Indiana, Maryland, Mississippi, and North Carolina. In Maryland, for example, at least 52 percent of capital judgments reviewed in state post-conviction proceedings during the study period were overturned due to serious error; the same was true for at least 25 percent of the capital judgments that were similarly reviewed in Indiana, and at least 20 percent of those reviewed in Mississippi.

- Of the death sentences that survived state direct and post-conviction review, 599 were finally reviewed on a first habeas corpus petition during the 23-year study period. Of those 599, 237 (40 percent) were overturned due to serious error.
- The "overall success rate" of capital judgments undergoing judicial inspection, and its converse, the "overall error-rate," are crucial factors in assessing the efficiency of our capital punishment system. The "overall *success* rate" is the proportion of capital judgments that underwent, and *passed,* the three-stage judicial inspection process during the study period. The "overall *error* rate" is the frequency with which capital judgments that underwent full inspection were *overturned* at one of the three stages due to serious error. Nationally, over the entire 1973–1995 period, the overall error-rate in our capital punishment system was 68 percent.
- Because "serious error" is error that substantially undermines the reliability of the guilt finding or death sentence imposed at trial, each instance of that error warrants public concern. The most common errors found at the state post-conviction stage (where our data are most complete) are (1) egregiously incompetent defense lawyering (accounting for 37 percent of the state post-conviction reversals), and (2) prosecutorial suppression of evidence that the defendant is innocent or does not deserve the death penalty (accounting for another 16 percent—or 19 percent, when all forms of law enforcement misconduct are considered). These two violations count as "serious," and thus warrant reversal, *only* when there is a "reasonable probability" that, but for the responsible lawyer's miscues, the outcome of the trial would have been different.

The result of very high rates of serious, reversible error among capital convictions and sentences, and very low rates of capital reconviction and resentencing, is the severe attrition of capital judgments. Figure 11.1 illustrates the sources of attrition, and the eventual disposition of cases where death sentences were reversed.

For every 100 death sentences imposed and reviewed during the study period, 41 were turned

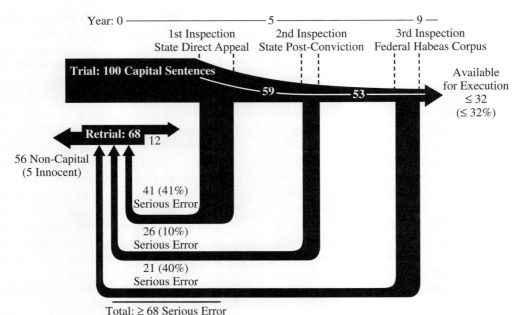

FIGURE 11.1   The Attrition of Capital Judgments

back at the state direct appeal phase because of serious error. Of the 59 that got through that phase to the second, state post-conviction stage, at least 10 percent—six more of the original 100—were turned back due to serious flaws. And, of the 53 that got through that stage to the third, federal habeas checkpoint, 40 percent—an additional 21 of the original 100—were turned back because of serious error. Overall, at least 68 of the original 100 were thrown out because of serious flaws, compared to only 32 (or less) that were found to have passed muster—after an average of nine to ten years had passed.

And for each such 68 individuals whose death sentences were overturned for serious error, 82 percent (56) were found on retrial *not* to have deserved the death penalty, including 7 percent (5) who were *cleared of the capital offense.*

• The seriousness of these errors is also revealed by what happens on retrial when the errors are supposed to be cured. In our state post-conviction sub-study where the post-reversal outcome is known, over four-fifths (56 out of 68) of the capital judgments that were reversed

were replaced on retrial with a sentence less than death, or no sentence at all. In the latter regard, fully 7 percent of the reversals for serious error resulted in a determination on retrial that the defendant was *not guilty* of the offense for which he previously was sentenced to die.

• High error rates pervade American capital-sentencing jurisdictions, and are geographically dispersed. Among the twenty-six death-sentencing jurisdictions in which at least one case has been reviewed in both the state and federal courts and in which information about all three judicial inspection stages is available:

1. 24 (92 percent) have overall error rates of 52 percent or higher;
2. 22 (85 percent) have overall error rates of 60 percent or higher;
3. 15 (61 percent) have overall error rates of 70 percent or higher;
4. Among other states, Georgia, Alabama, Mississippi, Indiana, Oklahoma, Wyoming, Montana, Arizona, and California have overall error rates of 75 percent or higher.

It is sometimes suggested that Illinois, whose governor declared a moratorium on executions in January 2000 because of the spate of death row exonerations there, generates less reliable death sentences than other states. Our data do not support this hypothesis: The overall rate of error found to infect Illinois capital sentences (66 percent) is slightly *lower* than the rate in capital-sentencing states as a whole (68 percent).

- High error rates have persisted for decades. More than 50 percent of all cases reviewed were found seriously flawed in twenty of the twenty-three study years, including in seventeen of the last nineteen years. In half of the years studied, the error rate was over 60 percent. Although error rates detected on state direct appeal and federal habeas corpus dropped modestly in the early 1990s, they went back up in 1995. The amount of error detected on state post-conviction has risen sharply throughout the 1990s.

- The 68 percent rate of *capital* error found by the three stage inspection process is much higher than the <15 percent rate of error those same three inspections evidently discover in *noncapital* criminal cases.

- Appointed federal judges are sometimes thought to be more likely to overturn capital sentences than elected state judges. In fact, state judges are the first and most important line of defense against erroneous death sentences. Elected state judges found serious error in and reversed 90 percent (2,133 of 2,370) of the capital sentences that were overturned during the study period.

- Under current state and federal law, capital prisoners have a legal right to one round of direct appellate, state post-conviction, and federal habeas corpus review. The high rates of error found at *each* stage, and at the *last* stage, and the persistence of high error rates over time and across the nation, confirm the need for multiple judicial inspections. Without compensating changes at the front-end of the process, the contrary policy of cutting back on judicial inspection would seem to make no more sense than responding to the impending insolvency of the Social Security System by forbidding it to be audited.

- Finding this much error takes time. Calculating the amount of time using information in published decisions is difficult. Only a small percentage of direct appeals decisions report the sentence date. By the end of the habeas stage, however, a much larger proportion of sentencing dates is reported in some decision in the case. It accordingly is possible to get an accurate sense of timing for the 599 cases that were finally reviewed on habeas corpus. Among those cases:

1. It took an average of 7.6 years after the defendant was sentenced to die to complete federal habeas corpus consideration in the 40 percent of habeas cases in which reversible error was found.
2. In the cases in which no error was detected at the third inspection stage and an execution occurred, the average time between sentence and execution was nine years.

As Figure 11.2 reveals, high rates of error frustrate the goals of the death penalty system. Figure 11.2 compares the overall rates of error detected during the state direct appeal and federal inspection process in the twenty-eight states with at least one capital judgment that has completed that process, to the percentage of death sentences imposed by each state that it has carried out by execution. In general, where the overall error rate reaches 55 percent or above (as is true for the vast majority of the states), the percentage of death sentences carried out drops below 7 percent.

Figure 11.2 illustrates another finding of interest: The pattern of capital outcomes for the State of Virginia is clearly an outlier—the State's high execution rate is nearly *double* that of the next nearest state and *five times* the national average, and its low rate of capital reversals is nearly *half* that of the next nearest state and less than *one-fourth* the national average. A sharp discrepancy between Virginia and other capital-sentencing jurisdictions characterizes most of our analyses. That discrepancy presents an important question for further study: Are Virginia capital judgments in fact half as prone to serious error as the next lowest state and four times less than the national average? Or, on the other hand, are its courts more

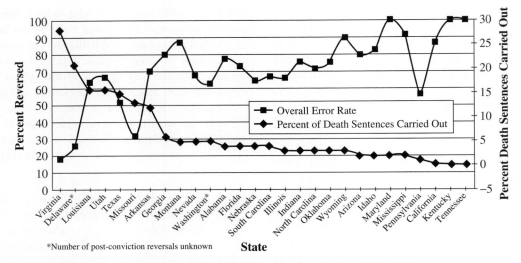

FIGURE 11.2 Overall Error Rate and Percent of Death Sentences Carried Out, 1973–1995

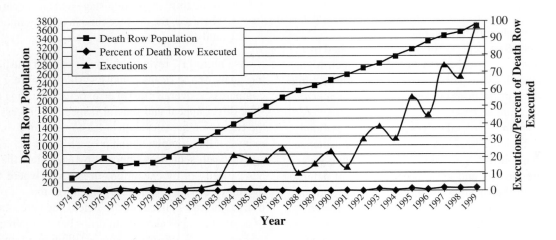

FIGURE 11.3 Persons on Death Row and Percent and Number Executed, 1976–1999

tolerant of serious error? Or, have Virginia's legislature and courts censored opportunities to inspect verdicts and detect error by procedurally constraining the definition of error and the time within which errors can be identified? We will address this issue below and in a subsequent report.

The rising number of executions nationally does not render these patterns obsolete. Instead of indicating improvement in the *quality* of death sentences under review, the rising number of executions may simply reflect how many *more* sentences have piled up awaiting review. If the error-induced pile-up of cases on death row is the *cause* of rising executions, their rise provides no proof that a cure has been found for disturbingly high and persistent error rates. The rising execution rate and the persistent error rate increase the likelihood of an increase in the incidence of wrongful executions. To see why this is true, consider a factory that produced 100 toasters in a year, only 32 of which worked. The factory's production problem would not be deemed fixed if the company simply raised its production run to 200 the next year in order to double the number of working toasters to 66. Thus, the real question isn't the *number* of death sentences carried out each year, but the *proportion*.

Figure 11.3 shows that in contrast to the annual *number* of executions (the middle line in the chart), the *proportion* of death row inmates executed each year (the bottom line in the chart) has remained remarkably stable—and extremely low. Since post-*Furman* executions began in earnest in 1984, the nation has executed only an average of about 1.3 percent of its death row inmates each year; in no year has it carried out more than 2.6 percent—or one in thirty-nine—of death sentences exposed to full review.

Figure 11.3 suggests that the rising number of executions (the middle line) is *not* caused by any improvement in the quality of capital judgments, but instead by the inexorable pile-up of people on death row (the top line in the chart) as judges struggle to exercise a degree of quality control over decade upon decade of error-prone capital judgments.

III. CONFIRMATION FROM A PARALLEL STUDY

Results from a parallel study by the U.S. Department of Justice suggest that our 32 percent figure for valid death sentences actually overstates the chance of execution. The 1998 Justice Department study includes a report showing the outcome of the 263 death sentences imposed in 1989. A final disposition of only 103 of the 263 death sentences had been reached nine years later. Of those 103, 78 (76 percent) had been overturned by a state or federal court. Only thirteen death sentences had been carried out. So, for every one member of the death row class of 1989 whose case was finally reviewed and who was executed as of 1998, six members of the class had their cases overturned in the courts. Because of the intensive review needed to catch so much error, 160 (61 percent) of

the 263 death sentences imposed in 1989 were still under scrutiny nine years later.

The approximately 3,500 people on death row today have been waiting an average of 7.4 years for a final declaration that their capital verdict is error-free—or, far more probably, that it is the product of serious error. Of the 6,700 people sentenced to die between 1973 and 1999, only 598—less than one in eleven—were executed. About three times as many had their capital judgments overturned or gained clemency.

IV. IMPLICATIONS OF CENTRAL FINDINGS

To help appreciate these findings, consider a scenario that might unfold any of the nearly 300 times a year that a death sentence is imposed in the United States. Suppose the defendant, or a relative of the victim, asks a lawyer or the judge, "What now?" Based on almost a quarter century of experience in thousands of cases in twenty-eight death-sentencing states in the United States between 1973 and 1995, a responsible answer would be: "The capital conviction or sentence will probably be overturned due to serious error. It'll take about nine years to find out, given how many other capital cases being reviewed for likely error are lined up ahead of this one. If the judgment is overturned, a lesser conviction or sentence will probably be imposed."

As any person hearing this statement would likely conclude as a matter of common sense, these reversals due to serious error, and the time it takes to expose them, are costly. Capital trials and sentences cost more than noncapital ones. Each time they have to be done over—as happens 68 percent of the time—some or all of that difference is doubled. The error-detection system all this capital error requires is itself a huge expense—evidently *millions of dollars* per case.

When retrial demonstrates that nearly four-fifths of the capital judgments in which serious error is found are more appropriately handled as non-capital cases (and in a sizable number of instances, as non-murder or even *non-criminal* cases), it is hard to escape the conclusion that most of the resources the capital system currently consumes are not buying the public, or victims, the valid death sentences for egregious offenses that a majority support. Rather, those resources are being wasted on the trial and review of cases that for the most part are not capital and are seriously flawed.

Public faith in the courts and the criminal justice system is another casualty of high capital error rates. When the vast majority of capital sentencing jurisdictions carry out fewer than 6 percent of the death sentences they impose, and when the nation as a whole never executes more than 3 percent of its death population in a year, the retributive and deterrent credibility of the death penalty is low.

When condemned inmates turn out to be *innocent,* the error is different in its consequences, but *not* evidently different in its causes, from the other serious error discussed here. There is no accounting for this cost: to the wrongly convicted; to the family of the victim, whose search for justice and closure has been in vain; to later victims whose lives are threatened—and even taken—because the real killers remain at large; and to the wrongly *executed,* should justice miscarry at trial, and should reviewing judges,

harried by the amount of capital error they are asked to catch, miss one.

If the issue was the fabrication of toasters (to return to our prior example), or the licensing of automobile drivers, or the conduct of any other private- or public-sector activity, neither the consuming public nor managers and investors would tolerate the error rates and attendant costs that dozens of states and the nation as a whole have tolerated in their capital punishment systems over the course of decades. Any system with this much error and expense would be halted immediately, examined, and either reformed or scrapped. We ask taxpayers, public managers, and policymakers whether that same response is warranted here, when the issue is not the content and quality of tomorrow's breakfast but whether society has a swift and sure response to murder and whether thousands of men and women condemned for that crime in fact deserve to die.

NOTE

1. For a fuller description of the findings presented in this article, see "A Broken System: The Persistent Patterns of Reversals of Death Sentences in the United States," by Andrew Gelman, James S. Liebman, Valerie West, and Alexander Kiss, *Journal of Empirical Legal Studies* 1 (July 2004), pp. 209–61.

READING QUESTIONS

1. How do the authors define overall success and failure rates? What were the overall success and error rates of convictions for capital murder? Cite some of the other relevant statistics mentioned by the authors regarding the error rates in capital cases.
2. What are the three stages of judicial review the cases in consideration can undergo? How do the authors define "serious error"? What are the two most common types of error found in capital murder cases?
3. Explain what the authors discovered about the average time involved in the review of capital cases. What effect does the length of the review process have on the criminal justice system?
4. What are some of the implications of these findings according to the authors? Why do the authors think that public faith in the courts is a casualty of these findings?

DISCUSSION QUESTIONS

1. Are the authors right to assume that knowledge of information regarding the overall success and failure rates of capital cases would undermine the public's faith in the court system? Why or why not? What other responses might the public have to this information?

2. What do the authors' findings suggest about the moral status of the death penalty? Consider and discuss whether the death penalty could be morally permissible even if there are serious errors made in capital cases.

ADDITIONAL RESOURCES

Web Resources

Amnesty International, <http://web.amnesty.org/pages/deathpenalty>. Pro-abolitionist site that reports data regarding the death penalty and its use worldwide.

Death Penalty Information Center, <http://www.deathpenaltyinfo.org/>. Pro-abolitionist forum.

The Pew Forum on Religion & Public Life, <http://pewforum.org/docs/>. An excellent, non-partisan resource for learning about the history of the death penalty in the United States and the current debate over its moral status.

Pro-Death Penalty.Com, <http://www.prodeathpenalty.com/>. A retentionist forum.

Bedau, Hugo Adam, "Punishment," <http://plato.stanford.edu/entries/punishment>. An overview of theories about the ethical justification of punishment.

Authored Books

Costanzo, Mark, *Just Revenge: Costs and Consequences of the Death Penalty* (New York: St. Martin's Press, 1997). An accessible, short book with emphasis on the social scientific research relevant to the death penalty.

Hanks, Gardner C., *Against the Death Penalty: Christian and Secular Arguments against the Death Penalty* (Scottdale, PA: Herald Press, 1997). A survey and defense of Christian and secular arguments against the death penalty.

Pojman, Louis, & Rieman, Jeffrey, *The Death Penalty* (Lanham, MD: Rowman & Littlefield, 1997). A debate between Pojman, a retentionist, and Rieman, an abolitionist.

van den Haag, Ernest, and Conrad, John P., *The Death Penalty: A Debate* (New York: Plenum Books, 1983). van den Haag defends the retentionist view and Conrad defends the abolitionist position.

Edited Collections

Baird, Robert M., and Rosenbaum, Stuart E. (eds.), *Punishment and the Death Penalty: The Current Debate* (Amherst, NY: Prometheus Books, 1995). Part I includes six essays by various philosophers over the justification of punishment and Part II contains twelve essays about the morality of the death penalty.

Bedau, Hugo Adam (ed.), *The Death Penalty in America: Current Controversies* (Oxford: Oxford University Press, 1997). A comprehensive anthology with thirty-three articles ranging over issues about the constitutionality, racial bias, public support, and morality of the death penalty in the United States.

12) War, Terrorism, and Torture

The contemporary world is besieged by acts of war, terrorism, and torture. The 9/11 destruction of the World Trade Center in New York and the coordinated attack on the Pentagon, as well as the terrorist bombings in Madrid (2004), London (2005), and Mumbai (2006, 2009), have ignited intense worldwide debate over the nature, causes, and morality of war and terrorism. This debate has been further intensified, particularly in the United States, as a result of the U.S. wars in Iraq and Afghanistan. Also, the deplorable abuse of prisoners by U.S. military personnel at the Abu Ghraib prison near the Iraqi capital of Baghdad, as well as so-called enhanced interrogation techniques including waterboarding, has sparked not only worldwide outrage, but also debate over the nature and morality of torture. Many people believe that at least some wars are, or could be, morally justifiable, even if many past and present wars are not justifiable. Terrorism and torture are widely condemned as morally wrong. The central moral questions these practices raise are these:

- Is (war), (terrorism), (torture) ever morally permissible?
- If any of these activities are ever morally permissible, what best explains why this is so?

I have inserted parentheses in the first question to indicate that for each of the three activities, we can raise the moral questions just mentioned, and so we should not just assume that their moral status—whether they are ever permissible and, if so, why—is the same. It may turn out, as some have argued, that, for instance, war is sometimes permissible but terrorism and torture never are.

In order to begin thinking about these moral issues, let us first consider questions and issues about the morality of war, and then turn to terrorism and torture in order.

1. WAR

As with all disputed moral issues, we must begin by specifying the subject of dispute—war. The *Merriam-Webster Online Dictionary* has this entry:

War

(1): a state of usually open and declared armed hostile conflict between states or nations;
(2): a period of such armed conflict[1]

There are also entries for both "hot" and "cold" wars. A **hot war** is defined as "a conflict involving actual fighting," whereas a **cold war** is described as "a conflict over ideological differences carried on by methods short of sustained overt military action and usually without breaking off diplomatic relations." The focus in this chapter is on so-called hot wars—which, in the twentieth century, include World Wars I and II, the Korean War, the Vietnam War, and the Gulf War—and are often the focus of contemporary moral discussions. More recently, of course, the U.S.-Iraq war has been subject to intense moral dispute.

2. TERRORISM

As with moral questions about war, a discussion of the morality of terrorism must begin with a working definition of terrorism. Here we immediately run into controversy, partly because some individuals make the moral wrongness of the violence associated with terrorism part of terrorism's very definition so that by definition terrorism is morally wrong. Such "question-begging" definitions—definitions that merely assume something controversial about what is being defined—are to be avoided here because for one thing, they inhibit asking legitimate moral questions about the sort of violent activity carried on in the name of some cause that we want to be able to ask. For another thing, merely defining terrorism as morally wrong will not solve any moral issues about this kind of violence. After all, those who might think that some forms of violence—for, say, political causes—are morally justified (or might be) can simply grant the morally loaded use of the term "terrorism" and call the kind of violence they might defend by some other name—"freedom fighting," for example. Again, mere verbal stipulation will not settle legitimate moral questions about various forms of violence carried out in the name of various causes.

One definition that avoids the sort of question begging just mentioned and that seems to capture what most people mean when speaking of terrorism is provided by James P. Sterba in his article included in this chapter:

> **Terrorism** is the use or threat of violence against innocent people to elicit terror in them, or in some other group of people, in order to further a political objective.

Three elements of this definition are worth noting. First, terrorism on Sterba's definition is not confined to nonstate groups and individuals; rather, it allows that states can engage in terrorism. In this way, Sterba's definition is broader than the one embraced by the U.S. State Department, which restricts terrorist activity to "subnational groups or clandestine agents." Second, Sterba's definition restricts the targets of terrorist activity to "innocent people," and similar definitions restrict targets to "noncombatants." But we find other definitions are not as restrictive in this way. For instance, Tomis Kapitan defines terrorism as being directed upon "civilians," where it is left open whether civilians are innocent.[2] Third, many if not most definitions of terrorism, like Sterba's, mention *political* goals and objectives as part of what terrorism is. This seems to be entirely in keeping with how the term is typically used. However, we do find definitions that are not restrictive in this way. For instance, in one of our readings, Haig Khatchadourian defines terrorism as involving "acts of coercion or of actual use of force, aiming at monetary gain (predatory terrorism), revenge (retaliatory terrorism), a political end (political terrorism), or a putative moral/religious end (moralistic/religious terrorism)." One implication of this definition is that acts of bank robbing for monetary gain, for example, count as acts of terrorism, thus greatly widening the scope of what is to count as terrorism. In any case, the important point here is that in reading about terrorism, one must keep an eye on how the term is being defined.

3. TORTURE

The main focus of discussion about the morality of torture is whether it is absolutely morally wrong or whether in certain "necessity" cases—often illustrated by "ticking bomb" cases—the use of torture to extract potentially life-saving information is morally permissible. Of course, we have to begin with the question "What is torture?"

According to article 1 of the 1984 United Nations Convention against Torture and Other Cruel, Inhuman or Degrading Treatment or Punishment:

> "**Torture**" means any act by which severe pain or suffering, whether physical or mental, is intentionally inflicted on a person for such purposes as [1] obtaining from him or a third person information or a confession, [2] punishing him for an act he or a third person has committed or is suspected of having committed, or [3] intimidating or coercing him or a third person, or [4] for any reason based on discrimination of any kind, when such pain or suffering is inflicted by or at the instigation of or with the consent or acquiescence of a public official or other person acting in an official capacity.[3]

Three observations about this definition are worth making here. First, the bracketed numbers (which I have inserted) indicate the various purposes or aims of acts of torture. Taking note of these various possible purposes is important because if torture is ever morally permissible, its permissibility will certainly depend in large measure upon the purposes of the torturer. For instance, in his article included in our readings, Henry Shue distinguishes between what he calls **terrorist torture** (which would presumably include acts of torture motivated by the sorts of purposes mentioned in 2, 3, and 4 in the previous definition) and **interrogational torture,** done for the purpose (mentioned in 1) of obtaining information from the victim in order, for example, to prevent or avert some impending terrorist attack.

Second, the UN Convention also distinguishes torture from what it refers to as "acts of cruel, inhuman, or degrading treatment or punishment which do not amount to torture as defined in article 1." This raises the obvious problem of distinguishing acts of torture from acts of cruel, inhumane, or degrading treatment. Here is not the place to delve into this difficult matter. Rather, for present purposes, it will suffice to list a few acts of what are widely taken to be torture: severe beatings, being made to stand for hours or days at a time, extended sleep deprivation, withholding food or water, being buried alive, electric shocks, having one's head forced underwater until nearly asphyxiated, rape, threatened rape, and threatened death. Such activities as slaps in the face that fall short of severe beatings, shouting obscenities at prisoners, and making prisoners engage in sexual acts are clearly instances of inhuman and degrading treatment, but they seem to fall short of torture.[4]

The third observation about the previous UN Convention definition is that to count as torture, the act must be performed by, initiated by, or consented to by a public official or someone acting in an official capacity. This rules out cases that we might ordinarily consider as torture, as when an individual, acting alone and for reasons of personal revenge, kidnaps and inflicts severe pain and suffering on his victim over an extended period of time. But this restriction is perfectly reasonable, given that the aim of the convention was to establish international law.

With a basic understanding of the concepts of war, terrorism, and torture now before us, let us turn to moral issues.

4. THEORY MEETS PRACTICE

Let us begin by distinguishing two sorts of questions we may ask about the morality of war. First, when (if ever) is a state or nation morally justified in going to war against another state or nation? Second, which sorts of military activities are morally permissible within war? In relation to both questions, we find what we may nonprejudicially refer to as extreme positions: moral nihilism and moral pacifism. Let us consider each of these in order, after which we will proceed to consider other, less "extreme," moral perspectives on war.

In discussions about the morality of war, **moral nihilism** is the view that moral considerations do not apply to war, that questions of moral right and wrong, good and bad do not apply because war creates a context in which "anything goes." Thus, to the question "Is war ever morally justified?" the nihilist in effect refuses to answer the question, claiming that questions about morality do not arise in connection with war. Of course, since there are two general sorts of questions about the morality of war—going to war and conduct within war— one might hold the view that although morality does apply to the decision to go to war and thus claim that some wars are morally justified and others are not, one might also hold that within war, anything goes morally speaking. Moral nihilism is the topic of the selection by Richard A. Wasserstrom included in this chapter.

At the other end of the moral spectrum is **antiwar pacifism,** according to which wars are always (or at least nearly always) morally wrong.[5] One basis for such a view is the idea that all intentional killing of human beings is morally wrong. But many individuals, including many moral philosophers, hold that some cases of intentionally killing human beings are morally justified—cases of self-defense being the most widely accepted. In the context of war, this would mean that wars of self-defense might sometimes be justified. But there is far more to the moral positions of those who would defend the morality of at least some wars, and here we find that perhaps the most prominent moral approach to war (or at least the most widely discussed) is **just-war theory,** to which we now turn.

Natural Law and Just-War Theory

Just-war theory is perhaps best understood as an extension of natural law ethics applied to the issue of war. One need not embrace natural law theory in order to accept the moral provisions of just-war theory, but in outlining this approach to the morality of war (and terrorism), appealing to some ideas from natural law theory—particularly the doctrine of double effect—is useful.[6]

Just-war theory makes the common distinction between questions about the morality of going to war, **jus ad bellum,** and about the morality of activities within a war, **jus in bello.** Each of these two parts is made up of various moral provisions. Here is a visual aid.

Jus ad Bellum

(Provisions governing going to war)

Legitimate Authority | Just Cause | Last Resort | Prospect of Success | Political Proportionality

Jus in Bello

(Provisions governing military activity within war)

Military Necessity | Discrimination | Military Proportionality

FIGURE 12.1   Just-War Theory

In what immediately follows, I will briefly state each of these provisions, at least as they are often understood.

Jus ad bellum

Here, then, is a statement of the five principles composing this part of just-war theory:[7]

Legitimate authority: War must be declared by a legitimate authority—typically understood as the officials of a recognized government. This condition is often understood as a requirement for violence or force to be considered war. So, for instance, spontaneous uprisings that result in violence do not count as wars.

Just cause: There must be a just cause for going to war. A very restrictive interpretation of this provision would require that the war be one of self-defense, in which a government is responding to violent aggression or is attempting to prevent imminent violent aggression by another state. This restrictive interpretation rules out any "aggressive" war that would, for example, forcefully interfere with the internal affairs of some state for "humanitarian" purposes.

Last resort: All reasonable alternatives to going to war must be exhausted. What counts as a "reasonable alternative" is left open to interpretation. Certainly, nonviolent diplomatic solutions are to be sought before going to war.

Prospect of success: In going to war, there must be a reasonable prospect of success. Again, what counts as reasonable is left open, as is the question of what counts as success. Clearly, winning a war counts as success, but in some cases a futile struggle to the death might be justified if the alternative is enslavement or extermination by a nation's opponent.

Political proportionality: The violence of war must be proportional to the wrong being resisted. Both here and in the provisions of jus in bello, considerations of consequences are relevant, though, unlike a pure consequentialist approach, this provision is but one requirement of the just-war approach to the morality of war.

Let us now turn to the provisions of jus in bello. Here my plan is to relate them to the **doctrine of double effect (DDE)**, which was presented in the moral theory primer (chapter 1) as part of natural law ethics. This doctrine is meant to address the question of whether it is ever morally permissible to knowingly bring about evil consequences in the pursuit of some good. According to DDE, in cases in which an action would produce (or likely produce) at least some good effects but at least one bad effect (where for present purposes we can restrict good and bad to the preservation and loss of human life respectively), the action in question is morally permitted only if all of the following conditions are met:

Intrinsic permissibility: The action, apart from its effects, must be morally permissible;
Necessity: The bad effect is unavoidable, and thus the action is necessary if the good effect is to be brought about;
Nonintentionality: The bad effect is not intended—it is neither one's end nor a means to one's end; and
Proportionality: The badness of the bad effect is not grossly out of proportion to the goodness of the good effect being sought.

The latter three principles, reformulated so that they each address aggression in war, yield the following provisions that compose jus in bello:

Jus in Bello

Military necessity: The military activity in question (e.g., the bombing of a military installation) must be judged to be *necessary* in order to bring about some justifiable military end.
Discrimination: The deaths of innocent noncombatants must not be directly intended either as an end of the military action or as a means to some further military purpose. Talk of innocent noncombatants here is meant to refer in particular to citizens of a state who are not actively engaged in that state's war efforts. Clearly, an unarmed young child counts as an innocent noncombatant, whereas armed soldiers do not. Other individuals—for example, those forced to work in a munitions plant—present hard cases requiring that this provision be more finely interpreted.
Military proportionality: Whatever good end the military action in question is supposed to serve, the likely evil that results from that activity (e.g., deaths and loss of property) must not be grossly out of proportion to the intended good ends of that activity.

To understand these provisions, consider cases of "tactical bombing," in which the aim of the mission is to destroy an enemy military base; however, in so doing, it is predictable (given the base's location) that a number of innocent noncombatants will be killed by the bombing. If the conditions of necessity and proportionality are met in a particular case of tactical bombing, then because the deaths of innocent civilians is not intended (either as an end or as a means to the tactical mission), this kind of activity would be morally permitted by just-war theory. Readers can contrast such tactical cases with cases of "terrorist bombing," in which the immediate aim is to kill innocent civilians in an effort to weaken enemy morale.

Finally, it is worth emphasizing that these provisions, as I have indicated in my presentation, require a good deal of interpretation in applying them to concrete cases. But, of course, this is true of all general moral principles.

Turning for a moment to our readings, in the selection from Khatchadourian, we find an argument for the absolute moral impermissibility of terrorist acts based partly on an appeal to the requirements of jus in bello. In another selection on terrorism, Michael Walzer also argues that terrorism is always morally wrong, though he explores this matter by considering various excuses someone might offer in an attempt to justify certain acts of terrorism. Again, Sterba appeals to just-war theory, but, interestingly, he defends what he calls "**just-war pacifism**"—a form of antiwar pacifism according to which, because of the stringent requirements of just-war theory, the massive use of lethal force, as in warfare, is almost always morally wrong.

Rights Approaches

As explained in chapter 1, section 2D, a rights-based moral theory takes the notion of moral rights as basic in approaching moral issues. Different rights-based theories disagree over which rights are fundamental. Khatchadourian, for example (who argues both from the perspective of just-war theory and from an appeal to human rights), denies that there is a right to life but claims that all human beings have a basic right to be treated as moral persons and that this right includes a right of "all to be free to satisfy their needs and interests." Of course, one need not suppose that rights are absolute, and so a rights approach need not by its very nature condemn all possible forms of terrorism. Nevertheless, some do, including the one defended by Khatchadourian.

Kantian Theory

The morality of torture is the topic of the selection by Henry Shue in which he brings to bear both just-war theory and Kantian moral principles in arguing against the moral permissibility of torture. We have already noted how the principles of just-war theory apply to war and to terrorism, and similar points apply to how it applies to torture. Kantian moral theory will appeal to either the Universal Law or the Humanity formulations of the categorical imperative (or both) in arriving at moral verdicts about various forms of torture.

Consequentialism

Consequentialist approaches to torture (as with any moral issue) may take either an act or a rule form. You may recall from chapter 1, section 2A, that act consequentialism focuses on the specific, concrete action being morally evaluated and considers the net intrinsic value of the consequences that would likely be caused by the action and compares them to the net intrinsic value of the likely consequences of some alternative action open to the agent at the time. By contrast, rule consequentialism considers not the values of the likely consequences of the specific, concrete actions under scrutiny, but rather the values of the likely consequences of the general acceptance of various alternative rules under which the action and its alternatives fall. So, on this version of consequentialism, a concrete action is permitted in a certain set of circumstances if a rule permitting acts of that type in the circumstances in question has at least as high an **acceptance value** as any other alternative rule for those circumstances.[8] So a specific, concrete act of torture would be wrong from a rule consequentialist perspective if a rule prohibiting torture in those circumstances would, if widely accepted, result in a greater level of net intrinsic value than would a rule permitting torture in those circumstances.

Alan M. Dershowitz, in our final reading selection of the chapter, briefly discusses this contrast between act and rule consequentialism, and goes on to defend an essentially act consequentialist (he calls it a "case utilitarian") approach—not to the whole of morality but to the morality of torture in "ticking bomb" cases—cases in which, for example, torture is used on a captured terrorist who has information about the whereabouts of a deadly explosive set to go off.

NOTES

1. As a third item, this dictionary includes "state of war," which is then linked to further definitions of this expression.

2. Tomis Kapitan, "The Terrorism of 'Terrorism,'" in *Terrorism and International Justice,* ed. James P. Sterba (New York: Oxford University Press, 2003).

3. A full text of this convention is available online at www.hrweb.org/legal/cat.html. This document goes on to state that "no exceptional circumstances whatsoever, whether a state of war or a threat of war, internal political instability or any other public emergency" would justify the use of torture: torture, according to this declaration, is *absolutely* prohibited. See article 16. It also prohibits the practice of "rendition" (article 3), whereby one country sends its prisoners to another country—often to a country known for harsh treatment of its prisoners. In 1994, the United States ratified the UN Convention, though in so doing it adopted a more restrictive definition of torture requiring that in order to be torture, the act "must be *specifically intended* to inflict *severe* physical or mental pain or suffering." For a useful discussion of the definition of torture generally as well as torture under U.S. law, see John T. Parry, "Escalation and Necessity: Defining Torture at Home and Abroad," in *Torture: A Collection,* ed. Sanford Levinson (New York: Oxford University Press, 2004).

4. In the wake of the Abu Ghraib prison scandal, U.S. senator (and former Vietnam War POW) John McCain proposed an amendment (attached to a defense spending bill) that protects anyone in U.S. custody from "cruel, inhuman, or degrading treatment." On December 15, 2005, the Bush-led U.S. White House, under pressure from members of both Republican and Democratic parties, agreed to the language of McCain's amendment.

5. There are other more restrictive forms of pacifism, including, for example, nonviolent pacifism, which maintains that any form of violence against human beings is wrong. See the reading by James P. Sterba for more on pacifism and its varieties.

6. For instance, Michael Walzer in *Just and Unjust Wars,* 2nd ed. (New York: Basic Books, 1992) defends a version of just-war approach to the morality of war, but is not a natural law theorist.

7. In presenting the provisions of jus ad bellum, I am following C. A. J. Coady's presentation of it in his "War and Terrorism," in *A Companion to Applied Ethics,* ed. R. G. Frey and Christopher Heath Wellman (Oxford: Blackwell Publishing, 2003).

8. The "acceptance value" of rule (in relation to some group) is defined as the net intrinsic value that would result were the rule accepted by a significant proportion of the members of the group in question.

RICHARD A. WASSERSTROM

Does Morality Apply to War?

Wasserstrom addresses the claim that when it comes to war, moral considerations are simply out of place—that given the nature of war, morality is irrelevant. Against this view—called moral nihilism—Wasserstrom considers three possible interpretations of the view that morality cannot be applied to war, and for each of them he argues that reasons for the nihilist position are unconvincing.

1. WAR AND MORAL NIHILISM

Before we examine the moral criteria for assessing war, we must examine the claim that it is not possible to assess war in moral terms. . . . For want of a better name for this general view, I shall call it moral nihilism in respect to war. If it is correct, there is, of course, no point in going further.

. . . During the controversy over the rightness of the Vietnam War there have been any number of persons, including a large number in the university, who have claimed that in matters of war (but not in other matters) morality has no place. The war in Vietnam may, they readily concede, be stupid, unwise, or against the best interests of the United States, but it is neither immoral nor unjust—not because it is moral or right, but because these descriptions are *in this context* either naive or meaningless or inapplicable.

Nor is this view limited to the Vietnam War. Consider, for example, the following passage from a speech given only a few years ago by Dean Acheson:

> [T]hose involved in the Cuban crisis of October, 1962, will remember the irrelevance of the supposed moral considerations brought out in the discussions. Judgment

centered about the appraisal of dangers and risks, and weighing of the need for decisive and effective action against considerations of prudence; the need to do enough, against the consequences of doing too much. Moral talk did not bear on the problem. Nor did it bear upon the decision of those called upon to advise the President in 1949 whether and with what degree or urgency to press the attempt to produce a thermonuclear weapon. A respected colleague advised me that it would be better that our nation and people should perish rather than be party to a course so evil as producing that weapon. I told him that on the Day of Judgment his view might be confirmed and that he was free to go forth and preach the necessity for salvation. It was not, however, a view which I would entertain as a public servant.[1]

. . . Whatever may be the correct exegesis of this text, I want to treat it as illustrative of the position that morality has no place in the assessment of war. There are several things worth considering in respect to such a view. In the first place, the claim that in matters of war morality has no place is ambiguous. To put it somewhat loosely, the claim may be descriptive, or it may be analytic, or it may be prescriptive. Thus, it would be descriptive if it were merely the factual claim that matters relating to war uniformly turn out to be decided on grounds of national interest or expediency rather than by appeal to what is moral. This claim I will not consider further; it is an empirical one better answered by students of American (and foreign) diplomatic relations.

It would be a prescriptive claim were it taken to assert that matters relating to war ought always be decided by appeal to (say) national interest rather than an appeal to the moral point of view. For reasons which have yet to be elucidated, on this view the moral criteria are capable of being employed but it is undesirable to do so. I shall say something more about this view in a moment.

The analytic point is not that morality ought not be used, but rather that it cannot. On this view the statement "The United States is behaving immorally in the way it is waging war in Vietnam" (or, "in waging war in Vietnam") is not wrong but meaningless.

What are we to make of the analytic view? As I have indicated, it could, of course, be advanced simply as an instance of a more sweeping position concerning the general meaninglessness of the moral point of view. What I find particularly interesting, though, is the degree to which this thesis is advanced as a special view about war and not as a part of a more general claim that all morality is meaningless. . . .

. . . [Consider now] the view that says there can be no moral assessment of war just because there is, by definition, no morality in war. If war is an activity in which anything goes, moral judgments on war are just not possible.

To this there are two responses. To begin with, it is not, as our definitional discussion indicates, a necessary feature of war that it be an activity in which everything is morally permissible. There is a difference between the view that war is unique because killing and violence are morally permissible in contexts and circumstances where they otherwise would not be and the view that war is unique because everything is morally permissible.

A less absolutist argument for the absurdity of discussing the morality of war might be that at least today the prevailing (although not necessary) conception of war is one that as a practical matter rules out no behavior on moral grounds. After all, if flame throwers are deemed perfectly permissible, if the bombing of cities is applauded and not condemned, and if thermonuclear weapons are part of the arsenal of each of the major powers, then the remaining moral prohibitions on the conduct of war are sufficiently insignificant to be ignored.

The answer to this kind of an argument requires, I believe, that we distinguish the question of what is moral in war from that of the morality of war or of war generally. . . . Paradoxically, the more convincing the argument from war's conduct, the stronger is the moral argument *against* engaging in war at all. For the more it can be shown that engaging in war will inevitably lead to despicable behavior to which no moral predicates are deemed applicable, the more this also constitutes an argument against bringing such a state of affairs into being.

There is still another way to take the claim that in matters of war morality has no place. That is what I have called the prescriptive view: that national interest ought to determine policies in respect to war, not morality. This is surely one way to interpret the remarks of Dean Acheson reproduced earlier. It is also, perhaps, involved in President Truman's defense of the dropping of the atomic bomb on Hiroshima. What he said was this:

> Having found the bomb, we have to use it. We have used it against those who attacked us without warning at Pearl Harbor, against those who have starved and beaten and executed American prisoners of war, against those who have abandoned all pretense of obeying international laws of warfare. We have used it in order to shorten the agony of war, in order to save the lives of thousands and thousands of young Americans.[2]

Although this passage has many interesting features, I am concerned only with President Truman's insistence that the dropping of the bomb was justified because it saved the lives "of thousands and thousands of young Americans."

Conceivably, this is merely an elliptical way of saying that on balance fewer lives were lost through the dropping of the bomb and the accelerated cessation of hostilities than through any alternative course of conduct. Suppose, though, that this were not the argument. Suppose, instead, that the justification were regarded as adequate provided only that it was reasonably clear that fewer *American* lives would be lost than through any alternative course of conduct. Thus, to quantify the example, we can imagine someone maintaining that Hiroshima was justified because 20,000 fewer Americans died in the Pacific theater than would have died if the bomb had not been dropped. And this is justified even though 30,000 more Japanese died than would have been killed had the war been fought to an end with conventional means. Thus, even though 10,000 more people died than would otherwise have been the case, the bombing was justified because of the greater number of American lives saved.

On this interpretation the argument depends upon valuing the lives of Americans higher than the lives of persons from other countries. As such, is there anything to be said for the argument? Its strongest statement, and the only one that I shall consider, might go like this: Truman was the President of the United States and as such had an obligation always to choose that course of conduct that appeared to offer the greatest chance of maximizing the interests of the United States. As President, he was obligated to prefer the lives of American soldiers over those from any other country, and he was obligated to prefer them just because they were Americans and he was their President.

Some might prove such a point by drawing an analogy to the situation of a lawyer, or a parent, or a corporation executive. A lawyer has a duty to present his client's case in the fashion most calculated to ensure his client's victory; and he has this obligation irrespective of the objective merits of his client's case. Similarly, we are neither surprised nor dismayed when a parent prefers the interests of his child over those of other children. A parent qua parent is certainly not behaving immorally when he acts so as to secure satisfactions for his child, again irrespective of the objective merits of the child's needs or wants. And, mutatis mutandis, corporate executive has a duty to maximize profits for his company. Thus, as public servants, Dean Acheson and Harry Truman had no moral choice but to pursue those policies that appeared to them to be in the best interest of the United States. And to a lesser degree, all persons qua citizens of the United States have a similar, if slightly more attenuated, obligation. Therefore, morality has no real place in war.

The analogy, however, must not stop halfway. It is certainly both correct and important to observe that public officials, like parents, lawyers, and corporate executives, do have special moral obligations that are imposed by virtue of the position or role they fill. A lawyer does have a duty to prefer his client's interests in a way that would be improper were the person anyone other than a client. And the same sort of duty, I think, holds for a parent, an executive, a President, and a citizen in their respective roles. The point becomes distorted, however, when it is supposed that such an obligation always, under all circumstances, overrides any and all other obligations that the person might have. The case of the lawyer is instructive. While he has an obligation to attend to his client's interests in very special ways, there are many other things that it is impermissible for the lawyer to do in furtherance of his client's interests—irrespective, this time, of how significantly they might advance that interest.

The case for the President, or for public servants generally, is similar. While the President may indeed have an obligation to prefer and pursue the national interests, this obligation could only be justifiable—could only be a moral obligation—if it were enmeshed in a comparable range of limiting and competing obligations. If we concede that the President has certain obligations to prefer the national interest that no one else has, we must be equally sensitive to the fact that the President also has some of the same obligations to other persons that all other men have—if for no other reason than that all persons have the right to be treated or not treated in certain ways. So, whatever special obligations the President may have cannot by themselves support the view that in war morality ought have no place. . . .

But the major problem with the national-interest argument is its assumption that the national interest not only is something immutable and knowable but also that it limits national interest to narrowly national concerns. It is parochial to suppose that the

American national interest really rules out solicitude for other states in order to encourage international stability.

Finally, national interest as a goal must itself be justified. The United States' position of international importance may have imposed on it a duty of more than national concern. The fact that such a statement has become hackneyed by constant use to justify American interference abroad should not blind us to the fact that it may be viable as an argument for a less aggressive international responsibility.

NOTES

1. D. Acheson, "Ethics In International Relations Today," in *The Vietnam Reader*, ed. M. Raskin and B. Fall (1965), p. 13.

2. Address to the Nation by President Harry S. Truman, Aug. 9, 1945, quoted in R. Tucker, *The Just War* (1960), pp. 21–22, n. 14.

READING QUESTIONS

1. What are the differences among the descriptive, analytic, and prescriptive interpretations of the claim that morality has no place in war, according to Wasserstrom?
2. Why does Wasserstrom reject the analytic view? Consider some possible responses in defense of this view.
3. Explain the argument from analogy that Wasserstrom considers in support of the prescriptive view.
4. Explain Wasserstrom's main objection to the argument for the prescriptive view that presidents have a special obligation to preserve and protect the national interest.

DISCUSSION QUESTIONS

1. Are there any other possible interpretations for the claim that morality has no place in war besides the ones suggested by Wasserstrom?
2. Do presidents and other officials have a special obligation to prefer the national interest? To what extent is the national interest knowable or unknowable?

HAIG KHATCHADOURIAN

Terrorism and Morality

After proposing a definition of terrorism, Khatchadourian distinguishes four main types of terrorism: *predatory, retaliatory, political,* and *moralistic.* He then proceeds to argue both from the perspective of just-war theory and from the perspective of rights that all forms of terrorism are morally wrong.

Recommended Reading: natural law theory, chap. 1, sec. 2B, particularly the doctrine of double effect. Also relevant are rights-focused approaches to moral issues, chap. 1, sec. 2D.

TERRORISM: WHAT'S IN A NAME?

What terrorism is or how the word should be employed is a much vexed question, and many definitions of it have been proposed. Some of the conceptual reasons for the lack of agreement on its meaning will become clearer as I proceed, but the fact that the term is almost invariably used in an evaluative—indeed, highly polemical and emotionally charged—way makes the framing of a neutral definition a difficult task. It is probably no exaggeration to say that, at present, it is as emotional a word as "war." In fact, some think of terrorism as a kind of war, and the mere mention of the word arouses similar anxieties and fears. This was particularly true at the time this was being written, against the backdrop of the Gulf War and President Saddam Hussein's repeated warnings of terrorism against American and European interests world-wide. Not surprisingly, therefore, terrorism is very widely condemned as a major evil plaguing the last decades of the Twentieth century, a century already drenched with the blood of the innocent and the noninnocent is a long series of wars, revolutions, civil wars, and other forms of violence.

The widespread condemnation of terrorism as an unmitigated evil stems in part from the fact that some of those governments or countries, political systems, or regimes, that are the main targets, particularly of state or state-sponsored political violence, use the word as a political-psychological weapon in their fight against the perpetrators and their avowed causes—for example, national liberation from foreign occupation or the overthrow of an oppressive indigenous system or regime. In fighting terrorism targeted at them, the victim groups or countries tend to indiscriminately label all their enemies as "terrorists," including those who practice the least violent kinds of protest, thus stretching the word's already loose usage and vague meaning beyond reason.[1] Despite its notorious vagueness and looseness, some overlap among the multiplicity of the word's definitions and characterizations exists. . . .

DEFINING "TERRORISM"

A fully adequate characterization or formal definition of "terrorism" must be as neutral as possible and not beg the issue of the morality of terrorism in general . . . notwithstanding the word's almost invariably negative connotations, particularly in the Western world. . . .

From Haig Khatchadourian, *The Morality of Terrorism* (New York: Peter Lang, 1998). Reprinted by permission of the publisher.

In the current literature the question of whether noninnocents can be included among the immediate victims of terrorism appears to be a very unsettled question. The absence of clarity and fixity—indeed, the ambivalence and uncertainty in current employments of the word—reflect the different users' stand on the *morality* of terrorism and the morality, especially, of the unlawful use of force in general. These uncertainties are intimately connected with uncertainties concerning the distinction between terrorism and "freedom fighting," such as a rebellion, a civil war, an uprising, or a guerrilla war aiming, for example, at national liberation. Those who consider the harming of innocent persons an essential feature of terrorism would tend to consider "freedom fighting" as invoking, inter alia, the maiming, killing or coercing of *non*innocents. That would allow "political assassination" to be classified as a species of "freedom fighting." . . .

The preceding discussion indicates that in addition to being open textured and vague, the various current evaluative concepts of terrorism, like all other evaluative concepts, are, in W. B. Gallie's phrase, "essentially contested."[2] Yet like most vague and unsettled expressions "terrorism" has a "common core of meaning" in its different usages. This core of meaning includes the notion that terrorist acts are acts of coercion or of actual use of force,[3] aiming at monetary gain *(predatory terrorism)*, revenge *(retaliatory terrorism)*, a political end *(political terrorism)*, or a putative moral/religious end *(moralistic/religious terrorism)*.[4]

What is absolutely essential for an adequate concept of terrorism and helps distinguish it from all other uses of force or coercion, but which most definitions I have come across lack, is what I shall call terrorism's "bifocal" character. I mean the crucial distinction between (a) the "immediate victims," the individuals who are the immediate targets of terrorism, and (b) "the victimized," those who are the indirect but real targets of the terrorist acts. Normally the latter are individual governments or countries or certain groups of governments or countries, or specific institutions or groups within a given country. The ultimate targets may also be certain social, economic or political systems or regimes which the terrorists dislike and hope to change or destroy by their terrorist activities. . . .

THE MORALITY OF TERRORISM AND A JUST WAR THEORY

Although the literature on terrorism is constantly growing, very little has been written about the morality of terrorism; perhaps because the writers take it for granted that terrorism is a scourge, always morally reprehensible and wrong: note for instance the common equation of terrorism with murder. . . .

This is not a very auspicious beginning for a moral evaluation of terrorism. From the fact that terrorist acts, including the killing of immediate victims, are prohibited in many if not all municipal legal systems, it does not follow that some or all such acts are *morally* wrong. Calling terrorist killings "murder" begs the complex ethical issues involved. . . .

Whether . . . some terrorists acts . . . are morally justified is an important question and will be discussed in relation to just war theory. . . .

The traditional conditions of a just war are of two sorts: conditions of justified going to war *(jus ad bellum)* and conditions of the just prosecution of a war in progress *(jus in bello)*. One of the fundamental conditions of the latter kind is that

> The destruction of life and property, even enemy life and property, is inherently bad. It follows that military forces should cause no more destruction than is strictly necessary to achieve their objectives. (Notice that the principle does not say that whatever is necessary is permissible, but that everything permissible must be necessary). This is the principle of necessity: that *wanton* destruction is forbidden. More precisely, the principle of necessity specifies that a military operation is forbidden if there is some alternative operation that causes less destruction but has the same probability of producing a successful military result.[5]

Another fundamental condition is the principle of discrimination or noncombatant immunity, which prohibits the deliberate harming—above all the killing—of innocent persons. In "Just War Theory" William O'Brien defines that condition as the principle that "prohibits direct intentional attacks on noncombatants and nonmilitary targets,"[6] and Douglas Lackey, in *The Ethics of War and Peace,* characterize it as "the idea that . . . civilian life and property should not be subjected to military force: military force must be directed only at military objectives."[7] A third fundamental condition is the principle of proportion, as "applied to discrete military ends."[8] That condition is defined by O'Brien as "requiring proportionality of means to political and military ends."[9] Or as Lackey states it, it is the idea that "the amount of destruction permitted in pursuit of a military objective must be proportionate to the importance of the objective. This is the *military* principle of proportionality (which must be distinguished from the *political* principle of proportionality in the *jus ad bellum*)."[10]

My contention is that these three principles, duly modified or adapted, are analogically applicable to all the types of terrorism, and that they are flagrantly violated by them. Indeed, all but the moralistic/religious type of terrorism violate a further condition of just war theory. I refer to the first and most important condition of *jus ad bellum* and one of the most important conditions of a just war in general: the condition of just cause. . . .

Of the four main types of terrorism, predatory, retaliatory and nonmoralistic/religious terrorism clearly run afoul of the just cause condition, understood—in a nutshell—as the self-defensive use of force. Conceivably only some acts of moralistic and moralistic-political/religious terrorism can satisfy that condition. It is clear that the former three types of terrorism violate that condition.

Let us begin with predatory terrorism, terrorism motivated by greed. Like "ordinary" acts of armed robbery, of which it is the terrorist counterpart, predatory terrorism is a crime and is morally wrong. Both cause terror and indiscriminately hurt whoever happens to be where they strike. Indeed, hostage-taking by armed robbers in hopes of escaping unscathed by forcing the authorities to give them a getaway car or plane is an additional similarity to terrorism. It can even be regarded as predatory terrorism itself, particularly if it is systematic and not a onetime affair, since both political and moralistic terrorism tend to be systematic. . . . Even then, armed robbery involving hostage-talking, must be distinguished from the kind of armed robbery that political or moralistic terrorists may indulge in to raise money for their particular political/moralistic/religious ends.

Nonetheless, bona fide predatory (and even retaliatory) terrorism is often unsystematic; like ordinary armed robbery, it may also be a one-time thing. Some well-known terrorist airplane hijackings in the United States for monetary gain have been one-time incidents, although in all but one instance I know of, that was simply because the hijackers were apprehended!

Like predatory terrorism, retaliatory terrorism may or may not be systematic. International terrorism usually includes a systematic policy of retaliation against a hated, enemy state or its citizens. A notorious example a few years ago was the retaliatory terrorism against the United States and its interests, sponsored by Libya, Syria, and/or Iran.

More important for the present discussion, retaliatory terrorism violates, among other moral rules, the just cause condition and the principles of justice, and is consequently wrong. For what is retaliation but another (more euphemistic?) word for revenge, which is incompatible with self-defense as well as due process. That is no less true in war, if retaliatory terrorism is practiced by a country in its efforts to defend itself against aggression. For example, if an attempt is made on the life of the aggressor country's head of state by agents of the victim state in retaliation for attacks on its territory, the assassination attempt would be (a) an act of *terrorism* if it is *intended* to pressure the aggressor's military to end the aggression. But despite its *goal* and the victim's perception of it as part of its national self-defense, it remains (b) an act of retaliation, not an act of self defense.

What I have said about predatory and retaliatory terrorism in relation to just cause applies to nonmoralistic political terrorism, to terrorism whose political goals are *not* moral. An example is when a revolutionary group commits acts of terrorism against a legitimate, democratically elected government it wants to overthrow out of lust for power.

By definition, moralistic terrorism satisfies just cause if "just cause" is interpreted broadly to mean a morally justifiable cause, for example, political terrorism strictly as part of a national liberation movement against a foreign occupier or indigenous oppressive regime. It *may* also satisfy the condition of right intention. Consequently, I shall turn to the other two conditions of just war I mentioned earlier, to ascertain whether even such terrorism can be morally justifiable.

Principle of Necessity and Terrorism

The principle of necessity states that "*wanton* destruction [in war] is forbidden. More precisely, the principle . . . specifies that a military operation is forbidden if there is some alternative operation that causes less destruction but has the same probability of producing a successful military result." *Pace* Lackey, who regards[11] it as a more precise form of the condition, it is distinct from, although closely related to, the principle that wanton destruction is forbidden in war. If a war *is* a last resort, it would follow that the destruction of life and property is necessary, not wanton. And if it is necessary, it *is* a last resort.

It is clear that predatory terrorism is always a wanton destruction of life or property, and the same is true of retaliatory terrorism; however, the concept of "last resort" is inapplicable to them. If Iran had chosen to sue the United States for compensation or reparation at the International Court of Justice at the Hague, for the shooting down an Iranian airbus during the Iraq-Iran war, that would have constituted a peaceful, nonviolent *alternative* to any terrorist retaliation against the United States Iran may have sponsored in its aftermath, such as the destruction of Pan Am Flight 103 over Lockerbie, Scotland, which some believe was instigated and financed by Iran and implemented by a notorious Palestinian terrorist. (The United States has steadfastly held Libya, and possibly Syria, responsible for that atrocity.) Logically, retaliation on the one hand and reparation, compensation, or restitution, or other peaceful ways of undoing or rectifying a wrong, are horses of very different colors.

Principle of Discrimination and Terrorism

In many acts of terrorism some or all of the immediate victims and/or victimized are innocent persons, in no way morally connected with or in any degree responsible for the wrong moralistic terrorism is intended to help rectify, hence for the physical or mental harm that the terrorists inflict on them. In predatory terrorism the immediate victims and the victimized are, almost without exception, innocent persons. That is also often true of retaliatory terrorism, at least as far as the immediate victims are concerned. Two very tragic examples in recent memory are the hijacking of the *Achille Lauro,* and the destruction of the Pan Am plane over Lockerbie. In political and political-moralistic terrorism, whether in wartime or in time of peace, some of the immediate victims or some of the victimized are likely to be innocent persons; but some may be noninnocents, such as members (especially high-ranking members) of the military, who are morally responsible for the real or imagined wrong that triggers the terrorism.

The problem of distinguishing innocent and noninnocent persons in relation to different types and forms of terrorism, except terrorism in war, is on the whole less difficult that the much-vexed corresponding problem relation to war. My position, mutatis mutandis in relation to war, simply stated, is this: (1) "Innocence" and "noninnocence" refer to *moral* innocence and noninnocence, relative to the particular acts, types, or forms of terrorism *T.* (2) Innocence and noninnocence are a matter of degree. (3) A perfectly innocent person is one who has no moral responsibility, a fortiori, no causal responsibility at all, for any wrong that gave rise to *T.* A paradigmatically noninnocent person is someone who has an appreciable degree of moral, hence direct or indirect causal responsibility for the wrong, triggering *T.*[12] Between that extreme and paradigmatic noninnocence there would be, theoretically, cases of decreasing moral responsibility corresponding to decreasing degrees of causal responsibility. Here the targets would be noninnocent in some but lesser degree than in paradigmatic cases of noninnocence. (4) Moral responsibility may be direct or indirect, by virtue of a person's direct or indirect role in *T*'s causation—where *T* is triggered or has its root cause(s) in some real injustice or wrong. The degree of a person's innocence may therefore also vary in that way. Everyone whose actions are a proximate cause of the wrong is noninnocent in a higher degree than those whose responsibility for it is indirect. In particular cases it is always possible in principle to ascertain whether an individual is, causally, directly involved. Generally it is also actually possible, although often quite difficult, to do so in practice. Ascertaining who is indirectly responsible and who is not at all responsible is another matter. Since we are mainly concerned with the theoretical problem of the morality of terrorism, that is not too disquieting. But it is of the essence from the point of view of would-be terrorists and that of the law—unless the terrorists happen to be deranged and target innocent individuals or groups they imagine to be morally responsible for the grievances they are out to avenge or redress. Further, the very life of some individuals may depend on the potential terrorists' ability to distinguish innocent from noninnocent persons or groups. Political, retaliatory, or moralistic terrorists, driven by passion or paranoia, often baselessly enlarge, sometimes to a tragically absurd extent, the circle of alleged noninnocent persons. They sometimes target individuals, groups or whole nations having only a tenuous relation, often of a completely innocent kind, to those who have wronged their compatriots or ancestors, stolen their land, and so on. The example given earlier of terrorists striking at the high-ranking officials of governments whose predecessors committed crimes against their people, illustrates this. Another example is terrorism targeting innocent persons presumed to be guilty by association, simply because they happen to be of the same race, nationality, or religion, or enjoy the same ethnic heritage as those deemed responsible for the hurt. . . .

Principles of Proportion and Terrorism

In addition to its violation of the moral principles considered above, terrorism may appear to violate two other principles of just war theory: (1) the *political* principle of proportion of *jus ad bellum* and (2) the *military* principle of proportion or *jus in bello*. . . . Lackey describes the political principle of proportionality as stipulating that "the war cannot be just unless the evil that can reasonably be expected to ensue from the war is less than the evil that can reasonably be expected to ensue if the war is not fought."[13]

The military counterpart of the political principle is described by Lackey as the idea that "the amount of destruction permitted in pursuit of a military objective must be proportionate to the importance of the objective. It follows from the military principle of proportionality that certain objectives should be ruled out of consideration on the ground that too much destruction would be caused in obtaining them."[14]

As in the case of war, the main problem facing any attempt to apply the *political* principle of proportion to terrorism is the difficulty of reaching even the roughest estimate of the total expected good vis-à-vis the total evil likely to be caused by a series of connected acts of political or *moralistic/religious* terrorism. The crudest estimates of the expected good of some political-moralistic/religious cause against the suffering or death of even one victim or victimized person are exceedingly difficult to come by. And if we turn from isolated acts of political-moralistic/religious terrorism to a whole series of such acts extending over a period of years or decades, as with Arab or IRA terrorism, the task becomes utterly hopeless. For how can we possibly measure the expected good resulting from the creation of, for example, an independent Catholic Northern Ireland or a Catholic Northern Ireland united with the Irish Republic, and compare it with the overall evil likely to be the lot of the Ulster Protestants in such an eventuality or on different scenarios of their eventual fate—then add the latter evil to the evils consisting in and consequent upon all the acts of terrorism that are supposed to help realise the desired good end? I see no possible way in which these factors can be quantified, hence added or subtracted.

It seems then that we cannot ascertain whether political or moralistic/religious terrorism sometimes or always violates the political principle of proportion. However, it is a patent fact that no political or moralistic/religious terrorist movement in this century—whether Palestinian, Lebanese, Libyan, Syrian, Iranian, Irish, or Algerians—has succeeded in realizing its ultimate or overall political or moralistic objectives. Moreover, these movements have no more chance of success in the future than they have had so far. Palestinian terrorism is typical. Since, in Israel and the West, terrorism is almost synonymous with murder, it is not surprising that instead of helping the eminently just Palestinian cause, Palestinian acts of terrorism (as distinguished from Palestinian resistance, e.g. the intifada) from the very start have hurt the cause almost beyond repair. Not only has terrorism failed to win the Palestinians their human and other rights or brought them any closer to self-determination: it has created strong public sympathy in the West for Israel and turned public attitudes strongly against the Palestinians, or at least their leadership, and has further increased Israeli security concerns.[15] This does enable us, I think, to conclude after all that the preceding types of terrorism are indeed in serious violation of the political principle of proportion. For the result of tallying the evils of terrorist acts in human pain and suffering, death and destruction, against the nonexistent overall benefits leaves a huge surplus of unmitigated evil on the negative side. I refer not only to the evil inflicted by the terrorists upon their victims and the victimized but also the evil they draw upon themselves and their families by risking loss of life, limb, or liberty in ultimately futile pursuit of their dangerous and violent objectives.

We now turn to the military principle of proportionality . . .

The present form of the principle *can* be applied, mutatis mutandis, to discrete acts of terrorism provided that their probable intermediate results can be roughly assessed. For example, in evaluating the morality of the *Achille Lauro* seajacking, the short-term and intermediate "political" gains the terrorists expected to receive must be weighed, if possible, against the killing of an innocent passenger and the terrorism visited on the other passengers on board. It can be safely said that apart from the damage the seajacking did to the PLO and to the Middle East peace process as a whole, whatever benefit the seajackers expected to reap from their acts, such as publicity and the dramatization of the plight of the Palestinians under Israeli military rule in the occupied territories, was vastly outweighed by the evils the seajacking resulted in. More important still, the actual and not . . . merely the expected outcome of acts of terrorism, good and bad, must be weighed,

if possible, against each other. That is, actual proportionality must obtain if, in retrospect, the acts are to be objectively evaluated. But to do so is precisely to assess the outcomes of the acts in terms of consequentialist criteria, and so will be left for later consideration.

The same general factors need to be weighed for the evaluation of other discrete acts of terrorism in relation to the military principle of proportionality; for example, the assassination of members of the Israeli Olympic team in Munich in 1972, the hijacking of TWA flight 847 in Athens, Greece, in 1985, the downing of Pan Am flight 103 over Lockerbie, Scotland, in 1989, and so on.

Terrorism and Human Rights

It can be safely said that the belief that all human beings have a (an equal) human right to life, at least in the minimal sense of a negative right to life—a right not to be unjustly or wrongly killed—is held by anyone who believes in the existence of human rights at all. That idea is also found in the United Nations *Universal Declaration of Human Rights*. Thus, Article 3 states, among other things, that "Everyone has the right to life." The importance of our acknowledging such a universal human right is evident: the protection of human life is the sine qua non of the individual's capacity to realize anything and everything—any and all values—a human being is capable of realizing in relation to himself or herself and others. But even if one does not acknowledge a distinct human right, a right to life as such, I believe that one is forced to acknowledge the existence of some protective norms, such as other human rights and/or principles of fairness and justice, that prohibit, except in very special circumstances, the taking of human life. For instance, justice prohibits the execution of an innocent person for a crime he or she has not committed. Or the moral protection of human life can be placed under the protective umbrella of, for example, a human right to be treated as a moral person rather than be used as an "object."

The special exceptional circumstances I have in mind are those in which the right to life is overridden by stronger moral or other axiological claims. They may include the protection of the equal rights of others, including others' right to life itself (such as in the case of soldiers sent by their country to war, to defend the lives and freedoms of their countrymen against an aggressor nation); or situations where a certain act is (1) the lesser of two evils and (2) violates no one's equal human or other moral rights, or the principles of fairness and justice. For instance, in some instances of passive or active euthanasia, or assisted suicide, such as in the case of terminal patients who are suffering unbearable physical pain (condition [1]) and the euthanasia or assisted suicide fulfils the patient's devout wish and desire to die (condition [2]). Except in such or similar exceptional cases, the deliberate or the knowing killing of innocent persons is morally wrong.

Elsewhere[16] I have argued that we must acknowledge a fundamental human right of all individuals to be treated as moral persons. Further, that that right includes an equal right of all to be free to satisfy their needs and interests, and to actualize their potentials: that is, to seek to realize themselves and their well-being.[17] In addition, I have argued that all human beings have an equal right to equal opportunity and treatment, to help enable them to realize the aforementioned values, either as part of or as implied by the right to be treated as a moral person.

A universal negative human right to life,[18] hence a right to one's physical and mental security and integrity, can be readily derived from the right to equal treatment and opportunity as a premise, if such a right is acknowledged,[19] as a condition of the very possibility of exercising that right at all or any other moral, legal, or other kind of right or rights, including the right to be treated as a moral person as a whole. The rights to equal treatment and opportunity would be empty or meaningless in practice if not in theory if one's security is not protected. . . .

It is clear that if a negative right to life is assumed, terrorists' killings of their immediate victims—unless they satisfy conditions (1) and (2) above—are always morally wrong. In reality, condition (1) may perhaps be sometimes satisfied, but condition (2) cannot ever be satisfied. In fact all types and forms of terrorism I have distinguished seriously violate the

human rights of their immediate victims and the victimized as moral persons.

Treating people as moral persons means treating them with consideration in two closely related ways. First, it means respecting their autonomy as individuals with their own desires and interests, plans and projects, commitments and goals. That autonomy is clearly violated if they are humiliated, coerced and terrorized, taken hostage or kidnapped, and above all, killed. Second, consideration involves "a certain cluster of attitudes, hence certain ways of acting toward, reacting to and thinking and feeling about" people.[20] It includes sensitivity to and consideration of their feelings and desires, aspirations, projects, and goals. That in turn is an integral part of treating their life as a whole—including their relationships and memories—as a thing of value. Finally, it includes respecting their "culture or ethnic, religious or racial identity or heritage."[21] These things are the very antithesis of what terrorism does to its victims and the victimized.

In sum, terrorism in general violates both aspects of its targets' right to be treated as moral persons. In retaliatory and moralistic/religious terrorism, that is no less true of those victims or those victimized who are morally responsible in some degree for the wrong that precipitates the terrorist strike than of those who are completely innocent of it. In predatory terrorism, the terrorist acts violate the human right of everyone directly or indirectly hurt by them. For the terrorists the life of the immediate victims and their human rights matter not in the least. The same goes for the victimized. The terrorists use both groups, against their will, simply as means to their own end. . . .

To sum up. The discussion of the nature of terrorism prepared the way for the central question: whether terrorism is ever morally right, morally justifiable. To answer that question two kinds of ethical principles/rules were deployed. (A) applicable human rights, and (B) applicable just war principles/rules. . . . On both (A) and (B), terrorism in general, in all its various types and forms, was found to be always wrong.

Since predatory and retaliatory terrorism, like predation and retaliation in general, are patently wrong, the inquiry was focused on political and moralistic/religious terrorism, which are held by some—with apparent plausibility—to be, in certain circumstances, morally justifiable. However, it was argued that terrorism of both types is wrong, since both violate certain basic human rights and applicable just war principles or rules.

NOTES

1. A notorious example, which carries this tendency to absurdity, is the late Mr. Rabin's calling the "stone children" of the Palestinian intifada "terrorists" in front of American television cameras. Mr. Rabin himself was murdered by a Jewish terrorist.

2. W. B. Gallie, "Essentially Contested Concepts," *Proceedings of the Aristotelian Society,* n.s., 56 (March 1956), 180ff. But Gallie maintains that a concept must have certain characteristics in addition to appraisiveness (he enumerates them on pp. 171–172) to be "essentially contested" in his sense.

3. Those who use "terrorism" as a condemnatory term would substitute "violence" for "force."

4. I borrow the categories "predatory" and "moralistic" from Edel, "Notes on Terrorism," in *Values in Conflict,* Burton M. Leiser, ed. (New York, 1981), 453.

5. Douglas P. Lackey, *The Ethics of War and Peace* (Englewood Cliffs, NJ, 1989), 59. Italics in original.

6. William O'Brien, "Just-War Theory," in Burton M. Leiser *Liberty, Justice, and Morals*, 2nd ed. (New York, 1979), 39. This section is in large measure reproduced from sections III–V of Haig Khatchadourian, "Terrorism and Morality," *Journal of Applied Philosophy,* 5, no. 2 (1958): 134–143.

7. Lackey, *Ethics,* 59.

8. Ibid., 37.

9. Ibid., 30.

10. Ibid., 59. Italics in original.

11. Lackey, *Ethics,* 59. Italics in original.

12. What constitutes an "appreciable degree" of moral responsibility would of course be a matter of controversy.

13. Lackey, *Ethics,* 40.

14. Ibid., 59.

15. A personal note: My own moral condemnation of terrorism and my conviction that it was bound to hurt rather than help the Palestinian cause led me, soon after the first Palestinian skyjacking, to send an open letter to the PLO leadership. In this letter I pointed these things out and pleaded that the PLO put an end to such acts. For rather obvious reasons the Beirut publication to which I sent the letter could not publish it.

16. Haig Khatchadourian, "Toward a Foundation for Human Rights," *Man and World,* 18 (1985): 219–240, and "The Human Right to be Treated as a Person," *Journal of Value Inquiry,* 19 (1985): 183–195.

17. Khatchadourian, "The Human Right," passim.

18. As distinguished from a positive human right to life, which includes—over and above the right not to be physically hurt or killed—a right to a minimum standard of welfare.

19. Such a right can also be derived from John Rawls' first and second principles of justice in *A Theory of Justice* (Cambridge, MA, 1971). *Indeed, the right to equal opportunity is part of his first principle.*

20. Khatchadourian, "The Human Right," 192.

21. Ibid.

READING QUESTIONS

1. Explain the differences among predatory, retaliatory, political, and moralistic/religious terrorism.
2. What does Khatchadourian mean by the "bifocal" character of terrorism?
3. Explain the distinction between *jus ad bellum* and *jus in bello.*
4. Describe the three principles violated by all forms of terrorism. Give examples of ways in which terrorist acts might violate each.
5. How does Khatchadourian distinguish between innocent and noninnocent persons?
6. What is one of the main difficulties that Khatchadourian cites regarding the application of the principle of proportion to terrorist acts?
7. Under what circumstances might Khatchadourian say that the taking of a human life is permissible? Provide specific examples.
8. What is a universal negative human right to life?
9. According to Khatchadourian, what is involved in treating people as moral persons?

DISCUSSION QUESTION

1. Suppose that both terrorist acts and certain acts of war violate human rights as well as the principles of just war. How might these types of actions differ? Compare and contrast.

MICHAEL WALZER

After 9/11: Five Questions about Terrorism

Written in the immediate aftermath of the 9/11 terrorist attacks, Walzer's essay explores a number of basic conceptual and moral issues about terrorism including its nature and probable causes. In particular, Walzer rejects what he calls the "culture of excuse and apology," which attempts to defend some acts of terrorism as morally legitimate.

This is not going to be a straightforward and entirely coherent argument. I am still reeling from the attacks of September 11, and I don't have all my responses in order. I will try to answer five questions about terrorism. Whether the answers add up to a "position"—theoretical or practical—I will leave to the reader.

1. What is terrorism?
2. How should we go about explaining it?
3. How is it defended or excused?
4. How should we respond?
5. What will be the signs of a successful response?

1. *What is it?* . . . Terrorism is the deliberate killing of innocent people, at random, in order to spread fear through a whole population and force the hand of its political leaders. But this is a definition that best fits the terrorism of a national liberation or revolutionary movement (the Irish Republican Army, the Algerian National Liberation Front [FLN], the Palestine Liberation Organization, the Basque Separatist Movement, and so on). There is also state terrorism, commonly used by authoritarian and totalitarian governments against their own people, to spread fear and make political opposition impossible: the Argentine "disappearances" are a useful example. And, finally, there is war terrorism: the effort to kill civilians in such large numbers that their government is forced to surrender. Hiroshima seems to me the classic case. The common element is the targeting of people who are, in both the military and political senses, noncombatants: not soldiers, not public officials, just ordinary people. And they aren't killed incidentally in the course of actions aimed elsewhere; they are killed intentionally.

From Michael Walzer, *Arguing about War* (New Haven & London: Yale University Press, 2004). Reprinted by permission.

I don't accept the notion that "one man's terrorist is another man's freedom fighter." Of course, the use of the term is contested; that's true of many political terms. The use of "democracy" is contested, but we still have, I think, a pretty good idea of what democracy is (and isn't). When communist Bulgaria called itself a "people's democracy," only fools were fooled. The case is the same with terrorism. In the 1960s, when someone from the FLN put a bomb in a café where French teenagers gathered to flirt and dance and called himself a freedom fighter, only fools were fooled. There were a lot of fools back then, and back then—in the sixties and seventies—was when the culture of excuse and apology was born (but I want to deal with that later).

2. *How should we go about explaining terrorism— and particularly the form of terrorism that we face today?* The first thing to understand is that terrorism is a choice; it is a political strategy selected from among a range of options. You have to imagine a group of people sitting around a table and arguing about what to do; the moment is hard to reconstruct, but I am sure that it is an actual moment, even if, once the choice is made, the people who opposed terror are commonly killed, and so we never hear their version of how the argument went. Why do the terrorists so often win the argument? What are the political roots of terror?

I don't think that a simple materialist explanation works, though there has been a lot of talk in the last couple of months about the human misery, the terrible poverty, the vast global inequalities in which terrorism is "ultimately rooted." Also about the terrible suffering, as someone wrote in one of our weeklies, endured by "people all over the world who have been the victims of American military action—in Vietnam, in Latin America, in Iraq . . ." The author of those words doesn't seem to have noticed that there are no terrorists coming from Vietnam and Latin America. Misery and inequality just don't work as explanations for any of the nationalist terrorist movements and certainly not for Islamic terror. A simple thought experiment in comparative politics helps explain why they don't work. Surely it is Africa that reveals the worst consequences of global inequality, and the involvement of the West in the production and

reproduction of inequality is nowhere more evident. There is a lot of local involvement too; many African governments are complicitous or directly responsible for the misery of their own people. Still, the role of the West is fairly large. And yet the African diaspora is not a friendly sea in which terrorists swim. And the same thing can be said for Latin America, especially Central America, where U.S. companies have played a significant part in exploiting and sustaining poverty; and yet the Latin diaspora is not a friendly sea. We need another explanation.

We need a combined cultural-religious-political explanation that has to focus, I think, on the creation of an Enemy, a whole people who are ideologically or theologically degraded so that they are available for murder: that's what the IRA did to Irish Protestants, the FLN to French Algerians, the PLO to Israeli Jews. This kind of Enemy is the special creation of nationalist and religious movements, which often aim not only at the defeat but at the removal or elimination of the "others." Wartime propaganda commonly has the same effect, demonizing the other side, even when both sides expect the war to end with a negotiated peace. Once the Enemy has been created, any of "them" can be killed, men, women, or children, combatants and noncombatants, ordinary folk. The hostility is generalized and indiscriminate. In the case of Islamic terrorism, the Enemy is the infidel, whose world leader is the United States and whose local representative is Israel.

Islamic terrorists don't call themselves freedom fighters; they have a different mission: to restore the dominance of Islam in the lands of Islam. Osama bin Laden, in the speech he delivered on video shortly before (it was broadcast after) the September 11 attacks, spoke about eighty years of subjection, which takes the story back to the establishment of European protectorates and trusteeships in the Middle East after World War I; the effort to create a Christian state in Lebanon; the effort to set up Western-style constitutional monarchies and parliamentary republics in the Arab world; the establishment of Israel as a Jewish state after the Second World War; and then the long series of military defeats from 1948 to 1991, not only in the Middle East but in East Asia, all of them experienced as terrible humiliations, at the hands of Jews,

Hindus, and Americans, who are not supposed to be warrior peoples at all.

But the military defeats are part of a larger story of the failure of state building and economic development in most of the Islamic world. The fundamentalist religious response to modernity, which is common across all the major world religions, comes up here against governments that are very far from admirable representatives of modernity: secular governments often, or governments that are ready for accommodation with the West and eager to absorb the latest technologies, but at the same time brutal, repressive, corrupt, authoritarian, unjust . . . and unsuccessful in providing either the symbols or the substance of a decent common life. And some of these governments, in order to maintain their own power, sponsor a kind of ideological and theological scapegoating, directed against external enemies: Israel, America, the West generally, who are blamed for the internal failures. Some of these governments are our allies, Islamic moderates or Arab secularists, but they have yet to take on the extremists in their midst; they have yet to commit themselves to an open struggle against the theological radicalism that inspires the terrorist networks. Jihad is a response not only to modernity but also to the radical failure of the Islamic world to modernize itself.

Earlier terrorist campaigns are also explicable, in part, by the internal authoritarianism and weakness of the "liberation movement," in this case, its refusal or inability to mobilize its own people for other kinds of political action. Terrorism, after all, doesn't require mass mobilization; it is the work of a tiny elite of militants, who claim to represent "the people" but who act in the absence of the people (that's why classical Marxism was always hostile to terrorism—the reason, alas, was strategic, not moral). When someone like Gandhi was able to organize a nonviolent mass movement for national liberation, there was no terrorism.

3. *How is terrorism defended?* In certain extremist Islamic groups today there is a straightforward defense, which is also a denial: there are no innocent Americans, hence attacks like those of September 11

are not terrorist in character. But the arguments that I want to consider are of a different sort: they don't justify the acts that we call terrorism. Instead, they are expressions of what I have already described as a culture of excuse and apology. There are basically two kinds of excuses. The first looks to the desperation of the "oppressed," as they are called (and as they may well be): terror, we are told, is the weapon of the weak, the last resort of subject nations. In fact, terror is commonly the first resort of militants who believe from the beginning that the Enemy should be killed and who are neither interested in nor capable of organizing their own people for any other kind of politics; the FLN and the PLO resorted to terror from the beginning, there was no long series of attempts to find alternatives. And as we have seen, there is at least one alternative—nonviolent mass mobilization—that has proven itself a far more effective "weapon of the weak."

The second kind of excuse looks to the guilt of the victims of terrorism. Here is how it works for Americans: we fought the Gulf War, we station troops on the sacred soil of Saudi Arabia, we blockade and bomb Iraq, we support Israel—what do we expect? Of course, the September 11 attacks were wrong; they ought to be condemned; but—a very big "but"—after all, we deserved it; we had it coming. Generally, this argument comes from people who before September 11 wanted us to stop protecting the Kurds in northern Iraq, to stop supporting Israel, and to get out of Saudi Arabia; and now they see a chance to use Islamic terrorism as a kind of "enforcer" for their own political agenda. They attribute their agenda to the terrorists (what else could terrorists have in mind but what Western leftists have always advocated?), and then call for a policy of appeasement in order to avoid further attacks. That is a policy, it seems to me, that would begin with dishonor and end in disaster. But I won't talk about that now; I want simply to deny the moral legitimacy of the excuse. Even if American policies in the Middle East and in East Asia have been or are wrong in many ways, they don't excuse the terrorist attack; they don't even make it morally comprehensible. The murder of innocent people is not excusable.

4. *How should we respond?* I want to argue for a multilateral response, a "war" against terror that has to be fought on many fronts. But who is the enemy here? Is it the people who planned or sponsored or supported the September 11 attacks or is it any and all other groups that practice a terrorist politics? I suggest that we think in terms of an analogy with humanitarian intervention. We (the United States, the United Nations, the North Atlantic Treaty Organization, the Organization of African Unity, and others) intervene, or ought to intervene, against genocide and "ethnic cleansing" wherever they occur. There are, of course, many different political and religious doctrines that inspire genocide and ethnic cleansing, and each intervention is distinct; each one requires its own calculations of morality and prudence. But our commitment should be general. The case is the same with terror: there are many terrorist ideologies and many terrorist organizations. We should oppose them all, but the different engagements will have to be considered one by one. We should imagine the "war" as including many possible engagements.

"War" is a metaphor here, but real war is a necessary part of the metaphorical "war." It may be the only part to which the frequently invoked doctrine of "just war" applies; we will have to look for other, though not unrelated, kinds of ethical guidance on the other fronts. The question about justice in the real war is a familiar one, and so is the answer—though the answer is easier in principle than in practice. In fighting against terrorists, we must not aim at innocent people (that's what the terrorists do); ideally we should get close enough to the enemy, or to his supporters, so that we are quite sure not only that we are aiming at them but also that we are hitting them. When we fight from far away, with planes and missiles, we have to get people in, on the ground, to select the targets, or we have to have very good intelligence; we must avoid overestimating the smartness of our smart bombs. Technological hubris isn't, I suppose, a crime, but it can lead to very bad outcomes, so it is better to leave a wide margin for error. And, finally, because even if we do all these things, we will still be imposing serious risks on the civilian population, we must reduce those risks as far as possible—and

take risks ourselves in order to do that. This last is the hardest thing I have to say, because I'm not the one who will have to take those risks. The proportionality rule is commonly invoked here: civilian deaths and injuries, euphemistically called "collateral damage," should not be disproportionate to the value of the military victory that is being sought. But because I don't know how to measure the relevant values or how to specify the proportionality, and because I don't think that anyone else knows, I prefer to focus instead on the seriousness of the intention to avoid harming civilians, and that is best measured by the acceptance of risk.

Assuming that we correctly identified the terrorist network responsible for the September 11 attacks and that the Taliban government was in fact its patron and protector, the war in Afghanistan is certainly a just one. The point of the war is prevention above all: to destroy the network and stop the preparation of future attacks. We shouldn't, in my view, think of the war as a "police action," aimed at bringing criminals to justice. We probably don't have the evidence to do that; and it may well be the case that evidence collected by clandestine means or by armed force in distant countries, evidence that doesn't come from official archives, such as the German records that figured in the Nuremberg trials, but from e-mail intercepts and similar unofficial sources, would not be admissible in an American court—and probably not in international courts either, though I don't know what rules of evidence apply in The Hague. In any case, do we really want trials now, while the terrorist networks are still active? Think of the hostage-takings and bomb threats that would almost certainly accompany them. The use of military courts would avoid these difficulties, because the rules of evidence could be relaxed and the trials held in secret. But then there will be costs to pay in legitimacy: for justice, as the saying goes, must not only be done, it must be seen to be done; it must be seen *being* done. So . . . there may be trials down the road, but we shouldn't focus on them now; the first object of the "war" against terrorism is not backward looking and retributive, but forward looking and preventive. If that's the point, then there is a sense in which Afghanistan is a sideshow, however necessary it is, however much attention the media give it, however focused on it our diplomats and soldiers have to be.

The most important battle against terror is being waged right here, and in Britain and Germany and Spain, and other countries of the Arab and Islamic diaspora. If we can prevent further attacks, if we can begin to roll up the terrorist cells, that will be a major victory. And it is very, very important, because "successes" like September 11 have energizing effects; they produce a rush of recruits and probably a new willingness to fund the terrorist networks.

Police work is the first priority, and that raises questions, not about justice, but about civil liberties. Liberals and libertarians leap to the defense of liberty, and they are right to leap; but when they (we) do that, we have to accept a new burden of proof: we have to be able to make the case that the necessary police work can be done, and can be done effectively, within whatever constraints we think are required for the sake of American freedom. If we can't make that case, then we have to be ready to consider modifying the constraints. It isn't a betrayal of liberal or American values to do that; it is in fact the right thing to do, because the first obligation of the state is to protect the lives of its citizens (that's what states are for), and American lives are now visibly and certainly at risk. Again, prevention is crucial. Think of what will happen to our civil liberties if there are more successful terrorist attacks.

Covert action is also necessary, and I confess that I don't know what moral rules apply to it. The combatant-noncombatant distinction is crucial to every kind of political and military activity; beyond that it is hard to know. Moral argument requires its cases, and here the cases are, deliberately and presumably rightly, concealed from view. Perhaps I can say a word about assassination, which has been much discussed in recent months. The killing of political leaders is ruled out in international law, even (or especially) in wartime—and ruled out for good reason—because it is the political leaders of the enemy state with whom we will one day have to negotiate the peace. There are obvious exceptions to this rule—no one, no moral person, would have objected to an allied effort to assassinate Hitler; we were in fact not prepared to negotiate

with him—but ordinary political leaders are immune. Diplomats are immune for the same reason: they are potential peacemakers. But military leaders are not immune, however high they stand on the chain of command. We have as much right to shell the enemy army's central headquarters as to shell its frontline positions. With terrorist organizations, this distinction between military and political leaders probably collapses; the two are hard to mark off, and we are not planning on negotiations. At any rate, it would seem odd to say that it is legitimate to attack a group of terrorists-in-training in a camp in Afghanistan, say, but not legitimate to go after the man who is planning the operation for which the others are training. That can't be right.

Diplomatic work comes next: right now it is focused on building support for military action in Afghanistan and for some kind of future non-Taliban regime. But over the long run, the critically important task will be to isolate and punish states that support terrorism. The networks look transnational; they exploit the globalist modernity that they so bitterly oppose. But make no mistake: neither the transnational networks, nor most of the more provincial ones, could survive without the physical shelter, the ideological patronage, and the funding provided by such states as Iran, Syria, Libya, and others. We are not going to go to war with those states; there is no *causus belli,* nor should we look for one. But there are many forms of legitimate political and economic pressure short of war, and it seems to me that we have to work hard to bring that kind of pressure to bear. This means that we have to persuade other countries—our allies in many cases, who have closer ties than we do with terrorist states and whose leaders have not been heroes in these matters—to bring pressure of their own to bear and to support disinvestment, embargo, and other sanctions when they are appropriate.

War, police work, covert action, and diplomacy: all these are tasks of the state. But there is also ideological work, which can't and shouldn't be directed or organized by the state, which will only be effective if it is carried on freely—and that means in the usual democratically haphazard and disorderly way. I suppose that the state can get involved, with the Voice of America and other media. But what I have in mind is different. Secular and religious intellectuals, scholars, preachers, and publicists, not necessarily in any organized way, but with some sense of shared commitment, have to set about delegitimizing the culture of excuse and apology, probing the religious and nationalist sources of terror, calling upon the best in Islamic civilization against the worst, defending the separation of religion and politics in all civilizations. This sort of thing is very important; argument is very important. It may sound self-serving for someone who makes his living making arguments to say this, but it is true nonetheless. For all their inner-directedness, their fanatical commitment and literal-minded faith, terrorists do rely on, and the terrorist organizations rely even more on, a friendly environment—and this friendly environment is a cultural/intellectual/political creation. We have to work to transform the environment, so that wherever terrorists go, they will encounter hostility and rejection.

5. *What will be the signs of a successful response?* How will we know when we have won this "war"? We have already been told by the secretary of defense that we are not going to get the conventional signs: formal surrender, signatures on a peace treaty. The measure of success will be relative: a decline in attacks and in the scope of attacks; the collapse of morale among the terrorists, the appearance of informers and defectors from their ranks; the rallying of opportunists, who have the best nose for who's winning, to our side; the silence of those who once made excuses for terror; a growing sense of safety among ordinary people. None of this is going to come quickly or easily.

There is one more measure: our ability to shape our foreign policies, particularly toward the Islamic world, without worrying about the terrorist response. Right now, we have to worry: we cannot do things that would lead someone like bin Laden to claim a victory, to boast that he had forced our hand. We have to walk a fine line: to sustain a defensible policy with regard, say, to the blockade of Iraq, the Arab-Israeli conflict, and the Kashmir dispute, and not to do anything that can plausibly be construed as appeasement. . . . There are American policies (not only in the Islamic world, but globally as well) that should be changed, but in politics one must not only do the right thing, one must do it for the right reasons; the attacks of September 11 are not a good reason for change. One day we will be free of this kind of constraint, and that will be another way of knowing that we have won.

READING QUESTIONS

1. What are the differences between the three types of terrorism mentioned by Walzer? Try to give an example of each.
2. Why does Walzer think that misery, poverty, and inequality cannot account for terrorism?
3. What are two types of excuse given to defend terrorism? Why does Walzer think that neither of these excuses is plausible?
4. Describe the extent to which Walzer thinks civil liberties should be considered in investigations into terrorist activity.
5. What role should intellectuals and scholars play in the response to terrorism, according to Walzer?
6. What will be some of the unconventional signs that a response to terrorism has been successful?

DISCUSSION QUESTION

1. Should a state put constraints on civil liberties in order to protect the lives of its citizens? Does the absence of successful terrorist attacks in the future guarantee the safety of our civil liberties?

JAMES P. STERBA

Terrorism and International Justice

Sterba argues that just-war theory, when properly interpreted, can be reconciled with antiwar pacifism, yielding a view he calls just-war pacifism. After setting forth the basic provisions of just-war pacifism, Sterba proceeds to apply this moral outlook to a variety of wartime and terrorist activities including the World War II U.S. bombing of Hiroshima and Nagasaki and the more recent U.S.-led war in Afghanistan. Sterba concludes by outlining how the United States ought to respond to the terrorist attacks of 9/11 if it is to satisfy the requirements of just-war pacifism.

Recommended Reading: natural law theory, chap. 1, sec. 2B, particularly the doctrine of double effect.

INTRODUCTION

How should we think about terrorism within a context of international justice? To answer this question it is helpful to start with a definition of terrorism. Since 1983, the U.S. State Department has defined terrorism as follows:

> Terrorism is premeditated, politically motivated violence perpetrated against noncombatant targets by subnational groups or clandestine agents, usually intended to influence an audience.[1]

In a recent U.S. State Department document in which this definition is endorsed, there is also a section that discusses state-sponsored terrorism.[2] It is clear then that the U.S. State Department does not hold that only subnational groups or individuals can commit terrorist acts; it further recognizes that states can commit terrorist acts as well. So let me offer the following definition of terrorism, which is essentially the same as the U.S. State Department's definition once it is

allowed that states too can commit terrorist acts, and once it is recognized that it is through attempting to elicit terror (that is, intense fear, fright or intimidation) that terrorists try to achieve their goals. The definition is:

> Terrorism is the use or threat of violence against innocent people to elicit terror in them, or in some other group of people, in order to further a political objective.

Using this definition, there is no problem seeing the attacks on New York City and Washington, DC, particularly the attacks on the World Trade Center, as terrorist acts.[3] Likewise, the bombing of the U.S. embassies in Kenya and Tanzania in 1998 as well as the suicide bombings directed at Israeli civilians are terrorist acts.[4]

But what about the U.S. bombing of a pharmaceutical plant in Sudan with respect to which the United States blocked a UN inquiry and later compensated the owner, but not the thousands of victims who were deprived of drugs;[5] or the U.S.-sponsored sanctions against Iraq that kill an estimated three thousand to five thousand children in Iraq each month;[6] or the United States's $4 billion a year support for Israel's occupation of Palestinian lands, now in its thirty-fifth year, which is illegal, that is, in violation of UN resolutions the same sort of resolutions over which the Bush administration now wants to go to war with Iraq that specifically forbid in the case of Israel "the acquisition of territory by force," and which has resulted in many thousands of deaths? If we want to go back further, what about the U.S. support for the Contras in Nicaragua and the death squads in El Salvador, especially during the Reagan years, and the United States's use of terrorist contra*city* threats of nuclear retaliation during the Cold War and its actual use of nuclear weapons against Hiroshima and Nagasaki at the end of World War II, resulting in over one hundred thousand deaths? Surely, all of these U.S. actions also turn out to be either terrorist acts or support for terrorist acts, according to our definition. How can we tell then, which, if any, of these terrorist acts, or support for terrorist acts, are morally justified?

THE PERSPECTIVE OF JUST WAR THEORY AND PACIFISM

My preferred approach to addressing this question is provided by pacifism and just war theory. This is because I think that pacifism and just war theory provide a very useful way to think morally about terrorism. Thinking morally about terrorism involves trying to think about it from the perspectives of all those involved, which is something we almost never fully manage to pull off, particularly when we are dealing with perspectives that are alien to our own. But the degree to which we fail to reach out and take into account the perspectives of all those involved is the degree to which we fail to reach a morally correct approach to the practical problems we face. That is why pacifism and just war theory are particularly helpful in this context; they tend to keep us focused on what we need to take into account if we are to achieve a morally correct

response to terrorism. So this is the approach that I will adopt here.

Most people identify pacifism with a theory of nonviolence. We can call this view "nonviolent pacifism." It maintains that *any use of violence against other human beings is morally prohibited.* Nonviolent pacifism has been defended on both religious and philosophical grounds. New Testament admonitions to turn the other cheek and to love one's enemies have been taken to support this form of pacifism. The Jains of India endorse this form of pacifism and extend it to include a prohibition of violence against all living beings. Philosophically, nonviolent pacifism has also seemed attractive because it is similar to the basic principle of "Do no evil" that is found in most ethical perspectives.

It has been argued, however, that nonviolent pacifism is incoherent. In a well-known article, Jan Narveson rejects nonviolent pacifism as incoherent because it recognizes a right to life yet rules out any use of force in defense of that right.[7] A strict nonviolence principle is incoherent, Narveson argues, because having a right entails the legitimacy of using force in defense of that right at least on some occasions. But nonviolent pacifism does not prohibit all force or resistance in defense of one's rights but only that which is violent.[8] Thus, Rosa Parks was nonviolently defending her rights when she refused to give up her seat in a bus to a white person in Montgomery, Alabama, in 1955.

Some pacifists have thought that the best way to respond to objections like Narveson's is to endorse a form of pacifism that clearly does not rule out all force but only lethal force. We can call this view "nonlethal pacifism." It maintains that *any lethal use of force against other human beings is morally prohibited.* This may have been the form of pacifism endorsed by Christians in the early church before the time of Constantine. Mahatma Gandhi is also often interpreted to be defending just this form of pacifism, as rooted in both Christianity and Hinduism. Cheyney Ryan, attempting to defend this form of pacifism, has argued that a difference between the pacifist and the nonpacifist is whether we can or should create the necessary distance between ourselves and other human beings in order to make the act of killing possible.[9] To illustrate, Ryan cites George Orwell's reluctance to shoot at an enemy soldier who jumped out of a trench and ran along the top of a parapet half-dressed and holding up his trousers with both hands. Ryan contends that what kept Orwell from shooting was that he couldn't think of the soldier as a thing rather than a fellow human being.

However, I do not believe that Ryan's example is compelling as a support for nonlethal pacifism. It is not clear that Orwell's inability to shoot the enemy soldier was because he could not think of the soldier as a thing rather than a fellow human being. Perhaps it was because he could not think of the soldier who was holding up his trousers with both hands as a threat or a combatant.

It also appears that Gandhi himself did not endorse this form of pacifism. In his essay "The Doctrine of the Sword," Gandhi wrote,

> I do believe that where there is only a choice between cowardice and violence, I would advise violence. Thus, when my eldest son asked me what he should have done, had he been present when I was almost fatally assaulted in 1908, whether he should have run away and seen me killed or whether he should have used his physical force which he could and wanted to use, and defended me, I told him that it was his duty to defend me even by using violence.[10]

There is, however, a form of pacifism that remains relatively untouched by the criticisms that have been raised against both nonviolent pacifism and nonlethal pacifism. This form of pacifism neither prohibits all uses of force nor even all uses of lethal force. We can call the view "anti-war pacifism" because it holds that *any massive use of lethal force, as in warfare, is morally prohibited.* Some historians claim that this is the form of pacifism endorsed by the early Christian church because, after 180 C.E., but not before, there is evidence of Christians being permitted to serve in the military, doing basically police work, during times of peace. Anti-war pacifism is also the form of pacifism most widely defended by philosophers today, at least in the English-speaking world. Two excellent defenses are Duane L. Cady, *From Warism to Pacifism,* and Robert L. Holmes, *On War and Morality.* Among the members of the primarily U.S. Canadian Concerned Philosophers for Peace, anti-war pacifism seems to be the most widely endorsed pacifist view.

In defense of anti-war pacifism, it is undeniable that wars have brought much death and destruction in their wake and that many of those who have perished in them are noncombatants or innocents. In fact, the tendency of modern wars has been to produce higher and higher proportions of noncombatant casualties, making it more and more difficult to justify participation in such wars. At the same time, strategies for nonbelligerent conflict resolution are rarely intensively developed and explored before nations choose to go to war, making it all but impossible to justify participation in such wars.

In my previous work, I attempted to further defend this form of pacifism by developing it along side of just war theory. I argue that when just war theory is given its most morally defensible interpretation then it too can be reconciled with the practical requirements of anti-war pacifism.[11]

In traditional just war theory, there are two basic elements: an account of just cause and an account of just means. Just cause is usually specified as follows:

1. There must be substantial aggression.
2. Nonbelligerent correctives must be either hopeless or too costly.
3. Belligerent correctives must be neither hopeless nor too costly.

Needless to say, the notion of substantial aggression is a bit fuzzy, but it is generally understood to be the type of aggression that violates people's most fundamental rights. To suggest some specific examples of what is and is not substantial aggression, usually the taking of hostages is regarded as substantial aggression while the nationalization of particular firms owned by foreigners is not so regarded. But even when substantial aggression occurs, frequently nonbelligerent correctives are neither hopeless nor too costly to pursue. And even when nonbelligerent correctives are either hopeless or too costly, in order for there to be a just cause, belligerent correctives must be neither hopeless nor too costly.[12]

Traditional just war theory assumes, however, that there are just causes and goes on to specify just means as imposing two requirements:

1. Harm to innocents should not be directly intended as an end or a means.
2. The harm resulting from the belligerent means should not be disproportionate to the particular defensive objective to be attained.

While the just means conditions apply to each defensive action, the just cause conditions must be met by the conflict as a whole.

Now, in previous work, I have argued that when just war theory is given its most morally defensible interpretation, it

1. Allows the use of belligerent means against unjust aggressors only when such means minimize the loss and injury to innocent lives overall.
2. Allows the use of belligerent means against unjust aggressors to indirectly threaten innocent lives only to prevent the loss of innocent lives, not simply to prevent injury to innocents.
3. Allows the use of belligerent means to directly or indirectly threaten, or even take the lives of, unjust aggressors when it is the only way to prevent serious injury to innocents.[13]

Obviously, just war theory, so understood, is going to place severe restrictions on the use of belligerent means in warfare. In fact, most wars throughout history have been unjustified either in whole or in part. For example, the U.S. involvement in Nicaragua, El Salvador, and Panama; the Soviet Union's involvement in Afghanistan; and Israeli involvement in the West Bank and the Gaza Strip all violate the just cause and just means provisions of just war theory as I defend them. Even the U.S.-led Gulf War against Iraq seems to have violated both the just cause and just means provisions of just war theory. In fact, one strains to find examples of justified applications of just war theory in recent history. Two examples that come to mind are India's military action against Pakistan in Bangladesh and the Tanzanian incursion into Uganda during the rule of Idi Amin. But, after mentioning these two examples, it is difficult to go

on. What this shows, I have argued, is that when just war theory and anti-war pacifism are given their most morally defensible interpretations, both views can be reconciled. In this reconciliation, the few wars and large-scale conflicts that meet the stringent requirements of just war theory are the only wars and large-scale conflicts to which a nti-war pacifists cannot justifiably object. We can call the view that emerges from this reconciliation "just war pacifism." It is the view that claims that because of the stringent requirements of just war theory, only very rarely will participation in a massive use of lethal force in warfare be morally justified.

Now one might think that from the perspective of just war pacifism acts of terrorism could never be morally justified. But this would require an absolute prohibition on intentionally harming innocents, and such a prohibition would not seem to be justified, even from the perspective of just war pacifism.[14] Specifically, it would seem that harm to innocents can be justified for the sake of achieving a greater good when the harm is

1. Trivial (e.g., as in the case of stepping on someone's foot to get out of a crowded subway)
2. Easily reparable (e.g., as in the case of lying to a temporarily depressed friend to keep her from committing suicide)
3. Nonreparable but greatly outweighed by the consequences of the action.

Obviously, it is this third category of harm that is relevant to the possible justification of terrorism. But when is intentional harm to innocents nonreparable yet greatly outweighed by the consequences?

Consider the following example often discussed by moral philosophers.[15] A large person who is leading a party of spelunkers gets himself stuck in the mouth of a cave in which flood waters are rising. The trapped party of spelunkers just happens to have a stick of dynamite with which they can blast the large person out of the mouth of the cave; either they use the dynamite or they all drown, the large person with them. Now it is usually assumed in this case that it is morally permissible to dynamite the large person out of the mouth of the cave. After all, if that is not done, the whole party of spelunkers will die, the large person with them. So the sacrifice imposed on the large person in this case would not be that great.

But what if the large person's head is outside rather than inside the cave, as it must have been in the previous interpretation of the case? Under those circumstances, the large person would not die when the other spelunkers drown. Presumably after slimming down a bit, he would eventually just squeeze his way out of the mouth of the cave. In this case, could the party of spelunkers trapped in the cave still legitimately use the stick of dynamite they have to save themselves rather than the large person?

Suppose there were ten, twenty, one hundred, or whatever number you want of spelunkers trapped in the cave. At some point, won't the number be sufficiently great that it would be morally acceptable for those in the cave to use the stick of dynamite to save themselves rather than the large person, even if this meant that the large person would be morally required to sacrifice his life? The answer has to be yes, even if you think it has to be a very unusual case when we can reasonably demand that people thus sacrifice their lives in this way.

Is it possible that some acts of terrorism are morally justified in this way? It is often argued that our dropping of atomic bombs on Hiroshima and Nagasaki was so justified. President Truman, who ordered the bombing, justified it on the grounds that it was used to shorten the war. In 1945, the United States demanded the unconditional surrender of Japan. The Japanese had by that time lost the war, but the leaders of their armed forces were by no means ready to accept unconditional surrender. While the Japanese leaders expected an invasion of their mainland islands, they believed that they could make that invasion so costly that the United States would accept a conditional surrender. Truman's military advisors also believed the costs would be high. The capture of Okinawa had cost almost 80,000 American casualties, while almost the entire Japanese garrison of 120,000 men died in battle. If the mainland islands were defended in a similar manner, hundreds of thousands of Japanese would surely die. During that time, the bombing of Japan would continue, and perhaps intensify, resulting in casualty rates that were no different from those that were expected from the atomic attack. A massive incendiary raid on Tokyo early in March 1945 had set off a firestorm and killed an estimated 100,000 people. Accordingly, Truman's Secretary of State James Byrnes admitted that the two atomic bombs did cause "many casualties, but not nearly so many as there would have been had our air force continued to drop incendiary bombs on Japan's cities."[16] Similarly, Winston Churchill wrote in support of Truman's decision "To avert a vast, indefinite butchery . . . at the cost of a few explosions seemed, after all our toils and perils, a miracle of deliverance."[17]

Yet the "vast, indefinite butchery" that the United States sought to avert by dropping atomic bombs on Hiroshima and Nagasaki was one that the United States itself was threatening and had already started to carry out with its incendiary attack on Tokyo. And the United States itself could have easily avoided this butchery by dropping its demand for unconditional Japanese surrender. Moreover, a demand of unconditional surrender can almost never be morally justified since defeated aggressors almost always have certain rights that they never are required to surrender. Hence, the United States's terrorist acts of dropping of atomic bombs on Hiroshima and Nagasaki cannot be justified on the grounds of shortening the war and avoiding a vast, indefinite butchery because the United States could have secured those results simply by giving up its unreasonable demand for unconditional surrender.

A more promising case for justified terrorism is the counter-city bombing by the British during the early stages of World War II. Early in the war, it became clear that British bombers could fly effectively only at night because too many of them were being shot down during day raids by German anti-aircraft fire. In addition, a study done in 1941 showed that of those planes flying at night recorded as having actually succeeded in attacking their targets, only one-third managed to drop their bombs within five miles of their intended target.[18] This meant that British bombers flying at night could reasonably aim at no target smaller than a fairly large city.[19]

Michael Walzer argues that under these conditions, the British terror bombing was morally justified because at this early stage of the war, it was the only way the British had left to them to try to avert a Nazi victory.[20] Walzer further argues that the time period when such terror bombing was justified was relatively brief. Once the Russians began to inflict enormous casualties on the German army and the United States made available its manpower and resources, other alternatives opened up. Unfortunately, the British continued to rely heavily on terror bombing right up until the end of the war, culminating in the fire-bombing of Dresden in which something like one hundred thousand people were killed. However, for that relatively brief period of time when Britain had no other way to try to avert a Nazi victory, Walzer argues, its reliance on terror bombing was morally justified.

Suppose then we accept this moral justification for British terror bombing during World War II. Doesn't this suggest a comparable moral justification for Palestinian suicide bombings against Israeli civilians? Israel has been illegally occupying Palestinian land for thirty-five years now in violation of UN resolutions following the 1967 Arab-Israeli War. Even a return to those 1967 borders, which the UN resolutions require, still permits a considerable expansion of Israel's original borders as specified in the mandate of 1947. Moreover, since the Oslo Peace Accords in 1993, Israeli settlements have doubled in the Occupied Territories. In the year that Sharon has been prime minister, some thirty-five new settlements have been established in the Occupied Territories.[21] In Gaza, there are 1.2 million Palestinians and four thousand Israelis, but the Israelis control 40 percent of the land and 70 percent of the water. In the West Bank, there are 1.9 million Palestinians and 280,000 Israelis, but the Israelis control 40 percent of the land and 37 percent of the water.[22] In addition, Israel failed to abide by its commitments under the Oslo Peace Accords to release prisoners, to complete a third redeployment of its military forces, and to transfer three Jerusalem villages to Palestinian control.[23] Moreover, at the recent Camp David meeting, Israeli's proposals did not provide for Palestinian control over East Jerusalem, upon which 40 percent of the Palestinian economy depends.[24] Nor did Israeli's proposals provide for a right of return or compensation for the half of the Palestinian population that lives in exile (President Clinton proposed that Chairman Arafat should just forget about them),

most of them having been driven off their land by Israeli expansion. So the Palestinian cause is clearly a just one, but just as clearly the Palestinians lack the military resources to effectively resist Israeli occupation and aggression by simply directly attacking Israeli military forces. The Israelis have access to the most advanced U.S. weapons and $4 billion a year from the United States to buy whatever weapons they want. The Palestinians have no comparable support from anyone. It is under these conditions that a moral justification for Palestinian suicide bombers against Israeli civilians emerges. Given that the Palestinians lack any effective means to try to end the Israeli occupation or to stop Israel's further expansion into Palestinian territories other than by using suicide bombers against Israeli civilians, why would this use of suicide bombers not be justified in much the same way that Walzer justifies the British terror bombing in the early stages of World War II? If the Israelis have the ultimate goal of confining most Palestinians to a number of economically nonviable and disconnected reservations, similar to those on which the United States confines Native American Indian nations, then surely the Palestinians have a right to resist that conquest as best they can.

Beginning with just war pacifism, I have argued that there are morally defensible exceptions to the just means prohibition against directly killing innocents. The cave analogy argument aims to establish that conclusion. British terror bombing at the beginning of World War II, but not the American dropping of atomic bombs on Hiroshima and Nagasaki at the end of that war, is offered as a real-life instantiation of that argument. The Palestinian use of suicide bombers against Israeli civilians is then presented as a contemporary instantiation of that very same argument.

Yet even if there is a moral justification for the Palestinian use of suicide bombers against Israeli civilians under present conditions, clearly most acts of terrorism cannot be justified, and clearly there was no moral justification for the terrorist attacks on New York City and Washington, DC, particularly the attacks on the World Trade Center.

Even so, the question remains as to whether the United States was morally justified in going to war against Afghanistan in response to these unjustified terrorist acts. According to just war pacifism, before using belligerent correctives, we must be sure that nonbelligerent correctives are neither hopeless nor too costly. The three weeks of diplomatic activity that the United States engaged in did not appear to be sufficient to determine whether it was hopeless or too costly to continue to attempt to bring Osama bin Laden before a U.S. court or, better, before an international court of law, without military action. We demanded that the Taliban government immediately hand over bin Laden and "all the leaders of Al Qaeda who hide in your land." But how could we have reasonably expected this of the Taliban, given that months after we have overthrown the Taliban government and installed a friendly one, we still have not been able to turn up bin Laden and most of his key associates? How could we have expected that the Taliban government, with its limited resources and loose control over the country, to do in three weeks what we still have not been able to accomplish in over a year?

It is conceivable that our leaders never really expected that the Taliban government would be able to meet our demands even if they had wanted to do so. After we began our military offensive, the Taliban government expressed a willingness to hand over bin Laden and his associates at least for trial in an international court if we would stop our military offensive. But we never took them up on their offer. Perhaps we knew that the Taliban government really lacked the resources to hand over bin Laden and his key associates, even while we used their failure to do so as the justification for our waging a war against them. . . .

In the United States, public opinion rather than the exhaustion of nonbelligerent options has served to motivate our military response to 9/11. The military response has been well received by at least a majority of American people, who want to see their government "doing something" to get bin Laden and fight terrorism. But satisfying public opinion polls is not the same as satisfying the requirements of just war pacifism. The United States first called its military action Infinite Justice and then later, in view of the religious connotations of that term, began calling it Enduring Freedom, but our

military action is neither just nor does it acceptably promote freedom unless nonbelligerent correctives are first exhausted, and they were not exhausted in this case. Nor has our military response yet delivered up for trial bin Laden or any of his top associates or even any of the top Taliban leaders, although some were killed by our military action, and some good detective and police work, not military action, has recently led to the capture in Pakistan of Abu Zubaydah, who is thought to be bin Laden's second or third lieutenant.

So, even if the United States itself had not engaged in any related terrorist acts or supported any related terrorist acts, there would still be a strong objection to its relatively quick resort to military force as a response to the terrorist attacks of 9/11. Given that the United States itself arguably has engaged in terrorist acts in Sudan, and through the UN against Iraqi children, as well as has supported terrorist acts through its political and financial support of Israel's illegal occupation of Palestinian lands, and given that these acts of terrorism, and support for terrorism, have served at least partially to motivate terrorist attacks on the United States itself, the United States surely needs to take steps to radically correct its own wrongdoing if it is to respond justly to the related wrongdoing of bin Laden and his followers. Unfortunately this is also something we have not yet done.

What then should we be doing if we are to respect the requirements of just war pacifism in our response to the terrorist attacks of September 11?

1. We should let Israel know in no uncertain terms that our continuing political and financial support depends upon its reaching an agreement with the Palestinians on the establishment of a Palestinian state in accordance with the relevant UN resolutions relatively quickly, within, say, three to six months. So many plans for a Palestinian state have been discussed over the years that it should not be that difficult to settle on one of them that accords with the relevant UN resolutions, once Israel knows that it can no longer draw on the political and financial support of the United States to resist a settlement. The evidence of serious negotiations between Israel and the Palestinians will be welcomed by people around the world.

2. The sanctions against Iraq imposed since 1991 must be radically modified to permit sufficient humanitarian assistance to the Iraqi people, particularly the children. (Obviously, I am opposed to a pre-emptive military strike against Iraq—one that does not exhaust nonbelligerent correctives.) According to a UNICEF study done in 1999, if the substantial reduction in child mortality throughout Iraq during the 1980s had continued through the 1990s, there would have been half a million fewer deaths of children under five in the country as a whole during the eight year the period of 1991 to 1998.[25] Moreover, the current oil-for-food program, which was only introduced in 1997 (six years into the sanctions), does not, by the UN's own estimate, provide sufficient food and medicine to prevent conditions in Iraq from getting even worse. This all has to change. The oil-for-food program must immediately be expanded to arrest and reverse the deteriorating humanitarian conditions in Iraq.

3. There should have been three to six months of serious diplomatic negotiations to bring Osama bin Laden and the leaders of his Al Qaeda network either before a U.S. court or, preferably, before an international court of law. Substantial economic and political incentives should have been offered to the relevant individuals and nations to help bring this about. Now that we have overthrown the Taliban in Afghanistan and helped establish a friendly government, we should end our military campaign immediately and return to nonbelligerent correctives, which can include the same sort of good detective and police work that has made possible the capture of Abu Zubaydah, the highest-ranking Al Qaeda member captured to date. This will even give us the unintended benefit of conveying to our enemies and to others that we are serious about engaging in belligerent correctives should the nonbelligerent ones prove ineffective.

One of the main lessons we should have drawn from the 9/11 terrorist attacks on the World Trade Center and the Pentagon is how vulnerable our costly high-tech military defenses are to smart, determined enemies using even the simplest of weapons imaginable—knives and boxcutters. And as bad as 9/11 was, it could have been far worse. There is little doubt that the terrorists who hijacked the airplanes and flew them into the World Trade Center and the Pentagon would not have hesitated to detonate a nuclear explosive, maybe one they would have hidden in the World Trade Center, if they could have done so.

It would also not be that difficult for terrorists to target chemical plants or, more easily, shipments of industrial chemicals such as chlorine that are transported in tank cars and trucks. Before 9/11, only about 2 percent of all the containers that move though U.S. ports were actually inspected. Currently, that number has been doubled, but that still means that 96 percent of such containers that are shipped from all over the world are not inspected when they enter the United States.[26] Detonating thousands of tons of ammonium nitrate loaded on a ship in a harbor would have the impact of a small nuclear explosion. Just last year, three hundred tons of ammonium nitrate apparently exploded in France, killing twenty-nine people and injuring more than twenty-five hundred.[27]

Building another layer of high-tech military defense, like the $238 billion George W. Bush proposes to spend on a missile defense system, does little to decrease our vulnerability to such terrorist attacks.[28] In fact, because such high-tech military expenditures divert money from projects that would significantly decrease our vulnerability to terrorist attacks, they actually have an overall negative impact on our national security.

What then should we do to prevent future terrorist attacks from being directed at the United States or U.S. citizens? In addition to the changes of policy I mentioned earlier with respect to Israel, Iraq, and Osama bin Laden's Al Qaeda network, there are many other things that the United States could do to project a more just foreign policy. For starters, there are a number of international treaties and conventions, for example, the Kyoto Climate Change Treaty, the Treaty Banning Land Mines, and the Rome Treaty for the establishment of an International Criminal Court, that the United States has failed to sign for reasons that seem to simply favor U.S. special interests at the expense of international justice or what would be of benefit to the world community as a whole.

Furthermore, looking at things from an international justice perspective can require a considerable modification of our usual ways of thinking about the relationships between nations and peoples. From an international justice perspective or, more generally, from a moral perspective, actions and policies must be such that they are acceptable by all those affected by those actions and policies (that is, the actions and policies must be such that they ought to be accepted, not necessarily that they are accepted by all those affected by those actions and policies). Thus, the fact that the United States, which constitutes 4 percent of the world's population while using 25 percent of its energy resources, refuses to sign the Kyoto Climate Change Treaty and make the cuts in its energy consumption that virtually all other nations of the world judge to be fair makes the United States, in this regard, something like an outlaw nation from the perspective of international justice.[29]

Yet the failure of the United States to accord with international justice cuts even deeper. According to the World Food Program, three-quarters of a billion people are desperately hungry around the world. According to that same program, even Afghanistan, the subject of so much of our recent attention, has received only 5 percent of the $285 million in emergency aid it needs to feed its people for the rest of the year.[30] One of two women ministers in the provisional Afghan government, Sima Samar, who is in charge of women's affairs, has an unheated office and no phone or money to effect policies in Afghanistan that would improve the situation for women.[31] There is no way that we can achieve international justice without a radical redistribution of goods and resources from rich to poor to eliminate hunger and desperation around the world. The United States needs to be a champion of this redistribution if it is to be perceived correctly as measuring up to the standard of international justice, and thus to be a just nation, whose resources and people should be respected. But the United States has not done this. In fact, its contribution to alleviate world hunger is (in proportion to its size) one of the smallest among the industrized nations of the world—roughly .11 percent, which President Bush proposes to increase to .13 percent; Britain's contribution is about three times as much, and Sweden, the Netherlands, and Norway proportionally give about eight times as much.[32]

Clearly, then, there is much that the United States can do if it wants to respond to the terrorist attacks of 9/11 in a way that accords with international justice. I have argued that the best account of pacifism and the best account of just war theory combined in just war pacifism requires that, as soon as possible, the United States put an end to its military response; that the U.S. make it clear that it is taking radical steps to correct for related terrorist acts of its own or of those countries it supports; and that it give nonbelligerent correctives a reasonable chance to work. I have further argued that the United States has to do more to be a good world citizen. It must stop being a conspicuous holdout with respect to international treaties, and it must do its fair share to redistribute resources from the rich to the poor as international justice requires. Only then would the United States be living up to the moral ideals that could make it what it claims to be. In turn, living up to those ideals may prove to be the best defense the United States has against terrorism directed against its own people.

NOTES

Earlier versions of this paper were presented to the Philosophy Department at the University of Illinois at Chicago, the Philosophy Department at the University of North Carolina at Charlotte, an Amnesty International Forum at the University of California at Irvine, and the University of Notre Dame. I wish to thank Thomas Bushnell, Bill Gay, Bernard Gert, Gary Gutting, Vittorio Hosle, Robert Johanson, Matthew Kennedy, Anthony Laden, Mark Levine, Deborah Marble, Charles Mills, Paul Quirk, James Rakowski, Kristin Shrader-Frechette, David Solomon, Rosemarie Tong, and Paul Weithman for their helpful comments.

1. *Patterns of Global Terrorism—2000.* Released by the Office of the Coordinator for Counterterrorism, April 2001.

2. *Patterns of Global Terrorism—2000.*

3. If we use the just war distinction between combatants and noncombatants, those killed at the Pentagon might be viewed as combatants in some undeclared war.

4. Since the bombings in Kenya and Tanzania were of U.S. government installations, they are only classified as terrorist acts by virtue of the fact that they were intended to maximize civilian casualties.

5. From an interview with Phyllis Bennis, *Z magazine,* September 12, 2001. While the bombing of the pharmaceutical plant may have involved unintentional harm to innocents, refusing to compensate the thousands of victims who were deprived of the drugs they needed is to intentionally harm innocents.

6. "Life and Death in Iraq," *Seattle-Post-Intelligencer,* May 11, 1999. See also Jeff Indemyer, "Iraqi Sanctions: Myth and Fact," *Swans Commentary,* September 3, 2002.

7. Jan Narveson, "Pacifism: A Philosophical Analysis," *Ethics* 75 (1965): 259–271.

8. We can understand "violence" here and throughout the paper as "the prima facie unjustified use of force."

9. Cheyney Ryan, "Self-Defense, Pacifism and the Possibility of Killing," in *The Ethics of War and Nuclear Deterrence,* ed. James P. Sterba (Belmont, CA: Wadsworth Publishing Co., 1985), pp. 45–49.

10. M. K. Gandhi, "The Doctrine of the Sword," in *Nonviolent Resistance* (New York: Schocken Books, 1961) p. 132.

11. James P. Sterba, *Justice for Here and Now* (Cambridge: Cambridge University Press, 1998), Chapter 7.

12. Built into the "too costly" requirement is the traditional proportionality requirement of just war theory. Clearly various nonbelligerent and belligerent measures can be either too costly to ourselves, to the other side, or to both sides together. When belligerent measures are too costly either to ourselves or to the other side or to both sides together, they are rightly judged disproportionate.

13. Sterba, Chapter 7.

14. This is because the requirements of just war pacifism, as I stated them earlier in this article, do not directly address the question of whether there are exceptions to the prohibition on intentionally harming innocents. Moreover, once that question is taken up by means of the same case-by-case analysis with which I defended the earlier stated requirements of just war pacifism (for the defense of these requirements, see my *Justice for Here and Now,* Chapter 7), certain exceptions to the prohibition on intentionally harming innocents turn out to be morally justified, as I go on to show.

15. See Philippa Foot, "The Problem of Abortion and the Doctrine of Double Effect," *Oxford Review* 5 (1967): 5–15.

16. James Byrnes, *Speaking Frankly* (New York: Harper Row, 1947), p. 264.

17. Winston Churchill, *Triumph and Tragedy* (New York: Houghton Mifflin, 1962), p. 639.

18. Noble Frankland, *Bomber Offensive* (New York: Ballantine Books, 1970), pp. 38–39.

19. As examples of how inaccurate night bombing was at the time, one oil installation was attacked by 162 aircraft carrying 159 tons of bombs, another by 134 aircraft carrying 103 tons of bombs, but neither suffered any major damage. See Charles Webster and Noble Frankland, *The Strategic Air Offensive Against Germany* 1939–45, Vol. I (London: HMSO, 1961) p. 164.

20. Walzer, pp. 255–262.

21. Editorial, *New York Times,* April 26, 2002, p. 26.

22. Avishai Margalit, "Settling Scores," *New York Review,* August 22, 2001, pp. 20–24.

23. See Robert Malley and Hussein, "Camp David: The Tragedy of Errors, *New York Review,* August 9, 2001, pp. 59–65; "A Reply to Ehud Barak," *New York Review,* June 11, 2002, pp. 46–49; "A Reply," *New York Review,* June 27, 2002, p. 48. See also Benny Morris and Ehud Barak, "Camp David and After: An Exchange," *New York Review,* June 13, 2002, pp. 42–45; "Camp David and After—Continued," *New York Review,* June 27, 2002, pp. 47–48.

24. Jeff Halper, The Israeli Committee Against House Demolitions, www.icahd.org.

25. "Life and Death in Iraq." See also Jeff Indemyer, "Iraqi Sanctions: Myth and Fact."

26. David Carr, "The Futility of Homeland Defense," *The Atlantic Monthly,* January 2002, pp. 53–55.

27. Richard Garwin, "The Many Threats of "Terror," *The New York Review,* October 2, 2001, pp. 17–19; Bruce Hoffman, *Terrorism and Weapons of Mass Destruction* (Santa Monica, CA: Rand, 1999). For numerous senerios by which terrorists could fairly easily create massive destruction, see Stephen Bowman, *When the Eagle Screams: America's Vulnerability to Terrorism* (New York: Birch Lane Press, 1994), especially Chapters 8–14.

28. James O. Goldsborough, "The Real Costs of Missile Defense," *San Diego Union-Tribune,* April 1, 2002.

29. Thomas Friedman, "Better Late Than Never," *New York Times,* March 17, 2002, p. 51.

30. Barbara Crossette, "Food Aid for Afghans Way Short of Need, U.N. Agency Says," *New York Times,* April 26, 2002, p. 12.

31. Ales Spillius, "'People, Say I Make Too Much Noise,' Dr. Sima Samar, Afghanistan's First Minister for Women's Affairs, Talks to Alex Spillus," *The Daily Telegraph* (London), February 22, 2002, p. 23.

32. Jon Sawyer, "U.S. Wrestles with Notions That Massive Aid Can Stop Terrorism: Nation Pledges More to Front-Line States, but Little Change for Others," *St. Louis Post-Dispatch,* December 3, 2001, p. 1 and Paul Krugman, "The Heart of Cheapness," *New York Times*, May 31, 2002, p. 23.

READING QUESTIONS

1. Explain the distinction between Sterba's definition of terrorism and the one formulated by the U.S. State Department in 1983.
2. What are the differences between nonlethal and nonviolent pacifism? What criticisms does Sterba raise against each of these views?
3. What reasons does Sterba offer in defense of anti-war pacifism?
4. What is just war pacifism and how does it represent a reconciliation between anti-war pacifism and just war theory?
5. Why are the bombings of Hiroshima and Nagasaki by the United States morally unjustifiable, according to Sterba?
6. Explain why the terrorist act of suicide bombing by the Palestinians against the Israelis is morally justifiable, according to Sterba.

DISCUSSION QUESTION

1. Should we agree with Sterba that the United States is "an outlaw nation from the perspective of international justice"?

HENRY SHUE

Torture

Shue explains the wrongness of torture by appeal to a general prohibition to protect the defenseless in the context of war—a prohibition that lies behind the moral importance that just-war theory attributes to noncombatants. He then proceeds to examine two types of torture—terrorist torture and interrogational torture—in order to determine whether either type might, under rare conditions, be morally justified. While willing to grant that it is imaginable that the evil that could be prevented by the use of torture might be so great as to outweigh the evil of using this means, Shue cautions against the use of such "artificial" cases in thinking about the morality of torture.

From Henry Shue, "Torture," *Philosophy and Public Affairs* 7 (1978). Reprinted by permission of Princeton University Press.

But no one dies in the right place
Or in the right hour
And everyone dies sooner than his time
And before he reaches home.

—*Reza Baraheni*

Whatever one might have to say about torture, there appear to be moral reasons for not saying it. Obviously I am not persuaded by these reasons, but they deserve some mention. Mostly, they add up to a sort of Pandora's Box objection: if practically everyone is opposed to all torture, why bring it up, start people thinking about it, and risk weakening the inhibitions against what is clearly a terrible business?

Torture is indeed contrary to every relevant international law, including the laws of war. No other practice except slavery is so universally and unanimously condemned in law and human convention. Yet, unlike slavery, which is still most definitely practiced but affects relatively few people, torture is widespread and growing. According to Amnesty International, scores of governments are now using some torture—including governments which are widely viewed as fairly civilized—and a number of governments are heavily dependent upon torture for their very survival.[1]

So, to cut discussion of this objection short, Pandora's Box is open. Although virtually everyone continues ritualistically to condemn all torture publicly, the deep conviction, as reflected in actual policy is in many cases not behind the strong language. In addition, partial justifications for some of the torture continue to circulate. . . .

ASSAULT UPON THE DEFENSELESS

The laws of war include an elaborate, and for the most part long-established, code for what might be described as the proper conduct of the killing of other people. Like most codes, the laws of war have been constructed piecemeal and different bits of the code serve different functions.[2] It would almost certainly be impossible to specify any one unifying purpose served by the laws of warfare as a whole. Surely major portions of the law serve to keep warfare within one sort of principle of efficiency by requiring that the minimum destruction necessary to the attainment of legitimate objectives be used.

However, not all the basic principles incorporated in the laws of war could be justified as serving the purpose of minimizing destruction. One of the most basic principles for the conduct of war (*jus in bello*) rests on the distinction between combatants and noncombatants and requires that insofar as possible, violence not be directed at noncombatants. Now, obviously, there are some conceptual difficulties in trying to separate combatants and noncombatants in some guerrilla warfare and even sometimes in modern conventional warfare among industrial societies. This difficulty is a two-edged sword; it can be used to argue that it is increasingly impossible for war to be fought justly as readily as it can be used to argue that the distinction between combatants and noncombatants is obsolete. In any case, I do not now want to defend or criticize the principle of avoiding attack upon noncombatants but to isolate one of the more general moral principles this specific principle of warfare serves.

It might be thought to serve, for example, a sort of efficiency principle in that it helps to minimize human casualties and suffering. Normally, the armed forces of the opposing nations constitute only a fraction of the respective total populations. If the casualties can be restricted to these official fighters, perhaps total casualties and suffering will be smaller than they would be if human targets were unrestricted.

But this justification for the principle of not attacking noncombatants does not ring true. Unless one is determined a priori to explain everything in terms of minimizing numbers of casualties, there is little reason to believe that this principle actually functions primarily to restrict the number of casualties rather than, as its own terms suggest, the *types* of casualties.[3] A more convincing suggestion about the best justification which could be given is that the principle goes some way toward keeping combat humane, by protecting those who are assumed to be incapable of defending themselves. The principle of warfare is an instance of a more general moral principle which prohibits assaults upon the defenseless.[4]

Nonpacifists who have refined the international code for the conduct of warfare have not necessarily viewed the killing involved in war as in itself any less terrible than pacifists view it. One fundamental function of the distinction between combatants and noncombatants is to try to make a terrible combat fair, and the killing involved can seem morally tolerable to nonpacifists in large part because it is the outcome of what is conceived as a fair procedure. To the extent that the distinction between combatants and noncombatants is observed, those who are killed will be those who were directly engaged in trying to kill their killers. The fairness may be perceived to lie in this fact: that those who are killed had a reasonable chance to survive by killing instead. It was kill or be killed for both parties, and each had his or her opportunity to survive. No doubt the opportunities may not have been anywhere near equal—it would be impossible to restrict wars to equally matched opponents. But at least none of the parties to the combat were defenseless.

Now this obviously invokes a simplified, if not romanticized, portrait of warfare. And at least some aspects of the laws of warfare can legitimately be criticized for relying too heavily for their justification on a core notion that modern warfare retains aspects of a knightly joust, or a duel, which have long since vanished, if ever they were present. But the point now is not to attack or defend the efficacy of the principle of warfare that combat is more acceptable morally if restricted to official combatants, but to notice one of its moral bases, which, I am suggesting, is that it allows for a "fair fight" by means of protecting the utterly defenseless from assault. The resulting picture of war—accurate or not—is not of victim and perpetrator (or, of mutual victims) but of a winner and a loser, each of whom might have enjoyed, or suffered, the fate of the other. Of course, the satisfaction of the requirement of providing for a "fair fight" would not by itself make a conflict morally acceptable overall. An unprovoked and otherwise unjustified invasion does not become morally acceptable just because attacks upon noncombatants, use of prohibited weapons, and so on are avoided.

At least part of the peculiar disgust which torture evokes may be derived from its apparent failure to satisfy even this weak constraint of being a "fair fight." The supreme reason, of course, is that torture begins only after the fight is—for the victim—finished. Only losers are tortured. A "fair fight" may even in fact already have occurred and led to the capture of the person who is to be tortured. But now that the torture victim has exhausted all means of defense and is powerless before the victors, a fresh assault begins. The surrender is followed by new attacks upon the defeated by the now unrestrained conquerors. In this respect torture is indeed not analogous to the killing in battle of a healthy and well-armed foe; it is a cruel assault upon the defenseless. In combat the other person one kills is still a threat when killed and is killed in part for the sake of one's own survival. The torturer inflicts pain and damage upon another person who, by virtue of now being within his or her power, is no longer a threat and is entirely at the torturer's mercy.

It is in this respect of violating the prohibition against assault upon the defenseless, then, that the manner in which torture is conducted is morally more reprehensible than the manner in which killing would occur if the laws of war were honored. In this respect torture sinks below even the well-regulated mutual slaughter of a justly fought war.

TORTURE WITHIN CONSTRAINTS?

But is all torture indeed an assault upon the defenseless? For, it could be argued in support of some torture that in many cases there is something beyond the initial surrender which the torturer wants from the victim and that in such cases the victim could comply and provide the torturer with whatever is wanted. To refuse to comply with the further demand would then be to maintain a second line of defense. The victim would, in a sense, not have surrendered—at least not fully surrendered—but instead only retreated. The victim is not, on this view, utterly helpless in the face of unrestrainable assault as long as he or she holds in reserve an act of compliance which would satisfy the torturer and bring the torture to an end.

It might be proposed, then, that there could be at least one type of morally less unacceptable torture. Obviously the torture victim must remain defenseless in the literal sense, because it cannot be expected that his or her captors would provide means of defense against themselves. But an alternative to a capability for a literal defense is an effective capability for surrender, that is, a form of surrender which will in fact bring an end to attacks. In the case of torture the relevant form of surrender might seem to be a compliance with the wishes of the torturer that provides an escape from further torture.

Accordingly, the constraint on the torture that would, on this view, make it less objectionable would be this: the victim of torture must have available an act of compliance which, if performed, will end the torture. In other words, the purpose of the torture must be known to the victim, the purpose must be the performance of some action within the victim's power to perform, and the victim's performance of the desired action must produce the permanent cessation of the torture. I shall refer to torture that provides for such an act of compliance as torture that satisfies the constraint of possible compliance. As soon becomes clear, it makes a great difference what kind of act is presented as the act of compliance. And a person with an iron will, a great sense of honor, or an overwhelming commitment to a cause may choose not to accept voluntarily cessation of the torture on the terms offered. But the basic point would be merely that there should be some terms understood so that the victim retains one last portion of control over his or her fate. Escape is not defense, but it is a manner of protecting oneself. A practice of torture that allows for escape through compliance might seem immune to the charge of engaging in assault upon the defenseless. Such is the proposal.

One type of contemporary torture, however, is clearly incapable of satisfying the constraint of possible compliance. The extraction of information from the victim, which perhaps—whatever the deepest motivations of torturers may have been—has historically been a dominant explicit purpose of torture is now, in world practice, overshadowed by the goal of the intimidation of people other than the victim.[5] Torture is in many countries used primarily to intimidate

potential opponents of the government from actively expressing their opposition in any form considered objectionable by the regime. Prohibited forms of expression range, among various regimes, from participation in terroristic guerrilla movements to the publication of accurate news accounts. The extent of the suffering inflicted upon the victims of the torture is proportioned, not according to the responses of the victim, but according to the expected impact of news of the torture upon other people over whom the torture victim normally has no control. The function of general intimidation of others, or deterrence of dissent, is radically different from the function of extracting specific information under the control of the victim of torture, in respects which are central to the assessment of such torture. This is naturally not to deny that any given instance of torture may serve, to varying degrees, both purposes—and, indeed, other purposes still.

Terroristic torture, as we may call this dominant type, cannot satisfy the constraint of possible compliance, because its purpose (intimidation of persons other than the victim of the torture) cannot be accomplished and may not even be capable of being influenced by the victim of the torture. The victim's suffering—indeed, the victim—is being used entirely as a means to an end over which the victim has no control. Terroristic torture is a pure case—the purest possible case—of the violation of the Kantian principle that no person may be used *only* as a means. The victim is simply a site at which great pain occurs so that others may know about it and be frightened by the prospect. The torturers have no particular reason not to make the suffering as great and as extended as possible. Quite possibly the more terrible the torture, the more intimidating it will be—this is certainly likely to be believed to be so.

Accordingly, one ought to expect extensions into the sorts of "experimentation" and other barbarities documented recently in the cases of, for example, the Pinochet government in Chile and the Amin government in Uganda.[6] Terroristic torturers have no particular reason not to carry the torture through to the murder of the victim, provided the victim's family or friends can be expected to spread the word about the price of any conduct compatible with disloyalty.

Therefore, terroristic torture clearly cannot satisfy even the extremely mild constraint of providing for the possibility of compliance by its victim.

The degree of need for assaults upon the defenseless initially appears to be quite different in the case of torture for the purpose of extracting information, which we may call *interrogational torture*.[7] This type of torture needs separate examination because, however condemnable we ought in the end to consider it overall, its purpose of gaining information appears to be consistent with the observation of some constraint on the part of any torturer genuinely pursuing that purpose alone. Interrogational torture does have a built-in end-point: when the information has been obtained, the torture has accomplished its purpose and need not be continued. Thus, satisfaction of the constraint of possible compliance seems to be quite compatible with the explicit end of interrogational torture, which could be terminated upon the victim's compliance in providing the information sought. In a fairly obvious fashion the torturer could consider himself or herself to have completed the assigned task—or probably more hopefully, any superiors who were supervising the process at some emotional distance could consider the task to be finished and put a stop to it. A pure case of interrogational torture, then, appears able to satisfy the constraint of possible compliance, since it offers an escape, in the form of providing the information wanted by the torturers, which affords some protection against further assault.

Two kinds of difficulties arise for the suggestion that even largely interrogational torture could escape the charge that it includes assaults upon the defenseless. It is hardly necessary to point out that very few actual instances of torture are likely to fall entirely within the category of interrogational torture. Torture intended primarily to obtain information is by no means always in practice held to some minimum necessary amount. To the extent that the torturer's motivation is sadistic or otherwise brutal, he or she will be strongly inclined to exceed any rational calculations about what is sufficient for the stated purpose. In view of the strength and nature of a torturer's likely passions—of, for example, hate and self-hate, disgust and self-disgust, horror and fascination, subservience toward superiors and aggression toward victims—no constraint is to be counted upon in practice.

Still, it is of at least theoretical interest to ask whether torturers with a genuine will to do so could conduct interrogational torture in a manner which would satisfy the constraint of possible compliance. In order to tell, it is essential to grasp specifically what compliance would normally involve. Almost all torture is "political" in the sense that it is inflicted by the government in power upon people who are, seem to be, or might be opposed to the government. Some torture is also inflicted by opponents of a government upon people who are, seem to be, or might be supporting the government. Possible victims of torture fall into three broad categories: the ready collaborator, the innocent bystander, and the dedicated enemy.

First, the torturers may happen upon someone who is involved with the other side but is not dedicated to such a degree that cooperation with the torturers would, from the victim's perspective, constitute a betrayal of anything highly valued. For such a person a betrayal of cause and allies might indeed serve as a form of genuine escape.

The second possibility is the capture of someone who is passive toward both sides and essentially uninvolved. If such a bystander should happen to know the relevant information—which is very unlikely—and to be willing to provide it, no torture would be called for. But what if the victim would be perfectly willing to provide the information sought in order to escape the torture but does not have the information? Systems of torture are notoriously incompetent. The usual situation is captured with icy accuracy by the reputed informal motto of the Saigon police, "If they are not guilty, beat them until they are."[8] The victims of torture need an escape not only from beatings for what they know but also from beatings for what they do not know. In short, the victim has no convincing way of demonstrating that he or she cannot comply, even when compliance is impossible. (Compare the reputed dunking test for witches: if the woman sank, she was an ordinary mortal.)

Even a torturer who would be willing to stop after learning all that could be learned, which is nothing at all if the "wrong" person is being tortured, would have difficulty discriminating among pleas. Any keeping of the tacit bargain to stop when compliance has been as complete as possible would likely be undercut by uncertainty about when the fullest possible compliance had occurred. The difficulty of demonstrating that one had collaborated as much as one could might in fact haunt the collaborator as well as the innocent, especially if his or her collaboration had struck the torturers as being of little real value.

Finally, when the torturers succeed in torturing someone genuinely committed to the other side, compliance means, in a word, betrayal: betrayal of one's ideals and one's comrades. The possibility of betrayal cannot be counted as an escape. Undoubtedly some ideals are vicious and some friends are partners in crime—this can be true of either the government, the opposition, or both. Nevertheless, a betrayal is no escape for a dedicated member of either a government or its opposition, who cannot collaborate without denying his or her highest values.

For any genuine escape must be something better than settling for the lesser of two evils. One can always try to minimize one's losses—even in dilemmas from which there is no real escape. But if accepting the lesser of two evils always counted as an escape, there would be no situations from which there was no escape, except perhaps those in which all alternatives happened to be equally evil. On such a loose notion of escape, all conscripts would become volunteers, since they could always desert. And all assaults containing any alternatives would then be acceptable. An alternative which is legitimately to count as an escape must not only be preferable but also itself satisfy some minimum standard of moral acceptability. A denial of one's self does not count.

Therefore, on the whole, the apparent possibility of escape through compliance tends to melt away upon examination. The ready collaborator and the innocent bystander have some hope of an acceptable escape, but only provided that the torturers both (a) are persuaded that the victim has kept his or her part of the bargain by telling all there is to tell and (b) choose to keep their side of the bargain in a situation in which agreements cannot be enforced upon them and they have nothing to lose by continuing the torture if they please. If one is treated as if one is a dedicated enemy,

as seems likely to be the standard procedure, the fact that one actually belongs in another category has no effect. On the other hand, the dedicated enemies of the torturers, who presumably tend to know more and consequently are the primary intended targets of the torture, are provided with nothing which can be considered an escape and can only protect themselves, as torture victims always have, by pretending to be collaborators or innocents, and thereby imperiling the members of these two categories.

MORALLY PERMISSIBLE TORTURE?

Still, it must reluctantly be admitted that the avoidance of assaults upon the defenseless is not the only, or even in all cases an overriding, moral consideration. And, therefore, even if terroristic and interrogational torture, each in its own way, is bound to involve attacks upon people unable to defend themselves or to escape, it is still not utterly inconceivable that instances of one or the other type of torture might sometimes, all things considered, be justified. Consequently, we must sketch the elements of an overall assessment of these two types of torture, beginning again with the dominant contemporary form: terroristic.

Anyone who thought an overall justification could be given for an episode of terroristic torture would at the least have to provide a clear statement of necessary conditions, all of which would have to be satisfied before any actions so extraordinarily cruel as terroristic torture could be morally acceptable. If the torture were actually to be justified, the conditions would, of course, have to be met in fact. An attempt to specify the necessary conditions for a morally permissible episode of terroristic torture might include conditions such as the following. A first necessary condition would be that the purpose actually being sought through the torture would need to be not only morally good but supremely important, and examples of such purposes would have to be selected by criteria of moral importance which would themselves need to be justified. Second, terroristic torture would presumably have to be the least harmful means of accomplishing the supremely important goal. Given how very harmful terroristic torture is, this could rarely be the case. And it would be unlikely unless the period of use of the torture in the society was limited in an enforceable manner. Third, it would have to be absolutely clear for what purpose the terroristic torture was being used, what would constitute achievement of that purpose, and thus, when the torture would end. The torture could not become a standard practice of government for an indefinite duration. And so on.

But is there any supremely important end to which terroristic torture could be the least harmful means? Could terroristic torture be employed for a brief interlude and then outlawed? Consider what would be involved in answering the latter question. A government could, it might seem, terrorize until the terror had accomplished its purpose and then suspend the terror. There are few, if any, clear cases of a regime's voluntarily renouncing terror after having created, through terror, a situation in which terror was no longer needed. And there is considerable evidence of the improbability of this sequence. Terroristic torture tends to become, according to Amnesty International, "administrative practice": a routine procedure institutionalized into the method of governing. Some bureaus collect taxes, other bureaus conduct torture. First a suspect is arrested, next he or she is tortured. Torture gains the momentum of an ingrained element of a standard operating procedure.

Several factors appear to point in the direction of permanence. From the perspective of the victims, even where the population does not initially feel exploited, terror is very unsuitable to the generation of loyalty. This would add to the difficulty of any transition away from reliance on terror. Where the population does feel exploited even before the torture begins, the sense of outrage (which is certainly rationally justified toward the choice of victims, as we have seen) could often prove stronger than the fear of suffering. Tragically, any unlikelihood that the terroristic torture would "work" would almost guarantee that it would continue to be used. From the perspective of the torturers, it is rare for any entrenched bureau to choose to eliminate itself rather than to try

to prove its essential value and the need for its own expansion. This is especially likely if the members of the operation are either thoroughly cynical or thoroughly sincere in their conviction that they are protecting "national security" or some other value taken to be supremely important. The greater burden of proof rests, I would think, on anyone who believes that controllable terroristic torture is possible. . . .

Much of what can be said about terroristic torture can also be said about instances involving interrogational torture. This is the case primarily because in practice there are evidently few pure cases of interrogational torture.[9] An instance of torture which is to any significant degree terroristic in purpose ought to be treated as terroristic. But if we keep in mind how far we are departing from most actual practice, we may, as before, consider instances in which the *sole* purpose of torture is to extract certain information and therefore the torturer is willing to stop as soon as he or she is sure that the victim has provided all the information which the victim has.

As argued in the preceding section, interrogational torture would in practice be difficult to make into less of an assault upon the defenseless. The supposed possibility of escape through compliance turns out to depend upon the keeping of a bargain which is entirely unenforceable within the torture situation and upon the making of discriminations among victims that would usually be difficult to make until after they no longer mattered. In fact, since any sensible willing collaborator will cooperate in a hurry, only the committed and the innocent are likely to be severely tortured. More important, in the case of someone being tortured because of profoundly held convictions, the "escape" would normally be a violation of integrity.

As with terroristic torture, any complete argument for permitting instances of interrogational torture would have to include a full specification of all necessary conditions of a permissible instance, such as its serving a supremely important purpose (with criteria of importance), its being the least harmful means to that goal, its having a clearly defined and reachable endpoint, and so on. This would not be a simple matter. Also as in the case of terroristic torture, a considerable danger exists that whatever necessary conditions were specified, any practice of torture once set in motion would gain enough momentum to burst any bonds and become a standard operating procedure. Torture is the ultimate shortcut. If it were ever permitted under any conditions, the temptation to use it increasingly would be very strong.

Nevertheless, it cannot be denied that there are imaginable cases in which the harm that could be prevented by a rare instance of pure interrogational torture would be so enormous as to outweigh the cruelty of the torture itself and, possibly, the enormous potential harm which would result if what was intended to be a rare instance was actually the breaching of the dam which would lead to a torrent of torture. There is a standard philosopher's example which someone always invokes: suppose a fanatic, perfectly willing to die rather than collaborate in the thwarting of his own scheme, has set a hidden nuclear device to explode in the heart of Paris. There is no time to evacuate the innocent people or even the movable art treasures—the only hope of preventing tragedy is to torture the perpetrator, find the device, and deactivate it.

I can see no way to deny the permissibility of torture in a case *just like this*. To allow the destruction of much of a great city and many of its people would be almost as wicked as purposely to destroy it, as the Nazis did to London and Warsaw, and the Allies did to Dresden and Tokyo, during World War II. But there is a saying in jurisprudence that hard cases make bad law, and there might well be one in philosophy that artificial cases make bad ethics. If the example is made sufficiently extraordinary, the conclusion that the torture is permissible is secure. But one cannot easily draw conclusions for ordinary cases from extraordinary ones, and as the situations described become more likely, the conclusion that the torture is permissible becomes more debatable.

Notice how unlike the circumstances of an actual choice about torture the philosopher's example is. The proposed victim of our torture is not someone we suspect of planting the device: he *is* the perpetrator. He is not some pitiful psychotic making one last play for attention: he *did* plant the device. The wiring is not backwards, the mechanism is not jammed: the device *will* destroy the city if not deactivated.

Much more important from the perspective of whether general conclusions applicable to ordinary cases can be drawn are the background conditions that tend to be assumed. The torture will not be conducted in the basement of a small-town jail in the provinces by local thugs popping pills; the prime minister and chief justice are being kept informed; and a priest and a doctor are present. The victim will not be raped or forced to eat excrement and will not collapse with a heart attack or become deranged before talking; while avoiding irreparable damage, the antiseptic pain will carefully be increased only up to the point at which the necessary information is divulged, and the doctor will then immediately administer an antibiotic and a tranquilizer. The torture is purely interrogational.

Most important, such incidents do not continue to happen. There are not so many people with grievances against this government that the torture is becoming necessary more often, and in the smaller cities, and for slightly lesser threats, and with a little less care, and so on. Any judgment that torture could be sanctioned in an isolated case without seriously weakening existing inhibitions against the more general use of torture rests on empirical hypotheses about the psychology and politics of torture. There *is* considerable evidence of all torture's metastatic tendency. If there is also evidence that interrogational torture can sometimes be used with the surgical precision which imagined justifiable cases always assume, such rare uses would have to be considered.

Does the possibility that torture might be justifiable in some of the rarefied situations which can be imagined provide any reason to consider relaxing the legal prohibitions against it? Absolutely not. The distance between the situations which must be concocted in order to have a plausible case of morally permissible torture and the situations which actually occur is, if anything, further reason why the existing prohibitions against torture should remain and should be strengthened by making torture an international crime. An act of torture ought to remain illegal so that anyone who sincerely believes such an act to be the least available evil is placed in the position of needing to justify his or her act morally in order to defend himself or herself legally. The torturer should be in roughly the same position as someone who commits civil disobedience. Anyone who thinks an act of torture is justified should have no alternative but to convince a group of peers in a public trial that all necessary conditions for a morally permissible act were indeed satisfied. If it is reasonable to put someone through torture, it is reasonable to put someone else through a careful explanation of why. If the situation approximates those in the imaginary examples in which torture seems possible to justify, a judge can surely be expected to suspend the sentence. Meanwhile, there is little need to be concerned about possible injustice to justified torturers and great need to find means to restrain totally unjustified torture.

NOTES

1. See Amnesty International, *Report on Torture* (New York: Farrar, Straus and Giroux, 1975), pp. 21–33.

2. See James T. Johnson, *Ideology, Reason, and the Limitation of War: Religious and Secular Concepts 1200–1740* (Princeton: Princeton University Press, 1975). Johnson stresses the largely religious origins of *jus ad bellum* and the largely secular origins of *jus in bello.*

3. This judgment is supported by Stockholm International Peace Research Institute, *The Law of War and Dubious Weapons* (Stockholm: Almqvist & Wiksell, 1976), p. 9: "The prohibition on deliberately attacking the civilian population as such is not based exclusively on the principle of avoiding unnecessary suffering."

4. To defend the bombing of cities in World War II on the ground that *total* casualties (combatant and noncombatant) were thereby reduced is to miss, or ignore, the point.

5. See Amnesty International, 69.

6. See United Nations, General Assembly, Report of the Economic and Social Council, *Protection of Human Rights in Chile* (UN Document A/31/253, 8 October 1976, 31st Session), p. 97; and *Uganda and Human Rights: Reports to the UN Commission on Human Rights* (Geneva: International Commission of Jurists, 1977), p. 118.

7. These two categories of torture are not intended to be, and are not, exhaustive.

8. Amnesty International, 166.

9. Amnesty International, pp. 24–25, 114–242.

READING QUESTIONS

1. What general principle makes torture wrong, according to Shue?
2. How does Shue define "the constraint of possible compliance"?
3. What is "terroristic torture," and how does Shue argue that terroristic torture cannot satisfy the constraint of possible compliance?
4. What is "interrogational torture," and how does Shue argue that its purpose is consistent with the constraint of possible compliance?
5. Shue claims that there are conceivable cases where torture is justified. How does he argue that this gives us no reason to relax legal prohibitions against torture?

DISCUSSION QUESTIONS

1. In discussing a conceivable case where torture is justified, Shue claims that "artificial cases make bad ethics." Do such "artificial" cases tell us *anything* about the morality of more realistic cases of torture?
2. How might Shue respond to the claim that torture should be legal under certain limited circumstances (such as those in which it would be morally permissible)? Would such a response be convincing?

ALAN M. DERSHOWITZ

Should the Ticking Bomb Terrorist Be Tortured?

The "ticking bomb" case refers to a hypothetical situation in which only by torturing a terrorist who knows the whereabouts of a ticking bomb can the bomb be found and defused before it detonates and kills many innocent people. Should the ticking bomb terrorist be tortured? Dershowitz argues from an act utilitarian moral perspective for an affirmative answer to this question. He then argues that a democratic society governed by the rule of law should never declare some action to be absolutely wrong, yet knowingly allow the military or other public officials to engage in that activity "off the books." But if torture is morally permissible in extreme "necessity" cases such as the ticking bomb case, democratic governments ought to change existing law to accommodate this practice. Dershowitz proposes that a system of judicial "torture warrants" be instituted as part of a legal system regulating the practice.

Recommended Reading: consequentialism, chap. 1, sec. 2a, particularly act utilitarianism.

HOW I BEGAN THINKING ABOUT TORTURE

In the late 1980s I traveled to Israel to conduct some research and teach a class at Hebrew University on civil liberties during times of crisis. In the course of my research I learned that the Israeli security services were employing what they euphemistically called "moderate physical pressure" on suspected terrorists to obtain information deemed necessary to prevent future terrorist attacks. The method employed by the security services fell somewhere between what many would regard as very rough interrogation (as practiced by the British in Northern Ireland) and outright torture (as practiced by the French in Algeria and by Egypt, the Philippines, and Jordan today). In most cases the suspect would be placed in a dark room with a smelly sack over his head. Loud, unpleasant music or other noise would blare from speakers. The suspect would be seated in an extremely uncomfortable position and then shaken vigorously until he disclosed the information. Statements made under this kind of nonlethal pressure could not be introduced in any court of law, both because they were involuntarily secured and because they were deemed potentially untrustworthy—at least without corroboration. But they were used as leads in the prevention of terrorist acts. Sometimes the leads proved false, other times they proved true. There is little doubt that some acts of terrorism—which would have killed many civilians—were prevented. There is also little doubt that the cost of saving these lives—measured in terms of basic human rights—was extraordinarily high.

In my classes and public lectures in Israel, I strongly condemned these methods as a violation of core civil liberties and human rights. The response that people gave, across the political spectrum from

From Alan M. Dershowitz, *Why Terrorism Works: Understanding the Threat, Responding to the Challenge* (New Haven and London: Yale University Press, 2002). Reprinted by permission.

civil libertarians to law-and-order advocates, was essentially the same: but what about the "ticking bomb" case?

The ticking bomb case refers to a scenario that has been discussed by many philosophers, including Michael Walzer, Jean-Paul Sartre, and Jeremy Bentham. Walzer described such a hypothetical case in an article titled "Political Action: The Problem of Dirty Hands." In this case, a decent leader of a nation plagued with terrorism is asked "to authorize the torture of a captured rebel leader who knows or probably knows the location of a number of bombs hidden in apartment buildings across the city, set to go off within the next twenty-four hours. He orders the man tortured, convinced that he must do so for the sake of the people who might otherwise die in the explosions—even though he believes that torture is wrong, indeed abominable, not just sometimes, but always."[1]

In Israel, the use of torture to prevent terrorism was not hypothetical; it was very real and recurring. I soon discovered that virtually no one was willing to take the "purist" position against torture in the ticking bomb case: namely, that the ticking bomb must be permitted to explode and kill dozens of civilians, even if this disaster could be prevented by subjecting the captured terrorist to nonlethal torture and forcing him to disclose its location. I realized that the extraordinarily rare situation of the hypothetical ticking bomb terrorist was serving as a moral, intellectual, and legal justification for a pervasive *system* of coercive interrogation, which, though not the paradigm of torture, certainly bordered on it. It was then that I decided to challenge this system by directly confronting the ticking bomb case. I presented the following challenge to my Israeli audience: If the reason you permit nonlethal torture is based on the ticking bomb case, why not limit it exclusively to that compelling but rare situation? Moreover, if you believe that nonlethal torture is justifiable in the ticking bomb case, why not require advance judicial approval—a "torture warrant"? That was the origin of a controversial proposal that has received much attention, largely critical, from the media. Its goal was, and remains, to reduce the use of torture to the smallest amount and degree possible, while creating public accountability

for its rare use. I saw it not as a compromise with civil liberties but rather as an effort to maximize civil liberties in the face of a realistic likelihood that torture would, in fact, take place below the radar screen of accountability. . . .

THE CASE FOR TORTURING THE TICKING BOMB TERRORIST

The arguments in favor of using torture as a last resort to prevent a ticking bomb from exploding and killing many people are both simple and simple-minded. Bentham constructed a compelling hypothetical case to support his utilitarian argument against an absolute prohibition on torture:

> Suppose an occasion were to arise, in which a suspicion is entertained, as strong as that which would be received as a sufficient ground for arrest and commitment as for felony—a suspicion that at this very time a considerable number of individuals are actually suffering, by illegal violence inflictions equal in intensity to those which if inflicted by the hand of justice, would universally be spoken of under the name of torture. For the purpose of rescuing from torture these hundred innocents, should any scruple be made of applying equal or superior torture, to extract the requisite information from the mouth of one criminal, who having it in his power to make known the place where at this time the enormity was practising or about to be practised, should refuse to do so? To say nothing of wisdom, could any pretence be made so much as to the praise of blind and vulgar humanity, by the man who to save one criminal, should determine to abandon 100 innocent persons to the same fate?[2]

If the torture of one guilty person would be justified to prevent the torture of a hundred innocent persons, it would seem to follow—certainly to Bentham—that it would also be justified to prevent the murder of thousands of innocent civilians in the ticking bomb case. Consider two hypothetical situations that are not, unfortunately, beyond the realm of possibility. In fact, they are both extrapolations on actual situations we have faced.

Several weeks before September 11, 2001, the Immigration and Naturalization Service detained Zacarias Moussaoui after flight instructors reported suspicious statements he had made while taking flying lessons and paying for them with large amounts of cash.[3] The government decided not to seek a warrant to search his computer. Now imagine that they had, and that they discovered he was part of a plan to destroy large occupied buildings, but without any further details. They interrogated him, gave him immunity from prosecution, and offered him large cash rewards and a new identity. He refused to talk. They then threatened him, tried to trick him, and employed every lawful technique available. He still refused. They even injected him with sodium pentothal and other truth serums, but to no avail. The attack now appeared to be imminent, but the FBI still had no idea what the target was or what means would be used to attack it. We could not simply evacuate all buildings indefinitely. An FBI agent proposes the use of nonlethal torture—say, a sterilized needle inserted under the fingernails to produce unbearable pain without any threat to health or life, or the method used in the film *Marathon Man,* a dental drill through an unanesthetized tooth.

The simple cost-benefit analysis for employing such nonlethal torture seems overwhelming: it is surely better to inflict nonlethal pain on one guilty terrorist who is illegally withholding information needed to prevent an act of terrorism than to permit a large number of innocent victims to die. Pain is a lesser and more remediable harm than death; and the lives of a thousand innocent people should be valued more than the bodily integrity of one guilty person. If the variation on the Moussaoui case is not sufficiently compelling to make this point, we can always raise the stakes. Several weeks after September 11, our government received reports that a ten-kiloton nuclear weapon may have been stolen from Russia and was on its way to New York City, where it would be detonated and kill hundreds of thousands of people. The reliability of the source, code named Dragonfire, was uncertain, but assume for purposes of this hypothetical extension of the actual case that the source was a captured terrorist—like the one tortured by the Philippine authorities—who knew precisely how and where the weapon was being brought into New York and was to be detonated. Again, everything short of torture is tried, but to no avail. It is not absolutely certain torture will work, but it is our last, best hope for preventing a cataclysmic nuclear devastation in a city too large to evacuate in time. Should nonlethal torture be tried? Bentham would certainly have said yes.

The strongest argument against any resort to torture, even in the ticking bomb case, also derives from Bentham's utilitarian calculus. Experience has shown that if torture, which has been deemed illegitimate by the civilized world for more than a century, were now to be legitimated—even for limited use in one extraordinary type of situation—such legitimation would constitute an important symbolic setback in the worldwide campaign against human rights abuses. Inevitably, the legitimation of torture by the world's leading democracy would provide a welcome justification for its more widespread use in other parts of the world. Two Bentham scholars, W. L. Twining and P. E. Twining, have argued that torture is unacceptable even if it is restricted to an extremely limited category of cases:

> There is at least one good practical reason for drawing a distinction between justifying an isolated act of torture in an extreme emergency of the kind postulated above and justifying the *institutionalisation* of torture as a regular practice. The circumstances are so extreme in which most of us would be prepared to justify resort to torture, if at all, the conditions we would impose would be so stringent, the practical problems of devising and enforcing adequate safeguards so difficult and the risks of abuse so great that it would be unwise and dangerous to entrust any government, however enlightened, with such a power. Even an out-and-out utilitarian can support an absolute prohibition against institutionalised torture on the ground that no government in the world can be trusted not to abuse the power and to satisfy in practice the conditions he would impose.[4]

Bentham's own justification was based on *case* or *act* utilitarianism—a demonstration that in a *particular case,* the benefits that would flow from the limited use of torture would outweigh its costs. The argument against any use of torture would derive from *rule* utilitarianism—which considers the implications of establishing a precedent that would inevitably be extended beyond its limited case utilitarian justification to other possible evils of lesser magnitude. Even terrorism itself could be justified by a case utilitarian approach. Surely one could come up with a singular situation in which the targeting of a small number of civilians could be thought necessary to save thousands of other civilians—blowing up a German kindergarten by the relatives of inmates in a Nazi death camp, for example, and threatening to repeat the targeting of German children unless the death camps were shut down.

The reason this kind of single-case utilitarian justification is simple-minded is that it has no inherent limiting principle. If nonlethal torture of one person is justified to prevent the killing of many important people, then what if it were necessary to use lethal torture—or at least torture that posed a substantial risk of death? What if it were necessary to torture the suspect's mother or children to get him to divulge the information? What if it took threatening to kill his family, his friends, his entire village? Under a simple-minded quantitative case utilitarianism, anything goes as long as the number of people tortured or killed does not exceed the number that would be saved. This is morality by numbers, unless there are other constraints on what we can properly do. These other constraints can come from rule utilitarianisms or other principles of morality, such as the prohibition against deliberately punishing the innocent. Unless we are prepared to impose some limits on the use of torture or other barbaric tactics that might be of some use in preventing terrorism, we risk hurtling down a slippery slope into the abyss of amorality and ultimately tyranny. Dostoevsky captured the complexity of this dilemma in *The Brothers Karamazov* when he had Ivan pose the following question to Alyosha: "Imagine that you are creating a fabric of human destiny with the object of making men happy in the end, giving them peace at least, but that it was essential and inevitable to torture to death only one tiny creature—that baby beating its breast with its fist, for instance—and to found that edifice on its unavenged tears, would you consent to be the architect on those conditions? Tell me the truth."

A willingness to kill an innocent child suggests a willingness to do anything to achieve a necessary result. Hence the slippery slope.

It does not necessarily follow from this understandable fear of the slippery slope that we can never consider the use of nonlethal infliction of pain, if its use were to be limited by acceptable principles of morality. After all, imprisoning a witness who refuses to testify after being given immunity is designed to be punitive—that is painful. Such imprisonment can, on occasion, produce more pain and greater risk of death than nonlethal torture. Yet we continue to threaten and use the pain of imprisonment to loosen the tongues of reluctant witnesses.

It is commonplace for police and prosecutors to threaten recalcitrant suspects with prison rape. As one prosecutor put it: "You're going to be the boyfriend of a very bad man." The slippery slope is an argument of caution, not a debate stopper, since virtually every compromise with an absolutist approach to rights carries the risk of slipping further. An appropriate response to the slippery slope is to build in a principled break. For example, if nonlethal torture were legally limited to convicted terrorists who had knowledge of future massive terrorist acts, were given immunity, and still refused to provide the information, there might still be objections to the use of torture, but they would have to go beyond the slippery slope argument.

The case utilitarian argument for torturing a ticking bomb terrorist is bolstered by an argument from analogy—an a fortiori argument. What moral principle could justify the death penalty for past individual murders and at the same time condemn nonlethal torture to prevent future mass murders? Bentham posed this rhetorical question as support for his argument. The death penalty is, of course, reserved for convicted murderers. But again, what if torture was limited to convicted terrorists who refused to divulge information about future terrorism? Consider as well the analogy to the use of deadly force against suspects fleeing from arrest for dangerous felonies of which they have not yet been convicted. Or military retaliations that produce the predictable and inevitable collateral killing of some innocent civilians. The case against torture, if made by a Quaker who opposes the death penalty, war, self-defense, and the use of lethal force against fleeing felons, is understandable. But for anyone who justifies killing on the basis of a cost-benefit analysis, the case against the use of nonlethal torture to save multiple lives is more difficult to make. In the end, absolute opposition to torture—even nonlethal torture in the ticking bomb case—may rest more on historical and aesthetic considerations than on moral or logical ones.

In debating the issue of torture, the first question I am often asked is, "Do you want to take us back to the Middle Ages?" The association between any form of torture and gruesome death is powerful in the minds of most people knowledgeable of the history of its abuses. This understandable association makes it difficult for many people to think about nonlethal torture as a technique for *saving* lives.

The second question I am asked is, "What kind of torture do you have in mind?" When I respond by describing the sterilized needle being shoved under the fingernails, the reaction is visceral and often visible—a shudder coupled with a facial gesture of disgust. Discussions of the death penalty on the other hand can be conducted without these kinds of reactions, especially now that we literally put the condemned prisoner "to sleep" by laying him out on a gurney and injecting a lethal substance into his body. There is no breaking of the neck, burning of the brain, bursting of internal organs, or gasping for breath that used to accompany hanging, electrocution, shooting, and gassing. The executioner has been replaced by a paramedical technician, as the aesthetics of death have become more acceptable. All this tends to cover up the reality that death is forever while nonlethal pain is temporary. In our modern age death is underrated, while pain is overrated.

I observed a similar phenomenon several years ago during the debate over corporal punishment that was generated by the decision of a court in Singapore to sentence a young American to medically supervised lashing with a cane. Americans who support the death penalty and who express little concern about inner-city prison conditions were outraged by the specter of a few welts on the buttocks of an American. It was an utterly irrational display of hypocrisy and double standards. Given a choice

between a medically administrated whipping and one month in a typical state lockup or prison, any rational and knowledgeable person would choose the lash. No one dies of welts or pain, but many inmates are raped, beaten, knifed, and otherwise mutilated and tortured in American prisons. The difference is that we don't see—and we don't want to see—what goes on behind their high walls. Nor do we want to think about it. Raising the issue of torture makes Americans think about a brutalizing and unaesthetic phenomenon that has been out of our consciousness for many years.[5]

THE THREE—OR FOUR—WAYS

The debate over the use of torture goes back many years, with Bentham supporting it in a limited category of cases, Kant opposing it as part of his categorical imperative against improperly using people as means for achieving noble ends, and Voltaire's views on the matter being "hopelessly confused."[6] The modern resort to terrorism has renewed the debate over how a rights-based society should respond to the prospect of using nonlethal torture in the ticking bomb situation. In the late 1980s the Israeli government appointed a commission headed by a retired Supreme Court justice to look into precisely that situation. The commission concluded that there are "three ways for solving this grave dilemma between the vital need to preserve the very existence of the state and its citizens, and maintain its character as a law-abiding state." The first is to allow the security services to continue to fight terrorism in "a twilight zone which is outside the realm of law." The second is "the way of the hypocrites: they declare that they abide by the rule of law, but turn a blind eye to what goes on beneath the surface." And the third, "the truthful road of the rule of law," is that the "law itself must insure a proper framework for the activity" of the security services in seeking to prevent terrorist acts.

There is of course a fourth road: namely to forgo any use of torture and simply allow the preventable terrorist act to occur.[7] After the Supreme Court of Israel outlawed the use of physical pressure, the Israeli security services claimed that, as a result of the Supreme Court's decision, at least one preventable act of terrorism had been allowed to take place, one that killed several people when a bus was bombed. Whether this claim is true, false, or somewhere in between is difficult to assess.[8] But it is clear that if the preventable act of terrorism was of the magnitude of the attacks of September 11, there would be a great outcry in any democracy that had deliberately refused to take available preventive action, even if it required the use of torture. During numerous public appearances since September 11, 2001, I have asked audiences for a show of hands as to how many would support the use of nonlethal torture in a ticking bomb case. Virtually every hand is raised. The few that remain down go up when I ask how many believe that torture would actually be used in such a case.

Law enforcement personnel give similar responses. This can be seen in reports of physical abuse directed against some suspects that have been detained following September 11, reports that have been taken quite seriously by at least one federal judge. It is confirmed by the willingness of U.S. law enforcement officials to facilitate the torture of terrorist suspects by repressive regimes allied with our intelligence agencies. As one former CIA operative with thirty years of experience reported: "A lot of people are saying we need someone at the agency who can pull fingernails out. Others are saying, 'Let others use interrogation methods that we don't use.' The only question then is, do you want to have CIA people in the room?" The real issue, therefore, is not whether some torture would or would not be used in the ticking bomb case—it would. The question is whether it would be done openly, pursuant to a previously established legal procedure, or whether it would be done secretly, in violation of existing law.

Several important values are pitted against each other in this conflict. The first is the safety and security of a nation's citizens. Under the ticking bomb scenario this value may require the use of torture, if that is the only way to prevent the bomb from exploding and killing large numbers of civilians. The second value is the preservation of civil liberties and human rights. This value requires that we not accept torture as a legitimate part of our legal system. In my debates with two prominent civil libertarians, Floyd Abrams and Harvey Silverglate, both have acknowledged that they would want nonlethal torture to be used if it could prevent thousands of deaths, but they did not want torture to be officially recognized by our legal system. As Abrams put it: "In a democracy sometimes it is necessary to do things off the books and below the radar screen." Former presidential candidate Alan Keyes took the position that although torture might be *necessary* in a given situation it could never be *right*. He suggested that a president *should* authorize the torturing of a ticking bomb terrorist, but that this act should not be legitimated by the courts or incorporated into our legal system. He argued that wrongful and indeed unlawful acts might sometimes be necessary to preserve the nation, but that no aura of legitimacy should be placed on these actions by judicial imprimatur.

This understandable approach is in conflict with the third important value: namely, open accountability and visibility in a democracy. "Off-the-book actions below the radar screen" are antithetical to the theory and practice of democracy. Citizens cannot approve or disapprove of governmental actions of which they are unaware. We have learned the lesson of history that off-the-book actions can produce terrible consequences. Richard Nixon's creation of a group of "plumbers" led to Watergate, and Ronald Reagan's authorization of an off-the-books foreign policy in Central America led to the Iran-Contra scandal. And these are only the ones we know about!

Perhaps the most extreme example of such a hypocritical approach to torture comes—not surprisingly—from the French experience in Algeria. The French army used torture extensively in seeking to prevent terrorism during a brutal colonial war from 1955 to 1957. An officer who supervised this torture, General Paul Aussaresses, wrote a book recounting what he had done and seen, including the torture of dozens of Algerians. "The best way to make a terrorist talk when he refused to say what he knew was to torture him," he boasted. Although the book was published decades after the war was over, the general was prosecuted—but not for what he had done to the

Algerians. Instead, he was prosecuted for *revealing* what he had done, and seeking to justify it.

In a democracy governed by the rule of law, we should never want our soldiers or our president to take any action that we deem wrong or illegal. A good test of whether an action should or should not be done is whether we are prepared to have it disclosed—perhaps not immediately, but certainly after some time has passed. No legal system operating under the rule of law should ever tolerate an "off-the-books" approach to necessity. Even the defense of necessity must be justified lawfully. The road to tyranny has always been paved with claims of necessity made by those responsible for the security of a nation. Our system of checks and balances requires that all presidential actions, like all legislative or military actions, be consistent with governing law. If it is necessary to torture in the ticking bomb case, then our governing laws must accommodate this practice. If we refuse to change our law to accommodate any particular action, then our government should not take that action.

Only in a democracy committed to civil liberties would a triangular conflict of this kind exist. Totalitarian and authoritarian regimes experience no such conflict, because they subscribe to neither the civil libertarian nor the democratic values that come in conflict with the value of security. The hard question is: which value is to be preferred when an inevitable clash occurs? One or more of these values must inevitably be compromised in making the tragic choice presented by the ticking bomb case. If we do not torture, we compromise the security and safety of our citizens. If we tolerate torture, but keep it off the books and below the radar screen, we compromise principles of democratic accountability. If we create a legal structure for limiting and controlling torture, we compromise our principled opposition to torture in all circumstances and create a potentially dangerous and expandable situation.

In 1678, the French writer François de La Rochefoucauld said that "hypocrisy is the homage that vice renders to virtue." In this case we have two vices: terrorism and torture. We also have two virtues: civil liberties and democratic accountability. Most civil libertarians I know prefer hypocrisy, precisely because it appears to avoid the conflict between security and civil liberties, but by choosing the way of the hypocrite these civil libertarians compromise the value of democratic accountability. Such is the nature of tragic choices in a complex world. As Bentham put it more than two centuries ago: "Government throughout is but a choice of evils." In a democracy, such choices must be made, whenever possible, with openness and democratic accountability, and subject to the rule of law.[9]

Consider another terrible choice of evils that could easily have been presented on September 11, 2001—and may well be presented in the future: a hijacked passenger jet is on a collision course with a densely occupied office building; the only way to prevent the destruction of the building and the killing of its occupants is to shoot down the jet, thereby killing its innocent passengers. This choice now seems easy, because the passengers are certain to die anyway and their somewhat earlier deaths will save numerous lives. The passenger jet must be shot down. But what if it were only *probable,* not certain, that the jet would crash into the building? Say, for example, we know from cell phone transmissions that passengers are struggling to regain control of the hijacked jet, but it is unlikely they will succeed in time. Or say we have no communication with the jet and all we know is that it is off course and heading toward Washington, D.C., or some other densely populated city. Under these more questionable circumstances, the question becomes *who* should make this life and death choice between evils—a decision that may turn out tragically wrong?

No reasonable person would allocate this decision to a fighter jet pilot who happened to be in the area or to a local airbase commander—unless of course there was no time for the matter to be passed up the chain of command to the president or the secretary of defense. A decision of this kind should be made at the highest level possible, with visibility and accountability.

Why is this not also true of the decision to torture a ticking bomb terrorist? Why should that choice of evils be relegated to a local policeman, FBI agent, or CIA operative, rather than to a judge, the attorney general, or the president?

There are, of course, important differences between the decision to shoot down the plane and the decision to torture the ticking bomb terrorist. Having to shoot down an airplane, though tragic, is not likely to be a recurring issue. There is no slope down which to slip. Moreover, the jet to be shot down is filled with our fellow citizens—people with whom we can identify. The suspected terrorist we may choose to torture is a "they"—an enemy with whom we do not identify but with whose potential victims we do identify. The risk of making the wrong decision, or of overdoing the torture, is far greater, since we do not care as much what happens to "them" as to "us." Finally, there is something different about torture—even nonlethal torture—that sets it apart from a quick death. In addition to the horrible history associated with torture, there is also the aesthetic of torture. The very idea of deliberately subjecting a captive human being to excruciating pain violates our sense of what is acceptable. On a purely rational basis, it is far worse to shoot a fleeing felon in the back and kill him, yet every civilized society authorizes shooting such a suspect who poses dangers of committing violent crimes against the police or others. In the United States we execute convicted murderers, despite compelling evidence of the unfairness and ineffectiveness of capital punishment. Yet many of us recoil at the prospect of shoving a sterilized needle under the finger of a suspect who is refusing to divulge information that might prevent multiple deaths. Despite the irrationality of these distinctions, they are understandable, especially in light of the sordid history of torture.

We associate torture with the Inquisition, the Gestapo, the Stalinist purges, and the Argentine colonels responsible for the "dirty war." We recall it as a prelude to death, an integral part of a regime of gratuitous pain leading to a painful demise. We find it difficult to imagine a benign use of nonlethal torture to save lives.

Yet there was a time in the history of Anglo-Saxon law when torture was used to save life, rather than to take it, and when the limited administration of nonlethal torture was supervised by judges, including some who are well remembered in history. This fascinating story has been recounted by Professor John Langbein of Yale Law School, and it is worth summarizing here because it helps inform the debate over whether, if torture would in fact be used in a ticking bomb case, it would be worse to make it part of the legal system, or worse to have it done off the books and below the radar screen.

In his book on legalized torture during the sixteenth and seventeenth centuries, *Torture and the Law of Proof,* Langbein demonstrates the trade-off between torture and other important values. Torture was employed for several purposes. First, it was used to secure the evidence necessary to obtain a guilty verdict under the rigorous criteria for conviction required at the time—either the testimony of two eyewitnesses or the confession of the accused himself. Circumstantial evidence, no matter how compelling, would not do. As Langbein concludes, "no society will long tolerate a legal system in which there is no prospect in convicting unrepentant persons who commit clandestine crimes. Something had to be done to extend the system to those cases. The two-eyewitness rule was hard to compromise or evade, but the confession invited 'subterfuge.'" The subterfuge that was adopted permitted the use of torture to obtain confessions from suspects against whom there was compelling circumstantial evidence of guilt. The circumstantial evidence, alone, could not be used to convict, but it was used to obtain a torture warrant. That torture warrant was in turn used to obtain a confession, which then had to be independently corroborated—at least in most cases (witchcraft and other such cases were exempted from the requirement of corroboration).[10]

Torture was also used against persons already convicted of capital crimes, such as high treason, who were thought to have information necessary to prevent attacks on the state.

Langbein studied eighty-one torture warrants, issued between 1540 and 1640, and found that in many of them, especially in "the higher cases of treasons, torture is used for discovery, and not for evidence." Torture was "used to protect the state" and "mostly that meant preventive torture to identify and forestall plots and plotters." It was only when the legal system loosened its requirement of proof (or introduced the "black box" of the jury system) and when perceived threats against the state diminished that torture was no longer deemed necessary to convict guilty defendants against whom there had previously been insufficient evidence, or to secure preventive information.[11] . . .

Every society has insisted on the incapacitation of dangerous criminals regardless of strictures in the formal legal rules. Some use torture, others use informal sanctions, while yet others create the black box of a jury, which need not explain its common-sense verdicts. Similarly, every society insists that, if there are steps that can be taken to prevent effective acts of terrorism, these steps should be taken, even if they require some compromise with other important principles.

. . . In deciding whether the ticking bomb terrorist should be tortured, one important question is whether there would be less torture if it were done as part of the legal system, as it was in sixteenth- and seventeenth-century England, or off the books, as it is in many countries today. The Langbein study does not definitively answer this question, but it does provide some suggestive insights. The English system of torture was more visible and thus more subject to public accountability, and it is likely that torture was employed less frequently in England than in France. "During these years when it appears that torture might have become routinized in English criminal procedure, the Privy Council kept the torture power under careful control and never allowed it to fall into the hands of the regular law enforcement officers," as it had in France. In England "no law enforcement officer . . . acquired the power to use torture without special warrant." Moreover, when torture warrants were abolished, "the English experiment with torture left no traces." Because it was under centralized control, it was easier to abolish than it was in France, where it persisted for many years.[12]

It is always difficult to extrapolate from history, but it seems logical that a formal, visible, accountable, and centralized system is somewhat easier to control than an ad hoc, off-the-books, and under-the-radar-screen nonsystem. I believe, though I certainly cannot prove, that a formal requirement of a judicial warrant as a prerequisite to nonlethal torture would decrease the amount of physical violence directed against suspects. At the most obvious level, a double check is always more protective than a single check. In every instance in which a warrant is requested, a field officer has already decided that torture is justified and, in the absence of a warrant requirement, would simply proceed with the torture. Requiring that decision to be approved by a judicial officer will result in fewer instances of torture even if the judge rarely turns down a request. Moreover, I believe that most judges would require compelling evidence before they would authorize so extraordinary a departure from our constitutional norms, and law enforcement officials would be reluctant to seek a warrant unless they had compelling evidence that the suspect had information needed to prevent an imminent terrorist attack. A record would be kept of every warrant granted, and although it is certainly possible that some individual agents might torture without a warrant, they would have no excuse, since a warrant procedure would be available. They could not claim "necessity," because the decision as to whether the torture is indeed necessary has been taken out of their hands and placed in the hands of a judge. In addition, even if torture were deemed totally illegal without any exception, it would still occur, though the public would be less aware of its existence.

I also believe that the rights of the suspect would be better protected with a warrant requirement. He would be granted immunity, told that he was now compelled to testify, threatened with imprisonment if he refused to do so, and given the option of providing the requested information. Only if he refused to do what he was legally compelled to do—provide necessary information, which could not incriminate him because of the immunity—would he be threatened with torture. Knowing that such a threat was authorized by the law, he might well provide the information.[13] If he still refused to, he would be subjected to judicially monitored physical measures designed to cause excruciating pain without leaving any lasting damage.

Let me cite two examples to demonstrate why I think there would be less torture with a warrant requirement than without one. Recall the case of the alleged national security wiretap placed on the phones of Martin Luther King by the Kennedy administration in the early 1960s. This was in the days when the attorney general could authorize a national security wiretap without a warrant. Today no judge would issue a warrant in a case as flimsy as that one. When Zacarias Moussaoui was detained after raising suspicions while trying to learn how to fly an airplane, the government did not even seek a national security wiretap because its lawyers believed that a judge would not have granted one. If Moussaoui's computer could have been searched without a warrant, it almost certainly would have been.

It should be recalled that in the context of searches, our Supreme Court opted for a judicial check on the discretion of the police, by requiring a search warrant in most cases. The Court has explained the reason for the warrant requirement as follows: "The informed and deliberate determinations of magistrates . . . are to be preferred over the hurried action of officers."[14] Justice Robert Jackson elaborated:

> The point of the Fourth Amendment, which often is not grasped by zealous officers, is not that it denies law enforcement the support of the usual inferences which reasonable men draw from evidence. Its protection consists in requiring that those inferences be drawn by a neutral and detached magistrate instead of being judged by the officer engaged in the often competitive enterprise of ferreting out crime. Any assumption that evidence sufficient to support a magistrate's disinterested determination to issue a search warrant will justify the officers in making a search without a warrant would reduce the Amendment to nullity and leave the people's homes secure only in the discretion of police officers.[15]

Although torture is very different from a search, the policies underlying the warrant requirement are relevant to the question whether there is likely to be more torture or less if the decision is left entirely to field officers, or if a judicial officer has to approve a request for a torture warrant. As Abraham Maslow once observed, to a man with a hammer, everything looks like a nail. If the man with the hammer must get judicial approval before he can use it, he will probably use it less often and more carefully.

There are other, somewhat more subtle, considerations that should be factored into any decision regarding torture. There are some who see silence as a virtue when it comes to the choice among such horrible evils as torture and terrorism. It is far better,

they argue, not to discuss or write about issues of this sort, lest they become legitimated. And legitimation is an appropriate concern. Justice Jackson, in his opinion in one of the cases concerning the detention of Japanese-Americans during World War II, made the following relevant observation:

> Much is said of the danger to liberty from the Army program for deporting and detaining these citizens of Japanese extraction. But a judicial construction of the due process clause that will sustain this order is a far more subtle blow to liberty than the promulgation of the order itself. A military order, however unconstitutional, is not apt to last longer than the military emergency. Even during that period a succeeding commander may revoke it all. But once a judicial opinion rationalizes such an order to show that it conforms to the Constitution, or rather rationalizes the Constitution to show that the Constitution sanctions such an order, the Court for all time has validated the principle of racial discrimination in criminal procedure and of transplanting American citizens. The principle then lies about like a loaded weapon ready for the hand of any authority that can bring forward a plausible claim of an urgent need. Every repetition imbeds that principle more deeply in our law and thinking and expands it to new purposes. All who observe the work of courts are familiar with what Judge Cardozo described as "the tendency of a principle to expand itself to the limit of its logic." A military commander may overstep the bounds of constitutionality, and it is an incident. But if we review and approve, that passing incident becomes the doctrine of the Constitution. There it has a generative power of its own, and all that it creates will be in its own image.[16]

A similar argument can be made regarding torture: if an agent tortures, that is "an incident," but if the courts authorize it, it becomes a precedent. There is, however, an important difference between the detention of Japanese-American citizens and torture. The detentions were done openly and with presidential accountability; torture would be done secretly, with official deniability. Tolerating an off-the-book system of secret torture can also establish a dangerous precedent.

A variation on this "legitimation" argument would postpone consideration of the choice between authorizing torture and forgoing a possible tactic necessary to prevent an imminent act of terrorism until after the choice—presumably the choice to torture—has been made. In that way, the discussion would not, in itself, encourage the use of torture. If it were employed, then we could decide whether it was justified, excusable, condemnable, or something in between. The problem with that argument is that no FBI agent who tortured a suspect into disclosing information that prevented an act of mass terrorism would be prosecuted—as the policemen who tortured the kidnapper into disclosing the whereabouts of his victim were not prosecuted. In the absence of a prosecution, there would be no occasion to judge the appropriateness of the torture.

I disagree with these more passive approaches and believe that in a democracy it is always preferable to decide controversial issues in advance, rather than in the heat of battle. I would apply this rule to other tragic choices as well, including the possible use of a nuclear first strike, or retaliatory strikes—so long as the discussion was sufficiently general to avoid giving our potential enemies a strategic advantage by their knowledge of our policy.

Even if government officials decline to discuss such issues, academics have a duty to raise them and submit them to the marketplace of ideas. There may be danger in open discussion, but there is far greater danger in actions based on secret discussion, or no discussion at all.

NOTES

1. Michael Walzer, "Political Action: The Problem of Dirty Hands," *Philosophy and Public Affairs*, 1973.

2. Quoted in W. L. Twining and P. E. Twining, "Bentham on Torture," *Northern Ireland Legal Quarterly*, Autumn 1973, p. 347. Bentham's hypothetical question

does not distinguish between torture inflicted by private persons and by governments.

3. David Johnston and Philip Shenon, "F.B.I. Curbed Scrutiny of Man Now a Suspect in the Attacks," *New York Times*, 10/6/2001.

4. Twining and Twining, "Bentham on Torture," pp. 348–49. The argument for the limited use of torture in the ticking bomb case falls into a category of argument known as "argument from the extreme case," which is a useful heuristic to counter arguments for absolute principles.

5. On conditions in American prisons, see Alan M. Dershowitz, "Supreme Court Acknowledges Country's Other Rape Epidemic," *Boston Herald*, 6/12/1994. . . .

6. John Langbein, *Torture and the Law of Proof* (Chicago: University of Chicago Press, 1977), p. 68. Voltaire generally opposed torture but favored it in some cases.

7. A fifth approach would be simply to never discuss the issue of torture—or to postpone any such discussion until after we actually experience a ticking bomb case—but I have always believed that it is preferable to consider and discuss tragic choices before we confront them, so that the issue can be debated without recriminatory emotions and after-the-fact finger-pointing.

8. Charles M. Sennott, "Israeli High Court Bans Torture in Questioning; 10,000 Palestinians Subjected to Tactics," *Boston Globe*, 9/7/1999.

9. Quoted in Twining and Twining, "Bentham on Torture," p. 345.

10. Langbein, *Torture and the Law of Proof*, p. 7.

11. Ibid., p. 90, quoting Bacon.

12. Langbein, *Torture and the Law of Proof*, pp.136–37, 139.

13. When it is known that torture is a possible option, terrorists sometimes provide the information and then claim they have been tortured, in order to be able to justify their complicity to their colleagues.

14. *U.S. v. Lefkowitz*, 285 U.S. 452, 464 (1932).

15. *Johnson v. U.S.* 333 U.S. 10, 13–14 (1948).

16. *Korematsu v. U.S.* 323 U.S. 214, 245–46 (1944) (Jackson, J., dissenting).

READING QUESTIONS

1. Explain the case for why the ticking bomb terrorist should be tortured according to Dershowitz. How did his visit to Israel impact his views on this matter?

2. What is the strongest argument against the view that the ticking bomb terrorist should be tortured? Explain how the distinction between act and rule utilitarianism is relevant to this argument.

3. What is the biggest problem for an act utilitarian justification of torture according to Dershowitz? What is a "torture warrant" and how does Dershowitz believe torture warrants could be implemented in order to overcome the relevant problem?

4. What are the four ways that Dershowitz considers for how we can resolve the dilemma between the conflicting values of security and abiding by the law? Why are accountability and visibility in democracy important according to Dershowitz? Consider in particular the possible consequences of a lack of accountability in a democracy.

DISCUSSION QUESTIONS

1. Should we agree with Dershowitz that the introduction of torture warrants would result in fewer terrorist attacks as well as allow for more government accountability? Why or why not? Consider and discuss some of the potential problems that might arise with the introduction of such warrants. Are there any better or additional alternatives that could be implemented in order to prevent terrorist attacks that would also result in greater accountability in a democracy?

2. Consider and discuss whether the act utilitarian argument that Dershowitz gives for the justification of torture fails to provide adequate reasons to support his view. Is Bentham's hypothetical case different in any morally relevant ways from the case of the ticking bomb terrorist that Dershowitz considers? If so, how?

ADDITIONAL RESOURCES

Web Resources

Amnesty International, <www.amnesty.org>. International organization that campaigns for recognition of human rights. A source of up-to-date news on torture.

The World Organization Against Torture, <www.omct.org>. Information about and opposition to torture and other human rights violations.

CIA Website, <www.cia.gov>. See "CIA & the War on Terrorism" link for the CIA's perspective on terrorism.

Anti-War.Com, <www.antiwar.com>. Site devoted to opposition to war. Critical of current and past U.S. administration positions on wars.

Fiala, Andrew, "Pacifism," *Stanford Encyclopedia of Philosophy*, <http://plato.stanford.edu/entries/pacifism>. An overview of types of pacifism with discussion of consequentialist, deontological, and religious approaches to the topic.

Miller, Seamus, "Torture," *Stanford Encyclopedia of Philosophy*, <http://plato.stanford.edu/entries/torture/>. An overview of the torture debate.

Orend, Brian, "War," *Stanford Encyclopedia of Philosophy*, <http://plato.stanford.edu/entries/war/>. An overview of the ethics of war and peace. Includes an extended treatment of the provisions of just war theory.

Authored Books and Articles

Allhoff, Fritz, "Terrorism and Torture," *International Journal of Applied Philosophy* 17 (2003): 105–18. A defense of torture for certain purposes only, including obtaining information regarding significant threats.

Davis, Michael, "The Moral Justification of Torture," *International Journal of Applied Philosophy* 19 (2005): 161–78. Critical of using ticking bomb scenarios in arguments over torture.

Dershowitz, Alan M., *Why Terrorism Works: Understanding the Threat, Responding to the Challenge.* (New Haven and London: Yale University Press, 2002). A lively exploration of the causes of and recommended responses to recent state-sponsored terrorism.

Holmes, Robert L., *On War and Morality* (Princeton, N.J.: Princeton University Press, 1989). Holmes defends a historically informed version of anti-war pacifism.

May, Larry, "Torturing Detainees During Interrogation," *International Journal of Applied Philosophy* 19 (2005): 193–208. Argues against the torture of captured suspected terrorists.

Miller, Seamus, "Is Torture Ever Morally Justified?" *International Journal of Applied Philosophy* 19 (2005): 179–92. Defense of the moral justification but not legalization of torture.

Waldron, Jeremy, "Torture and Positive Law," *Columbia Law Review* 105 (2005): 1681–750. Argues against the legalization of torture.

Walzer, Michael, *Just and Unjust Wars*, 2nd ed. (New York: Basic Books, 1992). An important book defending a just-war approach.

Walzer, Michael, *Arguing about War* (New Haven and London: Yale University Press, 2004). A collection of Walzer's essays in which he appeals to a version of just-war theory in examining a variety of issues including nuclear deterrence, humanitarian intervention, the recent wars in Afghanistan and Iraq, and terrorism.

Edited Collections

Cole, David (ed.), *The Torture Memos: Rationalizing the Unthinkable* (New York: The New Press, 2009). A collection of memos released by the U.S. Department of Justice describing interrogation techniques used by the CIA under the Bush administration.

Greenberg, Karen (ed.), *The Torture Debate in America* (Cambridge: Cambridge University Press, 2006). A collection of twenty essays, organized into four parts: "Democracy, Terror and Torture," "The Geneva Conventions and International Law," "On Torture," and "Looking Forward."

Levinson, Sanford (ed.), *Torture: A Collection* (New York: Oxford University Press, 2004). A collection of essays by different authors organized into four parts: (1) Philosophical Considerations, (2) Torture as Practiced, (3) Contemporary Attempts to Abolish Torture through Law, and (4) Reflections on the Post-September 11 Debate about Legalizing Torture. Part 4 includes articles by Elaine Scarry and Richard A. Posner that are critical of Dershowitz's views on the morality of torture.

Shue, Henry, and Rodin, David (eds.), *Preemption: Military Action and Moral Justification* (Oxford and New York: Oxford University Press, 2009). A collection of nine essays by scholars from the fields of history, law, political science, and philosophy debating the justifiability of preemptive war.

Sterba, James P. (ed.), *Terrorism and International Justice* (New York: Oxford University Press, 2003). A collection of essays by various authors covering basic questions about the natural causes and morality of terrorism.

13 } World Hunger and Poverty

The devastation caused by the Indian Ocean tsunami disaster in December 2004 prompted massive relief efforts by many nations including generous donations from many individuals. In 2005, parts of Alabama, Louisiana, and Mississippi were devastated by Hurricane Katrina, leaving many people without food, water, electricity, and shelter. According to a 2008 report by the World Bank, 1.4 billion of the world's population lives in extreme poverty, which it defines as not having enough income to meet one's most basic needs. These disasters and the World Bank's statistics call attention to the fact that disease, famine, poverty, and displacement are widespread evils that especially afflict the economically disadvantaged and may afflict those who live in relatively wealthy countries. Moral reflection on hunger, poverty, and other such evils prompts the following questions about the obligations of those more affluent countries and their citizens:

- Are economically advantaged people morally required to participate in a scheme of redistribution so that some of their wealth goes to people who are severely economically disadvantaged?
- If so, what best explains this obligation?

One way in which we can think about these questions is by focusing on the widely recognized duty of **beneficence** or charity, which is roughly the duty to help those in dire need.

1. THE DUTY OF BENEFICENCE

Let us assume there is a duty of beneficence, and let us assume further that this duty is a requirement only for those who are in a position to help others. There are three questions we can raise about this duty. First, there is the question of *scope*—to whom is this duty owed? Assuming for the sake of simplicity that we are concerned just with members of the current world population who are in need of help, does this obligation extend to distant strangers? The second question is about the duty's *content*—for those who can afford to do so, how much are they morally required to sacrifice? The third question is about *strength*—how strong is one's obligation to help those in need when doing so conflicts with other moral duties (such as educating one's own children) and with various nonmoral reasons for action including the pursuit of, say, expensive hobbies or various artistic endeavors? One can imagine a very strong duty of beneficence according to which the economically advantaged have an obligation to all disadvantaged individuals worldwide, which requires not only that they sacrifice a great amount of what they now have in an effort to help those in need, but also that this obligation to help is as strong as any conflicting duty they might have. On the other hand, one can easily imagine a moral code that includes a much weaker duty of beneficence along one or more of the three dimensions just described.

2. THEORY MEETS PRACTICE

Three main theoretical approaches to the moral issues of hunger and poverty are represented in this chapter's selections: consequentialism, the ethics of prima facie duty, and Kantian moral theory. Let us consider them in order.

Consequentialism

A purely consequentialist moral theory of the sort described in chapter 1, section 2A, is going to imply that one's moral obligation to help those in need will depend on the likely consequences of doing so compared to not doing so. Consequentialists can and do disagree about likely consequences, because they often disagree about the root causes of hunger and poverty. Thomas Robert Malthus (1766–1834) claimed that population necessarily outruns economic growth, which in turn necessarily leads to famine. Neo-Malthusians, as they are called, follow Malthus in claiming that the level of economic growth needed to sustain increases in population cannot be maintained, and that eventually unchecked population growth will lead to massive poverty and famine. This analysis of famine and poverty, together with a commitment to consequentialism, is the basis for Garrett Hardin's view that affluent countries and individuals have a moral obligation to *not* help those in overpopulated countries by giving food and other forms of aid. His claim is that doing so will in the long run likely be worse for humanity generally (including those who now have their basic needs met) than will be the likely consequences of refusing to help the needy in overpopulated countries. We can express Hardin's view on the morality of helping those in need by saying that for him, the scope, content, and strength of any such obligation depend entirely on the likely consequences on overall human welfare of engaging in such aid. Since the overall human welfare would likely be decreased by such aid, we have no obligation to help those in overpopulated countries; indeed, we have an obligation to not help.

Peter Singer also approaches the issue of helping those in need from a broadly consequentialist perspective—one that emphasizes one's moral obligation to reduce the level of human misery. On this basis, Singer reaches a different moral conclusion about giving aid from the one Hardin reaches. He argues that given the great evils of poverty and starvation, those who now enjoy an affluent life and who, by helping, would sacrifice nothing of genuine moral significance have a moral obligation to help those in need. As Singer points out, the scope, content, and strength of the duty to help would require a radical revision in how most people currently think about their obligations to others in need.

Another broadly consequentialist approach to moral questions about world hunger and poverty allows for the idea that rights in general and property rights in particular have intrinsic and not just instrumental value. (The idea that rights have only instrumental value is perhaps the most common view of rights held by consequentialists.) But, as Amartya Sen points out in one of our selections, recognizing the intrinsic value of a right does not rule out considering the consequences of adhering to the right. Sen's idea is that in thinking about our obligations to help those in need, we need to consider both the intrinsic value of holding some property right as well as the overall value of the consequences of adhering to that right. On this basis, Sen makes a case for the moral justification of redistribution of wealth in preventing famine.

Ethics of Prima Facie Duty

According to an ethics of prima facie duty, thinking about world hunger and poverty requires that we consider various competing prima facie duties. Suppose we grant that those living in affluence have a duty to help alleviate the evils of poverty and starvation. (Arguably, we might have this duty even if those to whom it is owed have no moral right against those who are in a position to help.) From this theoretical perspective, we have all sorts of prima facie duties—negative duties not to injure, lie, and break promises, as well as such positive duties as self-improvement and beneficence. When two or more of these prima facie duties conflict in some circumstance, we have to decide which of them is overriding and thus which of them is one's all-things-considered duty in that circumstance. This in turn requires that we think in detail about our circumstances and carefully weigh the relevant strengths of our prima facie obligations.

Kantian Moral Theory

Kant defended the claim that we have a duty of beneficence—a duty to help at least some of those in need on at least some occasions. Because it is up to those who are in a position to help to decide when and how to fulfill this duty—its fulfillment involves a good deal of latitude—Kant claimed that our duty of beneficence is a wide duty. (By contrast, duties to others to not inflict harm and duties to ourselves to not commit suicide are among the narrow duties—duties that do not involve the kind of latitude for choice that is characteristic of our wide obligations.)[1] What is the basis in Kant's theory for the wide duty of beneficence? In her article, Onora O'Neill explains that the Humanity formulation of Kant's fundamental moral principle—the categorical imperative—requires that we not treat others as mere means to our own ends and that we positively treat others as ends in themselves. It is this second, positive part of the categorical imperative that, according to O'Neill, is the basis for our wide duty of beneficence, which she explains and defends.

NOTE

1. For more on the distinction between wide and narrow duty in Kantian moral theory, see chapter 1, section 2C.

GARRETT HARDIN

Lifeboat Ethics

According to Hardin, in thinking about hunger and poverty as moral issues, it is useful to think of them in terms of the metaphor of a lifeboat. Each rich nation is to be thought of as occupying a lifeboat full of comparatively rich people, whereas each poor nation is thought of as a lifeboat containing mostly relatively poor people. Put in these terms, the question is what obligations do rich passengers in one boat have to their poorer counterparts in the less fortunate boats? Hardin rejects essentially Christian and Marxist approaches that would require rich nations to help poor ones, because he thinks that their ultimately unrealistic approaches to solving problems of hunger and poverty—problems of overpopulation—will lead to what he calls "the tragedy of the commons." Taking an essentially consequentialist perspective, Hardin argues that given the likely disastrous overall consequences of rich countries aiding poor countries, the moral implication is that the affluent ought not to help people in countries where overpopulation cannot realistically be brought under control.

Recommended Reading: consequentialism, chap. 1, sec. 2A.

No generation has viewed the problem of the survival of the human species as seriously as we have. Inevitably, we have entered this world of concern through the door of metaphor. Environmentalists have emphasized the image of the earth as a spaceship—Spaceship Earth. Kenneth Boulding (1966) is the principal architect of this metaphor. It is time, he says, that we replace the wasteful "cowboy economy" of the past with the frugal "spaceship economy" required for continued survival in the limited world we now see ours to be. The metaphor is notably useful in justifying pollution control measures.

Unfortunately, the image of a spaceship is also used to promote measures that are suicidal. One of these is a generous immigration policy, which is only a particular instance of a class of policies that are in error because they lead to the tragedy of the commons (Hardin 1968). These suicidal policies are attractive because they mesh with what we unthinkingly take

to be the ideals of "the best people." What is missing in the idealistic view is an insistence that rights and responsibilities must go together. The "generous" attitude of all too many people results in asserting inalienable rights while ignoring or denying matching responsibilities.

For the metaphor of a spaceship to be correct the aggregate of people on board would have to be under unitary sovereign control (Ophuls 1974). A true ship always has a captain. It is conceivable that a ship could be run by a committee. But it could not possibly survive if its course were determined by bickering tribes that claimed rights without responsibilities.

What about Spaceship Earth? It certainly has no captain, and no executive committee. The United Nations is a toothless tiger, because the signatories of its charter wanted it that way. The spaceship metaphor is used only to justify spaceship demands on common

From Garrett Hardin, "Living on a Lifeboat," *Science* 24 (1974). Reprinted by permission.

resources without acknowledging corresponding spaceship responsibilities.

An understandable fear of decisive action leads people to embrace "incrementalism"—moving toward reform in tiny stages. As we shall see, this strategy is counterproductive in the area discussed here if it means accepting rights before responsibilities. Where human survival is at stake, the acceptance of responsibilities is a precondition to the acceptance of rights, if the two cannot be introduced simultaneously.

LIFEBOAT ETHICS

Before taking up certain substantive issues let us look at an alternative metaphor, that of a lifeboat. In developing some relevant examples the following numerical values are assumed. Approximately two-thirds of the world is desperately poor, and only one-third is comparatively rich. The people in poor countries have an average per capita GNP (Gross National Product) of about $200 per year; the rich, of about $3,000. (For the United States it is nearly $5,000 per year.) Metaphorically, each rich nation amounts to a lifeboat full of comparatively rich people. The poor of the world are in other, much more crowded lifeboats. Continuously, so to speak, the poor fall out of their lifeboats and swim for a while in the water outside, hoping to be admitted to a rich lifeboat, or in some other way to benefit from the "goodies" on board. What should the passengers on a rich lifeboat do? This is the central problem of "the ethics of a lifeboat."

First we must acknowledge that each lifeboat is effectively limited in capacity. The land of every nation has a limited carrying capacity. The exact limit is a matter for argument, but the energy crunch is convincing more people every day that we have already exceeded the carrying capacity of the land. We have been living on "capital"—stored petroleum and coal—and soon we must live on income alone.

Let us look at only one lifeboat—ours. The ethical problem is the same for all, and is as follows. Here we sit, say 50 people in a lifeboat. To be generous, let us assume our boat has a capacity of 10 more, making 60. (This, however, is to violate the engineering principle of the "safety factor." A new plant disease or a bad change in the weather may decimate our population if we don't preserve some excess capacity as a safety factor.)

The 50 of us in the lifeboat see 100 others swimming in the water outside, asking for admission to the boat, or for handouts. How shall we respond to their calls? There are several possibilities.

One. We may be tempted to try to live by the Christian ideal of being "our brother's keeper," or by the Marxian ideal (Marx 1875) of "from each according to his abilities, to each according to his needs." Since the needs of all are the same, we take all the needy into our boat, making a total of 150 in a boat with a capacity of 60. The boat is swamped, and everyone drowns. Complete justice, complete catastrophe.

Two. Since the boat has an unused excess capacity of 10, we admit just 10 more to it. This has the disadvantage of getting rid of the safety factor, for which action we will sooner or later pay dearly. Moreover, *which* 10 do we let in? "First come, first served?" The best 10? The neediest 10? How do we *discriminate?* And what do we say to the 90 who are excluded?

Three. Admit no more to the boat and preserve the small safety factor. Survival of the people in the lifeboat is then possible (though we shall have to be on our guard against boarding parties).

The last solution is abhorrent to many people. It is unjust, they say. Let us grant that it is.

"I feel guilty about my good luck," say some. The reply to this is simple: *Get out and yield your place to others.* Such a selfless action might satisfy the conscience of those who are addicted to guilt but it would not change the ethics of the lifeboat. The needy person to whom a guilt-addict yields his place will not himself feel guilty about his sudden good luck. (If he did he would not climb aboard.) The net result of conscience-stricken people relinquishing their unjustly held positions is the elimination of their kind of conscience from the lifeboat. The lifeboat, as it were, purifies itself of guilt. The ethics of the lifeboat persist, unchanged by such momentary aberrations.

This then is the basic metaphor within which we must work out our solutions. Let us enrich the image step by step with substantive additions from the real world.

REPRODUCTION

The harsh characteristics of lifeboat ethics are heightened by reproduction, particularly by reproductive differences. The people inside the lifeboats of the wealthy nations are doubling in numbers every 87 years; those outside are doubling every 35 years, on the average. And the relative difference in prosperity is becoming greater.

Let us, for a while, think primarily of the U.S. lifeboat. As of 1973 the United States had a population of 210 million people, who were increasing by 0.8% per year, that is, doubling in number every 87 years.

Although the citizens of rich nations are outnumbered two to one by the poor, let us imagine an equal number of poor people outside our lifeboat—a mere 210 million poor people reproducing at a quite different rate. If we imagine these to be the combined populations of Colombia, Venezuela, Ecuador, Morocco, Thailand, Pakistan, and the Philippines, the average rate of increase of the people "outside" is 3.3% per year. The doubling time of this population is 21 years.

Suppose that all these countries, and the United States, agreed to live by the Marxian ideal, "to each according to his needs," the ideal of most Christians as well. Needs, of course, are determined by population size, which is affected by reproduction. Every nation regards its rate of reproduction as a sovereign right. If our lifeboat were big enough in the beginning it might be possible to live *for a while* by Christian-Marxian ideals. *Might*.

Initially, in the model given, the ratio of non-Americans to Americans would be one to one. But consider what the ratio would be 87 years later. By this time Americans would have doubled to a population of 420 million. The other group (doubling every 21 years) would now have swollen to 3,540 million.

Each American would have more than eight people to share with. How could the lifeboat possibly keep afloat?

All this involves extrapolation of current trends into the future, and is consequently suspect. Trends may change. Granted: but the change will not necessarily be favorable. If—as seems likely—the rate of population increase falls faster in the ethnic group presently inside the lifeboat than it does among those now outside, the future will turn out to be even worse than mathematics predicts, and sharing will be even more suicidal.

RUIN IN THE COMMONS

The fundamental error of the sharing ethics is that it leads to the tragedy of the commons. Under a system of private property the man (or group of men) who own property recognize their responsibility to care for it, for if they don't they will eventually suffer. A farmer, for instance, if he is intelligent, will allow no more cattle in a pasture than its carrying capacity justifies. If he overloads the pasture, weeds take over, erosion sets in, and the owner loses in the long run.

But if a pasture is run as a commons open to all, the right of each to use it is not matched by an operational responsibility to take care of it. It is no use asking independent herdsmen in a commons to act responsibly, for they dare not. The considerate herdsman who refrains from overloading the commons suffers more than a selfish one who says his needs are greater. (As Leo Durocher says, "Nice guys finish last.") Christian-Marxian idealism is counterproductive. That it *sounds* nice is no excuse. With distribution systems, as with individual morality, good intentions are no substitute for good performance.

A social system is stable only if it is insensitive to errors. To the Christian-Marxian idealist a selfish person is a sort of "error." Prosperity in the system of the commons cannot survive errors. If *everyone* would only restrain himself, all would be well; but it takes *only one less than everyone* to ruin a system of voluntary restraint. In a crowded world of less than perfect human beings—and we will never know any other—mutual ruin is inevitable in the commons. This is the core of the tragedy of the commons....

WORLD FOOD BANKS

In the international arena we have recently heard a proposal to create a new commons, namely an international depository of food reserves to which nations will contribute according to their abilities, and from which nations may draw according to their needs. Nobel laureate Norman Borlaug has lent the prestige of his name to this proposal.

A world food bank appeals powerfully to our humanitarian impulses. We remember John Donne's celebrated line, "Any man's death diminishes me." But before we rush out to see for whom the bell tolls let us recognize where the greatest political push for international granaries comes from, lest we be disillusioned later. Our experience with Public Law 480 clearly reveals the answer. This was the law that moved billions of dollars worth of U.S. grain to food-short, population-long countries during the past two decades. When P.L. 480 first came into being, a headline in the business magazine *Forbes* (Paddock 1970) revealed the power behind it: "Feeding the World's Hungry Millions: How it will mean billions for U.S. business."

And indeed it did. In the years 1960 to 1970 a total of $7.9 billion was spent on the "Food for Peace" program, as P.L. 480 was called. During the years of 1948 to 1970 an additional $49.9 billion were extracted from American taxpayers to pay for other economic aid programs, some of which went for food and food-producing machinery. (This figure does *not* include military aid.) That P.L. 480 was a give-away program was concealed. Recipient countries went through the motions of paying for P.L. 480 food—with IOU's. In December 1973 the charade was brought to an end as far as India was concerned when the United States "forgave" India's $3.2 billion debt (Anonymous 1974). Public announcement of the cancellation of the debt was delayed for two months: one wonders why....

What happens if some organizations budget for emergencies and others do not? If each organization is solely responsible for its own well-being, poorly managed ones will suffer. But they should be able to learn from experience. They have a chance to mend their ways and learn to budget for infrequent but certain emergencies. The weather, for instance, always varies and periodic crop failures are certain. A wise and competent government saves out of the production of the good years in anticipation of bad years that are sure to come. This is not a new idea. The Bible tells us that Joseph taught this policy to Pharaoh in Egypt more than 2,000 years ago. Yet it is literally true that the vast majority of the governments of the world today have no such policy. They lack either the wisdom or the competence, or both. Far more difficult than the transfer of wealth from one country to another is the transfer of wisdom between sovereign powers or between generations.

"But it isn't their fault! How can we blame the poor people who are caught in an emergency? Why must we punish them?" The concepts of blame and punishment are irrelevant. The question is, what are the operational consequences of establishing a world food bank? If it is open to every country every time a need develops, slovenly rulers will not be motivated to take Joseph's advice. Why should they? Others will bail them out whenever they are in trouble.

Some countries will make deposits in the world food bank and others will withdraw from it: there will be almost no overlap. Calling such a depository-transfer unit a "bank" is stretching the metaphor of *bank* beyond its elastic limits. The proposers, of course, never call attention to the metaphorical nature of the word they use.

THE RATCHET EFFECT

An "international food bank" is really, then, not a true bank but a disguised one-way transfer device for moving wealth from rich countries to poor. In the absence of such a bank, in a world inhabited by individually responsible sovereign nations, the population

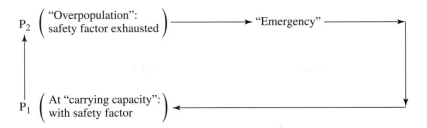

$$P_2 \begin{pmatrix} \text{``Overpopulation'':} \\ \text{safety factor exhausted} \end{pmatrix} \longrightarrow \text{``Emergency''} \longrightarrow$$

$$P_1 \begin{pmatrix} \text{At ``carrying capacity'':} \\ \text{with safety factor} \end{pmatrix} \longleftarrow$$

Figure 13.1

of each nation would repeatedly go through a cycle of the sort shown in Figure 13.1. P_2 is greater than P_1, either in absolute numbers or because a deterioration of the food supply has removed the safety factor and produced a dangerously low ratio of resources to population. P_2 may be said to represent a state of overpopulation, which becomes obvious upon the appearance of an "accident," e.g., a crop failure. If the "emergency" is not met by outside help, the population drops back to the "normal" level—the "carrying capacity" of the environment—or even below. In the absence of population control by a sovereign, sooner or later the population grows to P_2 again and the cycle repeats. The long-term population curve (Hardin 1966) is an irregularly fluctuating one, equilibrating more or less about the carrying capacity.

A demographic cycle of this sort obviously involves great suffering in the restrictive phase, but such a cycle is normal to any independent country with inadequate population control. The third century theologian Tertullian (Hardin 1969) expressed what must have been the recognition of many wise men when he wrote: "The scourges of pestilence, famine, wars, and earthquakes have come to be regarded as a blessing to overcrowded nations, since they serve to prune away the luxuriant growth of the human race."

Only under a strong and farsighted sovereign—which theoretically could be the people themselves, democratically organized—can a population equilibrate at some set point below the carrying capacity, thus avoiding the pains normally caused by periodic and unavoidable disasters. For this happy state to be achieved it is necessary that those in power be able to contemplate with equanimity the "waste" of surplus food in times of bountiful harvests. It is essential that those in power resist the temptation to convert extra food into extra babies. On the public relations level it is necessary that the phrase "surplus food" be replaced by "safety factor."

But wise sovereigns seem not to exist in the poor world today. The most anguishing problems are created by poor countries that are governed by rulers insufficiently wise and powerful. If such countries can draw on a world food bank in times of "emergency," the population *cycle* of Figure 13.1 will be replaced by the population *escalator* of Figure 13.2. The input of food from a food bank acts as the pawl of a ratchet, preventing the population from retracing its steps to a lower level. Reproduction pushes the population upward, inputs from the world bank prevent its moving downward. Population size escalates, as does the absolute magnitude of "accidents" and "emergencies." The process is brought to an end only by the total collapse of the whole system, producing a catastrophe of scarcely imaginable proportions.

Such are the implications of the well-meant sharing of food in a world of irresponsible reproduction. . . .

To be generous with one's own possessions is one thing; to be generous with posterity's is quite another. This, I think, is the point that must be gotten across to those who would, from a commendable love of distributive justice, institute a ruinous system of the commons. . . .

If the argument of this essay is correct, so long as there is no true world government to control reproduction everywhere it is impossible to survive in dignity if we are to be guided by Spaceship ethics. Without

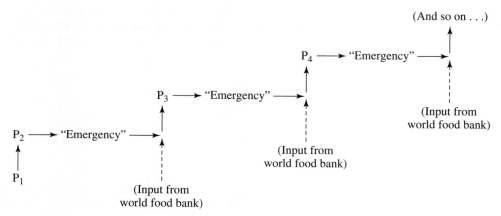

Figure 13.2

a world government that is sovereign in reproductive matters mankind lives, in fact, on a number of sovereign lifeboats. For the foreseeable future survival demands that we govern our actions by the ethics of a lifeboat. Posterity will be ill served if we do not.

REFERENCES

Anonymous. 1974. *Wall Street Journal,* 19 Feb.

Boulding, K. 1966. The economics of the coming spaceship earth. In H. Jarrett, ed. *Environmental Quality in a Growing Economy.* Johns Hopkins Press, Baltimore.

Hardin, G. 1966. Chap. 9 in *Biology: Its Principles and Implications,* 2nd ed. Freeman, San Francisco.

———. 1968. The tragedy of the commons. *Science* 162: 1243–1248.

———. 1969. Page 18 in *Population, Evolution, and Birth Control,* 2nd ed. Freeman, San Francisco.

Marx, K. 1875. *Critique of the Gotha program.* Page 388 in R. C. Tucker, ed. *The Marx-Engels Reader,* Norton, N.Y., 1972.

Ophuls, W. 1974. The scarcity society. *Harpers* 248 (1487): 47–52.

Paddock, W. C. 1970. How green is the green revolution? *Bioscience* 20: 897–902.

READING QUESTIONS

1. What are the problems with the metaphor of Earth as a spaceship according to Hardin?
2. Explain Hardin's lifeboat metaphor and the three possible responses that we might take toward the ethical problems it suggests.
3. Why does Hardin reject the first response to the ethical lifeboat problem? How does he respond to those who claim that the third possibility is unjust?
4. Why does Hardin think that an international food bank is an implausible solution to the problem of world hunger and poverty? What is the "ratchet effect" and how does it figure into his objections and proposed solution to the problem?

DISCUSSION QUESTIONS

1. Consider whether Hardin's lifeboat metaphor represents a plausible understanding of the way the nations of the world can or do operate. Are there any ways in which the metaphor could or should be modified?

2. Is Hardin correct to assume that the implementation of something like an international food bank would result in a vicious cycle of overpopulation accompanied by emergency scenarios? Consider some ways that a world food bank could operate more successfully in order to prevent such disasters.

PETER SINGER

The Life You Can Save

In this excerpt from his recent 2009 book, *The Life You Can Save,* Singer presents a basic argument for the claim that in not donating to human aid organizations, those in a financial position to do so are acting immorally—an argument he originally advanced in his influential 1972 article, "Famine, Affluence, and Morality." In the following selection, Singer presents recent empirical data about poverty and affluence, and he also responds to various objections to his basic argument that he has encountered over the years.

Recommended Reading: consequentialism, chap. 1, sec. 2A.

1. SAVING A CHILD

On your way to work, you pass a small pond. On hot days, children sometimes play in the pond, which is only about knee-deep. The weather's cool today, though, and the hour is early, so you are surprised to see a child splashing about in the pond. As you get closer, you see that it is a very young child, just a toddler, who is flailing about, unable to stay upright or walk out of the pond. You look for the parents or babysitter, but there is no one else around. The child is unable to keep his head above the water for more than a few seconds at a time. If you don't wade in and pull him out, he seems likely to drown. Wading in is easy and safe, but you will ruin the new shoes you bought only a few days ago, and get your suit wet and muddy. By the time you hand the child

over to someone responsible for him, and change your clothes, you'll be late for work. What should you do?

I teach a course called Practical Ethics. When we start talking about global poverty, I ask my students what they think you should do in this situation. Predictably, they respond that you should save the child. "What about your shoes? And being late for work?" I ask them. They brush that aside. How could anyone consider a pair of shoes, or missing an hour or two at work, a good reason for not saving a child's life?

In 2007, something resembling this hypothetical situation actually occurred near Manchester, England. Jordon Lyon, a ten-year-old boy, leaped into a pond after his stepsister Bethany slipped in. He struggled to support her but went under himself. Anglers managed to pull Bethany out, but by

From Peter Singer, *The Life You Can Save* (New York: Random House, 2009). Reprinted with permission of the author.

then Jordon could no longer be seen. They raised the alarm, and two police community support officers soon arrived; they refused to enter the pond to find Jordon. He was later pulled out, but attempts at resuscitation failed. At the inquest on Jordon's death, the officers' inaction was defended on the grounds that they had not been trained to deal with such situations. The mother responded: "If you're walking down the street and you see a child drowning you automatically go in that water…You don't have to be trained to jump in after a drowning child."[1]

I think it's safe to assume that most people would agree with the mother's statement. But consider that, according to UNICEF, nearly 10 million children under five years old die each year from causes related to poverty. Here is just one case, described by a man in Ghana to a researcher from the World Bank:

> Take the death of this small boy this morning, for example. The boy died of measles. We all know he could have been cured at the hospital. But the parents had no money and so the boy died a slow and painful death, not of measles but out of poverty.[2]

Think about something like that happening 27,000 times every day. Some children die because they don't have enough to eat. More die, like that small boy in Ghana, from measles, malaria, and diarrhea, conditions that either don't exist in developed nations, or, if they do, are almost never fatal. The children are vulnerable to these diseases because they have no safe drinking water, or no sanitation, and because when they do fall ill, their parents can't afford any medical treatment. UNICEF, Oxfam, and many other organizations are working to reduce poverty and provide clean water and basic health care, and these efforts are reducing the toll. If the relief organizations had more money, they could do more, and more lives would be saved.

Now think about your own situation. By donating a relatively small amount of money, you could save a child's life. Maybe it takes more than the amount needed to buy a pair of shoes—but we all spend money on things we don't really need, whether on drinks, meals out, clothing, movies, concerts, vacations, new cars, or house renovation. Is it possible that by choosing to spend your money on such things rather than contributing to an aid agency, you are leaving a child to die, a child you could have saved?

Poverty Today

A few years ago, the World Bank asked researchers to listen to what the poor are saying. They were able to document the experiences of 60,000 women and men in seventy-three countries. Over and over, in different languages and on different continents, poor people said that poverty meant these things:

- You are short of food for all or part of the year, often eating only one meal per day, sometimes having to choose between stilling your child's hunger or your own, and sometimes being able to do neither.
- You can't save money. If a family member falls ill and you need money to see a doctor, or if the crop fails and you have nothing to eat, you have to borrow from a local moneylender and he will charge you so much interest as the debt continues to mount and you may never be free of it.
- You can't afford to send your children to school, or if they do start school, you have to take them out again if the harvest is poor.
- You live in an unstable house, made with mud or thatch that you need to rebuild every two or three years, or after severe weather.
- You have no nearby source of safe drinking water. You have to carry your water a long way, and even then, it can make you ill unless you boil it.

But extreme poverty is not only a condition of unsatisfied material needs. It is often accompanied by a degrading state of powerlessness. Even in countries that are democracies and are relatively well governed, respondents to the World Bank survey described a range of situations in which they had to accept humiliation without protest. If someone takes what little you have, and you complain to the police, they may not listen to you. Nor will the law necessarily protect you from rape or sexual harassment. You have a pervading sense of shame and failure because you cannot provide for your children. Your poverty traps you, and you lose hope of ever escaping from a life of hard work for which, at the end, you will have nothing to show beyond bare survival.[3]

The World Bank defines extreme poverty as not having enough income to meet the most basic human needs for adequate food, water, shelter, clothing, sanitation, health care, and education. Many people are familiar with the statistic that 1 billion people are living on less than one dollar per day. That was the World Bank's poverty line until 2008, when better data on international price comparisons enabled it to make a more accurate calculation of the amount people need to meet their basic needs. On the basis of this calculation, the World Bank set the poverty line at $1.25 per day. The number of people whose income puts them under this line is not 1 billion but 1.4 billion. That there are more people living in extreme poverty than we thought is, of course, bad news, but the news is not all bad. On the same basis, in 1981 there were 1.9 billion people living in extreme poverty. That was about four in every ten people on the planet, whereas now fewer than one in four are extremely poor.

South Asia is still the region with the largest number of people living in extreme poverty, a total of 600 million, including 455 million in India. Economic growth has, however, reduced the proportion of South Asians living in extreme poverty from 60 percent in 1981 to 42 percent in 2005. There are another 380 million extremely poor people in sub-Saharan Africa, where half the population is extremely poor—and that is the same percentage as in 1981. The most dramatic reduction in poverty has been in East Asia, although there are still more than 200 million extremely poor Chinese, and smaller numbers elsewhere in the region. The remaining extremely poor people are distributed around the world, in Latin America and the Caribbean, the Pacific, the Middle East, North Africa, Eastern Europe, and Central Asia.[4]

In response to the "$1.25 a day" figure, the thought may cross your mind that in many developing countries, it is possible to live much more cheaply than in the industrialized nations. Perhaps you have even done it yourself, backpacking around the world, living on less than you would have believed possible. So you may imagine that this level of poverty is less extreme than it would be if you had to live on that amount of money in the United States, or any industrialized nation. If such thoughts did occur to you, you should banish them now, because the World Bank has already made the adjustment in purchasing power: Its figures refer to the number of people existing on a daily total consumption of goods and services—whether earned or home-grown—comparable to the amount of goods and services that can be bought in the United States for $1.25.

In wealthy societies, most poverty is relative. People feel poor because many of the good things they see advertised on television are beyond their budget—but they do have a television. In the United States, 97 percent of those classified by the Census Bureau as poor own a color TV. Three quarters of them own a car. Three quarters of them have air-conditioning. Three quarters of them have a VCR or DVD player. All have access to health care.[5] I am not quoting these figures in order to deny that the poor in the United States face genuine difficulties. Nevertheless, for most, these difficulties are of a different order than those of the world's poorest people. The 1.4 billion people living in extreme poverty are poor by an absolute standard tied to the most basic human needs. They are likely to be hungry for at least part of each year. Even if they can get enough food to fill their stomachs, they will probably be malnourished because their diet lacks essential nutrients. In children, malnutrition stunts growth and can cause permanent brain damage. The poor may not be able to afford to send their children to school. Even minimal health care services are usually beyond their means.

This kind of poverty kills. Life expectancy in rich nations averages seventy-eight years; in the poorest nations, those officially classified as "least developed," it is below fifty.[6] In rich countries, fewer than one in a hundred children die before the age of five; in the poorest countries, one in five does. And to the UNICEF figure of nearly 10 million young children dying every year from avoidable, poverty-related causes, we must add at least another 8 million older children and adults.[7]

Affluence Today

Roughly matching the 1.4 billion people living in extreme poverty, there are about a billion living at a level of affluence never previously known except in the courts of kings and nobles. As king of France, Louis XIV, the "Sun King," could afford to build the most magnificent palace Europe had ever seen, but he could not keep it cool in summer as effectively as most middle-class people in industrialized nations can keep their homes cool today. His gardeners, for all their skill, were unable to produce the variety of fresh fruits and vegetables that we can buy all year-round. If he developed a toothache or fell ill, the best his dentists and doctors could do for him would make us shudder.

But we're not just better off than a French king who lived centuries ago. We are also much better off than our own greatgrandparents. For a start, we can expect to live about thirty years longer. A century ago, one child in ten died in infancy. Now, in most rich nations, that figure is less than one in two hundred.[8] Another telling indicator of how wealthy we are today is the modest number of hours we must work in order to meet our basic dietary needs. Today Americans spend, on average, only 6 percent of their income on buying food. If they work a forty-hour week, it takes them barely two hours to earn enough to feed themselves for the week. That leaves far more to spend on consumer goods, entertainment, and vacations.

And then we have the superrich, people who spend their money on palatial homes, ridiculously large and luxurious boats, and private planes. Before the 2008 stock market crash trimmed the numbers, there were more than 1,100 billionaires in the world, with a combined net worth of $4.4 trillion.[9] To cater to such people, Lufthansa Technik unveiled its plans for a private configuration of Boeing's new 787 Dreamliner. In commercial service, this plane will seat up to 330 passengers. The private version will carry 35, at a price of $150 million. Cost aside, there's

nothing like owning a really big airplane carrying a small number of people to maximize your personal contribution to global warming. Apparently, there are already several billionaires who fly around in private commercial-sized airliners, from 747s down. Larry Page and Sergey Brin, the Google cofounders, reportedly bought a Boeing 767 and spent millions fitting it out for their private use.[10] But for conspicuous waste of money and resources it is hard to beat Anousheh Ansari, an Iranian-American telecommunications entrepreneur who paid a reported $20 million for eleven days in space. Comedian Lewis Black said on Jon Stewart's *The Daily Show* that Ansari did it because it was "the only way she could achieve her life's goal of flying over every single starving person on earth and yelling 'Hey, look what I'm spending my money on!'"

While I was working on this book, a special advertising supplement fell out of my Sunday edition of *The New York Times:* a sixty-eight-page glossy magazine filled with advertising for watches by Rolex, Patek Philippe, Breitling, and other luxury brands. The ads didn't carry price tags, but a puff piece about the revival of the mechanical watch gave guidance about the lower end of the range. After admitting that inexpensive quartz watches are extremely accurate and functional, the article opined that there is "something engaging about a mechanical movement." Right, but how much will it cost you to have this engaging something on your wrist? "You might think that getting into mechanical watches is an expensive proposition, but there are plenty of choices in the $500–$5000 range." Admittedly, "these opening-price-point models are pretty simple: basic movement, basic time display, simple decoration and so on." From which we can gather that most of the watches advertised are priced upward of $5,000, or more than one hundred times what anyone needs to pay for a reliable, accurate quartz watch. That there is a market for such products—and one worth advertising at such expense to the wide readership of *The New York Times*—is another indication of the affluence of our society.[11]

If you're shaking your head at the excesses of the superrich, though, don't shake too hard. Think again about some of the ways Americans with average incomes spend their money. In most places in the United States, you can get your recommended eight glasses of water a day out of the tap for less than a penny, while a bottle of water will set you back $1.50 or more.[12] And in spite of the environmental concerns raised by the waste of energy that goes into producing and transporting it, Americans are still buying bottled water, to the tune of more than 31 billion liters in 2006.[13] Think, too, of the way many of us get our caffeine fix: You can make coffee at home for pennies rather than spending three dollars or more on a latte. Or have you ever casually said yes to a waiter's prompt to order a second soda or glass of wine that you didn't even finish? When Dr. Timothy Jones, an archaeologist, led a U.S. government–funded study of food waste, he found that 14 percent of household garbage is perfectly good food that was in its original packaging and not out of date. More than half of this food was drypackaged or canned goods that keep for a long time. According to Jones, $100 billion of food is wasted in the United States every year.[14] Fashion designer Deborah Lindquist claims that the average woman owns more than $600 worth of clothing that she has not worn in the last year.[15] Whatever the actual figure may be, it is fair to say that almost all of us, men and women alike, buy things we don't need, some of which we never even use.

Most of us are absolutely certain that we wouldn't hesitate to save a drowning child, and that we would do it at considerable cost to ourselves. Yet while thousands of children die each day, we spend money on things we take for granted and would hardly notice if they were not there. Is that wrong? If so, how far does our obligation to the poor go?

2. IS IT WRONG NOT TO HELP?

Bob is close to retirement. He has invested most of his savings in a very rare and valuable old car, a Bugatti, which he has not been able to insure. The Bugatti is his pride and joy. Not only does Bob get pleasure from driving and caring for his car, he also knows that its rising market value means that he will be able to sell it and live comfortably after retirement. One day when Bob is out for a drive, he parks the Bugatti near the end of a railway siding and goes for a walk up the track. As he does so, he sees that a runaway train, with no one aboard, is rolling down the railway track. Looking farther down the track, he sees the small figure of a child who appears to be absorbed in playing on the tracks. Oblivious to the runaway train, the child is in great danger. Bob can't stop the train, and the child is too far away to hear his warning shout, but Bob can throw a switch that will divert the train down the siding where his Bugatti is parked. If he does so, nobody will be killed, but the train will crash through the decaying barrier at the end of the siding and destroy his Bugatti. Thinking of his joy in owning the car and the financial security it represents, Bob decides not to throw the switch.

The Car or the Child?

Philosopher Peter Unger developed this variation on the story of the drowning child to challenge us to think further about how much we believe we should sacrifice in order to save the life of a child. Unger's story adds a factor often crucial to our thinking about real-world poverty: uncertainty about the outcome of our sacrifice. Bob cannot be certain that the child will die if he does nothing and saves his car. Perhaps at the last moment the child will hear the train and leap to safety. In the same way, most of us can summon doubts about whether the money we give to a charity is really helping the people it's intended to help.

In my experience, people almost always respond that Bob acted badly when he did not throw the switch and destroy his most cherished and valuable possession, thereby sacrificing his hope of a financially secure retirement. We can't take a serious risk with a child's life, they say, merely to save a car, no matter how rare and valuable the car may be. By implication, we should also believe that with the simple act of saving money for retirement, we are acting as badly as Bob. For in saving money for retirement, we are effectively refusing to use that money to help save lives. This is a difficult implication to confront. How can it be wrong to save for a comfortable retirement? There is, at the very least, something puzzling here.

Another example devised by Unger tests the level of sacrifice we think people should make to alleviate suffering in cases when a life is not at stake:

> You are driving your vintage sedan down a country lane when you are stopped by a hiker who has seriously injured his leg. He asks you to take him to the nearest hospital. If you refuse, there is a good chance that he will lose his leg. On the other hand, if you agree to take him to hospital, he is likely to bleed onto the seats, which you have recently, and expensively, restored in soft white leather.

Again, most people respond that you should drive the hiker to the hospital. This suggests that when prompted to think in concrete terms, about real individuals, most of us consider it obligatory to lessen the serious suffering of innocent others, even at some cost (even a high cost) to ourselves.[16]

The Basic Argument

The above examples reveal our intuitive belief that we ought to help others in need, at least when we can see them and when we are the only person in a position to save them. But our moral intuitions are not always reliable, as we can see from variations in what people in different times and places find intuitively acceptable or objectionable. The case for helping those in extreme poverty will be stronger if it does not rest solely on our intuitions. Here is a logical argument from plausible premises to the same conclusion.

> First premise: Suffering and death from lack of food, shelter, and medical care are bad.
> Second premise: If it is in your power to prevent something bad from happening, without sacrificing anything nearly as important, it is wrong not to do so.
> Third premise: By donating to aid agencies, you can prevent suffering and death from lack of food, shelter, and medical care, without sacrificing anything nearly as important.
> Conclusion: Therefore, if you do not donate to aid agencies, you are doing something wrong.

The drowning-child story is an application of this argument for aid, since ruining your shoes and being late for work aren't nearly as important as the life of a child. Similarly, reupholstering a car is not nearly as big a deal as losing a leg. Even in the case of Bob and the Bugatti, it would be a big stretch to suggest that the loss of the Bugatti would come close to rivaling the significance of the death of an innocent person.

Ask yourself if you can deny the premises of the argument. How could suffering and death from lack of food, shelter, and medical care not be really, really bad? Think of that small boy in Ghana who died of measles. How you would feel if you were his mother or father, watching helplessly as your son suffers and grows weaker? You know that children often die from this condition. You also know that it would be curable, if only you could afford to take your child to a hospital. In those circumstances you would give up almost anything for some way of ensuring your child's survival.

Putting yourself in the place of others, like the parents of that boy, or the child himself, is what thinking ethically is all about. It is encapsulated in the Golden Rule, "Do unto others as you would have them do unto you." Though the Golden Rule is best known to most westerners from the words of Jesus as reported by Matthew and Luke, it is remarkably universal, being found in Buddhism, Confucianism, Hinduism, Islam, and Jainism, and in Judaism, where it is found in Leviticus, and later emphasized by the sage Hille.[17] The Golden Rule requires us to accept that the desires of others ought to count as if they were our own. If the desires of the parents of the dying child were our own, we would have no doubt that their suffering and the death of their child are about as bad as anything can be. So if we think ethically, then those desires must count as if they were our own, and we cannot deny that the suffering and death are bad.

The second premise is also very difficult to reject, because it leaves us some wiggle room when it comes to situations in which, to prevent something bad, we would have to risk something *nearly* as important as the bad thing we are preventing. Consider, for example, a situation in which you can only prevent the deaths of other children by neglecting your own children. This standard does not require you to prevent the deaths of the other children.

"Nearly as important" is a vague term. That's deliberate, because I'm confident that you can do without plenty of things that are clearly and inarguably not as valuable as saving a child's life. I don't know what *you* might think is as important, or nearly as important, as saving a life. By leaving it up to you to decide what those things are, I can avoid the need to find out. I'll trust you to be honest with yourself about it.

Analogies and stories can be pushed too far. Rescuing a child drowning in front of you, and throwing a switch on a railroad track to save the life of a child you can see in the distance, where you are the only one who can save the child, are both different from giving aid to people who are far away. The argument I have just presented complements the drowning-child case, because instead of pulling at your heartstrings by focusing on a single child in need, it appeals to your reason and seeks your assent to an abstract but compelling moral principle. That means that to reject it, you need to find a flaw in the reasoning....

3. COMMON OBJECTIONS TO GIVING

Charity begins at home, the saying goes, and I've found that friends, colleagues, students, and lecture audiences express that resistance in various ways. I've seen it in columns, letters, and blogs too. Particularly interesting, because they reflect a line of thought prevalent in affluent America, were comments made by students taking an elective called Literature and Justice at Glennview High (that's not its real name), a school in a wealthy Boston suburb. As part of the reading for the course, teachers gave students an article that I wrote for *The New York Times* in 1999, laying out a version of the argument you have just read, and asked them to write papers in response.[18] Scott Seider, then a graduate student at Harvard University researching how adolescents think about obligations to others, interviewed thirty-eight students in two sections of the course and read their papers.[19]

Let's look at some of the objections raised by these varied sources. Perhaps the most fundamental objection comes from Kathryn, a Glennview student who believes we shouldn't judge people who refuse to give:

There is no black and white universal code for everyone. It is better to accept that everyone has a different view on the issue, and all people are entitled to follow their own beliefs.

Kathryn leaves it to the individual to determine his or her moral obligation to the poor. But while circumstances do make a difference, and we should avoid being too black-and-white in our judgments, this doesn't mean we should accept that everyone is entitled to follow his or her own beliefs. That is moral relativism, a position that many find attractive only until they are faced with someone who is doing something really, really wrong. If we see a person holding a cat's paws on an electric grill that is gradually heating up, and when we vigorously object he says, "But it's fun, see how the cat squeals," we don't just say, "Oh, well, you are entitled to follow your own beliefs," and leave him alone. We can and do try to stop people who are cruel to animals, just as we stop rapists, racists, and terrorists. I'm not saying that failing to give is like committing these acts of violence, but if we reject moral relativism in some situations, then we should reject it everywhere.

After reading my essay, Douglas, another Glennview student, objected that I "should not have the right to tell people what to do." In one sense, he's correct about that. I've no right to tell you or anyone else what to do with your money, in the sense that that would imply that you *have* to do as I say. I've no authority over Douglas or over you. On the other hand, I do have the right of free speech, which I'm exercising right now by offering you some arguments you might consider before you decide what to do with your money. I hope that you will want to listen to a variety of views before making up your mind about such an important issue. If I'm wrong about that, though, you are free to shut the book now, and there's nothing I can do about it.

It's possible, of course, to think that morality is not relative, and that we should talk about it, but that the right view is that we aren't under any obligation to give anything at all. Lucy, another Glennview High student, wrote as follows:

> If someone wants to buy a new car, they should. If someone wants to redecorate their house, they should, and if they need a suit, get it. They work for their money and they have the right to spend it on themselves....

Lucy said that people have a right to spend the money they earn on themselves. Even if we agree with that, having a *right* to do something doesn't settle the question of what you *should* do. If you have a right to do something, I can't justifiably force you not to do it, but I can still tell you that you would be a fool to do it, or that it would be a horrible thing to do, or that you would be wrong to do it. You may have a right to spend your weekend surfing, but it can still be true that you ought to visit your sick mother. Similarly, we might say that the rich have a right to spend their money on lavish parties, Patek Philippe watches, private jets, luxury yachts, and space travel, or, for that matter, to flush wads of it down the toilet. Or that those of us with more modest means shouldn't be forced to forgo any of the less-expensive pleasures that offer us some relief from all the time we spend working. But we could still think that to choose to do these things rather than use the money to save human lives is wrong, shows a deplorable lack of empathy, and means that you are not a good person....

Libertarians resist the idea that we have a duty to help others. Canadian philosopher Jan Narveson articulates that point of view:

> We are certainly responsible for evils we inflict on others, no matter where, and we owe those people compensation...Nevertheless, I have seen no plausible argument that we owe something, as a matter of general duty, to those to whom we have done nothing wrong.[20]

There is, at first glance, something attractive about the political philosophy that says: "You leave me alone, and I'll leave you alone, and we'll get along just fine." It appeals to the frontier mentality, to an ideal of life in the wide-open spaces where each of us can carve out our own territory and live undisturbed by the neighbors. At first glance, it seems perfectly reasonable. Yet there is a callous side to a philosophy that denies that we have any responsibilities to those who, through no fault of their own, are in need. Taking libertarianism seriously would require us to abolish all state-supported welfare schemes for those who can't get a job or are ill or disabled, and all state-funded health care for the aged and for those who are too poor to pay for their own health insurance. Few people really support such extreme views. Most think that we do have obligations to those we can help with relatively little sacrifice—certainly to those living in our own country, and I would argue that we can't justifiably draw the boundary there. But if I have not persuaded you of that, there is another line of argument to consider: If we have, in fact, been at least in part a cause of the poverty of the world's poorest people—if we are harming the poor—then even libertarians like Narveson will have to agree that we ought to compensate them.... There are many ways in which it is clear, however, that the rich *have* harmed the poor. Ale Nodye knows about one of them. He grew up in a village by the sea, in Senegal, in West Africa. His father and grandfather were fishermen, and he tried to be one too. But after six years in which he barely caught enough fish to pay for the fuel for his boat, he set out by canoe for the Canary Islands, from where he hoped to become another of Europe's many illegal immigrants. Instead, he was arrested and deported. But he says he will try again, even though the voyage is dangerous and one of his cousins died on a similar trip. He has no choice, he says, because "there are no fish in the sea here anymore." A European Commission report shows that Nodye is right: The fish stocks from which Nodye's father and grandfather took their catch and fed their families have been destroyed by industrial fishing fleets that come from Europe, China, and Russia and sell their fish to well-fed Europeans who can afford to pay high prices. The industrial fleets drag vast nets across the seabed, damaging the coral reefs where fish breed. As a result, a major protein source for poor people has vanished, the boats are idle, and people who used to make a living fishing or building boats are unemployed. The story is repeated in many other coastal areas around the world.[21]

Or consider how we citizens of rich countries obtain our oil and minerals. Teodoro Obiang, the dictator of tiny Equatorial Guinea, sells most of his country's oil to American corporations, among them Exxon Mobil, Marathon, and Hess. Although his official salary is a modest $60,000, this ruler of a country of 550,000 people is richer than Queen Elizabeth II. He owns six private jets and a $35 million house in Malibu, as well as other houses in Maryland and Cape Town and a fleet of Lamborghinis, Ferraris, and Bentleys. Most of the people over whom he rules live in extreme poverty, with a life expectancy of forty-nine and an infant mortality of eighty-seven per one thousand (this means that more than one child in twelve dies before its first birthday).[22] Equatorial Guinea is an extreme case, but other examples are almost as bad. In 2005, the Democratic Republic of the Congo exported minerals worth $200 million. From this, its total tax revenues were $86,000. Someone was surely making money from these dealings, but not the people of the Congo.[23] In 2006, Angola made more than $30 billion in oil revenue, about $2,500 for each of its 12 million citizens. Yet the majority of Angolans have no access to basic health care; life expectancy is forty-one years; and one child in four dies before reaching the age of five. On Transparency International's corruption perception index, Angola is currently ranked 147th among 180 countries.

In their dealings with corrupt dictators in developing countries, international corporations are akin to people who knowingly buy stolen goods, with the difference that the international legal and political order recognizes the corporations not as criminals in possession of stolen goods but as the legal owners of the goods they have bought. This situation is, of course, profitable for corporations that do deals with dictators, and for us, since we use the oil, minerals, and other raw materials we need to maintain our prosperity. But for resource-rich developing countries, it is a disaster. The problem is not only the loss of immense wealth that, used wisely, could build the prosperity of the nation. Paradoxically, developing nations with rich deposits of oil or minerals are often worse off than otherwise comparable nations without those resources. One reason is that the revenue from the sale of the resources provides a huge financial incentive for anyone tempted to overthrow the government and seize power. Successful rebels know that if they

succeed, they will be rewarded with immense personal wealth. They can also reward those who backed their coup, and they can buy enough arms to keep themselves in power no matter how badly they rule. Unless, of course, some of those to whom they give the arms are themselves tempted by the prospect of controlling all that wealth…Thus the resources that should benefit developing nations instead become a curse that brings corruption, coups, and civil wars.[24] If we use goods made from raw materials obtained by these unethical dealings from resource-rich but money-poor nations, we are harming those who live in these countries.

One other way in which we in the rich nations are harming the poor has become increasingly clear over the past decade or two. President Yoweri Museveni of Uganda put it plainly, addressing the developed world at a 2007 meeting of the African Union: "You are causing aggression to us by causing global warming.…Alaska will probably become good for agriculture, Siberia will probably become good for agriculture, but where does that leave Africa?"[25]

Strong language, but the accusation is difficult to deny. Two-thirds of the greenhouse gases now in the atmosphere have come from the United States and Europe. Without those gases, there would be no human-induced global warming problem. Africa's contribution is, by comparison, extremely modest: less than 3 percent of the global emissions from burning fuel since 1900, somewhat more if land clearing and methane emissions from livestock production are included, but still a small fraction of what has been contributed by the industrialized nations. And while every nation will have some problems in adjusting to climate change, the hardship will, as Museveni suggests, fall disproportionately on the poor in the regions of the world closer to the equator. Some scientists believe that precipitation will decrease nearer the equator and increase nearer the poles. In any case, the rainfall upon which hundreds of millions rely to grow their food will become less reliable. Moreover, the poor nations depend on agriculture to a far greater degree than the rich. In the United States, agriculture represents only 4 percent of the economy; in Malawi it is 40 percent, and 90 percent of the population are subsistence farmers, virtually all of whom are dependent on rainfall. Nor will drought be the only problem climate change brings to the poor. Rising sea levels will inundate fertile, densely settled delta regions that are home to tens of millions of people in Egypt, Bangladesh, India, and Vietnam. Small Pacific Island nations that consist of low-lying coral atolls, like Kiribati and Tuvalu, are in similar danger, and it seems inevitable that in a few decades they will be submerged.[26]

The evidence is overwhelming that the greenhouse gas emissions of the industrialized nations have harmed, and are continuing to harm, many of the world's poorest people—along with many richer ones, too. If we accept that those who harm others must compensate them, we cannot deny that the industrialized nations owe compensation to many of the world's poorest people. Giving them adequate aid to mitigate the consequences of climate change would be one way of paying that compensation.

In a world that has no more capacity to absorb greenhouse gases without the consequence of damaging climate change, the philosophy of "You leave me alone, and I'll leave you alone" has become almost impossible to live by, for it requires ceasing to put any more greenhouse gases into the atmosphere. Otherwise, we simply are not leaving others alone.

America is a generous nation. As Americans, we are already giving more than our share of foreign aid through our taxes. Isn't that sufficient?

Asked whether the United States gives more, less, or about the same amount of aid, as a percentage of its income, as other wealthy countries, only one in twenty Americans gave the correct answer. When my students suggest that America is generous in this regard, I show them figures from the website of the OECD, on the amounts given by all the organization's donor members. They are astonished to find that the United States has, for many years, been at or near the bottom of the list of industrialized countries in terms of the proportion of national income given as foreign aid. In 2006, the United States fell behind Portugal and Italy, leaving Greece as the only industrialized country to give a smaller percentage of its national income in foreign aid. The average nation's effort in that year came to 46 cents of every $100 of gross national income, while the United States gave only 18 cents of every $100 it earned.

As % of GNI

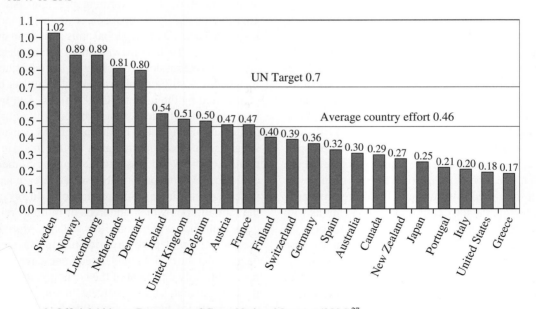

3 Official Aid as a Percentage of Gross National Income (2006)[27]

Philanthropic responses undermine real political change.

If those on the right fear that I am encouraging the state to seize their money and give it to the world's poor, some on the left worry that encouraging the rich to donate to aid organizations enables them to salve their consciences while they continue to benefit from a global economic system that makes them rich and keeps billions poor.[28] Philanthropy, philosopher Paul Gomberg believes, promotes "political quietism," deflecting attention from the institutional causes of poverty—essentially, in his view, capitalism—and from the need to find radical alternatives to these institutions.[29]

Although I believe we ought to give a larger portion of our income to organizations combating poverty, I am open-minded about the best way to combat poverty.[30] Some aid agencies, Oxfam for example, are engaged in emergency relief, development aid, *and* advocacy work for a fairer global economic order. If, after investigating the causes of global poverty and considering what approach is most likely to reduce it, you really believe that a more revolutionary change is needed, then it would make sense to put your time, energy, and money into organizations promoting that revolution in the global economic system. But this is a practical question, and if there is little chance of achieving the kind of revolution you are seeking, then you need to look around for a strategy with better prospects of actually helping some poor people.

Giving people money or food breeds dependency.

I agree that we should not be giving money or food directly to the poor, except in emergencies like a drought, earthquake, or flood, where food may need to be brought in to stop people from starving in the short term. In less dire situations, providing food can make people dependent. If the food is shipped in from a developed nation, for example the United States, it can destroy local markets and reduce incentives for local farmers to produce a surplus to sell. We need to make it possible for people to earn their own money, or to produce their own food and meet their other needs in a sustainable manner and by their own

work. Giving them money or food won't achieve that. Finding a form of aid that will really help people is crucial, and not a simple task, but as we'll see, it can be done.[31]

Cash is the seed corn of capitalism. Giving it away will reduce future growth.

Gaetano Cipriano contacted me after reading one of my articles because he thought that as an entrepreneurial capitalist, he could offer a helpful perspective. The grandson of immigrants to America, he owns and runs EI Associates, an engineering and construction firm based in Cedar Knolls, New Jersey, that has assets of around $80 million. "Cash is the seed corn of capitalism" is his phrase. Gaetano told me that he deploys his capital to the best of his ability to promote profits and enduring growth, and that giving more of it away would be "cutting my own throat." But he does not spend extravagantly. "I do not live in a splendid house," he told me. "I have no second home. I drive a 2001 Ford Explorer with 73,000 miles. I belong to a nice squash club, and have four suits and two pairs of black shoes. When I take vacations they are short and local. I do not own a boat or a plane." While he does give to charity, he does it "at a level which is prudent and balanced with sustainable growth." If he were to give much more money away, it would have to come out of sums that he now reinvests in his business. That, in turn, would reduce his future earnings and perhaps the number of people he is able to employ, or how well he can pay them. It would also leave him with less to give if, later in life, he decides that he wants to give more.

For similar reasons, we can agree that it's a good thing Warren Buffett did not give away the first million dollars he earned. Had he done so, he would not have had the investment capital he needed to develop his business, and would never have been able to give away the $31 billion that he has now pledged to give. If you are as skilled as Buffett in investing your money, I urge you to keep it until late in life, too, and then give away most of it, as he has done. But people with less-spectacular investment abilities might do better to give it away sooner....

What if you took every penny you ever had and gave it to the poor of Africa...? What we would have is no economy, no ability to generate new wealth or help anybody.

This objection comes from Colin McGinn, a professor of philosophy at the University of Miami.[32] It isn't clear whether McGinn's "you" is you, the individual reader, or the group an American Southerner might refer to as "y'all." If you [insert your name], took every penny you ever had and gave it to the poor of Africa, our national economy would not notice. Even if every reader of this book did that, the economy would barely hiccup (unless the book's sales exceed my wildest dreams). If *everyone* in America did it, the national economy would be ruined. But, at the moment, there is no cause for worry about the last possibility: there is no sign of it happening, and I am not advocating it.

Because so few people give significant amounts, the need for more to be given is great, and the more each one of us gives, the more lives we can save. If everyone gave significantly more than they now give, however, we would be in a totally different situation. The huge gulf between rich and poor means that if everyone were giving, there would be no need for them to take every penny they ever had and give it all to Africa. As you'll see before the end of this book, quite a modest contribution from everyone who has enough to live comfortably, eat out occasionally, and buy bottled water, would suffice to achieve the goal of lifting most of the world's extremely poor people above the poverty line of $1.25 per day. If that modest contribution were given, we would no longer be in a situation in which 10 million children were dying from poverty every year. So whether a small number of people give a lot, or a large number of people give a little, ending large-scale extreme poverty wouldn't cripple our national economy. It leaves plenty of scope for entrepreneurial activity and individual wealth. In the long run, the global economy would be enhanced, rather than diminished, by bringing into it the 1.4 billion people now outside it, creating new markets and new opportunities for trade and investment.

People do have special relationships with their families, their communities, and their countries.

This is the standard equipment of humanity, and most people, in all of human history, have seen nothing wrong with it.[33]

> —*Alan Ryan, philosopher and warden of*
> *New College, Oxford*

It is true that most of us care more about our family and friends than we do about strangers. That's natural, and there is nothing wrong with it. But how far should preference for family and friends go? Brendan, a Glennview High student, thought that instead of going to aid for the poor, money "can be better spent helping your family and friends who need the money as well." If family and friends really *need* the money, in anything remotely like the way those living in extreme poverty need it, it would be going too much against the grain of human nature to object to giving to them before giving to strangers. Fortunately, most middle-class people in rich nations don't have to make this choice. They can take care of their families in an entirely sufficient way on much less than they are now spending, and thus have money left over that can be used to help those in extreme poverty. Admittedly, saying just where the balance should be struck is difficult....

Kiernan, another Glennview High School student, made a point similar to Alan Ryan's:

> [*Giving what we don't need to the poor*] *would make the world a better, more equal place. But it is like a little kid buying a pack of candy, keeping one piece, and giving the rest away. It just doesn't happen.*

The issue raised by all these remarks is the link between what we humans are (mostly) like, and what we *ought* to do. When Brendan O'Grady, a philosophy student at Queen's University in Ontario, posted a blog about this issue, he got the following response from another Canadian philosophy student Thomas Simmons:

> Of course I do not want people to die, but I just feel generally unattached to them. I have no doubt that if I were to take a trip to places where people are starving then I might think differently, but as it stands now they are just too far removed. In not making these donations, I am implicitly valuing the affluence of my own life over

the basic sustenance of many others. And, well, I guess I do. Am I immoral for doing so? Maybe.[34]

When O'Grady queried this, Simmons clarified his position: "I don't intend to make a moral defense, but rather just reveal my personal feelings—that is, just to explain how I feel." The distinction between describing how things are and saying how they ought to be is also relevant to what Kiernan and Alan Ryan are saying. The fact that we tend to favor our families, communities, and countries may explain our failure to save the lives of the poor beyond those boundaries, but it does not justify that failure from an ethical perspective, no matter how many generations of our ancestors have seen nothing wrong with it.

NOTES

1. BBC News, September 21, 2007, http://news.bbc.co.uk/2/hi/uk_news/england/manchester/7006412.stm.

2. Deepa Narayan with Raj Patel, Kai Schafft, Anne Rademacher, and Sarah Koch-Schulte. *Voices of the Poor: Can Anyone Hear Us?* Published for the World Bank by Oxford University Press (New York, 2000), p. 36.

3. This is a compilation of things said by the poor, cited in ibid., p. 28.

4. World Bank Press Release, "New Data Show 1.4 Billion Live on Less Than US$1.25 a Day, But Progress Against Poverty Remains Strong," August 26, 2008, http://go.worldbank.org/ T0TEVOV4E0. The estimate is based on price data from 2005, and does not reflect increases in food prices in 2008, which are likely to have increased the number below the poverty line. For the research on which the press release is based, see Shaohua Chen and Martin Ravallion, "The Developing World Is Poorer Than We Thought, But No Less Successful in the Fight Against Poverty," Policy Research Working Paper 4073, World Bank Development Research Group, August 2008, www-wds.worldbank .org/external/default/WDSContentServer/IW3P/IB/2008/08/26/000158349_20080826113239/Rendered/PDF/WPS4703.pdf.

For further discussion of World Bank statistics, see Sanjay Reddy and Thomas Pogge, "How *Not* to Count the Poor," www.columbia.edu/-sr793/count.pdf, and Martin Ravallion, "How *Not* to Count the Poor: A Reply to Reddy and Pogge," www.columbia.edu/-sr793/wbreply.pdf.

5. Robert Rector and Kirk Anderson, "Understanding Poverty in America," Heritage Foundation Backgrounder #1713 (2004), www.heritage.org/Research/Welfare/bg1713.

cfm. Rector and Anderson draw on data available from the 2003 U.S. Census Bureau report on poverty and on various other government reports.

6. United Nations, Office of the High Representative for the Least Developed Countries, Landlocked Developing Countries and the Small Island Developing States, and World Bank, World Bank Development Data Group, "Measuring Progress in Least Developed Countries: A Statistical Profile" (2006), tables 2 and 3, pp. 14–15. Available at www.un.org/ohrlls/.

7. United Nations Development Program, *Human Development Report 2000* (Oxford University Press, New York, 2000) p. 30; *Human Development Report 2001* (Oxford University Press, New York, 2001) pp. 9–12, p. 22; and World Bank, *World Development Report 2000/2001,* overview, p. 3, www.worldbank.org/poverty/wdrpoverty/report/overview.pdf, for the other figures. The *Human Development Reports* are available at http://hdr.undp.org.

8. James Riley, *Rising Life Expectancy: A Global History* (New York: Cambridge University Press, 2001); Jeremy Laurance, "Thirty Years: Difference in Life Expectancy Between the World's Rich and Poor Peoples," *The Independent* (UK), September 7, 2007.

9. "Billionaires 2008," *Forbes*, March 24, 2008, www.forbes.com/forbes/2008/0324/080.html.

10. Joe Sharkey, "For the Super-Rich, It's Time to Upgrade the Old Jumbo," *The New York Times,* October 17, 2006.

11. "Watch Your Time," Special Advertising Supplement to *The New York Times,* October 14, 2007. The passage quoted is on p. 40.

12. Bill Marsh, "A Battle Between the Bottle and the Faucet," *The New York Times,* July 15, 2007.

13. Pacific Institute, "Bottled Water and Energy: A Fact Sheet," www.pacinst.org/topics/water_and_sustainability/bottled_water/bottled_water_and_energy.html.

14. Lance Gay, "Food Waste Costing Economy $100 Billion, Study Finds," Scripps Howard News Service, August 10, 2005, www.knoxstudio.com/shns/story.cfm?pk=GARBAGE-08-10-05.

15. Deborah Lindquist, "How to Look Good Naked," Lifetime Network, Season 2, Episode 2, July 29, 2009. As relayed by Courtney Moran.

16. Peter Unger, *Living High and Letting Die* (New York: Oxford University Press, 1996).

17. For further discussion see Peter Singer, *The Expanding Circle,* (Oxford: Clarendon Press, 1981), pp. 136, 183. For futher examples, see www.unification.net/ws/theme015.htm.

18. Peter Singer, "The Singer Solution to World Poverty," *The New York Times Sunday Magazine,* September 5, 1999.

19. Glennview High School is Seider's fictional name for the school, and the names of the students are also pseudonyms.

20. Jan Narveson, " 'We Don't Owe Them a Thing!' A Tough-minded but Soft-hearted View of Aid to the Faraway Needy," *The Monist,* 86:3 (2003), p. 419.

21. Sharon Lafraniere, "Europe Takes Africa's Fish, and Boatloads of Migrants Follow," *The New York Times,* January 14, 2008, and Elizabeth Rosenthal, "Europe's Appetite for Seafood Propels Illegal Trade," *The New York Times,* January 15, 2008.

22. See Leif Wenar, "Property Rights and the Resource Curse," *Philosophy & Public Affairs* 36:1 (2008), pp. 2–32. A more detailed version is available on Wenar's website: www.wenar.staff.shef.ac.uk/PRRCwebpage.html.

23. Paul Collier, *The Bottom Billion* (New York: Oxford University Press, 2007).

24. See Leonard Wantchekon, "Why Do Resource Dependent Countries Have Authoritarian Governments?" *Journal of African Finance and Economic Development* 5:2 (2002), pp. 57–77; an earlier version is available at www.yale.edu/leitner/pdf/1999-11.pdf. See also Nathan Jensen and Leonard Wantchekon, "Resource Wealth and Political Regimes in Africa," *Comparative Political Studies,* 37 (2004), pp. 816–841.

25. President Museveni was speaking at the African Union summit, Addis Ababa, Ethiopia, February 2007, and the speech was reported in Andrew Revkin, "Poor Nations to Bear Brunt as World Warms," *The New York Times,* April 1, 2007.

26. Andrew Revkin, op. cit., and "Reports from Four Fronts in the War on Warming," *The New York Times,* April 3, 2007; Kathy Marks, "Rising Tide of Global Warming Threatens Pacific Island States," *The Independent* (UK), October 25, 2006.

27. Organisation for Economic Co-operation and Development *(OECD), OECD Journal on Development: Development Co-operation Report 2007,* p. 134, www.oecd.org/dac/dcr. The table is reproduced by kind permission of OECD. See also *Statistical Annex of the 2007 Development Co-operation Report,* www.oecd.org/dataoecd/52/9/1893143.xls, Fig. 1e.

28. See, for example, Anthony Langlois, "Charity and Justice in the Singer Solution," in Raymond Younis (ed) *On the Ethical Life* (Newcastle upon Tyne: Cambridge Scholars, forthcoming); Paul Gomberg, "The Fallacy of Philanthropy," *Canadian Journal of Philosophy* 32:1 (2002), pp. 29–66.

29. Gomberg, *op. cit.*, pp. 30, 63–64.

30. See Andy Lamey's response to Anthony Langlois's paper in the volume referred to in n. 28, above.

31. Singer addresses the question of finding a form of aid that really works in chapter 7 of *The Life You Can Save,* "Improving Aid."

32. Colin McGinn, as quoted by Michael Specter in "The Dangerous Philosopher," *The New Yorker*, September 6, 1999.

33. Alan Ryan, as quoted by Michael Specter in "The Dangerous Philosopher," *The New Yorker*, September 6, 1999.

34. http://www.muzakandpotatoes.com/2008/02/peter-singer-on-affluence.html.

READING QUESTIONS

1. Explain what poverty and affluence are like today according to the information provided by Singer. Include in your explanation the World Bank's definition of "extreme poverty."
2. Describe the two main thought experiments utilized by Singer. Explain the differences between them.
3. What is Singer's basic argument for why failing to donate to aid organizations such as UNICEF is wrong? Why does Singer think that it is hard to reject each of the premises?
4. Describe a few of the common objections raised against the basic argument by high school students. How does Singer respond to each of these objections?
5. Explain the Libertarian view with respect to whether we have a duty to help others. How does Singer argue that wealthy nations and their citizens have caused harm to developing nations and their people?

DISCUSSION QUESTIONS

1. Are there any objections Singer fails to consider in response to his basic argument? Consider responses on his behalf to any further objections.
2. What do people spend money on that they either don't need or rarely use other than those things mentioned by Singer? What things might people be most easily convinced to do without?
3. How would you respond in the cases of the drowning child and the child on the train tracks? Consider and discuss differing reactions to these two thought experiments.

JOHN ARTHUR

World Hunger and Moral Obligation

One of the premises in Peter Singer's basic argument from the previous selection states: *If it is in your power to prevent something bad from happening, without sacrificing anything nearly as important, it is wrong not to do so.* Arthur labels this premise Singer's "greater moral evil rule," pointing out that it is meant to capture the idea that morality involves giving equal consideration to the interests of all, which is part of our moral code. However, as Arthur observes, such equality is only one part, and Singer's rule ignores other elements of our moral code including considerations of entitlement which involve both rights and desert. On the basis of considerations of entitlement, Arthur argues that our present moral code allows such considerations to qualify considerations of equality of interests. For example, our moral rights to life and to property represent entitlements that we can invoke as a moral justification for not helping strangers when the cost to us is substantial.

Of course, the fact that our current moral code includes such entitlements does not show that such entitlements are justified. Perhaps there is good reason to move to a new moral code that drops the sorts of entitlements mentioned above and includes Singer's greater moral evil rule. In the final section of his paper, Arthur considers this proposal and argues that an ideal moral code that is genuinely workable would include entitlements that justify the sort of rights to property that one can invoke as a moral justification for not helping strangers when the cost is substantial.

Recommended Reading: consequentialism, chap. 1, sec. 2A, see especially the discussion of rule consequentialism. Also relevant, the discussion of moral rights in chap. 1, sec. 2D.

INTRODUCTION

My guess is that everyone who reads these words is wealthy by comparison with the poorest millions of people on our planet. Not only do we have plenty of money for food, clothing, housing, and other necessities, but a fair amount is left over for far less important purchases like phonograph records, fancy clothes, trips, intoxicants, movies, and so on. And what's more we don't usually give a thought to whether or not we ought to spend our money on such luxuries rather than to give it to those who need it more; we just assume it's ours to do with as we please.

Peter Singer, "Famine, Affluence, and Morality" argues that our assumption is wrong, that we should not buy luxuries when others are in severe need. But [is he] correct? . . .

He first argues that two general moral principles are widely accepted, and then that those principles imply an obligation to eliminate starvation.

The first principle is simply that "suffering and death from lack of food, shelter and medical care are bad." Some may be inclined to think that the mere existence of such an evil in itself places an obligation on others, but that is, of course, the problem which Singer addresses. I take it that he is not begging the question in this obvious way and will argue from the existence of evil to the obligation of others to eliminate it. But how, exactly, does he establish this? The second principle, he thinks, shows the connection, but it is here that controversy arises.

This principle, which I will call the greater moral evil rule, is as follows:

> If it is in our power to prevent something bad from happening, without thereby sacrificing anything of comparable moral importance, we ought, morally, to do it.[1]

In other words, people are entitled to keep their earnings only if there is no way for them to prevent a greater evil by giving them away. Providing others with food, clothing, and housing would generally be of more importance than buying luxuries, so the greater moral evil rule now requires substantial redistribution of wealth.

Certainly there are few, if any, of us who live by that rule, although that hardly shows we are *justified* in our way of life; we often fail to live up to our own standards. Why does Singer think our shared morality requires that we follow the greater moral evil rule? What arguments does he give for it?

He begins with an analogy. Suppose you came across a child drowning in a shallow pond. Certainly we feel it would be wrong not to help. Even if saving the child meant we must dirty our clothes, we would emphasize that those clothes are not of comparable significance to the child's life. The greater moral evil rule thus seems a natural way of capturing why we think it would be wrong not to help.

But the argument for the greater moral evil rule is not limited to Singer's claim that it explains our feelings about the drowning child or that it appears "uncontroversial." Moral equality also enters the picture. Besides the Jeffersonian idea that we share certain rights equally, most of us are also attracted to another type of equality, namely that like amounts of suffering (or happiness) are of equal significance, no matter who is experiencing them. I cannot reasonably say that, while my pain is no more severe than yours, I am somehow special and it's more important that mine be alleviated. Objectivity requires us to admit the opposite, that no one has a unique status which warrants such special pleading. So equality demands equal consideration of interests as well as respect for certain rights.

But if we fail to give to famine relief and instead purchase a new car when the old one will do, or buy fancy clothes for a friend when his or her old ones are perfectly good, are we not assuming that the relatively minor enjoyment we or our friends may get is as important as another person's life? And that is a form of prejudice; we are acting as if people were not equal in the sense that their interests deserve equal consideration. We are giving special consideration to ourselves or to our group, rather like a racist does. Equal consideration of interests thus leads naturally to the greater moral evil rule.

RIGHTS AND DESERT

Equality, in the sense of giving equal consideration to equally serious needs, is part of our moral code. And so we are led, quite rightly I think, to the conclusion that we should prevent harm to others if in doing so we do not sacrifice anything of comparable moral importance. But there is also another side to the coin, one which Singer ignore[s]. . . . This can be expressed rather awkwardly by the notion of entitlements. These fall into two broad categories, rights and desert. A few examples will show what I mean.

All of us could help others by giving away or allowing others to use our bodies. While your life may be shortened by the loss of a kidney or less enjoyable if lived with only one eye, those costs are probably not comparable to the loss experienced by a person who will die without any kidney or who is totally blind. We can even imagine persons who will actually be harmed in some way by your not granting sexual favors to them. Perhaps the absence of a sexual partner would cause psychological harm or even rape. Now suppose that you can prevent this evil without sacrificing anything of comparable importance. Obviously such relations may not be pleasant, but according to the greater moral evil rule that is not enough; to be justified in refusing, you must show that the unpleasantness you would experience is of equal importance to the harm you are preventing. Otherwise, the rule says you must consent.

If anything is clear, however, it is that our code does not *require* such heroism; you are entitled to keep your second eye and kidney and not bestow sexual favors on anyone who may be harmed without them. The reason for this is often expressed in terms of rights; it's your body, you have a right to it, and that weighs against whatever duty you have to help. To sacrifice a kidney for a stranger is to do more than is required, it's heroic.

Moral rights are normally divided into two categories. Negative rights are rights of noninterference. The right to life, for example, is a right not to be killed. Property rights, the right to privacy, and the right to exercise religious freedom are also negative,

requiring only that people leave others alone and not interfere.

Positive rights, however, are rights of recipience. By not putting their children up for adoption, parents give them various positive rights, including rights to be fed, clothed, and housed. If I agree to share in a business venture, my promise creates a right of recipience, so that when I back out of the deal, I've violated your right.

Negative rights also differ from positive in that the former are natural; the ones you have depend on what you are. If lower animals lack rights to life or liberty it is because there is a relevant difference between them and us. But the positive rights you may have are not natural; they arise because others have promised, agreed, or contracted to give you something.

Normally, then, a duty to help a stranger in need is not the result of a right he has. Such a right would be positive, and since no contract or promise was made, no such right exists. An exception to this would be a lifeguard who contracts to watch out for someone's children. The parent whose child drowns would in this case be doubly wronged. First, the lifeguard should not have cruelly or thoughtlessly ignored the child's interests, and second, he ought not to have violated the rights of the parents that he helped. Here, unlike Singer's case, we can say there are rights at stake. Other bystanders also act wrongly by cruelly ignoring the child, but unlike the lifeguard they do not violate anybody's rights. Moral rights are one factor to be weighed, but we also have other obligations; I am not claiming that rights are all we need to consider. That view, like the greater moral evil rule, trades simplicity for accuracy. In fact, our code expects us to help people in need as well as to respect negative and positive rights. But we are also entitled to invoke our own rights as justification for not giving to distant strangers or when the cost to us is substantial, as when we give up an eye or kidney. . . .

Desert is a second form of entitlement. Suppose, for example, an industrious farmer manages through hard work to produce a surplus of food for the winter while a lazy neighbor spends his summer fishing. Must our industrious farmer ignore his hard work and give the surplus away because his neighbor or his family will suffer? What again seems clear is that we have more than one factor to weigh. Not only should we compare the consequences of his keeping it with his giving it away; we also should weigh the fact that one farmer deserves the food, he earned it through his hard work. Perhaps his deserving the product of his labor is outweighed by the greater need of his lazy neighbor, or perhaps it isn't, but being outweighed is in any case not the same as weighing nothing!

Desert can be negative, too. The fact that the Nazi war criminal did what he did means he deserves punishment, that we have a reason to send him to jail. Other considerations, for example the fact that nobody will be deterred by his suffering, or that he is old and harmless, may weigh against punishment and so we may let him go; but again that does not mean he doesn't still deserve to be punished.

Our moral code gives weight to both the greater moral evil principle and entitlements. The former emphasizes equality, claiming that from an objective point of view all comparable suffering, whoever its victim, is equally significant. It encourages us to take an impartial look at all the various effects of our actions; it is thus forward-looking. When we consider matters of entitlement, however, our attention is directed to the past. Whether we have rights to money, property, eyes, or whatever, depends on how we came to possess them. If they were acquired by theft rather than from birth or through gift exchange, then the right is suspect. Desert, like rights, is also backward-looking, emphasizing past effort or past transgressions which now warrant reward or punishment.

Our commonly shared morality thus requires that we ignore neither consequences nor entitlements, neither the future results of our action nor relevant events in the past. It encourages people to help others in need, especially when it's a friend or someone we are close to geographically, and when the cost is not significant. But it also gives weight to rights and desert, so that we are not usually obligated to give to strangers....

But unless we are moral relativists, the mere fact that entitlements are an important part of our moral code does not in itself justify such a role. Singer...can perhaps best be seen as a moral reformer advocating the rejection of rules which provide for distribution according to rights and desert. Certainly the fact that in the past our moral code condemned suicide and racial mixing while condoning slavery should not convince us that a more enlightened moral code, one which we would want to support, would take such positions. Rules which define acceptable behavior are continually changing, and we must allow for the replacement of inferior ones.

Why should we not view entitlements as examples of inferior rules we are better off without? What could justify our practice of evaluating actions by looking backward to rights and desert instead of just to their consequences? One answer is that more fundamental values than rights and desert are at stake, namely fairness, justice, and respect. Failure to reward those who earn good grades or promotions is wrong because it's *unfair;* ignoring past guilt shows a lack of regard for *justice;* and failure to respect rights to life, privacy, or religious choice suggests a lack of *respect for other persons.*

Some people may be persuaded by those remarks, feeling that entitlements are now on an acceptably firm foundation. But an advocate of equality may well want to question why fairness, justice, and respect for persons should matter. But since it is no more obvious that preventing suffering matters than that fairness, respect, and justice do, we again seem to have reached an impasse....

ENTITLEMENTS AND THE IDEAL MORAL CODE

The idea I want now to consider is that part of our code should be dropped, so that people could no longer invoke rights and desert as justification for not making large sacrifices for strangers. In place of entitlements would be a rule regarding that any time we can prevent something bad without sacrificing anything of comparable moral significance we ought to do it. Our current code, however, allows people to say that while they would do more good with their earnings, still they have rights to the earnings, the earnings are deserved, and so need not be given away.

The crucial question is whether we want to have such entitlement rules in our code, or whether we should reject them in favor of the greater moral evil rule....

I believe that our best procedure is not to think about this or that specific rule, drawing analogies, refining it, and giving counterexamples, but to focus instead on the nature of morality as a whole. What is a moral code? What do we want it to do? What type of code do we want to support? These questions will give us a fresh perspective from which to consider the merits of rules which allow people to appeal to rights and desert and to weigh the issue of whether our present code should be reformed.

We can begin with the obvious: A moral code is a system of rules designed to guide people's conduct. As such, it has characteristics in common with other systems of rules. Virtually every organization has rules which govern the conduct of members; clubs, baseball leagues, corporations, bureaucracies, professional associations, even *The* Organization all have rules. Another obvious point is this: What the rules are depends on why the organization exists. Rules function to enable people to accomplish goals which lead them to organize in the first place. Some rules, for example, "Don't snitch on fellow mafioso," "Pay dues to the fraternity," and "Don't give away trade secrets to competing companies," serve in obvious ways. Other times the real purposes of rules are controversial, as when doctors do not allow advertising by fellow members of the AMA.

Frequently rules reach beyond members of a specific organization, obligating everyone who is capable of following them to do so. These include costs of civil and criminal law, etiquette, custom, and morality. But before discussing the specific purposes of moral rules, it will be helpful to look briefly at some of the similarities and differences between these more universal codes.

First, the sanctions imposed on rule violators vary among different types of codes. While in our legal code, transgressions are punished by fines, jail, or repayment of damages, informal sanctions of praise, blame, or guilt encourage conformity to the rules of morality and etiquette. Another difference is that while violation of a moral rule is always a serious affair, this need not be so for legal rules of etiquette and custom. Many of us think it unimportant whether a fork is on the left side of a plate or whether an outmoded and widely ignored Sunday closing law is violated, but violation of a moral rule is not ignored. Indeed, that a moral rule has lost its importance is often shown by its demotion to status of mere custom.

A third difference is that legal rules, unlike rules of morality, custom, and etiquette, provide for a specific person or procedure that is empowered to alter the rules. If Congress acts to change the tax laws, then as of the date stated in the statute the rules are changed. Similarly for the governing rules of social clubs, government bureaucracies, and the AMA. Rules of custom, morals, and etiquette also change, of course, but they do so in a less precise and much more gradual fashion, with no person or group specifically empowered to make changes.

This fact, that moral rules are *in a sense* beyond the power of individuals to change, does not show that rules of morality, any more than those of etiquette, are objective in the same sense that scientific laws are. All that needs to happen for etiquette or morality to change is for people to change certain practices, namely the character traits they praise and blame, or the actions they approve and disapprove. Scientific laws, however, are discovered, not invented by society, and so are beyond human control. The law that the boiling point of water increases as its pressure increases cannot be changed by humans, either individually or collectively. Such laws are a part of the fabric of nature.

But the fact that moral rules, like legal ones, are not objective in the same sense as scientific ones does not mean that there is no objective standard of right or wrong, that one code is as good as another, or even that the "right thing to do" is just what the moral code currently followed in our society teaches is right. Like the rules of a fraternity or corporation, legal and moral rules can serve their purposes either well or poorly, and whether they do is a matter of objective fact. Further, if a moral code doesn't serve its purpose, we have good reason to think of a way to change it, just as its serving us well provides a good reason to obey. In important respects morality is not at all subjective.

Take, for example, a rule which prohibits homosexual behavior. Suppose it serves no useful purpose, but only increases the burdens of guilt, shame, and social rejection borne by 10% of our population. If this is so, we have good reason to ignore the rule. On the other hand, if rules against killing and lying help us to accomplish what we want from a moral code, we have good reason to support those rules. Morality is created, and as with other systems of rules which we devise, a particular rule may or may not further the shared human goals and interests which motivated its creation. There is thus a connection between what we ought to do and how well a code serves its purposes. If a rule serves well the general purposes of a moral code, then we have reason to support it, and if we have reason to support it, we also have reason to obey it. But if, on the other hand, a rule is useless, or if it frustrates the purposes of morality, we have reason neither to support nor to follow it. All of this suggests the following conception of a right action: Any action is right which is approved by an ideal moral code, one which it is rational for us to support. Which code we would want to support would depend, of course, on which one is able to accomplish the purposes of morality.

If we are to judge actions in this way, by reference to what an ideal moral code would require, we must first have a clear notion of just what purposes morality is meant to service. And here again the comparison between legal and moral rules is instructive. Both systems discourage certain types of behavior—killing, robbing, and beating—while encouraging others—repaying debts, keeping important agreements, and providing for one's children. The purpose which both have in discouraging various behaviors is obvious. Such negative rules help keep people from causing harm. Think, for example, of how we are first taught it is wrong to hit a baby brother or sister. Parents explain the rule by emphasizing that it hurts the infant when we hit him. Promoting the welfare of ourselves, our friends and family, and to a lesser degree all who have the capacity to be harmed is the primary purpose of negative moral rules. It's how we learn them as children and why we support them as adults.

The same can be said of positive rules, rules which encourage various types of behavior. Our own welfare, as well as that of friends, family, and others, depends on general acceptance of rules which encourage keeping promises, fulfilling contracts, and meeting the needs of our children. Just try to imagine a society in which promises or agreements mean nothing, or where family members took no concern for one another. A life without positive or negative rights would be as Thomas Hobbes long ago observed: nasty, brutish, and short.

Moral rules thus serve two purposes. They promote our own welfare by discouraging acts of violence and promoting social conventions like promising and paying debts, and second, they perform the same service for our family, friends, and others. We have reason to support a moral code because we care about our own welfare, and because we care about the well-being of others. For most of us the ideal moral code, the one we would support because it best fulfills these purposes, is the code which is most effective in promoting general welfare.

But can everyone be counted on to share these concerns? Think, for example, of an egoist, who only desires that *he* be happy. Such a person, if he existed, would obviously like a code which maximizes his own welfare. How can we hope to get agreement about which code it is rational to support, if different people expect different things from moral rules?...

There is also a line of reasoning which suggests that disagreement about which moral code to support need not be as deep as is often thought. What sort of code in fact *would* a rational egoist support? He would first think of proposing one which allows him to do anything whatsoever that he desires, while requiring that others ignore their own happiness and do what is in his interests. But here enters a family of considerations which will bring us back to the merits of entitlements versus the greater moral evil rule. Our egoist is contemplating what code to *support*, which means going before the public and trying to win general acceptance of his proposed rules. Caring for nobody else, he might secretly prefer the code I mentioned, yet it would hardly make sense for him to work for its public adoption since others are unlikely to put his welfare above the happiness of themselves and their families. So it looks as if the code an egoist would actually support might not be all that different from the ideal (welfare maximizing) code; he would be wasting his time to advocate rules that serve only his own interests because they have no chance of public acceptance.

The lesson to be learned here is a general one: The moral code it is rational for us to support must be practical; it must actually work. This means, among other things, that it must be able to gain the support of almost everyone.

But the code must be practical in other respects as well. I have emphasized that it is wrong to ignore the possibilities of altruism, but it is also important that a code not assume people are more unselfish than they are. Rules that would work only for angels are not the ones it is rational to support for humans. Second, an ideal code cannot assume we are more objective than we are; we often tend to rationalize when our own interests are at stake, and a rational person will also keep that in mind when choosing a moral code. Finally, it is not rational to support a code which assumes we have perfect knowledge. We are often mistaken about the consequences of what we do, and a workable code must take that into account as well.

I want now to bring these various considerations together in order to decide whether or not to reject entitlements in favor of the greater moral evil rule. I will assume that the egoist is not a serious obstacle to acceptance of a welfare maximizing code, either because egoists are, like angels, merely imaginary, or because a practical egoist would only support a code which can be expected to gain wide support. We still have to ask whether entitlements would be included in a welfare maximizing code. The initial temptation is to substitute the greater moral evil rule for entitlements, requiring people to prevent something bad whenever the cost to them is less significant than the benefit to another. Surely, we might think, total welfare would be increased by a code requiring people to give up their savings if a greater evil can be prevented.

I think, however, that this is wrong, and that an ideal code would provide for rights and would

encourage rewarding according to desert. My reasons for thinking this stem from the importance of insuring that a moral code really does, in fact, work. Each of the three practical considerations mentioned above now enters the picture. First, it will be quite difficult to get people to accept a code which requires that they give away their savings, extra organs, or anything else merely because they can avoid a greater evil for a stranger. Many people simply wouldn't do it: they aren't that altruistic. If the code attempts to require it anyway, two results would likely follow. First, because many would not live up to the rules, there would be a tendency to create feelings of guilt in those who keep their savings in spite of having been taught it is wrong, as well as conflict between those who meet their obligations and those who do not. And, second, a more realistic code, one which doesn't expect more than can be accomplished, may actually result in more giving. It's a bit like trying to influence how children spend their money. Often they will buy less candy if rules allow them to do so occasionally but they are praised for spending on other things than if its purchase is prohibited. We cannot assume that making a charitable act a requirement will always encourage such behavior. Impractical rules not only create guilt and social conflict, they often tend to encourage the opposite of the desired result. By giving people the right to use their savings for themselves, yet praising those who do not exercise the right but help others instead, we have struck a good balance; the rules are at once practical yet reasonably effective.

Similar practical considerations would also influence our decision to support rules that allow people to keep what they deserve. For most people, working is not their favorite activity. If we are to prosper, however, goods and services must be produced. Incentives are therefore an important motivation, and one such incentive for work is income. Our code encourages work by allowing people to keep a large part of what they earn, indeed that's much the point of entitlements. "I worked hard for it, so I can keep it" is an oft-heard expression. If we eliminate this rule from our code and ask people to follow the greater moral evil rule instead, the result would likely be less work done and so less total production. Given a choice between not working and continuing to work knowing the efforts should go to benefit others, many would choose not to work.

Moral rules should be practical in a third sense, too. They cannot assume people are either more unbiased or more knowledgeable than they are. This fact has many implications for the sorts of rules we would want to include in a welfare maximizing code. For example, we may be tempted to avoid slavish conformity to counterproductive rules by allowing people to break promises whenever they think doing so would increase total welfare. But again we must not ignore human nature, in this case our tendency to give special weight to our own welfare and our inability to be always objective in tracing the effects of our actions. While we would not want to teach that promises must never be broken no matter what the consequences, we also would not want to encourage breaking promises any time a person can convince himself the results of doing so would be better than if he kept his word.

Similar considerations apply to the greater moral evil rule. Imagine a situation where someone feels he can prevent an evil befalling himself by taking what he needs from a large store. The idea that he's preventing something bad from happening (to himself) without sacrificing anything of comparable moral significance (the store won't miss the goods) would justify robbery. Although sometimes a particular act of theft really is welfare maximizing, it does not follow that we should support a *rule* which allows theft whenever the robber is preventing a greater evil. Such a rule, to work, would require more objectivity and more knowledge of long-term consequences than we have. Here again, including rights in our moral code serves a useful role, discouraging the tendency to rationalize our behavior by underestimating the harm we may cause to others or exaggerating the benefits that may accrue to ourselves.

The first sections of this paper attempted to show that our moral code is a bit schizophrenic. It seems to pull us in opposite directions, sometimes

toward helping people who are in need, other times toward the view that rights and desert justify keeping things we have even if greater evil could be avoided were we to give away our extra eye or our savings account. This apparent inconsistency led us to a further question: Is the emphasis on entitlements really defensible, or should we try to resolve the tension in our own code by adopting the greater moral evil rule and ignoring entitlements? In this section I considered the idea that we might choose between entitlements and the greater moral evil rule by paying attention to the general nature of a moral code; and in particular to the sort of code we might want to support. I argued that all of us, including egoists, have reason to support a code which promotes the welfare of everyone who lives under it. That idea, of an ideal moral code which it is rational for everyone to support, provides a criterion for deciding which rules are sound and which ones we should support.

My conclusion is a conservative one: Concern that our moral code encourages production and not fail because it unrealistically assumes people are more altruistic or objective than they are means that our rules giving people rights to their possessions and encouraging distribution according to desert should be part of an ideal moral code. And since this is so, it is not always wrong to invoke rights or claim that money is deserved as justification for not giving aid, even when something worse could be prevented by offering help. The welfare maximizing moral code would not require us to maximize welfare in each individual case.

I have not yet discussed just how much weight should be given to entitlements, only that they are important and should not be ignored... Certainly an ideal moral code would not allow people to overlook those in desperate need by making entitlements absolute, any more than it would ignore entitlements. But where would it draw the line?

It's hard to know, of course, but the following seems to me to be a sensible stab at an answer. Concerns about discouraging production and the general adherence to the code argue strongly against expecting too much; yet on the other hand, to allow extreme wealth in the face of grinding poverty would seem to put too much weight on entitlements. It seems to me, then, that a reasonable code would require people to help when there is no substantial cost to themselves, that is, when what they are sacrificing would not mean *significant* reduction in their own or their families' level of happiness. Since most people's savings accounts and nearly everybody's second kidney are not insignificant, entitlements would in those cases outweigh another's need. But if what is at stake is trivial, as dirtying one's clothes would normally be, then an ideal moral code would not allow rights to override the greater evil that can be prevented. Despite our code's unclear and sometimes schizophrenic posture, it seems to me that these judgments are not that different from our current moral attitudes. We tend to blame people who waste money on trivia when they could help others in need, yet not to expect people to make large sacrifices to distant strangers. An ideal moral code thus might not be a great deal different from our own.

NOTE

1. Singer also offers a "weak" version of this principle which, it seems to me, is *too* weak. It requires giving aid only if the gift is of *no* moral significance to the giver. But since even minor embarrassment or small amounts of happiness are not completely without moral importance, this weak principle implies little or no obligation to aid, even to the drowning child.

READING QUESTIONS

1. What part of our moral code does Arthur think is being ignored by Peter Singer?
2. Explain Arthur's argument for why our moral code does not require the sort of heroism involved in actions such as giving up one's kidney or eye.
3. Explain the distinction between negative and positive moral rights according to Arthur. Give examples of each.
4. How does Arthur explain the difference between positive and negative forms of desert?
5. What two purposes do moral rules serve, according to Arthur?
6. Arthur mentions three ways in which a moral code must be practical. State those three ways.

DISCUSSION QUESTIONS

1. Does Peter Singer's greatest moral evil rule require that persons act in heroic ways or go above and beyond the call of duty as Arthur suggests?
2. How might Peter Singer respond to Arthur's claim that he has ignored the notion of entitlements in his argument for why we should give to charity?
3. In the final paragraph of his article, Arthur suggests that "to allow extreme wealth in the face of grinding poverty would seem to put too much weight on entitlements. It seems to me, then, that a reasonable code would require people to help when there is no substantial cost to themselves, that is, when what they are sacrificing would not mean *significant* reduction in their own or their families' level of happiness." How might one go about determining what counts as a "significant" reduction in one's level of happiness?

Amartya Sen

Property and Hunger

According to Sen, starvation and famine result from failures of entitlements to property that would otherwise provide the resources for the starving to afford life's necessities including food. This "entitlement" analysis suggests a redistributive economic policy to deal with famine that would increase the entitlements of severely deprived groups while reducing the entitlements of those in economically advantaged groups. Would such redistributive intervention represent a morally wrongful violation of the property rights of the advantaged? Does one's entitlement right to one's own property justify refusing to contribute to the alleviation of poverty and hunger of strangers? One might suppose that if rights have intrinsic value, then such redistribution is not justified. However, Sen proposes a moral system which, unlike a purely consequentialist view of rights, recognizes their intrinsic value, but like consequentialism insists that an overall moral assessment of any right must include a consideration of its likely consequences. If the value of the consequences of limiting or abridging a right are of very great benefit in helping to fulfill morally important goals, such limits are morally justified. The importance of avoiding starvation and famine is the basis for a moral claim or right not to be hungry, which can justify limiting the property entitlements of the economically advantaged. Sen concludes by exploring the likely practical implications of recognizing this right.

Recommended Reading: rights-focused approach to moral issues, chap. 1, sec. 2D. Also relevant is consequentialism, chap. 1, sec. 2A.

...[T]he claims of property rights, which some would defend and some...would dispute, are not just matters of basic moral belief that could not possibly be influenced one way or the other by any empirical arguments. They call for sensitive moral analysis responsive to empirical realities, including economic ones.

Moral claims based on intrinsically valuable rights are often used in political and social arguments. Rights related to ownership have been invoked for ages. But there are also other types of rights which have been seen as "inherent and inalienable," and the American Declaration of Independence refers to "certain unalienable rights," among which are "life, liberty and the pursuit of happiness." The Indian constitution talks even of "the right to an adequate means of livelihood."[1] The "right not to be hungry" has often been invoked in recent discussions on the obligation to help the famished.

RIGHTS: INSTRUMENTS, CONSTRAINTS, OR GOALS?

Rights can be taken to be morally important in three different ways. First, they can be considered to be valuable *instruments* to achieve other goals. This is

From Amartya Sen, "Property and Hunger," *Economics and Philosophy* 4 (1988): 57–68. Reprinted by permission of Cambridge University Press.

the "instrumental view," and is well illustrated by the utilitarian approach to rights. Rights are, in that view, of no intrinsic importance. Violation of rights is not in itself a bad thing, nor fulfillment intrinsically good. But the acceptance of rights promotes, in this view, things that are ultimately important, to wit, utility. Jeremy Bentham rejected "natural rights" as "simple nonsense," and "natural and imprescriptible rights" as "rhetorical nonsense, nonsense upon stilts." But he attached great importance to rights as instruments valuable to the promotion of a good society, and devoted much energy to the attempt to reform appropriately the actual system of rights.

The second view may be called the "constraint view," and it takes the form of seeing rights as *constraints* on what others can or cannot do. In this view rights *are* intrinsically important. However, they don't figure in moral accounting as goals to be generally promoted, but only as constraints that others must obey. As Robert Nozick has put it in a powerful exposition of this "constraint view": "Individuals have rights, and there are things no person or group may do to them (without violating their rights)." Rights "set the constraints within which a social choice is to be made, by excluding certain alternatives, fixing others, and so on."[2]

The third approach is to see fulfillments of rights as goals to be pursued. This "goal view" differs from the instrumental view in regarding rights to be intrinsically important, and it differs from the constraint view in seeing the fulfillment of rights as goals to be generally promoted, rather than taking them as demanding only (and exactly) that we refrain from violating the rights of others. In the "constraint view" there is no duty to help anyone with his or her rights (merely not to hinder), and also in the "instrumental view" there is no duty, in fact, to help unless the right fulfillment will also promote some other goal such as utility. The "goal view" integrates the valuation of rights—their fulfillment and violation—in overall moral accounting, and yields a wider sphere of influence of rights in morality.

I have argued elsewhere that the goal view has advantages that the other two approaches do not share, in particular, the ability to accommodate integrated moral accounting including inter alia the intrinsic importance of a class of fundamental rights. I shall not repeat that argument here. But there is an interesting question of dual roles of rights in the sense that some rights may be *both* intrinsically important and instrumentally valuable. For example, the right to be free from hunger could—not implausibly—be regarded as being valuable in itself as well as serving as a good instrument to promote other goals such as security, longevity or utility. If so, both the goal view and the instrumental view would have to be simultaneously deployed to get a comprehensive assessment of such a right....

The instrumental aspect is an inescapable feature of every right, since irrespective of whether a certain right is intrinsically valuable or not, its acceptance will certainly have other consequences as well, and these, too, have to be assessed along with the intrinsic value of rights (if any). A right that is regarded as quite valuable in itself may nevertheless be judged to be morally rejectable if it leads to disastrous consequences. This is a case of the rights playing a *negative* instrumental role. It is, of course, also possible that the instrumental argument will *bolster* the intrinsic claims of a right to be taken seriously....

There are two general conclusions to draw, at this stage, from this very preliminary discussion. First, we must distinguish between (1) the intrinsic value of a right, and (2) the overall value of a right taking note inter alia of its intrinsic importance (if any). The acceptance of the intrinsic importance of any right is no guarantee that its overall moral valuation must be favorable. Second, no moral assessment of a right can be independent of its likely consequences. The need for empirical assessment of the effects of accepting any right cannot be escaped. Empirical arguments are quite central to moral philosophy.

PROPERTY AND DEPRIVATION

The right to hold, use and bequeath property that one has legitimately acquired is often taken to be inherently valuable. In fact, however, many of its defenses seem to be actually of the instrumental type, e.g., arguing that property rights make people more free to choose one kind of a life rather than another. But even if we do accept that property rights may have some intrinsic value, this does not in any way amount to an overall justification of property rights, since property rights may have consequences which themselves will require assessment. Indeed, the causation of hunger as well as its prevention may materially depend on how property rights are structured. If a set of property rights leads, say, to starvation, as it well might, then the moral approval of these rights would certainly be compromised severely. In general, the need for consequential analysis of property rights is inescapable whether or not such rights are seen as having any intrinsic value....

...I have tried to argue elsewhere...that famines are, in fact, best explained in terms of failures of entitlement systems. The entitlements here refer, of course, to legal rights and to practical possibilities, rather than to moral status, but the laws and actual operation of private ownership economies have many features in common with the moral system of entitlements analyzed by Nozick and others.

The entitlement approach to famines need not, of course, be confined to private ownership economies, and entitlement failures of other systems can also be fruitfully studied to examine famines and hunger. In the specific context of private ownership economies, the entitlements are substantially analyzable in terms, respectively, of what may be called "endowments" and "exchange entitlements." A person's endowment refers to what he or she initially owns (including the person's own labor power), and the exchange entitlement mapping tells us what the person can obtain through exchanging what he or she owns, either by production (exchange with nature), or by trade (exchange with others), or a mixture of the two. A person has to starve if neither the endowments, nor what can be obtained through exchange, yields an adequate amount of food.

If starvation and hunger are seen in terms of failures of entitlements, then it becomes immediately clear that the total availability of food in a country is only one of several variables that are relevant. Many famines occur without any decline in the availability of food. For example, in the Great Bengal famine of 1943, the total food availability in Bengal was not particularly bad (considerably higher than two years earlier when there was no famine), and yet three million people died, in a famine mainly affecting the rural areas, through rather violent shifts in the relative purchasing powers of different groups, hitting the rural laborers the hardest. The Ethiopian famine of 1973 took place in a year of average per capita food availability, but the cultivators and other occupation groups in the province of Wollo had lost their means of subsistence (through loss of crops and a decline of economic activity, related to a local drought) and had no means of commanding food from elsewhere in the country. Indeed, some food moved *out* of Wollo to more prosperous people in other parts of Ethiopia, repeating a pattern of contrary movement of food that was widely observed during the Irish famines of the 1840s (with food moving out of famine-stricken Ireland to prosperous England which had greater power in the battle for entitlements). The Bangladesh famine of 1974 took place in a year of *peak* food availability, but several occupation groups had lost their entitlement to food through loss of employment and other economic changes (including inflationary pressures causing prices to outrun wages). Other examples of famines without significant (or any) decline in food availability can be found, and there is nothing particularly surprising about this fact once it is recognized that the availability of food is only one influence among many on the entitlement of each occupation group. Even when a famine *is* associated with a decline of food availability, the entitlement changes have to be studied to understand the particular nature of the famine, e.g., why one occupation group is hit but not another. The causation of starvation can be sensibly sought in failures of entitlements of the respective groups.

The causal analysis of famines in terms of entitlements also points to possible public policies of prevention. The main economic strategy would have to take the form of increasing the entitlements of the deprived groups, and in general, of guaranteeing minimum entitlements for everyone, paying particular attention to the vulnerable groups. This can, in the long run, be done in many different ways, involving both economic growth (including growth of food output) and distributional adjustments. Some of these policies may, however, require that the property rights and the corresponding entitlements of the more prosperous groups be violated. The problem, in fact, is particularly acute in the short run, since it may not be possible to engineer rapid economic growth instantly. Then the burden of raising entitlements of the groups in distress would largely have to fall on reducing the entitlements of others more favorably placed. Transfers of income or commodities through various public policies may well be effective in quashing a famine (as the experience of famine relief in different countries has shown), but it may require substantial government intervention in the entitlements of the more prosperous groups.

There is, however, no great moral dilemma in this if property rights are treated as purely *instrumental*. If the goals of relief of hunger and poverty are sufficiently powerful, then it would be just right to violate whatever property rights come in the way, since—in this view—property rights have no intrinsic status. On the other hand, if property rights are taken to be morally inviolable irrespective of their consequences, then it will follow that these policies cannot be morally acceptable even though they might save thousands, or even millions, from dying. The inflexible moral "constraint" of respecting people's legitimately acquired entitlements would rule out such policies.

In fact this type of problem presents a reductio ad absurdum of the moral validity of constraint-based entitlement systems. However, while the conclusions to be derived from that approach might well be "absurd," the situation postulated is not an imaginary one at all. It is based on studies of actual famines and the role of entitlement failures in the causation of mass starvation. If there is an embarrassment here, it belongs solidly to the consequence-independent way of seeing rights.

I should add that this dilemma does not arise from regarding property rights to be of intrinsic value, which can be criticized on other grounds, but not this one. Even if property rights *are* of intrinsic value, their violation may be justified on grounds of the favorable consequences of that violation. A right, as was mentioned earlier, may be intrinsically valuable and still be justly violated taking everything into account. The "absurdum" does not belong to attaching intrinsic

value to property rights, but to regarding these rights as simply acceptable, regardless of their consequences. A moral system that values both property rights and other goals—such as avoiding famines and starvation, or fulfilling people's right not to be hungry—can, on the one hand, give property rights intrinsic importance, and on the other, recommend the violation of property rights when that leads to better overall consequences (*including* the disvalue of rights violation).

The issue here is not the valuing of property rights, but their alleged inviolability. There is no dilemma here either for the purely instrumental view of property rights or for treating the fulfillment of property rights as one goal among many, but specifically for consequence-independent assertions of property rights and for the corresponding constraint-based approaches to moral entitlement of ownership.

That property and hunger are closely related cannot possibly come as a great surprise. Hunger is primarily associated with not owning enough food and thus property rights over food are immediately and directly involved. Fights over that property right can be a major part of the reality of a poor country, and any system of moral assessment has to take note of that phenomenon. The tendency to see hunger in purely technocratic terms of food output and availability may help to hide the crucial role of entitlements in the genesis of hunger, but a fuller economic analysis cannot overlook that crucial role. Since property rights over food are derived from property rights over other goods and resources (through production and trade), the entire system of rights of acquisition and transfer is implicated in the emergence and survival of hunger and starvation.

THE RIGHT NOT TO BE HUNGRY

Property rights have been championed for a long time. In contrast, the assertion of "the right not to be hungry" is a comparatively recent phenomenon. While this right is much invoked in political debates, there is a good deal of skepticism about treating this as truly a right in any substantial way. It is often asserted that this concept of "right not to be hungry" stands essentially for nothing at all ("simple nonsense," as Bentham called "natural rights" in general). That piece of sophisticated cynicism reveals not so much a penetrating insight into the practical affairs of the world, but a refusal to investigate what people mean when they assert the existence of rights that, for the bulk of humanity, are not in fact guaranteed by the existing institutional arrangements.

The right not to be hungry is not asserted as a recognition of an institutional right that already exists, as the right to property typically is. The assertion is primarily a moral claim as to what should be valued, and what institutional structure we should aim for, and try to guarantee if feasible. It can also be seen in terms of Ronald Dworkin's category of "background rights—rights that provide a justification for political decisions by society in abstract."[3] This interpretation serves as the basis for a reason to change the existing institutional structure and state policy.

It is broadly in this form that the right to "an adequate means of livelihood" is referred to in the Constitution of India: "The state shall, in particular, direct its policy towards securing . . . that the citizens, men and women equally, have the right to an adequate means of livelihood." This does not, of course, offer to each citizen a guaranteed right to an adequate livelihood, but the state is asked to take steps such that this right could become realizable for all.

In fact, this right has often been invoked in political debates in India. The electoral politics of India does indeed give particular scope for such use of what are seen as background rights. It is, of course, not altogether clear whether the reference to this right in the Indian constitution has in fact materially influenced the political debates. The constitutional statement is often cited, but very likely this issue would have figured in any case in these debates, given the nature of the moral and political concern. But whatever the constitutional contribution, it is interesting to ask whether the implicit acceptance of the value of the right to freedom from hunger makes any difference to actual policy.

It can be argued that the general acceptance of the right of freedom from acute hunger as a major goal has played quite a substantial role in preventing famines in India. The last real famine in India was in 1943, and while food availability per head in India has risen only rather slowly (even now the food availability per head is no higher than in many sub-Saharan countries stricken by recurrent famines), the country has not experienced any famine since independence in 1947. The main cause of that success is a policy of public intervention. Whenever a famine has threatened, a public policy of intervention and relief has offered minimum entitlements to the potential famine victims, and thus have the threatening famines been averted. It can be argued that the quickness of the response of the respective governments (both state and central) reflects a political necessity, given the Indian electoral system and the importance attached by the public to the prevention of starvation. Political pressures from opposition groups and the news media have kept the respective governments on their toes, and the right to be free from acute hunger and starvation has been achieved largely because it has been seen as a valuable right. Thus the recognition of the intrinsic moral importance of this right, which has been widely invoked in public discussions, has served as a powerful political instrument as well.

On the other hand, this process has been far from effective in tackling pervasive and persistent undernourishment in India. There has been no famine in post-independence India, but perhaps a third of India's rural population is perennially undernourished. So long as hunger remains non-acute and starvation deaths are avoided (even though morbidity and mortality rates are enhanced by undernourishment), the need for a policy response is neither much discussed by the news media, nor forcefully demanded even by opposition parties. The elimination of famines coexists with the survival of widespread "regular hunger." The right to "adequate means" of *nourishment* does not at all seem to arouse political concern in a way that the right to "adequate means" to *avoid starvation* does.

The contrast can be due to one of several different reasons. It could, of course, simply be that the ability to avoid undernourishment is not socially accepted as very important. This could be so, though what is socially accepted and what is not is also partly a matter of how clearly the questions are posed. It is, in fact, quite possible that the freedom in question would be regarded as a morally important right if the question were posed in a transparent way, but this does not happen because of the nature of Indian electoral politics and that of news coverage. The issue is certainly not "dramatic" in the way in which starvation deaths and threatening famines are. Continued low-key misery may be too familiar a phenomenon to make it worthwhile for political leaders to get some mileage out of it in practical politics. The news media may also find little profit in emphasizing a non-spectacular phenomenon—the quiet survival of disciplined, non-acute hunger.

If this is indeed the case, then the implications for action of the goal of eliminating hunger, or guaranteeing to all the means for achieving this, may be quite complex. The political case for making the quiet hunger less quiet and more troublesome for governments in power is certainly relevant. Aggressive political journalism might prove to have an instrumental moral value if it were able to go beyond reporting the horrors of visible starvation and to portray the pervasive, non-acute hunger in a more dramatic and telling way. This is obviously not the place to discuss the instrumentalities of practical politics, but the endorsement of the moral right to be free from hunger—both acute and non-acute—would in fact raise pointed questions about the means which might be used to pursue such a goal....

NOTES

1. This is presented as a "Directive Principle of State Policy." It does not have a direct operational role in the working of the Indian legal system, but it has considerable political force.

2. Robert Nozick, *Anarchy, State, and Utopia* (New York: Basic, 1974), pp. ix, 166.

3. Ronald Dworkin, *Taking Rights Seriously* (Cambridge, Mass.: Harvard University Press, 1977), p. 93.

READING QUESTIONS

1. Explain how rights can be instruments, constraints, or goals according to Sen. What does he think the advantages of the goal view of rights are?
2. What are the two conclusions about rights that he draws from the distinction among the three different views? How does he distinguish between the intrinsic value of a right and the overall value of a right?
3. What is the best explanation for the cause of famines according to Sen? Explain the difference between endowments and entitlements.
4. Explain what Sen means when he talks about the right not be hungry. How does he use the notion of background rights to argue for his view?

DISCUSSION QUESTIONS

1. How does Sen's solution to the problem of world hunger compare to the others proposed in this chapter? Discuss whether there are any potential problems with his view that he fails to consider.
2. What are some of the ways that private citizens could work to implement the sort of strategies suggested by Sen?

Onora O'Neill

A Kantian Approach to World Hunger

O'Neill approaches questions about our obligations to the hungry and poor through Kant's Humanity formulation of his fundamental moral principle, the categorical imperative: *So act that you use humanity, whether in your own person or that of another, always at the same time as an end, never merely as a means.* In requiring that we never treat others merely as means, the principle in question imposes requirements of justice. But in requiring that we treat humanity as an end, it goes further and imposes requirements of beneficence. After explaining the rudiments of Kant's Humanity principle, O'Neill proceeds to explore the implications of Kantian justice and beneficence regarding obligations to help those in need.

> *Recommended Reading*: Kantian moral theory, chap. 1, sec. 2C, particularly the humanity formulation of the categorical imperative.

We use others as *mere means* if what we do reflects some maxim *to which they could not in principle consent.* Kant does not suggest that there is anything wrong about using someone as a means. Evidently every cooperative scheme of action does this. A government that agrees to provide free or subsidized food to famine-relief agencies both uses and is used by the agencies; a peasant who sells food in a local market both uses and is used by those who buy it. In such examples each party to the transaction can and does consent to take part in that transaction. Kant would say that the parties to such transactions use one another but do not use one another as *mere* means. Each party assumes that the other has its own maxims of action and is not just a thing or prop to be used or manipulated.

But there are other cases where one party to an arrangement or transaction not only uses the other but does so in ways that could only be done on the basis of a fundamental principle or maxim to which the other could not in principle consent. If a false promise is given, the party that accepts the promise is not just used but used as a mere means, because it is *impossible* for consent to be given to the fundamental principle or project of deception that must guide every false promise, whatever its surface character. Those who accept false promises *must* be kept ignorant of the underlying principle or maxim on which the "undertaking" is based. If this isn't kept concealed, the attempted promise will either be rejected or will not be a *false* promise at all. In false promising the deceived party becomes, as it were, a prop or tool—a *mere* means—in the false promisor's scheme. Action based on any such maxim of deception would be wrong in Kantian terms, whether it is a matter of a breach of treaty obligations, of contractual undertakings, or of accepted and relied upon modes of interaction. Maxims of deception *standardly* use others as mere means, and acts that could only be based on such maxims are unjust.

From Onora O'Neill, "The Moral Perplexities of Famine and World Hunger," in Tom Regan, ed., *Matters of Life and Death,* 2nd edition, New York, Random House, 1986, pp. 322–329.

Another standard way of using others as mere means is by coercing them. Coercers, like deceivers, standardly don't give others the possibility of dissenting from what they propose to do. In deception, "consent" is spurious because it is given to a principle that couldn't be the underlying principle of *that* act at all; but the principle governing coercion may be brutally plain. Here any "consent" given is spurious because there was no option *but* to consent. If a rich or powerful landowner or nation threatens a poorer or more vulnerable person, group, or nation with some intolerable difficulty unless a concession is made, the more vulnerable party is denied a genuine choice between consent and dissent. While the boundary that divides coercion from mere bargaining and negotiation varies and is therefore often hard to discern, we have no doubt about the clearer cases. Maxims of coercion may threaten physical force, seizure of possessions, destruction of opportunities, or any other harm that the coerced party is thought to be unable to absorb without grave injury or danger. A moneylender in a Third World village who threatens not to make or renew an indispensable loan, without which survival until the next harvest would be impossible, uses the peasant as mere means. The peasant does not have the possibility of genuinely consenting to the "offer he can't refuse." The outward form of some coercive transactions may *look* like ordinary commercial dealings: but we know very well that some action that is superficially of this sort is based on maxims of coercion. To avoid coercion, action must be governed by maxims that the other party can choose to refuse and is not bound to accept. The more vulnerable the other party in any transaction or negotiation, the less their scope for refusal, and the more demanding it is likely to be to ensure that action is noncoercive.

In Kant's view, acts done on maxims that coerce or deceive others, so therefore cannot in principle have the consent of those others, are wrong. When individuals or institutions, or nation states act in ways that can only be based on such maxims they fail in their duty. They treat the parties who are either deceived or coerced unjustly. To avoid unjust action it is not enough to observe the outward forms of free agreement and

cooperation; it is also essential to see that the weaker party to any arrangement has a genuine option to refuse the fundamental character of the proposal.

TREATING OTHERS AS ENDS IN THEMSELVES

For Kant, as for utilitarians, justice is only one part of duty. We may fail in our duty, even when we don't use anyone as mere means (by deception or coercion), if we fail to treat others as "ends in themselves." To treat others as "Ends in Themselves" we must not only avoid using them as mere means but also treat them as rational and autonomous beings with their own maxims. If human beings were *wholly* rational and autonomous then, on a Kantian view, duty would require only that they not use one another as mere means. But, as Kant repeatedly stressed, but later Kantians have often forgotten, human beings are *finite* rational beings. They are finite in several ways.

First, human beings are not ideal rational calculators. We *standardly* have neither a complete list of the actions possible in a given situation nor more than a partial view of their likely consequences. In addition, abilities to assess and to use available information are usually quite limited.

Second, these cognitive limitations are *standardly* complemented by limited autonomy. Human action is limited not only by various sorts of physical barrier and inability but by further sorts of (mutual or asymmetrical) dependence. To treat one another as ends in themselves such beings have to base their action on principles that do not undermine but rather sustain and extend one another's capacities for autonomous action. A central requirement for doing so is to share and support one another's ends and activities at least to some extent. Since finite rational beings cannot generally achieve their aims without some help and support from others, a general refusal of help and support amounts to failure to treat others as rational and autonomous beings, that is as ends in themselves. Hence Kantian principles require us not only to act justly, that is in accordance with maxims that don't coerce or deceive others, but also to avoid manipulation and to lend some support to others' plans and activities. Since famine, great poverty and powerlessness all undercut the possibility of autonomous action, and the requirement of treating others as ends in themselves demands that Kantians standardly act to support the possibility of autonomous action where it is most vulnerable, Kantians are required to do what they can to avert, reduce, and remedy famine. On a Kantian view, beneficence is as indispensable as justice in human lives.

JUSTICE AND BENEFICENCE IN KANT'S THOUGHT

Kant is often thought to hold that justice is morally required, but beneficence is morally less important. He does indeed, like Mill, speak of justice as a *perfect duty* and of beneficence as an *imperfect duty*. But he does not mean by this that beneficence is any less a duty; rather, he holds that it has (unlike justice) to be selective. We cannot share or even support *all* others' maxims *all* of the time. Hence support for others' autonomy is always selective. By contrast we can make all action and institutions conform fundamentally to standards of nondeception and noncoercion. Kant's understanding of the distinction between perfect and imperfect duties differs from Mill's. In a Kantian perspective justice isn't a matter of the core requirements for beneficence, as in Mill's theory, and beneficence isn't just an attractive but optional moral embellishment of just arrangements (as tends to be assumed in most theories that take human rights as fundamental).

JUSTICE TO THE VULNERABLE IN KANTIAN THINKING

For Kantians, justice requires action that conforms (at least outwardly) to what could be done in a given situation while acting on maxims neither of deception nor of coercion. Since anyone hungry or destitute is more than usually vulnerable to deception and coercion, the possibilities and temptations to injustice are then especially strong.

Examples are easily suggested. I shall begin with some situations that might arise for somebody who happened to be part of a famine-stricken population. Where shortage of food is being dealt with by a reasonably fair rationing scheme, any mode of cheating to get more than one's allocated share involves using some others and is unjust. Equally, taking advantage of others' desperation to profiteer—for example, selling food at colossal prices or making loans on the security of others' future livelihood, when these are "offers they can't refuse"—constitutes coercion and so uses others as mere means and is unjust. Transactions that have the outward form of normal commercial dealing may be coercive when one party is desperate. Equally, forms of corruption that work by deception—such as bribing officials to gain special benefits from development schemes, or deceiving others about their entitlements—use others unjustly. Such requirements are far from trivial and frequently violated in hard times; acting justly in such conditions may involve risking one's own life and livelihood and require the greatest courage.

It is not so immediately obvious what justice, Kantianly conceived, requires of agents and agencies who are remote from destitution. Might it not be sufficient to argue that those of us fortunate enough to live in the developed world are far from famine and destitution, so if we do nothing but go about our usual business will successfully avoid injustice to the destitute? This conclusion has often been reached by those who take an abstract view of rationality and forget the limits of human rationality and autonomy. In such perspectives it can seem that there is nothing more to just action than meeting the formal requirements of nondeception and noncoercion in our dealings with one another. But once we remember the limitations of human rationality and autonomy, and the particular ways in which they are limited for those living close to the margins of subsistence, we can see that mere conformity to ordinary standards of commercial honesty and political bargaining is not enough for justice toward the destitute. If international agreements themselves can constitute "offers that cannot be refused" by the government of a poor country, or if the concessions required for investment by a transnational corporation or a development project reflect the desperation of recipients rather than an appropriate contribution to the project, then (however benevolent the motives of some parties) the weaker party to such agreements is used by the stronger.

In the earlier days of European colonial penetration of the now underdeveloped world it was evident enough that some of the ways in which "agreements" were made with native peoples were in fact deceptive or coercive or both. "Sales" of land by those who had no grasp of market practices and "cession of sovereignty" by those whose forms of life were prepolitical constitute only spurious consent to the agreements struck. But it is not only in these original forms of bargaining between powerful and powerless that injustice is frequent. There are many contemporary examples. For example, if capital investment (private or governmental) in a poorer country requires the receiving country to contribute disproportionately to the maintenance of a developed, urban "enclave" economy that offers little local employment but lavish standards of life for a small number of (possibly expatriate) "experts," while guaranteeing long-term exemption from local taxation for the investors, then we may doubt that the agreement could have been struck without the element of coercion provided by the desperation of the weaker party. Or if a trade agreement extracts political advantages (such as military bases) that are incompatible with the fundamental political interests of the country concerned, we may judge that at least some leaders of that country have been "bought" in a sense that is not consonant with ordinary commercial practice.

Even when the actions of those who are party to an agreement don't reflect a fundamental principle of coercion or deception, the agreement may alter the life circumstances and prospects of third parties in ways to which they patently could not have not consented. For example, a system of food aid and imports agreed upon by the government of a Third World country and certain developed countries or international agencies may give the elite of that Third World country access

to subsidized grain. If that grain is then used to control the urban population and also produces destitution among peasants (who used to grow food for that urban population), then those who are newly destitute probably have not been offered any opening or possibility of refusing their new and worsened conditions of life. If a policy is imposed, those affected *cannot* have been given a chance to refuse it: had the chance been there, they would either have assented (and so the policy would not have been *imposed*) or refused (and so proceeding with the policy would have been evidently coercive).

BENEFICENCE TO THE VULNERABLE IN KANTIAN THINKING

In Kantian moral reasoning, the basis for beneficent action is that we cannot, without it, treat others of limited rationality and autonomy as ends in themselves. This is not to say that Kantian beneficence won't make others happier, for it will do so whenever they would be happier if (more) capable of autonomous action, but that happiness secured by purely paternalistic means, or at the cost (for example) of manipulating others' desires, will not count as beneficent in the Kantian picture. Clearly the vulnerable position of those who lack the very means of life, and their severely curtailed possibilities for autonomous action, offer many different ways in which it might be possible for others to act beneficently. Where the means of life are meager, almost any material or organizational advance may help extend possibilities for autonomy. Individual or institutional action that aims to advance economic or social development can proceed on many routes. The provision of clean water, of improved agricultural techniques, of better grain storage systems, or of adequate means of local transport may all help transform material prospects. Equally, help in the development of new forms of social organization—whether peasant self-help groups, urban cooperatives, medical and contraceptive services, or improvements in education or in the position of women—may help to extend possibilities for autonomous action. Kantian thinking does not provide a means by which all possible projects of this sort could be listed and ranked. But where some activity helps secure possibilities for autonomous action for more people, or is likely to achieve a permanent improvement in the position of the most vulnerable, or is one that can be done with more reliable success, this provides reason for furthering that project rather than alternatives.

Clearly the alleviation of need must rank far ahead of the furthering of happiness in the Kantian picture. I might make my friends very happy by throwing extravagant parties: but this would probably not increase anybody's possibility for autonomous action to any great extent. But the sorts of development-oriented changes that have just been mentioned may *transform* the possibilities for action of some. Since famine and the risk of famine are always and evidently highly damaging to human autonomy, any action that helps avoid or reduce famine must have a strong claim on any Kantian who is thinking through what beneficence requires. Depending on circumstances, such action may have to take the form of individual contribution to famine relief and development organizations, of individual or collective effort to influence the trade and aid policies of developed countries, or of attempts to influence the activities of those Third World elites for whom development does not seem to be an urgent priority. Some activities can best be undertaken by private citizens of developed countries; others are best approached by those who work for governments, international agencies, or transnational corporations. Perhaps the most dramatic possibilities to act for a just or an unjust, a beneficent or selfish future belong to those who hold positions of influence within the Third World. But wherever we find ourselves, our duties are not, on the Kantian picture, limited to those close at hand. Duties of justice arise whenever there is some involvement between parties—and in the modern world this is never lacking. Duties of beneficence arise whenever destitution puts the possibility of autonomous action in question for the more vulnerable. When famines were not only far away, but nothing could be done to relieve them, beneficence or charity may well have begun—and stayed—at home. In a global village, the moral significance of distance has shrunk, and we may be able to affect the capacities for autonomous action of those who are far away.

THE SCOPE OF KANTIAN DELIBERATIONS ABOUT FAMINE AND HUNGER

In many ways Kantian moral reasoning is less ambitious than utilitarian moral reasoning. It does not propose a process of moral reasoning that can (in principle) rank *all* possible actions or all possible institutional arrangements from the happiness-maximizing "right" action or institution downward. It aims rather to offer a pattern of reasoning by which we can identify whether *proposed action or institutional arrangements* would be just or unjust, beneficent or lacking in beneficence. While *some* knowledge of causal connections is needed for Kantian reasoning, it is far less sensitive than is utilitarian reasoning to gaps in our causal knowledge. The conclusions reached about particular proposals for action or about institutional arrangements will not hold for all time, but be relevant for the contexts for which action is proposed. For example, if it is judged that some institution—say the World Bank—provides, under present circumstances, a just approach to certain development problems, it will not follow that under all other circumstances such an institution would be part of a just approach. There may be other institutional arrangements that are also just; and there may be other circumstances under which the institutional structure of the World Bank would be shown to be in some ways deceptive or coercive and so unjust.

These points show us that Kantian deliberations about famine and hunger can lead only to conclusions that are useful in determinate contexts. This, however, is standardly what we need to know for action, whether individual or institutional. We do not need to be able to generate a complete list of available actions in order to determine whether proposed lines of action are not unjust and whether any are beneficent. Kantian patterns of moral reasoning cannot be guaranteed to identify the optimal course of action in a situation. They provide methods neither for listing nor for ranking all possible proposals for action. But any line of action that is considered can be checked.

The reason this pattern of reasoning will not show any action or arrangement the most beneficent one available is that the Kantian picture of beneficence is less mathematically structured than the utilitarian one. It judges beneficence by its overall contribution to the prospects for human autonomy and not by the quantity of happiness expected to result. To the extent that the autonomous pursuit of goals is what Mill called "one of the principal ingredients of human happiness" (but only to that extent), the requirements of Kantian and of utilitarian beneficence will coincide. But whenever expected happiness is not a function of the scope for autonomous action, the two accounts of beneficent action diverge. For utilitarians, paternalistic imposition of, for example, certain forms of aid and development assistance need not be wrong and may even be required. But for Kantians, whose beneficence should secure others' possibilities for autonomous action, the case for paternalistic imposition of aid or development projects without the recipients' involvement must always be questionable.

In terms of some categories in which development projects are discussed, utilitarian reasoning may well endorse "top-down" aid and development projects which override whatever capacities for autonomous choice and action the poor of a certain area now have in the hopes of securing a happier future. If the calculations work out in a certain way, utilitarians may even think a "generation of sacrifice"— or of forced labor or of imposed population-control policies not only permissible but mandated. In their darkest Malthusian moments some utilitarians have thought that average happiness might best be maximized not by improving the lot of the poor but by minimizing their numbers, and so have advocated policies of "benign neglect" of the poorest and most desperate. Kantian patterns of reasoning are likely to endorse less global and less autonomy-overriding aid and development projects; they are not likely to endorse neglect or abandoning of those who are most vulnerable and lacking in autonomy. If the aim of beneficence is to keep or put others in a position to act for themselves, then emphasis must be placed on "bottom-up" projects, which from the start draw on, foster, and establish indigenous capacities and practices of self-help and local action....

READING QUESTIONS

1. Under what circumstances does one individual use another as a means according to O'Neill? Explain why false promises and coercion involve using someone as a means.
2. How can we treat others as ends in themselves according to O'Neill? In what ways are human beings limited by their finitude?
3. Explain the role of justice and beneficence in Kant's thought. Why do justice and beneficence require helping the vulnerable?
4. What reasons does O'Neill give for thinking that a Kantian approach to the problem of hunger is less ambitious but more successful than the utilitarian approach?

DISCUSSION QUESTIONS

1. Is O'Neill right to claim that the Kantian approach does not face the same sorts of difficulties as the utilitarian approach to the problem of world hunger? Why or why not? What sorts of problems might the Kantian approach face that the utilitarian approach does not?
2. Consider and discuss whether the Kantian argument for helping the vulnerable is more or less convincing than the traditional utilitarian arguments. What kinds of arguments would be the most likely to persuade people to help those in need?

ADDITIONAL RESOURCES

Web Resources

Hunger Notes, <www.worldhunger.org>. Established in 1976 by the World Hunger Education Services features information about world hunger.

The World Food Programme, <www.wfp.org>. A branch of the United Nations whose objectives include reducing hunger.

OXFAM, <http://www.oxfam.org/>. An international organization devoted to helping the world's poor.

Beauchamp, Tom, "The Principle of Beneficence in Applied Ethics," *Stanford Encyclopedia of Philosophy*, <http://plato.stanford.edu/entries/principle-beneficence>. A useful discussion of the place of a principle of beneficence in various ethical theories including those of Kant, Mill, and Hume, as well as how considerations of beneficence figures in discussions of applied ethics.

Authored Books & Articles

Cullity, Garrett, *The Moral Demands of Affluence* (Oxford: Oxford University Press, 2004). Cullity argues that the obligations of the affluent to help those in desperate need are modestly demanding.

O'Neill, Onora, *Faces of Hunger: An Essay on Poverty, Justice, and Development* (London and Boston: Unwin Hyman, 1986).

Pogge, Thomas, *World Poverty and Human Rights: Cosmopolitan Responsibilities and Reforms* (Cambridge: Polity Press, 2002). Pogge argues that our current economic order is morally indefensible and that those who are relatively economically well off are responsible for serious global injustices.

Murdoch, William W., & Oaten, Allan, "Population and Food: Metaphors and the Reality," *Bioscience* 25 (1975). A reply to Hardin's "lifeboat ethics."

Sen, Amartya, *Poverty and Famines: An Essay on Entitlement and Deprivation* (Oxford: Oxford University Press, 1984). A penetrating analysis of the causes of poverty and famine.

Unger, Peter, *Living High and Letting Die: Our Illusion of Innocence* (Oxford: Oxford University Press, 1996). An examination of the incongruity between basic moral principles most people do accept and their attitudes toward those in need.

Edited Collections

Aiken, William, & LaFollette, Hugh, eds., *World Hunger and Moral Obligation*, 2nd ed. (Englewood Cliffs: Prentice Hall, 1996). An extensive and important collection of essays.

Crocker, David, A., and Toby Linden (eds.), *Ethics of Consumption: The Good Life, Justice, and Global Stewardship* (Lanham, MD: Rowman & Littlefield, 1997). A collection of essays from renowned scholars from many disciplines that cover many aspects of morality and consumption.

14 The Environment, Consumption, and Global Warming

On March 15, 2005, the U.S. Senate voted (51–49) to approve a measure that would allow oil companies to drill for oil beneath the coastal plain of the Arctic National Wildlife Refuge (ANWR) in the northeastern region of Alaska. But in December 2005, the Senate voted to strip language from a defense appropriations bill that would have allowed drilling for gas and oil in the ANWR. Legal battles between pro-drilling interests and environmentalists over this refuge are likely to continue. Environmentalists opposed to this measure argue that drilling and laying pipelines would harm various forms of wildlife and the wilderness of the region generally. This is but one of a long list of environmental concerns that raise both legal and ethical issues.

One reason one might take up environmental causes is purely instrumental, namely, that human life depends crucially on the environment and so, out of concern for human welfare, we ought to preserve what we need to survive. But many environmentally concerned individuals think there is more to an ethical concern for the environment than how the welfare of human beings might be affected. Their thought is that at least some so-called lower forms of life (nonhuman and non-higher-animal life) have intrinsic value and thus some degree of **direct moral standing**. Their moral concern for the environment thus goes beyond a concern for how changing the environment might impact human beings. The moral claims of such environmentalists raise a number of fundamental ethical questions, including the following:

- Do biological entities other than humans and higher nonhuman animals have at least some degree of direct moral standing?
- What about nonliving things such as mountains and streams? What sort of direct moral standing (if any) do they have?
- If either some nonhuman biological creatures or nonliving things have direct moral standing, what does this imply about how human beings ought to treat such things?

1. EXPANDING THE SCOPE OF DIRECT MORAL STANDING?

As in the chapter on the ethical treatment of animals, the main philosophical issue in this chapter concerns what we are calling the scope of *direct* moral standing. You may recall that for something to be within the scope of direct moral standing is for it itself to count morally because of its own nature and not merely because it is of instrumental value to human beings or any other creature. If anything is clear in the realm of disputed moral issues it is that human beings have direct moral standing—each of us possesses a kind of standing that imposes requirements on others and how they treat us. We can put the point in terms of reasons: that your action would cause me serious injury is a reason for you not to do that action. Granted, there may be cases in which this reason is overridden by an even more important moral reason. But still, because of the fact that I am the sort of creature I am, I am of direct (not just indirect) moral concern.

Those who would ascribe moral rights to (at least some) nonhuman animals, or who would claim that human beings have obligations *to* nonhuman animals, advocate expanding the sphere of direct moral standing beyond the realm of human beings to include some nonhuman animals. As we shall see in this chapter, some philosophers propose that we expand the scope of direct moral standing even further and include a wider range of entities. These "expansionists" differ among themselves as to how inclusive this scope should be. In order to get a sense of the issues and arguments featured in some discussions about ethics and the environment, let us first introduce some terminology that is often used to pick out different positions one might take on this issue of scope, and then consider some of the arguments featured in debates over environmental ethics.

2. FOUR APPROACHES

Here, then, are four general approaches to questions about the scope of direct moral standing, organized from least to most inclusive:

- **Anthropocentrism:** The only beings who possess direct moral standing are human beings. All other beings (living and nonliving) are of mere indirect moral concern.
- **Sentientism:** All and only sentient creatures—creatures who have the capacity to experience pleasure and pain—have direct moral standing. Thus, morality includes requirements that include direct moral concern for all sentient beings.
- **Biocentrism:** All living beings *because they are living* possess direct moral standing. Thus, morality includes requirements that include direct moral concern for all living beings.
- **Ecocentrism:** The primary bearers of direct moral standing are ecosystems in virtue of their functional integrity. An **ecosystem** is a whole composed of both living and nonliving things including animals, plants, bodies of water, sunlight, and other geological factors. Hence, morality involves moral obligations to maintain the functional integrity of ecosystems and because, according to this view, ecosystems are *primary* bearers of direct moral standing, their preservation takes moral precedence over concern for individual things and creatures that compose the system.

One basic difference between the first three approaches and ecocentrism is the contrast between **atomism** and **holism** regarding the primary bearers of direct moral standing—a distinction implicit in the previous characterizations. Atomism in this context is the view that the primary items of moral appraisal are individuals—only individuals can be properly judged as intrinsically valuable, or rights holders, or as having obligations. By contrast, holism maintains that wholes or collectives are bearers of value, or of rights, or of obligations. Of course, the view that wholes are bearers of direct moral standing is compatible with the atomistic view that individual members of a whole also have direct moral standing. Thus, one view, sometimes called **ecoholism,** maintains that both ecosystems and at least some individual items that make up an ecosystem have direct moral standing. But notice that the eco*centrist* makes a stronger holistic claim: the *only* bearers of direct moral standing are wholes, and not the individual items of which they are composed.

3. THE VERY IDEA OF AN ENVIRONMENTAL ETHIC

Having described four basic positions about the scope of moral concern, we are now in a position to clarify the very idea of an environmental ethic. Here it is important to distinguish between an ethic *of* the environment and an ethic *for the use of* the environment. The latter kind of "management ethic" for the environment is consistent with anthropocentrism, and so it does not count as an environmental ethic. Thus, an environmental ethic must accord direct moral standing to beings other than humans. But this minimum necessary condition is not enough—not sufficient—for an ethic to be an environmental ethic. After all, an ethical theory that accorded some direct moral standing to humans and to apes, but nothing else, would not, strictly speaking, count as an **environmental ethic**. So, with some modification, let us follow philosopher Tom Regan's characterization of an environmental ethic:

1. An environmental ethic must hold that there are nonhuman beings that have direct moral standing.
2. An environmental ethic must hold that the class of beings that have direct moral standing is larger than the class of conscious beings—that is, this sort of ethic must ascribe direct moral standing to nonconscious beings.[1]

This characterization of an environmental ethic, while perhaps not airtight, does at least properly categorize the three basic approaches we discussed in the previous section. Clearly, anthropocentric and sentientist accounts of direct moral standing ethic are ruled out by Regan's definition, even if they allow for a management ethic in dealing with environmental issues. However, both biocentric and ecocentric views do count as versions of an environmental ethic. So, on this way of understanding ethical issues concerning treatment of the environment, the fundamental issue is over the scope of those beings (including living, nonliving, individuals, and collectives) that possess direct moral standing. And this issue brings us in direct contact with one of the most fundamental questions of ethical theory: *in virtue of what does something have direct moral standing?*

4. CONSUMPTION AND GLOBAL WARMING

Perhaps the most publicized contemporary ethical issue associated with the environment is that of global warming. Many have recently argued that excessive human consumption that produces emissions of greenhouse gasses (GHGs), including in particular high emission levels of carbon dioxide (CO_2),[2] has brought about certain undesirable climactic changes: global warming, severe weather, and changes in ocean currents. For instance, according to a 2007 report by the Intergovernmental Panel on Climate Change (IPCC).[3]

> Global atmospheric concentrations of CO_2, CH_4 and N_2O have increased markedly as a result of human activities since 1750 and now far exceed pre-industrial values determined from ice cores spanning many thousands of years. The atmospheric concentrations of CO_2 and CH_4 in 2005 exceed by far the natural range over the last 650,000 years. Global increases in CO_2 concentrations are due primarily to fossil fuel use, with land-use change providing another significant but smaller contribution. It is very likely that the observed increase in CH_4 concentration is predominantly due to agriculture and fossil fuel use. The increase in N_2O concentration is primarily due to agriculture.[4]

The IPCC report contains projections for the 21st century about the likely effects of global warming on four categories of concern: (1) agriculture, forestry, and ecosystems; (2) water resources; (3) human health; and (4) industry, settlement, and society. These projections are based on the assumption that GHGs will continue to be emitted at the same rate or higher than 2007 emission levels. Figure 14.1 presents the 2007 IPCC report that summarizes their projections.[5] (Note: Reference to SRES scenarios [Special Report on Emissions Scenarios] in the top row of the second column refers to various possible projections regarding demographic, economic, and technological changes on the basis of which predictions about global warming are projected. For example, one of the four basic scenarios "assumes a world of very rapid economic growth, a global population that peaks in mid-century and rapid introduction of new and more efficient technologies."[6])

Two comments are in order here. First, notice that not all of the predicted effects mentioned in this table are negative. For instance, one likely human health benefit from warmer temperatures is a decrease in mortality rates from exposure to cold. Also, reduced energy demand for purposes of heating homes and increased yields in agricultural products in areas whose temperatures will increase are among the projected positive effects of global warming. However, when put side to side with the number of projected negative effects (some of them, e.g., increased energy demand for cooling), the likely positive effects seem to be seriously outweighed by the likely negative effects.

Second, although most experts seem to agree that global warming is a genuine phenomenon, questions have been raised about the accuracy of the predictions featured in the IPCC report. Some have argued that the projections are faulty or misleading. Such critics include those who argue that the severity of the projected negative effects are exaggerated, while others have argued that such projections are too conservative, that the IPCC report underestimates the harm that will likely result from global warming.[7] Questions have also been raised about the extent to which global warming is due to human activities and how much is due to other, naturally occurring factors.

But assuming that global warming is a genuine phenomenon and assuming, too, that much of it is due to human activity including, for instance, the use of fossil

Examples of major projected impacts by sector

Phenomena and direction of trend	Likelihood of future trends based on projections for 21st century using SRES scenarios	Agriculture, forestry, and ecosystems	Water resources	Human health	Industry, settlement, and society
Over most land areas, warmer and fewer cold days and nights, warmer and more frequent hot days and nights.	Virtually certain	Increased yields in colder environments; decreased yields in warmer environments; increased insect outbreaks.	Effects on water resources relying on snowmelt; effects on some water supplies.	Reduced human mortality from decreased cold exposure.	Reduced energy demand for heating; increased demand for cooling; declining air quality in cities; reduced disruption to transport due to snow, ice; effects on winter tourism.
Warm spells/heat waves. Frequency increases over most land areas.	Very likely	Reduced yields in warmer regions due to heat stress; increased danger of wildfire.	Increased water demand; water quality problems, e.g., algal blooms.	Increased risk of heat-related mortality, especially for the elderly, chronically sick, very young and socially isolated.	Reduced in quality of life for people in warm areas without appropriate housing; impacts on elderly, very young and poor.
Heavy precipitation events. Frequency increases over most areas.	Very likely	Damage to crops; soil erosion, inability to cultivate land due to waterlogging of soils.	Adverse effects on quality of surface and groundwater; contamination of water supply; water scarcity may be relieved.	Increased risk of deaths, injuries and infectious respiratory and skin diseases.	Disruption of settlements, commerce, transport and societies due to flooding: pressures on urban and rural infra-structures; loss of property.
Area affected by drought increases.	Likely	Land degradation; lower yields/crop damage and failure; increased livestock deaths; increased risk of wildfire.	More widespread water stress.	Increased risk of food and water shortage; increased risk of malnutrition; increased risk of water- and food-borne diseases.	Water shortage for settlements, industry and societies; reduced hydropower generation potentials; potential for population migration.
Intense tropical cyclone activity increases.	Likely	Damage to crops; windthrow (uprooting) of trees; damage to coral reefs.	Power outages causing disruption of public water supply.	Increased risk of deaths, injuries, water- and food-borne diseases; post-traumatic stress disorders.	Disruption by flood and high winds; withdrawal of risk coverage in vulnerable areas by private insurers; potential for population migrations; loss of property.
Increased incidence of extreme high sea level (excludes tsunamis).	Likely	Salinisation of irrigation water, estuaries and fresh-water systems.	Decreased fresh-water availability due to saltwater intrusion.	Increased risk of deaths and injuries by drowning in floods; migration-related health effects.	Costs of coastal protection versus costs of land-use relocation; potential for movement of populations and infrastructure.

FIGURE 14.1 Examples of possible impacts of climate change due to changes in extreme weather and climate events, based on projections to the mid- to late 21st century. These do not take into account any changes or developments in adaptive capacity. The likelihood estimates in column 2 relate to the phenomena listed in column 1.

fuels that emit high levels of CO_2 into the atmosphere, the main ethical questions are these:

- What ethical implications does global warming have for individuals who live in a consumer society?
- What ethical implications does global warming have for governments, particularly those such as the United States whose consumer population apparently contributes a high percentage of the greenhouse gasses that contribute to the phenomenon of global warming?

These questions receive attention from Peter Wenz, Walter Sinnott-Armstrong, and Bjørn Lomborg in their contributions to this chapter.

5. THEORY MEETS PRACTICE

Kantian moral theory extended

Many defenders of an environmental ethic base their view (whether biocentric or ecocentric) on the claim that intrinsic value is possessed by such things as nonsentient life forms, features of the environment, perhaps whole species, and the ecosystem itself. Thus, on their view, some or all of these items have direct moral standing. If we now add the idea that creatures and things having direct moral standing require that they be treated with an appropriate kind and level of respect, we arrive at a Kantian ethical theory, extended in scope.

Consequentialism

A consequentialist might go a number of ways with regard to an environmental ethic. If she follows the utilitarian tradition and accords direct moral standing only to sentient creatures—creatures who have the developed capacity to have experiences of pleasure and pain—then she is going to deny that nonsentient creatures and nonliving things have direct moral standing. This view will thus deny that there is or can be a genuine environmental ethic as we defined it earlier.

However, recall that the main consequentialist idea is that the rightness or wrongness of an action depends entirely on the net intrinsic value of the likely consequences of the various alternative actions or policies under consideration. It is open to a nonutilitarian consequentialist to hold that nonsentient creatures and perhaps nonliving things have intrinsic value and thus embrace the central tenets of an environmental ethic. If a consequentialist goes this route, there is still a difference between consequentialism so extended and a Kantian environmental ethic: the consequentialist maintains that what has intrinsic value is something *to be promoted,* while the Kantian holds that respecting what has intrinsic value is not simply a matter of promoting more of it. For instance, it is open to a Kantian to claim that proper respect for the environment requires of us that we *appreciate* and *preserve* it (or certain of its elements) where doing so is not a matter of (but may sometime include) promoting in the sense of increasing the items having intrinsic value.

Thus, consequentialists as such need not reject the main tenets of an environmental ethic, and those who do embrace such an ethic need not worry about collapsing their view into an essentially Kantian view.

Virtue Ethics

Suppose one is skeptical of the idea that nonsentient creatures and/or nonliving things have direct moral standing, and thus skeptical of the idea of an environmental ethic. And suppose one rejects any form of consequentialism, including utilitarianism. What sense might one make of the idea that responsible moral agents morally ought to have a certain noninstrumental regard for the environment? One answer is provided by a virtue-centered approach to ethics, according to which to fail to have a proper noninstrumental regard for the environment might involve one or more failures of character. This is the approach taken by Thomas E. Hill Jr. in his article included in this chapter.

NOTES

1. See Tom Regan, "The Nature and Possibility of an Environmental Ethic," *Environmental Ethics* 3 (1981): 19–34. I have broadened Regan's conception by not requiring that an environmental ethic attribute direct moral standing to conscious beings. Clearly, a holistic ethic of the sort described earlier counts as an environmental ethic, but it *need not* attribute any direct moral standing to the individuals (both living and nonliving) that compose a whole ecosystem. It should also be noted that Regan's conception of an environmental ethic excludes both anthropocentrism and sentientism from counting as environmental ethics. But other writers define "environmental ethics" more generally as the study of the ethics of human interactions with, and impact upon, the natural environment. On this broader definition, neither anthropocentrist nor sentientist views are excluded.

2. In addition to CO_2, other greenhouse gasses include methane (CH_4), nitrous oxide (N_2O) and halocarbons (a group that includes fluorine, chlorine, and bromine).

3. Established in 1988, the IPCC is a scientific intergovernmental body whose main task is to study the effects of human activity on climate.

4. From IPCC, *Climate Change 2007: Synthesis Report*, p. 15.

5. IPCC, *Climate Change 2007: Synthesis Report*, p. 31.

6. IPCC, *Climate Change 2007: Synthesis Report*, p. 44.

7. See, for instance, ch. 7 of the Wikipedia entry on the IPCC, "Criticisms of IPCC," <http://en.wikipedia.org/wiki/Intergovernmental_Panel_on_Climate_Change>.

William F. Baxter

People or Penguins: The Case for Optimal Pollution

Baxter defends an anthropocentric approach to ethical issues concerning the environment by specifying four goals that are to serve as criteria for determining solutions to problems of human organization. On the basis of these "people-oriented" criteria, Baxter argues that we should view our treatment of the environment as a matter of various trade-offs whose aim is to promote human welfare. Two of Baxter's criteria appeal to the Kantian idea that all persons are to be treated as ends in themselves, and so his view represents one way in which Kant's ethics can be extended to environmental concerns.

Recommended Reading: Kantian moral theory, chap. 1, sec. 2C, particularly the humanity formulation of the categorical imperative.

I start with the modest proposition that, in dealing with pollution, or indeed with any problem, it is helpful to know what one is attempting to accomplish. Agreement on how and whether to pursue a particular objective, such as pollution control, is not possible unless some more general objective has been identified and stated with reasonable precision. We talk loosely of having clean air and clean water, of preserving our wilderness areas, and so forth. But none of these is a sufficiently general objective: each is more accurately viewed as a means rather than as an end.

With regard to clean air, for example, one may ask, "how clean?" and "what does clean mean?" It is even reasonable to ask, "why have clean air?" Each of these questions is an implicit demand that a more general community goal be stated—a goal sufficiently general in its scope and enjoying sufficiently general assent among the community of actors that such "why" questions no longer seem admissible with respect to that goal.

If, for example, one states as a goal the proposition that "every person should be free to do whatever he wishes in contexts where his actions do not interfere with the interests of other human beings," the speaker is unlikely to be met with a response of "why." The goal may be criticized as uncertain in its implications or difficult to implement, but it is so basic a tenet of our civilization—it reflects a cultural value so broadly shared, at least in the abstract—that the question "why" is seen as impertinent or imponderable or both.

I do not mean to suggest that everyone would agree with the "spheres of freedom" objective just stated. Still less do I mean to suggest that a society could subscribe to four or five such general objectives that would be adequate in their coverage to serve as testing criteria by which all other disagreements might be measured. One difficulty in the attempt to construct such a list is that each new goal added will conflict, in certain applications, with each prior goal listed; and thus each goal serves as a limited qualification on prior goals.

Without any expectation of obtaining unanimous consent to them, let me set forth four goals that I generally use as ultimate testing criteria in attempting to frame solutions to problems of human organization.

From William F. Baxter, *People or Penguins: The Case for Optimal Pollution*, Columbia University Press, 1974, pp. 1–13. Reprinted with permission of the publisher.

My position regarding pollution stems from these four criteria. If the criteria appeal to you and any part of what appears hereafter does not, our disagreement will have a helpful focus: which of us is correct, analytically, in supposing that his position on pollution would better serve these general goals. If the criteria do not seem acceptable to you, then it is to be expected that our more particular judgments will differ, and the task will then be yours to identify the basic set of criteria upon which your particular judgments rest.

My criteria are as follows:

1. The spheres of freedom criterion stated above.
2. Waste is a bad thing. The dominant feature of human existence is scarcity—our available resources, our aggregate labors, and our skill in employing both have always been, and will continue for some time to be, inadequate to yield to every man all the tangible and intangible satisfactions he would like to have. Hence, none of those resources, or labors, or skills, should be wasted—that is, employed so as to yield less than they might yield in human satisfactions.
3. Every human being should be regarded as an end rather than as a means to be used for the betterment of another. Each should be afforded dignity and regarded as having an absolute claim to an evenhanded application of such rules as the community may adopt for its governance.
4. Both the incentive and the opportunity to improve his share of satisfactions should be preserved to every individual. Preservation of incentive is dictated by the "no-waste" criterion and enjoins against the continuous, totally egalitarian redistribution of satisfactions, or wealth; but subject to that constraint, everyone should receive, by continuous redistribution if necessary, some minimal share of aggregate wealth so as to avoid a level of privation from which the opportunity to improve his situation becomes illusory.

The relationship of these highly general goals to the more specific environmental issues at hand may not be readily apparent, and I am not yet ready to demonstrate their pervasive implications. But let me give one indication of their implications. Recently scientists have informed us that use of DDT in food production is causing damage to the penguin population. For the present purposes let us accept that assertion as an indisputable scientific fact. The scientific fact is often asserted as if the correct implication—that we must stop agricultural use of DDT—followed from the mere statement of the fact of penguin damage. But plainly it does not follow if my criteria are employed.

My criteria are oriented to people, not penguins. Damage to penguins, or sugar pines, or geological marvels is, without more, simply irrelevant. One must go further, by my criteria, and say: Penguins are important because people enjoy seeing them walk about rocks; and furthermore, the well-being of people would be less impaired by halting use of DDT than by giving up penguins. In short, my observations about environmental problems will be people-oriented, as are my criteria. I have no interest in preserving penguins for their own sake.

It may be said by way of objection to this position, that it is very selfish of people to act as if each person represented one unit of importance and nothing else was of any importance. It is undeniably selfish. Nevertheless I think it is the only tenable starting place for analysis for several reasons. First, no other position corresponds to the way most people really think and act—i.e., corresponds to reality.

Second, this attitude does not portend any massive destruction of nonhuman flora and fauna, for people depend on them in many obvious ways, and they will be preserved because and to the degree that humans do depend on them.

Third, what is good for humans is, in many respects, good for penguins and pine trees—clean air for example. So that humans are, in these respects, surrogates for plant and animal life.

Fourth, I do not know how we could administer any other system. Our decisions are either private or collective. Insofar as Mr. Jones is free to act privately, he may give such preferences as he wishes to other forms of life: he may feed birds in winter and do with less himself, and he may even decline to resist an advancing polar bear on the ground that the bear's appetite is more important than those portions of himself that the bear may choose to eat. In short my basic premise does not rule out private altruism to competing life-forms. It does rule out, however, Mr. Jones' inclination to feed Mr. Smith to the bear, however hungry the bear, however despicable Mr. Smith.

Insofar as we act collectively on the other hand, only humans can be afforded an opportunity to participate in the collective decisions. Penguins cannot vote now and are unlikely subjects for the franchise—pine trees more unlikely still. Again each individual is free to cast his vote so as to benefit sugar pines if that is his inclination. But many of the more extreme assertions that one hears from some conservationists amount to tacit assertions that they are specially appointed representatives of sugar pines, and hence that their preferences should be weighted more heavily than the preferences of other humans who do not enjoy equal rapport with "nature." The simplistic assertion that agricultural use of DDT must stop at once because it is harmful to penguins is of that type.

Fifth, if polar bears or pine trees or penguins, like men, are to be regarded as ends rather than means, if they are to count in our calculus of social organization, someone must tell me how much each one counts, and someone must tell me how these life-forms are to be permitted to express their preferences, for I do not know either answer. If the answer is that certain people are to hold their proxies, then I want to know how those proxy-holders are to be selected: self-appointment does not seem workable to me.

Sixth, and by way of summary of all the foregoing, let me point out that the set of environmental issues under discussion—although they raise very complex technical questions of how to achieve any objective—ultimately raise a normative question: what *ought* we to do? Questions of *ought* are unique to the human mind and world—they are meaningless as applied to a nonhuman situation.

I reject the proposition that we *ought* to respect the "balance of nature" or to "preserve the environment" unless the reason for doing so, express or implied, is the benefit of man.

I reject the idea that there is a "right" or "morally correct" state of nature to which we should return. The word "nature" has no normative connotation. Was it "right" or "wrong" for the earth's crust to heave in contortion and create mountains and seas?

Was it "right" for the first amphibian to crawl up out of the primordial ooze? Was it "wrong" for plants to reproduce themselves and alter the atmospheric composition in favor of oxygen? For animals to alter the atmosphere in favor of carbon dioxide both by breathing oxygen and eating plants? No answers can be given to these questions because they are meaningless questions.

All this may seem obvious to the point of being tedious, but much of the present controversy over environment and pollution rests on tacit normative assumptions about just such nonnormative phenomena: that it is "wrong" to impair penguins with DDT, but not to slaughter cattle for prime rib roasts. That it is wrong to kill stands of sugar pines with industrial fumes, but not to cut sugar pines and build housing for the poor. Every man is entitled to his own preferred definition of Walden Pond, but there is no definition that has any moral superiority over another, except by reference to the selfish needs of the human race.

From the fact that there is no normative definition of the natural state, it follows that there is no normative definition of clean air or pure water—hence no definition of polluted air—or of pollution—except by reference to the needs of man. The "right" composition of the atmosphere is one which has some dust in it and some lead in it and some hydrogen sulfide in it—just those amounts that attend a sensibly organized society thoughtfully and knowledgeably pursuing the greatest possible satisfaction for its human members.

The first and most fundamental step toward solution of our environmental problems is a clear recognition that our objective is not pure air or water but rather some optimal state of pollution. That step immediately suggests the question: How do we define and attain the level of pollution that will yield the maximum possible amount of human satisfaction?

Low levels of pollution contribute to human satisfaction but so do food and shelter and education and music. To attain ever lower levels of pollution, we must pay the cost of having less of these other things. I contrast that view of the cost of pollution control with the more popular statement that pollution control will "cost" very large numbers of dollars.

The popular statement is true in some senses, false in others; sorting out the true and false senses is of some importance. The first step in that sorting process is to achieve a clear understanding of the difference between dollars and resources. Resources are the wealth of our nation; dollars are merely claim checks upon those resources. Resources are of vital importance; dollars are comparatively trivial.

Four categories of resources are sufficient for our purposes: At any given time a nation, or a planet if you prefer, has a stock of labor, of technological skill, of capital goods, and of natural resources (such as mineral deposits, timber, water, land, etc.). These resources can be used in various combinations to yield goods and services of all kinds—in some limited quantity. The quantity will be larger if they are combined efficiently, smaller if combined inefficiently. But in either event the resource stock is limited, the goods and services that they can be made to yield are limited; even the most efficient use of them will yield less than our population, in the aggregate, would like to have.

If one considers building a new dam, it is appropriate to say that it will be costly in the sense that it will require *x* hours of labor, *y* tons of steel and concrete, and *z* amount of capital goods. If these resources are devoted to the dam, then they cannot be used to build hospitals, fishing rods, schools, or electric can openers. That is the meaningful sense in which the dam is costly.

Quite apart from the very important question of how wisely we can combine our resources to produce goods and services, is the very different question of how they get distributed—who gets how many goods? Dollars constitute the claim checks which are distributed among people and which control their share of national output. Dollars are nearly valueless pieces of paper except to the extent that they do represent claim checks to some fraction of the output of goods and services. Viewed as claim checks, all the dollars outstanding during any period of time are worth, in the aggregate, the goods and services that are available to be claimed with them during that period—neither more nor less.

It is far easier to increase the supply of dollars than to increase the production of goods and services—printing dollars is easy. But printing more dollars doesn't help because each dollar then simply becomes a claim to fewer goods, i.e., becomes worth less.

The point is this: many people fall into error upon hearing the statement that the decision to build a dam, or to clean up a river, will cost $X million. It is regrettably easy to say: "It's only money. This is a wealthy country, and we have lots of money." But you cannot build a dam or clean a river with $X million—unless you also have a match, you can't even make a fire. One builds a dam or cleans a river by diverting labor and steel and trucks and factories from making one kind of goods to making another. The cost in dollars is merely a shorthand way of describing the extent of the diversion necessary. If we build a dam for $X million, then we must recognize that we will have $X million less housing and food and medical care and electric can openers as a result.

Similarly, the costs of controlling pollution are best expressed in terms of the other goods we will have to give up to do the job. This is not to say the job should not be done. Badly as we need more housing, more medical care, more can openers, and more symphony orchestras, we could do with somewhat less of them, in my judgment at least, in exchange for somewhat cleaner air and rivers. But that is the nature of the trade-off, and analysis of the problem is advanced if that unpleasant reality is kept in mind. Once the trade-off relationship is clearly perceived, it is possible to state in a very general way what the optimal level of pollution is. I would state it as follows:

People enjoy watching penguins. They enjoy relatively clean air and smog-free vistas. Their health is improved by relatively clean water and air. Each of these benefits is a type of good or service. As a society we would be well advised to give up one washing machine if the resources that would have gone into that washing machine can yield greater human satisfaction when diverted into pollution control. We should give up one hospital if the resources thereby freed would yield more human satisfaction when devoted to elimination of noise in our cities. And so on, trade-off by trade-off, we should divert our productive capacities from the production of existing goods and services to the production of a cleaner, quieter, more pastoral nation up to—and no further than—the point at which we value more highly the next washing machine or hospital that we would have to do without than we value the next unit of environmental improvement that the diverted resources would create.

Now this proposition seems to me unassailable but so general and abstract as to be unhelpful—at least unadministerable in the form stated. It assumes we can measure in some way the incremental units of human satisfaction yielded by very different types of goods. . . . But I insist that the proposition stated describes the result for which we should be striving— and again, that it is always useful to know what your target is even if your weapons are too crude to score a bull's eye.

READING QUESTIONS

1. What are the four goals Baxter proposes in order to develop a solution to the problems of human organization?
2. How does Baxter respond to the objection that it is selfish to act as if one person counts as one unit of importance? Mention at least four of the six reasons he gives in defense of his starting position.
3. What are the four categories of resources mentioned by Baxter? What is the difference between resources and dollars according to Baxter?
4. Explain Baxter's argument for why there is no "morally correct" state of nature to which we should return.
5. What is the ultimate goal toward which we should be striving according to Baxter?

DISCUSSION QUESTIONS

1. Should we go along with Baxter and reject the idea that we should not strive to protect and preserve nature and the environment unless doing so is a benefit to humans?
2. Is there such a thing as an optimal state of pollution? Is Baxter right to claim that part of our goal should be to achieve some optimal state of pollution?
3. What should our goals be regarding nature and the environment other than the one Baxter mentions here?

ALDO LEOPOLD

The Land Ethic

This essay is from the final chapter of Aldo Leopold's classic in environmentalism, *A Sand County Almanac*. Leopold proposes an ecocentric ethic whose basic principle is "A thing is right when it tends to preserve the integrity, stability, and beauty of the biotic community [including soils, waters, plants, animals]. It is wrong when it tends otherwise."

When god-like Odysseus returned from the wars in Troy, he hanged all on one rope a dozen slave-girls of his household whom he suspected of misbehavior during his absence.

This hanging involved no question of propriety. The girls were property. The disposal of property was then, as now, a matter of expediency, not of right and wrong.

Concepts of right and wrong were not lacking from Odysseus' Greece: witness the fidelity of his wife through the long years before at last his black-prowed galleys clove the wine-dark seas for home. The ethical structure of that day covered wives, but had not yet been extended to human chattels. During the three thousand years which have since elapsed, ethical criteria have been extended to many fields of conduct, with corresponding shrinkages in those judged by expediency only.

THE ETHICAL SEQUENCE

This extension of ethics, so far studied only by philosophers, is actually a process in ecological evolution. Its sequences may be described in ecological as well as in philosophical terms. An ethic, ecologically, is a limitation on freedom of action in the struggle for existence. An ethic, philosophically, is a differentiation of social from antisocial conduct. These are two definitions of one thing. The thing has its origin in the tendency of interdependent individuals or groups to evolve modes of co-operation. The ecologist calls these symbioses. Politics and economics are advanced symbioses in which the original free-for-all competition has been replaced, in part, by co-operative mechanisms with an ethical content.

The complexity of co-operative mechanisms has increased with population density, and with the efficiency of tools. It was simpler, for example, to define the antisocial uses of sticks and stones in the days of the mastodons than of bullets and billboards in the age of motors.

The first ethics dealt with the relation between individuals; the Mosaic Decalogue is an example. Later accretions dealt with the relation between the individual and society. The Golden Rule tries to integrate the individual to society; democracy to integrate social organization to the individual.

There is as yet no ethic dealing with man's relation to land and to the animals and plants which grow upon it. Land, like Odysseus' slave-girls, is still property. The land-relation is still strictly economic, entailing privileges but not obligations.

From *A Sand County Almanac, with Other Essays on Conservation from Round River*, Aldo Leopold, Oxford: Oxford University Press (1949, reprinted in 1981). Reprinted by permission of Oxford University Press, Inc.

The extension of ethics to this third element in human environment is, if I read the evidence correctly, an evolutionary possibility and an ecological necessity. It is the third step in a sequence. The first two have already been taken. Individual thinkers since the days of Ezekiel and Isaiah have asserted that the despoliation of land is not only inexpedient but wrong. Society, however, has not yet affirmed their belief. I regard the present conservation movement as the embryo of such an affirmation.

An ethic may be regarded as a mode of guidance for meeting ecological situations so new or intricate, or involving such deferred reactions, that the path of social expediency is not discernible to the average individual. Animal instincts are modes of guidance for the individual in meeting such situations. Ethics are possibly a kind of community instinct in-the-making.

THE COMMUNITY CONCEPT

All ethics so far evolved rest upon a single premise: that the individual is a member of a community of interdependent parts. His instincts prompt him to compete for his place in that community, but his ethics prompt him also to co-operate (perhaps in order that there may be a place to compete for).

The land ethic simply enlarges the boundaries of the community to include soils, waters, plants, and animals, or collectively, the land.

This sounds simple: do we not already sing our love for and obligation to the land of the free and the home of the brave? Yes, but just what and whom do we love? Certainly not the soil, which we are sending helter-skelter downriver. Certainly not the waters, which we assume have no function except to turn turbines, float barges, and carry off sewage. Certainly not the plants, of which we exterminate whole communities without batting an eye. Certainly not the animals, of which we have already extirpated many of the largest and most beautiful species. A land ethic of course cannot prevent the alteration, management, and use of these "resources," but it does affirm their right to continued existence, and, at least in spots, their continued existence in a natural state.

In short, a land ethic changes the role of Homo sapiens from conqueror of the land-community to plain member and citizen of it. It implies respect for his fellow-members, and also respect for the community as such.

In human history, we have learned (I hope) that the conqueror role is eventually self-defeating. Why? Because it is implicit in such a role that the conqueror knows, ex cathedra, just what makes the community clock tick, and just what and who is valuable, and what and who is worthless, in community life. It always turns out that he knows neither, and this is why his conquests eventually defeat themselves.

In the biotic community, a parallel situation exists. Abraham knew exactly what the land was for: it was to drip milk and honey into Abraham's mouth. At the present moment, the assurance with which we regard this assumption is inverse to the degree of our education.

The ordinary citizen today assumes that science knows what makes the community clock tick; the scientist is equally sure that he does not. He knows that the biotic mechanism is so complex that its workings may never be fully understood. . . .

SUBSTITUTES FOR A LAND ETHIC

When the logic of history hungers for bread and we hand out a stone, we are at pains to explain how much the stone resembles bread. I now describe some of the stones which serve in lieu of a land ethic.

One basic weakness in a conservation system based wholly on economic motives is that most members of the land community have no economic value. Wildflowers and songbirds are examples. Of the 22,000 higher plants and animals native to Wisconsin, it is doubtful whether more than 5 percent can be sold, fed, eaten, or otherwise put to economic use. Yet these creatures are members of the biotic community, and if (as I believe) its stability depends on its integrity, they are entitled to continuance.

When one of these non-economic categories is threatened, and if we happen to love it, we invent subterfuges to give it economic importance. At the beginning of the century songbirds were supposed to be disappearing. Ornithologists jumped to the rescue with some distinctly shaky evidence to the effect that insects would eat us up if birds failed to control them. The evidence had to be economic in order to be valid.

It is painful to read these circumlocutions today. We have no land ethic yet, but we have at least drawn nearer the point of admitting that birds should continue as a matter of biotic right, regardless of the presence or absence of economic advantage to us.

A parallel situation exists in respect of predatory mammals, raptorial birds, and fish-eating birds. Time was when biologists somewhat overworked the evidence that these creatures preserve the health of game by killing weaklings, or that they control rodents for the farmer, or that they prey only on "worthless" species. Here again, the evidence had to be economic in order to be valid. It is only in recent years that we hear the more honest argument that predators are members of the community, and that no special interest has the right to exterminate them for the sake of a benefit, real or fancied, to itself. . . .

Some species of trees have been "read out of the party" by economics-minded foresters because they grow too slowly, or have too low a sale value to pay as timber crops: white cedar, tamarack, cypress, beech, and hemlock are examples. In Europe, where forestry is ecologically more advanced, the non-commercial tree species are recognized as members of the native forest community, to be preserved as such, within reason. Moreover, some (like beech) have been found to have a valuable function in building up soil fertility. The interdependence of the forest and its constituent tree species, ground flora, and fauna is taken for granted.

Lack of economic value is sometimes a character not only of species or groups, but of entire biotic communities: marshes, bogs, dunes, and "deserts" are examples. Our formula in such cases is to relegate their conservation to government as refuges, monuments, or parks. The difficulty is that these communities are usually interspersed with more valuable private lands; the government cannot possibly own or control such scattered parcels. The net effect is that we have relegated some of them to ultimate extinction over large areas. . . .

To sum up: a system of conservation based solely on economic self-interest is hopelessly lopsided. It tends to ignore, and thus eventually to eliminate, many elements in the land community that lack commercial value, but that are (as far as we know) essential to its healthy functioning. It assumes, falsely, I think, that the economic parts of the biotic clock will function without the uneconomic parts. . . .

THE LAND PYRAMID

An ethic to supplement and guide the economic relation to land presupposes the existence of some mental image of land as a biotic mechanism. We can be ethical only in relation to something we can see, feel, understand, love, or otherwise have faith in.

The image commonly employed in conservation education is "the balance of nature." For reasons too lengthy to detail here, this figure of speech fails to describe accurately what little we know about the land mechanism. A much truer image is the one employed in ecology: the biotic pyramid. I shall first sketch the pyramid as a symbol of land. . . .

Plants absorb energy from the sun. This energy flows through a circuit called the biota, which may be represented by a pyramid consisting of layers. The bottom layer is the soil. A plant layer rests on the soil, an insect layer on the plants, a bird and rodent layer on the insects, and so on up through various animal groups to the apex layer, which consists of the larger carnivores.

The species of a layer are alike not in where they came from, or in what they look like, but rather in what they eat. Each successive layer depends on those below it for food and often for other services, and each in turn furnishes food and services to those above. Proceeding upward, each successive layer decreases in numerical abundance. Thus, for every carnivore there are hundreds of his prey, thousands of their prey, millions of insects, uncountable plants. The pyramidal form of the system reflects this numerical progression from apex to base. Man shares an intermediate layer with the bears, raccoons, and squirrels which eat both meat and vegetables.

The lines of dependency for food and other services are called food chains. Thus soil-oak-deer-Indian is a chain that has now been largely converted to soil-corn-cow-farmer. Each species, including ourselves, is a link in many chains. The deer eats a hundred plants other than oak, and the cow a hundred plants other than corn. Both, then, are links in a hundred chains. The pyramid is a tangle of chains so complex as to seem disorderly, yet the stability of the system proves it to be a highly organized structure. Its functioning depends on the co-operation and competition of its diverse parts.

In the beginning, the pyramid of life was low and squat, the food chains short and simple. Evolution has added layer after layer, link after link. Man is one of thousands of accretions to the height and complexity of the pyramid. Science has given us many doubts, but it has given us at least one certainty: the trend of evolution is to elaborate and diversify the biota.

Land, then, is not merely soil; it is a fountain of energy flowing through a circuit of soils, plants, and animals. Food chains are the living channels which conduct energy upward; death and decay return it to the soil. The circuit is not closed; some energy is dissipated in decay, some is added by absorption from the air, some is stored in soils, peats, and long-lived forests; but it is a sustained circuit, like a slowly augmented revolving fund of life. There is always a net loss by downhill wash, but this is normally small and offset by the decay of rocks. It is deposited in the ocean and, in the course of geological time, raised to form new lands and new pyramids.

The velocity and character of the upward flow of energy depend on the complex structure of the plant and animal community, much as the upward flow of sap in a tree depends on its complex cellular organization. Without this complexity, normal circulation would presumably not occur. Structure means the characteristic numbers, as well as the characteristic kinds and functions, of the component species. This interdependence between the complex structure of the land and its smooth functioning as an energy unit is one of its basic attributes.

When a change occurs in one part of the circuit, many other parts must adjust themselves to it. Change does not necessarily obstruct or divert the flow of energy; evolution is a long series of self-induced changes, the net result of which has been to elaborate the flow mechanism and to lengthen the circuit. Evolutionary changes, however, are usually slow and local. Man's invention of tools has enabled him to make changes of unprecedented violence, rapidity, and scope. . . .

THE OUTLOOK

It is inconceivable to me that an ethical relation to land can exist without love, respect, and admiration for land, and a high regard for its value. By value, I of course mean something far broader than mere economic value; I mean value in the philosophical sense. . . .

The "key-log" which must be moved to release the evolutionary process for an ethic is simply this: quit thinking about decent land-use as solely an economic problem. Examine each question in terms of what is ethically and esthetically right, as well as what is economically expedient. A thing is right when it tends to preserve the integrity, stability, and beauty of the biotic community. It is wrong when it tends otherwise.

It of course goes without saying that economic feasibility limits the tether of what can or cannot be done for land. It always has and it always will. The fallacy the economic determinists have tied around our collective neck, and which we now need to cast off, is the belief that economics determines *all* land-use. This is simply not true. An innumerable host of actions and attitudes, comprising perhaps the bulk of all land relations, is determined by the land-users' tastes and predilections, rather than by his purse. The bulk of all land relations hinges on investments of time, forethought, skill, and faith rather than on investments of cash. As a land-user thinketh, so is he.

I have purposely presented the land ethic as a product of social evolution because nothing so important as an ethic is ever "written." Only the most superficial student of history supposes that Moses "wrote" the Decalogue; it evolved in the minds of a thinking community, and Moses wrote a tentative summary of it for a "seminar." I say tentative because evolution never stops.

The evolution of a land ethic is an intellectual as well as emotional process. Conservation is paved with good intentions which prove to be futile, or even dangerous, because they are devoid of critical understanding either of the land, or of economic land-use. I think it is a truism that as the ethical frontier advances from the individual to the community, its intellectual content increases.

The mechanism of operation is the same for any ethic: social approbation for right actions; social disapproval for wrong actions.

By and large, our present problem is one of attitudes and implements. We are remodeling the Alhambra with a steamshovel, and we are proud of our yardage. We shall hardly relinquish the shovel, which after all has many good points, but we are in need of gentler and more objective criteria for its successful use.

READING QUESTIONS

1. How does Leopold distinguish an ethic from a philosophical ethic? Explain the ethical sequence in terms of ecological evolution.
2. How does Leopold characterize the idea of a land ethic? What is the main substitute for a land ethic and what are its weaknesses according to Leopold?
3. Explain the land pyramid structure characterized by Leopold. What role does evolution play in this system?
4. How does Leopold suggest we change the way we think about land use?
5. When is an action considered right in Leopold's view?

DISCUSSION QUESTIONS

1. Leopold suggests that economics should not be our only concern when it comes to the use of land. To what extent should economic considerations play a part in our treatment of nature and the environment? Are there any situations in which economic concerns might trump environmental ones?
2. Should we adopt the land ethic suggested by Leopold? What sorts of difficulties might arise if we consider things like soil, water, and plants as members of the same moral community to which we belong?

Thomas E. Hill Jr.

Ideals of Human Excellence and Preserving the Natural Environment

Hill rejects those attempts to explain proper environmental concern that appeal either to rights, to intrinsic value, or to religious considerations. Rather, Hill advocates an alternative to such views that focuses on ideals of human excellence as a basis for understanding proper moral concern for the natural world. In particular, Hill claims that insensitivity to the environment reflects either ignorance, exaggerated self-importance, or a lack of self-acceptance that are crucial for achieving the human excellence of proper humility. Hill's approach to environmental issues can be understood through the lens of a virtue ethics approach.

Recommended Reading: virtue ethics, chap. 1, sec. 2E. Also relevant are consequentialism, chap. 1, sec. 2A, and rights-based moral theory, chap. 1, sec. 2D.

I

A wealthy eccentric bought a house in a neighborhood I know. The house was surrounded by a beautiful display of grass, plants, and flowers, and it was shaded by a huge old avocado tree. But the grass required cutting, the flowers needed tending, and the man wanted more sun. So he cut the whole lot down and covered the yard with asphalt. After all it was his property and he was not fond of plants.

It was a small operation, but it reminded me of the strip mining of large sections of the Appalachians. In both cases, of course, there were reasons for the destruction, and property rights could be cited as justification. But I could not help but wonder, "What sort of person would do a thing like that?"

Many Californians had a similar reaction when a recent governor defended the leveling of ancient redwood groves, reportedly saying, "If you have seen one redwood, you have seen them all."

Incidents like these arouse the indignation of ardent environmentalists and leave even apolitical observers with some degree of moral discomfort. The reasons for these reactions are mostly obvious. Uprooting the natural environment robs both present and future generations of much potential use and enjoyment. Animals too depend on the environment; and even if one does not value animals for their own sakes, their potential utility for us is incalculable. Plants are needed, of course, to replenish the atmosphere quite aside from their aesthetic value. These reasons for hesitating to destroy forests and gardens are not only the most obvious ones, but also the most persuasive for practical purposes. But, one wonders, is there nothing more behind our discomfort? Are we concerned solely about the potential use and enjoyment of the forests, etc., for ourselves, later generations, and perhaps animals? Is there not something else which disturbs us when we witness the destruction or even listen to those who would defend it in terms of cost/benefit analysis?

From Thomas E. Hill Jr., "Ideals of Human Excellence and Preserving the Natural Environment," *Environmental Ethics* 5 (1998). Reprinted by permission.

Imagine that in each of our examples those who would destroy the environment argue elaborately that, even considering future generations of human beings and animals, there are benefits in "replacing" the natural environment which outweigh the negative utilities which environmentalists cite.[1] No doubt we could press the argument on the facts, trying to show that the destruction is shortsighted and that its defenders have underestimated its potential harm or ignored some pertinent rights or interests. But is this all we could say? Suppose we grant, for a moment, that the utility of destroying the redwoods, forests, and gardens is equal to their potential for use and enjoyment by nature lovers and animals. Suppose, further, that we even grant that the pertinent human rights and animal rights, if any, are evenly divided for and against destruction. Imagine that we also concede, for argument's sake, that the forests contain no potentially useful endangered species of animals and plants. Must we then conclude that there is no further cause for moral concern? Should we then feel morally indifferent when we see the natural environment uprooted? . . .

II

The problem, then, is this. We want to understand what underlies our moral uneasiness at the destruction of the redwoods, forests, etc., even apart from the loss of these as resources for human beings and animals. But I find no adequate answer by pursuing the questions, "Are rights or interests of plants neglected,?" "What is God's will on the matter?" and "What is the intrinsic value of the existence of a tree or forest?" My suggestion, which is in fact the main point of this paper, is that we look at the problem from a different perspective. That is, let us turn for a while from the effort to find reasons why certain *acts* destructive of natural environments are morally wrong to the ancient task of articulating our ideals of human excellence. Rather than argue directly with destroyers of the environment who say, "Show me why what I am doing is *immoral*," I want to ask, "What sort of person would want to do what they propose?" The point is not to skirt the issue with an ad hominem, but to raise a different moral question, for even if there is no convincing way to show that the destructive acts are wrong (independently of human and animal use and enjoyment), we may find that the willingness to indulge in them reflects the absence of human traits that we admire and regard morally important.

This strategy of shifting questions may seem more promising if one reflects on certain analogous situations. Consider, for example, the Nazi who asks, in all seriousness. "Why is it wrong for me to make lampshades out of human skin—provided, of course, I did not myself kill the victims to get the skins?" We would react more with shock and disgust than with indignation, I suspect, because it is even more evident that the question reveals a defect in the questioner than that the proposed act is itself immoral. Sometimes we may not regard an act wrong at all though we see it as reflecting something objectionable about the person who does it. Imagine, for example, one who laughs spontaneously to himself when he reads a newspaper account of a plane crash that kills hundreds. Or, again, consider an obsequious grandson who, having waited for his grandmother's inheritance with mock devotion, then secretly spits on her grave when at last she dies. Spitting on the grave may have no adverse consequences and perhaps it violates no rights. The moral uneasiness which it arouses is explained more by our view of the agent than by any conviction that what he did was immoral. Had he hesitated and asked, "Why shouldn't I spit on her grave?" it seems more fitting to ask him to reflect on the sort of person he is than to try to offer reasons why he should refrain from spitting.

III

What sort of person, then, would cover his garden with asphalt, strip mine a wooded mountain, or level an irreplaceable redwood grove? Two sorts of answers, though initially appealing, must be ruled out. The first is that persons who would destroy the environment in these ways are either shortsighted, underestimating the harm they do, or else are too little concerned for the well-being of other people. Perhaps too they have insufficient regard for animal life. But these considerations have been set aside in order to refine the controversy. Another tempting response might be that we count it a moral virtue, or at least a human ideal, to love nature. Those who value the environment only for its utility must not really love nature and so in this way fall short of an ideal. But such an answer is hardly satisfying in the present context, for what is at issue is *why* we feel moral discomfort at the activities of those who admittedly value nature only for its utility. That it is ideal to care for nonsentient nature beyond its possible use is really just another way of expressing the general point which is under controversy.

What is needed is some way of showing that this ideal is connected with other virtues, or human excellences, not in question. To do so is difficult and my suggestions, accordingly, will be tentative and subject to qualification.

The main idea is that, though indifference to nonsentient nature does not *necessarily* reflect the absence of virtues, it often signals the absence of certain traits which we want to encourage because they are, in most cases, a natural basis for the development of certain virtues. It is often thought, for example, that those who would destroy the natural environment must lack a proper appreciation of their place in the natural order, and so must either be ignorant or have too little humility. Though I would argue that this is not necessarily so, I suggest that, given certain plausible empirical assumptions, their attitude may well be rooted in ignorance, a narrow perspective, inability to see things as important apart from themselves and the limited groups they associate with, or reluctance to accept themselves as natural beings. Overcoming these deficiencies will not guarantee a proper moral humility, but for most of us it is probably an important psychological preliminary. . . .

Consider first the suggestion that destroyers of the environment lack an appreciation of their place in the universe. Their attention, it seems, must be focused on parochial matters, on what is, relatively speaking,

close in space and time. They seem not to understand that we are a speck on the cosmic scene, a brief stage in the evolutionary process, only one among millions of species on Earth, and an episode in the course of human history. Of course, they know that there are stars, fossils, insects, and ancient ruins; but do they have any idea of the complexity of the processes that led to the natural world as we find it? Are they aware how much the forces at work within their own bodies are like those which govern all living things and even how much they have in common with inanimate bodies? Admittedly scientific knowledge is limited and no one can master it all; but could one who had a broad and deep understanding of his place in nature really be indifferent to the destruction of the natural environment?

This first suggestion, however, may well provoke a protest from a sophisticated anti-environmentalist. "Perhaps *some* may be indifferent to nature from ignorance," the critic may object, "but *I* have studied astronomy, geology, biology, and biochemistry, and I still unashamedly regard the nonsentient environment as simply a resource for our use. It should not be wasted, of course, but what should be preserved is decidable by weighing long-term costs and benefits." "Besides," our critic may continue, "as philosophers you should know the old Humean formula, 'You cannot derive an *ought* from an *is*.' All the facts of biology, biochemistry, etc., do not entail that I ought to love nature or want to preserve it. What one understands is one thing; what one values is something else. Just as nature lovers are not necessarily scientists, those indifferent to nature are not necessarily ignorant."

Although the environmentalist may concede the critic's logical point, he may well argue that, as a matter of fact, increased understanding of nature tends to heighten people's concern for its preservation. If so, despite the objection, the suspicion that the destroyers of the environment lack deep understanding of nature is not, in most cases, unwarranted, but the argument need not rest here.

The environmentalist might amplify his original idea as follows: "When I said that the destroyers of nature do not appreciate their place in the universe, I was not speaking of intellectual understanding alone, for, after all, a person can *know* a catalog of facts without ever putting them together and seeing vividly the whole picture which they form. To see oneself as just one part of nature is to look at oneself and the world from a certain perspective which is quite different from being able to recite detailed information from the natural sciences. What the destroyers of nature lack is this perspective, not particular information."

Again our critic may object, though only after making some concessions: "All right," he may say, "*some* who are indifferent to nature may lack the cosmic perspective of which you speak, but again there is no *necessary* connection between this failing, if it is one, and any particular evaluative attitude toward nature. In fact, different people respond quite differently when they move to a wider perspective. When *I* try to picture myself vividly as a brief, transitory episode in the course of nature, I simply get depressed. Far from inspiring me with a love of nature, the exercise makes me sad and hostile. You romantics think only of poets like Wordsworth and artists like Turner, but you should consider how differently Omar Khayyám responded when he took your wider perspective. His reaction, when looking at his life from a cosmic viewpoint, was 'Drink up, for tomorrow we die.' Others respond in an almost opposite manner with a joyless Stoic resignation, exemplified by the poet who pictures the wise man, at the height of personal triumph, being served a magnificent banquet, and then consummating his marriage to his beloved, all the while reminding himself, 'Even this shall pass away.'[2] In sum, the critic may object, "Even if one should try to see oneself as one small transitory part of nature, doing so does not dictate any particular normative attitude. Some may come to love nature, but others are moved to live for the moment; some sink into sad resignation; others get depressed or angry. So indifference to nature is not necessarily a sign that a person fails to look at himself from the larger perspective."

The environmentalist might respond to this objection in several ways. He might, for example, argue that even though some people who see themselves as part of the natural order remain indifferent to nonsentient nature, this is not a common reaction. Typically,

it may be argued, as we become more and more aware that we are parts of the larger whole we come to value the whole independently of its effect on ourselves. Thus, despite the possibilities the critic raises, indifference to nonsentient nature is still in most cases a sign that a person fails to see himself as part of the natural order.

If someone challenges the empirical assumption here, the environmentalist might develop the argument along a quite different line. The initial idea, he may remind us, was that those who would destroy the natural environment fail to *appreciate* their place in the natural order. "Appreciating one's place" is not simply an intellectual appreciation. It is also an attitude, reflecting what one values as well as what one knows. When we say, for example, that both the servile and the arrogant person fail to *appreciate* their place in a society of equals, we do not mean simply that they are ignorant of certain empirical facts, but rather that they have certain objectionable attitudes about their importance relative to other people. Similarly, to fail to appreciate one's place in nature is not merely to lack knowledge or breadth of perspective, but to take a certain attitude about what matters. A person who *understands* his place in nature but still views nonsentient nature merely as a resource takes the attitude that nothing is *important* but human beings and animals. Despite first appearances, he is not so much like the pre-Copernican astronomers who made the intellectual error of treating the Earth as the "center of the universe" when they made their calculations. He is more like the racist who, though well aware of other races, treats all races but his own as insignificant.

So construed, the argument appeals to the common idea that awareness of nature typically has, and should have, a humbling effect. The Alps, a storm at sea, the Grand Canyon, towering redwoods, and "the starry heavens above" move many a person to remark on the comparative insignificance of our daily concerns and even of our species, and this is generally taken to be a quite fitting response.[3] What seems to be missing, then, in those who understand nature but remain unmoved is a proper humility.[4] Absence of proper humility is not the same as selfishness or egoism, for one can be devoted to self-interest while still viewing one's own pleasures and projects as trivial and unimportant. And one can have an exaggerated view of one's own importance while grandly sacrificing for those one views as inferior. Nor is the lack of humility identical with belief that one has power and influence, for a person can be quite puffed up about himself while believing that the foolish world will never acknowledge him. The humility we miss seems not so much a belief about one's relative effectiveness and recognition as an attitude which measures the importance of things independently of their relation to oneself or to some narrow group with which one identifies. A paradigm of a person who lacks humility is the self-important emperor who grants status to his family because it is *his,* to his subordinates because *he* appointed them, and to his country because *he* chooses to glorify it. Less extreme but still lacking proper humility is the elitist who counts events significant solely in proportion to how they affect his class. The suspicion about those who would destroy the environment, then, is that what they count important is too narrowly confined insofar as it encompasses only what affects beings who, like us, are capable of feeling.

This idea that proper humility requires recognition of the importance of nonsentient nature is similar to the thought of those who charge meat eaters with "speciesism." In both cases it is felt that people too narrowly confine their concerns to the sorts of beings that are most like them. But, however intuitively appealing, the idea will surely arouse objections from our nonenvironmentalist critic. "Why," he will ask, "do you suppose that the sort of humility I *should* have requires me to acknowledge the importance of nonsentient nature aside from its utility? You cannot, by your own admission, argue that nonsentient nature *is* important, appealing to religious or intuitionist grounds. And simply to assert, without further argument, that an ideal humility requires us to view nonsentient nature as important for its own sake begs the question at issue. If proper humility is acknowledging the relative importance of things as one should, then to show that I must lack this you must first establish that one *should* acknowledge the importance of nonsentient nature."

Though some may wish to accept this challenge, there are other ways to pursue the connection between humility and response to nonsentient nature. For example, suppose we grant that proper humility requires only acknowledging a due status to sentient beings. We must admit, then, that it is logically possible for a person to be properly humble even though he viewed all nonsentient nature simply as a resource. But this logical possibility may be a psychological rarity.

It may be that, given the sort of beings we are, we would never learn humility before persons without developing the general capacity to cherish, and regard important, many things for their own sakes. The major obstacle to humility before persons is self-importance, a tendency to measure the significance of everything by its relation to oneself and those with whom one identifies. The processes by which we overcome self-importance are doubtless many and complex, but it seems unlikely that they are exclusively concerned with how we relate to other people and animals. Learning humility requires learning to feel that something matters besides what will affect oneself and one's circle of associates. What leads a child to care about what happens to a lost hamster or a stray dog he will not see again is likely also to generate concern for a lost toy or a favorite tree where he used to live. Learning to value things for their own sake, and to count what affects them important aside from their utility, is not the same as judging them to have some intuited objective property, but it is necessary to the development of humility and it seems likely to take place in experiences with nonsentient nature as well as with people and animals. If a person views all nonsentient nature merely as a resource, then it seems unlikely that he has developed the capacity needed to overcome self-importance.

IV

This last argument, unfortunately, has its limits. It presupposes an empirical connection between experiencing nature and overcoming self-importance, and this may be challenged. Even if experiencing nature promotes humility before others, there may be other ways people can develop such humility in a world of concrete, glass, and plastic. If not, perhaps all that is needed is limited experience of nature in one's early, developing years; mature adults, having overcome youthful self-importance, may live well enough in artificial surroundings. More importantly, the argument does not fully capture the spirit of the intuition that an ideal person stands humbly before nature. That idea is not simply that experiencing nature tends to foster proper humility before other people; it is, in part, that natural surroundings encourage and are appropriate to an ideal sense of oneself as part of the natural world. Standing alone in the forest, after months in the city, is not merely good as a means of curbing one's arrogance before others; it reinforces and fittingly expresses one's acceptance of oneself as a natural being.

Previously we considered only one aspect of proper humility, namely, a sense of one's relative importance with respect to other human beings. Another aspect, I think, is a kind of *self-acceptance*. This involves acknowledging, in more than a merely intellectual way, that we are the sort of creatures that we are. Whether one is self-accepting is not so much a matter of how one attributes *importance* comparatively to oneself, other people, animals, plants, and other things as it is a matter of understanding, facing squarely, and responding appropriately to who and what one is, e.g., one's powers and limits, one's affinities with other beings and differences from them, one's unalterable nature and one's freedom to change. Self-acceptance is not merely intellectual awareness, for one can be intellectually aware that one is growing old and will eventually die while nevertheless behaving in a thousand foolish ways that reflect a refusal to acknowledge these facts. On the other hand, self-acceptance is not passive resignation, for refusal to pursue what one truly wants within one's limits is a failure to accept the freedom and power one has. Particular behaviors, like dying one's gray hair and dressing like those 20 years younger, do not *necessarily* imply lack of self-acceptance, for there could be reasons for acting in these ways other than the wish to hide from oneself what one really is. One fails to accept oneself when the patterns of behavior and emotion are rooted in a desire to disown and deny features of oneself, to pretend to oneself that they are not there. This is not to say that

a self-accepting person makes no value judgments about himself, that he likes all facts about himself, wants equally to develop and display them; he can, and should feel remorse for his past misdeeds and strive to change his current vices. The point is that he does not disown them, pretend that they do not exist or are facts about something other than himself. Such pretense is incompatible with proper humility because it is seeing oneself as better than one is.

Self-acceptance of this sort has long been considered a human excellence, under various names, but what has it to do with preserving nature? There is, I think, the following connection. As human beings we are part of nature, living, growing, declining, and dying by natural laws similar to those governing other living beings; despite our awesomely distinctive human powers, we share many of the needs, limits, and liabilities of animals and plants. These facts are neither good nor bad in themselves, aside from personal preference and varying conventional values. To say this is to utter a truism which few will deny, but to accept these facts, as facts about oneself, is not so easy—or so common. Much of what naturalists deplore about our increasingly artificial world reflects, and encourages, a denial of these facts, an unwillingness to avow them with equanimity.

Like the Victorian lady who refuses to look at her own nude body, some would like to create a world of less transitory stuff, reminding us only of our intellectual and social nature, never calling to mind our affinities with "lower" living creatures. The "denial of death," to which psychiatrists call attention, reveals an attitude incompatible with the sort of self-acceptance which philosophers, from the ancients to Spinoza and on, have admired as a human excellence. My suggestion is not merely that experiencing nature causally promotes such self-acceptance, but also that those who fully accept themselves as part of the natural world lack the common drive to disassociate themselves from nature by replacing natural environments with artificial ones. A storm in the wilds helps us to appreciate our animal vulnerability, but, equally important, the reluctance to experience it may *reflect* an unwillingness to accept this aspect of ourselves. The person who is too ready to destroy the ancient redwoods may lack humility, not so much in the sense that he exaggerates his importance relative to others, but rather in the sense that he tries to avoid seeing himself as one among many natural creatures. . . .

NOTES

I thank Gregory Kavka, Catherine Harlow, the participants at a colloquium at the University of Utah, and the referees for *Environmental Ethics,* Dale Jamieson and Donald Scherer, for helpful comments on earlier drafts of this paper.

1. When I use the expression "the natural environment," I have in mind the sort of examples with which I began. There is also a broad sense, as Hume and Mill noted, in which all that occurs, miracles aside, is "natural." As will be evident, I shall use "natural" in a narrower, more familiar sense.

2. T. Tildon, "Even This Shall Pass Away," in *The Best Loved Poems of the American People,* ed. Hazel Felleman (Garden City, New York: Doubleday, 1936).

3. An exception, apparently, was Kant, who thought "the starry heavens" sublime and compared them with "the moral law within," but did not for all that see our species as comparatively insignificant.

4. By "proper humility" I mean that sort and degree of humility that is a morally admirable character trait. How precisely to define this is, of course, a controversial matter; but the point for present purposes is just to set aside obsequiousness, false modesty, underestimation of one's abilities, and the like.

READING QUESTIONS

1. What is Hill's "strategy," mentioned in section II, for addressing cases that involve problematic treatment of the environment?
2. Why does Hill think that pointing to the shortsightedness or lack of proper concern with other people and animals does not really help explain what is morally problematic about the person who would cover his garden with asphalt, strip mine a wooded mountain, or level an irreplaceable redwood grove?
3. How does Hill understand the attitude of humility? What role does proper humility play in the case Hill makes for acknowledging the importance of nonsentient nature? How, according to Hill, does one learn to become humble?
4. Another theme in Hill's essay is the importance of self-acceptance. What does Hill mean by self-acceptance? How does he connect self-acceptance with preserving nature?

DISCUSSION QUESTIONS

1. Should we agree with Hill that considerations of self-acceptance are important in thinking about how we ought to treat the environment?
2. How might a utilitarian respond to Hill's appeals to humility and self-acceptance in explaining what is wrong with the person who would pave over his front yard in asphalt? Can a utilitarian appeal to these same sorts of considerations (humility and self-acceptance) in explaining on utilitarian grounds what is wrong with the person who paves over his garden? If so, would there be any significant difference between the views of Hill and the utilitarian with regard to how they would explain what is morally problematic about destroying (within one's rights) some part of the environment?

PETER WENZ

Synergistic Environmental Virtues: Consumerism and Human Flourishing

Wenz argues that consumerism—the ideology of maximizing consumption without limit—leads to various social harms affecting not only residents of third world countries, but people who live in industrialized countries as well. He then proceeds to argue that consumerism promotes the traditional vices of greed, avarice, envy, and gluttony, while such traditional virtues as frugality and temperance oppose this ideology and promote human flourishing. He further argues that both anthropocentric and nonanthropocentric approaches to environmental ethics offer, in their own distinctive ways, complementary support to the traditional virtues as well as opposition to the traditional vices.

Recommended Reading: virtue ethics, chap. 1, sec. 2E.

There is no conflict at this time between anthropocentric and nonanthropocentric goals in the moral development of people in industrial countries. Exercising the traditional virtues of frugality, appreciation, temperance, self-development, dedication, benevolence, generosity, empathy, and justice fosters human flourishing around the world and protects nature. Traditional vices, on the other hand, including six of the seven deadly sins—greed, avarice, gluttony, envy, luxury, and pride—as well as intemperance, selfishness, and indifference, foster lifestyles among current industrial people that diminish human well-being and harm the environment. The linchpin is consumerism, as currently understood and practiced in industrial countries, because it relies on vices that harm both people and nature. Traditional virtues oppose such consumerism.

I begin by defining consumerism and illustrating its harmful environmental effects. I argue next that consumerism harms poor people in the Third World.

I then contend that it harms industrial people. Finally, I argue that consumerism promotes and relies on the cultivation of traditional vices whereas traditional virtues foster human flourishing and environmental protection.

If I am correct about consumerism, then nonanthropocentric environmentalists have reasons to favor traditional virtues because their exercise tends to protect the nonhuman environment. Anthropocentrists have reason to support the same virtues because their exercise promotes human flourishing. Nonanthropocentric and anthropocentric considerations regarding human virtue and vice are thus mutually reinforcing. Each is stronger in combination with the other than alone, a relationship I define as synergistic.[1] In addition, if I am correct, defenders of traditional virtues have reason to embrace nonanthropocentric environmentalism because it supports many traditional virtues. I conclude by suggesting how synergistic environmental virtues should be manifest in practice.

CONSUMERISM HARMS THE ENVIRONMENT

Current environmental problems stem largely from consumerism in industrial countries, such as the United States. Consuming goods and services is not the problem. Human beings, like all living systems, require material throughput. We need food, clothing, shelter, and, because we are culture-oriented primates, education. Many products of modern technology make life easier or more fun, such as washing machines, CD players, trains, and cars. Consumerism differs from the consumption of such items, however, in treating consumption as good in itself. Consumerism is the ideology that society should maximize consumption, pursue consumption without limit.

Consumerism dominates American politics. No candidate for national office ever suggests maintaining or reducing the American economy. Everyone supports economic growth. The economy is never large enough. Life would be better if more people had more jobs producing more goods and services and earning more money to spend on consumption. "Enough" is politically subversive in a consumerism-dominated culture.

Attempts at unlimited consumption, pursued as an end in itself, degrade the environment. Global warming, for example, threatens species with extinction because of rapid climate change.[2] The warming results primarily from increased emissions of greenhouse gases, such as carbon dioxide. The United States, with less than 5 percent of the world's population, emits 24 percent of carbon into the atmosphere, caused significantly by consumer preference for gas-guzzling light trucks and sport utility vehicles (SUVs).[3] Such vehicles promote economic growth more than efficient alternatives—fuel-efficient cars and public transportation—through increased gasoline sales and required expansion of parking facilities. Commitment to unlimited economic growth favors inefficient transportation that threatens biodiversity through global warming.

Consumerism harms nonhumans in other ways as well: "Aquatic songbirds, called dippers, for example, disappear from stream waters acidified by pine plantations and acid rain."[4] Pine plantations are monocultures created to serve a growing market for wood pulp and building materials. The size of the average American home increased more than 50 percent between the 1960s and the 1990s, adding to economic growth and to the demand for building materials from pine plantations.[5] Acid rain results primarily from burning fossil fuels rich in sulfur, most often to generate electricity to run increasing numbers of electric appliances and air conditioners. The economy grows when people build larger houses, buy and use more appliances, and use more air conditioning. But pine plantations and acid rain harm the environment and endanger many species.

Development economist David Korten explains why environmental decline tends to accompany the rise in production required by increasing consumption: "About 70 percent of this productivity growth has been in...economic activity accounted for by the petroleum, petrochemical, and metal industries; chemical-intensive agriculture; public utilities; road building; transportation; and mining—specifically, the industries that are most rapidly drawing down natural capital, generating the bulk of our most toxic waste, and consuming a substantial portion of our nonrenewable energy."[6] Environmental researcher Alan Durning agrees that consumer-oriented societies are most responsible for impairing environmental quality: "Industrial countries' factories generate most of the world's hazardous chemical wastes....The fossil fuels that power the consumer society are its most ruinous input. Wresting coal, oil, and natural gas from the earth permanently disrupts countless habitats; burning them causes an overwhelming share of the world's air pollution; and refining them generates huge quantities of toxic wastes."[7]

CONSUMERISM HARMS POOR PEOPLE IN THE THIRD WORLD

Anthropocentrists would not care that environmental decline accompanies consumerism so long as people flourish. Advocates of global free market capitalism, such as Thomas Friedman, believe that growing economies will help all people in the long run, so consumerism, the engine of economic growth in capitalist societies, is good for people. He writes: "When it comes to the question of which system today is the most effective at generating rising standards of living, the historical debate is over. The answer is free-market capitalism.... In the end, if you want higher standards of living in a world without walls, the free market is the only ideological alternative left."[8] And all people can share in the cornucopia, according to Friedman:

> Countries...can now increasingly choose to be prosperous. They don't have to be prisoners of their natural resources, geography or history. In a world where a country can plug into the Internet and import knowledge, in a world where a country can find shareholders from any other country to invest in its infrastructure..., where a country can import the technology to be an auto producer or computer maker even if it has no raw materials, a country can more than ever before opt for prosperity or poverty, depending on the policies it pursues.[9]

Unfortunately, Friedman is wrong. The whole world cannot consume at the level of citizens of industrial nations. Friedman seems to have missed the difference between *anyone* being able to do something and *everyone* being able to do it. If I order twenty texts for a class of twenty-five students, anyone could have bought the book at the university store, but everyone could not. Similarly, even if Friedman were correct that any country may become rich like industrial countries (which is already problematic), environmental limits preclude most of the world's people living consumer lifestyles. David Korten writes: "If the earth's sustainable natural output were shared equally among the earth's present population, the needs of all could be met. But it is...clear that it is a physical impossibility, even with the most optimistic assumptions about the potential of new technologies, for the world to consume at levels even approximating those in North America, Europe, and Japan."[10] According to environmental researchers Mia MacDonald and Danielle Nierenberg, "If every person alive today consumed at the rate of an average person in the United States, three more planets would be required to fulfill these demands."[11]

Korten cites a study by William Rees, an urban planner at the University of British Columbia: "Rees estimates that four to six hectares of land are required to maintain the consumption of the average person living in a high-income country—including the land required to maintain current levels of energy consumption using renewable sources. Yet in 1990, the total available ecologically productive land area (land capable of generating consequential biomass) in the world was only an estimated 1.7 hectares per capita."[12] What is worse, the world's human population is expected to increase more than 50 percent over its 1990 level by 2050, whereas Earth remains stubbornly resistant to growth.[13]

This environmental analysis suggests what international economists actually observe: economic globalization, intended to increase world economic growth so that everyone can be prosperous consumers, impoverishes many people in the Third World. Some examples illustrate how this occurs. One goal of consumer society is to grow food efficiently so that more resources are available for optional consumer items. The United States often claims to have the world's most efficient agriculture because less than 2 percent of the population is engaged directly in farming.[14] Agricultural research to improve efficiency resulted in the high-yield varieties (HYVs) of wheat and rice behind the Green Revolution of the 1960s and 1970s.

Agriculture and food security are central to many Third World countries. HYVs were marketed to the Third World partly out of humanitarian concern for human nutrition and partly to make a profit from the sale of agricultural inputs. Such sales help the economy grow. The unintended result, however, was to impoverish many people in the Third World, explains Vandana Shiva, a physicist and the director of the Research Foundation for Science, Technology and Natural Resource Policy in India. HYVs yielded substantially more cash crops of wheat and rice per hectare than traditional varieties, which helped the economy to grow. But HYVs require much more water per bushel. Unfortunately, many poor countries, including India, suffer from water shortage. So

HYVs required deeper wells, which only relatively wealthy farmers could afford. With more water being pumped, water tables lowered beyond the reach of poor farmers, who could no longer get enough water even for traditional varieties. Many farmers lost their farms and became landless peasants seeking work.

HYVs also need more artificial fertilizer than traditional varieties. This again helped the economy grow but limited access to poorer farmers who could not afford such fertilizer. Worse yet, the fertilizer made *bathau*, a wild plant freely harvested for its vitamin A, a weed that threatened cash crops. Herbicides, another bought input that spurs economic growth, became necessary. Not only could poor farmers ill afford herbicides, but the intended result of their application, killing *bathau*, deprived many poor people of a free source of vitamin A. As a result, tens of thousands of children in India go blind each year for lack of vitamin A.

Dependence on free sources of food and materials is common in the Third World. Equally common is their reduction by globalization efforts aimed at turning traditional societies into "emerging markets." Worldwatch researcher Aaron Sachs compares rural Thailand with areas in the Amazon rain forest:

> Many of the villagers, like the peoples of the Amazon rainforest, used to derive their income from forest products—charcoal, bamboo shoots, wild mushrooms, squirrels, even edible toads. Small-scale subsistence farmers also depended on the forests to provide breaks against soil erosion and to regulate natural irrigation systems.
>
> Because they get much of what they need free, traditional peasants add little to the GDP of Thailand. In addition, they are too poor to buy goods produced in industrial countries, so they add little to the economic growth that consumerism requires. Thailand is better integrated into a consumer-oriented world economy when its land is taken from peasants, its trees are sold to logging interests, and its agriculture produces goods for export.
>
> But logging projects...have laid waste to the area's hillsides over the last three decades. Economists often point to Thailand as a clear success—and the country's lucrative exports, consisting mostly of agricultural products grown on previously forested land, have certainly helped boost the Thai economy....However..., the poorest people...lost...their livelihoods.[15]

Shiva similarly criticizes monocultural commercial forestry in India for depriving poor people of free forest products:

> An important biomass output of trees that is never assessed by foresters who look for timber and wood is the yield of seeds and fruits. Fruit trees such as jack, jaman, mango, tamarind etc. have been important components of indigenous forms of social forestry as practiced over the centuries in India.... Other trees, such as neem, pongamia and sal provide annual harvests of seeds which yield non-edible oils.... The coconut,... besides providing fruits and oil, provides leaves used in thatching huts and supports the large coir industry.[16]

David Korten gives examples of Third World industrialization that fosters economic growth as measured in purely monetary terms, ties poor countries ever closer to global consumerism, and is supposed to help the world's poor. In each case, however, such development harms poor people more than it helps them. Japan, for instance, wanting to avoid domestic pollution from smelting copper, financed the Philippine Associated Smelting and Refining Corporation:

> The plant occupies 400 acres of land expropriated by the Philippine government from local residents at give-away prices. Gas and wastewater emissions from the plant contain high concentrations of boron, arsenic, heavy metals, and sulfur compounds that have contaminated local water supplies, reduced fishing and rice yields, damaged the forest, and increased the occurrence of upper-respiratory diseases among local residents. Local people...are now largely dependent on the occasional part-time or contractual employment they are offered to do the plant's most dangerous and dirtiest jobs.
>
> The company has prospered. The local economy has grown.... The Philippine government is repaying the foreign aid loan from Japan that financed the construction of supporting infrastructure for the plant. And the Japanese are congratulating themselves for...their generous assistance to the poor of the Philippines.[17]

Korten claims that this case is typical of Third World industrialization:

> Rapid economic growth in low-income countries brings modern airports, television, express highways, and air-conditioned shopping malls...for the fortunate few. It rarely improves living conditions for the many. This

kind of growth requires gearing the economy toward exports to earn the foreign exchange to buy the things that wealthy people desire. Thus, the lands of the poor are appropriated for export crops. The former tillers of these lands find themselves subsisting in urban slums on starvation wages paid by sweatshops producing for export. Families are broken up, the social fabric is strained to the breaking point, and violence becomes endemic.[18]

And Aaron Sachs discusses one effect of desperate poverty and social disruption brought on by integrating traditional societies into the consumer-oriented global economy—child prostitution:

> Brazil alone has between 250,000 and 500,000 children involved in the sex trade, and a recent study conducted by the Bogota Chamber of Commerce concluded that the number of child prostitutes in the Colombian capital had nearly trebled over the past three years.... But the center of the child sex industry is Asia: children's advocacy groups assert that there are about 60,000 child prostitutes in the Philippines, about 400,000 in India, and about 800,000 in Thailand.[19]

Income and nutrition statistics also indicate that integrating Third World countries into the economic system that supports First World consumerism hurts the world's poor:

> In 1960, the per capita gross domestic product (GDP) in the 20 richest countries was 18 times that in the 20 poorest countries, according to the World Bank. By 1995 the gap between the richest and poorest nations had more than doubled—to 37 times.
>
> To a large extent, these vast income gaps drive global consumption patterns. Disproportionate consumption by the world's rich often creates pollution, waste, and environmental damage that harm the world's poor. For example, growing demand for fish for non-food uses, mainly animal feed and oils, is diminishing the source of low-cost, high-protein nutrition for a billion of the world's poor people.[20]

In the year 2000, at least 1.2 billion people were hungry, and roughly half the human population lacked sufficient vitamins and minerals.[21] The World Health Organization reports that six million people die each year as a result of hunger and malnutrition.[22]

Environmental change brought on by consumerism could exacerbate this problem. Although global warming is not yet responsible for hunger and malnutrition, a one-meter rise in sea level, which such warming may cause, would inundate much cropland used by poor people for subsistence.[23] Global warming is also expected to lower soil moisture during the growing season in the world's breadbaskets—the U.S. Great Plains, Western Europe, northern Canada, and Siberia—reducing yields and increasing the price of grain in world markets beyond the means of many people in the Third World.[24]

In sum, First World consumerism tends to harm people in the Third World, except for local elites. The environment could never support industrial lifestyles for all humanity, so the promise of currently poor people living consumer lifestyles is chimerical. Second, the pattern of development in Third World countries that ties those lands to consumerism in industrial countries tends to benefit only local elites and leave the vast majority much worse off than before, both materially and socially. Finally, gross statistics show that on balance consumerism increases income gaps between the world's rich and poor and jeopardizes food supplies for the poor.

CONSUMERISM HARMS INDUSTRIAL PEOPLE

Industrial people suffer from consumerism because it fosters perpetual discontent, social isolation, and depression. Here is how. A consumer society must have a growing economy to provide jobs and incomes needed for more consumption. Advertising whets people's appetites for consumption. Radio talk show host Dave Ramsey writes in his 1999 book *More Than Enough* that these ads work largely by sowing discontent: "Professional marketers and advertisers understand that they have to point out a need to you so you will recognize a need you didn't know you had. When you recognize that need, [a] process...has started [that] will end in frustration and finally purchase.... If you are a good marketer or advertiser your job is to bring dissonance or a disturbance to the person receiving your message.... That is the essence of marketing, to create an emotional disturbance."[25]...

Discontent also motivates consumers to work more hours to earn the money needed for desired purchases. One result is social isolation because people have less time for leisure, friends, and family. As a social species, people flourish only when they have close personal relationships, but the work time that consumerism demands interferes with such relationships. Ramsey writes:

> A workaholic gerbil in a wheel invented the stupid phrase "quality time." There is no question that quantity time is what is needed to develop strong fruitful relationships. We are failing miserably in this culture by not slowing down enough to enjoy each other....
>
> When I was growing up in the sixties, my mom would often be at a neighbor's kitchen table having a cup of coffee at midmorning while the kids played....The evenings would find half the neighborhood gathered on a deck or patio to enjoy a night of interaction. We camped together, the men fished together, and as a kid you could get your butt busted by any adult in the neighborhood. There was a real sense of community.
>
> What has stolen our ability to find those luxurious hours to invest in family and friends? Several things have stolen that time. We are so marketed to that we have started to believe that more stuff will make us happy. But in this country, more stuff has resulted in more debt. What debt means is that we end up spending our every waking hour working to pay off our bills.[26]

Vicki Robin and Joe Dominguez, authors of the bestseller *Your Money or Your Life* concur: "It would seem that the primary 'thing' many people have sacrificed in 'going for the gold' is their relationships with other people. Whether you think of that as a happy marriage, time with the children, neighborliness, a close circle of friends, shopkeepers who know you, civic involvement, community spirit, or just living in a place where you can walk to work and the beat cop is your friend, it's disappearing across the country."[27]...

Consumer items can also impair the sense of community. Air conditioning is one example. Older homes had porches, which were the coolest spots on hot summer days. Neighbors talked or visited porch to porch while avoiding indoor heat. Now people remain in their houses, isolated from neighbors, to avoid the heat. Air conditioning is wonderful and a lifesaver for some, but it does detract from a sense of community.

The car is [an] example. Cars are here to stay, but that does not tell us how many we should have or how best to use them. Cars have enabled people to move to suburbs where they live farther from neighbors and where neighbors commute in different directions to their respective jobs. The economy grows because more production is needed per capita when each person has his and her own car. "By 1990," [Robert] Putman notes, "America had more cars than drivers." What is more, "the fraction of us who travel to work in a private vehicle rose from 61 percent in 1960 to 91 percent in 1995, while all other forms of commuting...declined."[28] Unlike private vehicle commuting, public transportation and walking foster the kind of community involvement that people need to flourish. As Putnam found:

> The car and the commute...are demonstrably bad for community life. In round numbers the evidence suggests that *each additional ten minutes in daily commuting time cuts involvement in community affairs by 10 percent*—fewer public meetings attended, fewer committees chaired, fewer petitions signed, fewer church services attended, less volunteering, and so on....
>
> Strikingly, increased commuting time among the residents of a community lowers average levels of civic involvement even among noncommuters.[29]

Gary Gardner, the director of research for the Worldwatch Institute, cites research showing that consumerism does not foster human flourishing. He notes

> the failure of advanced industrial societies to deliver widely their most hyped product: well-being, or happiness. Studies of societal happiness show that income growth and happiness, which once marched upward together, have been uncoupled. In the United States, for example, the share of people describing themselves as "very happy" declined from 35 percent in 1957 to 30 percent today [2001], despite a more than doubling of income per person. For many of us, it seems, the more we ask consumption to fill our lives, the emptier we feel.[30]

Increasing rates of depression also show that the social isolation that consumerism fosters interferes with human flourishing: "Today, a quarter of Americans live alone, up from 8 percent in 1940, and at least 20 percent of the population is estimated to have poor mental health. By contrast, the Old Order Amish people of ... Pennsylvania, who have a strong community life made possible in part by their car-free, electricity-free lifestyles, suffer depression at less than one-fifth the rate of people in nearby Baltimore."[31].... So in sum, consumerism degrades the environment, further impoverishes poor people in the Third World, and impairs the ability of industrial people to lead fulfilling lives.

CONSUMERISM PROMOTES RECOGNIZED VICES

In 1956 Lewis Mumford pointed out a transformation in accepted virtues and vices that accompanies industrial civilization: "Observe what happened to the seven deadly sins of Christian theology. All but one of these sins, sloth, was transformed into a positive virtue. Greed, avarice, envy, gluttony, luxury and pride were the driving forces of the new economy: if once they were mainly the vices of the rich, they now under the doctrine of expanding wants embrace every class in [industrial] society."[32] Consumer society cultivates *greed*, the unlimited desire for more. Without greed consumer demand would flag, the economy would slump, and people would lose their jobs. *Avarice*, an inordinate desire for wealth, is implied by greed. People who want more and more of what money can buy desire unlimited amounts of money.

Gluttony is excessive food consumption. It seems that immoderate consumerism spawns overeating Worldwatch researchers Gary Gardner and Brian Halweil report:

Today [2000] it is more common than not for American adults to be overweight: 55 percent....Moreover, the share of American adults who are obese has climbed from 15 to 23 percent just since 1980. And one out of five American children are now overweight or obese, a 50 percent increase in the last two decades.

Treating the effects of obesity in the United States...costs more than $100 billion annually—more than 10 percent of the nation's bill for healthcare.[33]

In England adult obesity doubled during the 1990s to 16 percent.[34]

Envy is essential in a consumer society. Advertisers portray people with a product as having a better life than those without it. Consumers must envy the life of those with the product, or they would not buy it. Envy must often be strong enough to motivate hard work or long working hours to afford the product.

Pride is a factor in such motivation. Advertisers invite consumers to take pride in their ability to afford expensive or attractive goods and services. Ads often show others admiring a new car, window treatment, or hair color. If the item is a true *luxury*, then pride is enhanced. Luxury is no vice in a consumer society because, after all, you are worth it....

Sloth is the only one of the seven deadly sins that is not considered a virtue in a consumer society, perhaps because people must work more and more hours to produce the increasing volume of goods and services that consumerism requires. In addition to making virtues of what medieval Christians considered vices, consumerism fosters character traits that most people consider vices today. These include intemperance, selfishness, and indifference.

Intemperance is a lack of moderation or restraint. Consumerism cultivates and relies on intemperate consumers when economic growth rests in part on rich people creating jobs for others by, for example, building $2 million houses with six bedrooms for only two people. Even more consumers buy SUVs that are far larger than they need, cars with "performance" designed for professional racing, and mountain-climbing all-terrain vehicles to use in the flat Midwest. (Whose corn or soybean field do they imagine driving through?)

Selfishness is insufficient regard for the welfare of others. Consumerism fosters selfishness along with envy and greed. Envious people want the jobs, income, luxuries, recognition, and so forth that others have. They habitually compare themselves with those who have more and lament or resent their inferior position. This catalyzes greed. Such people have little mental energy to compare themselves with those who have less, so they tend selfishly to ignore occasions for helping the poor: hence the continuing appeal of middle-class tax cuts that reduce government programs needed by poor people.

As the tax cut example suggests, *indifference* follows selfishness. As people become more preoccupied with themselves, they pay less attention to other people's needs. Dramatic evidence comes from First World consumer indifference to the plight of poor people in the Third World who increasingly produce what we wear. According to David Korten, the footwear company Nike, for example,

> leaves production [of its shoes] in the hands of some 75,000 workers hired by independent contractors. Most of the outsourced production takes place in Indonesia, where a pair of Nikes that sells in the United States or Europe for $73 to $135 is produced for about $5.60 by girls and young women paid as little as fifteen cents an hour. The workers are housed in company barracks, there are no unions, overtime is often mandatory, and if there is a strike, the military may be called to break it up. The $20 million that basketball star Michael Jordan reportedly received in 1992 for promoting Nike shoes exceeded the entire annual payroll of the Indonesian factories that made them.[35]

This is typical, yet American consumers are so preoccupied with "stuff" that they ignore information about the near slave conditions of production that keep prices low. At the same time, however, our culture condemns the indifference of Germans during World War II who failed to help Jews. This is perverse. Opposing Nazi policies could be harmful to your health; buying domestically manufactured clothing is perfectly safe.

TRADITIONAL VIRTUES OPPOSE CONSUMERISM AND PROMOTE HUMAN FLOURISHING

Traditional virtues inhibit the consumerism that impairs human flourishing and degrades the environment. Consider *frugality*, which is, write Robin and Dominguez, "getting good *value* for every minute of your life energy and from everything you *have the use of*.... Waste lies not in the number of possessions but in the failure to enjoy them.... To be frugal means to have a high joy-to-stuff ratio. If you get one unit of joy for each material possession, that's frugal. But if you need ten possessions to even begin registering on the joy meter, you're missing the point of being alive."[36] Such frugality is closely allied to *appreciation*, the ability to appreciate and enjoy what you have. People who joyfully appreciate what they have are less likely to envy people who have more. They avoid the frustration and anger characteristic of envy and live happily without the compulsive consumption inherent in consumerism. Without compulsive consumption, they have fewer worries about money and more time to spend in meaningful relationships with family and friends. It is a win–win–win–win thing.

Temperance is another traditional virtue that opposes consumerism. When people have a sense of what is enough, they are more rational consumers. They have houses that are big enough but not so big as to waste space, money, and natural resources. Temperate consumers know when to stop eating, when they have enough clothing, and when a fancy wine is just too expensive. Advertisers and neoclassical economists oppose temperance. According to the economic theory dominant in consumer societies, people's wants are infinite, and there is no distinction between wants and needs, so any want can be considered a need. Hence, people are continually frustrated because they cannot have all that they are induced to think they need.

Practicing frugality, appreciation, and temperance creates opportunities to exercise another traditional virtue, *self-development*. At least some of the time saved from working to afford items that give little joy can be used to develop hobbies and skills. People can learn to play tennis, play the guitar, speak a foreign language, or knit. The sense of accomplishment from personal improvement in such pursuits cannot be bought. Of course, these pursuits also require some consumption, but it is not compulsive consumption. Practicing most sports and hobbies is much less expensive than acquiring material goods without sense or limit, especially when self-development is combined with frugality, appreciation, and temperance.

Dedication is another traditional virtue that stands between self-development and overconsumption. People who go quickly from one activity to another without the dedication needed for a reasonable chance of improvement or success may become major consumers of equipment, books, materials, and training. Embarking on a new activity often requires many purchases. On the other hand, those who, after some trial and error, dedicate themselves for years to one or more projects of self-development find long-term joy in the same books, equipment, and instruction. Such people tend to avoid overconsumption, especially, again, when their dedication is combined with frugality, appreciation, and temperance so that they avoid dedication to inherently wasteful or environmentally destructive pursuits, such as off-road racing.

People who avoid compulsive consumption find it easier to practice the virtue of *generosity* because they are not living on the edge of bankruptcy and can more easily live without the money and possessions that compete with generosity for personal resources. The possibility of generosity, in turn, promotes *empathy* with the plight of less fortunate people. Overspent and overworked Americans find empathy difficult because, lacking the means to be helpful (money and time), their insight into other people's troubles, which can be painful for anyone, is unrelieved by the joy of participating in improvement. Frugal, appreciative, and temperate people, by contrast, have the resources to be helpful and therefore the incentive to empathize with and help those less fortunate than themselves. The virtue of dedication can be used in projects of *benevolence* motivated by empathy.

Dedicated, empathic people engaged in projects of benevolence avoid the twin vices of indifference and injustice. Empathy itself opposes indifference. Injustice often results from people taking advantage of others, directly or indirectly, knowingly or unknowingly, as when Americans buy inexpensive clothing produced by child or near-slave labor. People whose sense of self-worth is tied to the amount of "stuff" they own resist paying the higher prices needed if workers are to receive just wages. By contrast, frugal, appreciative, temperate consumers can make justice a condition of purchase. Working conditions will improve in the Third World if enough consumers exercise these virtues.

TRADITIONAL VIRTUES AND ENVIRONMENTALISM ARE MUTUALLY REINFORCING

I have argued that traditional virtues oppose consumerism and that consumerism is a major impediment to human flourishing and a major cause of environmental degradation. This makes traditional virtues an ally of both anthropocentrism and nonanthropocentric environmentalism. It means that anthropocentrism and nonanthropocentrism are mutually supporting through their different but complementary support for many traditional virtues and their different but complementary opposition to many traditional vices.

Imagine an anthropocentrist who is most interested in human flourishing. If the arguments given above are correct, such a person should promote traditional virtues as a means to human flourishing. At the same time, the exercise of these virtues will reduce human consumption and associated environmental degradation, a result favored on other grounds by nonanthropocentrists (who consider nature valuable in itself).

Now imagine a nonanthropocentric environmentalist who values nature for itself. She can argue that nonanthropocentrism among industrial people at this time calls for reduced consumption and therefore opposition to consumerism. If the arguments given above are correct, then consumerism is effectively opposed by traditional virtues, so the environmentalist has a nonanthropocentrically based argument for traditional virtues. These arguments reinforce anthropocentrically based arguments for these virtues. There is synergy here because the two sets of arguments for environment-friendly traditional virtues are stronger together than either set is alone.

An illustration may help to clarify the point. Consider nonanthropocentrists opposed to people driving gas-guzzling SUVs because such vehicles contribute greatly to rapid climate change that threatens many species with extinction. Such nonanthropocentrists have reason to oppose the vices of envy, pride, luxury, indifference, and selfishness because these vices are implicated in decisions to own SUVs. Advertisements for SUVs induce envy. Drivers take pride in owning a vehicle larger and more expensive than most others on the road. SUV owners seek the luxury of extra room in the vehicle and are selfishly indifferent to the effects of its greenhouse gas emissions on nature. So nonanthropocentrists oppose the traditional vices of envy, pride, luxury, indifference, and selfishness and support the traditional virtues of appreciation, frugality, and temperance, which incline people to reject SUVs in favor of more modest vehicles.

Anthropocentrists also have reasons to oppose SUVs on the ground that they promote climate change, which is likely to harm many poor people around the world by increasing vector-born diseases and reducing food availability.[37] Domestically, SUVs endanger people in smaller cars. SUVs also exacerbate dependence on foreign sources of oil, which motivates attempts to control oil-rich areas of the world, resulting in conflicts that take human lives. Finally, people trying to find happiness and fulfillment in the kind of car they drive are doomed to frustration because human flourishing cannot rest on any such basis. So anthropocentrists have their own reasons to oppose vices that promote SUV ownership and to favor virtues that discourage the purchase of an SUV.

The two sets of reasons against SUV ownership are compatible, complementary, and additive, as they are mediated by opposition to the same vices and promotion of the same virtues. Together these two sets of reasons are stronger than either set is by itself. Thus, there is synergy between them....

PRACTICAL IMPLICATIONS

In light of the arguments above, the following questions must be addressed: How should we expect people with the traditional virtues discussed above to act differently from most other people in society? How thoroughly should we expect them to reject consumerism? Must a virtuous person abjure automobile ownership? Must a virtuous person be a vegetarian? What are the practical implications of synergistic environmental virtues?

If virtue is to promote human flourishing, it cannot often require lifestyles so out of harmony with mainstream social expectations that virtuous people lack the companionship and camaraderie that flourishing as a social animal requires. To promote human flourishing, virtue must also avoid prescribing behavior that is impractical in the human-built environment, such as life without a car in many American communities.

I suggest addressing such matters with what I call the Principle of Anticipatory Cooperation (PAC). The PAC calls for actions that deviate from the social norm in the direction of the ideal that virtuous people aspire to for themselves and others but which do not deviate so much that virtue impairs instead of fosters flourishing. Consider, for example, car ownership and use. If life without a car is nearly crippling, the PAC does not require that virtuous people abjure car ownership and use. It requires only that they try to arrange their lives so that their car use and its adverse impacts are substantially less than is common in that society at that time. If most cars get twenty miles to the gallon, but good cars are available at reasonable cost that get thirty miles to the gallon, the virtuous person will, other things being equal, choose the more fuel-efficient car. She will also use public transportation and carpool more than is common when she can do so without bending her life out of shape. Her behavior anticipates more widespread participation in such practices and therefore helps to move society in a desirable direction.

If behavior like this becomes more common in society—average fuel efficiency approaches thirty miles to the gallon, for example, and car makers come out with reasonably priced cars that are even more fuel efficient—the virtuous person should, when finances permit, choose a car that is again considerably more fuel efficient than average. Absent some special need or problem, the virtuous person buying a new car today would choose a gas/electric hybrid that gets at least forty-five miles to the gallon. Similarly, if the transportation infrastructure changes to make public transportation more convenient and popular, the virtuous person will increase her use of public transportation so that it still exceeds the norm for people with similar transportation needs. A virtuous couple would likely be among the first to get by with only one car....

The spirit of compromise in the PAC stems from two considerations. One, already mentioned, is that virtue should promote human flourishing; it would not if it requited heroic sacrifice. The second consideration is justice. There is no justice in virtuous people trying to be perfect in social circumstances that make such attempts nearly self-destructive. Of course, the virtues considered here may require some short-term sacrifice. If my arguments are correct, however, the long-term result will be a better life. People who reject consumerism (without becoming utterly at odds with society) will flourish better than people whose lives are dominated by envy, greed, work, money worries, and separation from family and friends. People who reject consumerism in favor of traditional virtues will also lead more environmentally friendly lives.

In conclusion, people in industrial, consumer-oriented societies should cultivate traditional virtues to benefit themselves, other human beings, and the nonhuman environment. Anthropocentric and nonanthropocentric arguments for cultivating and exercising these virtues are mutually reinforcing, and their combination is synergistic. However, because the arguments for this conclusion depend on the baleful effects of consumerism, I draw no conclusions about virtue in nonconsumer-oriented societies.

NOTES

1. For a more complete exposition of environmental synergism, see Peter S. Wenz, "Environmental Synergism," *Environmental Ethics* 24 (2002): 389–408.

2. Linda Starke, ed., *Vital Signs 2003* (New York: W. W. Norton, 2003), 84.

3. Starke, *Vital Signs 2003*, 40.

4. Starke, *Vital Signs 2003*, 82.

5. Dave Ramsey, *More Than Enough* (New York: Viking Penguin, 1999), 24.

6. David C. Korten, *When Corporations Rule the World* (West Hartford, CT: Kumarian Press, 1995), 37–38.

7. Alan Thein Durning, *How Much Is Enough?* (New York: W. W. Norton, 1992), 51–52.

8. Thomas L. Friedman, *The Lexus and the Olive Tree* (New York: Fartar, Straus and Giroux, 1999), 85–86.

9. Friedman, *The Lexus and the Olive Tree*, 167.

10. Korten, *When Corporations Rule the World*, 35.

11. Mia MacDonald with Danielle Nierenberg, "Linking Population, Women, and Biodiversity," in *State of the World 2003*, ed. Linda Starke (New York: W. W. Norton, 2003), 43.

12. Korten, *When Corporations Rule the World*, 33.

13. MacDonald with Nierenberg, "Linking Population, Women, and Biodiversity," 40.

14. For a critique of this view, see Peter S. Wenz, "Pragmatism in Practice: The Efficiency of Sustainable Agriculture," *Environmental Ethics* 21 (1999): 391–410.

15. Aaron Sachs, "The Last Commodity: Child Prostitution in the Developing World," *WorldWatch* 7, no. 4 (July–August 1994): 26–27.

16. Vandana Shiva, *Monocultures of the Mind* (London: Zed Books, 1993), 36.

17. Korten, *When Corporations Rule the World*, 31–32.

18. Korten, *When Corporations Rule the World*, 42.

19. Sachs, "The Last Commodity," 26.

20. Starke, *Vital Signs 2003*, 88.

21. Gary Gardnet and Brian Halweil, "Overfed and Underfed: The Global Epidemic of Malnutrition," in *Worldwatch Paper 150* (Washington, DC: Worldwatch Instirure, 2000), 7.

22. World Health Organization, *World Health Report 1998*, in Lester R. Brown, "Challenges of the New Century," *State of the World 2000*, ed. Linda Starke (New York: W. W. Norton, 2000), 7.

23. Grover Foley, "The Threat of Rising Seas," *The Ecologist* 29, no. 2 (March–April 1999): 77.

24. Peter Bunyard, "A Hungrier World," *The Ecologist* 29, no. 2 (March–April 1999): 87.

25. Ramsey, *More Than Enough*, 234.

26. Ramsey, *More Than Enough*, 22–23.

27. Vicki Robin and Joe Dominguez, *Your Money or Your Life* (New York: Penguin Books, 1992), 142.

28. Robert D. Putnam, *Bowling Alone* (New York: Penguin Books, 2000), 212.

29. Putnam, *Bowling Alone*, 213.

30. Gary Gardner, "The Virtue of Restraint," *WorldWatch* 14, no. 2 (March–April 2001): 14.

31. Gardner, "The Virtue of Restraint," 15.

32. Lewis Mumford, *The Transformation of Man* (New York: Harper and Row, 1956), 104–5.

33. Gardner and Halweil, "Overfed and Underfed," 14, 8.

34. Gardner and Halweil, "Overfed and Underfed," 14.

35. Korten, *When Corporations Rule the World*, 111.

36. Robin and Dominguez, *Your Money or Your Life*, 167–68.

37. See Paul Kingsnorth, "Human Health on the Line," *The Ecologist* 29, no. 2 (March–April 1999): 92–94; Bunyard, "A Hungrier World"; and Korren, *When Corporations Rule the World*, 31–32.

READING QUESTIONS

1. How does Wenz define "consumerism"? How does he believe that consumerism harms the environment?
2. How does consumerism harm people in the third world according to Wenz? How does it harm people in the industrialized world?
3. What vices are promoted by consumerism according to Wenz? Explain the three other bad character traits that Wenz believes are promoted by consumerism.
4. Explain the seven traditional virtues that oppose consumerism and promote human flourishing according to Wenz. What reasons does Wenz offer for thinking that traditional virtues and environmentalism are mutually reinforcing?
5. Explain Wenz's Principle of Anticipatory Cooperation. What are the two major consequences of this principle's application according to Wenz?

DISCUSSION QUESTIONS

1. Discuss which of the traditional virtues opposed to consumerism are the most important and useful ones to develop. Are there any other virtues that are in opposition to consumerism not considered by Wenz? Consider and discuss some of the practical ways in which any of these virtues can work to oppose the vices promoted by consumerism? Are there any other vices promoted by consumerism that Wenz fails to mention?
2. Suppose that individuals start working together to apply the Principle of Anticipatory Cooperation in their daily lives. How successful do you think such a project would be? Consider and discuss the sorts of practical and theoretical problems that might arise and how we might overcome such problems in order to increase the chances of a successful implementation of the principle.

WALTER SINNOTT-ARMSTRONG

It's Not *My* Fault: Global Warming and Individual Moral Obligations

Sinnott-Armstrong addresses the question: Given the enormity of the problem of global warming, what moral obligations does an *individual* (living in relative affluence) have in light of all this? To focus his question, he considers whether it is morally wrong for him to take a Sunday drive in a gas-guzzling car just for fun. In answering this question, Sinnott-Armstrong

This article was published in *Perspectives on Climate Change*, Walter Sinnott-Armstrong and Richard B. Howarth, "It's Not *My* Fault: Global Warming and Individual Moral Obligations," 295–315. Copyright Elsevier (2006).

appeals to a wide range of moral principles, including principles familiar from consequentialist, natural law (double effect), Kantian, and virtue ethics traditions. He argues that applying the various principles do not imply that he (or similarly situated individuals) has a *moral obligation* to refrain from taking the Sunday drive, though he admits that it is still "morally better or ideal" for individuals not to engage in such activities. Governments, however, do have a moral obligation to address the problem of global warming partly because only they are in a position to help fix the problem.

Recommended Reading: consequentialism, natural law theory, Kantian moral theory, virtue ethics, chap. 1, secs. 2A, 2B, 2C, and 2E.

Previous chapters in this volume have focused on scientific research, economic projections, and government policies. However, even if scientists establish that global warming is occurring, even if economists confirm that its costs will be staggering, and even if political theorists agree that governments must do something about it, it is still not clear what moral obligations regarding global warming devolve upon individuals like you and me. That is the question to be addressed in this essay.

1. ASSUMPTIONS

To make the issue stark, let us begin with a few assumptions. I believe that these assumptions are probably roughly accurate, but none is certain, and I will not try to justify them here. Instead, I will simply take them for granted for the sake of argument.[1]

First, global warming has begun and is likely to increase over the next century. We cannot be sure exactly how much or how fast, but hot times are coming.[2]

Second, a significant amount of global warming is due to human activities. The main culprit is fossil fuels.

Third, global warming will create serious problems for many people over the long term by causing climate changes, including violent storms, floods from sea level rises, droughts, heat waves, and so on. Millions of people will probably be displaced or die.

Fourth, the poor will be hurt most of all. The rich countries are causing most of the global warming, but they will be able to adapt to climate changes more easily.[3] Poor countries that are close to sea level might be devastated.

Fifth, governments, especially the biggest and richest ones, are able to mitigate global warming.[4] They can impose limits on emissions. They can require or give incentives for increased energy efficiency. They can stop deforestation and fund reforestation. They can develop ways to sequester carbon dioxide in oceans or underground. These steps will help, but the only long-run solution lies in alternatives to fossil fuels. These alternatives can be found soon if governments start massive research projects now.[5]

Sixth, it is too late to stop global warming. Because there is so much carbon dioxide in the atmosphere already, because carbon dioxide remains in the atmosphere for so long, and because we will remain dependent on fossil fuels in the near future, governments can slow down global warming or reduce its severity, but they cannot prevent it. Hence, governments need to adapt. They need to build seawalls. They need to reinforce houses that cannot withstand storms. They need to move populations from low-lying areas.[6]

Seventh, these steps will be costly. Increased energy efficiency can reduce expenses, adaptation will create some jobs, and money will be made in the research and production of alternatives to fossil fuels. Still, any steps that mitigate or adapt to global warming will slow down our economies, at least in the short run.[7] That will hurt many people, especially many poor people.

Eighth, despite these costs, the major governments throughout the world still morally ought to take some of these steps. The clearest moral obligation falls on the United States. The United States caused and continues to cause more of the problem than any other country. The United States can spend more resources on a solution without sacrificing basic necessities. This country has the scientific expertise to solve technical problems. Other countries follow its lead (sometimes!). So the United States has a special moral obligation to help mitigate and adapt to global warming.[8]

2. THE PROBLEM

Even assuming all of this, it is still not clear what I as an individual morally ought to do about global warming. That issue is not as simple as many people assume. I want to bring out some of its complications.

It should be clear from the start that "individual" moral obligations do not always follow directly from "collective" moral obligations. The fact that your government morally ought to do something does not prove that "you" ought to do it, even if your government fails. Suppose that a bridge is dangerous because so much traffic has gone over it and continues to go over it. The government has a moral obligation to make the bridge safe. If the government fails to do its duty, it does not follow that I personally have a moral obligation to fix the bridge. It does not even follow that I have a moral obligation to fill in one crack in the bridge, even if the bridge would be fixed if everyone filled in one crack, even if I drove over the bridge many times, and even if I still drive over it every day. Fixing the bridge is the government's job, not mine. While I ought to encourage the government to fulfill its obligations,[9] I do not have to take on those obligations myself.

All that this shows is that government obligations do not "always" imply parallel individual obligations. Still, maybe "sometimes" they do. My government has a moral obligation to teach arithmetic to the children in my town, including my own children.

If the government fails in this obligation, then I do take on a moral obligation to teach arithmetic to my children.[10] Thus, when the government fails in its obligations, sometimes I have to fill in, and sometimes I do not.

What about global warming? If the government fails to do anything about global warming, what am I supposed to do about it? There are lots of ways for me as an individual to fight global warming. I can protest against bad government policies and vote for candidates who will make the government fulfill its moral obligations. I can support private organizations that fight global warming, such as the Pew Foundation,[11] or boycott companies that contribute too much to global warming, such as most oil companies. Each of these cases is interesting, but they all differ. To simplify our discussion, we need to pick one act as our focus.

My example will be wasteful driving. Some people drive to their jobs or to the store because they have no other reasonable way to work and eat. I want to avoid issues about whether these goals justify driving, so I will focus on a case where nothing so important is gained. I will consider driving for fun on a beautiful Sunday afternoon. My drive is not necessary to cure depression or calm aggressive impulses. All that is gained is pleasure: Ah, the feel of wind in your hair! The views! How spectacular! Of course, you could drive a fuel-efficient hybrid car. But fuel-efficient cars have less "get up and go." So let us consider a gas-guzzling sport utility vehicle. Ah, the feeling of power! The excitement! Maybe you do not like to go for drives in sport utility vehicles on sunny Sunday afternoons, but many people do.

Do we have a moral obligation not to drive in such circumstances? This question concerns driving, not "buying" cars. To make this clear, let us assume that I borrow the gas-guzzler from a friend. This question is also not about "legal" obligations. So let us assume that it is perfectly legal to go for such drives. Perhaps it ought to be illegal, but it is not. Note also that my question is not about what would be "best." Maybe it would be better, even morally better, for me not to drive a gas-guzzler just for fun. But that is not the issue I want to address here. My question is whether I have a "moral" obligation not to drive a gas-guzzler just for fun on this particular sunny Sunday afternoon.

One final complication must be removed. I am interested in global warming, but there might be other moral reasons not to drive unnecessarily. I risk causing an accident, since I am not a perfect driver. I also will likely spew exhaust into the breathing space of pedestrians, bicyclists, or animals on the side of the road as I drive by. Perhaps these harms and risks give me a moral obligation not to go for my joyride. That is not clear. After all, these reasons also apply if I drive the most efficient car available, and even if I am driving to work with no other way to keep my job. Indeed, I might scare or injure bystanders even if my car gave off no greenhouse gases or pollution. In any case, I want to focus on global warming. So my real question is whether the facts about global warming give me any moral obligation not to drive a gas-guzzler just for fun on this sunny Sunday afternoon.

I admit that I am "inclined" to answer, "Yes." To me, global warming does "seem" to make such wasteful driving morally wrong.

Still, I do not feel confident in this judgment. I know that other people disagree (even though they are also concerned about the environment). I would probably have different moral intuitions about this case if I had been raised differently or if I now lived in a different culture. My moral intuition might be distorted by overgeneralization from the other cases where I think that other entities (large governments) do have moral obligations to fight global warming. I also worry that my moral intuition might be distorted by my desire to avoid conflicts with my environmentalist friends.[12] The issue of global warming generates strong emotions because of its political implications and because of how scary its effects are. It is also a peculiarly modern case, especially because it operates on a much grander scale than my moral intuitions evolved to handle long ago when acts did not have such long-term effects on future generations (or at least people were not aware of such effects). In such circumstances, I doubt that we are justified in trusting our moral intuitions alone. We need some kind of confirmation.[13]

One way to confirm the truth of my moral intuitions would be to derive them from a general moral principle. A principle could tell us why wasteful driving is morally wrong, so we would not have to depend on bare assertion. And a principle might be supported by more trustworthy moral beliefs. The problem is "which" principle?

3. ACTUAL ACT PRINCIPLES

One plausible principle refers to causing harm. If one person had to inhale all of the exhaust from my car, this would harm him and give me a moral obligation not to drive my car just for fun. Such cases suggest:

The harm principle: We have a moral obligation not to perform an act that causes harm to others.

This principle implies that I have a moral obligation not to drive my gas-guzzler just for fun "if" such driving causes harm.

The problem is that such driving does "not" cause harm in normal cases. If one person were in a position to inhale all of my exhaust, then he would get sick if I did drive, and he would not get sick if I did not drive (under normal circumstances). In contrast, global warming will still occur even if I do not drive just for fun. Moreover, even if I do drive a gas-guzzler just for fun for a long time, global warming will not occur unless lots of other people also expel greenhouse gases. So my individual act is neither necessary nor sufficient for global warming.

There are, admittedly, special circumstances in which an act causes harm without being either necessary or sufficient for that harm. Imagine that it takes three people to push a car off a cliff with a passenger locked inside, and five people are already pushing. If I join and help them push, then my act of pushing is neither necessary nor sufficient to make the car go off the cliff. Nonetheless, my act of pushing is a cause (or part of the cause) of the harm to the passenger. Why? Because I intend to cause harm to the passenger, and because my act is unusual. When I intend a harm to occur, my intention provides a reason to pick my act out of all the other background circumstances and identify it as a cause. Similarly, when my act is unusual in the sense that most people would not act that way, that also provides a reason to pick out my act and call it a cause.

Why does it matter what is usual? Compare matches. For a match to light up, we need to strike it so as to create friction. There also has to be oxygen. We do not call the oxygen the cause of the fire, since oxygen is usually present. Instead, we say that the friction causes the match to light, since it is unusual for that friction to occur. It happens only once in the life of each match. Thus, what is usual affects ascriptions of causation even in purely physical cases.

In moral cases, there are additional reasons not to call something a cause when it is usual. Labeling an act a cause of harm and, on this basis, holding its agent responsible for that harm by blaming the agent or condemning his act is normally counterproductive when that agent is acting no worse than most other people. If people who are doing "no" worse than average are condemned, then people who are doing "much" worse than average will suspect that they will still be subject to condemnation even if they start doing better, and even if they improve enough to bring themselves up to the average. We should distribute blame (and praise) so as to give incentives for the worst offenders to get better. The most efficient and effective way to do this is to reserve our condemnation for those who are well below average. This means that we should not hold people responsible for harms by calling their acts causes of harms when their acts are not at all unusual, assuming that they did not intend the harm.

The application to global warming should be clear. It is not unusual to go for joyrides. Such drivers do not intend any harm. Hence, we should not see my act of driving on a sunny Sunday afternoon as a cause of global warming or its harms.

Another argument leads to the same conclusion: the harms of global warming result from the massive quantities of greenhouse gases in the atmosphere. Greenhouse gases (such as carbon dioxide and water vapor) are perfectly fine in small quantities. They help plants grow. The problem emerges only when there is too much of them. But my joyride by itself does not cause the massive quantities that are harmful.

Contrast someone who pours cyanide poison into a river. Later someone drinking from the river downstream ingests some molecules of the poison. Those molecules cause the person to get ill and die. This is very different from the causal chain in global warming, because no particular molecules from my car cause global warming in the direct way that particular molecules of the poison do cause the drinker's death. Global warming is more like a river that is going to flood downstream because of torrential rains. I pour a quart of water into the river upstream (maybe just because I do not want to carry it). My act of pouring the quart into the river is not a cause of the flood. Analogously, my act of driving for fun is not a cause of global warming.

Contrast also another large-scale moral problem: famine relief. Some people say that I have no moral obligation to contribute to famine relief because the famine will continue and people will die whether or not I donate my money to a relief agency. However, I could help a certain individual if I gave my donation directly to that individual. In contrast, if I refrain from driving for fun on this one Sunday, there is no individual who will be helped in the least.[14] I cannot help anyone by depriving myself of this joyride.

The point becomes clearer if we distinguish global warming from climate change. You might think that my driving on Sunday raises the temperature of the globe by an infinitesimal amount. I doubt that, but, even if it does, my exhaust on that Sunday does not cause any climate change at all. No storms or floods or droughts or heat waves can be traced to my individual act of driving. It is these climate changes that cause harms to people. Global warming by itself causes no harm without climate change. Hence, since my individual act of driving on that one Sunday does not cause any climate change, it causes no harm to anyone.

The point is not that harms do not occur from global warming. I have already admitted that they do. The point is also not that my exhaust is overkill, like poisoning someone who is already dying from poison. My exhaust is not sufficient for the harms of global warming, and I do not intend those harms. Nor is it the point that the harms from global warming occur much later in time. If I place a time bomb in a building, I can cause harm many years later. And the point is not that the harm I cause is imperceptible. I admit that some harms can be imperceptible because they are too small or for other reasons.[15] Instead, the point is simply that my individual joyride does not cause global warming, climate change, or any of their resulting harms, at least directly.

Admittedly, my acts can lead to other acts by me or by other people. Maybe one case of wasteful driving creates a bad habit that will lead me to do it again and again. Or maybe a lot of other people look up to me and would follow my example of wasteful driving. Or maybe my wasteful driving will undermine my commitment to environmentalism and lead me to stop supporting important green causes or to harm the environment in more serious ways. If so, we could apply:

The indirect harm principle: We have a moral obligation not to perform an act that causes harm to others indirectly by causing someone to carry out acts that cause harm to others.

This principle would explain why it is morally wrong to drive a gas-guzzler just for fun if this act led to other harmful acts.

One problem here is that my acts are not that influential. People like to see themselves as more influential than they really are. On a realistic view, however, it is unlikely that anyone would drive wastefully if I did and would not if I did not. Moreover, wasteful driving is not that habit forming. My act of driving this Sunday does not make me drive next Sunday. I do not get addicted. Driving the next Sunday is a separate decision.[16] And my wasteful driving will not undermine my devotion to environmentalism. If my argument in this chapter is correct, then my belief that the government has a moral obligation to fight global warming is perfectly compatible with a belief that I as an individual have no moral obligation not to drive a gas-guzzler for fun. If I keep this compatibility in mind, then my driving my gas-guzzler for fun will not undermine my devotion to the cause of getting the government to do something about global warming.

Besides, the indirect harm principle is misleading. To see why, consider David. David is no environmentalist. He already has a habit of driving his gas-guzzler for fun on Sundays. Nobody likes him, so nobody follows his example. But David still has a moral obligation not to drive his gas-guzzler just for fun this Sunday, and his obligation has the same basis as mine, if I have one. So my moral obligation cannot depend on the factors cited by the indirect harm principle.

The most important problem for supposed indirect harms is the same as for direct harms: even if I create a bad habit and undermine my personal environmentalism and set a bad example that others follow, all of this would still not be enough to cause climate change if other people stopped expelling greenhouse gases. So, as long as I neither intend harm nor do anything unusual, my act cannot cause climate change even if I do create bad habits and followers. The scale of climate change is just too big for me to cause it, even "with a little help from my friends."

Of course, even if I do not cause climate change, I still might seem to contribute to climate change in the sense that I make it worse. If so, another principle applies:

The contribution principle: We have a moral obligation not to make problems worse.

This principle applies if climate change will be worse if I drive than it will be if I do not drive.

The problem with this argument is that my act of driving does not even make climate change worse. Climate change would be just as bad if I did not drive. The reason is that climate change becomes worse only if more people (and animals) are hurt or if they are hurt worse. There is nothing bad about global warming or climate change in itself if no people (or animals) are harmed. But there is no individual person or animal who will be worse off if I drive than if I do not drive my gas-guzzler just for fun. Global warming and climate change occur on such a massive scale that my individual driving makes no difference to the welfare of anyone.

Some might complain that this is not what they mean by "contribute." All it takes for me to contribute to global warming in their view is for me to expel greenhouse gases into the atmosphere. I do "that" when I drive, so we can apply:

The gas principle: We have a moral obligation not to expel greenhouse gases into the atmosphere.

If this principle were true, it would explain why I have a moral obligation not to drive my gas-guzzler just for fun.

Unfortunately, it is hard to see any reason to accept this principle. There is nothing immoral about greenhouse gases in themselves when they cause no harm. Greenhouse gases include carbon dioxide and water vapor, which occur naturally and help plants grow. The problem of global warming occurs because of the high quantities of greenhouse gases, not because of anything bad about smaller quantities of the same gases. So it is hard to see why I would have a moral obligation not to expel harmless quantities of greenhouse gases. And that is all I do by myself.

Furthermore, if the gas principle were true, it would be unbelievably restrictive. It implies that I have a moral obligation not to boil water (since water vapor is a greenhouse gas) or to exercise (since I expel carbon dioxide when I breathe heavily). When you think it through, an amazing array of seemingly morally acceptable activities would be ruled out by the gas principle. These implications suggest that we had better look elsewhere for a reason why I have a moral obligation not to drive a gas-guzzler just for fun.

Maybe the reason is risk. It is sometimes morally wrong to create a risk of a harm even if that harm does not occur. I grant that drunk driving is immoral, because it risks harm to others, even if the drunk driver gets home safely without hurting anyone. Thus, we get another principle:

The risk principle: We have a moral obligation not to increase the risk of harms to other people.[17]

The problem here is that global warming is not like drunk driving. When drunk driving causes harm, it is easy to identify the victim of this particular drunk driver. There is no way to identify any particular victim of my wasteful driving in normal circumstances.

In addition, my earlier point applies here again. If the risk principle were true, it would be unbelievably restrictive. Exercising and boiling water also expel greenhouse gases, so they also increase the risk of global warming if my driving does. This principle implies that almost everything we do violates a moral obligation.

Defenders of such principles sometimes respond by distinguishing significant from insignificant risks or increases in risks. That distinction is problematic, at least here. A risk is called significant when it is "too" much. But then we need to ask what makes this risk too much when other risks are not too much. The reasons for counting a risk as significant are then the real reasons for thinking that there is a moral obligation not to drive wastefully. So we need to specify those reasons directly instead of hiding them under a waffle-term like "significant."

4. INTERNAL PRINCIPLES

None of the principles discussed so far is both defensible and strong enough to yield a moral obligation not to drive a gas-guzzler just for fun. Maybe we can do better by looking inward.

Kantians claim that the moral status of acts depends on their agents' maxims or "subjective principles of volition"[18]—roughly what we would call motives or intentions or plans. This internal focus is evident in Kant's first formulation of the categorical imperative:

The universalizability principle: We have a moral obligation not to act on any maxim that we cannot will to be a universal law.

The idea is not that universally acting on that maxim would have bad consequences. (We will consider that kind of principle below.) Instead, the claim is that some maxims "cannot even be thought as a universal law of nature without contradiction."[19] However, my maxim when I drive a gas-guzzler just for fun on this sunny Sunday afternoon is simply to have harmless fun. There is no way to derive a contradiction from a universal law that people do or may have harmless fun. Kantians might respond that my maxim is, instead, to expel greenhouse gases. I still see no way to derive a literal contradiction from a universal law that people do or may expel greenhouse gases. There would be bad consequences, but that is not a contradiction, as Kant requires. In any case, my maxim (or intention or motive) is not to expel greenhouse gases. My goals would be reached completely if I went for my drive and had my fun without expelling any greenhouse gases. This leaves no ground for claiming that my driving violates Kant's first formula of the categorical imperative.

Kant does supply a second formulation, which is really a different principle:

The means principle: We have a moral obligation not to treat any other person as a means only.[20]

It is not clear exactly how to understand this formulation, but the most natural interpretation is that for me to treat someone as a means implies my using harm to that person as part of my plan to achieve my goals. Driving for fun does not do that. I would have just as much fun if nobody were ever harmed by global warming. Harm to others is no part of my plans. So Kant's principle cannot explain why I have a moral obligation not to drive just for fun on this sunny Sunday afternoon.

A similar point applies to a traditional principle that focuses on intention:

The doctrine of double effect: We have a moral obligation not to harm anyone intentionally (either as an end or as a means).

This principle fails to apply to my Sunday driving both because my driving does not cause harm to anyone and because I do not intend harm to anyone. I would succeed in doing everything I intended to do if I enjoyed my drive but magically my car gave off no greenhouse gases and no global warming occurred.

Another inner-directed theory is virtue ethics. This approach focuses on general character traits rather than particular acts or intentions. It is not clear how to derive a principle regarding obligations from virtue ethics, but here is a common attempt:

The virtue principle: We have a moral obligation not to perform an act that expresses a vice or is contrary to virtue.

This principle solves our problem if driving a gas-guzzler expresses a vice, or if no virtuous person would drive a gas-guzzler just for fun.

How can we tell whether this principle applies? How can we tell whether driving a gas-guzzler for fun "expresses a vice"? On the face of it, it expresses a desire for fun. There is nothing vicious about having fun. Having fun becomes vicious only if it is harmful or risky. But I have already responded to the principles of harm and risk. Moreover, driving a gas-guzzler for fun does not always express a vice. If other people did not produce so much greenhouse gas, I could drive my gas-guzzler just for fun without anyone being harmed by global warming. Then I could do it without being vicious. This situation is not realistic, but it does show that wasteful driving is not essentially vicious or contrary to virtue.

Some will disagree. Maybe your notions of virtue and vice make it essentially vicious to drive wastefully. But why? To apply this principle, we need some antecedent test of when an act expresses a vice. You cannot just say, "I know vice when I see it," because other people look at the same act and do not see vice, just fun. It begs the question to appeal to what you see when others do not see it, and you have no reason to believe that your vision is any clearer than theirs. But that means that this virtue principle cannot be applied without begging the question. We need to find some reason why such driving is vicious. Once we have this reason, we can appeal to it directly as a reason why I have a moral obligation not to drive wastefully. The side step through virtue does not help and only obscures the issue.

Some virtue theorists might respond that life would be better if more people were to focus on general character traits, including green virtues, such as moderation and love of nature.[21] One reason is that it is so hard to determine obligations in particular cases. Another reason is that focusing on particular obligations leaves no way to escape problems like global warming. This might be correct. Maybe we should spend more time thinking about whether we have green virtues rather than about whether we have specific obligations. But that does not show that we do have a moral obligation not to drive gas-guzzlers just for fun. Changing our focus will not bring any moral obligation into existence. There are other important moral issues besides moral obligation, but this does not show that moral obligations are not important as well.

5. COLLECTIVE PRINCIPLES

Maybe our mistake is to focus on individual persons. We could, instead, focus on institutions. One institution is the legal system, so we might adopt.

The ideal law principle: We have a moral obligation not to perform an action if it ought to be illegal.

I already said that the government ought to fight global warming. One way to do so is to make it illegal to drive wastefully or to buy (or sell) inefficient gas-guzzlers. If the government ought to pass such laws, then, even before such laws are passed, I have a moral obligation not to drive a gas-guzzler just for fun, according to the ideal law principle.

The first weakness in this argument lies in its assumption that wasteful driving or gas-guzzlers ought to be illegal. That is dubious. The enforcement costs of a law against joyrides would be enormous. A law against gas-guzzlers would be easier to enforce, but inducements to efficiency (such as higher taxes on gas and gas-guzzlers, or tax breaks for buying fuel-efficient cars) might accomplish the same goals with less loss of individual freedom. Governments ought to accomplish their goals with less loss of freedom, if they can. Note the "if." I do not claim that these other laws would work as well as an outright prohibition of gas-guzzlers. I do not know. Still, the point is that such alternative laws would not make it illegal (only expensive) to drive a gas-guzzler for fun. If those alternative laws are better than outright prohibitions (because they allow more freedom), then the ideal law principle cannot yield a moral obligation not to drive a gas-guzzler now.

Moreover, the connection between law and morality cannot be so simple. Suppose that the government morally ought to raise taxes on fossil fuels in order to reduce usage and to help pay for adaptation to global warming. It still seems morally permissible for me and for you not to pay that tax now. We do not have any moral obligation to send a check to the government for the amount that we would have to pay if taxes were raised to the ideal level. One reason is that our checks would not help to solve the problem, since others would continue to conduct business as usual. What would help to solve the problem is for the taxes to be increased. Maybe we all have moral obligations to try to get the taxes increased. Still, until they are increased, we as individuals have no moral obligations to abide by the ideal tax law instead of the actual tax law.

Analogously, it is actually legal to buy and drive gas-guzzlers. Maybe these vehicles should be illegal. I am not sure. If gas-guzzlers morally ought to be illegal, then maybe we morally ought to work to get them outlawed. But that still would not show that now, while they are legal, we have a moral obligation not to drive them just for fun on a sunny Sunday afternoon.

Which laws are best depends on side effects of formal institutions, such as enforcement costs and loss of freedom (resulting from the coercion of laws). Maybe we can do better by looking at informal groups.

Different groups involve different relations between members. Orchestras and political parties, for example, plan to do what they do and adjust their actions to other members of the group in order to achieve a common goal. Such groups can be held responsible for their joint acts, even when no individual alone performs those acts. However, gas-guzzler drivers do not form this kind of group.

Gas-guzzler drivers do not share goals, do not make plans together, and do not adjust their acts to each other (at least usually).

There is an abstract set of gas-guzzler drivers, but membership in a set is too arbitrary to create moral responsibility. I am also in a set of all terrorists plus me, but my membership in that abstract set does not make me responsible for the harms that terrorists cause.

The only feature that holds together the group of people who drive gas-guzzlers is simply that they all perform the same kind of act. The fact that so many people carry out acts of that kind does create or worsen global warming. That collective bad effect is supposed to make it morally wrong to perform any act of that kind, according to the following:

The group principle: We have a moral obligation not to perform an action if this action makes us a member of a group whose actions together cause harm.

Why? It begs the question here merely to assume that, if it is bad for everyone in a group to perform acts of a kind, then it is morally wrong for an individual to perform an act of that kind. Besides, this principle is implausible or at least questionable in many cases. Suppose that everyone in an airport is talking loudly. If only a few people were talking, there would be no problem. But the collective effect of so many people talking makes it hard to hear announcements, so some people miss their flights. Suppose, in these circumstances, I say loudly (but not too loudly), "I wish everyone would be quiet." My speech does not seem immoral, since it alone does not harm anyone. Maybe there should be a rule (or law) against such loud speech in this setting (as in a library), but if there is not (as I am assuming), then it does not seem immoral to do what others do, as long as they are going to do it anyway, so the harm is going to occur anyway.[22]

Again, suppose that the president sends everyone (or at least most taxpayers) a check for $600. If all recipients cash their checks, the government deficit will grow, government programs will have to be slashed, and severe economic and social problems will result. You know that enough other people will cash their checks to make these results to a great degree inevitable. You also know that it is perfectly legal to cash your check, although you think it should be illegal, because the checks should not have been issued in the first place. In these circumstances, is it morally wrong for you to cash your check? I doubt it. Your act of cashing your check causes no harm by itself, and you have no intention to cause harm. Your act of cashing your check does make you a member of a group that collectively causes harm, but that still does not seem to give you a moral obligation not to join the group by cashing your check, since you cannot change what the group does. It might be morally good or ideal to protest by tearing up your check, but it does not seem morally obligatory.

Thus, the group principle fails. Perhaps it might be saved by adding some kind of qualification, but I do not see how.[23]

6. COUNTERFACTUAL PRINCIPLES

Maybe our mistake is to focus on actual circumstances. So let us try some counterfactuals about what would happen in possible worlds that are not actual. Different counterfactuals are used by different versions of rule-consequentialism.[24]

One counterfactual is built into the common question, "What would happen if everybody did that?" This question suggests a principle:

The general action principle: I have a moral obligation not to perform an act when it would be worse for everyone to perform an act of the same kind.[25]

It does seem likely that, if everyone in the world drove a gas-guzzler often enough, global warming would increase intolerably. We would also quickly run out of fossil fuels. The general action principle is, thus, supposed to explain why it is morally wrong to drive a gas-guzzler.

Unfortunately, that popular principle is indefensible. It would be disastrous if every human had no children. But that does not make it morally wrong for a particular individual to choose to have no children. There is no moral obligation to have at least one child.

The reason is that so few people "want" to remain childless. Most people would not go without children even if they were allowed to. This suggests a different principle:

The general permission principle: I have a moral obligation not to perform an act whenever it would be worse for everyone to be permitted to perform an act of that kind.

This principle seems better because it would not be disastrous for everyone to be permitted to remain childless. This principle is supposed to be able to explain why it is morally wrong to steal (or lie, cheat, rape, or murder), because it would be disastrous for everyone to be permitted to steal (or lie, cheat, rape, or murder) whenever (if ever) they wanted to.

Not quite. An agent is permitted or allowed in the relevant sense when she will not be liable to punishment, condemnation (by others), or feelings of guilt for carrying out the act. It is possible for someone to be permitted in this sense without knowing that she is permitted and, indeed, without anyone knowing that she is permitted. But it would not be disastrous for everyone to be permitted to steal if nobody knew that they were permitted to steal, since then they would still be deterred by fear of punishment, condemnation, or guilt. Similarly for lying, rape, and so on. So the general permission principle cannot quite explain why such acts are morally wrong.

Still, it would be disastrous if everyone knew that they were permitted to steal (or lie, rape, etc.). So we simply need to add one qualification:

The public permission principle: I have a moral obligation not to perform an act whenever it would be worse for everyone to know that everyone is permitted to perform an act of that kind.[26]

Now this principle seems to explain the moral wrongness of many of the acts we take to be morally wrong, since it would be disastrous if everyone knew that everyone was permitted to steal, lie, cheat, and so on.

Unfortunately, this revised principle runs into trouble in other cases. Imagine that 1000 people want to take Flight 38 to Amsterdam on October 13, 2003, but the plane is not large enough to carry that many people. If all 1,000 took that particular flight, then it would crash. But these people are all stupid and stubborn enough that, if they knew that they were all allowed to take the flight, they all would pack themselves in, despite warnings, and the flight would crash. Luckily, this counterfactual does not reflect what actually happens. In the actual world, the airline is not stupid. Since the plane can safely carry only 300 people, the airline sells only 300 tickets and does not allow anyone on the flight without a ticket. If I have a ticket for that flight, then there is nothing morally wrong with me taking the flight along with the other 299 who have tickets. This shows that an act is not always morally wrong when it would (counterfactually) be disastrous for everyone to know that everyone is allowed to do it.[27]

The lesson of this example applies directly to my case of driving a gas-guzzler. Disaster occurs in the airplane case when too many people do what is harmless by itself. Similarly, disaster occurs when too many people burn too much fossil fuel. But that does not make it wrong in either case for one individual to perform an individual act that is harmless by itself. It only creates an obligation on the part of the government (or airline) to pass regulations to keep too many people from acting that way.

Another example brings out another weakness in the public permission principle. Consider open marriage. Max and Minnie get married because each loves the other and values the other person's love. Still, they think of sexual intercourse as a fun activity that they separate from love. After careful discussion before they got married, each happily agreed that each may have sex after marriage with whomever he or she wants. They value honesty, so they did add one condition: every sexual encounter must be reported to the other spouse. As long as they keep no secrets from each other and still love each other, they see no problem with their having sex with other people. They do not broadcast this feature of their marriage, but they do know (after years of experience) that it works for them.

Nonetheless, the society in which Max and Minnie live might be filled with people who are very different from them. If everyone knew that everyone is permitted to have sex during marriage with other people as long as the other spouse is informed and agreed to the arrangement, then various problems would arise. Merely asking a spouse whether he or she would be willing to enter into such an agreement would be enough to create suspicions and doubts in the other spouse's mind that would undermine many marriages or keep many couples from getting married, when they would have gotten or remained happily married if they had not been offered such an agreement. As a result, the society will have less love, fewer stable marriages, and more unhappy children of unnecessary divorce. Things would be much better if everyone believed that such agreements were not permitted in the first place, so they condemned them and felt guilty for even considering them. I think that this result is not unrealistic, but here I am merely postulating these facts in my example.

The point is that, even if other people are like this, so that it would be worse for everyone to know that everyone is permitted to have sex outside of marriage with spousal knowledge and consent, Max and Minnie are not like this, and they know that they are not like this, so it is hard to believe that they as individuals have a moral obligation to abide by a restriction that is justified by other people's dispositions. If Max and Minnie have a joint agreement that works for them, but they keep it secret from others, then there is nothing immoral about them having sex outside of their marriage (whether or not this counts as adultery). If this is correct, then the general permission principle fails again.

As before, the lesson of this example applies directly to my case of driving a gas-guzzler. The reason why Max and Minnie are not immoral is that they

have a right to their own private relationship as long as they do not harm others (such as by spreading disease or discord). But I have already argued that my driving a gas-guzzler on this Sunday afternoon does not cause harm. I seem to have a right to have fun in the way I want as long as I do not hurt anybody else, just like Max and Minnie. So the public permission principle cannot explain why it is morally wrong to drive a gas-guzzler for fun on this sunny Sunday afternoon.[28]

One final counterfactual approach is contractualism, whose most forceful recent proponent is Tim Scanlon.[29] Scanlon proposes:

The contractualist principle: I have a moral obligation not to perform an act whenever it violates a general rule that nobody could reasonably reject as a public rule for governing action in society.

Let us try to apply this principle to the case of Max and Minnie. Consider a general rule against adultery, that is, against voluntary sex between a married person and someone other than his or her spouse, even if the spouse knows and consents. It might seem that Max and Minnie could not reasonably reject this rule as a public social rule, because they want to avoid problems for their own society. If so, Scanlon's principle leads to the same questionable results as the public permission principle. If Scanlon replies that Max and Minnie "can" reasonably reject the anti-adultery rule, then why? The most plausible answer is that it is their own business how they have fun as long as they do not hurt anybody. But this answer is available also to people who drive gas-guzzlers just for fun. So this principle cannot explain why that act is morally wrong.

More generally, the test of what can be rejected "reasonably" depends on moral intuitions. Environmentalists might think it unreasonable to reject a principle that prohibits me from driving my gas-guzzler just for fun, but others will think it reasonable to reject such a principle, because it restricts my freedom to perform an act that harms nobody. The appeal to reasonable rejection itself begs the question in the absence of an account of why such rejection is unreasonable. Environmentalists might be able to specify reasons why it is unreasonable, but then it is those reasons that explain why this act is morally wrong. The framework of reasonable rejection becomes a distracting and unnecessary side step.[30]

7. WHAT IS LEFT?

We are left with no defensible principle to support the claim that I have a moral obligation not to drive a gas-guzzler just for fun. Does this result show that this claim is false? Not necessarily.

Some audiences[31] have suggested that my journey through various principles teaches us that we should not look for general moral principles to back up our moral intuitions. They see my arguments as a "reductio ad absurdum" of principlism, which is the view that moral obligations (or our beliefs in them) depend on principles. Principles are unavailable, so we should focus instead on particular cases, according to the opposing view called particularism.[32]

However, the fact that we cannot find any principle does not show that we do not need one. I already gave my reasons why we need a moral principle to back up our intuitions in this case. This case is controversial, emotional, peculiarly modern, and likely to be distorted by overgeneralization and partiality. These factors suggest that we need confirmation for our moral intuitions at least in this case, even if we do not need any confirmation in other cases.

For such reasons, we seem to need a moral principle, but we have none. This fact still does not show that such wasteful driving is not morally wrong. It only shows that we do not "know" whether it is morally wrong. Our ignorance might be temporary. If someone comes up with a defensible principle that does rule out wasteful driving, then I will be happy to listen and happy if it works. However, until some such principle is found, we cannot claim to know that it is morally wrong to drive a gas-guzzler just for fun.

The demand for a principle in this case does not lead to general moral skepticism. We still might know that acts and omissions that cause harm are morally wrong because of the harm principle. Still, since that principle and others do not apply to my wasteful driving, and since moral intuitions are unreliable in cases like this, we cannot know that my wasteful driving is morally wrong.

This conclusion will still upset many environmentalists. They think that they know that wasteful driving is immoral. They want to be able to condemn those who drive gas-guzzlers just for fun on sunny Sunday afternoons.

My conclusion should not be so disappointing. Even if individuals have no such moral obligations, it is still morally better or morally ideal for individuals not to waste gas. We can and should praise those who save fuel. We can express our personal dislike for wasting gas and for people who do it. We might even be justified in publicly condemning wasteful driving and drivers who waste a lot, in circumstances where such public rebuke is appropriate. Perhaps people who drive wastefully should feel guilty for their acts and ashamed of themselves, at least if they perform such acts regularly; and we should bring up our children so that they will feel these emotions. All of these reactions are available even if we cannot truthfully say that such driving violates a moral "obligation." And these approaches might be more constructive in the long run than accusing someone of violating a moral obligation.

Moreover, even if individuals have no moral obligations not to waste gas by taking unnecessary Sunday drives just for fun, governments still have moral obligations to fight global warming, because they can make a difference. My fundamental point has been that global warming is such a large problem that it is not individuals who cause it or who need to fix it. Instead, governments need to fix it, and quickly. Finding and implementing a real solution is the task of governments. Environmentalists should focus their efforts on those who are not doing their job rather than on those who take Sunday afternoon drives just for fun.

This focus will also avoid a common mistake. Some environmentalists keep their hands clean by withdrawing into a simple life where they use very little fossil fuels. That is great. I encourage it. But some of these escapees then think that they have done their duty, so they rarely come down out of the hills to work for political candidates who could and would change government policies. This attitude helps nobody. We should not think that we can do enough simply by buying fuel-efficient cars, insulating our houses, and setting up a windmill to make our own electricity. That is all wonderful, but it neither does little or nothing to stop global warming, nor does this focus fulfill our real moral obligations, which are to get governments to do their job to prevent the disaster of excessive global warming. It is better to enjoy your Sunday driving while working to change the law so as to make it illegal for you to enjoy your Sunday driving.

NOTES

1. For skeptics, see Lomborg (1998, chapter 24) and Singer (1997). A more reliable partial skeptic is Richard S. Lindzen, but his papers are quite technical. If you do not share my bleak view of global warming, treat the rest of this essay as conditional. The issue of how individual moral obligations are related to collective moral obligations is interesting and important in its own right, even if my assumptions about global warming turn out to be inaccurate.

2. See the chapters by Mahlman, Schlesinger, and Weatherly in this volume.

3. See the chapter by Shukla in this volume.

4. See the chapter by Bodansky in this volume.

5. See the chapter by Shuc in this volume.

6. See the chapter by Jamieson in this volume.

7. See the chapter by Toman in this volume.

8. See the chapter by Driver in this volume.

9. If I have an obligation to encourage the government to fulfill its obligation, then the government's obligation does impose some obligation on me. Still, I do not have an obligation to do what the government has an obligation to do. In short, I have no parallel moral obligation. That is what is at issue here.

10. I do not seem to have the same moral obligation to teach my neighbors' children when our government fails to teach them. Why not? The natural answer is that I have a special relation to my children that I do not have to their children. I also do not have such a special relation to future people who will be harmed by global warming.

11. See the chapter by Claussen in this volume.

12. Indeed, I am worried about how my environmentalist friends will react to this essay, but I cannot let fear stop me from following where arguments lead.

13. For more on why moral intuitions need confirmation, see Sinnott-Armstrong (2005).

14. Another difference between these cases is that my failure to donate to famine relief is an inaction, whereas my driving is an action. As Bob Fogelin put it in conversation, one is a sin of omission, but the other is a sin of emission. But I assume that omissions can be causes. The real question is whether my measly emissions of greenhouse gases can be causes of global warming.

15. Cf. Parfit (1984, pp. 75–82).

16. If my act this Sunday does not cause me to drive next Sunday, then effects of my driving next Sunday are not consequences of my driving this Sunday. Some still might say that I can affect global warming by driving wastefully many times over the course of years. I doubt this, but I do not need to deny it. The fact that it is morally wrong for me to do all of a hundred acts together does not imply that it is morally wrong for me to do one of those hundred acts. Even if it would be morally wrong for me to pick all of the flowers in a park, it need not be morally wrong for me to pick one flower in that park.

17. The importance of risks in environmental ethics is a recurrent theme in the writings of Kristin Shrader-Frechette.

18. Kant (1785/1959, p. 400, n. 1).

19. *ibid*, 424. According to Kant, a weaker kind of contradiction in the will signals an imperfect duty. However, imperfect duties permit "exception in the interest of inclination" (421), so an imperfect obligation not to drive a gas-guzzler would permit me to drive it this Sunday when I am so inclined. Thus, I assume that a moral obligation not to drive a gas-guzzler for fun on a particular occasion would have to be a perfect obligation in Kant's view.

20. *ibid*, 429. I omit Kant's clause regarding treating others as ends because that clause captures imperfect duties, which are not my concern here (for reasons given in the preceding note).

21. Jamieson (n.d.)

22. Compare also standing up to see the athletes in a sporting event, when others do so. Such examples obviously involve much less harm than global warming. I use trivial examples to diminish emotional interference. The point is only that such examples share a structure that defenders of the group principle would claim to be sufficient for a moral obligation.

23. Parfit (1984, pp. 67–86) is famous for arguing that an individual act is immoral if it falls in a group of acts

that collectively cause harm. To support his claim Parfit uses examples like the Harmless Torturers (p. 80). But torturers intend to cause harm. That's what makes them torturers. Hence, Parfit's cases cannot show anything wrong with wasteful driving, where there is no intention to cause any harm. For criticisms of Parfit's claims, see Jackson (1997).

24. Cf. Sinnott-Armstrong (2003) and Hooker (2003).

25. Cf. Singer (1971).

26. Cf. Gert (2005). Gert does add details that I will not discuss here. For a more complete response, see Sinnott-Armstrong (2002).

27. The point, of course, depends on how you describe the act. It would not be disastrous to allow everyone "with a ticket" to take the flight (as long as there are not too many tickets). What is disastrous is to allow everyone (without qualification) to take the flight. Still, that case shows that it is not always morally wrong to do X when it would be disastrous to allow everyone to do X. To solve these problems, we need to put some limits on the kinds of descriptions that can replace the variable X. But any limit needs to be justified, and it is not at all clear how to justify such limits without begging the question.

28. The examples in the text show why violating a justified public rule is not sufficient for private immorality. It is also not necessary, since it might not be disastrous if all parents were permitted to kill their children, if no parent ever wanted to kill his or her children. The failure of this approach to give a necessary condition is another reason to doubt that it captures the essence of morality.

29. Scanlon (1998).

30. Scanlon's framework still might be useful as a heuristic, for overcoming partiality, as a pedagogical tool, or as a vivid way to display coherence among moral intuitions at different levels. My point is that it cannot be used to justify moral judgments or to show what makes acts morally wrong. For more, see Sinnott-Armstrong (2006, chap. 8).

31. Such as Bill Pollard in Edinburgh.

32. Developed by Dancy (1993, 2004). For criticisms, see Sinnott-Armstrong (1999).

ACKNOWLEDGMENTS

For helpful comments, I would like to thank Kier Olsen DeVries, Julia Driver, Bob Fogelin, Bernard Gert, Rich Howarth, Bill Pollard, Mike Ridge, David Rodin, Peter Singer, and audiences at the University of Edinburgh, the International Society for Business, Economics, and Ethics, and the Center for Applied Philosophy and Public Ethics in Melbourne.

REFERENCES

Dancy, J. (1993). *Moral reasons.* Oxford: Blackwell.

Dancy. J. (2004). *Ethics without principles.* New York: Oxford University Press.

Gert, B. (2005). *Morality: Its nature and justification* (Revised ed.). New York: Oxford University Press.

Hooker, B. (2003). Rule consequentialism. In: *The Stanford Encyclopedia of Philosophy.* Available at: http://plato.stanford.edu/entrics/consequentialism-rule

Jackson, F. (1997). Which effects? In: J. Dancy (Ed.), *Reading Parfit* (pp. 42–53). Oxford: Blackwell.

Jamieson, D. (n.d.). When utilitarians should be virtue theorists. Unpublished manuscript.

Kant, I. (1959). *Foundations of the metaphysics of morals* (L. W. Beck, Trans.). Indianapolis. IN: Bobbs-Merrill. (Original work published in 1785).

Lomborg, B. (1998). *The skeptical environmentalist.* New York: Cambridge University Press.

Parfit, D. (1984). *Reasons and persons.* Oxford: Clarendon Press.

Scanlon, T. (1998). *What we owe to each other.* Cambridge, MA: Harvard University Press.

Singer, M. (1971). *Generalization in ethics.* New York: Atheneum.

Singer, S. F. (1997). *Hot talk, cold science.* Oakland, CA: The Independent Institute.

Sinnott-Armstrong, W. (1999). Some varieties of particularism. *Metaphilosophy, 30,* 1–12.

———. (2002). Gert contra consequentialism. In: W. Sinnott-Armstrong & R. Audi (Eds), *Rationality, rules, and ideals: Critical essays on Bernard Gert's moral theory* (pp. 145–163). Lanham, MD: Rowman and Littlefield.

———. (2003). Consequentialism. In: *The Stanford Encyclopedia of Philosophy.* Available at: http://plato.stanford.edu/entries/consequentialism

———. (2005). Moral intuitionism and empirical psychology. In: T. Horgan & M. Timmons (Eds), *Metaethics after Moore* (pp. 339–365). New York: Oxford University Press.

———. (2006). *Moral skepticisms.* New York: Oxford University Press.

READING QUESTIONS

1. How does Sinnott-Armstrong argue that individual moral obligations do not always follow directly from collective moral obligations (e.g., obligations of the government)?
2. What is the harm principle, and how does Sinnott-Armstrong argue that it does not imply that he has a moral obligation not to drive his gas-guzzler just for fun? Why does he think the principle implies this only if his driving the gas-guzzler is both unusual and done with the intent to harm?
3. One of Sinnott-Armstrong's objections to the risk principle is that it is too restrictive, and one possible response to this objection involves distinguishing significant from insignificant risks. What is the risk principle, and what does Sinnott-Armstrong believe is wrong with this response to his objection?
4. How does Sinnott-Armstrong interpret Kant's means principle, and why does he think the principle cannot explain why he has no moral obligation not to drive his gas-guzzler just for fun?
5. In his discussion of the group principle, Sinnott-Armstrong presents a hypothetical case where the president sends everyone a $600 check. What is the group principle, and how is Sinnott-Armstrong's case supposed to show that the group principle fails?
6. What is the contractualist principle, and how does Sinnott-Armstrong use the case of Max and Minnie to show that the principle cannot explain why driving gas-guzzlers just for fun is wrong?
7. How does Sinnott-Armstrong argue that we cannot know whether driving gas-guzzlers just for fun is wrong unless we can provide a defensible general moral principle that implies that it is wrong?

DISCUSSION QUESTIONS

1. Is Sinnott-Armstrong right that the virtue principle "cannot be applied without begging the question"? How might one argue, without begging the question, that driving gas-guzzlers just for fun is contrary to virtue?
2. Sinnott-Armstrong suggests that there is no contradiction in claiming that (i) people who drive wastefully should feel guilty and ashamed for doing so and that (ii) there is no moral obligation not to drive wastefully. But how could it be the case that one *should* feel guilty and ashamed for doing something even when what one did violates no moral obligation?

BJØRN LOMBORG

Let's Keep Our Cool about Global Warming

Lomborg argues that drastic reductions in CO_2 emissions that some have proposed as a way of curbing global warming is not politically realistic. Instead he advocates a balanced approach to the problem that involves economically feasible taxing of CO_2 emissions along with expenditures on the research and development of noncarbon emitting technologies.

Recommended Reading: consequentialism, chap. 1, sec. 2A.

There is a kind of choreographed screaming about climate change from both sides of the debate. Discussion would be on much firmer ground if we could actually hear the arguments and the facts and then sensibly debate long-term solutions.

Man-made climate change is certainly a problem, but it is categorically not the end of the world. Take the rise in sea levels as one example of how the volume of the screaming is unmatched by the facts. In its 2007 report, the United Nations estimates that sea levels will rise about a foot over the remainder of the century.[1] While this is not a trivial amount, it is also important to realize that it is not unknown to mankind: since 1860, we have experienced a sea level rise of about a foot without major disruptions.[2] It is also important to realize that the new prediction is lower than previous Intergovernmental Panel on Climate Change (IPCC) estimates and much lower than the expectations from the 1990s of more than two feet and the 1980s, when the Environmental Protection Agency projected more than six feet.[3]

We dealt with rising sea levels in the past century, and we will continue to do so in this century. It will be problematic, but it is incorrect to posit the rise as the end of civilization. We will actually lose very little dry land to the rise in sea levels. It is estimated that almost all nations in the world will establish maximal coastal protection almost everywhere, simply because doing so is fairly cheap. For more than 180 of the world's 192 nations, coastal protection will cost less than 0.1 percent GDP and approach 100 percent protection.[4]

The rise in sea level will be a much bigger problem for poor countries. The most affected nation will be Micronesia, a federation of 607 small islands in the West Pacific with a total land area only four times larger than Washington, D.C.[5] If nothing were done, Micronesia would lose some 21 percent of its area by the end of the century (Tol 2004, 5). With coastal protection, it will lose just 0.18 percent of its land area. However, if we instead opt for cuts in carbon emissions and thus reduce both the sea level rise and the economic growth, Micronesia will end up losing a larger land area. The increase in wealth for poor nations is more important than sea levels: poorer nations will be less able to defend themselves against rising waters, even if they rise more slowly. This is the same for other vulnerable nations: Tuvalu, the Maldives, Vietnam, and Bangladesh. The point is that we cannot just talk about CO_2 when we talk about climate change. The dialogue needs to include both considerations about carbon emissions and economics for the benefit of humans and the environment. Presumably, our goal is not just to cut carbon emissions, but to do the best we can for people and the environment.

Used by permission of the Skeptical Inquirer (http://www.csiop.org).

We should take action on climate change, but we need to be realistic. The U.K has arguably engaged in the most aggressive rhetoric about climate change. Since the Labour government promised in 1997 to cut emissions by a further 15 percent by 2010, emissions have *increased* 3 percent.[6] American emissions during the Clinton/Gore administration increased 28 percent. Look at our past behavior: at the Earth Summit in Rio in 1992, nations promised to cut emissions back to 1990 levels by 2000 (UNFCCC 1992, 4.2a). The member countries of the Organisation for Economic Cooperation and Development (OECD) overshot their target in 2000 by more than 12 percent.

Many believe that dramatic political action will follow if people only knew better and elected better politicians.[7] Despite the European Union's enthusiasm for the Kyoto Protocol on Climate Change—and a greater awareness and concern over global warming in Europe than in the United States—emissions per person since 1990 have remained stable in the U.S. while E.U. emissions have increased 4 percent (EIA 2006). Even if the wealthy nations managed to reign in their emissions, the majority of this century's emissions will come from developing countries—which are responsible for about 40 percent of annual carbon emissions; this is likely to increase to 75 percent by the end of the century.[8]

In a surprisingly candid statement from Tony Blair at the Clinton Global Initiative, he pointed out:

> I think if we are going to get action on this, we have got to start from the brutal honesty about the politics of how we deal with it. The truth is no country is going to cut its growth or consumption substantially in the light of a long-term environmental problem. What countries are prepared to do is to try to work together cooperatively to deal with this problem in a way that allows us to develop the science and technology in a beneficial way. (Clinton Global Initiative 2005, 15)

Similarly, one of the top economic researchers tells us: "Deep cuts in emissions will only be achieved if alternative energy technologies become available at reasonable prices" (Tol 2007, 430). We need to engage in a sensible debate about how to tax CO_2. If we set the tax too low, we emit too much. If we set it too high, we end up much poorer without doing enough to reduce warming.

In the largest review of all of the literature's 103 estimates, climate economist Richard Tol makes two important points. First, the really scary, high estimates typically have not been subjected to peer review and published. In his words: "studies with better methods yield lower estimates with smaller uncertainties." Second, with reasonable assumptions, the cost is very unlikely to be higher than $14 per ton of CO_2 and likely to be much smaller (Tol 2005).[9] When I specifically asked him for his best guess, he wasn't too enthusiastic about shedding his cautiousness—as few true researchers invariably are—but gave the estimate of $2 per ton of CO_2.[10]

Therefore, I believe that we should tax CO_2 at the economically feasible level of about $2/ton, or maximally $14/ton. Yet, let us not expect this will make any major difference. Such a tax would cut emissions by 5 percent and reduce temperatures by 0.16°F. And before we scoff at 5 percent, let us remember that the Kyoto protocol, at the cost of 10 years of political and economic toil, will reduce emissions by just 0.4 percent by 2010.[11]

Neither a tax nor Kyoto nor draconian proposals for future cuts move us closer toward finding better options for the future. Research and development in renewable energy and energy efficiency is at its lowest for twenty-five years. Instead, we need to find a way that allows us to "develop the science and technology in a beneficial way," a way that enables us to provide alternative energy technologies at reasonable prices. It will take the better part of a century and will need a political will spanning parties, continents, and generations. We need to be in for the long haul and develop cost-effective strategies that won't splinter regardless of overarching ambitions or false directions.

This is why one of our generational challenges should be for *all nations to commit themselves to spending 0.05 percent of GDP in research and development of noncarbon emitting energy technologies.* This is a tenfold increase on current expenditures yet would cost a relatively minor $25 billion per year (seven times cheaper than Kyoto and many more times cheaper than Kyoto II). Such a commitment could include all nations, with wealthier nations paying the larger share, and would let each country focus on its own future vision of energy needs, whether that means concentrating on renewable sources, nuclear energy, fusion, carbon storage, conservation, or searching for new and more exotic opportunities.

Funding research and development globally would create a momentum that could recapture the vision of delivering both a low-carbon and high-income world. Lower energy costs and high spin-off innovation are potential benefits that possibly avoid ever stronger temptations to free-riding and the ever tougher negotiations over increasingly restrictive Kyoto Protocol-style treaties. A global financial commitment makes it plausible to envision stabilizing climate changes at reasonable levels.

I believe it would be the way to bridge a century of parties, continents, and generations, creating a sustainable, low-cost opportunity to create the alternative energy technologies that will power the future.

To move toward this goal we need to create sensible policy dialogue. This requires us to talk openly about priorities. Often there is strong sentiment in any public discussion that we should do *anything* required to make a situation better. But clearly we don't actually do that. When we talk about schools, we know that more teachers would likely provide our children with a better education.[12] Yet we do not hire more teachers simply because we also have to spend money in other areas. When we talk about hospitals, we know that access to better equipment is likely to provide better treatment, yet we don't supply an infinite amount of resources.[13] When we talk about the environment, we know tougher restrictions will mean better protection, but this also comes with higher costs.

Consider traffic fatalities, which are one of the ten leading causes of deaths in the world. In the U.S., 42,600 people die in traffic accidents and 2.8 million people are injured each year (USCB, 2006, 672). Globally, it is estimated that 1.2 million people die from traffic accidents and 50 million are injured every year (Lopez, Mathers, Ezzati, Jamison, and Murray 2006, 1751; WHO 2002, 72; 2004, 3, 172).

About 2 percent of all deaths in the world are traffic-related and about 90 percent of the traffic deaths occur in third world countries (WHO 2004, 172). The total cost is a phenomenal $512 billion a year

(WHO 2004, 5). Due to increasing traffic (especially in the third world) and due to ever better health conditions, the World Heath Organization estimates that by 2020, traffic fatalities will be the second leading cause of death in the world, after heart disease.[14]

Amazingly, we have the technology to make all of this go away. We could instantly save 1.2 million humans and eliminate $500 billion worth of damage. We would particularly help the third world. The answer is simply lowering speed limits to 5 mph. We could avoid almost all of the 50 million injuries each year. But of course we will not do this. Why? The simple answer that almost all of us would offer is that the benefits from driving moderately fast far outweigh the costs. While the cost is obvious in terms of those killed and maimed, the benefits are much more prosaic and dispersed but nonetheless important— traffic interconnects our society by bringing goods at competitive prices to where we live and bringing people together to where we work, and lets us live where we like while allowing us to visit and meet with many others. A world moving only at 5 mph is a world gone medieval.

This is not meant to be flippant. We really could solve one of the world's top problems if we wanted. We know traffic deaths are almost entirely caused by man. We have the technology to reduce deaths to zero. Yet we persist in exacerbating the problem each year, making traffic an ever-bigger killer.

I suggest that the comparison with global warming is insightful; we have the technology to reduce it to zero, yet we seem to persist in going ahead and exacerbating the problem each year, causing temperatures to continue to increase to new heights by 2020. Why? Because the benefits from moderately using fossil fuels far outweigh the costs. Yes, the costs are obvious in the "fear, terror, and disaster" we read about in the papers every day.

But the benefits of fossil fuels, though much more prosaic, are nonetheless important. Fossil fuels provide us with low-cost electricity, heat, food, communication, and travel.[15] Electrical air conditioning means that people in the U.S. no longer die in droves during heat waves (Davis, Knappenberger, Michaels, and Novicoff 2003). Cheaper fuels would have avoided a significant number of the 150,000 people that have died in the UK since 2000 due to cold winters.[16]

Because of fossil fuels, food can be grown cheaply, giving us access to fruits and vegetables year round, which has probably reduced cancer rates by at least 25 percent.[17] Cars allow us to commute to city centers for work while living in areas that provide us with space and nature around our homes, whereas communication and cheap flights have given ever more people the opportunity to experience other cultures and forge friendships globally (Schäfer 2006).

In the third world, access to fossil fuels is crucial. About 1.6 billion people don't have access to electricity, which seriously impedes human development (IEA 2004, 338–40). Worldwide, about 2.5 billion people rely on biomass such as wood and waste (including dung) to cook and keep warm (IEA 2006, 419ff). For many Indian women, searching for wood takes about three hours each day, and sometimes they walk more than 10 kilometers a day. All of this causes excessive deforestation (IEA 2006, 428; Kammen 1995; Kelkar 2006). About 1.3 million people—mostly women and children—die each year due to heavy indoor air pollution. A switch from biomass to fossil fuels would dramatically improve 2.5 billion lives; the cost of $1.5 billion annually would be greatly superseded by benefits of about $90 billion.[18] Both for the developed and the developing world, a world without fossil fuels—in the short or medium term—is, again, a lot like reverting back to the middle ages.

This does not mean that we should not talk about how to reduce the impact of traffic and global warming. Most countries have strict regulation on speed limits—if they didn't, fatalities would be much higher. Yet, studies also show that lowering the average speed in Western Europe by just 5 kilometers per hour could reduce fatalities by 25 percent—with about 10,000 fewer people killed each year (WHO, 2002, 72; 2004, 172). Apparently, democracies in Europe are not willing to give up on the extra benefits from faster driving to save 10,000 people.

This is parallel to the debate we are having about global warming. We can realistically talk about $2 or even a $14 CO_2 tax. But suggesting a $140 tax, as Al Gore does, seems to be far outside the envelope.

Suggesting a 96 percent carbon reduction for the OECD by 2030 seems a bit like suggesting a 5 mph speed limit in the traffic debate. It is technically doable, but it is very unlikely to happen.

One of the most important issues when it comes to climate change is that we cool our dialogue and consider the arguments for and against different policies. In the heat of a loud and obnoxious debate, facts and reason lose out.

NOTES

1. (IPCC, 2007b:10.6.5). Notice that the available report (IPCC 2007a) has a midpoint of 38.5 cm.

2. Using (Jevrejeva, Grinsted, Moore, and Holgate 2006), 11.4 inches since 1860.

3. 1996: 38–35 cm (IPCC and Houghton 1996:364), 1992 and 1983 EPA from Yohe and Neumann 1997, 243; 250.

4. (Nicholls and Tol 2006, 1088), estimated for 2085. Notice low-lying undeveloped coasts in places such as Arctic Russia, Canada and Alaska are expected to be undefended. Notice that the numbers presented are for loss of dry land, whereas up to 18 percent of global wetlands will be lost.

5. "Micronesia" (CIA 2006).

6. Labour has urged a 20 percent CO_2 emission cut from 1990 in 2010 in three election manifestos (BBC Annon. 2006a); this translates into a 14.6 percent reduction from 1997 levels. From 1997 to 2004, CO_2 emissions increased 3.4 percent (EIA 2006).

7. Take, for instance, both Gore's "we have to find a way to communicate the direness of the situation" and Hansen's "scientists have not done a good job communicating with the public" (Fischer 2006).

8. Developing countries emitted 10.171 Gt of the global 26 Gt in 2004 (IEA, 2006, 513, 493) (OECD countries 51 percent in 2003 (OECD 2006, 148), Weyant estimates 29 percent from industrialized countries (1998, 2286), IPCC emission scenarios from 23 in the business-as-usual A1 to 36 percent (Nakicenovic and IPCC WG III 2000).

9. Based on a cost of $50 per ton of carbon (Tol 2005:2071).

10. From the Environmental Assessment Institute we asked him in July 2005: "Would you still stick by the conclusion that $15/tC seems justified or would you rather only present an upper limit of the estimate?" He answered: "I'd prefer not to present a central estimate, but if you put a gun to my head I would say $7/tC, the median estimate

with a 3 percent pure rate of time preference" ($7/tC = $1.9/tCO$_2$). This is comparable with Pearce's estimate of $1–2.5/tCO$_2$ ($4–9/tC) (2003:369).

11. There are many advantages to taxes over emission caps, mainly that with taxes, authorities have an interest in collecting them (because it funds the government), whereas with caps, individual countries have much less interest in achieving goals with such an effort, because the benefits are dispersed (global) and the damages localized (to local industries).

12. (Akerhielm 1995; Angrist and Lavy 1999; Graddy and Stevens 2005). Of course, this could be modified in many ways, such as by focusing on paying teachers better, more resources for books, computers, etc. It is also important that we should be saying "more teachers will at least not make schools worse and will likely make them better," as most studies show some or no effect from extra resources but very few show negative results.

13. E.g., (Fleitas et al. 2006; Gebhardt and Norris 2006). On the other hand, it is less clear that (after a certain limit) more doctors and bed space is the answer, since they may just make for more visits and increase the possibility of infections and harm (Weinberger, Oddone, and Henderson 1996; Wennberg et al. 2004).

14. (WHO 2002, 129) puts it second, whereas (WHO 2004, 5) puts it third.

15. This only looks at the marginal benefit of fossil fuels—which is the relevant one for our discussion. On a basic level, though, it is important to remember that they have fundamentally changed our lives. Before fossil fuels, we would spend hours gathering wood, contributing to deforestation and soil erosion—as billions in the third world still do today (Kammen 1995). We have electric washing machines that have cut domestic work dramatically. The historical economist Stanley Lebergott wrote only semi-jokingly: "From 1620 to 1920 the American washing machine was a housewife" (Lebergott 1993, 112). In 1900, a housewife spent seven hours a week laundering, carrying 200 gallons of water into the house and using a scrub board. Today, she spends 84 minutes with much less strain (Robinson and Godbey 1997, 327). We have a fridge that has both given us more spare time and allowed us to avoid rotten food and eat a more healthy diet of fruit and vegetables (Lebergott 1995, 155). By the end of the nineteenth century human labor made up 94 percent of all industrial work in the U.S. Today, it constitutes only 8 percent (Berry, Conkling, Ray, and Berry 1993, 131). If we think for a moment of the energy we use in terms of "servants," each with the same work power as

a human being, each person in Western Europe has access to 150 servants, in the U.S. about 300, and even in India each person has 15 servants to help (Craig, Vaughan, and Skinner 1996:103).

16. Steve Jones, "Help the Aged," said: "Many pensioners still agonize about whether or not to heat their homes in the cold weather. In the world's fourth richest country, this is simply shameful" (BBC Annon. 2006b).

17. The World Cancer Research Fund study estimates that increasing the intake of fruit and vegetables from an average of about 250 g/day to 400 g/day would reduce the overall frequency of cancer by around 23 percent (WCRF 1997:540).

18. Mainly from fewer deaths and less time use.

REFERENCES

Akerhielm, K. 1995. "Does class size matter?" *Economics of Education Review* 14(3), 229–41.

Angrist, J. D., and V. Lavy. 1999. "Using Maimonides' rule to estimate the effect of class size on scholastic achievement." *Quarterly Journal of Economics* 114(2), 533–75.

BBC Annon. 2006a, March 28. UK to miss CO$_2$ emissions target. BBC. Available at http://news.bbc.co.uk/2/hi/science/nature/4849672.stm. Accessed January 29, 2007.

———. 2006b, October 27. "Winter death toll" drops by 19%: Deaths in England and Wales fell to 25,700 last winter, a decline of 19% on the previous year. BBC Web site. Available at http://news.bbc.co.uk/2/hi/uk_news/6090492.stm. Accessed November 13, 2006.

Berry, B. J. L., E. C. Conkling, and D. M. Ray. 1993. *The Global Economy: Resource Use, Locational Choice, and International Trade.* Englewood Cliffs, N.J.: Prentice Hall.

CIA. 2006. *CIA World Fact Book.* Central Intelligence Agency, December 12.

Clinton Global Initiative. 2005, September 15. Special Opening Plenary Session: Perspectives on the Global Challenges of Our Time. Available at http://attend.clintonglobalinitiative.org/pdf/transcripts/plenary/cgi_09_15_05_plenary_1.pdf. Accessed January 29, 2007.

Craig, J. R., D. J. Vaughan, and B. J. Skinner. 1996. *Resources of the Earth: Origin, Use and Environmental Impact.* Upper Saddle River, N.J.: Prentice Hall.

Davis, R. E., P. C. Knappenberger, P. J. Michaels, and W. M. Novicoff. 2003. "Changing heat-related mortality in the United States". *Environmental Health Perspectives* 111(14), 1712–18.

EIA. 2006. International Energy Annual 2004. Energy Information Agency. Available at http://www.eia.doe.gov/iea/. Accessed November 30, 2006.

Fischer, D. 2006, December 15. Gore urges scientists to speak up. Contra Costa Times. Available at http://www.truthout.org/cgi-bin/artman/exec/view.cgi/67/24524. Accessed January 29, 2007.

Fleitas, I., et al. 2006. The quality of radiology services in five Latin American countries. *Revista Panamericana De Salud Publica-Pan American Journal of Public Health* 20(2–3), 113–24.

Gebhardt, J. G., and T. E. Norris 2006. Acute stroke care at rural hospitals in Idaho: Challenges in expediting stroke care. *Journal of Rural Health* 22, 88–91.

Graddy, K., and M. Stevens. 2005. The impact of school resources on student performance: A study of private schools in the United Kingdom. *Industrial & Labor Relations Review* 58(3), 435–51.

IEA. 2004. World Energy Outlook 2004: IEA Publications.

———. 2006. World Energy Outlook 2006: IEA Publications.

IPCC. 2007a. Climate Change 2007: WGI: Summary for Policymakers.

———. 2007b. Climate Change 2007: WGI: The Physical Science Basis. Cambridge (UK): Cambridge University Press.

IPCC and J. T. Houghton. 1996. Climate Change 1995: The Science of Climate Change. Cambridge, New York: Cambridge University Press.

Jevrejeva, S., A. Grinsted, J. C. Moore, and S. Holgate. 2006. Nonlinear trends and multiyear cycles in sea level records. *Journal of Geophysical Research-Oceans* 111(C9).

Kammen, D. M. 1995. Cookstoves for the Developing-World. *Scientific American* 273(1), 72–75.

Kelkar, G. 2006, May 8. The Gender Face of Energy. Presentation at CSD 14 Learning Centre, United Nations. Available at http://www.un.org/esa/sustdev/csd/csd14/lc/presentation/gender2.pdf. Accessed January 30, 2007.

Lebergott, S. 1993. Pursuing Happiness: American Consumers in the Twentieth Century. Princeton, N.J.: Princeton University Press.

———. 1995. Long-term trends in the US standard of living. In J. Simon (Ed.), State of Humanity (pp. 149–60). Oxford: Blackwell.

Lopez, A. D., C. D. Mathers, M. Ezzati, D. T. Jamison, and C. J. L. Murray. 2006. Global and regional burden of disease and risk factors, 2001: systematic analysis of population health data. Lancet 367(9524), 1747–57.

Nakicenovic, N., and IPCC WG III. 2000. Special Report on Emissions Scenarios: a Special Report of Working Group III of the Intergovernmental Panel on Climate Change. Cambridge, New York: Cambridge University Press.

Nicholls, R. J., and R. S. J. Tol. 2006. "Impacts and responses to sea-level rise: a global analysis of the SRES scenarios over the twenty-first century." *Philosophical Transactions of the Royal Society A—Mathematical Physical and Engineering Sciences* 364(1841), 1073–95.

OECD. 2006. *OECD factbook* 2006 (p. v.). Paris: Organization for Economic Co-operation and Development.

Pearce, D. 2003. "The social cost of carbon and its policy implications." *Oxford Review of Economic Policy* 19(3), 362–84.

Robinson, J. P., and G. Godbey. 1997. *Time for Life: The Surprising Ways Americans Use Their Time.* University Park, PA.: Pennsylvania State University Press.

Schäfer, A. 2006. "Long-term trends in global passenger mobility." *Bridge* 36(4), 24–32.

Tol, R. S. J. 2004. The double trade-off between adaptation and mitigation for sea level rise: an application of FUND. Hamburg University and Centre for Marine and Atmospheric Science, Hamburg.

———. 2005. "The marginal damage costs of carbon dioxide emissions: An assessment of the uncertainties." *Energy Policy* 33(16), 2064–74.

———. 2007. "Europe's long-term climate target: A critical evaluation." *Energy Policy* 35(1), 424–32.

UNFCCC. 1992. United Nations Framework Convention on Climate Change: United Nations Framework Convention on Climate Change.

USCB. 2006. Statistical Abstract of the United States: 2007. U.S. Census Bureau. Available at http://www.census.gov/prod/www/statistical-abstract.html. Accessed January 30, 2007.

WCRF. 1997. *Food, Nutrition and the Prevention of Cancer: A Global Perspective.* Washington, D.C.: World Cancer Research Fund & American Institute for Cancer Research.

Weinberger, M., E. Z. Oddone, and W. G. Henderson. 1996. "Does increased access to primary care reduce hospital readmissions?" *New England Journal of Medicine* 334(22), 1441–47.

Wennberg, J. E., et al. 2004. "Use of hospitals, physician visits, and hospice care during last six months of life among cohorts loyal to highly respected hospitals in the United States." *British Medical Journal* 328(7440), 607–610A.

WHO. 2002. The world health report 2002—reducing risk, promoting healthy life. World Health Organization.

———. 2004. World report on road traffic injury prevention: World Health Organization.

Wigley, T. M. L. 1998. "The Kyoto Protocol: CO_2, CH_4 and climate implications." *Geophysical Research Letters* 25(13), 2285–88.

Yohe, G., and J. Neumann. 1997. "Planning for sea level rise and shore protection under climate uncertainty." *Climatic Change* 37, 243–70.

READING QUESTIONS

1. How will climate change affect the poorest countries like Micronesia? How will it affect the richest countries? Where should our focus be regarding climate change according to Lomborg?
2. Why does Lomborg think we need to be more realistic about climate change? How have current governments failed with respect to their past promises to reduce emissions?
3. What two points does Lomborg raise for the statistical research that has been done so far on the costs of reducing CO_2 emissions? What should the goal of each nation be according to Lomborg? How does he think the nations of the world can achieve this goal?
4. Explain the traffic analogy considered by Lomborg. How does this case illustrate why it is unlikely that the nations and people of the world will be able to meet the reduced emissions goals set by Al Gore?

DISCUSSION QUESTIONS

1. Lomborg claims that climate change is not the end of the world but that it will be bad for some people. How realistic is this claim? What reasons could be offered in support of the view that climate change does pose a significant threat to the majority of people in the world?
2. Lomborg suggests that we need to consider arguments for and against different policies in order to combat the effects of climate change successfully. Is he right to suggest that the nations of the world are not currently engaged in this type of project? Why or why not? Are there any sorts of policies that deserve more consideration than others? What kinds of policies should be rejected?

ADDITIONAL RESOURCES

Web Resources

Global Issues, <www.globalissues.org/>. Site featuring many articles on global ethical issues (most of them written by the site's creator, Anup Shah).

The World Watch Institute, <www.worldwatch.org>. Features independent research on the environment and its protection.

Wikipedia, <http://en.wikipedia.org/wiki/Main Page>. Contains useful entries on global warming and on the International Panel of Climate Change (IPCC).

Brennan, Andrew and Yeuk-Sze Lo, "Environmental Ethics," *Stanford Encyclopedia of Philosophy*, <http://plato.stanford.edu/entries/ethics-environmental/>. An overview of the topic including a discussion of traditional ethical theories and environmental ethics.

Authored Books and Articles

Attfield, Robin, *Environmental Ethics: An Overview for the Twenty-First Century* (Cambridge: Polity Press, 2003). An introduction to environmental ethics that usefully surveys major positions and defends what the author calls "biocentric consequentialism."

Gardiner, Stephen M., "Ethics and Global Climate Change," *Ethics* 114 (2004): 555–600. A critical evaluation of the arguments by Lomborg and other like-minded skeptics.

Gore, Al, *An Inconvenient Truth* (Emmaus, PA: Rodale Books, 2006). Former U.S. Vice President's book version of his documentary film of the same name about the dangers of global warming.

Houghton, John, *Global Warming: The Complete Briefing*, 4th. (Cambridge: Cambridge University Press, 2009). An undergraduate textbook that provides a comprehensive scientific guide to global warming.

Lomborg, Bjørn, *Cool It: The Skeptical Environmentalist's Guide to Global Warming* (New York: Random House, 2007, reprinted: Vintage, 2008). An overview by economist and statistician of the problems produced by global warming and how best to address them. This book and Lomborg's previous books on global warming have stirred much controversy.

Anthologies

Hayward, Tim, and Carol Gould (eds.), *The Journal of Social Philosophy* 40 (2009), special issue: The Global Environment, Climate Change, and Justice. Eight articles exploring ethical and political implications of global climate change, including issues of intra- and inter-generational justice.

Jameison, Dale (ed.), *A Companion to Environmental Philosophy* (Oxford: Blackwell Publishing, 2003). Contains thirty-six articles written for this volume, which covers a wide variety of cultural, legal, political, and ethical issues relating to the environment.

Kaufman, Frederick, A. (ed.), *Foundations of Environmental Philosophy* (New York: McGraw–Hill, 2003). Combines text written for students with selected readings covering a wide range of topics, including biocentrism, ecocentric ethics, anthropomorphism, deep ecology, and ecofeminism.

Light, Andrew, and Rolston Holmes III (eds.), *Environmental Ethics: An Anthology* (London: Blackwell, 2002). Classical and contemporary selections covering a wide range of topics organized into six parts: (1) What Is Environmental Ethics?, (2) Who Counts in Environmental Ethics?, (3) Is Nature Intrinsically Valuable?, (4) Is There One Environmental Ethics?, (5) Focusing on General Issues, and (6) What on Earth Do We Want? Human Social Issues and Environmental Values.

Pojman, Louis P., *Environmental Ethics: Readings in Theory and Application,* 4th ed. (Belmont, CA: Wadsworth, 2004). A collection of eighty-two articles debating most every aspect of ethical concern for the environment including new articles for this edition on ecorealism, world hunger, population, and city life.

Sandler, Ronald, and Cafaro, Philip (eds.), *Environmental Virtue Ethics* (Lanham, MD: Rowman & Littlefield, 2005). Thirteen essays organized into four parts: (1) Recognizing Environmental Virtue Ethics, (2) Environmental Virtue Ethics Theory, (3) Environmental Virtues and Vices, and (4) Applying Environmental Virtue Ethics.

Schmidtz, David, and Elizabeth Willott (eds.), *Environmental Ethics: What Really Matters, What Really Works* (New York: Oxford University Press, 2001). This comprehensive anthology features sixty-two selections organized into two major parts: (1) What Really Matters: Essays on Value in Nature, and (2) What Really Works: Essays on Human Ecology.

Quick Guide to Moral Theories

Central ideas from each of the six types of moral theory surveyed in chapter 1 are included here.

A. CONSEQUENTIALISM

Basic idea:

C   Right action is to be understood entirely in terms of the overall intrinsic value of the consequences of the action compared to the overall intrinsic value of the consequences associated with alternative actions an agent might perform instead. An action is right if and only if (and because) its consequences would be at least as good as the consequences of any alternative action that the agent might perform instead.

Types of consequentialist theory:

Utilitarianism: A version of consequentialism that construes intrinsic value in terms of happiness or welfare.

U   An action is right if and only if (and because) it would (if performed) likely produce at least as high a utility (net overall balance of welfare) as would any other alternative action one might perform instead.

Perfectionist consequentialism: a version that construes intrinsic value in terms of human perfections, the most general of which are knowledge and achievement.

PC   An action is right if and only if (and because) it would (if performed) likely bring about a greater net balance of perfectionist goods than would any alternative action one might perform instead.

Rule consequentialism: a version that evaluates competing rules in terms of their acceptance value and then evaluates particular actions by reference to the acceptance value of associated rules.

> **RC** An action is right if and only if (and because) it is permitted by a rule whose associated acceptance value is at least as high as the acceptance value of any other rule applying to the situation.

B. NATURAL LAW THEORY

Basic principle:

> **NLT** An action is right if and only if (and because) in performing the action one does not *directly* violate any of the basic values (human life, procreation, knowledge, and sociability).

Doctrine of double effect

> **DDE** An action that would bring about at least one evil effect and at least one good effect is morally permissible if (and only if) the following conditions are satisfied:
>
> *Intrinsic permissibility.* The action in question, apart from its effects, is morally permissible;
>
> *Necessity:* It is not possible to bring about the good effect except by performing an action that will bring about the evil effect in question;
>
> *Nonintentionality:* The evil effect is not intended—it is neither one's end nor a chosen means for bringing about some intended end;
>
> *Proportionality:* The evil that will be brought about by the action is not out of proportion to the good being aimed at.

A violation that satisfies all of the provisions of the DDE counts as an indirect violation and is thus not prohibited by NLT.

C. KANTIAN MORAL THEORY

Humanity formulation of Kant's fundamental principle, the categorical imperative:

> **H** An action is right if and only if (and because) the action treats persons (including oneself) as ends in themselves and not as a mere means.

Universal Law formulation

> **UL** An action is right if and only if one can both (a) consistently conceive of everyone adopting and acting on the general policy (that is, the maxim) of one's action, and also (b) consistently will that everyone act on that maxim.

D. RIGHTS-BASED MORAL THEORY

As the name suggests, a rights-based moral theory takes the notion of moral rights as basic and defines or characterizes the rightness or wrongness of actions in terms of moral rights.

> **R** An action is right if and only if (and because) in performing it either (a) one does not violate the fundamental moral rights of others, or (b) in cases in which it is not possible to respect all such rights because they are in conflict, one's action is among the best ways to protect the most important rights in the case at hand.

Typical moral rights taken as fundamental include the Jeffersonian rights to life, various liberties, and the freedom to pursue one's own happiness.

E. VIRTUE ETHICS

A type of moral theory that takes considerations of virtue and vice to be the basis for defining or characterizing the rightness and wrongness of actions.

> **VE** An action is right if and only if (and because) it is what a virtuous agent (acting in character) might choose to do in the circumstances under consideration.

Commonly recognized virtues include honesty, courage, justice, temperance, beneficence, humility, loyalty, and gratitude.

F. ETHICS OF PRIMA FACIE DUTY

This sort of moral theory features a plurality of principles of prima facie duty. To reach an all-things-considered moral verdict in cases in which two or more principles apply and favor conflicting actions, one must use moral judgment to figure out which duty is most stringent.

Ross's list of prima facie duties:

Justice: prima facie, one ought to ensure that pleasure is distributed according to merit.

Beneficence:	prima facie, one ought to help those in need and, in general, increase the virtue, pleasure, and knowledge of others.
Self-improvement:	prima facie, one ought to improve oneself with respect to one's own virtue and knowledge.
Nonmaleficence:	prima facie, one ought to refrain from harming others.
Fidelity:	prima facie, one ought to keep one's promises.
Reparation:	prima facie, one ought to make amends to others for any past wrongs one has done them.
Gratitude:	prima facie, one ought to show gratitude toward one's benefactors.

Audi's proposed additions to Ross's list:

Veracity:	prima facie, one ought not to lie.
Enhancement and preservation of freedom:	prima facie, one ought to contribute to increasing or at least preserving the freedom of others with priority given to removing constraints over enhancing opportunities.
Respectfulness:	prima facie, one ought, in the manner of our relations with other people, treat others respectfully.

Glossary

Each entry in the glossary indicates the chapter and section in which the term is first introduced and, in some cases, additional places where the term occurs. Cross-references are in italics.

Abolitionist   Someone who is opposed to the death penalty and advocates its abolition. (chap. 11, intro.)

Abortion   Cases in which a pregnancy is intentionally interrupted and involves (as part of the process or aim of interruption) the intentional killing of the fetus. (chap. 9, sec. 2)

Acceptance value   The value of the consequences that would likely be brought about through the acceptance of some rule. See *rule consequentialism.* (chap. 1, sec. 2A)

Act consequentialism   Any version of *consequentialism* according to which it is the net intrinsic value of the consequences of particular alternative actions open to an agent in some situation that determines the rightness or wrongness of those alternative actions. See *rule consequentialism.* (chap. 1, sec. 2A)

Active euthanasia   Cases of euthanasia in which one party actively intervenes to bring about the death of another. See *euthanasia, passive euthanasia.* (chap. 7, sec. 1)

Addiction   A type of compulsive behavior involving dependence on some substance or activity that is undesirable. It is common to distinguish between physical and psychological addiction. (chap. 5, sec. 2)

Adult stem cell   Stem cell of a fully formed individual. See *stem cell.* (chap. 10, sec.1)

Adultery   The act of voluntary sexual intercourse between a married person and someone other than his or her legal spouse. (chap. 3, sec. 3)

Anthropocentrism   The only beings who possess *direct moral standing* are human beings. All other beings (living and nonliving) are of mere indirect moral concern. (chap. 14, sec. 2)

Antiwar pacifism   The view that wars are always or nearly always morally wrong. (chap. 12, sec. 4)

Assisted suicide   A suicide in which another party helps an individual commit suicide by providing either the information or the means, or by directly helping the person who commits the act. See *suicide.* (chap. 7, sec. 2)

Atomism   The view according to which the primary items of moral appraisal are individuals—it is only individuals that can be properly judged as intrinsically valuable, or rights holders, or as having obligations. (chap. 14, sec. 2)

Basic right   Any right of particular importance within the realm of rights. So, for instance, the right to life is a basic right. (chap. 1, sec. 2D)

Beneficence, duty of   The duty to help those in dire need. (chap. 13, intro. and sec. 1)

Biocentrism   The view that all living beings because they are living possess *direct moral standing*. Thus, morality includes requirements of direct moral concern for all living beings. (chap. 14, sec. 2)

Categorical imperative   The fundamental moral principle in the moral theory of Immanuel Kant. As this principle is employed in reasoning about moral issues, it takes two forms: the *Universal Law* and the *Humanity* formulations. (chap. 1, sec. 2C)

Civil unions   A legal category that grants some rights to same-sex couples. (chap. 3, sec. 3)

Clone   An individual that comes about as a result of cloning. Also referred to as an SCNT individual. (chap. 10, sec. 1)

Cloning   The process of "asexually" producing a biological organism that is virtually genetically identical to another organism. (chap. 10, sec. 1)

Cold war   A conflict over ideological differences carried on by methods short of sustained overt military action and usually without breaking off diplomatic relations. (chap 12, sec. 1)

Consequentialism (C)   A type of moral theory according to which the rightness and wrongness of actions is to be explained entirely in terms of the intrinsic value of the consequences associated with either individual concrete actions or rules associated with actions. See *act consequentialism, rule consequentialism, intrinsic value, utilitarianism, perfectionist consequentialism.* (chap. 1, sec. 2A)

Consequentialist theory of punishment   A theory of punishment according to which (C1) punishment as a response to crime is morally justified if and only if this practice, compared to any other response to crime, will likely produce as much overall intrinsic value as would any other response, and (C2) a specific punishment for a certain crime is morally justified if and only if it would likely produce at least as much overall intrinsic value as would any other alternative punishment. See *retributive theory of punishment.* (chap 11, sec. 2)

Conservatism   A political ideology that maintains that it is proper for a government to advocate and sometimes enforce a particular conception of the good life. This ideology tends to attach great importance to various cultural traditions, in contrast to Liberal ideology. See *liberalism.* (chap. 4, sec. 2)

Conservative position on some issue   A moral position on some issue which, in contrast to moderate and liberal positions, is restrictive in what it holds to be morally permissible behavior with regard to the issue. For example, with regard to issues of sexual morality, a typical conservative position holds that sexual intercourse is morally wrong except between married couples of the opposite sex. (chap. 3, sec. 1; chap. 9, sec. 5)

Context sensitivity thesis (CS)   The thesis that the rightness or wrongness of an action may depend in part on facts about the agent and her circumstances, including facts about such socially variable norms for what counts as an insult, a person's privacy, proper respect for others, and so forth. Not to be confused with *ethical relativism.* (chap. 1, appendix)

Deterrence   Someone is deterred from committing murder by the threat of the death penalty only if his recognition of the death penalty as a possible consequence of committing murder explains why he does not commit it. (chap. 11, sec. 2)

Direct moral standing   For something to have direct moral standing is for it to possess features in virtue of which it deserves to be given moral consideration by agents who are capable of making moral choice. See *indirect moral standing.* (chap. 8, sec. 1; chap. 9, sec. 3; chap. 14, sec. 1)

Divine command theory (DCT)   A moral theory according to which what makes an action right or wrong, or makes something intrinsically good or bad are the commands of God. (chap. 1, appendix)

Doctrine of double effect (DDE)   This doctrine is composed of a set of provisions under which it is morally permissible to knowingly bring about evil in the pursuit of the good. DDE is associated with *natural law theory.* (chap. 1, sec. 2B)

DOMA   An abbreviation for the 1997 U.S. Defense of Marriage Act which, for purposes of U.S. Federal law, defines "marriage" as a legal union between one man and one woman. (chap. 3, sec. 3)

Domestic partnerships   A legal category that extends some rights to unmarried couples, including same-sex couples. (chap. 3, sec. 3)

Drug   Any chemical substance that affects the functioning of living organisms. See also *psychotropic drug.* (chap. 5, sec. 1)

Drug abuse   Excessive nonmedical use of a drug that may cause harm to oneself or to others. (chap. 5, sec. 2)

Drug criminalization/decriminalization   The former refers to having legal penalties for the use and possession of small quantities of drugs; the latter refers to not having such legal penalties. (chap. 5, sec. 4)

Drug prohibition/legalization   The former refers to having legal penalties for the manufacture, sale, and distribution of large quantities of drugs; the latter refers to lack of such penalties. (chap. 5, sec. 4)

Duty-based moral theory   Any moral theory that takes the concept of duty to be basic and so characterizes or defines right action independently of considerations of intrinsic value and independently of considerations of moral rights. Examples include the ethics of prima facie duty and Kantian moral theory. Duty-based moral theories contrast with *value-based moral theories* and with *rights-based moral theories.* (chap. 1, sec.1)

Ecocentrism   The view according to which the primary bearers of *direct moral standing* are ecosystems in virtue of their functional integrity. Hence, morality involves moral obligations to maintain the functional integrity of ecosystems, and because, according to this view, ecosystems are primary bearers of direct moral standing, their preservation takes moral precedence over concern for individual things and creatures that compose the system. See *ecosystem, ecoholism.* (chap. 14, sec. 2)

Ecoholism   The view that both ecosystems and at least some individual items that make up an ecosystem have direct moral standing. (chap. 14, sec. 2)

Ecosystem   A whole composed of both living and nonliving things including animals, plants, bodies of water, sunlight, and other geological factors. See *ecocentrism.* (chap. 14, sec. 2)

Embryo   The term used to refer to a stage in prenatal development which in humans begins at roughly the second week of pregnancy and lasts until roughly the eighth week. See *zygote, fetus.* (chap. 9, sec.1; chap. 10, sec.1)

Embryonic stem cell   Stem cells found in an embryo. See *stem cell.* (chap. 10, sec.1)

Environmenal ethics   The view that (1) there are nonhuman beings that have direct moral standing, and (2) the class of such beings is larger than the class of conscious beings. (chap. 14, sec. 3)

Erotica   The depiction of erotic behavior (as in pictures or writing) intended to cause sexual excitement, but that either does not describe or portray sexual behavior that is degrading, or does not endorse such degrading behavior. See *pornography.* (chap. 4, sec. 1)

Ethical (moral) relativism (ER)   A type of moral theory which, in one of its most popular forms, claims that the rightness or wrongness of an action (performed by a member of some culture) is to be explained by reference to the moral code of the culture in question. (chap. 1, appendix)

Ethics of prima facie duty   A moral theory, originally developed by W. D. Ross, that features a plurality of moral principles that express *prima facie duties.* (chap. 1, sec. 2F)

Eugenics, human   The aim of improving the human race through genetic manipulation. (chap. 10, sec. 3)

Euthanasia   The act or practice of killing or allowing someone to die on grounds of mercy. (chap. 7, sec. 1)

Explanatory power, principle of   A principle for evaluating how well a moral theory does at satisfying the *theoretical aim* of such theories. According to this principle, a moral theory should feature principles that explain our more specific considered moral beliefs, thus helping us to understand why actions and other items of evaluation have the moral status they have. See *theoretical aim.* (chap. 1, sec. 3)

Extrinsic value   Something has extrinsic value when its value (good or bad) depends on how it is related to something having *intrinsic value.* (chap. 1, sec. 1)

Fetus   Used in a strict biological sense, a fetus is an unborn vertebrate animal that has developed to the point of having the basic structure that is characteristic of its kind. This stage is characterized by growth and full development of its organs. Also spelled "foetus." See *zygote, embryo.* (chap. 9, sec. 1)

Gambling   Betting on an uncertain outcome in which one risks something of value with the hope of receiving something of greater value. (chap. 5, sec. 5)

Genetic enhancement   The process of manipulating genetic material in order to enhance the talents and capacities of living creatures. See *cloning.* (chap. 10, sec. 3)

Golden rule   Do unto others as you would have them do unto you. (chap. 1, sec. 2C)

Harm principle   A liberty-limiting principle according to which a government may justifiably pass laws to limit the liberty of its citizens in order to prohibit individuals from causing harm to other individuals or to society. See *liberty-limiting* principle. (chap. 4, sec. 2; chap. 5, sec. 3)

Hate speech   Language (oral or written) that expresses strong hatred, contempt, or intolerance for some social group, particularly social groups classified according to race, ethnicity, gender, sexual orientation, religion, disability, or nationality. (chap. 4, sec. 4)

Hedonistic utilitarianism (HU)   A version of *utilitarianism* featuring a hedonistic theory of intrinsic value. See *value hedonism*. (chap. 1, sec. 2A)

Holism   The view that wholes or collectives are bearers of value, or of rights, or of obligations. (chap. 14, sec. 2)

Homosexuality   Sexual activity, particularly intercourse, between members of the same sex. (chap. 3, sec. 3)

Hot war   A conflict involving actual fighting. (chap. 12, sec. 1)

Humanity formulation   A particular formulation of Kant's categorical imperative according to which an action is morally permissible if and only if (and because) the action treats humanity (whether in oneself or others) never as a mere means but as an end in itself. (chap. 1, sec. 2C)

In vitro fertilization (IVF)   The process through which a sperm fertilizes an egg outside a woman's body and is later implanted in a woman's uterus. (chap. 10, intro.)

Indirect moral standing   For something to have indirect moral standing is for it to deserve moral consideration only because it is related to something with direct moral standing. See *direct moral standing*. (chap. 8, sec. 1; chap. 9, sec. 3; chap. 14, sec. 1)

Induced pluripotent stem cells (iPSC)   Adult stem cells that have been genetically reprogrammed so as to have the capacity to develop into cells of most any type. (chap. 10, sec. 4)

Instrumental value   See *extrinsic value*.

Interrogational torture   Torture whose aim is to gain information from the victim. See *torture*. (chap. 12, sec. 3)

Intrinsic value   To say that something has intrinsic positive value—that it is intrinsically good—is to say that its goodness is grounded in features that are inherent in that thing. Similarly for intrinsic negative value. See *extrinsic value*. (chap. 1, sec. 1)

Involuntary euthanasia   Cases of euthanasia in which the individual has expressed a desire not to be the subject of euthanasia, but others act in violation of that desire. See *euthanasia, voluntary euthanasia, nonvoluntary euthanasia*. (chap. 7, sec. 1)

Jus in bello   That part of *just-war theory* that sets forth moral requirements for military activities within a war. (chap. 12, sec. 4)

Jus ad bellum   That part of *just-war theory* that sets forth moral requirements for going to war. (chap. 12, sec. 4)

Just-war theory   A moral theory about the conditions under which a government is morally justified in going to war (*jus ad bellum*) and what military activities are morally permissible within a war (*jus in bello*). (chap. 12, sec. 4)

Just-war pacifism   The moral view that all or nearly all wars fail to meet the demands of just-war theory and are therefore morally wrong. (chap. 12, sec. 4)

Kantian moral theory   A type of moral theory first developed by German philosopher Immanuel Kant (1724–1804) that features the notions of respect for persons and universality. These two guiding ideas are expressed in Kant's *Humanity formulation* of his fundamental moral principle—*the categorical imperative*—and in the *Universal Law formulation,* respectively. (chap 1, sec. 2C)

Legal moralism principle   A liberty-limiting principle according to which a government may justifiably pass laws to limit the liberty of its citizens in order to protect common moral standards, independently of whether the activities in question are harmful to others or to oneself. See *liberty-limiting principle.* (chap. 4, sec. 2; chap. 5, sec. 3)

Legal paternalism principle   A liberty-limiting principle according to which a government may justifiably pass laws to limit the liberty of its citizens in order to prohibit individuals from causing harm to themselves. See *liberty-limiting principle.* (chap. 4, sec. 2; chap. 5, sec. 3)

Legal punishment   Punishment administered by a legal authority. (chap. 11, sec. 1)

Legal rights   Rights that result or come into existence as the result of the activities of a legal statute or some other form governmental activity. To be contrasted with *moral rights.* (chap. 1, sec. 2D)

Lex talionis (law of retribution)   A principle of punishment for specific offenses according to which the appropriate punishment for a crime involves doing to the wrongdoer the same kind of action that he or she did to his or her victim(s). See *retributive theory of punishment.* (chap. 11, sec. 2)

Liberal position on some issue   A moral position on some issue which, in contrast to conservative and moderate positions, is not as restrictive in what it holds to be morally permissible behavior with regard to the issue. For example, on issues of sexual morality, a typical liberal position holds that sexual intercourse is morally permissible so long as those involved do not violate any general moral rules such as rules against deception and coercion. See *conservative position, moderate position.* (chap. 3, sec. 1; chap. 9, sec. 5)

Liberalism   A political ideology that puts strong emphasis on liberty and equality of individuals, maintaining in particular that proper respect for the liberty and equality of individuals requires that governments remain as neutral as possible over conceptions of the good life. See *conservatism.* (chap. 4, sec. 2)

Liberty-limiting principle   A principle that purports to set forth conditions under which a government may be morally justified in passing laws that limit the liberty of its citizens. (chap. 4, sec. 2; chap. 5, sec. 3)

Moderate position on some issue   A moral position on some issue which is less restrictive than a conservative position and more restrictive than a liberal position. For example, with regard to issues of sexual morality, a typical moderate, in contrast to a typical conservative, will hold that marriage is not a necessary condition for morally permissible sexual intercourse. In contrast to a typical liberal, a moderate will hold that there are such requirements as being committed to a relationship with one's sexual partner that must be observed in order for sexual intercourse to be morally permissible. See *conservative position, liberal position.* (chap. 3, sec. 1; chap. 9, sec. 5)

Moral criteria   Features of an action or other item of evaluation in virtue of which the action or item is morally right or wrong, good or bad. Moral criteria for an action's rightness or wrongness are often expressed in *principles of right conduct,* while criteria for something's being intrinsically good or bad are often expressed in *principles of value.* (chap. 1, sec. 1)

Moral judgment   An acquired skill at discerning what matters the most morally speaking and coming to an all-things-considered moral verdict, where this skill cannot be entirely captured by a set of rules. (chap. 1, secs. 2D and 2F)

Moral nihilism (regarding war)   The view that morality does not apply to war. (chap. 12, sec. 4)

Moral principle   A general statement that purports to set forth conditions under which an action or other item of evaluation is right or wrong, good or bad, virtuous or vicious. (chap. 1, sec. 1)

Moral rights   Rights that an individual or group has independently of any legal system or other conventions. Such rights have also been called "natural rights." To be contrasted with *legal rights.* (chap. 1, sec. 2D)

Moral standing   See *direct moral standing, indirect moral standing.*

Moral theory   An attempt to provide well-argued-for answers to general moral questions about the nature of right action and value. Typically, answers to such questions are expressed as *moral principles.* See *theory of right conduct, theory of value.* (chap. 1, intro. and sec. 1)

Natural law theory   A type of nonconsequentialist moral theory that attempts to ground morality on objective facts about human nature. See *doctrine of double effect, consequentialism.* (chap. 1, sec. 2B)

Natural right   See *moral right.* (chap. 1, sec. 2D)

Negative right   A right corresponding to a negative duty on the part of rights addressees to refrain from certain actions that would violate the right in question. For instance, the right to free speech is a negative right demanding that others not interfere with one's attempt to express oneself in speech. (chap. 1, sec. 2D)

Nonvoluntary euthanasia   Cases of euthanasia in which the individual has not given his consent to be subject to euthanasia because he has not expressed a view about what others may do in case, for example, he goes into a persistent vegetative state. See *euthanasia, voluntary euthanasia, involuntary euthanasia.* (chap. 7, sec. 1)

Offense principle   A liberty-limiting principle according to which a government may justifiably pass laws to limit the liberty of its citizens in order to prohibit individuals from offending others. See *liberty-limiting principle.* (chap. 4, sec. 2; chap. 5, sec. 3)

Oocyte   An unfertilized egg whose fertilization results in a *zygote.* (chap. 9, sec. 1)

Pacifism (regarding war)   See *antiwar pacifism.*

Passive euthanasia   Cases of euthanasia in which the death of the individual in question resulted from (or was hastened by) withholding or withdrawing some form of treatment which, had it been administered, would likely have prolonged the life of that individual. See *euthanasia, active euthanasia.* (chap. 7, sec. 1)

Perfectionist consequentialism   A version of *consequentialism* that accepts a perfectionist theory of value. See *value perfectionism.* (chap. 1, sec. 2A)

Pornography   The depiction of erotic behavior (as in pictures or writing) intended to cause sexual excitement. See *erotica.* (chap. 4, sec. 1)

Positive right   A right corresponding to a positive duty on the part of rights addressees to perform certain actions called for by the right in question. For instance, the right to an education corresponds to an obligation, presumably of a state, to engage in certain activities to help ensure that its citizens receive (or have the opportunity to receive) an education. (chap. 1, sec. 2D)

Practical aim (of a moral theory)   To offer *practical guidance* for how we might arrive at correct or justified moral verdicts about matters of moral concern. See *theoretical aim.* (chap. 1, sec. 1)

Practical guidance, principle of   A principle for evaluating how well a moral theory does at satisfying the practical aim of such theories. According to this principle, a moral theory should feature principles that are useful in guiding moral deliberation toward correct or justified moral verdicts about particular cases which can in turn be used to help guide choice. See *practical aim.* (chap. 1, sec. 3)

Prevention   Someone is prevented by execution from committing a particular murder only if had the individual not been executed he or she would have committed the murder. (chap. 11, sec. 2)

Prima facie duty   An action which (1) possesses a duty-relevant feature where (2) this feature is a defeasibly sufficient condition for the action being an all-things-considered duty. (chap. 1, sec. 2F)

Principle of proportionality   A principle of punishment according to which the appropriate moral measure of specific punishments requires that they be in "proportion" to the crime: that the severity of the punishment should "be commensurate" with the gravity of the offense. See *retributive theory of punishment, lex talionis.* (chap. 11, sec. 2)

Principle of right conduct   A general moral statement that purports to set forth conditions under which an action or a practice is morally right and, by implication, when an action is morally wrong. (chap. 1, sec. 1)

Principle of utility   The fundamental moral principle of the utilitarian moral theory, according to which (in its "act" version) an action is morally right (not wrong) if and only if (and because) it would likely produce as high a utility as would any available alternative action open to the agent. See *utility.* (chap. 1, sec. 2A)

Principle of value   A general statement that purports to set forth conditions under which some item of evaluation (a person, experience, or state of affairs) is intrinsically good and, by implication, when any such item is intrinsically bad (or evil). (chap. 1, sec. 2)

Psychotropic drug   A drug that produces changes in mood, feeling, and perception, including opiates, hallucinogens, stimulants, cannabis, and depressants. (chap. 5, sec. 1)

Racism   Racial prejudice or discrimination based on a belief that race is the primary determinant of human traits and capacities and that racial differences produce an inherent superiority of a particular race. (chap. 6, sec. 1)

Reparation   Activities involved in making up for past wrongs. (chap. 6, sec. 2)

Reproductive cloning   Cloning whose main purpose is to produce an individual member of the species. Human reproductive cloning has as its aim the production of a child. See *cloning, therapeutic cloning.* (chap. 10, intro.)

Retentionist   Someone who favors the death penalty and wants states that have it to retain it. (chap. 11, intro.)

Retributive theory of punishment   A theory of punishment according to which (R1) what morally justifies punishment of wrongdoers is that those who break the law (and are properly judged to have done so) *deserve* to be punished, and (R2) the punishment for a particular offense against the law should "fit" the crime. See *lex talionis, principle of proportionality.* (chap. 11, sec. 2)

Right   An entitlement (either moral or legal) to be free to engage in some activity or exercise some power or to be given something. See *legal rights, moral rights, negative rights, positive rights, rights addressee, rights content, rights holder.* (chap. 1, sec. 2D)

Rights   See *moral rights.*

Rights-based moral theory (R)   A type of moral theory according to which moral rights (claims) are the basis for explaining the rightness and wrongness of actions. See *moral rights, rights-focused approach.* (chap. 1, sec. 2D)

Rights-focused approach   An approach to moral issues that focuses primarily on moral rights. Such an approach need not be committed to a rights-based moral theory. See *moral rights, rights-based moral theory.* (chap. 1, sec. 2D)

Rights addressee   The individual or group against whom a right is held and who thus has an obligation toward the holder of the right. (chap. 1, sec. 2D)

Rights content   What a moral or legal right is a right to. (chap. 1, sec. 2D)

Rights holder   The individual or group that possesses rights. (chap. 1, sec. 2D)

Rights infringement   An action that goes against the rights of a rights holder but which in the circumstances is justified. A moral rights infringement is morally justified, a legal rights infringement is legally justified. (chap. 1, sec. 2D)

Rights, strength of   The strength of a right corresponds to how strong the moral or legal justification must be in order for the right to be justifiably overridden. The stronger the right, the stronger the justification must be in order to override the right. See *rights infringement.* (chap. 1, sec. 2D)

Rights violation   An action that goes against the rights of a rights holder and which is either not morally justified (and hence moral wrong) or not legally justified (and hence illegal). (chap. 1, sec. 2D)

Rule consequentialism (RC)   Any version of consequentialism according to which the rightness or wrongness of some particular action that is (or might be) performed in some situation depends on the *acceptance value* of the rule corresponding to the action in question. A right action is one falling under a rule with at least as high an acceptance value as any other rule governing the situation in question. See *act consequentialism.* (chap. 1, sec. 2A)

Same-sex marriage   A legal marriage between members of the same sex. (chap. 3, sec. 3)